C000133372

£1

BRONZES
OF THE 19TH CENTURY

Bronzes
Of The 19th Century

Dictionary of Sculptors

by Pierre Kjellberg

---

translated by Kate D. Loftus, Alison Levie
& Leslie Bockol

Westminster Libraries

3 0417 0366 0801 2

Schiffer Publishing Ltd

77 Lower Valley Road, Atglen, PA 19310

ACKNOWLEDGEMENTS

We express our thanks to all those who, through their scholarship, their information or their documents, contributed to the realization of this work. We would especialy like to thank Simone Bersier (Le Louvere des Antiquaires), Geneviève Bonté, conservator and staff for the Library of Decorative Arts, Marie Bouchard, Marie-Cécile Commère, Rhodia Dufet-Bourdelle, Gilioli, Marie-Noelle de Grandry, conservator at the Museum of Decorative Arts, Pascale Grémont, conservator of collections at the Coubertin Foundation, Françoise Guitter, Danielle Heude, conservator of the Museum of France, Viviane Huchard, conservator of the Louvre, Antoinette Lenormand-Romain, conservator at the Museum of Orsay, Laure de Margerie and the documentary service of the Orsay, Anne Pingeot, conservator at the Orsay, and Dina Vierny.

Alain Beausire, archivist at the Rodin Museum, Jean Bernard, François Bouchard, Pierre Cadet, Jean Coudane (Museum of Orsay), Pierre Dintillac, business manager of the Susse Foundry and the staff at the foundry, Fabius frères, Jacques Ginepro, André Guiral (Le Louvre des Antiquaires), François Pérot, conservator of the musée du Petit Palais, Philippe Sorel, conservator of the Carnavalet Museum, Jacques Spiess, Armand Torossian, Michel Vangheluwe, municipal archivist of Valenciennes.

The conservators of the museums of the province.

The auctioneers of Paris and the province.

Christie's and Sotheby of London and New York.

Copyright © 1994 by Schiffer Publishing, Ltd.
Original edition in French published by
Les Editions de l'Amateur
Library of Congress Catalog Number: 94-66376

All rights reserved. No part of this work may be reproduced or used in any forms or by any means graphic, electronic or mechanical, including photocopying or information storage and retrieval systems without written permission from the copyright holder.

Printed in The United States of America
ISBN: 0-88740-629-7

We are interested in hearing from authors with book ideas on related topics.

Published by Schiffer Publishing Ltd.
77 Lower Valley Road
Atglen, PA 19310
Please write for a free catalog.
This book may be purchased from the publisher.
Please include $2.95 postage.
Try your bookstore first.

CONTENTS

THE MAGIC OF BRONZE

It all starts with clay—kneaded by the hand, molded by the thumb, hollowed out and grooved by the sculptor's tools. The work takes form through a mysterious alchemy within the mold; through the irresistible power of fire, the fragile clay becomes set forever into the hardest, most resistant alloy—bronze. The clay gives birth to the bronze.

No material can translate the spontaneity of thought and gesture in three dimensions better than clay can, and in no other material than bronze can this indestructible image be preserved and multiplied. Bronze, it is essential to remember, is first and foremost a medium of reproduction. Bronze has been used to reproduce "premier casts," sketches from the studios, which are often fired after the death of their author in order to perpetuate the artist's creative genius. In addition to these works of fine art, bronze has also given birth to a number of skillfully molded and shaped objets d'art, not always original, but certainly pleasant and stylish. Popular themes for these objects were drawn from a wide variety of sources, sometimes cast into hundreds of copies; portraits in bust or medallion form are less numerous but very widely distributed. Reductions of the monumental works erected in city squares and gardens were also cast for distribution.

Bronze is a means of reproduction; when small works are involved, the nature of collectors destines it to be a means of mass production as well. Except in certain rare instances, it would be risky indeed, to consider bronzes as unique pieces, unlike autographed works which were protected by the determined and sometimes sole intervention of the founders. Even at the end of the Renaissance, in the second half of the sixteenth century, the studio of the great sculptor Jean Boulogne at Borgo Pinto in Florence was thought to have multiplied the works of the master as he attracted more and more international customers. The English author A. Radcliff (*European Bronze Statuettes*, 1966) also mentions the studio of Antonio Susini, one of Jean Bologne's assistants, who copied the bronze castings of the great sculptor and other contemporary Italian masters. He made simple "reproductions," certainly with high-quality casting, but of a "conventional finish."

7

The same author also cites the example of major works from Bernini, reduced reproductions of very variable quality. Some of them are unquestionably old, and without them it could not be proved that the celebrated Baroque sculptor had anything to do with their execution.

THE PRINCIPAL ROLE OF THE FOUNDER

The considerable number of small bronzes made in the course of the nineteenth century provides strong evidence that the original artists did not intervene in the process of duplication. This lack of intervention, which goes without saying for old works or those of absent artists, is equally evident for those of living sculptors.

For every David d'Angers who disapproved of bronzes "retouched without his participation," how many of his colleagues entrusted their molds to the founder without much concern for the quality or the quantity of the proofs to be cast from them? A mold limited to a few copies allowed a sculptor to personally control each of them, but no one limit was obliged to limit themselves. Moreover, the notion of limiting and numbering proofs did not arrive until the end of the nineteenth century, and then only gradually and partially began to command attention. For many artists, the primary concern was to meet demand; indeed, Rodin himself did not limit his production.

Successful bronzes, like *Le Chanteur florentin* (The Florentine Singer) by Paul Dubon, were distributed throughout Europe, and other examples abound. Hardly a month passed in France without a casting of *L'Accolade* by Mène appearing in a showroom. It was the same with many of the bronzes by Barye, Carpeaux, and many others. Frequently, skilled artisans, provided with the appropriate tools, reworked these molds into many different sizes. These tools were fashioned after the pantograph, but were adapted to work with three-dimensional objects. The famous founder Barbedienne frequently used the process on a reduction machine, invented in 1836 by Achille Collas and conceived of by Frederic Sauvage. (The instrument, in iron and in bronze, is preserved at the Industrial Museum of Boulogne-sur-Mer.) Similar processes were used elsewhere in France and in many other countries. Thus, a number of subjects can be reproduced with precision for a relatively low price.

Paul Dubois, Le Chanteur florentin, 61 cm (F. Barbedienne), mechanical Collas reduction

As a result of this process and of huge demand, bronze 'editions' experienced a boom in the second half of the nineteenth century. Sculptors sold a certain number of models, along with the the right to be reproduce them, to an 'editor.' In the beginning, the editor was often a dealer who had the bronzes made by the foundry. Soon, the founders themselves became the editors, directly signing contracts with artists, and publishing catalogs offering bronzes from a number of sculptors in many versions and dimensions. The importance of the sculptors' names was minimal; these catalogs were sometimes organized in alphabetical order not by sculptor, but by subject.

In the report on the Exposition des Produits de l'Industrie in 1839 (the same year that Achille Collas presented his reduction machine there), the title of editor is mentioned for the first time: "M. Debraux d'Englures is, so to speak, the 'Editor' of art bronzes, entering under this title for the first time, and practising that profession exclusively."

Alexandre Falguière, Le Vainqueur au combat de coqs, 85 cm (Thiébaut), J. Ginepro Collection, Monaco.

THE DEBUT OF THE EDITIONS

Ferdinand Barbedienne, who founded his enterprise in 1838 in association with Collas, went on to become (along with Susse Frères) the great specialist in casting unlimited bronze editions which soon could be found in every lobby. Before long, he employed several hundred workers. He signed one of the first contracts, for an edition of a work by Rude, on March 22nd, 1843. The very first contract seems to have been that between Susse and Pradier, dated June 14, 1841. Others followed, with a number of sculptors. Contracts were for one or several works, or for the complete production of the artist (sometimes for life, and sometimes just for a limited time). The clauses varied, of course, from one contract to another, and some editors unscrupulously modified and distorted the models provided by sculptors in order to adapt them to the tastes (more often, whims) of their customers.

This democratization of sculpture, apurred by the boom of bourgeois business, had its detractors and its supporters from the very beginning. Among the latter is Arsine Alexandre, one of the biographers of Barye, who boldly settles the debate. Understanding that artists must put themselves within reach "of new realities" he responded to the critic Alexandre Decamps, who had lamented that Barye did not decorate the public plazas: "One wonders a little whether great art will be killed if twenty people of taste each possess a proof of a master-piece within their homes, under their attentive eyes, or if this masterpiece will be killed when produced as a unique specimen in colossal proportions to be exhibited in the street, for the curiosity of one hundred imbeciles and twenty thousand indifferent people."

How can one assume that a bronze made without the artist present is necessarily of mediocre quality? Far from it. Even if the founders do not aspire to the role of creator—they are, essentially, executors—most of them have manual skills, sensibility, and knowledge of the artist and of his work, which often permits them to translate perfectly the spirit and intentions of the artist. Certain people are preoccupied with this delicate problem of translation. After raising the possibility of artists executing their bronzes themselves, the founder Albert Susse, in his report on the Chicago exposition of 1893, questions: "But can one ask our contemporary sculptors to devote themselves to such a task? To do this, it would be necessary to enlarge the framework of their formal education, which is already very full." He concludes, "The manufacturers of bronzes must help our artists, in this respect, by making themselves in measure the artists' vigilant collaborators, clever at interpreting their works without betraying them." A few lines further, he wonders "if we could not do better in this than we are doing now, and if it is not possible, through narrower agreements and more precise collaboration between sculptors and founder, to realize desirable improvements in an industry so indisputably tied to the highest manifestations of art."

WHO MADE THIS BRONZE?

There is still some question about when a work in bronze can be considered an original work, and if one has the right to write in a sales or exhibition catalog that a bronze is "by" an artist or if it is necessary to say that the bronze is "fashioned after" the work of the artist. In the strictest sense, using the word "original" is limited (using the standards of bibliophiles) to reproductions in the first edition, limited in number and controlled by the artist. It is necessary to provide the proof of the artist's control and supervision, to show certain interventions of the sculptor; this is practically never possible. The case of Barye is a typical example. It is known that in 1838 he

Eutrope Bouret, Pierrot or Au clair de la lune, 45 cm.

opened his own foundry, from which came some bronzes of remarkable quality, the most sought after today. Did he intervene directly during the course of the work? Did he confide in his workers? Is it not the known quality of these bronzes that matters? In his turn, Ferdinand Barbedienne produced the works from these sketches, perhaps during the lifetime of Barye (and of sculptors) but in even greater quantity after his death. Some other founders, while producing just as many castings and in diverse circumstances, while Barye still lived, made sure that his works were cast out of his reach. For this reason, works by Barye can now be found of widely varying qualities.

So we return to the question, bronze "by" or "fashioned after?" With rare exceptions, the first expression does not correspond with reality. As for the second, it risks implying a slightly pejorative meaning, suggesting an imitation. It would seem that the best form is to indicate the name of the sculptor, but accompany it, as in book and stamp catalogs, with information as precise as possible on the approximate time period and the circumstances of casting, even if they are assumed. Why not have a code for quality as exists for money and medallions? Some descriptions, like "ancient casting" or "casting from an edition," which are not sorted by dates, are too vague. Thorough research remains to be done in this domain, which is still explored very little, perhaps because of the disappearance of the archives from the oldest foundries.

THE TRUE CRITERIA OF VALUE

It is good that a bronze must be judged first and foremost by its plastic art qualities and the quality of manufacture. "It is the eye which speaks," says an expert, and this eye must be trained. A bronze from a collection is not evaluated by its function in its environment, as a statue, but for itself, as an object. In the majority of cases, one can hold it, turn it over, feel it, weigh it in one's hand, and examine it from all faces and different angles. And thus, one distinguishes many essential elements of quality which give it its value, as much aesthetic as commercial.

Chiseling: The chiseling is precise, forceful, but without curtness. According to the style of the subject, the details are either rendered with great precision or they are obliterated by the shaping. Thus, when the bronze reproduces a clay studio model, the work of the fingers that molded the earth, even the least gesture of the artist is faithfully restored. On the other hand, the works of certain sculptors are sought for the abundance and the detail of their chiseled motifs.

Patina: This is a very important quality for connoisseurs. From the very beginning of a work, the patina undergoes the trials of time. Fine, translucent, revealing

Gustave Dussart, Inconsciente, 68 cm.

11

Pierre Bonnard, Baigneuse au rocher, 14.5 cm (Valsuani, Sagot-Le-garrec edition).

the quality of the alloy, patina continues to live and give life to the bronze. Many and subtle are its nuances. The tonalities varied greatly during the nineteenth century, including black, brown, or green patinas, metallic patina, and very valuable gilded or silvered patinas which are rather rare and greatly sought after.

Casting: The best is usually slender, hence slight, particularly in the nineteenth century. This finesse with metal implies great skill on the part of the casters, and is a sign of quality. Pay attention, however; some bronze statuettes are encountered that, though they are thick and heavy, are nonetheless perfectly chiseled and of excellent bearing.

Other Materials: Certain sculptors, principally at the end of the nineteenth century and in the 1900s, readily incorporated marble, ivory, quartz, and semi-precious stones with their bronze work. In principle, these works, which are representative of a certain affectation and extreme stylishness, have higher values than the works of the same subjects and quality done in plain bronze.

Dimensions: Except for the purely aesthetic criteria enumerated above, when the quality of execution is similar, the value of a bronze from a collection is usually proportionate to its height.

Signature of the sculptor: It is necessary to consider the condition of the pieces, and not grant an excessive importance to the signature; collectors are buying a beautiful bronze, not a great signature. The name of a renowned sculptor can appear important on a mediocre work in bad condition, on a casting from another already molded, or even on a complete fake. The signature can be inscribed on the original model, or it can be insccribed in the wax. If the wax is lost, the signature can be traced in the bronze with the aid of a special chisel and a hammer. Before 1820, sculptors' signatures rarely appeared on bronzes, only the founders' seals. In about 1820, Susse decided to affix the name of the artist next to his own. This became a general practice after 1850. (Note that the sculptors frequently changed their signatures during the course of their careers.)

Name of the founder: This mark appears as a seal, or again from a signature traced like that of the sculptor. It can establish a precise indication of the date of the casting if one knows the succession of founders to whom certain artists have awarded the conversions of their bronzes. The great founders of the nineteenth century and the beginning of the twentieth century, like Susse, Thiébault, Rudier, Hébrard, Velsuani, and a few others, were known for the beauty of most of their castings. But, to maintain the reputation of the sculptor's signature, the quality of each bronze which carries their name must be equal to this reputation.

State of preservation: Accidents, overly-pronounced wear and tear on the surface of the patina, repairs which are more or less skilled, missing parts, and additions which do not conform to the original model obviously depreciate a bronze to different extents.

THE NUMBERED SKETCHES

The founders Valsuani, Hébrard and Rudier are said to have produced the first works of limited and numbered editions at the end of the nineteenth century. As with prints, each proof carries a number indicating its place in the sequence, and usually the total number of casts which (in principle) must not be exceeded. Fraudulent casts are always possible, but they risk devaluing the work of the sculptor who is either responsible for it or a victim of it. A numbered bronze is, theoretically, worth more than a copy from an unlimited casting.

On March 3, 1981, a decree was issued in order to provide a better understanding of the term "original" edition. It defined a first edition of a limited casting as a casting of at most eight works, numbered from 1/8 to 8/8, to which can be added four works outside of the trade, likewise numbered in Roman numerals from I to IV. The twelve pieces can thus profit from the fiscal rules reserved for works considered originals. Any works beyond these twelve, the supplementary works, must, in principal, be marked "reproduction."

Although very recent, this ruling is not without interest, especially considering that some casts of works from the nineteenth and beginning of the twentieth century are currently produced by the heirs of certain artists. Rodin is one such case. The celebrated sculptor bequeathed the whole of his work to the state; thus granting the Rodin museum all rights. The museum owns most of the molds made during Rodin's life, and continues with the casts in the quantities provided for by the law, always of a remarkable quality.

THE POSTHUMOUS SKETCHES

Had Rodin not left very precise instructions as to the edition of his sculptures, one might nevertheless presume that the celebrated artist's intentions were to transform a great number of his works into bronze. This is not always the case. Consider Dalou: except for some bronzes that he retouched and cast in London in 1871, Dalou did not envision reproducing his sculptures in any but the orginial material. His heirs, after his death in 1902, wanted to pay him homage by reproducing some of his works themselves, first in very careful, limited castings by Hébrard, then in a more important series, and finally in unlimited editions by Susse. For Degas, who died in 1917, seventy-two original statuettes in wax were found in his studio, and twenty-two copies of each were fired in bronze in 1922. Would he have wanted this?

Alfred Grévin and Friedrich Beer, Oh! Eh!, 52 cm.

The same situation ensued with Daumier, who died in 1879. His famous *Ratapoil* was made the object of many sketches in 1891, 1925 and 1960. These castings were made from two plasters issued during his lifetime from his original terra cotta statuette. As for his other figurines and his satirical busts, they also were cast long after his death. Finally, and so as not to mention only the most famous cases, Gaugin left some amazing wooden sculptures which he undoubtedly never envisioned being reproduced in bronze—an outlook his heirs did not share.

These speculation are not intended to cast doubt on the quality of works issued by heirs after a sculptor's death; indeed, in most cases, the works are flawless. Rather, we speculate whether the decision to make reproductions, undoubtably well-intended but not reflecting the artist's wishes, is well-founded.

FORGERS AND CASTING FROM OTHER MOLDS

The original raw clay modeled by the artist cannot withstand the diverse operations which will give birth to a bronze. A model in plaster is therefore cast from the clay one. When the production involves a very large number of copies, the plaster is replaced by a "master model" in bronze specially made for this process. This master model, meticulously chiseled to transmit the maximum finesse to each reproduction, is sometimes made with screwed detachable pieces to facilitate the manufacture of the mold.

Those who cast fraudulent copies did not take so many precautions. A work from an existing edition serves simply as a model for new castings—to make reproductions of reproductions, in a sense. Theoretically, the hoax is verifiable. As a result of metal's contraction during cooling, the new proofs obtained are slightly smaller than those used as models. Yet it would be necessary to know the exact dimensions, to the nearest millimeter, of the model. In reality, it is often the mediocre quality of these clandestine castings, the softness of form, the stickiness, the absence of finesse in the details (recapturing them by chiseling would increase the cost, in an operation whose essential purpose is to be lucrative) which allows them to be identified.

Confusion sometimes occurs, deliberately or through ignorance, between copied castings and the correctly executed castings, though experts are not deceived. For the simple amateur, however, caution is advisable. Should you buy a copy casting if you like it? There is no reason not to—as long as you pay for it as a copy. And do not forget that a seal of a founder or a signature of a sculptor does not prove the authenticity of a sketch. For example: the seal of the founder Siot-Decauville is regularly set in bronze, like a conforming piece. A copy casting makes only a reproduction of the seal. It is important to distinguish one from the other.

Honoré Daumier, Ratapoil, 44 cm, (Siot-Decauville 17).

The practice of casting from other molds has been exercised, more or less openly, since the Renaissance, and it is still practiced today. At the end of the nineteenth century, a great number of bronzes that had been bought in France were reproduced in the United States. In 1893, Albert Susse protested vigorously against this "piracy," citing the American foundries who were guilty. Susse furnished a list of the pieces most easily copied, among them *L'amour victorieux* (Victorious love) of Grégoire; more than 100 million copy castings of this work had been sold in different countries.

CHEAP IMITATIONS

Remaining in this discussion are bronzes which are not actually bronze! These pieces appear to be made of bronze, but are made of a much lighter and less costly zinc-based alloy, called "white metal" by Amercians and "composition" by the French. Different procedures exist, some using galvanoplasty, which deposits a thin layer of copper on the work produced in zinc. These imitations were also ambiguously classified under the name "art bronzes." Following a lawsuit initiated by the manufacturers of these pieces, a court order from 1910 revoked the requirement that the label "imitation bronze" be shown on this type of article. Between the years 1860 and 1870, a number of sculptors cast some of their works in bronze and some in zinc. In a report on the exposition of Brussels in 1910, the founder Jacques Susse described these cheap imitations, which were sometimes great successes: "a good reproduction in zinc is much superior to a bad bronze, but a beautiful bronze, a true work of art, cannot be compared even with a very beautiful reproduction in zinc."

BRONZE THROUGH THE AGES

The Bronze Age, one of the key stages in the technological and social evolution of humanity, began in the third millennium before the era of Christianity. The original process of manufacturing the alloy of copper and tin for which this period was named was lost in the Dark Ages. From the beginning, this technique established a means of mass production. Weapons, jewelry, figurines, vessels and all sorts of items were produced.

Reproductions, as well as innumerable statuettes in bronze (often of a funereal origin), have been found in Mesopotamia, in Egypt, among the Minoans and the ancient Greeks, and also at the other end of the world, in China. Unquestionably, the great statues of Olympian gods and certain monumental effigies of Roman emperors were made as unique pieces, intended to eternally record in an imperishable material the revered traits of divinities and sovereigns. But there were also those who reproduced "multiples" in smaller sizes for the veneration of a greater number of people. It is believed that Greek and Roman studios inundated the Mediterranean

Armand Toussaint, Femme orientale porte-torchère, 153 cm (Graux-Marly, founder).

La Vénus de Milo (casting from the 19th century according to the marble from the museum of the Louvre).

basin with small bronzes, to such an extent that identical models have been discovered in regions as far apart as the Near Orient and France.

With the Renaissance artistic statuettes appeared, a piece sometimes cast fas one-of-a-kind objects for important collectors, but they did not stay one-of-a-kind for long. From the second half of the sixteenth century, foundries (principally in Italy, but also in Flanders, Germany, and France, produced innumerable statuettes to contend for the attention of art-lovers of that period and those of today. A number of greatly-admired ancient Greek and Roman sculptural masterpieces were faithfully reproduced in reduced sizes, with a small or large number of copies. As noted by a distinguished specialist, M. Georges Salmann, a quantity of small bronzes from the fifteenth and sixteenth centuries was long confused with authentic antique pieces until scholars studied and identified them at the end of the nineteenth or beginning of the twentieth century. (*Connaissance des Arts*, April 1975).

In the seventeenth and eighteenth centuries, public attention turned towards royal images which were erected in the center of towns. Allegorical or mythological groups also appeared, large ones placed in parks, and smaller ones decorating vestibules and lobbies of hotels and important buildings.

François Girardon's life-size or larger-than-life works *le Louis XIV* and *l'Enlèvement de Proserpine* were transformed into bronze reductions of at least a meter high. All these without speaking of other usages for bronze, all also reproducers, like the ornaments of furniture, the luminaries, the objects of furnishings. One thinks of Caffieri, of Gouthière, and of many other little-known or totally obscure bronziers, as well as their imitators of yesterday and today, who incessantly produce keyholes, *chutes d'angles*, handles, and sides for wall brackets in a rococo or neoclassical style.

ANCIENT AND MODERN IN THE NINETEENTH CENTURY

Craftsmen in the nineteenth century did not fail to pursue and increase the reproduction of models from antiquity. Clever practicioners most often copied a quantity of masterpieces from centuries past, sometimes identically, sometimes with variations. Indeed, famous works of the past and their styles were copied. Examples included *Vénus de Milo*, originally done in marble, discovered in 1820, and offered to King Louis XVIII for the Louvre museum, *Moïse* of Michel-Ange, *Persée* of Benvenuto Cellini, *Mercure* and *Enlèvement de Proserpine* of Jean Bologne, *Louis XIV* and *Chevaux de Marly* of

Guillaume Coustou, in short, the most celebrated works of the universal sculpture that everyone desires to have under his eyes in the format which suits him best.

The successful reproductions of ancient works continued throughout the nineteenth century. In 1862, reproductions outnumbered contemporary creations in the catalog of the Barbedienne foundry, the most prolific at that time. In reality, their manufacture still continues.

The "modern" sculptors, however, were not forgotten, and one will see that a number of them executed reductions of their monumental statues and groups, while others—Barye first—also completed works in small sizes specifically designed to be copied in great quantity. However, at the beginning of the century, when the neoclassical spirit was revered, sculpture did not indulge in this proliferation. If the majority of traditional sculptors remained faithful to the study of nature, realism, and the gracious themes appreciated just a short time before, they were no longer up to date and their careers came to an end. Only later, when the past came back into vogue, could one begin to reproduce their works: the bust of Madame Du Barry of Pajou (1730-1809), the innumerable children musicians, bacchantes, satires or loves of Clodion (1738-1814), *La Frileuse*, the bust of Voltaire of Houdon (1785-1828), some busts of young women of Chinard (1756-1813), to name only a few of the most sought after.

L'Education de Bacchus (casting from the 19th century according to Clodion).

Some artists of the same generation, particularly Chaudet (1763-1810) and Bosio (1768-1845), were influenced by the Italian sculptor Canova, who had been twice summoned to France by Napoleon I and who then had the audacity to sculpt an effigy of the emperor naked. Like Canova, they practiced the antique cult of the "beautiful ideal," better accomodated by the whiteness of stone and especially of marble than by the somber reflections of bronze. More than portraits and amiable scenes, they sculpted the heroes and gods of Olympia, eternal and disincarnate, to serve formal allegories.

The Restoration no longer provoked a radical change in sculpture. It was the artists who still served the imperial mystique of the past who were entrusted with replacing the royal statues destroyed at the time of the Revolution. Bosio, called the "French Canova," sculpted the Louis XIV [ital?]* of the place des Victoires in 1822, and in 1828, le quadrige de la Paix [ital?]* of l'arc de Triomphe of Carrousel. The academic Cartellier, for his part, completed Louis XV [ital?]* of Reims in 1818. While romanticism spread to all forms of expression for a longtime, neoclassicism and academicism resisted, thereby contributing to make the nineteenth century the most eclectic period in the history of art.

THE GREAT TURN OF ROMANTICISM

Gustave Doré, L'Effroi or L'Amour maternel, 59.5 cm.

The romantic movement profoundly influenced the first half of the nineteenth century. It developed first among the writers, poets and painters prone to expressing, whether by pen or by paint brush, the most exacerbated, dramatic, heroic and painful sentiments. These artists sought to question all that the preceding era had adored, and to exalt all it had ignored or combated. The romantics' line of conduct was a reaction against the immediate past, but an embrace of the more distant past. The classicists of the eighteenth century, the artists of the Revolution and of the Empire, saw only Antiquity, either directly or through the perspective of the Renaissance. The romantics, however, chose to rehabilitate the Middle Ages. The classicists considered reason above all else; the romantics accorded predominance to the imagination, sensibility, and feelings. They opposed Christianity and history in favor of free thought and mythology, preferred individualism to collective acts, and responded to sterile rules and precision with lyricism and freedom of expression.

Le Génie du christianisme by Chateaubriand was a precursor to Romanticism as early as 1803, and then *Notre Dame de Paris* by Victor Hugo in 1831, and the works of Lamartine, Alfred de Vigny, Alfred de Musset, and many others, all were responsible for provoking and sustaining the movement. Everyone participated in it, including Eugène Delacroix, whose canvases overflowed with color and fire to describe the dramas of the war of independence of Greece, and Géricault, who is known for his 1819 portrayal of the tragic shipwreck of La Méduse.

Confronted with three dimensions and with materials that are often difficult to work, sculptors naturally displayed a certain reserve compared to the exaggerations of some of their painter colleagues. Sculptors sometimes adhered to the new ideas more in their choice of themes than in the manner of treating it.

This adherence to new ideas occurred during the 1830s, when the production of a series of small bronzes was in full force. The individual portrait became a respected form again, as did scenes showing feats of weaponry, the splendid deeds of national heroes. Also important was the representation of simple human and family virtues, no longer symbolized by the far-off and impersonal deities of Olympia, but by flesh-and-blood people, who lived in the world—David victorious over Goliath, Joan of Arc saving the country, a young fisherman sitting on the bank of a river, a peasant carrying his last born child, the marshal Ney charging at the head of his troops, a famous dancer appearing in her favorite role.

18

Two artists with very different, but not opposing, temperaments were in the forefront, dominating romantic sculpture: David d'Angers and Rude. One more name, just as prestigious, also comes to mind: Antoine-Louis Barye, a true promoter of animal sculpture who would remain very important throughout the entire second half of the century.

The success that Barye gained from the Salon of 1831 marks the birth of a style; it is evident that the proliferation of his imitators and their works corresponds to an urgent and lasting demand from a vast public. Deer, lions, race horses, and hunting dogs, either alone or in groups, sitting peacefully together or fighting among themselves, were soon enthroned on every mantle. A number of animal sculptors following Barye's example appeared, among many others, Pierre-Jules Mène, Auguste Cain, Alfred Barye (the sculptor's own son), Christophe Fratin, Isidore Bonheur, Edouard Delabrière, Jules Moigniez, Prosper Lecourtier, the count Du Passage, the count of Ruillé, Georges Gardet, Jean Joire, Louis de Monard, Navelier, and, in the beginning of the twentieth century, Rembrandt Bugatti and François Pompon.

ABUNDANCE AND ECLECTICISM

The Second Empire, and then the Third Republic, experienced a true fever of construction. The decoration of a number of buildings furnished artists with a considerable amount of work. Moreover, there were great universal expositions. It was a time for excellence through official commissions. A number of works that had been executed for the new Louvre, city hall, and the opera were made into smaller versions cast in bronze, , beginning with the famous *Danse* by Carpeaux; "statue-mania" reigned. Historical personages, artists and contemporary personalities from Duguesclin to Napoléon III, Joan of Arc to Bourbaki, and Watteau to Alexandre Dumas, appeared everywhere as busts and statues, in groups along the avenues, squares and gardens, and as statuettes for apartments.

It is impossible to categorize the majority of sculptors from the second half of the nineteenth century in a precise genre. A number of them were enticed by the multitude of themes then in style, embarking upon one or the other indiscriminately according to the whim of fashion and the demand of art-lovers. All genres, subjects, and styles were used, and this eclecticism, of which we have already talked, conferred on the sculpture of this period its diverse character, including some confusion but also a richness.

Boleslas Biégas, L'Effroi, 175 cm (A. Rudier).

The use of history, which was precious to the romantics, was among the most successful of themes. Barye himself, in spite of his predilection for the art of animal figures, yielded to the portrayal of historic personages from the near or distant past, like kings Charles VI and Charles VII, Gaston de Foix, and Bonaparte. A number of other sculptors, Emmanuel Frémiet for example, whether animal sculptors or not, followed the same practice. The animal, in particular the horse, was still present in this type of work since very often the work involved equestrian portraits.

Exoticism, born from more and more frequent contacts with the Orient and Africa (this was the era of progress for the steamship and colonial conquests) had also seduced more than one sculptor. Barye again, and Mène and Frémiet did not escape from exotic influences, nor did Lèon Gérôme, who did more than just painting, as well as Charles Cordier, and Albert-Ernest Carrier-Belleuse, among many others. Arab cavaliers and Oriental dancers were thus a considerable success.

More or less linked to this vague Orientalism, polychromy strongly affected sculpture, and with bronzes involved the use of different patinas and gilt or the contribution of other materials: marble, onyx, ivory, or semi-precious stones. Some of those using the oriental style were: Cordier, Gérôme, and Barrias with his famous *Nature se dévoilant devant la Science,* sometimes cast entirely in bronze, sometimes with the head and the hands in white marble.

A number of sculptors crossed frequently from the Orient to Greece. Heirs of classical works, mythological scenes, and in their wake, allegories, scenes of this genre extolled childhood, adolescence, maternal love, successfully spanning the fluctuations in taste. They were usually treated with more realism and freedom than their predecessors by sculptors such as Mathurin Moreau, the other members of this great Dijon family, Auguste, and especially Hippolyte Moreau, Alexandre Faiguiére, Antonin Mercié, etc.

Louis Ernest Barrias, La Nature se dévoilant devant la Science, bronze with two patinas and white marble, 60 cm.

TRADITION AND RENEWAL

These stylish themes were redone to the point of satiation and could invariably be found again each year at the Salon. Paul Mantz, a critic, reputed to be conservative, wrote about the Salon of 1865 : "The monotony of the subjects treated by our statues implicates those who made them of a persistent somnolence, a perfect sterility of the imagination. Today, as yesterday, a young girl in conference with a colombian, a child stung by a snake, the soldier of the Marathon, etc. , shepherdess, seasons, muses. . .!"

Therefore, it is not surprising that in reaction, a desire to leave the beaten paths and find new sources of inspiration took form. Some sculptors stuck to translating exactly what the world offered from life, from movement, from strains, and from anecdotes. One truly original theme appeared: that of work. Factory workers, miners, laborers, peasants, and scenes from popular life multiplied under the influence of the social and somewhat contentious ideas of the era. Alfred Boucher and Edouard Drouot, as well as Henri Bouchard and the Belgian Constantin Meunier, particularly illustrate this tendency. Dalou, in the latter years of his life, worked on a monument to workers which like the Tour of Work envisioned by Rodin did not come to fruition.

In this sphere, a conscientious naturalism was imposed, but it came only after the precision of Rodin, and under his influence, an impressionist trend developed, favoring movement with the spontaneity of gestures and attitudes, more than attention to detail. The bronzes exhibited in Paris by the prince Paul Troubetzkoy were notably of this style.

At the end of the century, Art Nouveau, which literally exploded in decoration, and furniture, and did not remain a stranger to sculpture. It permeates certain works and certain artists like Louis-Ernest Barrias, Agathon Léonard and Raoul Larche with its lyricism, and sometimes its ecstacy. The name of the Larch remains linked with the famous representation of the *Loïe Fuller*

FROM CARPEAUX TO RODIN TO RENOIR

The names of Dalou and of Rodin have just been mentioned. Chronologically, the name of Jean-Baptiste Carpeaux would have been cited first. These three artists, with their extraordinary talent, dominated the second half of the nineteenth century, just as the trio David d'Angers, Rude, and Barye had done for the first half. Their talents were so exceptional that they cannot be classed in any category whatsoever, or in any particular style. They surpassed any category and their imprint, in particular that of Rodin, will mark the sculpture of the twentieth century for a longtime.

Antoine Bourdelle was among the practitioners who worked in Rodin's studio. First influenced by the master, Bourdelle then forged his own robust, sometimes expressionistic, style, which placed him at the juncture of two concepts of plastic arts, straddling two centuries.

Georges Guittet, Le Grand Porteur d'eau arabe, 86 cm (Slot 91 E.).

At the brink of the twentieth century some other great sculptors, including Maillol and Joseph Bernard, while assimilating the teaching of their mentors, tried to liberate themselves, rediscovering without imitating, the purity, and stylized balance of the ancient works. Most of them lived far into the twentieth century. While the latter part of their careers built upon a framework from the nineteenth century, the influence did not extend beyond the First World War.

In the years which preceded or immediately followed the turn of the century just as Rosa Bonheur, Léon Gérôme and especially Daumier had earlier, some painters produced sculpture as well. This was the case with August Renoir, whose works, do not forget, were executed by Richard Guino under his direction. Other painters who produced sculpture were Henri Matisse, who is credited with about seventy bronzes, Edgar Degas and Paul Gauguin to cite not only the most famous.

SCHOOLS, REWARDS AND SALONS

The sculptors usually accomplished their studies in a specialized school, the most prestigious being the School of Fine Arts of Paris (l'Ecole des Beaux-Arts de Paris). In the nineteenth century, this institution was placed under the powerful authority of The Academy of Fine Arts (l'Académie des Beaux-Arts). At first limited to drawing and theoretical studies, in 1863, it was provided with a variety of studios, of which three were for sculpture.

The specialized school for drawing and mathematics, better known as Petite Ecole, preoccupied itself more with what was then called the arts applied to industry. The school was frequented by such famous artists as Dalou, Carpeaux and Rodin. Finally, private studios were opened by renowned sculptors such as David d'Angers, Rude, Pradier, Jouffroy, etc. (Catalog of the exposition "French Sculpture in the Nineteenth Century," Grand Palais, 1986).

The ambition of the majority of sculptors was the first grand prize of Rome, which was truly venerated by them. The candidate awarded a prize as a result of the competition was assigned to stay for what was then five years at the Médicis villa (four years starting in 1863). During the course of his sojourn he was required to produce a certain assigned number of works which were sent to Paris to be exhibited there. It was left to each artist to make himself known to the public and the critics. The Salon could offer him this opportunity. Certainly the works sent to the Alson did not represent the entirety of his work, but they remained no less a witness to his style and choice of themes.

What is referred to simply as the Salon is none other than the official exposition which has taken place since the seventeenth century every other year at the Louvre in the Carré parlor (whence its name). It become annual in 1863. In 1881, the Society of French Artists took responsibility for it.

Arthur Beourgeois, Danseuse nubienne à la cruche, 113 cm.

The Society of Independent Artists was formed, in its turn, in 1884 and organized its own exposition. After the Exposition Universelle of 1889, the National Society of the Fine Arts was born as a result of a schism at the center of the Society of French artists. From then on it held its exposition at the Champ-de-Mers. Finally the Salon d'Automne was founded in 1903 and the Salon des Tuileries (the Exposition of Tuileries) in 1922.

During the course of the nineteenth century, the jury of the Salon, composed of the members of the Academy of the Fine Arts, who were conservative by nature, frequently refused to admit the work of certain sculptors. Barye had this bitter experience in 1837. It is here that one finds again the fundamental role of the bronzes and of those who reproduce them, the founders-editors. Their intervention sometimes proved to be truly decisive for the rejects of the Salon. Almost alone in the power to assure the connection between the artist and the art-lover, certain editors, who had their own gallery, exhibited the works of sculptors with whom they had a contract. Without doubt the unheard-of success of a collection of bronzes does sometimes occur with castings of a very low quality. On the whole, the big foundries knew how to avoid this mediocrity in order to create innumerable bronzes of all sizes, found on the market. Without these bronzes many of the sculptors would never have known the fame that was theirs during their lifetime, and which they are getting again today with the return to favor of the nineteenth century.

Auguste Rodin, L'Age d'airain, 175 cm.

=THE BIRTH OF BRONZE=

From the starting point, there are many delicate operations which together give life to a bronze: the original work to the reproduction. It most often starts with a plaster—itself fired from a raw earth—but sometimes sculptures in all sorts of other material are used.

There are two techniques for making a bronze. They carry some intriguing names: lost wax, sand casting. In fact, they both rest on the same principal: to introduce the alloy to fusion (from 75 to 90% of copper, the rest of tin, zinc and lead) in a thin space corresponding to the thickness that is desired for the bronze.

A form is first fired from the model. It faithfully reproduces the slightest details, but in a hollow or negative form. (If this mold were filled completely with bronze, the resulting statue would be very heavy and not very economical for an oppressive alloy.) Then, in their semi-total form, the works in bronze are dug out. Also a compact nucleus is introduced, to the interior of the mold, and it is between this nucleus and the mold that the small space used to form the bronze is created.

In order to reach this, the two procedures diverge. We describe the stages succinctly here. The techniques are classic. Certain recent changes in the methods have modified the process without challenging the fundamental principals.

There is still a common experience shared by the two types of manufacture: in the foundries where they are practiced, the moment the bronze is poured assumes a particular solemnity. This is the decisive stage which rewards the long work of the whole team. Not one error is allowed. One imagines being present at an ancient sacrifice. At the far end of the studio, in a kind of sanctuary, a menacing monster sits in state, the frightening splendor imposes respect and dread: the crucible. Attentively, the men observe it, watching for the dazzling flash, the signal which will unleash their movements. From these slow, precise motions, without a hitch, thanks to which the metal in fusion will spread out to create a single cast—this is essential—into the mold, giving life to a bronze. This is the key operation, perhaps not the most difficult but the one that determines all. Here, all succeeds or all fails.

Lost wax and sand casting have been known for a long time. The lost wax has been practiced from the earliest antiquity, in the Mediterranean as well as in the Near- and Far-East. In Africa it was also used beginning in the twelfth century with the bronzes of Bénin and the admirable heads of Ifé.

This technique casts works of all dimensions, even the most complicated forms, in one piece. Some famous examples of monumental statues cast using the lost wax method, are known, notably that of Persée by Benvenuto Cellini, described by the sculptor himself.

The two techniques were used concurrently during the nineteenth century, the sand casting more frequently because it cost less, and therefore sold better (the reverse would be true today because hand-work plays a more important part in this procedure). In 1893, in his report on the exposition of Chicago, the caster Albert Susse indicated that for some years, a movement in favor of the lost wax had appeared, "a very artistic process to tell the truth" but which can be employed "only under exceptional conditions and extreme knives." He concluded in favor of the sand casting which, with the repetition of the chiseling, "gives excellent results."

Today sand casting is most often chosen for works of simple form with a smooth outer layer, as well as for some pieces that are not very thick, such as medals or bas-reliefs. It is however important to specify that the method of manufacturing a bronze does not in any way influence its value.

*The photographic report which follows, showing the two techniques of casting, was made in the studios of the caster Susse, in Arcueil, by Michel Kempf.

CASTING WITH LOST WAX

One imagines sometimes that a bronze by lost wax is a unique work fired from an original in wax that disappears in the course of casting. This is not so. If such were the case, an entire statuette made of wax would produce, in effect, an entire bronze, which is practically never the case as we will point out. To the contrary, the model, as well as the molds which are fired from them, are preserved and can be used to make a greater or lesser number of works. As for the wax, it is essentially destined to create the narrow space that the bronze, in taking the place of it, will occupy later on. It is indeed lost at the time of each draft, which is where the procedure gets its name.

①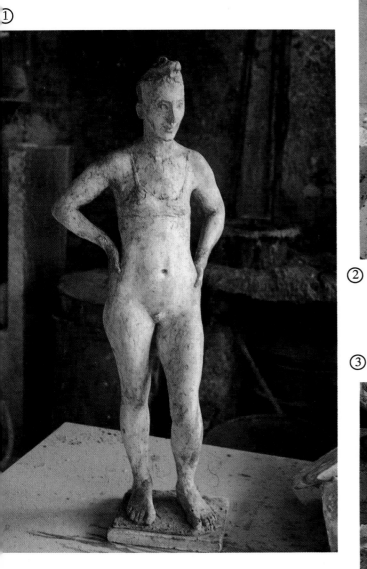

②

The mold, formerly in plaster or gelatin, today is very often made from elastomere reinforced by a plaster shell. (2) (3) It is composed of two or more parts depending on the form of the model.

③

From a plaster model—here *Lucette* or *Le Cirque*, by Germaine Richier (1)—a mold is fired called "in good hollow" which reproduces the statue faithfully in negative.

25

④   ⑤

The mold is opened again (6) and one can see a sculpture (7) for which the outer covering in wax exactly reproduces the original model. It is at this moment that the sculptor, if he so desires, or a practicioner, can intervene in order to alter the wax.

The model is placed upright and the mold is closed again. It is filled (then emptied) with a cold wax liquid (4) which, while cooling, leaves a layer of a certain thickness on the inside. The operation is repeated several times until the layer of wax has the thickness desired for the bronze (when the volume and the weight of the mold render its handling impossible, the wax is "stamped" with a pencil).

Once it is coated with the wax, the mold is filled to the brim with a refractory (5) liquid material which, in solidifying, will make up the nucleus.

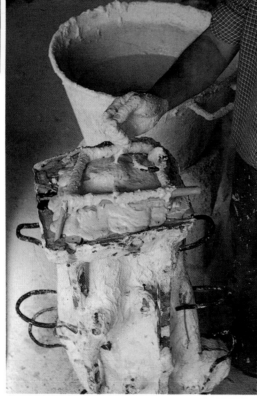

⑧

⑨

Thus prepared, the wax is gradually recovered with the aid of a very fine refractory material (9), capable of faithfully reproducing even a digital imprint. This is the "imprinting."

⑩

⑪

A whole network of wax sticks are put into place. (8) During casting, they will form drains: the "drainages" whereby the wax will drain itself, the "gushes" (casts, jets) by which the metal in fusion will be introduced, and the "vents" which will allow the air and gas to escape.

The "drains" the "vents" and the "jets" are then bound by the creation of some canals (10). New layers of refractory material thicker than the first, are then deposited in order finally to create a sort of compact block, the " mold of the foundry" (11), which will support the high temperatures of bronze in fusion. The foundry mold is then subjected, in a drying room, to a temperature of 200 to 300 degrees celcius—the wax casts and drains itself—then the mold is cooked at 500 degrees celcius which hardens the mold and the nucleus. Thanks to the shafts of iron previously inserted, the nucleus stays in place, once the wax has disappeared.

A decisive stage: the casting. The alloy in fusion (about 1000 degrees celcius, sometimes more) is first poured from the crucible into the "casting pocket" (12) then, from this in a single throw (13), into the interior of the foundry mold where it spreads into the space left free by the wax. After cooling, the foundry mold withdrawn from the pit where it had been buried for the casting, is broken. This is where you "let it fly." The work in bronze appears grayish, rough, bristly from tubulars and roughness. The nucleus, which stayed in the interior, is extracted from the bronze in pieces.

(14)

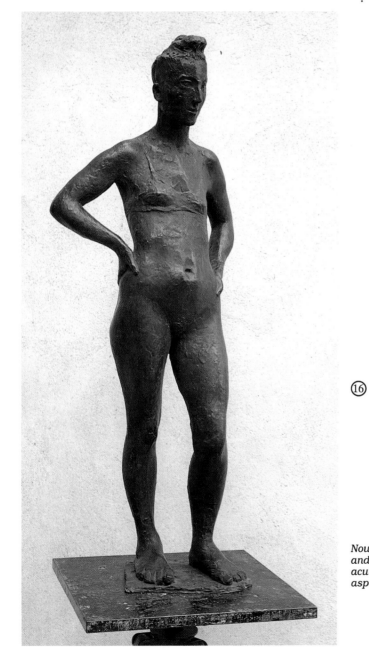

(15)

(16)

Now starts the long work of smoothening, of filling in, of chiseling (14) and finally, the particularly delicate stage of the patina, here in the acute stage (15), before the work appears finally in its definitive aspect (16) : a bronze in every way conforms to the initial model.

SAND CASTING

This type of manufacture is less complex than casting from lost wax in the sense that (if one considers only the principal operations) it demands only a limited number of transfers: from the original model to the mold and from the mold to the work in bronze. But the mold must be reconstructed for each casting. On the other hand, this procedure more directly requires skill on the part of the molder and the reliability of an exceptional hand. The silicon-claylike sand utilized for this technique comes in large part from the southern suburbs of Paris (it is found in other countries also). A number of French foundries were established in this region close to the capital. Some of them are still there. Today synthetic sands are also used. The advantage to synthetic sand is that it is solidified—polymerized—by spraying it with carbonic gas, whereas drying room heating is necessary to solidify natural sand.

②

On the original model in plaster—La Caravane, by Émile Gilioli (1)— some lines were traced in pencil in order to facilitate the execution of the mold.

Held by the metal frame in several places, this mold, here in synthetic sand (2), surrounds the model in order to reproduce it in a hollow form. Because of the irregular form of the so-called model, it includes some pieces which are mobile, both the sand and the "wrought pieces" (dark parts), which can be taken off and put back in place without difficulty.

In the hollow of the mold, the model has been replaced by a double, always made with the same sand. This reproduction will serve as the nucleus. But it is necessary "to draw from it the thickness," in other words reduce it (3), in order to make room for the thin space needed for the metal in fusion to spread out.

nce it is reduced, a protective layer is put on the nucleus with a
aint brush (4), this layer will escape when the metal adheres and
e sand crumbles.

The nucleus is "positioned" inside the mold
(5). It is held in place with iron shafts. These
shafts clearly separate the nucleus from the
mold, creating (6) a space which corresponds
to the thickness of the bronze, as well as the
supplying drains which have been prepared
in the mold.

The frame is closed around the mold and its
nucleus again (7). They are solidly held
between them in order to withstand the
pressure of the alloy in fusion at the moment
of the casting.

In the crucible, the alloy develops (8). Reaching the required temperature, it is poured into the casting pocket (9) then from this into a "basin" (10). A distaff, which closed off the opening of the latter, is then raised and the alloy spreads itself from a jolt between mold and nucleus by the canals prepared in the sand.

⑧

⑨

⑩

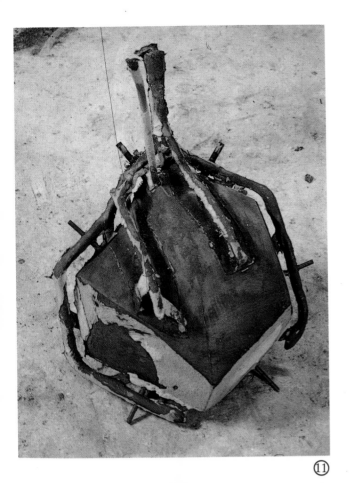

⑪

⑫

⑬

Cooling. The metal frames are open, the mold is broken and the work in bronze appears, crude from the foundry, surrounded by the tubes (11). It is subjected to the same operations of finishing, polishing (12), and application of patina that a cast made with lost wax is before reaching the perfect quality of the completed work (13).

FOREWORD

This dictionary essentially concerns the French sculptors of the nineteenth century (from the First Empire to the war of 1914-1918) some of whose works, either during their lifetime or after their death, were cast in collections of bronze. Foreign sculptors who traveled and exhibited in France are also included.

By collections of bronze, we mean casts of reduced dimensions suitable for homes or the lobbies of public buildings and hotels, as opposed to the monumental bronzes designed for squares and public gardens. These latter—at least the most important ones—are nevertheless mentioned in the descriptions devoted to each artist, and whether they still exist or disappeared during the army occupation during the last war.

In the same way, sculptures in various materials—plaster, terra cotta, marble, stone—are also cited if, because of the appeal of their subject, they gave rise to editions in bronze.

The summaries in this book do not pretend to retrace every detail of the life and career of each sculptor, but seeks to approach their work based on their use of bronze. However, some research has permitted us to discover useful data on certain artist, in particular, dates of birth or death which until now were not known.

TIME LIMITS

The sculptors whose career, started in the nineteenth century, and continued between the two wars, indeed beyond, are fairly numerous. The arbitrary but indispensable limits imposed on this book, do not allow us to approach this second part of their activity. In principal, to the extent it is possible to date the works those which had been made before the end of the first World War are indexed. On the other hand, bronzes drawn from these works are mentioned whatever the date of their casting. An example is Rodin's bronze, cast recently from an original plaster for the Rodin Museum; it is still a Rodin.

LISTS OF WORKS

The list of bronzes indexed for each artist does not pretend to be exhaustive. As we have specified, the numbered drawings became common only in the twentieth century without putting an end to the unlimited editions. In addition, it cannot be forgotten that the work of an artist enters into the public domain fifty years (to which we add the years of the war) after his death. Furthermore, several times after the death of a sculptor, a number of works, including models in plaster or bronze and also some molds, were put up for sale along with their right of reproduction, thus favoring the proliferation of castings in bronze. Under these conditions, no control was possible as far as the number of works cast in bronze.

TITLES OF WORKS

With the titles of some works, we enter the domain of the greatest fantasy. The same work is often called different names by the author himself in the course of successive exhibitions, then by the founder-editor, without counting the names given by the museums, the appraisers and experts, the gallery directors and the art historians. If one takes as an example a sculpture of an animal, it is not unusual for a group entitled Panther Attacking a Deer (which can also become Deer Attacked by a Panther) to become A Springing Tiger (or Lion) in Struggle. Tigers, jaguars, panthers, lions are easily confused as are crocodiles or alligators as well as camels and dromedaries. To the degree possible, we have tried to unify the titles or indicate the connection between one and the other.

DIMENSIONS

The numbers mentioned without other data always indicate height. L. means width. 30 x 70 cm reads 30 centimeters of height by 70 centimeters width.

As with the titles, the measurments of sculptures are very imprecise. It is indeed not unusual for differences of many centimeters to appear in the description of works clearly part of the same edition.

EDITIONS

In the catalogs published by the founder/editors (Barbedienne, Susse, Hébrard, Siot-Decauville, Thiébaut Valsuani, etc.), a number of subjects were proposed in many dimensions. It is clear that some of the castings had not been made in all the sizes indicated. In effect, most of the time, each work was executed on demand.

SALONS

The word Salon (exposition), unless otherwise indicated has for a long time applied only to the official exposition under the direction of the Société des Artistes Français since 1881. The other salons are indicated by their complete name. The Salon de la Société Nationale des Beaux-Arts is often designated, in summary, by the Nationale des Beaux-Arts.

MUSEUMS

With some exceptions, the museums identified are those in France. They are listed in alphabetical order by city (if a particular name is not given, they are the municipal museum of fine arts). The bronze works that a museum owns are indexed singly, mentioned here by purely suggestive title, in function from information that we have been able to find in the catalogs or which we had been furnished by the curator's office. The bronzes, as with all of the nineteenth century sculpture, were disregarded for a long time. A number of them are still languishing in the storerooms. Certain museum catalogs, when they exist, show up from the nineteenth century and the inventories have not all been restored to this day. The recent catalogs are still very rare, It is necessary in the first place to mention those catalogs of the collections of sculptures from the museum d'Orsay, published from its opening in December 1986. In the North—Pas-de-Calais, a methodical inventory of all the nineteenth century sculptures including the bronzes, preserved in the region's museums, was recently published in the catalog of the exposition "From Carpeaux to Matisse" in 1982. It will be necessary to wait for the achievement (anticipated in other regions) of such an initiative in order to have a more complete idea of the heritage of the bronzes from the nineteenth century in the public French collections.

PUBLIC SALES

Under this title we give a selection of bronzes presented in the bidding sales, in France and the principal places outside of France during the last few years. When similar works are sold frequently, only the most recent sales are noted. The designations and information about the works are taken from the sales catalogs. After the title, some important bids are mentioned in parentheses.

DICTIONARY OF
SCULPTORS

*Eugéne Aizelin,
Femme drapée
à l'antique
(Barbedienne).*

*Eugène Aizelin,
Le Jeune Pâtre,
87 cm.*

36

AIGON, ANTONIN

Montpellier, 1837
Paris, 1885

A sculptor of animal figures, Aigon exhibited at the Salon from 1867 to 1878. Of note among his bronzes are *Nature morte*, a silvered panel (1868), *Le Coup double, canards blessés* (1877), and *Chat sauvage et faisan* (1878).

MUSEUMS
Le Mans
Judith, statuette.
Montpellier
Chat sauvage et faisan, 50 cm.

AIRE, PAUL D'

Some of the bronzes by this sculptor, whose work seems to have bridged two periods, are well known, including *Le Faucheur*, 45 cm, *Femme âgée*, 21 cm, and *Cyrano de Bergerac*, in bronze and in ivory, 27 cm. An example of this last work was put on sale at the Drouot Hotel on June 15, 1981, room 4.

AIZELIN, EUGÈNE

Paris, July 10, 1821
Paris, 1902

A student of Ramey and of Dumont at the Ecole des Beaux-Arts in 1844, Aizelin made his debut at the Salon of 1852 with a plaster work entitled *Sapho*, which he exhibited in bronze the next year. It was displayed regularly at the Salon until 1897 and again at the Exposition Universelle of 1900, along with some biblical and mythological subjects, genre scenes, people from the opera, effigies of saints, etc. Among these large statues and groups were some works executed for the Parisian churches of the Trinity and Saint-Roch, for the Châtelet Theater, the Opéra, the Hôtel de Ville, and the Louvre. The following bronze statuettes were sent to the Salon: *Vestale* (1891), *Esclave* (1896), *Suzanne* (1897), as well as others in marble: *Hébé* (1865), *l'Enfant et sablier* and *Merveilleuse en tenue de bal* (1866).

Ferdinand Barbedienne was the editor for a great number of this sculptor's works in bronze. For the most part, they are offered in many sizes:

Amazone vaincue, 112, 74, 46, 37 cm.
Bergers d'Arcadie, 105, 62, 53, 42, 30 cm.
Buste de Jeune Fille, 32, 28, 22 cm.
Buste de Jeune Fille Renaissance, 56, 44, 34, 29 cm.
Buste de jeune fille Louis XVI, 24 cm.
Buste de jeune fille aux liserons, 50, 28, 24 cm.
Buste de la duchesse d'Etampes, 68, 40, 34 cm.
Buste de femme Louis XVI (with rose), 33, 26 cm.
Buste de Mignon, 56 cm.

L'Enfance de Tacite, 104, 64, 52, 42, 32 cm.
Hébé (after the marble of 1865), 60, 50, 40 cm.
Marguerite, 85, 69, 51 cm.
Mignon, 80, 67, 54, 40, 34 cm.
Orphée, 85, 54 cm.
Pandore debout (after the marble of 1864), 60, 50, 40 cm.
Pandore assise, 135, 90, 70, 53, 45, 33, 27 cm.
Psyché, 129, 86, 76, 51, 43, 31, 25 cm.
Vierge, 34, 28, 22 cm.

Other statuettes in bronze without an identified founder:

Brodeuse, 45 cm.
Glaneuse, 84 and 70 cm.
Jeune Berger et son chien, 40 cm.
Jeune Faucheur, 61 cm.
Jeune Femme assise à la cruche, 75 cm.
Jeune Femme au panier fleuri, 65 cm (founder, E. Colin)
Merveilleuse en tenue de bal and *Merveilleuse en tenue de ville*, a pair of statues
Nyssia au bain, 94 cm (Gautier edition)

MUSEUMS
Narbonne
La Sortie de l'église, bust, 37.5 cm (Salon of 1875).

SALES
Berger, Bergère, two statuettes (1878), Drouot,
  December 18, 1985, room 11.
Bergers d'Arcadie, 53 cm (Barbedienne), Drouot, May
  24, 1986, room 6.
Femme drapée à l'antique (Barbedienne), Christie's
  London, May 15, 1986; Beaune, October 19,
  1986.
Le Jeune Pâtre, 87 cm, Clermont-Ferrand, April 24,
  1986.
Mignon, 80 cm (Barbedienne), Sotheby London,
  November 7, 1985.
Nymphe de Diane, 77 cm (Barbedienne), Drouot,
  December 9, 1982, room 8; Sotheby London,
  March 20, 1986.
Le Penseur, Lyon, April 24, 1985.
Suzanne au bain, 64 cm (Barbedienne), Drouot, June
  16, 1983, room 10.

ALAPHILIPPE, CAMILLE
Tours August 13, 1874—?

After having frequented the studio of Barrias,
he won the grand prize in Rome in 1898, and
exhibited a pewter medallion with the portrait of a
child the same year at the Salon. He continued to
participate at the Salon with works such as *Lanceur
d'épervier*, a plaster statue (1903), *La Femme au
singe*, made in sandstone and bronze, 175 cm
(Petit Palais), and *Le Premier Miroir*, plaster (1908).
Other exhibited works include *L'Amour pélerin*, a
statue in plaster (1911), some works in sandstone,
and two statuettes in plaster entitled *L'Amour à
l'arc* and *Bacchante* (1913). A dancing figure, his
last contribution, appeared in 1914. His work
appeared again in 1935, when the bronze *Danseuse
aux thyrses*, 103 cm high, went on sale to the
public. Alaphilippe worked for different towns in
Algeria and Tunisia and was married in 1906 in
Dusseldorf. It is unknown, however, when he died.
A bronze entitled *Les Mains*, 51 cm, is found at the
museum of Alger.

ALBERT-LEFEUVRE, LOUIS ÉTIENNE
1845
August 11, 1924

There is very little information available about
this artist, though he is known to have studied
under Dumont and Falguière. He exhibited at the
Salon from 1875 to 1908 with such works as
Jeanne d'Arc, a statue in plaster (1875), *Pour la
patrie* (plaster in 1881, marble in 1890), *Frère et
Soeur*, a group in stone, (1888), *La Muse des bois*,
(plaster in 1892, marble in 1893), *La Chanson des
blés*, statuette in marble (1902), and finally two
statuettes: *L'Adolescence* in 1903 and *La Muse des
bois* in 1904.
   The Siot-Decauville foundry produced bronze
editions of *La Muse des bois*, 77 cm, and *Fondeur
du Moyen Age*, a vase carried by two men, 47 x 44
cm. *L'Adolescence*, 62 cm, was cast by H. Blanchet.
Other works are *Faneuse*, 47 cm, and *La Causerie*
or *Mère et enfant*, 62 cm.
   La Muse des bois, 77 cm, was sold in Avignon
on February 26, 1984.

ALDEBERT, ÉMILE
Born in Millau

Aldebert studied at the drawing school of
Marseille under the direction of the painter Loubon.
He established himself in that town and worked on
the decoration of the court house and the police
station; in 1874 became a teacher at the local
school of fine arts. Between 1868 and 1886, he
exhibited at the Salon de Paris, submitting such
works such as *Pêcheur à la ligne*, plaster (1874),
Tentation, a statuette in marble (1875), *Le Bateleur*,
plaster (1883), *Les Deux Amis*, plaster (1886), and
La Vocation (1891) and *Au bord de l'eau* (1911), two
statuettes in plaster. He is noted among living
artists until 1932. The museum of Marseille owns
the bronze *Pêcheur à la ligne*, 130 cm, cast from the
plaster of 1874.

ALLAR, ANDRÉ JOSEPH
Toulon, August 22, 1845
Toulon, August 6, 1926

André Joseph Allar won the grand prize of
Rome in 1869 after having studied under Guillaume
and Cavelier. He was the winner of numerous other
distinctions, and became a member of the Institut
in 1905. He exhibited regularly at the Salon from
1873 until 1914. Among his works are *Enfant des
Abruzzes*, a statue in bronze executed in Rome,
and *Hécube et Polydor*, bas-relief in plaster (1873),
La Tentation, a group in marble (1876), *L'Université*,
a group in marble for the Sorbonne (1890), *Jeanne
d'Arc*, marble for the basilica of Domrémy (1891),
Isis se dévoilant, a statue in marble (1901),
L'Architecture, a statue in bronze (1912), etc. A
statue of *L'Elouence* was displayed at the Church
of the Sorbonne. Allar also worked on the courthouse, the Opéra-Comique, the anatomy gallery at
the Jardin des Plantes, and the Grand Palais (a
group of plastic arts).
   Jeanne d'Arc à Domrémy, 60, 46 and 16 cm,
and a reduction of *L'Enfant des Abruzzes* were cast
by Thiébaut; a statuette entitled *La Science* was
cast by by Susse.

MUSEUMS
Marseille
Hécube et Polydor, after the base-relief from the Salon
  of 1873.
Paris, Orsay
Enfant des Abruzzes, 130 cm, cast by C. Matifat.

ALLIOT, LUCIEN
Paris, November 16, 1877
March 9, 1967

A student of Barrias and Coutan, Lucien Alliot
exhibited at the Salon from 1896 until the 1930s,
with works including *Violoncelliste*, plaster (1905),
Le Cantique, a statuette in plaster (1908), *Maternité*,
a group in marble, and five small bronzes: *Age des
roses, Bonne Vieille, Part à deux, Enfant au capuchon
et Rêverie* (1910). He also contributed *L'Echo de la
mer*, a sandstone fountain (1912). A number of
these works date from between the two world wars.

Louis Étienne Albert-Lefeuvre,
Muse des bois, 77 cm
(Siot-Decauville).

Lucien Alliot, *Don Quichotte et Sancho*,
silvered bronze and ivory,
25 x 53 cm.

SALES

Diane chasseresse, 79 cm, Sotheby London, June 7, 1984; Madrid, May 23, 1985.

Don Quichotte et Sancho Pança, silvered bronze and ivory, 25 x 53 cm, Lille, January 27, 1986.

Femme au cerceau, 31 cm, Drouot, February 8, 1983, room 2.

Jeune Femme accroupie, 58 cm L., Drouot, September 24, 1985, room 1.

Jeune Fille à l'écharpe, symmetrical, 43 cm, Madrid, October 25, 1983.

Nu allongé, 31 x 78 cm, Christie's New York, October 1, 1983.

Pierrot, gilded bronze, 16 cm, Drouot, December 2, 1983.

ALLOUARD, HENRI ÉMILE

Paris, July 11, 1849
August 12, 1929

From 1865 until 1928, Allouard exhibited paintings and sculpture, including a number of busts in plaster, marble and bronze, at the Salon. Among the bronzes were *Marguerite*, silvered and gilded bronze (1880), *Femme Foulah* (Guinea), in bronze ornamented with jewelry (1904), and *Le Cardinal de Richelieu* (1912). Other objects that were exhibited are *Molière mourant*, a marble statue (1885), *Souviens-toi*, a group in plaster (1886), *Lutinerie*, a group in marble (1888), *Héloïse au paraclet*, a statuette in stone, marble and ivory (1896), *Une Source* and *Pater Noster*, two statues in marble (1899), *Richelieu à La Rochelle*, a large statue in

bronze, 220 cm (1905), *La Sieste*, a statuette in ivory, marble and bronze (1907), *Le Gué*, a statuette in bronze, marble and ivory (1909). *Réprimande*, a group in bronze, marble and ivory (1912), *La Cruche cassée*, a statuette in ivory, marble and stone.

Many of Allouard's works have been produced in porcelain by the Sèvres factory, and in bronze by the following founders:

Barbedienne: *Artilleur*, 45 cm, *Marin*, 43 cm, *Soldat colonial*, 45 cm, *La Sieste*, 35 cm.

Siot-Decauville: *Pater Noster*.

Susse: *Porte-Drapeau équestre*, 80 cm, *La Source*, 49 cm.

Thiébaut: *Loin du monde*, 73 adn 29 cm.

MUSEUMS
Marseille
Femme Foulah, 57 cm.

SALES

Pierrot intimidé, 39.5 cm, Drouot, November 28, 1985, rooms 5 and 6.

Maquette de fontaine, metal and terra cotta, 32 cm (1881), reserved at the White House in Washington,

Drouot, March 10, 1986, room 16.

AMANN, LÉOPOLD LOUIS

Paris, December 17, 1848
Epinal, March 29, 1908

The Epinal Museum possesses a bronze medallion dated 1902, 19 cm in diameter, which symbolizes *La Moselle*; it is signed by this artist, who is described as a painter, sculptor, and decorator.

AMY, JEAN BARNABÉ

Tarascon, June 11, 1839
Tarascon, March 1907

In 1874, in collaboration with his colleague Boisseau, Jean Barnabé Amy made a work entitled *Figaro* in bronze, three meters high, for the headquarters of the newspaper of the same name. He is also the creator of a number of masks, busts, and statues of historic and contemporary personnages. At the Salon of 1883, he exhibited a relief in bronze entitled *La Tarasque,* and at the Salon of 1896, a small version of his *Tambour d'Arcole* in bronze (the earlier version had been unveiled the preceding year at Cadenet). Some small bronzes by Amy sometimes appear on the market, such as a group representing two children fighting over a drum, or *L'Homme prisonnier de l'Amour.*

MUSEUMS
Aix-en-Provence
Frédéric Mistral, medallion.

Avignon
Buste de Marc Bonnefoy, 63 cm (1870).
Montpellier
Tête de chien, 65 cm.

SALES
Deux Enfants jouent du tambour, 77 cm (1876),
    Drouot, November 28, 1986, room 14.

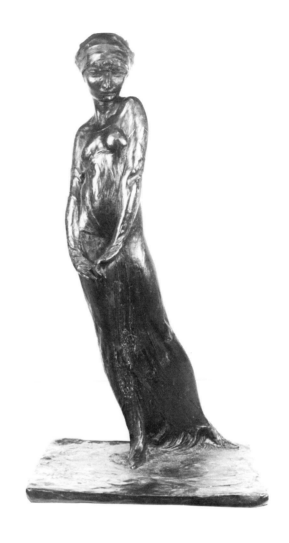

Libero Andreotti, Jeune Femme,
55 cm (Hébard).

Jean Barnabé Amy,
Deux Enfants jouant avec un tambour,
77 cm (1876).

ANDREOTTI, LIBERO

1877
Florence, 1933

Of Italian nationality, Andreotti worked alternatively in Paris and in Milan until 1914 before returning to Florence. He exhibited some bronzes at the Salon d'Automne in 1910-1911 and exhibited at the Salon de la Société Nationale des Beaux-Arts between 1909 and 1913. His work was influenced by Donatello, Ghiberti and other Florentines from the Renaissance, whom he admired greatly. One bronze by this artist, *Jeune Femme,* 55 cm (Hébrard cast), was sold at Saint-Germain-en-Laye on June 5, 1983.

ANFRIE, CHARLES

Born in 1833

C. Anfrie

Though there is little available information about this artist's life, an important piece in bronze and his composition merit attention. Charles Anfrie exhibited at the Salon between 1883 and 1895. His work includes French military subjects and figures of young women and children, as well as medals chiseled with a great deal of minute detail. Among his military subjects are some small casts in bronze: *Les Dernières Cartouches, Le Porte-Drapeau, Fusilier marin, Estafette* (a plaster exhibited at the Salon of 1888), *Cuirassier soutenant un soldat blessé, Zouave*, etc. His works portraying young women include *Le Premier Prix* and *La Clé des champs*; and his portrayals of children include *Le Lance-Pierres, Enfant à la toupie, Le Petit Furneur, Un accident*, etc. Other statuettes in bronze that appeared in sales at the beginning of the century are *Gymnase, Le Gymnasiarque, Promenade*.

SALES

Les Dernières Cartouches, 68 cm, Avignon, February 25, 1978.
Nymphe debout, 44 cm, Sotheby London, November 10, 1983.
Paysanne appuyée à un tronc d'arbre, 63.5 cm, Sotheby London, June 23, 1983.
Zouave, 47 cm, Le Havre, December 5, 1983; Orléans, December 22, 1984.

Charles Anfrie,
Le Zouave,
47 cm.

Charles Anfrie,
Chapitaine de chasseur,
25.5 cm (1886).

Charles Anfrie,
Les Dernières Cartouches,
68 cm.

ARNOLD, HENRY

Paris, 1879
Paris, 1945

A painter and sculptor, Henry Arnold was a member of the 'band of Schnegg', the group of Rodin's practicioners. Through his quest for pure and unadorned forms, he quickly attempted to distinguish himself from the famous sculptor. Moreover, he was very active in the social sphere to help other sculptors and artists. He exhibited at the Société Nationale des Beaux-Arts in 1906, and between the two wars at the Salon des Tuileries and the Salon d'Automne. He is known for a number of busts and some female figures.

MUSEUMS
Blois
Femme à sa toilette, 38 cm (1900; H. Gonon, caster).

SALES
Femme assise, 39 cm (1911), Drouot, December 4, 1981.
La Paix, 62 cm (1929; Susse), Drouot, March 28, 1985.

ARSON, ALPHONSE ALEXANDRE

Paris, January 11, 1822
1880

ARSON

A sculptor of animals, Arson exhibited at the Salon between 1859 and 1880. He left a number of genre scene groups, some of which are humorous, but his works most often portray animals, particularly wild or domestic birds. Among the works shown at the Salon are *Pule et poussins, Coqs combattant*, bronze (1859), *Groupe de faisans*, wax (1863), *Faisan et ses petits*, bronze (1864), *Perdrix et sa couvée surprise par une belette* (wax, 1865), *Perdrix* (wax, 1870), *Faisans et leurs petits* (silvered bronze, 1870), *Dispute de perdrix* (silvered bronze, 1874), *Coq et poule de prairie* (bronze, 1877), *Famille de faisans surprise par des oiseaux de proie* (bronze medallion, 1877), etc. A certain number of Arson's works were made into editions in bronze. In addition to some recent works sold at public sales, notable pieces include *Coq*, 15 cm, *Grenouille chevauchant un lapin*, 8 cm, *Le Martin-Pêcheur*, 24 cm, *Oiseau aquatique*, 24 cm, *Oiseau sur un coquillage*, 24 cm, *Les Deux Oiseaux au nid*, 20 cm.

SALES
Chien avec perroquet, 52 cm, Sotheby London, November 25, 1982.
Faisan, 47 cm, Sotheby London, November 8, 1984.
Le Lièvre, gilded bronze, 8 cm, Drouot, December 7, 1983, room 14.
Œuf frais, poule et poussin portant un panier, 16 cm, Drouot, December 7, 1983; Angers, April 16, 1986.
Souris jouant au golf, 10 cm, Sotheby London, March 8, 1984.

ARTHEZ, PHILIPPE D'

Born in Paris

A student of Frémiet, Arthez is known for a bronze bust portraying the painter Grandsire (1907). An edition of this piece, cast by Rudier, 55 cm, is owned by the museum of Clermont-Ferrand.

ASCOLI, JOSEPH

Epernay, January 25, 1847
February 17, 1929

This student of Chapu is mentioned at the Salon from 1890 to 1909, noted for statuettes in plaster such as *Petit Pêcheur ardennais* (1890), *Clytie* (1896), *Gringoire* (1898), *Auto-portrait* (1901), and *Mon père et La Nuit semeuse d'étoiles* (1907), as well as the bronze statue *Pelotari basque* (1905), some bronze plaques including *Rêverie* (1902), and bust and medallion portraits, some of which are in bronze. His *Gringoire*, 62 cm, was cast by Susse in bronze and in pewter.

ASTANIÈRES EUGÈNE NICOLAS, COUNT OF CLÉMEN

Paris, March 3, 1841
Cap-Breton, January 30, 1918

This military officer from the School of Saint-Cyr was wounded and imprisoned in 1870, but upon returning to France he nonetheless continued his military career for some time. Eventually, however, his wounds caused him to give up the military, and he devoted himself to sculpture, to which he had been introduced when he was very young. He studied with Falguière and was, like his teacher, very academic. He exhibited regularly and successfully at the Salon of Paris between 1878 and 1907, at the Expositions Universelles of 1889 and 1900, and in different foreign towns. The state comissioned many works by him. In 1897, he set up shop at Cap-Breton, in the Landes, where he built a house and a studio which he called 'The Wreckage' and 'The Prairie', respectively. A number of his works were inspired by the sea, especially by fishing. Works noted at the Salon include *La Régénération* and *Cheval de chasse*, two bronzes (1878), *Bouboule*, the head of a dog in bronze (1879), *L'Espiègle*, a statue in marble, and *Martin*, a young fisherman at the line, in bronze (1886), *L'Enfant à la vague*, marble (also seen in one bronze and two plaster versions), *Pêcheur à la ligne*, a statuette in marble, *Pêcheur à l'épervier*, a statuette in bronze (1889). *Un coup manqué*, a statuette in marble (1892), two statuettes in marble entitled *Jongleur* (1897) and *Un moine* (1898), and a statue in bronze entitled *Acrobate* (1899), etc. Of further note are *La Cuisson des crevettes, Mousse à Cap-Breton*, and *Jeune Pêcheur*.

Le *Pêcheur à la ligne* was cast in bronze by Susse in three dimensions, 77, 62 and 52 cm.

ASTE, JOSEPH D'

Born in Naples

Joseph D'Aste came to Paris around 1900, and exhibited at the Salon beginning in the year 1905. He produced a number of groups and statuettes of children, especially representing some popular and rural scenes, studies of animals, and busts. At the Salon some groups in plaster are of particular note: *Fillette aux dindons* (1905), *Au bord du lac* (1906), and *Jeune Faune jouant* (1913). Some statu-

Joseph d'Asté, Dehors ou Jeunes Hollandais dans la neige,
gilded bronze and marble, 27 x 41 cm.

ettes in marble also appeared there, including *Le Retour du bois* (1907) and *Danseuse* (1908), as did a statuette in bronz entitled *Le Dimanche des Rameaux en Bretagne*, cast by Montagutelli. Some other works cast in bronze are *La Porteuse de bois, La Petite Fleuriste, Chant des moissonneuses,* and *Première Caresse* (cast by A. Goldscheider), as well as *Berger et bergère avec leurs moutons*, a group in gilded bronze, 60 cm L.

SALES
Jeune Bergère et ses quatre moutons, 30 x 40 cm, Drouot, March 1, 1985, room 7.
Jeunes Faunes et bouc, 39 cm L., Drouot, December 6, 1984, room 5.
Cinq Jeunes Hollandais or *Dehors*, gilded bronze, 27 x 41 cm, Drouot, March 16, 1983.
Mère et ses quatre enfants sur un tronc d'arbre, 33 cm, Sotheby London, November 6, 1986.
Satyre et chèvre, 39.5 cm, Christie's New York, May 15, 1984.

ASTRUC, ZACHARIE

Angers, February 8, 1835
Paris, May 24, 1907

Originally a writer, journalist, and art critic, Zacharie Astruc founded a journal entitled *Le Salon* in 1863, and published several works. He also practiced painting and sculpture. He went to Spain and brought back with him a print of the painting by Alonso Cano, *Saint François d'Assise* which would be reproduced in bronze by the Christofle house. He participated in the Salon from 1869 to 1906 and in 1883 he exhibited there his best-known work, *Le Marchand de masques*, which can be seen in the Luxemburg gardens. The pedestal of this 2-meter bronze statue shows the masks of Corot, Alexandre Dumas' son, Berlioz, Carpeaux, J.-B. Faure, Delacroix, Balzac, Barbey d'Aurevilly, Gambetta, Gounod, and Victor Hugo. Among the works Astruc sent to the Salon are several busts in bronze, including those of Barbey d'Aurevilly (1876), Edouard Manet (1881), and Carmen (1892), a bas-relief in bronze entitled *L'Aurore* made for the School of Saint-Cyr (1878), and a statue in bronze entitled *Le Roi Midas*, made for a square in Nice (1888).

MUSEUMS
Angers
Buste d'Isabelle Doria, 67 cm.
Carcassonne
Buste du comte Fabre de l'Aude, 70 cm (1887).
Paris, Orsay
Buste de Barbey d'Aurevilly, 82 cm.
Saint-Sauveur-le-Vocomte
Le Marchand de masques, 94 cm (reduction of the statue from the Luxembourg gardens).

AUBÉ, JEAN-PAUL

Longwy, July 3, 1837
Cap-Breton, August 23, 1916

Aubé made his debut at the Salon of 1861, after having studied statuary at the Ecole des Beaux-Arts with Duret and Dantan Sr., and decorative sculpture in Italy. His first exhibited work, a bust of Merimée, was bought by the Institute. He also participated at the Salon of the Société Nationale des Beaux-Arts from 1891 to 1914. His work includes a number of busts, some decorative vases, and some statues. He also made many monuments, including that of Gambetta (placed recently at the Carousel in Paris) and the bronze statue of Dante in front of the preparatory school of France. He exhibited at the Salon most notably with a group in bronze entitled *La Sirène* (1875), the marble statues *Galatée* (1880) and *L'Agriculture* (1881), the plaster statuettes *Le Corail* and *Bailly* (1883), a plaster group representing *François Boucher* (1888), and a bronze study entitled *Tête d'enfant* (1889). The portrait of François Boucher appeared again at the Société Nationale des Beaux-Arts in 1891, this time in marble. Aubé also sculpted a statue in bronze of Colbert (1895) for the Gobelins, and many busts, among them *Colbert* (1894). A statuette in marble of *L'Agriculture*, 115 cm, was presented at the Exposition Nationale des Beaux-Arts in 1883.

Aubé, who worked for the Rose Palace of Count Boni of Castellane, made a number of decorative objects, such as vases and some dishes decorated with motifs in relief. He provided models to the Sèvres factory and to the Haviland factory in Paris.

Bronze castings have been found of *La Brise* and *La Force et l'endurance*, small plaques by Aubé, and of the statuettes *Dante Alighieri*, 42 cm, *Etienne Marcel à cheval*, 60 cm (E. Jullien, founder), *François Boucher*, 48 cm, *Flore* or *L'Espoir*, 6.5 cm, and *La Peinture*, 6.5 cm. The Thiébaut house cast *Dante*, 84, 62, 45, 22 cm, and *Shakespeare*, 82 cm.

MUSEUMS
Dijon
Buste du préfect Gaston Joliet, 42 cm.
Nancy
François Boucher, 48 cm.
Paris, Orsay
Buste de la comtesse Hallez, 50 cm.
Buste d'Henry Kistemaeckers, 52.5 cm.

SALES
La Peinture, 63 cm, Drouot, June 27, 1983, room 5.

AUBERT, ANTOINE PIERRE

Lyon, January 26, 1853
October 18, 1912

Son of the Lyon sculptor Jean-Antoine Aubert, Antoine Aubert studied at the school of fine arts in his hometown, where he became a teacher, and then in Paris with Dumont and Bonnassieux. He specialized in sculpting portraits in the bust format. He first exhibited in Lyons in 1876, then participated at the Salon de Paris from 1879 to 1911. He also made some bas-reliefs and some medallions in terra cotta, some of which were cast in bronze. Among his works exhibited at the Salon are *La Musique*, cast in plaster (1882), *La Folie de Marguerite*, in bronze (1883), *Mimi*, a medallion in plaster (1888), etc. The bronze statuette *Philosophe grec*, 37 cm high, is also noteworthy.

AUBERT, JEAN ANTOINE

Digne, April 4, 1822
Lyon, December 11, 1883

This sculptor worked primarily on the decoration or restoration of buildings in the Lyon region, especially the churches and the chapel of the Hôtel-Dieu of Lyon. He also sculpted a certain number of figurines representing young children.

AUVRAY, LOUIS

Valenciennes, April 7, 1810
Paris, 1890

In his simultaneous career as a writer, this sculptor founded the *Revue artistique et littéraire* (Artistic and Literary Review) and finished the *Dictionnaire des artistes français* (Dictionary of French Artists) that had been started by Bellier de la Chavignerie. He had begun hos studies in sculpture in 1830 at the Ecole des Beaux-Arts, in the studio of David d'Angers. He worked on different monuments in Paris and in Valencienne. His work includes a number of busts and medallion portraits, several of which are at the museum of Valenciennes. The bronze medallions that Auvray sent to the Salon include *Portrait d'homme*, *Portrait de femme* (1852), *Monsieur Auvray père* (1874), *H. Catenucci, dessinateur* (1879), and *Portrait de femme* (1882); he also sent some busts, including *L'Abbé de l'Epée*, marble (1853), from which was cast a smaller bronze, *Solon*, a bronze study of a head (1876), and *A. Dubois, architecte* (1876).

MUSEUMS
Lille
Buste de Solon, 49 cm (H. Molz, caster)
Valenciennes
Profil féminin, medallion, 16.5 cm diam., marked
  Munich, 1844. (Eck and Durand, founders).

BAFFIER, JEAN-EUGÈNE

Neuvy-le-Barrois (Cher), November 18, 1851
Paris, April 19, 1920

Jean-Eugène Baffier was still very young when a visit to the cathedral of Nevers determined his vocation. After having studied at the school of fine arts in Nevers, then at the Ecole Nationale des Arts Décorative in Paris, he participated at various salons with busts, statues, and groups—historic figures or typical peasant scenes—in terra cotta or bronze. Two of his monumental works can be seen at Bourges: *L'Homme-taureau*, a bronze dedicated to the glory of the fighters of 1870, and *Louis XI assis*. In Paris, his monument to Michel Servet (1900) and a bust of the Republic (1886) are found at Ferdinand-Brunot Square.

A number of bronzes by Baffier were exhibited at the Salon des Artistes Français, inlcuding the statue of Marat (1885), the busts of his mother (1886) and his father (1887), of Louis XI (1887), etc.; at the Salon de la Nationale des Beaux-Arts were shown *Moissonneur berrichon*, *Le Paradis de la terre*, *Compagnon niverhais* (1890) and *Jardinier arrosant* (1893), as well as an ensemble of Art Nouveau-style decorative objects. These objects had been produced alternately in bronze and in pewter by the Siot-Decauville foundry. They include flat candlesticks, pitchers, goblets, salt cellars, sugar bowls, etc.

Some notable bronze sketches by Baffier are *A la régalade* (man drinking), *Paysan et sa femme nourrissant un veau*, bas relief, 41 x 28 cm, and *Le Vieux Paysan blessé*, 50 cm.

MUSEUMS
Bourges
L'Epine or *Femme soignant son mari*, bas-relief.
P'tit Jean le greffeux (1886).
Châteauroux
P'tit Jean le greffeux, 48 cm.
Le Maître sonneur, 86 cm.
Paris, Orsay
Buste of M. Baffier père, 57 cm (Salon of 1887).
Buste de Mme Baffier mère, 55 cm (Salon of 1886).

The museum of Nevers also has some works by this artist.

SALES
Louis XI, 55 cm, Drouot, April 30, 1984, room 5.

BAILLEUL, JEAN

Lille, July 18, 1878
March 14, 1949

Bailleul began to exhibit at the Salon in 1902 after having worked in the studios of Barrias and of Coutan. His first consignment, a statue in plaster, represented the former secretary of Verlaine, known by the nickname *Maître Bibi-la-purée, etudiant de quarante-cinquième année!* Also of note are *Les Terrassiers*, agroup in bronze (1904), *Joie maternelle*, a bust in bronze (1905), *Après le grisou*, a group in plaster, and *Glaneuse au repos*, a statuette in marble (1910), *Le Carrier*, a statue in stone (1912).

MUSEUMS
Amiens
Terrassiers se rendant à leurs travail, 40 x 45 cm.
Narbonne
Maître Bibi-la-Purée, 47.5 cm.

BAILLY, CHARLES ÉLOY

Reménoville (Meurthe), January 7, 1830
Paris, August 6, 1895

Entering the Ecole des Beaux-Arts in 1855, Bailly exhibited for the first time at the Salon in 1863 with a plaster work entitled *Saint-Sébastien*, later exhibiting *La Besace*, plaster (1867), *Porteuse d'amphores*, plaster (1869), and a statue of the town of Brest for the Hôtel de Ville of Paris (1880), a statue of Voltaire in plaster (1895), a statue in plaster entitled *Diogène*, and *L'Abbé Grégoire*, statue in bronze for Lunéville. Also of note are the statuette *Jeanne d'Arc* in bronze and ivory, with a height of about 20 cm, and *Eve à la fontaine*, a work cast by Barbedienne in two sizes, 35 and 17 cm.

BARALIS, LOUIS

Toulon, July 7, 1862
1940

The museum of Toulon has some plaster casts by this artist who, after having studied with Barrias and Cavelier, debuted at the Salon in 1888 with a statue in marble, *Philoctète*. Next came some works in plaster—groups including *Un sauvetage* (1894), *Bacchanale* (1907, exhibited in bronze in 1909) *Nageuses* (1913), and *L'Amour capturé* (1914), and the statuettes *Danseuse* (1906), *Chasseur d'aigles* (1908), and *Léda* (1910). An allegorical bas-relief by Baralis, *La Mécanique*, decorates the facade of the Lyon station. Finally, a statuette in bronze entitled *Le Voleur de nids*, 80 cm, appeared in the catalog of the Siot-Decauville foundry.

BAREAU, GEORGES MARIE VALENTIN

Paimboeuf, April 11, 1866
Nantes, January 4, 1931

Among the works shown at the Salon of 1889 were *La Gloire*, a statuette in plaster (1892), *David chantant devant Saül*, a statuette in bronze, and *Mort de Léandre*, a statuette in plaster (1893), *Vox pacis*, a statuette in plaster, and *La Fortune*, a statuette in bronze (1894), *Pour le drapeau*, a

Georges Bareau,
Le Temps et la Sagesse, 82 cm.

group in plaster (1895), *L'Histoire*, a statuette in silver (1898), *Diane chasseresse*, a statue in marble (1899), *Le Temps et la Sagesse*, a statuette in bronze (1903), *Le Réveil de l'Humanité*, a statue in marble (1906), *Le Semeur*, a statue in bronze (1910). Georges Bareau also sculpted a group in stone entitled *L'Art asiatique* for the Grand Palais in Paris, and the *Monument à Jacques Cartier* for Saint-Malo.

The following subjects were cast by Barbedienne: *L'Appel aux armes*, 50 cm, *L'Histoire*, 60 and 25 cm, *Le Semeur*, 54 cm, *Le Travail*, 95 cm, and *Diane Chevauchant un aigle*, 84 cm.

SALES

Diane chasseresse chevauchant un aigle, 83 cm (Barbedienne), Drouot, May 11, 1982, room 4; Christie's New York, March 30, 1985.
Le Forgeron, 93 cm (Barbedienne), Cologne, June 24, 1983.
Le Temps et la Sagesse, 82 cm, Tours, November 25, 1985.

BARILLOT EUGÈNE

There is no available information on the life of this late-nineteenth-century artist, who seems to have specialized in sculpting small subjects, with meticulous attention to detail.

SALES

Cornac monté sur un éléphant, bronze paint, 32 cm, Drouot, April 4, 1984.
Jeune Femme, ivory torso, gilded bronze skirt, 33.5 cm, Sotheby Monaco, December 7, 1981.

BARON, VINCENT ALFRED

Meximieux (Ain), June 11, 1820—?

A sculptor, engraver of medallions, and an actor at the same time, he entered the Ecole des Beaux-Arts beginning in 1837 and participated at the Salon from 1849 to 1861, essentially with medallions. Two of them, both portraits of actors, belong to the Carnavalet Museum: *Rachel*, 16.1 cm diam., and *Joseph Isidore Samson, de la Comédie française*, 16.1 cm diam.

BARRAU, THÉOPHILE EUGÈNE VICTOR

Carcassonne, October 3, 1848
Paris, April 1913

Barrau frequented the schools of fine arts in Toulouse and then in Paris, where he became a student of Jouffroy and of Falguière. Busts and statues of people (some contemporary and others not) as well as some decorative works are attributed to him. He participated at the Salon from 1874 to 1912, as well as at the Expositions Universelle of 1889 and 1900. Those remaining from among the exhibited pieces are *Caprice*, a group in plaster (1878), *La Vanneuse*, plaster (1885), *Salomé*, marble (1889), *Léda*, silvered bronze (1896), *Le Sommeil de l'"Innocence*, a statue in bronze (1897), and *Bacchante et satyre*, a small group in bronze (1912).

La Vanneuse was cast in bronze by Susse in two sizes, 47 and 31 cm, and *Salomé* by Thiébaut, 77.5 cm.

The Carcassonne Museum preserves a bust in bronze of the Senator Marcou (Salon of 1896) by Barrau .

Eugène Barillot,
Cornac montésur un éléphant,
painted bronze, 32 cm.

BARRE, JEAN AUGUSTE

Paris, November 25, 1811
February 5, 1896

The chiseler Jean-Jacques Barre, sculptor and maker of medallions, was educated by his father. He worked initially for Louis-Philippe, and during the Second Empire became the appointed portraitist of Napoléon III. He completed about twenty busts in marble of the imperial family as well as the tomb for the queen Hortense at the church of Rueil. He received important commissions from the State and from the city of Paris, including a group of four children in bronze, 60 cm, symbolizing the seasons, made for the Cirque Fountain at the Champs-Elysées (1840), *La Prudence*, for the Saint-Michel Fountain (1860), *Saint Luc* for the church of Saint-Vincent-de-Paul, as well as the monumental statue in bronze of Pierre Antoine Berryer for the city of Marseille. He exhibited at the Salon from 1831 to 1886. He modeled a number of effigies as busts and standing figures, portraying famous people and actresses like Miss Mars and Hortense Schneider. Among the works attributed to him are the statuettes in bronze of Fanny Elssler, Marie Taglioni in the role of Sylphide (1837), Rachel as well as the Duke of Orléans (1842), the Count of

Jean Auguste Barre, Fanny Elssler, 43.5 cm
(1837; Richard, Eck and Durand, founders).
Fabius frères Collection, Paris.

47

Nieuwerkerque (silvered bronze, 1868), a portrait of *Mater dolorosa* (1852), some medallions in bronze with the head of Apollo (1881), and a portrait of Miss Jeanne Hoding.

The Susse foundry cast *Berryer à la tribune* in bronze, 44 and 30 cm, *L'Empereur*, 20 cm, *Napoléon 1er debout*, 25 and 15 cm, *Le Duc d'Orléans*, 47 cm, and *Marguerite de Bourgogne équestre*, 58, 35 and 18 cm.

In his thesis (*La Petite Sculpture d'édition au XIXe siècle*, 1944), C.B. Metman indicates that a number of statuettes by Barre were cast by Richard, Eck and Durand as well, in particular *Marie Taglioni*, *Fanny Essler*, and *La Reine Victoria à l'âge de dix-huit ans*, 41 cm. A casting of *Napoléon 1er debout*, 11.5 cm, which was sold in London in 1980, also had the seal of this foundry. Finally, C.B. Metman cites some other statuettes in bronze belonging to private collectors: *Madame Degove*, 35 cm (H. Gonon and his son, founders), *La duchesse de Fitz-James*, 46 cm, and *Emma Livry dans le "Papillon"*, 49 cm.

MUSEUMS

Ajaccio, Napolean Museum
L'Empereur debout, un chapeau à ses pieds, 29 cm.
Buste de la princesse Clotilde de Savoie, (Salon of 1861).
Buste du prince Napoléon Jérôme, 69 cm (Salon of 1855).

Lille
Casimir Périer, medallion, 17 cm diam.

Nice
La Bayadère Amany (1838).

Paris, Decorative Arts
L'Avocat Berryer, 30 cm (Susse).
Le Duc d'Orléans, 48 cm (Susse).
Fanny Elssler dansant la Cachuca, 47 cm.
Marie Taglioni en Sylphide, 45 cm (Richard, Eck and Durand).
La Reine Victoria, 41 cm (1837).

Paris, Carnavalet
Rachel, 42 cm (1847, formerly silver plated).

Paris, Petit Palais
Le Duc d'Orléans, 32 cm.

Valence
Rachel, statuette.

SALES

Rachel en Hermione, silvered bronze, 61 cm (1847), Sotheby London, June 9, 1983.
Marie Taglioni en Sylphide, 43 cm (1837), Sotheby London, October 29, 1981.
Reine à cheval chassant au faucon, 52 cm, Christie's London, July 17, 1984.

BARREAU, AUGUSTE MARIE

Died in 1922

Born in Paris, this sculptor is very little known except for one bronze entitled *La Jeune Fille grecque*, 43 cm, owned by the Museum of Calais—a reduction of a statue presented at the Exposition des Beaux-Arts in 1865. The preceding year he had sent a statue in plaster entitled *L'Espérance déçue* to the Salon, which has also been cast as a reduction in bronze. The museum of Clermont-Ferrand owns a copy, 15.5 cm high.

Louis Ernest Barrias,
La Renommée,
gilded bronze and ivory,
85 cm (Susse).

BARRIAS, LOUIS ERNEST

Paris, April 13, 1841
Paris, February 4, 1905

Barrias, drawn to the charm of the Renaissance, was realistic and meticulous with details (even slightly affected, according to his biographer Georges Lafenestre). He belonged to the generation of sculptors who "following the innovative or preservation masters of the Romantic period, strove to

Louis Ernest Barrias,
Jeune Fille de Bou Saada,
gilded bronze, 31 cm.

reconcile their teachings in a free and productive eclecticism." The son of a miniaturist, Barrias entered the studio of Jouffroy at the Ecole des Beaux-Arts in 1858. He won the second prize of Rome in 1861 with a bas relief entitled *Chryssis rendu à son père par Ulysse*, and four years later won the first prize on the theme *La Fondation de Marseille*. His first appearance at the Salon was in 1861. In 1870, he exhibited his *Fileuse de Mégare*, a marble that he brought back from his visit to Rome. Displaying a great deal of activity, he was soon entrusted with a number of commissions for commemorative or funereal monuments, busts, statues, and groups, not only for the mother country but for the colonies as well. The bearer of a number of medals and distinctions, Barrias became a member of the Institut and succeeded Cavelier as a professor at the Ecole des Beaux-Arts.

Among Barrias's most important monumental works, is it worthwhile to mention *Le Serment de Spartacus* (Salon of 1872), today in the Tuileries gardens, the monument of the *Défense de Paris* in Courbevoie (Barrias had fought during the siege of 1870, in the mobile batallion of the Marne), the emotional group *Premières Funérailles*, 220 cm (1883), acquired by the Petit Palais museum, the gigantic monument to Victor Hugo, 11 meters high (1902), built for the plaza of the same name in Paris (today destroyed), and the tomb of the duchess of Alençon in the royal chapel of Dreux (1904). In addition, he sculpted a number of statutes in bas relief for diverse monuments: the Opéra, the Louvre, the church of the Sorbonne, and the Hôtel de Villes of Paris, Poitiers, and Neuilly. The group *La Défense de Paris*, 4 meters high, was completed after Barrias won a competition against various sculptors, among them Rodin and Gustave Doré; the commision was unveiled in 1883, and was returned to its original site in the middle of the buildings in the new quarter of the Défense, in 1983.

From 1865 to 1904, Barrias exhibited regularly at the Salon. A number of his works were later made successfully into editions, namely: *Le Printemps*, a statuette in marble for the Païva Hotel on the Champs-Elysées (1865), *La Fortune et l'Amour* and *Italienne et enfant*, two small groups in bronze (1872), *Bernard Palissy*, a statue in bronze (1881), *Mozart enfant*, in bronze (1887), *Jeune Fille de Bou-Saada*, bronze for the tomb of the painter Guillaumet at the Montmartre cemetery (1890), *Bacchante courant*, a statuette in silver (1891), *Jeanne d'Arc prisonnière*, in marble for Bonsecours near Rouen (1892), *La Nature mystérieuse et voilée se dévoilant devant la Science*, a statue in marble for the faculty of medicine of Bordeaux (1893), *Famille de Nubiens se défendant contre un crocodile*, haut-relief in bronze for the lateral facade of the Museum (1894), *Danseuse* in bronze (1894), *La Lumière*, a statuette in bronze, and *La Renommée*, a statuette in silver and ivory (1902), etc.

Barrias sometimes a number of variations on one theme, and then cast them in bronze in several sizes. An example is the *Jeune Fille de Bou-Saada*, which was created from the *Fileuse de Mégare*. As for *La Nature se dévoilant devant la Science*, his best-known work and a harbinger of the Art Nouveau movement, the statue was first portrayed as a marble nude in 1893 in Bordeaux, but was shown draped with clothing in 1902 at the old medical school in Paris. While reductions were made, more often in marble than in bronze, the latter differed according to their dimensions, their patina, and the inclusion of parts in marble or ivory.

Louis Ernest Barrias,
La Nature se dévoilant devant la Science,
polychrome patina, 60 cm (Susse),
See a proof in bronze and marble, page **20***).

Bronzes cast by Barbedienne
Amphore femme ailée, 14 cm.
Bernard Palissy, 103, 80, 60, 40, 20 cm.
Les Deux Soeurs, 27 cm.
Deux Enfants sur un tortue, 27 cm.
Enfant au coquillage, 15 cm.
Enfant à l'escargot, 13 cm.
Enfant à l'amphore, 14 cm.
Enfant au panier, 14 cm.
Engant à la tirelire, 21 cm.
Enfant aux lianes (small vase) 11 cm.
Fée aux lézards (flower stand) 22 x 34 cm.
Fleurs d'hiver (woman sitting), 59, 46, 38 cm.
Mozart enfant, 115, 89, 66, 47 cm.
Bronzes cast by Susse
Jeanne d'Arc prisonnière, 110, 71, 50, 33, 21 cm.
Jeune Fille de Bou-Saada, 70, 52, 31 cm.
Jeune Fille de Bou-Saada, (bust), 37, 28, 19 cm.
Jeunesse (bust), 22 cm.
La Nature se dévoilant devant la Science, 97, 73, 58,
    43, 24 cm.
La Reconnaissance, 103, 78, 52, 47 cm.
La Renommée, 85, 43 cm.
Les Tablettes de l'Histoire, 46 cm.
Bronzes cast by Siot-Decauville
La Nature se dévoilant devant la Science.
Fille d'Eve.
Bronze cast by A. Rudier
La Liseuse, 22 cm.
Bronzes cast by Thiébaut
Le Chant, 100, 75, 33, 15 cm.
La Musique, 100, 75, 33, 15 cm.
Les Premières Funérailles, 85, 71, 51 cm.

MUSEUMS
Calais
La Nuit du 4 Août, high relief, 128 x 198 cm (monu-
    ment to Victor Hugo).
Châteauroux
La Nature se dévoilant devant la Science, bronze and
    marble, 97.5 cm.
Le Mans
La Nature se dévoilant devant la Science, 73 cm.
Meaux
Jeune Fille de Bou-Saada.
Nice
Les Premières Funérailles, Dryade.
Paris, Carnavalet
Buste du peintre Regnault, 51.5 cm.
Paris, Orsay
Le Peintre Guillaumet, medallion, 17 cm diam.
Le Peintre Henri Regnault, bust, 53 cm.
Paris, Petit Palais
Le Peintre Henri Regnault, bust, 53 cm.
The museum also owns a number of terra cotta pieces
    by this artist.
Pithiviers
La Nature se dévoilant devant la Science, 73 cm.

SALES
L'Aurore, 75 cm (Susse), Drouot, May 27, 1982,
    rooms 5 and 6.
Enfant dessinant, gilded bronze, 43 cm, Drouot, June
    15, 1981, rooms 5 and 6.
Enfant au coquillage, 18 cm, (Barbedienne), Drouot,
    December 13, 1986, room 7.
Enfant au panier, gilded bronze, 14 cm,
    (Barbedienne), Drouot, March 16, 1983, room9.
Fleurs d'hiver, 62 cm (Barbedienne), Drouot, Decem-
    ber 2, 1983, room 5.
Jeanne d'Arc, Saint-Quentin, March 10, 1985.
Jeune Fille de Bou-Saada, 31 cm, (Susse), Chartres,
    June 2, 1984; Christie's New York, December 13,
    1985.

Louis Ernest Barrias,
Jeune Fille de Bou Saada,
31 cm (Susse).

Jeune Fille de Bou-Saada, 50 cm, Bourg-en-Bresse,
    March 25, 1984.
Jeune Fille jouant du violoncelle or La Musique, 73 cm
    (Thiébaut), Sotheby Londres, June 12, 1986.
Mozart, 48 cm, Sotheby London, November 8, 1984.
La Nature se dévoilant devant la Science, 24 cm,
    Drouot, July 2, 1984, room 4; Drouot, November
    29, 1985, room 9.
La Nature se dévoilant devant la Science, 43 cm,
    Drouot, November 9, 1984.
La Nature se dévoilant devant la Science, 58 cm,
    Saint-Germain-en-Laye, March 10, 1985.
La Nature se dévoilant devant la Science, 73 cm,
    Drouot, November 23, 1983; Sotheby New York,
    September 13, 1986.
La Nature se dévoilant devant la Science, bronze and
    marble, 58 cm, Drouot, May 20, 1983, room 7;
    Drouot, December 7, 1983.
La Nature se dévoilant devant la Science, bronze and
    marble, 97 cm, Drouot, December 10, 1980.
A work in silvered patina and ivory, 40 cm, marked P,
    cast by Siot-Decauville, was sold for119,000
    Francs at the Drouot Hotel, April 23, 1984, room
    1.
Premières Funérailles, 85 cm, (Thiébaut), Sotheby
    London, June 17, 1986.
Putti à la tortue, 15 cm (Barbedienne), Drouot, De-
    cember 13, 1986, room 7.
La Renommée, 85 cm (Susse), Christie's London, April
    3, 1985.
La Renommée, gilded bronze and ivory, 85 cm,
    (Susse), Christie's London, May 15, 1986.

BARTHOLDI, FRÉDÉRIC AUGUSTE

Colmar, April 2, 1834
Paris, October 4, 1904

La Liberté éclairant le monde (The Statue of Liberty), at the entrance to the port of New York, and *Le Lion de Belfort* (to a lesser degree) have become more famous than the man who made them. Still, his work is hardly limited to these two gigantic accomplishments. Bartholdi certainly has worked on a monumental scale, but a number of his best-known sculptures, including those listed here, were cast in a reduced formats, frequently in many sizes.

After some architectural study in Colmar, Bartholdi studied in the studio of the painter Ary Scheffer in Paris, and then in the studio of the sculptor Soitoux. Around 1855 he travelled to Greece with yet another painter, Jean-Léon Gérôme. From this era, two of his works (both small groups) were cast in bronze: *Le Bon Samaritain* and *Les Sept Souabes* (inspired by a Germanic legend). In 1857, he finally began participating at the Salon, with a large bronze entitled *La Lyre chez les Berbères, souvenir du Nil*.

Bartholdi is the author of a number of busts, medallions, and statues of famous men, commemorative monuments, and fountains. He donated several statues to his hometown, Colmar, including *Le Général Rapp*, bronze (1855), *Le Peintre Martin Schongauer*, stone (Salon of 1861), and *L'Amiral Bruat*, bronze (Salon of 1863). He is also responsible for *Vauban d'Avallon*, the *Vercingétorix* of Clermont-Ferrand (1870), the *Champollion* in marble from the courtyard of the College of France, and the group in bronze entitled *Washington et La Fayette* (1890) from the Plaza of the Untied States (*Etats-Unis*) in Paris. A small statue in bronze, *Génie funèbre*, 78 cm, destined for the tomb of Nefftzer at the Montmartre cemetery, was shown at the Salon of 1866.

After the war of 1870 (during the course of which he was assigned to the headquarters of Garibaldi), Bartholdi began to devote himself to great patriotic themes, culminating in the Lion and the Liberty. *Le Lion de Belfort*, hewn into the red sandstone rock that overhangs the citadel, measures 22 meters long and 11 meters high. Executed from 1875 to 1880, it symbolizes the resistance of the city during the war. The model in plaster, a third of the size, was presented at the Salon of 1878. A model of the same dimensions in hammered copper, exhibited at the Salon of 1880, is located at the center of Denfert-Rochereau Square in Paris. A number of smaller editions in bronze were cast from it.

A colossal statue in thinly-plated beaten copper entitled *La Liberté éclairant le monde* ("Liberty Lighting up the World"), 33 meters tall, was erected in New York in 1886 to celebrate the American centennial of independence; the work had been made possible by a subscription launched simultaneously in France and the United States. Starting in 1878, a 1/16th-size model was exhibited at the Salon. Several smaller statues in bronze would be cast from it. The one which stands in the middle of Grenelle Bridge in Paris, 8.6 meters high, was donated by America. Another, much smaller at 2.87 meters high, is found in the Luxembourg gardens. Both were cast by Thiébaut Frères. Finally, some reductions in several dimesions were cast in bronze and in terra cotta.

By the end of his life, Bartholdi had also completed the monument of the *Trois Sièges de Belfort* (plaster, exhibited at the Salon of 1903), and unveiled it in that town in 1912; he also completed the monument *Aux aéronautes du sièges de Paris* (sketch from the Salon of 1904), unveiled at Neuilly-sur-Seine in 1906.

Bronzes cast by the Thiébaut house
Borne frontière, 44 cm.
Lion de Belfort, 46, 21 and 10 cm.
Bronzes cast by Barbedienne (1897 contract)
Le Général Gribeauval, 57 cm.
Otia Pacism 38 cm.
Vercingétorix, 42 cm.
Washington et La Fayette, group, 94 cm.
Washington et La Fayette, bas relief, 83 x 52 and 25 x 16 cm.
Washington et La Fayette, medallion, 25.5 cm diam.

MUSEUMS
Belfort
Lion de Belfort, first model of the study, 55 x 90 cm.
Clermont-Ferrand
Vercingétorix, 17 cm (Barbedienne).
Nantes
Le Général Mellinet, 68 cm (1865).
Paris, Petit Palais
Reconnaissance du secours apporté en 1870 par la Suisse aux Strasbourgeois assiégés, reduction, 80 cm, from the monument erected in Bâle.
Les Zurichois apportent à leurs amis de Strasbourg une soupe de millet en témoignage de leur attachement, bas relief, 19 x 39 cm (1905).
Strasbourg
Buste d'homme, 40 cm (1858).
Le Vigneron buveur d'eau or *L'Assoiffé*, 55 cm (1869).

SALES
La Liberté éclairant le monde, 48.5 cm, Christie's New York, December 6, 1985.
La Liberté éclairant le monde, 87 cm, Christie's New York, May 31, 1985.
La Liberté éclairant le monde, 128 cm, Christie's New York, May 31, 1985.
La Liberté éclairant le monde, 128 cm, (cast by Avoiron Clément, Paris), Christie's New York, December 6, 1985.
La Liberté éclairant le monde, 131 cm (probably a unique model in "metal" cast by Avoiron), Christie's New York, June 15, 1985.

BARTHOLOMÉ, ALBERT

Thiverval, August 29, 1848
Paris, 1928

Bartholmé

Bartholemé's first discipline was painting; he studied first in Switzerland, and then in the Gérôme's studio at the Ecole des Beaux-Arts in Paris, and exhibited his paintings at the Salon from 1879 to 1886. In that last year, however, crushed by sorrow after the death of his young wife, he devoted himself to sculpture—without ever having learned it—while making her tomb for the Bouillant cemetery, near Crépy-en-Valois. The

Albert Bartholomé,
Fillette pleurant, 40 cm.
Musée d'Orsay.

BARYE, ALFRED
Paris, January 21, 1839—?

Although he was the son, the student, and frequently the imitator of the famous Antoine-Louis Barye, this artist remains little known. It is thought that he died around 1882, the date of his last submission to the Salon. An animalist himself, he worked in the studio of his father to produce a number of race horses, his greatest successes, though he also contributed some groups of birds and genre figures, most of them in bronze. Although his work was not as creative as that of Antoine-Louis, his sculpture, nevertheless survived as well. On the whole, they were of good quality, and are noted for their great attention to details. While they are generally signed "A. Barye son," some are marked simply "Barye," leading them to be confused (intentionally or not) with those of his father.

touching melancholy which emerges from this work is also found in the artist's masterpiece, the monument to the dead of Père-Lachaise—Bartholemé had worked on it for ten years before it was unveiled in 1899. The extraordinary success of this important ensemble established his reputation throughout Europe, and he won the grand prize for sculpture at the Exposition Universelle in 1900. He also sculpted other funerary monuments, including those of Meilhac at the Montparnasse cemetery (1906) and of Benoît Malon at the Pére-Lachaise, as well as the monument to Jean-Jacques Rousseau commissioned in 1907 for the Panthéon.

Bartholomé began exhibiting at the Salon de la Nationale des Beaux-Arts in 1891; in particular he submitted female figures in different poses. Of note among the bronzes are the figures *Petite Fille pleurant* (1894), *Jeune Fille dansant* (1896), and *Baigneuse* (1903), as well as *Tête de jeune homme* (1892) and *L'Enfant mort* (1903).

The Siot-Decauville house made bronze castings of a number of studies, and reductions of different portraits from the Père-Lachaise monument: *Jeune Fille se lamentant* (the central group), *Petite Fille pleurant,* and some other isolated figures in ronde-bosse or in bas-relief. The same founder also offered *Nu de dos,* a study for a fountain. Hébrard cast a statuette of *Jeune Baigneuse* in bronze.

MUSEUMS
Calais
Masque du Japonais Tadamasa Hayashi, 28.5 cm (1892).
Paris, Orsay
Fillette pleurant, 40 cm.
Central haut-relief from the monument to the dead of Père-Lachaise, 58 cm.

SALES
Buste de femme, 51 cm (Hébrard No. 2.), Sotheby Monaco, October 25, 1982.
Jeune Baigneuse assise, 35 x 44 cm (Hébrard), Epernay, March 3, 1985.
Jeune Fille au serpent, bronze and ivory, Christie's London, June 29, 1983.

Alfred Barye,
L'Eleveuse
de poules,
80 cm.

Alfred Barye, Le Cheval "Gladiator,", 51 x 70 cm, (1864, Chantilly).

*Alfred Barye,
Le Faisan.*

Alfred Barye debuted at the Salon of 1864 with a statuette in bronze entitled *Walter Scott, cheval de selle de l'empereur*, after which he exhibited sporadically until 1882. Some other bronzes which can be mentioned are *Vermont, cheval de course*, dated 1864, 25 cm, perhaps his best work (1865), *Cheval de course monté par son jockey* (1866), a medallion portrait of a man (1866), *Perdrix effrayées* (1874), and finally *Bouffon italien du XVIe siècle*, 28 cm (1882). Some slightly different versions of this last work were cast in many dimensions. *Un Cavalier arabe* in bronze was listed as being made in collaboration with the sculptor Emile Guillemin. Other bronzes by Alfred Barye include *Jeanne d'Arc à cheval*, 80 cm, *Paysanne éleveuse de poules*, 80 cm, *Eléphant et son cornac*, 16 cm, and *Enfant et son chien*, 18 cm, etc.

MUSEUMS
Agen
Paysanne éleveuse de poules.
Compiègne, château
Walter Scott, cheval de selle de l'empereur, 33 cm.

SALES
Bouffon italien, 28 cm, Drouot, March 17, 1982.
Le Cheval "Gladiator" (1864, Chantilly), 51 x 70 cm, Rambouillet, March 9, 1986; Sotheby London, March 20, 1986.
Le Cheval Vermont, 50 cm, Enghien, October 6, 1985.
Eléphant, 28 cm, Drouot, February 29, 1984.
Eléphant et son cornac, 16 cm, Rambouillet, March 25, 1984.
Eléphant déracinant un arbre, 15.5 cm, Rambouillet, November 18, 1984.
L'Eleveuse de poules, Fontainebleau, January 30, 1983.
Lévrier, 28 cm, Sotheby London, November 8, 1984.
Lion debout, 18 x 24 cm, Drouot, October 24, 1984, room 9.
Sanglier, 8.5 cm, Rambouillet, November 18, 1984.

*Alfred Barye,
Eléphant, 28 cm.*

BARYE, ANTOINE LOUIS

Paris, September 24, 1795
Paris, June 25, 1875

In the trilogy of great masters of Romantic sculpture, Antoine Louis Barye follows immediately after David d'Angers and Rude. Only slightly their junior, he stands out for the theme which dominates most of his work: animals. Any mention of Barye today calls instantly to mind his innumerable statuettes of big game, deer, dogs, and fowl, cast in bronze. This is understandable; although the famous sculptor was certainly not limited to this genre and and this technique, he remains nonetheless the first and greatest animal sculptor of the nineteenth century, as well as one of the promotors of the bronze edition to which he gave tremendous impetus.

The son of Pierre Barye, a goldsmith from Lyon who came to Paris after the unrest of 1793, Antoine Barye was born (we have determined precisely) not in 1796, as most authors claim, but on the "second vendémiaire of the year IV," in other words, in 1795, as shown by research done at the archives of the Seine (Charles Otto Ziessenis, *Les Aquarelles de Barye*, 1954). At the age of fourteen, he was apprenticed at the home of a certain metal en-

BARYE

Antoine Louis Barye,
Gaston de Foix,
34.5 x 30 cm
(Barye casting).
Fabius frères
Collection,
Paris.

graver named Fourier, who manufactured accessories for military clothing; he also worked for the famous goldsmith Biennais. In 1815, enlisted in the topographical brigade of the army, he took part in drafting maps. Returning to civilian life in 1816, he entered the studio of the sculptor Bosio; in 1817, he entered that of the painter Gros; and in 1818, he enrolled in the Ecole des Beaux-Arts. Finally, from 1823 to 1831, he collaborated with the goldsmith Fauconnier, furnishing models of small animals for the ornamentation of table centerpieces.

All of these experiences contributed to the Antoine Barye's artistic training. Gros's spirited and romantic temperament was not without influence, while two other painters, Géricault and Delacroix, romantics and lovers of horses as well, also made a strong impression on him. Barye's stay at Fauconnier's smithy allowed him to familiarize himself with the crafts of the foundery and of chiseling, which he would later practice independently.

Barye's only remaining task was to study the nature of the animals themselves, especially wild animals, whose power, contained strength, and suppleness captivated him. He achieved this in the Jardin des Plantes, thanks to the friendship of an old caretaker, and completed some very elaborate studies of living animals (and even dead animals) which he observed in actual anatomical detail. The Ecole des Beaux-Arts owns some astonishing drawings (reproduced in May 1972 by the review *Connaissance des Arts*) in which Barye had ultiplied the measurements, showing at which point his study of nature surpassed quasi scientific knowledge.

DECIDED BY THE PUBLIC

Barye's career had a modest start; only after some time would it grow into a tremendous success. He obtained a mere second prize for his sculpture *Cain maudit par Dieu* in 1820 (while he was still just a student at the Ecole des Beaux-Arts), and during the next three years he failled repeatedly to win the first prize of Rome; finally, in 1824, he departed from the Ecole des Beaux-Arts.

His career continued its modest advance at the Salon of 1827, where he exhibited several busts which attracted little attention and were not saved for posterity. His career finally brightened when his plaster *Tigre dévorant un gavia* (41 x 103 cm) was presented with some other sculptures at the Salon of 1831; it was cast in bronze the next year. While the jury awarded this work only a second prize, Barye's success with the public was considerable. Despite the reticence of a certain circle which considered the animal world an unworthy subject for great art, critics flooded Barye with praise. While Charles Lenormant said that he felt pursued "by an odor from a menagerie" in the presence of so much realism, Delecluze more seriously noted that this group, "where life is rendered with so much force and passion. . . .[was] the most forceful and best work of sculpture of the Salon."

This was undoubtedly the true point of departure for Barye's career. He continued to confront unshakable hostility from the establishment for many years, but his work would not be diminished; overall, his work was brilliant, despite some fleeting difficulties.

Antoine Louis Barye,
Le Duc d'Orléans,
37 cm
(Barye casting).

1) *Antoine Louis Barye, Charles VI dans le forêt du Mans, 49 x 42 cm. Musée d'Orsay.*

2) *Antoine Louis Barye, Charles VII victorieux, 36 cm.*

3) *Antoine Louis Barye, Le Général Bonaparte, 36 cm (Barye casting).*

4) *Antoine Louis Barye, Guerrier tartare arrêtant son cheval, 35 cm.*

Charles Saunier remarked that in the work *Tigre dévorant un favial*, which Barye dedicated to the great goldsmith Fauconnier, the abundance of accessory detail and the minute precision with which they were rendered are evidence of Bayre's long stay at Fauconnier's home. However, the sculptor soon freed himself from the fastidious refinement inherent to the goldsmith trade, releasing all the evocative strength and power of his art.

At the Salon of 1833, the plaster model of *Lion écrasant un serpent* (135 x 180 cm) again earned him a second prize and the acclaim of art-lovers. The bronze he exhibited at the Salon of 1836 elicited cries of admiration from Alfred de Musset, who wrote in the *Revue des Deux-Mondes* "What vigor and what truth! This roaring lion, this hissing serpent. . .What power in this paw posed on its prey!. . .Where indeed did Mr. Barye find such models? Is his studio a desert in Africa or a forest in Hindustan?"

Barye had sent other animals and two figures in bronze to the Salon of 1833, very much in corformity with the love of history so dear to romantics: *Charles VI dans la forêt du Mans* and *Charles VII le Victorieux*, also called *Cavalier du XVe siècle*. The following year one of his admirers, and not the least of them, the Duke of Orléans, commissioned him to do an important table centerpiece, to include five hunting groups and four smaller representations of animals in combat. In 1837, the Salon's jury, always hesitant about animal art in general and sculpture in particular, refused to admit the hunting groups. Exasperated by the quarrel, Barye (who, moreover, had still not obtained his admission to compete for the prize of Rome) decided that he would no longer participate at the Salon. He did not return for thirteen years.

THE OFFICIAL COMMISSIONS

Despite some critics' lack of appreciation and, as we will see later, concerns and setbacks that led Barye to open his own bronze foundry in 1838, the sculptor's work continued to make him rich. He received a number of official commissions, including, in 1836, a bronze lion in bas relief for the pedestal of the Juillet column, unveiled in 1840 at the plaza of the Bastille; in 1846, another sitting lion, also in bronze, in ronde-bosse for the gardens of the Tuileries (since 1867 placed with a counterpart made for the occasion, to flank the Seine side of the pavilion of Flore); and in 1847, the eagles of the Iéna Bridge.

In 1850, for his return to the Salon, Barye exhibited a plaster, *Jaguar dévorant un lièvre*, which elicited praise from another of his admirers, the painter Léon Bonnat: "I believe that this will be the unanimous masterpiece of masterpieces from this man, who has produced so many of them. He evokes from this marvelous bronze. . .an impression of ferocity and extraordinary savagery. This is from a genius." The Exposition Universelle of 1855 was yet another triumph. He sent only a single piece to the fine arts section, the *Jaguar dévorant un lièvre*, but exhibited an imposing ensemble of sculptures of all sorts and sizes in the section industrial products. He was awarded the grand medal of honor and the cross of the officer of the Légion of Honor.

As he had demostrated with his early portraits of historic personages, Barye did not scorn the human figure. He also sculpted nudes, effectively conveying human grace, muscular power, and exertion. In this vein he was commissioned by the Duke of Monpensier in 1840 to produce *Roger et Angélique* for a mantle trim; he sculpted *Thésée et le Minotaure* and *Thésée combattant le centaure Biénor* (the latter presented in plaster at the Salon of 1850); the four groups in stone entitled *La Paix, La Guerre, L'Ordre, La Force*, which were executed in 1854 for the Denon and Richelieu pavilions of the new Louvre (where they can still be seen, very high up and very damaged). He was commissioned by Isaac Pereire in 1858 to execute a mantle trim including the figure *Apollon conduisant le char du soleil* (executed in only two models), and also sculpted *Napoléon III équestre* in haut-relief for the entrances of the Carrousel in 1860 (replaced after

Antoine Louis Barye,
Paysan du Moyen Age, 31 cm.
Musée d'Orsay.

Antoine Louis Barye,
Hercule
et le sanglier
d'Erymanthe,
13 cm.

central union of Industrial Applied Arts (later called the Decorative Arts). On January 25th of the following year, he married Amélie Antoinette Houdart (his first wife had died in 1834), simultaneously legitimizing their eight children. In 1868, after an fruitless first attempt, and this time without having solicited it, he entered the Institute. In 1869 he was commissioned to sculpt four colossal animals for the palace of Longchamp in Marseille, which would be executed according to his plaster models.

A UNIVERSAL RENOWN

Until the war of 1870, Barye had barely travelled farther than Barbizon, where he loved to meet with his friends Millet, Daumier, Rousseau, Diaz, and others. Afterwards, however, he retreated to

Antoine Louis Barye,
Néréide, 34 cm.

1870 by the *Génie des arts d'Antonin Mercié*), as well as the *Napoléon 1er en empereur romain* of Ajaccio in 1865.

A number of Barye's works cited here were cast as large bronzes, sometimes with variations. However, he also modeled a quantity of small subjects, mostly animal figures—big game, elephants, horses, deer, dogs, rabbits, and birds—specifically for commercial editions. There were those who deplored this practice. The critic Decamps, one of Barye's supporters, regretted that the artist was "reduced to the manufacture of paperweights." The phrase caught on, and Barye's detractors did not miss the opportunity to use it ironically.

In 1848, Ledru-Rollin, then a member of the provisory government of the Second Republic, procured for Barye the post 'chief of the castings studio and preservationist of the plasters gallery' at the Louvre Museum, a post that he occupied for two years. In 1854, he was named professor of zoological drawing at the Museum of Natural History. In 1893, he acceded to the presidency of the

Cherbourg with his family. In 1873, upon returning to the capital, he sold a bronze model of each of his works (about one hundred and twenty pieces) to an American art lover from Baltimore named William Thomson Walters; these pieces were destined for the Corcoran Gallery in Washington. A great admirer of the sculptor, Walters had previously bought an important ensemble of bronzes for his own collection, today the Walters Art Gallery of Baltimore. Toward the end of his life, Barye's reputation across the Atlantic increased, and many museums and important collectors acquired his sculptures. Among the main American public museums with collections of Barye's bronzes, in addition to the Corcoran and the Walters Art Galleries, are the Metropolitan Museum of New York and the museums of Brooklyn, Philadelphia and Cambridge (Massachusetts).

In Paris, an exhibition of Barye's works was organized a short time after his death, at the Ecole des Beaux-Arts in 1875. The sale of his studio took place at the Drouot Hotel from the 7th to the 12th of June, 1876. The sale comprised two hundred and twenty bronzes, some unedited, to which were added more than one hundred and fifty models in bronze, some sold with their plasters. Only later did they become a part of the Louvre's collection thanks to donations by Zoubaloff, Thomy-Thiéry, and Chauchard. As we will see, many other French museums own some of Barye's works, notably the Bonnat museum in Bayonne, which, along with the Louvre, preserves some paintings and some remarkable watercolors as well.

The sculptor's extensive body of work and the abundance of the bronzes which were cast (mostly after his death) ought not to obscure his exceptional and unique genius. In his representations of animals, certain authors detected "the same energy as in the studies of Delacroix" (Anthony Radcliff). All emphasize his romantic spirit, his realism, his passion for accuracy, "his search for figures very much like us" (Pierre Pradel). It is gratifying to see in his works the qualities which so many 19th-century animal sculptors so rarely achieved: the art of creating accurate portraits of animals, of capturing, if it is possible to do so, their feelings of ferocity, terror, suffering, and tragedy. Whether he was portraying animals or people, working in the largest or the smallest of formats, Barye was able to confer on almost all of his sculptures an impression of the *monumental*—the mark of a true genius.

A SCULPTOR & A FOUNDER

Beginning in 1838, Barye himself made the first castings of his own works. Until this date, he had entrusted the fulfillment of his major works to many founders, in particular to Honoré Gonon,

Antoine Louis Barye, Minerve, 33 cm.

Antoine Louis Barye, Junon, 28 cm (Barye casting). Fabius Frères Collection, Paris

60

1) Antoine Louis Barye, Thésée et le Minotaure, 44.5 cm
(Barbedienne).

2) Antoine Louis Barye, Thésée combattant le centaure
Biénor, 34 cm (Barye casting), Fabius frères, Paris.

3) Antoine Louis Barye, Thésée combattant le centaure
Biénor, 75 cm (Barbedienne).

Antoine Louis Barye,
Angélique et Roger
montés sur l'hippogriffe,
from the centerpiece of
the duc de Montpensier,
53 x 67 cm (Barye casting).

Antoine Louis Barye,
La Paix, 50 cm
(Leblanc-Barbedienne).

Antoine Louis Barye,
La Guerre, 50 cm
(Barbedienne).

Antoine Louis Barye,
Tigre dévorant un gavial,
20 x 51 cm (Barye casting).
Fabius frères Collection, Paris.

Antoine Louis Barye,
Tigre marchant,
23 x 40 cm
(Barbedienne, gilded FB seal).

Antoine Louis Barye,
Panthère surprenant un zibeth,
11 x 23 cm.

Antoine Louis Barye,
Tigre surprenant une antilope,
35 x 53 cm
(Barbedienne).

Antoine Louis Barye,
Lionne du Sénégal, 33 x 37 cm.

only registered signature and would alone be responsible for the direction of the affairs of the company." Finally, article five foresaw that, "being placed under the management of the director, all the models would remain forever with the current company, or be exploited for the factory." These models were thus cast by different founders, outside of Barye's control. It was not until 1857 that the company could be dissolved and the sculptor could recover his models after reimbursing Emile Martin. Living at the time at 13 Rue des Fossés-Saint-Victor, Barye himself cast the bronzes in his own studio. There is every reason to think that he executed them with the same standards of quality as he had before. Eugène Guillaume confirmed this in 1868, during a conference given at the Central Union of Decorative Arts: "Mr. Barye," he said, "depended on no one for the care of casting his works; he truly left them only to be finished off."

Barye published many catalogs (practically impossible to find today) of the bronzes castings that he offered his clientele. The first was dated 1847, issued while he resided at 6 Rue de Boulogne, and consisting of the works made before his association with Emile Martin. It included a hundred and seven different subjects: the numbers of the pieces for which he had received the most requests were indicated. The next two catalogs had addresses, one at 10 Rue Saint-Anastase, where Barye opened a store in 1854, the other at 12 Rue Chaptal. They seem to have been issued during the period of collaboration with Emile Martin.

The last four catalogs are clearly from a later period, since they mention the great medal of honor awarded to Barye at the Exposition Universelle of 1855. They indicate the following addresses: 13 Rue des Fossés-Saint-Victor, then 10 Quai des Célestins (where Barye had his store), and finally 4 Quai des Célestins (where he lived at the end of his life). The number of models offered for sale increased considerably, exceeding two hundred and thirty at the last location.

As has already been noted, between 1845 and 1857 Emile Martin arranged to have castings executed by different founders. His account book (Glenn F. Benge, *A. L. Barye, Sculptor of Romantic Realism, 1984.*) attests that, at that time, Ferdinand Barbedienne was among these founders. Some other names were cited, inlcuding Eck and Durand, Gayrard, Lévéque, Richard, and Liénard.

who casted works including *Tigre dévorant un gavial*, *Lion au serpent*, and *Charles VII*. In 1838, however, intending to distribute his own works and to follow their execution more closely, Barye opened his own foundry. The first bronzes made this way, or at least supervised and controlled by the artist, are evidently the most coveted. They can be distinguished by a stamp with the name of the sculptor in very small capitals, to which a number is sometimes added, though not always. According to a preciseness described in a letter signed by him, each model had a number based on its relative order. Barye's conscientious professionalism and the perfectionism cited in every biography implies that he affixed his seal only on the proofs which fully satisfied him, explaining the reputation of these signed pieces. The numbers seem to have been rapidly abandoned, as certain customers hesitated to buy the higher ones. To be precise, numbers starting at zero, that one finds on certain bronzes in different spots, are only marks for assembling them.

Several years after opening his foundry, Barye, undoubtedly overwhelmed by management difficulties for which he was not prepared, was forced to enter into a partnership with Emile Martin, a manufacturer specializing in casting decorative iron. By an agreement dated May 15, 1845, a company was formed between the two men under the trade name Barye et Cie (Barye and Co.). It was housed "in the headquarters where the manufacturing was established," 6 Rue de Boulogne in Paris. Article four of the contract specifies that while "M. Barye desired to occupy himself exclusively with his art, M. Emile Martin would have the

THE POSTHUMOUS CASTINGS

All of these bronzes, including some that the sculptor never cast during his lifetime, were reissued in even greater numbers after his death. When Barye's studio was sold in 1876 after his death, Ferdinand Barbedienne bought one hundred and twenty-five models, along with the reproduction rights. This famous founder, and after 1892 his nephew and successor Leblanc-Barbedienne, produced increasing numbers of castings until the beginning of the twentieth century, and then transferred the rights to the great collector Zoubaloff. Zoubaloff later donated them to the Louvre.

The 1887 Barbedienne catalog offered a hundred and twenty subjects in bronze, from 3 to 128 cm in height, from 12 Francs (*Tortue* No. 2) to 10,000 Francs (*Grand Lion assis des Tuileries*, in

Antoine Louis Barye,
Lion marchant,
bas-relief,
20 x 40 cm
(Brame edition).

Antoine Louis Barye,
Lion assis
des Tuileries,
19 cm
(Brame edition).

Antoine Louis Barye,
Lion marchant, 23 cm
(Barbedienne, gilded FB seal).

Antoine Louis Barye,
Cheval srupris par un lion,
40 cm.

65

*Antoine Louis Barye,
Lion au serpent,
22 x 31 cm
(Barye No1 seal),
Fabius frères Collection,
Paris.*

original dimensions). A number of these subjects were sold in many sizes. *Thésée et le centaure Biénor* was offered in its original full size for 6000 F, and in four reductions priced from 550 to 3200 F, not to mention a draft priced at 390 F.

Some bronzes by Barbedienne were marked with a small seal in copper reading "FB". To certain collectors, this suggests that the castings were made during the lifetime of the sculptor. One of Barye's more recent biographers, Stuart Pivar (*The Barye Bronze*, 1974) contents himself with specifying that this seal corresponds "to a certain era" but not necessarily to a better quality. According to André Fabious, a leading expert on Barye, it was used by Barbedienne between 1876 to 1889.

Also in the posthumous sale of 1876, painting dealer Hector Brame bought seventy-eight other models, which he resold at the Drouot Hotel on April 24, 1884. During the eight years he possessed these works, he cast them (some quite large) marked with a small H, the initial of his first name (though possibly it indicated Henri, the master of Barye's studio, with whom Brame surely collaborate).

Other plasters, waxes, and bronzes fell to various purchasers who made castings of them. Thus we find works cast by Vever, the great jeweler (including a small casting in silver of *Hercule portant un sanglier*), by Delafontaine (primarily dogs), by the sculptor and founder Hippolyte Peyrol, etc. Some other castings, all anonymous, have

undoubtedly been made, and as early as the end of the nineteenth century Arsène Alexandre placed protections against "the unbridled gimmicking of Barye's old works which has occurred in the trade. It has become difficult," he added, "not to say impossible, to assign a precise date to certain pieces." This ambiguity and confusion makes the "works stamped by Barye himself," the bronzes known to have been published by his own foundry, especially interesting.

THE CASTINGS

The last catalogs published during Barye's life, as well as catalogs from editors and founders like Barbedienne and the inventories drawn up by Stanislas Lami and Stuart Pivar, made it possible to establish a relatively complete list of the bronzes of castings of the famous sculptor (remembering that the production of Barye had long been part of the public domain). His works are classified by subject in the list below, with the names of the works, the names of the editors (including Barye himself), and the dimensions.

Historic People

Charles VI effrayé dans la forét du Mans, Barye,
  Barbedienne, 49 x 42 cm.
Charles VII victorieux, Barye, 30 x 24 cm;
  Barbedienne, 39 x 30 cm.
Le Duc d'Orléans à cheval, Barye, Barbedienne, 37 x
  30 cm.
Gaston de Foix à cheval, Barye, Brame, 37 x 30 cm.
Le Général Bonaparte à cheval, Barye, Barbedienne,
  36 x 29 cm.

Anonymous People

L'Amazone en costume de 1830, Barye, Buissot, 40 x
  38 cm.
Arabe montant un dromadaire, Barye, Delafontaine,
  24 x 16 cm.
Cavalier africain surpris par un serpent, Barye,

Barbedienne, 22 x 22 cm.
Cavalier arabe tuant un lion, Barye, Brame, 39 x 29
  cm.
Cavalier arabe tuant un sanglier, Barye, Brame, 25 x
  35 cm.
Deux Cavaliers arabes tuant un lion, Barye, Brame, 37
  x 40 cm.
Petit Fou de Rome, Barye, Barbedienne, 18 x 8 cm.
Guerrier du Caucase, Barye, Delafontaine, 20 x 16
  cm.
Guerrier tartare arrêtant son cheval, Barye,
  Barbedienne, 35 x 32 cm.
Indien monté sur un éléphant écrasant un tigre, Barye,
  Brame, 29 x 35 cm.
Paysan du Moyen Age, Barye, Piet, 31 x 20 cm.
Piqueur en costume Louis XV, Barye, Barbedienne, 19
  x 16 cm.

Antoine Louis Barye,
Cheval turc,
antérieur droit levé,
29 x 31 cm
(Barye No4 seal).

CATALOGUE
DES BRONZES
DE BARYE,
Statuaire.
Rue des Fossés St Victor, 13.
PARIS.

Exposition universelle de 1855. *La grande Médaille d'Honneur.*

Figures.

Hauteur du Bronze m/m	Longueur de la Plinthe m/m				F
36	29		1	Le Général Bonaparte	170.
37	30		2	Le Duc d'Orléans	170.
40	38	Équestre.	3	Amazone, Costume moderne	165.
37	30		4	Gaston de Foix	250.
30	24		5	Charles VII. le Victorieux	170.
35	32		6	Guerrier Tartare arrêtant son cheval	200.
22	22		7	Cavalier Africain surpris par un serpent	150.
37	40		8	Cavalier Arabe tuant un lion	350.
29	38		9	Indien monté sur un Éléphant, terrassant un tigre	220.
53	6.		10	Angélique et Roger montés sur l'Hippogriphe	700.
20	9		11	Les Grâces	120.
			12	Trois femmes assises, Vénus, Minerve et Junon, qui supportent une vasque.	

Catalogue des bronzes édités par Antoine Louis Barye, vers 1860.

47	31		13	Thésée combattant le Minotaure	300.
28	12	Musée du Roi	14	Thésée combattant le Centaure Bienor	600.
35	35	de la Ville Loire	15	Esquisse du même sujet	220.

Animaux.

23	25		16	Singe monté sur un Antilope	80.
25	12		17	Ours debout	45.
23	17		18	Groupe d'Ours	80.
14	21		19	Ours assis	35.
7	26		20	Lévrier couché	30.
10	18	Pendant	21	Épagneul	20.
9	18		22	Braque	20.
12	22	Pendant	23	Épagneul en arrêt sur un Faisan	35.
11	22		24	Braque en arrêt sur un Lapin	35.
13	25	Pendant	25	Deux Chiens en arrêt sur des Perdrix	70.
13	25		26	Deux Chiens en arrêt sur des Faisans	70.
14	26	Pendant	27	Basset assis	45.
14	26		28	autre Basset assis	45.
16	25	Pendant	29	Basset debout	45.
16	25		30	autre Basset debout	45.

11	15		31	petit Chien Basset debout	20.
21	37		32	Loup tenant un Cerf à la gorge	140.
23	17		33	Deux jeunes Lions	80.
14	31		34	Lion dévorant une Biche	60.
12	27		35	Lion tenant un Gnou	50.

— 3. —

56	73	Jardin des Tuileries	36	Lion au Serpent	
26	35		37	réduction du même sujet	150.
18	21		38	petite réduction	70.
15	16	Jardin des Tuileries	39	Esquisse du même	35.
37	31		40	Lion assis	150.
21	16		41	réduction du même	40.
19	15		42	petite réduction	33.
21	23	Pendant	43	Lionne du Sénégal	50.
21	23		44	Lionne d'Algérie	50.
23	40	Pendant	45	Lion qui marche	140.
23	40		46	Tigre qui marche	140.
			47	les mêmes sans plinthes — chaque	100.
35	53		48	Tigre surprenant un Antilope	400.
16	32		49	réduction du même sujet	120.
42	5	Ministère de l'Intérieur	50	Tigre dévorant un Gavial	
20	51		51	réduction du même sujet	240.
11	27	Pendant au N° 35.	52	petite réduction	55.
13	33	Pendant au N° 34.	53	Tigre dévorant une Gazelle	60.
39	54	Pendant au N° 48.	54	Panthère saisissant un Cerf	350.
39	53		55	le même avec profil	300.
7	18		56	Panthère couchée	18.
10	20	Pendant	57	Panthère de l'Inde	25.
10	20		58	Panthère de Tunis	25.
11	23		59	Panthère surprenant un gibet	40.
13	21		60	Jaguar qui marche, N° 1.	40.
11	22	Pendant	61	Jaguar qui marche, N° 2.	35.
13	20		62	Jaguar debout	50.

— 4. —

8	22		63	Jaguar couché	30.
8	18		64	Jaguar et Caïman	38.
44	5	Musée du Luxembourg	65	Jaguar dévorant un Lièvre	
7	23		66	Jaguar dévorant un Agouti, Esquisse de la précédente	36.
9	32		67	Jaguar dormant	50.
1	32		68	Ocelot emportant un Héron	135.
4	8	Pendant	69	Lapin les oreilles couchées	3.
4	8		70	Lapin les oreilles dressées	3.
			71	les mêmes sans terrasse — chaque	2.

14	16	Pendant	72	Éléphant d'Asie	35,
14	16		73	Éléphant d'Afrique	35,
23	35		74	Éléphant écrasant un Tigre	150,
				—	
40	41		75	Cheval surpris par un Lion	150,
20	25		76	Cheval la tête baissée	65,
14	17	Pendant	77	réduction du même	25,
14	17		78	Cheval demi sang .	25,
30	26	Pendant	79	Cheval Turc	90,
30	26		80	Second cheval Turc	90,
20	32		81	Les mêmes sur plinthe carrée . . Chaque	95,
				—	
15	14		82	Dromadaire d'Égypte	35,
15 8				Dromadaire (1)	45
22	31		83	Élan surpris par un Lynx	135,

— 5. —

139 Daim . . . 40

8	14		84	Daim couché	10,
5	9		85	Faon de Daim	7,
36	61		86	Cerf terrassé par deux Lévriers . . .	500,
20	16		87	Cerf qui marche . . .	35,
24	19		88	Cerf au repos . . .	35,
20	18		89	Cerf qui écoute . . .	30,
20	16	Pendant	90	Cerf la jambe levée	30,
			91	Cerf s'frottant ses bois contre un arbre	60
22	26		92	Cerf Biche et Faon . . .	75,
10	15		93	Biche couchée	15,
7	18		94	Faon couché . . .	12,
14	20	Pendant	95	Axis . . .	22,
14	16		96	Cerf de Java . . .	25,
17	14	Pendant	97	Cerf Axis . . .	25,
17	17		98	Cerf du Gange . . .	25,
26	41		99	Cerf de Virginie, couché . . .	120,
				—	
9	11		100	Gazelle d'Éthiopie . . .	15,
11	8		101	Kevel	15,
				—	
17	29		102	Taureau	75,
22	22		103	Taureau cabré . . .	60,
23	23		104	le même groupé avec un Tigre .	85,
15	30		105	Taureau terrassé par un Ours .	890,
				—	
29	32		106	Aigle tenant un Héron . . .	190,
26	18		107	Aigle les ailes étendues	100,

— 6. —

21	11		108	Perruche posée sur un arbre . .	25,
13	21	Pendant	109	Faisan sur plinthe	14,
13	21		110	Autre Faisan sur plinthe	14,

7	3		111	Cigogne .	5,
7	3		112	Cigogne disposée pour cachet	6,
3	6		113	Cigogne posée sur une Tortue	10,
				—	
3	11		114	Tortue N° 1	9,
5	14		115	la même sur plinthe ou marbre. N° 2	15,
2	6		116	réduction N° 1	3,
3	8		117	réduction du N° 2	4,
3	11		118	Tortue à charnière, disposée pour boîte	8,
4	20		119	Crocodille sans terrasse	13,
17	42		120	Crocodille dévorant un Antilope . . .	200,
9	31		121	Serpent Python avalant une Biche	50,
16	40	Pendant	122	Python enlaçant une Gazelle	110,
19	39		123	Python étouffant un Crocodille	120,

Bas reliefs.

22	44		124	Lion de la Colonne de Juillet	70,
15	21		125	Léopard	10,
		Pendant	126	Panthère . . .	10,
			127	Genette . . .	10,
			128	Cerf de Virginie . . .	10,
10	16			les mêmes sans Cadre . . . Chaque	6,

— 7. —

Ornements.

		La Paire	129	Coupe ornée d'Arabesques et de feuilles de Vigne	
			130	Coupe, pied de Faune et Raisins	45,
			131	Coupe à bords renversés, haute tige	45,
		La Pièce	132	Brûle parfums	15,
			133	Brûle parfums supporté par trois petites figures	20,
			134	Brûle parfums orné de Chimières	20,
			135	Lustre à 30 lumières orné de 10 petites figures et d'un groupe d'oiseaux	1400,
51	21		136	Candélabre à 3 lumières	110,
55	17		137	Candélabre à 3 lumières décoré d'Arabesques et surmonté d'une Cigogne	125,
94		La Paire	138	Candélabre à 12 lumières, composé de fruits, feuilles et racines de pavots avec Serpent à la tige et surmonté d'un Oiseau	600,
95	40		139	Candélabre à 9 lumières décoré de 6 figures mascarons et Chimières	1000,
19	9		140	Flambeaux	25,
24	10	La Paire	141	Flambeaux ornés de Volubilis, raisins, pied de Faune et Serpent à la tige	35,
			142	Flambeaux décorés de feuillages et clochettes avec insecte à la tige	60,

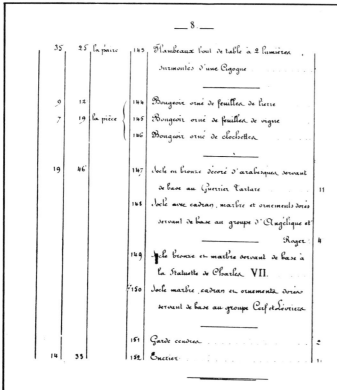

*Antoine Louis Barye,
Eléphant du Sénégal
courant,
14 x 19 cm.*

*Antoine Louis Barye,
Cheval turc
antérieur gauche levé,
31 cm (Barbedienne).*

Allegorical People
La Guerre, La Paix, L'Ordre, La Force, based on four
    groups at the Louvre, Barbedienne, 100, 50 and
    36 cm.

Mythological People
Angélique et Roger montés sur l'hippogriffe, a center-
    piece for the Duke of Montpensier, Barye, Brame,
    53 x 67 cm.
Candélabre à neuf lumières (from the same center-
    piece), Barye, 95 cm.
Les Trois Grâce supportant un brûle-parfum (drawn
    from candelabras from the same centerpiece),
    Brame, 20 x 9 cm.
Junon (from the same centerpiece), Barye, Peyrol, 31
    x 13 cm.
Minerve (from the same centerpiece), Barye,
    Barbedienne, Thiébaut, 33 x 13 cm.
Hercule et le sanglier d'Erymanthe, Vever, 13 x 7 cm.
Une Néréide, Thiébaut, 31 cm L.
Thésée et le Minotaure, Barye, 47 x 13 cm;
    Barbedienne, 60 and 47 cm.
Thésée combattant le centaure Biénor, Barye, 128 x
    112 cm; Barbedienne, 128, 95, 75, 56 and 42 cm.
Thésée combattant le centaure Biénor (sketch), Barye,
    Barbedienne, 35 x 35 cm

Wild Beasts
Jaguar couché tenant une tête de cheval, Barye,
    Barbedienne, 8 x 22 cm.
Jaguar debout No. .1, Barye, Barbedienne, 13 x 21
    cm.
Jaguar debout No. .2, Barye, Brame, 11 x 19 cm.
Jaguar dévorant un crocodile, Barye, Barbedienne, 8 x
    32 cm.
Jaguar dévorant un agouti (sketch), Barye, Brame, 7 x
    23 cm.
Jaguar dévorant un lièvre, Barye, 44 x 105 cm;
    Barbedienne, 95, 44, 18 and 11.
Jaguar dormant, Barye, Barbedienne, 9 x 32 cm.
Jaguar marchant No. .1, Barye, Brame, 13 x 21 cm.
Jaguar marchant No. .2, Barye, Barbedienne, 11 x 22
    cm.
Jaguar tenant un caïman, Barye, Barbedienne, 8 x 13
    cm.
Léopald, Barye, Heilbroner, 10 x 16 cm.
Léopald, bas-relief, Barye, 15 x 21 cm.
Lion assis No. .1, Barye, Graech-Marly, 37 x 31 cm.
Lion assis No. .2, Barye, Delafontaine, 21 x 16 cm.
Lion assis No. .3, Barye, Brame, 19 x 15 cm.
Lion assis No. .4, Barye, Brame, 19 x 15 cm.
Lion assis (sketch), Barye, Barbedienne, 28 x 30 cm.
Lion couché, Thiébaut, 16 cm L.
Lion debout, Thiébaut, 12 cm.
Lion dévorant une biche, Barye, Barbedienne, 14 x 31
    cm.
Lion dévorant un sanglier, Barye, Heilbroner, 19 x 32
    cm.
Lion marchant, Barye, Barbedienne, 23 x 40 cm.
Lion marchant, Barye, Brame, 28 x 36 cm.
Lion marchant (bas-relief), Brame, 20 x 40 cm.
Lion de la colonne de Juillet, Barye, 22 x 44 cm;
    Barbedienne, 27 x 55, 22 x 44 cm.
Lion au serpent, Barbedienne, 42 cm.
Lion au serpent No. .1, Barye, Brame, 26 x 35 cm.
Lion au serpent No. .2, Barye, Brame, 18 x 21 cm.

Antoine Louis Barye,
Eléphant écrasant un tigre,
23 x 35 cm.

30, boulevard Poissonnière

BRONZES D'ART

F. BARBEDIENNE

OEUVRES
DE
A.-L. BARYE

PARIS
1880

Lion au serpent (sketch), Barye, Brame, 15 x 36 cm.
Lion tenant un guib, Barye, Barbedienne, 12 x 27 cm.
Deux Jeunes Lions, Barye, Peyrol, 23 x 17 cm.
Lion et lionne, Thiébaut, 12 cm.
Lionne d'Algérie, Barye, Barbedienne, 21 x 33 cm.
Lionne couchée, Thiébaut, 8 cm.
Lionne du Sénégal, Barye, Barbedienne, 21 x 33 cm.
Lionne emportant un héron, Barye, Barbedienne, 17 x 32 cm.
Panthère, Barye, Heilbroner, 10 x 16 cm.
Panthère bas-relief, Barye, 15 x 21 cm.
Panthère attaquant un cerf, Susse, 15 x 25 cm.
Panthère couchée, Barye, Barbedienne, 7 x 18 cm.
Panthère couchée tenant un cerf muntjac, Barye, Delafontaine, 11 x 21 cm.
Panthère de l'Inde, Barye, Barbedienne, 13 x 25 cm.
Panthère saisissant un cerf, Barye, Barbedienne, 39 x 51 cm.
Panthère surprenant un zibeth, Barye, Peyrol, 11 x 23 cm.
Panthère de Tunis, Barye, Barbedienne, 13 x 25 cm.
Tigre dévorant un gavial, Barye, 42 x 105 cm and 20 x 51 cm; Brame, 13 x 33 cm.
Tigre dévorant une gazelle, Barye, Barbedienne, 13 x 33 cm.
Tigre dévorant un paon, Barbedienne, 16 x 43 cm.
Tigre dévorant un pélican, Barbedienne, 19 x 38 cm.
Tigre marchant, Barye, Barbedienne, 23 x 40 cm.

*Pages from the catalog of bronzes
by Antoine Louis Barye
cast by Ferdinand Barbedienne
around 1880.*

— 2 —

fr.

THÉSÉE COMBATTANT LE CENTAURE BIENOR.
Grandeur originale 6,000
    h. 1.25 c.; l. 1.12 c.
La réduction N° 1 3,200
    h. 0.95 c.; l. 0.82 c.
La réduction N° 2 1,500
    h. 0.75 c.; l. 0.65 c.
La réduction N° 3 800
    h. 0.56 c.; l. 0.50 c.
La réduction N° 4 550
    h. 0.42 c.; l 0.35 c.
Esquisse du même sujet 390
    h. 0.36 c.; l. 0.35 c.
THÉSÉE COMBATTANT LE MINOTAURE.
Augmentation de la grandeur originale 950
    h. 0.60 c.; l. 0.40 c.
Grandeur originale 480
    h. 0.46 c.; l. 0.30 c.
GUERRIER TARTARE ARRÊTANT SON CHEVAL. 350
    h. 0.37 c.; l. 0.33 c.
LE GÉNÉRAL BONAPARTE 300
    h. 0.38 c ; l. 0.29 c.
LE DUC D'ORLÉANS 280
    h. 0.37 c.; l. 0.30 c.
PIQUEUR COSTUME LOUIS XV 140
    h. 0.19 c.; l. 0.16 c.
CHARLES VII LE VICTORIEUX.
Augmentation de l'original 400
    h. 0.39 c.; l. 0.30 c.
Grandeur originale 290
    h. 0.30 c.; l. 0.24 c.
MINERVE 160
    h. 0.38 c.; l. 0.13 c.
PETIT FOU DE ROME 50
    h. 0.14 c.; l. 0.08 c.

— 3 —

ANIMAUX

fr.

GROUPE D'OURS 150
    h. 0.22 c.; l. 0.13 c.
OURS ASSIS 75
    h. 0.14 c.; l. 0.21 c.
OURS DANS SON AUGE 65
    h. 0.11 c.; l. 0.15 c.
BASSET ASSIS, POIL RAS 85
    h. 0.14 c.; l. 0.26 c.
BASSET ASSIS, POIL LONG 85
    h. 0.14 c.; l. 0.26 c.
BASSET DEBOUT, N° 1 85
    h. 0.16 c ; l. 0.24 c.
BASSET DEBOUT, N° 2 45
    h. 0.11 c.; l. 0.14 c.
BASSET ANGLAIS 80
    h. 0.16 c.; l. 0.22 c.
LOUP TENANT UN CERF A LA GORGE 225
    h. 0.23 c.; l. 0.38 c.
LION TENANT UN GUIB 95
    h. 0.12 c.; l. 0.28 c.
LION DÉVORANT UNE BICHE 110
    h. 0.14 c.; l. 0.31 c.
LIONNE DU SÉNÉGAL 100
    h. 0.21 c.; l. 0.23 c.
LIONNE D'ALGÉRIE 100
    h. 0.21 c ; l. 0.23 c.
LION QUI MARCHE 185
    h. 0.23 c.; l. 0.40 c.
TIGRE QUI MARCHE 185
    h. 0.23 c.; l. 0.40 c.
TIGRE DÉVORANT UNE GAZELLE 140
    h. 0.14 c.; l. 0.40 c.

Antoine Louis Barye,
Indien monté
sur un éléphant
écrasant un tigre,
28.5 x 36.5 cm
(Barye seal No.3).
Fabius frères Collection,
Paris.

Tigre marchant, Barye, Brame, 25 x 36 cm.
Tigre surprenant une antilope, Barye, Brame, 35 x 53 cm.
Tigre surprenant un cerf, Barye, Brame, 16 x 32 cm.
Large Animals
Buffle, Barye, Barbedienne, 15 x 20 cm.
Chameau, Thiébaut, 12 cm.
Petit Chameau de Perse, Barye, Servant, 12 x 9 cm.
Cheval demi-sang, Barye, Brame, 14 x 17 cm.
Cheval demi-sang la tête baissée, Barye, Brame, 20 x 25 cm, 14 x 17 cm; Brame, 20 cm.
Cheval percheron, Barye, 20 x 16 cm; Thiébaut, 41 x 20 cm.
Cheval pur-sang d'Arabie, Barye, Delafontaine, 28 x 24 cm.
Cheval surpris par un lion, Barye, Brame, 40 x 41 cm.
Cheval turc, Barye, 30 x 26 cm; Barbedienne, 31, 19 and 14 cm.

Cheval turc (variant), Barye, 30 x 26 cm.
Cheval turc No. .3, Barye, 20 x 19 cm.
Cheval turc No. .4, Barye, 13 x 12 cm.
Dromadaire d'Algérie, Barye, 19 x 18 and 15 x 14 cm; Lefèvre, 19 cm.
Dromadaire harnaché d'Egypte, Barye, Brame, 24 x 19 cm.
Eléphant d'Afrique, Barye, Jacquette, 14 x 16 cm.
Eléphant a'Asie, Barye, Brame, 14 x 16 cm.
Eléphant de Cochinchine, Barye, Brame, 14 x 19 cm.
Eléphant écrasant un tigre, Barye, Brame, 23 x 35 cm.
Eléphant du Sénégal or *Eléphant courant*, Barye, 14 x 19 cm; Barbedienne, 14 and 7 cm.
Hémione (mule), Barye, Barbedienne, 21 x 18 cm.
Ours assis, Barye, Barbedienne, 14 x 21 cm.
Ours debout, Barye, Brame, 25 x 12 cm.
Ours debout No. .2, Barye, Brame, 24 x 12 cm.
Ours fuyant des chiens, Barye, Brame, 31 x 39 cm.

Ours monté sur un arbre mangeant un hibou, Barye, Brame, 20 x 14 cm.
Ours terrassé par des chiens de grande race, Barye, Brame, 27 x 36 cm.
Groupe d'ours, Barye, Barbedienne, 23 x 17 cm.
Taureau, Barye, Barbedienne, 17 x 29 cm.
Taureau cabré, Barye, Barbedienne, 22 x 22 cm.
Taureau cabré avec un tigre, Barye, Barbedienne, 23 x 23 cm.
Taureau terrassé par un ours, Barye, Brame, 15 x 30 cm.
Taureau avec tigre, Barye, Barbedienne, 23 x 23 cm.
Petit Taureau, Barye, Brame, 10 x 13 cm.

Horned animals
Axis, Barye, Barbedienne, 14 x 20 cm.
Biche couchée, Barye, Barbedienne, 10 x 15 cm.
Bouquetin mort, Barye, Barbedienne, 15 x 30 cm.
Cerf, dating from 1829; according to Stuart Pivar, the only works known carrying the seal of Susse and to have been cast perhaps during Barye's lifetime.
Cerf axis, Barye, Barbedienne, 17 x 14 cm.
Cerf bramant, Barye, Barbedienne, Brame, 21 x 18 cm.
Cerf couché, Susse, 45, 17 and 11 cm.
Cerf debout, Susse, 77, 42, 25 and 18 cm.
Cerf qui écoute, Barye, Barbedienne, 20 x 16 cm.
Cerf s'élançant, Brame, 27 x 33 cm.
Cerf frottant ses bois contre un arbre, Barye, Barbedienne, 20 x 21 cm.
Cerf du Gange, Barye, Barbedienne, 17 x 17 cm.
Cerf la jambe levée, Barye, Barbedienne, 20 x 16 cm.
Cerf au jaguar, Susse, 33, 19 and 12 cm.
Cerf de Java, Barye, Barbedienne, 14 x 16 cm.
Cerf qui marche, Barye, Barbedienne, 20 x 16 cm.
Cerf au repos, Barye, Brame, 24 x 19 cm.
Cerf de Virginie, Barye, Barbedienne, 10 x 16 cm.
Cerf de Virginie couché, Barye, Barbedienne, 26 x 41 cm.
Cerf de Virginie couché, bas-relief, Barye, 15 x 21 cm; Barbedienne, 10 x 15 cm.
Cerf, biche et faon, Barye, Barbedienne, 22 x 26 cm.
Cerf dix cors terrassés par deux lévriers d'Ecosse, Barye, Brame, 50 x 40 cm.
Daim, Barye, Barbedienne, 11 x 15 cm.
Daim terrassé par trois lévriers d'Algérie, Brame, 27 x 36 cm.
Daim, daine et deux faons, Barye, Barbedienne, 14 x 27 cm.
Daine couchée, Barye, Barbedienne, 8 x 14 cm.
Daine et son faon, Barye, Barbedienne, 8 x 14 cm.
Elan surpris par un lynx, Barye, Barbedienne, 22 x 31 cm.
Faon couché, Barye, Barbedienne, 7 x 8 cm.
Faon de daim, Barye, Barbedienne, 5 x 9 cm.
Gazelle d'Ethiopie, Barye, Barbedienne, 9 x 11 cm.
Gnou, Barye, Barbedienne, 19 x 22 cm.
Kevel, Barye, Barbedienne, 8 x 11 cm.

Dogs
Basset anglais, Barye, Barbedienne, 16 x 25 cm.
Basset assis (two versions), Barye, Barbedienne, 14 x 26 cm.
Basset debout (two versions), Barye, Barbedienne, 16 x 25 cm.
Braque, Barye, Delafontaine, 9 x 18 cm.
Braque en arrêt sur faisan, Barye, Delafontaine, 11 x 21 cm.
Chien d'arrêt, Thiébaut, 15 cm.
Chien au canard, Delafontaine, 14 x 21 cm.

Deux Chiens en arré sur des faisans, Barye, Delafontaine, 13 x 25 cm.
Deux Chiens en arrét sur des perdrix, Barye, Delafontaine, 13 x 25 cm.
*Epagneul*Barye, Delafontaine, 10 x 18 cm.
Epagneul No. .2, Barye, Delafontaine, 10 x 16 cm.
Epagneul en arrét sur un lapin, Barye, Delafontaine, 11 x 21 cm.
Levrette rapportant un lièvre Barye, Brame, 21 x 22 cm.
Lévrier couché, Barye, Gerbaut, 7 x 26 cm.
Tom, lévrier d'Algérie, Barye, Susse, 20 x 36 cm.
Diverse Animals
Bouc, Thiébaut, 9 cm L.
Chat assis, Barye, Brame, 9 x 6 cm.
Chimère, Vial, 12 x 6 cm.
Chimpanzé, head, Barbedienne, 7 x 3 cm.
Crocodile, Barye, Barbedienne, 4 x 20 cm.
Crocodile dévorant une antilope, Barye, Brame, 17 x 42 cm.
Genette emportant un oiseau, Barye, Barbendienne, 10 x 16 cm.
Genette emportant un oiseau, bas-relief, Barye, 15 x 21 cm; Barbedienne 7 x 14 cm.

Antoine Louis Barye,
Taureau,
17 x 29 cm.

Lapin oreilles dressées, Barye, Barbedienne, 4 x 8 cm.
Lapin oreilles couchées, Barye, Barbedienne, 4 x 8 cm.
Groupe de lapins, Barye, 6 x 8 cm.
Lièvre assis, Barye, Barbedienne, 8 x 5 cm.
Lièvre effrayé, Barye, Barbedienne, 4 x 5 cm.
Loup marchant, Barye, Brame, 24 x 32 cm.
Loup pris au piège, Barye, Piet, 12 x 13 cm.
Loup tenant un cerf à la gorge, Barye, Barbedienne, 21 x 37 cm.
Ratel dénichant des oeufs, Barye, Barbedienne, 11 x 11 cm.
Sanglier blessé No. . 1, Barye, Brame, 16 x 25 cm.
Sanglier blessé No. . 2, Barye, Brame, 16 x 25 cm.
Serpent python avalant une biche, Barye, Barbedienne, 9 x 31 cm.
Serpent python enlaçant une gazelle, Barye, Barbedienne, 16 x 42 cm.

Serpent python étouffant un crocodile, Barye, Barbedienne, 19 x 39 cm.
Serpent python et gnou (from the centerpiece of the Duke of Orleans) Barbedienne, 29 x 37 cm.
Singe monté sur un gnou, Barye, Brame, 23 x 25 cm.

Fowl

Aigle les ailes étendues, Barye, Barbedienne, 26 x 18 cm.
Aigle les ailes étendues, le bec ouvert, Barye, 26 x 18 cm.
Aigle emportant un serpent, Barye, Brame, 13 x 6 cm.
Aigle tenant un héron, Barye, Barbedienne, 29 x 32 cm.
Cigogne posée sur un piédouche, Barye, Barbedienne, 8 x 4 cm.
Cigogne posée sur une tortue, Barye, Barbedienne, 8 x 6 cm.
Faisan (two versions), Barye, Brame, 7 x 14 cm.
Faisan blessé, Barye, Barbedienne, 13 x 21 cm.

*Antoine Louis Barye,
Taureau cabré,
22 cm.*

75

Faisan doré de Chine, Barye, Brame, 11 x 12 cm.
Hibou, Barye, Barbedienne, 10 x 4 cm.
Marabout, Barye, Barbedienne, 13 x 4 cm.
Perruche posée sur un arbre, Barye, 21 x 11 cm.
Perruche sur un arbre (variant), Barye, Brame, 21 x 11 cm.
Milan emportant un héron, Brame, 31 x 13 cm.
Milan emportant un lièvre, Barye, Brame, 17 x 7 cm.

Miscellaneous Objects
We mention here the most important among them:
Bout de table avec faisan endormi, Brame, 20 cm.
Candélabre à trois lumières, style Charles VII, Barye, 57 cm.
Candélabre antique à trois lumières, surmonté d'une cigogne, Barye, 55 cm.
Candélabre à six lumières, avec cerf, biche, faon, milan, Barbedienne, 57 cm.
Candélabre à neuf lumières, six figures, mascarons et chimères, Barye, 95 cm.
Candélabre grec à dix lumières, surmonté d'un hibou, Barye, 60 cm.
Candélabre à douze lumières, fruits, feuilles et racines de pavot, serpent et oiseau, Barye, 94 cm.
Coupe, pied de faune et raisins, Barye, Brame, 10 cm.
Encrier, Brame, 15 x 34 cm.
Flambeau avec médaillon antique, Barye, 26 cm.
Flambeau volubilis, racines, pied de faune, Barye, 24 cm.
Flambeau à deux lumières avec paon, Barye, 22 cm.

MUSEUMS
Ajaccio, Napoleon Museum
Napoléon I équestre, 45.5 cm.
Agen
Taureau cabré, Tiger resting.
Amiens
Aigle enlevant un chamois, bas-relief, 10.5 x 14.5 cm.
Aigle tenant un serpent, bas-relief, 10.5 x 14.5 cm.
Cheval demi-sang, 12 x 17 cm.
Dromadaire d'Algérie, 15 x 17.5 cm.
Eléphant du Sénégal, 15 x 19 cm (Barbedienne).
Famille de cerfs, 20 x 23 cm.
Jaguar dévorant un crocodile, 8 x 23 cm (Barbedienne).
Jaguar dormant, 7 x 22 cm (Barbedienne).
Jaguar tenant un caïman, 10 x 25 cm.
Lion au serpent, 13 x 17 cm (Barbedienne).
Lion au serpent, (another version), 13.5 x 21 cm.
Deux Jeunes Lions se battant, 18 x 17 cm.
Lionne couchée, 13 x 27 cm, (Barbedienne).
Lionne couchée, 10 x 19 cm.
La Paix, 36 x 30 cm (Barbedienne).
Tigre couché, 11 x 20 cm (Barbedienne).
Tigre marchant, bas-relief, 6 x 13 cm.
Vautour, 13 x 8 cm.
Angers
Grand Cerf terrassé par deux lévriers (No. 2), 37 cm.
Autun
Apollon, Taureau.
Bayonne
Angélique et Roger montés sur l'hippogriffe, 52 cm.
Cavalier africain surpris par un serpent (model), 24 cm.
Cerf aux écoutes.
Cheval turc, antérieur droit levé.

Antoine Louis Barye,
Candelabre à neuf lumières
from the centerpiece of the duc of Montpensier,
95 cm (Brame edition).

Eléphant du Sénégal.
Eléphant écrasant un tigre.
Gaston de Foix à cheval, two proofs, 40 and 34 cm.
Lion assis, three works of different dimensions.
Lion marchant.
Lion au serpent, two works, 22 and 21 cm.
Lion au serpent, cast, 10 cm.
Lion de la colonne de Juillet.
Singe monté sur un gnou.
Thésée combattant le centaure Biénor, two works, 46 and 34 cm.
Tigre dévorant un gavial, three works, 37, 19 and 11 cm.
Tigre surprenant une antilope, 36 cm.
Paire de candélabres à douze lumières, décor serpents et oiseaux.
  The museum of Bayonne has a total of ninety-three bronzes by Barye. Certain subjects are represented by many models or in many sizes.

Belfort
Hercule et le sanglier d'Erymanthe, 12.6 cm.
Jaguar tenant un caiman (Barbedienne), 8.2 x 23.5 cm.
Lionne couchée (Barbedienne), 10 x 20 cm.
Bernay
Chat, Lapin, Lion.
Bordeaux
Charles VII victorieux à cheval, gilded bronze, 30 x 24 cm (Gonon).
Lion dévorant sa proie, 14.5 x 30.5 cm.
Guerrier tartare arre*tant son cheval, 38 x 33 cm.
Panthère saisissant un cerf du Gange, 36 x 53.5 cm.
Thésée combattant le Minotaure, 40 x 30 cm.
Tigre et antilope, 33 x 52 cm.

Antoine Louis Barye,
Singe monté sur un gnou,
23 cm.

Boulogne-sur-Mer
Tigre marchant.
Calais
Napoléon 1er en redingote, à cheval (1866), 92.5 cm.
Châteauroux
Cerf couché, 26.5 x 41 cm.
Lion marchant, 29 x 45.5 cm.
Lion terrassant un boa, 18 x 17 cm.
Lion terrassant un sanglier, 30.5 x 40.2 cm.
 Lion terrassant un serpent, 17.5 x 20.5 cm.
Loup pris au piège, 12 x 13 cm.
Petit Lièvre, 8 x 5 cm.
Petit Lièvre, 4.5 x 5.7 cm.
Cognac
Aigle sur rocher tenant un héron, 32 cm.
Dijon
Biche, 8 cm.
Chevrette, 7 cm.
Eléphant debout, 14 cm.
Eléphant courant, 14 cm.
Faon de daim, 6.4 cm.
Jaguar dormant, 8.5 x 31 cm.
Kevel, 10.4 cm.
Léopard, 11 x 22 cm.
Lion marchant, 23 cm.
Lion au serpent, 26 cm.
Panthère dévorant une gazelle, 11 cm.
Tigre marchant (Barye No. 1 stamp), 20 x 45 cm.
Tortue, 3 cm.
Gray
Eléphant du Sénégal, 14 cm.
Le Fou du roi, 13 cm.

Antoine Louis Barye,
Loup tenant un cerf
à la gorge,
21 x 37 cm.

Antoine Louis Barye,
Elan surpris
par un lynx,
22 x 31 cm
(Barye casting).

Antoine Louis Barye,
Le Cerf debout,
50 cm
(Susse).

Grenoble
Cerf, 17 x 24 cm.
Chien de chasse en arrêt devant un lièvre, 10 x 16 cm.
Panthère dévorant une gazelle, 12 x 31 cm.
Libourne
Basset debout, 16.5 x 24 cm.
Lyon
Combat de lions, *Lion au serpent*, *Tigre* (two bas-reliefs).
Marseille, Cantini
Aigle sur rocher déchirant un oiseau (Barbedienne), 32 cm.
Amazone (duchesse d'Angoulême), 37 cm.
Caïman et serpent (Barbedienne), 39 x 17 cm.
Cavalier circassien, 17 x 19.5 cm.
Chameau, 15.5 x 18 cm.
Chiens et ours (two works), 44 and 34 cm.
Eléphant et son cornac, 18 cm.
Girafe, 12.8 x 25.5 cm.
Grue tenant un serpent (Barbedienne), 6 x 17 cm.
Lièvre accroupi (Barbedienne), 6 x 4.5 cm.
Lièvre assis, (Barbedienne), 5 x 8 cm.

Tigre (Barbedienne), 22 cm.
Tortue, 10 cm.
Eight plaques, 14 x 10 cm., representing various animals.
Marseille, Grobet-Labadie
Chien et oie, 16 x 22 cm.
Eléphant marchant, 14 x 20 cm.
Lion assis, 21 x 16 cm.
Lion marchant, 23 x 39 cm.
Lion au serpent, 17.5 x 20 cm.
Meaux
Chameau, 15 cm (Brame cast).
Mont-de-Marsan
Thésée combattant le centaure Biénor (Barbedienne), 41.5 cm.
Montpellier
Le Centaure et le Lapithe, 34 cm.
Cerf bramant, 23 cm.
Cheval turc, two proofs, 29 and 30 cm.
Cheval surpris par un lion, 48 cm.
Chien basset, 12 x 30 cm.

79

Eléphant d'Asie, 14 x 16 cm.
Eléphant d'Afrique.
Hercule portant le sanglier d'Erymanthe, 12 cm.
Jaguar couché tenant un caiman, two proofs, 10 x 19
   and 9 x 23 cm.
Jaguar dévorant un agouti, 10 x 19 cm.
Lion assis, 35 x 24 cm.
Lion marchant, 22 x 37 cm.
Lion au serpent, 26 x 30 cm.
Lionne d'Algérie, 20 x 18 cm.
Lionne couchée, 9 x 19 cm.
Lionne debout, 13 x 20 cm.
Lion du Sénégal, 20 x 19 cm.
Napoléon équestre, 35 x 30 cm.
Singe monté sur un gnou, 20 x 24 cm.
Taureau cabré, 20 x 28 cm.
Taureau attaqué par un tigre, 21 x 22 cm.
Thésée combattant le Minotaure, 46 cm.
Tigre marchant, 24 x 37 cm.
Nîmes
Panthère attaquant un cerf (Susse), 32.6 cm.
Orléans
Charles VII victorieux, 36 cm.
Paris, Decorative Arts
Bonaparte à cheval (Barbedienne), 36 cm.
Charles VII victorieux (Barbedienne), 30 cm.
Cheval turc (Barbedienne), 30 cm.
Le Duc d'Orléans (Barbedienne), 37 cm.
Groupe d'ours (Barbedienne), 20 cm.
Jaguar dormant (Barbedienne), 8 x 31 cm.

*Antoine Louis Barye,
L'Aigle, ailes étendues,
bec ouvert,
26 x 35 cm
(Barye casting),
Fabius frères Collection,
Paris.*

*Antoine Louis Barye,
Le Cerf de Virginie couché,
26 x 41 cm
(Barye No. 1 seal)
Fabius frères Collection,
Paris.*

Lion marchant, 23.5 x 39.5 cm.
Panthère de l'Inde (Barbedienne), 12.5 cm.
Panthère saissant un cerf (Barbedienne), 38 cm.
Taureau tête baissée, 19 x 30 cm.
Serpent python enlaçant une gazelle, 15 x 39 cm.
Thésée combattant le centaure Biénor (Barbedienne), 35 cm.
Tigre et alligator, 20 x 50 cm.
Tigre dévorant un gavial, 10 x 27.5 cm.
Tigre marchant, 21 x 39 cm.

Paris, Louvre
Aigle sur un rocher, 25 cm.
Angélique et Roger montés sur l'hippogriffe, 52 cm.
Cerf marchant, 20.5 cm.
Cerf écoutant, tête haute (Brame), 19 cm.
Cheval pur-sang d'Arabie, 29 cm.
Eléphant d'Afrique, 13 cm.
Eléphant d'Asie, 13.5 cm.
Eléphant de Cochinchine, 15 cm.
Eléphant du Sénégal chargeant, 14 cm.
Faon de cerf couché, tête au sol, 4 x 15 cm.
Jaguar couché tenant une tête de cheval, 7 x 22 cm.
Jaguar dévorant un lièvre, 42 cm.
Lion assis, 145 x 190 cm (Salon of 1836; at Tuileries until 1916).
Lion marchant, bas-relief in the style of the pillar of July, L.40 cm
Lion au serpent, several smaller versions, height about 12 cm.
Lionne debout, 19 cm.
Milan emportant un lièvre
Ours debout, 24 cm.
Panthère saisissant un cerf, 36 cm.
Panthère de Tunis, 10 x 20 cm.
Spatule dévorant un poisson, 17 cm.
Tigre couché en sphinx, 13 cm.
Tigre dévorant un gavial, 41 x 103 cm.
Tigre dévorant une gazelle, 12 cm.
Tigre marchant gueule ouverte, 21 cm.
Les Trois Grâces.
The museum also has a series of medallions and small plaques in bronze as well as a number of plasters and some waxes.

Paris, Orsay
Biche couchée, 9 x 15 cm.
Cerf qui écoute, 20 x 16.5 cm. (Barye 50).
Cerf la jambe levée, 18 x 16 cm (Barye 18).
Cerf marchant, 19 x 22.5 cm (Barye 34).
Charles VII victorieux, 30 cm.
Crocodile dévorant une antilope, 17 x 41.5 cm (Barye 2).
Guerrier tartare à cheval, 35 x 36 cm (Barye 3).
Jaguar couché tenant une tête de cheval, 7 x 22 cm.
Lévrier couché, 6.5 x 26 cm.
Lion marchant, 23 x 41.5 cm.
Lion au serpent, 13.5 x 18 cm.
Lion tenant un gulb, 9.5 x 26 cm.
Loup défendant sa proie, 24.5 x 39 cm.
Ours terrassé par des chiens, 26 x 33 cm.
Deux ours, 23 cm.
Python enlaçant une gazelle, 17 x 40 cm.
Tigre marchant, 21 x 44 cm.

Paris, Petit Palais
Aigle tenant un chamois, bas-relief, 9 x 11.5 cm.
Basset debout, 15 x 25 cm.
Biche couchée, 16 cm.
Biche au repos, 11 cm.
Cerf de France qui écoute, 20 cm L.
Cerf de Virginie, bas-relief, 10.3 x 14 cm.
Chien de chasse, 11 x 21 cm.
Cigogne, 8 cm.
Daim, 16 cm.
Deux Jeunes Lions, 18 cm.
Dromadaire monté par un Arabe, 24 cm.
Faon au repos, 15 cm.

Gnou, 19 x 23 cm.
Lapin assis, 8 cm.
Lapin broutant, 4.5 x 7 cm.
Lapin broutant oreilles dressées, 8 cm L.
Lion accroupi, 20 cm.
Lion assis, 10 cm.
Lion au serpent, 16 x 20 cm.
Lionne couchée, 15 x 28 cm.
Lionne debout, 18 x 22 cm.
Panthère marchant à gauche, bas-relief, 8 x 14 cm.
Thésée combattant le Minotaure, 44 cm.
Tigre, bas-relief, 14 cm L.
Tigre et caïman, 9 x 23 cm.
Tigre marchant, 20 x 39 cm.
Tigre surprenant un cerf, 16 x 31 cm.
Tortue, 7.5 cm L.
Poitiers
Cheval demi-sang tête baissée, 20 x 30 cm.
Lion dévorant une biche, 14 x 31 cm.
Singe monté sur un gnou, 23 x 25 cm.
Reims
Aigle ailes déployées, 28 x 26 cm.
Cheval cabré attaqué par un lion, 40 x 37 cm.
Lion assis, 197 x 182 cm.
Lion marchant, 23.3 x 39.6 cm.
Lion écrasant un serpent, 27.2 x 34 cm.
Tigre attaquant un crocodile, 20.2 x 50 cm.
Tigre marchant gueule ouverte, 21 x 43 cm (Barye stamp 04).
Thésée et le centaure Biénor, 35.6 x 36 cm.
Thésée combattant le Minotaure, 45.5 x 29.5 cm.
Quatre groupes, reductions of four works from the Louvre (Barbedienne seal in gilded metal), as follows:
La Force protégeant le Travail, 72 x 84 cm.
La Guerre, 97 x 91.5 cm.
L'Ordre protégeant les nations industrielles, 98 x 80 cm.
La Paix, 98 x 84 cm.
Rouen
Cheval turc, 28.5 x 29 cm.
Lion assis, 36 x 32 cm.
Lion écrasant un serpent, 31.5 x 48 cm.
Lion marchant, 23 x 40 cm.
Lion au serpent, 13 x 17 cm.
Thésée combattant le centaure Biénor, 38 x 40 cm.

Antoine Louis Barye,
Levrette rapportant un lièvre, 21 cm.

Saint-Denis de la Réunion
Aigle et chamois, 10 x 14 cm.
Aigle et serpent, 9 x 13 cm.
Cerf, 10 x 14 cm.
Jaguar, 8 x 13 cm.
Panthère, 8 x 13 cm.
Saint-Etienne
Aigle tenant un héron, 21 x 31.5 cm.
Cavalier africain surpris par un serpent (No. 3), 24 x 29 cm.
Elan surpris par un lynx, 23 x 33 cm.
Lion au serpent, 26 x 35.5 cm.
Thésée combattant le Minotaure, 46 x 30 cm.
Strasbourg
Aigle sur un rocher, bec ouvert, 25.5 cm.
Aigle sur un rocher, bec fermé, 28 cm.
Cavalier arabe tuant un lion, 38 cm.
Cavalier tartare, 39.5 cm.
Cerf arrêté la tête haute, 19 cm.
Cerf de Java, 14.5 cm.
Charles VII victorieux.
Chat assis, 9.3 cm.
Cheval au repos, 9.7 x 16.5 cm.
Cheval surpris par un lion, 37.5 cm.
Cheval turc, antérieur droit levé, 29.3 cm.
Cheval turc, antérieur gauche levé, 29.3 cm.
Chien basset assis, 14 x 25.5 cm.
Eléphant monté par un Indien, 27.5 cm.
Gaston de Foix à cheval, 32 cm.
Levrette rapportant un lièvre, 20.5 x 32.5 cm.
Lion assis, two proofs, 31.5 and 21 cm.
Lion dévorant un serpent, 17 cm.
Lion marchant, 21 x 39.5 cm.
Lion tenant un cerf à la gorge, 23 x 38 cm.
Ours debout, 24.5 cm.
Panthère couchée, 10 x 19.5 cm.
Panthère saisissant un cerf, 36 cm.
Python étouffant un crocodile, 15.5 x 39 cm.
Singe monté sur un gnou, 23.3 cm.
Taureau cabré, 21.5 x 27.5 cm.
Taureau chargeant, 15.3 x 28 cm.
Thésée combattant le centaure Biénor, 35 cm.
Tigre dévorant un crocodile, 26 x 50 cm.
Tigre dévorant un crocodile, 8.4 x 23 cm.
Tigre dévorant une gazelle, 12.5 x 33 cm.
Tigre marchant, 21.5 x 39 cm.
Troyes
Dromadaire, 26 x 26 cm.
Valence
Tigre dévorant un gavial.
Vernon
Cerf, 14.5 cm.

Of further note at the museum of Alger are the works *Grande Panthère saisissant un cerf*, 34 cm, *Tigre surprenant une antilope*, 36 cm, *La Guerre*, 30 cm (Barbedienne), and *La Paix*, 30 cm (Barbedienne).

SALES
Historic People
Charles VII victorieux, 30 cm, Versailles, May 13, 1984; 38 cm (Barbedienne), Christie's London, July 17, 1984.
Gaston de Foix à cheval, 35 cm, Enghien, October 6, 1985; Sotheby London, June 17, 1986.
Godefroy de Bouillon, 33 cm, Drouot, December 17, 1984, rooms 5 and 6.
Le Général Bonaparte à cheval, 36 cm (Barbedienne), Dijon, November 27, 1983; Sotheby London, July 5, 1985.
Napoléon 1er à cheval, 45 cm, Rambouillet, December 8, 1985.
Anonymous People
Cavalier arabe tuant un lion, 41 cm, Christie's New York, June 19, 1984.
Guerrier arabe à cheval, 35 cm, Christie's New York, June 19, 1984.
Méhariste sur sa monture or *Arabe montant un dromadaire*, 28 cm, Enghien, June 26, 1983.

Picador, 72 cm, Dijon, November, 27, 1983.
Allegorical People
La Guerre, 48 cm (Leblanc-Barbedienne), Enghien, December 18, 1983.
La Paix, 52 cm (Leblanc-Barbedienne), Enghien, December 18, 1983, Divonne-les-Bains, July 27, 1984.
Mythological People
Hercule et le sanglier d'Erymanthe, 13 cm, Drouot, June 4, 1986, room 2.
Minerve, 32 cm, Dijon, March 18, 1984; Orléans, November 17, 1984.
Une Néréide, 34 cm, Rambouillet, November 30, 1986.
Thésée et le Minotaure, 18 in. (Barbedienne), Drouot, June 15, 1984, room 4; Christie's New York, June 19, 1984.
Thésée et le centaure Biénor, 45 cm (Barbedienne), Lokeren, February 16, 1985; Sotheby New York, April 26, 1986.
Thésée et le centaure Biénor, 48 cm (Barbedienne, gilded seal), Drouot, February 10, 1985, room 1.
Thésée et le centaure Biénor, 56 cm (Barbedienne), Drouot, June 10, 1985, room 10.
Thésée et le centaure Biénor, 75 cm (Barbedienne), Drouot, March 20, 1985, room 4; Compiègne, June 1, 1986; Sotheby London, June 20, 1986; Lyon, July 3, 1986.
Thésée et le centaure Biénor, sketch, 35 cm, Drouot, November 26, 1986, room 9; Drouot, December 4, 1986, rooms 5 and 6.
Vénus, 15.2 in., Rambouillet, November 30, 1986.
Big Game
Jaguar dévorant un crocodile, 8 x 23.5 cm, Drouot, December 16, 1985, room 11.
Jaguar dévorant un lièvre, 95 cm (Barbedienne), Christie's New York, June 19, 1984.
Jaguar dévorant un lièvre, 44 cm (Barbedienne), Drouot, February 10, 1986.
Lion assis, 18.5 cm, Sotheby London, June 7, 1984.
Lion assis, 37 cm, Saint-Germain-en-Laye, December 9, 1984.
Lion debout, 18 x 24 cm, Drouot, October 24, 1984, room 9.
Lion dévorant une biche, 14 x 31 cm, Versailles, June 19, 1985; Rambouillet, October 20, 1985; Christie's London, May 15, 1986.

30	BRONZES FONDUS, ETC.

422 — Daine couchée. Deux épreuves.

423 — Biche couchée. Trois épreuves.

424 — Faon de cerf. Six épreuves.

425 — Lapins groupés. Trois épreuves.

426 — Élan emportant un lièvre. Deux épreuves.

427 — Fou de Rome, bronze de la Renaissance. Quatre épreuves.

———

BRONZES

FONDUS SUR LE PLATRE AYANT SERVI DE MODÈLE

428 — Thésée combattant le Minotaure.

429 — Cerf dix cors terrassé par deux lévriers.

430 — Taureau. Deux épreuves.

431 — Lionne debout.

432 — Lion au serpent, n° 2.

433 — Lion au serpent, n° 3.

434 — Tigre dévorant une gazelle.

CATALOGUE
DES
ŒUVRES DE FEU BARYE
BRONZES
AQUARELLES — TABLEAUX
CIRES, TERRES CUITES, MARBRES, PLATRES
MODÈLES
AVEC DROIT DE REPRODUCTION
Dépendant de la Succession de M. BARYE

DONT LA VENTE AURA LIEU

HOTEL DROUOT, SALLES Nᵒˢ 8 & 9,
Les Lundi 7, Mardi 8, Mercredi 9, Jeudi 10,
Vendredi 11 et Samedi 12 Février 1876,
A UNE HEURE ET DEMIE

Par le ministère de Mᵉ CHARLES PILLET, Commissaire - Priseur,
10, rue de la Grange-Batelière,
Assisté de M. DURAND-RUEL, Expert, 16, rue Laffitte,
Et de M. WAGNER fils, 2 bis, passage Vaucouleurs,
Chez lesquels se trouve le présent Catalogue.

EXPOSITIONS { PARTICULIÈRE : le Samedi 5 Février 1876,
             { PUBLIQUE : le Dimanche 6 Février 1876.

*Pages from the estate sale
of Antoine Louis Barye.*

BRONZES INÉDITS   31

435 — Cerf qui marche.

436 — Cerf qui écoute.

437 — Chien épagneul.

438 — Faon de cerf.

439 — Cerf de la Virginie. Bas-relief.

440 — Genette emportant un oiseau. Bas-relief.

441 — Jaguar dormant. Épreuve en plomb, fondu sur le plâtre.

442 — Panthère de l'Inde. Épreuve en galvano.

443 — Panthère de Tunis. Épreuve en galvano.

BRONZES INÉDITS

MODÈLES EN PLATRE, MARBRES & CIRES

444 — Cavalier du moyen-âge. Bronze inédit.

445 — Cavalier du moyen âge. Modèle en plâtre.

446 — Serpent python saisissant un gnou à la gorge. Bronze inédit.

447 — Serpent python saisissant un gnou à la gorge. Modèle en plâtre.

Lion dévorant un sanglier, 19 x 35 cm, Drouot, February 18, 1985, room 2.

Lion marchant, 23 x 40 cm, Roubaix, March 11, 1984; Avranches, April 29, 1984; Drouot, November 28, 1985, rooms 5 and 6.

Lion marchant, 23 x 40 cm (Barbedienne), Drouot, June 19, 1985, room 9; Christie's London, January 22, 1986; Neuilly, November 19, 1986.

Lion au serpent, 27 cm Drouot, July 19, 1984, room 9; Sotheby London, November 8, 1984; Drouot, March 22, 1985, rooms 5 and 6.

Lion au serpent, 42 cm (Barbedienne), Saint-Germain-en-Laye December 9, 1984.

Lionne couchée, 8 cm, Pont-Audemer, April 20, 1986.

Lionne debout, 20.5 cm, (Barbedienne, gilded seal), Sotheby London, November 8, 1984.

Lionne dévorant une antilope, 31 cm L., Drouot, March 14, 1985, room 1.

Lionne du Sénégal, 21 cm (Barbedienne), Enghien, October 6, 1985.

Panthère attaquant un cerf, 33 cm, Sotheby London, March 20, 1986.

Panthère couchée, 7 x 18 cm (Barbedienne, gilded seal), Drouot, October 8, 1986, room 1.

Panthère de l'Inde, 13 cm (Barbedienne), Lokeren, October 20, 1984; Sotheby, November 8, 1984.

Panthère saisissant un cerf, 39 x 51 cm, Angers, June 11, 1985.

Panthère de Tunis, 13 cm (Barbedienne), Drouot, October 24, 1984; Sotheby London, November 8, 1984.

Tigre dévorant un gavial, 11 cm, (Barye stamp No.1), Dijon, March 8, 1983.

Tigre dévorant un gavial, 20 cm, Nantes, June 24, 1986.

Tigre dévorant un gavial, 45 cm, Semur-en-Auxois, February 16, 1986.

Tigre dévorant un gavial, 100 cm, (work of the artist dated 1837), Dijon, March 28, 1984 (sold at auction at 76,000 F).

Tigre dévorant une gazelle, 13 x 33 cm, Drouot, March 10, 1984, room 8.

Tigre dévorant une gazelle, 26.5 cm, London, March 8, 1984.

Tigre marchant, 23 x 40 cm (Barbedienne), Drouot, June 19, 1985, room 1; Enghien, October 6, 1985; Bayeux, December 5, 1985; Drouot, November 17, 1986, room 1.

Tigre surprenant une antilope, 35 x 53 cm, Drouot, November 26, 1984, rooms 5 and 6; Neuilly, November 19, 1986.

Large Animals

Cheval arabe, 34 cm, Lokeren, April 20, 1985.

Cheval attaqué par un tigre, 25 x 35 cm, Nice, November 14, 1984.

Cheval demi-sang, 12 cm, (Barbedienne), Sotheby, November 8, 1984.

Le Cheval Gladiator, 51 x 70 cm, Rambouillet, March 9, 1986.

Cheval normand, 12 cm, Dijon, March 18, 1984.

Cheval percheron, 20 cm, (Thiébaut, Furnière, and Gavignot succ.), Sotheby, March 30, 1986.

Cheval surpris par un lion, 27 x 39 cm, Lokeron, February 25, 1984.

Cheval turc, antérieur droit levé, 20 cm, Semur-en-Auxois, October 12, 1986.

Cheval turc, antérieur droit levé, 28.5 cm, Rambouillet, November 30, 1986.

Cheval turc, antérieur droit levé, 29.5 cm (Barbedienne, gilded seal), Enghien, November 23, 1986.

Cheval turc, antérieur droit levé, 29 cm (Barye No. 4), Enghien, November 23, 1986 (sold at auction for 236,000 F).

Cheval turc, antérieur gauche levé, 12.5 cm, Sotheby London, November 6, 1986.

Cheval turc, antérieur gauche levé, 29 cm (Barbedienne, gilded seal), Enghien, October 6, 1985, (sold for 130,000 F).

Cheval turc, antérieur gauche levé, 29 cm, (Barbedienne), Sotheby New York, April 26, 1986; Drouot, July 22, 1986, rooms 5 and 6; Enghien, November 23, 1986.

Dromadaire, 15 cm, Drouot, December 6, 1984, room 5.

Dromadaire sellé, 30 cm, Enghien, June 26, 1983.

Eléphant marchant, 37 cm, (Barbedienne), Rouen, December 7, 1986.

Eléphant du Sénégal, 14 cm, (Barbedienne), Dijon, March 18, 1984; Drouot, May 11, 1984, room 5; Sotheby London, June 7, 1984; Drouot, March 20, 1985, room 4.

Eléphant et son cornac, 28 cm (Barye seal No. 2), Saint-Germain-en-Laye, December 9, 1984.

Ours couché, 10 cm, Dijon, March 18, 1984.

Ours debout, 24.5 cm, Dijon, March 18, 1984.

Ours terrassé par des chiens de grande race, 27 cm, Drouot, December 8, 1983, rooms 5 and 6; Drouot, March 26, 1984, room 9.

Couple d'ours jouant, 20 cm, (Barbdienne), Drouot, April 4, 1984, room 1.

Taureau, 18 cm, Drouot, April 16, 1984, room 1; Sotheby London, November 8, 1984.

Taureau cabré, 22 cm, (Barbedienne), Sotheby London, March 20, 1986.

Taureau cabré attaqué par un tigre, 23 cm (Barbedienne), Drouot, March 20, 1985, room 4.

Fowl

Aigle emportant un lièvre, 16 cm, Drouot, December 4, 1985, room 14.

Jeune Coq, 21 cm, Christie's London, May 15, 1986.

Coq de bruyère, 13 cm, Grenoble, June 25, 1984.

Mid-size animals

Cerf, 51 cm, Meaux, June 22, 1986.

Cerf, 48 cm (Susse), Sotheby London, March 20, 1986.

Cerf bramant, 21 cm (Barbedienne), Drouot, March 20, 1985, room 4.

Cerf attaqué par des chiens, 47 cm (Victor Paillard, founder), Sotheby London, June 17, 1986.

Cerf, biche et faon, 22 cm (Barbedienne), Dijon, March 18, 1984.

Cerf dix cors terrassé par deux chiens, 50 cm, Christie's London, January 22, 1986; Manosque, March 11, 1986.

Cerf et loup, 22 x 46 cm, Bourg-en-Bresse, March 2, 1986. Chiens

Basset, 14 x 26 cm (Barbedienne), Troyes, October 1984; Sotheby London, November 8, 1984.

Basset anglais, 16 x 25 cm, Versailles, June 16, 1984.

Braque à l'arrêt, 9.5 x 19 cm, Drouot, November 21, 1985, room 13.

Chien de chasse à l'arrêt, 18 cm (Barye seal No. 41), Drouot, October 8, 1986, room 1.

Various animals

Crocodile dévorant une antilope, Rambouillet, November 30, 1986.

Lapin, 4 x 8 cm, Drouot, December 5, 1984; Drouot, December 5, 1986, room 10.

Loup marchant, 24 x 32 cm, Drouot, May 3, 1985, room 4.

Mulet, 18.5 cm, Drouot, October 28, 1985, room 15.

Python étouffant un crocodile, 19 cm (Barbedienne), Christie's New York, September 28, 1985.

Singe monté sur un gnou, 23 cm, Sotheby London, March 8, 1984; Rambouillet, November 30, 1986.

Objects

Paire de candélabres à neuf lumières, décor mascarons et chimères, 95 cm, Drouot, November 18, 1986, rooms 5 and 6 (sold for 162,000 F).

BASSET, URBAIN

Grenoble, December 3, 1842
December, 1924

Basset made several decorative works for the Hôtel de Ville of Paris and for the schools of medicine and science at Grenoble. At the Salon, where he exhibited from 1870 until his death, three bronzes appeared: *Le Torrent* (1878), *Les Premières Fleurs*, 100 cm (1880), and a statuette entitled *La Source* (1882). Many reductions are known of *Torrent*, so apparently it achieved a certain success.

MUSEUMS

Grenoble

Les Premières Fleurs, 141 cm.

Le Torrent, cast of a fountain, 250 cm (1878).

Le Torrent, reduction, 86 cm (1895).

SALES

Le Torrent, 67 cm, Drouot, February 27, 1985, room 5.

BASTET, VICTORIEN ANTOINE

Bollène (Vaucluse), January 17, 1853
Bollène, May 2, 1905

From a peasant family, Bastet started at the school of design of Avignon before entering the Ecole des Beaux-Arts of Paris in 1874. According to Stanislas Lami, he left a large number of works, including busts of contemporaries and some statues and statuettes. Among his consignments at the Salon, starting in 1879, are the plasters *La Source du Vaucluse* (1882), *Le Paradis perdu* (1884), *Danseuse*, and *Eve* (1901); the bronzes include *Abandonnée* (1891), *Le Réveil de Manon* (1899), *Manon* (1905); and finally, two statuettes in marble entitled *Cigale* (1891) and *Sensitive* (1902). Also reported on the Parisian market in 1978 is *Porteuse d'eau mauresque* in regulation polychrome, 55 cm.

MUSEUMS

Avignon

Buste d'Armand de Pontmartin, 81 cm (Thiébaut).

Buste de Pourquery de Boisserin, life-size.

Buste de P.J. Yvaren, 66 cm.

BASTIEN-LEPAGE, JULES

Damvillers (Meuse), November 1, 1848
Paris, December 10, 1884

Among the well-known painter Bastien-Lepage's known sculptural works are several rare pieces executed in a very impressionistic style at the end of his life. A statuette in bronze entitled *Jeanne d'Arc écoutant les voix*, 32.5 cm, from a previewed edition of twelve models, was sold in London by Sotheby on June 17, 1986. Another bronze, *Orphée*, 25 cm (Coubertin 1/8), was sold at the Drouot Hotel on July 1, 1987.

BAUDICHON, RENÉ

Tours, March 26, 1878
Paris, July 18, 1963

This sculptor and medallion engraver entered the Ecole des Beaux-Arts in 1879. He is best known for his plaques representing genre scenes, including *Paysanne vue de dos*, 13 x 9 cm, *Breton au cimetière*, 16 x 9 cm, *Amore socio via secura* (a couple sitting on a bench, cast by Susse), 31 x 26 cm, etc. The museum of Tours has two of his works, *La Moisson* and *La Route de la vie*. A plaque in gilded bronze entitled *Philémon et Baucis*, 20 x 23.5 cm, also cast by Susse, was sold at the Drouot Hotel on December 2, 1983. The museum of Angers has a small plaque in bronze, 6.7 cm high, entitled *Noces d'argent*.

BAUDOT, ÉMILE MARCEL

Paris?
Verdun, March 24, 1916

This sculptor, who died on the battlefield, is best known for portraits (busts or statues, most often in plaster), which he exhibited in different salons starting in 1910. Also of note are several bronzes: *Tête de femme* and *Buste de jeune fille* at the Nationale des Beaux-Arts in 1914, *Femme assise sur une draperie* and *Femme drapée*, two statuettes at the Salon d'Automne in 1912, and *Tête de jeune homme* at the same Salon in 1913. Three bronzes, *Tête de jeune homme*, *Buste de jeune homme* and *Femme accroupie*, were sold at Bayeux on December 8, 1985.

Emile Marcel Baudot:
Tête de jeune homme,
Femme accroupie,
Buste de jeune homme.

BAUJAULT, JEAN-BAPTISTE

La Crèche (Deux-Sèvres), April 19, 1828
La Crèche, September 27, 1899

Having revealed his talent for drawing and sculpture at a very young age, Baujault entered the Ecole des Beaux-Arts in 1852, and took classes with Jouffroy. He began exhibiting his works at the Salon in 1859. The best-known, a statuette in marble representing a young Gaulois entitled *Au gui l'an neuf* (Salon de 1875), is in the Tuileries gardens. Also notable are three statuettes in plaster, *L'Eloquence, La Foi patriotique, La Justice* (Salon of 1866), a plaster statue entitled *Baigneuse surprise*, a bust in marble of Meyerbeer for the Institut (1870), *Le Premier Miroir*, a statue in marble (1873, with a reduction in silvered bronze at the Salon of 1875), *Le Rêve*, a statue in marble (1883), and *L'Education de Vercingétorix*, a group in plaster (1896), made for the Hôtel de Ville of Niort, where Baujault's sculptures appeared in a retrospective exhibition in 1902. This artist is also responsible for many commemorative monuments, including a statue in bronze of the colonel Denfert-Rochereau (3 m. high) unveiled at Saint-Maixent in 1880.

The catalog of the Barbedienne house offered *Le Premier Miroir* in five sizes, 174, 85, 68, 51 and 34 cm.

The museum of Niort has a number of Baujault's works, including some busts in plaster of contemporaries, and a bust in bronze entitled *François Airault*, 59 cm.

BAUSSAN, SÉBASTIEN AUGUSTE

Avignon, May 24, 1829
Montpellier, 1907

Baussan studied under his father, the sculptor Joseph Baussan, and would himself become a teacher at the school of fine arts in Montpellier. The museum of this city has a bas-relief in bronze, *L'Assomption*, 36 x 19 cm, the door for a tabernacle of the Notre-Dame-des-Tables church, as well as some medallion portraits: *Monsieur d'Albènas*, 25 cm diam., *F. Bazille*, 20 cm diam., and *Madame Bertrand*, 19 cm diam.

BAYARD DE LA VINGTRIE, PAUL ARMAND

Paris, May 22, 1846
Paris, May 2, 1900

After having fought for the defense of Paris in 1870, Bayard de la Vingtrie made his debut at the Salon in 1876, and there received a first prize medal for *Charmeur de serpent*, 176 cm, the bronze of which appeared for a time at Monceau Park. He continued to do consignments until 1892, including some busts and statues of personalities and allegorical figures. A statuette in bronze by this artist, *Jeanne d'Arc écoutant les voix*, was sold at Parthenay on May 25, 1986.

Paul Armand Bayard de la Vingtrie,
Jeanne d'Arc écoutant les voix.

BAYSER, MARGUERITE GRATRY DE

Lille, 1884
Lille, February 1975

At the beginning of the century, Marguerite Gratry de Bayser modeled animals—dogs, cats, and horses—before meeting Vital Cornu, who gave her some tips. She received her first award at the Salon of 1908. In 1915, she settled in Paris, perfected her art, and then traveled to Africa, Egypt, and America and participated in a number of expositions. In 1952, at the new Bernheim Gallery, she showed an entire series of animals, *Gazelle*, *Chatte*, *Chouette*, *Epervier*, *Poisson*, etc., as well as some figures, *Coureur indien*, *Indochinoise*, *Mariniquaise* and others. The great majority of her work was done between the two world wars. One of her bronzes, *Gazelle*, has been situated in Henri-Bataille Square, near the hippodrome of Auteuil, since 1930. The museum of Mans has a bronze from 1912 entitled *Tête de femme*, 32 cm. The museum of the Petit Palais has a bust, also in bronze, *Lysica*, 45 cm. A samll bronze, *Poisson-lune*, 19 cm, cast by Susse, was sold at the Drouot Hotel on October 22, 1986, room 1.

BECQUET, JUSTIN

Besançon, June 17, 1829
Paris, February 28, 1907

Becquet was the oldest surviving student of Rude, whose teachings he conscientiously applied. He debuted at the Salon of 1853. His abundant work includes statues and biblical or allegorical groups, busts of people, and some animals, sometimes of monumental size. A number of his sculptures were erected at sites in different French cities, including Paris's Hôtel de Ville, the National Library (a statue entitled *Numismatique*, under the portal), and in the garden of Galliéra Palace (*Le Dieu Pan et un tigre*, a bronze dedicated to his master Rude). Notable among the works Becquet sent to the Salon are *Lion* in terra cotta (1874), *Vache* in terra cotta (1875), *Penseur*, a statuette in bronze (1883), *Lion*, a study in bronze (1887), *La Source*, a statuette in marble, and *Masque*, a study in bronze (1890). *La Source*, also called *La Source de la Seine*, was cast in bronze by Barbedienne, 70 cm L.

MUSEUMS
Dijon
La France courtoise, 25 cm.

SALES
La Source de la Seine, 70 cm L. (Barbedienne), Reims, April 28, 1985.

BEER, FRÉDÉRIC

Brno (Moravia), September 2, 1845
Circa 1912

Born in Moravia, at that time an Austrian possession, Frédéric Beer studied at the Academy of Vienna in 1865, and then in Rome in 1870. Five years later, he established himself in Paris and obtained French citizenship. He exhibited at the Salon from 1876 to 1908, notably with *Aurore*, a statue in plaster (1880), *Albert Dûrer enfant*, a statue in bronze (1885), *Tête d'étude* in bronze (1889), *Amour maternel*, a statuette in terra cotta (1895), *Laurier*, a statuette in bronze, and *Pitié*, a statuette in marble (1908), as well as a number of busts. A certain number of his works also carry the signature of Alfred Grévin, who had supplied him with the sketches.

The Susse foundry cast a bust entitled *Luther enfant*, 30 cm, and a statuette entitled *Escholier du XVe siècle*, 71 and 49 cm. Thiébaut cast the statuette *Albert Dûrer assis*, 38 cm. Of final note is the work *Aurore*, in gilded bronze and equipped with electricity.

BEGUINE, MICHEL

Uxeau (Saône-et-Loire), August 9, 1855
April 1929

A very active sculptor, a student of Dumont and of A. Millet, Beguine is especially well-known for allegorical statues such as *La Douleur, Le Printemps,* and *L'Art grec* (a statue in stone for the façade of the Grand Palais in Paris), as well as some groups and statues of historic people. At the Salon of 1883, he showed *David vainqueur,* a statue in plaster (in bronze in 1887, and in a smaller bronze in 1890), *Charmeuse,* a statue in marble (1891), *Le Printemps,* a statuette in bronze (1892), *Tricoteuse bretonne,* a statuette in bronze (1912), and *Jeune Fille au miroir,* a statuette in marble (1914). *La Charmeuse* was cast in bronze by Siot-Decauville.

MUSEUMS
Paris, Carnavalet
Buste de Louis Charles Delescluze, 61.5 cm (1890).

SALES
La Charmeuse, 81 cm (Colin, founder), Sotheby New York, September 13, 1986.
Idylle, 82 cm, Barcelona, March 26, 1985.
Paysanne, 66 cm, Drouot, March 4, 1983, room 1.

BELIN, JOSEPH FRANÇOIS

Paris?
1902

A student of Jouffroy, Belin began to send busts, allegories and genre scenes to the Salont in 1890. A statuette in bronze entitled *La Vague* was exhibited at the Salon of 1898. Some other subjects cast in bronze are known, including a bust of a child.

BELLOC, JEAN-BAPTISTE

Pamiers?
Paris, January 23, 1919

After being taught by Marcié and Thomas, Jean-Baptiste Belloc exhibited at the Salon from 1888 until 1913, most notably contributing *Temps futurs,* a statue in bronze, *Tobie et l'ange,* a group in bronze (1896), *Brunehilde,* a statue in silver, gold, bronze, ivory and precious stones, *Buste de Mme Desbordes-Valmore* in silver and ivory (1897), *Porte-Etendard tunisien* and *La Paix,* two bronzes (1903), *Guerrier mogol,* a statuette in bronze, and *Douleur,* a statuette in marble (1907), and *Le Général Gallieni équestre,* a statuette in bronze (1911). Two statuettes in bronze entitled *Douleur* and *Danseuse* were exhibited at the Salon d'Automne in 1903. Belloc worked in North Africa, particularly on the decoration of the theater of Tunis. He is also the author of a monument to General Lamoricière, unveiled in Constantine in 1909.

Joseph François Belin,
Fleurs d'Automne,
49 cm.

Jean-Baptiste Belloc,
Méhariste triomphant,
45 cm.

Jean-Baptiste Belloc, J eune Arabe debout tenant une lance.

Temps futurs was cast in bronze by Susse in four sizes, 88, 66, 44 and 29 cm. Also of note are *Cavalier marocain*, cast by Barbedienne, and without an ascertained founder, a statuette entitled *Touareg*.

SALES

Arabe sur un cheval cabré, gilded bronze, 99 cm, Sotheby London, June 7, 1984.
Arabe sur un dromadaire enlevant une femme or *Méhariste triomphant*, 45 cm, L'Isle-Adam, September 29, 1985.
Jeune Arabe debout tenant une lance, Issoudun, June 25, 1978.

BERNARD, ANTOINE LOUIS

Paris, March 5, 1821
1900

At the Ecole des Beaux-Arts in 1839, Bernard studied in the studio of Duret, and then in the studio of Klagmann before making his debut at the Salon of 1847. The following year, he exhibited a statuette in bronze at the Salon entitled *Napolitain jouant avec une écrevisse*. Until 1865, his consignments consisted of a series of portraits in bust and medallion form, some in plaster and others in bronze.

BERNARD, EDMOND

Toulouse, 1849—?

At the museum of Tourcoing is found a small bust entitled *Homme barbu*, 40 cm, signed by this sculptor; the piece won the second prize in Rome in 1874.

BERNARD, EUSTACHE

Grenoble, July 15, 1836
December 20, 1904

This artist, who became director of the school of sculpture in Grenoble, worked primarily on monuments for his hometown: the cathedral, the courthouse, and the museum. The latter has a statuette in bronze entitled *Barnave*, 30 cm.

BERNARD, JOSEPH

Vienna (Isère), January 17, 1866
Boulogne-sur-Seine, January 7, 1931

Since his father was a stonecutter who worked on the restoration of monuments in the Rhône Valley, the young Joseph Bernard began to accompany his father to the building sites at the age of twelve, and learned the craft of direct cutting that he would practice all his life. He first entered the school of fine arts of Lyon, but in 1885 transfered to the school in Paris to study in the studio of Cavelier. He stayed there only six months. A serious artist with a talent for great accuracy, he worked alone from this point onward. He soon accomplished a number of studies, often monumental—*Le Fardeau de la Vie*, the *Monument à la Paix*—which he destroyed when he moved to Boulogne in 1921. This early period was marked by a rather dramatic style reminiscent of Rodin, and only a single work is left: *L'Espoir vaincu*, sculpted in marble for a public garden, but now held at the museum of Vienna.

In 1908, Joseph Bernard exhibited some small sculptures at the Adrien Hébrard Gallery, with which he had signed an exclusive contract for the casting of his works. Most of these editions are dated from before 1914. It is also in this period that he sculpted in marble and stone, or sometimes modeled directly in plaster, resulting in several important works: *La Jeunesse charmée par l'Amour*,

Jospeh Bernard,
Torse de femme,
first study for
La Victoire, 28 cm
(Hébrard),
Coubertin Foundation.

J. BERNARD

Joseph Bernard,
Jeune Fille à la cruche,
184 cm
(A. Rudier).

Joseph Bernard,
Jeune Fille
à la draperie,
138 cm.
Coubertin Foundation.

which would be acquired by the city of Paris, *Chants immortels*, *Plénitude*, *La Rieuse*, *La Femme à la cruche*, *jeune Fille à sa toilette*, *La Femme et l'enfant* (young woman dancing with a child, one of his best-known sculptures), the monument to Michel Servet unveiled in Vienna in 1911, and the frieze in marble of the *Danse*, completed in 1913. Photographs of the Manzi and Joyant Gallery in Paris, taken in 1914 during one of the sculptor's first major exhibitions, are proof that the works which are mentioned below and which are often dated much later did exist during these earlier years.

After the First World War, Joseph Bernard achieved international renown. A new series of statuettes was cast in the last years of his life. He worked frequently for the great decorator Ruhlmann, completing the sculpted decoration of his *Hôtel du collectionneur* at the Exhibition of Decorative Arts in 1925.

The feminine body has an important place in the work of Joseph Bernard. The full forms that he liked always reveal a studied elegance of movement, harmony of proportions, and grace of gestures and position. His sense of the monumental appears even in the works of reduced size.

Bernard's 1907 contract with Hébrard incorporated some verbal clauses which, in principle, limited the editions to ten works. While it seems that this limit was frequently exceeded, many castings were actually sanctioned for a higher number of proofs. This contract expired in 1918, and was later denounced by Bernard on several occasions. Afterwards, he worked with several other founders, primarily C. Valsuani and Rudier, but never accomplishing true editions. After 1970, the foundry of the Coubertin foundation cast some of Joseph Bernard's works in series limited to twelve original works established by the law of 1981, and under the control of Mr. Jean Bernard, the sculptor's son and heir.

The chronological list below mentions the majority of Joseph Bernard's works cast in bronze. The names of the founders who executed these bronzes are not always known, and the number of proofs made is often difficult to determine. In the castings of Hébrard, the ten models planned for were not always cast. For the more important editions, the total number of castings intended or the number of works which could be inventoried have been noted. Finally, it is necessary to remember that some works made by the foundry of Coubertin can be added to the list of successful castings.

1904
Groupe à la clochette, 18 cm.
Danseuse voilée, 32 cm.
Danseuse nue, 32 cm.

1905
La Danse des roses, 36 cm.
Danseur et danseuse, 32 cm.
Erinnye, 23 cm.
Faune et bacchante, in busts, 35 x 43 cm.
Tête de jeune fille, 18 cm.
Tête de Salomé, 17 cm.

1906
De l'Aurore à l'apothéose, three heads of women, 52 cm.
Charmeuse, femme au serpent, 31.5 cm.
La Chute, femme se coiffant, 31 cm.
L'Effort vers la nature, head, 32 cm.
L'Étreinte, 19 cm.
Frileuse, 23 cm.
L'Harmonie, 250 cm (public garden at Bourges).
Jeunes Faunesse, 55 cm.
Le Poète, head, 18 cm.
Premier bijou 24 cm.

1907
Souvenir Rabelaisien, 19.8 cm.

1908
Femme chantant, study for *De l'Aurore à l'apothéose*, 26 cm (two variations).
Portrait du poète André Rivoire, 35 cm.
Portrait de Jean Bernard, fils du sculpteur, 27.5 cm.
Le Sphinx moderne, 34 cm.

1909
Madame Gabriel Faure, head, 26 cm.
Monument à la gloire de l'aviation (not finished), small model, 23 cm.
Tête de fillette, 20 cm.

1909-1910
Studies for the monument to Michel Servet:
Avant l'Essor, study of a young girl, 34 cm; 25 works planned for by Hébrard.
Avant l'Essor, 63 cm.
Groupe de la Jeunesse, 32.5 cm; 25 works planned for by Hébrard.
Groupe de la Jeunesse, second state, 59.5 cm.
Tête de la Jeunesse, 44 cm.
Tête de jeune homme, 44 cm.
Tête de Michel Servet, 53 cm.
La Tendresse, 36 cm; 25 proofs previewed by Hébrard.
La Tendresse, last state, 64 cm.
La Tendresse, 68.5 cm.
Tête du Remord, 12 cm.
La Gloire, torso, first study for the Victoire, 28 cm. 50 proofs planned by Hébrard, a number of proofs located.
Etude drapée pour la Victoire, 55 cm.
Etude drapée sans tête, 47 cm.
Three bronzes cast after the monument in stone of Michel Servet:
La Jeunesse et la Raison, 270 cm.
Michel Servet. 265 cm.
Le Remord, 260 cm.

1910
Jeune Fille à la cruche or the *Porteuse d'eau*, 54 cm; 50 proofs planned by Hébrard, more than 35 proofs located.
Jeune Fille à la cruche, torso of the sketch, 33 cm.
Jeune Fille à la cruche, 184 cm; 12 proofs made.
Jeune Fille à la cruche, torso, 97 and 48 cm.
Jeune Fille à la cruche, bust, 64 cm.
Jeune Fille à la cruche, head, 30 cm.
Jeune Fille à la cruche, reduction, 64 cm; 28 proofs located.

*Joseph Bernard,
Jeune Fille assise
à sa toilette,
64 cm
(Valsuani).*

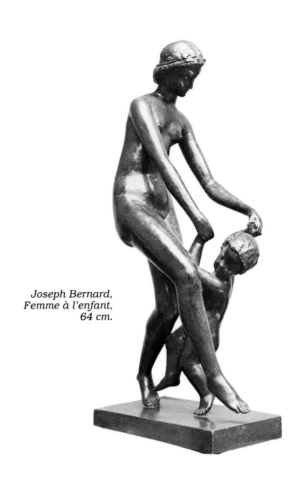

*Joseph Bernard,
Femme à l'enfant,
64 cm.*

*Joseph Bernard,
Couple assis,
first state
for La Jeunesse,
30 cm
(Hébard 3/25).*

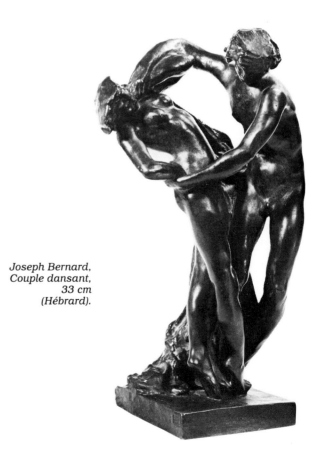

*Joseph Bernard,
Couple dansant,
33 cm
(Hébrard).*

Joseph Bernard,
L'Enfant dansant
aux castanettes,
26.5 cm,
Coubertin
Foundation.

In addition to these works are several objects in bronze—some sections adorned with female shapes, an ashtray *La Vague*, a mirror frame, an inkwell, etc.

MUSEUMS
Calais
Sphinx moderne, head, 32 cm (1908).
Cambrai
Jeune Fille à la cruche, 178 cm (1912).
Lyon
Femme dansant, 185 cm (C. Valsuani).
Jeune Fille assise se coiffant, 157 cm (Rudier).
Jeune Fille à la draperie, 64 cm.
Paris, Orsay
Femme à la cruche, 175 cm (1912; Hébrard).
Femme dansant avec un enfant, 183 cm (1912; Rudier cast 1925).
Madame Gabriel Faure, bust, 39 cm (1909; Hébrard).

The museum of the Coubertin foundation at Saint-Rémy-les-Chevreuse is devoted to publicizing the work of Joseph Bernard; it owns some great bronzes, marbles, and stone works, as well as fifteen hundred sketches donated by the sculptor's son. Some works by Bernard are exhibited elsewhere, in museums in Vienna (Isère), Montauban, Bruxelles, Venice, Lisbon, and Prague. The museum of Alger owns *Deux Danseuses*, 54 cm (C. Valsuani No. 2, 1928) and *Jeune Fille à la cruche*, 64 cm (C. Valsuani No. 19, 1927).

1911
Les Voix, 38 cm.
1912
Buste de jeune fille, 27.5 cm; cast planned at 10 works.
Les Deux Danseuses, 54 cm; 17 proofs located, certain of them from Valsuani.
Enfant dansant, 26.5 cm; cast planned for 15 proofs.
Faune dansant, 42 cm.
Faune dansant, 73 cm; cast planned for 25 proofs.
Faune dansant, 185 cm.
Femme à l'enfant, 184 cm.
Femme à l'enfant, 64 cm.
Femme à l'enfant, study, 55 cm; cast planned by Hébrard at 25 models, a number of proofs located.
Grande Bacchante, 172 cm.
Jeune danseuse, 63.5 cm, cast planned for 25 proofs.
Jeune Danseuse or *Jeune Fille à la draperie*, 138 cm (1912-1926).
Jeune Fille assise à sa toilette, 155 cm.
Jeune Fille assise à sa toilette, study, 65 cm; cast planned for 25 models, a number of proofs located.
La Pureté, head, 25 cm.
La Pureté, bust, 45 cm.
Tête de Jeune fille coiffée en bandeau, 32 cm.
Tête de poète ou de penseur, 50 cm.
1916 to 1930
Groupe de danseuses, 60 cm (1916).
Tête de faune, 25 cm (1918).
La Petite Bacchante, 70 cm (1919); cast planned for 25 models.
Buste aux deux mains, 50 cm (1920).
Jeune Fille debout se coiffant, first state, 66 cm (1922).
Jeune Fille debout se coiffant, second state, 68 cm.
Jeune Fille debout se coiffant, 102 cm.
Jeune Fille aux tresses, 158 cm (1923).
Couple dansant, 60 and 78 cm (1926).
Figure pour un athlète, unfinished, 195 cm (1927-1930).
1930
Boxeur, 47 cm.
Femme allongée, 23 cm.
Femme au bracelet, 49 cm.
Femme couchée avec un enfant, 27 x 51 cm.
Homme portant une haltère, 49.5 cm.
Petite tête de femme, 8 cm.
La Victoire, study without arms, 58 cm.
La Victoire, winged study, 58 cm.

Sarah Bernhardt,
Autoportrait en chauve-souris,
inkwell, 30 cm (1880; Thiébaut frères).
See reproduction in color **on the back cover.**

SALES

Couple assis, 30 cm (Hébrard 3/25), Dijon, May 20, 1984.
Couple dansant, 33 cm, (Hébrard), Drouot, December 5, 1985, room 1.
La Danse, 35 cm (Hébrard), Drouot, October 19, 1983, room 9.
Eve au serpent, 30 cm (Hébrard), Drouot, July 7, 1983, room 9.
Jeune Fille en buste, 40 cm (Valsuani No. 8), Drouot, December 14, 1984, room 10.
Jeune Fille à la cruche, 65 cm (C. Valsuani No. 21), Enghien, June 26, 1983; (C. Valsuani), Lille, October 25, 1986.
Nu (Hébrard No. 2), Grenoble, December 9, 1985.
Cadre de miroir orné de femmes voilées, 37 cm L., Drouot, February 3, 1986.

BERNHARDT, ROSINE BERNARD,

ALSO KNOWN AS SARAH

Paris, October 22, 1845
Paris, March 26, 1923

The celebrated dramatic performer also practiced sculpture. She produced a series of busts of actors, writers, and poets, statuettes and small groups of animals, and some works inspired by the sea—about forty pieces in all, of which only a small number are now known. The great animal sculptor François Pompon would have elaborated on some of these sculptures. Bernhardt exhibited at the Salons of 1874 to 1897, contributing *Après la tempéte*, a group in plaster (1876), *Ophélie*, basrelief in marble (1881), *Bellone*, a bust in marble (1890), and *Souvenir*, a head in marble (1891), as well as different busts in bronze.

In the sale organized in Paris after the actress's death, the work *Masque de Jacques Damala mort*, 24 x 27 cm appeared. Of further note are some castings in bronze from her sculptures: *Après la tempéte*, 75 cm, *Autoportrait in chauve-souris* (inkwell), cast by Thiébaut, 26 cm, (1880; a model of the piece belongs to the Boston Museum), *Le Fou de la mort* cast by G. Martin, 31 cm (1877). A certain number of other pieces were sold recently at auction (see below).

MUSEUMS
Paris, Carnavalet
Buste d'Emile de Girardin, 20.5 cm (Casse and Delpy, editors).
Paris, Petit Palais
Buste de Victorien Sardou, 72 cm.

SALES
Après la tempeté, bust, 75 cm (1876), Christie's Oklahoma (United States), September 24, 1981.
Autoportrait en chauve-souris, inkwell, 30 cm (Thiébaut), Drouot, June 23, 1986, room 1 and 7 (sold for 460,000 F).
Emile de Girardin, 21 cm Versailles, November 18, 1984.
Poisson, 36 cm (Hébrard), Christie's New York, April 3, 1982.

BERNSTAMM (BERSTAMM), LÉOPOLD

Riga, April 20, 1859
1939

Bernstamm was trained at the academy of Saint-Petersburg in 1873, then in Florence, and finally in Paris with the sculptor Mercié. In 1886 he became director of the Grévin museum, and at the same time

Léopold Bernstamm,
Coquelin cadet or Le Malade imaginaire,
37 cm (Siot-Decauville),
Musée d'Orsay.

began exhibiting at the Salon with a number of busts (most in bronze) of personalities, especially artists: *Jules Chéret* (1895), *Jules Lemaître* and *L'Ambassadeur de Chine* (1897), *J.-L. Gérôme* (1898), *Edmond Rostand* and *Paul Deschanel* (1899), *Edmond Detaille* and *François Coppée* (1903), *Léon Bonnat* (1904), *Albert Carré* (1907), *Louis Blériot* (1910), *Branly* (1912), etc. He is also responsible for *Pierre-le-Grand charpentier*, a statue in bronze commissioned by the Russian emperor (1909). A smaller version, also in bronze, appeared at the Salon of 1911. Berstamm, sometimes spelled Bernstamm, is also the author of the monument *Edouard Pailleron* in Monceau Park (Salon of 1905). The Siot-Decauville foundry cast his *Buste florentin* in bronze, as well as many other busts and statuettes.

MUSEUMS
Châlons-sur-Marne
Léon Bourgeois, 55.5 cm (1903).
Nice
Buste de Jules Chéret.

Paris, Orsay
Coquelin cadet or *Le Malade imaginaire*, 37 cm (Siot-Decauville).
Reims
Buste d'homme, 63.5 cm (1902).
Versailles
Bustes d'Ernest Renan et de Léon Bonnat.
Vesoul
Buste à mi-corps de J.-L. Gérôme, 76 cm (Siot-Decauville).

SALES
Portrait présumé de Tolstoi assis sur un bac, 35 cm. (Hébrard), Drouot Hotel, November 18, 1986, rooms 5 and 6.

BERTAUX, HÉLÉNA
Paris, July 4, 1825
Château de Lassay (Sarthe), April 20, 1909

Bertaux studied sculpture with her father, Pierre Hébert, and with Augustin Dumont. Using the pseudonym Allélit, she exhibited for the first time at the Salon of 1848, with a statue in plaster of a female. Her submissions to the Salon became regular starting in 1857, at which time she used her real name. Best-known from her prolific output are her large works, notably for numerous monuments: the Saint-Laurent and Sain-François-Xavier churches, the Louvre, the Tuileries, city hall, the Senate, the Opera, the monumental fountain at Amiens (unveiled in 1864), the facade of the Grenoble museum, the Saint-Gratien church (a font in bronze entitled *Les Trois Vertus théologales*, and a group representing a poor box entitled *Pour les pauvres s'il vous plaît*).

The founder and president of the Union des Femmes Peintres et Sculpteurs (Union of Women Painters and Sculptors), Héléna Bertaux was one of the first artists to demand the admission of women to the Ecole des Beaux-Arts and to the competition for the prize of Rome.

The museum of the Petit Palais has a bronze, 179 cm high, entitled *Psyché sous l'empire du mystère*.

BERTHIER, PAUL
Rueil, 1879-1916

The animal sculptor Paul Berthier is the author of statuettes and small groups, especially of deer and other animals from Africa and Asia. In 1903, he sent *Tigre* in plaster to the Salon, and a group in wax entitled *Le Sirocco*, representing an Arab and his dromedary caught in the wind. In 1904 he sent two plasters entitled *Les Fauves* and *Ours combattant*; in 1905, the bronze *Méhari et fargui*; and in 1906, another bronze, *Poursuite*. The Thiébaut house cast *Le Fauconnier arabe*, 42 cm tall. The museum of Tours preserves a proof in bronze of *Sirocco*, 38 x 29 cm. A model of *Faucconier arabe à cheval*, 42 cm (Thiébaut), was sold at the Drouot Hotel on November 29, 1985, room 9.

BERTHOUD, PAUL FRANCOIS
Paris, May 17, 1870-?

A sculptor, painter, and engraver, Berthoud exhibited at the Salon starting in 1889. He also participated at the Salon d'Automne from 1907 to 1931 and at the Salon de la Société Nationale des Beaux-Arts, where he exhibited again in 1939. His submissions seem to be primarily limited to busts. One, *Tête de Femme*, 35.5 cm (cast by Montagutelli), was sold at Drouot Hotel and November 26, 1982, room 4.

BERTRAND-BOUTÉE, RENÉ
Maubeuge, 1877
1950

Bertrand-Boutée was a student of Barrias and Coutan. He began to exhibit at the Salon in 1898. Among his pieces exhibited were *Mondaines*, two statuettes in plaster (1905), *Pour la race*, a plaster group (1906), *Première Traîne*, a statuette in silver and gold (1907), *Mabuse*, a bust in bronze, and *Sous le charme*, a statuette in marble (1908), *Bébé boit* and *Bébé a bu*, two statuettes in bronze (1913), and *Enfant à la fontaine*, a statue in stone and bronze(1914). Bertrand-Boutée continued his art after World War I, and contributed a statuette in bronze representing *Joueur de football*(Soccer player) to the Salon of 1924. The museum of Maubeuge has some works in plaster as well as a bronze, *La Première Traîne*, 43 cm.

BEYLARD, CHARLES LOUIS
Bordeaux, May 4, 1843
July 28, 1925

Beylard specialized in historical genre portrayals. From 1876 to 1914 he exhibited works at the Salon such as *Méléagre*, a group in bronze (1877), *Maria Magdalena*, a statue in plaster, 125 cm (1880), *Jeanne d'Arc*, a statue in plaster (1889), as well as the statuettes *Peau d'âne*, plaster (1892), *Taquinerie*, marble (1895), *Souvenir de thèse*, bronze, and *A la toilette*, gilded bronze (1905). His monumental group in stone entitled *La Ville de Paris* tops the facade of the Lyon Station in Paris. *Buste de Jeanne d'Arc* in bronze, 31 cm, appears in the catalog of the Susse foundry. The museums of Clermont-Ferrand and of Troyes each have a large bronze version, 170 cm high, of *Méléagre*, cast by Jaboeuf and Bezont.

BIEGAS BOLESLAS
March 29, 1877
Paris, 1954

Born in Poland, Biegas was a sculptor, painter, and author of plays for the theater. He practiced his art in Paris in a style combining symbolism, surrealism, and the fantastic. He exhibited at the Salon

Boleslas Biegas,
Adam or Le Penseur,
170 cm
(A. Rudier).

Bleslas Biegas,
L'Effort, 175 cm
(1910; A. Rudier).
See reproduction
in color page 19?)

d'Automne in 1910 (*Adam* or *Le Penseur*) and at the Nationale des Beaux-Arts from 1902 to 1927, with works including *L'Avenir*, bronze (1907), *Titanic*, bronze (1913), and some busts and terra cottas. The founders Rudier, Valsuani, Susse, and Blanchet cast a certain number of his sculptures in bronze, often in rather large dimensions. Of particular note are *Les Chevaux de l'Enfer*, 53 cm, *Détresse*, a woman standing, 170 cm, *Le Printemps*, gilded bronze, 89 cm, etc. Two bronzes completed in France are indicated as belonging to the Poznan Museum: *L'Avenir*, 67 cm, and *Dernier Coucher de soleil*, 58 cm.

SALES

Adam or *Le Penseur*, 170 cm (Rudier), Enghien, June 27, 1982 (sold for 145,000 F).
Adam or *Le Penseur*, 56 cm, L'Isle-Adam, June 16, 1985.
L'Ange à la couronne d'épines, 104 cm (Valsuani), Drouot Hotel, June 27, 1984, room 6.
Le Compositeur et l'Inspiration, 58 cm (Valsuani), Drouot Hotel, October 19, 1983, room 9.
Le Coup de vent, 48.5 cm (recent Susse cast 3/4), Sotheby Monaco, March 11, 1984.
L'Effroi, 175 cm (A. Rudier), Enghien, March 29, 1987.
Pressentiment, 61 cm (Valsuani; 1903), Sotheby Monaco, March 6, 1983.
La Puissance de la Volonté, 210 cm (Blanchet 1/8), Enchien, April 17, 1983.
Le Repos, 50 cm (Blanchet 2/8; 1920), Enghien, April 17, 1983.
Le Réveil de la Pensée, 74 cm, Christie's New York, May 24, 1984.
La Vie, 195 cm (Blanchet 1/8), Drouot Hotel, March 23, 1984, room 6.
Wagner, 75 cm (1904), Enghien, March 21, 1982.

BIGONET, CHARLES

Paris, July 11, 1877
Paris, June 21, 1931

In 1897 Bigonet began exhibiting busts in plaster of genre subjects at the Salon, including *La Colombe et la fourmi* and *Premier Pas*. Then, after a sojourn in Algeria as resident student of the Villa Abd-el-Tif (in 1912), he did statues of people from that country, including small bronzes such as *Mauresque accroupie*, 45 cm, and *Buste de jeune Israélite*, 37 cm. These two works belong to the museum of Algiers.

BLANCHARD, JULES

Puiseaux (Loiret), May 25, 1832
May 3, 1916

A number of allegorical or mythological figures were completed by Blanchard, including *L'Architecture*, a statue in bronze placed at the entrance to the city hall, *Les Arts plastiques*, a group in stone on the facade of the Grand Palais, the front of the courthouse of Angers, a statue in stone entitled *La Bocca della Verita* in the Luxembourg garden, etc. The Thiébaut house cast one of his works, *Jeune Equilibriste*, in two sizes, 85 and 47 cm. The museum of Châlons-sur-Marne owns a large bronze, 230 cm high, entitled *Faune dansant* (1873), and the museum of Orsay owns *Buste de femme arabe*, 69 cm (1901), cast by Jaboeuf and Cie.

BLANCHOT, LÉON

Bordeaux, November 25, 1868
Paris, June 27, 1947

Blanchot worked simultaneously as a sculptor and an illustrator. (Under the pseudonym of Ivan Loewitz, he illustrated Hector Malot and Jules Simon.) He studied at the school of fine arts in Bordeaux, then went to Paris where, at the Salon, he exhibited busts, medals, and statues: *Sainte Agnès*, plaster (1893), *Pierre Gringoire*, plaster (1894), *Lorelei*, plaster (1895), *Le Regret*, plaster (1896), *Petite Maman*, a group in plaster (1908), etc. He also submitted pieces—including statuettes in plaster and a group in stone entitled *Jeune Mère*—to the Salon de la Société Nationale des Beaux-Arts from 1906 to 1914.

SALES

Elégante en chapeau à plumes or *Femme au boa*, 32 cm (Eugène Blot, founder), Drouot Hotel, November 28, 1984, room 13; Sotheby Monaco, October 6, 1985.

Jules Blanchard,
Buste de femme arabe,
69 cm (1901).
Musée d'Orsay.

BLAVIER, ÉMILE VICTOR

Born in Crespin (North)

Blavier made his debut at the Salon in 1852, after having started studying sculpture at the academic school of Douai, and continuing it in Paris at the studios of Toussaint and Calmel. Until 1876, he exhibited a number of busts and statues, among them *Devineresse*, a group in bronze (Salon of 1857), *Egyptienne et son enfant attaqués par un crocodile*, a small group in plaster preserved at the museum of Douai with many of his other works (some of them very large), and some statuettes in bronze including *Le Départ* and *Le Retour* (1870). The museum of Douai also owns two large medallions in bronze, *Portraits de Louis Potiez*, a former curator, 73 x 60 cm, dated 1852.

SALES

Jeunes Voyageurs, two pendants, 53 cm Sotheby London, November 8, 1984.
Paysan and *Paysanne*, two pendants, 30 cm, Sotheby London, November 25, 1982.

BLOCH, ARMAND LUCIEN

Montbéliard (Doubs), July 1, 1866
March 1932

Busts, masks, and animals, sculpted easily in wood, characterize the work of this student of Falguière and Antonin Mercié. He exhibited at the Salon from 1888 to 1933. A mask in bronze of Eugène Carrière, 45 cm, is displayed at the museum of Belfort. The museum of Reims has a profile of a man in medallion, 25 cm diam.

BLONDAT, MAX

Crain (Yonne), November 30, 1872
Boulogne-sur-Seine, 1926

MAX-BLONDAT

Max Blondat exhibited at the Salon between 1890 and 1914, and then again from 1920 to 1925, after being influenced by contact with the sculptors Thomas, Mathurin Moreau, and Valton. His work, often very much in the Art Nouveau spirit, includes commemorative monuments, fountains, patriotic statues and groups, allegorical figures, and even burlesques. This last genre includes a statue entitled *Victor Hugo chevauchant un Pégase à tête d'âne*, completed in 1880 for a banquet of artists, as well as a group of three children contemplating a frog made for a fountain, and a group entitled *Jeunesse*, exhibited at the Salon of 1907. Blondat produced a number of figurines of women and children, some of which decorated vases and other furnishings.

Max Blondat,
Le Tourbillon,
trophy cup in bronze, 56 cm.

Some pieces were cast by Siot-Decauville: *Buste de vieillard*, a statuette, *La Femme*, a tall draped figure which is one part of a piece entitled *Le Tourbillon*, another trophy entitled *Les Vagues*, some vases, flower stands, and trays, a lamp entitled *Les Cloches de pâques*, and a door knocker entitled *Femme nue*, 34.5 cm.

Valsuani cast some figurines of soldiers made during the First World War, as well as a figure for a clock (see the collections of the museum of Beauvais).

MUSEUMS

Beauvais
L'Aumônier, 35 cm (Valsuani; 1916).
Le Coeur qui bat clock in bronze and lapis-lazuli, 32 cm (Valsuani; 1917).
La Femme, gilded bronze, 28 cm (Siot-Decauville).
La Pensée, inkwell, 33 cm (Siot-Decauville).
Le Pinard, 35 cm (Valsuani).
La Soupe, 32 cm (Valsuani).

The museum of Beauvais, which orgainzed an exhibition of works by Max Blondat in 1979, owns some later pieces executed in the 1920s.

Boulogne-Billancourt
A recent donation from the family of the sculptor includes two bronzes of note: *La Soupe*, 39 cm (1916), and *Silhouette*, 33 cm (1917).

SALES

Amour endormi, gilded bronze, 36 x 47 cm (Valsuani), Drouot Hotel, March 5, 1983, room 10.
Les Bottes de sept lieues (the Petit Poucet astride a globe), 16 cm, Drouot Hotel, May 19, 1982, room 1.

BOFILL, ANTOINE

Born in Barcelona

Bofill studied at the school of fine arts of the Catalanian capital. In Spain and France he exhibited some small figures and groups that he had cast in bronze; he exhibited as often in Germany or Austria as he did in France. He began to participate at the Salon in 1894. His submissions included *En Triomphe*, a statuette in bronze, and *Le Repos*, a group in bronze (1896), *Enfant arabe au singe*, a group in terra cotta (1902), *Pauvre Moineau*, a statue in plaster (1904), some groups in plaster, *Une prière*, (1905), *Caresse* (1906), a statuette in bronze, *Fondeur* (1906), and two other plasters, *Peau-rouge à cheval* and *Campagnard à cheval* (1910).

Among the works cast in bronze are *En Triomphe*, cast in two sizes, 75 and 51 cm, *Jeune Pêcheur*, 25 cm, *Le Travail*, 38 cm, *Faneuse*, 36 cm, *Indien à cheval*, 40 cm, *Jeanne d'Arc*, 33 cm, *Enfant et taureau*, 33 cm, *L'Epave*, 75 cm, *Le Dernier d'une race*, 50 cm,

Antoine Bofill,
Retour des champs,
39.5 cm.

Antoine Bofill,
Le Dernier
d'une race,
50 cm.

Antoine Bofill,
Sirène sur un
cheval cabré,
77 cm.

Antoine Bofill,
Bohémienne,
bronze and ivory.

Antoine Bofill,
Pêcheur
lançant
une amarre,
72 cm.

Labor, 70 cm, Sommeil de la jeunesse, bust, 34 cm, Le Trot attelé, 70 cm, La Source, a vase in gilded bronze, 37 cm. Certain pieces were executed with ivory ornamentation.

Bofill was listed among living artists as late as 1939.

SALES
Arabe en prière, 49.5 cm, Sotheby London, June 7, 1984.
Bohémienne, bronze and ivory, Douamenez, March 28, 1982.
Cri de liberté, young man brandishing his chains, 105 cm, Drouot Hotel, October 29, 1986, room 14.
Le Dernier d'une race, 50 cm, Rambouillet, November 18, 1984.
Le Faneur, Le Havre, November 26, 1984.
L'Hiver, bronze and ivory, 22 cm, Barcelona, March 17, 1983.
Jeanne d'Arc, bronze and ivory, 58 cm, Sotheby London, March 17, 1983.

Mascotte automobile, 13.5 cm, (Etling), Drouot Hotel, June 14, 1985, room 14.
Nymphe chevauchant un papillon, gilded bronze, 30.5 cm Christie's New York, May 24, 1984.
Pêcheur landant une amarre, 72 cm, Drouot Hotel, June 13, 1983; room 10.
Le Travail, 38 cm, Lokeren (Belgium), June 1, 1985.

BOISHERAUD, SÉBASTIEN DE
Maisdon (Loire-Atlantic), November 1, 1847
La Montagne (Loire-Atlantic), 1927

The museum of Nantes has a statuette in bronze entitled Hébé, 76 cm high, by this artist. The piece was exhibited at the Salon of 1891.

BOISSEAU, ÉMILE ANDRÉ
Varzy (Nièvre), March 29, 1842
Paris, November 17, 1923

BOISSEAU

After having studied sculpture at the Ecole des Beaux-Arts under the direction of Dumont and Bonnassieux, Boisseau exhibited regularly at the Salon starting in 1870. He particularly liked to cut marble, which he joined facilely to bronze, and even to onyx and other materials. Among his numerous commissions were L'Amour captif, plaster (1876; bronze in 1891), Le Génie du mal, marble (1880), Japonaise, bust in marble and bronze (1882), Le Crépuscule, a group in marble (1883), Echo, a statuette in bronze (1885), La Défense du foyer, a group in marble (1887), (today in the square of Ajaccio, in front of the Invalides in Paris), Aréthuse, compagne de Diane, a statuette in marble (1888), Les Fruits de la guerre, a group in marble (1895), Mousmé, a bust of a Japanese in bronze and onyx (1897), Oyser, le troubadour du pays bleu, a statuette in marble, onyx and bronze (1898), Les Fils de Clodomir, a group in marble, onyx, bronze, silver, and precious stones (1899), Fleurs de printemps, a statuette in marble (1905), La Jeunesse entre l'amour et l'amitié, a group in bronze (1907), Lever de l'aurore, a group in bronze and onyx (1911), and Messagère du printemps, a statuette in marble (1912).

Le Crépuscule a été was cast in bronze by Thiébaut, in three sizes, 72, 58 and 43 cm. Other bronzes include Enfant sortant d'un oeuf, Les Deux Minets (a child and two cats), Figaro (in collaboration with Amy), and Vercingétorix, 40 cm.

MUSEUMS
Varzy
La Défense du foyer, 60 cm reduction (Barbedienne).
La Jeunesse entre l'amour et l'amitié.

SALES
La Défense du foyer, 60 cm, Fontainebleau, March 3, 1985; Christie's New York, September 27, 1986.
La Défense du foyer, 87 cm (Society of Bronzes of Paris), Sotheby London, March 20, 1986.
Jeune Fille en costume médiéval, 81 cm, Christie's London, March 20, 1984.
Jeune Fille romantique, 57 cm, Brussels, March 23, 1983.
La Nuit, Charlevilee-Mézières, December 1, 1985.
Vercingétorix, 40 cm, Drouot Hotel, June 15, 1981, room 4.

BONHEUR, ISIDORE
Bordeaux, May 15, 1827-1901

I.BONHEUR

The two lions crouched in stone which flank the stairs on the Dauphine Plaza side of the Paris courthouse are far from Bonheur's best-known works, but they attest well to the talent of this sculptor, who produced quite a series of statuettes and small groups of animals in bronze.

Like his sister Rosa Bonheur, Isadore was very gifted at drawing and making models; he was taught first by his father, the painter Raymond Bonheur, and then at the Ecole des Beaux-Arts. He excelled at realistically capturing the attitudes and spontaneous movements of animals, even of man—a mare caressing her colt, a lion playing with his young, a horse leaping over a hedge, a polo player. The founder Hippolyte Peyrol, who married Bonheur's youngest sister Juliette Bonheur (he was indeed Isadore's brother-in-law, not his uncle, as is sometimes written), cast the majority of his works into bronzes of a very good quality. His career came to an end with the completion of a monument designed to commemorate his sister, a monument which was unveiled at Fontainebleau in 1901, the same year as her death.

Isadore Bonheur appeared for the first time at the Salon of 1848 with a painting and a plaster, both representing a *Cavalier africain attaqué par un lion*. He continued his career with a number of groups and figures of horses and horsemen including *Le Jockey à cheval* which seems to have brought him immediate success. There are many versions of this which were exhibited at the Salon at different times (1864 and 1879) and at the Exposition Universelle of 1889. Today it is sometimes confused because a number of different titles were used, including *Le Grand Jockey* and *Retour du pesage*. In the most often recognized of these versions, called *Le Grand Jockey*, the rider is stroking the neck and withers of his mount. The group entitled *Le Retour du pesage* shows the jockey looking back. In other variants, the jockey's mount is sometimes shown at a walk, and sometimes standing still.

Other bronzes sent to the Salon include *Cheval, Deux Gazelles* (1853), *Zèbre attaqué par une panthère*, completed for the gardens of Fontainebleau (1855), *Taureau et ours* (1857), *Chien et brebis* (1859), *Etalon anglais* (1863), *Postillon* (1866), *Dromadaire* (1868), *Lion et ses petits* (1869), *Boeuf et chien* (1870), *Pépin le Bref dans l'arène* (1874), *Cora, chienne d'arrêt* (1876), *Cavalier Louis XV, Cavalier arabe, Maquignon* (1881), *Le Saut de la haie* (1884 and Exhibition of 1889), *Porte-Etendard d'époque Henri II, Cerf faisant tête* (1885), *Trompette sous Louis XIII* (1886), *Relais de chiens* (1889), *Taureaux de combat espagnols* (1891), *Cuirassier, Chasseur d'Afrique* (silvered bronze, 1892), *Famille de lions* (1895), *Cavalier Louis XV* (silver, 1896), *Jeu de polo* (1897), and *Chevaux* (1898).

In addition to recent sales, a list below records the artist's works appearing in older sales or business sales. The list acquaints us with some of the works cast (the majority by Peyrol, but the name of the

Emile André Boisseau,
La Défense du foyer,
64 cm.

101

Isidore Bonheur,
Retour au pesage,
54 cm.

founder is rarely specified), and with their sizes. As always, it is often very difficult to match them with the works exhibited at the Salon because of the great variety of titles used. Those listed first are the bronzes of Isidore Bonheur belonging to his sister Rosa Bonheur, sold in 1900 after her death.

Bourricaire espagnol, 36 x 25 cm.
Bison courant, 18 x 35 cm.
Bison lancé, 16 x 24 cm.
Cheval de selle, 35 x 38 cm.
Chien de chasse gueule ouverte, 8 x 13 cm.
Lion assis, 42 x 31 cm.
Mendiant espagnol sur sa mule, 39 cm.
Taureau, 16 x 24 cm.
Vache combattant, 22 x 37 cm.

Isidore Bonheur,
Jockey à cheval,
71 cm.

Isidore Bonheur,
Le Grand Jockey,
95 cm.

Other works in bronze
Antilope à la course, 10.5 x 13.5 cm.
Cavalier africain attaqué par une lionne, 27 cm.
Cavalier chassant le buffle, 60 cm L.
Cavalier Louis XV, 100 cm.
Cerf, 80.5 cm.
Chat jouant avec sa queue, 6 x 12.5 cm.
Chat et singe (from a fable by La Fontaine), 8 x 16.5 cm.
Cheval arrêté, 69 x 84 cm.
Cheval libre au pas, 71 x 115 cm.
Cheval au trot, 46 x 72 cm.
Cheval et cerf, 24 cm.
Course de steeple (three horses jumping a hedge), 85 x 150 cm.
Cuirassier à cheval, 51 cm.
Dromadaire en marche, 22 cm.
Jument et étalon, 97 cm L.
Lièvre se grattant, 6.5 cm.
Lionne à l'affût, 21 cm.
Lionne et lionceaux, 32 x 68 cm.
Taureau combattant un ours, 22 x 37 cm.
Taureau debout, 31 cm.

Isidore Bonheur,
Veneur en costume Louis XV,
45 cm.

Cheval près d'un piquet, 36.5 cm, Sotheby London, November 8, 1984.
Chien de chasse tenant un lièvre, 19 cm, Epinal, December 14, 1986.
Dromadaire sellé, 27 cm, Enghien, June 26, 1983.
Guetteur arabe ou Cavalier arabe au fusil, 33 cm, Enghien, October 16, 1983.
Guetteur arabe ou Cavalier arabe au fusil, 60 cm, L'Isle-Adam, September 29, 1985.
Jockey à cheval, 36 cm, Sotheby London, July 5, 1986.
Jockey à cheval, 53 cm (Peyrol), Sotheby London, March 21, 1985.
Jockey à cheval, 61 cm, Christie's New York, March 30, 1985; Drouot Hotel, June 20, 1985, room 4; L'Isle-Adam, July 7, 1985; Washington, December 8, 1985.
Jockey à cheval, 71 cm, Christie's London, July 3, 1985; Le Havre, December 1, 1985.
Jument et poulain, 18 cm, Sotheby London, November 6, 1986.
Lion guettant, 20 cm (Griffoul, founder in Newark, United States), Sotheby London, June 12, 1986.
Le Lion et la souris, 22 cm, Sotheby London, March 8, 1984.
Lionne aux aguets, 42 cm, Nantes, November 24, 1984.
Postillon avec deux chevaux, 35.5 cm, Sotheby London, November 6, 1986.
Sanglier courant, Epinal, December 14, 1986.
Le Saut de l'obstacle, 49 cm, Christie's New York, September 28, 1985; Enghien, October 6, 1985.

Isidore Bonheur,
Guetteur arabe or Cavalier arabe au fusil,
60 cm.

Veneur en costume Louis XV et ses trois chiens, 38 cm.
Zèbre (or onagre) attaqué par une panthère, 55 cm.

To this list, it is naturally fitting to add a number of works of the *Jockey à cheval* in different versions and sizes, as well as various animals—horses (stallions, thoroughbreds, draft horses, etc.), sheep, goat, chickens, geese, ducks, etc.

MUSEUMS
Fontainebleau, château
Onagre attaqué par un jaguar (E. Vittoz, founder).
Paris, Orsay
Le Jockey à cheval ou Le Retour au pesage, 54 cm.
Le Grand Jockey, 61 cm.
Le Jockey à cheval à l'arrêt, 36 cm.
Périgueux
Cerf, 204 x 148 cm (H. Peyrol, founder).

SALES
Le Canard, 7 cm, Drouot Hotel, March 20, 1985, room 4.
Cerf sur un rocher, 21 cm (Peyrol), Sotheby London, June 12, 1986.
Grand cerf debout, 82 x 67 cm (1893), Christie's London, May 15, 1986.
Cheval de course, 40 cm, Sotheby London, June 12, 1986.
Cheval de course arrêté, 29 cm, Chartres, June 5, 1983.
Cheval au galop, 24 cm, Lokeren, February 16, 1985.
Cheval et palefrenier, 42 cm, Sotheby London, June 8, 1984.

Isidore Bonheur,
Sanglier courant,
19 cm.

Isidore Bonheur,
Cheval de course, 29 cm.

Isidore Bonheur,
Postillon et
deux cheveaux,
35.5 cm.

Isidore Bonheur,
Lionne à l'affût, 21 x 42 cm.

Isidore Bonheur,
Taureau, 35 x 63 cm
(Peyrol, founder).

Taureau, 11 cm, Sotheby London, November 7, 1985.
Taureau, 35 cm, Drouot Hotel, April 3, 1985.
Taureau à l'arrêt, 71 cm, Christie's New York, September 27, 1986.
Teaureau cabré, Pithiviers, May 19, 1985.
Taureau chargeant, 35 cm, Christie's New York, February 19, 1985.
Taureau marchant, 38 cm, (Peyrol), Christie's New York, September 27, 1986.
Taureau et ours, Le Havre, April 20, 1986.
Veneur Louis XV, 45 cm, Rambouillet, November 18, 1984.

BONHEUR, ROSA

Bordeaux, March 16, 1822
Thomery (Seine-et-Marne), 1899

Rosa B

Very well known as a painter of animals, Rosa Bonheur was also a sculptor. She studied with her father, the painter Raymond Bonheur, and with Léon Cogniet. Very early on she proved to have a talent for

drawing, at the same time displaying an independent and original character. She came to Paris when she was very young, where she was soon buried in a dressmaking studio where her father had placed her for apprenticeship. She preferred to draw nature in the woods of Boulogne and animals at the fairs and even in the slaughterhouses. She haunted these places, freely dressed as a man. Her debut took place at the Salon of 1841 with some paintings, but the following year she exhibited a terra cotta sculpture depicting a sheared sheep as well, and then a bull in plaster in 1843. She practiced sculpture only until the 1850s, producing a small body of work—several plasters, terra cottas, and waxes which, like her paintings, achieved great success for their realism and individualism. They primarily portrayed certain breeds of animals: bulls—one of her favorite themes—and steer, sheep, horses, deer, and wild boar. Some of the works evoke memories of Scotland, which she had visited.

Highly esteemed in England, and a protegé of the queen, Rosa Bonheur received numerous honors, in France and abroad equally. According to her wishes, her works were dispersed after she died suddenly at By Castle, near Thomerie, where she had established her studio. A number of her sculptures, like those of her brother Isidore Bonheur, had been cast in bronze by her brother-in-law, the founder Hippolyte Peyrol. In the work which he dedicated to Rosa Bonheur in 1900, Roger-Milès listed these pieces: *Cerf traversant un espace couvert, Razzia* (Scotland)*Chevreuil au repos, Poneys de l'île de Skys, en Ecosse, Berger écossais, Boeuf couché, Bélier couché, Brebis debout, Taureau marchant,* and *Taureau beuglant.* Also on this list is a unique edition of *Taureau debout* cast for the author.

Other specifications, especially the sizes, were given in the sales catalog made after the artist's death on May 30, 1900. The following bronzes appeared at that sale: *Bison courant,* 18 x 35 cm, *Bison lancé au galop,* 25 x 37 cm, *Cheval,* 17 x 19 cm, *Chien de chasse,* 8 x 13 cm, *Taureau,* 16 x 24 cm, and *Vache combattant,* 22 x 37 cm.

Some different pieces, some of them cast by founders other than Peyrol, were presented in 1973 at the Gallery of Decorative Arts in Lausanne, as part of the exhibition *Les Animaliers du XIXe siècle.* Included were *Bélier couché,* 9.5 x 22.5 cm, *Brebis couchée* (Cottet founder), 10 x 23 cm, *Brebis paissant,* 15 x 21 cm, *Taureau beuglant,* 15 x 22 cm, and *Taureau couché,* 15 x 29 cm.

MUSEUMS
Bordeaux
Bélier, 9 x 22 cm.
Jeune Taureau, 15 x 21 cm.
Mouton broutant, 15 x 21.5 cm.
Mouton couché, 15 x 27 cm.
Fontainebleau
Bélier couché, 9 cm (Peyrol, founder)
Boeuf couché, 14.5 cm (Peyrol)
Brebis couchée, 10.5 cm (Peyrol)
Brebid rondue, 14.5 cm (Peyrol)
Taureau beuglant, 15 cm (Peyrol)
Taureau marchant, 17 cm (Peyrol).

SALES
Bélier couché, 9 cm, Enghien, October 10, 1982.
Le Mouton, 15 cm, Drouot Hotel, March 20, 1985;
    Bruxelles, April 23, 1985.
Taureau, 17 cm, Drouot Hotel, April 4, 1984, room 1;
    Drouot Hotel, November 7, 1985, room 1.
Taureau beuglant, 15 cm, Dijon, March 18, 1984;
    Bergerac, November 16, 1986.
Taureau couché, 14 x 27 cm, Lokeren, October 20, 1984.
Vache couchée, Drouot Hotel, November 7, 1985, room 1.

BONNARD, PIERRE
Fontenay-aux-Roses, October 3, 1867
Le Cannet (Alpes-Maritimes), January 23, 1947

The son of a civil servant, Bonnard studied the law and painting simultaneously, but after 1889 he devoted himself exclusively to painting. At the Julian Academy and at the Académie des Beaux-Arts, he became friends with Vuillard, K.-X. Roussel, Maurice Denis, Vallotton, and Sérusier, who formed the group 'the Nabis'. He worked and exhibited first with Vuillard and Maurice Denis, and then developed a personal style in which color played an increasingly important role. He lived in Paris starting in 1902, and in Saint-Germain-en-Laye, in the south's Seine valley. Encouraged by the merchant Ambroise Vollard, he tried modeling and made about ten figures, mostly of females. These works, of a very impressionistic spontaneity, were cast in bronze by the lost wax method, the majority in numbered castings by Valsuani. The following bronzes can be named:

Baigneuse, 17.5 cm; works numbered to 12.
Baigneuse, 27 cm.
Les Deux Baigneuses, 18 cm (Valsuani); works numbered to 15.
Le Cheval marin, 11 x 17 cm; works numbered to 24.
Femme assise appuyée sur un rocher, 16.5 cm; one series of works numbered to 8, another to 24.
Femme assise à sa toilette, 15 cm (Valsuani); works numbered to 30.
Femme nue debout appuyée sur un rocher, 19 cm; works numbered to 12.
Le Printemps, 19 cm (Valsuani); works numbered to 15.
Le Printemps, table centerpiece, 33.5 x 22 cm.
Suzanne au bain, bas-relief, 19 x 28 cm (Valsuani); works numbered to 12.
Surtout en bronze et glace, 15 x 83 cm, cast in several models for Ambroise Vollard.

MUSEUMS
Bordeaux
Les Deux Baigneuses, 18 cm.
Paris, Orsay
Surtout en bronze et glace, 15 x 83 cm (Vollard edition)
Troyes, Museum of Modern Art
Nu debout, 19 cm (4/12)

SALES
Baigneuse, 17.5 cm (9/12), Copenhagen, May 14, 1985.
Baigneuse au rocher, 15 cm (Valsuani, cast by Sagot-Legarrec), Enghien, November 24, 1985.
Le Cheval marin, 11 x 17 cm (17/24), Drouot Hotel, December 8, 1982.
Suzanne au bain or *Suzanne et les vieillards*, bas-relief, 19 x 28 cm, Drouot Hotel, December 1, 1983;
    (Valsuani 12/12), Copenhagen, October 15, 1985.

Pierre Bonnard,
Baigneuse, mains derrière la nuque,
35 cm.

Pierre Bonnard,
Baigneuse au rocher, 14.5 cm
(Valsuani, Sagot-Legarrec edition).

Pierre Bonnard,
Les Deux Baigneuses, 18 cm
(Valsuani No4).

BONNASSIEUX, JEAN-MARIE

Panissières (Loire), Spetember 19, 1810
Paris, June 3, 1892

Bonnassieux's father was a carpenter, and at a very young age the boy was apprenticed to a manufacturer of ornaments for the church to sculpt figurines in wood. Later he became the student of the Lyonnais sculptor Legendre-Héral, who made him enroll at the municipal school of drawing. In 1834, he was admitted to the Beaux-Arts, and in 1836 won the first grand prize of Rome with a bas-relief entitled *Socrate buvant la cigué*. As a fervent Catholic, he specialized in religious sculpture and received a number of commissions in Paris and Lyon. He was strongly influenced by antiquity, so although his work includes busts of contemporaries it also includes several mythological or allegorical scenes. He is the author of the colossal (12 meteres high) statue of *Notre Dame* at Puy, cast with bronze from cannons taken at Sébastopol. This artist's work also includes a bust in bronze entitled *Le Père Lacordaire*, dating from Rome in 1840, *David tendant la fronde*, a large (2 meters high) bronze exhibited in 1878 and owned by the Troyes museum, *Le Baptême du Christ*, another bronze for a fountain in Lyon (1846), and *Henri IV*, also in bronze for La Flèche.

BONNEMÈRE, LIONEL

Angers, 1843
Paris, November 28, 1905

After working with Barye, Lionel Bonnemère devoted himself primarily to animal sculpture, which he exhibited at the Salon between 1869 and 1878. Of note is *Pigeon voyageur blessé* in bronze (1877). This artist was president of the Société Artistique et Littéraire de l'Ouest (Artistic and Literary Society of the West) for a long time.

BONNET, GUILLAUME

Saint-Germain-Laval (Loire), June 27, 1820
Lyon, April 26, 1873

Bonnet studied in Lyon, and was admitted to the Ecole des Beaux-Arts in Paris in 1843. In 1848, he won the second prize of Rome for medal engraving and went to Italy. Upon returning to France in 1853, he established himself in Lyon. His important works increased, particularly beginning in 1860. He provided a number of statues, groups, and bas-reliefs for the landmarks of the city like the city hall, the stock market building, churches, the court house, Hôtel-Dieu, etc. He also did portraits of his contemporaries in busts and medallions and some statuettes in plaster, including *Le Père Lacordaire* and *Monsieur de Chateaubriand* (exhibited at the Salons of 1847 and 1848). The museum of Lyon owns some of his works. There are also reductions in bronze of the muses Erato and Thalie, whose statues rise above the facade of Lyon's main theater.

BOSIO, BARON FRANÇOIS (JOSEPH)

Monaco, March 19, 1768
Paris, July 29, 1845

Bosio (signature)

The neo-classical aspect of Bosio's work earned him the nickname 'the French Casanova'. However, Bosio was not limited to this style, and he did much work for Napoleon I and the imperial court. He also quite easily placed himself in the service of the Bourbons, and then in the service of Louis-Philippe, collecting many commissions and distinctions first from one and then the others. As for his most famous work, *Henri IV enfant*, the sculpture is more evocative of historic romanticism than of antiquity.

Bosio came to Paris in 1786 to study with Pajou. He next traveled to Florence and Naples, and then to Rome, where he stayed for seventeen years. Bosio returned to Paris in 1808, and worked there for the rest of his life. His reputation as a great decorative sculptor brought him a certain number of official commissions; a segment of the bas-relief work surrounding the Vendôme column (1807-1810), the majestic quadrige in bronze of the Arc de Triomphe of the Carrousel (unveiled in 1828 by Charles X), the recently restored equestrian statue of Louis XIV at Victoires Plaza (1822), and *l'Hercule combattant Acheloüs transformé en serpent* in bronze (1824) at the Tuileries gardens.

After sculpting a number of busts and statues of the emperor, members of his family, and those close to him, Bosio sculpted an equal number of representational effigies of the Bourbons and their ancestors. His *Henri IV enfant* in marble, commissioned by the city of Paris, was sent to the Salon of 1824. Its success quickly led to a number of replicas in marble and in bronze (one of those in bronze was exhibited at the Salon of 1843). A model in silver is today preserved by the Louvre museum. Another important work, also reproduced in bronze, is *La Nymphe Salmacis sortant du bain*, originally exhibited in marble at the Salon of 1837.

François-Joseph Bosio,
Henri IV enfant,
42 cm.

The catalogs of the Barbedienne house mention the following pieces cast in bronze, each in three sizes: *Henri IV enfant*, 50, 36, 24 cm, *Jeune Indienne*, 25, 20, 15 cm, *La Nymph Salmacis*, 32, 24, 19 cm, *Vénus endormie*, 8.4, 6, and 4.4 in. *Henri IV enfant* was also cast by Susse in three sizes, 42, 35, and 25 cm, as well as by other founders including Eck and Durand, L. Marchand, and Delafontaine.

MUSEUMS
Le Puy
Henri IV enfant, 60 cm (1828).
Buste de Charles Crozatier, 58 cm.
Lille
Henri IV enfant.
Nantes
Buste de Louis XVIII, 83 cm.
Orléans
Buste de Henri IV et de Marie de Médicis, 27 cm.
Paris, Decorative Arts
Henri IV enfant, silvered bronze, 41 cm.
Versailles
Enfant au papillon.
Henri IV enfant, 41 cm.
Buste du duc de Berry.

SALES
Henri IV enfant, 116 cm, Saint-Etienne, September 21, 1986.
Vénus accroupie, 75 cm, Christie's London, March 25, 1982.

BOTTÉE, LOUIS ALEXANDRE
Paris, 1852
November 14, 1940

A sculptor and a decorative engraver, this winner of the grand prize of Rome in 1878 began to appear at the Salon in 1882. His works exhibited there include *Timidezza*, a bust in marble (1884), *Le Génie des récompenses*, a medallion in bronze (1886), *L'Amour*, a statuette in marble (1888), *Nuit de printemps*, a statuette in plaster (1892), and a bronze entitled *L'Amour à l'affût* (1895). This last work was cast by Susse in three sizes, 83, 67, 42 cm. The museum of Angers has two plaques, *Le Service de santé, Paris*, and *L'Ecole d'art, Paris*; the Carnavalet Museum owns another plaque, *Albert Léon Lambert, acteur du Français*, 24 x 15 cm.

BOUCHARD, HENRI
Dijon, December 18, 1875
Paris, September 1, 1960

H. Bouchard

Strongly encouraged by his parents despite the fact that his carpenter father was a modest artisan, Bouchard entered the studio of an ornamentalist from Dijon at the age of fourteen while taking evening courses at the municipal school. He went to Paris in 1895 and attended the Julian Academy, and then

Henri Bouchard,
Paysan romain de la Sabine, 35 cm
(1902; Italian casting 1906)
Private collection, Paris.

entered the studio of Barrias at the Ecole des Beaux-Arts. In 1901, he won the first grand prize for sculpture and lived in Rome from 1902 to 1906. However, the heroes of antiquity interested him less than the daily lives of workers; this became the subject of the works he sent to the Salon from the Médicis Villa, including *Le Faucheur* and *Les Bardeurs de fer* in 1905, and *Le Forgeron au repos* in 1906.

Upon returning to Paris, Bouchard established himself in the Montparnasse quarter and pursued his career in the same realistic style, describing the nature of men and of animals. He traveled in different countries, including Italy, Greece, Spain, North Africa, England, Germany, and Belgium. In 1907, he affirmed his strong personal style with *Le Grand Forgeron au repos*, made of large planes on which the light played. After this work, which was exhibited in bronze at the Salon of 1910, came *Claus Sluter* of Dijon (plaster at the Salon of 1911, bronze at the Salon of 1913), *Nicolas Rolin* and *Guigone de Salins* of Beaune (plaster in 1912), *Le Défrichement*, a monument in bronze cast by Malesset (Salon of 1912, intended for the Champs-de-Mars but placed in Charleville in 1932 and destroyed during the German Occupation), and finally, the great *Monument de la Réformation* of Geneva, accomplished in collaboration with Paul Landowski and unveiled in 1917.

Meanwhile, after Bouchard was married in Paris, he was mobilized for military action; after the war, he returned to sculpt many monuments for the dead. In 1924, he established himself in a studio which has been preserved by his son and his daughter-in-law on Rue d'Yvette in Paris. The Saint-Pierre-de-Chaillot Church, for which he made many sculptures (including the immense front pediment) between 1932 to 1935, was his most important work between the two world wars. Also noteworthy is the monumental bronze group *Apollon*, 8 meters high, placed facing the Seine at the foot of one of the pavillons of the Chaillot Palace, as well as some statues and groups for different churches.

Henri Bouchard continued to be active until his death, and left a number of statuettes in different materials, notably in bronze. He almost never concerned himself with creating editions of his works, contenting himself with creating one or several castings, which he himself sold from his studio. As a result of this, only two or three numbered subjects are known, and his bronzes primarily exist in very quantities. Furthermore, the works thus made were mended with each casting, resulting in a certain number of variations among them.

The chronological list below mentions the bronzes in the repertoire of the Bouchard museum and those cast from works executed before 1914, along with the names of the museums owning them (when that information is available). The dates indicated are those of the execution of the original model (the dates that one finds on the bronzes are usually those of the casting). Nearly all the different founders who cast these works used the lost wax method (especially Bisceglia and Siot) with the exception of a series cast in sand by Rudier in 1911.

Henri Bouchard,
Négresse à la corbeille, 51 cm (1914; Siot).
Private collection, Paris.

Henri Bouchard,
Plocheur bourguignon,
manches longues,
43 cm (1901;
Bisceglia casting 1905).
Musée d'Orsay.

Henri Bouchard,
Le Fardier,
bas-relief,
25 x 103 cm
(1903; italian
casting 1905).
Private collection,
Paris.

1900
Le Chemineau, 35 cm.
Maternité paysanne, 41 cm, Bouchard Museum.
1901
Tête de Jules Dutar, doctor, 37 cm.
Buste de paysan bourguignon, 35 cm., Bouchard Museum, Dijon Museum (casting 1935).
Piocheur bourguignon, manches courtes, 43 cm, Dijon Museum.
Piocheur bourguignon, manches longues, 43 cm, Orsay Museum.
Vendangeur bourguignon, about fifteen models known, in many dimensions and with variations. One proof of 45 cm at the Dijon museum.
1902
Vieux Paysan romain, 41 cm, Bouchard Museum.
Paysan romain de la Sabine, 35 cm, museums of Bouchard and Dijon.
Joueur de zamponia, 16 cm, Bouchard Museum (two models).
Jeune Romaine dansant, 48 cm, Bouchard Museum and the Metropolitan Museum, New York.
1903
Le Piqueux de boeufs, 30 cm, Dijon.
Le Fardier, bas-relief, 25 x 103 cm, Bouchard Museum.
Les Femmes de Campanie, bas-relief, 47 x 65 cm, Bouchard Museum.
Les Débardeurs du port de Naples, bas-relief, 50 x 65 cm, Orsay Museum.
Les Débardeurs du port de Naples, detail, plaque, 49 x 17 cm, Bouchard Museum.
Les Bardeurs de fer, bas-relief.
Le Laboureur, sketch for the Défrichement, 15 x 30 cm, Bouchard Museum.

Henri Bouchard,
Retour du travail,
41 x 49 cm
(1908; Bisceglia).
Private collection,
Paris.

1) Henri Bouchard, Le Débardeur, 70 cm (Bisceglia 1905). Musée d'Orsay.

2) Henri Bouchard, La Faneuse, 39 x 47 cm (1911; A. Rudier 1911). Private collection, Paris.

3) Henri Bouchard, Diane à l'aurore, 35 x 80 cm (1914; Siot 1914). Private collection, Paris.

Le Mineur au travail, 32 cm, Bouchard Museum.
Le Mineur marchant.
Le Débardeur, 70 cm, Orsay Museum.
Fillette à la cruche, 56 cm, many models known including one at the Bouchard Museum.
Le Mendiant, 20 cm, two models known.
Le Berger romain.
Femme drapée marchant, 21 cm.
Aissaoua, femme tunisienne, 36 cm.
Le Marabout, 18 cm.
Couple arabe avec un âne.
Chameau agenouillé, 38 cm, Dijon Museum.
Retour de marché arabe, three variations including one of 20 cm at the Dijon Museum.

1904

Porteur d'eau marocain.
Le Picador attaqué, 28 cm.
Buste de jeune Romain, 42 cm, Bouchard Museum.
Le Faucheur, 61 cm, cast 12 works of which two are at the Bouchard Museum.
Le Faucheur (Rome 1904), 160 cm, cast by H. Jamais, Dijon Museum.
Le Laboureur au repos, 55 cm, a model Siot 1/5.
Le Forgeron au repos, 157 cm, Metropolitan Museum, New York.

Henri Bouchard, Vendangeur bourguignon, 73 cm (1901; Siot casting 1903). Private collection, Paris.

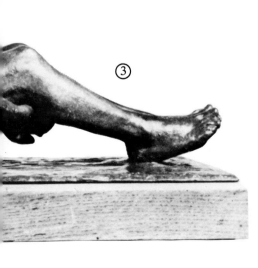

③

1905
Le Puddleur.
Le Débardeur adossé, 73 cm, Bouchard Museum.
Buste du peintre Victor Guétin, 43 cm, Dijon Museum.

1906
Buste à la rose, 60 cm.
Charles le Téméraire, 67 cm, two models known.
Course de chevaux, bas-relief, 13 x 72 cm, Bouchard
    Museum.

1907
Pierre de Montereau, 64 cm.
Etienne Avenard, head, 29 cm.
Faneuse, 27 cm, Dijon Museum.
Maternité, 55 cm.

1908
Retour des champs, 27 cm.
Retour du travail, 41 cm, Dijon Museum.
Couple de gazelles, 35 cm.

1909
Jeune Fille et le faon, 53 cm.
Chien, 25 cm.
Cinq Poulains d'un an, group, 29 cm.
Saint-Damien, cheval, 67 cm, unique work for the
    proprietor of the horse at the Perray stud farm.
Jument, 23 cm.
Poulain courant, 19 cm.
Deux Chevaux cabrés, 39 cm.
Cheval dressé, avec personnage, 44 cm, Bouchard
    Museum.

1910
Henri Martin, head, 48 cm, National Museum of Modern
    Art.
Boeufs au labour, 17 cm.
Jeune Fille et gazelle, 55 cm, Metropolitan Museum,
    New York.
Le Défrichement, for the monument of Charleville, 17 x
    60 cm.
Danseuse, 40 cm.

1911
Claus Sluter, study of the head, 42 cm, Dijon Museum.
Claus Sluter, study for the statue of Dijon, 68 cm,
    museums of Dijon and of Algiers.
Jeux maternels, 18 cm.
Jeux maternels, variation, 19 cm.
La Faneuse, 39 cm.
Le Faneur.
Le Soir de labour, six works cast.
Le Pâturage, 23 cm, nineteen works cast, three of which
    are at the Bouchard Museum.
En vendange, 31 cm, Bouchard Museum.
Le Bûcheron.

Henri Bouchard,
Cheval dressé,
44 cm
(1909; Godard casting).
Private collection,
Paris.

Henri Bouchard, Jeune Fille et le faon, 53 x 57 cm
(1909; Bisceglia casting 1909). Private collection, Paris.

Henri Bouchard,
Chevaux cabrés,
39 x 42 cm
(1909; Bisceglia 1910).
Private collection, Paris.

117

Henri Bouchard,
Jeune Romaine dansant, 47 cm
(1902; Siot-Decauville casting 1906).
Bouchard Museum, Paris.

Pendule, 20 cm, Bouchard Museum.
Le Temps, in front of a clock, bas-relief, 156 cm,
    Bouchard Museum.
1912
Guigone de Salins, 72 cm (Valsuani cast 1968), Dijon
    Museum.
Nicolas Rolin, head, 43 cm (Valsuani cast 1968), Dijon
    Museum.
Jeune Fille à la gazelle, 65 cm, many works including a
    number 1/10, a work at the Bouchard Museum.
1914
Négresse à la corbeille, 52 cm, two works including one
    at the Bouchard Museum.
Diane à l'aurore, 35 cm, two works including one at the
    Bouchard Museum.
Buste de Charles Cottet, painter, 44 cm, Dijon Museum.

SALES

The bronzes of Bouchard appear only very rarely at public sales. A small bas-relief dating around 1918, L'Heure de l'attaque, 7.5 x 20 cm, sold at the Drouot Hotel November 18, 1985, room 6, bought by the Bouchard Museum.

BOUCHER, ALFRED

Bouy-sur-Orvin (Aube), September 23, 1850
Aix-les-Bains, August 17, 1934

A. BOUCHER

Alfred Boucher received his first lessons in sculpture while he was still very young, taught at Nogent-sur-Seine by Marius Ramus. He worked with another sculptor from Nogent, Paul Dubois, and with Antoine Dumont after he entered the Ecole des Beaux-Arts of Paris in 1869. Though he did not win the competition for the prize of Rome, Boucher nevertheless traveled to Florence and Rome, from which he sent his first works, in particular a statue of Eve. Upon returning to France in 1878, he established himself in Paris. Later, he also worked in Aix-les-Bains. He left a number of portraits of artists and personalities, some statues and groups, allegorical or otherwise, often made for funerary or commemorative monuments, as well as some figures of workers. The abundance and diversity of his work is apparent from a list of some of his most characteristic works exhibited at the Salon starting in 1874: Enfant à la fontaine, plaster (1874), Eve après sa faute, plaster, 180 cm (1878), L'Amour filial, a group in bronze (1883), Laënnec découvrant l'auscultation (1884), the bronze group Au but !, his best-known and most reproduced work (1887), and Vaincre ou mourir, a work in plaster of the group crowning the monument to children of the Dawn at Troyes (1887), Sculpteur florentin, a statue in bronze (1888). He also made some statues in marble such as A la terre!, a nude man weilding a shovel (1890) which, like Au But!, was very successful, Le Repos (1892), Nymphe à la coquille and Diane surprise (1893), La Naissance de la terre (1895), Aux Champs (1897), Le Bûcheron (1906), and La Rêverie (1912); he also made some busts in bronze including that of his mother (1905), a statue in bronze of his wife (1914), and another bronze statue entitled S'il le faut.

All of Boucher's works stand out for their natural quality and a very highly developed sense of expression and movement, which led them to be greatly appreciated during the lifetime of the sculptor. Captivated by social ideas, in 1902 he founded Rue de Vaugirard, a foyer for young artists, the 'Beehive of the Arts' through which passed the artists Soutine, Chagall, and Laurens, among others. The building, which still exists, is none other than the old Rotonde des Vins (rotunda of wines) from the 1900 Exposition Universelle. Two years later, Boucher founded the Dubois-Boucher museum at Nogent-sur-Seine, to which he donated nearly fifty of his sculptures (Cf. Dominique Canaud, Les Sculptures du XIXe siècle dans le département de l'Aube, La Vie à la campagne, September 1982).

Alfred Boucher does not seem to have practiced much direct cutting. A number of his works were reproduced in bronze by different founders, often in many dimensions.

Barbedienne
Au but! many sizes.
La Chasseresse, 135 and 54 cm.
Terrassier or *L'Effort*, 67, 56 and 41 cm.

A.A. Hébrard
Satyre et Bacchante, 83 and 40 cm.

Siot-Decauville
Au but! (many sizes).
La Bourrasque, a couple of reapers.
Faneuse or *Paysanne à la fourche*, 90 and 57 cm.
Jeune Fille à la fontaine.

Alfred Boucher,
Au but!
102 cm
(Siot, founder).

119

Susse
L'Amour boudeur, 47, 32 and 16 cm.
Faneuse.
Hirondelle blessées, 93, 80, 68 and 46 cm (this last
    theme recaptured on an ashtray and a plate).
Jeanne d'Arc dans sa prison (four sizes).
Renommée, in pewter, 27 cm.

Of note also are two statuettes in bronze with no mention of the founder, Enfant au lézard, 20 cm, and La Musique, 58 cm.

Some works by Boucher were treated in sandstone by Müller, and the Sèvres factory cast many of his works. In the last years of his life, Boucher also sculpted in cement, most notably in 1921, when he made the monument to the dead from the two wars of Nogent-sur-Seine.

Alfred Boucher,
Le Terrassier, 60 cm.

MUSEUMS
Aix-en-Provence
Au but!, 69 cm.
Avignon
Buste de vieillard, 47 cm.
Besançon
La Faneuse, 57 cm (Siot-Decauville).
Paris, Orsay
Buste d'Antonin Dubost, 55 cm.
Reims
Au but!, 102 x 151 cm (Barbedienne).
Toulon
Faneuse au repos, 70 cm.
Troyes
Amours jouant, bas-relief.
Buste d'Auguste Mortier, medallion, 8 cm diam.
Buste de M. Trumet de Fontarce, 41 cm.

The museum of Troyes also owns some plasters, some terra cottas, and some marbles. One other series of plasters belongs to the museum of Nogent-sur-Seine. Moreover, some original plasters of major works including Laënnec, La Piété filiale, Au but!, and A la terre can be found at the city hall of Sainte-Savine.

SALES
Au but!, 33 cm, Christie's New York, March 30, 1985.
Au but!, 51 cm(Siot-Decauville), Sotheby London, November 8, 1984.
Au but!, 100 cm(Siot-Decauville), Sotheby London, November 26, 1986.
La Faneuse, 57 cm (Siot-Decauville), Troyes, November 28, 1986.
Femme ailée, 63 cm, Drouot Hotel, June 10, 1983, room 15.
Jeune Femme songeuse, 39 cm, Drouot Hotel, February 19, 1982, room 6.
Jeune Fille à la fontaine, 52 cm (Siot-Decauville), Sotheby New York, September 13, 1986.
Nymphe ailée, gilded bronze, 68 cm, Christie's New York, June 15, 1985.
Paysanne, 90 cm (Siot-Decauville), Christie's New York, June 14, 1983.
Le Terrassier, 41 cm (Barbedienne), Tourcoing, July 3, 1986.
Le Terrassier, 60 cm (Barbedienne), Sotheby London, March 8, 1984; Deauville, April 26, 1985; Troyes, June 29, 1986.
Le Terrassier, 67 cm (Barbedienne), Sotheby London, March 20, 1986.

BOUCHER, JEAN

Cesson (Ille-et-Vilaine), November 20, 1870
Paris, June 17, 1939

Boucher was a teacher at the Ecole des Beaux-Arts and a member of the Insitut beginning in 1889. Of a very romantic temperament, he exhibited groups in plaster and in marble at the Salon such as Un soir (1899), L'Eté (1900), and Devant la mer (1901), as well as multiple busts of comtemporaries. He also exhibited various pieces and fragments of the Victor Hugo monument that he executed for Guernesey, considered to be one of his major works. He is also the author of the statue of Ernest Renan at Tréguier and of the monument Victoire, unveiled at Verdun in 1929.

MUSUEMS
Paris, Orsay
La Peste or Chinoise au brûle-parfum, 65 cm (C. Valsuani).
    A bronze cast from a project for the monument to Victor Hugo at Guernesey, 70 cm, belongs to the city of Paris (exhibition Victor Hugo, Grand Palais, 1985).

Rennes
Tête de poilu.

SALES
Un soir, a couple sitting, 71 cm, Christie's Oklahoma
    (USA), September 24, 1981.
Victor Hugo debout, 68 cm, Christie's Oklahoma (USA),
    September 24, 1981.
Victor Hugo, mask, 35 cm, Sotheby Monaco, December 7,
    1983.
Victor Hugo, project for the monument for Guernesey, 70
    cm, Geneva, December 11, 1985.

BOUCHERON, ALEXANDRE
Sens, 1847
1887

From 1880 to 1885 Boucheron exhibited some small figures of animals in wax and in bronze at the Salon: *Eléphant d'Asie*, bronze (1880), *Rhinocéros femelle de Nubie*, bronze, and *Deux ânesses*, wax (1883), and *Combat de tigres de Chine*, wax (1884). Another statuette, *Hirondelle blessée*, was cast in bronze by the founder Susse in four sizes: 93, 80, 68, 46 cm.

BOUILLON, HENRI THÉOPHILE
Saint-Front (Charente), April 21, 1864
Saint-Front, 1934

This sculptor is known for some busts and figures, including *L'Amour fuyant la Misère*, a plaster exhibited at the Salon of 1892. The museum of Bordeaux has a bronze copy of this work, 125 cm high, cast by E. Gruet Jr., as well as a bust of a woman, 52 cm.

BOURDELLE, ANTOINE
Montauban, October 30, 1861
Le Vésinet, October 1, 1929

A practicioner and collaborator with Rodin from 1893 to 1908, Antoine Bourdelle was also the great sculptor's friend. Working intimately with Rodin, Bourdelle was naturally influenced by him for a time. However, he quickly realized that he needed to create a personal style, an original style conforming to his temperament; this development led him to be a precursor of the principal trends of twentieth century sculpture. From a southwestern family of artisans and peasants, Bourdelle had always been very influenced and attracted by the forces of nature, by their incessant power, and by the renewal of creation. "I have followed the great art of the times on the rocks," he said. He translated this power of creation in his sculpture, made of large vigorously cut designs, simplified shapes, strong gestures, and architectural severity. His was an art of freedom and invention, infused with a certain archaism that was reproached by some, to whom he responded: "All that which is synthesized is archaism; the archaic is the opposite of the word 'copy', the born enemy of the lie, of all stupidly odious fake art." (*Ecrits sur l'art and sur la vie* (Writings on art and on life)).

BOURDELLE

*Antoine Bourdelle,
La Force, from the Alvear monument,
122 cm (Susse).*

Antoine Bourdelle,
Pénélope sans fuseau,
61 cm,
(Peterman, founder, Brussels),
dedicated "to my wife."

Antoine Bourdelle,
Femme en blouse, bras au dos, 54 cm (1909).

122

While Bourdelle often cut statues and monuments of a very large size in stone or marble, he also modeled a great deal in clay, though only for making inumerable preparatory studies. His production is considerable, and a number of the sketches, variations, and successive projects of increasing dimensions were cast in bronze, both during the artist's life and after his death.

Fascinated with drawing, the young Emile Antoine Bourdelle had abandoned his studies at the age of thirteen in order to work with his father, a carpenter and cabinet-maker in Montauban. The sculpture with which the young artist adorned the furniture brought him recognition, and he obtained a scholarship for the school of fine arts of Toulouse. In 1884, at the school of fine arts in Paris, he was admitted to the studio of Falguière. Incapable of enduring the rules and the style of teaching at the institution, he abandoned it two years later. The same year, he rented a studio on the dead-end Rue d'Maine, where he would work for the rest of his life. Dalou, with whom he became friends, was one of his neighbors. The dead-end street was later renamed in his honor, and in 1949 the Bourdelle Museum was opened near the original studio.

Starting in 1880 in Montauban and in Toulouse, Bourdelle sculpted some busts; fittingly, it was a bust which became his first submission to the Salon des Artistes Français in 1884. The following year, he obtained an honorable mention with a statue in plaster entitled *La Première Victoire d'Hannibal*. In 1887, he started the long series of portraits of Beethoven, whose tumultuous and tragic face fascinated him as much as his music did. By the time he died in 1929, the sculptor had made nearly fifty busts and statues of the composer. His collaboration with Rodin, which began in 1893, did not hinder him from pursuing his own work. He worked eagerly at the work *Monument aux morts de 1870*, which had been commissioned by Montauban. The model, presented in 1896, was accepted only thanks to the intervention of Rodin, who would later say of it: "This is an epic work, one of the best outbursts of modern sculpture." At the time of the unveiling of the monument in 1902, the reactions to it were very divided, if the descriptions published by certain newspapers are any indication: it was called a "hottentot monstruosity" and a work of "singular excess."

In addition to exhibiting at the Salon des Artistes Français, Bourdelle began in 1891 to exhibit regularly at that of the Société Nationale des Beaux-Arts. His notoriety increased. In 1900, his *Tête d'Apollon* marked an important stage in the evolution of his art. "The exaltation of shapes," (Raymond Cogniat) of his first period, during which the influence of Rodin remained very real, progressively gave way to a spirit of order and synthesis. Rodin himself was not mistaken when he said to Bourdelle about his sculpture: "You part from me!"

In 1905, the Hébrard Gallery devoted a personal exhibition to Bourdelle, in which not only sculptures but some very remarkable paintings and drawings were exhibited. A statue which would be very successful appeared in its first version here, Bourdelle's rendition of *Pénélope*. It is important to note that a number of subjects would be successively reworked and presented in many versions, with some variations of pose, modeling, and size (this was not limited to enlargements or mechanical reductions). Among

*Antoine Bourdelle,
Madeleine Charnaux
au chignon,
46 cm
(Busato No8).*

these is *Sapho, which* reverted to the original of 1887 and for which the last version would not be finished until 1925. *Drame intérieur* (1899), *Le Fruit* (1902/1911), *L'Hymne intérieur* (1905/1908), *Jeune Sculpteur au travail* (1906/1918), *Femme bras au dos* (1909), *Héraclés archer* (Bourdelle's first great success, at the Salon of 1910), *Paysanne à l'enfant* (1910), *Centaure mourant* (which he considered the high point of his work, 1911/1917), and *Madeleine Charnaux*, one of his students (1917), etc.

At the same time, Bourdelle started work on the great commissions which, for the most part, came from foreign governments or private citizens. He is known for *Monument à Mickiewicz* (first model in 1909, unveiled at Alma Plaza in 1929); the facade of the theater of the Champs-Elysées, Avenue Montaigne, that he not only adorned with a large mythological epic in high relief, but which he himself drew for the architect Auguste Perret (1910-1913); the colossal *Général Alvear équestre* of Buenos Aires with, flanking the pedestal, effigies of *La Victoire, La Force, L'Éloquence* and *La Liberté* (1912-1922, unveiled in 1925); *Vierge à l'offrande* in stone on the hill of Niederbrück in Alsace (1919-1922); and the tall statue of *La France* (1925), of which there is a model figure on the terrace of the Palace of Tokyo in Paris, another at Fort Vauban in Briançon, and a third on the monument to the dead of World War I in Montauban.

It is fitting to mention a decoration for the Grévin museum (1900), the coronation in stucco polychrome, of the scene at the opera of Marseille (1924), works made in ceramic by the factories of Haviland and Limoges and by Bigot, as well as the numerous remarkable busts of people including Ingres, Rodin, Vincent of Indy, Anatole France, Auguste Perret, and Beethoven.

The majority of these sculptures, their multiple versions and projects, and other less well-known works (including some statuettes, groups of children, and studies of animals, etc.) were cast in bronze at the request of Bourdelle. The castings, un-numbered but produced in limited quantities, were made at the foundries of Eugène Rudier (who signed with the name of his father, Alexis Rudier), Hébrard, and in Belgium, where casting was less expensive.

Antoine Bourdelle,
Maternité, bust,
63 cm.

After the death of the sculptor, his studio and the works it contained were futilely offered to the State by his widow for about twenty years. The donation was finally accepted by the city of Paris, which opened the museum in 1949. A contract was then signed with Mme Bourdelle and her daughter, Mme Dufet-Bourdelle (today curator of the museum), stipulating that each of the sculptures could be cast in ten bronze copies, by two artists who would be selected through a competition. Works which had already been made, as could be determined by a general inventory, were exempt from this contract. Produced by different founders—Susse, Godard, Valsuani, Hohwiller, the Coubertin Foundation, Clémenti, etc., the proofs thus obtained were numbered and carry the note "Copyright by Bourdelle." A number of them also carry a stylized star, the artist's monogram made of an A and a B reversed.

Bourdelle made many trips to Italy, first in 1914 when his nearly thirty sculptures were remarkably successful at the Biennale of Venice, and then in 1921, in the company of August Perret. In 1925, he exhibited in Pittsburgh, New York, Chicago, and Cleveland. He benefitted, in 1928, from a retrospective which marked the opening of the Fine Arts Palace in Brussels (a large posthumous retrospective would be organized in Orangerie of the Tuileries in 1931.) He married a Flemish woman, Stéphanie Van Parys, who served as his model for several pieces, including *Pénélope, Femme bras au dos, Femme bras levés*, etc. One of his original Greek students, Cléopâtre Sevastos, became his second wife. She also served as a model for a number of works, including *Femme sculpteur au repos, L'Offrande, Femme au compas, Femme sculpteur au travail, Sainte Barbe*, as well as for *L'Architecture*, from the bas-reliefs of the Champs-Elysées theater. From this union his daughter was born. She inspired him to do some charming small pieces: *Poucette Bourdelle, Poucette à la pomme, Amourette*, etc.

Dying at the height of his fame in 1929, Bourdelle had already transmitted not only his personal style but also his concept of sculpture to his students of the Grande Chaumière ("the great thatched cottage"), where he had taught since 1909. Among them were artists as well-known as Alberto Giacometti, Germaine Richier, Matisse, Vieira da Silva, Auricost, and Hajdu.

The list of bronzes by Bourdelle provided below, though not exhaustive, was established starting with the work published in 1975 by Ionel Jianou and Michel Dufet. The chronological inventory developed by the authors identified the status of the number of works cast at the time and the places where they could be found. As with Rodin, it is astonishing to see that most monumental works were made in many models. Between them, eight models of the first version of the *Héraclès archer* (2.5 meters high) and ten from the second version are enumerated. Seven works of *Centaure mourant*, 2.88 meters high were counted, and three tall bronzes of *La France* exist, none of which measure less than 4.5 meters high. Also, as with Rodin but more so it seems, not only the finished works were cast but the successive studies, the different versions, and the isolated fragments as well.

Since 1975, other works have been (or in the future can be) cast up to the maximum number of ten works as stipulated in the contract of 1949. For this reason, we are content to note here the titles of some works (classed in alphabetical order) and their dimensions with, for each subject, the date of its first appearance. In order not to divide a production into fractions which form a rather insoluble picture, the list below continues only until the death of Bourdelle in 1929.

Adam, 65 and 232 cm.(1889)
Adam, head, 51 cm.
Adam, hand, 35 cm.
Adam, torso, 80 cm.
Adolescente, mask with bust , 38 cm.(1890)
Adolescente, mask with neck, 38 cm.
Adolescente, mask without neck, 20 cm.
A la rivière (1890), 16.5 x 29 cm.
Les Amants or *Pelléas et Mélisand* or *Vague*, 29 cm.(around 1900)
Amazone blessées (1929), 5 x 9 cm.
L'Amour agonise (1886), 40 x 98 cm.
Amourette, Poucette (1914), 105 cm.
Amourette, small bust, 36 cm.
Anatole France, bust (1919), 70 cm.
Anatole France, bust without drapery (1919), 58 cm.
André Rouveyre, mask (1909), 32 cm.
Angèle, bust, model for *La Bacchante* (1906), 28 cm.
Angèle, head, 14 cm.
Angélique (1891), 13 cm.
Aphrodite accroupie (1890), 9 cm.
Aphrodite (1900), 20 cm.
Apollon, head with neck (1900), 43 cm.
Apollon, head with large pedestal, 67 cm.

Antoine Bourdelle,
La Vierge à l'offrande, 66 cm
(A. Rudier).

Antoine Bourdelle,
Paysanne à l'enfant,
38 cm
(A. Rudier).

Antoine Bourdelle,
Héraclès archer,
third study,
63.6 cm
(A. Rudier).

Apollon, head with a small pedestal, 42 cm.
Apollon, mask with neck, 47.5 cm.
Apollon, mask without neck, 35 cm.
Arlane (1929), 12 cm.
Arlequin (1905), 40 cm.
Asclépios (1929), 36 cm.
Auguste Perret, bust (1922), 55 cm.
Augusta or *La Parisienne* (1907), 80 cm.
Augusta, head, 20 cm.
L'Aurore, bas-relief (1895), 190 cm.
L'Aurore à la rose (1898), 35 cm.

Bacchanale, mask (1907), 12.5 cm.
Bacchante aux jambes croisées (1906), 37 and 53 cm.
Bacchante aux jambes croisées, study of a torso, 25 cm.
Bacchante (1907), 81 cm.
Bacchante portant Eros (1923), 60 cm.
Bacchante portant Eros, torso, 26.5 and 51 cm.
Bacchante endormie (1903), 16 cm.
Baigneuse accroupie (1906-1907), 26, 52 and 105 cm.
Baigneuse, Vénus à sa toilette (1906), 36 and 27 cm.
Baigneuse, variant, 27 cm.
Baigneuse, head, 14 cm.
Le Baiser (1907), 22 and 27 cm.
Le Baiser aux nattes (1912), 12 and 21 cm.
Le Baiser aux volubilis (1907), 43 cm.
Batteur de faux (1907), 18 cm.
Beethoven, la joue appuyée sur une main (1887), 57.5 cm.
Beethoven, la joue appuyée sur une main (1888), 54 cm.
Beethoven pensif (around 1888), 40 cm.
Beethoven aux grands cheveux, first study (1889), 47 cm.
Beethoven aux grands cheveux second study (1889), 47.5 cm.
Beethoven aux grands cheveux, head (1891), 60 cm, inscription: "My domain is the air, the great wind raises me, my soul whirls."
Beethoven aux grands cheveux, head, variant (1891), 60 cm, inscription: "Me, I am Bacchus who presses out delicious nectar for men."
Beethoven aux grands cheveux, head (1891), 30 cm, inscription: "My domain. . ."
Beethoven aux grands cheveux, head, romantic study (around 1891), 31 cm.
Beethoven aux grands cheveux, head, variant with scarf (1891), 48 cm.
Beethoven aux petits cheveux (1890), 30 cm.
Beethoven aux petits cheveux, small mask on a shaft (1890), 27 cm.
Beethoven aux petits cheveux, mask, definitive study (1890), 32 cm.
Beethoven à la cravate (1890), 38 cm.
Beethoven à la cravate, 35 cm.
Beethoven, grand masque tragique (1901), 50, 76, 78 cm.
Beethoven, tête dite Hébrard (1901), 58 cm, inscription: "Me, I am Bacchus. . ."
Beethoven à la colonne, eyes closed (1901), 61 cm.
Beethoven à la colonne, eyes open (1902), 44 and 51 cm.
Beethoven dit métropolitain (1902), 104 cm.
Beethoven dit métropolitain, study, 64 cm.
Beethoven, petite tête, study for Beethoven standing (1903), 14 cm.
Beethoven, petit buste, (1903), 20 cm.

Beethoven, torse avec tête (1905), 38 cm.
Beethoven, torse avec tête droite, variant, 37 cm.
Beethoven avec deux mains (1908), 53 cm, inscription: "I am all that was, all that is, all that will be, no mortal man has raised my veil."
Beethoven à une main, study for the preceding subject, 47 cm.
Beethoven, main, 20 cm.
Beethoven drapé (1910), 47 cm.
Beethoven, étude de buste, 14.5 cm.
Beethoven, étude de main, 6 cm.
Beethoven, petite étude de tête, 14 cm.
Beethoven, tête aux raisins (1924-1925), 46 cm.
Beethoven, masque sans raisins, 31 cm.
Beethoven aux raisins, head, variant called Bacchus with closed eyes, 43 cm.
Beethoven à l'architecture (1924-1925), 40 cm.
Beethoven à l'architecture, study of the head, 36 cm.
Beethoven à l'architecture, mask, 24 cm.
Beethoven à l'architecture, mask called, with ruffle, 29.5 cm.
Beethoven à la croix, dit la Pathétique (1929), 38 and 73 cm.
Beethoven à la croix, small bust, 10 cm.
Beethoven à la croix, large bust, 19 cm.
Bélier couché (1908), 53 cm.
Bélier au rocher (1908), 30 cm.
Le Bélier rétif (1909), 30 and 54 cm.
La Belle Américaine (1928), 37 cm.
Bergère au mouton blessé (1929), 13 cm.
Bourdelle père (1906), 47 cm.
Pierre Bourdelle enfant (1907), 37 cm.
Pierre Bourdelle, small study, 23 cm.
Bourdelle, bust, (1908), 28 and 34 cm.
Bourdelle, statuette without arms (1908), 58 cm.
Madame Bourdelle (1912), 36 cm.
Bourdelle musicien, bust (1916), 14 and 32 cm.
Bourdelle musicien, study, 72 cm.
Bourdelle grand musicien, 72 cm.
Bourdelle, grand violon, 60 cm.
Bourdelle, petit violon, 60 cm.
Bourdelle, masque (1925), 38 cm.
Bourdelle (1921), 11 cm.

Antoine Bourdelle,
L'Hymne intérieur, 3
7 cm.

Cardeuse de laine (1899), 30 cm.
Cariatide, bust (1900), 60 cm.
Carpeaux au travail (1909), 246 cm.
Carpeaux, main tenant la glaise (1909), 31 cm.
Carpeaux, main tenant la statuette (1909), 34 cm.
Carpeaux, large bust (1910), 63 cm.
Cavalier avec draperie, study for the monument to General Alvear (1913-1914), 10.5 and 14.5 cm.
Cavalier à la chimère (1929), 22 cm.
Le Centaure mourant, first study (1911), 38 cm.
Le Centaure mourant, second study (1911), 69 71, and 288 cm.
Le Centaure mourant, torso (1914), 131 cm.
Le Centaure mourant, study of right hand (1914), 52.5 cm.
Le Centaure mourant, study of left hand (1914), 55.5 cm.
Petit Cheval et cavalier, Alvear monument (1913-1920), 56 and 69 cm.
Cheval, head (1913-1920), 17.5, 45, 54 and 160 cm.
Cheval sans selle (1915), 45. 47. 148 cm.

Beethoven, debout, sketch (1903), 75 cm.
Beethoven assis sur un rocher (1903), 28 cm.
Beethoven, grand accoudé (1903), 50 and 123 cm.
Beethoven dans le vent, sans draperie (1904-1908), 126 cm, inscription: "To the man and to the god Beethoven."
Beethoven dans le vent, avec draperie (1904-1908), 126 cm.
Beethoven dans le vent, study of the head (1904), 23 cm.
Beethoven dans le vent, study of the bust, 29 and 32.5 cm.

Chèvre et mouton (1907), 26 cm.
La Chilienne, Mme Vargas (1921), 47 cm.
La Chilienne, mask, 69 cm.
La Chilienne, statuette (1928), 51 cm.
La Chute (1890), 15 x 33 cm.
Combat des héros et des dieux (1929), 14 x 23 cm.
Coquelin cadet en Mascarille, mask (1891), 46 and 52
    cm.
Le Cruchon, femme agenouillée (1929), 25 cm.
Cuirassier (1893), 16 cm.

La Danse du marbre, Mme Bourdelle (1908), 28 cm.
La Danse dans les ailes (1929), 21 cm.
Danseuse du 14 Juillet (1906), 27 and 37 cm.
Danseuse à la draperie (1913), 29 cm.
Daphné devient laurier (1910), 85 cm.
Daphné devient laurier, study of a torso, 40 cm.
Daumier, project for a monument (1927), 26 cm.
Daumier, head, 22 and 68 cm.
Les Deux Amis (1908), 23 cm.
Les Deux Soeurs (1892), 27 cm.
Deux Soeurs (1911), 16cm.
Docteur Koeberlé, bust (1914), 68 cm.
Docteur Koeberlé, head, 45 cm.
Dragon bras levé (1893), 65 cm.
Dragon bras levé, large study without sword (1893-
    1900), 53.5 cm.
Dragon bras levé, study without sword, 52 cm.
Dragon sur un rocher, study (1897), 102 cm.
Dragon, bust, 16 cm.
Dragon, head, 26 cm.
Drame intérieur (1899), 48 and 62 cm.
Dziady, bas-relief for the monument at Mickiewicz
    (1909), 11 and 15 cm.

L'Effroi, study of the head, high relief for the monument
    to the dead at Montauban (1909), 46 cm.
L'Elève allemande or *La Fiancée*, bust (around 1900), 25
    cm.
L'Elève allemande, mask, 30 cm.
L'Elève allemande, torso, 42 cm.
L'Eloquence, for the Alvear monument, first version
    (1913), 38 cm.
L'Eloquence, second version (1923), 112 cm.
L'Eloquence, torso (1914-1915, 52.5 cm.
L'Eloquence, study of the head (1918), 45 cm.
L'Eloquence, study for the monument of doctor Soca at
    Montevideo (1927), 23 and 26.5 cm.
Enfant à la rose (1898), 29 cm.
Enfant endormi, mask (1905), 18 and 22 cm.
Enfant endormi, mask with shoulders, 28 cm.
Enfant endormi, head, 21 cm.
Enfant qui pleure (1900), 35 cm.

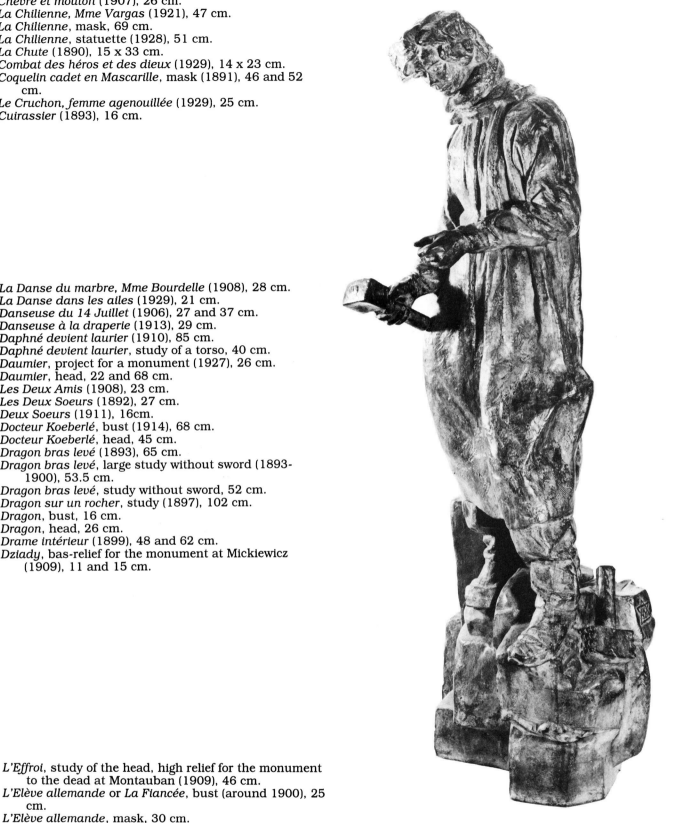

Antoine Bourdelle,
Jeune Sculpteur au travail, 130 cm
(A. Rudier).

Enfant qui rit (1900), 40 cm.
Enfant rieur à la houpette (1891), 14 cm.
L'Enlèvement d'Europe (1929), 21 cm.
L'Epopée polonaise, for the monument to Mickiewicz (1909), 33 and 55 cm.
L'Epopée polonaise, torso, 110 cm.
L'Epouvante de la guerre, for the monument to the dead of Montauban (1899), 38 x 148 cm.
L'Epouvante de la guerre, study of the head (1909), 33 cm.
L'Esprit maîtrisant la matière (1910), 72 cm.
Etude de femme, (1906), 20 cm.
Etude de nu or *Nu diptère* (1902), 21 cm.
Etude de tête, d'après Isadora Duncan, for the monument to Mickiewicz (1912), 24 cm.
Eve (1908), 21 cm.
Eve, high relief, 25 cm.

Garçonnet, bust (1885), 18 cm.
Génie ailé (1887), 42 cm.
Génie inconnu (1929), 15 cm.
Le Génie médical, for the monument of doctor Soca (1927), 23 and 26.5 cm.
Grand Baiser aux nattes (1891), 21 cm.
Grand guerrier de Montauban, for the monuments to the dead (1893-1902), 180 cm.
Grand Guerrier, study of a torso, 82 cm.
Grand Guerrier, sudy of a bust, 62 cm.
Grand Guerrier, put down with a sword, 41 x 77 and 83 x 148 cm.
Grand Guerrier, hand and arms (1898), 32.5 and 56 cm.
Grand Guerrier, hand and arms holding a section of a sword, 30 cm.
Guerrier, without bas-relief, for the monument to the dead of Montauban (1889), 34 cm.

Femme nue adossée au mur (1890), 28 cm.
Femme sculpteur au travail (1906), 50 cm.
Femme sculpteur au travail, bust, 20.5 cm.
Femme sculpteur au travail, hand, 8.5 cm.
Femme sculpteur au repos (1906), 33 and 68 cm.
Femme bras levé (1909), 59 and 105 cm.
Femme bras au dos (1909), 17 and 54 cm.
Femme au compas, Mme Bourdelle (1909), 43 cm.
Femme au compas, bust, 12 cm.
Femme à la fontaine, Mme Bourdelle (1909), 34 cm.
Femme avec chevelure aux fruits, small head (1909), 19.5 cm.
Femme et enfant, maman et Poucette (1912), 20 cm.
Femme assise dite jupe plissée (1919), 26 cm.
Femme couchée sur une amphore (1929), 15 x 25 cm.
Femme nue allongée (1929), 7 x 20 cm.
Figure hurlante, for a monument to the dead (1896-1899), 93 cm.
Fillette rieuse, head (1890), 21 cm.
Fillette rieuse, mask, 27.5 cm.
Fillete à la branche (1900), 13 cm.
Le Fondeur (1929), 36 cm.
La Force, for the monument Alvear (1918-1923), 38, 122 and 372 cm.
La Force, head, 68 cm.
La Force head with mane, 80 cm.
La Force, bust with mane, 81 cm.
La Force, hand (1914), 45 cm.
La France, for the monument to the dead of Montauban (1893-1896), 120 cm.
La France, mask, 44 cm.
La France (1925), 136, 460 and 900 cm.
La France, head, 47 and 92 cm.
Le Fruit (1906), 60, 76 and 100 cm.
Le Fruit, variante (1911), 226 cm.
Le Fruit, torso, 30 and 102 cm.
Le Fruit, torso with head, 63.5 and 131 cm.
Le Fruit, mask, 38 cm.
Le Fruit, head, 14 and 51 cm.
Le Fruit, right hand, 29 cm.
Le Fruit, left hand, 40 cm.

Antoine Bourdelle,
Héraclès à la biche, 63 cm
(A. Rudier).

Guerrier, a single arm, study in bas-relief (1893-1900), 36 cm.
Guerrier au casque or *Dragon moustachu* (1893-1900), 60, 67 and 85 cm.
Guerrier au casque, variant, 82 cm.
Guerrier au casque, mask with chin strap, 20 cm.
Guerrier hurlant, for the monument of Montauban, 46 cm.
Guerrier hurlant, bust stated with epaulet, 65 cm
Guerrier mourant, for the monument of Montauban, study of a head, 33 cm.
Guerrier mourant, hand, 36 cm.
Hamadryade (1929), 29 and 44 cm.
Hamlet, study (1881), 45.5 cm.
Hamlet, (1891), 36 cm.

Héraclès archer (1909), 250 cm.
Héraclès archer, second version, 248 cm.
Héraclès archer, study, 64 and 58 cm.
Héraclès archer, intermediate study, 77 cm.
Héraclès archer, study without arc, 38.5 cm.
Héraclès archer, incomplete study, 30 cm.
Héraclès archer, torso, 94 cm.
Héraclès archer, head, 6, 9, 11, 41 and 44 cm.
Héraclès archer , mask, 8, 6 and 35 cm.
Héraclès archer, right hand, 36.5 cm.
Héraclès archer , left hand, 35 cm.
Héraclès à la biche (1910), 63 cm.
Hercule et Cacus, study (1882), 59 cm.
Hercule, head (1905), 38 cm.
Homère, study for the bust of doctor Koeberlé (1914), 36 cm.
L'Homme suspendu (1884), 53 cm.
L'Homme à la guitare, incomplete sketch (1890), 41.5 cm.
L'Homme à la cruche (around 1900), 37 cm.
L'Hymne intérieur (1905), 32, 37 and 73 cm.

Icare (1887), 33 cm.
Infirmière (1916), 72 cm.
Ingres, bust (1908), 59 and 82 cm.
Irlandaise, mask (1913), 26 cm.
Isadora Duncan for the monument to Mickiewicz (1912), 19 cm.
Italienne à genoux (1900), 28 cm.
Italienne à genoux, small buste, 14 cm.

James Frazer, bust (1922), 68 cm.
Jane Avril (1900), 27.5 cm.
Jeanne d'Arc pastoure, (1898), 74 cm.
Jeanne d'Arc en prière, (1898), 15.5 cm.
Jeanne d'Arc à l'étendard (1910), 77 and 126 cm.
Le Jeu du voile (1910), 68 and 70 cm.
Jeux d'enfants (around 1900), 18 cm.
Jeune Bacchante (1907), 13.5 and 23 cm.
Jeune Bergère (1882), 33 cm.
Jeune Fille cueillant des pommes (1895), 26 and 54 cm.
Jeune Fille aux épaules (1898), 33 cm.
Jeune Fille de La Roche-Posay (1926), 55 cm.

Jeune Fille aux violettes et aux roses (1890), 23 cm.
Le Jeune Sculpteur, Pierre Bourdelle (1908), 29 cm.
Jeune Sculpteur au travail (1918), 65 and 126 cm.
Jeunesse, (1911), 45 and 46.5 cm.
Le Jour et la nuit (1904), 70 cm.

Krishnamurti, head with cap decorated with lotus (1927), 76 cm.

La Liberté, for the monument Alvear (1913), 33 cm.
La Liberté, definitive version (1915), 38 and 122 cm.
La Liberté, head (1914), 64 cm.

Madeleine Charnaux au chignon (1917), 24, 46, 49 and 63 cm.
Madeleine Charnaux sans chignon (1917), 45 cm.
Main désespérée (around 1900), 34 cm.
Marie Laprade à la capeline (1897), 38 cm.
Marie Laprade en tenue de ville (1897), 41 cm.
Mademoiselle Markovitch, Russian student (1914), 53 and 65 cm.
Marocain assis (1924), 24.5 cm.
La Marquise de Silvia de Mari, head (1887), 39 cm.
Marsyas (1890), 22 cm.
Masque, profile (1896-1900), 33 cm.
Masque, 30 cm.
Masque dit bras troué, 62 cm.
Masque dit penché en arrière, 47 cm.
Masque (around 1905), 38 cm.
Maternité (1893), 63 cm.
Maternité, variant, 63 cm.
Maternité, mask, 25 cm.
Mauviette à la cruche (1929), 31 cm.
Mélancolie (1909), 57 cm.
Mélancolie, small mask, 11 cm.
Mélisande (around 1900), 13.5 cm.
Mère et fille (1891), 45 cm.
Mickiewicz (1909-1924), 30, 33 and 262 cm.
Modèle timide (1910), 53 and 71 cm.
Monogramme de Bourdelle (1919), 26 cm.
Monsieur Eros (1929), 15 cm.
Monument aux morts de Montauban, small model (1893-1896), 85 cm.
La Mort du cygne (1929), 30 cm.
Mouton penché (1907), 25 cm.
Muse courant, bas-relief for the theatre of the Champs-Elysées (1911), 19 x 31 cm.
Muse, small mask, 9 x 17.5 cm.

Naissance de Vénus (1927), 21 cm.
Nativité (1929), 12 and 23 cm.
Noble Fardeau (1910), 127 and 220 cm.
Noble Fardeau, study, 84 cm.
Noble Fardeau, child with hand, 29 cm.
Noble Fardeau, single bust, 23 cm.
La Nonne (1888), 25 cm.
Nostalgie, head of a faun (1909), 30 cm.
Nu pilier (1906), 37 cm.
Nu pilier (1918), 79 cm.
Le Nuage or *L'Aurore* (1907), 30 and 50 cm.
Le Nuage, torso of Vénus, 28 cm.
La Nuit, a profile (1904), 50 cm.
La Nuit, front view, 61 cm.

L'Offrande, Mme Bourdelle jeune fille (1905), 70 cm.
L'Offrande, study, 51 cm.
L'Offrande, head, 11 cm.
L'Offrande, buste, 11 and 13 cm.

Pallas drapée (1889), 29 cm.
Pallas, bust, 29 cm.
Pallas, torso, 65 and 92 cm.
Pallas, mask, 35 cm.
Pallas guerrière, torso (1889), 97 cm.
Passion (around 1900), 17 cm.
La Patrie soutenant le héros, project of the monument
    (1906), 21 cm.
La Patrie soutenant le héros, variant, 15 cm.
Paysanne à l'enfant (1910), 38, 52 and 75 cm.
Pénélope au fuseau (1905), 42.5 and 55 cm
Pénélope sans fuseau (1907-1912), 61, 120, 240 cm.
Pénélope sans fuseau, head, 12 and 19 cm.
Pénélope sans fuseau, study of a head, 16.5 cm.
Petit Bonhomme, Eros (1905), 68 cm.
Petit Bonhomme, torso, 27 cm.
Petit Bonhomme, bust, 30.5 cm.
Petit Bonhomme, head, 16 cm.
Petit Enfant et sa mère (1910), 29 cm.
Petit Faune, head (1905), 18 cm.
Petit Garçon à la branche (1900), 13 cm.
Petite Nymphe (1886), 10 x 15 cm.
Petite Tête avec raisin (1910), 20 cm.
Phryné (1929), 32 cm.
Pierre et sa mère (1903), 19 cm.
La Polonaise (1911), 51 cm.
Les Pommes (1907), 32, 38.5 and 46 cm.
Poucette à la pomme (1911), 61 cm.
Poucette Bourdelle (1912), 18 cm.
Le Prophète (1888), 34 cm.

Rembrandt jeune (1909), 66 cm.
Rembrandt vieux (1909), 50 cm.
Rembrandt, tête penchée, 50 cm.
Rieuse cheveux sur l'épaule (1889), 39 cm.
Rieuse (1889), 36 cm.
Rieuse (1891), 23 cm.
Rieuse (1903), 25, 27 and 32 cm.
Rieuses, group called *Rires et roses* (1903), 38 cm.
Rieuse au grand chignon (1909), 19 and 24 cm.
Riri, study of a head for the statue of *Vénus* (1901), 11.5
    cm.
Riri, study with neck, 18 cm.
Riri, torso (1904), 34 cm.
Rodin au travail (1909), 69 cm.
Rodin, bust, 57 and 67 cm.
Madame Roussel au chapeau (1895), 35 and 46 cm.
Madame Roussel au chapeau, head, 17 cm.

Sainte Barbe, d'après Mme Bourdelle (1916), 100 cm.
Saint Sébastien (1883), 71 cm.
Salammbô (1890), 30 cm.
Sapho, first composition (1887), 28 and 30 cm.
Sapho, second composition (1887), 70 adn 208 cm.
Sapho, bust, 97 cm.
Sapho, head, 55 cm.
Séléné couchée (1916), 85 cm.
Petite Séléné couchée (1916), 43 cm.
Petite Séléné couchée, study of a head, 11 cm.
Grande Séléné debout (1916), 126 cm.
Séléné, right hand, 17.5 cm.
Séléné, left hand, 18.5 cm.
La Sieste sous l'arbre (1887), 40 cm.
La Sieste, homme endormi (1894), 22 x 42 cm.
Miss Sinclair Breckens (1910), 58 cm.
Souffrance, head (1893-1902), 32 and 44 cm.
Source vive (1929), 24 cm.
Sphinge, head of a woman (1903), 29 cm.

Tête de bébé, bas-relief (1880), 10.5 cm.
Tête d'enfant de Montauban (1885), 22 cm.
Tête de femme avec poisson (1892), 28 cm.
Tête de gorgone, door knocker (1925), 67 cm.
Tête de gorgone, study, 21 cm.
Tête de jeune fille aux macarons (1890), 25 cm.
Tête de Raymond (1918), 20 cm.

Antoine Bourdelle,
Le Nuage, 30.5 cm
(A. Rudier No 14).

Antoine Bourdelle,
Bacchante aux jambes croisées,
37 cm
(A. Rudier).

Antoine Bourdelle,
Bacchante au raisins,
83.5 cm
(A. Rudier).

Tête de vieille femme (1904), 17 cm.
Tireuse à l'arc (1929), 29 cm.
Tolstoi (1906), 58 cm.
Les Trois Soeurs or *Les Trois Grâces*, bas-relief (1892), 43 x 67 cm.
La Truie (1909), 19 cm.

L'Urne, study of a nude (1927), 98 cm.
L'Urne, torso, 38 cm.

La Vague (1887), 12.5 x 29.5 cm.
Vase avec femme nue (1892), 28 and 38 cm.
Vendangeuse (1912-1927), 69 and 88 cm.
Le Vent, project of a monument (1906), 24 cm.
Vénus baigneuse, small head (1905), 9 cm.
La Victoire (1921), 38, 122 and 172 cm.

La Vie blessée (1886), 13 and 42 cm.
Vieille Bacchante (1903), 85 cm.
Vieille Femme assise aux pommes (around 1903), 17 cm.
Vierge à l'offrande, for the monument of Niederbrück (1919), 64, 66 and 250 cm.
Vierge à l'offrande, study of a head (1921), 38 cm.
Vierge à l'Enfant sur colonnette (1929), 19 cm.
Vincent d'Indy (1927), 65 cm.
Violoncelle voilé (1914), 35 cm.
Violoncelliste (1914), 30 cm.

Antoine Bourdelle,
Petite Tête de femme
avec chevulure aux fruits, 19.6 cm
(A. Rudier).

MUSEUMS
Albi
Jeanne d'Arc, 67.
Tête d'Apollon, 58 cm.
Arles
Le Fondeur, 36 cm.
Le Génie médical, 54 cm.
Gorgone, doorknocker, 67 cm.
James Frazer, bust, 68 cm.
Krishnamurti, head on a capital, 76 cm.
Bordeaux
Jeanne d'Arc, 290 cm (A. Rudier).
Belfort
Coquelin cadet en Mascarille, 52 cm.
Calais
Le Bélier rétif, 53 cm (A. Rudier).
Héraclès archer, torso, 91 cm (E. Godard).
Cambrai
Anatole France, bust, 70 cm (A. Rudier).
Dijon
La Force, study of a head for the Alvear monument at Buenos Aires, gilded bronze, 65 cm.
Grenoble
Bacchante, 83 cm.
Le Havre
Beethoven, 58 cm. (1901).
Beethoven aux grands cheveux, bust, 90 cm.
Drame intérieur, 62 cm.
Ingres, bust, 82 cm.
Lille
Pénélope sans fuseau, 118 cm (Hohwiller).
Lyon
Carpeaux au travail, 246 cm.
Drame intérieur, 62 cm.
Mont-de-Marsan
La France, 460 cm (1923).
Montauban
Armand Saintis, bust, 98 cm (1884).
Docteur Koeberlé, bust, 68 cm.
Emile Garisson, bust, 60 cm.
Femme sculpteur au repos, 60 cm.
Ingres, bust, 80 cm.
James Frazer, bust, 68 cm.
Jeanne d'Arc pastoure, 58 cm.
Krishnamurti, bust, 66 cm.
Léon Cladel, bust, 126 cm.
La Nuit, full-faced, 61 cm.
Rembrandt vieux, 50 cm.
Tête de combattant, 35 cm.
La Victoire aptère, 235 cm.
    Several bronzes by Bourdelle are exhibited out of doors in the city of Montauban.

Antoine Bourdelle,
Tête de Beethoven aux grands cheveux,
30 cm (1891).

Montpellier
Apollon, head with neck, 43 cm.
L'Eloquence, head, 45 cm.
Morlaix
Tristan Corbière, bust, 113 cm. (1912).
Narbonne
Pierre Laprade enfant, 37 cm.
Nice
Beethoven, mask, 24 cm.
Orléans
Noble Fardeau, 127 cm (A. Rudier).
Orléans, historical museum
Jeanne d'Arc à l'étendard, 126 cm.
Paris, Decorative Arts
Les Nuées, upper part of the scene, bas-relief, 55 x 104 cm.
Paris, Bourdelle museum
The museum preserves nearly all of the works of the sculptor, as many in plaster as in bronze.
Paris, Carnavalet
Coquelin cadet en Mascarille, 52 cm.
L. H. Marais, acteur, 71 cm.
Paris, Orsay
Anatole France, nude torso, 70 cm.
Auguste Perret, bust, 55 cm.
Baigneuse sur un rocher, 36 cm. (Hébrard).
Beethoven, bust, inscription: "I am Bacchus. . .", 22 cm.
Le Bélier rétif, 53.2 cm.
Le Docteur Koeberlé, bust, 68 cm (A. Rudier).
La Force, for the monument Alvear, 372 cm (A. Rudier).
Héraclès archer, second version, gilded bronze, 248 cm.

Héraclès, head, 34.5 cm.
L'Offrande, 69 cm (Hébrard).
Pénélope, second version, 60 cm (1926).
Paris, Petit Palais
La Mort du dernier centaure, 287 cm.
Pénélope sans fuseau, 120 cm.
Paris, Rodin Museum
Rodin, bust, 57 cm.
Rodin, project of the monument, 90 cm.
Rodin au travail, 69 cm.
Rouen
Le Fruit, 226 cm.
Toulouse
Docteur Koeberlé, bust, 68 cm.
Tours
Anatole France, bust, 70 cm.
Valence
Noble Fardeau, 127 cm (Susse).

Many foreign museums have works by Bourdelle. The principal ones include Anvers, Bruxelles, Gand, Amsterdam, Rotterdam, Lausanne, Zurich, Cologne, Stuttgart, Copenhagen, Helsinki, Stockholm, Goteborg, Oslo, Rome, Lisbon, Dresden, Prague, Bucharest, Warsaw, Sofia, Moscow, Baltimore, Boston, Detroit, Los Angeles, New York, New Orleans, Minneapolis, Buenos Aires, and Tokyo. Some monumental bronzes appear at outdoor sites in Dallas, Seoul, at the Hakone museum, and in Japan.

The Algiers museum owns the second version of *Héraclès archer*, 248 x 240 cm, and *Buste du docteur Koeberlé*, 68 cm.

SALES
Adolescente au fichu, 39 cm (Susse No. 1), Drouot Hotel, December 15, 1983, rooms 5 and 6.
Bacchante aux jambes croisées, 37 cm (A. Rudier), Sotheby London, June 27, 1984.
Batteur de fer, 17.5 cm (Valsuani No. 3), Christie's New York, May 18, 1983.
Beethoven aux grands cheveux, 60 cm (J. Peterman, Brussells), Sotheby New York, July 21, 1985.
Beethoven, grand masque tragique, 78 cm (Hohwiller), Sotheby New York, November 14, 1985.
Beethoven, bust, 21 cm (Valsuani), Rambouillet, October, 12, 1986.
Le Bélier, 31 cm (Hébrard), Drouot Hotel, December 7, 1983, room 9.
Danseuse du 14 Juillet, 27 cm (A. Valsuani), Sotheby New York, November 14, 1985.
Danseuse du 14 Juillet, 37 cm (A. Valsuani No. 4), Christie's New York, November 13, 1985.
L'Enfant endormi, 28 cm (Valsuani No. 5), Drouot Hotel, December 15, 1983, rooms 5 and 6.
Femme bras au dos, 54 cm, Drouot Hotel, April 15, 1986, room 6.
Femme avect chevelure aux fruits, small head, 19.5 cm (A. Rudier), Neuilly, February 1, 1983.
Buste de femme, 46 cm, Drouot Hotel, November 28, 1984, rooms 5 and 6.
Le Fondeur, 36 cm (Susse 5/8), Sotheby London, October 23, 1985.
Le Fruit, femme nue debout, 75.5 cm (A. Rudier), Bernay, June 23, 1984 (taken for 260,000 F).
Le Général Bolivar équestre, study, 116 cm (Susse, 1984), Christie's New York, November 20, 1986.
Guerrier, mask, 35 cm (Hébrard No.4), Sotheby London, June 30, 1983.
Héraclès archer, 30 cm (Susse No. 5), Sotheby London, November 19, 1986.
Héraclès archer, 54.5 cm (Susse No. 6), Sotheby New York, November 13, 1985 ($210,000).
Héraclès archer, 64 cm (A. Rudier), Sotheby New York, May 13, 1986; Christie's New York, November 19, 1986.

Antoine Bourdelle,
Buste de Rembrandt, 50 cm.

Héraclès archer, 81 cm (Valsuani No. 4), Christie's New York, November 13, 1985.
Hymne intérieur, 37 cm (Susse No. 7), Drouot Hotel, December 15, 1983, rooms 5 and 6.
Jeune Fille aux pampres, 20 cm (A. Rudier), Drouot Hotel, March 19, 1984, room 5 and 6.
Jeune Sculpteur au travail, 126 cm (A. Rudier), Drouot Hotel, November 27, 1984, rooms 5 and 6.
La Liberté, 38 cm (Susse), Drouot Hotel, March 28, 1985, room 2; Sotheby London, June 25, 1986.
La Main, 34 cm (Hébrard), Drouot Hotel, September 26, 1986, room 8.
Maternité, 16 cm, Drouot Hotel, March 19, 1984, rooms 5 and 6.
Mélancolie, 57 cm (A. Rudier), Sotheby New York, October 18, 1985.
Nativité, 11.5 cm, Sotheby London, February 13, 1985.
Le Nuage, 30 cm, (A. Rudier), Enghien, June 23, 1985.
Pallas, mask, 35 cm, Sotheby London, February 23, 1983.
Paysanne à l'enfant, 38 cm (A. Rudier), Neuilly, February 1, 1983.
Pénélope, 60 cm, dedicated "to my wife" (Peterman, Brussels), Drouot Hotel, March 16, 1983.

Riri, high pedestal, 26.7 cm (A. Vasuani), Christie's New York, October 9, 1986.
Madame Roussel au chapeau, 35 cm (Susse 5/10), Sotheby New York, November 14, 1985.
Sainte Barbe, 100 cm (A. Rudier), Sotheby London, June 26, 1985.
Tête d'homme, 28 cm (Bisceglia), Drouot Hotel, December 5, 1985, room 1.
La Victoire, 122 cm (A. Rudier), dedicated to Marshal Pétain, Enghien, March 24, 1985 (332,500 F).
La Vierge à l'offrande, 64 cm, Sotheby London, June 26, 1985.
La Vierge à l'offrande, 66 cm (A. Rudier), Sotheby London, March 26, 1986.

BOURET, EUTROPE

Paris, April 16, 1833
October 5, 1906

BouRet

Bouret submitted a number of pieces to the Salon from 1875 to 1903, including *Petite Baigneuse*, terra cotta (1881), *La Source*, marble (1882), *Sarah la baigneuse* and *Mercure*, plasters (1883), some groups and statuettes in bronze including *Les Confidences* and *Les Orphelins* (1886), *Mercure* (1889), *La Pudeur* and *La musique légère* (1892), *Le Cirque, Terpsichore* (1894), *La Libellule* (1898), and *L'Espérance* (1899).

Eutrope Bouret,
Figaro, 37 cm.

Eutrope Bouret,
Pierrot or Au clair de la lune, 45 cm.
See reproduction in color page 10*.

A number of works by Bouret were cast in bronze, principally feminine figures including L'Amour vainqueur, Baigneuse, 70 cm, Bonaparte debout, 31.5 cm, Au clair de la lune, 67 and 45 cm, Diane, 56 cm, Femme égyptienne, 32.5 cm, L'Histoire, Jeanne d'Arc à cheval, 62 cm, Jeanne d'Arc debout tenant son épée, La Libellule, Lulli, 80 and 60 cm, Pierrot debout, 50 cm, and Poésie des champs, 39 cm. The museum of Meaux has one work in bronze entitled La Liseuse.

SALES

Au cirque, 77 cm, Sotheby London, March 17, 1983.
Déesse égyptienne, Déesse romaine, two statuettes in gilded bronze, 39 cm, Sotheby London, November 7, 1985.
Figaro, bronze and ivory, 28 cm, Sotheby London, June 20, 1985.
La Grâce de Dieu, Sans famille, two statuettes, 49 and 48 cm, Sotheby London, November 10, 1983.
Jeune Femme en robe du soir, 79 cm, Christie's New York, March 1, 1983.
Pêcheuse de crabes, Epernay, March 3, 1985.
Pierrot, 46 cm, Sotheby London, March 20, 1986.
Le Travail, jeune forgeron, 61 cm, Drouot Hotel, December 1, 1986, room 14.

BOURGEOIS, BARON CHARLES ARTHUR

Dijon, May 19, 1938
Paris, November 11, 1886

A student of Duret and of Guillaume at the Ecole des Beaux-Arts, Bourgeois received the grand prize of Rome in 1836 for Nisus et Euryale. His work is composed of statues, groups, and bas-reliefs, some of them executed to decorate Parisian monuments, the city hall, the Sorbonne, and churches. His most important artistic accomplishments are some very realistic busts and statues of an exotic character. Many of them were shown at the Salon between 1863 and 1886, including Charmeur de serpents, bronze, 2 meters high (1864, with a number of reductions in many sizes), Laveuse arabe, bronze (1868), Sphinx, bronze for the monument erected in Brussels in honor of French soldiers who died in the war of 1870-1871 (1881), Chasseur de crocodile, 190 cm, a statue in plaster (1883; also made in bronze), and Danseuse égyptienne, a statuette in bronze (1886). Also of note is L'Acteur grec in bronze, 210 cm, in the garden of Luxembourg. The two best-known bronzes by Bourgeois, Le Charmeur de serpents and Le Chasseur de crocodile, are today found in the Jardin des Plantes in Paris.

SALES

Le Charmeur de serpents, 56.5 cm, Drouot Hotel, May 23, 1984, rooms 5 and 6; Sotheby London, June 7, 1984; Enghien, April 28, 1985.
Le charmeur de serpents, 80 cm, Drouot Hotel, December 5, 1985, rooms 5 and 6; Marseille, November 29, 1986.
Le Charmeur de serpents, 112 cm, Enghien, October 16, 1983.
Le Charmeur de serpents, Porteuse d'eau nubienne, 111 and 113 cm, Enghien, November 23, 1986.
Danseur nègre, Sotheby London, June 7, 1984.
Danseuse égyptienne or Esméralda, gilded and silvered bronze, 56 cm, Drouot Hotel, May 23, 1984.
Danseuse égyptienne or Esméralda, 120 cm, Drouot Hotel, December 9, 1981, room 16.
Femme noire au pagne, 68 cm, Enghien, October 16, 1983.

Charles Arthur Bourgeois,
Charmeur de serpents
or Danseur nubien, 56.5 cm.

BOURGEOIS, LOUIS MAXIMILIEN

Paris, February 11, 1893
Paris, October 1901

Louis Maximilien Bourgeois was a sculptor and medal-engraver who exhibited a number of bust and medallion portraits, often in bronze, as well as some allegorical and mythological statues, among them La Guerre, a statue in marble (1873), L'Imagination, a statue in plaster designed for the grand lobby of the Opera of Paris, 250 cm (1874), Mercure, a statue in marble (1877), Premier Collier, a statuette in plaster (1897) and two statuettes in bronze entitled Muse des trophées (1897) and Harmonie (1898). Bourgeois also worked on the decoration of the Louvre, Paris's city hall, and the old Trocadéro.

MUSEUMS
Angers

This museum owns seven medallions in bronze, for the most part portraits of members of the Bourgeois family, 11.9 to 20 cm diam.

Arras
Portrait du sénateur A. Paris, medallion, 16.5 cm diam.
  (1885).
Bordeaux
Mercure, 180 cm (1877).

BOURGOIN, EUGÈNE

Reims, 1880
Paris, 1924

Bourgouin

Bourgoin started to exhibit in 1905 and 1906 at
the Salon des Artistes Français, and in 1907 began to
show his works at the Salon of the Société Nationale
des Beaux-Arts. He exhibited primarily works in
bronze. In 1907 these included *La Résignation*, a bust
in gilded bronze, a mask entitled *La Prière*, another
bust entitled *Vers l'au-delà*, and a statuette called
Désespérance. His other statuettes include *La Fleur
brisé* in 1909, *Ad Sidera* and *Lacrymasque fundebam*
in 1911, etc.

MUSEUMS
Reims
Buste de Léon Harman, 46 cm.

*Eugène Bourgoin,
Femme nue accroupie.*

Troyes
La Liberté, homme nu enchaîné (journey of the prisoners
  of war, 1917), plaque 6.1 x 6.2 cm.
La Prière, mask, 29 cm.

SALES
Petite Fille à l'oiseau, 40 cm (Susse), Drouot Hotel, June
  27, 1983, room 6.

*Robert Bousquet,
Le Taureau,
23.5 x 41 cm.*

BOUSQUET, ROBERT

1888
1917

During the course of his very brief career—he died
in combat during the First World War—this animal
sculptor produced some statuettes of horned animals, such as *Etude de zébu*, exhibited in bronze at
the Salon of 1913. Also in bronze are his works *Lionne
terrassant un serpent*, 37.5 cm, and *Jeanne d'Arc
brandissant son épée*, a spirited equestrian of 52.5
cm.

BOUTELLIER, JEAN ERNEST

Toulouse, August 6, 1851
Circa 1920

After studying under Jouffroy and Falguière in
Paris, Boutellier became the director of the school of
fine arts in Dijon. He exhibited regularly at the Salon
from 1880 to 1903, and his work includes the plasters *Jeune Mendiant aveugle* (1881), *Avant le combat*
(1882), *Retour de l'enfant prodigue* (1884), *Nymphe
victorieuse* (1891), and *En péril* (1894). He also modeled some busts in bronze, and a statuette in marble
entitled *Bataille de fleurs* (1892). *Étienne Marcel
équestre* was cast in bronze, 50 cm, by Valsuani.

BOUTRY, EDGAR HENRI

Lille, January 13, 1857
Levallois-Perret, February 1, 1938

Boutry, the winner of the prize of Rome in 1887, had learned his craft at the academic schools of Lille and then in Paris at Cavelier's studio in the Beaux-Arts. Boutry was the author of a group in stone entitled *L'Art au Moyen Age,* ornamenting the facade of the Grand Palais. He primarily left portraits in the form of busts, medallions, plaques, and statuettes. At the Salon, he also exhibited works entitled *L'Amour et la Folie,* bas-relief in plaster (1891), *Chasseurs,* a group in bronze (1892), *Au bain,* marble (1903), *Heure joyeuse,* a group in plaster (1911), etc. His abundant work is characterized by a graceful style evocative of the Art Nouveau years. He worked on many monuments in Lille, the city hall of Roubaix, and some commemorative monuments.

MUSEUMS
Lille
L'Architecte Emile Vanderbergh, medallion, 38 cm (1898).
Le Peintre Alfred Agache, bust, 70 cm (1916, Godard Sr., founder).
Portrait d'A. Mourcou, bas-relief, 63 x 52 cm (1910).

Maurice Bouval,
Le Secret,
67 cm.

Jean Ernest Boutellier,
Etienne Marcel équestre,
50 cm.

BOUVAL, MAURICE

Toulouse, March 9, 1863
March 20, 1916

After having studied at the studio of Faluière, Maurice Bouval produced a number of bronzes, which he exhibited at the Salon from 1891 to 1914. A certain number of them carry the seal of founders such as Jollet, Thiébaut Frères, Colin, and Goldscheider. Among these bronzes are a bust of his father (1892), and some statuettes including *Les Parfums des fleurs* (1900), *Les Feuilles d'Automne* (1902), *Majesté* (1905), and *Rêve d'automne* in bronze and ivory (1907). He also crafted articles including a piece of a table entitled *L'Obsession,* a plant stand entitled *Le Pavot* (1897), and an gilded bronze ashtray in an Art Nouveau style (1899). Finally, among his works are a group entitled *L'Orgueil* and a statue entitled *La Flamme* (1903).

Some bronzes by Bouval were cast by Thiébaut, specifically *Femme au nénuphar, Femme au pavot,* 20 cm, *Feuille d'automne,* 48 cm and 24 cm, as well as some lamps, candlesticks, sconces, chandeliers including *Aurore et Crépuscule,* two 50 cm candelabras, a candlestick called *Capucine,* 46 cm, and a candlestick called *Rose trémière,* 47 cm.

Notable works from the foundery of Colin and Cie are *Carmencita, Les Parfums des fleurs, Buste de Ruth,* 47.5 cm, in gilded bronze, and a vase ornamented by a nude woman, 20 cm.

A number of the bronzes which appeared for sale include Le Secret, 38 cm, the busts of *Ondine,* 38 cm in. and of *Ophélie,* 36 cm, and a bas-relief symbolizing *La Joie et la Douleur.*

MUSEUMS
Paris, Carnavalet
Henri Feulard, médecin, plaque 24.5 x 12 cm (1897).

SALES
Nymphe, gilded bronze, 46 cm (E. Colin, founder), Christie's New York, May 24, 1984.
Nu debout (seal), 12.5 cm, Sotheby London, Aprile 28, 1983.
Ophélie, gilded bronze, 18 cm, Sotheby Monaco, March 11, 1984.
Le Secret, gilded bronze, 67 cm, Sotheby Monaco, April 13, 1986.
Le Sommeil, femme aux pavots, gilded bronze, 43 cm (E. Colin, founder), Christie's London, June 29, 1983.

BOVERIE, EUGÈNE JEAN
Paris, May 6, 1869
Paris, December 15, 1910

Boverie's work includes a number of busts and statues of contemporary or historical people designed for commemorative monuments. Some of his pieces are *Caïn* and *L'Abandonnée,* two groups in plaster presented to the Salon, respectively in 1893 and in 1895, *Griserie,* a statuette in marble (1903), and *Recueillement,* a small group in bronze (1907). The museum of the Petit Palais owns a group in bronze representing a couple leaning on their elbows on a wall entitled *Recueillement,* 43.5 cm. Another bronze group, *Amoureux sur un banc,* 46 cm, was sold at the Drouot Hotel on May 10, 1985, room 7.

BOVY, JEAN ANTOINE
Geneva, December 14, 1795
1877

Bovy was an engraver in medals as well as a sculptor. He studied in the studio of Pradier and produced a number of medallions with portraits and historic scenes. The museum of Carnavalet owns one of these medallions, *Portrait de François Arago,* 21 cm diam.

BRETON, PAUL-EUGÈNE
Toulouse, May 21, 1868
January 4, 1932

This student of Falguière began submitting works to the Salon in 1896. These works included sculptures in plaster and in marble such as *Gladiateur,*

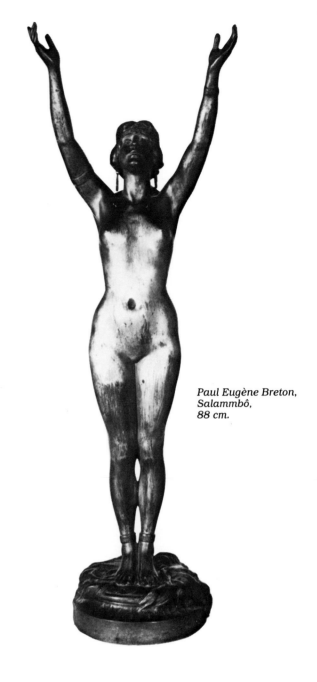

Paul Eugène Breton, Salammbô, 88 cm.

plaster (1896), *Martyr,* plaster (1898), *Salammbô,* marble (1900), *Enlèvement d'Eurydice* and *Les Perles,* two groups in marble (1903), and *Suggestion,* a statuette in plaster (1913), etc.

SALES
Salammbô, 33.5 cm, Drouot Hotel, November 18, 1985, room 6.
Salammbô, 88 cm, La Flèche, June 26, 1983.

BRIDEN, DÉSIRÉ
La Chapelle-Saint-Luc (Aube), 1850
Troyes, 1936

Désiré Briden studied first at the school of drawing in Troyes, and then at the Beaux-Arts in Paris. After having worked in the capital, he returned to Troyes in 1897 to become director of the Ecole Municipale des Beaux-Arts, a position he held from 1904 until his death. He exhibited at the Salon only from 1881 to 1913, from which period date his important works, primarily busts and medallions. Aside from the busts of contemporaries, some of which were cast in bronze, Briden's works include Jeanne d'Arc devant ses juges (1885), *A la patrie* (1887), *Dernier Sommeil* (1889), and *L'Alarme* (1894), all in plaster, as well as a vase, also in plaster, decorated on the theme of wine (1903).

Briden also completed many commemorative monuments. From the monument dedicated to the children of Aube, two haut-reliefs still exist, including *La Charge de Reichshoffen* (1890).

MUSEUMS
Troyes

This museum owns a number of works by Briden, busts and sketches for the most part in plaster, as well as some bronzes:
Buste du docteur Raoul Hervey, 47 cm (Gruet, founder).
Buste de M. Jeaunet père, 60.5 cm.
Le Docteur Jules Hervey, medallion, 32 cm diam.
Monsieur Emile Vaudé, medallion, 31 cm diam.

BROU, FRÉDÉRIC

Ile Maurice, December 11, 1862
May 15, 1925

Born of French parents, Brou was the author of statues in plaster entitled *Eve, La Chrysalide* (Salon of 1897), and *Au bord d'une fontaine* (1905), a bust in bronze of Léon Bloy (1905), some statuettes in plaster entitled *Première Poupée* (1902) and *Thérèse* (1903), the bronze statuette *Enfant* (1904), and the bronze and ivory statuette *Petite Hollandaise* (1909; Goldscheider, founder). Brou is also responsible for two bas-reliefs in bronze, *Franklin à la cour de France* and *Franklin signant le traité de Paris* (1906), designed for the pedestal of J. J. Boyle's statue of Franklin in Paris's Trocadéro Plaza.

MUSEUMS
Cognac
Femme nue se coiffant, 28 cm.
Paris, Petit Palais
Portrait d'enfant, 90 cm (1903).

BRUCHON, ÉMILE

Born in Paris in the nineteenth century, this student of Mathurin Moreau sent a model of a tomb for the Père-Lachaise to the Salon in 1880. Nothing else is known about him, other than that there are some statuettes of children and young women cast in bronze or régule, entitled *Le Génie du progrès*, 80 cm, *Le Lâcher des pigeons*, 50 cm, and *Le Vainqueur* (holding a laurel crown and a pigeon), 53 cm. A statuette in régule, *Femme-fleur*, 33 cm, was sold at the Drouot Hotel on May 17, 1984, room 7.

BUGATTI, REMBRANDT

Milan, October 16, 1885
Paris, January 8, 1916

The Bugatti name is known throughout the world—primarily because Rembrandt's brother Ettore was the famous automobile maker. However, Rembrandt's genius as an animal sculptor places him among the great masters whose influence bridged the transition from the 19th to the 20th century. Today, his works, nearly all bronzes, achieve fetch high prices in public sales. The son of Carlo Bugatti (a painter and creator of very odd furniture which is eagerly sought today, among other things), Rembrandt came to Paris with his family at the age of seventeen. Drawn to sculpture while still very young, he received direction from Paul

Rembrandt Bugatti,
Madame Bugatti,
55 cm.

Troubetzkoy. He exhibited his first works—of animals of the creation—in Milan, Venice, Turin, and finally in Paris, at the Salon de la Société Nationale des Beaux-Arts of 1904. That same year, he met the founder Adrien Hébrard, a meeting which determined the future of his whole career. Hébrard, who also owned a gallery at 8 Rue Royale, contracted with Bugatti for the exclusive right to cast his sculptures. This contract, says Mary Harvey *(The Bronzes of Rembrandt Bugatti,* 1979) was signed by Carlo Bugatti, since Rembrandt was still a minor. Also in 1904, the Hébrard gallery organized the first exhibition of his works. The exhibition would be followed by many others, as well as a large posthumous retrospective in 1920. Moreover, he continued to exhibit regularly at the National of Fine Arts as well as at the Salon d'Automne.

Bugatti was passionate about sculpting the animals which he studied at the Jardin des Plantes. With the same intent, he went to Anvers in 1907 and worked diligently in the famous zoo of that Flemish metropolis. He was still there at the beginning of the war, and placed himself at the disposal of the Croix-Rouge (Belgian Red Cross), and then returned to Paris in 1914 to establish himself in Montparnasse. His work had become more refined, and was profoundly touched by the horrors of the war. His physical health and morale declined, and he committed suicide on the 8th of January, 1916. The sculptures of Bugatti reveal an exceptional temperament. He observed animals and their behavior in the manner of the impressionist painters, and made only a few human figures and portraits. He described animals without the least affectation, without transformation, just as he saw them in the zoos or elsewhere. Able to maintain the spontaneity of the sketches even in his most finished pieces, he portrayed the nervous, tense, sometimes tragic attitudes of big game, the tender gestures, the gentle timidity of a doe, the blind power of a water buffalo. His bronzes also benefited

*Rembrandt Bugatti,
Chien et chiots, 36 x 43 cm.*

from the remarkable casting quality and patinas peculiar to the Hébrard foundry, though for unknown reasons some rare works exist that carry the seal of the Valsuani foundry and the Palazzolo.)

A number of subjects were then cast in bronze, usually in a large sizes, sometimes with variations. A certain number of animals were extracted from groups of two or three in order to be cast separately. Although the archives of the Hébrard house are only partial, Jacques and Véronique des Cordes (in their work devoted to the sculptor) were able to draft an incom-

*Rembrandt Bugatti,
Bouledogue, 14 cm.*

*Rembrandt Bugatti,
Deux Loups d'Egypte, 23 x 35 cm.*

plete inventory of Bugatti's bronzes. This inventory specified the exact titles of the works (often approximations in the earlier works and the sales catalogs) as well as the numbers of the castings in bronze. The majority of them did not exceed a dozen models, and sometimes only five; several unique works are indexed. Only those few pieces in the greatest demand, such as *Bouledogue français* and the *Jaguar accroupi*, were cast in series of more than thirty works. Nearly all of the proofs were numbered.

The following list of Bugatti's bronzes, which is not exhaustive, was developed from various sources of information, especially from three of the most recent works published on the sculptor: *The Bronzes of Rembrandt Bugatti*, by Mary Harvey (1979), *Bugatti* by Philippe Dejean (1981), and, most recently, *Rembrandt Bugatti sculpteur, catalogue raisonné* by Jacques Chalom des Cordes and Véronique Fromanger des Cordes (1987). The dates noted are those of the casting or of the exhibition of the work at the Salon de la Société Nationale des Beaux-Arts (SNBA) or at the Salon d'Automne (SA).

*Rembrandt Bugatti,
Le Grand Fardier,
50 x 255 cm.*

143

Big Game
Deux Chacals (1905), 24 x 34 cm.
Jaguar accroupi (SA 1908), 10 x 20 cm.
Jaguar assis (SA 1908), 14 x 20 cm.
Jaguar courant, 15 x 38 and 22 x 52 cm.
Jaguar rampant, 14 x 26 cm.
Deux jaguars, 32 x 86 cm.
Léopard, 31 x 42 cm.
Léopard à l'arrêt, 32 x 67 cm.
Léopard assis (1912), 19 x 12 cm.
Léopard marchant, 21 x 51 cm.
Deux Léopards, le second queue baissée, 32 x 110 cm.
Deux Léopards, le second queue levée, 56 x 59 cm.
Deux Léopards marchant (1904), 25 x 103 cm.
Lion couché (1909), 17 x 31 cm.
Lion debout, tête dans sa crinière (1908), 30 x 54 cm.
Lion et lionne face à face, 22 x 104 cm.
Lion et lionne de Nubie (SA 1911), 44 x 115 cm.
Lion de Nubie (part of the preceding group), 44 x 71 cm.
Lionne de Nubie (part of the preceding group), 41 x 71
    cm.
Lionne à la boule (1903).
Lionceau et lévrier assis (1906), 30 x 33 cm.
Panthère dévorant (SNBA 1906), 22 x 71 cm.
Panthère étendue, 31 x 68 cm.
Panthère marchant, 19 x 49 and 22 x 52 cm.
Panthère moustachue grognant (1907), 33 x 64 cm.
Petite Panthère (1911).
Petite Panthère assise (1907).
Petite Panthère se léchant la patte, 15 x 37 cm.
Deux Panthères, la première, patte levée, 26 cm.
Deux Panthères marchant, 23 x 93 cm.
Trois Panthères marchant.
Puma marchant (1908), 28 x 60 cm.
Tigre baillant, 28 x 54 cm.
Grand Tigre stylisé, 42 x 73 cm.
Tigresse et serpent, 50 x 41 cm (inscription: "Last work
    by my brother, Paris, January 8, 1916, Ettore
    Bugatti").

Rembrandt Bugatti,
Singe cynocéphale or Babouin sacré, 43 x 45 cm.

Rembrandt Bugatti,
Léopard,
32 x 41 cm
(Hébrard No 3).

Large animals
Bison d'Amérique (1910), 41 x 74 cm.
Bison européen (SNBA 1908), 35 x 50 cm.
Deux Bisons (1907), 32 x 89 cm.
Boeuf, 38 x 48 cm (Palazzolo, founder).
Buffle Gayal (1911), 39 x 56 cm.
Cheval sauvage (1907), 34 x 44 cm.
Dromadaire buvant.
Deux Dromadaires, côte à côte, 35 x 45 cm.
Couple de dromadaires et leur petit tétant, 36 x 86 cm.
Eléphant, 29 x 38 cm.
Eléphant, 45 x 49 cm.
Eléphant blanc trompe allongée, 42 cm.
Eléphant blanc trompe baissée, 42 cm.
Eléphant dressé (1904), 19 cm, model utilized for the
    radiator plug of the royal Bugatti.
Eléphant avec feuillage, 52 x 61 cm.
Eléphant marchant, 15 x 22 and 21 x 26 cm.
Eléphant trompe allongée (1907), 20 x 10 cm.
Eléphant trompe levée, les pattes avant sur un rocher, 60
    cm.

Rembrandt Bugatti,
Deux Jaguars,
32 x 86 cm.

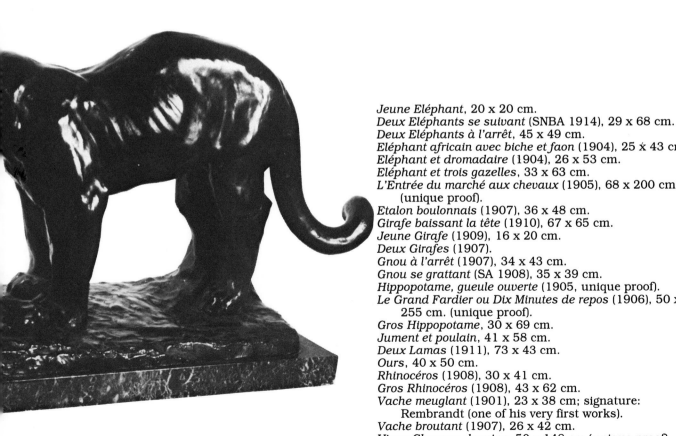

Jeune Eléphant, 20 x 20 cm.
Deux Eléphants se suivant (SNBA 1914), 29 x 68 cm.
Deux Eléphants à l'arrêt, 45 x 49 cm.
Eléphant africain avec biche et faon (1904), 25 x 43 cm.
Eléphant et dromadaire (1904), 26 x 53 cm.
Eléphant et trois gazelles, 33 x 63 cm.
L'Entrée du marché aux chevaux (1905), 68 x 200 cm.
    (unique proof).
Etalon boulonnais (1907), 36 x 48 cm.
Girafe baissant la tête (1910), 67 x 65 cm.
Jeune Girafe (1909), 16 x 20 cm.
Deux Girafes (1907).
Gnou à l'arrêt (1907), 34 x 43 cm.
Gnou se grattant (SA 1908), 35 x 39 cm.
Hippopotame, gueule ouverte (1905, unique proof).
Le Grand Fardier ou Dix Minutes de repos (1906), 50 x
    255 cm. (unique proof).
Gros Hippopotame, 30 x 69 cm.
Jument et poulain, 41 x 58 cm.
Deux Lamas (1911), 73 x 43 cm.
Ours, 40 x 50 cm.
Rhinocéros (1908), 30 x 41 cm.
Gros Rhinocéros (1908), 43 x 62 cm.
Vache meuglant (1901), 23 x 38 cm; signature:
    Rembrandt (one of his very first works).
Vache broutant (1907), 26 x 42 cm.
Vieux Chevaux de mine, 50 x 148 cm (unique proof)
Yack sans cornes, 37 x 48 cm.

Rembrandt Bugatti,
Deux Léopards marchant,
25 x 103 cm.

Rembrandt Bugatti,
Lion de Nubie,
46 x 64 cm
(Valsuani).

Rembrandt Buga
Lion et lion
de Nub
46 x 116 c

146

*Rembrandt Bugatti,
Panthère marchant,
19.5 x 47 cm.*

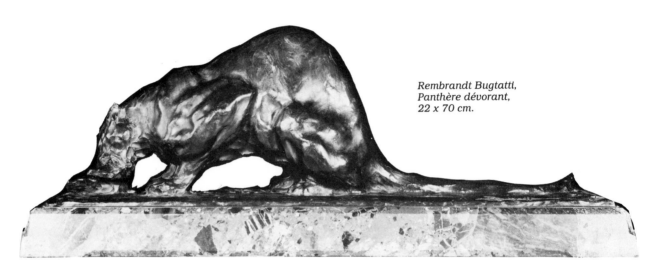

*Rembrandt Bugtatti,
Panthère dévorant,
22 x 70 cm.*

Deux Yacks, dont un couché (1908), 28 x 76 cm.
Trois Yacks (1910), 47 x 93 cm (unique piece).
Zèbre ou Hémione, 22 x 34 cm.
Zèbre et antilope, 38 x 62 cm.
Zèbre et autruche or *Hémione et émeu* (also cast sepa-
  rately).
Zébu, 32 x 50 cm.
Zébu femelle et son petit, 27 x 61 cm.
Zébu nain, 30 cm.
Zébu et oies, 33 x 58 cm.

Horned Animals

Antilope Canna (SA 1911), 50 x 52 cm.
Deux Antilopes Goudou ou La Caresse (1905), 22 x 45
  cm.
Deux Antilopes se caressant (1908).
Trois Antilopes ou Mère malade (1912), 60 x 137 cm.
  (unique piece on a wood pedestal).
Biche allaitant ses faons (SA 1905), 34 x 51 cm.
Deux Biches (base of irregular form), 20 x 43 cm.
Deux Biches se caressant, 22.5 x 33 cm.
Deux Biches et un faon (1905), 22 x 49 cm (Palazzolo,
  founder).
Trois Biches (1906), 25 x 81 cm.

Rembrandt Bugatti,
Petite Panthère assise, 19 cm.

148

Petit Buffle Anoa (1911), 38 cm.
Cerf, 44 x 37 cm.
Grand Cerf bramant, 45 x 51 cm.
Jeune Cerf, 33 x 28 cm.
Cerf se grattant (1906), 25 cm.
Cerf et biche chinois, cinq animaux (1907), 42 x 130 cm
    (unique piece).
Cerf, deux biches et un faon.
Deux Cerfs, 46 x 46 cm.
Deux Cerfs, 28 x 48 cm.
Grand Elan, 77 x 75 cm (unique proof).
Faon, 31.5 x 28 cm.
Faon, 34 x 38 cm.
Faon marchant, 49 x 58.5 cm.
Gazelle à l'arrêt (1906), 38 x 38 cm.
Renne allaitant, 32 x 58 cm.

Assorted animals
Les Deux Anes (1909), 51 x 44 cm.
Basset (1906), 25 x 53 cm.
Bélier marchant (1909), 23 x 32 cm (Valsuani).

Rembrandt Bugatti,
Puma marchant,
28 x 60 cm.

Rembrandt Bugatti,
Deux Panthères marchant,
23 x 93 cm.

*Rembrandt Bugatti,
Eléphant et gazelles,
133 x 63 cm.*

*Rembrandt Bugatti,
Eléphant, 46 x 37 cm.*

*Rembrandt Bugatti,
Eléphant blanc
trompe allongée,
43 cm
(Anvers 1908;
Hébrard).*

*Rembrandt Bugatti,
Eléphant blanc
trompe baissée,
42 cm (Anvers 1907;
Hébrard).*

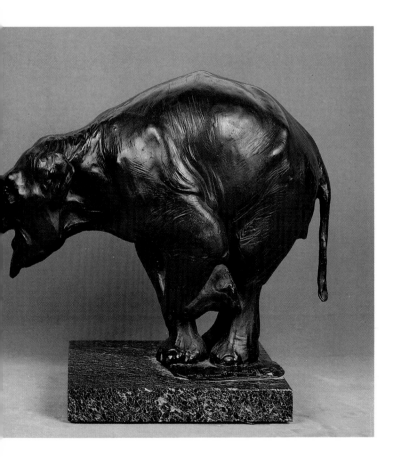

*Rembrandt Bugatti,
Eléphant dressé,
19 cm.*

Rembrandt Bugatti,
Eléphant,
biche et faon,
40 x 75 cm.

Rembrandt Bugatti,
Trois Yacks,
47 x 93 cm.

Rembrandt Bugatti,
Deux Bisons, 32 x 89 cm.
(Hébrard 1922)

Rembrandt Bugatti,
Gnou se grattant,
35 x 39 cm (No 3).

Bouledogue (1906), 14 x 14 cm.
Bouledogue (1905), 35 x 35 cm.
Braque couché (1904), 16 cm.
Chat assis, 24 x 15 cm.
Petit Chat à l'écuelle, 20 x 36 cm.
Chèvre contre un tronc d'arbre, 30 x 23 cm.
Chèvre, bouc et bouquetin (1904).
Chien annamite (1905), 24.5 x 22 cm.
Chien pointer (1905), 31 x 34 cm.
Chien lévrier debout (1907), 28 x 29 cm.
Chien et chiots (1908), 36 x 43 cm.
Chienne et ses petits (1905), 40 x 32 cm.
Fourmilier, 38 x 48 cm.
Deux Kangourous (1906), 35 x 80 cm.
Deux Loups d'Egypte (1906), 23 x 35 cm.
Mouton, 20 x 43 cm.
Deux Sangliers (1905), 16 x 22 cm.
Serpent python (1910), 20 x 53 cm.
Singe à la boule, 28 x 25 cm.
Singe à la carotte, 19 x 33 cm.
Singe cynocéphale ou Babouin sacré, 43 x 45 cm.
Deux Tapirs, 29 x 71 cm.

Birds
Autruche tête baissée (SA 1908), 40 x 45 cm.
Autruche tête droite, 26 cm.
Petite Autruche, 10 x 12 and 13 x 14 cm.
Trois Casoars, 43 x 87 cm.
Deux Casoars (part of the preceding group), 43 x 60 cm.
Casoar (part of the preceding group), 40 x 27 cm.
Combat de coqs (1905).
Coq et grenouille (1913), 25 x 34 cm.
Echassier, 46 x 35 cm.
Echassier cigogne (SA 1912), 46 x 23 cm.
Echassier cigogne (1909), 43 cm.
Echassier Jabiru, 33 x 27 cm.
Echassier Jabiru, 26 x 18 cm.
Flamant, cou replié (1907), 35 x 21 cm.
Deux Flamants (1905), 28 x 29 cm (unique piece).
Marabout (1913).
Deux Marabouts (1907, unique proof).
Oie (1912), 14 x 14 cm.
Pélican, 26 x 18 cm.
Pélican se grattant (1904), 22 x 21 cm.
Pélican au repos (1904), 15 cm.

Deux Pélicans dont un aux ailes déployées, 25 x 50 cm.
Deux Pélicans se disputant (1906), 29 x 59 cm.
Deux Grands Pélicans, 56 x 37 cm.
Trois Pélicans, 25 x 35 cm.
Deux Pélicans (same group without the central pelican).
Secrétaire mâle (1911), 33 x 35 cm.
Secrétaire femelle (SA 1912), 33 x 28 cm.
Vautour (1907), 45 x 25 cm.
Deux Vautours, 33 x 36 cm.

Personages
Athlète allongé (1907), 42 x 75 cm.
Athlète debout (1906), 62 cm.
Atlas portant le monde.
Christ en croix, 79 x 60 cm; one of his last works
    (Valsuani).
Femme assise, bras croisés (1907).
Femme au chat (1906).
Femme au chien ou Diane (unique piece).
Femme drapée en robe longue (1907), 59 cm.
Femme à genoux, bras dernière la tête, 35 cm.
Femme debout, une main sur la hanche (1912), 69 cm.
Jeune Fille assise (1907), 55 cm.
Jeune Fille nue (1906), 62.5 cm.
Jeune Fille à genoux se coiffant (1906).
Jeune Garçon nu (1906), 13 cm.
Jeunesse, jeune fille assise, bras sur la tête (1907).
La Marchande de pommes (SNBA 1913), 66 x 36 cm.
Montreur d'ours (SNBA 1906), 52 cm.
Sam White, portrait à mi-corps, 32 cm.

MUSEUMS
Paris, Decorative Arts
Madame François Crozier, avec chapeau, called *La
    Parisienne*, 70 cm.
Madame François Crozier, nue tête, 65.5 cm.
*Monsieur François Crozier, ministre plénipotentiaire à
    Anvers.*
Paris, Orsay
Biche, allaitant ses deux faons, 35.5 cm.
Christ en croix, 58.5 cm.
Deux Lamas (Hébrard No. 1), 35 cm.
    The museum also owns a number of plasters, some of
which were given to the Louvre in 1981 by Mr. Desbordes,
heir of Mlle L'Ebé Bugatti, daughter of the automobile
maker and niece of Rembrandt.
Paris, Petit Palais
Les Pélicans, 30 x 25 cm.
Reims
Chienne et ses petits, 36.5 cm.
    A certain number of Rembrandt Bugatti's works belong
to some foreign museums, especially those in Anvers,
Brussels, Rome, Cleveland, Los Angeles, San Francisco,
etc.

SALES
Big Game
Jaguar accroupi, 29 cm, Christie's New York, March 31,
    1984.
Léopard, 32 cm, Rambouillet, October 20, 1985.
Léopard et lionne, 35 x 115 cm, Sotheby London, Decem-
    ber 3, 1986.
Le Lion, 47 x 64 cm, Drouot Hotel, March 18, 1986,
    rooms 1 and 7.
Lion assis, Sotheby Monaco, October 9, 1983.
Lion et lionne de Nuble, 46 cm, Enghien, March 24,
    1984.
Lionne couchée, 19 cm L., Drouot Hotel, May 21, 1984.
Panthère marchant, 19 x 49 cm, Drouot Hotel, December
    10, 1984, room 7.
Panthère marchant, 22 x 52 cm, Drouot Hotel, June 12,
    1985, rooms 5 and 6.
Deux Panthères marchant, 23 x 93 cm, Enghien, October
    23, 1983; Drouot Hotel, May 22, 1985, room 1.
Puma dévorant, 23 x 68 cm, Espace Cardin, November
    26, 1984.

*Rembrandt Bugatti,
Vache broutant,
36 cm (No 3).*

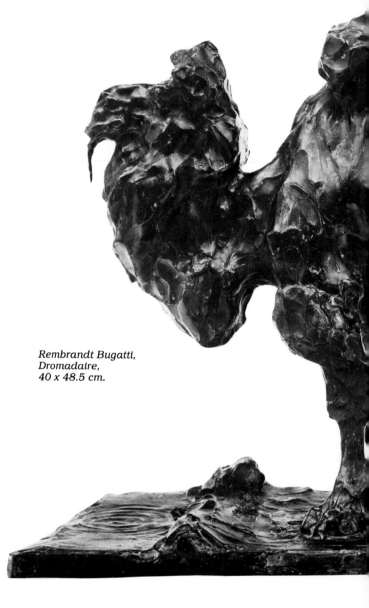

*Rembrandt Bugatti,
Dromadaire,
40 x 48.5 cm.*

154

Rembrandt Bugatti,
Gros Rhinocéros,
43 cm.

Rembrandt Bugatti,
Le Grand Fourmillier, 38 x 48 cm.

*Rembrandt Bugatti,
Grand Ours
marchant,
38 x 57 cm.*

*Rembrandt Bugatti,
Grand Cerf bramant,
45 cm.*

*Rembrandt Bugatti,
Grand Elan, 77 cm.*

Rembrandt Bugatti,
Cerf et biches chinois,
42 x 130 cm
(unique piece).

Rembrandt Bugatti,
Le Faon,
33 x 39 cm.

Rembrandt Bugatti,
Les Deux Biches,
21 x 34 cm.

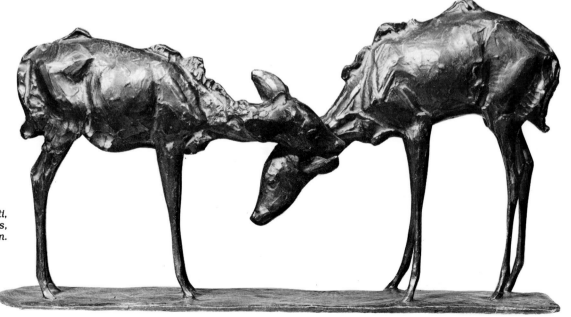

Rembrandt Bugatti,
Deux Biches,
22.5 x 33 cm.

157

Rembrandt Bugatti,
Biche allaitant ses faons,
34 x 51 cm.

Rembrandt Bugatti,
Grand cerf et biche,
44 x 56 cm (No 3).

Puma marchant, 28 x 60 cm, Enghien, November 24, 1985.

Le Repas des fauves, 35 x 84.5 cm, Enghien, December 18, 1983.

Large animals

Cheval, 36.5 cm (Palazzolo, founder), Dijon, April 27, 1986.

Dromadaire, 40 cm, Saumur, June 8, 1985.

Eléphant, 45 x 49 cm, Drouot Hotel, April 7, 1986, rooms 5 and 6.

Eléphant à l'arrêt, 43 x 46 cm, Drouot Hotel, April 7, 1986, rooms 5 and 6.

Eléphant à l'arrêt, 46 x 57 cm, Enghien, December 18, 1983.

Eléphant d'Asie, 20 cm, Enghien, March 24, 1984.

Eléphant blanc trompe allongée, 42 cm, Drouot Hotel, May 7, 1986, room 4.

Eléphant blanc trompe baissée, 42 cm, Drouot Hotel, May 7, 1986, room 4. (sold with the preceding statue for 2, 261,000 F).

Eléphant dressé, 19 cm, Enghien, June 19, 1986.

Eléphant marchant, 15 x 22 cm, Drouot Hotel, November 27, 1986, rooms 1 and 7.

Jeune Eléphant, 14 cm, Drouot Hotel, December 5, 1986, room 1.

Deux Eléphants indiens, 30 x 65.5 cm, Sotheby London, December 3, 1986.

Eléphant et trois gazelles, 30 x 56 cm, Enghien, November 25, 1984.

Eléphant avec biche et faon, 40 x 75 cm, Enghien, June 19, 1986 (taking 720,000 F).

Gnou se grattant, 36 cm, Brussels, October 15, 1984; Rambouillet, November 30, 1986 (price awarded: 450,000 F).

Le Gros Hippopotame, 21.5 x 57 cm, Christie's Geneva, November 9, 1986.

Les Deux Hémiones, 48 x 44 cm, Drouot Hotel, December 5, 1986, rooms 5 and 6 (sold 428,000 F).

Ours, 20.5 x 35 cm, Drouot Hotel, March 19, 1985, room 1.

Grand Ours marchant, 38 cm, Enghien, April 13, 1986.

Rhinocéros, 41 cm, Enghien, June 19, 1986 (bringing 850,000 F).

*Rembrandt Bugatti,
Renne allaitant,
32 x 58 cm.*

*Rembrandt Bugatti,
L'Echassier cigogne,
45 cm.*

*Rembrandt Bugatti,
Trois Antilopes Goudou
or Mère malade,
60 x 137 cm.*

Rembrandt Bugatti,
Autruche tête baissée, 40 cm
(Hébrard No 6).

Rembrandt Bugatti,
Marabout, 22.5 x 29 cm
(Hébard No 5, casting 1925).

Rembrandt Bugatti,
Les Casoars,
43 x 87 cm.

*Rembrandt Bugatti,
Secrétaire mâle,
Secrétaire femelle,
33 cm.*

Horned Animals

Antilopes Goudou or La Caresse, 24 cm, Enghien,
November 24, 1985; Dijon, November 9, 1986;
Drouot Hotel, November 13 1986.
Antilopes Goudou ou La Caresse, 90 cm (unique piece),
Enghien, March 24, 1984 (prize: 1, 680,000 F).
Deux Biches, 20 x 43 cm, Drouot Hotel, November 13,
1986.
Deux Biches se caressant, 22.5 x 33 cm, Drouot Hotel,
March 14, 1985, room 1; Enghien, November 24,
1985.
Biche et deux faons, 34 x 51 cm, Drouot Hotel, November
18, 1985, room 6.
Deux Biches et faon, 22 x 49 cm (Palazzolo, founder),

Enghien, November 25, 1984.
Grand cerf bramant, 45 x 51 cm, Enghien, November 25,
1984; Sotheby London, December 3, 1986.
Cerf et biche, 23.5 cm, Enghien, November 25, 1984.
Cerf et biche chinois, 42 x 130 cm (Hébrard, unique
piece), Enghien, June 23, 1985 (awarded 1,135,000
F).

*Rembrandt Bugatti,
Serpent python,
20 x 53 cm.*

Cerf et faon, 23 x 48.5 cm, Sotheby London, December
3, 1986.
Daim têtant sa mère, 32 x 56.5 cm, Lyon, October 19,
1986.
Faon, 33 cm, Drouot Hotel, February 6, 1984, room 7;
Sotheby London, December 3, 1986.

Assorted Animals

Anesse et ânon, 38 cm, Enghien, November 24, 1985
(500,000 F).
Bouledogue, 14 x 14 cm, Drouot Hotel, March 16, 1983,
room 9.
Bouledogue, 35 x 35 cm, Christie's New York, March 30,
1985.
La Brebis pleine, 19.5 cm, Enghien, November 24, 1985.
Chat lapant son écuelle, 14.3 x 16 cm, Christie's, Sep-
tember 28, 1985.
Chien annamite, 25 cm, Enghien, March 24, 1984.
Chien couché, 50 cm L. long, Sotheby London, June 26,
1985.
Le Grand Fourmilier, 38 x 48 cm, Enghien, November 24,
1985, (1,855,000 F).
Deux Kangourous, 35 x 80 cm, Sotheby New York, May
21, 1984.
Poney, 21 cm, Rambouillet, June 8, 1986.

Birds

Autruche tête baissée, 40 cm, Rambouillet, November 30,
1986 (taken for 430,000 F).
Casoar, 40 cm, Drouot Hotel, December 10, 1985, rooms
5 and 6.
Trois Casoars, 43 x 87 cm, Sotheby London, March 27,
1985.
Cigogne, 35.5 cm, Drouot Hotel, March 7, 1985.
Cigogne, 45 cm, Versailles, November 18, 1984; New
York, June 12, 1985.
Coq et grenouille, 25 cm, Sotheby London, December 7,
1983.
Echassier Jabiru, 33 x 27 cm, Les Andelys, April 13,
1986.
Héron marchant, 35.5 cm, Drouot Hotel, March 7, 1986,
room 10.
Deux Vautours, 33 cm, Enghien, November 24, 1985.

Personages

Madame Bugatti, 55 cm, Drouot Hotel, March 18, 1986,
rooms 5 and 6 (550,000 F).

161

BUHOT, LOUIS CHARLES HIPPOLYTE

Paris, September 8, 1815
Paris, October 20, 1865

Buhot, a student of David d'Angers, participated at the Salon between 1837 and 1865, and is known for a number of medallions, busts, statues, and groups. A few of the bronzes among his submissions were part of a group entitled *La Vendange*, exhibited in 1853, and another group, *Jupiter et Hébé*, 60 cm, cast from a plaster exhibited in 1865. One statue in plaster entitled *Sarah la baigneuse* (1850) was cast in bronze (a proof, 156 cm high, appeared at a 1979 exhibition in London). This artist also sculpted some decorative vases. A small bust of *Napoléon III*, in régule, 14 cm, was sold in 1978 at the Drouot Hotel.

BUREAU, LÉON

Limoges, September 17, 1866
Limoges, May 26, 1906

BUREAU

A specialist in exotic animals, Bureau apprenticed with Falguière and appeared at the Salon for the first time in 1884. There he exhibited the following plasters, some of which were cast in bronze: *Caille aux écoutes* (1885), *Ménélas et Grondeur*, Saint-Hubert dogs (1886), *Les Amoureux transis* (lion and lionnesse, 1890), *Tigre royal du Cambodge* (1891) *Combat de tigre et de sepents* (1894), *Enfant au crabe* (1896), and *Jaguar dévorant un aigle* (1899).

Léon Bureau,
Deux Chiens de chasse,
28 cm.

Some works in bronze have appeared on the market. In addition to the recent models that have been sold are *Cheval et son jockey*, 68 cm, *Chien d'arrêt*, 27 x 34 cm, *Faison royal*, 28.5 cm, *Lion et lionne*, 75 cm, *Lionne rampant*, 7 x 25 cm, *Ménélas et Grondeur*, two dogs, 28 x 37.5 cm, and *Panthère et oiseau mort*.

SALES
Cheval à l'arrêt, Tours, March 24, 1986.
Chien de chasse, 28 cm, Sotheby London, June 7, 1984.
Deux Chiens, 28 cm, Epinal, December 14, 1986.
Faisan, Limoges, October 20, 1985.
Jeune Femme à la branche fleurie, 71 cm, Sotheby London, March 8, 1984.

Léon Bureau,
Lion et lionne,
75 cm.

BUZONNIÈRES, LOUIS MICHEL GASTON

Born in Orléans

This animal artist worked principally in his hometown, and is especially known for his portrayals of birds. At the Salon, where he exhibited between 1866 and 1889, the following bronzes appeared: *Héron pris au piège* (1867), *Oiseau avec sa proie* and *Vache* (1868), *Echassier d'Amérique* and *Aigle pygargue de Sologne* (1870), *Busard et sa proie* (1873), *Flore, chienne d'arrêt, race française* (1883), and *Héron cendré* (1889).

CABET, JEAN-BAPTISTE

Nuits-Saint-Georges, February 1, 1815

Cabet entered the Beaux-Arts in 1835 after having attended the school of drawing in Dijon. He perfected his style as a student in Rude's studio, where he became his teacher's favorite collaborator. After Rude's death, Cabet completed some of the sculptor's marbles. In 1846, his hostility toward the regime of Louis-Philippe forced him to seek exile in Russia, where he travelled to Saint Petersburg and Odessa. In Odessa, he sculpted a monumental fountain. Upon returning to Paris in 1852, he married Rude's niece, and established himself on Denfert Street in Rude's old house. He worked for the Louvre, the Opera, the Tribunal de Commerce, and the church of the Sorbonne (a statue entitled *Théologie*), among others. He made the bronze bust of Rude, 72 cm, for the sculptor's tomb at Père-Lachaise, and sent it to the Salon of 1857. (It is said that Rude might have collaborated on this work before his death.) In 1880 he sent another significant work to the Salon—a monumental statue in marble entitled *La Résistance*, 250 cm, a reproduction of a stone statue erected in Dijon in 1875 to commemorate the defense of the city in 1870. This work was destroyed a short time after by the government, which thought it contained hidden allusions to the Commune.

MUSEUMS
Dijon
La Résistance, 116 cm (according to the model of the statue commissioned by the city).
Paris, Carnavalet
Buste de François Rude, 27 cm (1856, Eck and Durand, founders).

SALES
La Résistance, 116 cm, Christie's Oklahoma (USA), September 24, 1981.

CACHEUX, LOUIS ÉMILE

Paris, January 26, 1874-?

The works of this artist are few and seem to have been rarely made into editions. We know only of some very rare bronzes by him, but they show substantial talent and great skill in molding.

Louis Emile Cacheux,
La Nuit, 12 x 24 cm
(Godard Sr., founder),
J. Ginepro Collection, Monaco.

CADE, NICOLAS CONSTANT

Corcieux (Vosges), April 19, 1846
Besançon, February 25, 1887

After studying in Paris, Nicolas Cade established himself in Besançon to teach at the school of fine arts. He exhibited some busts and statuettes in marble, plaster and bronze at the Salon between 1868 and 1880. They included *Le Poète Gilbert*, a statuette in bronze, *Saint Jérôme*, a statuette in plaster, and *Le Gladiateur mourant*, another statuette in plaster (46 x 60 cm). This last work is preserved at the museum of Besançon. The museum of Epinal owns a proof in bronze of *Poète Gilbert*, 30 cm, cast by Barbedienne. A version of *Buste d'homme de lettres*, 23 cm (E. Gruet, founder), was sold at the Drouot Hotel on March 13, 1981.

CAHIEUX, HENRY (OR CAILLEUX)

Paris ?
1854

This little-known artist exhibited at the Salon only in 1850 and 1853. The Barbedienne house cast his works entitled *L'Automne*, *L'Emir*, *Jardinier*, *Jeune Femme romaine*, and *Le Printemps*.

CAILLÉ, JOSEPH MICHEL

Nantes, March 27, 1836
Nantes, August 18, 1881

Joseph Caillé studied first in Nantes, and then in Paris with Duret and Guillaume. He debuted at the Salon in 1863, and exhibited there until his death. His work includes busts and statues, and some bas-reliefs, including the plaster bas-relief *La Fondation de Marseille* (1865), the marble statue *Aristée pleurant ses abeilles* (1866), the plaster group *Bacchante jouant avec une panthère* (exhibited in marble at the Salon of 1870, in bronze at the Salon of 1875; some versions are owned by the museum of Nantes), and the stone group entitled *Cain* (Salon of 1876), sculpted for the gardens of Ranelagh in Paris. The bronze group *Bacchante jouant avec une panthère*, 180 cm (H. Molz, founder), was sold at the Drouot Hotel on March 27, 1985 for 160,000 F.

CAIN, AUGUSTE

Paris, November 10, 1821
Paris, August 6, 1894

A. CAIN

An obituary of sculptor Pierre Jules Mène, published in 1879, made mention of his son-in-law August Cain, "the sculptor of the lions and tigers..."—suggesting that Cain focused upon big game. By examining his work, however, it becomes clear

Nos		Prix bronze
1	GRAND COMBAT DE COQS, Nº 1	1000 fr.
	hauteur 61 c., longueur 65 c., profondeur 43 c.	
2	GRAND COMBAT DE COQS, Nº 2	500 »
	h. 53 c., l. 40 c., p. 25 c.	
3	LION ET LIONNE SE DISPUTANT UN SANGLIER	800 »
	h. 39 c., l. 63 c., p. 31 c. Argenté	1400 »
4	TIGRESSE RAPPORTANT UN PAON A SES PETITS, Nº 1	600 »
	h. 43 c., l. 63 c., p. 20 c.	
5	TIGRESSE RAPPORTANT UN PAON A SES PETITS, Nº 2	350 »
	h. 52 c., l. 47 c., p. 16 c.	
6	PANNEAU, FAISANS	1400 »
	h. 78 c., l. 128 c.	
7	PANNEAU, RENARD SAISISSANT UN CANARD	1400 »
	h. 78 c., l. 128 c.	
8	PANNEAU, AIGLE SAISISSANT UNE PERDRIX	1400 »
	h. 78 c., l. 128 c.	
9	PANNEAU, FAUCON CHASSANT LE LAPIN	1400 »
	h. 78 c., l. 128 c.	
	Ces panneaux avec cadre bois . . . en plus.	125 »
	— — bronze . —	400 »
10	NID DE FAISANS	1000 »
	h. 66 c., l. 62 c., p. 38 c.	
11	GRAND FAISAN SEUL	500 »
	h. 57 c., l. 46 c., p. 28 c.	
12	GROUPE DE FAISANS	80 »
	h. 20 c., l. 33 c.	
13	GROUPE FAISANS	45 »
14	COQ FAISAN	25 »

Catalog of bronzes by Auguste Cain cast by Susse frères (Susse brothers) end of the 19th century.

— 13 —

Nos		Prix bronze
15	PETIT FAISAN	20 fr.
16	RELAIS DE CHIENS DE MEUTE (race de la Saintonge)	900 »
	h. 62 c., l. 51 c., p. 40 c.	
17	GROUPE CHIENS DE MEUTE (race Anglaise)	400 »
	h. 33 c., l. 42 c., p. 26 c.	
18	GROUPE CHIENS DE MEUTE (race Saint-Hubert)	400 »
	h. 33 c., l. 42., p. 26 c.	
19	CHIEN DE MEUTE (Caron)	350 »
	h. 40 c., l. 45 c., p. 20 c.	
20	FAISANE ET SES PETITS	350 »
	A la base h. 28 c., l. 40c., p. 20 c.	
21	BŒUF DU TROCADÉRO . Nº 1	900 »
	h. 68 c., l. 68 c., p. 31 c.	
22	COQ FRANÇAIS CHANTANT Nº 1	1200 »
	h. 92 c., l. 65 c., diam. 40 c.	
23	COQ FRANÇAIS CHANTANT Nº 2	360 »
	h. 47 c., l. 32 c., diam 23 c.	
24	COQ FRANÇAIS CHANTANT Nº 3	180 »
	h. 30 l.	
25	VAUTOUR SUR UNE TÊTE DE SPHINX	250 »
	h. 49 c., l. 24 c., p. 20 c.	
26	FAMILLE DE PERDRIX	200 »
	h. 24 c., l. 43 c., p. 24 c.	
27	PERDRIX	15 »
28	IBIS A LA CHASSE AUX GRENOUILLES	120 »
	h. 45 c., l. 39 c. Argenté	160 »

No		Prix bronze
29	BASSE-COUR COQ ET POULE.	80 »
	h. 18 c., l. 25 c.	
30	GROUPE COQ ET POULES DU MANS	70 »
	h. 16 c., l. 19 c. Argenté	90 »
31	PETIT COQ ET POULE	30 »
32	COQ COCHINCHINOIS, N° 1.	80 »
33	COQ COCHINCHINOIS, N° 2.	25 »
34	BÉCASSE MORTE	75 »
	h. 10 c., l. 30 c.	
35	PLAQUE PERDREAUX MORTS (avec cadre) . . .	60 »
	argenté. . . .	80 »
36	PLAQUE CANARD MORT (avec cadre)	60 »
	argenté. . . .	80 »

Bœuf du Kroudero n° 2 haut 56 %m
« « « n° 3 haut 35 %m

(handwritten in right margin: Et le Coq Faisan Chantant n° 4)

— 14 —

Nos		Prix bronze
37	PIERROT PRIS AU PIÈGE	50 fr.
	argenté. . . .	70 »
38	ANE D'AFRIQUE AVEC PANIERS	55 »
39	ANE D'AFRIQUE	50 »
40	CIGOGNE SUR TORTUE.	50 »
41	GROUPE DE CANARDS	40 »
42	FAMILLE DE LAPINS	25 »
43	LAPIN SURPRIS, Porte-Allumettes.	30 »
44	LAPIN A LA CAROTTE.	15 »
45	LAPIN SUR TERRIER	15 »
46	GRENOUILLE MUSICIENNE.	25 »
47	POULE FAISANE.	25 »
48	PETITE POULE ET POUSSINS.	20 »
49	POULE COCHINCHINOISE DROITE	15 »
50	POULE COCHINCHINOISE ALLONGÉE.	15 »
51	POULE HUPPÉE.	15 »
52	POULE ORDINAIRE	15 »
53	COQ SUR PANIER, Porte-Allumettes.	35 »
	h. 18 c. Argenté. . . .	50 »
54	STAPULE.	20 »
55	GRAND ENCRIER OISEAUX MÉSANGES	150 »
	Argenté. . . .	220 »
56	PETIT ENCRIER OISEAUX	75 »
57	PAON, Porte-Allumettes	60 »
	h. 23 c.	
58	RUINE COLONNE, Porte-Allumettes	45 »
59	CENDRIER GRENOUILLE.	25 »
	Argenté . . .	35 »
60	CENDRIER RAT	20 »
	Argenté. . . .	25 »
61	CENDRIER LAPIN.	20 »
	Argenté. . . .	40 »
62	CACHET HERCULE ET ANTÉE avec Marbre . .	50 »
	Argenté. . . .	90 »
63	BOUGEOIR AU POISSON	25 »

— 15 —

Nos		Prix bronze
64	BOUGEOIR, Pied antique.	15 fr.
	Argenté. . . .	30 »
65	NID D'OISEAUX, Porte-Cigares	90 »
66	OURS CHIFFONNIER, Porte-Cigares.	75 »
67	VASE RUINE ANTIQUE, Porte-Cigares	65 »
68	FEUILLE OISEAUX COMBATTANT.	65 »
69	FEUILLE AU HÉRON PHILOSOPHE.	60 »
70	FEUILLE AU COQ SUR PANIER	60 »
	Argenté. . . .	80 »

71	FEUILLE AU HÉRON	50 »
72	COFFRET GENRE SAXE.	250 »
	h. 19 c., l. 31 c. Argenté. . . .	309 »
73	COFFRET AUX MURONS.	190 »
	h. 20 c., l. 26 c. Argenté . . .	250 »
74	PAIRE CANDÉLABRES, Gibier, 6 lumières. . . .	340 »
	h. 80 c. Argentés . . .	650 »
75	— CANDÉLABRES Grecs, 6 lumières.	270 »
	h. 82 c.	
76	— CANDÉLABRES Œillets, 5 lumières.	250 »
77	— CANDÉLABRES Cor de chasse 3 lumières. .	275 »
	h. 45 c. Argentés . . .	400 »
78	— CANDÉLABRES Nids de Fauvette 3 lumières	240 »
	h. 50 c. Argentés . . .	350 »
79	— BOUTS DE TABLE Ours, 3 lumières. . . .	180 »
	l. 31 c. Argentés . . .	290 »
80	— BOUTS DE TABLE HÉRONS 2 lumières. .	130 »
81	— BRAS GRECS 3 lumières	210 »
82	— BRAS ŒILLETS 4 lumières	230 »
83	— FLAMBEAUX COLONNE	80 »
84	— FLAMBEAUX HÉRONS.	80 »
85	— FLAMBEAUX CANARDS.	80 »
86	— FLAMBEAUX GRECS.	75 »
87	— FLAMBEAUX MÉDAILLES.	75 »
88	— FLAMBEAUX GRENOUILLES	60 »
89	— Petits FLAMBEAUX GRECS	55 »
90	— VASES RENARD ET LES RAISINS	400 »

— 16 —

Nos		Prix bronze
91	PAIRE VASES GRECS.	170 fr.
92	— VASES AUX MURONS	170 »
93	— VASES INDIENS.	170 »
94	— VASES-BUIRES, Renaissance	130 »
	Argentés . .	200 »
95	— VASES LIERRES.	120 »
96	— VASES GRECS, Petit Modèle.	120 »
97	— VASES LÉZARDS.	120 »
98	— VASES AUX FRAISES	70 »
99	GRAND PLATEAU FAISANS.	125 »
	Diamètre 35 c. Argenté. . . .	180 »
100	GRAND PLATEAU LAPINS.	125 »
	Diamètre 35 c. Argenté. . . .	180 »
101	PAIRE COUPES ŒILLETS.	250 »
102	— COUPES FAUCONS, Grands Plateaux . . .	220 »
103	— COUPES FAUCONS, Petits Plateaux	180 »
104	— COUPES CHASSE, Milieux unis.	150 »
105	— COUPES CHASSE, BASSES, N° 2	90 »
106	— COUPES AU HÉRON	160 »
107	— COUPES GRECQUES.	80 »
108	— COUPES RATS, Pieds Fleur de Lys. . . .	60 »
109	— COUPES CANARDS.	60 »
110	— GROUPE DE PIGEONS.	25 »

Courbevoie. — Imprimerie E. BERNARD et Cie, 14, rue de la Station.

Auguste Cain,
Le Sphinx et le vautour, 49 cm
(Susse).

that though he was devoted to depicting animals in dramatic situations, he began by representing birds and some small mammals. His debut work at the Salon was *Fauvettes défendant leur nid contre un loir*, and his other works include *Aigle se préparant à défendre sa proie, Furet terrassant un lapin,* and *Combat de coqs.* Only later did he begin to portray large game and elephants. Furthermore, it is worth noting that August Cain also sculpted animals in more pleasant situations, in such works as *Famille de perdrix, Lion assis, Cerf couché,* and his great *Coq français.*

Beginning as an apprentice butcher with his father, August Cain was introduced to sculpture in the studio of a wood sculptor, Alexandre Guionnet, before entering the studio of Rude. In 1852, he married the daughter of Pierre Jules Mène, who clearly influenced him.

Although many writers and the Susse catalog indicate that Cain produced many small bronzes, relatively few of them appear on the art market today compared to those of Mène or Barye. Most of them were produced only circa 1846 through 1868; after this date, Cain received a number of commissions from the State for monumental works in bronze. Cain's predilection for wild game and their continual struggle for survival is evident in these large works, which include the two groups which flank the Rue de Castiglione entrance to the Tuileries, entitled *Lion et lionne se disputant un sanglier* (1882) and *Rhinocéros attaqué par des tigres* (1884), as well as *Tigre terrassant un crocodile* (1869) and *Tigresse apportant un paon à ses petits* (1876) inside the garden. Other significant works are *Lion de Nubie et sa proie* (1870) in the Luxembourg gardens, and *Lions assis,* which flanks one of the doors of the city hall on the Rue Lobau (1884); at the Louvre, Cain's four *Lionne* pieces decorate the two doors of the south wing, adjacent to the garden of Carrousel (1867). Also memorable are the two groups in bronze entitled *Chiens de meute* in the gardens of Chantilly Castle. Some of these great bronzes were also cast in smaller sizes.

Auguste Cain participated regularly at the Salon from 1846 until his death. Here, in addition to the monumental works which will be named, his submissions included three groups in wax, *Fauvettes défendant leur nid contre un loir* (1846), *Faucon surpris par un crotale* (1847), and *Bécasse et musaraigne* (1850); a plaster entitled *Aigle se préparant à défendre sa proie* (1852), cast in bronze the following year for the Minister of the Interior; and another plaster entitled *Vautour brun d'Egypt* (1855), cast by Gonon in four bronze versions to serve as the feet of a porphyry slab table for the Egyptian exhibit of the Louvre. Lastly, he submitted to the Salon an entire series of bronzes: *Famille de perdrix* (1953), *Furet terrassant un lapin* (1857), *Faucon chassant des lapins* and *Faisans surpris par une fouine,* two bas-reliefs, 99 x 145 cm (1861), *Combat de coqs* (1864), *Le Sphinx et le vautour* (1865; the marble exhibited in 1863 is currently at Thann, in Alsace),

*Auguste Cain,
Coq sur un panier,
17 cm (after the
Coq français chantant).*

*Augstue Cain,
Lionne portant
un sanglier
à ses lionceaux,
49 cm L.
(Susse).*

*Auguste Cain,
Tigresse portant
un paon
à ses petits,
45 x 78 cm
(Susse; after
the group from
the Tullieries).*

167

Auguste Cain,
Deux Chiens de meute,
40 cm.

Nid de faisans (1874), Relais de chiens bâtards français, and Cerf couché (1894). As for Coq français, exhibited in wax at the Salon of 1883, it was made in bronze for tennis room at Versailles. Auguste Cain's works were cast bronze in the personal foundry of his father-in-law, Pierre Jules Mène, during his lifetime. After his death, they were cast by Susse Brothers. Only his monumental groups were made by other founders, including Barbedienne, Thiébaut, A. Rolland, and Gonon. On page 164 appear some excerpts from the Susse foundry's catalog, describing the complete edition of Auguste Cain's works. Other bronzes by Cain carrying the seal of Barbedienne are Tête de basset Saint-Hubert, 44 cm, and Deux Braques, Lumineau et Séduisant, 32 cm.

MUSEUMS
Fontainebleau, château
Aigle se préparant à défendre sa proie (E. Vittoz, founder).
Paris, Decorative Arts
Tigresse apportant un paon à ses petits, 47 cm (reduction of a group from the Tuileries).
Paris, Orsay
Sphinx et vautour.
Riom
Lion et lionne se dispurant un sanglier, 32 cm (reduction of a group from the Tuileries).
Strasburg
Coq gaulois, 65 cm (Susse).
Versailles, tennis room
Coq gaulois, gilded bronze, 65 cm.

SALES
Ane d'Afrique, 14 cm, Enghien, October 6, 1985.
Chien de meute à l'attache, Orléans, May 26, 1984.

Chien de Saint-Hubert, 44 cm, Versailles, June 16, 1984, Enghien, October 6, 1985.
Deux Chiens de chasse, Orléans, June 16, 1984.
Deux Chiens de meute attachés, 40 cm, Gien, June 24, 1984.
Coq de l'Inde, Drouot, November 28, 1985, rooms 5 and 6.
Héron et grenouille, 21 cm (Susse), Enghien, February 22, 1981.
Groupe de lièvres, 16 cm, Rambouillet, November 18, 1984.
Lion à l'autruche, 35 cm, Drouot, June 21, 1981.
Lion et lionne se disputant un sanglier, 38 cm, Sotheby London, June 7, 1984; Drouot, June 14, 1985, room 1.
Lionne apportant un sanglier à ses petits, 35 cm, Drouot, October 19, 1983, room 9.
Poule, 7 cm, Drouot, March 10, 1984, room 8.
Tigresse apportant un paon à ses petits, 45 cm (Susse), Drouot, March 16, 1983, room 9.
Vautour sur une tête de sphinx, Nanterre, October 28, 1986.

CAMBOS, JEAN JULES
Castres, April 28 1828
Castres, May 2, 1917

La Cigale, one of the major works of this sculptor, belongs to the museum of Castres. Cambois entered the Ecole des Beaux-Arts of Paris in 1853. Starting in 1857, he exhibited busts and statues including Portrait de M. Henri T.L., a statuette in bronze (1857), La Douleur, a statue in plaster, Portrait du maréchal de Pérignon, a statuette in silvered bronze (1859), La Cigale (plaster in 1864, marble in 1865, and bronze in 1868), Jeune Chef gaulois, bronze (1868), La Femme adultère, bronze (1870), Eve (1872), La Fourmi (1874), La Paix (1879), La Poésie for the city hall of

Auguste Cain,
Deux Chiens de chasse,
33 cm.

Paris (1882), *Jeune Mère* and *Musique vocale* (1887), and *Le Printemps* (1895). He also submitted some statuettes, including *Jeune Fille à la tortue* (1905), *Constellation de Bérénice* (1906), and *La Reconnaissance* (1907), all in plaster, and a bust in bronze entitled *Jeune Fille en Minerve* (1907). Bronzes encountered on the market include *Chanteur de ballades*, 85 cm, and *Ecrivain du Moyen Age*, 71 cm.

MUSEUMS
Paris, Orsay
La Femme adultère, 87 cm (Boyer and Rolland, founders).

Pierre Campagne,
Phryné devant ses juges, 85.5 cm.

SALES
Baigneuse, 77 cm, Sotheby London, November 8, 1984.
La Danse, 86 cm, Drouot, July 7, 1983.

CAMPAGNE, PIERRE

Gontaud (Lot-et-Garonne), 1851-?

Campagne was a student of Falguière. He exhibited at the Salon beginning in 1889, showing works including *Autour du drapeau*, a group in bronze (1891), *Vénus désarmant l'Amour endormi*, a group in plaster (1892), *Phyrné*, a statue in plaster (1893, marble in 1894; it was apparently cast in bronze in many sizes); *L'Epave*, marble (1895), *Phylis de la Tour du Pin*, an equestrian statue in bronze (1901), *Chouan*, a bust in bronze (1905), and *Miroir de Diane*, a statuette in plaster (1906). Pierre Campagne was listed among the living artists in the Société des Artistes Français until 1938.

SALES
Mozart debout, 76 cm, Christie's Oklahoma (USA), September 24, 1981.
Phryné devant ses juges, 35 cm, Drouot, December 2, 1983.
Phryné devant ses juges, 85.5 cm, Christie's London, September 25, 1986.

CAMUS, JEAN-MARIE

Clermont-Ferrand, November 12, 1877
June 15, 1955

Jean-Marie Camus made his debut at the Salon of 1900 with a group of children in plaster; he produced a certain number of busts and statues for his hometown, as well as some monuments to the dead for Bort-les-Orgues and La Tour-d'Auvergne. Many bronzes by this artist have been sold at auction at various times, including *Groupe de trois enfants formant écritoire*, 26 cm (Goldscheider, founder, 1903), *Buste d'enfant*, 11.5 cm, and *Femme nue se courbant*, 65 cm (Bisceglia, founder). The museum of Clermont-Ferrand owns *Groupe d'enfants en classe*, bronze, 18 x 27 cm (1903), and, also in bronze, the bust of Frédéric Cohendy, 58 cm (1904).

CANA, LOUIS ÉMILE

Paris, October 21, 1845
1895

The animal sculptor Louis Émile Cana was a student of Arson, and like his teacher was particularly attracted by birds. Cana exhibited at the Salon from 1863 to 1887, showing works in wax including *Caille et ses petits* (1863), *Perdrix* (1869), and *Querelle de pigeons* (1887), and the bronzes *Héron* (1865), *Buse et lapin* (1867), *Combat de coqs* (1868), *Perdrix d'Amérique dite Cupido* (1870), *Perdrix glaneuse* (1872), and *Faisans* (1873). Also known is a group in bronze, 41 cm high, representing a horse tied next to a dog. One very small bronze entitled *Moineau*, 5.5 cm, was sold at the Drouot Hotel on June 17, 1985, room 9.

CANIEZ, BARTHÉLEMY

Valenciennes, March 29, 1854
1910

Caniez took courses at the Académies in Valenciennes, and then from 1876 to 1880 studied at the Ecole des Beaux-Arts of Paris in the studio of Cavelier. In 1894, he was hired to teach at the school of industrial arts in Geneva. From at least 1882 to 1906, he exhibited busts and statues in bronze and plaster at the Salon of Paris, including, in 1895, a plaster model for the statue of the Grand Condé, designed for the military school in Paris. His works also include *La Source*, a statue in bronze and marble (1890), and *Un résigné*, a bust in bronze (1903). The museum of Valenciennes preserves *Buste de vieillard*, 54 cm, cast in bronze by Siot-Decauville (1901).

CARABIN, RUPERT

Saverne, March 17, 1862
Strasbourg, November 28, 1932

R.Carabin

R.Carabin

Rupert Carabin is most famous for his wooden furniture in oak, pear, or sculpted walnut, oddly ornamented with female figures. However, he also left a certain number of statuettes and groups characteristic of the Art Nouveau style which reigned at the very end of the 19th century. Born of Alsacian parents, he came to Paris at the age of eight; his family left their country after the defeat of 1870, refusing to adopt German nationality. When Carabin was very young, he apprenticed with an engraver, and became a workman there at the age of sixteen. Next he worked as an ornamental sculptor with a furniture manufacturer in a Saint-Antoine suburb.

According to his daughter, Mme Colette Merklen Carabin, in the catalog of the Carabin exhibition at the Luxembourg Gallery in 1974, the artist frequented the school of medicine, where he modeled mortuary masks while perfecting his knowledge of anatomy. He met the art critic Gustave Geffroy, and through him met impressionist and post-impressionist painters like Monet, Toulouse-Lautrec, and Seurat. He executed some pieces of furniture, notably for the great Alsacian art aficianado Albert Kahn, and participated in the formation of the Société des Artistes Indépendants in 1884. His sculpted work is profoundly marked with his love of dance. He admired Cléo de Mérode, the Belle Otéro, Loïe Fuller and made a series of statuettes of dancers in bronze which he exhibited in 1897 at the new Bernheim Gallery. He also participated at the Salon des Indépendants from 1884 to 1891, and then at the Société Nationale des Beaux-Arts. After World War I, he was named director at the school of decorative arts in Strasbourg. He completed many monuments to the dead, including the monument in Saverne that was destroyed in 1942.

The catalog of Carabin's works (compiled for the 1974 exhibition dedicated to him at the Luxembourg Gallery) mentions a certain number of small bronzes, without indicating the number of castings. For the most part, these were exhibited at the Salon de la Société Nationale des Beaux-Arts between 1897 and 1920, and include:

La Loïe Fuller, a series of seven statuettes presenting different poses, from 17 to 22.5 cm high.
Femme au chat, four different types, 19.5, 19.5, 23, and 49 cm.
Danseuse, five statuettes with different attitudes, from 14 to 21 cm.

*Rupert Carabin,
Sirène et pieuvre,
25 cm.*

Rupert Carabin,
*Au Moulin
de la Galette,
50 cm
(Susse).*

Rupert Carabin,
*Femme portant
un tronc d'arbre,
54 cm.*

Portrait de Léandre, plaque, 31 x 15.5 cm.
Sirène et pieuvre, bronze and onyx, 29 cm.
La Posada (four Spanish dancers), high-relief, 24.5 x 29 cm.
Joueur de biniou, 26 cm.
Danse bretonne (four people), 19 cm.
Danse bretonne (a couple), 19.5 cm.
Lutteurs bretons, 17 cm.
Bougeoir constitué d'une femme nue, 19.5 cm.
Femme portant un tronc d'arbre (for a soccer tournament).
Au Moulin de la Galette (a couple dancing), 20 cm.
Danseuse aux crotales, six different statuettes, from 19 to 24.5 cm.
La Belle Otéro, silvered bronze, 17 cm.
La Foi (woman carrying a sick little girl), 14 cm.
En Alsace, vers le marché de Saverne, 58 cm.
Danse bretonne (vase).
Envolée de femmes nues (clock), bronze and amethyst.
Moulin-Rouge, plaque, 22 x 32.5 cm.
La Paix, La Guerre, Pro patria mortis, Pro aris et focis, four plaques, 20 cm diam.
Joueuse au tambourin, 22.5 cm.
Nu au tambourin, 25 cm.
Joueuse à la raquette, 23 cm.
Nu au javelot, 28.5 cm.
Sirène à la coquille, 30 cm.
Masque mortuaire de la soeur de l'artiste, 30 cm.
La Comtesse du Chaylard, 57 cm.
Marie Darzens, 57 cm.

Some of these bronzes, belonging to a Parisian collector, appeared at the 1985 Exhibition Les Chemins de Gauguin, at the museum of Prieuré in Saint-Germain-en-Laye. It is fitting to mention various objects, such as mirrors, inkwells, pommels of canes, plaques, and jewelry (in bronze, pewter, and silver), as well as some statuettes in sandstone (gritstone) and in enameled ceramic.

MUSEUMS
Paris, Petit Palais
Joueuse à la raquette, 23 cm.

SALES
Au Moulin de la Galette, 50 cm (Susse), Drouot, June 12, 1985, rooms 5 and 6.
Femme portant un tronc d'arbre, 54 cm, Drouot, May 27, 1983, room 4.
Sirène et pieuvre, 25 cm, Drouot, May 5, 1986, room 7.

CARDONA, JOSÉ
Born in Barcelona

After studying at the school of fine arts in Barcelona, José Cardona began exhibiting in Paris—in 1902 at the Salon des Artistes Français, in 1903 at the Nationale des Beaux-Arts, and in 1904 at the Salon d'Automne. He exhibited primarily statuettes in bronze, especially portraits: *Monsieur Louis Cazaux* (Salon of 1902), *Mademoiselle Parade* (1905), and *Alphonse XIII roi d'Espagne* (1906). Two statuettes in bronze appeared at the Salon d'Automne in 1904, entitled *Chiffonnier* and *Bonjour Madame*. Cardona was still listed among the living artists of the Société des Artistes Français in 1939. His statuettes of *Chiffonnier* and *Bonjour Madame* were cast by Goldscheider. One statue in plaster, exhibited at the Salon of 1907 under the title *Au travail*, was cast in reduction, 55 cm, by Emile Pinédo. This sculpture was also known by the names of *Laboureur* or *Terrassier* and exists in other dimensions.

SALES
Jeune Garçon, 17 cm, Angers, April 16, 1985.
Le Terrassier, 39 cm, Drouot, January 10, 1985, room 9.

CARL, JULES ANTOINE
Sainte-Croix-aux-Mines (Haut-Rhin), June 6, 1863-?

A teacher at the school of fine arts in Nancy, Carl began exhibiting at the Salon in 1892, in 1910 showing a statuette in bronze entitled *Jeanne d'Arc*. He began exhibiting at the Nationale des Beaux-Arts in 1896, when he submitted two busts in bronze, *Le Vieux Tailleur de pierre* (1901) and *Un poète d'autrefois* (1902), as well as a statuette in plaster, *La Liseuse* (1902).

MUSEUMS
Belfort
La Liseuse, 23.5 cm.
Châteauroux
La Liseuse, 23.5 cm.
Nancy
Pierre de Blarru, bust, 66 cm.
Madame D., medallion, 30 x 24 cm.
Volonté, bust of a woman, 63 cm.
Narbonne
Jeanne d'Arc, 19 cm (cast of a statue for the city of Epinal).

CARLÈS, ANTONIN
Gimont (Gers), July 24, 1851
Paris, February 18, 1919

Carlès participated at the Salon from 1878 to 1914 after his training in Marseille, in Toulouse, and with Jouffroy and Hiolle at the École des Beaux-Arts in Paris. His most characteristic works include *La Cigale*, a bust in plaster (Salon of 1878), *Abel*, a statuette in plaster, 65 cm (1881), *La Jeunesse*, a statue in plaster (1883), *Retour de chasse*, a statue in bronze now at the Tuileries, and a bust in bronze of his father (1888). Other typical works include *Minerve* in bronze, sculpted for the front of the New York Herald building in New York (1894), *Fortunata*, a bust in bronze (1895), *L'Humanité reconaissante*, bronze for the monument to Pasteur in Dole (1902), a statuette of *Bacchus* (plaster in 1904, marble in 1905), and a number of busts. One bust of *Junon* was cast in bronze by Susse in two sizes, 65 and 48 cm, while *La Jeunesse*, 28 cm, *Retour de chasse* (similar to the statue in the Tuileries), and *Gladiateur* appeared in the catalog of Siot-Decauville.

MUSEUMS
Amiens
Buste d'Abel, haut-relief, 44 x 53 cm.
Auch, museum of Jacobins
Le Père de l'artiste, bust, 42 cm.
Le Peintre Théobald Chartran, bust, 43 cm.
    The majority of Carlès' other works given to the museum by his widow were stolen during World War II.
Besançon
Buste du peintre Théobald Chartran, 62 cm.
Dijon
Bacchus, 105 cm.
Paris, Petit Palais
Armand Berton, bust, 45 cm.
Reims
Bacchus adolescent, 58.4 cm (Siot-Decauville).

SALES
Bacchus adolescent, 47.5 cm, Sotheby London, March 8, 1984.

CARLI, AUGUSTE HENRI

    Marseille, July 2, 1868
    Paris, January 1930

    Among the busts, statues, and groups that this artist sent to the Salon starting in 1899, there are two notable busts in bronze entitled *Maître vénitien* and *Jeune Sénégalais* (1914), and one plaster statue entitled *Chloé* (1899). *Chloé* reappeared as a plaster statuette in 1904, and was cast in bronze in two sizes, 68 and 50 cm, by Thiébaut.

CARLIER, ÉMILE FRANÇOIS

    Paris, January 3, 1827
    Paris, 1879

    Carlier, a student of Feuchère, exhibited some genre scenes, allegories, and different portraits of distinction. He submitted several statuettes including *L'Ivresse*, bronze (1850), *La Tempérance, La Cruche cassée* (bronzes, 1865), *L'Industrie française, Jeune Femme offrant une couronne*, silver (1870), *Frileuse*, marble (1872), and *Pierrot*, marble (1876), as well as a statue in bronze, also on the theme of the *Frileuse* (1879).
    After 1865, Carlier collaborated with the goldsmith François-Désiré Froment-Meurice, to whom he furnished some models in different styles.

CARLIER, ÉMILE JOSEPH NESTOR

    Cambrai, January 3, 1849
    Paris, April 11, 1927

    Carlier made his debut at the Salon of 1874 after studying in Cambrai, in Valenciennes and at the Ecole des Beaux-Arts in Paris. His work includes some allegories, genre scenes, a number of busts (many of which are in bronze), and several animals.

Emile Joseph Carlier,
Le Contrebandier, 63 cm.

    His submissions to the Salon include *Gilliat et la pieuvre*, a group in plaster (1879), in bronze (1880), and in marble (1890), *La Fraternité* or *L'Aveugle et le paralytique* in bronze (1884), *La Famille*, a group in plaster (1887), *La Brise*, a statuette in bronze (1896), *La Vierge et l'Enfant*, in bronze (1904), *Baigneuse*, bronze (1905), and many statuettes in marble including *Jeunesse* (1912), *La Vague* (1913), and *Pannyre aux talons d'or* and *Danseuse au voile* (1914). Carlier is moreover the author of the allegory *L'Histoire naturelle* ornamenting the facade of the Sorbonne.
    Several of Carlier's works were cast in régule, and others in bronze, such as *Jeune Fille embrassant sa mère*, 83 cm, *Jeune Femme au chat*, 75 cm, and *Jeune Paysan*, 23 cm.

MUSEUMS

Cambrai

Gilliat et la pieuvre, 214 cm (A. Rudier, founder).

Le Miroir, group in marble and bronze, 234 cm (Salon of 1897).

Buste d'Abel Berger, 72 cm (Hohwiller, founder).

Buste d'Eugène Bouly, 80 cm (1885).

Buste d'Auguste Dorchain, 73 cm (1899, Molz, founder).

Portrait de Louis Blériot, medallion, 48.5 cm diam.

    The Cambrai museum also owns some plasters, terra cottas, and marbles by the same sculptor.

CARON, ALEXANDRE AUGUSTE

Paris, April 16, 1857
June 21, 1932

*Alexandre Caron,
Femme nue
se coiffant,
19.7 cm.*

    Caron was greatly influenced by the dominant spirit of end of the 19th century. His works, most of which are mythological or symbolic and small in size, were made up of various precious materials: ivory, gems, silver, gold, bronze, etc.

    Some of them were cast by the Sèvres factory. At the Salon, where he exhibited beginning in 1894, some statuettes are especially noteworthy: *Eve*, ivory and gold (1899), *Esclave à vendre*, ivory, gold, enamels, and fine stones (1900), *Eros à l'affût* (1901), *Du haut de l'Olympe* and *Charmeuse* (1902), all three in ivory and gold with precious stones, *Désillusion* (1906), *Atalante* (1907), *Surprise* (1908), *La Mouche* (1910), all in ivory, and *Danse antique* (1914) in ivory and fine stones, etc.

    Du haut de l'Olympe was translated into bronze and exhibited in 1903. A group in plaster entitled *Après le bain* (1900) was made into a smaller (46.5 cm) version in silver, ivory and fine stones, and was sold in Monte-Carlo in 1977. A statuette in silvered bronze entitled *Jeune Fille au macaron*, 33 cm, was sold at the Drouot Hotel in 1976.

CARPEAUX, JEAN-BAPTISTE

Valenciennes, May 11, 1827
Courbevoie, October 12, 1875

    Three masterpieces alone—*La Danse* from the Opera of Paris, the decoration on the Flore pavillion at the Louvre, and *La Fontaine des quatre parties du monde* on the Avenue of the Observatory—guarantee Carpeaux's place among the greatest masters of 19th century French sculpture. However, his brief career gave birth to many other sculptures, all of which provide additional evidence of his vivid and non-conformist genius. A relentless, spirited, tormented worker, Carpeaux produced a host of drawings, drafts, paintings, rough sketches in plaster and in terra cotta, busts, statuettes and groups in marble and in bronze, in addition to his great monumental accomplishments, all in the space of about twenty years, from 1855 until his death.

    At the age of 11, when he already dreamed of being a sculptor, Carpeaux went to Paris with his family; soon afterward, they left him there alone in order to seek their fortune in America. By chance, Carpeaux's cousin Victor Liet understood his aspirations, and in 1842 enrolled him in the Petite Ecole, where he learned sculpture in the company of Davioud, Garnier, Chapu, and Carriès. Later, he became an assistant teacher in a drawing class, and had Dalou and Rodin as students.

THE FIRST SCULPTURES

    In 1844, when he was only seventeen years old, Carpeaux entered the Ecole des Beaux-Arts, working in the studios of Abel, of Pujol, and then of Rude. Rude, whom Carpeaux revered and considered his master all his life, advised the young sculptor to leave for another studio—that of Francisque Duret, a more prudent artist, in better favor, and therefore, in a better position to help Carpeaux in the competition for the prize of Rome. When Carpeaux first entered the trial for admission in 1846, his bas-relief representing *Joseph reconnu par ses frères* was ranked sixteenth of fifty-three entries. This result, together with the recommendations of a certain number of faithful friends (including the lawyer Jean-Baptiste Foucart) and testimonials full of praise from Abel de Pujol and Rude, won Carpeaux an annual scholarship from the Conseil Général du Nord, ameliorating a very precarious financial situation.

    In 1853, Carpeaux made his debut at the Salon, exhibiting *La Soumission d'Abd-el-Kader à l'Empereur,* a bas-relief in plaster which received little notice. He decided to present his work to Napoléon III, whom he followed from city to city during the ruler's official trip through the north. He finally succeeded at Amiens, and received a commission for a marble piece, to be carried out by a practicioner, Charles Romain Capellaro.

    In 1855, Carpeaux finally achieved success. The first grand prize of Rome for a sculpture was awarded to his *Hector implorant les Dieux en faveur de son fils Astianax.* The following year, he was able to go to the Villa Médicis. Soon, having difficulty tolerating the discipline of the Ecole and the constraints of official academicism, he came to prefer wandering about the streets of Rome, which swarmed with life, or admiring the frescoes of Michelangelo at the Sistine Chapel. "When an artist feels pale and cold," he wrote, "he runs to Michelangelo in order to warm himself, as with the rays of the sun."

Carpeaux's work did not diminish, and from Rome he sent to Paris the plaster of *Jeune Pêcheur à la coquille* or *Pêcheur napolitain*, which was exhibited in 1858 at the Ecole des Beaux-Arts (the bronze appeared at the Salon of 1859 and the marble at the Salon of 1863, where it was bought by the Empress). While the work owes much to Rude's *Petit Pêcheur napolitain*, the vitality revealed in the tension of its contours gave proof that Rude's student had, in his turn, become a master.

THE MAJOR WORKS

Enthralled by Dante's *Divine Comedy*, Carpeaux devoted himself to presenting the theme of Ugolin; it occupied him for four years, from 1857 to 1861—, or rather, it preoccupied him, for soon obstacles appeared in his path. The rules of the Académie de France in Rome required that the subjects chosen by resident students be drawn exclusively from Scripture or from ancient history. Schnetz, the stern director of the Villa Médicis, actually advised Carpeaux to transform his *Ugolin* into Saint Jérome! The sculptor refused, and did not hesitate to travel to Paris to solicit—and obtain— authorization to finish his work from the Minister of Fine Arts, M. Achile Fould. The resultant work, a 195 cm high plaster, was a triumph in Rome in 1861, but provoked an absolute uproar the following year in Paris at the exposition of the Ecole des Beaux-Arts. Although the Institut refused an execution of it in marble (which did not appear until the Exposition Universelle of 1867), the State commissioned a bronze; it was cast by Victor Thiébaut and exhibited at the Salon of 1863, then placed in the Tuileries (today it is at the Orsay museum). Carpeaux had the

J. B. Carpeaux

Jean-Baptiste Carpeaux,
Ugolin et ses enfants,
sketch, 44 cm
(Susse).

Jean-Baptiste Carpeaux,
Ugolin et ses enfants,
48 cm.

luck of arriving back in France during a period when new large works were in great demand, and he received important commissions. The first of these was the sculpted ornamentation in the Flore pavillion at the Louvre, which occupied him from 1863 to 1866 and for which he executed the admirable *Triomphe de Flore*, this time welcomed by the critics without the least reticence. Next, Charles Garnier, who constructed the new Opera, entrusted to him one of the groups for the facade, for which Carpeaux sculpted the famous, universally known *Danse*. In 1964 this was replaced with a copy by the sculptor Paul Belmondo, and the original was put in shelter first in the Louvre and then in the Orsay. When Carpeaux's original was first unveiled on July 27, 1869, the audacity of the nude bodies and the mischieveous circle provoked a veritable scandal. On the 8th of December, the decision was made to have Charles Gumery sculpt another Danse, "treated with decency, in conformity with the desires of the public," but the declaration of war in July 1870 saved the masterpiece by Carpeaux.

Carpeaux received another large commission in 1867: the fountain for the Avenue of the Observatory, on the theme *Quatre Parties du monde* (the four sides of the world). After seven years of working—frequently interrupted, especially by the war—the plaster's splendid nature was presented at the Salon of 1872 alone; the bronze was put in place in 1874.

Since his return from Rome, Carpeaux's notoriety had never been in doubt; the intrigues that continually mounted around his various works did nothing to dispell it. He counted, amoung his admirers, a number of people like the Count of Nieuwerkerque, the Superintendant des Beaux-Arts, and the prince Demidoff. The princess Mathilde introduced him to the court. He attended, painting and drawing the balls at the Tuileries. He sculpted effigies of Empress Eugénie and the young imperial prince, for whom he became the drawing teacher. His studio overflowed with work, and yet, several times, he found himself confronted by tragic financial difficulties. Indeed, during the years following the design and execution of the *Danse* he was literally bankrupt. As a result, he quickly became interested in casting his works, which he believed was the only way of providing himself with the liquid assets necessary for pursuing his sculpture. Because of this, a great number of bronzes carrying his signature are more or less the direct heirs of some of his great works.

"I had no resources other than the sale of bronzes," wrote Carpeaux, still in Rome in 1855, to his patron, Jean-Baptiste Foucart. A few years later, in 1858, while still in Rome, he asked his parents in the United States to advance him the money needed for an edition of his *Pêcheur à la coquille:* "I have the chance of doubling, tripling the gain by the reproductions...It is not a question of working six months just to earn enogh for bread; it is necessary also to think of capitalizing. Bronze is a material which will work very well with this statue—it was conceived with this in mind...." A little bit later, in another letter, he described his fear of being dispossessed of his right of reproduction: "I want to guard the ownership of this work and to manage its reduction to a scale that would fit on a mantle as the original sits on a pedestal..." (Catalog from the exposition "De Carpeaux à Matisse, trésors des musées du nord de la France," 1982). In fact, it is interesting to note, the first bronze model of *Pêcheur à la coquille* was reputedly exhibited at the Salon of 1859, cast by Victor Thiébaut without the presence of the sculptor.

The adventure of the *Pêcheur à la coquille* was far from over. To follow the story as it unfolded, it is necessary to travel through the career of the sculptor until his death, and even beyond. During the last years of his life, after the war of 1870 and his return from England (where he had retired temporarily), Carpeaux decided to increase the distribution of his works. This time, his family (who had returned from America several years earlier) was interested in being involved with his fame. He entered into a partnership with his brother, Emile Carpeaux, who served as a kind of commercial director. At Emile's demand, and "in order to add efficiency to his studio," Carpeaux produced a number of replicas and variants of his earlier works, also multiplying it in marble (very often sculpted by the practicioners), in terra cotta (cast in his own studio at Auteuil), and naturally the bronzes, which he entrusted to many foundries which did not always include a mark on the proofs.

Jean-Baptiste Carpeaux,
Buste du Génie de la Danse,
54 cm.

1) Jean-Baptiste Carpeaux, Flore accroupie, 52 cm (Carpeaux propriety seal). J. Ginepro Collection, Monaco.

2) Jean-Baptiste Carpeaux, Le Génie de la Danse, 101 cm (Carpeaux propriety seal).

3) Jean-Baptiste Carpeaux, Flore accroupie, 22 cm (Susse).

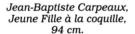

Jean-Baptiste Carpeaux,
Jeune Fille à la coquille,
94 cm.

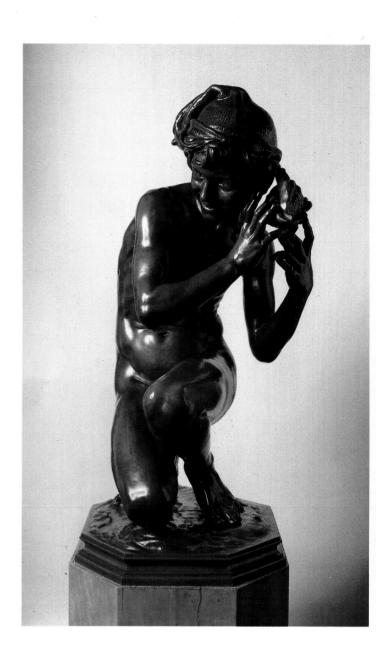

Jean-Baptiste Carpeaux,
Le Pêcheur napolitain, 89 cm
(Carpeaux propriety seal).
Fabius frères Collection, Paris.

LE PÊCHEUR AND ITS DERIVATIVES

During this period between 1872 and 1875, new proofs in bronze of the *Pêcheur* in the dimensions of the original plaster (91 cm) were produced, along with some reductions. A contract, signed for this purpose with Barbedienne as early as 1863, is preserved in the archives of Valenciennes (Catalog *De Carpeaux à Matisse*, already cited). In one of the sales organized by the sculptor in order to salvage his finances yet again, on April 29, 1873, a proof in bronze in the original dimensions appeared. In a second sale, December 20th of the same year, there appeared a 91 cm bronze and four 45 cm reductions. In another sale, on May 23, 1874, and again on

December 28, 1874—indeed, at all the sales during the lifetime of Carpeaux—a 91 cm bronze and a 35 cm reduction were listed for sale.

Carpeaux did not stop here. He sculpted a variant of his work, this time with a net placed on the left leg. Called *Jeune Pêcheur avec filet*, it was also cast by him in bronze. Then he sculpted (or ordered it to be sculpted) in marble, and edited in bronze the single bust which became the *Rieur napolitain*, 55 cm, for which different proofs were sold on April 29, December 20, 1873, May 23, 1874 (in a reduction of 26 cm), and December 28, 1874 (55 and 26 cm).

Moreover, a pendant version of the *Jeune Pêcheur* entitled *Jeune Fille à la coquille*, 40 in, had been

178

Jean-Baptiste Carpeaux,
Le Rieur napolitain, La Rieuse napolitaine,
two busts, 26 cm
(Carpeaux propriety seal).

Jean-Baptiste Carpeaux,
Jeune Pêcheur avec filet,
60 cm (Susse).

Jean-Baptiste Carpeaux,
Buste de la Rieuse napolitaine,
model from the foundry, 52.5 cm
(Carpeaux sale, June 2, 1894).
Fabius frères Collection, Paris.

presented in plaster at the Salon of 1864, and in marble (to be bought by the Empress) at the Salon of 1867. He made the piece into many replicas in marble and castings in terra cotta and in bronze (proofs in bronze April 29, and December 20, 1873). The single bust, *La Rieuse napolitaine,* would be reproduced in bronze in many dimensions.

La Rieuse in turn engendered variations: *Espiègle, Rieuse aux roses,* and *Rieuse aux pampres.* One proof of each of these three busts appeared in the catalog of December 20, 1873.

After Carpeaux's death, his descendants continued to exploit his work. On May 31 and June 1 and 2 of 1894, large numbers of paintings and designs,

179

*Jean-Baptiste Carpeaux,
Bacchante aux roses, 65 cm
(Carpeaux propriety seal).*

not to mention the replicas in marble and the editions in terra cotta. They can be judged while reviewing a chronological history of Carpeaux's career, as brief as it was prolific.

As for *Le Pêcheur* and its derivatives, a number of proofs in bronze of these different works were sold at public sales organized by Carpeaux in 1873 and 1874. But other bronzes which did not appear in these sales were cast no less frequently by the sculptor himself while he lived, continuing after his death, and, for a certain number of them, even today. In principle, the mark "propriété Carpeaux" indicates the works cast during his lifetime; however, it would be necessary to ascertain that this seal was not used posthumously by his heirs.

As early as 1855, before leaving for Rome, Carpeaux made some statuettes, including *La Toilette* and *La Tendresse maternelle*. In 1856, as a resident of the Villa Médicis and even before his *Jeune Pêcheur à la coquille*, he sculpted a small bust in marble entitled *L'Enfant boudeur*. Interestingly, in this same time period he sculpted another bust in plaster entitled *La Palombella*, which he shipped to Paris (his first submission from Rome) in order to be exhibited at the Ecole des Beaux-Arts; the marble appeared at the Salon of 1864. It was essentially a portrait of a certain Barbera Pasquarelli, a native of the village of Palombella near Rome, for whom he had indulged a brief passion. Many variations of this bust are known, including *L'Eté*. In 1963 the town of Palombella inaugurated a street named Carpeaux to commemorate the sculptor).

Following *Jeune Pêcheur*, the monumental group entitled *Ugolin* (195 cm, exhibited in Paris in 1862) also became an object of replicas and further editions. One replica in terra cotta in the original dimensions was executed in 1873. It belongs today to the glyptothèque of Copenhagen. During the same period, reductions in bronze and in terra cotta were sold. According to Madame Annie Braunwald, a specialist on Carpeaux, it was after the death of Carpeaux that the draft itself was cast in many sizes, at the demand of his daughter, Madame Louise Clément-Carpeaux.

After having finished a group in stone entitled *La Tempérance* for the church of the Trinity in Paris, Carpeaux exhibited *Le Prince impérial et son chien Néro* (56 in.), a statue in plaster, at the Salon of 1866. In 1867 he showed a marble version at the Exposition Universelle, and in 1868 showed a variation without the dog, in silvered bronze. This work gave birth to a number of reductions in all materials, notably in bronze, but also in an unglazed porcelain version from Sèvres, under the name *L'Enfant au chien*.

several marbles, nearly forty models in bronze, and about twenty terra cottas and plasters—preserved until then in his studio—were sold at the Drouot Hotel. Importantly, all of them, from the models in bronze (intended as editions) to the terra cottas and plasters, were sold with the reproduction rights in bronze and marble. Thus, even before Carpeaux's work entered the public domain, it faced the possibility of unlimited reproductions and editions. Two additional sales took place on May 30 and December 8 of 1913, this time without the rights to reproduction. Items for sale included numerous original plasters and some models in bronze, comprising almost half of his cast works and their different reductions. Of further note is the contract signed in 1914 with the Susse foundry for the edition of a certain number of works. *Le Pêcheur avec filet*, while being made, had been previewed in three reductions.

The desire to disperse his works, which Carpeaux had so often expressed and had effectively accomplished during his lifetime, was, to put it mildly, pursued at a frantic pace after his death.

The long story of *Jeune Pêcheur à la coquille* and its proliferation offers a shortened account, as gripping as it is instructive, of the production of this famous sculptor's work. Nearly all his pieces were issued in more or less abundant castings in bronze,

The Salon of 1866 also saw the presentation of Carpeaux's half-sized plaster of the front of the Flore pavillion, *La France impériale portant la Lumière dans le monde et protégeant l'Agriculture et les Sciences*. In addition, he exhibited his freize of children carrying palms and the famous *Triomphe de Flore*. Carpeaux drew upon this latter work to make several altered versions in bronze, including the *Flore accroupie*, and a bust entitled *Le Printemps*.

Jean-Baptiste Carpeaux,
L'Amour à la folie,
80 cm.

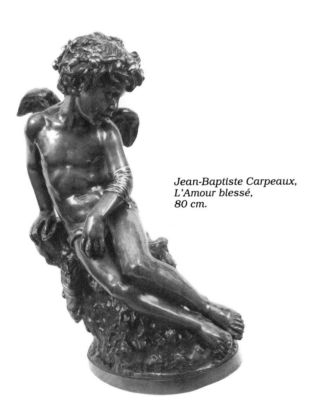

Jean-Baptiste Carpeaux,
L'Amour blessé,
80 cm.

Jean-Baptiste Carpeaux,
L'Amour désarmé,
90 cm.

Carpeaux had made some partial studies as early as 1868 for the fountain of the *Quatre Parties du monde*, which was not finished until 1874. These included two busts in plaster: *Le Chinois* and *La Négresse*.

THE YEAR OF *LA DANSE*

In 1869, Carpeaux married Amélie de Montfort, twenty years his junior, daughter of the General Viscount de Montfort. Carpeaux's intrusive, conniving family hardly appreciated his marriage, says the artist's daughter Madame Clément-Carpeaux, to the extent that they kept him apart from his wife and children in the last years of his life. As for *La Danse*, the group from the Opera which, also in 1869, unleashed the agitation previously described, it was reused and divided into separate elements and many sizes. Derivative works that can be found include *Le Génie de la Danse*, the bust of the spirit *L'Amour à la folie*, the child appearing at the feet of the spirit, "madness" in hand.

Some preparatory studies were also cast, specifically the busts *Bacchante aux lauriers* and *Bacchante aux roses*, three heads entitled *Bacchante aux yeux baissés*, *Bacchante criant*, and *Faune* (which would be cast posthumously in a limited edition by Hébrard), and finally *Les Trois Grâces*.

Also from 1869 were the works *Buste de Mme Carpeaux en toilette de mariée* and *Eugénie Fiocre, danseuse étoile de l'Opera*, from which, the following year, the sculptor cast *L'Amour désarmé*, also called *Psyché désarmant l'Amour*. This piece eventually evolved into the statue of *Watteau* for the future monument of Valenciennes, on which he worked intermittently for nine years and which was not unveiled until 1884.

In 1870, Carpeaux sculpted the front of the city hall of Valenciennes on the theme of *La Ville de Valenciennes défendant la patrie*. Some reductions in bronze were later made of it. At the beginning of the siege of Paris, he modeled a small group in plaster entitled *Maternité* or the *Enfant malade*, which portray his wife and his first child, Charles, born on April 23.

After the disaster of September 1870, Carpeaux sought exile in London. Carpeaux sculpted some busts including those of the painter Gérome and of the musician Gounod, as well as some statuettes entitled *Frères et soeur* and *La Frileuse*. Always confronted with financial difficulties, he and Carrier-Belleuse jointly organized a sale of their works at Christie's.

THE ERA OF THE EDITIONS

Upon his return to France, Carpeaux collaborated with his brother to begin a period of intense commercialization of his works. Still, new subjects continued to emerge, including *Suzanne surprise* in 1872 and the group entitled *Daphnis et Chloé* in 1873 (some reductions in bronze of this group were cast later), commissioned by Lord Ashburton when the the sculptor was again sojourning in London, called there by the Empress Eugénie at the time of Napoléon III's death, and finally, *L'Amour blessé* and *Figaro*.

In 1874, though he was undermined by a devastating and lingering illness, Carpeaux continued to work on many projects. He sculpted *Eve au serpent* or *Eve tentée*, and during the course of a stay with

Jean-Baptiste Carpeaux,
Les Trois Grâces, 84 cm
(Carpeaux propriety seal).

Jean-Baptiste Carpeaux,
Figaro, 54 cm.

Jean-Baptiste Carpeaux,
Notre-Dame-de-Saint-Cordon,
33 cm
(Valsuani 4/12).

Jean-Baptiste Carpeaux,
La Frileuse, 40.5 cm
(Carpeaux propriety seal).
Fabius frères Collection,
Paris.

183

Jean-Baptiste Carpeaux,
La Ville de Valenciennes
défendant la patrie, 55 cm.

Jean-Baptiste Carpeaux,
Eve au serpent, 72 cm
(cast during Carpeaux's lifetime).

Alexandre Dumas Jr. in Puys, near Dieppe, he sculpted *La Pêcheuse de vignots*. After a trip to Nice, he reached the home of Prince Stirbey in Courbevoie, where he died, alone, at the age of forty-eight.

Carpeaux's body of work was immense. It is impossible to pass in silence his paintings and drawings of amazing quality, and the innumerable sketches which preceded the completion of most of his statues and groups. Some religious sculptures remain to be mentioned, though they are less interesting, and a number of accurate and lifelike busts, among which are that of Anna Foucart (1860), the princess Mathilde (1863), the small bust of the Empress (37 cm), Charles Garnier (1869), and Alexander Dumas Jr (1873), in addition to those of people already mentioned. Some of them, particularly the bust of Dumas, were cast in bronze in many sizes.

184

The proliferation of Carpeaux's subjects—reissued in various materials and sizes, modified or divided into several pieces—is regrettable, whether a particular example was reproduced by Carpeaux himself at the end of his life, or after his death, when his bronzes were cast many times by Barbedienne, Susse, Thiébaut, Hébrard and other founders. Though the master did not earn his glory through the reproductions, they can never diminish the greatness that is obvious in his major works, his universally-known masterpieces, the sketches molded by hand from his brilliant imagination, and even the bronzes themselves—as long as their own qualities are worthy of the original model—especially those which were cast during his lifetime.

THE PRINCIPAL BRONZES

Carpeaux's bronzes were cast during his lifetime and after his death by a variety of founders. An exhaustive list makes clear that his work has been in the public domain for a long time. It is no less certain that a certain number of these works can be considered improper, or even fraudulent, for they were made based on works which were never intended to be reproduced in materials other than that of the original. For this reason, some specialists caution against a few small female figures recently executed in bronze, reproductions of simple studies in unbaked clay purchased from the studio at the Drouot Hotel in the 1960s. Below is a list of the best-known bronzes by Jean-Baptiste Carpeaux.

Statuettes and groups

L'Amour blessé, 80 cm; some proofs edited by Susse, 51 cm.
L'Amour désarmé, 90 cm.
L'Amour à la folie, 80cm.
Christ, 28 cm.
Daphnis et Chloé, posthumous reductions.
Eve accroupie, 41 cm.
Eve au serpent or Eve tentée, 72 cm.
Figaro, 80 and 54 cm.
Flore accroupie, 52 and 22 cm.
Frère et soeur, 68 cm.
La Frileuse, 41 cm.
Le Génie de la danse, 105 and 58 cm.
Jeune Fille à la coquille, 100 cm.
Jeune Pêcheur à la coquille or Pêcheur napolitain, 91, 45, and 35 cm.
Jeune Pêcheur avec filet, edited by Susse (contract of 1914), 63, 35, and 23 cm.
Le Marchand de poissons, 110 cm.
La Pêcheuse de vignots, 74 in.
Le Prince impérial or L'Enfant au chien, 64, 47, 32, and 15 cm (many variants).
Le Printemps, 67 cm.
Suzanne surprise, 70 cm.

*Jean-Baptiste Carpeaux,
La Pêcheuse de vignots, 74 cm
(Carpeaux propriety seal).*

La Toilette, 69 cm.
Les Trois Grâces, 84 and 52 cm.
Ugolin et ses enfants, 48 cm; some proofs Hébrard of
52.5 cm; other reductions edited by Susse.
Ugolin et ses enfants, sketch, posthumous editions in
many dimensions including 44 cm.
La Ville de Valenciennes défandant la patrie, 55 cm.

Busts

Alexandre Dumas fils, 82, 66, 47, 35 cm.
Bacchante criant, limited posthumous edition by
Hébrard.
Bacchante aux lauriers, 65 and 36 cm.
Bacchante aux roses, 65 cm.
Bacchante aux yeux baissés, limited posthumous edition
by Hébrard.
Candeur, 69 cm.
Chinois, 69 cm.
L'Enfant boudeur, 33 cm.
Espiègle, 53 cm.
Faune, limited posthumous edition by Hébrard.
Fiancée, 68 cm.
Le Génie de la danse, 104, 66, and 54 cm.
Négresse, 64 cm.
Le Printemps, 58 cm.
Le Rieur napolitain, 55 and 26 cm.
La Rieuse napolitaine, 53 and 26 cm.
La Rieuse aux pampres, 55 cm.
La Rieuse aux roses, 55 cm.

MUSEUMS
Angers
Buste d'Anna Foucart, 58 cm (1860).
Bayonne
Buste de Bacchante.
Beauvais
Buste de Mme V. Thiébaut, 78 cm.
Boulogne-sur-Mer
Buste de l'impératrice Eugénie (Thiébaut).
Calais
Le Prince impérial, 15 cm (1865).
Cambrai
Jeune Fille à la coquille, 98 cm.
Jeune Pêcheur à la coquille, 90 cm.
Compiègne, château
L'Impératrice protégeant les orphelins et les arts, 34 cm.
Le Prince impérial, bust, 31 cm.
Le Prince impérial et son chien Néro, 45 cm.
Le Prince impérial, 64 cm. (Barbedienne).
Dijon
Buste de Charles Tissot, ambassadeur de France, 57
cm. (Thiébaut).
Buste de Joseph Tissot, doyen de la faculté des lettres,
52 cm (Barbedienne).
Le Génie de la danse, 104 cm.
Grenoble
Christ en croix, 35 x 21 cm.
Lille
Edouard Reynart, directeur du musée de Lille, octagonal
medallion, 25 x 22 cm (1867).
Lyon
Palombella.

Jean-Baptiste Carpeaux,
Le Prince impérieal et son chien Néro, 27.5 cm
(Carpeaux propriety seal).

Maubeuge
Le Prince impérial, bust, 64.5 cm (1865).
Nice
L'Amour à la folie.
La France impériale éclairant le monde, 36 cm.
Le Génie de la danse, 104 cm.
Le Prince impérial et son chien Néro, 45 cm.
Notre-Dame de saint Cordon, 34 cm (Hébrard).
La Tempérance, 34 cm (Hébrard)
Paris, Carnavalet
Le Prince impérial, bust, 31 cm (1865).
Paris, Orsay
Le Prince impérial et son chien Néro, 69 cm (1865).
Ugolin et ses enfants, 195 cm (1860).
Watteau, sketch for the statue of Valenciennes, 123 cm.
Buste d'Anna Foucart, 47.5 cm.
Buste d'Eugène Giraud, 64.6 cm (1862).
Buste de Charles Garnier, 67.6 cm (1869).
Buste de Gérome, 60 cm.
Buste du notaire Beauvois, 65.4 cm (1862).
The museum also owns a number of works, sketches and models in plaster, terra cotta and marble.
Paris, Petit Palais
L'Amour à la folie, 70.5 cm.
Confidence, mother and child, 14.5 cm.
Désespoir, 22 cm.
Enfant pleurant, 13.5 cm.
L'Espiègle, bust of a young woman, 50 cm (1860).
Le Génie de la danse, 104 cm.
Napoléon 1er assis à Sainte-Hélène, 20 cm.
Trait d'union, group, 19 cm.
A number of works in plaster and in terra cotta also belong to the museum of the Petit Palais.
Saint-Omer
Le Prince impérial, bust, 32 cm. (1865).
Valenciennes
L'Amour désarmé, 68 cm.
Joseph reconnu par ses frères, bas-relief, 22.5 x 29.5 cm.
Main de jeune fille tenant un oiseau, 28 cm.
La Ville de Valenciennes défendant la patrie, reduction, 54 x 44 cm (1873).
Buste d'Anna Foucart, 48 cm (1860).
Buste de Bacchante aux roses, 59 cm (Susse).
Buste de Bacchante aux yeux baissés, 32 cm (unique proof).
Buste de Bruno Chérier, 62 cm (1875).
Buste de Charles Garnier, 67.6 cm (E. Gruet, founder).
Buste de faune, 34 cm (1869; unique proof).
Buste de Louis Maximilien Beauvois, 26 cm.
Buste de Victor Liet, 47 cm.
L'Architecte Joseph Vaudremer, medallion, 16 x 12 cm.
Edouard Reynart, medallion, octagonal, 25 x 22 cm.
Madame Delpy, medallion, 18 cm diam.
Louis Joseph Foucart à soixante ans, medallion, 19.6 cm diam. (1850).
Madame L.J. Foucart à cinquante-deux ans, medallion, 19.2 cm (1850).
Le Peintre Félix Giacomotti, medallion, 18 cm diam.
Le Peintre Emile Lévy, medallion, 19 cm diam.
Numerous plasters by Carpeaux as well as some terra cottas and marbles make up part of the collections of the museum.

Other museums have some sculptures by Carpeaux, in particular the Roybet-Fould museum, in Courbevoie near Paris, and abroad, the National Gallery of Washington, the glyptotheque Ny Carlsberg of Copenhagen, etc.

SALES
L'Amour blessé, 51 cm (Susse), Vougeot, November 24, 1984.
L'Amour à la folie, 40 cm, Valenciennes, November 24, 1986; Drouot, June 2, 1986, room 2.

Jean-Baptiste Carpeaux,
Suzanne surprise, 76 cm
(Carpeaux propriety seal).
J. Ginepro Collection, Monaco.

L'Amour moqueur, 71 cm (Susse), Drouot, June 2, 1986, room 2; Drouot, November 19, 1986, room 10; Drouot, December 4, 1986, rooms 5 and 6.

Automne, bust, 56 cm, Christie's London, May 15, 1986.

Bacchus, 15 cm, Drouot, June 25, 1984, room 6.

Christ, 30 cm, Valenciennes, April 9, 1984.

Eve tentée, 72 cm, Drouot, February 3, 1986, room 2.

Figaro, 54 cm, Bergerac, March 28, 1984.

Flore, 38 cm (Susse), Valenciennes, May 26, 1986; Drouot, June 2, 1986, room 2.

Flore accroupie, 22 cm, Verrières-le-Buisson, December 14, 1985.

La Frileuse, 41 cm, Drouot, June 2, 1986, room 2.

Le Génie de la danse, 58 cm, Sotheby London, June 7, 1984; Drouot, February 3, 1986.

Le Génie de la danse, 58 cm (Carpeaux property seal), Drouot, June 2, 1986, room 2.

Le Génie de la danse, 69 cm, Sotheby London, November 7, 1985.

Le Génie de la danse, 84 cm, (Carpeaux property seal), Drouot, June 2, 1986, room 2.

Le Génie de la danse, 101 cm (Carpeaux property seal), Enghien, March 24, 1985; Drouot, June 2, 1986, room 2; Sotheby London, June 12, 1986; Pau, October 26, 1986.

Le Génie de la danse, bust, 54 cm, Bourg-en-Bresse, March 2, 1986.

Jeune Fille à la coquille, 94 cm, Dijon, April 27, 1986.

Jeune Pêcheur napolitain, 35 cm, Valenciennes, March 24, 1986.

Jeune Pêcheur napolitain, 91 cm (Susse), Drouot, March 16, 1983; Angers, June 11, 1985.

Jeune Pêcheur napolitain, 91 cm (Susse), Christie's New York, March 13, 1984; Rambouillet, March 9, 1986.

Jeune Pêcheur napolitain au filet, 60 cm (Susse, chiseler of art Jules Barbier), Christie's London, May 15, 1986.

Maternité, 18 cm, Drouot, June 2, 1986, room 2; Chartres, October 26, 1986.

Notre-Dame-de-Saint-Cordon, 34 cm (Hébrard No.4), Sotheby London, November 27, 1984; Drouot, June 2, 1986, room 2.

La Pêcheuse de vignots, 74 cm (Carpeaux property seal), Bourg-en-Bresse, March 2, 1986; Sotheby London, March 20, 1986.

Le Poète breton, 56 cm, Sotheby London, June 20, 1985.

Le Prince impérial, 31 cm, (Barbedienne), Drouot, March 28, 1985, room 2.

Le Rieur napolitain, bust, Bordeaux, June 24, 1986.

Le Rieuse, bust, 32.5 cm Valenciennes, December 1, 1986.

Les Trois Grâces, 52 cm (1/10), Nantes, February 24, 1986.

Les Trois Grâces, 80 cm (Susse), Christie's New York, June 15, 1985.

Ugolin et ses enfants, 52.5 cm (Hébrard), Christie's London, July 17, 1984.

Ugolin et ses enfants, sketch, 44 cm, Drouot, November 30, 1983.

Valenciennes défendant la patrie, Valenciennes, November 26, 1984.

CARPENTIER, PAUL

Rouen, November 17, 1787
Paris, May 10, 1877

Carpentier painted historical scenes and portraits. He also left some sculptures, including *Louis XVI donnant ses instructions à La Pérouse*, exhibited at the Salon of 1838. The museum of Troyes has a bust in bronze of *Paillot de Montabert*, 50 cm high.

Jean-Baptiste Carpeaux, Buste de Chinois, 59 cm.

Jean-Baptiste Carpeaux, Jeune Homme assis, 72 cm (Susse).

CARRIER-BELLEUSE, ALBERT ERNEST, ALSO KNOWN AS CARRIER DE BELLEUSE

Anisy-le-Château (Aisne), June 12, 1824
Sèvres, June 4, 1887

A·CARRIER

*Albert
Carrier-Belleuse,
La Liseuse,
bronze and ivory,
58 cm.*

Carrier-Belleuse has been nicknamed 'the Clodion of the 19th century', but this comparison with the famous sculptor is not unanimously considered a compliment. The Goncourt brothers, in regards to a centerpiece executed in 1867 for the Païva, called Carrier-Belleuse the "junker of the 19th century...a copier of Clodion." What exactly is meant by this? Carrier-Belleuse had come to Paris as a child, and at the age of thirteen became an apprentice to an engraver by the name of Bauchery. He worked next with the goldsmith Fauconnier, and then with the Fannières brothers, also goldsmiths. In 1840, thanks to an endorsement from David d'Angers, he entered the Ecole des Beaux-Arts, but he was ill-suited for formal training. More attracted by the decorative arts, he took courses at the Petite Ecole, and debuted at the Salon of 1850 with two medallions in bronze. In 1851, he was employed by an English porcelain factory, Minton China Works in Staffordshire. There he created models and directed a school of drawing until 1855. Upon returning to Paris, he reappeared at the Salon in 1857, and his fame increased. He worked in Paris for the church of Saint-Augustin, the Tuileries, the Louvre, the city hall, the Opera, the French Theater, the Tribunal de Commerce, the casino of Vichy, etc. He also sculpted the graceful caryatids for the facade of the Renaissance Theater in Paris, the pediment of the Bank of France, the statue of Masséria in Nice, the statue of Dumas, Sr. in Villers-Cotterêts, and the statue of General San Martino in the cathedral of Buenos Aires. He was exceptionally prolific—"virtually a sculpting machine," wrote Edouard Lockroy of him in the journal *L'Artiste*, in 1865—and was moreover the author of a quantity of busts, small groups, statuettes, potraits of historical or contemporary people, nudes, allegories, and genre scenes, as well as ornaments, candelabras, vases, and furnishings, all achieving considerable success during the Second Empire. His works were made in terra cotta, plaster, marble, and bronze, often with some unexpected elements in porcelain or ivory. "He cuts everything, he shapes everything, he forms everything," wrote Edouard Lockroy in *L'Artiste*, adding: "...but what spirit, imagination, and verve this machine has! Sometimes, one would think him a genius.

These statements by his contemporaries accurately identified the merits and limits of Carrier-Belleuse's art, a naturalistic, easygoing, and seductive art, full of vivacity and movement. "For a long time," Paul Mantz would later write, "Carrier had been a tireless artisan of amiable elegances and lively graces;" in this sense, he can be considered one of the precursors of Art Nouveau. Winner of a number of awards, he was named director of works of art at the Sèvres factory in 1875. He gave a new impetus to the manufacture of unglazed porcelain, for which his figures and his groups often served as models.

Among the most remarkable works by Carrier-Belleuse, are a considerble quantity of busts. The names of all the great (and not so great) members of the artistic and literary world—painters, musicians, writers, and poets—and most of the political, financial, and mercantile nobility are encountered. But it is in his busts from the realm of fantasy—*L'Automne, Le Printemps, La Douleur, La Frileuse, Diane,* etc.—that his virtuosity is fully displayed. Nearly a dozen busts were cast in bronze after his death by the founder Pinedo, at the request of his widow.

At the Salon of 1857, along with several busts, Carrier-Belleuse exhibited a group entitled *L'Amour et l'Amitié*, then, in 1859, another group entitled *Jupiter et Hébé*, and a statuette entitled *Béranger assis lisant*, all of which had been executed in bronze. In 1861, his plaster work entitled *Salve Regina* added greatly to his fame. Next came *Bacchante*, a statue in marble which created a sensation at the Salon of 1863 (for the Tuileries), then a curious group in bronze and marble with the pretentious title *L'Industrie apportant au monde la lumière, le pain et l'abondance*, commissioned in 1865 by the people of Creusot for presentation to M. Schneider. *Le Messie*, a 2 meter high group in marble designed for the Chapel of the Virgin in the church of Saint-Vincent-de-Paul in Paris, appeared at the Salon of 1867 at the same time as *Entre deux amours*, a marble of which bronze reductions were subsquently cast. Also at the Salon were a centerpiece for the hotel of the Païva (1867), the *Nymphe marine* in bronze (1874), to be placed on top of one of the fountains of the French Theatre Plaza in 1885, and *Diane victorieuse*, a statuette in plaster made in marble in 1887, in bronze in 1888.

Carrier-Belleuse primarily used terra cotta, ordering a large number of busts and especially statuettes to be cast by assistants in his own studio. Oddly enough, a number of these statuettes in multiple repetitions were surrendered for auction in 1874 and in 1883 by the artist himself, and then again after his death, in 1887. Notable sculptures involved in this were *La Confidence*, 60 cm, *Le Baiser d'amour*, 60 cm, *Bacchanale*, 40 cm, *Les Deux Amours*, 40 cm, *Eve et ses enfants*, 75 cm, *La Jeune Mère*, 50 cm, *Psyché et l'Amour*, 50 cm, *Léda*, 50 cm, *La Liseuse*, 75 cm, *La Fileuse*, 70 cm, and *L'Harmonie*, 55 cm.

La Liseuse and *La Fileuse* are among the subjects most often cast in bronze, usually with some elements in ivory. Other works that were frequently cast, often in many sizes, are *Jeune Pêcheur dansant*, *Soldat de la Renaissance* and its counterpart *Hallebardier*, *Danseurs napolitains*, *L'Harmonie*, *Mélodie*, busts including portraits of Michelangelo and Rembrandt, and some statuettes: *Salvator Rosa*, 61 cm, *Michel-Ange*, 65 cm (Denière, founder), and *Apollon à la lyre*, 48 cm.

Many works by Carrier-Belleuse, notes C.B. Metman (*La Petite Sculpture d'édition du XIXe siècle*), were cast around 1855 by the founder E. de Labroue, including *Albert Dürer*, *L'Arioste*, *Dante*, *Le Highlander*, *Rembrandt*, *Le Zouave*.

The Barbedienne catalog mentions *Deux Femmes debout de style Louis XVI* in three dimensions, 200, 98 and 78 cm, as well as the marble *La Victoire*, a woman carrying a torch, mounted on a pillar for a total height of 225 cm. In the Thiébaut house can be found *Le Baiser d'une mère* in two sizes, 48 and 39 cm.

1) *Albert Carrier-Belleuse, Hallebardier, 57 cm.*

2) *Albert Carrier-Belleuse, Soldat de la Renaissance, 47 cm.*

3) *Albert Carrier-Belleuse, La Source, 56 cm.*

4) *Albert Carrier-Belleuse, Diane chasseresse, 80 cm.*

5) *Albert Carrier-Belleuse, Danseur napolitain, 29 cm.*

MUSEUMS
Angoulême
Faune et bacchante, 92 cm (1900).
Chambéry
La Liseuse, gilded bronze, 60 cm.
Laon
Béranger assis, 25 cm.

③ ④ ⑤

Langres
La Liseuse, bronze and ivory, 25.5 cm.
Paris, Orsay
La Bonne Mère, 55 cm.
Hébé et l'aigle de Jupiter, silvered bronze, 51 cm (1858).
Reims
Les Bacchantes, 92 cm.
Troyes
Frédéric Eugène Piat, bust, 70 cm.
A. Thiers, bust, (cast white iron), 28 cm.

SALES
L'Amour et l'Amitié, 85 cm, Gien, December 7, 1986.
Automne, 79 cm, Sotheby London, November 8, 1984.
Deux Bacchantes au tambourin dansant, 89 cm., Christie's London, May 15, 1986.
La Cigale, 81 cm, Sotheby London, march 21, 1985.
Cupidon et Psyché, 44 x 53 cm, Drouot, May 21, 1983.
La Danse, 72 cm, rennes, May 14, 1985.
Danseur napolitain, 29 cm, Avranches, November 2, 1986.
Danseurs napolitains, two statuettes, 51 cm, Sotheby London, March 8, 1984.
Danseur napolitain au luth, 100 cm, Christie's London, September 25, 1986; Sotheby London, November 6, 1986.
Danseur napolitain au tambourin, 104 cm, Christie's London, September 25, 1986.
Danseuse aux violes, 68 cm Sotheby London, June 12, 1986.
Deux Danseuses, Bergerac, July 5, 1986.

Diane chasseresse, 80 cm, L'Aigle, May 31, 1986.
L'Enlèvement, Manosque, March 23, 1986.
Femme à la rose, bust, 61.5 cm, Enghien, December 2, 1984.
La Fileuse debout, bronze and ivory, 36 cm, Troyes, October 20, 1985.
La Fileuse, gilded and silvered bronze and ivory, 45 cm, Lokeren, October 20, 1984.
La Fileuse, gilded and silvered bronze and ivory, 76 cm, Christie's New York, October 16, 1984.
La Fileuse, brass and ivory, 32.5 cm, Brussels, March 1, 1984.
L'Harmonie, 62 cm, Drouot, December 20, 1983.
Léonard de Vinci, bust, 52 cm, Christie's New York, September 27, 1986.
La Liseuse, 61 cm, Orléans, May 19, 1984; Sotheby London, March 20, 1986; Saint-Etienne, September 21, 1986; Troyes, November 23, 1986.
La Liseuse, bronze and ivory, 40 cm, Grenoble, December 3, 1984; Saint-Germain-en-Laye, March 10, 1985; Drouot, April 26, 1985; Drouot, October 25, 1985 room 4; Dijon, December 15, 1985; Sotheby London, March 20, 1986; Morlaix, May 19, 1986.
Mélodie, 73 cm, Lille, September 22, 1986.
La Musique, Bordeaux, October 23, 1986.
Nu aux roseaux, 76 cm, Sotheby New York, September 13, 1986.
Rubens, bust, 52 cm, Christie's New York, September 27, 1986.
Soldat de la Renaissance and *Hallebardier*, two statuettes, 47 cm, Drouot, October 19, 1983, room 9.
La Source, 56 cm, Bayeux, October 6, 1985.

Albert Carrier-Belleuse, Mélodie, 80 cm.

Albert Carrier-Belleuse, L'Enlèvement de Déjanire, 68 cm.

Albert Carrier-Belleuse, Cupidon et Psyché, 44 x 53 cm.

CARRIER-BELLEUSE, LOUIS ROBERT

Paris, July 4, 1848
Paris, June 14, 1913

The son and student of Albert Ernest Carrier-Belleuse, this artist initially studied painting. His first sculptures did not appear at the Salon until 1889. He made some vases in terra cotta and executed models in sandstone, and eventually became the artistic director of the Choisy-le-Roi pottery factory. He completed a number of busts, genre figures, and mythological or allegorical statues. All of his works, full of charm and elegance, show the influence of his father. In addition to projects for several monuments commissioned by some states in Central America, his contributions to the Salon include *La Charmeuse de panthère*, a statuette in marble and bronze (1892), *Le Char des amours*, a group in marble and bronze edited by Goldscheider (1908), and some works entirely in marble (also edited by Goldscheider) such as *Méditation* and *Retour des vandanges* (1914). One proof in bronze of *La Charmeuse de panthère*, 74 cm, was sold at the Drouot Hotel on May 30, 1985, room 5.

CARRIÈS, JEAN JOSEPH MARIE

Lyon, February 15, 1855
Paris, July 1, 1894

Carriès is known primarily as a ceramicist, thanks to the exceptional collection of busts and masks owned by the museum of the Petit Palais in Paris. However, a certain number of his sculptures were cast in bronze, rounding out a remarkable production in which utmost realism is combined with symbolic intentions. After working for two years with an industrial sculptor, Carriès went to Paris in 1873. While he studied at the Petite Ecole, he did not manage to enter the Ecole des Beaux-Arts. His first submissions to the Salon date from 1875, though he did not become famous until the 1880s, the period which saw the execution of the majority of his sculptures. Carriès met the founder Pierre Bingen, known for his castings using the lost wax method, who made some high quality bronzes for him. The patinas are admirable, and many of the editions seem to have been strictly limited. Some may even be unique models.

Beginning in 1888, Carriès devoted himself primarily to ceramics, and soon retired in the Nivernais in Cosne, in Saint-Amand-en-Puisaye, and then in Montriveau. He died in Paris at the home of his friend Georges Hoentschel, who welcomed him when he was sick. Later Hoentschel offered the artist's works to the museum of the Petit Palais.

Among the sculptures by Carriès cast in bronze are the busts *Charle 1er*, plaster (Salon of 1881), *L'Evêque*, plaster (Salon of 1883), *Le Guerrier* (cast in 1881, exhibited at the Société Nationale des

*Jean Carriès,
Le Gentilhomme français
called Le Callot, 34 cm
(P. Bingen, founder).*

*Jean Carriès,
Buste de jeune fille, 68 cm.*

Beaux-Arts in 1895), *Tête de moine, Monsieur de Galhau, Monsieur Villeroy* (1884), *Franz Hals, Femme de Hollande dite Madame Hals, Gambetta* (1885), *Auguste Vacquerie, Loyse Labé* (1887), *Vélasquez* (1889), *Le Mendian russe, L'Epave de théâtre dit le Cabotin, Jules Breton avec un chapeau* (1892), and finally a statuette, *L'Enfant au pantin* (exhibited in bronze at the Nationale des Beaux-Arts in 1895). Pieces lacking a casting date or exhibition date are a statuette entitled *Saint Louis enfant,* some medallions entitled *Mademoiselle Favier* (the granddaughter of Mr. Villeroy), *Le Fils du général Lewal, La Fille du général Lewal,* and *La Soeur du sculpteur,* as well as the busts *Le Cuisinier, La Dame à la colerette* (1887), 60 cm, and *Tête de Satyre*, 35 cm.

MUSEUMS
Lyon
Loyse Labé, bust.
Paris, Decorative Arts
*Enfant tenant un polichine*lle, 69 cm.
Paris, Orsay
Charles 1er, bust, 33 cm (P. Bingen).
L'Evêque, bust, 52 cm (P. Bingen).
Tête de faune, 35 cm (P. Bingen).
Tête de Jules Breton, 50 cm.

Thomas François Cartier,
Lion sur un rocher, 53 x 67 cm,
pedestal in stone.

Jean Carriès,
Tête de faune, 35 cm
(1883; Bingen, single proof),
Musée d'Orsay.

Paris, Petit Palais
Buste de femme, bas-relief, 43 x 35 cm.
Epave de théâtre or le Cabotin, 44 cm.
Tête de faune, 35 cm.

SALES
Le Gentilhomme français dit le Callot, 34 cm (P.
    Bingen), Drouot, December 4, 1986, rooms 5 and
    6.
Tête de faune, 35 cm, Drouot, November 28, 1984,
    rooms 5 and 6 (taking 95,000 F, preempted for the
    museum of the Petit Palais).

CARTIER, THOMAS FRANÇOIS

Marseille, February 21, 1879
1943

THOMAS CARTIER

   Cartier, an animal sculptor who was trained by
the animal sculptor George Gardet, displayed a
predilection for hunting dogs, terriers, and wolves,
but on occasion sculpted big game, including fighting deer and birds of prey. He worked at the Ruche,

1) Thomas François Cartier,
Combat de cerfs.

2) Thomas François Cartier,
Setter à l'arrêt, 41 x 58 cm.

3) Thomas François Cartier,
Chien de chasse tenant un
renard.

②

①

③

195

and exhibited at the Salon des Artists Français at the beginning of the 20th century as well as at the Salon d'Automne. His works include, from 1904, a statuette in bronze entitled *Chat se léchant* and a group of dogs in plaster entitled *La Sieste*, from 1911 *Kroumir, chat persan* in marble, from 1912 *Lionne en furie* in marble, and from 1914 *Tigre parmi les ruines*, a group in marble.

SALES
L'Aigle blessé, 22.5 cm, Drouot, June 27, 1983.
Cerf dix cors, 45.5 cm, Drouot, June 14, 1985, room 14.
Chien-loup, 48 cm, Drouot, October 19, 1983, room 9.
Combat de cerfs, Vienna, December 14, 1986.
Lion debout sur un rocher, 44 cm, Saint-Brieuc, May 13, 1984; Nancy, October 19, 1986.
Lionne, 27 cm, Sotheby London, March 20, 1986.
Lionne rugissant, Drouot, March 26, 1986, room 9.
Louve et louveteaux, 50 cm, Drouot, March 27, 1984, room 8.
Setter à l'arrêt, 41 cm, Calais, March 24, 1985.
Tigre blessé, Drouot, June 3, 1986, room 10.

CARVIN, LOUIS ALBERT

Paris, August 7, 1875
January 6, 1951

L.CARVIN

Carvin was a student of Frémiet and of Gardet. He primarily depicted animals, especially from episodes of La Fontaine's *Fables*, but occassionally composed genre scenes as well. His submissions to the Salon, spanning from 1891 until the 1930s, were mainly executed in marble: *Cochon d'Inde à poil frisé*

(1892), *Le Rat et l'huître* (1893), *Le Rat et l'oeuf*, (1894), *Le Chat et le vieux rat* (1896), *Défense de la famille* (1899), *Lassitude* (1905), and *Panthère à l'affût* (1908). Some works were submitted in plaster as well, including *Les Singes et le léopard* (1895), *Ecureuil et serpent* (1898), *Affamés, chat et oiseau* (1901), and *Pigeons voyageurs belges* (1908). His contributions in wax include *Caresse matinale bengalis*, 4.4 in. (1902), edited in bronze by Susse, and his bronzes include *Chien setter* (1907), *Lionne mourant*, and paperweights decorated with swallows entitled *Amour de printemps* (1914), etc.

SALES
L'Accolade, 42 x 60 cm, Drouot, April 3, 1985.
Lévrier, 60 cm long, Versailles, June 16, 1984.
Lévrier debout, 31 x 60 cm, Lokeren, February 16, 1985.
Lévrier Saluki persan, Brussels, October 15, 1984.

CAUDRON, THÉOPHILE

Combles (Somme), March 21, 1805
Paris, February 18, 1848

Historical bas-reliefs related to the lives of Childebert and Louis XIV, a colossal statue of Saint Sébastien for the church of his birthplace, various works for the cathedral of Amiens and for the obelisk of Arles, and some statues of contemporaries constitute the work of this sculptor, who exhibited at the Salon starting in 1831.

MUSEUMS
Amiens
Archimède, géomètre syracusain, 115 cm (Barbedienne), according to the plaster of 1836.
Les Arènes d'Arles, bas-relief, 151 x 153 cm (commissioned by the city of Amiens to Barbedienne in 1877).

Louis Albert Carvin,
L'Accolade, 42 x 60 cm.

CAUNOIS, AUGUSTIN

Bar-sur-Ornain (Meuse), June 13, 1787
Paris 1859

Caunois won the second prize for medallion engraving in 1813, and between 1819 and 1849 exhibited at the Salon with busts, medallions, bas-reliefs in plaster, and statues, including the plaster *Jeune Spartiate*, 103 cm, in 1819. He is also the author of statues in stone, including *Charles Le Brun* for the city hall and *Sainte Marguerite* for the church of Madeleine. The museum of Troyes owns a medal (5.5 cm in diameter) commemorating March 16, 1830, and three medals in bronze: *Perrot-Prailly*, 18 cm diam., *Perrot, ancien colonel de la garde nationale de Troyes*, 18 cm diam., both cast by Quesnel, and *Profil d'homme*, 19.5 cm diam.

CAUNOIS, CHARLES JOSEPH

Troyes 1815
1878

From 1848 to 1850 Charles Joseph Caunois exhibited medallions in plaster and portraits of dramatic actors and others at the Salon. The museum of Troyes has four medallions in bronze: *E. Régnier*, 17.2 cm diam., *Geneviève Gégnier*, 18 cm diam., *L. J. M. Richard*, 13.5 cm diam., *Tête d'homme*, 21 cm diam., and a plaque entitled *La Duchesse de Berry*, 29 x 22 cm.

*Julien Caussé,
Perrette et le pot au lait,
regule, 44 cm.*

CAUSSÉ, JULIEN

Bourges, January 28, 1869-?

Julien Caussé was among the students of Falguière and started to exhibit at the Salon in 1888. Among his commisions are various statuettes: *Hébé* and *L'Histoire* (plasters, 1895), *Monsieur F., peintre* (bronze, 1897), *Rêverie* (marble, 1900), *Torrent*, (plaster, 1908), *Source* (plaster, 1910), as well as some statues of larger dimensions: *Euterpe* (plaster, 1892), *Exilée* (marble) and *Soldat blessé* (plaster, 1894), *Martyr* (plaster, 1896), *Eve* (stone 1903), *Nymphéa* (stone, 1910), and finally, two busts in marble: *Chrysanthème* (1911) and *Petite Maman* (1912). Many of his sculptures, principally of feminine subjects, were cast in bronze, and sometimes also in régule, as was *La Fée des glaces* (posed on a glass pedestal; the model in bronze was cast by Blot around 1900). Another bronze statuette, *Femme à demi-drapée*, had a decidedly Art Nouveau spirit, as did most of Caussé's works.

SALES
Femme à la grande cape, 19 cm., Rouen, March 18, 1984.
Jeune Femme aucroissant de lune, 75 cm, Reims, March 24, 1985.
Perrette et le post au lait, régule, 44 cm, Drouot, October 19, 1983.

CAVAILLON, ELISÉE

Nimes, March 8, 1873
Paris, May 5, 1954

Cavaillon exhibited at the beginning of the 20th century at the Salon de la Société Nationale des Beaux-Arts, submitting a number of bronzes, including the statuettes *Un besogneux* (1902), *Lessiveuse* (1904), *Etude de nu* (1905), *Chemineau* (1906), *Femme au bas* and *Femme à la bottine* (1907), *Femme courbée* (1910); the bas-reliefs *Femme au panier, Femme aulacet, Chiffonier* (1903), *Marchande de fleurs* (1904), and *Amoureux* (1906); and the bronze statues *Joueur de biles* (1908), *Baigneuse* (1909), and *Enfant aux billes* (1914). He also exhibited at the Salon d'Automne and at the Salon des Tuileries. One of his bronzes, *Rembrandt*, 58 cm, was cast by the founder Eugène Blot.

MUSEUMS
Amiens
Marché des halles, bas-relief, 48 x 40 cm (given in 1905).
Châteauroux
Un besogneux, 36 cm (1903).
Nimes
Au repos.
Périgueux
Un travailleur, 42 cm.

CAVELIER, PIERRE JULES

Paris, August 30, 1814
Paris, January 28, 1894

Entering the Ecole des Beaux-Arts in 1831, Cavalier worked with David d'Angers and in 1842 obtained the grand prize for sculpture with his group *Diomède enlevant le Palladium*. Upon returning to Paris after a five year stay in Rome, he received commissions from the Louvre (many pediments), the city hall, the Opera, the Palais Galliéra, the churches of Notre Dame, Saint-Augustin, and the Trinity, the Tour Saint-Jacques (a marble statue of Blaise Pascal), the Gare du Nord (a statue of the city of Paris), the old Trocadero, and finally, his principal accomplishment, the Palais de Longchamp in Marseille.

As a teacher at the Ecole des Beaux-Arts, Cavalier trained a number of students, including Barrias. He was elected to be a member of the Institut in 1865. His work, largely inspired by mythology and old stories, includes some busts and medallions.

At the Salon of 1840, he exhibited *Jeune Grec remportant aux jeux olympiques le prix de la course à pied*, a statue in bronze cast by Richard, Eck and Durand, and in 1842, a statue in plaster, *Femme grecque edormie*, which reappeared in marble under the name of *Pénélope* at the Salon of 1849 and which was the object of reductions (including one in silver which appeared at the Exposition Universelle of 1900). He also executed some models of pieces for a centerpiece for the Duke of Orléans, which was executed in gilded bronze by Denière. At the Exposition Universelle of 1855, he presented two bronzes: a study of a head entitled *La Tragédie,* and *Buste de Dante*; at the Salon of 1869 he exhibited a statue, also in bronze, entitled *François 1er.*

The statuette of *Pénélope* was listed in the Barbedienne catalog in the following dimensions: 95, 62, 36, 31 and 25 cm. He also executed two other statuettes in bronze, both nearly fifty centemeters in height, representing *Paul et Virginie.*

CAZAUBON, PIERRE NOËL

Born in Paris

The Museum of Pau has preserved a bust in bronze, *Jeune Fille*, 50 cm, unusual because this artist sculpted primarily in wood. Another bronze cast by Valsuani, *Jeune Femme nue au chignon*, 107 cm, was sold in Clermont-Ferrand on November 19 1986, and *L'Eurasienne*, 107 cm (A. Valsuani), was sold on February 1, 1987 in Granville; both pieces stemmed from the same subject.

CAZIN, MARIE

Paimboeuf (Loire-Atlantique), 1844
Equihen (Pas-de-Calais), 1924

This painter and sculptor was the wife and student of Jean-Charles Cazin, himself a painter, engraver, and (most notably) a very reputable ceramicist. Beginning in 1876, Marie exhibited some landscapes, as well as statues and busts, at the Salon. She also participated at the expositions of the Royal Academy of London and at the Salon de la Société Nationale des Beaux-Arts. Of particular note among the bronzes she sent to the Artistes Français are a mask entitled *Tristesse* (1882), two busts entitled *David* and *La Fortune* (1883), a statue entitled *Le Regret* (1885), and a group entitled *Jeunes Filles* (1886). Of further note at the Nationale des Beaux-Arts in 1899 are some bas-reliefs in bronze designed for different commemorative monuments, including *Boeuf du Nivernais*, in bronze (1893), and the group *Jeunes Filles*, also in bronze. Marie Cazin sent another bronze, the group entitled *Jeunes Garçons*, to the Exposition Universelle of 1889, and two bronze bas-reliefs, *Saint Marc* and *Saint Jean*, to the Exposition of 1900.

MUSEUMS
Paris, Orsay
Buste de David, 37 cm.
Saint-Quentin
Jeune Fille, 73 cm.

*Pierre Cazaubon,
Jeune Femme nue
au chignon,
107 cm
(A. Valsuani).*

CHALON, LOUIS

Paris, January 15, 1866-?

A painter, a book illustrator, and a sculptor, Louis Chalon exhibited at the Salon between 1898 and 1911, showing busts and subjects from antiquity and mythology (Agamemnon, Mort de Sardanapale, Orphée), as well as Wagnerian characters. His work includes *Tannhauser au Venusberg*, a group in plaster (Salon of 1899), *Le Repos*, a paperweight in bronze, and *La Lyre*, a statuette in plaster (1907), *Au soleil*, a statuette in plaster (1908), and *Femme au bas*, a statuette in bronze (1911). His work also includes some vases, flat candlesticks, and flower urns, ornamented with the sort of female figures (*Les Filles des vagues, La Fée des glaces*) that were so appealing in Art Nouveau. Some of them also bear the signature of the chisel-worker Louchet. Of note among the small groups and statuettes in bronze are *Tannhauser au Venusberg*, 65 cm, some models of *La Walkyrie* in different sizes (sometimes with a bronze patina, sometimes in gilded bronze), *La Loie Fuller*, 22 cm, and *Femme papillon*, 62 cm.

SALES

Femme jouant de la harpe, 103 cm, Christie's New York, September 27, 1986.
Femme libellule, gilded bronze, enamel and ceramic, 47 cm, Drouot, December 13, 1986, rooms 1 and 7 (fetching 71,000 F).
La Walkyrie, 73 cm, Sotheby London, March 21, 1985.
La Walkyrie, bronze polychrome, 94 cm, Christie's New York, May 24, 1984.

CHAMBARD, LOUIS LÉOPALD

Saint-Amour (Jura), August 25, 1811
Neuilly-sur-Seine, March 10, 1895

A student of David d'Angers, Chambard won the first grand prize for sculpture in 1837 with a work on the theme *Marius sur les ruines de Carthage*, and went to Rome. From Rome he shipped his first submissions to the Salon in 1841. Returning to Paris, he completed two fonts in marble for the chapel of the Luxembourg Palace and two statues and a bas-relief for the chapel of Dreux. He worked also for the city hall, the churches of Saint-Augustin and Notre-Dame-de-la-Croix of Ménilmontant, the Louvre, etc. His abundant production includes some allegorical, mythological, and religious statues of a large size, as well as some busts of friends and contemporary personages. Among the reductions presented at the Salon are La Par*ure*, a small marble (1850), *Une suppliante*, a statuette in bronze (1852), *Enfant portant une coquille*, marble, 100 cm high (1863), and *Follette*, terra cotta (1882). A 104 cm high bronze entitled *Le Bûcheron* was sold in London by Sotheby on June 7, 1984.

CHAPLAIN, JULES CLÉMENT

Mortagne, July 12, 1839
Paris, July 13, 1909

Winner of the prize of Rome in 1863, Chaplain worked simultaneously as a sculptor and as a medal- and print-engraver. His sculpted work dates primarily from the end of his life. It consists mostly of statues, busts and medallions—usually portraits—often designed as funerary monuments. He was made a member of the Institute in 1881.

MUSEUMS
Angers
Gustave Larroumet, plaque, 7 cm.
Bordeaux
Portrait de Léon Bonnat, medallion, 9.8 cm diam.
Scène de famille, medallion, 60 cm diam.
Zeus et Prométhée, medallion, 8.3 cm diam.
   The museum has a number of other small medallions and medals, portraits and allegories.
Paris, Carnavalet
Marie Henriette Pauline Bucquet, medallion, 22.5 diam.
Troyes
Portrait du docteur Millard, medallion, 22.5 cm diam. (1893).

CHAPU, HENRI MICHEL

Le Mée (Seine-et-Marne), September 29, 1833
Paris, April 21, 1891

Chapu was one of the official court sculptors of the Third Republic. Son of a coachman who became a concierge in Paris, he began to study at the Petite Ecole; then, starting in 1849, he studied at the Ecole des Beaux-Arts, where he was taught by Pradier and Duret. He successfully carried off the second grand prize for medal-engraving in 1851, and the second grand prize for sculpture in 1855. He then went to Rome, where he remained until 1861. His abundant production, often inspired by antiquity, won him a number of honors and distinctions. He was elected to be a member of the Institut in 1880. His *Jeanne d'Arc à Domrémy*, the marble of which was exhibited at the Salon in 1872, gained him recognition with the public and considerable success. Many replicas were made in plaster, marble, and bronze. Another successful marble was La Jeuness*e* (Salon of 1875), sculpted for the monument of Henri Regnault erected in the courtyard of the Ecole des Beaux-arts.

The works of Chapu appear in a number of museums as well as on some monuments in Paris, including the city hall, the Sorbonne, the Palais de Justice, the Opera, the Gare du Nord, many churches, the Printemps department stores, and in some parks. Some of them, in particular *Jeanne D'Arc*, were cast in bronze in smaller sizes. He also made some small groups and statuettes, notably of dancers, as well as some busts and medallion portraits of contemporaries—painters, engravers, sculptors, architects, etc. His work also includes a statuette executed in 1885 in silver entitled *Victoire*, which won the grand prize of Paris, and a table centerpiece commissioned by the princess Amélie de Bragance.

Henri Chapu,
Jeanne d'Arc, 70 cm
(F. Barbedienne, Collas reduction).

Félicien David, sketch for his monument, 30 cm.
Femme pleurant sur une stalle ornée d'un médaillon, sketch for a funerary monument, 34 cm.
Héro et Léandre, two sketches, 52 cm.
La Jeunesse, sketch for the monument to Henri Regnault, 53 cm (Barbedienne).
La Semeuse, 43 cm.
   Four portraits in medallion including two of the painter Léon Bonnat, 21.5 and 11.5 cm diam.
Bordeaux
Baron de Carayon La Tour, bust, 88 cm.
Châlons-sur-Marne
Jeanne d'Arc à Domrémy, 117 cm (1872, Barbedienne).
Le Mée
   The museum of Chapu's hometown owns an ensemble of his works.
Marseille
Ten medallion portraits
Moret-sur-Loing
La Jeunesse, 60 cm.
Paris, Decorative Arts
Ferdinand Barbedienne, bust, 15.5 cm (Barbedienne).
Paris, Carnavalet
Sadi Carnot, bust, 81 cm.
Paris, Orsay
Léon Bonnat, bust.
   A number of medallion portraits including Léon Bonnat, Mme Chapu, Sully Prud'homme, Auguste Vacquerie, the founder Victor Thiébaut, the architect Vaudremer, etc.
Valenciennes
Portraits en médaillon d'Emile Trélat, 19 cm diam, of *Emile Vaudremer*, 18 cm, of the architect E. Guillaume, 29.5 cm diam. (Rome, 1861).

SALES
Jeanne d'Arc, 70 cm (Barbedienne), Cologne, October 26, 1984; Sotheby London, November 6, 1986.
Jeunesse, femme drapée cueillant une fleur, Drouot, March 26, 1986, room 9.
La Renommée, 135 cm, Copenhagen, November 12, 1984.

Edited by the Barbedienne house
Jeanne d'Arc à Domrémy, 117, 72, 60, 47, 36, 30, 23 cm.
La Jeunesse, 118, 95, 60 cm.
Jeune Fille à la branche de laurier, high relief, 60 cm.
Marie, 60 cm.
La Science, bas-relief.

The Thiebaut house
   Among others, three bas-reliefs: *L'Aurore*, *La Pensée*, and *La Vérité*, these last two in many sizes, from 125 to 20 cm high.

   Other works edited in bronze and appearing at sales include *Chasseur poignardant un ours*, *Danseuse au tambourin*, 34 cm, and *Flore accroupie*, a statuette in gilded bronze, etc.

MUSEUMS
Angers
Charles Questel, medallion, 22 cm diam.
Bayonne
Danseuses, two sketches, 33 and 42 cm.
Danseuses, two sketches, 45 cm (Barbedienne).
Dédale et Icare, sketch, 45 cm (Barbedienne).

CHARDIGNY, PIERRE JOSEPH

Aix-en-Provence, February 20, 1794
Paris 1866

   A sculptor and a medal-engraver, Chardigny studied first with his father, and then, starting in 1814, with Bosio and Cartelier at the Ecole des Beaux-Arts. He made his debut at the Salon in 1819. He lived in London and exhibited at the Royal Academy in 1842 and 1843. He executed a statue in bronze of Ferdinand VII of Spain in Barcelona.

MUSEUMS
Compiègne, château
Buste de l'impératrice Eugénie, 12.5 cm (1855)
Buste de Napoléon III, 13 cm (1855).
Périgueux
Buste de Dante, 13 cm.
Troyes
Buste de P.J. de Béranger, 12.5 cm.
Buste de Louis Ulbach, 63 cm.

Charon, Alfred

Poitiers, July 8, 1863
Ville-d'Avray, September 21, 1955

Son of the sculptor Amédée Charon and a student of Cavelier, Barrias, and Coutan, Alfred Charon began to exhibit at the Salon in 1883, showing some plasters and bronzes including *Jeune Equilibriste*, bronze (1886), *L'Amour moderne*, a statuette in bronze (1891), *Chérubin*, a statuette in bronze and onyx (1898), as well as some medallions in bronze.

Charpentier, Alexandre

Paris, January 10, 1856
Neuilly-sur-Seine, March 3, 1909

Alexandre Charpentier started exhibiting at the Salon in 1879, but in 1890 left the Société des Artistes Français to join the newly-forming Société National des Beaux-Arts. He left a host of medal-

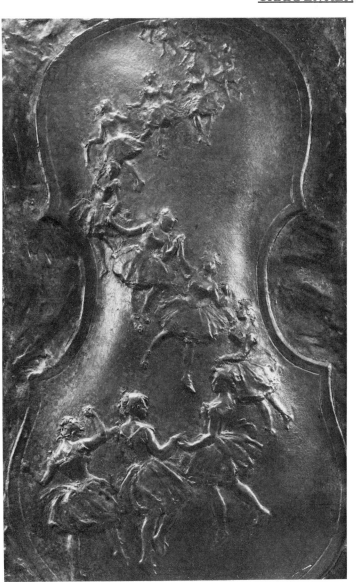

Alexandre Charpentier,
Fantaisie sur le dos d'un violon,
bas-relief, 37 x 21 cm

Alexandre Charpentier,
Jeune Mère allaitant son enfant,
bas-relief, 16 x 24 cm.
J. Ginepro Collection, Monaco.

lions, plaques, bas-reliefs, statuettes, and groups in bronze, pewter, terra cotta, and glazed earth. His work featured themes from everyday life, mothers with children, the dance, and some portraits of artists, writers, and actors. He was also interested in the decorative arts, producing furnishings, candlesticks, coffee services, locks, door handles, etc. He sought to free himself from traditional concepts, and some of his works clearly evoke the Art Nouveau spirit. Among his more typical submissions to the Salon de la Société National des Beaux-Arts were *Femme montant dans sa baignoire*, bas-relief in plaster, *Nourrice* and *Femme au parapluie*, figurines in terra cotta (1891), *La Sonate*, bas-relief in bronze, *Fantaisie sur le dos d'un violon*, a plaque in bronze (1892), *Les Boulangers*, a monumental haut-relief rendered in sandstone by Emile Muller (1897, today located at the Scipioin square in Paris), *La Fuite de l'heure*, a small group in gilded bronze (1899), furnishing for a string quartet decorated with four bas-reliefs in gilded bronze (1901, Museum of Decorative Arts), *Cérès*, a statuette in bronze, and *Etude de nu pour une figure drapée*, bronze (1907).

MUSEUMS
Paris, Decorative Arts
Sodome and *Gomorrhe*, two bas-reliefs, 36 x 28 cm.
Paris, Orsay
Gomorrhe, bas-relief in galvanized bronze, 34 x 27 cm. (1892).

SALES
Fantaisie sur le dos d'un violon, plaque, 37 x 21 cm, Drouot, March 8, 1982.
Mère allaitant, 24.5 cm, Drouot, March 16, 1983, room 9.
Femme nue au laurier, 49 cm, Sotheby Monaco, April 13, 1986.

CHARPENTIER, FÉLIX MAURICE

Bollène, January 10, 1858
Paris, December 7, 1924

The author of a group in stone entitled *L'Art contemporain* decorating the facade of the Grand Palais, and of two bas-reliefs entitled *La Navigation* and *Le Vapeur* for the facade of the Lyon train station in Paris, Félix Charpentier began in 1882 to exhibit a certain number of allegories at the Salon. The best-known of these, a statue in plaster entitled *L'Improvisateur* (1887), was reproduced many times in bronze. Other statues and groups include *Le Repos*, plaster (Salon of 1882), *Jeune Faune*, bronze (1887), *La Chanson*, marble (1890), *Les Lutteurs*, marble, and *Les Hirondelles*, plaster (1893), *Les Adieux d'une hirondelle*, bronze (1894), *Etoile filante*, marble (1897), *Volupté*, marble (901), *Enfant*, statuette in plaster (1903), two stauettes in marble polychrome, *Jeanne d'Arc* (1905) and *Coup de vent* (1907), and another statuette in marble, *Source* (1912), etc.

Some works by Félix Charpentier were cast in bronze by Colin and Cie, such as *L'Improvisateur*, *Etoile filante*, and *La Jeunesse*. Of further note are *Le Chasseur d'oiseaux*, *Les Hirondelles*, *Jeanne d'Arc*, 28 cm, and *Bacchante sur les flots*, 94 cm.

MUSEUMS
Avignon
Autoportrait de profil, medallion, 6 cm diam.
Le Puy
Vieux Berger, 41 cm.
Paris, Decorative Arts
L'Improvisateur, (E. Colin, founder), based on the plaster of 1887.
Paris, Carnavalet
Femme nue accroupie tenant un serpent, 39 cm.

*Félix Charpentier,
Muse.*

*Félix Charpentier,
L'Emprovisateur,
78 cm.*

*Félix Charpentier,
Brise.*

Paris, Orsay
Jean Henri Fabre, statuette, 41 cm.
L'Improvisateur, 190 cm (Siot and Persinka, founders).

SALES
Brise, Douarnenez, April 28, 1982.
Femme au bain, vase, 61 cm (E. Colin, founder),
 Fontainebleau, November 24, 1985.
L'Improvisateur, 60 cm, Drouot, June 19, 1985, room
 9; Drouot, October 25, 1985, room 5.
Muse, Bordeaux, October 28, 1982.
Nu debout, 72 cm, Sotheby London, March 8, 1984.

CHATROUSSE, ÉMILE FRANÇOIS
Paris, March 6, 1829
Paris, November 12, 1896

Apprenticed to a jewelry engraver at the age of eleven, and later enrolling as a student of the painter Abel of Pujol, Chatrousse was attracted to sculpture at a very young age. He exhibited for the first time at the Salon of 1848, and entered Rude's studio three years later, to become Rude's last student. He is the author of a number of busts and medallions, and received many commissions for the Louvre, the Tuileries, the city hall, the churches of Saint-Eustache, Saint-Leu, and the Trinity, etc. He also became an art critic and published some commentaries about the Salon of 1861 and on the statuary at the Universal Exposition of London in 1862. After his death, many of his works were cast in bronze in small sizes, but their rarity on the market suggests that they were cast as limited editions.

This artist's principal works at the Salon and at the universal expositions include *Hortense Eugénie, reine de Hollande et son troisième fils, futur Napoléon III*, marble, 85 cm high, commissioned by the Emperor for the Museum of Versailles (Exposition 1855), *La Résignation*, marble, 100 cm, for the Saint-Eustache church (Salon of 1859), *Héloïse et Abélard*, marble (Salon of 1859), *Petite Vendangeuse*, marble, 96 cm, (1863), *La Muse grave, La Muse comique*, two statuettes in terra cotta (1868), *La Source et le ruisseau*, a group in marble, 140 cm, for the Luxembourg gardens (1869), *Une jeune Parisienne*, a statue in marble also made for the Luxembourg garens (1877), *La Lecture*, marble (1877), *Jeanne d'Arc*, bronze, erected on the Saint-Marcel Boulevard in Paris (1887), *Madame Roland*, bronze, 110 cm (1882), and *Source endormie*, a statue in plaster (1897).

Chatrousse is also the author of a statue in stone entitled *L'Histoire*, placed in 1899 in Adolphe-Chérioux Square in Paris, and an allegory entitled *Le Drame*, executed for the theater of Châtelet, and for which a 50 cm reduction in bronze was made. Other known bronzes are *L'Histoire*, 60 cm, edited by Thiébaut, and *La Source*, 92 cm, by Nymphe et Amour.

MUSEUMS
Paris, Carnavalet
Alfred de Liesville, bust, 65 cm (Thiébaut).
Reims
La Lecture, 58 cm.

SALES
Femme et enfants nus, 61 cm, Sotheby London, March
 8, 1984.
La Lecture, 65 cm, Drouot, November 26, 1985, room
 8.

Emile François Chatrousse,
La Lecture,
65 cm.

CHAUVET, LOUIS FLORENTIN
Béziers, March 4, 1878
Paris, May 3, 1958

This sculptor and painter started exhibiting at the Salon in 1902, most notably showing busts and statuettes, often in bronze. He is well-known for a 1908 series of figurines in bronze including *Cruche cassée, Deux Têtes de faunes, Rieuse, Abruti*, and *Epave*; in 1911, he executed a statuette in marble entitled *L'Eveil*; the following year, two statuettes in gilded bronze entitled *Méditation* and *Diane*; and in 1913, another statuette in gilded bronze entitled *Portrait de Madame H.* After the war, Chauvet also belonged to the Société Nationale des Beaux-Arts. A statuette in gilded bronze, *Femme nue sur un rocher*, 43 cm, was sold at the Drouot Hotel on December 2, 1983.

CHAVALLIAUD, LÉON
Reims, 1858
1921

For the most part, this artist modeled busts of people from his hometown. The museum of Reims owns the following busts in bronze:

Adolphe Hubinet, 69 cm (1895, Thiébaut).
Camille Lenoir, député de la Marne, 66.3 cm (1915).
Le Chef d'orchestre E. Lefebvre-Dérodé, sketch, 28.5 cm (1913).
Le Docteur H. Henrot, 75 cm.
Henri Vasnier, 45 cm (1886; Bingen).
Jean-Baptiste Pérot, bas-relief, 90 cm (1909).
Jean-Pierre Lundy aîné, 58 cm (1888; Bingen).
Victor Diancourt, 47.5 cm (1897; Bingen).
Victor Portevin, 46 cm (1887).

CHEMELLIER, GEORGES PETIT DE
Born in Angers
Died in 1908

Chemellier began participating at the Salon in 1882, with *Get up!*, a plaster statue portraying a clown with a poodle (1882); this work evolved into a bronze statuette exhibited the following year entitled *L'Arrivée*. Chemellier also exhibited a statuette in silver for a prize at Longchamp (1884), a silver statuette for a steeple-chase in Auteuil entitled *Heur et malheur* (1885), and *Avant le bain*, a group in bronze (1886), etc.

SALES
Get up!, 38.5 cm, Drouot, October 5, 1984, room 2.
Get up!, 60 cm, Drouot, March 11, 1983; Christie's London, May 15, 1986.

CHEMIN, VICTOR
Pairs, August 25, 1825
Neuilly-sur-Seine, 1901

V. CHEMIN

A student of animal sculpture under Barye, Chemin regularly exhibited at the Salon between 1857 and 1894; his contributions included a number of animals, often domestic ones, predominantly dogs, foxes, and monkeys. His works were presented in wax, plaster, terra cotta and bronze. Among the bronzes are *Chiens terriers aux prises* (1857), *Chevreuil* (1859), *Tom, chien terrier* (1861), *Tacks, chien basset de race hongroise* (1863), *Lièvre blessé* (1868), *Le Singe cuisinier* (1879), *Chasse au renard* (1880), *Le Loup et la cigogne, La Dispute* (1881), *Le Cerf aux abois* (1882), *Chasse au cerf* (1887), *Daim au repos* (1888), *Chien* (1891), *Taureau au combat* (1892), and *Verrat aux champs* (1894).

Among the bronzes that have appeared on the market at various times are *Cheval sellé*, 12.5 cm, *Chien à l'arrêt*, 20 cm long, *Deux Chiens et un loup*, 23 cm, *Grand Chien*, 120 cm, *Héron et renard*, 23 cm, and *Le Singe musicien*, 32 cm.

SALES
Cheval et son jockey, 27 cm, Sotheby London, November 7, 1985.
Le Chien, 8.5 x 17.5 cm, Drouot, March 20, 1985, room 4.
Chien à l'affût, 9 cm, Valenciennes, May 26, 1986.
Deux Chiens de chasse attachés, 45 cm, Verrières-le-Buisson, June 2, 1985.
Le Héron et le chien, 39 cm, Drouot, June 19, 1985, room 9.
Levrette, 21 cm, Drouot, March 27, 1984, room 8; Pont-Audemer, April 20, 1986.
Le Saut d'obstacle, 24 cm, Enghien, October 10, 1982.
Vache au champ, 22 cm long, Drouot, November 7, 1985, room 1.

Georges de Chemillier,
Get up!,
60 cm.

CHENILLON, JEAN LOUIS
Auteuil, November 15, 1810
Paris, October 30, 1875

Chenillon spent part of his youth in the Sarthe at the Lude Castle, at the home of his guardian, the Marquis of Talhouët. His studied at Paris's Ecole des Beaux-Arts with David d'Angers. His work includes

Victor Chemin,
Deux Chiens de chasse attachés,
45 cm.

after the death of Carrier-Belleuse, Chéret took the older artist's place as director of works of art at the Sèvres factory. Henceforth his work was composed primarily of small sculptures, groups, and statuettes, as well as vases, jugs, plates, and candlesticks. These pieces were ornamented with people, scenes, and various motifs including children, frogs, masks, garlands, butterflies, etc. He also is responsible for some decorations, fountains, and monumental mantlepieces executed for individual hotels.

After his death, Chéret's works were exhibited at the Ecole des Beaux-Arts, then dispersed at the Drouot Hotel on December 26 to 29, 1894. This sale included numerous terra cottas from 15 to 70 cm high, such as *La Petite Charmeuse* (plaster from the Salon of 1881), *Le Coup de vent, Le Sommeil* (marble at the Salon of 1888), *La Voyageuse, La Corbeille, La Marchande, Bacchus, Le Petit Déjeuner,* and *Enfant aux masques,* as well as numerous bronzes, primarily vases and furniture. Among the vases are:

Femmes poursuivies par des papillons, 62 cm.
Enfants et masques, 62 cm.
Les Surprises de l'Amour, 43 cm.
Enfant jouant au cerceau, 35 cm.
La pêche est ouverte, 78 cm.
Le Vernissage, 37 cm.
Guirlandes et masques, 34 cm.
Les Enfants et les grenouilles, 38 cm.

The sale also included some bronze candlesticks including *L'Espiègle*, 16 cm, and *Bonsoir*, 22 cm, and some large electric sconces decorated with seven children carrying flowers, 180 cm, and their reductions of 115 cm high. Some other sconces also appeared at his sale: *Les Fuchsias*, 70 cm, *Les Libellules*, 55 cm, *La Danseuse Empire*, 85 cm, and *Le Porteur de bijoux*, 75 cm. Among other items appearing were a plant stand decorated with four children carrying baskets, 25 cm, part of a centerpiece composed of six children carrying baskets, 35 cm, and two groups entitled *La Voyageuse*, 50 cm, and *La Peinture*, 32 cm. Only two groups in bronze, *Le Jour* and *La Nuit*, appeared at the Salon in 1883.

A vase decorated with young women and children, 57 cm, was put up for sale in London by Sotheby, November 8, 1984.

a number of busts of political figures from the July Monarchy. He collaborated with Viollet-le-Duc in the restoration of Notre-Dame in Paris, and also worked on the Hôtel de Ville, the Sainte-Clotilde church, the Tour Saint-Jacques, and for the cathedrals of Mans and Moulins. He exhibited at the Salon, starting in 1835 with a bust in bronze entitled *Monseigeur Bouvier, évêque du Mans* (1848). Chenillon's later contributions included a bronze portrait statuette of his father, Pierre Chenillon (1850), *Le Pêcheur de Villerville* (1872), *Brasseur alsacien* (1874), and finally *Jeune Berger soignant son chien blessé*, a bronze of 110 cm height now owned by the museum of Chartres. This last work was cast by Thiébaut (34 x 48 cm).

CHÉRET, GUSTAVE JOSEPH

Paris, September 12, 1838
Paris, June 13, 1894

Less well-known than his older brother (the famous decorator and painter Jules Chéret), Gustave Chéret first studied sculpture in the home of an ornamentalist, and then with Albert Ernest Carrier-Belleuse, whose daughter he married. He particpated at the Salon in 1863 and 1865, but did not exhibit there again until 1875; he gave it up entirely in 1891. From then on, he exhibited in the art object section of the Société Nationale des Beaux-Arts. In 1887,

CHEVRÉ, PAUL ROMAIN

Brussels, July 5, 1867
February 20, 1914

Born of French parents in Belgium, Chevré studied with Cavelier and Barrias, and participated at the Salon from 1891 to 1913. He is the author of a bronze statue portraying Samuel Champlain designed for the city of Quebec. His most appreciated work seems to have been the *Combat de coqs*, which he presented in plaster to the Salon of 1891, in bronze in 1893, and in marble in 1903. A reduction in bronze of this piece, 75 cm, was sold in Oklahoma in 1981.

CHOPPIN, PAUL FRANÇOIS

Paris, February 26, 1856
June 13, 1937

Among the bronzes exhibited at the Salon by this student of Jouffroy and Falguière were a certain number of busts and statues, including *Seize Ans* (1891) and *Laveuse* (1897), as well as some statuettes: *Suzanne surprise au bain* (1886), *Un volontaire de 1792* (1889), and *Le Commandant Marchand* (1899). Among his works in other materials are statuettes in plaster entitled *La France militaire* (1902) and *Amour lutinant un crabe* (1904), statuettes in terra cotta entitled *Amour porte fleur* (1895), *Châtelaine sous Henri II* (1903), and *Joyeux Bambin* (1913); he also contributed some busts in terra cotta entitled *Cupidon* (1900), *Chérubin* (1902), *Ondine* (1903), *Bacchus enfant* (1906), *Druidesse* (1907), and *Innocence* (1914).

A statuette entitled *Un volontaire de 1792*, a reduction of the statue designed for Parmentier Square in Paris, was also known by the name of *Vainqueur de la Bastille*, or *L'Appel aux armes*. One proof, 54.5 cm high, belongs to the museum of Reims.

CHOREL, JEAN-LOUIS

Lyon, January 28, 1875
After 1946

Chorel studied at the school of fine arts in Lyon, and then in Paris. Beginning in 1903 he exhibited at the Salon, contributing most notably a number of bronzes: *Le Docteur Ollier*, a small group made in collaboration with the Dijonaise doctor Destot (1905), *Le Maître d'armes*, a statuette (1907), *Le Sablonnier*, a statuette (1912), etc. A bronze entitled *Centaure*, 23 x 23 cm was sold at the Drouot Hotel on October 18, 1985, room 3.

CHRÉTIEN, EUGÈNE ERNEST

Elbeuf, June 14, 1840
Paris, 1909

Chrétien studied at the school of fine arts in Marseille, and then in Paris. A group entitled *Un suivant de Bacchus* marks his debut at the Salon of 1868. He exhibited there regularly until his death, contributing allegories, scenes of everyday life, and busts, particularly *Guerrier forgeant son épée*, a statue in bronze of 225 cm, designed for the Cours-la-Reine in Paris (1883). A reduction of this piece in bronze appeared at the Salon of 1890. Other pieces exhibited at the Salon include *Gaulois au siège d'Alésia*, a statue in plaster (1883), *La Jeunesse et l'Amour*, a group in marble (1891), *Petite Liseuse*, a statuette in terra cotta (1894), *Jeune Bacchante*, a reduction in bronze of a statue (1894), *La Cigale et la fourmi*, a group in plaster (1898), and finally, a series of statuettes in plaster: *Arion* (1899), cast in bronze, *Diane* (1902), *Faneuse des fleurs* (1904), *Echo* (1907), *Le Matin* or *Le Chant du coq* (1908), *La Liseuse* (1909). Other notable bronzes include *Le Voile* or *Annabelle*, 90 cm, *Guerrier forgeant son épée*, 70 cm, and *Le Printemps*, 85 cm, cast by Thiébaut.

MUSEUMS
Amiens
Un suivant de Bacchus, 168 cm (1869).

SALES
Arion, jeune violoniste, 37 cm, Christie's Oklahoma (United States), September 24, 1981.

CHRISTOPHE, ERNEST

Loches, January 1827
Paris, January 16, 1892

The remarkable effigy in bronze of Godefroy Cavaignac at the Montmartre Cemetery, executed in 1847, is signed "Rude and Christophe, his young student," although it is said that the student had actually contributed very little to the effort. Ernest Christophe, whose collection of works is scanty, exhibited irregularly at the Salon starting in 1850. However, he made a few personal works of genuine worth, such as his statue in marble entitled *La Comédie humaine* or *La Femme au masque* from the Garden of the Tuileries (1874), today at the Orsay museum, and a group in bronze of 2.2 meters high, *La Fatalité*, cast by Gonon, exhibited at the Salon of 1885 and acquired by the museum of Luxembourg before being sent to the warehouse at Bagnères-de-Luchon.

MUSEUMS
Chambéry
Esclave enchaîné, 31 cm (1850; Eck and Durand).
Dijon
Rude sculptant la Marseillaise, sketch for a monument to Rude, 66 cm.
Montpellier
La Comédie humaine, 55 cm.
Paris, Orsay
Esclave enchaîné, 31 cm (1851; Eck and Durand).

CHRISTOPHE, PIERRE

Saint-Denis, July 16, 1880
Bordeaux, January 13, 1971

Certain works by this animal sculptor were cast in sandstone by Müller. Beginning in 1897, when he was still very young, Pierre Christophe participated at the Salon with a number of plasters such as *Chienne bull dog* and *Chienne prise au piège* (1899), *Groupe de chèvres* (1900), *Chat* (1903), *Cynocéphale mandrill et pélican* (1904), *Coq et poules* (1907), *Chevaux et paysans* and *Chevreuil au temps des amours* (1910). He also exhibited some waxes and some bronzes: *Daguet et biche japonais* (1904), *Cormorans, Cerf japonais* (1905), *Biche sika du Japon* (1908), *Retour des champs* (1912), etc. In 1913, he sent a whole series of small statuettes of animals to the first salon of animal artists, as well as a small group entitled *Deux Juments et paysan bas-normand*. The review *L'Art et les Artistes* then wrote that his works are characterized by a certain rusticity, "a direct feeling of the homeland."

MUSEUMS
Nice
Jeunes Biches au repos (1904)
Paris, Decorative Arts
Chèvre au repos, 22 cm (1906)
Chèvre debout, 19.5 cm (Bingen et Costenoble,
    founders).
Chien couché, 9 x 18 cm.
Chienne basset, 15 cm.
Pélican debout, 15 cm. (Hébrard).

SALES
Chien assis, 15.5 cm, *Chien Greyhound debout*, 34 cm,
    Le Coq, 36 cm, *Pélican*, 18 cm, *Le Poulain*, 22 cm,
    Enghien, February 22, 1981.

CLARA, JOSÉ

Olot (Spain), December 16, 1878
Barcelona, 1958

José Clara spent some time at the schools of fine
arts in Olot, in Toulouse, and finally in Paris, where
Rodin noticed his work. Clara displayed a decided
preference for the female form and the graceful
movement of dancers. At the Salon, starting in 1903,

José Clara,
La Diosa,
37.5 cm (7/8).

José Clara,
Femme nue debout,
120 cm.

207

José Clara,
L'Esclave,
82 cm (6/8).

José Clara,
Tête de femme, 36 cm
(Godard père).

he exhibited some inspiring sculptures which were particularly literary, even mystical; these included *Extase* (1903), *Jésus* (1905), *Simon de Montfort* (1906), *Le Tourment* (1907). In 1908, he moved to the Nationale des Beaux-Arts with *Le Crépuscule* (1908), a nude female with a pure and harmonious form, and then a statue in bronze entitled *Jeunesse* and a head of a woman in bronze and marble (1909); the nezxt year, he showed two other bronzes, *Femme accroupie* and *Figurine drappée*. His bronzes were usually made in limited and numbered castings. A certain number of proofs carrying the seal of A. Valsuani were numbered from a series of 8.

MUSEUMS
Paris, Decorative Arts
Tête de jeune femme souriante au chignon, 34 cm. (Godard, founder).

SALES
La Baigneuse or *Femme à sa toilette*, 45 cm (1/8), Drouot, May 18, 1984, room 1; Drouot, April 21, 1985, room 1; Drouot, March 24, 1986, room 1; (6/8), Bayeux, May 19, 1986.
La Diosa, 37.5 cm (3/8), Drouot, May 18, 1984, room 1; (5/8), Enghien, November 25, 1984; (7/8), Drouot, December 9, 1985, room 1.
L'Esclave, 81 cm (2/8), Drouot, May 18, 1984, room 1; (6/8), Enghien, November 25, 1984; (7/8), Drouot, June 17, 1985.
Femme agenouillée, 17 cm, Rambouillet, June 8, 1986.
Jeune fille à la toilette, 46 cm (Valsuani 5/8), L'Isle-Adam, June 15, 1986.
Femme nue debout, 45 cm, Barcelona, December 19, 1984.
Femme nue debout, 120 cm, Rambouillet, July 27, 1986.
Maternité, 32 cm (Valsuani 1/8), Drouot, December 9, 1985, rooms 1 and 7.
Muses, 121 cm (Valsuani 2/8), Drouot, June 17, 1985, rooms 5 and 6.
Ronde enfantine, 44 cm (Valsuani 2/8), Drouot, June 17, 1985, rooms 5 and 6.
Tête de femme, 36 cm (Godard Sr., founder), Drouot, November 27, 1986, rooms 1 and 7.

CLARA, JUAN

Born in Olot (Spain), 1875

This artist is sometimes confused with José Clara, undoubtedly his brother; like his brother, he began exhibiting at the Société Nationale des Beaux-Arts in 1903. A student of Barrias, he seems to have specialized in statuettes and small anecdotal groups of young children. Of note is *Musique*, a statuette in plaster (1904), *Premier Pas*, bronze and marble (1906), *Enfant taquin*, bronze, and *Au guignol*, plaster (both 1907), *Lever de Lolotte*, bronze cast by Goldscheider (1908), *Jour de fête* and *Enfant au biberon*, two bronzes (in 1909), and *L'Auto à Lolotte* and *Gazoullis*, two plasters. Also cast by Goldscheider are *Group de trois enfants assis sur un banc*, 22.5 cm, *Premier Chausson*, and *Nénette*, as well as *Enfant et chien*, 27 cm, *Fillette assise sur un tabouret*, 24.5 cm, and *Fillette escaladant une chaise*, 24 cm. A bronze entitled *La Petite Comédienne assise*, 19.5 cm, was sold on March 10, 1985 at L'Isle-Adam.

Juan Clara,
Jeune Enfant à la poupée,
20.5 cm (No 12).

CLAUDEL, CAMILLE

Fère-en-Tardenois (Aisne), December 8, 1864
Montdevergues (Gard), October 19, 1943

C. Claudel

Camille Claudel's collaboration and relationship with Rodin played a small part in obscuring the personality and originality of this artist. A long incarceration, which lasted the final thirty years of her life, sometimes make us forget the thirty preceding years during the course of which her career unfolded as a sculptor. The sister of the writer Paul Claudel and his elder by four years, Camille expressed her artistic temperment and talent for models very young age. She came to the attention of the sculptor Alfred Boucher in Nogent-sur-Seine, where she resided with her parents, and went to Paris with her mother in 1882. In a private academy, she studied sculpture with the same Alfred Boucher then with Rodin for whom,beginning in 1885, she became the preferred model, collaborator and friend.

The influence of the great sculptor on the young artist was felt principally in the works of her first ten years of activity, during the period before their separation. Biographies of Claudel, especially the one by curator M. Bruno Gaudichon of the Poitiers museum (Catalogue of the Camille Claudel Exposition, museum of Poitiers and the Rodin Museum, 1984), distinguish four major tendencies in her work. One of these, naturalism, was illustrated by some works of uncompromised realism, such as the bust of the family's servant *La Vieille Hélène*, or the famous group *L'Age mûr*.

In the long series of busts of her family, her surroundings, and various comtemporaries, another tendency sometimes comes to light—a kind of theatrical expressionism which inspired her to dress her people in the clothing of antiquity. This is evident in one of the four portraits she made of her thirteen-year-old brother Paul and another made some years later, known by the name *Jeune Romain*.

Next came some anecdotal scenes taken from life, like *Les Causeuses, La Femme à sa toilette, La Vague*. In these works, the artist freed herself from Rodin's control. She herself noticed it, writing to her brother Paul: "You see that this is no longer has anything of Rodin." In the last years of the 19th century, she finally returned to more classical styles and subjects; Camille Claudel readily called on God and the heroes of antiquity, but still preserved her characteristic realism and extreme sensitivity, the bases upon which all of her work rests.

At the age of nineteen, barely established in Paris, Camille Claudel made her debut at the Salon of 1883 with a bust in plaster. She had already modeled many works, including the bust of her brother Paul at thirteen years of age, called *Le Jeune Romain*, and *Vieille Hélène*, which she sent, in terra cotta, to the Salon of 1885. She continued to exhibit, particularly with the Artistes Français; she showed the study in bronze, 32 cm, (1885) of a work that was to become *Giganti* or *Tête de brigand*; *Jeune Fille*, the bust in bronze (47 cm) of her sister Louise (1886); the bust in bronze (44 cm) of *Paul en jeune Romain* (1887, the year in which she collaborated with Rodin on the group the *Bourgeois de Calais*); a group in plaster, *Çacountala* (1888) which, in marble, would become *Vertumne et Pomone*, and the bronze *L'Abandon*; the bust in bronze (32 cm) of Charles Lhermitte, the son of the painter (1889).

In 1891, though she was increasingly neglected by Rodin, she accompanied him to Anjou and Touraine before exhibiting the bust in bronze (40.7 cm) at the Salon de la Société Nationale des Beaux-Arts in 1892. At the same Salon, one of her major works appeared the following year—*La Valse*, a plaster full of vitality and movement which won great success and critical acclaim. In 1894, she sent to this salon a bust in bronze (33 cm), entitled *La Petite Châtelaine*, or *Jeanne enfant*, or *La Petite de l'Islette*; in addition she sent *Le Dieu envolé*, in plaster, a preliminary stage of *L'Implorante* from the famous group *L'Age mûr*. In 1895 she sent a plaster entitled *La Confidence* which was later called *Les Causeuses* or *Les Bavardes*. In 1897, she contributed a group in plaster entitled *La Vague*, and in 1898, *La Profonde Pensée*, a bronze representing a woman kneeling in front of a fireplace; in 1899 she contributed *Persée et la Gorgone*, in plaster.

Upon returning to the Salon des Artistes Français in 1903, she sent the bronze of *L'Age mûr*, 114 cm (her customer, the captain Tissier, had the piece cast by the Thiébaut house at his own expense), and in 1905 she sent to the Salon a bronze (45 cm) entitled *La Petite Sirène*. Frequently—in 1905, 1907, and

②

①

1) Camille Claudel, *Tête de jeune fille au chignon*, 17 cm (Coubertin 3/8).

2) Camille Claudel, *La Valse*, 46 cm (unique model in gilded patina).

3) Camille Claudel, *L'Abandon* or *Çacountala*, 43 cm (Eugène Blot). J. Ginepro Collection, Monaco.

1908—the founder Eugène Biot exhibited those works of Camille Claudel which he had cast in his gallery. She also received some commissions from the State including *La Niobide blessée*, a bronze 90 cm high, in 1907; it was to be one of her last works, today in the garden of the marine headquarters of Toulon.

Camille Claudel's, relentless work, her emotional quarrels with Rodin, and her financial difficulties altered the physical and mental health of the artist, who cloistered herself in her studio at 19 Bourbon Quay. In 1913, complaints from the building's other tenants (apparently more worried than really inconvenienced by her strange behavior) led to her confinement first at Ville-Evard and then at Montde-vergues near Villeneuva-lès-Avignon. She died there thirty years later.

Camille Claudel's bronze works were cast by different founders: the bust of Rodin and *La Prière* were cast by Gruet, *L'Age mûr* by Thiébaut and another version by Carvelhani, *Tête de femme âgée* by Rudier, the *Buste de Paul Claudel à trente-sept ans* by P. Converset, *La Niobide blessée* by Eugène Blot, and *Chien affamé* (the only animal subject by the artist with a cat) by Alexis Rudier. The castings, on the other hand, were primarily undertaken by Eugène Blot, starting in 1905, in limited and numbered castings.

Some valuable information on this subject was furnished in a document written in 1937 or 1938 by Blot himself, when he yielded to Leblanc-Barbedienne "...his rights to manufacture and of the castings on several models of the statuary..." Among these models were those of Camille Claudel. Particularly interesting data, Eugène Blot listed them with the number of castings planned for and for the most part, the number of proofs sold by him up until this date (between parentheses in the list below):

③

L'Abandon or *Çacountala* or *Vertumn et Pomone*, 63 cm, 25 proofs (18); 42 cm, 25 proofs (14). Eugène Blot notes that some sculptors like Hoetger and Bartholomé had acquired some models of this work.

L'Aurore, bust, 34 cm, 25 proofs (not of the number of models sold).

La Fortune, 48 cm, 50 proofs (15). According to Mme Reine Marie Paris (*Camille Claudel*, 1984), the casting would have been reduced to 25 proofs.

L'Implorante or *Suppliante*, 69 cm, 10 proofs (5); 29 cm, 100 proofs (59). In another text written on December 17, 1936, Eugène Blot recalled the castings of this bronze and made a statement about a third dimension: ". . .I first bought from her the figure *Imploration*...This kneeling figure was part of a group of three people that she called *Le Chemin de la vie* or *La Jeunesse et l'âge mûr*...In the original cut, called no 1, I limited the casting to ten proofs. I immediately made of it a reduction no 2, that I limited to one hundred proofs. Since, having bought the entire group... I have had it reduced by the reductor of Rodin. I thus found myself the owner of a mid-size version of *L'Imploration* that I called no 1 1/2 and that I limited to twenty models."

L'Age mûr or *Le Chemin de la vie* or *La Destinée*, 6 proofs (not the number of models sold) Blot, who exhibited then in his gallery in 1907, adds that these bronzes were of the same dimensions as the proofs cast by Rudier, about 120 cm in length (not from data on the castings of Rudier).

Persée et Gorgone, about 50 cm, 25 proofs (not the number of models sold).

La Petite Sirène or *La Joueuse de flûte*, 45 cm, 25 proofs (6).

La Valse, 50 cm, 50 proofs (24); 23 cm, 25 proofs (4). According to Eugène Blot, this work, conceived with some variants in the base and the clothes, would have at first been entrusted to Siot-Decauville but it is not clear if the latter effected some castings of it: "This model was originally bought on the advice of M. Armand Dayot, inspector of the Beaux-Arts, by the editor Siot-Decauvile, and Claudel, always in need of money, wanted to resell it to me. Upon my response that this was impossible, M. Siot-Decauville, with whom I was on very good terms, wanted also to write me a letter in which he renounced his rights."

Other models, which do not seem to have been given to Leblanc-Barbedienne, appeared on of Eugène Blot's list: *Femme assise devant une cheminée* or *Au coin du feu Cendrillon*, 22 cm, unlimited casting (65). *Femme assise devant une cheminée* or *Rêve au coin du feu*, 26 cm, 25 proofs (10). *Femme agenouillée devant une cheminée* or *Profonde Pensée*, 45 cm, 25 proofs (6). This is a question of what is called "works for food" as testified to in the commentaries of the founder: "... the *Cendrillon*, woman sitting close to a fireplace, that I had the good idea not to limit the number. As she had sold many and the great artist was always in need of money, she made me another figure in front of a fireplace called *La Bûche de Noël*, that I limted. I was very successful selling them by placing behind the logs of these fireplaces, especially the first, a red bulb in order to make it a nightlight."

It is necessary still to note among the castings of Eugène Blot:

Les Causeuses, version with folding screen, 33 cm, 50 proofs.

Vieil Homme, study for La Vieillesse, 25 proofs, and *Deux bustes de femme*, 25 proofs (these three works exhibited at the Blot Gallery in 1908).

Finally, in her work on Camille Claudel, Mme Reine Marie Paris notes 15 numbered models of the *Buste de Rodin*, cast from the *Mercure de France* and cast by Rudier, as well as some recent castings of the Jeune Fille à la gerbe, made by the Coubertin Foundry in 1983.

MUSEUMS
Abbeville
Psaume or La Prière or *L'Inspirée*, 45 cm (A. Gruet, founder).
Aurillac
Auguste Rodin, bust, 40 cm.
Avignon
Mon frère or *Jeune Romain*, 44 cm.
Bagnols-sur-Cèze
L'Imploratne, 28.6 cm (E. Blot 32/100).
Calais
Mon frère, bust, 44 cm.
Châteauroux
Buste de Paul Claudel enfant à l'antique, 43 cm.
Château-Thierry
Paul Claudel à trente-sept ans, 48 cm.
Cherbourg
Giganti or *Tête de brigand*, 32 cm.
Clermont-Ferrand
Louise de Masary, bust, 47 cm (1886)

Camille Claudel,
L'Age mûr, 114 x 163 cm
(Thiébaut-Fumière and Gavignot).
Musée d'Orsay.

Camille Claudel,
L'Implorante, 58 cm
(Blot, founder).

Guéret
Auguste Rodin, bust, 40 cm.
Lille
Giganti or Tête de brigand, 32 cm (1886).
Paris, Orsay
L'Age mûr 114 x 163 cm (Thiébaut - Fumière et
    Gavignot).
Paris, Petit Palais
Auguste Rodin, bust, 40 cm.
Paris, musée Rodin
L'Age mûr, 121 x 181 cm (Carvelhani, founder).
Auguste Rodin, bust, 40 cm (Gruet, founder).
Les Causeuses, 24 cm (G. Rudier).
Les Causeuse, onyx and bronze, 45 cm.
L'Implorante, 28.6 cm (E. Blot, founder).
Paul Claudel à trente-sept ans, 48 cm (P. Converset,
    founder).
La Valse, 43 cm (Siot-Decauville).
Poitiers
L'Abandon or Çacountala, 43 cm (E. Blot 9/50).
La Fortune, 48 cm (E. Blot).
La Valse, 46 cm (E. Blot).
Reims
Giganti or Tête de brigand, 47 cm.
Toulon
Mon fre're or Jeune Romain, bust, 44 cm.
Toulouse
Jeune Homme, 51 cm.

SALES

L'Abandon or *Çacountala*, 42 cm (E. Blot), Drouot, June 20, 1984, rooms 5 and 6; Drouot, May 22, 1985.

Les Causeuses, 33 cm (E. Blot No.1), Sotheby London, June 29, 1983.

Le Chat, 3 x 15 cm, Drouot, June 25, 1984, room 6.

L'Implorante or *La Suppliante*, 28.5 cm (E. Blot), Drouot, March 22, 1985; Drouot, May 3, 1985; Drouot, November 28, 1986, room 10; Rambouillet, November 30, 1986.

La Valse, gilded bronze, 46 cm (E. Blot No.2), Drouot, March 18, 1986, room 7 (taking 311,000 F).

CLAUDET, MAX

Fécamp (Seine-Maritime), Auguste 18, 1840
Salins (Jura), May 25, 1893

Also a painter, ceramicist, and writer, this sculptor lived and worked in Salins, the original home of his parents. He sculpted statues and busts of contemporaries for this town and others in the region. He exhibited a small number of works at the Salon after 1864. His work there includes some bronzes: a statuette entitled *Robespierre à la Convention* (1874), a group entitled *Le Jour de la fête de saint Jean-Baptiste* (1876), a statue entitled *Hoche enfant* (1878), a medallion entitled *Une bonne pipe* (1888), and a bust entitled *Un petit Roi mage* (1892). Among the works not exhibited at the Salon is another statuette in bronze, *La Mère Lantimèche*. A bust entitled *Femme âgée*, cast by Boyer and Rolland (1875), was sold in Lyon on October 19, 1986.

CLAUSADE, LOUIS

Toulouse, 1865
Paris, December 19, 1899

Louis Clausade died at the site of the Exposition Universelle of 1900, on which he had worked. His signature can be found on the bronze statue of *Beaumarchais* (1895) which stands on the Rue Saint-Antoine in Paris, the stone group *Art romain* (1899) from the facade of the Grand Palais, and a monument to *Carnot* (1897) for the city of Limoges. A student of Falguière, he exhibited at the Salon beginning in 1884, and is also responsible for a number of busts, especially in plaster, and some medallions. His *Beaumarchais* was cast in bronze, 50 cm, by Thiébaut.

CLÉMENCIN, FRANÇOIS ANDRÉ

Lyon, October 7, 1878
Paris, March 6, 1950

Starting in 1907, he exhibited some genre scenes at the Salon, including *Les Murmures de la forêt*, a group in plaster (1907), *Fleurs et ris*, plaster (1908), *Celuy quy fut pris* (a horseman carrying a woman), a statuette in bronze, 38 cm, and *Avant le tournoi*, a group in bronze (1910), *Baigneuse* and *Enigme*, two statuettes in gilded bronze (1911), *Jeune Bacchante tenant des pampres*, 57 cm, etc.

SALES

Celuy quy fut pris, 38 cm, Sotheby London, November 6, 1985.

Danseuse au lierre, silvered bronze, 47 cm, Drouot, October 19, 1983.

François André Clémencin, Danseuse au lierre, silvered bronze, 47 cm

CLÈRE, GEORGES PROSPER

Nancy, November 9, 1819
1901

Georges Prosper Clère intended to become a doctor, but instead turned to sculpture and studied at the school of fine arts first in Dijon and then, in Paris, in the studio of Rude. He soon made a number of works for the decoration of the Louvre, the Tuileries, the préfecture of Versailles, etc. Starting in 1853, he exhibited at the Salon some busts and figures in bronze: *Faune gymnaste* (1859), *Histrion* (1861), *Hercule étouffant le lion de Némée* (1864), *Un garçon boucher*, a statuette (1864), and *Le Baron Larrey, chirurgien de l'empereur*, medallion (1867). Thiébaut had cast a bust entitled *Jeune femme du Moyen Age* in gilded bronze, and a group entitled *Homme étouffant un lion*, 60 cm L, based on *Hercule* from the Salon of 1864.

François André Clémencin, Celuy guy fut pris, 38 cm.

CLÉSINGER, JEAN-BAPTISTE, KNOWN AS AUGUSTE

Basançon, October 20, 1814
Paris, January 6, 1883

CLESiNGER

This sculptor and painter studied with his father, the academic sculptor George Philippe Clésinger, who took him to Rome in 1832. He entered the studio of the Danish neo-classical artist Thorvaldsen, who strongly influenced a part of his work. He returned to Paris in 1838, but spent time in Switzerland, Florence, and Besançon before returning to the French capital in 1845. In 1847, he married Solange Gabrielle Dudevant, the daughter of George Sand, from whom he was separated five years later. The year 1847 also marked his first success at the Salon, with a marble entitled *Femme piquée par un serpent.*

Afflicted with a streak of vanity, Clésinger did not seem to engage the affections of those around him. According to Stanislas Lami, Clésinger considered himself superior to all of his colleagues. It was during the course of his first stay in Rome that he changed his name to Auguste, as he no doubt considered that more in line with his talent. In 1856, the critics railed at his *François 1er à cheval*, a commission for the courtyard of the Louvre; the piece was quickly removed from the site. Vexed, he returned to Rome, from which he sent a number of very neo-classical marbles as well as the Roman bulls, *Combat de taureaux*, large steers which represented a new aspect of his work. He returned to Paris in 1864. From that time on, his mythological or allegorical compositions, his equestrian effigies, his busts of the personalities of the art world, and his few statues of animals (for the most part in marble) earned him multiple distinctions. However, his fame seemed to decline considerably after the war of 1870.

Among the works which especially typify Clésinger are the monument of Gustave Flaubert in the Luxembourg gardens and some marbles: *La Jeunesse de Sapho* (Salon of 1859), *Cornélie et ses deux fils, Cléopatre mourant* (1861), *Bacchante* (1863), *Combat de taureaux romains*, red marble, 49 cm (1864), and *Taureau romain* (1878). The most sought-after was reduced by the Collas process and cast in bronze in different formats by Barbedienne. The marbles, mostly sent from Italy, include

Automne, 94, 55, 45, and 37 cm.
Bacchante, 83, 41, 33, and 17 cm.
Cléopâtre mourant, 82, 42, 33 and 18 cm.
Cornélie et ses dux fils (Les Gracques), five unspecified sizes.
Diane au repos, 77, 38.5, and 25 cm.
Femme couchée, piquée par un serpent, 59 cm long.
Hélène, 85, 69, and 44 cm.
Hercule enfant, 40 and 16.5 cm.
Printemps, 100, 58, 47, and 39 cm.
Sapho au rocher, 74, 58, 42, and 29 cm.
Sapho en méditation, 85, 65, and 45 cm.
Satyre, 82, 42, 33, and 18 cm.
Taureau romain, 115, 85, 44, 33, 23, and 17 cm.
Zingara, danseuse napolitaine, 132, 105, 84, and 55 cm.

CLERGET, ALEXANDRE

Saint-Palais (Pyrénées-Atlantiques), September 26, 1856
December 21, 1931

This student of Falguière exhibited at the Salon from 1889 to 1924, contributing medallions and busts in bronze or plaster as well as the following statues in plaster or marble: *Faucheur* (1891), *Avant la lutte* (1893), *Fleurs des bois* (1899), and *Consultation* (1897). He also contributed some statuettes in bronze: *Révérance* (1902), *Sortie de chapelle*, gilded bronze (1903), *La Dame à l'écharpe*, bronze and ivory (1907), *Onésime Reclus* (1912), and a vase, also in bronze: *Fête des fleurs*. Some models were made by the factory of Sèvres. The foundry Siot-Decuaville cast the following works by Clerget: *Liseuse, Consultation, Femme à l'iris sur une feuille de nénuphar*, 26 cm, *La Fiancée*, gilded bronze, an inkwell, and some gladiola vases.

Auguste Clésinger,
Buste de femme,
gilded bronze,
68 cm (1868).

Auguste Clésinger,
Buste de juene femme
au collier,
82 cm (Barbedienne).

Auguste Clésinger,
Cléopâtre mourant, 78 cm L.
(Rome 1861; F. Barbedienne).

Auguste Clésinger,
Bacchante, 83 cm
(Rome 1862; Barbedienne, Collas reduction).

Auguste Clésinger,
Sapho, 47.5 cm.
J. Ginepro Collection,
Monaco.

217

*Auguste Clésinger,
Combat de taureaux romains,
85 cm L.*

*Auguste Clésinger,
Taureau romain, 85 cm
(F. Barbedienne).*

The following busts also appeared in the Barbedienne catalog:

Automne, 75, 29, and 14 cm.
Bacchante, 31, 19, and 15 cm.
Charlotte Corday, 75, 35, 29, 21, and 15 cm.
Hélène, 78, 54, 40, 32.5, 24, 16, and 11 cm.
Jeune Femme romaine, six sizes.
Pâris, 90, 45, 35, 26, 18 and 13 cm.
Printemps, 75, 31, 14.5 cm.
Rachel (comédie), 31 and 19.5 cm.
Rachel (tragédie), 31 and 19.5 cm.
Sapho jeune, 68, 34, 27 cm.
Tête de Christ, seven sizes.

MUSEUMS
Angoulême
Sapho, 59 cm.
Compiègne, château
Hélène de Troie, 81.5 cm (Barbedienne; Rome 1860).
Thomas Couture, bust, 80 cm (Barbedienne).
Grenoble
Danseuse au tambourin, 55 cm (Barbedienne).

Nice
Ariane.
Niort
Euterpe, 85 cm (Barbedienne).
Paris, Decorative Arts
Ariane étendue sur le dos d'un tigre, 98 cm.
Paris, Orsay
La Dame aux roses, bust, 68 cm.
Troyes
Taureau, 15 cm.

SALES
Bacchante, 83 cm (Rome, 1862; Barbedienne), Drouot,
    December 13, 1986, room 7.
Buste de femme, gilded bronze, 68 cm (1868), La
    Flèche, November 16, 1986.
Buste de famme au collier, 82 cm (Barbedienne), Tours,
    June 2, 1986.
Cléopâtre, 45 cm (Barbedienne), Drouot, February 28,
    1984, room 5; Engien, December 2, 1984.
Cléopâtre, 78 cm (Barbedienne), Drouot, March 22,
    1985.
Combat de taureaux romains, 33 x 68 cm, Bourg-en-
    Brasse, March 2, 1986.
Jeune Femme au tambourin, 43 cm, Sotheby London,
    march 20, 1986.
Sapho, Fontainebleau, November 10, 1985.
Taureau romain, 17 cm (Barbedienne), Drouot, July 7,
    1983.
Taureau romain, 44 cm, Fontainebleau, April 29, 1984.
Taureau romain, 85, Enghien, March 7, 1982.
Taureau romain, 115 cm, Clermont-Ferrand, December
    16, 1985 (sold for 160,000 F).

COINCHON, JACQUES ANTOINE THÉODORE

Moulins, September 10, 1814
Paris, 1881

This sculptor studied with David d'Angers, and
the museum of Moulins owns some of his works. He
is known for a group in bronze entitled *Alexandre
tuant un lion sur les rives du Bosphore*, and four
statuettes in plaster: *Jeune Enfant endormi sous un
arbre* (Salon of 1844), *Bacchus* (1848), *Pythagore*
(1870), and *Lumen* (1878).

A contract was signed with the Susse foundry for
the castings of the following works:

Bacchus, 58 cm.
Les Buveurs, 30 cm.
Frère et soeur, 23 cm.
Homère assis, 55 and 30 cm.
Jeanne Hachette, 44 cm.
Jeune Fille à la fontaine, 48 cm.
La Leçon de flûte, 55, 42, and 33 cm.

One statuette in bronze entitled *David* was sold
in London in 1972. Another bronze, *Joueur de flûte
double*, 85 cm (with an inscription indicating that it
was cast and chiseled by Armand Vétu, 1858), was
sold at the Drouot Hotel on July 11, 1985.

COLIN, GEORGES

Vincennes, April 26, 1876
July 15, 1917

From 1899 to 1914 Georges Colin exhibited at
the Salon, notably *La Course à l'abîme*, a group in
wax (1901), the model in plaster of *Santos-Dumont*
(1914) designed for the city of Saint-Cloud, and the

Auguste Clésinger,
Hercule enfant
subtitled "Au prince impérial,"
gilded bronze, 40 cm
(1857; Barbedienne).

following statuettes in plaster: *Elégie* (1905), *Femme
au sablier* (1907), *Danseuse aux marionnettes* and
Ulysse (1910), *L'Art industriel* (1912). Finally, in
bronze, he contributed a statuette entitled *Chrysis*
(1912), a group entitled *L'Age d'or* (1911), and a
statue entitled *Le Pilote* (1913), cast by Arthur
Goldscheider. Another bronze, *Pour la patrie*, representing the soldier of the Marathon dying, 109 cm,
is found at the museum of Bar-le-Duc; a second
model of the same work appears at the city hall of
Paris.

SALES
Le Chemin parcouru, 50 cm, Vitry-le-François, March
    24, 1985.
Le Chemin parcouru, 65 cm, Drouot, June 6, 1984,
    room 2.

COLIN, PAUL HUBERT

Paris, August 3, 1801
Nîmes, ?

Paul Hubert Colin exhibited at the Salon from
1833 to 1840 and became a teacher of sculpture and
ornamentation in Nîmes. In Paris, he worked for the
Palais de Justice, the church of Saint-Paul, for the
préfecture and the city hall of Avignon, and for the
courthouse in Montpellier. Two small figures in
plaster were exhibited, one, *Femme endormie*, at the
Salon of 1834, and the other, *Jeune Italienne*, at that
of 1840, while a statuette in bronze entitled *Talma
dans le rôle de Néron* appeared at the Exposition
Centennale de l'Art Français in 1900.

COLLE, ALPHONSE

Chaleville, May 21, 1857
December 28, 1935

Author of a monumental fountain in his birth-place, Alphonse Colle participated at the Salon after 1880 with some busts in terra cotta and bronze, and some statues and groups in plaster: *L'Enfant prodigue* (1886), *Souvenir* (1889), *Le Menuet* (1892), *Orphée mourant* (1893), *Idylle* (1909), *L'Epave* (1913); some groups in bronze: *Le Temps de l'amour* (1891), *Combat de coqs* (1897); and finally some statuettes: *Flirt*, marble (1895), *Dernier Viole*, plaster (1902), *Feuilles d'automne*, marble (1903), and *Portrait de M.C.*, bronze (1914). Alphonse Colle continued to exhibit after the war, in particular some statuettes in bronze: *Napoléon 1er* in 1928 and *Sous Verdun, 1916*, in 1932. One statuette in bronze, *L'Espagnole à l'éventail*, 40 cm (The Bronze Society of Paris), was sold in Reims on October 13, 1985.

Paul Comolera,
Le Combat de coqs, 60 cm.
Two pigeons in love.

COLOMBO, RENZO

Died in 1885

Born in Milan, and a student of the Académie de Florence, Colombo exhibited only for a few years at the Salon of Paris, contributing most notably the terra cotta *Socrate devant ses juges* (1884), the plaster bas-relief *Pro patria* designed for a monument to the dead of the Battle of Champigny, a bust in plaster of *Napoléon 1er* (1885), and finally, *Le Retour du calvaire*, a statue in plaster exhibited after his death in 1886. Some bronzes were sold at different times: *Bohême orientale*, 40 cm, *Juge au conseil des dix à Venise*, statuette, and finally, three busts: *La Frileuse*, *La Vénitienne* and *Napoléon 1er*. The last (60 cm) was cast by the founder Pinedo in four dimensions.

COMOLERA, PAUL

Paris, 1818
Paris, 1897

An animal sculptor, student of Rude, and the master of Moigniez, Paul Comolera primarily exhibited wild birds and barnyard animals at the Salon, from 1846 until his death. Of particular note is *Chien barbet agaçant un coq indien*, plaster (1848), *Caille prise au piège*, plaster (1849), *Héron blesé par une flèche*, *Bécassine morte*, bronzes (1852), *Faisan*, *Sarcelle*, bronzes (1863), *Perdrix blessée*, bronze (1865), *Perdrix morte*, terra cotta (1866), *Famille de perdrix*, silvered bronze (1870), *Combat de coqs*, bronze, *Bécasse*, silvered bronze (1873), *Deux pigeons s'aimaient d'amour tendre* and *L'Ouverture de la chasse*, bronzes (1886), as well as some busts in bronze.

Paul Comolera,
Coq, 63 cm.

Paul Comolera,
Le Héron
et la grenouille,
polychrome bronze,
80 cm.

Jules Félix Constant,
Le Jardinier,
31 cm.

Many of his works were repoduced in faience by the Hippolyte Boulenger factory of Choisy-le-Roi, while others were cast in bronze by different founders. Aside from his pieces which have appeared at public sales during recent years, one can mention *Bécasse*, 31 cm, *Combat de coqs*, 60 cm, *Faisan*, 32 cm, *Flamboyant, cheval de course, Hirondelle en vol*, 18 cm (Susse), *Lévrier*, 37 cm (cast by Tiffany), *Martin-pêcheur ramenant une grenouille*, 18.5 cm, and *Taureau chargeant*, 28 cm. A group, *Le Coq vainqueur*, 51 cm, was also cast in composition.

SALES

Coq, 63 cm, Meaux, November 16, 1986.
Héron blessé, 66 cm, Sotheby London, November 6, 1986.
Oiseau défendant son nid, gilded bronze, 65 cm, Christie's New York, December 13, 1985.

CONSTANT, JULES FÉLIX

1848-1939

This artist's bronze entitled *L'Allégorie de l'amour*, 96 cm high, was sold in Marseille on May 24, 1986. Another bronze representing a *Jardinier* is also known.

CONSTANT, NOÉMIE

see Vignon

CONVERS, LOUIS

Paris, September 4, 1860
October 1915

Winner of the prize of Rome in 1888, and the author of one of the stone groups (*Les Quatre Saisons*) which flanks the main entrance to the Petit Palais in

Paris, this artist left a number of sketches in terra cotta, plaster, and wax, now owned by the museum of the Petit Palais. A statuette in bronze entitled *La Comédie*, 26 cm and dated from 1910, is also found there. He also sent some statuettes in bronze to the Salon: *La Justice*, a reduction of a statue in marble designed for the courthouse in Grenoble (1898), *Salomé* (1899), *La Victoire* (1902), and *Biblis changée en source* (1913), as well as some works in marble. Susse cast in bronze the work entitled *La Victoire*, 62 cm, as well as a bell entitled *Servante*, 12 cm. In the catalogs for the Thiébaut foundry the following bronzes are found: *La Justice*, 61 cm, *Nymphe se coiffant*, 35 cm, *Nymphe ouvrant une coquille*, 30 cm, *Nymphe roulant un coquillage*, 30 cm, and *Salomé*, 75 and 52 cm.

CORDIER, CHARLES HENRI JOSEPH

Cambrai, November 1, 1827
Alger, May 1905

Cordier left his hometown at the age of nineteen and debuted two years later at the Salon after having passed through the Ecole des Beaux-Arts and the studio of Rude. Attracted by ethnography, he made many trips—to Algeria (1856), Greece (1858), and Egypt (1865)—and brought back from them a taste for the exotic. He sought to represent the different human types that he had glimpsed, and he is known for nearly fifty busts and statues of indigenous peoples from different parts of the world. He was also one of the promoters of polychromy in sculpture, utilizing different materials and unfired patinas for his bronzes. His success among a wealthy clientele, including the Queen of England, was considerable. Today, some of his works fetch high prices at auctions.

Cordier, who died bankrupt in Algiers, also left some statues of famous men, including *Maréchal Gérard, Ibrahim pacha* in Cairo and *Christophe Colomb* in Mexico (10 m, 1874) as well as some busts of comtemporaries. He is also the author of decorative works and restorations at the Tour Saint-Jacques, the Louvre, the Opera, and the Ferrière Castle. One of his sons, Henri Cordier, also became a sculptor.

The list of Charles Cordier's submissions at the Salon provides evidence of his favorite themes, while simultaneously revealing his preference for combining diverse and often precious materials: *Guerrier*

CORDIER

Charles Cordier,
Buste de négresse,
40 cm.

Charles Cordier,
Buste de Nubien,
82 cm.

Charles Codier,
Duex porteuses d'eau, polychrome bronze,
89 cm (Cairo 1861).

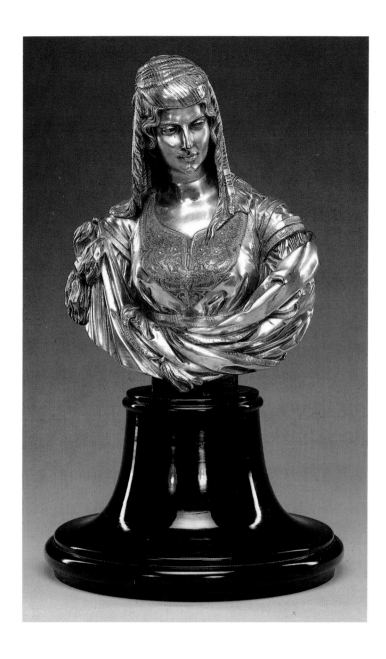

Charles Cordier,
Buste de Juive d'Alger,
silvered bronze, 92 cm (1862).

blessé, a statuette in plaster, 45 cm (1847), *Nubien*, a bust in bronze, 80 cm (1848), *Nègre de Tombouctou*, a bust in bronze (1850), *Homme et femme de type mongol*, two busts in bronze (1853), many busts in bronze or in bronze and onyx, *Mauresque, Arabe, Nègre, Maltais, Nègre en costume algérien* (1857), *Danseuse juive*, a statuette in enameled bronze (1859), *Femme des îles de l'archipel, Femme de l'Araucamie*, two statuettes in bronze (1860), *Juive d'Alger*, a bust in bronze, onyx and porphyry (1863), *Jeune Mulâtresse*, a statue in bronze, enamels and onyx, *Jeune Négresse portant une urne*, a statue in marble polychrome, bronze and enamels (1864), *Fellah en costume de harem*, a bust in bronze, gold, silver, turquoise, and porphyry (Exposition Universelle of 1867), *Fellah*, a lamp post in marble, onyx and bronze (1870), *Prêtresse d'Isis jouant de la harpe*, a statue in enameled bronze (1874 and Exposition Universelle of 1878), *Christoph Colomb*, a reduction in silver and onyx of the monument of Mexico (1876), and some statuettes in marble: *Psyché* (1877), *L'Aurore* (1878), and *Arianne abondonnée* (1883).

MUSEUMS
Dijon
Chelk arabe d'Egypte, bust, 90 cm.
Paris, musée de la Marine
Christophe Colomb, silvered bronze, 30 cm (reduction of the monument of Mexico)
Paris, Orsay
Arabe d'El Aghouat en burnou, bust in bronze and onyx, 72 cm.
Câpresse or *Négresse des colonies*, bust in bronze and onyx, 96.5 cm.

Nègre du Soudan, bust in bronze and onyx, 67.5 cm.
Nègre en costume algérien, bust in bronze and marble,
   96 cm.
Troyes
Juive d'Alger, bust in bronze, marble and onyx, 74 cm.
Versailles, château
Eugène Lamy, bust.

SALES

Arabe à la chéchia, bust, 82 cm, Enghien, October 21,
   1984 (price of sale: 147000 F).
Juive d'Alger, bust in silvered bronze and enamel, 61
   cm (1862), Sotheby London, March 20, 1986.
Négresse, bust, 40 cm, Dijon, October 27, 1985.
Nubien, bust in silvered bronze, 83.5 cm (1848),
   Drouot, April 25, 1986, room 6.
Petits Arabes, two statuettes in gilded bronze, onyx,
   porphyry, 106 and 109 cm, Versailles, May 27,
   1984 (sold for 465,000 F).
Porteuses d'eau, two bronzes with polychrome patina,
   89 cm, dated Cairo 1866, Enghien, October 21,
   1984.
Prêtresse d'Isis jouant de la harpe, 188 cm, Enghien,
   March 4, 1984 (sold for 800,000 F).
Victoire équestre, haut-relief, 75 x 52 cm, Drouot,
   November 20, 1985, room 11.

CORDIER, HENRI

    Paris, October 26, 1853
    1926

    Though he had studied under his father, the
sculptor Charles Henri Joseph Codier (and also
under Gérôme, Frémiet, and Mercié), this artist
distinguished himself from the elder Cordier with
his choice of subjects—portraits of historical people,
allegories, and animals. However, some of his exotic
works sometimes cause the two artists to be confused with each other. Remembered among his
submissions to the Salon, which started in 1876, are
Esquimaux, two busts in plaster (1878), *Le Ralliement*,
an equestrian statue in plaster (1879), *Nubien et
Nubienne*, two busts in plaster, 60 cm which were
later cast in bronze (1880), *Salomé*, a statue in
plaster (1881), *Etienne Marcel*, an equestrian statue
in plaster (1882), *Les Frères Montgolfier*, a group in
bronze for the city of Annonay (1885), *Ballerine*,
bronze (1886), *Eve*, a statue in plaster (1890), *Charles
Lebrun*, statue in marble (1907), *Taureau espagnol*,
bronze (1910), and *Paon*, bronze (1912), etc. Henri
Cordier was also the author of one of the four groups
in stone (*La Littérature*) which crowns the portal of
the Grand Palais on the Avenue Franklin-Roosevelt.
His other bronzes include *Assad, cheval arabe,
Boeuf au labour, Bouvier à la charrue, Cheval à la
sphère* and four equestrian statuettes of 65 cm in
height designed for the Versailles museum: *Artilleur,
Chasseur, Cuirassier*, and *Spahis*.

MUSEUMS
Libourne
Taureau des domaines de l'Etat, 32.5 cm.
Paris, musée de l'Armée
Coq vainqueur, gilded bronze.

SALES
Nubien et Nubienne, two busts, 43 and 46 cm, Drouot,
   December 10, 1984.

*Charles Cordier,
Prêtresse d'Isis jouant de la harpe,
188 cm.*

CORDONNIER, ALPHONSE AMÉDÉE

    La Madeleine-lez-Lille, February 2, 1848
    Paris, October 28, 1930

    After studying at the academic schools of Lille
and the Ecole des Beaux-Arts of Paris, Cordonnier
made two visits to Rome. During the course of the
first visit, from 1873 to 1875, he sent his first
sculptures to the Salon of Paris: the plaster *Persée* in
1874 and *Réveil*, also a plaster, in 1875. He received
the grand prize for sculpture in 1877 and returned
to Rome from 1878 to 1881 before establishing
himself permanently in Paris, where he found incontestable notoriety. His style, forceful and vigorous,
tended towards greater simplicity at the end of the

century. At this time he dealt eagerly with subjects related to the life and labor of the common people. He received a number of commissions: a group in bronze of *L'Electricité* for the facade of the Galerie des Machines in Paris, some statues and groups for the Sorbonne (a statue of *L'Histoire*), the city hall, the Grand Palais, the city hall of Tours (a pediment), different monuments of Lille (including the monument to Pasteur composed of figures in bronze cast by Thiébaut Frères in 1897) and of Roubaix. He is also the author of a group in stone entitled *Maternité*, today placed in Adolphe-Chérioux Square in the fifteenth district of Paris. Some bronzes were among his submissions to the Salon: *Bénédictin*, a statuette (1886), *Archéologie*, a bust in bronze and marble (1887), *Silène*, a statuette (1896), *Le Gui*, a statuette (1903), *Les Pauvres Gens*, a small group (1904), and a certain number of bust portraits.

The Susse foundry cast *Le Marchand de dieux antiques*, 66 cm, in bronze, modeled after the statue in plaster exhibited at the Salon of 1896.

MUSEUMS
Lille
François Becquart, bust, 68 cm.
Homme âgé, bust, 40 cm.
Pierre le Grand, bust, 64 cm.
This museum owns other works by Cordonnier, the majority in plaster.

Cormier,
Danseuse
orientale,
59 cm.

Cormier,
Femme
aux roses,
42 cm.

CORMIER, JOSEPH DESCOMPS

Clermont-Ferrand, January 18, 1869
Paris, April 24, 1950

Female figures characterize the production of this artist, who readily mixed marble and ivory and sometimes utilized lithographic stone for small pieces. He sent statuettes (for the most part) from his studio in La Charité-sur-Loire to the Salon starting in 1883; those in bronze include *Diane* (1898), *Femme des bois* or *La Sorcière* (1911), and *L'Epouvante* (1913); others in lithographic stone include *Nonia* (1903), *Bilitis* (1905), and *Bruit de printemps* (1906); others in marble or other materials include *Nonia au bain*, in ivory and fine stones (1904), *Maria de Padilla*, in marble (1905), *La Chanson de Pan*, in stone (1913), and *Femme des bois*, in marble (1914). He continued his activity after the First World War and resumed his submissions to the Salon. Some of his works were cast in bronze. He also produced some terra cottas and ceramics and furnished some models to the Sèvres factory.

225

SALES

L'Archère, gilded bronze and ivory, 39.5 cm, Christie's New York, May 23, 1984.

Bacchante chèvre, gilded bronze, 76.2 cm, Christie's New York, October 1, 1983.

Danseuse, bronze and ivory, 53 cm, Brussels, June 17, 1985.

Danseuse orientale, rehauts (re-raised) polychromes, 59 cm, Lille, April 21, 1986.

Femme nue debout, 19 cm, Drouot, March 22, 1985, room 3.

Jeune Femme assise, Drouot, May 20, 1985, room 1.

Jeune Femme à la robe fleurie, 37.5 cm, Drouot, March 23, 1984, room 1.

Jeune Femme aux roses, Nanterre, May 13, 1986.

Jeune Femme et enfant musicien, 27 x 60 cm (Barbedienne, around 1920), Drouot, November 5, 1986, room 7).

Lion, L'Isle-Adam, February 16, 1986.

Masque de danse, 45 cm, Rio de Janeiro, October 24, 1984.

Personnage de la Commedia dell'arte, bronze and ivory, 36 cm, Versailles, January 30, 1983.

COSTA DE BEAUREGARD, MARQUIS ALBERT

La Motte-Servolex (Savoie), May 24, 1835
Paris, February 16, 1909

A politician, historian, painter, and member of the Académie Française, Costa occasionally practiced the art of sculpture he had learned with Gumery. His participation at the Salon consisted only of one bust in bronze (a portrait of his father the Marquis Costa de Beauregard) exhibited in 1864, a group in bronze entitled *Hamlet et le fossoyeur,* and a plaster head of a monk in plaster, exhibited at the Salon of 1865.

The museum of Chambéry owns the bronze bust of the Marquis Pantaléon Costa de Beauregard, father of the artist and founder of the Musée Savoisien in Chambéry, 80 cm.

CORTOT, JEAN-PIERRE

Paris, August 20, 1787
Paris, August 12, 1843

At the age of thirteen, Jean-Pierre Cortot had already studied sculpture with Antoine Bridan and worked with various sculptors. In 1809 he obtained the prize of Rome with a work in ronde-bosse entitled *Marius sur les ruines de Carthage*. He stayed in Rome for ten years. His extremely academic style was applied to a number of statues and mythological and religious groups, often of very large dimensions and, for the most part, executed as offical commissions. *L'Apothéose de Napoléon 1er* or the *Triomphe de 1810* (1833, 5.85 m.), one of the four groups of the Arc de Triomphe, and the pedestal of the Chambre des Députés (1842), were considered his major works (although the first was under-appreciated and violently criticized at the time). Also significant are the works *Louis XIII équestre* in stone from the Vosges Plaza(1829), the statue in bronze of *Casimir Périer* (1837) at the Père-Lachaise, and some decorative works for the Louvre and many churches in Paris and the provinces. A certain number of projects executed in plaster by Cortot were never completed. This is the case with *L'Immortalité*, a colossal statue designed for the Pantheon, the plaster model of which was made into some reductions in bronze entitled *La Victoire*.

The Barbedienne catalog notes two works by Cortot cast in many sizes: *Le Soldat de Marathon* (based on the marble of the Salon of 1834, today at the Louvre museum), 98, 66, 51, 40 cm, and *Sainte Catherine* (based on the statue of the church of la Madeleine), 70, 35, 17 cm.

MUSEUMS
Louvre

Le Soldat spartiate or *Soldat de Marathon*, reduction, 40 cm.

La Victoire or *L'Immortalité*, 130 cm.

La Victoire, sketch, 45 cm.

SALES

Le Soldat de Marathon (Barbedienne), Bergerac, April 26, 1986.

*Georges Charles Coudray,
Kidda, 75 cm
(Société des bronzes of Paris).*

COUDRAY, GEORGES CHARLES

Born in Paris

A student of Falguière, this artist produced statues, busts, and medallions which often revealed an eastern influence. He exhibited his work at the Salon from 1883 to 1903. Among his most characteristic works are *Aquila*, a statuette in bronze (1892), *Les Nénuphars*, a bust in terra cotta (1899), and *Iris*, a statue in marble (1902). His most famous work, however, and the most widely reproduced, is a statuette in plaster entitled *Tahoser*, inspired by *Roman de la Momie* of Théophile Gautier, representing an Egyptian playing the harp. The statuette was exhibited at the Salon of 1892 and has been reproduced many times in bronze.

SALES
Arabe au cimeterre, 91 cm, Christie's Oklahoma (United States), September 24, 1981.
Kidda, 75 cm (Société des Bronzes de Paris), Sotheby London, March 20, 1986.
Tahoser, 53 cm, Drouot, June 18, 1986, room 9.
Tahoser, 70 cm, Sotheby London, November 7, 1985; Nancy, December 8, 1985; Semur-en-Auxois, March 30, 1986; Drouot, May 21, 1986, room 14; Reims, October 26, 1986.
Tahoser, 85 cm, Christie's New York, October 16, 1984; Lille, April 21, 1986.

COURTET, AUGUSTIN

Lyon, 1821
Paris, 1891

Groups and statuettes with subjects from antiquity are typical of works produced by this sculptor. He studied first at the school of fine arts in Lyon, then at the École des Beaux Arts in Paris with Pradier, Ramey Jr., and Dumont. Courtet's debut at the Salon was in 1847. He is the author of a group in bronze, *Centauresse et faune*, for the park of the Tête-d'or in Lyon. Some reductions in bronze of this work are known. The Thiébaut house cast *Danseuse romaine*, 39 cm, and *Faune sautant à la corde*, 37 cm. The museum of Blois owns a statuette entitled *Faune sautant à la corde*, 37 cm, cast by Thiébaut et fils (1849).

COUTAN, JULES

Paris, September 22, 1848
Paris, February 23, 1939

A student of Cuvelier and the winner of the prize of Rome in 1871, Coutan debuted at the Salon in 1876. He also participated in the decoration of the Exposition Universelle of 1889, and directed the Sèvres factory from 1891 to 1894 before replacing Falguière at the Académie des Beaux-Arts in 1900. He received some commissions for the ornamentation of different monuments in Paris. He is responsible for some statues, primarily allegorical, for the Paris courthouse (*La Clémence*), the city hall, and the National Library (*La Calligraphie*). He also made a haut-relief in bronze entitled *L'Attaque des aigles* for the side facade of the anatomy gallery at the Jardin des Plantes, and the large sandstone portico executed by Sèvres for the factory's pavillion at the 1900 Exposition Universelle; today this work is located in Félix-Desruelles Square, the apse of the

Georges Charles Coudray,
Tahoser, 70 cm.

Jules Coutan,
Renommée équestre,
haut-relief
on pillar
in onyx,
75 cm.

Jules Coutan,
La Paix armée,
98 cm.

Saint-Germain-des-Prés Church. Many of Coutan's allegories were reduced and cast in bronze, sometimes in many dimensions; Thiébaut cast its version of the haut-relief *Renommée* in two sizes, 122 x 88 cm and 80 x 57.5 cm, *La Paix armée* in 78, 47, and 19 cm, and two candelabras, *La Danse* and *Le Chant*, in 210, 155, 130, and 50 cm.

MUSEUMS
Paris, Decorative Arts
Homme en costume de travail portant un sac et un panier (part of a centerpiece).
Paris, Petit Palais
La Paix armée, 98.5 cm.

SALES
Paix, Travail, Union, gilded bronze, 62 cm, Drouot, May 19, 1982, room 1.
La République, 99.5 cm (Thiébaut—Fumière and Gavignot), Christie's New York, June 19, 1984.
La Victoire or *Renommée*, 75 cm (support in onyx), Drouot, November 13, 1985, room 4.

COUTHEILLAS, HENRI FRANÇOIS

Limoges, December 16, 1862
October 31, 1927

A student in the schools of decorative arts first in Limoges and then in Paris, Henri François Coutheillas exhibited at the Salon starting in 1890. He first exhibited some busts, and then figures: *Chasseresse*, plaster (1894), *Nymphe aux roseaux*, a statuette in marble (1895), *Le Chêne et le roseau*, a group in marble (1900), some statuettes in bronze including *Débardeur* (1901), *Roseau* (1902), *Le Bûcheron* and *Naïveté* (1903), and *Dans la colline* (1909), and a small group in plaster entitled *Aux champs* (1914). He continued to be an active artist after the war, always prefering to sculpt allegorical nude female figures. He is also the author of a monument to the dead in the city of Guéret. A cross section entitled *Les Pavots* was cast in bronze by the Thiébaut house.

MUSEUMS
Guéret
Canéphore, 22 cm.
André Porthault, ami du sculpteur, medallion, 32 cm (1905).
Tête d'homme au capuchon, 10 cm.

CRAUK, GUSTAVE

Valenciennes, July 16, 1827
Meudon, November 17, 1905

Expressing his artistic tendencies at a young age, Gustave Crauk began his studies at the academy of Valenciennes and pursued them, starting in 1845, at the Ecole des Beaux-Arts of Paris with Ramey Jr., Dumont, and then Pradier. He won the

1851 prize of Rome with a bas-relief entitled *Les Grecs et les Troyens se disputant le corps de Patrocle*, and starting in 1853 sent some works to the Salon from Italy before his return to Paris in 1856. At that time he received numerous commissions from the state and from the city of Paris. His very abundant works include bust and medallion portraits of comtemporaries, statues, and allegorical groups. He worked for the Louvre, the palace of Luxembourg, the museum of Luxembourg (the front), the Opera, the city hall, the Gare du Nord, the Sèvres factory (pediment), the school of medicine, and the churches of the Sacré-Coeur and the Trinité among others. He is the author of the statue of the Admiral of Coligny (1892), and the apse of the temple of the Oratoire.

Among the submissions by Crauk to the Salon were a number of bronzes, as well as busts of contemporaries including Mac Mahon executed for the Ecole de Saint-Cyr (1861), and of Casimir-Perier (1867). He also made the statues entitled *Femme à l'amphore*, 185 cm (1861), *La Victoire couronnant le drapeau français*, 200 cm, for the Crimée Column of Arts-et-Métiers Square (1864), *La Douleur*, 125 cm, for a tomb to Père-Lachaise, and finally a statuette entitled *Le Maréchal Pélissier, duc de Malakoff* (1859). Also of note is a bronze, *Enfant Nègre sénégalais*, dating from 1896.

At the end of his life, in 1903, the sculptor opened the Crauk Museum in Valenciennes, created by the donation of a large number of his works, notably models. This collection was integrated with the Musée des Beaux-Arts after World War II.

MUSEUMS
Amiens
Satyre assis, 185 cm (1860).
Cambrai
Auguste Herlin, medallion, 81 cm diam.
Le Général Garibaldi, medallion, 18 cm diam.
Compiègne, château
Le Maréchal Pélissier, 32 cm.
Grenoble
Buste de Casimir-Perier, 75 cm.
Paris, Carnavalet
Poulin, architecte des palais nationaux, medallion, 17 cm diam. (Barbedienne).
Roubaix
Constantin Mils, bust.
Troyes
Buste de Casimir-Perier, 59 cm (Thiébaut).
Valenciennes
Le Général Faidherbe, 187 cm (Barbedienne).
La Victoire, reduction in gilded bronze, 40 cm (Siot-Decauville).
Some busts: *Emile Signol*, 57 cm, *Portrait d'une femme*, 71 cm (Barbedienne), *Portrait d'homme*, 51 cm, *Le Général Derroja*, 73 cm (Barbedienne), *Le Général Saget*, 32 cm (Thiébaut Frères), *Jules Potier*, 28 cm, *Le Shah de Perse Nasser Eddim*, 89 cm.
Some medallions: *Adrien Marc, notaire*, 45.5 cm diam, *Cardinal Lavigerie*, 62 cm diam (Thiébaut Frères), *Edouard Fromentin*, 39.5 cm diam, *Emile Dusart, architecte*, 40 cm diam (Barbedienne), *Giuseppe Garibaldi*, 19 cm diam.

SALES
Bacchante et Silène, 86 cm, Drouot, October 28, 1985, room 4.

CRISTESCO, CONSTANTIN

Born in Romania, Cristesco studied sculpture in Paris with Victor Peter and Raoul Verlet. At the Salon, he exhibited in 1908 a group in bronze entitled *Victimes* in 1908 and a group in plaster entitled *Chevaux du prince Ghika* in 1911. The Susse house cast the bronze *Question d'amour-propre*, representing the fall of a horse on a hurdle. One proof on a marble base, 47 cm, was sold in London by Sotheby on March 20, 1986. One other work was sold in Lille on January 26, 1987.

Constantin Cristesco,
Cheval sautant une haie
or Question d'amour-propre, 47 cm
(support in marble).

CROISY, ARISTIDE
Fagnon (Ardennes), March 31, 1840
Paris, November 6, 1899

Attracted to sculpture at an early age, Aristide Croisy went to Paris when he was sixteen years old, and was admitted to the Ecole des Beaux-Arts just one year later. In 1863, he was awarded the second prize of Rome for his bas-relief *Nysus et Euryale*, and in 1867 he exhibited at the Salon for the first time. In addition to some restorations at the chapel of the château of Versailles, he worked in Paris for the city hall, the Louvre, the Bourse, and the 19th district's

*Aristide Croisy,
Baigneuse au rameau,
60 cm.*

city hall. He is also the author of many commemorative statues and monuments, including *Chanzy* in Buzancy in the Ardennes, *Le Chevalier Bayard* in Mézières, the monument to the dead of Sedan, etc. Of note among his submissions to the 1870 Salon are *La Prière d'Abel*, a statue in bronze cast by Thiébaut, and to the 1898 Salon, a statuette in bronze entitled *Baigneuse*.

The Susse foundry cast the following works in different dimensions:

Chasseur à pied, 40, 30, 19 cm.
La Défense du drapeau, 120, 80, 58 cm.
La Défense du dreapeau, avec deux marins, 58 cm.
Le Général Chanzy, 100, 69, 40 cm.
Marin, 68, 49, 33 cm.
Mobile, 68, 49, 33 cm.
Patrie, 111, 85, 55, 42 cm.
Tirailleur, 60, 40, 30 cm.
Zouave et chasseur, 66, 53, 35 cm.
Zouave pontifical, 66, 48 cm.
Une Baigneuse au rameau, 60 cm, was sold at the Drouot Hotel on March 23, 1987, room 3.

CROZATIER, CHARLES
Le Puy, 1795
Paris, February 8, 1855

Although he had studied sculpture with Cartelier, Crozatier worked primarily as a founder and an engraver. In this role, he is responsible for the production of important bronzes, among which are some monumental works. On the other hand, his personal work as sculptor seems to have been very small.

MUSEUMS
Bayonne
Prométhée enchaîné, 75 cm.
Le Puy
Main symbolique de Crozatier, 20 x 10 cm.
Vierge à l'Enfant, 69 cm (1854).
Vierge à l'Enfant assise, 69 x 40 cm.
This museum also has some works in different materials.

CUGNOT, LOUIS LÉON
Paris, October 7, 1835
Paris, August 19, 1894

Son of the sculptor Etienne Cugnot, Louis Léon Cugnot entered the Ecole des Beaux-Arts in 1854 and in 1859 shared the first grand prize of Rome with Falguière, for a work on the theme *Mézence blessé secouru par son fils Lausus*. In 1863, while still in Rome, Cugnot made his debut at the Salon with one of his major works, *Corybante étouffant les cris de Jupiter enfant* (the marble of which was placed in the gardens of the Tuileries). Some other allegorical or mythological compositions followed, such as *Cérès rendant la vie à Triptolème*, a group in marble (1865), and then some bronzes: *Fileuse de Procida*, a souvenir of Italy (1867), *Retour d'une fête de Bacchus*, a group of 145 cm high designed for the garden of the Palais des Arts in Lyon (1870), *Fileuse* (1873), *Mercure messager d'amour* (1879), *Jeanne d'Arc à ses derniers moments* (1882), and finally some decorative vases, including *Les Quatre Saisons* for the garden of the archbishop of Bourges and for the Niort garden (1884). Cugnot worked on different Parisian monuments: the city hall, the Opera, the Louvre, the churches of the Sorbonne and of the Trinité, the Hotel de la Paiva, the courthouse (*La Loi protégeant l'Innocence* and *La Loi punissant le coupable* for the north facade), and finally for the palace of Saint-Cloud and for the city of Lima (the monument of the *Victoire des Péruviens sur l'escadre espagnole* in 1866).
MUSEUMS
Amiens
Corybante étouffant les cris de Jupiter enfant, 216 cm (based on the plaster sent from Rome, 1862).
Lyon
Faune ivre.
Saint-Etienne
Corybante étouffant les cris de Jupiter enfant, reduction, 92 cm.

CUMBERWORTH, CHARLES
Verdun, February 17, 1811
Paris, May 19, 1852

Cumberworth

Busts of women and children and allegorical statues in a classical style were sent by this artist to the Salon between 1833 and 1848. Most memorable are a statue in bronze entitled *Pêcheur napolitain jouant de la mandoline* (1838), another statuette in bronze, *Marie* (1846), some statues in marble, *La Modestie* and *La Générosité* (1837), and a group in plaster entitled *Paul et Virginie* (1844).

The following works were included in contracts for castings by the Susse foundry:

Le Comte de Paris et l'ange gardien, 25 cm.
Danseuse au tambourin, 42 cm.
Domingo, 75, 41, and 32 cm.
Enfants se disputant pour une corbeille de fleurs, 100, 65, and 52 cm.
Jeune Fille endormie et l'ange gardien, 25 and 20 cm.
Jeune Fille à l'oiseau, 30 cm.
Marie, 90, 41, and 32 cm.
Mère de famille, 30 and 12 cm.
Moïse sauvé des eaux, 42 cm.
Odalisque couchée (according to Ingres), 25 and 10 cm.
Odalisque couchée habillée, 25 cm.
Paul et Virginie, 50, 35, 30 and 25 cm.
Tom-Pouce, 12 cm.
Vierge immaculée, 40 and 25 cm.

In his thesis *La Petite Sculpture d'édition* (1944), C.B. Metman notes that *Le Passage du torrent*, first cast by Boyer, was also cast by Susse after the death of Cumberworth.

The catalog of the Thiébaut house offers *Le Lever*, 22 cm, *Le Coucher*, 20 cm, *La Joie d'une mère*, 33 cm, and *La Peine d'une mère*, 32 cm.

Also according to C.B. Metman, the founder Daubrée, who was a friend of the sculptor, made the posthumous castings of *Agar et Ismael, Amours fixées, L'Amour de soi, Gage d'amour, Indienne, Négresse, Printemps, Souvenir, Vénus aux fleurs*, etc. Finally, many other subjects including *Cléopatre* and *Lesbie* were cast in bronze by Léon Marchand.

MUSEUMS
Chartres
Pudeur.
Paris, Decorative Arts
Le Duc de Montpensier debout, 54 cm (Susse).
Innocence, 30 cm (E. Quesnel).
Paris, Louvre
L'Amour de soi, 34.5 cm
Femme à demi nue tenant un médaillon sur sa poitrine, 35 cm.
Lesbie ou la Jeune Femme à l'oiseau mort, 34.5 cm.

Joseph Cuvelier,
Deux Chevaux
de course montés,
25 cm
(H. Luppens, founder).

SALES

Moise sauvé des eaux, 39 cm, Sotheby London, November 8, 1984.
Paul et Virginie, 36 cm (based on the group of 1844, with clothed people), Sotheby London, November 8, 1984.
Encrier, oiseau et fleur, 11 cm, Enghien, 1981.

CURILLON, PIERRE

Tournus, March 6, 1866
La Jumellière (Maine-et-Loire), March 2, 1954

After beginning his studies at the school of fine arts in Lyon in 1886, Pierre Curillon arrived in Paris in 1890 and exhibited at the Salon from 1893 to 1942. His works there were almost all statues and groups in plaster, including *La Liseuse* (1894), *Victime du devoir*, *Résignation* (1896), *Surprise* (1897), *Découragement* (1900), *Piété filiale* (1902), *Frisson de la vague* (1911), etc. There are also several replicas in marble and some bronzes, including a statue entitled *Le Bon Berger* for a tomb of Père-Lachaise. The works from the first part of Curillon's career have elongated and graceful forms. He also participated in the decoration and restoration of many public monuments, and after the First World War he made a number of monuments to the dead. His work entitled *Glaneuse* was cast in bronze by Siot-Decauville.

CUVELIER, JOSEPH

Commines (Nord), ?
Malmaison, October 21, 1870

Cuvelier died in combat while defending Paris. He had started to exhibit at the Salon in 1867, contributing a number of studies of animals, particularly horses and ponies, as well as wax medallions with equestrian portraits. His works include *Carrossier, cheval demi-sang*, a statuette in bronze (1867), and *La Sortie du pesage*, a group in wax (1870).

SALES

Cheval à l'arrêt, 38 cm (H. Luppens, founder), Sotheby London, March 20, 1986.
Cheval et son jockey, 24.5 cm, Sotheby London, March 20, 1986.
Cheval de trait, 36.5 cm (H. Luppens, founder), Sotheby London, March 20, 1986.
Deux Chevaux de course montés, 25 cm (H. Luppens), Sotheby London, March 20, 1986.
Jockey tombant de cheval, 18 cm, Sotheby London, November 7, 1985.

Joseph Cuvelier,
Cheval à l'arrêt, 38 cm
(H. Luppens, founder).

DAGONET, CHARLES ERNEST

Châlons-sur-Marne, May 4, 1856
Châlons-sur-Marne, July 30, 1926

Primarily an animal sculptor, Dagonet was also a very good portrait artist, though he did not neglect to sculpt religious, historical, and allegorical subjects as well. He became devoted to representing violent or painful scenes. The work *Eve chassée du paradis*, sent to the Salon of 1894, is considered to be his masterpiece. Initially studying painting under Jean-Paul Laurens, Dagonet soon chose to devote himself to sculpture after receiving instruction from Moreau-Vauthier (whose daughter he married in 1885). In 1913 he established himself permanently in Châlons-sur-Marne, and there experienced a difficult era of German occupation. He made his debut at the Salon in 1883, and exhibited a number of busts there, some of them in bronze. Also at the Salon were some plasters, including *Christ au tombeau* (1886), *Valet de chiens* (1887), *Chevrette prise au collet* (1888), *La Nuit* (1890; marble in 1892), and *Chasseur d'ours de l'âge de pierre* (1899). He also submitted to the Salon a group in wax entitled *Capture* (1898), and finally the bronzes *Chevreuil mort* (1892), *A Gergovie* (1899), *La Marseillaise* (1903), *Cerf pris par les loups* (1904), and *Combat de cerfs* (1906).

Dagonet is also the author of a monument in honor of Carnot in Châlons-sur-Marne and of many monuments to the dead executed after the First World War. There are a fair number of bronzes by Dagonet made by different founders. In an exhibition of his works, organized in 1982 at the museum of Châlons-sur-Marne, the following proofs were shown:

Buffle attaqué par un couple de lions, 49 x 76 cm.
La Capture, 30 x 56 cm (cast to 20 models).
Chasseur d'ours de l'âge de pierre, 20.5 cm.
Combat de cerfs, 22 x 42 cm (Hohwiller, founder; exists in many sizes).
La Marseillaise (cast by Thiébaut Frères in 80, 58, and 37 cm).
Buste de La Marseillaise, 30 cm.
Neptune, 17.5 cm (one of his last works).

La Nuit, 83 cm (Houdebine, founder).
Some medallions and busts, including that of his father, Léon Dagonet, 73 cm, and that of his grandson Maurice, 36 cm, and finally, a bas-relief representing his daughter Thérèse, 37 x 30 cm.

Other notable bronzes by the sculptor are *Danseuse au triangle*, 94 cm, cast by Barbedienne, *Diane*, *Actéon*, two statues of 160 cm high (sold in Versailles in 1976), *Valet de chiens*.

MUSEUMS
Châlons-sur-Marne
L'Aurore, 67 cm (Houdebine, founder).

SALES
Chien forçant un cerf, 60 cm, Marseille, November 29, 1986.
Piqueux à cheval chargé par un sanglier, 36 cm, Christie's London, January 22, 1986.

DALOU, JULES

Paris, December 31, 1838
Paris, April 15, 1902

The opposite of Carpeaux, his teacher who stayed intimately tied to the period of the Second Empire, he became the sculptor par excellence of the Third Republic. From 1871 to the amnesty of 1879 he was even forced into exile in England as a result of his politics and his position in charge of preservation at the Louvre, a position to which he was named by the Commune of Paris. Originally from a common thoroughly republican environment, Dalou, at a very young age, was influenced by Carpeaux, assistant teacher at the Petite Ecole where he met Rodin. When he was sixteen years old, Dalou was admitted to the Ecole des Beaux-Arts where the very academic teachings of Duret scarcely suited him. In order to earn a living, he worked for some goldsmiths, applying himself to engraving the minute detail on miniscule subjects. He also did ornamental sculpture on the facades of buildings and funeral monuments. In 1861 he sent his first submission to the Salon, *Dame romaine jouant aux osselets*, which he himself later destroyed.

Before enumerating the works and the facts of Dalou's career, it is important to determine what significance the numerous bronzes carrying his signature had for the artist's work. Details indicate that the large majority were executed after his death. Except for some subjects cast under his control during his visit to London, and later, between 1898 and 1899, two or three figurines and the bust of Henri de Rochefort (as well as some rare castings in sandstone made by Haviland in Limoges), Dalou never envisioned his works being reproduced in a material other than the one he had initially chosen. Moreover, he opposed it: "A work," he said, "is made for one material and one dimension; to change it is to distort it."

But he had named Orphelinat des arts of Courbevoieas residuary legatee, on the condition that they take care of his only handicapped daughter. In possession of more than three hundred sculptures from the sculptor's studio, principally sketches and studies in plaster and in terra cotta, this establishment resold them in 1905 for 30,000 F, to the city of Paris (they belong today to the museum of the Petit Palais). The executors of Dalou's will made the decision to authorize the reproduction of these works, according to them in order to enhance the glory of the artist and to insure the revenues of the Orphelinat des Arts (which they did).

These posthumous bronzes were first cast by the lost wax method by Hébrard. Some proofs carry the notation "unique piece;" others were numbered, generally from 1 to 10. Some were cast in a greater number, which is doubtlessly the reason for their success; they were also numbered, but by series of ten or twelve, each series designated with a letter of the alphabet. It remains to be known how many letters were used. Finally, some more abundant, numberless castings were made by the Susse house, not to mention the unglazed porcelain and sandstones produced by the Sèvres factory).

Dalou failed twice to take the prize of Rome, and never went to Italy. Instead, he traveled to London, and from there to Belgium in 1875, and thus felt the influence of Rubens and of Flemish baroque; these styles combined with Carpeaux's, and appear in a number of Dalou's works. Two opposing forces met in the sculptor's work: a conscientious realism— sometimes harsh, and sometimes delicate—most notable in his extensive series of seated young women (embroiderers, readers, mothers nursing, etc.), and a much freer, lyrical baroque tendency, represented notably by the *Triomphe de Silène, Les Petits Enfants de la reine Victoria*, and the

Bacchanales. The baroque aspects of Dalou's style (and this was not unique to Dalou) manifested itself more in the early sketches than in the finished works.

At the beginning of his career, Jules Dalou pursued his work by sculpting ornaments. He worked at the hotel of the Paiva on the Champs-Elysées, for which he executed some bas-reliefs, some statues, and four consoles which each had two figures of women. Shortly thereafter, he began to participate in the decoration of many hotels belonging to the rich bourgeosie, including the Hotel Menier in Monceau Park. The artist married in 1866, and in 1869 finally experienced success at the Salon with his group *Daphnis et Chloé*; even greater success was to come at the Salon of 1870, with *Brodeuse*. After Dalou's flight to London with his wife and daughter, he cast a bronze of *Brodeuse* based on a reduction in plaster that he had taken into exile. This bronze would be shown in 1873 at the salon of

Jules Dalou,
Lavoisier, 42 cm (Susse),
J. Ginepro Collection, Monaco.

the Royal Academy. Another bronze was cast when he returned to France, this one by Legrain.

Among the most noteworthy worksfrom the artist's long stay in London are *La Boulonnaise au rameau*, a terra cotta from 1871, 60 cm, bought by the Count of Carlisle (to whom Dalou had been introduced by his friend, the painter Alphonse Legros), as well as *Jeune Mère allaitant* or the *Parisienne allaitant*, a marble presented in 1872 at the Royal Academy under the title *Maternal Joy*. Next on this list are *Paysan française allaitant*, 125 cm, a terra cotta from 1874, *La Leçon de lecture*, actually a portrait of Madame Dalou and her daughter, a plaster, 48 cm (dated 1874), *Boulonnaise allaitant son enfant*, a variant of *La Paisanne*, 66 cm (1877), *La Liseuse*, 47 cm, and a study for this last work, *Femme nue lisant dans un fauteuil*, 34 cm.

In 1877, Dalou made a group in marble entitled *La Charité*, which was erected behind the stock exchange in London, to be replaced by a bronze in 1897. In 1878, he gave the chapel of Windsor Castle a monument in memory of Queen Victoria's grandchildren who had died young. The following year, one year before returning to France, he sent the model of *Triomphe de la République* to the open competition held by the city of Paris. Even though it did not meet the requirements imposed for the plaza of the same name, the work was so successful that it was finally chosen to be raised in the center of the Plaza of the Nation. The sculpture was unveiled provisionally under the design of a plaster tinted bronze in 1889, and permanently, in bronze, ten years later.

Upon returning to Paris, Dalou exhibited at the Salon of 1883 two haut-reliefs in plaster, *La Fraternité* and *Mirabeau répendant à Dreux-Brézé*. The latter was cast in bronze by Eugène Gonon for the salon of the Paix du Palais-Bourbon. At the Salon of 1885 the plaster of the *Triomphe de Silène* appeared, the bronze version of which, cast by Thiébaut, has stood in the gardens of Luxembourg since 1898. Also in 1885, the tomb of Auguste Blanqui was unveiled at Père-Lachaise with the recumbent bronze statue of the politician. In 1886, the statue of Lavoisier took its place at the Sorbonne.

The *Monument à Delacroix*, cast in the lost wax method by Bingen, was in turn unveiled in the gardens of Luxembourg in 1890. That same year the sculptor left the Société des Artistes Français to participate in the formation of the Société Nationale des Beaux-Arts, at which Salon he would henceforth exhibit. Also unveiled in 1891, for the tomb of Victor Noir at the Père-Lachaise, was a recumbent bronze effigy sculpted with astonishing realism, just like the fountain of the flower garden for the gate of Auteuil, with its stone medallion in high-relief representing a graceful bacchanal.

The pediment of the Dufayel stores in Paris, decorated on the theme of *Le Progrès entraînant le Commerce et l'Industrie*, dates from 1894; the *Monument à la mémoire d'Alphand* on Avenue Foch, from 1899; and the two lions on the left bank of the Alexandre III Bridge, from 1900. Other sculptures were unveiled after Dalou's death, including the

Jules Dalou,
Lazare Hoche, 75 cm.

monument to Hoch in Quiberon (1902), to Gambetta in Bordeaux (finished by Camille Lefèvre in 1905), of Levassor or the *Automobile*, at Maillot Gate in Paris (1907, also finished by Camille Lefèvre), and finally of August Scheurer-Kestner in the Luxembourg Garden (1908).

It is necessary to mention Dalou's official commissions. In addition to the multiple sketches and preliminary studies made for these works, Dalou produced some statuettes and some small groups which inspired different posthumous castings by Hébrard and Susse, as discussed above. They include, among others, *Châtiments*, a haut-relief exhibited at the Société Nationale des Beaux-Arts in 1890, the *Nymphe et faune*, sometimes called *Le Baiser* (around 1892), *Bacchus consolant Ariane* (1892), *La Frileuse* (around 1892), and *La Vérité méconnue*, also called *Le Miroir brisé* (around 1900).

One enormous project occupied Dalou for the twelve last years of his life. He had planned the building of a gigantic monument to the working man, but it did not get beyond the stage of studies. There remain only about a hundred figurines representing all the types of work carried out by men: *Semeurs et Semeuses, Batteur de faux, Faneuse, Retour des champs, Botteleur, Marin au filet, Paveur au repos, Homme retroussant ses manches, Soudeur, Terrassier*, etc. From 1889 on, the sculptor dreamed of this work as the crown of his career, a way to make concrete his social and political ideas. He had studied the types of peasants, miners, factory men, and sailors while traveling in different regions of France. Only the *Grand Paysan* was finished, with a raw grandeur. Some of the very small (10 to 20 cm high) terra cotta sketches, today existing as bronze castings at the Petit Palais, release an exceptional sense

Jules Dalou,
La Vérité méconnue
or le Miroir brisé,
35 cm.

DALOU

Jules Dalou,
Femme nue
s'essuyant le pied,
34 cm
(Hébrard No 6).

Jules Dalou,
Baigneuse surprise,
55 cm.

of the monumental, with a power and feeling far surpassing the idealistic character typical of other works commenting on the social issues of that period. A remarkable and talented craftsman, Dalou (according to the biography by Henriette Caillaux) devoted himself "to the cult of human forms, harmonious and beautiful." Eclectic—sometimes classical, sometimes baroque—he remained, as another author wrote, "the most gifted of the official artists of the end of the 19th century."

From the general inventory of Dalou's works compiled by Henriette Caillaux in the 1935 work devoted to the sculptor, it is possible to draft a list of bronzes made through the lost wax method by the founder Hébrard (to which can be added the more abundant castings noted above). They are classed below by subject matter.

Feminine figures
Baigneuse, also called *Avant le bain,* 56 cm.
Baigneuse, also called *Surprise,* 55 cm.

La Berceuse, after the terra cotta exhibited in 1874 at the Royal Academy under the name of *Rocking Chair,* 56 cm. (unique proof).
La Brodeuse (plaster at the Salon of 1870), 28 cm.
La Fileuse nue, les bras croisés, 39 cm (10 proofs).
La Liseuse, 47 cm.
Femme allaitant, (10 proofs).
Femme assise, sans bras, study for a monument to justice, not finished, 30 cm (10 proofs).
Femme cousant, 22 cm.
Femme à la jambe levée, 18 cm (10 proofs).
Femme au drapeau, sketch for the haut-relief of *Fraternité,* 40 cm.
Femme sans tête, study for the statue of Lavoisier.
Torse de femme se pressant le sein, 12 cm (10 proofs).
Femme nue assise, study for the monument to justice, 28 cm (10 proofs).
Femme nue assise dans un fauteuil, retirant son bas, 19 cm (10 proofs).
Femme nue assise sans bras, study for the monument to Gambetta, 27 cm (10 proofs).
Femme nue baissée s'essuyant le pied, 36 cm.
Femme nue s'essuyant le pied, 34 cm (10 proofs).

Femme nue lisant dans un fauteuil, 1878, study for *La Liseuse*, 34 cm (unique proof).
Femme nue retirant son bas, 34 cm.
Femme nue se courbant called *La Mère*, sketch for the haut-relief of the *Fraternité*, 25 cm (unique proof).
Femme nue accroupie, bas-relief, 22 x 15 cm (10 proofs).
Femme nue assise, bas-relief, 30 x 17 cm (10 proofs).
Femme nue vue de dos, bas-relief, 41 x 16 cm.
Femme nue, study for the *Triomphe de la République*, 49 cm (10 proofs).

Children

Enfant portant un livre, study for the *Triomphe de la République*, 47 cm (unique proof).
Protection de l'Enfance, sketch for the group of Queen Victoria's grandchildren, 47 cm.
Enfant couché, study for the same group, 33 cm (unique proof).
Enfant, study for the same group, 45 cm (10 proofs).
Bébé endormi, bust for the same group, 31 cm.
Tête de jeune garçon, for the same group, 31 cm.
Ange à l'enfant, first project for the same group, 33 cm.
Ange et cinq enfants, sketch for the same group.

Jules Dalou,
Study for La République, 49 cm
(Hébrard).

Jules Dalou,
Buste d'enfant endormi, 31 cm
(Hébrard).

Jules Dalou,
La Chute d'Icare, 16.5 x 51 cm
(Hébrard No 4).

Jules Dalou,
Tête de juene garçon,
31 cm.

Jules Dalou,
Le Chasseur, sketch, 22 cm
(Hébrard).

239

Jules Dalou,
Tête de Silène, 4 cm,
(Hébrard).

Jules Dalou,
Le Triomphe de Silène,
study, 66 cm
(recent casting by Susse).
J. Ginepro Collection, Monaco.

Masculine figures
Homme assis, 19 cm (10 proofs).
Masque d'homme, 22 cm (unique proof).
Homme les bras levés, sketch for the *Triomphe de Silène*, 40 cm (unique proof).
Homme nu allongé, sketch for the same group, 20 x 52 cm (5 proofs).
Le Charretier lorrain, bust, 1893, 47 cm (10 proofs).
Le Chasseur, project for a group not executed designed for the duke of Gramont, 65 cm (10 proofs).
Le Chasseur, sketch for the same group, 22 cm (10 proofs).
Ecorché, study for the same group, 37 cm (10 proofs).

Paysan à la blouse, 52 cm.
Le Paysan italien, bust, 1897, 40 cm (10 proofs).

Mythology, allegory
Bacchanale, reduction of the haut-relief of the Jardin Fleuriste, 63 cm diam. (unique proof).
Bacchus consolant Ariane, 1892, 84 cm (unique proof).
Bacchus consolant Ariane, sketch, 25 cm.
Bacchus consolant Ariane, first project, 20 cm (10 proofs).
Centaure lapidant un homme, 20 cm (10 proofs).
Centaure enlevant une femme, 26 cm.
Torse de centaure, 23 cm (10 proofs).
La Charité, 91 cm.

240

*Jules Dalou,
Buste
de Silène,
23 cm
(Hébrard
No 18, 1923).*

Diane au carquois, sketch, 15 cm (10 proofs).
Mélancolie, 24 cm.
Nymphe et faune called wrongly *Le Baiser*, 42 cm.
Le Progrès entraînant le Commerce et l'Industrie, sketch
   for the pediment of the Dufayel store, in Paris,
   1894, 32 x 71 cm (10 proofs).
Le Rapt à tête de faune, 14 cm.
Supplication wrongly called, *Tentation*, 27 cm (10
   proofs).
Le Triomphe de Silène, sketch for the group of the
   Luxembourg Garden, 68 cm (unique proof).
Silène seul, 54 cm (unique proof).
Masque de Silène, 14 cm (50 proofs).

People

Alphand, 28 cm, *L'Ingénieur*, 27 cm, *Le Peintre*, 28 cm,
   Le Sculpteur, 20 cm, four studies of nudes for the
   monument to Alphand (10 proofs each).
L'Amiral Courbet, project of the monument not ex-
   ecuted, 16 cm (10 proofs).
La Courtisane, sketch for a monument not accom-
   plished, 21 cm.
Delacroix, model of the monument of the Luxembourg
   Garden, 90 cm (unique proof).

*Jules Dalou,
Centaure
lapidant
un homme,
20 cm
(Hébrard).*

*Jules Dalou,
Centaure
enlevant
une femme,
26 cm
(Hébard).*

Charles Floquet, sketch for his monument to Père-Lachaise, 47 cm.
Lazare Hoche, model for his monument in Quiberon, 1902, 40 cm.
Lazare Hoche, model of the statue, 75 cm.
Victor Hugo, bust based on the marble of the Comédie-Française.
Les Orateurs de la Restauration, project for the monument designed for the Pantheon, 66 cm.
Emile Levassor, sketch for the monument of the Maillot Gate in Paris, 1907, 20 cm.

Animals
Cheval étude, 31 cm (10 proofs).
Deux Lions conduits par des enfants, sketch for the Alexandre III Bridge, 24 x 10 cm.
Tête de lion, 10 cm.
Patte de lionne, high-relief, 11 x 34 cm.
Tête de lionne, high-relief, 40 x 51 cm (unique proof).
Tête de mouton, 24 x 35 cm.
Tête de singe, 21 cm (10 proofs).

Sketches for the monument to the working man
Débardeur poussant un bloc, 14 cm.
Homme portant une corbeille, 12 cm.

Jules Dalou,
Le Baiser du faune,
43 cm
(Hébrard).

Homme soulevant un sac, 10 cm.
Marlin au filet, 29 cm.
Ouvrier au repos, 14 cm.
Paveur avec chapeau.
Paveur courbé avec demoiselle, 13 cm.
Paveur droit sans chapeau, 17 cm.
Paveur tête nue, 15 cm.
Terrassier s'appuyant sur sa pelle, tête à gauche, 16 cm.
Terrassier s'appuyant sur sa pelle, 20 cm.
Terrassier chargeant, 19 cm.
Tueur saignant un boeuf, 7 x 18 cm.
Tueur saignant un boeuf, fragment, 25 cm.

Bas-reliefs
Botteleuse, medallion, 10 cm diam.
Chantier de tailleurs de pierre, 19 x 57 cm.
Maréchal-ferrant, 21 x 18 cm.
Moissonneurs, 17 x 57 cm.
Pêcheurs, 17 x 57 cm.
Travaux à la campagne, freize in 3 registers, 22 x 18 cm.

Castings in bronze made by Susse
Bacchanale, reduction of the high-relief of the Jardin fleuriste, 63 cm.
Boulonnaise allaitant son enfant, 1877, 66 cm.

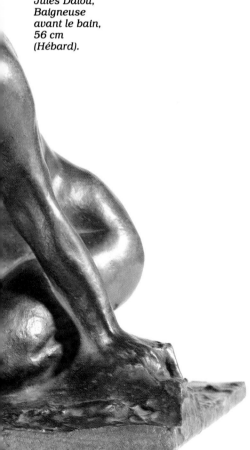

Jules Dalou,
Baigneuse
avant le bain,
56 cm
(Hébard).

Jules Dalou,
Baigneuse
se lavant le pied,
54 cm
(Hébrard A 2).

243

1) Jules Dalou, La Sagesse soutenant la Liberté, study for the monument in Gambetta, 57 cm (1889).

2) Jules Dalou, Moissonneur affûtant sa faux, 12 x 15.5 cm (Susse).

3) Jules Dalou, Retour des champs, 13 cm (Susse).

③

Jules Dalou, Botteleuse,
11 cm (Susse).

Les Châtiments, 1890, bas-relief, 33 x 23 cm.
Femme nue, torso, 49 cm.
La Fraternité, bas-relief, 44 x 28 cm.
La Fayette, sketch, 1881, 36 cm.
Lavoisier, 103, 51, 42, and 29 cm.
La Liseuse, 47 cm.
Mirabeau répondant à Dreaux-Brézé, sketch for the
   high-relief, 26 x 60 cm.
Nymphe et faune called *Le Baiser*.
La Parisienne (or *Jeune Mère*) *allaitant*, 1872.
Le Grand Paysan, diverse reductions based on the
   statue (H. 1.95 m.), the statue itself cast by Susse.
Paysanne française allaitant, reduction of the terra
   cotta exhibited at the Royal Academy in 1874, 50
   cm.
Paysanne française allaitant, sketch, 39 cm.
Silène, mask, 14 cm.
Le Travail, 61 and 30 cm.
La Vérité méconnue or *Le Miroir brisé*, 35 adn 22 cm.

Sketches for the monument to the working man
Bineur debout, 14 cm, *Botteleur*, 11 cm, *Botteleuse*, 11
   cm, *Casseur de pierres*, 10 cm, *Glaneuse*, 8 cm,

Retour de l'herbe, 11 cm, *Retour des champs*, 13
cm, *Retour du bois*, 13 cm, *Semeur sur piédestal*,
82 cm, *Petit Semeur sur piédestal*, 41 cm,
Terrassier, 20 cm, *Tonnelier*, 15 cm, etc.

MUSEUMS
Arras
Les Epousailles or *Passage du Rhin*, group, 26.5 cm
   (Hébrard).
Autun
   This museum owns a torso portrait of a woman and
twenty-one small bronzes cast from terra cotta sketches
for the monument to the working man: *Balayeur au
capuchon*, *Batteur de faux*, *Couvreur*, *Faneuse*, *Homme
piochant*, *Homme retroussant ses manches*, *Moissonneur*,
Paveur au repos, *Soudeur*, etc.
Belfort
Ouvrier portant un panier de pierres, 11 cm (Hébrard).
Le Paveur, sketch, 12 cm (Hébrard).
Mont-de-Marsan
La Brodeuse, 67.5 cm (1870).
La Défense de la patrie (Hébrard, unique piece, 1901).
Le Grand Paysan, 79 cm (Susse).

245

Jules Dalou,
Terrassier s'appuyant sur sa pelle, 16 cm
(Hébrard A 15).

Paysan, mains sur les hanches, 13 cm
(Susse).

Paris, Decorative Arts
Général Hoche, 72 cm (Hébrard).
Grande console de l'hôtel de la Paiva (1864), supported
    by two figures of nude men in bronze (which would
    have been modeled for Dalou by Carrier-Belleuse).
Paris, Orsay
Bacchanale, medallion in high-relief, 63 cm diam.
Baigneuse, sketch, 17.7 cm (Hébrard).
Le Baiser du faune, 42 cm (Hébrard).
Centaure enlevant une femme, 28.5 cm.
Georgette Dalou, fille du sculpteur, bust, 51.5 cm
    (1876).
Tête d'enfant endormi, 19 cm (Hébrard).
Etude de femme lisant, 33 cm (1878; Hébrard, unique
    piece).
Homme couché, study for the *Triomphe de Silène*, 22 cm
    (Hébrard, one of the five proofs cast in 1906).
Homme soulevant un sac, 9 cm (Hébrard No 8).
Jeune Homme, bust, 47 cm (1884).
Lavoisier, 103 cm.
Parisienne allaitant, 46 cm (Hébrard).
Le Grand Paysan, 197 cm (Susse).
Etude pour le Grand Paysan, man standing, 14.5 cm
    (Susse).
Henri Rochefort, bust, 71.5 cm (1888; Bingen, founder).
Paris, Petit Palais
Ariane et Bacchus, 20 cm.
Centaure enlevant une femme, 25 cm (Hébrard).
Centaure lapidant, study of a torso, 23 cm (Hébrard).
Femme tenant sa jambe levée, 18 cm (Hébrard).
Torse de femme, study for a statue of *L'Abondance*, 50
    cm.
Femme tombant en avant, study for the *Triomphe de
    Silène*, 27 x 35 cm (Hébrard).
Homme à terre, study for the same group, 16 x 51 cm
    (Hébrard).
Junon, torso, 18 cm (Hébrard).
La Paix, study for the monument to Victor Hugo, 26 cm
    (Hébrard).

Jules Dalou,
Paysan relevant ses manches,
42 cm (Susse).
J. Ginepro Collection, Monaco.

246

Jules Dalou,
La Paysanne française,
sketch, 39 cm
(Susse).

Jules Dalou,
La Paysanne française allaitant,
50 cm (Susse).
J. Ginepro Collection, Monaco.

Le Peintre, Le Sculpteur, studies for the monument of
    Alphand, 28, and 23 cm (Hébrard).
Supplication, 31 cm (Hébrard).
Tête de lionne, haut-relief, 40 x 51 cm.
Busts: Charcot, 45 cm, Jean Gigoux, painting, 57 cm
    (unique proof), Francis Magnard, directeur du
    Figaro, 54 cm, Albert Siouville, 60 cm, Auguste
    Vacquerie, 47 cm, Portrait d'homme anonyme, 48
    cm.
    The museum of the Petit Palais also has some studies
in plaster and a very large number of sketches in terra
cotta, among which are those designed for the monument
to the working man.

    Works by Dalou also appear in many foreign muse-
ums, including the Victoria and Albert Museum of London.

SALES
L'Aiguiseur de faux, 30 cm (Susse), L'Isle-Adam, April
    28, 1985.
Ariane abandonnée, 20 cm (Susse), Drouot, February
    18, 1985, room 2.
Baigneuse assise sur un rocher, 55.5 cm, Argentan,
    May 25, 1986.
Baigneuse, called Avant le bain, 56 cm (Hébrard),
    Enghien, November 25, 1984 (sold for 178,000 F).
Baigneuse se lavant le pied, 34.5 cm (Hébrard), Drouot,
    July 1, 1985, room 4; Christie's London, January
    22, 1986; Drouot, June 18, 1986, room 4 (taking
    110,000 F).
Le Baiser du faune, 41.5 cm (Hébrard), Sotheby New
    York, April 26, 1986; Christie's London, May 15,
    1986.
Le Batteur de faux, 12.5 x 16 cm (Susse), Versailles,

247

*Jules Dalou,
Femme allaitant
or Maternité,
32 cm.*

*Jules Dalou,
La Boulonnaise,
35 cm
(Susse).*

*Jules Dalou,
Femme nue accroupie,
34.5 cm
(Hébrard A 7).*

Jules Dalou,
La Brodeuse,
64 cm
(edited by E. Legrain).

Jules Dalou,
La Liseuse,
55 cm
(1874; C. Valsuani),
J. Ginepro Collection, Monaco.

Jules Dalou,
Les Châtiments,
bas-relief, 33 x 23 cm
(Susse).

February 16, 1984.
La Botteleuse, 11.5 cm, Neuilly, May 10, 1983.
La Boulonnaise, 35 cm (Susse), Neuilly, December 4, 1984.
Boulonnaise allaitant, 65 cm (Susse), Drouot, May 25, 1984, rooms 5 and 6.
La Brodeuse, 21.5 cm (Hébrard), Drouot, November 28, 1985, rooms 1 and 7.
Centaure lapidant un homme (Hébrard No 2), Drouot, December 14, 1984.
Le Chasseur, 21 cm (Hébrard), Drouot, April 18, 1986, room 5.
Le Châtiment, bas-relief, 35 x 26 cm, Drouot, December 12, 1983.
La Chute d'Icare, 16.5 x 51 cm (Hébrard No 4), Drouot, May 19, 1982, room 1.
Combat d'hommes, 34 cm (Gaensien, founder), Drouot, May 30, 1984.
La Couseuse, 28 cm, Drouot, March 23, 1984, room 5; Sotheby London, June 17, 1986.
Enfant, bust, 38 cm, Roubaix, March 23, 1986.
Enfant endormi, bust, 18 cm (Hébrard), Drouot, March 25, 1985, room 7.
L'Enlèvement d'Europe, 27 cm (Hébrard), Roubaix, March 23, 1986.
Etude de nu, 20 cm, Rouen, December 7, 1986.
Faune, head, 15 cm (Hébrard No 23), Drouot, June 25, 1984, room 6.
Femme allaitant, 40 cm (Susse), Granville, June 13, 1986.
Femme assise bras levés, 20 cm (Susse), Rouen, December 7, 1986.
Femme au fagot, Rambouillet, October 12, 1986.
Femme, torso, 50 cm, Saint-Dié, March 17, 1985.
Le Général Hoche, 72 cm (Hébrard), Drouot, December 17, 1986, room 10.
Jeune Femme allaitant, 35 cm (Hébrard), Calais, November 10, 1985; Saint-Germain-en-Laye, November 29, 1985.
Jeune Fille, bust, 38 cm (Hébrard), Drouot, November 27, 1986, rooms 1 and 7.

La Marseillaise, 51.5 cm (Hébrard No 1), Drouot, November 29, 1985, room 9.
Maternité, 21.5 cm (Hébrard), Drouot, November 28, 1985, rooms 1 and 7.
Le Miroir brisé, 22 cm (Susse), Lokeren, October 20, 1986, Saint-Dié, November 30, 1986.
Le Moissonneur, bas-relief, 17.3 x 56 cm (Hébrard No 3), Drouot, February 27, 1985, room 1.
Le Paysan français, 39 cm (Susse), Neuilly, November 18, 1985.
Le Paysan à la moisson, 10.5 cm (Susse), Valenciennes, May 26, 1986.
Le Paysan remontant sa manche, 43 cm (Susse), Drouot, July 7, 1983, room 9.
Le Paysan remontant sa manche, 78 cm (Susse), Drouot, October 29, 1984, room 6.
Le Philosophe, 51 cm (Susse), Drouot, march 25, 1985, room 9.
La Porteuse de lait, 12 cm (Susse), Drouot, March 25, 1985, room 9.
La Ravaudeuse, 21 cm (Hébrard), Drouot, December 19, 1984.
La République, nude woman, 50 cm (Hébrard), Christie's London, May 15, 1986.
Retour des champs, 13 cm (Susse), Neuilly, May 10, 1983.
Silène a' mi-corps, 23 cm (Hébrard No 18, 1923), Drouot, May 19, 1982, room 1.
Silène, head, 44 cm (Hébrard), Drouot, July 1, 1986, room 15.
Le Terrassier, 60 cm (Susse), Rambouillet, October 20, 1985, Neuilly, November 19, 1986; Douai, December 7, 1986.

DAMERON, FRANÇOIS

Dijon, 1837
August 13, 1900

Dameron was a teacher at the school of fine arts in Dijon and a student of Jouffroy. From 1873 to 1886, he exhibited some busts and medallions representing contemporaries at the Salon. The museum of Dijon has a certain number of them, in marble and in plaster, as well as a medallion in bronze entitled *Emile Gleize*, a portrait of the curator of the museum (1876), 21 cm diam., and a bust in bronze, *Le Docteur Jules Lassalle* (1855), 71 cm.

DAMPT, JEAN-BAPTISTE AUGUSTE

Vénarey (Côte-d'or), January 2, 1854
Dijon, 1945

A student of the schools of fine arts in Dijon and then in Paris, this sculptor had lived in North Africa, and was often tempted by eastern themes. He began to exhibit at the Salon in 1876, contributing a certain number of busts as well as statues and groups, including *Ismaël*, plaster (1879), *Jeune Fille*, bronze (1884), *A la forge*, bronze (1885), *Avant la fantasia, souvenir de Tanger*, bronze (1887), etc.

The most characteristic period of his production was around 1900, when he made small busts and groups with symbolic meanings, often executed in ivory combined with wood or silver. Dampt was also asked to sculpt many monuments to the dead of World War I in Bourgogne.

Barbedienne cast a bronze casting of Dampt's *Saint Jean à genoux* in five sizes, 50, 38, 30, 23, and 14.5 cm.

MUSEUMS
Paris, Orsay
Cavalier arabe or *Avant la fantasia*, 52 cm (Tanger 1885), cast by Bingen.
Semur-en-Auxois
Enfant menant un boeuf (1904).

The museum of Dijon owns nearly thirty works by this artist in different materials.

DANTAN, ANTOINE LAURENT

Saint-Cloud, December 8, 1789
Saint-Cloud, May 25, 1878

Known as 'Dantan the elder', in 1816 he entered the Ecole des Beaux-Arts where he was taught by Bosio. Very attracted to mythological scenes, he known for the purity of his style, which was full of classical themes. In 1828, he won the first grand prize for sculpture with *La Mort d'Hercule*, and went to Rome. He returned to Paris in 1833, but even as early as 1819 he was exhibiting his works at the Salon, notably contributing such pieces as *Tête de*

nègre, in bronze (1837), *Jeune Fille napolitaine jouant du tambourin*, a statue in bronze (1838), *Mademoiselle Anaïs, du Théâtre français*, a statuette in plaster (1842), and a group of children in bronze (1852). Furthermore, a statue in bronze entitled *Vendangeuse* was sent to the Exposition Universelle of 1855, along with a bust in bronze of *Pierre Ligier dans le rôle de Richard III*, dated 1852. Dantan the elder also left a number of bronze busts and statues by Malherbe for the city of Rouen. He participated in the decoration of the Louvre, the city hall and many other Parisian churches. The Barbedienne catalog mentions the casting of a *Sainte Madeleine*, reduction in bronze of the statue from the church of la Madeleine, in 70, 35, and 17 cm in height.

MUSEUMS
Paris, Decorative Arts
Monsieur Dumas, industriel lyonnais, 35 cm (1839).
Paris, musée de l'Assistance publique
Buste de Velpeau (1857).

DANTAN, JEAN-PIERRE

Paris, December 28, 1800
Bade, September 6, 1869

Jean-Baptiste Dampt,
Cavalier arabe or Avant la fantasia,
souvenir de Tanger,
52 cm (1885; Bingen).
Musée d'Orsay.

Jean-Pierre Dantan was initiated by his father, a sculptor of wood, and as early as 1819 worked on the restoration of the ornamentation on the basilica of Saint-Denis. He entered the Ecole des Beaux-Arts in 1823, and, like his older brother Antoine Laurent, studied with Bosio. He debuted at the Salon of 1827 and went to Italy the following year with his brother, who had won the first prize of Rome. In order to differentiate between them, Jean-Pierre is called 'Dantan the younger'.

Considered to be the creator of the caricature genre of scultpure, Jean-Pierre Dantan made innumerable portrait-caricatures in terra cotta (close to three hundred), a certain number of which were cast in bronze. These very humorous, often unmerciful works target French and foreign personalities, and brought the sculptor great success, notably in Great Britain and with the critics. In Paris, he exhibited them in different locations, in particular with Susse at the Bourse. Moreover, he executed some three hundred and twenty busts in a more serious genre, among which were a number of musicians, some statues for churches in Paris and for the Louvre, and finally nearly twenty statuettes including *Madame Alexis Dupont de l'Opera dans le pas styrien*, 47 cm, which was cast in gilded bronze by the Lerolle brothers in 1837 (C.B. Metman, *La Petite Sculpture d'édition*, 1944).

Jean-Pierre Dantan,
Portrait-charge de l'architecte Hippolyte Lebas,
52 cm (Victor Thiébaut),
Fabius frères collection, Paris.

Dantan drew his inspiration from different countries; he visited London in 1833-1834, returned there in 1842, went to Algeria in 1844, and to Egypt in 1848. When he died, his widow donated the majority of his busts and caricature-portraits to the Carnavalet Museum. Also of note, cast by Susse, are the busts of *Beethoven*, 45 cm, *Glück*, 17 cm, *Mozart*, 17 cm, and *Haydn*, 17 cm.

MUSEUMS

Grenoble
Buste de Clot Bey, 36 cm.
Nancy
Buste du maréchal Canrobert, 70 cm.
Paris, Carnavalet
Forty-two busts in caricature.
Paris, Hébert museum
Le Peintre Hébert, caricature statuette, 27.2 cm.
Paris, Louvre
Buste-charge de Carle Vernet (1824).
Buste-charge de Talleyrand, 31 cm (1833).

DARBEFEUILLE, PAUL
Toulouse, October 5, 1852
October 27, 1933

This artist, who was both a sculptor and painter, produced allegories including *L'Avenir,* a statue in bronze, 14 cm, exhibited at the Salon of 1883, as well as *Enfant à la coquille,* another bronze, 75 cm, at the Salon of 1888. Other works include *L'Enfant qui rit,* a bust in plaster (1881) and *La Libellule,* in marble (1896). One bronze, *Femme lisant,* 63 cm, was sold in Meaux on June 22, 1986.

Paul Darbefeuille,
Femme lisant,
63 cm.

DARCQ, ALBERT

Lille, September 8, 1848
Lille, March 8, 1895

Darcq's entire career unfolded in his hometown, where he frequented the Ecoles Académiques from the age of seven. After tackling painting, he turned permanently to sculpture and started to exhibit in Lille in 1867. In 1871, he entered the Beaux-Arts of Paris in the studio of Cavelier, but, abandoning the contest for the prize of Rome, he returned to Lille in 1874. He obtainted the chair of sculpture at the Ecoles Académiques, which he held until his death. Starting in the same year, he participated at the Salon of Paris with some busts and statues in plaster, including *Vulcain travaillant* (1881), *Faucheur au repos* (1882), and *La Victoire* (1886). At the Salon of 1888, he presented the plaster model of a vast, semi-circular bas-relief entitled *Leçon sur la vie et la mort*, 200 x 410 cm, the bronze of which was cast the following year to be placed at the front of the Lille medical school. In 1878, he had already made the pediment for Rameau Palace, also in Lille.

MUSEUMS
Lille
Bacchante, bust, 80 cm (Engels, founder in Lille),
    based on the plaster of the Salon of 1875.
Buste de Géry Legrand, 70 cm (1881).
Buste d'homme, 47 cm (1875).
Buste d'Edouard Van Heude, 35 cm (1886).

DAUMIER, HONORÉ

Marseille, February 26, 1808
Valmondois, February 10, 1879

An observer who was simultaneously merciless and full of humor about the world of politics, law, and finance, Daumier was a painter of society's mores, a brilliant cartoonist, a fervent republican, and, as the engraved epitaph on his tomb at Père-Lachaise reads, a "good man, a great artist, and a great citizen," Daumier was universally celebrated for the innumerable lithographies appearing in the journals of his time. His paintings—nearly one hundred—were less well-known. His sculpted work is better-known thanks to the bronzes which have been cast from them. He never saw them, and no doubt never anticipated them, but nonetheless they bear a precious witness to the particularities of his art.

Daumier's father was a glazier—others say a framer—with aspirations to be a poet. Honoré Daumier went to Paris with his family at the age of six, and then entered the home of a lithographer, where he was introduced to the stone "engraving" technique which would win him fame if not fortune. Passionate about drawing and sculpture, he was encouraged in them by Alexandre Lenoir, the founder of the Museum of Monuments Français, with whom his father had struck up an acquaintance. Daumier made his debut in journalism in 1830 while furnishing some lithographs to *La Silhouette*, and then in 1832, to *La Caricature* and to *Charivari*, opposition

Honoré Daumier,
Autoportrait, bust, 72 cm
(Valsuani E 1).

Honoré Daumier,
Charles Philippon
or Le Rieur édenté, 15.5 cm
(Barbedienne 11/25 MLG).

Honoré Daumier,
Charles Guillaume Etienne
or Le Vaniteux, 15 cm
(Barbedienne 11/25 MLG).

Honoré Daumier,
Charles Léonard Gallois
or l'Ironiste,
21 cm.

Honoré Daumier,
Le Baron Delort
or Le Moqueur,
23 cm.

Honoré Daumier,
Claude Baillot
or L'Infatué de soi, 18 cm
(Barbedienne 4/25 MLG).

Honoré Daumier,
Jean Auguste Chevandier de Valdrome
or Le Stupide, 18 cm (
C. Valsuani, Mme H).

journals founded by Charles Philippon. One of his caricatures, representing Louis-Philippe and entitled *Gargantua,* led him to serve six months in prison in Sainte-Pélagie that same year.

1832 also marked the first publication of caricature-masks portraying the defenders of the "order of things"—that is, the parlementarians who served as targets of his journal. In order to observe the objects of his attention, Daumier attentively followed the sessions of parliament. Upon returning to his studio to make preliminary versions of his lithographs, Daumier molded the famous clay busts, today made in bronze, of which we will speak later on.

After the disappearance of *La Caricature,* prohibited by the government in 1835, Daumier continued to collaborate on *Charivari,* and later on *Boulevard, Journal amusant,* and *Monde illustré.* The public welcomed his lithographs but seemed to consider him primarily a humorous caricaturist. By chance, his very fine sensitivity and his immense talent were recognized by his friends—among them, Delacroix, Corot, Millet, Michelet, Balzac, and Baudelaire—who tirelessly supported and encouraged him. Indeed, Corot bought him the small house that he had rented in Vamondois, in which he would end his life, poor and nearly blind. Buried first in the village cemetery, his body was later transferred to Père-Lachaise where he lies between Corot and Daubigny. In most of his busts of parliamentarians, Daumier modeled or would have modeled (because sometimes protests were raised against the busts) figurines which constitute true studies of attitudes. But his most famous work remains the foreign silhouette of *Ratapoil,* a burlesque caricature of a pensioned officer, a recruiting agent for the Bonapartists. Daumier is also responsible for the two bas-reliefs of the *Emigrants,* and two large busts, including his self-portrait. It is probable that other works were cast by the artist. The majority were executed in unfired earth, and a number of them undoubtedly disintegrated. Others are known only by the plasters which have been cast from them.

By referring to the most recent research, it is possible to inventory the bronze castings made since the death of the artist.

Honoré Daumier,
Ratapoil, 43.5 cm
(A. Rudier).
J. Ginepro Collection, Monaco.

THE BUSTS OF THE PARLIAMENTARIANS

Modeled in terra cotta and paint at the beginning of the 1830s, the parliamentarians measure between 12.5 and 23.5 cm high. There are thirty-six caricature portraits whose identification is sometimes uncertain. In 1927, a print merchant and editor named Maurice Le Garrec bought these busts from the descendants of Philippon, to whom Daumier had recently sold them. Le Garrec had them repaired by the sculptor Fix-Masseau, then had them cast in bronze, in lost wax, by Barbedienne. Here the names of Daumier's subjects appear in alphabetical order; in parentheses are the names by which the artist's biographer Maurice Gobin designated them:

Le Comte d'Argout (*Spirituel et malin,* witty and cunning), 13 cm.
Claude Baillot (*L'Infatué de soi,* infatuated with himself), 18 cm.
Félix Barthe (*L'Important personnage,* The important personage), 16.5 cm.

Jean-August Chevandier de Valdrome (*Le Stupide,* The stupid), 18 cm.
Laurent Cunin (*Le Mauvais,* The evil one), 15 cm.
Benjamin Delessert (*Le Têtu borné,* The narrow stubborn one), 17.5 cm.
Le Baron Delor (*Le Moqueur,* The liar), 23 cm.
Hippolyte-Abraham Dubois (*Le Gros, gras et... satisfait,* The big, fat and... satisfied), 19.2 cm.
André-Marie-Jean-Jacques Dupin (*L'Orateur,* The Orator), 15 cm.
Charles-Guillaume Etienne (*Le Vaniteux,* The Vain), 15 cm.
Le Comte de Falloux (*Un malin,* A sly one), 23.5 cm.

255

① ② ③

Jean-Marie Fruchart (*Le Dégoût personnifié*, Distaste personified), 13.5 cm.
Jean-Claude Fulchiron (*Le Tartuffe*, The hypocrite), 15 cm.
August-Hippolyte Ganneron (*Le Timide*, The timid), 18 cm.
Joachim-Antoine J. Gaudry (*Triste jusqu'à la mort*, Sad until death), 17 cm.
François-Pierre Guizot (*L'Ennuyeux*, The bored), 22.5 cm.
Jean-Marie Harlé père (*Le Gâteux*, The senile dotard), 12 cm.
Le Comte de Kératry (*L'Oséquieux*, The Obsequious), 12.5 cm.
Charles-Malo-François de Lameth (*L'Indécis*, The indecisive), 14.5 cm.
Lecomte (*Le Subtil*, The clever), 17 cm.
Jacques Lefebvre (*L'Esprit fin et tranchant*, The secret and glaring spirit), 20 cm.
Le Comte de Montlosier (*Le Fourbe et rusé*, The deceiver and sly one), 18 cm.
Antoine Odier (*Le Méprisant*, The contemptuous), 15 cm.
Alexandre-Simon Pataille (*Le Gourmet*, The gourmet), 17 cm.
Jean-Charles Persil (*Le Scrupuleux*, The scrupulous), 19 cm.
Le Baron de Podénas (*L'Important malicieux*, The important malicious one), 21 cm.
Docteur Clément François Victor Gabriel Prunelle (*Le Dédaigneux*, The disdainful one), 13 cm.
Pierre-Paul Royer-Collard (*Le Vieux Finaud*, The old sly fox), 13 cm.
Comte Horace Sébastiani (*Le Fat*, The conceited), 13 cm.
Jean Vatout (*L'Entêté*, The obstinate), 20 cm.
Charles-Henri Verhuel, comte de Sevehear (*Le Niais*, The foolish), 13 cm.
Jean-Pons-Guillaume Viennet (*Le Rusé*, The sly one), 20 cm.
Inconnu, sometimes called *Pelet de la Lozère* (*L'Homme à la tête plate*, The man with the flat head), 14 cm.
Inconnue, called sometimes *Le Maréchal Soult* or *De Broglie* (*Le Hargneux*, The bad-tempered), 15 cm.

The two last busts make an exception in the sense that they do not represent parliamentarians. They are:

Charles-Léonard Gallois, journalist and historian (*L'Ironiste*, The ironic), 21 cm.
Charles Philippon, founder of *La Caricature et du Charivari* (*Le Rieur édenté*, The toothless laugher), 15.5 cm.

Twenty-six of these busts were cast in twenty-five models apiece; ten others—Le Comte d'Argout, Fulchiron, Guizot, Harlé père, Lameth, Odier, Pataille, Prunelle, Verhuel and Viennet—were each cast in thirty models. All were numbered and carry the seal of the editor, M.L.G. (for Maurice Le Garrec). The casting was started in 1929, and was finished in 1952. Complete series appear in many French and foreign collections, as well as in the musuems of Marseille and Lyon.

In the 1970s, Valsuani made three new castings of each of the thirty-six busts, for Mme Le Garrec and her two daughters, Mme Henyer and Mme Cordier. The proofs were marked LG, Mme H or Mme C according to their destination. As for the original works that had been sculpted in earth (terra crue), they were twice—first in the 1960s and then in 1980—before being sold at the Orsay museum. They were the focus of an exposition at the Sagot-Le Garrec Gallery in 1979.

Two other busts, also in earth, appear at the Glyptotèque Ny Carlsberg of Copenhagen—*Tête d'homme souriant*, 9 cm, and *Tête d'homme au chapeau haut-de-forme*, 11.5 cm, each of which was also cast in fifteen bronze models. Maurice Gobin, the author of the first catalog of Daumier bronzes (in 1952), pointed out the existence of some fraudulent copy castings; they are of an inferior quality, and while not numbered they do carry the initials HD in a semi-circle. These castings from other molds were destroyed shortly after World War II.

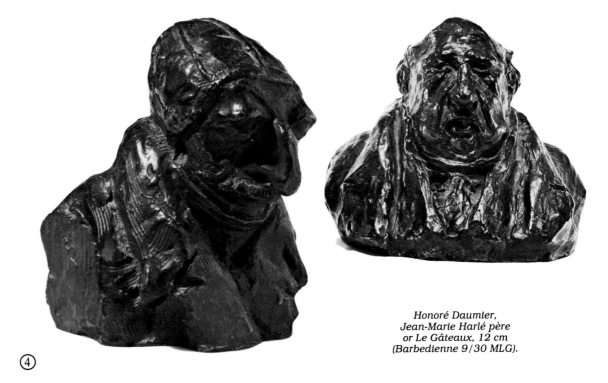

1) Honoré Daumier, Jean Pons Guillaume Viennet or Le Rusé, 20 cm (Barbedienne 18/30 MLG).

2) Honoré Daumier, Inconnu, called le maréchal Soult or de Broglie, or Le Hargneux, 15 cm (Barbedienne MLG).

3) Honoré Daumier, Lecomte or Le Subtil, 17 cm (Barbedienne 9/25 MLG).

4) Honoré Daumier, Inconnu, called Pelet de la Lozère, or L'Homme à la tête plate, 14 cm.

④

Honoré Daumier, Jean-Marie Harlé père or Le Gâteaux, 12 cm (Barbedienne 9/30 MLG).

THE FIGURINES AND *RATAPOIL*

Unlike the busts, Daumier's figurines were made not in terra crue but in terra cotta. Twenty-four of them represent typical characters of the bourgeoisie. Certain critics, notably Americans, believe that these statuettes, with their rather mysterious origins, were modeled belatedly by an anonymous sculptor, modeled after Daumier's lithographs and wood-engravings. The strongest proponent of this theory is Jeanne L. Wasserman, who discussed it in an article published by the *Gazette des Beaux-Arts* in February 1983.

Starting in the 1930s, Valsuani produced bronze castings of twenty-three of these figurines, using the lost wax method. Thirty numbered models (and three or four trial proofs marked EE1, EE2, etc.) were cast of each subject. Eighteen of them are known by the names given to them by Maurice Gobin:

L'Amateur d'art, 16.5 cm.
L'Amoureux, 18 cm.
L'Avocat saluant, 15.2 cm.
Le Bon Vivant, 15.9 cm.
Le Bourgeois en attente, 15.5 cm.
Le Bourgeois qui flâne, 18.7 cm.
Le Bourgeois en promenade, 16.5 cm.
Le Confident, 18.5 cm.
Le Dandy, 18.5 cm.
L'Homme d'affaires, 19.3 cm.
Le Lecteur, 17.1 cm.
Le Monsieur qui ricane, 18.6 cm.
Le Petit Propriétaire, 17. cm.
Le Poète, 15.3 cm.
Le Portier parisien, 16.2 cm.
Le représentant noue sa cravate, 17.8 cm.
Rôdeur ou le ramasseur de bouts de cigares, 14.6 cm.
Le Visiteur, 17.2 cm.

The five last figurines have been identified since the appearance of Maurice Gobin's volume. They are named:

L'Amateur en contemplation, 17.9 cm.
L'Amateur surpris (avec sa canne), 18.3 cm.
Coquetterie, 17 cm.
L'Elégant, 17 cm.
Provincial à Paris, 18.5 cm.

The sketch in unbaked clay of the famous Ratapoil dates from 1851. Daumier then asked his sculptor friend Victor Geoffroy-Dechaume to make a molding from it; the sketch seems to have been destroyed in the process, but the two resulting plaster models allowed the artists to proceed with three castings in bronze. Beginning in 1890, Siot-Decauville cast twenty numbered models, 43.5 cm, marked with the name of the sculptor and the seal of the founder. In 1925, Eugène Rudier cast twenty new proofs (and some trial proofs) for H. Bing, which were signed H. Daumier with the seal of the founder (that of his father Alexis Rudier). In 1960, yet another new casting, this time by C. Valsuani—twelve models (and three artist's proofs), without a signature, but numbered and marked with a founder's seal reading "Lost wax Valsuani."

Two very similar versions of *The Emigrants* were modeled in terra cotta around 1851-1852 to portray the deportation of nearly forty-eight people. Some plaster versions were cast, which gave rise to many castings in bronze. Five numbered proofs, 37 x 76.5 cm, were cast from the second version in 1893 by Siot-Decauville; also from that version, ten other numbered works, 33 x 72 cm, were cast by Eugène Rudier around 1935, each marked with the seal of Alexis Rudier. Finally, in 1955, ten proofs from the first version, 31 x 66 cm, were made by Georges Rudier for members of the Geoffroy-Dechaume family, descendants of Daumier's friend.

The bust *L'Autoportrait* was modeled around 1855, also in terra crue. A plaster was cast, without doubt by Geoffroy-Dechaume, from the now-missing original. In 1954-1955, Valsuani used these to make a casting of a dozen bronze proofs, plus three artist's proofs, each 72 cm. Please note that the quality of this self-portrait has been questioned by specialists including Jeanne L. Wasserman and Jacques de Caso (*Gazette des Beaux-Arts*, February 1983).

Of final note is the bust called *Louis XIV* or *L'Homme à la perruque,* 57 cm, thought to be a portrait of the actor Pierre Bernard, known as Bernard Léon. The earthen original, modeled around 1846-1850, still exists, and a plaster made from it was used in turn to produce Valsuani's bronze sketches in 1960—ten proofs, each 43.5 cm, including eight numbered and two trial proofs.

*Honoré Daumier,
Le Bon Vivant,
15.9 cm
(Valsuani 14/30).*

MUSEUMS
Lyon
This museum possesses a complete series of thirty-six busts of the parliamentarians.
Marseille
This museum possesses a complete series of thirty-six busts of the parliamentarians as well as a model of *Ratapoil,* 43 cm, one of the proofs cast by Siot-Decauville.
Paris, Orsay
Ratapoil, 43 cm (Siot-Decauville).
Paris, Petit Palais
Buste de M. Odier.

SALES
Busts
(Prices of adjudication of these were between 30,000 and 60,000 F).
Le Comte d'Argout, 13 cm (Barbedienne 26/30), Christie's New York, November 20, 1986.
Claude Baillot, 18 cm (Barbedienne 4/25), Christie's New York, October 9, 1986.
Chevandier de Valdrome, 18 cm (Valsuani), Drouot, March 19, 1984, rooms 5 and 6; Drouot, March 4, 1985.
Charles-Guillaume Etienne, 15 cm (Barbedienne 11/25), Christie's New York, October 9, 1986.
Le Comte de Falloux, 23.5 cm (Barbedienne 14/25), Christie's London, June 26, 1984.
Le Comte de Falloux, 23.5 cm (Valsuani), Drouot, December 14, 1984, room 6.
Jean-Marie Fruchart, 13.5 cm (Barbedienne), Drouot, November 23, 1984, rooms 5 and 6.
Charles Léonard Gallois, 21 cm (Barbedienne 15/25), Drouot, June 27, 1983.
Auguste-Hippolyte Ganneron, 18 cm (Barbedienne 21/25), Drouot, May 25, 1984, rooms 5 and 6.
Jean-Marie Harlé père, 12 cm (Barbedienne), Drouot, November 23, 1984, rooms 5 and 6.
Le Comte de Kératry, 12.5 cm (Barbedienne 17/25), Drouot, June 20, 1984, rooms 5 and 6.
Le Comte de Montlosier, 18 cm (Barbedienne 17/25), Drouot, june 20, 1984, rooms 5 and 6.
Charles Philippon, 15.5 cm (Barbedienne 11/25), Christie's New York, October 9, 1986.
Charles Philippon, 15.5 cm (Valsuani), Drouot, December 14, 1984, room 6.
Le Baron de Podénas, 21 cm (Valsuani, Mme H.), Christie's New York, November 20, 1986.

*Honoré Daumier,
L'Elégant,
17 cm
(Valsuani 10/30).*

*Honoré Daumier,
L'Amoureux,
18 cm
(Valsuani 23/30).*

*Honoré Daumier,
L'Homme d'affaires,
19.3 cm
(Valsuani).*

*Honoré Daumier,
Le Monsieur
qui ricane,
18.6 cm
(Valsuani).*

*Honoré Daumier,
L'Amateur d'art,
16.5 cm
(Valsuani 29/30).*

*Honoré Daumier,
Le Provincial à Paris,
18.5 cm
(Valsuani 10/30).*

*Honoré Daumier,
Le Bourgeois
qui flâne,
18.7 cm
(Valsuani 23/30).*

Comte Sébastiani, 13 cm (Barbedienne 10/25), Versailles, April 1, 1984.
Jean Vatout, 20 cm (Barbedienne 24/25), Drouot, November 29, 1984, rooms 5 and 6.
Jean-Pons-Guillaume Viennet, 20 cm (Barbedienne 20/30), Drouot, November 29, 1984, rooms 5 and 6).
Le Maréchal Soult, 15 cm (Barbedienne 15/25), Christie's New York, May 15, 1986.

Figurines
L'Amateur d'art, Le Bourgeois, Grenoble, December 8, 1986.
L'Amoureux, 18 cm (Valsuani 23/30), Drouot, December 1, 1983.
Le Bourgeois qui flâne, 18.7 cm (Valsuani 23/30), Drouot, January 23, 1984, room 1.
Le Bourgeois en promenade, 16.5 cm (Valsuani 8/30), Sotheby New York, June 7, 1984; (Valsuani No. 5), Grenoble, December 8, 1986.
L'Elégant, 17 cm (Valsuani 10/30), Drouot, December 1, 1983.
Le Monsieur qui ricane, 18.6 cm (Valsuani), Drouot, April 16, 1986, rooms 5 and 6.
Le Portier parisien, 16.2 cm (Valsuani 7/30), Christie's New York, October 9, 1986.
Le Provincial à Paris, 18.5 cm (Valsuani), Drouot, January 23, 1984, room 1; Valenciennes, April 9, 1984.
(Price of adjudication: between 40,000 and 78,000 F).
Ratapoil, 43.5 cm (Siot-Decauville No12), Soissons, December 10, 1983 (taking 500,000 F); (Siot-Decauville No. 17), Sotheby London, November 27, 1984 (£70,000).

Honoré Daumier,
L'Avocat saluant, 15.2 cm
(Valsuani 2/30).

Ratapoil, 43.5 cm (Rudier 10/20), Drouot, April 29, 1985; (Rudier), Drouot, May 18, 1985, rooms 5 and 6; Sotheby London, December 3, 1986.
Ratapoil, 43.5 cm (C. Valsuani, EE1), Sotheby New York, May 14, 1986; (C. Valsuani, EE2), Christie's New York, November 20, 1986.
Les Emigrants, bas-relief, 31 x 70 cm, Drouot, March 18, 1984.
Les Emigrants, bas-relief, 34 x 72.5 cm, Sotheby London, June 27, 1984.
Les Emigrants, bas-relief, 29 x 64.5 cm, Saint-Brieuc, July 20, 1985.

DAUTEL, PIERRE VICTOR
Valenciennes, March 19, 1873
November 12, 1951

A sculptor and a medal-engraver who won the prize of Rome in 1902, Dautel seems to have produced medals, medallions, and bas-relief plaquettes. The museum of Valenciennes possesses a medallion in bronze entitled *Portrait du peintre Henri Harpignies*, 24.5 cm diam, dated from 1909.

DAVID, FERNAND
Paris, September 3, 1872
December 13, 1926

At the Salon, where Fernand Davis began exhibiting in 1893, appear some busts, medallions, groups, statues in plaster entitled *Inquiétude maternelle* (1899), *La Musique* (1902), *Femme au bain* (1908), and *Jeunesse* (1910), and statuettes in bronze entitled *Le Coup de vent* (1907), *Baigneuse*, and *Le Comte R... de R... en tenue de chasseur* (1909). David also made statuettes in terra cotta and projects for many monuments and fountains. Of further note is a statuette in bronze entitled *Flore assise*, 56 cm high.

MUSEUMS
Paris, Orsay
Buste de l'acteur Silvain, 58 cm
Buste d'homme, 44 cm.
Tête de Négresse, 48.5 cm
Paris, Petit Palais
Bacchus, 90 cm.

DAVID D'ANGERS, ALSO CALLED
DAVID, PIERRE JEAN

Angers, March 12, 1788
Paris, January 6, 1856

Born into a modest family, David d'Angers learned drawing from his father, a wood-sculptor. But it was to his mother and his drawing teacher at the Ecole Centrale of Angers that he owed his departure for Paris in 1808. He entered the studio of the sculptor Roland and made the acquaintance of his namesake, the famous painter Jacques Louis David. Thanks to the encouragement of the latter, the young artist won the first prize of Rome in 1811. At the Académie de France, he met the sculptor Canova,

*David d'Angers,
Ambroise Paré,
50 cm.*

*David d'Angers,
La Liberté,
57 cm.
Museum of Decorative Arts.*

and with him learned about neo-classicism in all its fullness. Around 1830, at the peak of his glory, David d'Angers frequently visited Victor Hugo, who introduced him to sculpting nudes, as well as Alfred de Vigny and Sainte-Beuve.

This contact with artistic environments of opposing styles provides a good explanation of David d'Angers' art, halfway in between them. He so defies categorizing that although certain authors consider him to be one of the most outstanding personalities of sculpture in the romantic tradition, others are more inclined to place him within the classic tradition, even though they acknowledge that the artist did "bump into" romanticism in his desire to liberate sculpture "from the academic scholarly constraints" (André Fontaine and Louis Vauxcelles). David d'Angers himself confirms this double relationship in the notebooks—published in 1958—in which he recorded his thoughts and impressions. He noted there his simultaneous admiration for the Greeks and for the gothics, without dismissing as irrelevant the disparate concepts that distinguish and separate them from one another.

In 1817, upon returning to France, d'Angers received the commission for a statue of the Grand Condé designed for the Louis XVI Bridge, now the Concorde Bridge. The model in plaster was exhibited at the Salon. This audacious work, sculpted with haughty gestures and modern costumes that infringed on the rules of classicism—made d'Anger famous, and developed his reputation as an innovator.

After that, the artist was flooded with so many commissions that it would be impossible to take a census of them here. The following list includes only the most notable, in particular those which engendered some reductions in bronze: the statue in marble of Bonchamps (Salon of 1824) for his tomb at Saint-Florent-le-Vieil, in the Maine-et-Loire (in 1793, before his death, General Vendéen Bonchamps had ordered, the liberation of 5 million republican prisoners including David's father); the statue in marble of Racine (1827); that of Thomas Jefferson in Washington (1834); and the front of the Pantheon, commissioned after the days of July 1830 (in which he had taken part), inaugurated in 1837. Also on the list are a quantity of statues, sometimes of enormous size, for Paris and various cities in the province: *Bichat,* for the school of medicine, *Dominique Larrey* for the court of the Val-de-Grâce, *Armand Carrel* for his tomb at the cemetery of Saint-Mandé, *Cuvier* for Montbéliard, *Ambroise Paré* for Laval, *Pierre Paul Riquet* for Béziers, *Jean Gutenberg* for Strasbourg, *Le Roi René* for Angers, *Jean Bart* for Dunkerque, etc., as well as the funereal monuments in marble of the general Foy and of the general Gobert to Père-Lachaise, and finally more than one hundred busts and seven hundred fifty medallions in bronze representing particularly some contemporaries.

David d'Angers became a member of the Institut in 1826, and a professor at the Ecole des Beaux-Arts the following year; he also took up politics and became mayor of the eleventh district of Paris and deputy of the Maine-et-Loire in 1848. After the coup d'etat of December 1851, however, he was convicted as republican, sentenced first to prison and then to exile in Brussels and Greece. He did not re-enter France until 1853, and passed away just three years later.

Like most sculptors, David d'Angers' personality is better conveyed in his smaller works and in his sketches than in his statues and monumental groups. His purity of line and pursuit of ideal beauty is the mark of classicism in his work; however, his forceful, expressive, "vigorous and powerful technique" (especially in his busts and medallions) indicates an ardent spirit, largely open to the generous concepts of romanticism.

Produced primarily in bronze, d'Angers' medallions constitute an astonishing gallery of portraits of contemporary writers, musicians, scholars, painters, and politicians. Those encountered include Victor Hugo, Goethe, La Fayette, Bonaparte, Thiers, Géricault, Cherubini, and Achille Collas (who invented the sculpture reduction procedure that bears his name). Some medallions measure up to 50 cm in diameter, but the great number of them do not go beyond 20 cm. Many museums possess them, but the most important collections are found at the museum of Angers and at the Louvre.

Unlike the countless medallions, statuettes occupy a relatively unimportant place in d'Angers' production. The museum of Angers' catalog mentions only about forty sketches and maquettes in terra cotta and plaster and some castings in bronze, most of which are reductions of the statues: *Jefferson, Gutenberg, La Liberté*. The museum of the Louvre possesses some of them as well. It is interesting to note a letter by Mme David d'Angers written in October 1867 and published by Henry Jouin, which discusses the origin of the small bronzes by the sculptor:

"I know from a certain manner that among the statuettes by David, those of Jefferson, Armand Carrel, Cuvier (the statue of Montbéliard), and of Saint Cécile are only sketches; Condé, Foy, Jean Bart, and Talma are also some sketches, but much more polished. The statuettes of Gutenberg, the young Greek, and Fénelon had been obtained by the Collas reduction procedure. The statuettes by David, as I just explained, are for the most part only trial runs for the statues. He never had the desire nor the patience to recopy a work already finished. He yielded to the demand of the founders who wanted to reproduce some of his statues by the Collas procedure, which is far from perfect since it must be followed by a complicated touch-up by chiseling which often harms the faithfulness of the reproduction. Among the repeated requests, it is certain that he himself retouched his sketches of Condé and of Jean Bart as well as a reduction of Bonchamps that Froment-Meurice had chiseled, and of which M. Théobald de Soland posseesses a model, but (with the exception of the three statues of which I just spoke) David prefered many of his own sketches to the bronzes retouched without his participation."

The reproduction of certain works by David d'Angers did not decline after his death. Susse announced a *Gutenberg* in two dimensions, 40 and 16 cm, and in the catalogs of the Barbedienne house can be found the following bronzes:

David d'Angers,
Balzac, medallion,
19.5 cm diam.
Louvre Museum.

Fénelon (bending down), 54, 27, 20 cm.
Jeune Fille grecque (after a marble destined to the tomb of Botzaris in Missolonghi, exhibted at the Salon of 1827), 24, 20 cm.
Ambroise Paré (reduction of the statue in bronze by Laval), 49, 28, 23, 16 cm.
A series of busts:
Arago, 25 and 9 cm, Balzac, 24 cm, Béranger, 23, 16, 11 and 9 cm, Berzélius, 26 cm, Bichat, 26 cm, Chateaubriand, 21 and 8 cm, André Chénier, 24 and 9 cm, Cuvier, 25 and 14 cm, Delavigne, 30 and 6 cm, Desgenettes, 27 cm, Duméril, 25 cm, L'Abbé Grégoire, 25 cm, De Humbolt, 25 cm, Victor Hugo couronné, 25 cm, Victor Hugo non couronné, 21 and 8 cm, La Fayette, 19 cm, Lamartine, 24 and 19 cm, Lamennais, 24 cm, Schiller, 43, 29 and 12 cm, and Siéyèa, 25 cm.

Of final note are the works cast by the Thiébaut house: La Liberté, cast in a 24 cm high casting, and the 548 medallions portraying famous men, made from 1785 to 1850.

MUSEUMS
Alençon
Two medallions: Ambroise Paré and Louis Proust, chimiste angevin.
Angers
During his lifetime, David d'Angers donated to his hometown all the works from his studio, including the plaster models of his statues and monumental groups. This collection of nearly 700 pieces includes many hundreds of medallions in bronze. Since 1984 it has been remarkably presented in the ancient Toussaint church, which was restored especially for the purpose.
Of note here, in addition to the medallions, are:
Bonaparte, profile, 35 cm, according to a fragment from the front of the Pantheon.
Gutenberg, statuette.
La Liberté, 57.5 cm (sketch from a project for the Arc de Triomphe).
La France et l'Allemagne, bas-relief.
Paganini, bas-relief.
Les Quatre Ages de l'enfance, bas-relief.

Thomas Jefferson, 39.5 cm, according to the maquette of the statue erected in Washington.
Voltaire, profile, according to a fragment of the front of the Pantheon.
The busts displayed here include:
Comte de Volney.
François de Salignac Fénelon, 65 cm (Crozatier, founder).
François 1er, 73 cm.
Jean-François Bodin.
Jean Racine, 53 cm (Eck and Durand).
Louis Larevellière-Lepeaux.
Louis Proust.
Paganini, 57 cm (H. Gonon and his son).
Pierre Corneille (H. Gonon).
Prosper Ollivier (Eck and Durand).

Bayonne
Bonaparte, 35 cm, profile from the front of the Pantheon.
Ludwig Tieck, poete allemand, 30 cm (Eck and Durand).
This museum also possesses nearly fifty bronze medallions, among which are Bonaparte, Delacroix, Alexandre Dumas, Géricault, Houdon, Victor Hugo, Ingres, L'Impéatrice Joséphine, Kléber, La Fayette, Marat, Alfred de Musset, and Robespierre.
Béziers
Tête de Pierre Paul Riquet.
Besançon
Portrait de Jean Gigoux, medallion, 16.5 cm diam (1844).
Bordeaux
Six medallions: César Faucher, 17.5 cm diam. (Eck and Durand).
César et Constantin Faucher, 21.5 cm diam. (Eck and Durand).
Charles Dupaty, 16.5 cm diam.
Constantin Faucher, 17.5 cm diam. (Eck and Durand).
François Magendi, 16 cm diam.
Rosa Bonheur, 17 cm diam. (Eck and Durand).
Châlons-sur-Marne
Horace Vernet, medallion, 13.2 cm diam.
Chartres
Two medallions: Kléber and Le Sergent Marceau.
Dijon
La Liberté, 57 cm, and 25 medallions in bronze.
Grenoble
Casimir-Perier, medallion, 16 cm diam.
Morlaix
Edouard Corbière, medallion, 18 cm diam.
Nancy
Armand Carrel and J.J. Granville, two medallions.
Le Comte Boulay de la Meurthe, colossal bust, 69 cm.

Paris, Decorative Arts
La Liberté, 57 cm.
Paris, Assistance publique
Ambroise Paré, 48 cm.
Paris, Carnavalet

Three hundred and fifty-two medallions, the majority in bronze, including a medallion of large dimensions, Portrait de Jacques-Antoine Manuel, 58 cm diam. (1831).
Paris, Louvre
Ambroise Paré, 48 cm.
Armand Carrel
Bonchamps, 20 cm.
Cuvier, 37 cm.
Fénelon, 26 x 42 cm.
Le Grand Condé, 37 cm.
Gutenberg, 41 cm.
Jean Bart, 41 cm (after the sketch of the statue).
Jefferson, 41 cm.
La Liberté, 57 cm.
Racine, 40 cm (after the sketch of the marble statue from the Salon of 1827).
The museum of the Louvre owns also a large number of medallions in bronze.

Pau
Le Géologue Elie de Beaumont, medallion, 16 cm diam.
Laure Devéria, medallion, 9.5 cm diam.
Périgeaux
Napoléon 1er en buste, medallion, 13.5 cm diam.
Reims
Les Massacres de Galicie, medallion, 23 cm diam.
(1846).
Rouen
Buste d'Armand Carrel
Géricault, medallion.
Saumur
Tête de Bonchamps, nature grandeur.
Strasbourg
Buste de Bonaparte, haut-relief, 36 cm.
Toulon
Madame Roland, medallion, 23 cm diam.
Robespierre, medallion, 13.5 cm diam. (1836).
Samuel Haharmann, medallion, 23 cm diam.
Toulouse
Le Baron Larrey, medallion, 16 cm.
Troyes
Lazare Carnot, medallion, 17.4 cm diam.

SALES

Alexandre Dumas père, medallion, 12 cm diam.,
Sotheby Monaco, June 14, 1982.
Ambroise Paré debout, 60 cm, Nantes, December 17,
1986.
Le Lutteur (Thiébaut), Alençon, December 16, 1984.
Four medallions: *Balzac, Byron, Goethe,* and *Schiller,*
Epinal, December 18, 1983.
La République debout, 34.5 cm, Drouot, May 13, 1982,
room 4.

DAVIN, AUGUSTE

Saint-Michel-en-Beaumont (Isère), December 6,
1866
1928

This artist, who was active both in Paris and in
Grenoble, produced portraits which he began to
exhibit at the Salon in 1889. The museum of Grenoble
preserves two medallions in bronze, *Le Sculpteur
Rubin,* 29 cm diam., and *Concours musical de
Grenoble,* 30 cm diam.

DEBAY, AUGUSTE HYACINTHE

Nantes, April 2, 1804
Paris, March 24, 1865

Debay studied sculpture with his father Joseph,
and painting with the Baron Gros. After winning the
grand prize of Rome for painting in 1823, he decided
to devote himself permanently to sculpture. He
worked for the church of Saint-Etienne-du-Mon (*La
Résurrection* on the front of the facade), the fountain
of Saint-Michel (figures bending down entitled *Puissance* and *Modération*), and one of the fountains of
the Plaza de la Concorde (*L'Océan* and *La
Méditerranée*). At the Salon of 1845, he exhibited a
group in marble entitled *Le Berceau primitif* or *Eve et
ses enfants,* which would be cast in bronze by
Barbedienne.

DEBAY, JOSEPH

Malines, October 16, 1779
Paris, June 14, 1863

Joseph Debay went to Paris when he was still
quite young, in order to study sculpture first at the
Académie Royale and then with Chaudet. In the very
first years of the 19th century he went to Nantes,
where he worked for nearly fifteen years on a number
of the city's monuments, including the stock exchange, the city hall, and the cathedral. His debuts
at the Salon began in 1817, and they prompted
commissions for the decoration of the Louvre, the
Arc de Triomphe, the Bourse, and the churches of
Saint-Merri, Saint Nicolas-du-Chardonnet, Sainte-
Marguerite, and Notre-Dame-de-Bonne-Nouvelle. He
also sculpted a statue of Louis XV on horseback for
Montpellier. In 1845, he was called direct a studio to
repair the statues at the Louvre museum. His two
sons, Jean (1802-1862) and Auguste (1804-1865)
also became sculptors, so Josegph Debay is frequently called Debay Sr. At the Salon of 1822 he
exhibited a statue in plaster entitled *Mercure
saisissant son épée pour trancher la tête d'Argus,*
110 cm, the marble of which was exhibited two years

Auguste Debay,
Torse d'homme.
Louvre Museum.

Auguste Debay,
Le Berceau primitif, 44.5 cm.
J. Ginepro Collection, Monaco.

DEBUT, DIDIER

Moulins, June 4, 1824
Paris, April 1893

Debut

A student of David d'Angers, Didier Debut won the second prize of Rome in 1851. He sent a number of works (mainly plasters) to the Salon from 1848 until his death, in particular *Une leçon de flûte* (1848), *Petite Fille fellah* (1868), *Bouvier*, 100 cm (1875), and a series of plaster statuettes including *Sommeil de l'Amour* (1870), *Faneuse* (1887), *Gaulois* (1888), *Callot en Italie* (1889), *Ruy Blas* (1893), and finally statuettes entitled *Nemrod*, in bronze (1889) and *Eros*, in marble (1892). Another statuette, *Porteur*

Didier Debut,
Le Barde,
78 cm.

later and now belongs to the Louvre. At the Salon of 1842 appeared the marble *Vierge à l'Enfant*, and at the Salon of 1863, his last work, *Faustulus*, a 60 cm high bronze group. Two of the works by Debay Sr. are noted among the castings by Barbedienne: *Vierge à l'Enfant*, 50, 38, and 25 cm, and *Le Chancelier de l'Hospital*, 90, 67, and 45 cm. Another work, *Repos du monde*, 25 cm, appears in the catalog of the Thiébaut house. Susse cast *Le Génie de la chasse*, 60 and 44 cm.

MUSEUMS
Compiègne, château
Hallali, 16 cm (Quesnel, founder).
Nantes
Mercure saisissant son épée, 110 cm (Carbonneaux, founder).

Didier Debut,
Le Porteur d'eau arabe,
32 cm.

DEBUT, MARCEL
Paris, March 27, 1865
1933

DEBUT

This painter and sculptor studied with his father, Didier Debut, and began to exhibit at the Salon in 1883. The works he exhibited there are reminiscent of his father's subjects and style, and include some statuettes in plaster entitled *Sommelier du XVe siècle* (1889), *Petit Pêcheur au harpon* (1893), *Actéon* (1897), *Le Génie des arts* (1898), a statuette in

d'eau arabe, appears to have been successful, as proofs in bronze were rather frequently dispersed in public sales; data shows that this figure carries an urn in each hand, while the figure of an Arab water-carrier made by his son Marcel carries a single urn on the shoulder. Of further note re the bronzes *Couple dansant,* 75 cm, and *Joueur de vielle,* 45 cm.

MUSEUMS
Bordeaux
Gaulois, 57 cm.

SALES
Le Barde, 78 cm, Nogent-le-Rotrou, November 17,
    1985; Lille, January 27, 1986.
Janissaire, guerrier arabe, 32 cm, Drouot, June 17,
    1985, room 9; Christie's London, January 22,
    1986.
Le Jeune Artiste, 24 cm, Drouot, May 27, 1983, room 4.
Le Porteur d'eau arabe, 32 cm, Drouot, February 27,
    1985; Reims, March 24, 1985; Christie's London,
    January 22, 1986.

Marcel Debut,
Fantassin arabe,
37 cm.

marble entitled *Une gueuse* (1905), numerous statues, groups, and bas-reliefs in plaster, and finally the bronzes *Watteau*, a statuette (1890), a vase on the theme of *Persée et Andromède* (1896), *Labourage*, a group (1898), and *L'Hiver*, bas-relief, (1913).

Many works by Marcel Debut were cast in bronze, particularly his *Porteur d'eau arabe*, 31 cm, in which the figure carries a vase on his shoulder (whereas the similarly titled figure by his father holds an urn in each hand). Also cast in bronze are *Le Fauconnier*, 85 cm, as well as different vases and flower stands. Some subjects were cast in composition.

SALES

Fantassin, 37 cm, Enghien, April 28, 1985.
Fatima, 80 cm, Vienna, November 24, 1985; Lyon, July 3, 1986.
Le Porteur d'eau arabe, 32 cm, Madrid, October 23, 1985.
Le Porteur d'eau arabe, 65 cm, Brussels, December 10, 1985.
Vercingétorix, 86 cm, Drouot, December 9, 1982, room 8.
Le Violoniste and *Le Flûtiste*, two statuettes, 50 cm, Sotheby London, March 17, 1983.

DEGAS, EDGAR CALLED DE GAS

Paris, July 19, 1834
Paris, September 26, 1917

Degas

Known and admired all over the world for his paintings, pastels, and lithographs, this famous artist also sculpted (actually, modeled), principally in wax. Aside from a single statuette entitled *La Petite Danseuse de quatorze ans*, exhibited in 1881, this aspect of his work was revealed only after his death.

At the time of Edgar Degas' birth, his father was the manager of the Parisian branch of a bank founded in Naples by his grandfather, who had sought refuge there during the Revolution. After some studies at the Louis le Grand school, Degas entered the Ecole

Edgar Degas, Grande arabesque, deuxième temps, 43 cm (15/J).

Edgar Degas,
Danseuse attachant le cordon de son maillot,
42.5 cm (33/P).
Musée d'Orsay.

des Beaux-Arts in 1855. He made the acquaintance of Ingres, worked with a student of his named Louis Lamothe, admired Delacroix, and discovered Japanese stamps. He became an integral part of the impressionist group, and from 1874 to 1886 participated in all their exhibitions. But, unlike the friends who had originally interested him in landscapes, Degas was primarily intrigued by the gestures, movement, and attitudes of horses, which he studied beginning in the 1860s at his friend Valpinçon's place in Normandie and then at the race track, or of women, particularly of dancers in their different positions.

Self-educated in sculpting materials, Degas practiced it throughout his life only from an empirical standpoint, in spite of the advice from his friend, the sculptor Bartholomé. This brought him a number of difficulties and disappointments; he would much later find fault with his works (which he had readily abandoned in the midst of their execution) when they yielded to disintegration, or cracked, and fell to dust.

His first attempts concerned horses, which he often modeled from memory. According to Léonard von Matt and John Rewald (in *L'Œuvre sculpté de Degas*), *La Petite Danseuse de quatorze ans*, a young girl from the lower class of the Opera, was his first representation of the human body. He molded it in wax but dressed it in a real gauze tutu, a blouse, and shoes, and attached natural hair. The 80 cm work provoked some very diverse reactions at the exhibition of the impressionists in 1881. For J.-K. Huysmans, it was "the single truly modern attempt...at sculpture."

The other feminine statuettes, including some nudes, are not dated. They were never exhibited during the lifetime of the artist, nor was a bas-relief entitled *La Cueillette des pommes*. Degas' overwhelming sensitivity and acuity of vision brought him to repeat some nearly identical poses, with very minute, intricate details. These statuettes measure between 10 and 50 cm high; only a very few are larger. Unlike *Petite Danseuse de quatorze ans,* they were conceived not as completed works but as studies, full of spontaneity and suppleness. Whenever they appear in modern auctions, they provoke resounding bids.

Degas spent the end of his life in his studio and his apartment on Paris's Rue Victor-Massé. As his eyesight progressively failed, he began to devote himself almost exclusively to sculpting his figurines. In 1912, his building was to be demolished, and he was compelled to move to the Boulevard de Clichy, where he worked very little until his death in 1917; two years before Renoir who considered him as the greatest sculptor of his time, and the same year that Rodin who, after having dealt "entirely with touch" would one day declare: "I am mistaken, Degas is a great sculptor. He is better than me!"

It was indeed only in 1917 that Paul Durand-Ruel, drafting the posthumous inventory of Degas' works, counted 150 figurines—the majority in wax, some in dried clay, and nearly all in bad shape. In all, seventy-four statuettes could be saved and minutely restored; they portrayed dancers, women at their dressing tables, and seventeen studies of horses. Seventy-two of these were cast by the lost wax method in 1919-1921 by Adrien Hébrard, each in twenty-two proofs, twenty of which were trade proofs. Besides the signature of Degas and the seal of the founder, each proof carries a number and a letter. The letter, one of the first twenty of the alphabet (this is, from A to T), replaces the usual number of the proof. As for the number, it identifies the subject (from 1 to 72).

Bought in 1930, a complete series carrying the letter P is now part of the collections of the Orsay museum. The original waxes were acquired by the American collector Mellon, who gave four of them to the Louvre in 1956,.

Edgar Degas,
La Révérance,
33 cm (34).

Edgar Degas,
Danse espagnole,
43 cm (45/F).

Below, numbered in the order of the Hébrard casting, are listed the seventy-two subjects that were each cast in twenty-two bronze models (as discussed above, and according to the work of Léonard von Matt and Georges Rewald):

1. *Arabesque ouverte sur la jambe droite, le bras gauche en avant*, 28.5 cm.
2. *Arabesque sur la jambe droite, la main droite près de terre, le bras gauche en dehors*, 27 cm.
3. *Arabeesque sur la jambe droite, le bras gauche dans la ligne*, 28.5 cm.
4. *Cheval se cabrant*, 30.5 cm.
5. *Position de quatrième devant sur la jambe gauche*, 56.5 cm.
6. *Position de quatrième devant sur la jambe gauche*, 40.5 cm.
7. *Tête, étude pour le portrait de Madame S.*, 16 cm.
8. *Danseuse au repos, les mains sur les hanches, la jambe gauche en avant*, 37.5 cm.
9. *Danseuse saluant*, 22 cm.

Edgar Degas,
Danseuse,
position de 4e devant
sur la jambe gauche,
57 cm
(Hébrard 58/C).

10. *Cheval en marche*, 21 cm.
11. *Cheval marchant au pas relevé*, 22 cm.
12. *Danseuse au tambourin*, 27.5 cm.
13. *Cheval à l'abreuvoir*, 16 cm.
14. *Arabesque ouverte sur la jambe droite, le bras gauche en avant*, 20 cm.
15. *Grande Arabesque, deuxième temps*, 43 cm.
16. *Grande Arabesque, troisième temps*, 40 cm.
17. *Femme se lavant la jambe gauche*, 14.5 cm.
18. *Grande Arabesque, premier temps*, 48 cm.
19. *Danseuse s'avançant, les bras levés*, 35 cm.
20. *Danse espagnole*, 40.5 cm.
21. *Etude de cheval*, 22 cm.
22. *Cheval faisant une "descente de main,"* 19 cm.
23. *Danseuse tenant son pied droit dans la main droite*, 52 cm.
24. *Femme enceinte*, 43 cm.
25. *Cheval au galop sur le pied droit, le pied gauche arrière seul touchant terre* (see 35).

26. *Le Tub*, 47 x 42 cm.
27. *Tête, étude pour le portrait de Madame S.*, 27 cm.
28. *Torse de femme se frottant le dos avec une éponge*, 48.5 cm.
29. *Danseuse mettant son bas*, 46 cm.
30. *Cheval de trait*, 10 cm.
31. *Danseuse saluant*, 21 cm.
32. *Cheval au galop tournant la tête à droite, les pieds ne touchant pas la terre* (see 36).
33. *Danseuse attachant le cordon de son maillot*, 42.5 cm.
34. *La Révérence*, 33 cm (in the series A, this proof is numbered 24 by error; there are indeed in this series two proofs numbered 24).
35. *Jockey monté sur le cheval no 25*, H. total 24 cm.
36. *Jockey monté sur le cheval no 32*, H. total 28.5 cm.
37. *Cueillette des pommes*, bas-relief, 45 x 47.5 cm.
38. *Cheval arrêté*, 29 cm.
39. *Danseuse se frottant le genou*, 31 cm.

*Edgar Degas,
Danseuse tenant
son pied droit
dans la main droite,
52 cm (23).*

*Edgar Degas,
Femme sortant du bain,
42 cm (71/G).*

40. *Danseuse regardant la plante de son pied droit,* 45.5 cm.
41. *Danseuse au repos, les mains sur les reins, la jambe droite en avant,* 44.5 cm.
42. *Femme surprise,* 40.5 cm.
43. *Femme assise dans un fauteuil, s'essuyant l'aisselle,* 31.5 cm.
44. *Femme assise dans un fauteuil, s'essuyant la nuque,* 31.5 cm.
45. *Danse espagnole,* 43 cm.
46. *Femme assise s'essuyant le côté gauche,* 35 cm.
47. *Cheval au galop sur le pied droit,* 30 cm.
48. *Cheval s'enlevant sur l'obstacle,* 28.5 cm.
49. *Cheval au trot, les pieds ne touchant pas le sol,* 22 cm.
50. *Femme se coiffant,* 46 cm.
51. *Danseuse habillée au repos, les mains sur les reins, la jambe droite en avant,* 42.5 cm.
52. *Danseuse mettant son bas,* 45.5 cm.

53. *Femme s'étirant,* 36.5 cm.
54. *Femme assise s'essuyant la hanche gauche,* 44.5 cm.
55. *La Masseuse (groupe de deux femmes),* 41 x 38 cm.
56. *Etude de nu pour la danseuse habillée,* 72 cm.
57. *Préparation à la danse, le pied droit en avant,* 55.5 cm.
58. *Position de quatrième devant sur la jambe gauche,* 57 cm.
59. *Danseuse regardant la plante de son pied droit,* 49.5 cm.
60. *Grande Arabesque, troisième temps,* 43.5 cm.
61. *Femme se lavant la jambe gauche,* 20 cm.
62. *Tête appuyée sur une main, bust,* 12 cm.
63. *Danseuse au repos, les mains sure les rins, la jambe droite en avant,* 43.5 cm.
64. *Danseuse agrafant l'épaulette de son corsage,* 35 cm.
65. *Cheval caracolant,* 26.5 cm.
66. *Cheval pur-sang marchant au pas,* 13 cm.
67. *Danseuse regardant la plante de son pied droit,* 45.5 cm.
68. *Danseuse tenant son pied droit dans la main droite,* 49.5 cm.
69. *Danseuse regardant la plante de son pied droit,* 48 cm.
70. *Danseuse mettant son bas,* 43 cm.
71. *Femme sortant du bain (fragment),* 42 cm.
72. *Danseuse s'avançant les bras levés, la jambe droite en avant,* 69 cm.

The two figurines remaining were subsequently cast in bronze, *La Petite Danseuse de quatorze ans* in proofs marked by letter, 99 cm, and *L'Ecolière,* first in five models reserved for the heirs, and then in 1956, in twenty models again by Hébrard, the first two unnumbered, the others numbered from 3 to 20, 26.6 cm. This last casting was commissioned by the Knoedler Gallery in New York, proprietor of the original wax.

MUSEUMS
PARIS, ORSAY
La Petite Danseuse de quatorze ans, bronze, tulle, and satin, 80 cm.

This museum also possesses a complete collection of the bronzes (series P), as well as four original waxes donated by the collector Paul Mellon in 1956. (65 of the bronzes were exposed in 1983 at the Centre culturel du Marais.)
Valenciennes
Femme sortant du bain, 42 cm (71 HER, model reserved to the heirs).

Bronzes by Degas appear in many foreign museums, particularly in Great Britain, New York's Metropolitan Museum of Art, Washington's National Gallery, Copenhagen's Ny Calsberg Glyptotheque, as well as in a number of particular collections, particularly in Switzerland (Cf. catalogue of the exposition of the Swiss collections of Manet to Picasso, Lausanne 1964).

SALES
Arabesque sur la jambe droite, 28.5 cm (1/E), Sotheby London, December 2, 1986.
Position de quatrième devant sur la jambe gauche, 40.5 cm (6/B), Drouot, November 27, 1986, rooms 1 and 7 (taking 621,000 F).
Danseuse au repos, 37.5 cm (8/B), Sotheby London, December 3, 1986.
Danseuse saluant, 22 cm (9/HER), Sotheby London, March 27, 1985.
Arabesque ouverte sur la jambe droite, 20 cm (14/Q), Sotheby London, December 4, 1984; (14/HER), Sotheby London, June 24, 1986.

Edgar Degas,
Femme se coiffant,
46 cm (50/E).

Edgar Degas,
Cheval pur-sang
au pas,
13 cm (66/M).

Edgar Degas,
Cheval au galop
sur le pied droit,
30 cm (47/P).
Musée d'Orsay.

273

Grande Arabesque, troisième temps, 40 cm (16/T),
  Sotheby London, December 2, 1986.
Danseuse s'avançant, bras levés, 35 cm (19/K),
  Sotheby London, June 24, 1986; (19/E), Sotheby
  London, December 2, 1986.
Etude de cheval, 22 cm, (21/I), Sotheby New York,
  November 19, 1986.
Danseuse tenant son pied droit, 52 cm (23/J), Christie's
  New York, May 14, 1986.
Femme enceinte, 43 cm (24/E), Christie's New York,
  May 14, 1986.
Torse de femme se frottant le dos, 48.5 cm (28/HER),
  Sotheby New York, November 19, 1986.
Danseuse mettant son bas, 46 cm, (29/B), Sotheby New
  York, May 15, 1985.
Danseuse saluant, 21 cm (31/F), Sotheby London,
  March 28, 1984.
Cheval arrêté, 29 cm (38/M), Drouot, June 4, 1982
  (496,000 F).
Danseuse au repos, les mains sur les reins, 44.5 cm
  (41/B), Christie's New York, May 16, 1984.
Femme surprise, 40.5 cm (42/Q), Sotheby New York,
  May 15, 1985; (42/E), Sotheby New York, Novem-
  ber 14, 1985.
Femme assise dans un fauteuil, 31.5 cm (44/F),
  Sotheby London, June 24, 1985.

Edgar Degas,
Cheval arrêté,
29 cm (38/M).

Edgar Degas,
Cheval au galop
sur le pied droit
et son jockey,
24 cm (25 and 35).

274

Cheval au galop, 30 cm (47/D), Sotheby London, June 24, 1986 (£230,000).
Femme se coiffant, 46 cm (50/E), Drouot, November 26, 1984, rooms 5 and 6 (480,000 F); (50/G), Sotheby London, March 27, 1985.
Danseuse habillée au repos, 42.5 cm (51/J), Christie's New York, May 16, 1984.
La Masseuse, 41 cm (55/D), Sotheby New York, may 15, 1985; (55/F), Christie's New York, November 19, 1986.
Position de quatrième devant sur la jambe gauche, 57 cm (58/C), Sotheby London, December 2, 1986.
Danseuse regardant la plante de son pied, 49.5 cm (59/H), Christie's New York, May 16, 1984.
Grande Arabesque, troisième temps, 43.5 cm (60/M), Sotheby New York, May 15, 1984.
Femme la tête appuyée sur une main, 12 cm (62/E), Sotheby London, December 3, 1985.
Danseuse agrafant l'épaulette de son corsage, 35 cm (64/C), Versailles, June 26, 1985; (64/G), Sotheby London, December 4, 1985.
Cheval pur-sang, 13 cm (66/M), Enghien, June 19, 1986.
Danseuse tenant son pied droit, 49.5 cm (68/F), Sotheby New York, November 19, 1986.

DEGEORGE, CHARLES JEAN MARIE

Lyon, March 31, 1837
Paris, November 2, 1888

Admitted to the Ecole des Beaux-Arts in 1858 and winning the grand prize of Rome for medal-engraving in 1866, Degeorge participated at the Salon from 1864 to 1888. Of note among his works displayed there are *Jeune Vénitien du XVe siècle,* a bust in bronze (1872), *La Jeunesse d'Aristote,* a statue in marble, 125 cm (1875), *Souvenir d'Italie,* a small bronze (18 79), and *Un petit Florentin,* a study in terra cotta (1888). *La Jeunesse d'Aristote* was cast in bronze by Susse in four dimensions, 80, 60, 40, and 30 cm.

MUSEUMS
Amiens
Buste de Paul Emile Sautai, 50 cm.
Paris, Orsay
Three medallions: *L'Architecte Pascal,* 14 cm diam, *Henri Regnault,* 12.3 cm diam, *P. Sautai,* 10.2 cm diam.
Strasbourg
Buste de Jules Claretie, 54.5 cm (1874).

DEJEAN, LOUIS EUGÈNE

Paris, June 9, 1872
Nogent-sur-Marne, 1953

Dejean worked as a practician with Carlès and with Rodin after following the courses at the Ecole Nationale des Arts Décoratifs. He exhibited his works at the Salon des Artistes Français (particularly some medallions) from 1890 to 1893, and especially at the Nationale des Beaux-Arts beginning in 1899. Undoubtedly influenced by the Greek statuettes at the Louvre, he modeled a number of feminine figurines in terra cotta that the art critic A.H. Martinie described as "tanagras modernes." His art, initially precise and studied, evolved under the influence of Rodin to express greater power, before drawing closer to the style of Maillol. Dejean carried off his first success in 1904 with *La Parisienne,* and was

Louis Eugène Dejean,
La Parisienne,
32 cm.

particularly fond of this and other statuettes of young women living in the style of the times. *La Femme à sa toilette* constituted another of his favorite subjects. Among a number of statuettes that he sent to the Salon de la Société Nationale des Beaux-Arts are *Femme assis, Femme au chapeau,* and *Femme à l'ombrelle,* all terra cottas, *En promenade,* bronze (1902), *Douce Oisiveté,* bronze (1903), *La Dame au grand manteau,* terra cotta (1904), *Sortie de spectacle,* stone, (1906), *Le Menuet,* bronze (1907), *L'Amour et les ombres,* bronze (1908), *Femme en soirée,* marble (1911), *Jeune Fille nue,* bronze, and *Femme se coiffant,* marble (1914), etc. Dejean pursued his career after the First World War. He made the monument to the dead of the city of Saint-Ouen, a monumental statue of *Paix* for the grand dining room of the ocean liner *Normandie,* and *Nymphe couchée* for the artificial lake of the Tokyo palace.

Many founders, including Valsuani, Hébrard, and Rudier, cast in bronze some works by Louis Dejean. Of note from the Valsuani house are *Femme agenouillée,* 72 cm, and *Vénus,* 83 cm; from the Hébrard house, *Femme assise à l'éventail,* 27 cm; from the Rudier house, *Femme en robe a' crinoline* and *Jeune fille debout se coiffant,* 75 cm; and without note of the founder, *Femme bras levé,* 30.5 cm, *Torse de femme nue,* 82 cm, as well as *Buveur à la gargoulette,* 39 cm.

MUSEUMS
Douai
En soirée, 31 cm.
Paris, Decorative Arts
Femme à la cape, 33 cm.
La Senseitive, femme décolletée, 38.5 cm
Paris, Orsay
La Parisienne, 45 cm.
Poitiers
Jeune Fille debout se coiffant, 75 cm (A. Rudier).

SALES
Femme nue à genoux se coiffant, 48 cm, Enghien,
    March 29, 1981.
Jeune Fille se coiffant, 40 cm (L. Gatti, founder),
    Zurich, November 30, 1985.
Jeune Fille se coiffant, 75 cm (A. Rudier), Drouot, June
    10, 1985, room 1.
La Parisienne, 32 cm, Drouot, July 7, 1983, room 9;
    Saint-Maur, December 11, 1985.

Edouard Delabrière,
Lion sur calman, 50 x 80 cm.

DELABRIÈRE ÉDOUARD

    Paris, March 29, 1829
    1912

E. DELABRIERE

Almost nothing is known of this artist's life
besides his works, which exist in plaster, wax, terra
cotta, and often cast in bronze, and appeared regularly at the Salon from 1848 to 1898. They reveal a
marked penchant for hunting scenes made up of
men or of animals. Like many other animal sculptors, Delabrière submitted to the influence of Barye,
but he did not push the plastic research nearly as far
as his renowned colleague had, devoting himself
more to rendering anecdotes of the events. Among

Edouard Delabrière,
Le Premier Gibier,
50 x 64 cm.

Edouard Delabrière,
Lion du Sénégal sur antilope, 48 cm.

Edouard Delabrière,
Tigre marchant, 45 cm L.

Edouard Delabrière,
Taureau attaqué par un ours.

Edouard Delabrière,
Chameau, 30 cm.

Edouard Delabrière,
Grand Cerf, 22 cm L.

his principal consignments to the Salon were *Lévrier tenant un lièvre sous sa patte*, wax (1848), *Combat de cerfs* and *Le Dernier Pas, chasse au cerf*, plasters (1849), *Tigre royal déchirant un jeune crocodile*, plaster (1852), *Cerf d'Amérique blessé*, bronze (1853), *Panthère de l'Inde dévorant un héron*, bronze (1861), *Cerf de Cochinchine*, bronze (1864), *Tigre du Bengale*, bronze (1865), *Tiercelet sur perdrix*, bronze (1873), *Vache et son veau*, bronze (1874), *L'Hallali* and *Coq faisan effrayé par une belette*, bronzes (1875), *Le Pas-perdu, chasse au renard*, bronze (1876), *Retour de chasse, époque Louis XV* and *Chien braque et lièvre*, bronzes (1877), *Piqueur de Charles IX*, bronze (1881), *Picador*, bronze (1882), *Le Premier Gibier, group de lions*, plaster (1892), *Chien sur perdrix*, bronze (1898), *Chiens courants*, bronze (1904), etc. Delabrière is also the author of a model on the theme of horseback riding, designed for the front of the Louvre.

In addition to the bronzes presented in public sale during the course of recent years, it is possible to note very numerous groups and statuettes of animals such as horses, hunting dogs, deer and large mammals, birds and diverse subjects, in particular: *Cheval, antérieur gauche levé*, 29 cm, *Cheval attaqué par une lionne, Chien braque et épagneul sur faisan*, 30 x 47 cm, *Lion en marche*, 9.5 x 13 cm, *Lion du Sénégal sur une antilope*, 48 x 72 cm, *Panthère attaquant un cerf, Sanglier des Ardennes*, 8 x 18 cm, *Chameau*, 29 cm (exhibited in 1985 at the Shepherd Gallery in New York), *Perdrix appelant sur ses emblavures*, 22 cm, *Taureau fonçant sur un picador*, 44 x 57 cm, *Hercule et le taureau*, 18 x 11 cm, *Thésée terrassant un lion*, two statuettes entitled *Le Troubadour* and *La Rose*, and a pair of andirons in gilded bronze ornamented by sitting lions.

Edouard Delabrière,
Chien de chasse rapportant un canard,
20.5 cm.

Edouard Delabrière,
Deux Chiens de relais, 57 cm.

MUSEUMS
Amiens
Panthère de l'Inde et héron, 65 x 140 cm (1858).

SALES
Bécasse, Drouot, January 16, 1985, room 13.
Chasseur à cheval et ses deux chiens, 27 cm, Sotheby London, November 8, 1984.
Chevreuil, 9 cm, Troyes, April 20, 1986.
Chien de chasse, 21 cm, Troyes, November 24, 1985.
Chien de chasse tenant un canard, 20.5 cm, Meaux, October 21, 1984.
Chien de chasse tenant un lièvre, 31 cm, Sotheby London, March 8, 1984.
Chien de relais, 46 cm, Pont-Audemer, July 28, 1985, Meaux, June 22, 1986.
Dromadaire, 30 cm, Enghien, June 26, 1983.
Eléphant trompe levée, 20 cm, Sotheby London, April 28, 1982.
Epagneul et braque sur faisan, 22.5 cm, Bergerac, October 11, 1986; Sotheby London, June 12, 1986.
Etalon debout, 19 cm, Enghien, October 6, 1985.
Grand Cerf, 22 cm. L, Drouot, July 7, 1983, room 9.
Lion sur caïman, 48 cm, Sotheby London, June 20, 1985.
Lion du Sénégal sur antilope, 48 cm, Enghien, October 6, 1985; Christie's London, September 25, 1986.
Le Premier Gibier (lion and two cubs with a peacock), 62 cm L, Christie's Oklahoma (United States), September 24, 1981.
Renard tenant un faisan, 25 cm, Versailles, December 14, 1980.
Le Retour de la chasse, 45 cm, Lille, June 4, 1984.
Tigre attaquant une antilope, 40 x 55 cm, Drouot, March 12, 1982.
Tigre marchant, 45 cm, Drouot, July 7, 1983, room 9.
Tigre rugissant, 28 x 45 cm, Drouot, June 21, 1981.

DELAGRANGE, LÉON NOËL
Orléans, March 13, 1872
January 4, 1910

This student of Barrias and of Vital-Cornu exhibited at the Salon from 1894 to 1907, but abandoned sculpture in 1908. He was also a pioneer of aviation, and disappeared in a flying accident near

Edouard Delabrière,
Le Retour de la chasse, 48 cm.

Léon Delagrange,
Le Chevalier, 66 cm.

and leaving for Rome. The works that he sent from Italy to Paris, principally marble figures of women, established his notoriety. Upon returning to the capital he furnished some sculptures for the Opera, the Sorbonne, the churches of Saint-Eustache and Saint-Joseph, and the cathedral of Bordeaux, among others. Of a number of works exhibited it is necessary to mention *Enfant monté sur une tortue*, bronze, 135 cm, dated 1866 (Exposition universelle 1867), *Il Pecoraro*, a statue in bronze, 170 cm, cast by Thiébaut (Salon of 1869), *Eve après le péché*, a statue in marble (1870), *La Vierge au lys*, a statue in marble (1878), *La Musique*, a statue in marble for the Opera (1878; a drawing in silvered bronze at the Exposition Universelle of 1878), *L'Aurore*, a statue in marble (1884), *Paysanne debout lisant un livre*, a statuette for a centerpiece executed by Christofle (Exposition Universelle of 1889), and *Eve avant le péché*, a statue in marble (Salon of 1891). A group in marble entitled *L'Education maternelle* (1875) ornaments Samuel-Rousseau Square in the seventh district of Paris.

Bordeaux. His work is made up of medallions, bas-reliefs, busts, statues, and groups in different materials, a certain number of them in bronze. Of note from the Salon are *Le Mystère des ruines*, a statuette in marble (1901), *L'Amour soucieux*, a bust in wax (1906), and *Amour et Jeunesse*, a group in marble (1907).

SALES
Les Amoureux, gilded bronze, chiseled by Louchet, Drouot, December 2, 1983.
Le Chevalier de Malte, bronze and ivory, 46 cm, Drouot, June 14, 1982, room 7.

DELAPLANCHE, EUGÈNE

Paris, February 28, 1836
Paris, January 10, 1891

After his studies at the Ecole des Beaux-Arts, Delaplanche exhibited for the first time at the Salon of 1861. He worked for the hotel of the Païva, before winning the first grand prize of sculpture in 1864

Eugène Delaplanche,
Zéphyr, gilded bronze, 115 cm
(Barbedienne).

Many works have been cast in bronze in different dimensions, particularly by Barbedienne. These include:

La Musique, 171, 102, 85, 68, 56, 34 cm
L'Education maternelle, 116, 63, 53, 42, 31 cm.
La Vierge, after the statue from the Saint-Joseph church, 97, 67, 50, 34 cm.
La Libellule, 61 and 98 cm.

The Thiébaut house, for its part, cast *Enfant sur une tortue,* 80 and 42 cm, as well as *La Sécurité,* 63 cm.

MUSEUMS
Marseille
Enfant monté sur une tortue, 135 cm.
Il Pecoraro, 170 cm (Rome 1868).
Saint-Denis
Danse, 115.

SALES
La Libellule, 98 cm (Barbedienne), Drouot, January 21, 1983; Reims, May 25, 1986.
La Libellule, 116 cm (Barbedienne), Drouot, June 27, 1983, room 5.
Zéphir, gilded bronze, 115 cm (Barbedienne), Biarritz, April 13, 1986.

DELBET, DOCTEUR PIERRE

La Ferté-Gaucher, November 15, 1861
La Ferté-Gaucher, July 17, 1957

The museum of Orsay possesses a work by this artist entitled *La Douleur,* a small bronze, 10.7 cm high.

DELECOLLE, LOUIS AUGUSTE

Troyes, March 24, 1828
Grenoble, May 21, 1868

Louis Auguste Delecole's production was limited almost exclusively to busts, in particular a series of portraits of people from his native Troyes. At the end of his life, he established himself in Grenoble, where he married. He worked particularly for the churches of Chambéry. Two of his busts in bronze appeared at the museum of Troyes: *Pierre Pithon,* 23.5 cm, and *F. Pithon,* 24.5 cm, both cast by Quesnel.

DELHOMME, LÉON ALEXANDRE

Tournon-sur-Rhône, July 20, 1841
Paris, March 16, 1895

Delhomme studied sculpture first at the academic school of Lyon, and then in Paris at the Ecole des Beaux-Arts. In 1867, after this training, he debuted at the Salon with a plaster entitled *Gaulois blessé implorant Teutates.* Many statues in bronze were exhibited here later on, including *Démocrite méditant sur le siège de l'âme,* 160 cm (1869), bought by the city of Lyon, *Le Défi* (1879), *L'Age du bronze* (1891), and *Lazare Carnot* (1891), destined for Algeria. Delhomme also made a statue in bronze of Louis Blanc (1887) which is presently found at Monge

Plaza in Paris, and a group in stone entitled *La République* for the stairway of the Sorbonne, as well as some busts in stone or in marble of musicians, painters and other artists. The Thiébaut house cast *Le Défi* in two dimensions, 75 and 55 cm.

The museum of Lyon possesses Delhomme's bronze *Déomcrite.* A proof in bronze of *Gaulois,* 56 cm (1878), was sold in New York by Christie's on March 20, 1981.

DELHOMMEAU, CHARLES

Paris, March 21, 1883—?

Charles Delhommeau produced busts before he decided to specialize in animal sculpture, which he exhibited at the Société Nationale des Beaux-Arts. A mandrille (African monkey) in bronze, 44 cm, appeared at an exposition of the Antiquaires du Louvre in 1983. *Groupe de félins,* 23.5 cm, cast by Leblanc-Barbedienne, was sold in Enghien in 1981, and *Rongeur,* 25 cm, cast by Scudéri, was sold at the Drouot Hotel on July 7, 1983, room 9.

DELOYE, JEAN-BAPTISTE

Sedan, April 30, 1838
Paris, February 1899

Some busts, medallions, statues of contemporary personalities, more than two hundred medals, and some statuettes constitute the essential works

Jean-Baptiste Deloye, Berger et son chien, 61 cm.

by this artist, who stayed for many years in Vienna after the war of 1870-1871. Upon returning to Paris in 1879, he worked for the city hall and received some important commissions from the commander Hériot for the chateau of La Boissière, and by Mme Pelouze for that of Chenonceaux. He also furnished some models of unglazed porcelain to the Sèvres factory. His participation at the Salon, starting in 1865, includes some statuettes in marble entitled *La Source de Trianon* (1884), *Le Prix du tournoi and Diane*, 48 cm (1885), *Diane chasseresse*, 66 cm (1887), *Bacchant*, 41 cm (1888), *Caton* (1895), *La Vendange* (1897), *Hébé*, 55 cm, and *Evohé* (1898), and *Minerve* (1899). Of further note, in 1888, are forty-five medallions in bronze; in 1897, *Fleur de pêcher*, a bust in marble and bronze; and in 1898, *La Part du capitaine*, a statuette in marble and bronze, 54 cm. A pair of statuettes in bronze entitled *Les Bienfaits de la civilisation*, 55 cm, were made part of the sale after the death of the sculptor in 1899.

MUSEUMS
Amiens
This museum possesses forty medallions in bronze, portraits of sculptors, painters, and other artists, including Carrier-Belleuse and Eugène Carrière, as well as diverse works in plaster and in terra cotta.
Angers
Carrier-Belleuse, medallion, 12 cm diam.
Paris, Decorative Arts
La Part du capitaine, marble and bronze, 54 cm.

SALES
Frédéric Lemaître, 47 cm, Drouot, October 28, 1985, rooom 14.

Séraphin Denecheau,
Diane sur un croissant de lune,
60 cm.

DELPERIER, GEORGES

Paris, November 20, 1865
November 30, 1936

A student of Thomas and Falguière in Paris, Georges Delperier established himself in Tours in 1898 and there unfolded an active career. A portion of his work was inspired by the Middle Ages, and correspond to the neo-gothic style he used for the decoration of a number of monuments. He produced a number of busts for exhibition at the Salon starting in 1885. It was a statuette, however, entitled *Le Maréchal-ferrant*, 26 cm, which was cast by Barbedienne. The museum of Tours possesses a statuette entitled *L'Aviation*, also in bronze, and in an Art Nouveau spirit. Another bronze, *Allégorie de la France*, 59 cm (1898), was sold in London at Sotheby's on November 25, 1982.

DEMAY, GERMAIN

1819-1886

Germain Demay showed some animal figures at the Salon only in 1844 and 1848, before being employed by the state at the Archives Nationales. He had first undertaken medical studies, and then worked for Barye for nearly ten years. He sent a plaster to the Salon of 1844 entitled *Jaguar apercevant un proie*, and a series of bronzes to the Salon of 1848: *Panthère, Chien de Terre-Neuve, Cerf, Daim, Biche, Faon, Cigogne*, and *Courlis*. He apparently also produced some medallions in bronze, since there are two of them at the museum of Guéret, both dated 1839; they are portraits of the deputy Jean-François Barailou of the Creuse, 18 cm diam., and of his son, the doctor and colonel Barailou, 18.5 cm diam. The museum of Reims preserves a medallion portait of Victor Noir, 25.5 cm diam. (1870). A statuette, *Coq de bruyère*, 21 cm L., was sold at the Drouot Hotel on March 13, 1981.

DENECHEAU, SÉRAPHIN

Vihiers (Maine-et-Loire), October 21, 1831
1912

A student of Rude and of David d'Angers, this artist worked on diverse Parisian buildings, including the Louvre, the Opera (busts of musicians), the Gare du Nord, and the churches of the Trinity and of Saint-Etienne-du-Mont. Author of portraits and of mythological and allegorical scenes, Denecheau exhibited on a regular basis at the Salon, starting in

1859. Of note is the bronze group entitled *Femme caressant une chimère,* shown at the Exposition Universelle of 1867, and a statue entitled *Jules César,* shown at the Salon of 1869.

MUSEUMS
Angers
Femme caressant une chimère, 115 x 185 cm (1867).

SALES
Diane sur un croissant de lune, 60 cm, Christie's London, September 25, 1986.
Diane sur un croissant de lune, 99 cm, Sotheby New York, April 26, 1986.
Vénus, 68 cm, Sotheby London, November 7, 1985.

DEPAULIS, ALEXIS JOSEPH
Paris, August 30, 1792
Paris, September 15, 1867

This sculptor and medal-engraver exhibited at the Salon from 1815 to 1855. The museum of Périgueux possesses a medallion in bronze by him entitled *Portrait d'A.C. Quatremère de Quincy,* 14.5 cm diam.

DEPLECHIN, VALENTIN EUGÈNE
Roubaix, May 27, 1852
Thiais, March 4, 1926

Born into an aristocratic family, Deplechin worked first as an engineer, practicing sculpture merely as an amateur before devoting himself to it entirely. Studying at the academic schools in Lille and then at the Beaux-Arts in Paris, he also undertook some trips through Europe and to North Africa. From these travels he brought back an obvious taste for the exotic, tempered by the influence of the classical antiquity. He established himself in Lille and sent his works to the Salon of Paris, first in 1873, and then regularly from 1881 to 1901. In addition to a number of busts, his subjects clearly reveal his sources of inspiration: *Jeune Nubien,* a statue in plaster (1882), *Charmeur,* a statue in plaster (1886), *Le Penseur* and *Fellah au bord du Nil,* two statuettes in plaster (1890), *Amphitrite,* a statue in marble (1893, later cast as a bronze reduction), *Fontaine de Bacchus,* plaster (1894; marble in 1901), and *Peine de coeur,* a statue in marble (1896). Of further note, a medallion in bronze entitled *Un vieux de la vieille* appeared at the Salon of 1877. Another of Deplechin's major works is the monument to the songwriter Desrousseaux, inaugurated in Lille in 1902.

MUSEUMS
Lille
Buste de Desrousseaux, 33 cm (1892).
Buste de Verly, 58 cm (1905).
Un vieux de la vieille, medallion, 14 cm diam.
　　This museum also possesses some plasters, terra cottas, and marbles.

SALES
Amphitrite, 51 cm, Christie's London, February 23, 1981.

DERRÉ, ÉMILE
Paris, October 22, 1867—?

The signature of this artist can be found on the *Chapiteau des baisers* in the gardens of Luxembourg, and on the stone fountain *Innocents* (1906) in Willette Square at the foot of the Montmartre butte. Émile Derré exhibited at the Salon starting in 1895, and a bronze entitled *Le Baiser,* 57 cm, was sold at the Drouot Hotel on June 27, 1983, room 6.

DESBOEUFS, ANTOINE
Paris, October 13, 1793
Paris, July 12, 1862

A student of Cartellier at the Beaux-Arts, Antoine DesBoeufs won the first grand prize for medal-engraving in 1814. He did not really start his career

Antoine Desboeufs,
L'Amour maternel, 42 cm
(Quesnel, founder).
Louvre Museum.

as a sculptor until 1820, all the while serving as the engraver of the cabinet of the duke of Angoulême. He recieved some commissions from the city of Paris and from the state, and produced statues and groups for the churches of Saint-Laurent, Saint-Germain-des-Près, Saint-Sulpice, Notre-Dame-de-Lorette, and la Madelaine, for one of the fountains of the Concorde Plaza, and for the base of the columns of the Trône. He also executed some busts and statues of contemporaries, as well as plaster statuettes in which his classicism is apparent: *Petite Vénus,* destined to be cast in bronze in a unique model (Salon of 1831), and *La Duchesse d'Orléans* (Salon of 1836). One other work, *L'Ange gardien,* was cast by Barbedienne in 48, 30, and 20 cm. A small group in bronze, *Jeune Mère et ses deux enfants* or *l'Amour maternel,* 42 cm (Quesnel, founder, 1835), was acquired by the Louvre at the Drouot Hotel on October 19, 1983.

DESBOIS, JULES

Parçay (Maine-et-Loire), December 20, 1851
Paris, October 2, 1935

Jules Desbois' initiation to sculpture occured in Tours, where he was taught by an artistic priest, the abbot Brisacier; Desbois continued his studies at the school of fine arts in Angers, and lastly, from 1874 to 1877, at Cavalier's studio at the Beaux-Arts in Paris. In 1875, he debuted at the Salon with a bust of *Orphée.* In 1878, he worked with Rodin for an business that made ornaments. He spent two years in New York in the studio of the American sculptor John Quincy Adams Ward, with whom he collabo-

Jules Desbois,
Eve tentée, 30.5 cm
(Hébrard).
J. Ginepro Collection,
Monaco.

Jules Desbois,
Léda,
37 x 55 cm
(Gruet, founder).

rated. He soon grew discouraged and abandoned sculpture, only to devoted himself to it anew three years later, working as a practician with his colleagues. On Rodin's recommendation, a collector commissioned him to execute a statue; after this, Desbois would have a consistently brilliant career. The commissioned statue, *Acis changé en source,* was exhibited in plaster at the Salon of 1886, and in marble the following year.

Desbois preferred to sculpt with the direct cut method, in wood as much as in ivory (Cf. catalog of the "Exposition De Carpeaux à Matisse" in the Musées du Nord, 1982). He is the author of a statue entitled *L'Hiver* which is found in the Tuileries gardens, and of *Puvis de Chavannes* in Paul-Painlevé Square in Paris. His production is marked by expansive virtuosity and extremely elaborate realism. His work also includes a number of plates, vases, gourdes, tobacco pots, pewter pitchers, all ornamented with bas-relief nudes or animals. These works, of an Art Nouveau spirit, were exhibited at the Salon du Champ-de-Mars in 1911. At the Salon des Artistes Français were exhibited (in addition to *Tête d'Orphée* of 1875 and *Acis changé en source,*) a statue in plaster entitled *Othryade* in 1877 and a group in marble entitled *Satyre et nymphe* in 1887. At the Nationale des Beaux-Arts, where he started to exhibit in 1890, the following works were among those exhibited: *La Mort du bûcheron,* plaster (1890), *Le Baiser* and *Narcisse,* two groups executed in gritstone by Delaherche (1890), *La Misère,* plaster (1891), *La Mort, Le Baiser,* and *Dryade au saule,* three bronzes, the latter gilded, and a marble entitled *Léda* (1896), *Femme à l'arc,* a statuette in silver (1903), *Fantaisie,* a bust (1906), and *Masque de femme* (1908), both in bronze, the second carrying the seal of Hébrard.

Many works by Jules Desbois have been cast by the Sèvres factory.

Siot-Decauville is among the founders who cast the artist's works; their contributions include *Buste de filette,* and diverse objects like inkwells, champagne glasses, plates, carafes, and candy dishes.

Hébrard also cast some subjects by Desbois, as can be discerned by some statuettes carrying the

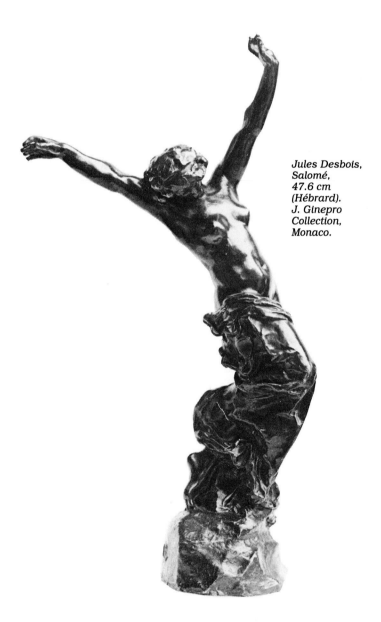

*Jules Desbois,
Salomé,
47.6 cm
(Hébrard).
J. Ginepro
Collection,
Monaco.*

*Jules Desbois,
La Comédie,
32 cm
(Hébard).
J. Ginepro
Collection,
Monaco.*

seal of this founder: *La Danse*, 32.5 cm (sometimes called *La Comédie* or, improperly, *Le Jour et la Nuit*), *Le Couple*, 56 cm, *La Bique*, 18 cm, *Eve tentée*, 30 cm, *Salomé*, 49 cm, and *La Vigne*, bust, 18 cm. Of further note is *Torse d'homme incliné*, 128 cm, carrying the mark of Alexis Rudier.

MUSEUMS
Besançon
Léda et le cygne, 36 x 56 cm.
Paris, Orsay
Orgueil, bust of a woman, 50 cm (Hébrard).
Salomé, 49 cm (Hébrard).
Torse d'homme, gilded bronze, 128 cm (A. Rudier).
Paris, Petit Palais
Jeune Fille dansant, 35 cm.
Sisyphe, 165 cm.

SALES
Baigneuse sur un rocher, 24.5 cm (Hébrard), Versailles, October 17, 1982.
Femme à la conque, vase, 40 cm (Siot-Decauville), Versailles, October 17, 1982.
Le Jour et la Nuit or *La Comédie*, 32.5 cm, (Hébrard), Enghien, November 27, 1983.
Léda et le cygne, 36 x 56 cm (Gruet, founder), Drouot, March 16, 1983, room 9.
Tête de femme, 28 cm, Sotheby London, November 24, 1982.
La Vigne, 18 cm, Sotheby London, June 7, 1984.

DESCA, EDMOND

Vic-de-Bigorre, November 26, 1855
June 22, 1918

Beginning as a marble apprentice, and continuing on to become a student of the sculptor Jouffroy at the Ecole des Beaux-Arts, Edmond Desca exhibited regularly at the Salon from 1879 to 1914. His contributions there include allegories, genre and historical scenes, as well as diverse personages. Among the most notable are *Le Chasseur d'aigles*, bronze, 250 cm, placed at the Buttes-Chaumont (1883), *On veille!*, a group in marble (1887), *Le Nègre Jonas*, a bust in bronze (1907), *La Résistance*, a group in marble (1908), *Officier méhariste*, bronze (1911), *La Mort du lion*, a group in marble (1913) today in Montsouris Park, and *La Lutte pour la vie*, a group in plaster (1914). There are also some statuettes to add to the list: *La Matador*, bronze (1886), *Danton*, plaster, and *Carrier de la vallée d'Ossau*, marble (1890), *A la princesse!* bronze (1897), *Alice Desca*, plaster (1909), and *Le Dessin (Mme Alice Desca)*, marble (1913). Desca collaborated in the building of a monumental fountain in Tarbes, and also made a bronze statue of Danton for this city.

Desca is also known for some bronzes of reduced dimensions, including *L'Inquisiteur*, 60 cm, and a reduction of *La Mort du lion*, 71 cm. The museum of Saint-Maur-des-Fossés, near Paris, possesses a proof of this latter work, cast by Valsuani in 1920.

DESCHAMPS, FRÉDÉRIC

Born in Saint-Erblon (Ille-et-Vilaine)

An animal sculptor and a watercolorist, Deschamps sent to the Salon of 1894 a group in plaster entitled *Cocorico, gloire au vainqueur!;* a bronze version of the piece, cast by Siot-Decauville, would be shown the following year. At the Salon of 1901 appeared a work entitled *Héron* in bronze, and at the Nationale des Beaux-Arts in 1892 appeared *La Défense du nid*, a bas-relief in marble for a fireplace. *Cocorico*, cast in bronze by Siot-Decauville, 64 cm, was sold by Christie's London on March 20, 1984.

DESCHAMPS, LÉON JULIEN

Paris, May 26, 1860
September 1928

The harvest seems to have particularly inspired this artist, if one judges by some of his consignments to the Salon, starting in 1888: *En moisson (A Harvest)*, a statue in marble (1891; presented also in 1903), *Moissonneuse (Harvester)*, a study of a bust in plaster (1895), and *Moissonneuse*, a statuette in bronze (1904). Yet another piece exploring the theme of the harvest is a stone group by Deschamps that was inaugurated in Paris's nineteenth district (today at the Rhin-et-Danube Plaza). Of further note are some medallions in bronze, including the portrait of *Emile Combes* in gilded bronze, and *L'Enfant* at the Salon of 1902. The Susse house cast in bronze the work *En moisson* (from the Salon of 1903), 62 cm, and *Moissonneuse*, a bust of 73 cm.

DESCOMPS, JOSEPH
SEE CORMIER

DESPIAU, CHARLES ALBERT

Mont-de-Marsan, November 4, 1874
Paris, October 28, 1946

Though he worked as a practician with Rodin from 1907 to 1914, Despiau had started to show his own original works long before, at the Salon des Artistes Français between 1898 and 1900, and at the Nationale des Beaux-Arts starting in 1901. The son and grandson of plaster artists, he was attracted to sculpture while he was still very young. His artistic identity evolved under the tutelage of Hector Lemaire at the Ecole des Arts Decoratifs, and later by Barrias at the Ecole des Beaux-Arts. Some plasters and marbles constitute his first consignments to the Salon, principally clothed female figures portrayed in full length or in bust; these were not very successful. However, at the Salon of 1907 his notoriety began to grow. He received a number of official commissions from his hometown, and from other towns as distant as Buenos Aires. At the same time, Rodin noticed him, and drew the younger artist into his studio. Nonetheless, Despiau's style differs profoundly from that of the master who sculpted *Bourgeois de Calais*—in its aspect of selectivity and calm, a sense of measure and equilibrium, and finally in a certain rusticity that appears when his peasant origins burst through. Despiau left a thousand sketches, statues, and bas-reliefs, and some two hundred remarkable busts. It would seem that bronze editions of his works were not very abundant.

An exposition of Despiau's work was held in 1974 at the Rodin Museum. The catalog of this exposition and some other sources of information (including the biography written in 1930 by Léon Deshairs) allow us to establish a chronological list of the principal Despiau bronzes cast in 1920 from older works; the date in parentheses is that of the original from which the model was cast. The numbers of proofs indicated here are evidently not definitive.

Marc Worms, head, 32 cm (1901).
Petite Fille des Landes, bust, 46 cm (1904); some proofs in bronze, a certain of them in gilded bronze, carry the seal of Valsuani and are numbered to 3.
Fillette de la rue Batelière tenant un enfant par la main, 34 cm (1905).
Petit Groupe d'enfants (1905); some proofs signed.
Paulette, bust, 33 cm (1907); cast by Meroni Radice, proofs not numbered.
Paulette, bust in gilded bronze, 50 cm (1907); some proofs carrying the seal of Bisceglia are numbered to 10.
Docteur André Weill, bust, 34 cm (1909).
La Jeune Fille des Landes, head, 56 cm (1909); some proofs are numbered; other proofs in pewter, also numbered, were made in 1929).
La Bacchante, 31 cm (1909); some proofs, a certain number of fragmentaries or with some variants, such as pieces without the right leg, with the left leg raised (8 numbered proofs), with a single torso.
La Bacchante, 59 cm, enlargement made by Despiau in 1929; 6 signed proofs.
Le Faune, 100 cm (1912), cast by Valsuani.
Madame Etienne, bust called *La Dame au nez pointu* (1913); some proofs not numbered.
Figure de faunesse, first version of the female faun in stone of 1925 (1913); some proofs not numbered.
Cra-Cra (Mademoiselle Mouveau), 26 cm (1917); 8 numbered proofs by Alexis Rudier.
Jacquot, 28 cm (1917); some proofs cast by Sasportas and numbered to 8; other proofs not numbered from the first and second stage.
Léda, plaque, 16 x 12 cm (1917).
Lucien Lièvre, head, 54 cm (1918); some proofs not numbered.
A number of works executed starting in 1920 were also made the object of castings and editions, most of which are numbered. Notable are many of the portraits and some figures such as *Nu allongé*, 35 x 80 cm (1922), *Athlète au repos*, 34 cm (1923), *Eve*, 190 cm (1925), *La Bacchante*, 143 cm (1929), *Adolescente*, 63 cm (1929), *Assia*, 185 cm (1937), *Dionysos*, 54 cm (1939), and *Apollon*, 110 cm (1939-1946).

MUSEUMS
Bordeaux
La Jeune Fille des Landes, head, 56 cm (1909).
Lucien Lièvre, head, 54 cm (1918).
Mont-de-Marson
This museum possesses a number of bronzes from all time periods, some of them cast specifically to his intention in the 1970s.

Petite Fille des Landes, bust, 46 cm (1904; A. Rudier).
Femme nue assise se lavant les pieds (around 1906; Susse cast 1976).
Paulette, gilded bronze (head from 1907, bust completed in 1939), 50 cm (Bisceglia 2/10).
Jeune Fille des Landes, 31 cm (1909; Valsuani cast 1976).
La Bacchante, 30 cm (1909; Valsuani).
Le Faune, 100 cm (1912; Susse cast 1978).
Buste du docteur Fabre, 41 (1912; Susse cast 1978).
Buste de Madame Etienne called *La Dame au nez pointu*, 47.5 cm.
Other bronzes after 1920: *Athlète au repos*, *Nu assis*, *Eve*, *Odette assise*, *Odette debout*, *Apollon*, etc. as well as a number of busts.

Some other French museums and foreign museums preserve bronzes by Despiau, in particular the museum of Algiers.

SALES
Cra-Cra, 26.5 cm (A. Rudier), Christie's London, December 3, 1985.
La Femme au turban, 35 cm (A. Rudier), Drouot, November 26 1984, rooms 5 and 6.
Paulette debout, 38.5 cm (C. Valsuani 5/9), Sotheby London, June 30, 1983.
Mademoiselle Simon, bust (Valsuani), Drouot, November 26, 1984, rooms 5 and 6.

DESPREY, LOUIS ANTONIN
Châtillon-sur-Saône (Côte-d'Or), March 22, 1832
1892

Enrolled in the Ecole des Beaux-Arts in 1851, this artist produced busts of contemporaries, mythological scenes, and allegorical subjects. The bust, *Monseigneur Coeur*, bishop of the city, 46 cm; a replica in bronze of the marble exhibited at the Salon of 1861 is at the museum of Troyes.

DESPREZ, LOUIS
Paris, July 7, 1799
Paris, November 15, 1870

Powerfully influenced by his great predecessors, this artist, who had studied with Bosio at the Beaux-Arts beginning in 1813, made copies after the works of Michelangelo and Puget. After winning the grand prize of sculpture in 1826 with *La Mort d'Orion*, he sent from Rome *Les Bergers d'Arcadie* a bas-relief in marble destined for the tomb of Poussin. He exhibited at the Salon between 1824 and 1865, most notably with two bronzes in 1835: *Jeune Fille* and *Buste de Puget*. He also worked for the Chamber of Deputies, the churches of the Madeleine, Saint-Augustin, Saint-Germain-l'Auxerrois (the 16 statues of the portal), Saint-Merri, and Saint-Gervais, as well as for the Louvre and the Tour Saint-Jacques. He also sculpted the statue *Fléchier* for the Saint-Sulpice fountain.

MUSEUMS
Aix-en-Provence
Milon de Crotone, 97 cm (according to the statue of Puget).
Avignon
Milon de Crotone, 97 cm (according to Puget).
Moïse assis tenant les Tables de la Loi, 97 cm (according to the statue by Michelangelo).
Le Puy
Milon de Crotone, 97 cm.
Moïse assis, 95 cm.

DESRUELLES, FÉLIX

Valenciennes, June 7, 1865
La Flèche, 1943

Félix Desruelles is best-known in the north of France for his many monuments to the dead, including that of Arras, erected after the war of 1914-1918. He also made a statue in gilded bronze entitled *Les Fruits* for the esplanade of the palace of Chaillot (1937). He is also responsible for some busts and diverse figures which he exhibited at the Salon starting in 1883: *Job,* a statue in plaster (1896) which won him a gold medal at the Exposition Universelle of 1900, *Bust du peintre Le Sidaner* (1904), *Jeune Fille,* a statuette in gilded bronze (1905), *La Cigale,* a statuette in marble (1912), *Vendangeuse,* a statuette in plaster (1914), etc. The museum of Maubeuge possesses a portrait-medallion in bronze of Georges Paillot, 31 cm diam. Some works in marble or in stone by Desruelles appear in many museums of northern France, including that of Valenciennes. *Europe et le taureau,* a bronze cast by Jaboeuf and Rouard, 34 cm, was sold in London by Sotheby on March 20, 1986.

DESTREEZ, JULES CONSTANT

Gisors (Eure), April 5, 1831—?

This student of Triqueti participated sporadically at the Salon from 1855 to 1882, contributing some busts and figures in plaster. The museum of Amiens preserves his statuette in bronze entitled *Jeune Femme au pigeon,* 78 cm.

DETRIER, PIERRE LOUIS

Vougécourt (Haute-Savoie), July 25, 1822
1897

Pierre Louis Detrier exhibited at the Salon from 1866 to 1896, submitting some works in bronze: *Ulysse reconnu par Pénélope* (1870), *L'Innocence et l'Amitié* (1875), *Le Caprice,* bas-relief (1879), *Amour maternel* (1883), *Jeune Fille au nid* (1887), *Les Gaudes* (1890), *Grande Soeur* (1892), and *Amateur Louis XVI* (1896). Bronzes were cast from many of his works, in particular *Un Amateur,* 35 cm, modeled from a plaster exhibited in 1888, *Déesse vestale, Merveilleuse, Le Muscadin,* the bust of *Printemps,* and *Femme et enfant,* 55 cm. The founder Raingo was employed by him. A statuette in gilded bronze, *L'Angélus, paysanne priant,* 67 cm, was sold at the Drouot Hotel on December 2, 1983, room 5.

DEVAULX, FRANÇOIS THÉODORE

Paris, April 15, 1808
January 21, 1870

Winning the second prize of Rome in 1833 after studying under Ramey Jr. at the Ecole des Beaux-Arts, Devaulx worked for the Val-de-Grâce and for the Louvre. In 1849, he exhibited at the Salon the work *Cavalier grec et son cheval,* plaster, one-third of the group in stone destined to ornament the Iéna Bridge. A statuette in bronze entitled *George Washington,* 46 cm, was sold by Christie's in London on July 17, 1984. A bust in regule, *Victor-Emmanuel II,* dated 1859, 13 cm, belongs to the Chambéry museum.

DEVILLEZ, LOUIS HENRY

Mons (Belgique), July 19 1855—?

Though he seems to have produced little, this student of the academy of fine arts in Brussels and the Ecole des Beaux-Arts in Paris, this sculptor exhibited at the Artistes Français beginning in 1879, at the Exposition Universelle of 1889, and at the Nationale des Beaux-Arts starting in 1893. His work includes some busts and medallions, particularly many busts in bronze of historical people and famous artists, as well as some mythological figures. He was the friend of the painter Eugène Carrière, a number of whose works he owned.

MUSEUMS
Avignon
Jeune Femme sortant du bain, 80 cm.
Belfort
Buste d'Emilienne, 40 cm (dedicated to Camille Lefèvre).

DEVREESE, GODEFROY

Courtrai, August 19, 1861
Brussels, August 31, 1941

While this Belgian sculptor and medal-engraver studied in Brussels, he nonetheless exhibited in Paris—with the Artistes Français in 1892 and at the Nationale des Beaux-Arts starting in 1895. His work is made up primarily of medals, but also of some bronzes of animals or other subjects. Among his consignments of bronzes, it is necessary to note *Portrait équestre* (1892), *Lutteur en garde* (1895), *Etalon flamand* (1896), *Porteuse de pommes de terre* (1898), etc. Also of note are some bronzes cast by the Société des Bronzes in Brussels or by Petermann: *Le Baiser,* 45 cm, *Buste d'enfant,* 30.5 cm, and *Femme à cheval en amazone,* a statuette. The Orsay museum possesses *Pêcheur de La Panne,* 39.5 cm.

DIÉBOLT, GEORGES

Dijon, May 6, 1816
Paris, November 7, 1861

Diébolt is the sculptor responsible for *Zouave du pont de l'Alma,* which is now in place on that current-day bridge, and of its companion *Grenadier,* transported to Dijon, near Lake Kir. He is also the author of *La Victoire maritime* which decorates the center of the bridge at the Invalides and of decorative sculptures for the Louvre (front of the Rohan pavillion), the city hall, and the Tour Saint-Jacques. A student of the Ecole des Beaux-Arts beginning in 1835, and the winner of 1841's first grand prize of sculpture, Diébolt remained in Rome, from whence he sent some works which attracted the attention of the public, particularly *L'Enlèvement de Déjanire* and *La Méditation*. He also made a colossal statue, *La France rémunératrice*, which was placed in 1851 at the intersection of the Champs-Elysées for the distribution of awards won by French industry at London's Exposition. The bronze sketch of this work was exhibited at the Exposition Universelle of 1855 and acquired by the government ten years later.

Diébolt also executed large haut-reliefs in bronze symbolizing *La Loi, La Force,* and *La Justice* for the city of Lyon. A group in marble entitled *Héro et Léandre,* presented at the Salon of 1863, was cast in bronze in two dimensions, 42 and 25 cm, by the Thiébaut house.

The museum of Dijon, the Museum of Decorative Arts in Paris, and the Orsay museum each possesses a proof in bronze, 36 cm high, of *La France rémunératrice.*

DING, HENRI MARIUS

Grenoble, 1844
Grenoble, August 24, 1898

Henri Marius Ding was the son of an industrial inventor who created a stove which carries the family name. He developed an attraction for sculpture while he was still young, and sojourned in Italy in 1871 and 1872. Upon returning to France, he worked primarily in his hometown (the museum of which possesses many of his works) and in the rest of that region. He sculpted *La Liberté,* a statue in marble destined for the monument inaugurated in 1888 in Vizille to celebrate the centennial of the Dauphinoise revolution. He executed another monument to the revolution in Dauphine while he was in Grenoble in 1897. Ding participated for only three years at the Salon of Paris, exhibiting a statuette in plaster entitled *Mendiant aveugle* (1876), and two statues in plaster, *Enfant à la source* (1877) and *Ecce Homo* (1878). One of his major works, *La Muse de Berlioz* or *Stella Montis,* the marble of which belongs to the museum of Grenoble, represents a woman playing the harp. The statue was cast in bronze by Thiébaut in two dimensions. A model, 94 cm high, was sold at the Drouot Hotel on February 3, 1986, room 2 (for 69,500 F). The museum of Grenoble possesses a bronze entitled *La Pogne,* 43 cm high.

DORÉ, GUSTAVE

Strasbourg, January 6, 1832
Paris, January 23, 1883

This man was brilliant, fascinating, provocative, and at the same time adulated by his contemporaries. He is best known for his work as a cartoonist, as a lithographer, and as an illustrator of *Contes drolatiques, Don Quixote,* the *Bible,* and other landmark works of literature. He is also known to have been a great painter and a remarkable watercolorist. On the other hand, his sculpted work is virtually unknown, aside, perhaps, from the bronze monument to Alexandre Dumas Sr. at Malesherbes Plaza

Gustave Doré,
L'Effroi
or L'Amour maternel,
59.5 cm.
See reproduction
in color on
page 18 .

Gustave Doré,
La Défense nationale, 62 cm. Saute-mouton, 37 cm (Thiébaut).
Cronos fauchant, 60 cm.

in Paris (1883). It was not until the end of his life that Gustave Doré devoted himself to sculpture, producing about forty-five groups, statues, and bas-reliefs, most often allegories. Some models were exhibited at the Salon, provoking surprise and diverse reactions, often favorable. Among his groups in plaster are *La Parque et l'Amour,* the first consignment (1877), then *La Gloire* (1878; today in the museum of Maubeuge), *Le Temps,* a project of a clock, and *Madone* (1879), and *Christianisme* (1881). Of further note at the Salon of 1879 is a group in plaster entitled *L'Effroi* or *l'Amour maternel,* representing a Nubian woman lifting her child away from the menace of a snake. Made in marble, this work was placed on the tomb of the dramatic artist Alice Ozy in Père-Lachaise.

In 1878, Gustave Doré presented to the Exposition Universelle a colossal vase in plaster, two meters high, luxuriantly decorated on the theme of vines and the vineyard. Cast in bronze by Thiébaut Frères, this work was next exposed at the Salon of 1882, and then at the international exhibition of Chicago in 1893; the following year it was bought by the palace of the Legion of Honor in San Francisco, which possesses it still. Doré's sculptures of smaller dimensions often reveal the imagination and the wit of the illustrator; frequently cited is a work entitled *A saute-mouton,* a scene featuring two characters dear to Rabelais—a knight in armor and a monk—the first leaping over the other.

During the course of the posthumous sale which took place from the 10th to the 15th of April, 1885,

289

a number of models in plaster, terra cotta, and bronze were sold, for the most part with the right of reproduction, and sometimes with the molds. The most significant of the works thus sold were *L'Effroi* or *l'Amour maternel* (reduction), *Pyramide humaine* or the *Saltimbanques, Puck* (owl), *Le Déclin,* and *La Parque et l'Amour.*

The same bronzes (as well as some others originating from private collections) appeared at the time of the Gustave Doré exhibition organized in 1983 at the Museum of Modern Art of Strasbourg, and then in Paris at the Pavillon des Arts:

La Belle et la bête, 33 cm.
La Défense nationale, 62 cm, after the plaster made for the competition for the monument to the siege of Paris, won by Barrias (a proof of 142 cm high was sold in Paris in 1969).
L'Effroi or *l'Amour maternel,* 58 cm.
La Madone, 79 cm, reduction by Thiébaut Frères of the plaster exposed at the Salon of 1880.
Miroir, framework in gilded bronze made up of a drapery and of angelots making an about-face, 103 x 63 cm (a model, intended for the Empress of Russia, was bought by Jean Cocteau,; another belongs to the museum of Bourg-en-Bresse).
Pyramide humaine, 58.8 cm (a first proof, 129 cm high, is found at the museum of Sarasota in Florida).
Puck, silvered bronze, 27 cm.
Saute-mouton, 37.6 cm, cast by Thiébaut.

These different works, described and discussed in the exposition catalog, offer a rather complete panorama of the bronzes by Gustave Doré. Still remaining to be mentioned, however, are the Thiébaut house castings in many dimensions of *La Danse,* 102 and 78 cm, and of *La Madone,* 82, 71, 49 and 30 cm, as well as a clock in gilded bronze, 130 cm, executed in 1879 for Alice Ozy, today owned by the Museum of Decorative Arts in Paris.

SALES
A saute-mouton, 35 cm (Thiébaut), Drouot, June 3, 1986, room 4 (sold for 79,000 F).
Cronos fauchant ses enfants, 60 cm, Drouot, June 3, 1986, room 4.
La Défense nationale, 60 cm, Drouot, June 30 1982; Drouot, June 3, 1986, room 4.
L'Effroi or *l'Amour maternelle,* 59.5 cm, Enghien, April 28, 1985.
Nymphe poursuivre par l'Amour, 112 cm (Thiébaut), Versailles, June 18, 1985.
Vénus jouant avec l'Amour, 21 cm L. (Thiébaut), Drouot, June 3, 1986, room 4.

DOUBLEMARD, AMÉDÉE DONATIEN
Beaurain (Aisne), July 8, 1826
Paris, 1900

Doublemard began his studies in sculpture with Duret, and won successively the third, the second, and finally the first grand prize of Rome, the last in

*Edmond Drappier,
Cavalier chargeant,
40 cm.*

Edmond Drappier,
Homme faisant reculer un cheval,
34 x 50 cm.

1855. He is credited with the great monument to Marshall Moncey which stands on Clichy Plaza in Paris, the statue of Camille Béranger on Temple Square, some busts and some statues of famous contemporary people executed for different cities of France, a monument to Bolivar for Ecuador, and finally some genre scenes and allegories, often of excellent quality. Some works in bronze were exhibited at the Salon: *Jeune Fille étonnée à la vue d'un lézard* (1861), *L'Education de Bacchus* (1865), *Génie funéraire* for a tomb to Père-Lachaise (1880). Of further note, at the Salon of 1875, is one of his most remarked-upon works, the group in plaster entitled *Jeune Faune et panthère.*

L'Education de Bacchus was cast in bronze by the Thiébaut foundry in two dimensions, 71 and 52 cm. Also known is a statuette of *Scapin,* 47 cm.

The Carnavalet museum in Paris owns a statuette entitled *L'Acteur Coquelin dans le rôle de Figaro,* 85 cm (1874).

DRAPPIER, EDMOND

Born in Viterne (Meurthe-et-Moselle)

Edmond Drappier is known only by his participation at the Salon in the beginning of the 20th century, at which time he was domiciled at the Siot-Decauville foundry. During this period he exhibited some bronzes, in which the horse is clearly his favorite theme: *Passage difficile,* an equestrian group (1906), *Epave,* a horse (1907), *Pour vaincre,* an equestrian group (1910), *Forgeron* (1911), and *Après la parade* (1912).

SALES
Cavalier chargeant, 40 cm, Saint-Maur, April 27, 1986.
Cheval de trait et paysan, 49 cm (Siot-Decauville),
    Christie's Oklahoma (United States), September 24, 1981.

DREUX, PAUL EDOUARD

Paris, October 5, 1855
June 8, 1947

Dogs are the almost exclusive theme of this animal sculptor, who worked for the Sèvres factory and exhibited a number of subjects at the Salon. The Museum of Decorative Arts possesses a bronze statuette finished by Dreux in 1911 entitled *Chien griffon debout,* 21 cm, carrying the seal of the Club Français du Griffon.

DROUET, CHARLES

Paris, May 6, 1836
Paris, April 19, 1908

Starting in 1886, Charles Drouet devoted himself to the original collection of paintings and objets d'art which would be dispersed after his death. Before and during 1861, he exhibited bas-reliefs, busts, and medallions at the Salon, often showing a markedly Italian influence, particularly from Capri, where he seems to have visited. Some bronzes among his consignments are *Zaluca,* bas-relief (exhibited in 1874), *Femme de l'île de Capri,* a bust (in 1876), and a bas-relief portrait in silver of the king of Spain, *Alphonse XII* (1878). The Museum of Decorative Arts preserves a medallion in bronze entitled *Zaluca,* 58 cm diam., dated from Capri, 1867.

DROUOT, EDOUARD

Sommevoire (Haute-Marne), April 3, 1859
1945

A vast repertory, a variety of themes, and a sense of movement and expression made this artist an outstanding member of the sculpture community at the end of the 19th and beginning of the 20th centuries. A number of his works were made into plentiful bronze castings by different founders. A number of busts, figures (feminine as well as masculine), allegories, and mythological compositions appeared at the Salon, where he started to exhibit in 1889. Among his contributions were rather numerous statuettes in plaster: *Printemps* (1897), *Iris* (1901), *La Semeuse* (1902), *La Science* (1903), *Le Foregeron* (1904), and *La Reconnaissance* (1909); in bronze were the statuettes *Pax Labor* (1898), *Le Vainqueur* and *Vers la source* (1905), *L'Eveil du printemps* (1906), *Sur le rivage* (1908), *Le Poème du printemps* (1909), *Salammbô* and *Nymphe chasseresse* (1910), *Judith* (1911), *Andromaque* (1912), *L'Horizon,* and *Indien couché* (1913). Other works include *L'Amateur,* a statue in marble (Salon 1893), *Eternelle Lumière,* a group in bronze (1899), *Le Triomphe du siècle,* a group in bronze (1906), *Maréchal-ferrant,* a group in plaster (1908), and *Hommage et reconnaissance,* a group in bronze (1914).

A number of bronzes were cast modeled after the works of Edouard Drouot. In addition to pieces sold recently at auctions are those sold earlier, either at auction or in the marketplace: *L'Amour naturel* and *L'Amour légitime,* 33 cm, *Baigneuse,* 67 cm, *Duel de femmes,* 40 x 68 cm, *L'Echo, Buste d'Egyptienne, Femme et oiseau,* 82 cm, *La Fortune,* 90 cm, *Galathée,*

Edouard Drouot,
L'Echo,
55 cm.

Edouard Drouot,
La Muse des bois,
72.5 cm.

Edouard Drouot,
La Charmeuse
de serpents,
69 cm.

Edouard Drouot,
Libellule,
71 cm.

①

②

③

1) Edouard Drouot, Amour souffleur.

2) Edouard Drouot, Le Bretteur.

3) Edouard Drouot, Vercingétorix, 81 cm.

Edouard Drouot, Pousse-pousse, 34 cm.

Edouard Drouot,
Indien à cheval, 65 cm L.
(Etling, founder).

Gaulois, 82 cm, *Homme combattant un fauve*, 52 cm, *Indien couché*, 91.5 cm L, *Joueuse de pipeaux, Deux Lions affrontés*, 28 x 48 cm, Le Maréchal-ferrant, 50 x 71 cm, *Mercure*, 90 cm, *Nymphe*, 91.5 cm, *Ode à Pan*, 65 cm, *Paysan sur son cheval attelé à une herse*, 19 cm, *Prométhée et l'aigle*, 67 cm, *La Source*, 96 cm, and *Le Temps*, etc. Some bronzes carry the seal of the Thiébaut house. A number of them seem to have been cast in many dimensions.

SALES

Alsacien, 53.5 cm, Christie's Oklahoma (United States), September 24, 1981.

L'Aurore, 94 cm, Christie's New York, July 17, 1984.

Le Bretteur, Meaux, October 21, 1984.

Le Carrier, 43 cm, Christie's Oklahoma, September 24, 1981.

Le Casseur de pierres, 68 cm, Christie's London, July 18, 1983.

Cerf bramant, 53.5 cm, Christie's Oklahoma, September 24, 1981.

Le Chant du ruisseau, Reims, October 27, 1985.

Charmeuse d'oiseau, gilded bronze, 82 cm, Drouot, December 2, 1983, room 5.

Charmeuse de serpent, 69 cm, L'Isle-Adam, November 9, 1986.

Le Chasseur à cheval, 32 cm, Sotheby London, November 10, 1983.

Le Chasseur et son chien, 95 cm, Brussels, April 23, 1985.

Chef sioux à l'affût, 20 x 45 cm, Drouot, June 18, 1985, rooms 5 and 6.

Coq, Parthenay, December 20, 1986.

La Dernière Allumette, 51.5 cm, Sotheby New York, April 26, 1986.

Femme nue dans les roseaux, 53 cm, Sotheby London, April 28, 1982.

Fermier et son attelage de boeufs, 67 cm L., Christie's Oklahoma, September 24, 1981.

Gladiateur sur son char, 40 x 70 cm, Neuilly, April 10, 1984.

Edouard Drouot,
Gladiateur sur son char,
40 x 70 cm.

Edouard Drouot,
Le Maréchal-ferrant, 50 x 71 cm.

Edouard Drouot,
Coq.

Hercule et le lion de Némée, 72 cm, Sotheby London, June 12, 1986.

Homme en lutte avec un tigre, 61 cm, L'Isle-Adam, April 28, 1985; Drouot, December 6, 1986, room 10.

Indien à cheval, 65 cm L. (Etling, founder), Saumur, June 8, 1985; Sotheby New York, October 25, 1985.

Jeune Femme, 80 cm, Argenteuil, December 14, 1986.

Joueur de football, 33.5 cm, Sotheby London, November 7, 1985.

Méhariste à la lance, 58 cm, Enghien, October 16, 1983.

La Muse des bois, 72.5 cm, Sotheby London, June 7, 1984.

Ode à Pan, 65.5 cm, Sotheby London, April 28, 1982.

Pax labor, jeune homme bras droit levé, 98.5 cm, Sotheby London, November 8, 1984.

Pousse-pousse, 34 cm, Drouot, November 10, 1985, room 6.

Quatre Coureurs de marathon, 61 cm, Washington, June 10, 1984.

Tigres luttant, 35 x 64 cm, Christie's London, September 25, 1986.

Vercingétorix, 81 cm, Lille, January 27, 1986.

François Villon, Nogent-le-Rotrou, November 17, 1985.

DUBOIS, ERNEST HENRI

Dieppe, March 16, 1863
December 30, 1930

Ernest Dubois,
Le Pardon, 72 cm.

Dubois is the author of a monument in Bossuet raised in the cathedral of Meaux in 1907; he also sculpted busts and allegorical works which he started to exhibit at the Salon in 1892, and a statue in bronze of Mansart (Salon of 1908). The Orsay museum possesses a bronze medallion by Dubois, 15 cm diam., representing an elderly man; the museum of Bordeaux owns a bust of a man, 56 cm high.

SALES
Cavalier à l'épervier, 70 cm, Drouot, April 26, 1985, room 6.
Le Pardon, 72 cm, Cannes, November 18, 1986.

DUBOIS, PAUL

Nogent-sur-Seine, July 8, 1827
Paris, May 22, 1905

This son of a lawyer studied law before he succumbed to his attraction to sculpture, and in 1858 enrolled in the Ecole des Beaux-Arts. After only a year there, he left on a four year trip to Italy, particularly to Florence. The Florentine sculpture from the Renaissance impressed him greatly, and clearly influenced his art. The great-nephew of the famous sculptor Jean-Baptiste Pigalle, Paul Dubois used the name 'Dubois-Pigalle' for his debut at the Salon of 1857. However, it was his *Saint Jean-Baptiste enfant* (1864) and, even more, his *Chanteur florentin* (1865) which guaranteed the artist's glory. These two works were cast in a number of models, and a gilded bronze version of *Chanteur florentin* appeared at the Exposition Universelle in 1867.

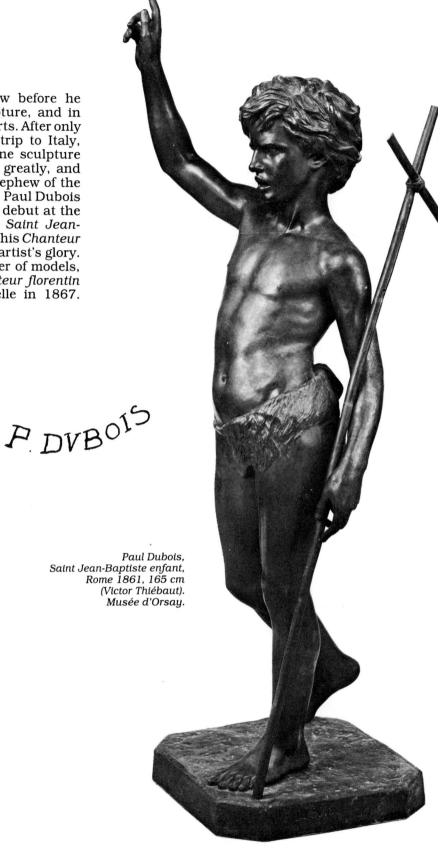

Paul Dubois,
Saint Jean-Baptiste enfant,
Rome 1861, 165 cm
(Victor Thiébaut).
Musée d'Orsay.

Paul Dubois,
Le Petit Porteur d'eau,
50 cm.

Paul Dubois,
Mozart, 62 cm.

Paul Dubois,
Le Chanteur florentin,
49 cm.

After executing *Eve naissante* for the Salon of 1873, Dubois sculpted another major work, the tomb of General Lamoricière in the cathedral of Nantes, in 1879; he also made the *Connétable de Montmorency* of the château de Chantilly (1886), the *Jeanne d'Arc* of Reims, a 4 meter high bronze inaugurated in 1869 (a bronze replica rests in the Saint-Augustin Plaza in Paris), and *Le Souvenir,* a group in bronze exhibited at the Salon of 1902. He is also responsible for a number of busts of contemporaries, including those of Bizet, Baudry, the Duke of Aumale, Pasteur, Saint-Saëns, and Bonnat, to list some of the best-known.

Dubois became curator of the museum of Luxembourg in 1873, a member of the Institut in 1876, and director of the Ecole des Beaux-Arts in 1878. After having worked with Henner, he also executed some work as a painter, and starting in 1880, he exhibited sculptures and paintings simultaneously.

Also on the list are bronzes such as *Arlequin*, 86 cm, *Colombine, La Danse, Buste de David, Diane au lévrier*, 33 cm, and a slightly modified version of the *Chanteur florentin*, as well as *Le Petit Marchand d'eau*, 68 cm, and finally *Le Souvenir*, 60 cm.

MUSEUMS

Angoulême
Le Chanteur florentin, 75 cm.
Bayonne
Léon Bonnat à cinquante-cinq ans, 36 cm (1889).
Châlons-sur-Marne
La Charité, 96 cm (Barbedienne).
Chartres
Le Chanteur florentin.
Epinal
L'Inspiration, 64 cm (Barbedienne).
Grenoble
Le Chanteur florentin, 39 cm.
Langres
Saint Jean-Baptiste adolescent (Barbedienne).
Niort
Le Courage militaire, 85 cm (Barbedienne).
Paris, Orsay
L'Alsace et la Lorraine, 142 cm (1905; Bingen-Costenoble).
Le Chanteur florentin, silvered bronze, 155 cm (Barbedienne).
La Charité, 96 cm (master-model of Barbedienne).
Saint Jean-Baptiste enfant, bust, 165 cm (Rome 1861; Thiébaut).
Camille Saint-Saëns, bust, 49 cm.
Paris, Petit Palais
Antoine Dubois, père du sculpteur, 39 cm.
Eve naissante, 180 cm.
Jean-Jacques Henner, bust, 45 cm.
Louis Pasteur, bust, 50 cm.
Périgueux
Docteur Jules Parrot, bust, 38 cm (Gruet, founder).
Troyes
La Charité, 64 cm.
La Foi, 65.5 cm (Barbedienne).
This museum also owns a number of original plasters and more than eighty waxes.
Versailles, château
Georges Bizet, bust, 65.5 cm.
Louis Pasteur, 50 cm.

Paul Dubois,
Maternité, 78 cm
(Barbedienne).

The catalogs of the Barbedienne house note the castings in bronze, in different dimensions, of the following works:

L'Alsace et la Lorraine, 66 cm.
Le Chanteur florentin, 115, 93, 76, 62, 49, 39 cm.
Deux femmes debout, porte-lumières, Renaissance style, 200, 164, 100, 77 cm.
Jeanne d'Arc équestre, three dimensions not specified.
Saint Jean-Baptiste, 120, 95, 80, 64 cm.
Four statuettes modeled after the tomb of the General Lamoricière:
La Charité, 96, 80, 64, 48, 36 cm.
Le Courage militaire, 105, 86, 68, 51, 39 cm.
L'Etude et la Méditation, 95, 80, 64, 48, 36 cm.
La Prière, 97, 82, 65, 49, 37 cm.

SALES

L'Arlequin, Toulouse, June 6, 1985.
Le Chanteur florentin, 62 cm (Barbedienne), Sotheby London, March 20, 1986.
Le Chanteur florentin, 76 cm (Barbedienne), Lille, November 25, 1985; Dijon, December 15, 1985.
Le Chanteur florentin, 93 cm (Barbedienne), Toulouse, June 24, 1986.
La Charité, 48 cm, Troyes, October 21, 1984.
Le Courage militaire, 51 cm (Barbedienne), Lokeren, April 20, 1985.
Le Courage militaire, 68 cm (Barbedienne), Sotheby London, March 20, 1986.
Le Forgeron, 41 cm, Drouot, January 23, 1984, room 1.
Jeanne d'Arc à cheval, 40 cm L. (Barbedienne No. 2), Reims, April 28, 1985.
Maternité, 78 cm (Barbedienne), Drouot, December 13, 1986, room 7.
Mozart, 62 cm, Tours, June 17, 1985; Sotheby London, June 12, 1986.
Porteur d'eau, 50 cm, Nantes, June 24, 1986.
Saint Jean-Baptiste enfant, 84.5 cm (Barbedienne), Christie's New York, October 5, 1982.
Saint Jean-Baptiste prêchant, 64 cm (Barbedienne; Rome, 1861), Troyes, November 23, 1986.

DUBRAY, VITAL GABRIEL

Paris, February 1813
Paris, October 1, 1892

The son of a wood sculptor, Vital Gabriel Dubray entered the Beaux-Arts to become the student of Ramey at the age of seventeen. He worked on many Parisian monuments, including the Louvre, the Opera, the city hall, the churches of Saint-Augustin, Saint-Roch, Saint-Etienne-du-Mont, and the Trinité. He also made some groups and statues of famous men for different cities of France: *Jeanne Hachette* (1851) for Beauvais, *Le Sacre de l'impératrice Joséphine*, bas-relief in bronze for Saint-Pierre-de-la-Martinique (Salon of 1857), *L'Histoire de Jeanne d'Arc*, ten bas-reliefs in bronze ornamenting the base of the statue of the heroine made by Foyatier for Orléans (1861), some medallions and a bas-relief in bronze for the general hospital of Orléans, the bronze statues of *Cardinal Fesch* and *Louis Bonaparte*, king of Hollande, for Ajaccio, and *Napoléon 1er équestre*, a 4.4 meter high bronze cast by Thiébaut for Rouen (1865). At the Salon, where he started exhibiting in 1840, his other works include *Spontini inspiré par le génie de la musique*, a group in bronze (1848), the bust in bronze of *Général Abbatucci* (1852), a reduction in bronze of the *Napoléon 1er* of Rouen (1866), and *Oedipe et le sphinx*, a group in plaster (1868) that was later cast in bronze by Thiébaut.

A casting of *Napoléon équestre*, 85 cm, was made by Thiébaut as well.

MUSEUMS
Chinon, château
L'Impératrice Eugénie et son fils.
Compiègne, château
Napoléon 1er équestre, reduction, 85 cm.
Paris, Carnavalet
L'Impératrice Joséphine, 51 cm (Charpentier, founder).

DUBUCAND, ALFRED

Paris, November 25, 1828
1894

DUBUCAND

Alfred Dubucand was taught by Barye. His work is composed mainly of waxes of small dimensions, and some plasters which, for the most part, were cast in bronze. He is most noted for eastern-style groups portraying horses and the hunt, which he did not start to exhibited at the Salon until 1867. Among the bronzes are *Valet retenant son chien* and *Griffon attaquant un canard* (1896), *Equipage de chasse pour la gazelle en Egypte* (1874), *Chasse dans le Sahara* (1875), *Chasse à l'autruche dans le Sahara* (1876), *Anier du Caire* (1876 and Exposition Universelle of 1878), *Chasseur persan au guépard*

Alfred Dubucand,
Kadlin, étalon pur-sang
aux haras du Pin, 13 cm.

Alfred Dubucand,
Cerf douze-cors, 30 cm.

(1879), *Le Trait de Parthe* (1881), and *Cavalier et femme arabes à la fontaine* (1883). Although he lived for another eleven years, Dubacand no longer participated at the Salon after this date.

Other bronzes by this sculptor remain to be mentioned, including *Autruche*, 24 cm, *Cavalier arabe en observation*, 51 cm, *Grand Cerf*, 37 cm, *Deux Chiens*, 30 cm L., *Chien et faisan*, 24.5 cm, *Eléphant*, 16 cm, *Niger, étalon demi-sang du haras du Pin*, 13 cm, *Bécasses et leurs bécasseaux*, 37 x 38 cm, etc.

SALES

Cavalier arabe chassant le lion, 25 cm, Sotheby London, March 20, 1986.
Cavalier arabe se désaltérant, gilded bronze, 50 cm, Saint-Dié, March 25, 1984.
Cavalier arabe avec deux lévriers, 52 cm, Dijon, April 17, 1986.
Cavalier arabe avec deux lévriers, 25.5 cm, Enghien, April 28, 1985.
Cavalier mexicain au lasso, 63 cm, Drouot, June 10, 1985, room 10.
Cerf, 29 cm, Rambouillet, November 18, 1984.
Le Cerf et la biche, 39 x 41 cm, Saint-Brieuc, December 9, 1984.
Chasseur berbère sur son dromadaire, 46 cm, Sotheby Monaco, December 11, 1984; Louviers, October 19, 1986; Sotheby London, June 12, 1986.
Chasseur berbère sur son dromadaire, 79 cm, Sotheby London, March 21, 1985 (taking £24,000).
Chasseur persan au guépard, 54 x 44 cm, Christie's London, march 20, 1984.
Le Faisan et le lézard, 71 cm, Drouot, February 6, 1984, room 7; Sotheby London, March 20, 1986.
Jeune Arabe et son âne, 34.5 cm, Enghien, October 16, 1983; Sotheby London, March 21, 1985.
Lièvre dressé, 9.5 cm, Rambouillet, March 25, 1984.
Deux Lièvres, 11 cm, Rambouillet, November 18, 1984.
Pur-sang arabe, 45 cm, Sotheby London, June 7, 1984.

Alfred Dubucand, Cavalier et femme arabe à la fontaine, 66 cm.

Alfred Dubucand,
Cavalier mexicain
au lasso,
63 cm.

Alfred Dubucand,
Cavalier arabe et deux lévriers,
25.5 cm.

Alfred Dubucand,
Chasseur berbère
sur son dromadaire,
avec deux lévriers,
46 cm.

Alfred Dubucand,
Ane et enfant,
34 cm.

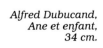

DUCHOISELLE

This artist sculpted some ceilings for the palace of the Louvre, and ios known for some bronzes recently sold at auction: *Indienne dans sa pirogue,* 92 cm L. (1866), sold in London by Sotheby on November 6, 1986; the same subject, 102 cm wide, sold in New York by Sotheby on April 26, 1986.

Duchoiselle,
Femme indienne dans sa pirogue,
61 cm (1866).

Duchoiselle,
Enfant au cerceau, 30 cm.

DUCUING, PAUL

Lannemezan, March 1, 1868
Toulouse, March 9, 1949

A student of the Toulouse natives Falguière and Mercié, Paul Ducuing furnished some models to the Sèvres factory and started exhibiting at the Salon in 1888. The works he showed there include a few bronzes, *Le Chanteur Jaliote* in 1902 and *Druidesse* in 1910. The Barbedienne seal appears on a small group entitled *Femme et Amour,* 25 cm, sculpted in a very 18th-century spirit. Other notable bronzes include *Comédien,* a statuette, 39 cm high, and *Femme et bacchante,* 53.5 cm, sold by Christie's in New York in 1979.

DUHOUSSET, EMILE

This officer—he was captain in the infantry in 1858—left a series of military statuettes treated in a very realistic style. Some bronzes were cast, a certain number of them by the Thiébaut house: *Le Caporal,* 30 cm, *Le Clairon,* 31 cm, *Le Sapeur,* 32 cm, *Le Tambour,* 30 cm, *Le Zouave,* 31 cm; (a contract with a six year duration was signed with the sculptor in 1858).

DUMAIGE, ETIENNE HENRI

Paris, January 16, 1830
Saint-Gilles-Croix-de-Vie, March 31, 1888

A student of Feuchère and of Dumont, Dumaige exhibited at the Salon from 1863 to 1886, showing busts, statues, and groups including *L'Age d'or,* a group in bronze (1864), *Héro,* a statue in bronze (1866), *Retour des champs,* a group in marble (1872), *Molière,* a statuette in terra cotta (1873), *François Rabelais,* a statue in marble for the plaza of the city hall in Tours (1880), *Camille Desmoulins,* a statue in plaster (1882), and *Patrie,* a group in bronze (1886). Different works by Dumaige were cast in bronze, in particular some statuettes of dancers, as well as works entitled *Salomé* and *Esméralda,* a statuette of a grenadier of 1792 entitled *Après le combat,* a reduction of *Camille Desmoulins,* a group symbolizing *Le Printemps,* another *La Source,* etc.

SALES
Après le combat (grenadier of 1792), founder's model, 68 cm, Drouot, December 14, 1984.
Après le combat, 68 cm, Sotheby London, March 20, 1986.
Avant le combat (volunteer of 1792), 68 cm, Sotheby London, March 21, 1985.
Aprè le combat, Avant le combat, two statuettes, 68 cm, Drouot, June 8, 1983, room 4.
Camille Desmoulins, 67 cm, Brussels, March 18, 1985.
Camille Desmoulins, 97 cm, Sotheby London, March 17, 1983.
Couple de jeunes Romains avec brûle-parfum, 86.5 cm, Christie's Oklahoma (United States), September 24, 1981.
Famille de la Renaissance, 70.5 cm, Christie's Oklahoma, September 24, 1981.
Femme et enfant, 74.5 cm, Sotheby New York, April 26, 1986.
Io et Mercure, 82 cm (on a clock), Sotheby London, April 28, 1982.
Jeune Femme, bust in regule, 64 cm, Drouot, May 4, 1984, room 10.

Etienne Henri Dumaige,
Les Deux Danseuses,
52 cm.

Etienne Henri Dumaige,
Après le combat,
grenadier de 1792,
68 cm.

DUMONT, AUGUSTIN ALEXANDRE

Paris, August 4, 1801
January 28, 1884

Dumont did a great deal of formal sculpting, but it does not seem that many bronzes were cast from his works. Having studied with his father, Jacques Edme Dumont, and with Cartellier, Dumont won the grand prize of sculpture in 1823. He entered the Institut in 1838. At the end of his life, stricken with paralysis, he devoted himself to teaching, and in 1852 was named professor at the Beaux-Arts, where he taught innumerable students. Having been born at the Louvre while his father was lodged there, this artist died at the Palais of the Institut, where he himself was lodged.

During Dumont's sojourn in Rome, he sent to Paris a number of works which were widely admired, drawing both popular and critical attention. *Jeune Faune jouant de la flûte* drew the first reactions, followed by *Alexandre étudiant pendant la nuit*, and

then *L'Amour tourmentant l'âme* (also called *Eros et le papillon*), a marble exhibited at the Salon of 1827 which would be replicated in bronze many times.

Upon returning to Paris in 1830, Dumont soon was entrusted with a number of commissions for the Institut, the Palais de Justice, the Sénat, the Bourse (a statue of *Commerce*), the Louvre (sculpture for the Lesdiguière Pavillion), and many churches including la Madeleine (the statue of *Sainte Cécile*). He executed a number of statues of famous men for the museum of Versailles (Louis-Philippe, François I, etc.), and for differnt cities, including a bronze of the prince Eugène de Beauhamais (1864), today placed in the gardens of the Invalides, and the portrayal of Saint-Louis from one of the columns of Trône. However, two major works dominate Dumont's production: *Le Génie de la liberté*, 4 meters high in gilded bronze, cast in 1835 and installed in 1840 at the top of the Juillet column on the Bastille Plaza (a half-size model appeared at the Salon of 1836), and the bronze *Napoléon 1er en César*, 3.57 meters high, crowning the Vendôme column since 1863, overturned in 1871 and put back in place four years later.

In 1843, Dumont contracted with the Barbedienne house, granting them the right to cast certain works in bronze. The catalogs of this house note versions of *Louis-Philippe*, 85 and 42 cm, and *Sainte Cécile*, 68, 32 and 17 cm.

MUSEUMS
Nice
Eros et le papillon.
Paris, Louvre
Le Génie de la liberté, modeled from the statue of the Bastille, 232 cm.
Semur-en-Auxois
Buste du chirurgien Pierre Nicolas Gerdy, 58 cm.
The museum of Semur also possesses almost all of the artist's original plasters, as well as some molds.

Dupuis, Daniel

Blois, February 15, 1849
Paris, November 13, 1899

Daniel Dupuis began his career with painting, but turned to sculpture and medal-engraving (for which he won the first grand prize of Rome in 1870). He participated at the Salon from 1867 to 1896, sending some busts, medallions (often in bronze), and medals. Some statuettes and groups of note are *Amoure au dauphin, Berceuse,* 66 cm, and *L'Echo,* 80 cm. A number of his works are preserved at the museum of Blois. The museum of Dijon possesses a medallion in bronze entitled *Portrait de Charles Quentin, directeur de l'Assistance publique,* 1882, 25 cm diam. At the museum of Grenoble, another medallion, 20 cm diam., commemorates the Exposition Universelle of 1889. Finally, a bust entitled *Le Comte Ange de Guernisac,* founder of the Morlaix museum, 63 cm, belongs to that museum.

Dupuy, Laurence

Born in Nimes

She worked at the beginning of the 20th century, and began in 1905 to exhibit people and genre scenes, primarily in plaster, at the Salon. Her career remained active between the two wars, and she was still a member of the Sociétaires des Artistes Français after the Second World War. The work *Danseuse aux cymbales* was cast by Susse in many dimensions. A proof, 63 cm high, was sold at the Drouot Hotel on December 10, 1980.

Duret, Francisque Joseph

Paris, October 19, 1804
Paris, May 26, 1865

Even though classical antiquity, tempered by the Florentine Renaissance, was his preferred authority, some of Duret's works reveal a much more anecdotal and familiar tendency, evoking the 'troubadour' style dear to the romantics. Among the best-known pieces revealing this tendency are his *Jeune Pêcheur dansant,* and *Improvisateur.* In regard to

Francisque Duret,
L'Improvisateur, 56 cm
(Delafontaine, founder).

Jeune Pêcheur dansant, Louis Gonse (*La Sculpture française*, 1895) speaks of a "sentiment of youth and a freshness of life which place it well above that which was produced by the Ecole." But the same author, in judging the entire body of this sculptor's work, adds: "Such a debut inspires great hopefulness. But the memory of antiquity gathered in Italy, which has filled the spirit of Duret with a beautiful breath of independence and vitality...extinguishes itself little by little in the stifling air of the studio."

Having studied with his father, François Joseph, and with Bosio, Duret obtained the first grand prize of sculpture in 1823, sharing it with Augustin Dumont. He began his travels in Italy in 1824. In Rome in 1831, he executeed his first consignments to the Salon, in particular *Mercure inventant la lyre.* Bought by the king, this statue in marble would be destroyed at the Palais-Royale in 1848; however, many replicas in bronze had been made of it.

It was during the course of a trip to Naples that Duret conceived of the famous *Jeune Pêcheur dansant la tarentelle* which, cast in bronze by Honoré Gonon, was exhibited at the Salon of 1833. Today it belongs to the Louvre; a large number of reductions were cast of it. *Le Vendangeur improvisant,* or *L'Improvisateur,* exhibited in 1839, was also made by him. Apparently this work was the object of fewer bronze castings, as were other lesser-known works including *Danseur napolitain,* presented at the Salon in 1838 as a pendant of the *Jeune Pêcheur.* Of further note, from the centennial exposition of French art in 1900, is a statuette in bronze entitled *Victoire.*

Duret was most facile at modeling clay with the intent of then casting bronzes from it; generally, he left direct-cut marble work to the practicians. His notoriety brought him many official commissions for monuments such as the Louvre (the front of the Richelieu pavillion), the Palais de Justice, the Bourse (a statue of *Justice*), the Théâtre Français, the fountain of Saint-Michel (a group portraying Saint Michel knocking down the dragon, bronze, 5.5 meters high), the Ambassadeurs fountain on the Champs-Elysées, the crypt in the dome of the Invalides (two caryatids in bronze from Napoléon's tomb), the churches of the Madeleine, Notre-Dame-de-Lorette, Sainte-Clotide, and Saint-Vincent-de-Paul, as well as some statues of Molière, Cardinal Richelieu, and Chateaubriand, etc. Heaped with honors and decorations, Duret entered the Institut in 1843 and was given the title of professor at the Ecole des Beaux-Arts in 1852. His teaching was tremendously well-respected, and his reputation brought him a number of students.

Duret signed a contract with the founder Quesnel for casting for the following works: *Jeune Pêcheur dansant la tarentelle, L'Improvisateur, Mercure inventant la lyre,* and *Danseur napolitain.* The rights granted in this contract, wrote C.B. Metman (*La Petite Sculpture d'édition,* 1944), were yieled by Quesnel to Delafontaine around 1855.

For its part, the Susse foundry cast *Danseur au tambourin* and *Danseur napolitain,* both 40 cm height.

Francisque Duret,
Danseur au tambourin
and *Danseur napolitain,* 53 cm.

MUSEUMS
Aix-en-Provence
Jeune Pêcheur dansant la tarentelle, 162 cm (Richard and Quesnel).
Lyon
Chactas sur la tombe d'Atala.
Macon
L'Improvisateur napolitain.
Montpellier
Danseur napolitain, reduction, 44 cm.
Jeune Pêcheur dansant la tarentelle, reduction, 44 cm.
Nîmes
Danseur napolitain aux castagnettes, 43.5 cm.
Danseur napolitain au tambourin, 42 cm.
Paris, Louvre
Jeune Pêcheur dansant la tarentelle, 158 cm (Honoré Gonon).

SALES
Bacchus à la mandoline, 56 cm, Sotheby London, March 8, 1984.
Danseurs napolitains, two statuettes, 53 cm, Angers, June 11, 1985.
Femme debout drapée à l'antique, 94 cm, Sotheby New York, September 13, 1986.
L'Improvisateur, 56 cm, Sotheby London, March 8, 1984.
Rachel en muse de la tragédie, gilded bronze (modeled after the marble of the Comédie Française), Drouot, June 4, 1986, room 7.

DUROUSSEAU, PAUL LÉONARD

Born in Paris

This artist started to exhibit at the Salon de la Société Nationale des Beaux-Arts in 1897, with a number of plaques in bronze, some works in plaster, and, in 1909, a large group in bronze entitled *Les Vaincus éternels*. A reduction of this bronze, 52 cm, cast by Hébrard, was sold in Rambouillet in 1982.

DUSEIGNEUR, JEAN BERNARD, CALLED JEHAN

Paris, June 23, 1808
Paris, March 6, 1866

Duseigneur, one of the most steadfast adherents to romantic styles in sculpture, drew eagerly from history or medieval legends, as can be seen in his favorite themes. His *Roland furieux*, a plaster which marked his debuts at the Salon in 1831, attracted attention to him. The statue was greatly admired by Victor Hugo, who dedicated a poem to its creator. Duseigneur was also knowledgable in the fields of archeology and writing. A student of Bosio at the Beaux-Arts beginning in 1822, he participated in the decoration of a number of monuments in Paris, most notably the churches of the Madeleine, Notre-Dame-des-Victoires, Sainte-Elisabeth, and Saint-Roch (some statues, groups, and Stations of the Cross) as well as the Louvre, the city hall, the cathedral of Bordeaux, and (near Rouen) the basilica of Bonsecours. In addition to the historical and religious works, Duseigneurs left some busts and more than eighty medallions, portraits of writers and artists. In 1833, after *Roland furieux*, he exhibited a group in plaster entitled *Une larme pour une goutte d'eau*, portraying two heroes from Victor Hugo's writings, Esméralda and Quasimodo. The sculptor's consistent and prolific contributions to the Salon continued until his death.

MUSEUM
Paris, Louvre
Roland furieux, 130 x 140 cm (Charnod, founder).
Théophile Gautier, oval medallion, 20 cm (1831).

DUSSART, GUSTAVE

Lille, September 26, 1875
Amiens, February 19, 1952

Cited for having sculpted the allegorical figures on the facade of the Palace of Monaco, Gustave Dussart exhibited at the Salon beginning in 1899; he contributed a number of works, for the most part allegorical and often in bronze, including *Danseuse* and *Inconsciente*, two statuettes (1908), *L'Offrande, Le Réveil, La Pensée*, and *Etude Louis XIII*, four statuettes in gilded bronze (1909), *Le Secours*, a statue (1912), as well as some busts. His style, inspired by the Art Nouveau, is sometimes reminiscent of impressionism in his treatment of clothing. Some works by Dussart were cast in bronze, without doubt in many dimensions, notably *Danseuse* and *Le Réveil*. One proof of *Réveil*, 65 cm high, was sold in Sainte-Germain-en-Laye on December 9, 1984; another bronze, *Inconsciente*, 68 cm, was sold in Lyon on May 18, 1987 **(see reproduction page 11).**

Paul Léonard Durousseau,
Les Vaincus éternels,
52 cm
(Hébrard).

Prosper d'Épinay,
La Jeunesse d'Hannibal, 130 cm
(Barbedienne).

ELSHOECHT, CARLE

Dunkerque, May 10, 1797
Paris, February 27, 1856

Son and student of a painter and sculptor from of Brussels, Elshoecht later worked in Paris with Bosio and participated at the Salon from 1824 to 1853. He worked on decorations for the Louvre, the church of Notre-Dame-de-Lorette, the fountains on Concorde Plaza, the church of Tourcoing, the church of Saint-Ouen in Rouen, the city hall of Laon, the Hotel Dieu in Lyon, and a wide range of funerary monuments. A number of busts and medallions by Elshoecht are found dispersed in museums. Some statuettes were exhibited at the Susse house, notably Thérèse *Elssler dans le rôle de Gipsy* in 1839, and *Frère Charles* in 1844. Other statuettes exist, portraying actresses and other people, such as the Duke of Orléans and the Prince of Joinville.

MUSEUMS
Paris, Decorative Arts
Femme en toilette de bal, galvanic bronze, 44 cm (1849).
Paris, Louvre
Thérèse Elssler dans le rôle de la reine Mab (1839).

ENDERLIN, JOSEPH LOUIS

Aesch (Switzerland), June 26, 1851
1941

Born in Switzerland to French parents, Enderlin participated in the Salon from 1878 to 1935 and worked on the decoration of the city hall and the Grand Palais. For the portal of the latter, he made a group in stone entitled *L'Art de la Renaissance.* His work also includes some busts and statues of artists, genre scenes, and groups of children. His noteworthy contributions to the Salon of 1880 include a statue in plaster entitled *Joueur de billes,* and at the Exposition Universelle of 1889, a bronze entitled *Bataille d'enfants.* The museum of Valence owns a bust in bronze of Adrien Didier, 50 cm high.

EPINAY, PROSPER D'

Ile Maurice, 1836
Saint-Cyr-sur-Loire, 1914

The son of a politician, Prosper D'Epinay studied in Paris and in Rome before exhibiting at the Salon from 1874 to 1902. His contributions included such diverse themes as *L'Enfant spartiate,* a statue in bronze (1875), a statue of *David* and a statuette of *La Fiancée d'Abydos,* both in marble (1876), a bronze statuette entitled *Saint Jean* and a marble statuette entitled *Evohé,* (1879), *Le Prince impérial* in terra cotta (1881), the marble statues *Harmonie* (1893) and *Jeanne d'Arc au sacre* (1902), and *Chasseresse grecque,* a bust in bronze (1902). Of further note are a number of busts and statues portraying Saint Jean in the desert, Sappho, Sarah Bernhardt, etc.

In 1885, 1893 and 1902, some works by Epinay were distributed through public sale, particularly the following bronzes: *Ange déchu*, 36 cm; *Bacchante endormie*, 36 cm; *Baigneuse grecque*, 95 cm; *Baigneuse se peignant*, 48 cm (indicated as being a unique proof); *Le Cardinal de Richelieu*, 50 cm; *Ceinture dorée*, 95 cm; *Le Duc d'Aumale*, 50 cm (unique proof); *L'Enfant spartiate*, 120 cm; *L'Entente cordiale*, 36 cm (unique proof); *Fantaisie, souvenir de Dresde, Henri IV*, 53 cm; *Incroyable*, 32 cm; *Jeanne d'Arc équestre*, 45 cm (cast in twelve models); *Merveilleuse*, 32 cm; *La Mort du prince impérial*, 38 x 40 cm (unique proof); *Neptune*, 27 cm; *Paul et Virginie*, 68 cm; *Le Prince impérial*, bust (unique proof); *Saint Jean-Baptiste*, 110 cm; *Satyre*, 35 cm (unique proof); and *Toinon*, bust, 85 cm.

MUSEUMS
Compiègne, château
Buste du prince impérial, 44 cm (Barbedienne).

SALES
La Jeunesse d'Hannibal, 130 cm (Barbedienne), Drouot, December 10, 1980.

ESCOULA, JEAN

Bagnère-de-Bigorre, October 26, 1851
Paris, August, 1911

Jean Escoula studied under his father, who was a marbler, until the age of twenty, and then under Gautherin. He worked first as a practician with Carpeaux, and for a number of years with Rodin, who gave him the responsibility of executing many marbles. Correspondingly, he began exhibiting at the Salon in 1876. In 1891, he left the Société des Artistes Français in favor of the Société Nationale des Beaux-Arts, where he exhibited henceforth. While a number of his sculptures appear in museums, one of his better-known pieces can now be found placed in Montsouris Park, a large bronze entitled Le Bâton de vieillesse, 170 cm high, presented at the Salon of 1883. Also among his remarkable works from the Salon are *Le Sommeil* (Salon of 1885), *Jeune Baigneuse* (1888), and *La Mort de Procris* (1890); his works from the Nationale des Beaux-Arts include *Satyre jouant de la flûte*, marble (1895), *La Douleur*, a marble bust sculpted with powerful realism (1897), *Amour pastoral*, a group in plaster (1905), and finally some marble statuettes, entitled *Berger de Lemnos* (1908), *Nymphe des sources*, and *La Jeune Fille à la chèvre* (1910).

Siot-Decauville cast many of Escoula's works in bronze, including the bust of *La Douleur, Amour pastoral*, and *Joueur de flûte*. One proof of a bust of *La Douleur*, 42 cm (Siot-Decauville), belongs to the museum of Valenciennes.

ETCHETO, JEAN-FRANÇOIS

Madrid, March 9, 1853
Paris, November 10, 1889

Born to French parents who established themselves in Bayonne in 1860, Etcheto left for Paris in 1872 to work in Carpeaux's studio, which was then at the Ecole des Beaux-Arts. He debuted at the Salon in 1881 with a statue of François Villon, executed in bronze. This work was later cast by Thiébaut in 75, 53 and 37 cm. A bust of François Villon, 23 cm, was also cast by the same founder.

ETEX, ANTOINE

Paris, March 20, 1808
Chaville, July 14, 1888

Antoine Etex, the son of an ornamentist sculptor, was an extremely prolific artist. He is the author of two colossal groups, *La Résistance de 1814* and *La Paix de 1815*, which adorn the west front of the Arc de Triomphe. He made then when he was twenty-five at the request of Thiers. A student of Pradier and of Dupaty, Etex also studied painting with Ingres and architecture with Duban, and was a writer as well. Entering the Ecole des Beaux-Arts in 1824, he obtained merely the second prize of Rome in 1829. He traveled to Italy nonetheless, and it was from Rome that he sent to the Salon of 1833 his group *Cain et sa race maudite de Dieu*, more than 2 meters high, which became a great success. He traveled next to Algeria and to Spain, and under the Second Empire was charged to undertake a mission to the United States. His considerable work was characterized by an extremely classical style, infused with an almost Davidian spirit. Aside from his groups for the Arc de Triomphe, Etex's work includes a number of statues for the church of the Madeleine, the church of Saint-Paul, the Invalides (*Vauban*), the Palais du Luxembourg (*Charlemagne*), and the tomb of Géricault at the Père-Lachaise, as well as the bronze *Philippe-Auguste* atop one of the columns of the Trône, and some effigies of famous men in many cities of the province.

It seems that Etex did not produce many sculptures in small formats, nor were his monumental works reduced and cast in large numbers. Nevertheless, his *Hyacinthe mourant*, 88 cm, brought him his second prize of sculpture in 1829, and a marble version of it was exhibited at the Salon of 1833. Later, a casting in bronze appeared at the Exposition Universelle of 1855 and a reduction, 40 cm, also in bronze, was part of the sale held in February of 1889 at the Drouot Hotel, after the death of the artist.

MUSEUMS
Marseille
Hyacinthe mourant, 88 cm (1829).
Nantes
Nyssia or Jeune Héro, 156 cm (modeled after the group in marble from the Salon of 1850).
Paris, Louvre
Buste du député Dornés, reduction, 26 cm.
Rossini, statuette.
Rouen
Buste de Théodore Géricault, 71 cm.
Versailles
Buste de Théodore Géricault, 71 cm.

FACHE, RENÉ

Douai, November 23, 1816
Valenciennes, March 1891

After studying under David d'Angers, Fache taught as a professor at the Academy of Valenciennes from 1857 to 1887. He executed a number of works in the north of France for the churches of Douai, Cambrai, and Anzin, among others. He produced busts and medallions, and exhibited at the Salon from 1874 to 1884. The museum of Douai possesses some of his works, including a bust in bronze of General Lhérillier, 73 cm, which appeared at the Salon of 1874.

FAGEL, LÉON

Valenciennes, January 30, 1851
Cousoire (North), March 20, 1913

Fagel studied at the academic school of Valenciennes and under the direction René Fache, as well as in Cavelier's studio at Paris's Ecole des Beaux-Arts. After winning the first grand prize of Rome in 1879 with *Tobie rendant la vue à son père*, he exhibited at the Salon des Artistes Français from 1878 to 1893, and then at the Société Nationale des Beaux-Arts from 1895 to 1911. He undertook a number of government commissions, as well as some monuments in Paris and in different cities in the north. Of note are the statues of *Lamarck* and *Chevreul* for the Jardin des Plantes, another of *Chevreul* for Roubaix, the monuments to the *Vainqueurs de Vattignies* and to the president *Carnot* (both from 1895), for Maubeuge, and the monument of *Talma* in Poix-du-Nord (1904). Two important works are preserved at the museum of Valenciennes: *La Première Ofrande d'Abel*, in marble, 137 cm (Salon of 1887), and *Le Petit Tambour de Wattignies*, a fragment of the monument of Maubeuge.

The small sculptures of Fagel are little known. Other pieces include the bronze *Page de Roméo* from the Salon (1891), and, from the Nationale des Beaux-Arts, the works *Printemps* (1897), *La Couture* in stone (1905), *Automne* in plaster (1910), and *Le Tambour de Wattignies* in plaster (1911). This last work was cast in bronze by Susse; Thiébaut cast *Jeanne d'Arc à genoux*, 46 and 24 cm (modeled after the marble executed for the church of the Sacré-Coeur in Paris) and *Page Stephano*, 87 and 65 cm.

FAIVRE, FERDINAND

Marseille, October 8, 1860
1937

Faivre was a student of Cavelier, and began exhibiting at the Salon in 1882. Of note among his works are some plaster pieces, including *Toilette* (1887), *Derniers Jeux* (1892), *Psyché sur le rocher* (1897; a replica in gritstone was executed by Müller the following year), and *Le Matin* (1910). He is also known for a number of statuettes in marble including *Eve, Biblis* (1901), *Baigneuse* (1904), *La Chatte métamorphosée en femme* (1906), *Diane endormie* (1907), *Evanouissement de Psyché* (1908), *L'Alsace* (1910), *Biblis changée en source* (1911), and *La Musique* (1912). There are also some notable bronzes: *Jeunesse* (1893), *Jean Ehrhard* (1895), *L'Enfance de Bacchus* (1899), *La Délivrance* (1904), a centerpiece in gilded bronze entitled *Divinités marines* (1906), a statuette in bronze and marble entitled *La Bacchante ivre* (1912), and *Conversation d'amour* (1914), among others. Faivre continued to participate at the Salon after the First World War. He sculpted a fountain decorated with people and shellfish, which was cast in bronze by Siot-Decauville. Three statuettes by Faivre appeared in the Thiébaut catalog: *Chatte métamorphosée en femme*, 15 cm, *Flore*, 62 cm, and *La Jeunesse* (or *Flore au cerceau*), 60 and 16 cm.

SALES

La Chatte métamorphosée en femme, gilded bronze, 15 cm, Drouot, February 10, 1982, room 2.
Jean, 133.5 cm (Thiébaut), Christie's New York, September 21, 1981.

FALCONNIER, LÉON

Ancy-le-Franc (Yonne), March 10, 1811
October, 1876

Beginning as a perfume apprentice in Paris, Falconnier went to Caen and became a wood sculptor. He returned to Paris in 1833 to work as an ornementalist sculptor at the church of the Madeleine and at the Arc de Triomphe. Joining the Beaux-Arts in 1837, he exhibited at the Salon from 1841 to 1874. He also contributed works of ornamental sculpture for the Louvre, the Ecole Militaire, a number of other buildings including some barracks, and for the city hall of Caen. He also practiced oil painting and pastel painting. For the most part, his works were allegorical or religious; notable examples at the Salon include the marble *Cain maudit*, 275 cm high (1853), a group in plaster entitled *L'Emancipation des esclaves par Abraham Lincoln*, 80 cm (1868), the plaster statue *Gaulois debout!* (1870), and a marble statuette entitled *Jeune Bourguignonne* (1874). A reduction in bronze of *L'Emancipation des esclaves*, 53 cm, was sold in New York at Christie's on September 27, 1986.

①

FALGUIÈRE, ALEXANDRE

Toulouse, September 7, 1831
Paris, 1900

Because he was born in Toulouse, and other renowned sculptors like Antonin Mercié and Injalbert, his contemporaries, were also natives of Languedoc, he is sometimes considred the leader of what is called the Toulouse School. He was, above all, one of the masters of realism, who in France during the second half of the 19th century became more and more skilled. According to his biographer Léonce Bénédite, his father, a mason by trade, sent him to Paris to learn drawing with Carrier-Belleuse.

In 1854, he entered the studio of Jouffroy at the Ecole des Beaux-Arts. The extremely classical training he received there is discernable in his early works, a statuette in plaster entitled *Thésée enfant*, with which he debuted at the Salon in 1857, and a bas-relief entitled *Mézence blessé par Enée et secouru par son fils Lausus*, with which he won the prize of Rome in 1859.

Falguière stayed at the Académie de France in Rome for five years. He worked there and sent many of his works to the Salon, particularly in 1864, when he submitted his work *Vainqueur au combat de coqs*. It was "one of the most successful debuts in memory," wrote the critic Paul de Saint-Victor, who was reminded of Jean de Bologne's *Mercure. Vainqueur*, a classic, lively work, was presented a second time at the Exposition Universelle of 1867. After his return to Paris, the sculptor's reputation was solidly established; he was elected to the Institut in 1882. At the Salon of 1868, he was awarded the medal of honor for his *Tarcicius*, a moving and realistic figure of a young Christian martyr, which he had begun while in Italy. The influence of the Florentine Renaissance is visible in this piece, as it is in the works of a number of earlier sculptors sensitive to the period, beginning with Duret, Rude and Paul Dubois.

In his studio on the Rue de l'Ouest (today the Rue d'Assas) this particularly gifted and prolific artist continually produced works of sculpture, as well as paintings which he exhibited for the first fime at the Salon of 1873. His care in rendering, precisely and simultaneously, the animation, gestures, and facial expression lead him to utilize "expedients which his genius knew how to transcend," wrote Léonce Bénédite. Another significant factor in his work was that he used living models (a street urchin from his neighborhood for *Tarcicius*) as much as type castings, even photographs. He liked to work in clay and to cast it into drafts, the boldness and vigor of which, he then sought to translate into marble.

It does not seem that Falguière was particularly attracted to monumental statuary, although he received and executed many important commissions, including the *Fontaine Sainte-Marie* in Rouen (1879), the *Gambetta* in Cahors (1883), the *Amiral Courbet* of Abbeville (1890), the *La Fayette* in Washington, and the *Cardinal Lavigerie* in Biskra (1900), as well as *Le Triomphe de la Révolution*, an immense and ephemeral project in plaster placed at the top of the Arc de Triomphe de l'Etoile from 1881 to 1885. Of further note are the works *Pierre Corneille*, in marble, of the Comédie Française (Salon of 1878); *L'Asie*, a decorative figure of the old Trocadéro (1878, today on the esplanade of the Orsay museum); some busts of contemporaries; *Saint Vincent de Paul*, commissioned for the Panthéon (1879); *Eve*, in marble, much admired at the Salon of 1880; *Diane*, presented at the Salon in plaster in 1882, and in marble in 1887; *Nymphe chasseresse* (1884); the two marble statuettes *La Musique* and *La Femme au paon*, exhibited respectively in 1889 and 1890; *Le Poète chevauchant Pégase*, a quite forgotten group in bronze in the square of the Opera in Paris (1897); the *Balzac* commissoned for the Avenue Friedland by

②

③

④

the Société des Gens de Lettres after they refused Rodin's famous version (Falguière's student Laurent Marqueste finished the work in 1902, after his teacher's death); and finally the portrayal of *Ambroise Thomas* in Monceau Park, the *Monument à Pasteur* on Breteuil Plaza, and a group in bronze entitled *L'Inspiration guidée par la Sagesse* at the western entrance to the Grand Palais.

A number of sculptures by Falguière were cast in bronze, principally by the Thiébaut Frères foundry. This was the case, naturally, with his most famous work, *Vanqueur au combat de coqs,* which was cast in a large number of models. Other founders, principally Hébrard, also diffused some works by Falguière.

Falguière

Works from the Thiébaut catalog
Calisto, 75, 48 and 13 cm.
Charmeuse, 76 and 56 cm.
Danseuse (Cléo de Mérode), 63, 47, and 14 cm.
Diane chasseresse, 103, 77, 46 and 13 cm.
Femme au paon, 77, 56 and 16.5 cm.
La Rochejaquelein, 61 cm.
Marguerite, 91 and 50 cm.
Nymphe chasseresse, 57, 43 and 13.5 cm.
La Poésie héroique, 81 cm.
Le Poète monté sur Pégase, 71 cm.
Saint Vincent de Paul, 57 cm.
Tarcicius, 31 x 71 and 19 x 45 cm.
Vainqueur au combat de coqs, 85, 70, 52, 38 and 13 cm.

1) Alexandre Falguière, Nymphe chasseresse, 40 cm (Thiébaut frères). J. Ginepro Collection, Monaco.

2) Alexandre Falguière, Esclave au collier, 71 cm (F. Goupil, editor).

3) Alexandre Falguière, Jeune Femme nue, 71.5 cm (Siot-Decauville).

4) Alexandre Falguière, Le Vainqueur au combat de coqs, 85 cm (Thiébaut). See reproduction in color page 9

Alexandre Falguière,
Buste de Diane,
60 cm
(Thiébaut frères).

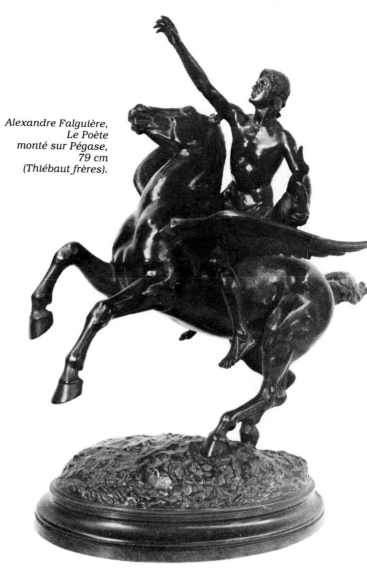

Alexandre Falguière,
Le Poète
monté sur Pégase,
79 cm
(Thiébaut frères).

Bustes de Cléo de Mérode, 60 and 26 cm, Diane, 60 and 43 cm, Gambetta, 54 cm, Nymphe chasseresse, 22 and 15 cm, Saint Vincent de Paul, 18 cm.

Bronzes cast by Hébrard
Femme nue tirant à l'arc, 40 cm.
Jeune Centaure se retournant, 23 cm.
Tête de blessé au bandeau, 16 cm.
Other subjects listed by Hébrard without indication of dimensions include Centaure enfant, Cigale, Circé, Défense nationale, Diane se dévêtant, Esméralda, bas-relief, Madame Chrysanthème, bas-relief, Résistance, as well as some medallions and some busts of artists, notably Bizet, Beethoven, and Rodin.

Bronzes cast by Susse
Renommée, 124, 95, 72 and 43 cm.
Bronzes cast by Siot-Decauville
Jeune Femme nue tirant à l'arc, 71.5 cm.

MUSEUMS
Amiens
Buste de Gambetta, 55 cm (Thiébaut).
Bayonne
Bustes du baron Daumesnil, 65 cm, and of Rodin, 50 cm (1900).
Calais
Bust de Gambetta, 55 cm (Thiébaut).
Carcassonne
Buste de Jacques Gamelin, 85 cm (1898; Thiébaut).
Nantes
Buste de M. Métayer, 61 cm.
Paris, Decorative Arts
Jeune Centaure se retournant, sketch, 23 cm (Hébrard).
Paris, Orsay
Vainqueur au combat de coqs, 174 cm (Thiébaut).
Petit Palais Museum
Possesses a number of terra cottas, some plasters and some waxes.
Toulouse
Balzac assis, 25 cm.
This museum also possesses many plasters by the sculptor.
Troyes
Buste du sculpteur Paul Dubois, 55 cm.

SALES

Balzac assis, 27 cm, Drouot, November 18, 1986, rooms 5 and 6.

Cléo de Mérode, 39 cm, Drouot, March 1, 1982, room 10.

Diane chasseresse, 46 cm, Lokeren, February 16, 1985.

Diane chasseresse, 77 cm, Christie's New York, June 19, 1984.

Diane chasseresse, 103 cm (Thiébaut), Drouot, November 9, 1984, room 6.

Buste de Diane, 43 cm (Thiébaut), Drouot, November 9, 1984, room 6.

Buste de Diane, 60 cm (Thiébaut), Drouot, October 26, 1984, room 1; Fontainebleau, June 2, 1985; Drouot, October 8, 1986, room 1.

Esclave au collier, 71 cm (F. Goupil, caster), Drouot, February 6, 1984, room 7.

Femme debout, 71.4 cm (Siot-Decauville), Drouot, February 2, 1983, room 4.

Femme à la cithare, 88 cm, Anvers, May 22, 1985.

Jeune Femme nue tirant à l'arc, 71.5 cm (Siot-Decauville), Drouot, February 2, 1983, room 4.

Junon et le paon, 77 cm (Thiébaut), Christie's London, May 15, 1986.

Nymphe chasseresse, 57 cm (Thiébaut), Christie's London, March 20, 1984.

Pégase, 79 cm (Thiébaut), Brest, November 5, 1985.

Phryné, 84 cm, Christie's London, March 20, 1984.

La Porteuse de flambeau, 93 cm (Goldscheider No4), Drouot, April 24, 1985, room 5.

La Renommée, gilded bronze, 46.5 cm, Drouot, June 13, 1983, room 10.

Tête de blessé au bandeau, 16 cm (Hébrard No 10), Drouot, May 19, 1982, room 1; (Hébrard), Drouot, April 15, 1983, room 7.

Le Vainqueur au combat de coqs, 43 cm, Drouot, December 2, 1983, room 5.

Le Vainqueur au combat de coqs, 85 cm (Thiébaut), Enghien, May 13, 1984; Montreuil-sur-Mer, February 23, 1985; Sotheby London, March 20, 1986; Toryes, June 29, 1986.

Le Vainqueur au combat de coqs, 96 cm, Lille, April 21, 1986.

Jacques Auguste Fauginet,
Le Chien et la souris,
18 x 21 cm.

FAROCHON, JEAN-BAPTISTE

Paris, March 10, 1812
Paris, July 1, 1871

A sculptor and a medal-engraver, Farochon won the 1835 first grand prize of Rome for his work in the latter discipline. He began participating in the Salon in 1833, contributing a number of medals, but also some busts and bas-reliefs. His career as sculptor, for which he prepared with David d'Angers at the Ecole des Beaux-Arts, started truly around 1845. He worked for a variety of churches in Paris, the Richelieu Pavillion in the Louvre, and the Palais de Justice of Reims, among others. At the Salon of 1845, he exhibited a series of statuettes destined for the principal door of the church of Saint-Vincent-de-Paul; these included figures of Christ, 95 cm, and eight of the twelve apostles, each 77 cm.

MUSEUMS

Chambéry
Jean-Jacques Rousseau, 97 cm (Jaboeuf and Rouard) reduction of the statue from the Richelieu Pavillion in the Louvre, exhibited at the Salon of 1857.

Paris, Carnavalet
Louis Maris Debelleyme, medallion, 21 cm diam.

Paris, Louvre
Three medallions in bronze, portraits of *Lefuel* (1840), of *Ingres* (Salon of 1868) and of *Corot*.

FAUGINET, JACQUES AUGUST

Paris, April 22, 1809
Paris, 1847

FAUGINET

Starting in 1826 at the Ecole des Beaux-Arts, Jacques August Fauginet first studied medal-engraving, and then sculpture. In 1831, he won the second prize of Rome for this art. His participation at the Salon started in the same year, and continued until 1846. He produced a number of busts, medallions, plaques, statues and statuettes of people, as well as some groups of animals, dominated by portrayals of horses. In 1833, Lord Seymour commissioned him to execute some plaques representing horses and ponies. He also sculpted a monument to *Florian* (1839, cemetery of Sceaux), and the statue of *Massillon* for the fountain of Saint-Sulpice (1843). Notable among the bronzes sent to the Salon are *Le Cheval Sylvia* (1834), *Pur-sang anglaisST1*, a bas-relief, and *Chien griffon*, (1835), *Chasseur africain combattant une lionne*, *L'Etalon arabe*, *Le Pur-sang anglais Sweeper*, *Le Cheval Hercule* (all at the Salon of 1836), *Enfant assis sur un cygne* (1839), *Etude de cheval anglais Beggarman* (1841), and *La Jument anglaise Volante* (1842). Also noteworthy are some plaster statuettes, including *Catherine de Médicis méditant la construction des Tuileries* (Salon of 1838), *Jeune Femme* (same Salon), and finally, the artist's last works, exhibited in 1846: a bas-relief in plaster entitled *Le Baptême du Christ,* and a bust in bronze of the *Docteur Champion*.

FAURE DE BROUSSE, VINCENT DÉSIRÉ

Paris—?
1908

Just two bronzes comprise de Brousse's consignments to the Salon starting in 1876: a bust of *Patricienne florentine* (1876), and another of *Damoiselle florentine du XVIe siècle* (1877). Other bronzes not presented at the Salon include *Jeune Femme et oiseaux*, 70 cm, *Mère et ses trois enfants*, 23 cm, and *Pandore et Mercure*, 68 cm.

SALES
L'Abondance, regule, 72 cm, Drouot, March 13, 1981, room 5.
Couple d'amoureux, 105.5 cm, Sotheby New York, June 19, 1981.
La Jeune Violoniste et son compagnon, 79 cm, Sotheby Chester, July 21, 1983.
Marie-Antoinette, 55 cm, Sotheby London, November 10, 1983.
Patricienne florentine, 38 cm, Christie's London, July 18, 1983.

FAVRE, MAURICE

Paris, July 1, 1875
1915

This sculptor and medal-engraver's participation at the Salon lasted just under twenty years, spanning from 1896 to 1914. He sent some medallions and busts there, most notably the bronze of *Camille Pelletan* (1908), a statue in marble entitled *Regret* (1907), a group in marble entitled *La Petite Fille et le pantin* (1914), and a group in bronze entitled *Edouard VII et la reine Alexandra* (1909). Some of his works in small format, like *Le Preux* or *Chant de la fileuse*, were cast in bronze and ivory, a certain number of them in many dimensions.

SALES
Buste de femme, 53 cm, Brussels, October 20, 1982.
Chant de la fileuse, bronze and ivory, 39.5 cm, Sotheby Monaco, October 25, 1982.
Lion, 35.5 cm, Sotheby London, November 25, 1982.
Taureau et chien, Christie's New York, May 17, 1983.

FEITU, PIERRE

Mûr-de-Bretagne, April 16, 1868
December 31, 1936

Pierre Feitu did not exhibit solely in Paris, but in different cities in the United States as well. He seems to have been well-established in the United States at the beginning of the century, living in New York as of 1909. At the Salon des Artistes Français and at the Nationale, his exhibited works were primarily busts. He is the artist responsible for the sword of Belgium's King Albert I. Another bronze is included in his repertory, a statuette entitled *Femme nue pêchant*.

SALES
Faneuse, rêvu..., 104 cm (1900), Christie's New York, May 17, 1983.
Portrait d'homme, plaque in gilded bronze, 38 cm (1899), Drouot, December 2, 1983.

FÉLON, JOSEPH

Bordeaux, August 21, 1818
Nice, 1896

A sculptor, painter, and lithographer, Joseph Félon worked in different cities in France, particularly Nîmes, Bordeaux and Nancy; in Paris, he worked on the Louvre, the Tuileries, the Sorbonne, the city hall, the Trocadéro, the churches of Sainte-Elisabeth and Sainte-Etienne-du-Mont, etc. He participated at the Salon from 1840 to 1896, contributing most notably the works *Galathée*, a bas-relief in bronze (1850), *Andromède*, a statuette in bronze, *Baigneuse*, a statuette in plaster (1850), *Amphitrite*, a bas-relief in bronze (1852), and *Nymphe tourmentant un dauphin*, a group in bronze placed in the Jardin des Plantes (1864), *L'Heure du repos*, a statuette in marble (1865), *Vanité*, a statuette in terra cotta (1866), *Arlésienne*, another statuette in terra cotta (1869), and *Amour porte-lumière*, a statuette in bronze (1894). Also credited to him are some portraits in bust and in medallion, for the most part in bronze.

MUSEUMS
Nîmes
Andromède sur les rochers, statuette.
Paris, Louvre
Blanche Félon et sa fille, 41 cm (1849; E. Vittoz, bronzier, Paris).

SALES
Andromède, 53 cm, Christie's London, March 20, 1984.

FERRAND, ERNEST JUSTIN

Paris, November 6, 1846
March 12, 1932

A regular participant at the Salon starting in 1882, this artist presented some people, diverse scenes, and allegories, notably *Retour des champs*, a bust in bronze (1884), *Le Bout de l'oreille*, a statuette in plaster (1886), *Le Repos de Diane*, another statuette in plaster (1888), *L'Indiscrète*, a statuette in bronze (1890), *Rose perdue*, a group in bronze (1892), and some other statuettes in plaster: *Le Lilas* (1895), *Le Guetteur* (1896), *Le Commerce* (1903), *Gloria Labor* (1905), *Dénicheur d'aigles* (1909), etc. A bronze entitled *Le Chasseur*, 117 cm, was sold in London by Sotheby on June 20, 1985; *Pêcheur au harpon* was also sold in London by Sotheby, on June 12, 1986.

FERRARY, MAURICE

Embrun, August 8, 1852
Neuilly-sur-Seine, September 24, 1904

A student of Cavelier, Ferrary exhibited at the Salon beginning in 1875, and obtained the first grand prize of Rome in 1882. In addition to some decorative sculptures for the city hall, the building of the Crédit Lyonnais, and the Petit Palais (*La Seine et ses rives*, a group in stone for the main stairway), some more refined works should be mentioned as evidence of Ferrary's predilection for playing with

Joseph Felon,
Blanche Félon et sa fille, 41 cm
(E. Vittoz, bronzier).
Louvre Museum.

MUSEUMS
Aix-en-Provence
Cyparisse pleurant la mort de son cerf, statue.
Avignon
Portrait d'Henriette Colet, medallion, 17.8 cm diam.

FERRIÈRES, LOUIS FRANÇOIS, GEORGES, COMTE DE

Paris, November 10, 1837
1907

This artist sculpted animals, primarily horses and dogs, with great realism. He exhibited his works in plaster, wax, and bronze at the Salon from 1865 to 1893, most notably *Chien lévrier,* plaster (1865), *Cheval et chien,* plaster (1868), *Chien d'arrêt,* bronze, (1874), *Chien ratier,* bronze (1877), *Prisonnier de guerre,* a group in wax, and *Retour de chasse,* bronze (1878), *Cheval avec son jockey,* wax (1879), *Cheval au dressage* and *Chien couchant en arrêt,* both bronze (1881), *Trois Amis,* a group in silvered bronze (1882), *L'Abandonné,* a group in bronze, *Chevalier du XVe siècle,* a statuette in plaster (1887), *L'Heure de l'avoine,* wax (1890), and *Chevaux de poste,* plaster (1892). A small group entitled *Deux Chiens de chasse et faisan* was cast in bronze by Thiébaut in two dimensions, 39 and 22 cm (modeled after a work exhibited in 1883 entitled *Un mort peu respecté*). A proof, 22 cm high, was sold in London at Sotheby's on March 8, 1984.

marble colors, and for using ivory and other precious materials: *Belluaire agaçant une panthère,* now in Batignolles Square (Salon of 1880), *Salomé,* a statuette in marble and bronze (1896), *La Sulamite,* a statuette polychrome in marble, ivory and gold, and *Favorite,* another polychrome statuette in different materials (1897), *Saint-Georges,* a statuette in bronze, and *Léda,* a statuette in marble and ivory (1898), *Roger et Angélique,* a statuette in bronze and ivory (1899), *Le Commerce,* a statuette in plaster (1903), and *Saint-Michel,* a statuette in bronze (1904). His work *Belluaire agaçant une panthère* was cast in bronze by Siot-Decauville. A proof, 67 cm high, was sold in Brussels on November 25, 1982.

FERRAT, HIPPOLYTE

Aix-en-Provence, April 22, 1830
Aix-en-Provence, February 27, 1882

Little is known about the important works of this artist, beyond the fact that a work entitled *Cyparisse pleurant la mort de son cerf* was exhibited in plaster at the Salon of 1859 and in bronze at that of 1861. Ferrat was a student of Duret.

FEUCHÈRE, JEAN-JACQUES

Paris, August 26, 1807
July 25, 1852

Feuchère was an eclectic artist, working simultaneously as a sculptor, painter, and enameler; to an even greater extent, he was a major collector. The son of an engraver, he worked while still in his youth for a number of bronziers and goldsmiths. Most notably, he executed some shields in embossed iron ornamented with the very elaborate decorations of the Renaissance. Studying sculpture under Cortot and Ramey, he exhibited at the Salon from 1831 until his death. He received some commissions for ornamenting the Arc de Triomphe, the fountain of Saint-Sulpice (the statue of *Bossuet*), the church of Saint-Denis-du-Saint-Sacrement (a small pediment), the Pont d'Iéna (*Guerrier arabe*), the fountain of Cuvier (the statue of *L'Histoire naturelle*), and the city hall of Rouen. His collection of objects d'art, as well as a certain number of his terra cottas, were sold after his death in a sale held March 8-10, 1853 in the Hôtel des Ventes on the Rue des Jeûneurs.

Through his style and his choice of subjects from antiquity, Feuchère demonstrated his faithfulness to classicism; at the same time, however, his choice to portray historic characters from other eras reveals his genuine effort to be open to new ideas. The following bronzes were among his consignments to the Salon: *Satan,* a statuette (1835), *Benvenuto Cellini,* a statuette (1837), *La Poésie* and *Enfants,* two groups cast by Vittoz (1841), *Léonard de Vinci,* a statuette (1843), and *Amazone domptant un cheval sauvage*, exhibited in plaster in 1843. This last small group was later made into many proofs in bronze, one of which appeared in the posthumous sale of 1853, noted in the catalog as being "cast and chiseled for Jean Feuchère and under his eyes." In the same sale, the statuette of *Satan* was presented, mounted in a clock. Lastly, Feuchère executed the following works in terra cotta: *Le Laocoon*, *Le Mauvais Génie*, *Combat d'amazones*, *Nymphe*, *Bacchus enfant domptant une panthère*, *Le Triomphe de Bacchus*, and *Vénus aux amours*, among others.

Two works by Feuchère were cast by the Susse house, *La Paix* and *La Force*, both 32 cm high.

MUSEUMS
Nemours
L'Acteur Bressant.
Paris, Decorative Arts
Les Ivresses, champagne bucket in silvered bronze, 13 cm.
Paris, Louvre
Amazone domptant un cheval sauvage, 44 cm (1843).

SALE
Satan, l'ange déchu, 34 cm, Cologne, June 29, 1984; Auch, June 29, 1986.

FIOT, MAXIMILIEN

Le Grand-Pressigny (Indre-et-Loire), January 22, 1886
Corbeil, September 19, 1953

This animal sculptor studied under Prosper Lacourtier, and left some statues and groups of dogs, deer and birds. At the Salon of 1912, he exhibited a bronze group with two dogs entitled *Loustalot et Rustaut*. Among his works in plaster are *Cerf aux écoutes* (1908), *Emballé*, a statuette (1910), and *Le Débuché*, a group composed of a deer and a doe (1914), etc. A number of his works were cast in bronze by Susse.

SALES
Albatros, 60 cm (Susse), Neuilly, May 10, 1983.
Bécasse, 65 cm, Epinal, December 14, 1986.
Cerf six-cors, 60 cm, Sotheby London, June 12, 1986.
Combat d'aigles, 45 cm, Belfort, November 18, 1984.
Couple de panthères au repos, 14 x 21 cm (Susse), Enghien, February 22, 1981; Rambouillet, November 7, 1982.
Deux Chevaux dont un cabré, 52 cm, Dijon, November 27, 1983.

Jean-Jacques Feuchère, Satan, l'ange déchu, 34 cm.

Jean-Jacques Feuchère, Amazone, 44 cm (1843).

Maximilien Fiot, Mouette, silvered bronze, 37 cm (Susse).

Maximilien Fiot,
Vol de perdreaux,
34 x 85 cm
(Susse).

Maximilien Fiot,
Mouette en vol,
65 cm.

Maximilien Fiot,
Echassier.

Maximilien Fiot,
Horde de sangliers, 80 cm L.

Echassier, Drouot, October 24, 1986, room 5.
Goéland, Drouot, September 30, 1986, room 10.
Le Grand Cerf, 46 cm (Susse), Drouot, December 3,
    1984, rooms 5 and 6.
Horde de sangliers, 80 cm L. (Susse), Lille, November
    17, 1986.
Mouette, silvered bronze, 37 cm (Susse), Lille, January
    26, 1987.
Trois Lévriers en course, 95 cm L. (Susse), Christie's
    Oklahoma (United States), September 24, 1981.

FIX-MASSEAU, PIERRE FÉLIX, KNOWN AS MASSEAU

Lyon, March 17, 1869
1937

A talented sculptor of busts, Masseau had the great foresight to save Daumier's raw terra cotta models from disappearance. Around 1925, he restored them to editions in bronze. Masseau's own work was first exhibited at the Salon de la Société Nationale des Beaux-Arts in 1893. A number of bronzes could be found there, including *Jouissance intime* (1895), *L'Attente, Le Passé,* two busts (1879), *Le Lunghino,* another bust (1899), *Beethoven* (1902), *Bilitis* and *L'Education d'un faune* (1905), *Femme se lavant* and *Vers la joie* (1906), *Convoitise,* a group (1910), as well as diverse works in plaster and marble. Siot-Decauville produced bronze editions of *Emprise, Petite Folle,* and *Le Secret,* 63 and 28 cm; Hébrard cast *Vers la joie,* 47 cm; and Hohwiller cast *Convoitise,* 30.5 cm. Also notable, though the founders are unknown, are *Faunesse,* 30 cm, *Femme au chat,* a plaque representing *Chopin,* 7 x 5 cm, a mask entitled *Réflexion,* 43 cm, and some inkwells ornamented with orchids and clustered florettes.

MUSEUMS
Paris, Petit Palais
Buste d'Eugène Dutuit, 54 cm.

SALES
Buste de Beethoven, 18 cm, Drouot, March 20, 1985,
    room 14.
Danseuse dégrafant son corsage, Versailles, April 25,
    1982.
Petite Folle, pewter, 32 cm (Siot-Decauville), Drouot,
    June 27, 1983, rooom 6.
Tête de femme, 20.5 cm, Christie's New York, April 3,
    1982.

Fix-Masseau,
Petite Folle, 32 cm
(Siot-Decauville).
J. Ginepro Collection, Monaco.

318

Fix-Masseau,
Vers la joie,
47 cm
(Hébrard).
J. Ginepro Collection,
Monaco.

Fix-Masseau,
Buste de Beethoven,
44 cm

Fix-Masseau,
Le Secret, 63 cm
(Siot-Decauville).

FONTAINE, EMMANUEL

Abbeville, December 8, 1856
Commercy, September 21, 1935

The essential pieces of this sculptor's work include medallions and a large number of busts, which he sent to the Salon over a twelve-year period starting in 1877. Afterwards he undertook works including a bronze entitled *A l'assaut!* for the tomb of Admiral Courbet (1890), the marble *A l'eau Porthos!* (1893; cast in bronze the following year), a group in plaster entitled *Fascination* (1895), a statue in marble entitled *Inspiration,* (1899), a head of *Liseron* in plaster (1901), a marble statuette on the same theme (1903), and a statuette in ivolry and gilded bronze entitled *Premier Frisson* (1907). His work *A l'eau Porthos!* was cast in bronze by Siot-Decauville in two dimensions, 79 and 40 cm. Susse cast *L'Inspiration,* 70 cm, *Le Matin,* 69 cm, and *Liseron,* a bust of 27 cm. The Vivenel Museum in Compiègne possesses a reduction of the group *A l'eau Porthos!.*

FORCEVILLE, GÉDÉON ALPHONSE CASIMIR DE

Saint-Maulvis (Somme), February 12, 1799
Amiens, January 30, 1886

Established in Amiens, Forceville cast in bronze a statue by Pierre l'Ermite for the city of Amiens in 1844. As a sculptor, he exhibited at the Salon from 1845 to 1880. The works he showed there include a number of busts, some in bronze, and statues, often in marble, including *Jeune Fille, L'Enfant heureux, Le Petit Pêcheur napolitain,* and *La Nuit.* At the Salon, he exhibited two bronzes: a statue entitled *Masaniello* (1865), and a statuette entitled *Sainte Cécile* (1869). At the museum of Amiens can be found two of his busts in bronze, *Le Docteur Rigollot,* 51 cm (1846), and *Le Docteur Barbier,* 60 cm (1867).

FORESTIER, ANTONIN CLAIR

Cannes, October 18, 1865
Fontenay, January 10, 1912

Forestier began exhibiting at the Salon in 1890 with statues in plaster and marble, including *Le Loup de mer* (1890), *Bacchante* (1891), *Premiers Désirs* (1894), *Le Désert* (1895), and a group in bronze, *L'Ouragan et la feuille* (1901). He also showed some statuettes in plaster, including *Batelier napolitain* (1899) and *Skating* (1910); his marbles included *Sortie de bal* (1901), *Béatrix* (1902), and *L'Attente* (1911); and lastly, his bronzes included the work entitled *Le Gui* (1908). Also notable among Forestier's sculpture are some busts of Australian personalities.

Works by this sculptor have been cast in bronze by Susse and by Valsuani. The Valsuani seal can be found on a statuette entitled *La Victoire,* 40 cm; this piece was also cast in a 27.5 cm high version by Richard, Eck and Durand.

Antonin Clair Forestier,
La Victoire, 40 cm
(Valsuani).

SALES
Nymphe, gilded bronze, 31 cm, Drouot, March 12, 1984, room 4.
La Victoire, 40 cm (Valsuani), Drouot, July 7, 1983.

FORETAY, ALFRED JEAN

Morges (Switzerland), January 12, 1861—?

This artist was fond of sculpting figures (and particularly busts) of young women, characterized by an Art Nouveau spirit. A student of Falguière, Foretay began participating at the Salon in 1891. Some of his works were cast in bronze. Also notable are some busts cast in regule, nearly thirty centimeters in height. A large statuette in bronze entitled *Etoile d'amour,* 127 cm, modeled after a marble exhibited at the Salon of 1903, was sold in 1979 by Christie's in New York.

FOUQUES, HENRI AMÉDÉE

Paris, April 21, 1857
Paris, April, 1903

This artist, who debuted at the Salon in 1881, primarily sculpted animals in isolated figures or in groups, as well as hunting and genre scenes. One of his monumental works from the Salon of 1891, a group cast in iron representing *Un drame dans le désert*, was erected in Cambronne Square in Paris. A marble entitled *Five O'Clock, chien de chasse* (1895) belongs to the museum of the Petit Palais. At the Salon, Fouques exhibited mostly plasters, most notably *Fox, chien d'arrêt* (1884 and Exposition Universelle of 1889), *Entre l'enclume et le marteau, chien et loup* (1886), the statuette *L'Electricité* (1889), the terra cotta statuette *Farniente*, the statuette *Trompette, chienne vendéenne* (1894), the bronze *Chienne de chasse* (1896), the plaster statuette *La Défensive* (1898), the bronze *Tom, chien de chasse* (1899), the bronze Amour conjugal, lion et lionne (1901), the plaster *Petit Chat guitariste* (1902), and the bronze *La Fiancée du lion* (1904). *Chien et chat*, 30 cm, also called *La Querelle* or *Trop tard!*, was cast in bronze by Thiébaut.

MUSEUMS
Dijon
Trop tard! chien et chat, reduction of a group exhibited in 1885, 30 cm.

SALES
Virtus Civica or *Défense du sol*, 77 cm (1899), Drouot, December 14, 1984, room 6.

FOUQUET, ÉMILE FRANÇOIS

Paris, June 13, 1817
1879

A student of Foyatier, Émile François Fouquet exhibited at the Salon only in 1870, 1876 and 1879, showing some busts, wax medallions, and a bas-relief treated in an academic style inspired by antiquity. Two notable works in bronze are *Femme debout lisant*, 35 cm, and *Pâris*, 28.5 cm.

FOUQUIER, ROBERT FRÉDÉRIC

Rouen, 1807
1870

The museum of Rouen possesses a bas-relief in bronze entitled *Mort du chevalier Bayard* by this artist.

FOURDRIGNIER, ÉDOUARD

1842 - 1907

Three bronzes by this sculptor appear at the museum of Beauvais: *Madame Fourdrignier*, a portrait in bas-relief, 18 x 12.7 cm, and the medallions *Jeux d'enfants*, 12.5 cm diam., and *La Ronde*, 12.5 cm diam.

FOURNIER, PIERRE ÉMILE

Paris, May 20, 1829
1896

This sculptor and painter studied with Barye and with Frémier. He exhibited at the Salon from 1864 to 1892, submitting statuettes, groups of animals, and equestrian figures, almost exclusively in wax. These include *Cavalier polonais* and *Chasseur de la garde* (1864), *Gazelle* (1866), *Dindon* (1867), *Mouton mérinos* (1868), *La Mort du faon et Cerg de Cochinchine* (1869), *Cerf attaqué par un ours* (1870), *Taureau et doguin* and *Gazelles* (1872), *Vautour et chauve-souris* (1878), *Zébus* (1890), and *Buffle du Cap* (1892). Fournier seems also to have made some bronzes and terra cottas.

FOURQUET LÉON

Saint-Forget (Seine-et-Oise), December 20, 1841—?

A student of Jouffroy, Fourquet exhibited at the Salon from 1866 to 1883. He contributed allegories and other subjects, such as *Source de l'Yvette* (plaster in 1874, marble in 1878), *Psyché évanouie*, statuette in marble (1875), *Cupidon* and *Flore*, statuettes in plaster (1879), etc. A statuette in bronze entitled *Femme à la tortue*, 44 cm, appeared at the museum of Alger.

FRAGONARD, ALEXANDRE ÉVARISTE

Grasse, October, 1780
Paris, November 10, 1850

Studying under his father, the famous Jean Honoré Fragonard, and also under David, Alexandre Fragonard was simultaneously a painter of history, a decorator, the creator of several large ensembles at the Louvre, a lithographer, an illustrator and a sculptor. Under the last title, he presented only a single work at the Salon, in 1833, though he did execute many decorative compositions which, peculiarly and unfortunately, have disappeared. These pieces include the pediment of the Chamber of Deputies, replaced after 1830 by a Cortot piece that can still be seen there today, and the fountain of the Marché aux Carmes which was found at Maubert Plaza, and the bronze statue of *Pichegru* which was erected in Besançon in 1829 and destroyed the following year. The museum of Besançon preserves a fragment of this work, the *Buste de Pichegru*, 41 cm high.

FRANCE, PAUL LECREUX, KNOWN AS JACQUES

Vers, 1826
Paris, July 3, 1894

This artist was the creator of a bust entitled *République*, a replica of which can be seen at the museum of Rouen. Another bust of the *République*, this one with masonry marks, 88 cm, belongs to the Grand Orient of France; it was exhibited at the Centenaire de la République, at Paris's Hotel de Rohan in 1978.

Fratin, Christophe

Metz, January 1, 1801
Le Raincy, August 16, 1864

FRATIN

Christophe Fratin,
Deux pintades, 17 cm.

Fratin studied drawing first in Metz, and then worked in the studio of Géricault in Paris. Perhaps it was his time with Géricault that inculcated in him a love of sculpting animals, to which his entire career was devoted. His father, who was a naturalist, is likely to have been another powerful influence.

Fratin received some commissions from the State, including many groups designed for the botanical garden and the esplanade of his hometown; these include two dogs, a deer at bay, a purebred horse, and some eagles. At Montrouge Square in Paris currently appears a colossal bronze group, 2 meters high, entitled *Cheval attaqué par un lion*, executed in 1852. He was popular not only in France but also in Germany, Austria, the United States, and especially in England. At the Universal Exposition of 1851 in London, he was acclaimed as the greatest contemporary animal sculptor. His works appeared in many foreign museums, particularly the Wallace Collection of London, while *Deux Aigles gardant leur proie* stood in Central Park in New York. He exhibited regularly until 1863. However, for unknown reasons, he put seventy-eight of his terra cottas up for sale in 1857. Among his works also figure a number of statuettes and small groups in bronze, greatly appreciated for their precise realism and vigor. Also warranting attention are the reductions of his monumental works and original creations.

Many of Fratin's pieces show horses, especially portraits of famous horses like *Fermer, cheval anglais pur-sang*, a wax with which he debuted at the Salon of 1831, the same exhibition in which Barye's *Tigre dévorant un gavial* was featured. Fratin also portrayed other horses, as well as game, elephants, deer, dogs, and birds, sometimes solitary portraits but sometimes in scenes of struggle with other animals. These works were executed primarily in bronze: *Ecorché de cheval* (1833), *Félix, cheval pur-sang du haras de Viroflay* (1834), *Rainbow, étalon appartenant à M. Rieussac, Vautour dévorant une gazelle, Tigre terrassant un jeune chameau, Lion dévorant un zèbre, Eléphant tuant un tigre, Lionne apportant une proie à ses lionceaux, Cheval mort* (all at the Salon of 1835), *Aigle et vautour se disputant une proie* (1839), and *Le Cheval Tomy*, 29 cm (1842). Also worth mentioning are Fratin's plasters, including the work *Cheval arabe*, 30 cm high (1863).

Different founders cast the bronzes of Fratin. Thiébaut advertised versions of *Lion portant un sanglier*, 55 cm, and *Lion et cerf*, 32 cm, as well as two ewers, one decorated with panthers, the other with a stork, both 14 cm high. Quesnel cast *Singe dansant* and *Ours jouant;* Daubrée cast *Chien de chasse, Condor et gazelle*, 13 cm, and *Jument*

Christophe Fratin,
Combat d'aigles.

*Christophe Fratin,
Taureau debout,
41 cm.*

*Christophe Fratin,
Lion marchant, 27 x 55 cm.*

*Christophe Fratin,
Lionne et sa proie, 27.5 cm L.
(Richard, Eck and Durand).*

*Christophe Fratin,
Lionne portant une gazelle
à ses petits,
58 cm.*

*Christophe Fratin,
Lion couché, 27.5 cm L.
(Richard, Eck and Durand).*

Christophe Fratin,
Lion marchant,
27 cm.

Christophe Fratin,
Chien de chasse tenant un lièvre,
21 x 29 cm.

Christophe Fratin,
Jument et son poulain,
37 x 43 cm.

Christophe Fratin,
Ours jouant
de la cornemuse,
10 cm.

défendant son poulain, 30 cm; Braux cast *Lévrier à l'arrêt avec lièvre,* 22.5 cm. Other bronzes carry the seals of Susse or of Richard, Eck and Durand. Other bronzes appear without indication of the founder; these pieces include:

Aigles attaquant un bouquetin, 48 cm (a reduction of a group from Central Park in New York).
Autruche, octagonal bas-relief, 20 x 14.5 cm, exhibited at the Shepherd Gallery in New York in 1980.
Braque courant, 12 x 25 cm.
Cavalier arabe chassant le lion, 38 cm.
Cerf attaqué par trois chiens, 38 cm.
Cerf couché, 30 cm.
Cerf dix-cors, 12 cm.
Cerf marchant, 55 cm.
Cheval cabré attaqué par un lion.
Cheval terrassé par un lion, 20 x 40 cm.
Deux Chevaux jouant.
Chien tenant une perdrix, 24 x 38 cm.
Couple de boeufs, 30 x 45 cm.
Eléphant monté par deux Indiens, 42 cm.
Epagneul couché, 7 x 18 cm.
Labrador courant, 40 cm L.
Lion attaquant un sanglier, 49 cm. L.
Lionne portant une gazelle, 58 cm.
Lionceaux, 7 x 15 cm.

Christophe Fratin,
Grand Cerf dix-cors marchant,
55 cm.

Lionne couchée, 7 x 16 cm.
Lionne portant une autruche, 56.5 cm.
Lionne portant un cerf, 25 x 42 cm.
Le Montreur de foire, 15 cm.
Ours jouant de la cornemuse, 10 cm.
Sanglier attaqué par quatre chiens, 43 cm. L.
Singe dansant.
Singe aux paniers.
Singe portant une hotte, 25 cm.
Taureau, octagonal bas-relief, 19 x 27 cm (exhibited at the Shepherd Gallery in New York in 1985).
Paire de bougeoirs aux pélicans, 30 cm.
Paire de bougeoirs aux oursons, 58 cm.
Paire de bougeoirs aux hérons, 30 cm.
Boîte ornée de cerfs, biches et chiens, 10 x 18 cm.

MUSEUMS
Comiègne, museum of Vivenel
Tony, cheval ayant appartenu à M. Vivenel, 29 cm (1842).
Lyon
Eléphant femelle défendant son petit contre un lion, 31 cm.
Metz
Autoportrait, statuette-charged, 45 cm.
Nîmes
Vache, 14 x 20 cm.
Paris, Louvre
Ours dentiste, 12 cm.
Strasbourg
Lion en marche, 30 x 52 cm.

SALES
Deux Aigles attaquant une chèvre, 23 cm, Sotheby London, November 10, 1983.
Autoportrait, 19.5 cm, Sotheby London, November 7, 1985.
Cerf couché, 36 cm, Sotheby London, June 7, 1984.
Grand Cerf dix-cors, 54 cm, Enghien, March 7, 1984.
Cheval arabe, 27 cm, (Richard, Eck and Durand), Sotheby London, July 5, 1985.
Cheval se frottant contre une branche, 37 cm, Rambouillet, March 25, 1984.

Christophe Fratin,
Cavalier en armure.

Christophe Fratin,
Eléphant monté
par deux Indiens,
42 cm.

Cheval hennissant, 25 cm, Drouot, December 3, 1982, room 7.
Chevaux, Drouot, January 10, 1985.
Chevaux cabrés, 35 cm, Enghien, October 10, 1982.
Deux Chevaux sauvages, 35.5 cm, Sotheby London, June 7, 1984.
Chien de braconnier et lièvre, 23 cm, Sotheby London, November 25, 1982.
Trois Chiens de chasse attaquant un cerf, 42 cm L., Christie's New York, September 28, 1985.
Coq, 12 cm, Drouot, March 10, 1984, room 8.
Deux Dindes, 16 cm L., Drouot, December 9, 1982, room 8.
Deux Etalons luttant, 37 cm, Sotheby London, November 8, 1984.
Jument et son poulain, 28 cm, Rambouillet, March 25, 1984.
Jument et son poulain, 36 cm, Sotheby London, March 20, 1986.
Levrette, 6 cm L., Drouot, October 5, 1984.
Lion couché, 27.5 cm L. (Richard, Eck and Durand), Drouot, July 7, 1983, room 9.
Lion dévorant une antilope, 36 cm, Drouot, April 23, 1986, room 9.
Lion dévorant un buffle, 19 x 40 cm, Drouot, December 10, 1982, room 4.
Lion marchant, 27.5 cm, Drouot, March 12, 1984, room 4.
Lion marchant, 27 cm, Sotheby London, March 20, 1986.
Lionne et sa proie, 27.5 cm L. (pendant of the lion couché), Drouot, July 7, 1983, room 9.
Loup attaquant un étalon, 25.5 cm, Sotheby London, June 12, 1986.
Le Mâtin à l'écuelle, 15.5 x 24 cm, Drouot, October 19, 1983, room 4.
Minerve à cheval, 46 cm, Enghien, October 10, 1982.
Ours acrobates et jongleurs, two candlesticks, 25 cm, Drouot, June 13, 1983, room 10.
Ours assis fumant sa pipe, 18 cm, Sotheby London, November 10, 1983.
Groupe d'ours, 15 cm, Sotheby London, November 10, 1983.
Deux Pintades, 10 x 17 cm, Drouot, July 7, 1983, room 9.
Pot à tabac, décor d'animaux, 31 cm (dedicated to Jean Nicot, 1842), Rambouillet, November 7, 1982.
Pur-sang arabe, 33 cm, Sotheby London, November 7, 1985.
Pur-sang arabe, 40 cm, Sotheby London, July 5, 1985.
Pur-sang et terrier, 28 cm, Sotheby London, March 8, 1984.
Rainbow, étalon anglais, 31 cm, (Quesnel, founder), Sotheby London, July 5, 1985.
Le Singe, 14 cm, Drouot, December 14, 1984, room 6.
Taureau, bas-relief, 19 x 27 cm, Drouot, November 13, 1985, room 1.
Taureau debout, 41 cm, Enghien, October 6, 1985, room 1.
Taureau tête dressée, Bordeaux, February 23, 1984.
Tigre couché sur un singe mort, 10 x 29 cm, Christie's London, May 15, 1986.
Tigresse dévorant une chèvre, 29 cm, Rouen, November 28, 1982.
Vache et taureau, 24 cm, Sotheby London, March 21, 1985.

FRÉMIET, EMMANUEL

Paris, December 6, 1824
Paris, September 10, 1910

If Frémiet's fame was not sufficiently established by his gilded bronze *Jeanne d'Arc équestre* in the Plaza of Pyramides in Paris, he would still be known for many other very interesting pieces, on two essential themes: animals, and historical or fictional

FREMIET

Emmanuel Frémiet,
Louis d'Orléans,
reduction of the statue
from Pierrefonds,
49 cm.

1) Emmanuel Frémiet, Jeanne d'Arc à cheval, 70 cm.

2) Emmanuel Frémiet, Schéhérazade, gilded bronze, 51 cm (Barbedienne).

3) Emmanuel Frémiet, La Saint-Hubert, 47 cm.

4) Emmanuel Frémiet, Le Grand Condé, 50 cm.

5) Emmanuel Frémiet, Saint Georges et le dragon, 52 cm (Barbedienne).

6) Emmanuel Frémiet, Louis XIII enfant, 46 cm.

③

④

⑤

⑥

329

characters of the past. Descended from a Bourgognese family, Frémiet received his first lessons from his aunt, Sophie Frémiet—also known as Mme Rude, the wife of the famous sculptor. He also studied at the Petite Ecole (which would later become the Ecole Nationale des Arts Décoratifs) and in the studio of the painter Jacques Christophe Werner, before entering Rude's studio. At the same time, he familiarized himself with animals and acquired a solid knowledge of anatomy by frequenting the Jardin des Plantes and the Museum, as did many of his contemporaries.

Frémiet's skill, widely renowned during his lifetime, won him numerous commissions. His historical accuracy is appreciable, as is his meticulous precision in rendering animals, human faces, and clothing. "M. Frémiet," reads the report of the international jury of the Exposition Universelle of 1900, "is one of those rare artists in whom talent is complemented by profound attention to craft." The same text explains that he prepares his models himself, "attends to the reductions, supervises the chiseling, and finally, decides the patinas...His small bronzes are the joyously delicate, his animals are exquisite, his statuettes in gilded and silvered bronze are of a precious forcefulness," wrote Louis Gonse. Phillipe Fauré-Frémiet, the great sculptor's descendent and biographer (the daughter of Frémiet had married the composer Gabriel Fauré), evaluated the abundant production of the great sculptor as a sort of legend of the centuries, "a virile art, not very voluptous, not very feminine, neither Classical nor Romantic—first and foremost, independent."

Despite his untiring activity, great success, and many honors, Emmanuel Frémiet lived an entirely simple and quiet family life. In a discouraged moment, at the beginning of the war of 1870, he considered abandoning sculpture. Finally, at the end of this period, he carried out his most important commissions. Named, in 1875, professor at the Museum of Natural History, replacing Barye, he was elected to the Académie des Beaux-Arts in 1892.

Frémiet made his debut at the Salon of 1843 with a study of a gazelle in plaster. During nearly a dozen years, he exhibited animals almost exclusively, in wax, terra cotta, and plaster as well as in bronze. One of them, *Marabout tenant un caïman* (Salon of 1850), was designed to serve as a model for the four feet of a table in porphyre for the Egyptian museum of the Louvre.

"You seem to have heard," Frémiet later wrote in response to a critique, "that I have made only some cats and other animals. Permit me, in an attempt to enlighten you, to send you a list of works I have produced beyond the speciality in which you appear to want to enclose me." Despite the sculptor's protestations, the animal occupies a considerable place in his work. They are also found combined with human figures in many groups, as in the equestrian figures.

Much impressed by the musculature and prodigious strength of large animals, particularly of bears and monkeys, Frémiet portrays them regularly as victors in struggles with man. *Après le Combat d'une ourse et d'un homme* (1850), a plaster which was later destroyed, created a scandal at the Salon of 1859; it represents again a *Gorille femell enlevant une Négresse*. In 1861 appeared *Le Centaure Térée emportant un ours*, also in plaster, a bronze of which would be exhibited at the Salon of 1863. Next was presented, in a much modified version, a new *Gorille enlevant une Négresse* (1887), as well as *Orang-Outang et sauvage de Bornéo* (marble of 1895, now at the Museum), *Le Chasseur d'ours* (1897), a haut-relief in bronze on the lateral facade of the anatomy gallery at the Jardin des Plantes, and a statue in bronze entitled *Dénicheur d'oursons*, also at the Jardin des Plantes.

In the category of the equestrian statues, it should be pointed out that the *Jeanne d'Arc* which stands on a (too low) pedestal at the center of the Plaza of Pyramides is not the same one which was inaugurated in 1874. While some work was being done on the subway in 1899, Frémiet, who had not been satisfied with the original, replaced it with a second version, which actually is not much different from the first.

Other major works by the sculptor include the *Napoléon 1er équestre* of Grenoble, inaugurated in 1866 and erected in 1870. Today it is located in Laffrey, in the Isère, on the edge of the lake where the emperor rallied to him the royal troups after he returned from the Isle of Elba. Another important work is *Louis d'Orléans équestre* (1869), located in

Emmanuel Frémiet,
Le Char de Minerve,
gilded bronze, 60 cm.

the court of the chateau of Pierrefonds. Frémiet's bronze sea horses, dolphins, and tortoises from the fountain of the Observatoire (1870), are frequently overlooked, no doubt because of the prestigious central group by Carpeaux entitled *Quatre Parties du monde;* nevertheless, Frémiet received 24,000 F for his work, only 1,000 F from the amount Carpeaux received for his. Frémiet's *Eléphant pris au piège* (1877), made for the cascade of the Trocadéro, stands today on the esplanade of the Orsay Museum; his *Homme de l'âge de pierre* (1872) was made for the menagerie of the Jardin des Plantes; *Saint Grégoire de Tours* (1878) is located at the Panthéon; *Porte-falot à cheval* in bronze, 285 cm, in the stairway of the city hall (1883); *Saint Michel terrassant le dragon,* in bronze, on the spire of the church of Mont-Saint-Michel (1896); a colossal statue of *Ferdinand de Lesseps* was erected in 1899 in Port-Said at the entrance of the Suez Canal; and *Pégase conduit par les Arts et les Scineces,* two groups in gilded bronze, surmount the two towers of the right bank of the Alexandre-III Bridge (1900). Other important works include *Duguesclin équestre* (1902, Dinan); *Simon Bolivar,* an equestrian group in bronze for Santa Fé de Bogota in Colombia (1910; another *Simon Bolivar équestre* was erected in Paris on the Cours de la Rien at the corner of the Alexandre-III Bridge); and finally a number of decorative works for some hotels, particularly in Paris.

In addition to his monumental works, Frémiet made innumerable statuettes and groups, usually in clay or in wax, intending to cast them in bronze, a material which he knew and appreciated. In 1855, Napoléon III (one of Frémiet's most faithful admirers) commissioned fifty-five wax statuettes of French army uniforms, destined for the young imperial prince. These statuettes were destroyed in the fire at the Tuileries in 1871, but some of them, cast in bronze, appeared at the Exposition Universelle of 1855 and at the Salon of 1859.

In addition to these works, there were a number of other bronzes exhibited at the Salon: *Héron* (1849), *Le Chien blessé* (1850 and Exposition of 1855), *Deux Chiens bassets, Ravageot et Ravageole* (1853), *Chevaux de halage* (Exposition of 1855), *Deux chevaux de course montés* (1866 and Exposition Universelle of 1889), three figurines from the series of the uniforms of the French army entitled *Carabinier, Voltigeur* and *Artilleur à cheval* (Exposition of 1855), six other figurines entitled *Cent-Garde, Artilleur de la garde, Zouave de la garde, Sapeur, Chasseur à cheval* and *Cheval de troupe* (1859), *Le Centaure Térée emportant un ours* (1863), *Cavalier gaulois* (1864) and *Cavalier romain* (1866), both in demi-grandeur for the chateau of Saint-Germain-en-Laye, and *Chef arabe à cheval,* 33 cm (1865). Next came a series of medieval personages, probably influenced by archaeological history, particularly developed in Pierrefonds by Viollet-le-Duc: *Fauconnier* and *Damoiselle,* two statuettes in silvered bronze (1873), *Ménestrel du XVe siècle,* a statuette in silvered bronze (1875), *Saint Michel* and *Spadassin,* two statuettes respectively in gilded and silvered bronze, exhibited in 1879, *Charmeur de serpents* (1883), *Chevaux de course* (1885), *Chiens courants* and *Lévriers* (1886), *Saint Louis* (1887 and Exposition of

Emmanuel Frémiet,
Conducteur de char romain, 40 cm.

1889), *L'Aieul* and *Incroyable,* two statuettes in silvered bronze (1888), *Credo* (Exposition of 1889), *Saint Georges équestre,* statuette (1891 and Exposition Universelle of 1900), *A Domrémy,* a statuette (1893), *La Poule aux oeufs d'or* (1897), *Louis XIII enfant à cheval,* a statuette (Exposition of 1900), and *Le Char de Minerve,* a model for a Sèvres centerpiece (1904).

The inventory of the bronzes by Frémiet is known to be incomplete. Outside of the Salon, other statuettes can be cited: *Jaguar et gorille* (1876), *Zouave pontifical* (1877), *Schéhérazade* (1878), *Mueletier espagnol* (1879), *Napoléon 1er en redingote* (1908), and *Napoléon 1er habit* (1909), as well as *Molière, Washington, La Fée aux chansons, Duelliste au manteau, Jeanne d'Arc à Orléans, Vierge de Bethléem, Sainte Cécile, Sainte Catherine de Sienne,* etc.

It is fitting, lastly, to remember a number of decorative objects and furnishings, such as the lamp from 1899 portraying *Singe faisant des bulles de savon* (the original of which ornaments the dining room of the hotel of M. Dervillé in Paris) and a bas-relief representing the *Triomphe de Mérovée,* decorating a medal cabinet of the cabinetmaker Diehl. This piece of furniture, which appeared at the Exposition Universelle of 1867, was bought in a public

Emmanuel Frémiet,
Saint Michel et le dragon, gilded bronze, reduction of the statue from Mont-Saint-Michel, 27 cm (Barbedienne).

sale by the Louvre in 1973. It was exhibited again in 1979 at the Grand Palais's "Exposition of French Art from the Second Empire" before permanently entering the Orsay's collection.

A catalog published by Frémiet around 1860, and now preserved in the national archives, indicates that beginning in that year the sculptor began casting his works commercially, in bronze as often as in plaster. This catalog listed a rather large number of animals and nearly a dozen of the French army figurines, without mention of the sizes. The bronzes were priced from three to over ten times the cost of the plasters. All of them were put up for sale at the original domicile of the artist, at 42 Boulevard du Temple in Paris.

Furthermore, many works by Frémiet were cast in bronze by Susse, including a cup entitled *Jeanne d'Arc*, 10 x 42 cm, another cup called *Vestal antique*, 11 x 45 cm, and a statuette entitled *Ourse et Finlandais*, 30 cm. Barbedienne, however, executed the largest number of editions of Frémiet's sculptures. In the collections of the Dijon museum can be found the list of most of the bronze 'master models' for these editions. According to a 1986 article by Catherine Chevillot in the review *L'Estampille*, Frémiet cast his own works until 1872. After this date, the founder Charles More became his caster, executing proofs that were sometimes numbered. The Barbedienne editions started only after the sculptor's death in 1910.

MUSEUMS
Abbeville
Chef arabe à cheval, 33 cm.
Bayonne
Centaure terrassant un ours, 34.5 cm.
Epagneul couché, 10 cm.
Bernay
Chat et Coq, two statuettes.
Béziers
Centaure terrassant un ours, 37 cm (Ch. More, caster of the works by Frémiet in Paris).
Blois
Carabinier de la Garde impériale, 37 cm.
Cuirassier de la Garde impériale, 37 cm.
Artilleur de la Garde impériale, 37 cm.
Carcassonne
Cheval arabe, 27 cm (1859).
Cheval de troupe, 30 cm (1859).
Cosaque, 25.5 cm (1859).
Héron, 21 cm (1849).
Saint Georges terrassant le dragon, 52 cm (1891).
Sapeur, 26 cm (1859).
Zouave de la Garde, 23.5 cm (1859).
Chalon-sur-Saône
Cavalier gaulois, 37 cm.
Cavalier romain, 33 cm (reductions of the statues of Saint-Germain-en-Laye).
Châteauroux
Cavalier romain, 41 cm.
Clermont-Ferrand
Sceau-cachet à la grenouille, 11.5 cm.

Emmanuel Frémiet,
Pan et oursons,
25 x 55 cm
(F. Barbedienne).

Compiègne, château
Napoléon III équestre, 36 cm.
Napoléon III, bust, 13.5 cm.
Ravageot et Ravageole, chiens bassets, 60 x 80 cm (Salon of 1853).
Soldats, 30 cm.
Dijon
Master models in bronze used for the Barbedienne editions:

Personages
L'Aïeul, equestrian group, 45 cm (1888).
L'Amour fustigeant un paon, 42 cm (1900).
L'Astronomie, 20 cm.
Le Centaure Térée emportant un ours, 45 cm (1861).
Char étrusque, 30 x 39 cm (1907).
Char de Diane, 72 cm (1900).
Char de Minerve, 83 cm (1900).
Chef arabe à cheval, 33 cm (1865).
Le Cheval primé monté, 42 cm.
Chevaux de course et leurs jockeys, 46 x 49 cm (1885).
Cocher romain, 40 cm.
Credo, 39 cm (1889).
Damoiselle, 44 cm (1873).
Duelliste, Charles IX, 34 cm.
Duelliste, Henri III, 34 cm.
Duguesclin, reduction of the statue of Dinan, 67 cm (1902).
Etienne Marcel, reduction of the statue from the city hall of Paris, 51 cm (1883).
Fauconnier, 44 cm (1873).
La Fée aux chansons, 47 cm.
Figure allégorique, 52 cm.

François 1er, 50 cm (1892).
Gorille enlevant une Négresse, 45 cm (1887).
Le Grand Condé équestre, 50 cm (1881).
Hommage à Corneille, 65 cm (1879).
Incroyable, 29 cm (1888).
Isabeau de Bavière à cheval, 46 cm (1892).
Jeanne d'Arc à Domrémy, 40 cm (1893).
Jeanne d'Arc équestre, reduction of the first statue in the Plaza of Pyramides, 75 cm (1874).
Jeanne d'Arc à genoux, 48 cm (1875).
Jeanne d'Arc à Orléans, 52 cm.
Louis XIII, sortie de manège, 46 cm (1900).
Louis d'Orléans, reduction of the statue of Pierrefonds, 49 cm (1873).
Maternité, 36 cm (1898).
Ménestrel, 29 cm (1875).
Molière, 39 cm.
Muletier espagnol, 33 cm (1879).
Napoléon 1er, 34 cm (1909).
Napoléon 1er debout en habit, 32 cm (1909).
Napoléon 1er debout en redingote, 32 cm (1908).
Nègre charmeur de serpents, 43 cm (1883).
Pan et oursons, 25 x 55 cm.
Porte-falot à cheval, reduction of the statue from the city hall, 133 x 111 cm (1883).
Sainte Catherine de Sienne, 46 cm.
Sainte Cécile, 54 cm.
Saint Georges équestre, 53 cm (1891).
Saint Hubert équestre, 47 cm.
Saint Louis, 40 cm.
Saint Michel terrassant le dragon, maquette of the statue from Mont-Saint-Michel, 60 cm (1879).
Schéhérazade, equestrian group, 51 cm (1878).

333

Emmanuel Frémiet,
Cheval de saltimbanque, 22 cm.

Cats
Chat assis, 8 cm.
Chat au collier assis, 6 cm.
Chat et fauvette, 14 x 39 cm.
Chat à la patte, 14 x 21 cm.
Chat au poulet, 7 x 26 cm (1889).
Buste de chat, 22 cm.
Chatte mangeant ses petits, 7 x 18 cm.
Chatte mangeant une souris, 7 x 14 cm.
Chatte et ses petits, 24 x 58 cm (1848).

Dogs
Chien basset assis, 15 cm.
Chiens bassets, 15 x 18 cm.
Chien blessé couché, 10 x 20 cm.
Chien courant blessé, 27 cm (1850).
Chien courant couché, 11 x 23 cm.
Chien griffon à la torture, 9 x 22 cm.
Chien limier assis, 25 cm.
Chiens limiers assis, 25 cm.
Chien loulou couché, 7 x 15 cm.
Chien pris au piège, 9 x 20 cm.
Chien Terre-Neuve couché, 14 x 25 cm.
Chien Terre-Neuve debout, 26 x 26 cm.
Chien terrier assis, 16 cm.
Tête de chien, seal, 8 cm.
Chienne griffon et ses petits, 14 cm (1850).
Lévriers, 26 x 35 cm (1886).

Diverse animals
Ane du Caire, 27 cm (1890).
Anon, 18 cm.
Chèvre et ses petits, 16 x 20 cm.
Grenouille, seal, 11 cm.
Mouton, 15 x 20 cm.
Renard, 8 x 19 cm.
Singe assis et escargot, 18 x 29 cm.
Singe, seal, 11 cm.
Souris à l'huître, 7 cm.

Soeur de charité, 23 cm (1859).
Vélasquez équestre, reduction of the bronze from the
    Casa Velasquez in Madrid, 57 cm (1891).
Vierge de Bethléem, 32 cm.
Washington, 39 cm.

Statuettes of the uniforms from the French army
Artilleur au manteau, 26 cm.
Brigadier des guides à cheval, 36 cm.
Cantinière, 23 cm.
Cent-Garde, 30 cm.
Chasseur à cheval, 35 cm.
Cheval de troupe, 31 cm.
Cuirassier à cheval, 36 cm.
Fantassin, 25 cm.
Gendarme à cheval, 38 cm.
Gendarme, 26 cm.
Grenadier, 29 cm.
Marin, 24 cm.
Napoléon III à cheval, 35 cm.
Sapeur, 26 cm.
Turco, 24 cm.
Zouave assis, 21 cm.
Zouave couché à l'affût, 14 x 21 cm.

Large animals
Chameau tartare, 30 x 33 cm (1849).
Cheval, 27 x 30 cm.
Cheval au corbeau, 12 x 22 cm (1859).
Cheval primé, 40 cm.
Cheval pur-sang, 36 x 43 cm.
Cheval de saltimbanque, 22 cm (1859).
Cheveaux de halage, 24 x 30 cm (1855).
Eléphant pris au piège, 17 cm.
Eléphant, seal, 7 cm.
Ours et ses petits, 12 x 24 cm.

Emmanuel Frémiet,
Deux Bassets, Ravageot et Ravageole,
gilded bronze, 15 x 17 cm.

334

Fowl
Canard, 4 x 10 cm.
Canards se disputant un rat, 10 x 24 cm.
Coq chantant, 12 cm.
Courlis et grenouille, 7 x 15 cm.
Fauvette, pin tray, 8 x 16 cm.
Héron, 22 cm.
Poule, 7 cm.
Poule aux oeufs d'or, 35 x 43 cm.
Poule et rat, 9 x 15 cm.

The museum of Dijon preserves also a statue in gilded bronze, *François Rude tenant le modèle de la Marseillaise*, 180 cm.

Epinal
Deux Bassets, 14 x 17 cm.
Chatte allaitant ses petits, 11 x 20 cm.
Grenoble
Cavalier romain à cheval, 33.5 cm.
Chatte et ses petits, 24 x 57 cm.
Napoléon 1er équestre, reduction of the statue from
    Laffrey Lake, 34 cm.
Guéret
Chat, 8.2 cm.
Chatte au collier, gilded bronze, 5.5 cm.
Courlis guettant une grenouille, 6.5 cm.
Grenouille liée sur une tige de bois, 11 cm.
Poule et poussins, 6.8 cm.
Souris sur une huître, 7.5 cm.
Four figurines from the French army:
Le Cent-Garde, 30 cm, *Le Fantassin*, 25, *Le Sapeur*, 26
    cm, *Le Zouave*, 23.5 cm.

Emmanuel Frémiet,
Cheval sellé, 31 cm.

Emmanuel Frémiet,
Couple de chiens attachés,
24 cm.

Emmanuel Frémiet,
Deux Chevaux de course montés, 45 cm
(Barbedienne).

335

Emmanuel Frémiet,
*Homme attaqué
par un oiurs.*

Emmanuel Frémiet,
*Gorille enlevant
une Négresse,*
44.5 cm.
J. Ginepro
Collection, Monaco.

Le Mans
Chevaux de halage, 22.5 cm.
Chien courant, 9 cm.
Chien de garde, 15.5 cm.
Le Puy
Chat dévorant un poulet, 8 x 34 cm.
Cheval, 27 x 29 cm.
Chien de berger, 13.5 cm.
Renard, 9 x 18 cm.
Lille
Chatte allaitant ses petits, 24 cm (1848).
Montpellier
Saint Michel terrassant le dragon, reduction of the
    statue from Mont-Saint-Michel, 30 cm.
Moulins
Le Grand Condé équestre.
Nantes
Chevaux de halage, 22.5 cm.
Chien courant au repos, 11.5 cm.
Niort
Chatte allaitant ses petits, 11 x 20 cm.
Chien au repos.
Paris, musée de l'Armée
Ten figurines of soldiers from the French army, from 23
    to 30 cm; *Artilleur de la Garde, Cantinière, Cent-
    Gard, Gendarme, Grenadier de la Garde, Matelot,
    Sapeur d'infanterie, Voltigeur d'infanterie, Zouave
    assis,* and *Zouave de la Garde.*
Paris, Decorative Arts
Le Duc d'Orléans à cheval, silvered bronze, 47 cm (Ch.
    More, caster).
Gendarme debout lisant, 26 cm.
Quartier-maître de la marine, mains sur les hanches, 24
    cm.

Saint Georges et le dragon, 47 cm (Ch. More, caster).
Saint Michel et le dragon, silvered bronze, 57 cm (Ch.
    More).
Paris, Carnavalet
Chien blessé, 69 cm (Gonon, founder).
Ferdinand de Lesseps, reduction of a monument of
    Port-Said, 64 cm (Barbedienne).
Marabouts enchaînés, 89 cm.
Saint Georges et le dragon, gilded bronze, 57 cm (1871).
Périgueux
Chat dans une pose contournée, 14.5 cm.
Coq en maraude, 8.5 cm.
Courlis poursuivant une grenouille, 7 cm.
Rennes
Three figurines of soldiers from the French army:
    Artilleur à cheval, Carabinier, and *Cuirassier.*
Saint-Germain-en-Laye, Antiquités nationales
Cavalier gaulois.
Cavalier romain.
Semur-en-Auxois
Chat, 25 cm.
Cheval au piquet, 31 cm.
Héron, 22 cm.
Griffon et ses petits, 13 cm.
Two figurines from the French army: *Artilleur de la
    Garde,* 26 cm, and *Zouave,* 21 cm.
Strasbourg
Saint Michel terrassant le dragon, 60 cm.
Toulouse
Isabeau de Bavière, 49 cm.
Troyes
Louis d'Orléans équestre, 46.5 cm.
Saint Michel terrassant le dragon, gilded bronze, 60 cm.

Emmanuel Frémiet,
*Le Singe
aux bulles de savon,*
luminary of
gilded bronze and
opalined glass on
a panel of wood,
H. of the bronze: 87 cm
(Thiébaut-Fumière).

Valence

Au voleur!, haut-relief oval, 25 cm.
Chienne griffon et ses petits.
Le Christ mort sur les genoux de la Vierge.
Héron
Zouave assis tenant son fusil.

Vernon

Courlis pousuivant une grenouille, 7 x 15 cm.

SALES

Personages

Cavalier gaulois, 36.5 cm, Christie's London, January 22, 1986; Guéret, September 28, 1986.
Cavalier romain, 33 cm, Drouot, March 26, 1986, room 9.
Char attelé de trois cerfs, Drouot, February 4, 1985.
Char de Minerve, gilded bronze, 60 cm, L'Isle-Adam, October 7, 1984.
Chasseur, 31 cm (Susse), Drouot, April 4, 1984, room 1.
Cheval de course et son jockey, 45.5 cm, Sotheby London, July 5, 1985.
Deux chevaux de course montés, 45 cm (Barbedienne), Enghien, October 6, 1985 (for 150,000 F); *L'Aigle,* May 31, 1986.
Chef arabe à cheval, 38.5 cm, Sotheby London, March 20, 1986.
Conducteur de char romain, 40 cm, Drouot, June 17, 1983, room 9; Sotheby London, March 20, 1986.
Credo, 39 cm (Barbedienne), Sotheby London, March 20, 1986.
François 1er à cheval, 46 cm, Sotheby London, November 6, 1986.
Isabeau de Bavière à cheval, gilded bronze, 46 cm, Sotheby London, March 8, 1984.
Jeanne d'Arc à cheval, 73 cm, Drouot, Devember 14, 1984, room 6.
Louis XIII à cheval, 50 x 37 cm, Agen, June 29, 1985.
Louis XV à cheval, silvered bronze, 49 cm, Sotheby London, June 7, 1984.
Louis d'Orléans à cheval, 46 cm, Sotheby London, July 5, 1985.
Louis d'Orléans à cheval, 69 cm, Compiègne, November 23, 1986.
Louis d'Orléans à cheval, 79 cm, Drouot, February 6, 1984, room 7.
Napoléon 1er à cheval, 33 cm, Sotheby London, November 8, 1984.
Pan et oursons, 25 cm, Drouot, February 6, 1984, room 7; Lyons-la-Forêt, June 16, 1985.
Saint Georges équestre et le dragon, 53 cm (Barbedienne), Drouot, July 1, 1986, room 15.
Saint Hubert équestre, 47 cm, Drouot, July 7, 1983, room 9.
Saint Michel terrassant le dragon, gilded bronze, 56 cm, Drouot, November 28, 1984, room 13.
Schéhérazade, gilded bronze, 51 cm, Drouot, March 12, 1982.

Animals

Cheval pur-sang, 30 cm (Barbedienne), Drouot, May 21, 1986, room 14.
Chevaux romains, 41 cm, Drouot, December 13, 1985, room 16.
Chèvre et chevreau, 18 cm, Vitry-le-François, April 21, 1986.
Chien couché, gilded bronze, 15.5 cm, (Barbedienne), Drouot, October 19, 1983, room 9.
Chien de meute, 24 cm (Barbedienne), Drouot, Aril 23, 1986, room 9.
Deux chiens assis attachés, 24 cm, Morlaix, May 27, 1985.
Couple de bassets, 15 cm, Drouot, March 27, 1984, room 8; Valenciennes, December 1, 1986.
Dogue, 20 cm, Drouot, March 27, 1984, room 8.
Dromadaire, 28 cm, Drouot, April 4, 1984, room 1.
Eléphant d'Asie, 16 cm, Drouot, March 23, 1985, room 13.
Eléphant entravé, 16.5 cm, Drouot, December 10, 1984, room 7.

FRÈRE, JEAN JULES

Cambrai, October 1, 1851
Paris, May 1906

After some studies in Cambrai, and then in Paris with Cavelier and Cordier at the Ecole des Beaux-Arts, Frère exhibited at the Salon of 1878. On this occasion he showed a plaster entitled *Chanteur oriental,* 110 cm, which was later cast in bronze by Hohwiller and bought by the city of Cambrai. However, the bronze that can now be seen in the Jardin aux Fleurs of this city might be a later version. In 1888, he sent a group in bronze, *Les Deux Pigeons,* to the Salon. A contract was arranged for Barbedienne to execute a bronze casting in 1902 of Frère's statue in marble entitled *L'Amour piqué,* 148 cm, preserved at the museum of Cambrai. His work *Chanteur oriental* was cast in bronze by Thiébaut in two dimensions, 91 and 43 cm.

FRIANT, ÉMILE

Dieuze (Moselle), April 16, 1863
Paris, 1932

This very skillful painter and designer maintained a strong reputation throughout his lifetime. The museum of Grenoble possesses a bust in bronze by him, entitled *La Foi,* 48 cm. This piece was exhibited at the Salon de la Société Nationale des Beaux-Arts in 1901.

FROMENT-MEURICE, JACQUES

Paris, October 7, 1864
Versailles, January 1948

From a family of famous goldsmiths, Jacques Froment-Meurice was the son of the Art Nouveau specialist Emile Froment-Meurice. He developed into a very skillful animal sculptor, very perceptive and discerning of the positions and attitudes of certain animals. He made a noteworthy series of studies called *Les Gestes des ânes,* and also sculpted a number of horses, equestrian figures, scenes of life in the Basque country, busts, and medallions. He executed many commemorative monuments, particularly the monument to *Chopin* located in Monceau Park in Paris.

A student of Chapu and of the Académie Julian, Froment-Meurice made some voyages across Europe and through Africa. He participated at the Salon des Artistes Français from 1891 to 1895, in 1892 exhibiting a study in bronze entitled *Nitouche, jument anglo-irlandaise,* and in 1894 a group in plaster entitled *Le Chien de Montargis.* He participated next at the Salon de la Société Nationale des Beaux-Arts, showing a number of works in different materials: *Meissonnier montant sur son cheval Rivoli* in plaster and *Géricault,* haut-relief in marble (1902), *Dragon à cheval* in plaster (1903), *A la foire de Bidache* and *La Ruade de l'ânesse,* plasters (1904), *Bouvillons et marchand de boeufs à Bidache,* haut-

Jacques Froment-Meurice, Atlas et Mercure enfant, inkwell in maillechort (an alloy made of copper, zinc and nickel which looks like silver) and marble, 30 cm L.

Jacques Froment-Meurice,
Le Lancier,
73 cm.

relief in bronze, *Le Retour du marché à Bayonne*, a group in plaster, *La Courbette*, bronze (from the series *Les Gestes des ânes*), *Le Duc d'Aumale sur sa ponette Pélagie* in plaster (all at the Salon of 1905), *Ane se roulant* and *Boby*, two statuettes in bronze, *Avant la corrida à Saint-Sébastien* in plaster (1906), *La Vieille Anesse tondue* in bronze (1907), *Le Flirt*, a group in bronze from the series *Les Gestes des ânes* (1908), *Etalon boulonnais* and *Poney du Gers*, two bronzes (1911), *Cheval de guerre* in bronze (1912), and *Cerf et biche*, a group in plaster (1913), etc.

Jacques Froment-Meurice continued to work between the two world wars. In 1934, obliged to abandon his studios of Brunoy for financial reasons, he offered many of his works to museums. Poitiers received one of his favorite works, the plaster of *Pèlerin*; Rouen received the *Géricault*; Chantilly, the *Duc d'Aumale* in bronze.

Many works by this sculptor have been cast in bronze. Of note are *Meissonier sur son cheval Rivoli*, 62 cm, *Retour du marché de Bayonne*, 54 cm, *Nitouche, jument anglor-irlandaise*, 32 cm, and *Dragon à cheval*, 52 cm, among others. The Hébrard foundry cast many models from the series *Les Gestes des ânes*, in particular *La Courbette*, 32 and 17 cm, and *La Ruade*, 33 and 18 cm.

MUSEUMS
Bordeaux
Allégorie du temps, group cast by Rudier the elder.

SALES
Ane s'ébrouant, 16 cm, Enghien, October 6, 1985.
Le Lancier, 73 cm, Nancy, September 25, 1983.
Meditantur praella ludo, 26 cm, Drouot, December 17, 1982, room 2.

FUGÈRE, HENRY

Saint-Mandé, September 7, 1872
January 13, 1944

The son of sculptor Léon Fugère and a student of Cavelier, Henry Fugère started exhibiting in 1893 with medallions, busts and (most notably) some statuettes, primarily in bronze: *La Fumée*, (1896), *L'Age d'or* (1899), *Etoile du berger* (1900), *Tentation* (1909), *Les Deux Amis* (1910), *Rieuse, Danseuse*, and *Saint Christophe* (1911). He also exhibited some statuettes in plaster, including *Espoir* (1903) and *L'Age de pierre* (1911) among others. He continued to sculpt after World War I, and much of his work from this time clearly reveals the influence of the then-popular Art Deco style.

Many works by Fugère were cast in bronze, among others *L'Age de pierre*, *Danseuse*, 51 cm, *Le Progrès*, 64 cm, and *Salomé*, as well as a stinging shellfish ornamented by a figure of a young woman, made by Siot-Decauville.

SALES
Chasseresse au lévrier, silvered bronze, 52 cm L., (after 1920), Drouot, October 19, 1983, room 9.
Domination, 85 cm, Drouot, May 30, 1984, room 5.

Jeune Femme à son miroir, gilded bronze and ivory, 30 cm, Sotheby London, March 21, 1985.

Jeune Musicienne, bronze and ivory, 33 cm, Sotheby Chester, July 21, 1983.

Proaris et focis, 64 cm (around 1890), Sotheby London, June 23, 1983.

Salomé, gilded bronze, 40.5 cm, Christie's New York, September 29, 1983.

FULCONIS, LOUIS GUILLAUME

Avignon, 1818
Paris, May 11, 1873

Fulconis frequented the school of fine arts of Avignon before exhibiting at the Salon from 1857 to 1872. Meanwhile, he visited Algeria, and a large number of his works portray different types of inhabitants of this country. Among these pieces are *Ouled-Naïet, bayadère* (Salon of 1861), *Le Retour du marché*, a statue in plaster (1861), *Canéphore algérienne*, a statue in plaster (1863), *Mauresque d'Algérie* and *Juive d'Alger*, two busts in plaster (1869), *Juif d'Alger essuyeur de métaux* and *Femme kabyle filant*, two other busts in plaster (1870).

In the Barbedienne catalog appears Fulconis' *Deux Femmes algériennes porte-lumières*, listed in three sizes: 200, 120 and 100 cm. Also notable in bronze are *Cérès et la Fortune*, 86 cm, and in the posession of a private collector, a statuette entitled *Le Prince impérial enfant en grenadier*, 29 cm, dated 1859.

Henry Fugère,
Aiguière Coquillage avec jeune femme
(Siot-Decauville).

GAILLARD, LÉON JACQUES

Preignac (Gironde)—?
World War I

This little-known sculptor, a student of Falguière and of Mercié, exhibited some statuettes at the Salon between 1892 and 1914: *La Cigale*, marble (1896), *Yolaine*, plaster (1898), *Frédégonde*, plaster (1905), and *Devant l'aréopage*, plaster (1914). A group in bronze of three personages, representing the kidnapping of a Sabine, 110 cm, was sold at the Drouot Hotel on June 25, 1984.

GALLAUD, MARIE

Paris, March 19, 1867
1945

Marie Gallaud started exhibiting at the Salon in 1890; she showed figurines and busts of villagers and peasants of Bretagne, scenes of everyday life, etc. The museum of Grenoble preserves a bust in bronze entitled *Vieux Vagabond*, 44 cm.

GANUCHAUD, PAUL

Born in Paris, 1881

This sculptor exhibited in different salons, and was known to be still working in 1936. A small bronze entitled *La Bergère*, 26 x 31 cm, was sold in Angers on June 19, 1985.

GARDET, GEORGES

Paris, October 11, 1863
February 6, 1939

The son of a sculptor and a student of Aimé Millet and of Frémiet at the Ecole des Beaux-Arts, Georges Gardet very quickly revealed himself to be an animal sculptor of great skill. Appreciated particularly for his groups of big game in powerful forms, he received

Léon Jacques Gaillard,
Enlèvement d'une Sabine, 110 cm.

Georges Gardet,
Drame au désert,
after the bronze
from Montsouris Park,
30 cm (Siot-Decauville).

Though he liked translating the muscular strength of large game in combat, Gardet did not disdain small animals, and executed such works as *Poussin et caneton*, marble (Salon of 1891), and *Singe et torture*, stone (1892). He is also the author of a monumental group in bronze entitled *Bison et jaguar* for the entrance of the museum of Laval (1892), *Chien danois* and *Chienne danoise*, two marbles for the château of Chantilly (1894), a group in marble entitled *Tigre et lion* for the château de Vaux-le-Vicomte (1898), some lions to ornament the stairways of the Alexandre III Bridge on the Right Bank (1900), the bronze *Lionne au guet* (Salon of 1909), the gilded bronze group *Cerf et biche* (Salon of a number of commissions. He debuted at the Salon at the age of twenty. In 1887, he won his first success with his group *Panthère et python*, also entitled *Drame au désert*. A plaster, this piece was cast in bronze to be placed at Montsouris Park, where it can still be seen. Gardet produced not only plasters, many of which would be translated into bronze, but also some works in marble, sometimes of many colors, and others in onyx or in diverse materials as commissioned by rich clients desiring to preserve "portraits" of family pets. Many of his sculptures were also replicated in unglazed porcelain by Sèvres. Gardet was considered to be the most talented animal sculptor of his time.

G.GARDET

Georges Gardet,
Couple de tigres,
53 x 69 cm
(Colin, founder).

Georges Gardet,
Lion allongé, 35 cm
(Valsuani).

Georges Gardet,
Sanglier,
35 x 53 cm
(Barbedienne).

Georges Gardet,
Les Deux Sangliers.

1910), etc. Certain of his works belong to foreign museums in Bucharest, Hamburg, and Oxford.

Almost regularly, Georges Gardet exhibited animals at the Salon before 1914, and then between the two wars until 1931. A number of them were cast in bronze in reduced dimensions by Thiébaut, Barbedienne, Siot-Decauville, and some other foundries.

Bronzes carrying the seal of Barbedienne:
Le Grand Cerf, 110 cm.
Deux Lévriers, 46 cm.
L'Idole, 27.5 cm.
Groupe de levrettes, 28 cm.
Groupe de perruches, 24 cm.
Oiseau sortant de l'oeuf, 12 cm.
Poussin, 13 cm.
Sanglier, 35 cm.
Souris et escargots, 8.5 x 29.5 cm.

Bronzes cast by Siot-Decauville:
Chien couché, 47 cm. L.
Drame au désert.
Lion et lionne.
Lionne attaquant un bison, 44 cm.
Panthère au guet.
Panthère au serpent, 29 cm.
Panthère grimpant, 46 cm. L.

Ours mendiant, 30 cm. (and other dimensions).
Deux Tigres.
Tigre et tortue.
Tigre se caressant, 37 cm.
Many objects including a tobacco can, cigar can, etc.

Other bronzes were cast by Valsuani (*Lion allongé*, 35 cm), Thiébaut (*Combat de panthères*, 73, 48 and 39 cm), the Société of Bronzes of Paris (*Lion dévorant une antilope*), and Colin (*Couple de tigres*), etc.

Of final note is Gardet's *Ours mendiant*, his most popular work. This piece was the object of a casting in unglazed porcelain by Sèvres, and was sold by this factory until 1930.

MUSEUMS
Avignon
Drame au désert, 175 x 260 cm.
Blois
Buffle et jaguar, 21 x 41 cm.
Lionne et tortue, 22 x 46 cm.
Boulogne-sur-Mer
Panthère, 27 cm.
Grenoble
Ours assis, 30 cm.
Louviers
Ours assis, 30 cm.

Georges Gardet,
Le Grand Cerf,
110 cm
(Barbedienne).

Georges Gardet,
Combat de cerfs,
40 cm.

Paris, Decorative Arts
Caneton et escargot, 8 x 25 cm.
Paris, Orsay
Panthère dévorant un mouton, 53 cm.
L'Ours mendiant, 30.6 cm (Siot-Decauville).

SALES
Cerf dix-cors, Drouot, June 15, 1981.
Le Grand Cerf, 110 cm (Barbedienne), Versailles, June 16, 1984; Enghien, October 6, 1985.
Combat de cerfs, 40 cm, Versailles, June 16, 1984; Vannes, January 26, 1986.
Drogues danois, 147.5 cm L., Christie's New York, October 16, 1984 (sold for 20,000 dollars).
Jaguar attaquant un serpent, 30 cm (Siot-Decauville), Christie's New York, December 15, 1985.
Laie et ses petits, 75 cm L. (Barbedienne), Versailles, June 16, 1983; Drouot, March 14, 1985, room 1.
Lion allongé, 35 cm (Valsuani), Drouot, November 5, 1985, room 6.
Lionne et tortue, 20 x 43 cm, Sotheby London, March 8, 1984; Nice, November 14, 1984.
Lionne attaquant un bison, 44 cm L. (Siot-Decauville), Sotheby Johannesburg, July 3, 1984.
Sanglier, 53 cm L. (Barbedienne), Drouot, July 7, 1983, room 9.
Les Deux Sangliers, Drouot, February 4, 1985, room 14.
Setter, 27.5 x 55 cm (Société des bronzes of Paris), Christie's London, May 15, 1986.
Singe assis sur une tortue, 19 cm, Enghien, October 10, 1982.
Tigre se caressant, 37 cm (Siot-Decauville), Drouot, November 9, 1984, room 6.
Tigre jouant avec un lézard, 11.5 cm, Drouot, October 19, 1983, room 9.
Tigresse, 33 x 64 cm, Enghien, October 10, 1982.
Couple de tigres, 52.5 cm (Colin, founder), Enghien, October 6, 1985.

GARNIER, JEAN

Mouzeuil (Vendée), March 24, 1853
Vers, 1910

This artist participated fairly regularly at the Salon from 1883 to 1905, with works in different materials, particularly statuettes: *Nymphe chantant*, terra cotta (1892), *Rêverie* (plaster in 1893, marble the following year), *Oh! la grenouille*, wax (1894), *Amazone victorieuse*, bronze (1896), *Le Corail*, tin (1897), and *Gladiateur*, plaster (1905). Also of note is his bronze statue entitled Amazone combattant, which was exhibited in 1892. Outside of the Salon, he is known for the gilded bronze work entitled *Amphitrite, La Bergère*, 47 cm, as well as *Le Chant du rossignol*, 80 cm, *Corail*, 70 cm, *Danse serpentine*, 40 cm, *La Fileuse, Jeune Femme voilée*, 75 cm, and *Lavandière, Le Terrassier*, 14 cm. He also made diverse objects, vases, and cups in tin, silver, and metal, often with an Art Nouveau spirit. Finally, he sculpted some statuettes in bronze, *Marin écossais dansant* and *Jeune Violoniste*, which are noted to have been cast by the Sanson foundry in Hamburg.

MUSEUMS
Bordeaux
Jeune Fille à la flèche, 58 cm.

SALES
L'Enfer des luxurieux, plate decorated in relief, 58.5 cm diam., Drouot, May 25, 1984, rooms 5 and 6.
Pierrot, 43 cm, Sotheby London, March 20, 1986.

Jean Garnier,
Petite Fermière,
22.5 cm.

Jean Garnier,
*Pêcheuse
de crevettes*,
32 cm.

GASQ, PAUL

Dijon, May 31, 1860
Paris, 1944

The winner of the first prize of Rome in 1890, Gasq became a member of the Institut in 1935. He principally sculpted classic and allegorical subjects, as well as some portraits in bust, medallion, bas relief, and statuette form. He portraited many members of the Joliet family from Dijon, among whom were curators of the museum, a mayor, and a prefect. Memorable works exhibited at the Salon, starting in 1880, include *Héro et Léandre*, a bas-relief in plaster (1893), *Orphée*, a statue in plaster (1894), and *La Gloire*, a statue in bronze for the monument of Carnot in Dijon (1898). Others include *Réveil de la source*, a statue in plaster (1899), *Volubilis*, a statuette in marble (1902), *Le Milieu du jour*, a figure in plaster (1908), *Monument à Houdon*, a group in marble (1909), *Aux volontaires de la Révolution*, a group in plaster (1911), etc. A statue in marble of *Médée* is found in the gardens of the Tuileries, a group in stone entitled *L'Art et la Nature* or *La Sculpture* ornaments the facade of the Petit Palais, and a bas-relief entitled *L'Electricité* appears on the facade of the Gare de Lyon in Paris.

MUSEUMS
Dijon
Les Deux Frères Joliet, bas-relief, 46 x 32 cm (1899).
Gaston Joliet, préfet, 48 cm (1904).
Persée foulant la tête de Méduse, door knocker, 38 x 20 cm.
Réveil de la source, according to the plaster of 1899, 200 cm.
Reims
Camille Lenoir, député de la Marne, bas-relief, 52 x 34 cm (1901).

SALES
Femme ailée, bust, half-exposed, 90 cm, Drouot, June 23, 1982, room 16.
La Paix, 88 cm, Sotheby London, March 17, 1983.

GATELET, EUGÈNE

Nancy, March 9, 1874
Nancy, January 1, 1932

This sculptor is best-known for his busts, including *Louis Majorel* in stone for the garden at the school's museum in Nancy, the bust in bronze of his father, and another bust in bronze entitled *Après l'effort*, which belongs to the Musuem of the Fine Arts in Nancy. A 20 x 15 cm placque in gilded bronze entitled *Portrait d'Emile Coué* bears the inscription "It is not the will of men but the imagination that...," and was sold at the Drouot Hotel on December 2, 1983.

GATTEAUX, JACQUES ÉDOUARD

Paris, September 4, 1788
Paris, February 8, 1881

Very well-off and a great lover of art, Jacques Édouard Gatteaux amassed an important collection which was partly destroyed at the time of the events of the Commune (1871), the rest were distributed by legacy, between the Louvre, the museum of Montauban, the Engraving Department of the National Library and the Ecole des Beaux-Arts, after his death. A sculptor and a medal-engraver, he learned drawing and engraving from his father, and sculpture in the studio of Moitte. He went to Rome in 1809 after winning the first grand prize for medal-engraving. Upon his return to Paris four years later, he received many commissions from the state for the Louvre, the Théâtre Français, and the Palais de l'Institut. He also made a number of medals, busts, and statues. His presentations at the Salon included a bust in plaster of *Michel-Ange* (1822, to be be cast in bronze in 1844), a statue in bronze entitled *Le Chevalier d'Assas*, 2 m high, for the city of Vigan (1827), a statue in marble entitled *Triptolème* (1831) which, along with a marble entitled *Pomone* (1844), is found today in the Tuileries. In 1839 he exhibited the bronze statue *Minerve après le jugement de Paris* at the Salon, and finally, in 1844, a reduction in bronze of the *Chevalier d'Assas*. After 1855 he no longer participated at the Salon. The museum of Nîmes possesses a bronze of the *Chevalier d'Assas* offered by the sculptor in 1849.

GATTI, JESUALDO

Naples, 1855
Vers, 1893

Gatti worked in Paris and exhibited between 1881 and 1887 at the Salon, contributing some busts, a statuette in plaster entitled *A Naples*, and a group in bronze entitled *Le Chat et la souris*, 155 cm. At the Exposition Universelle of 1878, he presented a statue in bronze entitled *Une impressions des temps pompéiens*. His *Chien de meute* was cast in bronze by the Susse house in two sizes, 17 and 8 cm. A work entitled *Chien couché*, 17 x 50 cm (Susse), perhaps the same work as *Chien de meute*, was sold in Enghien on March 2, 1980 and another proof in London by Sotheby on June 12, 1986.

GAUDEZ, ADRIEN ÉTIENNE

Lyon, February 9, 1845
Neuilly-sur-Seine, January 23, 1902

Enrolling in the Beaux-Arts in 1862, Adrien Gaudez debuted at the Salon two years later. In 1870, while a prisoner of war in Magdebourg, Germany, he sculpted the monument to the French soldiers dying in captivity that would be raised in the city's cemetery. He is also the author of the *Florian of Alès*, as well as of a monument to the dead of Remiremont, and *Moissonneur*, a statue in bronze destined for Monceau Park. At the Salon, his bronzes were few in number. In addition to *Moissonneur* (1880), he contributed *Pro Patria* (1884), *Les Premiers Imprimeurs* (1888), *Watteau* (1890), *Le Génie de l'électricité* (1897), and *Le Faucheur* (1899). However, it seems that a number of his works were cast in bronze, judging by the proofs noted in different works and catalogs, or dispersed in public sale, particularly in an organized sale held undoubtedly by Gaudez himself on October 3, 1883. In addition to some terra cottas, this sale included the following bronzes, for the most part in many models:

Béatrix, 106 and 69 cm (3 models of each).
Le Ciseleur du XVIe siècle, 65 cm, after the plaster from
    the Salon of 1881 (5 models).
Le Ciseleur, 35 cm (2 models).
Danseur, Danseuse, 50 cm (5 models of each).
Le Ferronnier du XVIe siècle, 50 cm (2 models).
L'Hirondelle, 17 cm (4 models).
Noce du Moyen Age, 61 cm (1 model).
Ondine, 80 cm (4 models).
Valet de chien, 39 cm (8 models).

Other bronzes must still be mentioned, for the
most part cast in many dimensions: *Bacchante*
(inscribed "Trésor des Mers," i.e. treasure of the
seas), 112.5 cm, *Le Belluaire, Défense du foyer,*

Adrien Etienne Gaudez,
Actéon,
51.5 cm.

Adrien Etienne Gaudez,
Roméo et Juliette,
64 cm.

Adrien Etienne Gaudez,
Défense du foyer,
30.5 cm.

347

Dénicheur d'aigles, Etoile du matin, Femme à la cruche, Flore, L'Industrie, Jeanne d'Arc équestre, 35 cm, *Jeanne d'Arc debout*, 75 cm, *Jeune Garçon assis lisant*, 65 cm, *Lulli enfant*, 74 cm, *Mignon, Les Patineurs, Pro Patria, Vainqueur*, 69 cm, etc.

Of final note are the works cast by Susse, *Benvenuto Cellini*, 80, 64, 52 cm, and *Molière enfant*, 78, 60, 40 cm.

MUSEUMS
Clermont-Ferrand
Actéon, 105 cm.
Louviers
Gambetta, reduction of a statue for Le Neubourg, 56 cm.
Valence
Paix et Abondance, 56 cm.

SALES
Actéon, 74 cm, Sotheby London, March 20, 1986.
Le Forgeron, 60 cm, Drouot, March 16, 1981.
La Fortune récompensant le Travail, 57.5 cm, Christie's Oklahoma (United States), September 24, 1981.
Jeune Garçon assis, 71 cm, Sotheby London, June 7, 1984.
La Leçon d'escrime ou l'Ecole d'honneur, 74 cm, Sotheby London, June 7, 1984.
Lulli enfant, 50 cm, Cannes, April 3, 1984; Sotheby London, November 7, 1985.
Marguerite, 61 cm, Drouot, December 20, 1983.
Mignon, 42 cm, Drouot, June 19, 1985, room 9.
Orphée et Cerbère, 76 cm, Christie's London, May 15, 1986.
Raphaël, 72 cm, Vitry-le-François, March 24, 1982.
Roméo et Juliette, 64 cm, Nice, April 14, 1982.
Sainte Cécile, 89 cm, Sotheby London, March 21, 1985.
Le Travail, 66 cm, Clermont-Ferrand, April 17, 1982.

GAUDISSARD, ÉMILE

Alger, December 15, 1872
1956

Both a sculptor and a painter, Gaudissard participated at the Salon starting in 1893, showing some busts, statues, and reliefs in different materials. These works include *Job*, a statue in plaster (1896), *Le Semeur*, a statue in plaster (1899), *La Bonté*, a statue in stone (1904), *Le Printemps*, a statue in marble (1906), *Monsieur Pacheco*, a statuette in bronze, and *La Jeunesse*, a group in plaster (1910). The Orsay Museum possesses a small bronze, *Mauresque*, 37.5 cm, dated from 1909 (H. Gonon, founder). At the museum of Alger is found another small bronze entitled *Le Printemps*, 32 cm.

GAUGUIN, PAUL

Paris, June 7, 1848
Atuana (îles Marquises), May 8, 1903

The bronzes "according to" Gauguin were cast more than half a century after his death, and it is likely that he never envisioned the execution of the majority of them. The expression "according to" is much more justified here where the proofs were cast, at the request of his beneficiaries, not from models designed to be cast but from some sculpted wood. It

Paul Gauguin,
La Luxure, 70 cm (Valsuani 7/12).

Paul Gauguin,
La Petite Parisienne, 27 cm.

Paul Gauguin,
Oviri, 74 cm (Valsuani 7/12).

Paul Gauguin,
Buste de Mme Schuffenecker, 60 cm.

office of a stockbroker. In 1873, he married a young Danish woman, Mette Sophie Gad, who bore him five children. However, a passion for painting soon overcame him. Influenced by the impressionists, he participated at their fourth exposition in 1879. Four years later, he left his job and was quickly impoverished. His wife returned to Denmark with their children. In 1886, during one of his many visits to Pont-Aven in Brittany, Gaugin met Emile Bernard, and soon became a leader of a school, separating himself from the impressionists in order to develop his own style. In the meantime, he went to Panama and to Martinique (1887), and then to Arles (1888) where he stayed with Van Gogh for two months. He also kept company with the poets known as the 'Symbolists'. Finally, in 1891, he installed himself in Polynesia, at first in Tahiti. After two visits, interrupted by a return to Paris in 1893, he reached Atuana in the Ile d'Hiva Oa, the Marquise island on which he passed away, unapproachable and alone. A number of his canvases, inundated by colors, evoke this last part of his life, as do the majority of his sculptures.

It is possible to draw up a list of the bronzes cast according to Gaugin's works if one refers to the catalog of Gaugin's sculptures and ceramics published by Christopher Gray in 1963, to the public sales of recent years, and to diverse sources of information including the certificates drafted in 1975 for five series of bronzes by Mme Spiess, proprietor of the Galerie de Paris in Toulouse. In the following list, the items referenced in the Christopher Gray catalog are indicated by the abreviation 'C.G.'.

is known that the famous painter had practiced clay modeling extensively (he produced numerous ceramics which sometimes appeared in his paintings) as well as wood sculpture. Except for some statuettes, busts and masks executed in France, most of his sculpted work dates from the long sojourn he took to Tahiti starting in 1891. It consists of some furniture, seats, objects ornamented with motifs directly inspired by Polynesian art, some symbolic bas-reliefs representing native women similar to those in his canvases, and finally cylindrical totems evoking Tahitian idols. These last were the particular objects of limited bronze editions cast by the lost wax method.

Gaugin's life story is well known, having been frequently told. Born in Paris, he lived until the age of seven with his mother's family in Pérou. At seventeen, he engaged himself as a simple sailor. Liberated from his military obligations a short time after the events of the Commune, he began work in the

La Petite Parisiene, 27 cm (C.G. No4), according to a wax original. Edition undoubtedly commisioned by Ambroise Vollard. The founder and the number of proofs are not mentioned.

Négresse martiniquaise à genoux, 20 cm, around 1888 (C.G. No61), according to a wax. According to Gray, an edition of six proofs were made by the Zac Gallery before 1939, another by the Modern Foundry, Astoria, Long Island, around 1957.

La Luxure, 70 cm, around 1890. (C.G. No88). Edition in twelve models by Valsuani.

Buste de Madame Schuffenecker, 60 cm, around 1889 (C.G. No.89), cast in 1960 by Valsuani for Maurice Malingue: two series of ten proofs, the second outside of market marked by letters.

Idole à la perle, 35 cm, around 1893 (C.G. No.94), six proofs numbered by Valsuani and six others marked by initials for the family of Monfreid.

Hina, around 1893 (C.G. No.95). Two editions, one of six proofs (1959), the other of twenty proofs, by Valsuani.

Hina et Te Fatou, 32 cm, around 1893 (C.G. No.96); six proofs Valsuani (1959).

Masque de jeune Tahitienne "Tehura", 20 cm, around 1893 (C.G. No.98). The other side, bas-relief representing Eve; seven proofs numbered from 0/6 to 6/6; eight proofs monogrammed As, SC, AH, JH, AM, JB, RS, DW, and a proofs for the museum Toulouse-Lautrec in Albi. Founder, Valsuani. Editions made from 1959 to 1968 by Mme Spiess, Galerie de Paris in Toulouse, in collaboration with Mme Agnès Huc de Monfreid, owner of the original woods of Gauguin by inheritance from his father, the painter Daniel de Monfreid, friend of the famous artist.

Paul Gauguin,
L'Après-midi d'un faune,
34 cm
(Valsuani HC).

Paul Gauguin,
Stèle du Christ,
face ornée
de figures polynésiennes,
50 cm
(Valsuani 0/6).

Paul Gauguin,
Hina et Te Fatou,
32 cm
(Valsuani).

Paul Gauguin,
L'Idole à la coquille, 27 cm
(Valsuani).

Idole à la coquille, 27 cm, around 1893 (C.G. No.99); seven proofs numbered from 0/6 to 6/6; eight proofs monogramed (like the preceding piece); a proof for the museum of Albi; Valsuani; editions Spiess/Huc de Monfried, from 1959 to 1968.

Oviri, 74 cm, around 1893 (C.G.No.113); thirteen proofs numbered from 0/12 to 12/12; five proofs monogrammed JB, DW, DM, JC, PS; one proof for the tomb of Gauguin in Atuana, where it would be placed in 1973; Valsuani; editions Spiess/Huc de Monfreid, from 1959 to 1968.

Stèle du Christ, 50 cm, around 1895 (C.G. No. 125). On the other side, Polynesian personages and motifs; seven proofs numbered from 0/6 to 6/6; seven proofs monogramed AM, JB, AS, PS, JC, DW, JH; a proof for the museum of Albi; Valsuani; editions Spiess/Huc de Nomfreid, from 1959 to 1968.

La Pirogue, 90 x 36 cm (C.G. No.103), according to the model in plaster cast from original wood. Casting previewed from 10 proofs numbered from 1/10 to 10/10; Valsuani; editions Spiess/Huc de Monfreid, from 1959 to 1968.

L'Après-midi d'un faune, 34 cm (C.G.No.100); ten proofs by Valsuani and ten proofs carrying the seal Alexis Rudier.

Masque d'homme, 25 cm (C.G. No.110). A casting would have been commissioned by Vollard. No indication of founder nor of the number of proofs.

Masque de femme Tahi Tian, 25 cm; six proofs, Valsuani.

Eve, according to a ceramic; ten proofs, Valsuani.

Vase maori. Casting by Valsuani not specified.

Some other sculptures by Gauguin had been cast in bronze including a cane and a bas-relief entitled *Les Cygnes.*

MUSEUMS
Albi
Le conteur parle, 32.5 cm.
Hina, 36 cm.
Idole à la coquille, 26.5 cm.
Idole à la perle, 22.5 cm.
Tehura, mask, 20 cm.

Mont-de-Marsan
Hina, 36 cm (Valsuani).
Tehura, 20 cm (other side: Eve).
Paris, Orsay
Madame Schuffenecker, bust, 60 cm (Valsuani 3/10).
Masque de femme Tahi Tian, 25 cm.

A certain number of Gaugin bronzes belonging to private collectors and to Geneva's museum of the Petit Palais (*La Petite Parisienne*) were exhibited in 1985 at the museum of Prieuré in Saint-Germain-en-Laye.

SALES
L'Après-midi d'un faune, 34 cm (Valsuani 3/10), Christie's New York, May 17, 1984.
Grand Plat, 91 cm L. (Valsuani 6/10), Drouot, October 24, 1986, room 7.
Hina et Te Fatou, 32 cm (Valsuani), Le Touquet, May 18, 1986.
L'Idole à la coquille, 27 cm (Valsuani), Brest, May 28, 1986.
La Luxure, 70 cm (Valsuani), Drouot, May 9, 1985, room 10.
Masque de femme, 40 cm (one of three proofs cast in 1956), Christie's New York, October 9, 1986.
Oviri, 74 cm (Valsuani 7/12), Brest, May 25, 191986; Lyon, September 23, 1986 (for 120,000 F); (Valsuani 8/12), Le Touquet, May 18, 1986.

Paul Gauguin,
Masque de jeune Tahitienne "Tehura," 20 cm
(Valsuani 0/6).

La Petite Parisienne, 27 cm, Honfleur, July 11, 1982;
    Poitiers, March 3, 1984; Brest, May 20, 1984; Gien,
    October 13, 1985; Rouen, December 3, 1985; Lyon,
    December 3, 1985; Christie's New York, November
    20, 1986.
Madame Schuffenecker, bust, 60 cm (Valsuani 7/10),
    Bourg-en-Bresse, March 2, 1986; Rambouillet,
    October 12, 1986.
Stèle du Christ, 50 cm (Valsuani), Dijon, November 27,
    1983.
Tehura, mask of a young Tahitien, 20 cm (Valsuani 0/
    6), Christie's New York, May 17, 1984.
Vase maori, 20 cm (Valsuani), Brest, December 8,
    1983.

Gauquié Henri

Flers-lès-Lille, January 16, 1858
Paris, August 1927

Henri Gauquié's major works include *Le Watteau*
from the Luxembourg gardens, four lampposts surrounded by cupids in bronze on the Alexandre-III
Bridge, and a number of funerary monuments,
including that of sculptor Gustave Crauk at the
cemetery of Valenciennes. A student of Cavelier, he
is mentioned in Salon records starting in 1880. A
number of his consignments appeared there, particularly *Persée vainqueur de Méduse,* a group in
plaster (1886), *Vae Victis,* plaster (1889), *Brennus,* a

statue in bronze (1890), *Diane,* a statuette in marble
(1891), *Le Réveil du printemps,* a statue in marble
(1892), *Bacchante et satyre,* a group in marble
(1895), and some statuettes, all in marble: *A Watteau*
(1900), *Vendangeuse* (1905), *Diane* (1906), and
Baigneuse au crabe (1907). Others statuettes exhibited, in bronze, include *Gloire et patrie* (1897), *Cigale,*
gilded bronze (1904), *Chasseur$ST* (1905), and
Samson (1909), among others. *Bacchante et satyre*
was cast by Siot-Decauville; *Diane Chasseresse,* 49
cm, by Thiébaut.

MUSEUMS
Reims
Brennus, Vae Victis, 54 cm.
Valenciennes
Buste de Loiseau, 62 cm (E. Groult, founder).
SALES
L'Esclave libéré, gilded bronze, 97 cm, Drouot, May 17,
    1984, room 7.
La Lutte pour la vie, 65 cm, Cologne, March 18, 1983.
Nil virtuti in vium, 59.5 cm, Christie's New York, Octo-
    ber 18, 1983.
Samson, 89 cm, Douai, November 16, 1986.
Vae victis, 54 cm, Drouot, June 14, 1985, room 1.

Gautherin, Jean

Ouroux (Nièvre), December 19, 1840
Paris, July 21, 1890

Gautherin enrolled at the Ecole des Beaux-Arts
in 1864, and began exhibiting at the Salon the
following year, principally showing busts, statues,
and allegorical groups. He worked on diverse monu-

Jean Gautherin,
Clotilde de Surville,
86 cm
(Barbedienne).

GAUTIER, JACQUES LOUIS
Paris, December 13, 1831—?

Although they appear only rarely in public sale, a number of works by Rude's student Gautier were cast as "bronze d'art," according to Stanislas Lami. Among Gautier's consignments to the Salon between 1850 and 1868, and to the Exposition Universelle of 1855, the following pieces are notable

Jean Gautherin, Renommée, 51.5 cm.

Jacques Louis Gautier, Macbeth, 88 cm.

ments in Paris including the city hall and the Palais du Trocadéro, on the cathedrals of Marseille and Nevers, and the casino of Monte-Carlo. The bronze work *Diderot* from the Boulevard Saint-Germain in Paris also carries his signature. He sent a piece entitled *Clotilde de Surville* to the Exposition Universelle of 1878 and to the Salon of 1879; it was later cast in bronze by Barbedienne in multiple formats, 175, 103, 86, 69, 52, 43 and 35 cm. Also cast in many sizes by Barbedienne is *Avant l'orage*, in 89, 70, 59, 44 and 36 cm. An allegory representing *L'Instruction éclairant le monde*, 45 cm, was made the object of an edition by Susse, and *La Séduction*, 84 cm, was cast by Thiébaut.

SALES
Clotile de Surville, 86 cm, Drouot, December 3, 1982.
Jeune Paysanne, 87.6 cm, Christie's New York, June 15, 1985.

additions to his busts and medallions: *La Misère*, a sketch in bronze (1850), *Méphistophélès*, a statuette in bronze (1855), *Marinette et Gros René*, *Le Départ pour l'école* and *La Leçon de danseST1*, three small groups in bronze (1856). Also noteworthy are some models in plaster, a clock, a foot for a champagne glass, and a vase destined to the Christofle house.

SALES
Macbeth, 88 cm, Drouot, December 4, 1985, room 3.
Méphistophélès, 84 cm, Sotheby London, June 17, 1986.

GAYRARD, PAUL

Clermont-Ferrand, September 3, 1807
Enghien, July 22, 1855

GAYRARD

The son and student of sculptor Raymond Gayrard, Paul Gayrard also studied with Rude and David d'Angers. After debuting at the Salon in 1827, he became successful with a wealthy clientele and produced some statues and busts of famous people, now located in different museums and at the Comédie Française. In addition, he sculpted the four evangelists for the Sainte-Clotide Basilica in Paris. His work also includes some animals—horses, dogs, and groups of race horses—which would be cast in bronze; of particular note among these pieces is *Cheval d'attelage harnaché et bridé*, 66 cm, of which the plaster was exhibited at the Salon of 1847 and the bronze at the Salon of 1848. One statuette in bronze, *Chien couché*, 8 x 16 cm, is dated London 1848, leaving one to suppose that Gayrard spent some time across the English Channel. This piece was sold in Enghien in 1980.

Paul Gayrard,
Chien couché,
6 x 15 cm.

SALES
Cheval monté par un singe, 12 cm, Sotheby London, November 7, 1985.
Chien de chasse, 12.5 cm, Sotheby London, March 21, 1985.
Chien couché, 6 x 15 cm, Christie's London, May 15, 1986.
Course de chevaux montés par des singes, 23 cm, Sotheby London, November 8, 1984.
Gens d'arme avec son mousquet, 58.5 cm, Drouot, December 14, 1984, room 6.
Jeune Couple regardant un serpent, 49.5 cm, Sotheby London, June 20, 1985.
Pinscher (chien) couché sur une terrasse, 22 x 31 cm, Drouot, October 25, 1985, room 14.

GAYRARD, RAYMOND

Rodez, October 25, 1777
Paris, May 4, 1858

After being enlisted in the army from 1796 until 1802, Raymond Gayrard went to work in Paris with the goldsmith Odiot. He studied sculpture with Boizot, as well as medal-engraving, the discipline in which he started his career. Moreover, in 1825 he received a license for medal-engraving from the chamber and from the office of the king. His first statue, a marble representing *L'Amour essayant ses flèches*, was exhibited at the Salon of 1819, where it was bought by the king for Saint-Cloud. His rather varied production situated itself in the academic tradition, composed of some groups, statues, bas-reliefs representing diverse scenes, allegories, saints, animals, busts, and in particular a number of bronze medallions representing some famous people. He sent no less than forty-five of them to the Expostition Universelle of 1855, not to mention those which made frequent appearances at the Salon, especially between 1838 and 1842. Also attributed to Raymond Gayrard are the two large statues of *Force* and *Suffrage universel* placed in the court of honor of the Chamber of Deputies, as well as the front of the courthouse in Rodez. Two works by this sculptor are noted as having been cast by the Susse house: *Le Départ pour la chasse*, 22 cm, and *Napoléon 1er à cheval en costume impérial*, 20 cm. The Carnavalet Museum in Paris possesses a medallion in bronze, 27 cm diam., entitled *Portrait du chimiste Théophile Jules Pelouze*.

GECHTER, JEAN-FRANÇOIS

Paris, 1796
Paris, December 11, 1844

A student of Bosio, Gechter signed the large bas-relief representing *La Bataille d'Aboukir* which ornaments the Arc de Triomphe de l'Etoile. He is also the author of a number of equestrian groups, and statues and statuettes of kings, saints, gladiators, knights from the Middle Ages, Indians, historic people, a certain number of which appeared at the Salon between 1824 and 1844. In the second part of his career, Gechter devoted himself especially to animal sculpture, for which he had shown a remarkable disposition. Particularly admirable is the model of his horses in the equestrian effigies. Among his consignments to the Salon are bronzes indicated as being "demi-nature": *Gladiator vaincu* and *Guerrier s'arrachant une flèche du talon* (1824), and *Castor*

Jean-François Gechter,
*Charles Martel combattant Abderame
roi des Sarrasins*, 75 cm.

Jean-François Gechter,
Cavalier indien chassant le fauve,
51 x 50 cm.

domptant un cheval (1831). At the Salon of 1833 he exhibited *Charles Martel combattant Abderame, roi des Sarrasins*, which was later the object of important editions in bronze. Some large bronzes were also exhibited at the Salon, including *La Mort de Tancrède* in 1837 and *Amazone blessée* in 1840.

Three bronzes by Gechter appeared in an exposition at the Shepherd Gallery in New York in 1985: *Cheval attaqué par une lionne* (1843), 16 cm, *Cheval et serpent* (1840), 26 cm, and *François 1er chassant le sanglier* (1843), 51 cm.

MUSEUMS
Bordeaux
Soldat avec son fusil, 43 cm.
Paris, Decorative Arts
Louis-Philippe 1er debout, 41 cm.
Paris, Louvre
La Mort de Tancrède, silvered bronze, 16.5 x 41 cm.

SALES
Amazone blessée, 27 x 38.5 cm, Sotheby London, April 28, 1982.
Cavalier arabe, 34.5 cm, Sotheby London, June 23, 1983.
Cavalier indien chassant le fauve, 51 cm, Dijon, October 27 1985.
Cheval de trait, 12 cm (1842), Sotheby London, March 17, 1983.
Cheval de trait, 30.5 cm, Sotheby London, November 7, 1985.
Combat de deux cavaliers or *Charles Martel combattant Abderame*, 38 cm, Sotheby London, June 12, 1986.
Combat de deux cavaliers or *Charles Martel combattan Abderame*, 48 cm, Drouot, December 14, 1984, room 6.
Combat de deux cavaliers or *Charles Martel combattant Abderame*, 75 cm, Drouot, July 1, 1986, room 15.
Lévrier et lièvre, 37 cm, Sotheby London, March 21, 1985.

GEOFFROY, ADOLPHE LOUIS VICTOR
Paris, February 27, 1844
Paris, December 17, 1915

The son and student of the sculptor Geoffroy-Dechaume and the collaborator of Viollet-le-Duc in the Notre-Dame-de-Paris, Geoffroy exhibited at the Salon from 1861 to 1910. There he showed busts, allegories including *La France et la République*, and most particularly animals, usually in plaster but often reappearing in bronze one or two years later. This was the case with *Lévrier d'Afrique* (Salon of 1863), *La Chienne Lolotte* (1873), *Lion du Soudan* (1880), *Panthère de Cochinchine* (Exposition Nationale des Beaux-Arts, 1883), and *Lion et lionne* (1890). This last group was cast by Siot-Decauville at the same time as *Tigre et antilope* and some other animals.

GÉRICAULT THÉODORE
Rouen, September 26, 1791
Paris, January 26, 1824

David d'Angers and Rude may have been the two greatest sculptors of the Romantic era, but according to some authors the famous painter Géricault was the first, producing small Romantic sculptures translated in bronze. To qualify this, it should be added that these translations were executed much later, well after the death of the artist. His works include *Satyre et bacchante* in plaster, 29 cm, and most notably the *Cheval écorché* in wax, 23 x 25.5 cm. Horses were Géricault's favorite subject (and indeed, at the age of thirty-three he died after falling from a horse). Géricault is known for drawing and painting horses of every breed, in every position and from all angles. According to one of his biographers, M. Charles Clément, *Cheval écorché* was bought by the Susse foundry in the posthumous sale of Géricault's work, before being yeilded, some years later, to a collector. In the meantime, specifies M. Clément, "it had been molded and was found in all the studios."

The same author enumerates the rare sculptures of Géricault, including, aside from *Cheval écorché*, the work *Cheval arrêté par un homme*, a bas relief in stone, 20 x 32 cm, dating from 1819. Other works include *Satyre et bacchante* in stone, 29 cm, *Boeuf terrassé par un tigre*, 25 cm, *Négre brutalisant*

une femme in terra cotta, and finally *L'Empereur Alexandre de Russie à cheval*, a maquette in wax, 30 cm.

The museum of the Louvre possesses the bronze *Satyre attaquant une nymphe*, donated in 1938 by the founder Rudier.

One proof of the *Cheval écorché*, 23.2 cm (C. Valsuani, 8/15), was sold in London by Sotheby, December 7, 1983.

GERMAIN, JEAN-BAPTISTE

Fismes (Marne), December 28, 1841
September 23, 1910

Aside from other sculptural groups, the bronzes exhibited between 1866 and 1909 at the Salon by this student of Dumont and Gumery are of particular interest: *Didon et Enée* (1876), *Une sirène* (1895), *Excelsior* (1896), *L'Etoile polaire* (1898), and a vase

Théodore Géricault,
Cheval écorché,
23 cm
(Valsuani).

357

entitled *Etoile du matin* (1894). He also exhibted some statuettes: *Jeanne d'Arc* (1879), *Printemps* (1889), *Rosée* (1897), *Le Travail* (1898), *Le Torrent, L'Industrie du feu* (1899), *Le Seveur* (1900), *La Nuit* (1901), *Forgeron de la paix, Pax Manu Victoris* (1904), *Le Génie des sciences, Défense de la patrie* (1906), *Dans les ruines, Si vis pacem, para bellum* (1907), *Frappeur* (1908), *La Métallurgie* (1909).

Certain works by Germain were cast in bronze, including *Allégorie de la danse et de la musique*, 88 cm (Susse), *Diane chasseresse*, 66 cm, *Jeanne d'Arc debout*, 70 cm, etc. Of note is an edition in regule of the *Forgeron de la paix*, 95 cm.

SALES

Esméralda, 54 cm, Vienna, November 24, 1985.
Joueur de flûte, 64.8 cm, Drouot, June 15, 1984, room 7; Sotheby London, November 1985.
Joueur de harpe, 62.5 cm, Drouot, June 15, 1984, room 7.

GÉRÔME, JEAN LÉON

Vesoul, May 11, 1824
Paris, January 10, 1904

J.L.GEROME

Jean Léon Gérôme,
La Danse or Danseuse à la pomme, 70 cm
(Siot-Decauville).

Best-known as a painter, this son of a goldsmith enjoyed a great notoriety during his lifetime. Forgotten for a time, his works have returned to favor today because of a number of collectors, principally in the United States. Gérôme came to Paris in 1841, enrolled in the Ecole des Beaux-Arts the following year, and took a trip to Italy in the company of his teacher, Paul Delaroche. He made his debut as a painter at the Salon in 1847, and won renown there that would only increase with time.

It was not until he was almost fifty that Gérôme became interested in sculpture, and he presented a sculpted work for the first time at the Exposition of 1878. This first group, *Gladiateurs*, is none other than the central motif of his famous painting *Pollice verso*, painted in 1874. It was not, however, his first attempt. "An admirer of Rude," wrote Charles Moreau-Vauthier, "he had already modeled two small gladiators, around 1859, statuettes of a surprisingly somber energy, two masterpieces known and admired by all his friends. One fine day, at the instigation of Fremiet and influenced by the surrounding countryside in Bougival, Gérôme resumed sculpture." Also according to Moreau-Vauthier, Gérôme's group of *Gladiateurs* from 1878 was not well understood by the public, but the body of his sculptural work—genre scenes, people, and allegories-would later win him just as many praises as his paintings had. Like his canvas work, his sculptures revealed his fascination with the east, or rather for stylish eastern motifs; in 1856 he had even traveled to Egypt, in the company of Bartholdi.

Accepted at the Institute in 1865, Gérôme is also the author of the equestrian statue of *Duc d'Aumale à Chantilly*, a monument of *Paul Baudry* in La Roche-sur-Yon, and *L'Aigle expirant* in bronze, 150 cm, from the battlefield of Waterloo. At his death, he was buried at the Montmartre cemetery. On his tomb stands a statue in bronze of *La Douleur*, 120 cm, which he had sculpted at the time of the death of his son.

Some castings in bronze of 40 cm high are known, starting with two of the first statuettes of gladiators entitled *Rétaire* and *Mirmillon*, modeled around 1859, as well as a 50 cm reduction of a group entitled *Gladiateurs;* furthermore, many subjects cast by the Sèvres factory are not to be overlooked. However, most works by Gérôme were cast in bronzes of excellent quality by the founder Siot-Decauville. A number of these bronzes (of which a list follows) were exhibited in 1974 by the Tanagre Gallery in Paris.

The indications given below come from a catalog from this exhibition and from the work on Gérôme published by Gérald M. Ackerman in 1986.

Bronzes cast by Siot-Decauville
L'Aigle de Waterloo, 72 and 20.5 cm.
Anacréon (1878-1881), proofs in many dimensions.
Bacchante (1892), 97 and 58 cm.
Bethsabée or *Femme à sa toilette* (1896), 32 cm.
Bonaparte à cheval entrant au Caire (Salon of 1897), 83 and 41 cm.
Bonaparte, bust, cast in two dimensions.
César franchissant le Rubicon, equestrian (around 1900), 80 and 38 cm.

Jean Léon Gérôme,
Tanagra, gilded bronze, 75 cm
(Siot-Decauville).

Corinthe (1903-1904), gilded or silvered bronze and semi-precious stones, 74.5 cm.
La Danse or *Danseuse à la pomme* (Salon of 1891), 95, 52, and 28 cm (some versions in bronze, marble and semi-precious stones).
Danseuse mauresque.
L'Entrée à Jérusalem or *Les Rameaux*, 90 and 30 cm.
Femme au cerceau (1891), 23 cm.
Femme au voile, 86, 66, and 48.5 cm (some proofs in bronze and marble or in bronze and ivory).
Frédéric le Grand à cheval (Salon of 1899), two dimensions including 41 cm.
La Fuite en Egypte (1897), 90 cm.
Jongleuse or *Joueuse de boules* (1902), 70, 27, and 19 cm.
La Madeleine (1897), 50 cm (another version in gilded bronze, opal, emerald, colored glass, etc.).
Martyre indienne, woman and tiger, (1891), 48.5 cm.
Mendiant avec lion (around 1898), 50 cm.
Plaudite Cives or *Belluaire* (Salon of 1898), 40 cm.
Saut d'obstacle or *Les Deux Jockeys* (Salon of 1903), posthumous edition, 130 x 28 cm.
Tamerlan (Salon of 1898), cast in one dimension.
Tanagra, 75 cm, (editions in gilded bronze or in silvered bronze according to the marble from the Orsay Museum).
La Victoire marchant (Salon of 1899), 98 and 41 cm.
La Victoire en péplum (1897), 98, 41 and 24 cm.
La Vitesse, 93 cm L.
Washington à cheval (Salon of 1901), 79.5 and 41 cm.
Buste de Bellone (1892), 87 cm.
Buste du Christ (1897), 62 cm.
Buste de Séléné (around 1895), 71 cm.

The Barbedienne house cast Anacréon in five sizes, 112, 93, 74, 54 and 40 cm. In 1926, the house surrendered to Paul Siot-Decauville the rights of reproduction for the works by Gérôme.

MUSEUMS
Châteauroux
Bonaparte à cheval entrant au Caire, 55.5 cm (Siot-Decauville).
Evreux
Philippe Rousseau, bust, 14 cm, (Gruet, founder).
Montpellier
Le Rétiaire, 30 cm.
Le Sagittaire, 30 cm.
Paris, Orsay
Bonaparte entrant au Caire, 83 cm, (Siot-Decauville).
Le Gladiateur sculpté par Gérôme, large group (the statue of Gérôme was added by Aimé Morot, Gérôme's son-in-law.
Rouen
Philippe Rousseau, bust, 64 cm.
Versailles, château
Le Duc d'Aumale, bust, 62 cm (1899).
Vesoul
Anacréon, Bacchus et l'Amour, 54 cm (Barbedienne).
Bacchante, 58 cm.
Bellone, bust in bronze, wood and glass of René Lalique, 87 cm (1892).
Bonaparte entrant au Caire, 41 cm.
La Douleur, 120 cm.
La Duc d'Aumale, bust, 62 cm.
Le Docteur Reclus, bust, 62 cm.
Tanagra, 152 cm.

SALES
Bacchante, gilded bronze, 58 cm, Christie's New York, October 16, 1984.
Bonaparte entrant au Caire, 41 cm (Siot-Decauville), Sotheby London, June 20, 1985.
Corinthe, gilded bronze, incrustations of opals, turquoises and enamel, 73 cm, Sotheby Monaco, June 24, 1985 (price of adjudication, 270,000 F).
La Danse, 70 cm, (Siot-Decauville), Cannes, November 18, 1986; Neuilly, November 19, 1986.
L'Etalon, 31.7 cm, (Siot-Decauville), Drouot, June 28, 1982, room 7.

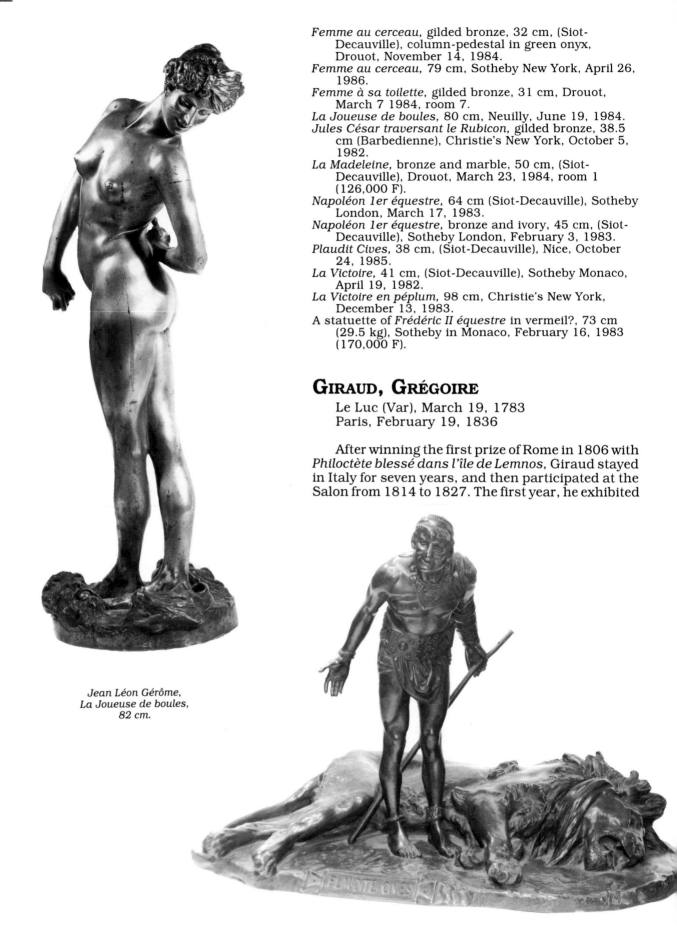

Femme au cerceau, gilded bronze, 32 cm, (Siot-Decauville), column-pedestal in green onyx, Drouot, November 14, 1984.

Femme au cerceau, 79 cm, Sotheby New York, April 26, 1986.

Femme à sa toilette, gilded bronze, 31 cm, Drouot, March 7 1984, room 7.

La Joueuse de boules, 80 cm, Neuilly, June 19, 1984.

Jules César traversant le Rubicon, gilded bronze, 38.5 cm (Barbedienne), Christie's New York, October 5, 1982.

La Madeleine, bronze and marble, 50 cm, (Siot-Decauville), Drouot, March 23, 1984, room 1 (126,000 F).

Napoléon 1er équestre, 64 cm (Siot-Decauville), Sotheby London, March 17, 1983.

Napoléon 1er équestre, bronze and ivory, 45 cm, (Siot-Decauville), Sotheby London, February 3, 1983.

Plaudit Cives, 38 cm, (Siot-Decauville), Nice, October 24, 1985.

La Victoire, 41 cm, (Siot-Decauville), Sotheby Monaco, April 19, 1982.

La Victoire en péplum, 98 cm, Christie's New York, December 13, 1983.

A statuette of *Frédéric II équestre* in vermeil?, 73 cm (29.5 kg), Sotheby in Monaco, February 16, 1983 (170,000 F).

Giraud, Grégoire

Le Luc (Var), March 19, 1783
Paris, February 19, 1836

After winning the first prize of Rome in 1806 with *Philoctète blessé dans l'île de Lemnos,* Giraud stayed in Italy for seven years, and then participated at the Salon from 1814 to 1827. The first year, he exhibited

*Jean Léon Gérôme,
La Joueuse de boules,
82 cm.*

*Jean Léon Gérôme,
Plaudite Cives,
38 x 56 cm
(Siot-Decauville).*

a bas-relief in marble entitled *Phalante et Ethra*, after a wax model he had executed in Rome in 1808. A statue in marble entitled *Chien couché*, his best-known work, was also modeled after a wax made in Italy to be presented at the Salon of 1827. *Pâris*, another statue in marble, 135 cm, appears at the museum of Nantes. Many works by Grégoire Giraud were cast in bronze, either in the full grandeur of the original size (*Philoctète blessé* and *Phalante et Ethra*) or in reduction (*Chien couché*). The majority appeared at the Exposition Centennale de L'Art Français in 1900.

MUSEUMS
Aix-en-Provence
Chien couché, reduction of the marble of 1827.
Riom
Chien couché, 26 cm, reduction of the marble of 1827.

GIRAUD, HENRI

Died in 1895

Born in Termonde, Belgium to French parents, Henri Giraud participated at the Salon from 1870 to 1894. He exhibited there most notably a statuette in wax entitled *Danseuse mauresque* (1872), and two statuettes in bronze, *Premier Hochet* (1889) and *Jeanne d'Arc* (1890). Also known are some other statuettes in bronze of animals, as well as *Jeune Femme portant un panier de fleurs*.

Roger Godchaux,
Lionceau assis, 19 cm.

SALES
Chien couché, 16 cm (Barbedienne), Versailles, March 9, 1981.
Cupidon, 53 cm, Barcelona, March 15, 1983.

GIRAULT, EUGÈNE

Toulon, 1886- ?

This artist began participating at the Salon in 1907, principally with some busts in plaster. He exhibited there again in 1931 and was listed among living artists until 1944. Some of his works have appeared in Algeria and Syria. A work in gilded bronze entitled *Poilu grenadier* that carries his signature, 9 cm, was sold in Drouot on December 2, 1983.

GODCHAUX, ROGER

Vendôme, December 21, 1878

An animal sculptor and a student of Gérôme, Godchaux started in 1905 to send a number of waxes to the Salon, including *Lion* (1905), *Etude de cheval* (1906), and *Jument surprise par un serpent* (1908). He also sent some plasters: *Le Vieux Cheval*, bas-relief (1907), *Retour des champs* (1909), *Chevaux de relais* (1913), and *Attila* (1914), etc. A single noteworthy bronze, the bas-relief *Misère*, was exhibited in 1908. Godchaux's activity continued after World War I, and he continued to appear among the members of the Société des Artistes Français until 1958. Many of his works were cast in bronze by Susse and by Valsuani.

Henri Giraud,
Il bat!,
56 cm.

MUSEUMS
Vernon
Chien griffon, 15 cm (Susse).
Eléphant, 20 cm.
Lapin, 18.5 cm (Valsuani).

SALES

Caniche à la boule, 12 cm, Drouot, March 27, 1984, room 8.
Cheval de course et son jockey, 24 cm (around 1920), Sotheby London, July 5, 1985.
Eléphant et son cornac, 58 cm (Susse), Sotheby London, June 23, 1983.
Lionne assise, 18 cm (Susse), Versailles, February 28, 1982.
Lionne couchée, 6 x 18 cm (Susse), Enghien, March 2, 1980.
Lionne tournant la tête, Nice, December 19, 1985.
Lionceau assis, 19 cm (Susse), Drouot, March 20, 1985; Drouot, June 14, 1985, room 1; Lille, June 24, 1985.
Lionceau assis, 39 cm (Susse), Drouot, February 6, 1984, room 7.
Panthères, book-ends, 21 cm, (Susse), Enghien, October 19, 1980.

Cyprien Godebski,
La Force étouffant le Génie, 93 cm.

GODEBSKI, CYPRIEN

Méry-sur-Cher, October 30, 1835
Paris, November 25, 1909

The son of a Polish writer and a student of Jouffroy, Godebski worked in cities in different countries, particularly in Sébastopol, Warsaw, and Krakow. In Paris, he sculpted the tomb of the *Théophile Gautier* at the Montmartre cemetery and that of *Constantin Guys* at the cemetery of Pantin. He is also the author of a number of busts of personalities, principally Polish. Finally, he exhibited at the Salon from 1857 to 1896. Of note is *Amour mendiant,* a statuette in silvered bronze (1882), of which there exist some castings in patinated bronze, a group in bronze entitled *La Persuasion* (1886), and a group in marble entitled *La Force brutale étouffant le Génie* (1888).

MUSEUMS
Carcassonne
Buste de la comtesse Fabre de l'Aude, 34 cm (and Company of the bronzes of Brussels).
Compiègne, Vivernel Museum
Two oval medallions, portraits.
Lille
La Persuasion, 176 cm (1885).

SALES
La Force brutale étouffant le Génie, 127 cm, Sotheby London, March 20, 1986.
La Force brutale étouffant le Génie, 93 cm, Sotheby London, November 6, 1986.

GODET, HENRI

Paris, March 5, 1863
Vincennes, 1937

A sculptor and medal-engraver, Godet is best-known for a number of small bronzes of women, in particular 'women-flowers', each nearly twenty centimeters in height, made in different materials and often cast in bronze. Thus, among the busts sent to the Salon starting in 1883, of note are *Petit Frileux* (1883) and *Vanité* (1886), both in terra cotta; *Printemps* and *Hiver* (1885), *Ophélie* in marble (1901). He made many busts in bronze, sometimes incorporating other materials: *Coquette Louis XV* in bronze (1894), *La Nymphe au roseau* in bronze and marble, cast by Houdebine (1896), *Le Rêve,* bronze and marble (1897), and *Liseron,* marble with applications of bronze (1900). Godet also exhibited some statuettes such as *Le Lever de l'aurore* in bronze (1895), *Le Froid* (1907) and *Eternel Printemps* (1911) in marble, *Fête champêtre, La Moisson,* and *La Muse* in marble (1908). He also showed some groups in bronze: *Le Ravissement de Psyché* after a painting by Bouguereau (1896), *L'Amour et Psyché* (1903), and *Le Génie des arts inspirant l'Industrie (1905).* Some sketches in clay were acquired recently by the Orsay Museum. Henri Godet himself cast some of the works. There exists a small publicity brochure in which he outlines the multiple facets of his activities in sculpture-statuary, namely his work as a decorative sculptor, a funereal architect, a sculptor of furnishings, busts, and medallions, a medal-engraver, a craftsman of stone and marble reproductions of ancient sculptures, etc. Under the heading "sculptor of furnishings," he enumerates some of his personal works such as *L'Amour et Psyché,* 100 cm, *La Brise,* 80 cm, and different busts including *Le Rêve,* 60 cm, which he executed indiscriminately in bronze, marble or terra cotta.

*Henri Godet,
Femmes-fleur, pair of busts
in gilded bronze and enamel, 20 cm.*

*Henri Godet,
Le Ravissement
de Psyché,
according to
a painting
by Bouguereau,
80 cm.*

SALES

Femmes-fleurs, two busts in gilded bronze and enamel, Avignon, July 2, 1983.

Glaneuse, 77 cm, Drouot, June 18, 1981.

Jeune Femme, mounted in lamp, 30.5 cm, Sotheby Monaco, October 6, 1985.

Napoléon 1er équestre, 56 cm, Christie's New York, April 16, 1985.

Ophélie, 38.5 cm (Société des Bronzes de Paris), Sotheby London, April 22, 1982.

Le Ravissement de Psyché, according to the painting by Bourguereau, 80 cm, Argentan, May 25, 1986.

GONON EUGÈNE

Paris, October 16, 1814
Paris, September 11, 1892

Son of the famous founder Honoré Gonon, this artist began to study sculpture in 1838 at the Ecole des Beaux-Arts, and worked with Pradier. He focused on modeling birds, while continuing to collaborate with his father on casting (by the lost wax method) the works of a number of contemporary artists, including Barye and Dalou. He exhibited at the Salon from 1852 to 1891, notably the bronzes *Nid de fauvettes inquiétées par un rat et une vipère, Rossignols et raisins* (1853), *Pinson mort* in bronze (1857), *Combat de merles* in wax (1859), *Combat de grives* in wax (1870), *Cresserelle attaquant un merle* in bronze (1879), and *Alouette prise au piège* in wax (1881).

GORY, AFFORTUNATO

Born in Florence

In the beginning of the 20th century, Afortunato Gory sent to the Salon a number of his works, in which bronze was frequently intermingled with marble or ivory. These include *Iris,* a bust in marble and bronze (1904), a statuette of *Michel-Ange* in marble (1912), *Bacchante aux amours,* a group in gilded bronze (1914), and in the same year a statuette in ivory and bronze entitled *Bouquetière.* Also attributable to him are some feminine statuettes, dancers, young girls, eastern or medieval people, as well as some busts of women and children. He continued his career after World War I.

SALES

La Bouquetière, gilded bronze, 35.5 cm, Drouot, December 2, 1983, room 5.

Danseuse, bronze polychrome, 51 cm, Christie's London, July 18, 1983.

Danseuse oriental, gilded bronze, 67 cm, Christie's London, April 17, 1984.

Danseuse orientale, gilded bronze and marble, 100 cm, Moulins, September 28, 1986.

Danseuse orientale, gilded bronze and ivory, 46.5 cm, Enghien, October 21, 1984.

Dante, gilded bronze, 66 cm, Christie's Oklahoma (United States), September 24, 1981.

①

②

③

1) Affortunato Gory, Guerrier
marocain, gilded bronze and
marble, 65 cm.

2) Affortunato Gory, Danseuse
orientale, gilded bronze and
ivory, 46.5 cm.

3) Affortunato Gory, Petite
Fille à la lettre, bust in gilded
bronze and white marble, 42 cm.

Elégante romantique, gilded bronze and ivory, 34 cm,
    Drouot, June 14, 1982, room 7.
La Filette à la coiffe, bust in bronze and marble, 43 cm,
    Drouot, May 14, 1982.
La Fillette et la grenouille, 21.5 cm, Madrid, March 26,
    1985.
Fillete portant deux paniers, gilded bronze and ivory, 20
    cm, Drouot, March 4, 1983, room 1.
Guerrier marocain, bronze and marble, 65 cm, Enghien,
    April 28, 1985; L'Isle-Adam, September 29, 1985.
Homme à la lance, Drouot, September 30, 1986.
Jeune Femme au cerceau, 40 x 50 cm, Brussels,
    September 17, 1984.
Jeune Femme à l'escalier, gilded bronze, ivory and
    marble, 41 cm, Orléans, December 14, 1985.
Jeune Femme, bust in gilded bronze and marble, 28
    cm, Drouot, January 23, 1984, room 1; Granville,
    November 3, 1985.
La Jongleuse à la balle, bronze and ivory, 58.5 cm,
    Brussels, June 17, 1982.
Pas de danse, bronze, ivory and marble, 27.5 cm,
    Madrid, March 26, 1985.
Petite Fille à la lettre, bust in gilded bronze and white
    marble, 42 cm, Lille, November 25, 1985.
Salomé, gilded bronze and ivory, 90 cm, Drouot, June
    10, 1981.

GOSSIN, LOUIS

Paris, June 6, 1846
1928

Gossin

This student of Mathurin Moreau exhibited a number of works regularly at the Salon starting in 1877. His submissions included some statuettes, particularly in bronze, including *Le Soir* (1888), *Défense du sol* (1900), *Le Ruisseau* (1910), *Dian au bain, La Semeuse,* bronze and ivory (1914), as well as two small groups in bronze, *L'Enlèvement* and *Colin-maillard* (1914). Other statuettes were also contributed by Gossin: *A la fontaine* (1892) and *Danseuse* (1909), both in marble; and in plaster, *Amour vainqueur* (1893), *Vainqueur* (1903), *Laveuse* and *Danseuse* (1908), and *L'Amour captif* (1909). Among the bronzes of the largest dimensions are *Joueur d'osselets* (1893), *Le Génie de la paix* (1894), *David vainqueur* (1898), *Dénicheur d'aigles* (1899), *La Science prend possession de l'Air* (1911), *Coquetterie* (1912), *Le Triomphe de l'amour* (1913), etc.

SALES

David vainqueur, 69 cm, Christie's Oklahoma (United States), September 24, 1981.
Groupe de cinq putti avec un char, 33 cm (Jollet, founder), Sotheby London, November 6, 1986.
Orphée, 60 cm, Meaux, March 10, 1986.

GOUGET, ÉMILE JOSEPH ALEXANDRE

Born in Bray-sur-Seine (Seine-et-Marne)

This animal sculptor, a student of Barye, exhibited the following works at the Salon: in 1868, *Lion couché* in plaster; in 1869, *Lion couché* and *Lionne et vipère* in bronze and marble; and in 1870, *Combat entre un lion et un tigre,* a group in plaster.

GRANDMAISON, NICOLAS

Toulouse, April 19, 1857
1931

A student of Falguière and of Mercié (both also from Toulouse), this artist began to exhibit at the Salon in 1893, with works entitled *La Science,* bas-relief in bronze (1900) and *Renommée,* a bronze statuette (1904).

GRANGER, GENEVIÈVE

Tulle, February 1, 1877
April 5, 1967

A sculptor and medal-engraver, Geneviève Granger began to exhibit at the Salon des Artistes Français in 1898, as well as at the Salon d'Automne. Her work includes some allegorical subjects, such as *Le Vent, La Musique, La Paix,* and *La Patrie,* some

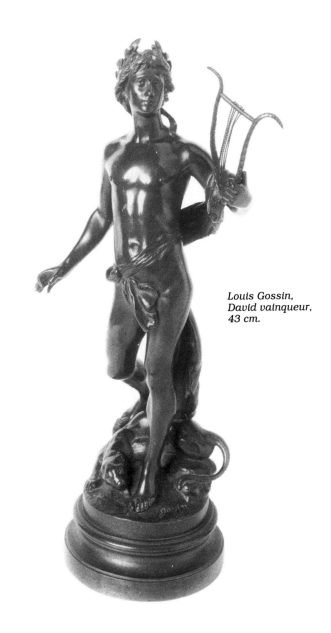

Louis Gossin,
David vainqueur,
43 cm.

feminine figures including *Femme tricotatn et son enfant* and *Nu assis,* some busts and some medals. Known to be the work of this artist is a statuette in bronze entitled *Regret,* 40 cm high. The museum of Périgueux possesses a bas-relief in bronze by Granger, *Le Docteur J. J. Peyrot en buste,* 50 x 43 cm.

GRASS, PHILIPPE

Wolxhelm (Bas-Rhin), May 6, 1801
Strasbourg, April 9, 1876

Grass worked for four years in the studio of the sculptor Ohmacht before entering Bosio's at the Ecole des Beaux-Arts. He produced principally some portraits, busts and statues, including that of *Kléber* for the city of Strasbourg. Moreover, he would become the sculptor of the cathedral, for which he would execute notably *Le Jugement dernier* for the large doorway. There are few bronzes among his consignments to the Salon from 1831 to 1873, with the exception of a study of a horse (1839) and a statue entitled *Icare essayant ses ailes* (1841) which was destroyed in 1870.

MUSEUMS
Aix-en-Provence
Portrait d'A.H. Frégier, medallion, 16 cm diam.
Morfaix
Buste d'Emile Souvestre, écrivain, 25 cm.
Strasbourg
André-Jung, ancien bibliothécaire, medallion.
Cheval de charge, 35 x 38.5 cm.
Le Sculpteur Ohmacht, statuette, 31.2 cm.

GREBER, HENRI

Beauvais, May 28, 1855
Paris, June 1941

H.GRÉBER

This artist participated in the decoration of the Grand Palais, contributing statues of *Industrie* and *Agriculture*, as well as working on the Gare d'Orsay and the church of Saint-Pierre-de-Montmartre. He is also known for the statue in bronze of *Emmanuel Frémiet* (1913) in the Jardin des Plantes, and for

Henri Gréber,
*Enfant
vendangeur,*
27 cm.

Bellovaque vainqueur, a work in bronze, 240 cm, destined for the city of Beauvais. The Thiébaut foundry cast the following works:

Jeanne d'Arc, 60 cm.
Naissance de la source, 50 cm.
Le Souvenir, 68, 57, 38 and 19 cm.
Le Vainqueur, 84, 70, 52 and 38 cm.

The museum of Beauvais possesses a standing portrait of the doctor Bauclon, deputy of the Oise, 36.5 cm. A statuette in bronze, *Narcisse*, 91.5 cm, was sold in London by Sotheby on April 12, 1985.

GRÉGOIRE, JEAN-LOUIS

Paris, December 15, 1840
1890

The son of a chiseler, Grégoire started to exhibit at the Salon in 1867, contributing some busts of contemporaries, mythological works, diverse scenes and, after the defeat of 1870, some patriotic subjects. Of note are a number of bronzes, including a bust of *L'Alsace* (1874), statues including *Psyché* (1880) and *La Surprise* (1881), groups including *L'Anneau de fiançailles* (1882), *La Valse* (1884), *Le Rabatteur de faux* (1886), and *La Défense du drapeau* (1888), and statuettes including *Le Souvenir* (1869) and *Marguerite* (1883). Also of note is a group entitled *La Danse* (1878), and a statuette entitled *Pêcheuse de crevettes* (1885), both in marble.

Many works by J.-L. Grégoire have been cast in bronze by Susse:

L'Alsace, bust, 48, 44, 34, 28, and 20 cm.
Amour charmeur, 64, 48, 31 cm.
L'Anneau de finaçailles, 51 cm.
La Chute de Carthage, 60 and 45 cm.
Clairon, la charge!, 51 cm.
La Lorraine, bust, 48 cm.
Pêcheuse de crevettes, 72, 62, 52 cm.
Tambour, en avant!, 51 cm.

Other bronzes listed on the market inlcude *L'Allégro*, 92 and 60 cm (Bernoux, founder), *Famille du temps de Louis XIII*, 81 cm, *Jeanne d'Arc équestre*, *Marguerite*, 95 cm, *Le Miroir brisé*, 39 cm, *Mozart enfant*, 35 cm, *Nymphe des bois*, 112 cm, *Persée et Andromède*, 60 cm, and *Triomphe de la joie*, 33 cm.

MUSEUMS
Louviers
Soldat de 1870, 56 cm.
Saint-Maur-des-Fossés
L'Alsace, 86 cm (1888).

SALES
L'Allégro, 92 cm (Bernoux, founder), Melun, April 10, 1983.
La Bergère au chevreau, gilded bronze, 70 cm (Boyer, founder), Drouot, December 2, 1983, room 5.
Cléopâtre, 74 cm, Drouot, February 18, 1983, room 7.
La Défense du drapeau, 92 cm, Amiens, November 14, 1985.
Jeanne d'Arc à cheval, 66 cm, Sotheby London, June 7, 1984.
Jeune Femme drapée tenant une urne, 54 cm, Sotheby London, November 10, 1983.
Jeune Femme tenant une branche avec deux oiseaux, 114 cm, Sotheby London, March 20, 1986.

1) *Jean-Louis Grégoire, L'Allégro, 92 cm (Bernoux, founder).*

2) *Jean-Louis Grégoire, La Défense du drapeau, 92 cm.*

3) *Jean-Louis Grégoire, Un artiste au XVII siècle, 56.5 cm.*

Jeune Fille à la guirlande de fleurs, 127 cm, Sotheby Chester, July 21, 1983.
Le Joueur de flûteau, 26 cm, Cologne, March 31, 1984.
Mozart enfant, avec violon, 37 cm, Sotheby London, November 8, 1984.
Mozart enfant, 56.5, Sotheby London, June 12, 1986.
Le Temps des cerises, 60 cm, Nantes, October 16, 1985.
Trois Amours, 80 cm, Sotheby London, March 8, 1984.

GRÉGOIRE, RENÉ

Saumur, June 4, 1871
April 1945

This sculptor and medal-engraver, the winner of the prize of Rome in 1899, had debuted at the Salon in 1895 and at the Nationale des Beaux-Arts in 1897. Attributed to him are some statuettes, busts and small plaques in bronze, among which are *Douceur de vivre, Le Baiser,* and *La Pitié,* executed around 1910. A group in bronze entitled *Sisyphe* portrays a man pushing a rock, 45 x 62 cm; this work was sold by Christie's in Oklahoma (United States) on September 24, 1981.

GRÉVIN, ALFRED

Epineuil (Yonne), 1827
Saint-Mandé, May 5, 1892

Curator of the famous wax museum which carries his name, Grévin was also a humorous cartoonist, a painter of costumes from the theatre, and a sculptor. For his work in this last discipline, he continued to draw inspiration from the people of the theatre then in vogue in Paris. Bronzes by this artist include *Femme costumée en lapin,* 33 cm, *Jeune Femme portant un panier,* 28 cm (sold in London in 1980), and *Ménestrel,* 41 cm (marked with the seal of A. Basset, a bronzier in Paris, and sold in London at Sotheby's on April 28, 1982). Certain works were made in collaboration with the sculptor Friedrich Beer, and thus carry his signature as well.

The museum of Chambéry possesses a bronze statuette, 53 cm high, entitled *Oh! eh!,* and the Périgueux holds a work entitled *Mulâtresse nue fumant,* 31 cm. A proof of *Oh! eh!,* signed Grévin and Beer, was sold in Corbeil-Essonnes on June 5, 1987 **(see reproduction page *13).**

GROOTAERS, LOUIS GUILLAUME

Nantes, August 19, 1816
Montaigu (Vendée), October 8, 1882

Of Belgian parentage but naturalized in France in 1837, Grootaers first went to Italy (though not under the auspices of the grand prize of Rome) before establishing himself in Nantes. He exhibited at the Salon from 1845 to 1881, contributing a number of busts, in particular a bronze bust of the *Général de Bréa* (1849), a person for whom he seemed to have marked a certain predilection. He also worked on many monuments in Nantes, including the church of Saint-Nicolas and the Passage Pommeraye. One of his busts in bronze of the *Général de Bréa*, 51 cm (1848), belongs to the Musuem of Decorative Arts in Paris.

GUENIOT, ARTHUR

Bournezeau (Vendée), May 1, 1866
Vitry-le-François, February 16, 1951

This artist exhibited at the Salon until 1933. The museum of Reims possesses one of his bronzes, a work entitled *La Douleur*, or *Deuil*, 18.3 cm, dating from 1907.

GUIGUES, LOUIS

Bessèges (Gard), April 30, 1873
1943

A student of Alfred Boucher, Louis Guigues exhibited in an irregular fashion at the Salon between 1897 and 1940. A statuette entitled *Femme au hennin*, 39 cm, cast by A. Bingen-Costenoble, appears at the museum of Châlons-sur-Marne.

GUILBERT, ERNEST

Paris, 1848—?

Some commemorative monuments (including that of Thiers in Nancy), the statue of *Poésie* for the facade of the Opera-Comique in Paris, and some busts of contemporaries and historic people (including *Etienne Dolet*, for Maubert Plaza) marked the career of this artist. A student of Dumont and of Chapu, he exhibited regularly at the Salon. Among his consignments are the bronzes *La Revanche*, a group destined for the Ecole de Saint-Cyr (1891), a bust of *Eugène Boudin* (1901), and a statuette of *Napoléon 1er* (1913). He also exhibited a group in marble entitled *Daphnis et Chloé* (1886), a statue in plaster entitled *Cancalaise* (1892) of which a reduction in bronze was cast by Siot-Decauville, and finally two plaster statuettes entitled *La Porteuse d'eau* and *Le Retour de la pêche* (1913). One bust of the painter *Victor Giraud*, 62 cm, belongs to the Carnavalet Museum in Paris. A group in bronze, *Daphnis et Chloé*, 76 cm, was sold by Christie's in Oklahoma (United States) on September 24, 1981.

GUILLAUME, EUGÈNE

Montbard (Côte-d'Or), July 4, 1822
Rome, March 1, 1905

Guillaume received his first lessons at the school of drawing in Dijon before moving on to the Ecole des Beaux-Arts of Paris to study under Pradier. Pradier's sponsorship won him a number of commissions and recompenses. In 1845 he obtained the grand prize of sculpture with his *Thésée retrouvant l'épée de son père*, and the following year went to Rome to stay for four years. Guillaume's consignments to the Salon were appreciated by the critics. *Le Faucheur*, a bronze 148 cm high, appeared in 1849. Also in bronze was *Les Gracques*, 81 cm, which he presented in 1853. He worked on the Louvre, the Opera (the group of *Musique instrumentale*), the Winter Circus (the freize of *Jeux du cirque*), the fountain of Saint-Michel (the statue *La Force*), the zoology gallery of the Jardin des Plantes (a seated figure entitled *L'Histoire naturelle*), some churches, and the stock exchange and the courthouse in Marseille. He made the statues of *Colbert* for Reims, *Pascal* for Clermont-Ferrand, *Rameau* for Dijon, as well as busts including some of *Napoléon 1er* at different ages. A statuette of *Jeune Pêcheur* was cast in bronze. He became a member of the Institut at the age of forty, and then the director of the Ecole des Beaux-Arts and of the Académie de France in Rome.

Eugène Guillaume,
Le Faucheur, Rome 1849, 168 cm
(Eck and Durand).
Musée d'Orsay.

Eugène Guillaume,
Délivrance,
72 cm
(Barbedienne).

Emile Guillemin,
and Alfred Barye Jr,
Cavalier arabe,
80 cm.

MUSEUMS

Bayonne
Buste d'Ingres, 37 cm.
Clermont-Ferrand
Pascal assis, 33 cm.
Gray
Anacréon couronné de roses, 39 cm (Delafontaine, founder), modeled after the marble from the Salon of 1852.
Montpellier
Portrait d'A. Bruyas, medallion, 18 cm diam.
Portrait d'A. Bruyas, dated Rome 1848 villa Médicis.
Paris, Orsay
Le Faucheur, 168 cm (Eck and Durand; Rome 1849).
Les Gracques, 85 cm (Eck and Durand).
Reims
Jean-Baptiste Colbert, 58.3 cm

SALES

Le Braconnier, 60 cm, Bourgoin-Jallieu, October 10, 1986.
Délivrance, nude woman raising a sword, 207 cm (Barbedienne), Sotheby London, November 6, 1986.

GUILLEMIN, ÉMILE CORIOLAN HIPPOLYTE

Guillemin focused his attention on heroic or exotic genres, pushing to the limits a served realism, which particularly in his bronzes, was assisted by using a remarkable quality of chiseling. Some statues are attributed to him, as are some groups of biblical heros, men of arms, conquistadors, and especially eastern people. These works display Guillemin's very lively workmanship in different dimensions, sometimes larger than nature. At the Salon, he presented *Rétiaire* and *Mirmillon*, two statuettes of Roman gladiators in bronze (1872), and then a series of busts in bronze: *Femme mauresque* (1877), *Jeune Fille kurde* (1879), *Janissaire du sultan* and *Jeune Fille du Caire* (1880), *Jeune Fille arabe du Caire* (1881), *Jeune Mulâtresse* and *Dame musulmane* (1882), *Jeune Fille mauresque d'Alger* and *Jeune Fille juive d'Alger* (1883), and *Femme*

Emile Guillemin,
Napoléon 1er debout,
97 cm.

Of final note is the bronze *Cavalier arabe,* some proofs of which are known to be 66 and 80 cm high. This work sometimes carries the signatures of Guillemin and of Barye Jr., suggesting that this piece was made in collaboration.

SALES

Arlequin, 101 cm, Christie's London, June 3, 1982.
Cavalier arabe, 66 cm, Castres, June 24, 1984; Les Andelys, October 7, 1984; Sotheby London, November 8, 1984.
Cavalier arabe, 80 cm, Enghien, October 16, 1983; Sotheby London, June 20, 1985.
Chien de guerre, man with his dog, 84.5 cm, Christie's New York, September 27, 1986.
Fauconnier arabe, 111 cm, Sotheby London, November 8, 1984.
Femme arabe, bust in bronze polychrome, 61 cm, Drouot, May 14, 1986, room 10.
Femme orientale porte-flambeau, 260 cm (Barbedienne), Enghien, October 16, 1983 (460,000 F).
Femme orientales prote-flambeaux, two floor lamps, 235 cm (Barbedienne),Enghien, March 4, 1984 (530,000 F).
Jeune Fille kurde, bust, 79 cm, Christie's New York, December 14, 1982.
Napoléon 1er debout, 97 cm, Deauville, May 4, 1986.
Rébecca et Eliézer, 81 cm, Christie's Oklahoma (United States), September 24, 1981.

GUILLOT, ANATOLE

Etigny (Yonne), February 23, 1865
Paris, February 1911

A sculptor and ceramist who studied under Gautherin and Falguière, Guillot made a number of ornamenmtal compostions, including the freize of the *Ravail* for the door of the Exposition of 1900, and the statues and bas-reliefs for the rotunda of the new Printemps department stores. Some of his works were cast by the Sèvres factory. He exhibited at the Salon from 1887 to 1911, showing some statuettes in bronze, including Coup de vent (1903), *Faneuse* and *Porteuse d'eau* (1907), as well as Le Réveil in gilded bronze (1911).

SALES

Arabe au fusil, 75 cm, Drouot, February 3, 1984, room 7.
Nu debout, gilded bronze, 41.5 cm, Sotheby London, June 7, 1984.
Paysan scrutant le ciel, 55 cm, Calais, March 2, 1986.

GUILLOUX, ALBERT GASTON

Rouen, October 9, 1871
1952

The museum of Bayonne preserves a plaque by this sculptor, a piece in silvered bronze commemorating the millennium of the city of Rouen. A group in bronze, *Mercure sur un char ailé,* 120 cm, was sold in London by Sotheby on November 7, 1985.

kabyle d'Algérie (1884). Moreover, at the Salon of 1881 was exhibited a statue in bronze entitled *Aide fauconnier indien, retour de chasse à la gazelle,* and in 1895, a bust in bronze and marble entitled *Type de femme algérienne de la tribu Ouled Nails.*

Still to be added to the list are a number of other works in plaster inspired by eastern motifs, and some other bronzes from outside of the Salon, including different versions of conquistadors, knights from the Middle Ages on foot or on horseback. These include *Janissaire en vedette tenant une lance, Joueuse de mandoline arabe, Danseuse turque, Judith,* etc.

The Barbedienne house cast in bronze some figures of women, forming a pair and carrying candelabrum:

Indienne et Persane, 200, 120, 95 and 78 cm.
Deux Femmes de la Renaissance, 120 cm.
Deux Femmes japonaises, 120 cm.

*Anatole Guillot,
Arabe au fusil,
75 cm.*

*Anatole Guillot,
Paysan scrutant le ciel,
56 cm.*

GUILLOUX, ALPHONSE EUGÈNE

Rouen, June 2, 1852
Bois-Guillaume (Seine-Maritime), November 19, 1939

After completing his studies at the schools of fine arts in Rouen then in Paris, Guilloux produced a number of busts and statues of contemporary personalities while undertaking various tasks for the restoration of historical monuments. Additionally, many monuments for the dead are to be credited to this sculptor. The museum of Rouen possesses some of his works, including a bust in bronze of *Jules Adeline.*

GUIMBERTEAU, RAYMOND

Angoulême, 1863
Angoulême, January 1905

A student of Cavalier and of Barrias, this artist is especially known for some busts in bronze or in plaster; he is also the author of the monument to

Président Carnot in Annecy (1897). The museum of Cognac features a medallion in bronze entitled *Portrait d'Adolphe Péré*, 17 cm high and dating from 1896.

GUINO, RICHARD

Gérone (Spain), May 26, 1890
February 2, 1973

Richard Guino is best-known as Auguste Renoir's practicioner, in which capacity he executed the majority of Renoir's sculpted works between 1913 and 1918. In 1973, a judgement was passed that designated him as the co-author of these sculptures. Hoever, Guino did produce a quantity of work independently. Born in Spain to French parents and later naturalized to French citizenship, Guino began his studies at Barcelona's school of fine arts. Then, at the instigation of Maillol, Guino went to Paris; under Maillol's continued direction, he soon demonstrated his undeniable gift. Analyzing his style, certain authors assert that he did not 'exploit' Renoir's style, or even the style of the statues which he had sculpted under the senior artist's direction. In fact, in Guino's bronzes from 1912-1920 that have appeared in public sales, the influence of the master of Cagnes and of Maillol are the most evident, both in the workmanship and in the subject matter (from nudes to ample forms).

The works by Guino which provide the best evidence of his talent were often sketches, and were frequently cast in limited editions by different founders. From 1919 to 1924, he worked under contract with A.A. Hébrard; later he collaborated with Susse, Colin, and Blanchet. Godard also worked for him.

As is clear in the list below, Guino's bronzes have frequently appeared in public sales during recent years, particularly in Enghien in 1984. Also of note are the works exhibited in 1977 during the course of a retrospective of the sculptor's work, organized at the Renoir Museum in Cagnes-sur-Mer: *Tête au chignon*, 13 cm (1912), *Femme à la mandoline*, 24 cm (1914-1915), *Femme à la pomme et draperie*, 33 cm (1915), *Vénus à la pomme*, 37 cm (1915), *Femme et enfant*, 12.5 cm (1916), *Petite Baigneuse assise*, 18 cm (1916), *Feme agenouillée à la toilette*, 24 cm (1916), *Centaure enlevant une femme*, 23 cm (1916), *Grande Maternité*, 100 cm (1918-1920), and some other pieces from later dates.

The Renoir Museum in Cagnes possesses a bust the bronze *Renoir à la casquette*, 45 cm.

SALES

L'Automne, 69 cm (Colin; around 1925), Enghien, March 24, 1985.

Enfant au perroquet, 63 cm (2/25), Versailles, November 18, 1984; Drouot, February 3, 1986, room 6.

Femme accroupie à la draperie, 27.5 cm (Susse 3/8, 1912), Enghien, June 17, 1984.

Femme accroupie à la draperie, 30 cm (Valsuani 3/10), Enghien, June 17, 1984.

Femme agenouillée à la toilette, 24 cm (Godard VIII/VIII, 1916), Enghien, June 17, 1984.

Femme assise à la draperie, 34 cm (Blanchet V/VIII, 1915), Enghien, June 17, 1984.

Femme assise à la toilette, 18 cm (Blanchet VIII/VIII, 1915), Enghien, June 17, 1984.

Femme à la corbeille, 29 cm (Blanchet VIII/VIII, 1914), Enghien, June 17, 1984.

Femme debout à la draperie, 41 cm (Taube EA 2, 1919), Enghien, June 17, 1984.

Femme et enfant au miroir, medallion, 13 cm diam (Susse V/VIII, 1915), Enghien, June 17, 1984.

Femme à la mandoline, 24 cm (Godard EA 3/4, 1912), Enghien, June 17, 1984.

Femme au miroir, 36 cm (Godard VI/VIII, 1914), Enghien, June 17, 1984.

Femme à la pomme, 28 cm (Godard VII/VIII, 1919), Enghien, June 17, 1984.

Femme aux raisins, 51 cm (Blanchet VII/VIII), Drouot, November 29, 1985, room 9.

Femme relevant ses cheveux, 69 cm (Susse EA 1/4, 1912), Enghien, June 17, 1984.

Femme au tambourin, 35 cm (Blanchet III/VIII, 1920), Enghien, June 17, 1984.

Femme au voile, 34 cm (Susse 6/8), Enghien, June 17, 1984.

Richard Guino,
*Femme assise
à la toilette*,
1915, 18 cm
(Blanchet VIII/VIII).

Richard Guino,
*Femme accroupie
à la draperie*,
1912, 27.5 cm
(Susse 3/8).

Richard Guino,
Femme à la courbeille,
1914, 29 cm
(Blanchet VIII/VIII).

Georges Guittet,
Le Grand Porteur
d'eau arabe,
86 cm (Siot).
See reproduction
in color page 21*.

Couple de femmes, rough sketches according to a wood,
   31 cm (Susse EA2, 1913), Enghien, June 17, 1984.
La Grande Maternité, 96 cm (Susse, around 1936),
   Enghien, June 17, 1984.
Léda et le cygne, 50 cm (Taube EA 2, 1919), Enghien,
   June 17, 1984.
Petite Baigneuse, 18 cm (Valsuani), Drouot, November
   30, 1982, room 9.
Petite Maternité, 24 cm (Susse 4/8, 1915), Enghien,
   June 17, 1984.
Les Premier Pas, 20 cm (Blanchet EA II/IV, 1916),
   Enghien, June 17, 1984.
Renoir peignant, 31 cm (Susse 1/8, 1916-1918),
   Drouot, November 30, 1982, room 9; (Susse 4/8),
   Enghien, June 17, 1984.
Renoir, profile, bas-relief in cut-out (découpe), 31 cm
   (Blanchet EA 1/4, 1915), Enghien, June 17, 1984.
Tête de Coco, 35 cm (Valsuani 3/10, 1913), Drouot,
   November 30, 1982, room 9.
Les Trois Grâces, 51.5 cm (Susse EA 3, 1919), Enghien,
   June 17, 1984.
Vénus à la pomme, 37 cm (Susse 8/8, 1913), Enghien,
   June 17, 1984.

GUITTET, GEORGES

   Cholet, March 13, 1871
   September 1902

   Georges Guittet exhibited at the Salon from 1894
to 1902, during which time he took a trip to Italy.
Throughout his very short career, Guittet seems to
have had a marked predilection for eastern characters. Because of this inclination, he exhibited a
plaster at the Salon of 1897 entitled Porteur d'eau
arabe, to be made in marble in 1901, and later cast
in bronze. Of further note is Enfant à la tortue,
presented in plaster at the Salon of 1894 (marble in
1898).

SALES
Jeune Arabe, head, bronze and marble, 36 cm,
   Saumur, June 16, 1984.
Le Porteur d'eau, 51 cm, Drouot, December 1, 1983.
Le Porteur d'eau, 88 cm (Siot-Decauville), Saumur,
   June 16, 1984; Enghien, October 21, 1984.

GUMERY, CHARLES

   Paris, June 14, 1827
   Paris, January 19, 1871

   Winning the grand prize of Rome in 1850 with La
Mort d'Achille, Charles Gunery sent a 2-meter high
bronze he had made in Italy, entitled Jeune Faune
jouant avec un chevreau, to the Exposition Universelle
of 1855. His first appearance at the Salon occured
two years later. He received a number of commis-

sions and executed some statues and monuments for diverse cities: *La Tempérance*, statue in bronze, 2.2 m, for the fountain of Saint-Michel; *L'Agriculture* and *L'Industrie*, two other bronzes, 1.2 m, for Arts-et-Métiers Square, today Camille-Chautemps Square; *La Nuit*, in stone, for the Avenue de l'Observatoire; *L'Harmonie* and *Poésie*, two monumental groups in gilded bronze, 7.5 m, at the top of the facade of the Opera; *Le Moissonneur*, in bronze, 1.7 m, formerly in Monceau Park; the statue in bronze of the president *Félix Faure* for Chambéry; that of *Lapeyronie* at the school of medicine in Montpellier; those of *La Science* and of *La Jurisprudence*, also for Chambéry; and other works for the Louvre, the Gare du Nord, the church of the Trinity in Paris, and for the city of Bordeaux, etc. Finally, in 1869, Gumery was entrusted to sculpt the group *La Danse*, destined to replace the scandalous version by Carpeaux on the facade of the Opera in Paris. The war of 1870 at least had the positive side-effect of preventing this substitution. *Le Faune jouant avec un chevreau*, a bronze of 2 meters in height, dated from Rome in 1854, belongs to the museum of Montpellier.

GUYOT, GEORGES

Paris, December 10, 1885
1973

Fascinated throughout his life by the behavior of animals, Guyot translated the results of his studies into paintings, illustrations, and engravings as well as into sculptures. A large part of his career unfolded after the First World War. A retrospective of his work took place at the Salon des Indépendants in 1943, but he did not organize his first personal exhibition until 1970, at the age of eighty-five years old. He is the author of a group in gilded bronze, *Chevaux et chien*, which dominates the large basin of the Palais de Chaillot (1937). However, he began sending his first sculptures to the Salon at the beginning of the century; these included the statuettes in plastiline entitled *Lionne surprise* and *Ours faisant le beau* (1906), *Etude de chien* and *Chimpanzé* (1907). Also among his contributions were some others in plas-

ter: *Panthère* (1908), *Lassitude*, a lionness (1909), *Lutte de chiens* (1912), *Bouledogue français* (1913), and *Setter anglais* (1914). He also contributed some bronzes: *Char* (1909), *Chienne danoise* (1910), *Chien de berger* (1913), and *Revanche* (1914).

A 1963 biography of Guyot by Guy Dornand permits the establishment of a chronology of Guyot's bronzes dating before World War I (in addition to those which will be listed here): *Ours brun* (1906), *Singe à la banane* (1907), *Chien bouledogue* (1908), *Lionne assise bâillant* (1909), *Buste de Roland Dorgelès* (1911), *Lutte de chiens* (1912), and *Lion emportant un homme* (1914). Many works by this artist were cast in bronze by Susse and by E. Godard.

MUSEUMS
Maubeuge
Etude de singe, 43 cm.

SALES
Babouin assis, 50 cm L. (E. Godard 1/8), Drouot, February 6, 1984, room 7.
Les Deux Chats, 50 x 65 cm, Enghien, March 2, 1980.
Labrador assis, 23 cm, Sotheby London, November 8, 1984.
Le Lion, 23 cm, Drouot, June 12, 1985, room 15.
Lionne couchée, 18.5 cm L. (Susse), Drouot, December 13, 1986, room 7.
Lionne et lionceau, 51 x 51 cm, Enghien, March 2, 1980.
Ours assis, 51 (Godard 0/8), Drouot, June 16, 1982, room 7.
Ours brun, 18 cm, Drouot, June 12, 1985, room 15.
Ours brun, 47 cm (Susse), Drouot, May 31, 1986, rooms 5 and 6.
Ours debout, 38 cm (Godard 0/8), Drouot, June 16, 1982, room 7.
Panthère aiguisant ses griffes, 77 cm (Susse), Neuilly, May 10, 1983.
Panthère, 33 x 50 cm, Rochefort-sur-Mer, June 23, 1985; Pau, October 27, 1985; Lyon, November 27, 1985.
Panthère noire tête levée, 33.5 cm (Susse), Enghien, March 7, 1982; Drouot, June 23, 1986, rooms 5 and 6.
Singe assis, 26 cm, Christie's New York, February 19, 1985.
Le Taureau de Laguiole, 29 x 47 cm (Susse 1/10), Douai, March 24, 1985.

Georges Guyot,
Le Taureau de Laguiole,
29 x 47 cm
(Susse 1/10).

Georges Guyot,
Panthère noire,
33 x 50 cm.

HABERT, ALFRED LOUIS

Paris, October 4, 1824
Paris, 1893

This student of Pradier exhibited only three times at the Salon, between 1850 and 1886, notably showing two statuettes in bronze, *L'Amour méditant (1861)* and *La Discipline* (1886). Also known by this sculptor is another statuette in bronze, *Cupidon, 25 cm high*, sold in London in 1977. Finally, *La Vierge aux raisins* is noted for having been cast by Susse in three sizes, 40, 33 and 23 cm.

HALÉVY, LÉONIE

Paris, January 31, 1820
Saint-Germain-en-Laye, July 16, 1884

Married to the composer Fromental Halévy, this student of Frémiet primarily sculpted busts in marble as well as some statues. She participated at the Salon only from 1877 to 1880. This last year, she sent a statue in stone of *Fromental Halévy*, intended for the city hall but never installed. The museum of Troyes possesses a bust in bronze entitled *Homme barbu, 63 cm*.

HALOU, ALFRED JEAN

Blois, June 20 1875
Paris 1939

A conscientious artist, Halou is the author of very delicate statuettes and groups which were very popular in their day. Certain works were cast in bronze, notably *Enfant à la guirlane*, 78 cm (1901), *Joie de l'Eté*, *Le Lever*, 78 cm, *Nalade à la source*, 20 cm, as well as a bust of *Saint Jean-Baptiste*, 50 cm, and a bas-relief, *Adam et Eve*, 84 x 63 cm. The museum of Lyon possesses a bronze representing a *Nymphe accroupie*. A version of *Nu accroupi*, 100 cm, is also noted at the museum of Alger.

HANNAUX, EMMANUEL

Metz, January 31, 1855
Paris, May 19, 1934

E. HANNAUX

Winner of the second prize of Rome in 1881, Hannaux was the student of Dumont and of Bonnassieux. He exhibited at the Salon starting in 1878, notably with the following bronzes: *Le Duc d'Harcourt*, a statuette (1887), *Mercure et Bacchus*

Emmanuel Hannaux,
Le Poète et la sirène,
57 cm.

(1892), *Bûcheron*, a statue (1893), two busts entitled *Le Poète* (1904) and *Victoire* (1905), some other busts, a statuette entitled *Patria non immemor* (1911), and two statuettes in bronze and ivory entitled *Vainqueur* (1910) and *L'Amour du drapeau* (1914), both cast by Goldscheider. Other works by this sculptor were cast in bronze, particularly *Le Drapeau* (shown as a plaster at the Salon of 1889), *Le Poète et la sirène* (shown as a marble at the Salon of 1903) by Susse, in three dimensions. *Mercure*, 61 cm, and *Buste de jeune femme casquée à l'antique* were both cast in bronze by E. Colin in many dimensions.

MUSEUMS
Metz
Buste de F. Curel (Hébrard, 1907).
Buste de L.N.L. Ladoucette (1893).
Le Poète et la sirène, 80 cm.

SALES
Femme tenant un casque, 56 cm, Drouot, February 8, 1983, room 2.
Le Poète et la sirène, 57 cm, Drouot, October 26, 1983, room 13.

HÉBERT, PIERRE EUGÈNE ÉMILE
Paris, October 12, 1828
Paris, October 20, 1893

HÉBERT

A student of his father (the sculptor Pierre Hébert) and of Feuchère, this artist participated at the Salon from 1846 to 1893 with bronzes such as *Toujours et jamais*, a group (1863), *La Pologne*, a medallion (1867), *Œdipe*, a statue (1869), *Belléroption vainqueur de la chimère*, another group (1874), *Sémiramis, reine d'Assyrie*, a bust (1874), a large statue of *Rabelais*, 240 cm, destined for the city of Chinon, and finally *L'Oracle*, bas-relief (1893). Of further note are some statuettes: *Méphistophélès* in plaster (1853) and *L'Amour suppliant* in marble (1859), as well as *Jeune Fille sauvant une abeille*, also in marble, presented at the Exposition Universelle of 1855. Hébert also had sculpted two allegorical figures in stone, *La Comédie* and *La Drame*, 130 cm, for the facade of the Théatre du Vaudeville in Paris.

Many bronzes by Hébert are noted in the United States and in Great Britain, in some public or private collections; these works include *Bellérophon*, 114 cm, *Le Champion d'aviron*, 81 cm L., *Toujours et jamais*, 150 cm (University of Kansas), *Méphistophélès*, 99 cm (Bowes museum), and *Œdipe*, 93 cm. A bust entitled *Egyptienne*, 48 cm, was exhibited at the Shepherd Gallery of New York in 1985. Also notable are *La Boxe*, *Les Captives*, *Le Fil de la Vierge*, *Le Jeu de cache-cache*, *Ondine*, and *Le Printemps*.

SALES
L'Amoureuse, gilded bronze, 56 cm, Sotheby London, June 7, 1984.
Œdipe, 93 cm, Christie's Oklahoma (United States), September 24, 1981.
Sémiramis, 60 cm, Christie's London, March 20, 1984.
Thétis debout, statuette, Drouot, April 8, 1981.

HÉBERT, THÉODORE MARTIN
Paris, July 29, 1829
Paris, 1913

Busts, mythological groups, and other subjects (the majority in plaster) were sent by this artist to the Salon between 1848 and 1886. A bronze entitled *L'Esclave*, 102 cm high (1880) was sold in London by Sotheby on April 28, 1982.

HEIZLER, HIPPOLYTE
Paris, April 19, 1828
Paris, October 20, 1871

An animal sculptor, Heizler participated at the Salon from 1846 until his death, regularly exhibiting portrayals of big game, dogs, and fowl, nearly exclusively in plaster. Some of his works were cast in bronze. He also worked in collaboration with other sculptors on the decoration of different Parisian monuments, including the Louvre, the Tuileries, and the Opera.

HENNET DE BUTTET, JEANNE
Valence, 1854
Le Bourget-du-Lac, 1926

This artist is known for her portraits in bust and medallion form, inlcuding a bust in bronze entitled *Jeune Italien*, sent to the Salon in 1877. The museum of Chambéry possesses a bust entitled *Macarille*, 59 cm, dating from 1880, and the medallion *Portrait du baron Marc de Buttet* from Bourget, a portrait of the sculptor's husband, 56 cm diam., made in 1881.

HERCULE, BENOÎT LUCIEN
Toulon, July 28, 1846
Paris, November 6, 1913

A very reputable medal-engraver, this student of Jouffroy also produced some busts, medallions, statuettes and plaster models of dishes and platters. Found among his consignments to the Salon are only a few bronzes: a bas-relief (for a fountain in Toulon) entitled *Buveur*, 100 x 180 cm (1881), a statuette entitled *Japonaise* (1889), and a bust entitled *Turenne enfant*, 150 cm (1891). On the other hand, quite a number of statuettes in plaster were shown at the Salon, including *Quêteuse* (1890), *Rêverie* (1893), *Parisienne*, *Sortie de bal*, *En promenade*, *Patineuse*, *Au bal*, *L'Attente*, *Marchande de fleurs* (all in 1904), *L'Orage* (1908), *Saïd Ali, sultan des Comores* (1910), and *En campagne* (1912). Of further note are *Primevère*, a statuette presented in terra cotta in 1892 and in biscuit in 1911, and

Hippolyte Heizler,
Chiens bassets artésiens
devant un lièvre,
12 x 32 cm.
J. Ginepro Collection,
Monaco.

L'Aurore, a marble statuette exhibited in 1906. Many works by Hercule belonged to the museum of Toulon. The bust of *Turenne enfant* was cast in bronze, 60 cm, by the Thiébaut house. Also noteworthy are two statuettes in bronze, *Pénélope* and *Phryné*.

HEURTEBISE, LUCIEN EUGÈNE OLIVIER

Le Mans, February 12, 1867
1944

Heurtebise participated at the Salon from 1889 to 1933. The bronze now possessed by the museum of Mans, *Centenaire vosgienne*, 46 cm, was first exhibited at the Salon in 1924. Another bronze, entitled *A qui le tour?*, 73.5 cm, was sold in London by Sotheby on March 20, 1986.

HIERHOLZ, GUSTAVE

Lausanne, August 5, 1877—?

Born of French parents, Hierholz seems to have lived until the 1950s. An animal sculptor, he started exhibiting at the Salon in 1907. The following bronzes appeared there, among others: *Bellérophon* and *La Chimère* (1909), *Chiens courants aux écoutes and Moutons* (1910), and *Labour kabyle* (1919). Also notable is another bronze, *Taureau sur les Alpes*, exhibited at the Nationale des Beaux-Arts in 1904.

SALES

L'Aigle, 80 x 120 cm (prize from the president of the Republic offered to Louis Biériot in 1910), Drouot, December 6, 1979.
Cheval, 42.5 cm (Susse), Sotheby London, November 8, 1984.

HINGRE, THÉOPHILE

Ecouen (Val-d'Oise), November 19, 1832
November 12, 1911

A sculptor and an engraver in medals, this artist, essentially an animal artist, made a number of plaques, of small groups, statuettes, and some bas-reliefs, representing bulls as well as mice. He debuted at the Salon in 1863, where he continued to exhibit some bronzes: *Poussin*, silvered bronze (1868), *Famille de perdrix* (1877), *Une Nichée de lapins*, bas-relief (1898), some plaques in silvered bronze showing different animals (1903 and 1906), and *Cheval à l'abreuvoir* (1907), etc. Also notable are many works in plaster. Thiébaut cast a vase entitled *Hirondelles* in two dimensions, 62 and 41 cm.

SALES

Le Courlis, Chalon-sur-Saône, March 24, 1984.
Le Dindon, 17 x 11 cm, Enghien, March 2, 1980.
Encrier aux libellules, 14 x 32 cm, Enghien, October 10, 1982.
Vide-poches vannerie, décor souris, 17 x 19 cm (Thiébaut), Drouot, June 14, 1985.

HIOLIN, LOUIS AUGUSTE

Septmont (Aisne), March 18, 1846
Silly-la-Poterie (Nord), May 1910

After some studies at the school of drawing in Soissons, Hiolin went to Paris in 1864 and entered the Ecole des Beaux-Arts the following year. Employed by Viollet-le-Duc, he sculpted some works for the château of Pierrefonds. Taken prisoner in 1870, he could resume and complete his studies at the Beaux-Arts only upon his return to France. He then received a certain number of commissions—for the Casino of Paris, the theater in Besançon, the cathedral of Tréguier, the chapel of la Rue Jean-Goujon in Paris, and the monument to the dead of Soissons. His best-known work, *Au loup!*, a group in bronze exhibited at the Salon of 1887, was acquired by the city of Paris for the Buttes-Chaumont. Hiolin, who exhibited at the Salon starting in 1874, also left a statue of *Racine enfant* for the Ferté-Milon, as well as some portraits in bust and in medallion.

SALES
Au loup!, 55 cm, Sotheby London, November 25, 1982.
Au loup!, 79 cm (Pinedo, founder), Sotheby London, June 12, 1986.
Au loup!, 85 cm, Le Puy, December 1, 1986.

HIOLLE, ERNEST EUGÈNE

Paris, May 5, 1834
Nois-le-Roi, October 6, 1886

Hiolle initiated his studies in Valenciennes, where he grew up, before entering the Ecole des Beaux-Arts in 1853. Nine years later he won the first grand prize of Rome with a statue in plaster entitled *Aristée pleurant ses abeilles*, 1.2 meters in height. His work, greatly inspired by antiquity, includes some busts in marble and in bronze, and a number of allegories or mythological scenes. He secured a number of commissions, and worked for the Opera, the old Trocadéro, the city hall (the groups of *Instruction* and *Travail* framing the clock), the Temple of the Visitation, Rue Saint-Antoine (the figures of *Religion* and *Charité* on the pediment), etc. Moreover, he executed the monument in Cambrai to the dead from the war of 1870, the front of Cambrai's city hall, the statue of *La Fayette* for Le Puy, and the statue of the *Général Foy* for Ham. The museum of Valenciennes possesses a large number of his models.

MUSEUMS
Abbeville
Brutus jeune, bust, 35 cm (according to the marble from the Salon of 1867).
Lyon
Buste de Carpeaux (for his tomb in Valenciennes; Salon of 1877).
Buste de Chenavard (Salon of 1874).
Buste de Jouffroy (Salon of 1877).
Paris, Orsay
Paul Aubé, sculpteur, medallion, 16 cm, diam.

SALES
Jeune Femme nue s'essuyant le pied, 90 cm (1885), Sotheby London, March 20, 1986.

HOETGER, BERNHARD

Hörde (Westphalie), May 4, 1874
Beatenburg (Switzerland), July 18, 1949

B. Hoetger
Paris

A visit to the 1900 Exposition Universelle of Paris convinced Hoetger to establish himself in the French capital. He apparently frequented the Académie de Düsseldorf after undertaking some studies in sculpture and wood-decoration. He was soon engaged as a practician by Rodin, and made himself known at the Salon of 1901 with an emotional group entitled *L'Aveugle*. This first work remained his most famous; it was the object of many replicas and reductions in bronze and would be cast in gritstone (sandstone) by Adrien Dalpayrat. Hoetger also worked for the Maison Moderne of Maïer Graefe and produced some figures—particularly of *Loïe Fuller*—in a more refined style, influenced by Art Nouveau. Alternatively, social concerns drew his interest to the working world. He sculpted a series of beggars, personages from Parisian life, musicians, *Vieille Bretonne* (1904), and a series of workers which are reminiscent of those by the Belgian sculptor Constantin Meunier. He became friends with a number of Montmartre artists, furnished drawings to the review *L'Assiette au beurre*, and exhibited his works not only to the Artistes Français and the Nationale des Beaux-Arts, but also at the house of founder Eugène Blot, who cast a certain number of them in bronze.

In 1907, Hoetger returned to Germany, where he pursued a triple career in sculpture, painting, and architecture. He left his country in 1933 and established himself in Switzerland.

After shutting down his operations in 1937 and 1938, Eugène Blot yeilded the rights to manufacture and cast the sculptures of many artists to Leblanc-Barbedienne. Not hesitating to call Hoetger "the Rodin of Germany," Leblanc-Barbedienne listed the works which had been cast, along with the number of the castings already made and the number of works already sold:

Torse de femme, 45 cm, 25 models, 10 sold.
Pleureuse, unlimited casting.
Aspiration, unlimited casting.
Semeur, 54 cm, 50 models, 9 sold.
Aveugle, 49 cm, 50 models, 14 sold.
Adieux, 58 cm, 25 models, 6 sold.
Jeunesse, bust, 44 cm, 50 models, 15 sold.
Silhouettes, unlimited casting.

Furthermore, he was interested in drawing up a list of the bronzes by Hoetger made in France, the majority, as we will come to see, cast by Eugène Blot. This list was established in chronological order at the time of the exposition of his plastic works from the Parisian years, 1900-1910, organized in 1977 in Bremen, Germany, by the Graphisches Kabinett Kunshandel.

Bernhard Hoetger,
Machine humaine, bas-relief, 44 x 37 cm.
Musée d'Orsay.

1901 (or around 1901)
Le Mineur.
L'Aveugel et sa compagne, 47.5 cm.
Enfant jouant, 15 x 24 cm.
Pleureuse, 27 cm.
Petites Nymphes, 29.5 cm.
Le Rêve, 23 cm.
L'Enfant au cerceau, 19 cm.
Enfant, bras droit levé, 21 cm.
Bacchante, 26.3 cm.
Loïe Fuller, 26 cm.
La Tempête, 31 cm.

Femme assise à la couronne, 14 x 21 cm.
La Fumée, gilded bronze, 6.5 x 33.5 cm.
Le Pardon, 29 cm.
Femme et fillette, 15 x 32.5 cm.
1902 (or around 1902)
Le Fondeur, bas-relief, 49.5 x 36 cm.
Machine humaine, bas-relief, 45 x 38 cm.
Le Haleur, 42 cm.
Portefaix.
Le Charbonnier, 36 cm.
Jeune Garçon au bâton, 19.5 cm.
Le Mendiant, 26.5 cm.

1903 (or around 1903)
Jeune couple, 21.2 cm.
Jeune Fille à la cruche, 23.5 cm.
Jeune Fille à l'ombrelle, 20.3 cm.
Porteuse d'eau, 16 cm.
Jeune Fille bottée, 25 cm.
Buste de femme (study for *La Fécondité*), 9.4 cm.
Buste de femme, 14 and 10 cm.
1904 (or around 1904)
Deux Femmes bretonnes, 14.7 cm.
Homme assis sur un banc, 12 cm.
Deux Vieux Pêcheurs, 14.5 cm.
Ramasseur de pommes de terre, 9.2 cm.
Emile (worker), 9 cm.
Moissonneuse, 17 cm.
Vieille Bretonne, 10.8 cm.
Tête d'enfant (study), 33 cm.
Tête de femme, 24 cm.
Jeunesse (head of woman), 43.5 cm.
Fécondité, bust (first version), 46 cm.
Fécondité, bust (second version), 43 cm.
1905 (or around 1905)
Torse de femme, 39 cm.
Masque de Lee Hoetger, 33 cm.
1906
Eve et le cygne, 116 cm.
Le Sourire (head of a man), gilded bronze, 58 cm.
L'Envol de la Pensée, gilded bronze, 47 cm.
1909
Torse de femme, 65 cm.
Torse de jeune fille, 103 cm.

MUSEUMS
Paris, Orsay
Machine humaine, relief, 44 x 37 cm (Eug. Blot; 1902).
Le Maître d'armes, 41 cm (Eug. Blot).
Torse de femme, 34.5 cm (Eug. Blot).
Poitiers
L'Aveugle, 48 cm (Eug. Blot No. 13).
Pleureuse, 27 cm (Eug. Blot).

SALES
Le Chemineau, 26 cm (Andro, founder), Drouot, March
    12, 1982, room 2.
La Couronne, régule, 14 cm (1901), Drouot, March 11,
    1983, room 4.
Elégante pensive, 29 cm, Drouot, June 10, 1985, room
    1.
Le Haleur, 35 cm (Eug. Blot), Semur-en-Auxois, April 4,
    1983.
Jeune Femme assoupie, 28.5 cm, Drouot, December 17,
    1982.
Le Mendiant, 26 cm (1902), Enghien, March 25, 1984.
Petite Nymphe, 28.6 cm, Christie's London, April 17,
    1984.
Torse, 30.5 cm (Eug. Blot No.15), Munich, December 6,
    1982.

Louis Holweck,
Le Vin, 48 cm.

HOLWECK, LOUIS

Paris, 1861
August 28, 1935

Holweck

Holweck's participation at the Salon spanned from 1882 until 1920. He primarily exhibited busts and diverse groups and figures there, including *L'Enfance de Bacchus*, a group in plaster (1887), *Le* *Vin*, a group in plaster (1888; exhibited as a bronze in 1891 and as a plaster reduction in 1899), *L'Architecture*, a statuette in plaster (1896), *Le Matin*, another statuette in plaster (1901), *Bernadin de Saint-Pierre*, a monument in bronze with the figures of Paul and Virginia on the pedestal, in a very Romantic style, destined for the Jardin des Plantes where it can still be found (1907), and a statue in stone and bronze entitled *Les Cendres* (1910). Some castings in bronze of *Vin* are known, 48 cm in height.

HOTTOT, LOUIS

Paris, May 12, 1829
Neuilly-sur-Seine, 1905

Eastern characters and scenes dominate the production of this sculptor, who participated at the Salon from 1885 to 1898. Of note are a statuette in bronze entitled *Fille d'Egypte* (1885) and a number of plasters such as *Almée du Caire* (1887), *Phoebé et Echo* (1888), *Alexandre III, empereur de Russie, à cheval* (1891), *Appel à la danse à Memphis* (1892), *Circé*, a statuette (1897), etc. Among the works cast in bronze, of note are *Jeune Harpiste orientale, Napoléon 1er*, 67 cm, *Tête d'Italienne, Buste de jeune fille*, etc. Some subjects were cast in composition as well.

SALES

Jeune Arabe, Jeune Fille arabe, two statuettes, 53 cm, Sotheby London, March 21, 1985.
Jeune Femme couchée, 43 cm, Sotheby London, June 20, 1985.
Jeune Orientale devant un guéridon, gilded metal, 145 cm, Christie's Oklahoma (United States), September 24, 1981.
Jeune Orientale à la harpe, bronze and marble, 46 cm, Enghien, October 16, 1983.
Paire de grands vases en métal ornés chacun de trois personnages orientaux, 110 cm, Sotheby New York, September 13, 1986.

HOUDAIN, ANDRÉ D'

Cambrai, 1860
Paris, February 15, 1904

Subjects from antiquity, allegories, scenes from everyday life, and animals compose Houdain's very eclectic work. A student of Cavelier, he began to exhibit regularly at the Salon in 1881. Attributed to him most notably are some plasters, including *Dompteur gaulois, Danaïde, Enlèvement d'une Sabine, Les vendanges sont faites, Faune, La Fatalité, Boeuf sous le joug, Les Haleurs,* etc. His monument to *Pasteur* was installed in Melun in 1897. Also known is a study in bronze entitled *Taureau,* dating from 1896. The Thiébaut house cast Houdain's sculpture *Montreur d'ours* at 32 cm in height.

HOUSSIN, EDOUARD

Douai, September 13, 1847
Paris, May 15, 1917

This artist, who became an instructor of sculpture and model-making at the Sèvres factory, was known for many monuments and statues in the north of France as well as a bronze representing *Phaéton,* 240 cm, erected in a public garden of Briançon. At the Salon, where he exhibited regularly from 1873 to 1914, he showed a number of busts, often in bronze and, also in bronze: *Enfant à la panthère,* a group (1881), *Esméalda,* a statuette (1883), *Phaéton,* a statue (1889), and *Le Bateau de sauvetage,* haut-relief (1904). He also executed some portraits of *Loïe Fuller* which were made in bronze, most notably a head of the famous dancer dated from 1897, 30.5 cm.

MUSEUMS
Douai
Buste d'Emile Dubois, sénateur, 65 cm.
Buste de Samuel Henry Berthoud, 55 cm (1873).

SALES
Le Départ pour la pêche, 80 x 200 cm (Jaboeuf and Rouard, founder, 1901).
Esméalda, 82 cm, Drouot, March 23, 1987, room 3.

Edouard Houssin,
Esméralda, 82 cm.

HUDELET, HENRY PAUL

Langres, December 20, 1849
1878

During the course of a very brief career, Hudelet exhibited at the Salon for only two consecutive years: in 1876, a statue in bronze entitled *Joueur de dés,* and in 1877, a medallion in bronze entitled *Portrait de femme.* A reduction of the *Joueur de dés,* 40 cm, was cast in bronze. One proof belongs to the museum of Langres.

HUGUENIN, JEAN-PIERRE VICTOR

Dole, February 21, 1802
Paris, January 8, 1860

This sculptor began his studies in Dijon, but in 1825 moved to Paris to study in Ramey's studio at the Ecole des beaux-arts. Hired to execute a number of official commissions, he produced busts and statues of historic personages. He worked for the Louvre, for the churches of the Madeleine, Saint-Paul-Saint-Louis, and Notre-Dame-des-Champs, and for the cathedral du Mans, among other landmarks. His statue in bronze of *Pascal Paoli,* 3 meters high, cast by Eck and Durand, was installed in Corte, Corsica in 1854. He exhibited at the Salon from 1835 to 1859, with a noteworthy bronze group inspired by a poem by Alfred de Vigny, *La Chute d'Eloa* (1842), and a statuette in marble entitled *Baigneuse surprise* (1845). At the museum of Dole is found the bust in bronze of the *Baron Delort* (1835), 75 cm.

*Dominique Hugues,
La Muse de la source,
marble and bronze, 165 cm.
Musée d'Orsay.*

HUGUES, DOMINIQUE JEAN-BAPTISTE

Marseille, April 15, 1849
October 28, 1930

This artist's work encompasses some very eclectic subjects from the realms of religion, allegory, and mythology. He is known for two statues in marble in Paris: *L'Homme et la Misère* (1907), located in the gardens of the Tuileries, and *La Gravure* under the portal of the national library, as well as a statue in stone, *La Ville de Nantes,* on the facade of the Gare d'Orsay

Winning the prize of Rome in 1875, Hugues started to exhibit at the Salon in 1878. His work features few bronzes, and those are often mixed with marble. Among these pieces are *Amphitrite,* a group in marble and bronze intended for a fountain (1900), and two statuettes in bronze, *Indolence,* indicated as being a unique proof (1909), and *Joueuse de flûte* (1912). Two other statuettes in bronze, *Un tireur* and *Jean-Louis,* were exhibited at the Nationale des Beaux-Arts in 1891, along with a statue in bronze entitled *L'Immortalité.*

The founder Siot-Decauville cast in bronze *La Muse de la source* and *Un potier* after the plasters exhibited respectively at the Salon of 1893 and 1895.

MUSEUMS
Arras
Ravenne, bust in marble and bronze, painted and
    encrusted with blue stones, 45 cm.
Belfort
Mélancolie, 56 cm.
La Rieuse, 55 cm.
Paris, Orsay
Muse de la source, marble and bronze, 165 x 140 cm.

HUSSON, HONORÉ JEAN ARISTIDE

Paris, July 1, 1803
Menton, July 30, 1864

The son of an engraver of metal, Husson chose instead to pursue sculpture, and perfected his art in the studio of David d'Angers. He won the second and then the first prize of Rome, the latter in 1830 with a bas-relief entitled *Thésée combattant le Minotaure.* He remained in Rome for five years, and from there he sent his first works to the Salon of 1832, including a plaster of 1.6 meters in height representing *Adam et Eve.* He received innumerable official commissions, furnishing a number of busts to ministers and diverse administrations, some statues of contemporary or historical people, some allegorical or mythological groups for the Luxembourg gardens (*Eustache Lesueur* and *Marguerite de Provence*), the city hall, and the Louvre. He is responsible for a fountain from the Concorde Plaza (statues in bronze of *La Moisson* and *La Vendange*), two angels in bronze, 90 cm, for the high altar of the Dôme des Invalides, etc. One of his busts, symbolizing *La Liberté,* was bought by the state, and twenty-five models were cast in galvanized zinc. The museum of Clermont-Ferrand possesses a bust, *La République,* 75 cm (1848), and a medallion, *Portrait de femme,* 21 cm diam. (1844).

IDRAC, JEAN ANTOINE

Toulouse, April 14, 1849
Paris, December 28, 1884

Idrac arrived at Paris at the age of seventeen in order to work at the Beaux-Arts in the studios of Cavelier, Guillaume, and Falguière. He won the first prize of Rome in 1873 and debuted at the Salon in 1877 with one of his best-known works, *L'Amour piqué* (or *blessé*), a plaster of 130 cm height executed in Rome the preceding year. In 1879 appeared *Mercure inventant le caducée*, in marble, 90 x 180 cm, a bronze model of which was placed in Capitole Square in Toulouse. In 1881, Idrac exhibited *Salammbô* in plaster, 180 cm, which was translated in marble the following year. He left his last work unfinished, a piece entitled *Etienne Marcel équestre* of 4.5 m high, to be completed by Marqueste, cast in bronze and erected before the lateral facade of the city hall of Paris. Many statues and groups by Idrac were made the object of reductions in bronze, particularly *Etienne Marcel*. Thiébaut cast *Premier Baiser*, 72, 53 and 12.5 cm, and *Salammbô*, 81 cm.

MUSEUMS
Lille
L'Amour piqué, 130 cm (according to the plaster from the Salon of 1877).
Paris, Petit Palais
Etienne Marcel équestre, 52.5 cm.

Some plasters and some marbles figured in many French museums as well as in Chicago and in Copenhagen.

ILLIERS, GASTON D'

Boulogne-sur-Seine, June 26, 1876
1952

An animal sculptor, Gaston d'Illiers devoted his work to one theme almost exclusively—the horse. His works portrayed them at the race track, the hunt, labor, and war, and in several breeds. A

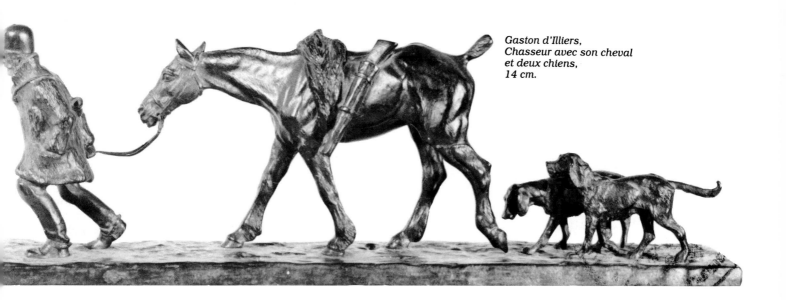

Gaston d'Illiers,
Chasseur avec son cheval
et deux chiens,
14 cm.

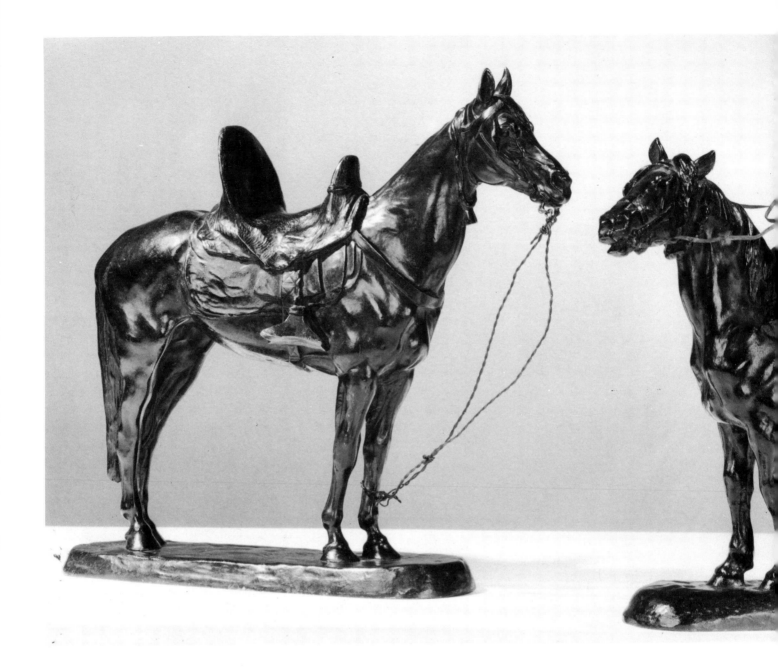

student of the Count of Ruillé, Illiers started to exhibit his works at the Salon in 1899, in particular some statuettes in bronze including *Incroyable* (1903), *Vieux Cheval* (1904), *Chien d'équipage* (1906), *Piqueur (or Piqueux)* and *Dolly* (1909), *Chien de berger belge* (1910), and *Etalon boulonnais* (1911). A number of other works were cast in bronze; the frequency of their appearance in public sales suggests that they were cast in multiple models.

SALES

Après la chasse, 19.5 cm, Rambouillet, March 25, 1984.

Avant la course, 21 cm, Sotheby London, March 8, 1984; L'Isle-Adam, July 7, 1985.

Chasseur, son cheval et deux chiens, 14 cm, Tours, November 25, 1985.

Cheval de cirque, 12 cm, Rambouillet, March 25, 1984.

Cheval de course, 21 cm, Sotheby London, November 7, 1985.

Cheval franchissant une haie, 19 cm, Rambouillet, March 25, 1984.

La Croupade, 10 cm, Drouot, March 20, 1985, room 4.

La Curée, 25 cm, Rambouillet, March 25, 1984.

Deux Chasseurs arabes avec chiens et faucons, 38 cm, Sotheby London, June 12, 1986.

Esméralda, mare at a stop, 12 cm, Rambouillet, March 25, 1984.

Esméralda, mare marching, 11 cm, Rambouillet, March 25, 1984.

Estafette montée, 29 cm, Drouot, December 14, 1984, room 6.

Etalon, 11 x 15 cm, Rambouillet, March 25, 1984.

Fauconnier près de son cheval, 29 cm, Drouot, May 19, 1982, room 1.

Fauconnier lâchant le faucon sur un lièvre, gilded bronze, 34 cm, Drouot, May 19, 1982, room 4.

Le Petit Ane, 10.5 cm, Drouot, March 20, 1985, room 4.

Le Piqueux, 22 cm, Rambouillet, March 25, 1984.

Prince, 11 x 14 cm, Drouot, December 10, 1984, room 7.

Pur-sang, 19 cm, Rambouillet, March 25, 1984.

Le Retour de la chasse, 14 cm (1926), Enghien, October 6, 1985.

Gaston d'Illiers,
Cheval arabe sellé,
26 cm.

Gaston d'Illiers,
Homme à cheval,
26 cm.

Jean Antoine Injalbert,
Buste de jeune fille
souriante, 27 cm.

INJALBERT, JEAN ANTOINE

Béziers, February 23, 1845
Paris, March 3, 1933

Well-respected during his lifetime for his skill in modeling the human body, Injalbert won the first grand prize of Rome in 1874, and would later train a number of French and foreign students. He worked on the Palais de Justice of Paris, the Sorbonne (a statue in stone of *La Chimie*), the Gare d'Orsay, the Petit Palais (the pediment *La Ville de Paris entourée des muses*), the Mirabeau Bridge (four colossal figures of marine divinities in bronze), and the Herault Police Station in Béziers. He is also the author of the monument to Auguste Comte in the Plaza de la Sorbonne in Paris, and two groups in stone entitled *Lion et enfant*, symbolizing Love and Strength, on the Peyrou Promenade in Montpellier. His consignments at the Salon des Artistes Français, starting in 1873, include a number of bronzes, busts, and medallions as well as some statues: *Le Christ* (1881), *Titan* (1884), *Le Coureur* (1885), *Hippomène* and *Un escrimeur moderne* (1886), and *Renommée*, hautrelief (1888).

Starting in 1891, Injalbert exhibited at the Salon de la Nationale des Beaux-Arts, showing numerous bronzes: *Tête de femme* and *Nymphes et satyres* (1891), *Nymphe surprise par n satyre*, *Eve après le péché*, *La Princesse Clémence*, *La Danse* (1893), *Berger de la Sabine* (1899), *Muse des bois*, cast by Hébrard (1903), *Jeune Faune ivre* (1905), *Faune* (1908), *Tête de faune*, *Une jeune fille*, *Saint-Saëns*, *Laloux* (1911), *Buste de Jeune Faune* (1913), *Nymphe à Tivoli* (1914), etc. Injalbert also participated at the Salon d'Automne.

The Thiébaut foundry cast two groups in bronze, representing a child and a lion: *L'Amour domptant la Force* and *La Force domptée par l'Amour*, both of 45 cm high, modeled after stone groups from Montpellier. Thiébaut also cast *La Renommée*, bas-relief, in two dimensions, 135 x 66 cm and 71 x 36 cm.

The Siot-Decauville catalog advertised *Amour aux colombes, Enfant au mascaron* and *Buste de Rieur*. Some other works were cast by Hébrard, Valsuani, Bingen, Goldscheider, etc. An important collection of Injalbert's work is kept at the museum of Béziers, but, rather curiously, the bronzes appear only rarely on the market and in public sales.

MUSEUMS
Angers
Buste de Lenepveu, 79 cm.

Béziers
L'Abondance, study of a woman standing, 28 cm.
Chanteur napolitain, head, 25 cm.
La Charité, 29 cm.
Douleur d'Orphée, 41 cm.
Enfant coiffé d'un chapeau, 49 cm.
Enfant martyr, head, 29 cm.
Enfant au masque, study for the Fountain du Titan in Béziers, 60 cm.
Femme ivre, 170 cm.
Femme ivre, 50 cm (Carvillon, founder in Paris).
Femme assise en costume moderne, 49 cm (Hébrard).
Femme assise mettant son bas, 34 cm.
Femme assise sur un rocher, 34 cm.
Femme drapée debout, 31 cm.
Femme nue debout, 41 cm.
Femme à la puce, 42 cm.
Hippomène, head, 25 cm.
Isabelle, bust, 28 cm.
Jeune Femme, bust, 38 cm.
Jeune Pâtre, 48 cm.
Malaria, 56 cm.
Marche funèbre, woman playing a violoncello, 37.2 cm.
Nymphe lutinant un satyre assis, 45 cm (Valsuani).
Pifferraro jeune, 39.5 cm.
Rieur, head, 49.5 cm.
Satyre assis jouant de la flûte, 34 cm.
Sibylle de Panzoult, 28 cm (Valsuani).
Sources du Tibre, 43.5 cm.
Ubriacone, head, 29 cm.
Victor Hugo aux Feuillantines, 15 x 33 cm (exposition Victor Hugo at the Grand Palais, 1985).

Louviers
Le Rieur, bust, 48 cm.

Moulins
Tête d'adolescent, life-size.

Nantes
L'Amour domptant la Force, 45.5 cm.

Nîmes
Hippomène, statue.

Paris, Orsay
Satyre et nymphe, 61 cm (P. Bingen).
Satyre et nymphe sur un chapiteau, 57.5 cm.
Vigeant or *Escrimeur moderne*, 33 cm (P. Bingen; 1885).

Paris, Petit Palais
Buste de M. Cameré, ingénieur des ponts et chaussées, 60 cm.

Reims
Buste de jeune fille, 22 cm.
Christ en croix, 296 cm (Rome 1877).

SALES
Buste d'adolescent, 38 cm, Drouot, December 16, 1985, room 11.
Buste de jeune femme, 39 cm, Sotheby London, November 25, 1982.
Le Petit Voleur de poires, 84 cm, Sotheby London, March 8, 1984.

ISELIN, HENRI FRÉDÉRIC
Claire-Goutte (Haute-Saône), December 14, 1825
Mars, 1905

Iselin's initiation to sculpture occurred in Rude's studio, as well as at the Ecole des Beaux-Arts. His production includes a number of busts and statues in different materials, portraying historical and contemporary people. Among his other works are many busts of *Napoléon III*, including one in bronze commissioned by the state in 1867, some busts of *Jean Goujon, Mirabeau, Joachim Murat*, and *Général Lamoricière*. At the Salon, where he made his debut in 1849, Iselin exhibited the busts in bronze of the *Duc de Morny* in 1863 and of the *Prosper Mérimée* in 1887. Moreover, he worked on diverse Parisian edifices including the Louvre, the Opera, and the city hall. The bust in bronze of the *Duc de Morny*, 85 cm, belongs to the museum of Clermont-Ferrand, and the bust of *Napoléon III*, 62 cm (1865), at the museum of the château of Compiègne.

ITASSE, JEANNE
Paris, November 25, 1867
January 12, 1941

The daughter and student of sculptor Adolphe Itasse, Jeanne Itasse began exhibiting at the Salon at the age of fourteen, most notably showing some bronzes: *Tête de vieille femme* (1886), *Jeune Ecolier*, a statue, and *Laure de Noves*, a medallion (1889), *Harpiste égyptienne*, a statue (1892), a fragment of the funerary monument of Adolphe Itasse at the Père-Lachaise (1894), *Buste d'Adolphe Itasse* (1897), *Etude de tête* (1898), etc. She also showed some statuettes in plaster: *Bacchante* (1896), *Léda* (1907), *Coquelin aîné* (1908), and *Le Faucheur* (1909). She submitted a bas-relief entitled *Mater Dei*, first in gritstone (sandstone) (1902), and then in plaster (1904). This bas-relief was cast in bronze by the Susse house, 53, 40, 24 and 15 cm; *Harpiste égyptienne* was cast by Barbedienne.

MUSEUMS
Avignon
Buste d'Adolphe Itasse, 55.5 cm (Thiébaut).
Paris, Carnavalet
L'Acteur Coquelin aîné dans l'Affaire des poisons de V. Sardou, 44 cm.

SALES
Enfant assis, 47.5 cm, Sotheby London, November 6, 1986.

JACOPIN, ACHILLE EMILE

Château-Thierry, November 2, 1874
Château-Thierry, February 5, 1958

A sculptor and a medal-engraver, Jacopin exhibited three amusing, small, animal bronzes at the Salon in 1913—*Les Deux Rats et l'oeuf* and *Le Rat et l'huître*, both cast by Jollet, and *Groupe de souris*, cast by Goldscheider. A bust in bronze of *Alexandre Granval*, 61.5 cm, belongs to the museum of Reims. A proof of *Le Rat et l'huître*, 14 cm in height, was sold by Christie's in New York on March 13, 1984.

JACQUE, CHARLES

Paris, May 23, 1813
May 7, 1894

A painter of the Barbizon school and an excellent etcher, Charles Jacque is especially known for his numerous (perhaps too numerous!) canvases representing barnyard animals, shepherds and shepherdesses with their herds of sheep, and sheepfolds. On the same themes, he executed some small bronzes, which appear from time to time in public sale. Six small barnyard animals (maximum height of 9 cm) were sold in Enghien on March 29, 1987.

Charles Jacque,
Vache marchant,
12 x 21 cm.

JACQUEMART, HENRI ALFRED

Paris, February 22, 1824
Paris, January 4, 1896

A·JACQUEMART

Jacquemart earned his reputation for groups and figures of animals, and statues of saints and historic people sculpted for different monuments. Among his works are the two griffins in bronze from the fountain of Saint-Michel, the two lions in bronze from one of the doors of the city hall, Rue Lobau, the *Rhinocéros* from the old Trocadéro (today on the esplanade of the Orsay Museum), the four evangelists from the church Saint-Augustin, the eight lions in bronze from the old fountain of the Château-d'Eau, today the plaza of Félix-Eboué, the four sphinx in stone from the fountain of the Châtelet, the portrait of *Louis XII* in bas-relief from the city hall of Compiègne, and the colossal statue of *Mehemet Ali* in Alexandria.

At the Beaux-Arts, Jacquemart studied painting with Delaroche, and sculpture, to which he would devote himself, with Klagmann. He participated at the Salon from 1847 to 1879 and received a number of distinctions. He traveled in Egypt and Turkey, and brought back from these visits impressions which he translated in his works. He made a number of small animal bronzes and furnished some models to the house of the Christofle goldsmith shop.

*Henri Jacquemart,
Cheval et chien,
22 x 35 cm.*

Cast in bronze by the Barbedienne house
Bonaparte en Egypte, 26 cm.
Groupe de boeufs, 24, 18 and 9.5 cm.
Cheval, 32 cm.
Chien, 22 cm.
Dromadaire nubien (improperly called chameau), 43 cm.
Lion assis, 34 cm.
Taureau, 24 cm.
Editions from the Susse house
Christ debout, 46, 30 and 13 cm.
Enfant au chat, 12 cm.
Enfant au chien, 12 cm.
Enfant à la poupée, 12 cm.
Enfant au tambourin, 12 cm.
Jeanne d'Arc, 35, 30, 25 and 12 cm.
Jeune Fille en prière, 18 cm.
Jeune Garçon en prière, 18 cm.

Also of note, though no founders are specified, are *Cerf paissant*, 27 x 35 cm, *Cheval et chien*, 22 x 35 cm, and *Epagneul*, 10 cm.

MUSEUMS
Belfort
Cerf, 20.3 x 23.5 cm.
Chien assis regardant une tortue, 15 x 18.5 cm.
Chien de chasse debout, 18.5 x 28 cm.
Faisan doré, 11.5 x 22 cm.
Lynx assis, 18.3 x 7 cm.
Poule faisane, 10 x 20 cm.
Chambéry
Cerf frottant ses bois.
Le Mans
Chien assis, 15 cm.
Montpellier
Cerf, 12.5 cm.
Nantes
Chameleier de l'Asie mineure, 157 cm (Le Caire 1869).
Nîmes
Chien à la tortue, 15.3 cm.

SALES
Cheval et chien, 22 cm, Enghien, October 6, 1985.
Chien et tortue, 16 x 18 cm, Drouot, June 12, 1981; Drouot, November 19, 1982, room 7; Versailles, January 30, 1983; Sotheby Chester, October 6, 1983.
Deux Chiens et un chiot, 22 cm, Sotheby London, June 7, 1984.
Cigogne, 15 cm, Rambouillet, March 25, 1984.
Coq faisan, 10.5 cm, Enghien, February 22, 1981.
Faisan, 12.5 cm, Rambouillet, March 25, 1984.
Valet de chiens, 170 cm, Ossages, July 23, 1984 (sold for 210,000 F).

JACQUOT CHARLES

Bains (Vosges), January 12, 1865
1930

In 1886 this student of Falguière began sending his works to the Salon, primarily in plaster; they included *La Prière aux champs* (1887; bronze in 1888), *Nymphe et satyre* (1888), *Jeanne d'Arc* (1890), *Ad Patriam* (1893), *Le Soir* (1905), *La Bergère de Domrémy* (1913), etc. Thiébaut cast *Ad Patriam*, 72 cm, and Siot-Decauville cast *Départ de Domrémy*. The Carnavalet museum possesses the 56 cm bust in bronze of one of the old curators, *Jules Cousin*, (1904).

JALEY, JEAN-LOUIS

Paris, January 27 1802
Neuilly-sur-Seine, May 30, 1866

To summarize the artist Jean-Louis Jaley's work and style, sculptor Augustin Dumont said at the artist's obsequies that "he best expressed delicate forms, tender sentiments, and moral abstractions." A student of his father and of Cartellier, Jaley entered the Ecole des Beaux-Arts in 1820, won the first grand prize of Rome in 1827, and succeeded David d'Angers to become a member of the Institute in 1856. He received commissions for many monuments, including the Louvre, the Palais de Justice, the city hall, the Gare du Nord, the church of the Madeleine, etc. Among his principal works exhibited at the Salon starting in 1824 were *La Prère* (1833), *La Pudeur* (1834), two marbles executed during his visit to Rome, *L'Amour enfant,* a statuette in marble (1847), *Bacchante,* a statuette in bronze (1848), *Jeune Fille* or the *Rêverie,* marble, 120 cm (1850), and *Danaïde,* bronze (1863).

La Prière was cast in bronze by Barbedienne in three dimensions, 37, 27 and 18 cm. A statuette in bronze of 26.5 cm high, *Jean Sylvain Bailly, maire de Paris,* belongs to the Carnavalet Museum.

JOIRE, JEAN

Lille, September 5, 1862
Lille, September 8, 1950

J. JOIRE

Born into a family of bankers, Jean Joire was still very young when he abandoned the milieu of finance for which he had been intended, in order to devote himself to animal sculpture, a pursuit which occupied him for his entire life.

It does not seem that his production, made up almost exclusively of plasters intended to be cast in bronze, was very abundant. His descendants remember that his work was cast by Susse, Valsuani,

Hébrard, Barbedienne and some others foundries, and very often he offered his works to his friends.

Others of his models were cast in greater or lesser numbers of copies. Rarely appearing in public sales, they obtained some rather high bids. They almost exclusively portray horses, and more seldom, dogs, treated with realism and an undeniable sense of movement. Joire was particularly drawn to sculpt-

Jean Joire,
Deux Chiens alsaciens,
49 x 66 cm (Susse).

Jean Joire,
Le Fardier à deux chevaux.

Jean Joire,
Groupe de huit chevaux
décomposant le pas du cheval.

Jean Joire,
Poney de cirque, 20.5 x 22 cm
(F. Barbedienne).
François Joire Collection, Paris.

Jean Joire,
Cheval attaché à la longe, 42 cm
(E. Bureau, chiseler).
François Joire Collection, Paris.

Jean Joire,
Idylle,
Salon of 1910.

Jean Joire,
Groupe de
quatre chevaux attelés,
41 x 116 cm
(E. Bureau, chiseler, 1892).
François Joire Collection, Paris.

ing many horses in harness, and was more interested in draft horses and labor horses than race horses. An excellent horseman and a great circus enthusiast, he also sculpted some circus horses in plumed crests. The work *Attelage à quatre* marks his debut at the Salon in 1891. Next came some other horses, singly or in groups, often in plaster, sometimes in wax or in bronze. Of note is *Scène hippique*, (Salon of 1903), *Flèche*, a horse in bronze (1905), *Frayeur*, a group of horses in plaster (1906), *Tom, chien de berger belge*, bronze (1907), *Chevaux de cirque*, a group in bronze cast by Valsuani (1908), *Taquinerie*, a group of horses in plaster (1909), *Idylle*, two horses in bronze (1910), *Fardier dans les Flandres*, a group of four horses pulling a stone, in bronze (1912), *En 1830, diligence à cinq chevaux*, bronze (1913), *On the road, mailcoach*, plaster, and *Percheron*, bronze (1914). Also known is a surprising group in bronze, an analysis of the pace of a horse showing eight horses side by side.

After the First World War, from 1918 to 1939, Jean Joire continued to exhibit regularly at the Salon, still primarily contributing horses. *Hussard à cheval*, a monumental figure by Joire, exists in the woods of Boulogne in Lille.

Jean Joire,
Cheval de labour boulonnais
monté par un enfant,
31.5 x 33 cm (Valsuani).
François Joire Collection, Paris.

MUSEUMS
Lille
Tom, chien de berger belge, 65 x 119 cm (1905).
Paris, Petit Palais
La Diligence en 1850, 40 cm.
Tourcoing
Le Grand Fardier, 70 x 280 cm (Jabeouf and Rouard, founders).

SALES
Cheval de parade, 20.5 cm (Barbedienne), Enghien, June 21, 1981.
Cheval au trot, 39.5 x 58 cm, Lille, November 22, 1982.
Cheval au trot, 47.5 cm (Verbeyst, founder), Sotheby London, June 7, 1984.
Deux Chiens alsaciens, 49 x 66 cm, Christie's London, September 25, 1986.

Jean Joire,
Cheval sellé au trot,
41 x 57 cm.
François Joire
Collection,
Paris.

JOUANT, JULES

Born in Paris—or in Neuilly-sur-Seine, according to certain authors—Jules Jouant made the monument to *Francs-tireurs des Ternes,* to be erected at the Plaza of Saint-Ferdinand in Paris. He collaborated with Rodin, as evidenced by a letter from the founder Eugène Blot in the national archives: "At Rodin's place, I met Jules Jouant, with whom he had traveled much, and for a very long time. He created at my place many models, he had some happy ideas..."

In 1911, Jouant exhibited a mask of *Beethoven* in bronze at the Société Nationale des Beaux-Arts; this piece would be presented again at the Salon des Artistes Français in 1914. This mask, as well as those of *Wagner, César Franck,* and *Chopin,* were cast by Eugène Blot, with whom Jouant worked almost solely. In the aforementioned letter, Blot confirmed that as soon as Jouant's sculpting career ended, he (Blot) had helped the sculptor to establish himself as a teacher at the Ecole Boulle. Noteworthy is the fact that Blot gave the rights of reproducing Jouant's four masks to Leblanc-Barbedienne in 1937.

The museum of Poitiers possesses the masks in bronze of *Beethoven* and of *Wagner,* 9 cm in height, cast by Eugène Blot in 1905. A mask of *Beethoven,* cast by Barbedienne, 37 cm, was sold at the Drouot Hotel on February 6, 1984, in room 7.

JOUFFROY, FRANÇAIS

Dijon, February 1, 1806
Laval, June 25, 1882

Jouffroy was among the government-sponsored artists guided by academic dogmas, and little inclined to free himself from them. Considered to be one of the best sculptors of his time, he was made a member of the Institut in 1857, and a professor at the Ecole des Beaux-Arts in 1863. At the end of his life, he devoted most of his energy to teaching, after having been honored with countless commissions. At the age of eleven, he had started his studies at the school of fine arts in Dijon, later advancing to that of Paris. He won the prize of Rome in 1832 with a work on the theme of *Capanée foudroyé sous les murs de Thèbes.* His first consignments to the Salon were sent from Rome in 1835.

Upon returning to France, Jouffroy worked for many churches in Paris, including Saint-Augustin (*Le Christ et les douze Apôtres* for the facade), Saint-Germain-l'Auxerrois, Saint-Gervais, la Madeleine, and Sainte-Clotilde. He also worked on the Palais de Justice, the Opera (*L'Harmonie,* a group from the facade), the Luxembourg, and the Gare du Nord. For the Louvre, he executed the two monumental groups (*La Marine de guerre* and *La Marine marchande*) on the windows of the carrousel on the Seine side, and the front and the caryatids from the Mollien Pavillion. Many statues of historic people—groups and commemorative monuments—were also destined for some cities of the province. Despite the extent of his career, Jouffroy's best-known work remains a very conventional statue in marble sent to the Salon of 1839, *Jeune Fille confiant son secret à Vénus,* today at the Louvre. In this sculpture, Edmond About saw evidence of a reaction against Romanticism, and "the vogue of antiquity recovered." A reduction in bronze of this statue was exhibited in 1900. Some editions of it would be made, particularly by Barbedienne, in four sizes, 81, 64, 55, 40 cm. Also known are some proofs in zinc. In addition, Barbedienne cast in bronze *Trois Enfants avec une croix,* 67, 52, 35, 22 cm, after a group sculpted for the church of Saint-Germain-l'Auxerrois.

The museum of Dijon preserves a bust in bronze of *Louis Dietsch,* a composer of Dijon music, 35 cm (1873), as well as some works in marble or in raw clay.

JOURJON, TOUSSAINT FRANÇOIS

Saint-Genest-Lerp (Loire), 1809
Rennes, 1857

This sculptor, who exhibited at the Salon from 1844 to 1849, seems to have focused on sculpting busts. The museum of Chambéry possesses a bust in bronze of *Général Dessaix,* cast in 1836 by Quesnel.

JOUVE, PAUL

Marlotte (Seine-et-Marne), March 16, 1878
Paris, March 13, 1973

P. Jouve

A painter, engraver, and the illustrator of books including Kipling's *The Jungle Book,* Paul Jouve was also a sculptor. His work is devoted almost exclusively to one theme: big game and other animals from the untouched forest and the bush. In the first years of the century, he visited the principal zoos of Europe, including those of Anvers and of Hamburg, and then stayed for many years in Algiers. Beginning in 1904, he had some small animals in bronze cast by Alexis Rudier, and exhibited them at the at the Salon at the beginning of the century, specifically in 1913 Bing Gallery and at the Société Nationale des Beaux-Arts. At the Société, his notable exhibitions included *Loup* and *Cheval de halage* (1905), *Chien fox-terrier* (1907), *Eléphant* (1913), *Lion marchant* and *Tigre de Java mangeant un sanglier* (1914), these last two subjects produced in a limited casting.

Paul Jouve pursued his activity after World War I. He is noted as the author of a bronze entitled *Lion tuant une chèvre,* placed in front of the group of big game of the Jardin des Plantes in 1937, and of another group in gilded bronze entitled *Taureau et daim,* executed the same year for one of the fountains of the basins of the Palais de Chaillot.

In addition to the animals executed in gritstone (sandstone), of further note among Jouve's bronzes are *Combat de mouglons,* 23 x 56 cm, *Le Hibou,* inkwell, 17 cm, *Panthère marchant,* 13 x 31 cm, and *Trois Singes,* 16 cm, etc.

MUSEUMS
Paris, Decorative Arts
Guenon protégeant ses deux petits, 16 cm.

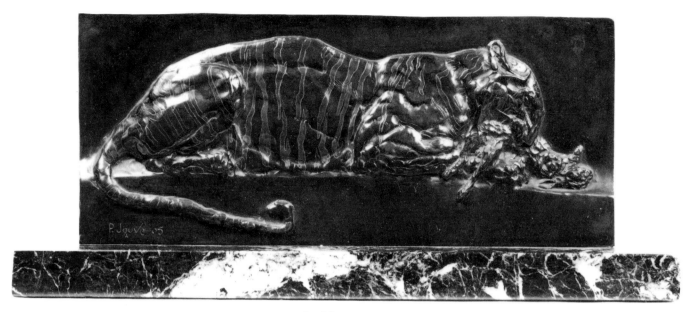

Paul Jouve,
Tigre du Bengale, bas-relief, 20 x 50 cm (1905).

SALES

Cléo, le chien à la dragée, 45 cm (A. Rudier; perhaps a
sole proof) Drouot, June 24, 1980.

Eléphants dans un décor de jungle, pair of doors, 274 x
198 cm each, Drouot, November 23, 1983, rooms 5
and 6 (320,000 F).

Lion dévorant un sanglier, 32 x 97 cm (A. Rudier),
Sotheby London, June 7, 1984.

Le Lion au marcassin, 43 cm, Enghien, October 25,
1982.

Panthère, bas-relief, 50 x 83.5 cm, Enghien, December
4, 1983.

Le Singe et l'idole, 19 cm L., Drouot, November 20,
1984, room 10.

Tigre dévorant sa proie, 32 cm L., Versailles, November
8, 1981.

Tigre emportant un cerf, 25.5 x 41.5 cm, Enghien, June
21, 1981.

JULLIEN, HIPPOLYTE ANDRÉ

Born in Gap, 1840

For nearly a dozen years, from 1866 to 1876,
Jullien exhibited at the Salon, showing busts and
some statues made primarily in plaster. Later he
taught in Switzerland, until 1887. The museum of
Bordeaux possesses a bust in bronze by this sculptor, entitled *Cambronne,* 23 cm high.

Paul Jouve,
Grand Lion
dévorant un marcassin,
43 x 82 cm.

K

KAMPF, LÉOPALD EUGÈNE

Born in Clairvaux (Aube)

Under the Second Empire, Léopald Kampf was commissioned into the Third Infantry in Courbevoie and resided in Paris in 1870. He ended his career at the rank of general. His sculpted work, apparently not very abundant, was devoted to military subjects, as can be seen in his some consignments at the Salon: *Zouave au combat*, a statuette in bronze (1864), and *Gaulois combattant* and *Franc combattant*, two statuettes in plaster (1870). At the cemetery of the Père-Lachaise is found the bust in bronze of *Affry de la Monnoie*, 37 cm. The founder Daubrée reproduced many works by this sculptor, including *Chasseur buvant à son bidon, Conscrit faisant du maniement d'arme avec un balai, Vivandière,*, and *Zouave assis sur un tambour* (Ref. C. B. Metman). The Museum of Decorative Arts in Paris possesses a small bronze by Kampf entitled *Vivandière debout*, 32 cm.

KINSBURGER, SYLVAIN

Paris, January 21, 1855
April 21, 1935

S. KINSBURGER

A sculptor, medal-engraver, and a designer, Kinsburger began exhibiting a number of bronzes at the Salon in 1878, including *Faucheur, Passeur* (1887), *La Chasse, Maraudeur* (1889), another group of the *Chasse* (1890), *Rêverie* (1892), *La Reconnaissance* (1905), *Sous la feuillée* (1909), and *Flore* (1914). It is also necessary to note some statuettes in plaster, including *La Chanson* (1883), *Le Clairon* (1884), *Printemps nouveau* (1892), *Diane* (1893), *Farniente* (1910), *Football* (1912) and a statuette in marble, *Amour vainqueur* (1902), etc. Also known are some works cast in bronze, particularly *Joueur de football*, 45 cm, *Psyché et l'Amour*, 62 cm, and *Femme à la mandoline*, 80 cm.

Sylvain Kinsburger,
Le Preux, 31.5 cm.

SALES
Jeune Femme au chapeau, 19 cm, Angers, April 16, 1986.
Jeunes Femmes décolletées, two busts, 29 and 27 cm, Sotheby London, April 28, 1982.
Les Vendanges, Reims, October 27, 1985.

KLEY, LOUIS

Sens, March 17, 1833
Sens, March 8, 1911

L.KLEY

This artist first studied jewelry, and then, while still very young, began to sculpt. He participated at the Salon beginning in 1853, with noteworthy statuettes in plaster.imitating ivory: *Rose du matin, Rose du soir* (1859), and *Egyptienne puisant de l'eau* (1861). Other plaster statuettes shown at the Salon include *Aspasie, Pandore* (1868), *L'Amour suppliant* (1877), *L'Amour mendiant* (1881), *L'Oubliée* (1888), *Enfant au baiser* (1889), *Jeanne d'Arc apprenant sa condamnation, La Marguerite effeuillée* (1890), and *Le Supplice de Jeanne d'Arc* (1897). He also exhibited statuettes in patinated bronze at the Salon, including *Perdrix* (Exposition of 1855) and *Bacchante* (Salon of 1857), and in silvered bronze, including *Petit Bandit* (1885) and *Amour méditant* (1886). Outside of the Salon, he is known for a certain number of statuettes ·and small groups of children, small animals, and birds. Particularly noteworthy are the following bronzes, which appeared on the market at different times: *L'Amour bondissant,* 15 cm, *L'Amour courant,* 15 cm, *L'Amour prisonnier, La Colère, L'Envie* (two figures of young boys), 15.5 cm, *Danseuse nue aux castagnettes, Danseuse nue au tambourin, Eve, Gavroche,* a statuette in gilded bronze, *Jeune Fumeur, Marquis,* a statuette in gilded bronze, and *Taureau,* etc.

MUSEUMS
Guéret
Lévrier en arrêt, 8.6 cm.

SALES
Amour perché sur une coloquinte, 14.5 cm, Drouot, June 17, 1985, room 9.
Femme nue accroupie, 23.5 cm,Toulouse, November 6, 1986.

*Korschmann,
Femme-fleur, lighted flower girl
in gilded and patinaed bronze, 64 cm
(Louchet, founder).*

KORSCHMANN, CHARLES, ALSO SPELLED

KORSCHANN

Brno (Czechoslovakia), 1872—?

Korschmann has been compared to his compatriot, the painter Alphonse Mucha, of whom he had executed a portrait in bust. Adept in Art Nouveau techniques like Mucha, Korschmann focused particularly on modeling feminine figures, busts, children, and peasant subjects. After some studies in Vienna, Berlin, and Paris, he established himself in the French capital and exhibited at the Salon between 1894 and 1906. His noteworthy contributions there include *Buste de Mucha* (plaster in 1902, marble in 1903), *La Comtesse de M.,* a statuette in bronze (1905), and *L'Assaut,* a group in plaster (1906). Many of his works were cast in bronze by Louchet. Also known among his works are *Berger et moutons,* a group in bronze, 30 cm, and *Femme nue se drapant,* gilded bronze, 51 cm, as well as some cups, vases, flower stands, and lamps in bronze and in composition, ornamented by figures in relief typical of the turn-of-the-century period.

SALES
Bergère et brebis, 38 cm (Eug. Blot), Christie's New York, December 13, 1983.
Bouquetière lumineuse, décor de femme-fleur en haut relief, gilded and patinated bronze, 64 cm (Louchet, founder), Drouot, May 14, 1986.

LABATUT, JULES JACQUES

Toulouse, July 31, 1851

Labatut won the first prize of Rome in 1881 and exhibited regularly at the Salon, where he showed a number of busts, including *Roland*, which was destined for the Carnot Plaza in Toulouse. The museum of this city preserves two bronzes by Labatut: *L'Architecte Esquié*, a bust of 58.2 cm, and *Les Heures*, a statue of 121 cm.

LACOMBE, GEORGES

Versailles, 1868
Alençon, 1916

Born to a family of artists and enjoying a certain fortune, this painter and sculptor did not really intend to sell his works. A member of the group of the Nabis of Pont-Aven starting in 1892, he painted a number of portraits and sculpted some busts, bas-reliefs, figurines for the theatre of marionettes, and types of Breton people. He preferred to sculpt in wood, and worked almost exclusively in it, especially mahogany. His style, very close to that of his painter friends, often evokes Emile Bernard and Gauguin. In a 1969 exhibition in Paris, organized by the Pacitti Gallery, only a single bronze entitled *Bûche* appeared, cast by Valsuani from a work in wood and numbered 6/12.

Also known are some busts and medallions in bronze, portraits of contemporaries, particularly of Nabis. Some editions were made after Lacombe's death by his inheritors.

SALES
Buste de Pierre Bonnard, 56 cm, (Valsuani 1/6), Brest, December 12, 1982.
Danse bretonne, 21 x 66.5 cm (Valsuani 1/12), Drouot, June 19, 1984, rooms 5 and 6.

LAFOND, EMILE

Paris, July 10, 1853
Paris, May 6, 1916

L'Art décoratif, a statue in stone ornamenting the entrance of the Grand Palais at the corner of the

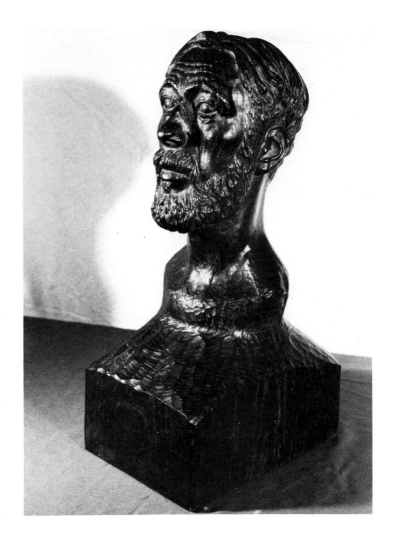

Georges Lacombe,
Buste de Pierre Bonnard, 56 cm
(Valsuani 1/6).

Cours la Reine (Queen's court), carries the signature of this sculptor and painter. Lafond exhibited at the Salon, in the sculpture section, from 1886 to 1902. Of note there are two bronzes, *Paysanne de l'Oise*, a bust from 1886, and *Tête de paysanne* from 1893. Lafond also sculpted some works in marble polychrome, incorporating different materials like onyx, fluorine spar (mineral), and lithographic stone.

LAFRANCE, JULES ISIDORE

Paris, December 16, 1841
Paris, January 16, 1881

The son of an ornamental sculptor, Lafrance also practiced painting. It was, however, his sculpted work which won him the most success—namely, the first prize of Rome in 1870. In 1861 he had started to exhibit at the Salon. Primarily, he produced works of religious character, with an apparent predilection for the personage of Saint Jean-Baptiste. Lafrance represented him many times, in full-length sculptures as well as in bust. He also worked on the decoration of some monuments (including the Louvre) and furnished models to some goldsmiths, among whom was Christofle. The Susse foundry cast, in bronze, his *Saint Jean-Baptiste enfant* in many dimensions: 95, 70, 59, 42 and 26 cm. A statuette in silver representing *Notre-Dame de Lourdes*, 1.10 meters high, belongs to the Vatican. The museum of Alençon possesses a bronze of 1.50 m, *Saint Jean-Baptiste* (1873).

Jules Isidore Lafrance,
Saint Jean-Baptiste enfant,
40 cm (Susse).
J. Ginepro Collection, Monaco.

LAITIE, CHARLES RENÉ

Paris, 1782
Paris, December 13, 1862

Laitie won the first prize of Rome in 1804 on the theme of *Méléagre refusant de secourir sa ville*, and then exhibited at the Salon from 1812 to 1838. He returned to Italy in the 1840s, and apparently stopped sculpting in this period. His work was composed of religious, historical or allegorical statues executed for diverse monuments, including the cathedral of Arras, the Parisienne churches of Saint-Merri, Saint-Etienne-di-Mont, Saint-Gervais, Notre-Dame-de-Lorette (*La Charité*), the Louvre, the Bourse, and the Arc de Triomphe. A statuette in bronze by this artist, *Homère*, 31 cm, appeared at the museum of Angers.

LAMBERT, EMILE PLACIDE

Paris, December 2, 1835
Paris, April 27, 1897

A rich artist and the proprietor of the château de Ferney (where Voltaire had lived), Lambert sculpted a number of busts of contemporaries for Swiss clients. He also sculpted statues of *Voltaire*, including that which ornamented the courtyard of city hall of the first district in Paris, and anecdotal works about rural life. At the Salon, where he exhibited starting in 1867, one notices some statues in bronze such as *Retour des champs* (1870), *Cléopâtre* (1875), *Innocence* (1880), *Premier Désir* (1884), and a statue in plaster, *Après la moisson* (1880).

Thiébaut cast an edition of *L'Italienne* in bronze, 75 and 44 cm. This piece was exhibited at the Salon under the title *Retour des champs* and was sometimes called *La Moissonneuse*.

LAMI, STANISLAS

Paris, November 30, 1858
February 1944

Grandson of the painter Bidault, Lami was simultaneously a sculptor and a writer. He was in effect the author of an important dictionary for sculptors, covering periods from antiquity to the 19th century. At the Salon he exhibited many busts and statues in plaster or in marble, some waxes and some bronzes, starting in 1882. Among the bronzes exhibited are a mask, *La Lune* (1885), and some busts, *Rembrandt* (1896), *Léonard de Vinci*, and *Le Titien* (1909). Some of his major works are in marble: *L'Epave* (1887), *La Première Faute* (1891), *Le Silence de la tombe* (1893), *Jeune Femme aux pigeons* (1897), and *Les Saisons de la vie* (1908). Also of note are some busts in wax: *Quentin de la Tour*, *Première communiante* (1905), *Souvenir de Florence* (1906), and some others in plaster including *Berlioz* (1884), which was cast in bronze.

SALES
Chien regardant un escargot dans son plat, 26 cm, Drouot, December 2, 1983, room 5.
Chien regardant un escargot dans son plat, 41 cm, Drouot, December 9, 1982, room 8.

Stanislas Lami,
Buste de Rembrandt
(Siot-Decauville).

LA MONACA, FRANCIS

Catanzaro (Italy), February 10, 1882
1926

La Monaca exhibited in Rome, London, and Paris, and his principal works were busts of contemporaries and figures of people, real or allegorical. In 1908, he sent to the Salon two statuettes in bronze, *Danseur* and *Siffleur;* in 1912, he sent a piece called *Napoléon 1er équestre* in bronze, and a group in plaster, *Les Héros de la mer;* in 1914, these were followed by a figure in bronze, *La Pauvreté.* Some of La Monaca's works were cast by Valsuani.

SALES
Danseuse nue, 38 cm (C. Valsuani), Brive, November 17, 1985.
Homme en smoking, 80 cm (Valsuani), Drouot, May 23, 1984, rooms 5 and 6.

LAMOURDEDIEU, RAOUL

Faugerolles (Lot-et-Garonne), February 2, 1877
Pierrefonds, May 8, 1953

A sculptor and an engraver of medals, this well-reputed artist worked a great deal after the First World War. Among his early works, which often have an anecdotal character, the following were exhibited at the Salon de la Société Nationale des Beaux-Arts:

Raoul Lamourdedieu,
Cheval attelé,
39 cm
(1903).

Francis La Monaca,
Danseuse nue,
38 cm
(C. Valsuani).

L'Esclave de la vie, a statue in plaster (1905), *Caïn*, a statue in plaster (1906), *Femme à la chemise* and *La Douleur*, two statuettes in bronze (1908), *Le Cordonnier* and *Le Terrassier*, two statuettes in plaster (1912), and *Diane*, bronze (1914). There are some statuettes in bronze which he exhibited at the same time at the Salon d'Automne: in 1905, *L'Eté*, *L'Esclave*, and *Pensive*, and in 1906, *Dernier Apprêt*, *L'Essayage*, *La Coiffure*, *La Chemise*, *La Toilette*, and *La Douleur*.

MUSEUMS
Albi
Le Soir, 84 cm.

SALES
L'Athlète, 30 cm, Drouot, 1977.
Cheval attelé, 39 cm (1903), Saint-Dié, February 27, 1983.

LANCELOT-CROCE, MARCELLE RENÉE

Paris, January 26, 1854
Around 1938

A sculptor and and an engraver of medals, Lancelot-Croce divided her activity between Paris and Rome, where she had married the Italian sculptor Croce. She also spent time in Troyes, the museum of which possesses many of her works, in particular some medals and placques. She participated at the Salon starting in 1878 with a rather large number of bronze medallions, busts that were often executed in bronze, and some figures. Especially notable are *Faune du bois de Clamart*, a bust in bronze (1882), *La Famille*, a bas-relief in plaster

(1891), *La Chasse*, a medallion in bronze (1895), and *Le Roi Victor-Emmanuel en Calabre*, a bas-relief in bronze (1906).

MUSEUMS
Lille
L'Amore sparso per tutto, bas-relief, 43 x 34 cm.
Narbonne
La Famille, bas-relief, 45 x 36 cm.
Troyes
This museum possesses nearly thirty works, medals, medallions and plaques representing contemporary personalities, particularly:

Adolfo Venturi, plaquette, 13.3 x 9 cm.
A. Boucher, plaquette, 12.7 x 8.5 cm.
Carolus Duran, plaquette, 11.2 x 8 cm.
Docteur J. Chompret, plaquette, 12 x 9.5 cm.
Ernest et Geroges Bonbon, plaquette, 22.5 x 16.5 cm.
Hans Saint-Lerche, plaquette, 12.5 x 8.5 cm.
Hommage au maréchal Foch, La Marne, 1918, medallion, 20 cm diam.
Lion couché avec arbustes, medallion, 21 cm diam.
Marcelle Lancelot, plaquette, 14 x 13.2 cm.
Renner Behmer, plaquette, 11.5 x 8.5 cm.
La Ville de Troyes, medallion, 20 cm diam (1919).
Vittorio-Emmanuele re d'Italia, plaquette, 21.3 x 13.7 cm (1925).
Wilhelm von Siemens, plaquette, 12.5 x 8.8 cm.

LANCERAY, EUGÈNE ALEXANDROVITCH

1848
Saint Petersburg, 1886

The very evocative production of this Russian artist, composed nearly entirely of horses, horsemen, and country people, is especially known by the

Eugène Alexandrovitch Lanceray, La Troïka, 30 cm L. (1880).

Eugène Lanceray,
Grande Fantasia arabe,
80 x 107 cm.

complete edition produced by the Susse foundry. The catalog includes more than a hundred statuettes and small groups in bronze. The following is a list of the most outstanding works, in the order in which they were presented:

Moujik au tonneau, 11 cm.
Pâtre couché, 7 x 14 cm.
Enfant à la brouette, 8 x 11 cm.
Petit batelier, 10 x 19 cm.
Enfants russes (pair of flat candlesticks), 8 cm.
Tcherkess en embuscade, 8 x 20 cm.
Etalon arabe, 15 x 18 cm.
Fellah à l'amphore, 14 cm.
Petit Saharien à cheval, 15 cm.

Ordonnance sous Grosnoye, 15 cm.
Arbalétrier sous Grosnoye, 18 cm.
Fauconnier sous Louis XIII, 15 cm.
Amazone sous Louis XIII, 14 cm.
Trompette de mousquetaire, 15 cm.
Petit cavalier russland, 12 cm.
Retour du labour, 18 cm.
Petit Napolitain sur un âne, 15 cm.
Courrier du désert sur dromadaire, 17 cm.
Petit Cavalier moujik, 21 cm.
Petit Cavalier tcherkess, 22 cm.
Fantasia tcherkess, 27 cm.
Ane d'Alger, 18 x 22 cm.
Type kabyle, 24 cm.

①

②

Bourriquier arabe, 22 cm.
Traîneau de ville à deux figures, 17 x 28 cm.
Baskire au lasso.
Fantasia arabe, 33 cm.
Circassien à cheval fumant, 27 cm.
Géorgien à cheval caracolant, 27 cm.
Tcherkess à cheval regardant en arrière, 27 cm.
Baskire à cheval, coup de vent, 27 cm.
Chasseur au départ (equestrian), 26 cm.
Chasseur au retour (equestrian), 25 cm.
La Fuite (horseman), 19 x 27 cm.
Hors de combat (fallen horseman), 13 x 32 cm.
Porte-Enseigne, 28 cm H.
Encrier, paysanne russe, 17 x 28 cm.
Adieux du cosaque (on horseback), 43 and 26 cm.
Chamelier et deux chameaux, 25 cm.
Troika au repos, 18 x 35 cm.
Gardien de troupeau à cheval, 40 cm.
Chasseur d'Afrique, 32 cm.
Attelage de boeufs du Caucase, 18 x 35 cm.
Kabyle marchand d'eau, 26 x 32 cm.

③

④

1) *Eugène Alexandrovitch Lanceray, Teleska, quatre paysans, 31 x 63 cm.*

2) *Eugène Alexandrovitch Lanceray, Taboun au repos, 30 x 45 cm (1880).*

3) *Eugène Alexandrovitch Lanceray, Paysanne russe à cheval.*

4) *Eugène Alexandrovitch Lanceray, Baskire au lasso, 22 cm.*

Le Koumiss, 24 x 37 cm.
Encrier Pouchkine (the head of Pushkin as an old man), 18 x 36 cm.
Arabe et son fils tué, 32 cm.
Cosaque poursuivant l'ennemi, 30 cm.
Cosaque du Don grand trot, 37 cm.
Trompette de hussard, 37 cm.
Boyard capitaine d'arme, 41 cm.
Opritchnick garde du corps, 40 cm.
Vachère et veau, 29 cm.
Pâtre et brebis, 30 cm.
Les Deux Mères, 30 cm.
Dans les steppes (two horsemen), 30 cm.
Troïka au départ, 23 x 43 cm.
Retour du vainqueur (a racehorse), 40 cm.
Cosaque à cheval et jeune fille, 38 cm.
Afghan du Nord, 43 cm.
Labour à quatre boeufs, 23 x 55 cm.
Fauconnier russe à cheval, 48 cm.
Teleska quatre paysans, 31 x 63 cm.
Arabe à cheval au lionceau, 49 cm.
Arabe à cheval avec deux faucons, 46 cm.

Chasse au Birkout, 54 cm.
Cheik arabe, 47 cm.
Hyde Park (a group of three horsemen).
Steeple-Chase (three racehorses), 31 x 45 cm.
Cosaque porte-drapeau, 63 cm.
Cosaque fourrageur, 52 cm.
Arabe à cheval, riche marchand, 58 cm.
Après le combat (an equestrian group), 49 cm.
Prise du cheval sauvage, 44 x 63 cm.
Passage des Balkans (an equestrian group), 38 x 52 cm.
Swiatoslaw (an equestrian character), 54 cm.
Grande Troïka d'hiver, 47 x 102 cm and 38 x 60 cm.
Guerrier épique (a horseman bearing a flag), 80 cm.
Taboun au repos (people and a group of horses), 41 x 87 cm.
Taboun en marche, 52 x 85 cm.
Les Trois Cosaques fourrageurs, 58 x 95 cm.
Grande Fantasia arabe (four horsemen), 80 x 107 cm.
Huntsmann, 51 cm.
Grande Charrette tarentasse, 50 x 97 cm.
Emir de Boukhara, 49 cm.

Lanceray also had certain of his works cast in Saint Petersburg by the founder Chopin, as well as in Poland. They were frequently signed in Cyrillic characters.

SALES

Cavalier algérien, 44.5 cm (Chopin, founder), Enghien, June 14, 1981.

Cavalier dressant un cheval, 44.5 cm, Sotheby London, March 20, 1986.

Cavalier à la lance, chargeant, Sotheby London, April 28, 1982.

Cavalier russe, 22.5 cm, Sotheby Amsterdam, June 25, 1982.

Chasseurs à cheval, deux statuettes, 27 cm, Sotheby London, March 21, 1985.

Chasseur à cheval tenant un faucon, 50 cm (Chopin), Drouot, January 24, 1983, room 1.

Chevaux de course sautant un obstacle, 27 cm, Sotheby London, November 8, 1984.

Chien de chasse, 18.5 cm, Sotheby London, March 8, 1984.

Clairon à cheval, 20 cm (Chopin), Enghien, October 6, 1985.

Cosaque, 45 cm, Brusells, September 15, 1986.

Cosaque debout sur sa selle, 28 cm, Enghien, June 14, 1981.

Cosaque au galop, 33 cm, Washington, December 8, 1985.

Cosaque prenant un cheval au lasso, 43 cm (Chopin), Sotheby London, Novmeber 8, 1984.

Fantasia arabe, quatre cavaliers, 63 cm, Enghien, October 21, 1984 (sold at auction for 300,000 F).

Femme russe à cheval, L'Isle-Adam, April 28, 1985.

Le Grand Fauconnier à cheval, 48.5 cm (Chopin), Drouot, May 6, 1981.

Jeune Cavalier conduisant deux chevaux et un poulain, 20 x 29 cm. (1878; Chopin), Enghien, October 19, 1980.

Jeune Cavalier embrassant sa fiancée, 21 cm, Sotheby London, April 28, 1982.

Jeune Cavalier quittant sa fiancée, 24 cm, Sotheby London, April 28, 1982.

Ours debout, 59 cm (1865), Sotheby London, March 17, 1983.

Soldats menant leurs montures à l'abreuvoir, 81 cm L., Sotheby London, February 15, 1984.

La Troïka, 30 cm L. (1880), Drouot, February 6, 1984, room 7.

Troïka avec couple de paysans, 51 cm, Sotheby London, March 8, 1984.

Trompette à cheval, 36 cm (Chopin), Enghien, June 14, 1981.

LANDOWSKI, PAUL

Paris, June 1, 1875
March 31, 1961

An official sculptor wityh a strong reputation, Landowski received innumerable commissions and made a quantity of monumental works and commemorative monuments all over the world. Notable, among others, are the *Mur de la Réformation* in Geneva (executed in collaboration with Henri Bouchard in 1917), the front of Paris's Institut océanographique, the door in bronze of the school of medicine in Paris, and some works in Vienna, Madrid, and Brazil. After spending part of his youth in Algiers, Landowski won the first prize of Rome in 1900 with *David combattant,* 120 cm, of which three proofs in bronze would be cast. His last consignment from Rome is one of his best-known and most remarkable groups, *Les Fils de Caïn,* 240 cm, which won great success when it was exhibited in plaster at the Salon of 1906. The bronze cast from it was placed at the time in Napóleon's court in the Louvre. This work summarizes the artist's style: a sense of

*Paul Landowski,
La Danseuse aux serpents,
70 cm (1914).*

the grandeur and of theatrical expression, and, simultaneously, a sense of realism and incontestable sobriety and moderation. Landowski was named director of the villa Médicis in Rome in 1933.

Beginning in the 1930s, some works of small dimensions were cast in bronze in limited and numbered castings (Cf. Raymond Isay, *Paul Landowski,* 1931). Notable among subjects made before 1914 are:

Bédouine à la cruche, 39 cm; some proofs carrying the seal of the founder L. Gatti.

Le Borgne, bust.

La Charmeuse de paons; 25 numbered proofs.

Combat de vautours (1908); 15 numbered proofs.

La Danseuse aux serpents (194); 6 numbered proofs.

David combattant, reduction of a group from 1900, 25 numbered proofs.

Enfant rieur, bust.

Fakir au serpent (1908); 25 numbered proofs.

Les Fils de Caïn (1906).

Le Haleur, bust.

Mademoiselle Paulette Landowski.

Petit Coureur arabe.

Porteur d'eau aveugle (1905), 43 cm.

Le Pugiliste; 15 proofs.

Soun, danseuse sacrée.

Le Voleur d'oranges (1905).

Mademoiselle Yvonne Behrendt.

It is necessary to mention Landowski's portraits as well; some were in medallion form, and others were in bronze.

MUSEUM
Boulogne-Billancourt

Part of Paul Landowski's studio and home in Boulogne were transformed into a museum-garden where a number of works were reunited, including some projects, maquettes, and drawings. Of particular note are the bronzes from before 1914, listed here with the names of the founders:

Combat de vautours, 48 cm (1908; Gatti).
Danseuse aux serpents, 70 cm (1914; Gatti).
David combattant, 120 cm (1900; Susse).
Fakir aux serpents, 50 cm (1908; Leblanc-Barbedienne).
Les Fils de Caïn, 72 cm (1906; Herbrandt).
L'Hymne à l'Aurore, 230 cm (1908; Rudier).
Porteur d'eau aveugle, 43 cm (1905; Leblanc-Barbedienne).
Porteuse d'eau arabe, 37 cm (1905; Gatti).
Le Voleur d'orange, 33 cm (1905; Gatti).

SALES
Bédouine à la cruche, 39 cm (L. Gatti), Drouot, June 22, 1983, room 1.
Le Charmeur de serpents, 50 cm (L. Gatti No.13), Drouot, June 6, 1984, room 2.
David combattant, 78 cm (Bisceglia frères No.13), Drouot, June 27, 1983, room 6.

LANFRANCHI, LAMPIERO (PIERRE LÉON)

Born in Paris

A sculptor of animals, Lanfranchi exhibited principally statuettes in plaster, in particular at the Société Nationale des Beaux-Arts. These pieces included: Vieux Jaguar sur la défensive and Ma petite chienne (1909), Après la lutte, Peau-Rouge et jaguar and Panthère dans l'attitude d'un sphinx (1910), Lion sur un rocher (1912). A bronze, Après la lutte, 49 cm (Gastini 9/12), was sold at the Drouot hotel on February 6, 1984, room 7.

LANSON, ALFRED DÉSIRÉ

Orléans, March 11, 1851
Paris, April 1898

Lanson won the first grand prize of Rome in 1876 with Jason rapportant la Toison d'or. His work includes some allegories, and figures inspired by antiquity. He is the author of decorative sculptures for the hotel de ville of Limoges, of a statue in bronze called Jeanne d'Arc blessée à la bataille de Jargeau (1898) for the city of Jargeau, and of a group in marble called Judith et Holopherne, then destined for the gardens of the Tuileries. He exhibited at the Salon from 1870 to 1897. He sent a statue in bronze of Jason to the Exposition Universelle of 1878. It was exhibited again in 1892 at the Société Nationale des Beaux-Arts, along with two statuettes in gilded bronze, Salammbô and Diane, and a statuette in marble, Coup de vent.

The Susse foundry cast Jason rapportant la Toison d'or in three dimensions, 100, 75 and 50 cm.

MUSEUMS
Calais
La Vierge et l'Enfant, medallion in bas-relief, 56.5 cm diam. (Rome 1880).
Orléans
Diane, statuette in gilded bronze (1892).
Salammbô, 54 cm (1892).

LANZIROTTI, ANTONIO GIOVANNI

Naples, May 9, 1839—?

Lanzirotti studied in Palerme, and then in Paris, where he exhibited a statue, La Vierge gauloise, at the Salon of 1859. He is also to be creast with some busts, some medallions, and a statue in bronze, L'Esclave grecque, which belongs to the museum of Nice.

SALES
Le Printemps de la vie, 85.5 cm, Sotheby London, November 10, 1983.
Satyre, 71 cm, Milan, April 22, 1982.

LAOUST, ANDRÉ LOUIS ADOLPHE

Douai, September 16, 1843
Paris, May 7, 1924

Starting in 1868, this student of Jouffroy was a regular and prolific contributor to the Salon. His submissions included a number of bronzes—some busts and statues—among which were the following: Spes, for a monument in Roubaix (1880), Le Chanteur indien Ganhai (1886), Lully, a statuette in silvered bronze, Buste de Pierrot, a personage whom he would frequently portray (1889), L'Inspiration, a statuette cast by Raingo frères (1892), L'Agriculture, a statue (1893), L'Inspiration and Pierrot, two busts (1894), and four statuettes: Le Menuet (1898), Chryséis (1906), Choisis, and Amour navigateur, the last in marble and bronze (1914). In 1913, he exhibited a statue symbolizing Electricité. It is necessary to mention some additional statues in plaster, including that of a violinist entitled Au clair de la lune or Fortune de Lully, 170 cm (1886; marble in 1888).

Lampiero Lanfranchi,
Lion terrassant un homme, 50 cm
(1910; Gustini casting).

Laplanche

Pierre-Albert Laplanche,
Cerf dix-cors,
hallali courant,
50 cm.

The Susse foundry cast *La Pavane* in two dimensions, 67 and 50 cm, whereas Thiébaut cast *L'Agriculture* and *L'Industrie*, each in 98, 59 and 38 cm. Also of note is a statuette of *Pierrot* or *Le Clown*, 85 cm.

MUSEUMS
Douai
Buste de Casimir Giroud, 50 cm (Barbedienne).
Lille
Louis Devémy, medallion, 39 cm diam. (1869).
Tourcoing
Le Menuet, 175 cm.

SALES
Le Joueur de cithare, Versailles, March 20, 1983.

LAPLANCHE, PIERRE-ALBERT

Lyon, 1826
Paris, 1873

Some works by this animal sculptor appeared at times on the market. At the Salon, he exhibited the terra cotta *Groupe d'oiseaux morts* in 1857, and two bronzes, *Etude de lama* in 1864 and *Cerf de France* in 1869.

MUSEUM
Reims
Chien basset, study, 14 x 28 cm.
Couple de chiens malinois, 40.2 x 45.8 cm.
Lévrier kurde en arrêt, 18.4 x 25 cm.
Martin-pêcheur sur un tronc d'arbre, 14 cm.
Sanglier blessé, 22 x 30.7 cm.

SALES
Berger allemand couché, 17 cm, Enghien, February 22, 1981.
Cerf dix-cors, hallali courant, 64 cm long, Reims, April 27, 1986.
Cerf poursuivi par deux chiens, 49 cm, Dijon, November 27, 1983.
Chien-loup assis, Vitry-le-François, April 21, 1986.
Combat de sangliers, 32 cm L., Versailles, June 16, 1984.

LAPORTE, EMILE

Paris, November 18, 1858
Paris, 1907

A genre and landscape painter, Laporte also made rather numerous sculptures which he exhibited at the Salon between 1881 and 1906. Particularly notable are *Buste de grand-mère*, in bronze, and *Départ pour le combat*, in plaster (1884), *Baiser maternel,* in bronze (1885), *Belluaire,* in bronze (1886 and Exposition Universelle of 1889), *Le Métal,* a statuette in plaster (1894), *A la fontaine,* a statuette in marble (1896), *Jeanne d'Arc recevant l'Épée de Robert de Baudricourt,* a group in marble and bronze (1899), and finally two busts in bronze: *Mon neveu* (1903) and *Portrait du petit Robert* (1905).

The Siot-Decauville foundry cast four bronzes by this artist: two statuettes, *Actéon* in 80, 53, 35 and 16 cm, and *Premières Armes,* and two busts, *Cigale* and *Hérodiade.* A work entitled *Gaulois* (or sometimes *Viking) avec son fils* is also designated under the title *Pro Patria. Premières Armes* and *Départ pour le combat,* seem to be a single work. The personage *Gaulois,* cast separately, is sometimes entitled *Vercingétorix.*

MUSEUMS
Angers
Buste de chef gaulois, 60 cm.
Autun
Pro Patria, 95 cm.
Clermont-Ferrand
Vercingétorix, 84 cm.
Tourcoing
Gaulois montrant le chemin à son fils, 45 cm.

SALES
Actéon, 35 cm (Siot-Decauville), Drouot, June 1, 1983, room 4.
La Défense du sol, 53 cm, Vitry-le-François, December 2, 1984.
La Défense du sol, 66 cm, Lokeren, April 20, 1985.
La Défense fu sol, 85.5 cm, Christie's London, July 18, 1983.
Jeune Femme au bouquet de roses, 118 cm (1889), Sotheby London, March 17, 1983.
Jeune Garçon et coq, 100 cm, Sotheby London, June 12, 1986.
Pro Patria, 61 cm, Nogent-le-Rotrou, November 28, 1982.

LAPORTE-BLAIRZY, LÉO
Toulouse, April 5, 1965
Paris, 1923

Laporte-Blairzy was the student of Falguière and of Antonin Mercié. The museum of Toulouse possesses a statuette of his work *Clémence Isaure,* 57.5 cm high. Also of note is another statuette in bronze representing a bather drying her leg.

LAQUIS, DOMINIQUE
Guebwiller, April 20, 1816- ?

An animal sculptor, Laquis sent some bronzes to the Salon, including *Chien d'arrêt* in 1859 and *Renard aux aguets* in 1868. The museum of Strasbourg possesses a small bronze, *Cigogne appuyée à des roseaux,* 15 cm high.

LARCHE, RAOUL
Saint-André-de-Cubzac (Gironde), October 22, 1860
Paris, June 2, 1912

RAOUL.LARCHE

Larche's activity corresponds with the pinnacle of the Art Nouveau period, of which he remains one of the most remarkable representatives. After some studies at the Ecole des Beaux-Arts, particularly

Emile Laporte,
Pro Patria, 61 cm.

under the direction of Jouffroy and of Falguière, he debuted at the Salon of 1884 and obtained the second prize of Rome in 1886.

In this era, Larche was greatly admired as a modern sculptor. He won one of his greatest successes with a sculpture of *Loïe Fuller*, in which she was enveloped in a whirlwind of sails. Fuller, a famous American dancer then performing with the beautiful Folies-Bergères troupe, inspired many editions of statuettes in bronze of different dimensions, often gilded, and often incorporating lamps with one or two lights.

At the Salon he successfully showed some works which were made the objects of subsequent castings: *Jésus enfant devant les docteurs*, marble (1891), *La Prairie et le ruisseau*, marble, *La Sève*, plaster (1893), and a group in bronze, *La Tempête* (1899).

Raoul Larche received some official commissions for monuments in Paris including the Grand Palais (the group of *La Musique*). Other commissions included those for the Exposition Universelle of 1900 and, in 1909, for a basin on the theme of *La Seine et ses affluents*, originally intended for the Carrousel but finally placed on the north corner of the Grand Palais. It still stands at that site, now facing the entrance of the Galeries nationales.

Siot-Decauville was Larche's usual founder, and cast *Loïe Fuller* in different sizes and patinas. Siot-Decauville cast a number of other works as well, mainly allegorical, and all displaying the abundant realism so typical of the era. These include:

L'Apôtre.
Bethsabée.
Douleur d'Oreste.
Fleur des prés, 95, 70, 50, 30 cm.
La Foi ou Jeanne d'Arc, 25 cm.

Raoul Larche,
Bacchanale,
gilded bronze, 44 cm.

Raoul Larche,
Petit Roi, 37 cm
(Siot-Decauville).

Raoul Larche,
Vingt Ans,
52 cm
(Siot-Decauville).

Raoul Larche,
Deux Jeunes Faunes,
45 cm.

Raoul Larche,
Les Roseaux,
73.5 cm
(Siot-Decauville).

1) Raoul Larche, Néréide sur un dauphin.

2) Raoul Larche, La Foi or Jeanne d'Arc, 24 cm (Siot-Decauville).

3) Raoul Larche, Bacchante jouant avec un enfant, gilded bronze, 60 cm.

*Raoul Larche,
La Sève
or Métamorphose
de Daphné, 32 cm
(Siot-Decauville).*

*Raoul Larche,
La Sève or
Métamorphose
de Daphné, 158 cm
(Siot-Decauville 1/3).*

*Raoul Larche,
Vannettes
aux cinq enfants,
16 x 50 cm
(Siot-Decauville).*

*Raoul Larche,
La Mer,
trophy in pewter,
76 cm
(Siot-Decauville).*

*Raoul Larche,
La Loïe Fuller,
33 cm.*

Raoul Larche,
La Loïe Fuller,
p in gilded bronze,
46 cm
(Siot-Decauville).

Raoul Larche,
La Loïe Fuller,
lamp in gilded bronze,
45.5 cm
(Siot-Decauville).

Jésus devant les docteurs, 37 cm.
Petit Roi, 30 cm.
La Prairie et le ruisseau, 53 cm.
Les Roseaux.
La Sève called also *La Métamorphose de Daphné* or
    Dryade.
La Tempête et les nuées.
Vingt Ans, 88, 70, 50 cm.
Les Violettes (a woman and two adolescents).
Les Blés, pair of lamps.

Some vases, cups, ashtrays, tobacco cans, table pieces, a centerpiece entitled *La Mer*, and another entitled *L'Etang* were made in pewter by the same founder. Also known are works of different materials, including bronze, marble, ivory, onyx, and rock crystal. Many major works by Larche were cast by the Sèvres factory.

MUSEUMS
Bordeaux
Bacchus enfant, 23 x 27.5 cm (Siot-Decauville).
La Garonne, 32 x 42 cm (Siot-Decauville).
Paris, Orsay
La Mer, table centerpiece in pewter (Siot-Decauville).
Paris, Petit Palais
Fleurs des prés, gilded bronze, 137 cm.
La Tempête et les nuées, 349 cm.

SALES
Bacchanale, gilded bronze, 44 cm, Cannes, November
    18, 1986.
Bacchante jouant avec un enfant, gilded bronze, 60 cm,
    Drouot, February 26, 1982, room 11.

Raoul Larche,
La Tempête et les nuées,
87 cm.

Raoul Larche,
Rêves,
pair of vases
in gilded bronze,
54 cm
(Siot-Decauville).

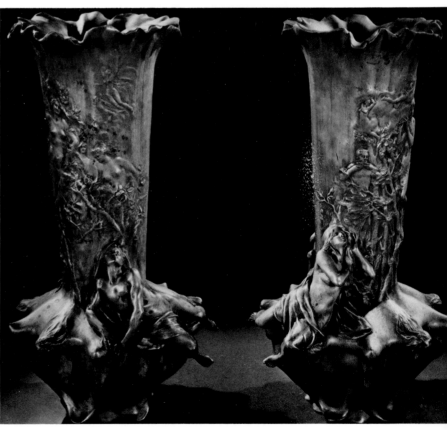

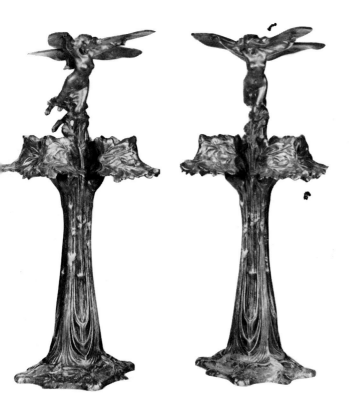

Raoul Larche, Les Blés,
pair of lamps in gilded bronze, 60 cm.

Deux Jeunes Faunes, *45 cm, Neuilly, April 15, 1986.*
Deux Jeunes Satyres, *44.5 cm, Sotheby London,*
November 10, 1983.
Faune sous une fleur, *lamp in gilded bronze, 40 cm*
(Siot-Decauville), Drouot, June 10, 1983, room10.
In nomine patris..., *95 cm, Drouot, June 11, 1987, room*
*7 (**see reproduction page* 652**).*
Jeanne d'Arc, *81 cm (Siot-Decauville), Morlaix, Novem-*
ber 3, 1986.
Jésus parmi les docteurs, *gilded bronze, 37 cm (Siot-*
Decauville), Drouot, February 6, 1984, room 7.
Jeune Fille, *bust, 37 cm (Siot-Decauville), Zurich,*
November 8, 1985.
Jeune Homme à l'épée, *90 cm, Lokeren, February 16,*
1985.
Loïe Fuller, *lamp in gilded bronze, 33 cm (Siot-*
Decauville), Drouot, February 15, 1984, room 7;
Corbeil-Essonnes, May 12, 1984; Sotheby Monaco,
October 7, 1984; Christie's New York, September
27, 1986.
Loïe Fuller, *lamp in gilded bronze, 46 cm (Siot-*
Decauville), Neuilly, May 19, 1984; Christie's New
York, May 24, 1984; Sotheby Monaco, March 17,
1985; Drouot, June 14, 1985, room 14; Drouot,
July 1, 1986, room 15.
Nu sur un rocher, *gilded bronze, 33.5 cm (Siot-*
Decauville), Sotheby London, May 2, 1985.
Petit Roi, *gilded bronze, 37 cm (Siot-Decauville),*
Drouot, May 23, 1984, room10.
Les Roseaux, *73.5 cm (Siot-Decauville), Drouot, Octo-*
ber 20, 1986, room 1.
Saint Jean-Baptiste, *37 cm, Drouot, June 14, 1982,*
room 7.
La Sève *or* Métamorphose de Daphné, *158 cm (Siot-*
Decauville 1/3), Enghien, January 31, 1982 (sold
for 245,000 F).
Trois Jeunes Filles entourant un jeune homme, *53 cm*
(Susse No. 2), Sotheby London, March 21, 1985.
Trois Nymphes, *lamp in gilded bronze, 62.5 cm (Siot-*
Decauville), Christie's New York, December 13,
1985.
Lampe au céleri, *gilded bronze, 71 cm, Tours, June 17,*
1985.

Paniers aux enfants, *five pieces of a table in gilded*
bronze, 46 cm L. max. (Siot-Decauville), Sotheby
Monaco, April 13, 1986.
Pendule ornée d'un globe surmonté d'une femme, *73.5*
cm (Siot-Decauville), Drouot, May 23, 1984.
Vannette aux cinq enfants, *centerpiece, 16 x 50 cm*
(Siot-Decauville), Drouot, May 23, 1984, room 10.
Paire de vases, Rêves, *gilded bronze, 54 cm (Siot-*
Decauville), Drouot, March 16, 1983, room 9.

LARROUX, ANTONIN
Toulouse, June 3, 1859
February 11, 1937

This student of Falguière participated rather
regularly at the Salon, starting in 1881, with figures
and groups evoking field work. Always on the same
theme, he made vases and inkwells in tin. Some
bronzes include the following: *Nymphe lutinant un
dauphin* (Salon of 1892), from a centerpiece; *Travaux
des champs;* two statuettes, *Moissonneur* and
Vendangeuse (1902); and other statuettes, including *Les Vendanges* (1905), *Travaux des champs* and
La Faneuse (1906), and *Les Foins* (1907).

Thiébaut cast *La Semeuse* in three dimensions,
78, 58 and 34 cm, and Siot-Decauville cast a bust of
a young girl smiling entitled *La Vigne.*

SALES
La Cribleuse de blé, *52 cm, Angers, March 23, 1983.*
La Vendangeuse, *91, Lokeren, April 14, 1984.*

Antonin Larroux,
La Cribleuse de blé, 52 cm.

LAURENT, EUGÈNE

Gray, April 29, 1832
Paris, 1898

The author of a statue in bronze of *Jacques Callot* for the city of Nancy, Laurent exhibited a number of busts and of medallions in plaster at the Salon between 1861 and 1893. He also exhibited there a statue in bronze of *Psyché* in 1886, and two statuettes, *Jeanne d'Arc* in marble in 1890, and *Jacques Callot* in terra cotta in 1893. Many of his works were cast in bronze, including the *Jeanne d'Arc*. Also notable are a statuette entitled *Jeune Faucheur* carrying the seal of Thiébaut and a statuette entitled *Pêcheuse* which was cast in many dimensions.

SALES

Buste de juene fille, 59 cm (Susse), Dunkerque, June 15, 1985; Sotheby London, March 20, 1986.
Jeanne d'Arc, 67 cm, Nancy, December 16, 1984.
Le Petit Faucheur, 36 cm, Sotheby London, March 26, 1980.

Eugène Laurent, Buste de jeune fille, 59 cm (Susse).

Adolphe Jean Lavergne, Gaulois, 73 cm.

LAURENT-DARAGON, CHARLES JOSEPH

Paris, February 12, 1833
Paris, September 1904

This artist was educated at the Ecole des Beaux-Arts and in the studio of Carpeaux. He made a number of portraits in bust and in medallion, often in bronze, as well as some full-length figures. Notable at the Salon, where he began exhibiting in 1863, are *Psyché*, a statuette in plaster (1874; statue in marble in 1892), and the following busts: *Raoul Duval, député* (1887), *Monsieur Céide* (1888), *L'Abbé Testary* (1890), and *Monsieur Emile Aimond, ingénieur* (1896). Laurent-Daragon seems also to have produced some animal subjects. *Taureau*, a statuette in bronze, was sold at the Drouot hotel on June 6, 1985, room 4.

LAVALETTE D'EGISHEIM, JACQUES

Born in Heidelberg

Lavalette d'Egisheim was the author of statues, statuettes and busts representing some famous artists, particularly singers and dancers; his works include representations of the dancer *Camille Leroux* (1844) and *Mademoiselle George dans le rôle de Lucrèce Borgia* (a statuette in plaster at the Salon of 1850). A casting in bronze, 40 cm, of *Mademoiselle Camille Leroux* appeared at the museum of decorative arts of Paris.

LAVERGNE, ADOLPHE JEAN

Born in Hautefort (Dordogne)

A student of Jouffory, Lavergne exhibited principally genre scenes and some busts at the Salon, starting in 1863: *Joueur de palet*, plaster (1863),

Perplexité, bronze (1893), and *Jeune Fille rieuse*, a bust in bronze (1894). Other known works by this artist are some statuettes cast in bronze, including *Jeune Pêcheur, Escrimeur, Gaulois, Jeune Homme et Jeune Femme en costume du XVIIIe siecle*, etc. A bust of *Léon Dierx*, 69 cm (1903), belongs to the museum in Saint-Denis de la Réunion which bears Lavergne's name. A statuette in bronze, *Charmeur de lézard*, 47 cm, was sold at the Drouot hotel on December 2, 1983, room 5.

LAVIGNE, HUBERT

Cons-la-Granville (Moselle), July 11, 1818
Paris, January 12, 1882

Admitted to the Ecole des Beaux-Arts in 1835, Lavigne next made works of sculpture for a number of monuments: the Louvre, the Palais-Royal, the city hall, the fountain Saint-Michel, the church of the Sorbonne, many bridges of Paris, the old Trocadéro, the chapelle royale of Dreux, and the cathedral of Bayeux. Notable at the Salon are *Jeune Faune*, a figurine in bronze (1859), *L'Amour*, a statue in marble, 90 cm, (1863), *Mercure inventant la lyre*, a statue in plaster (1877), *Daphnis*, a statue in bronze, 155 cm, for a park in Nancy (1879), etc. Lavigne published an interesting collection on the civil state of French artists, with the notes of decease or of burial since 1823.

Maurice Lebeau, Méhariste africain, 60 cm (Susse).

Adolphe Jean Lavergne, Jeune Pêcheur, 49 cm.

LEBEAU, MAURICE

Beauvais, March 11, 1885
Châtillon-sous-Bagneux, May 19, 1961

LEBEAU

Before the war of 1914-1918, Lebeau had exhibited at the Salon only in 1906, 1907 and 1909. His *Méhariste africain* was cast by Susse in many dimensions. A proof of 60 cm was sold in Melun on August 21, 1983; another, 86 cm, was sold in Enghien on October 16, 1983.

LEBOEUF, LOUIS JOSEPH

Lons-le-Saunier?
Paris, 1870

This artist, who participated at the Salon starting in 1857, is known for his works in plaster, including some statuettes: *Portrait d'un chasseur* (1859), *Portrait de M. Courbet* (1861), and *Le Docteur Meyniès, naturaliste,* as well as for a bust in bronze of *Victor Hugo* (1866), a model of which is owned by the museum Victor Hugo in Paris. The museum of Reims preserves a medallion by Leboeuf, *Portrait de Victor Diancourt,* 21.5 cm diam. (1868).

Charles Auguste Lebourg,
Le Travail, 48 cm.

LEBOURG, CHARLES AUGUSTE

Nantes, February 20, 1829
Paris, February 1906

Lebourg came to Paris in 1851 and received instruction from Rude. Although ignored by most Parisiens, he is nevertheless present in all the quarters of the capital. He is in effect the author of the caryatids of the fountains Wallace. These figures, inspired by the *Trois Grâces* of Germain Pilon, symbolize *La Simplicité, La Bonté, La Sobriété* and *La Charité.* Lebourg also worked for the Louvre, the city hall, and the church of the Trinity. Among the works which he sent to the Salon between 1852 and 1906 are some statues in bronze: *Joueur de biniou dansant la nigouce* (1857), *Jeune Oiseleur rendant la liberté à une hirondelle* (1868), and *Lion au repos* (1896), *Jeanne d'Arc* (1906). He also sent some statuettes and small groups, also in bronze: *Enfant nègre gouant avec un lézard* (1853), *Théodore Masonneuve* and *Le Printemps* (1889), *Le Baron d'Espeleta* (1893), and *Tête de setter Laverack* (1896). Also of note are some statuettes in terra cotta: *La Rosée, Le Parfum* (1861), and *L'Aurore* (1868). Finally, outside of the Salon, are his works of *Napoléon 1er* and of *Joséphine,* 51 cm. The museum of Nantes possesses a bust in bronze of *M. Cossé,* 79 cm (1889).

SALES

Le Forgeron or *Le Travail,* 48 cm, Sotheby London, November 7, 1985; Brest, November 18, 1986.
Jeune Oiseleur libérant une hirondelle, 165 cm (V. Thiébaut), Christie's London, March 20, 1984.
Joueur de biniou dansant, 97 cm (1856), Christie's Oklahoma (United States), September 24, 1981.

LECHESNE, AUGUSTE JEAN-BAPTISTE

Caen, 1815
Caen, November 2, 1888

AUGUSTE LECHESNE

An ornamentalist sculptor, Lechesne worked on the decoration of a number of facades. In Paris, where he established himself in 1840, he sculpted particularly the freize of the Maison Dorée, Boulevard des Italiens, and animals for a house in the Renaissance style at the Saint-Georges Plaza, as well as some groups representing dragons being trained by children for the railing around the basin of Neptune in Versaille. He readily combined young children and big animals in his compositions. At the Salon, he debuted in 1848 with *Amour et jalousie, combat d'oiseaux,* a group in terra cotta, and then exhibited *Effraie défendant sa proie,* a group in wood (1849), *Combat et frayeur,* and *Victoire et reconnaissance,* two groups in marble (1853), *Dénicheur,* a group in bronze destined for a square in Caen (1857), and *Terre-Neuve expirant sur la tombe de son maître,* plaster (1878). A group in bronze, *Chasse au sanglier,* appeared at the Exposition Universelle of 1855.

Auguste Lechesne,
Chiens attaquant un sanglier,
35 x 53 cm.

The museum of Caen possesses a life-size bust in bronze of *M. Bertrand, ancien maire de la ville* by this artist. At the château of Compiègne is found a group cast by Eck and Durand, *Chiens attaquant un sanglier,* 35 x 53 cm (1853).

SALES
Chiens attaquant un sanglier, 35 x 53 cm, château d'Echailly, near Saumur, June 23, 1985.
Deux Perroquets sur une branche, 111 cm, Sotheby London, June 12, 1986.

LECOINTE, LÉON
Paris, April 9, 1826
Paris, 1913

Lacointe's consignments to the Salon, where he debuted in 1850, include a number of bronzes. Of note are, in 1863, an ornamented vase in bas relief entitled *Les Arts de la paix* (presented also at the Exposition Universelle of 1867); in 1869, a bust, *Il Vecchio;* in 1870, a cup, *Le Départ d'Endymion;* in 1874, a statuette, *L'Adieu;* in 1876, a statue, *La Pêche;* in 1877, a vase, *Le Printemps et l'Automne;* in 1882 and in 1886, two statues then destined for the square of Anvers, *Sedaine* and *Diderot.* The museum of Grenoble possesses Lecointe's bust in bronze, *Vieillard,* 49 cm, cast by Gruet.

LECORNET, NICOLAS
Born in Gourgeon (Upper-Saône)

Lecornet's work includes allegories, nymphs, and figures of children and young girls which he exhibited at the Salon from 1880 to 1884. His signature somtimes reads "Lecorney."

SALES
Le Baiser de l'enfant, gilded bronze, 32 cm (Susse), Drouot, December 2, 1983, room 5.
Espagnol à la guitare, 83 cm, Orléans, May 19, 1984.

LECOURTIER, PROSPER
Grémilly (Meuse), July 12, 1851
Paris, January 19, 1924

The life of this sculptor, who studied in Paris under the direction of Frémiet and Coutant, is little known. His work, on the other hand, is known to be abundant, and is entirely devoted to animals, including dogs, horses, birds, and big game. He participated at the Salon almost each year from 1875 to his death in 1924; indeed, a consignment of his work appeared at the Salon in 1925, crcast to the late Lecourtier. Memorable contributions to the Salon include a number of bronzes: *Cheval arabe* (1879), *Chien et ses petits, Chien bull-terrier* (1882), *Chienne* (1883), *Marchand de volaille* (1884), *Chien d'arrêt*

419

Prosper Lecourtier,
Chien de meute, 48 cm.

Prosper Lecourtier,
Deux Chiens de chasse attachés, 65 cm.

Prosper Lecourtier,
La Fantasia arabe,
78 cm.

Prosper Lecourtier,
Prenez garde au chien!,
45 cm (1878).

(1886), *Chiens bassets* (1889), *Cheval de trait* (1901), *Course de char romain,* gilded bronze (1904), *Départ pour le marché* (1905), *En arrêt,* a group of dogs (1906), *Lionne* (1907), *Tempête,* gilded bronze, and *Lion* (1907), *Cerf* (1909), *Lionne au repos* (1911), etc. Some characteristic works of note in other materials are *Mouette rieuse* (1875) and *Pigeon voyageur au repos* (1876), both in wax; *Tigre guettant sa proie,* plaster (1877); *Famille de tigres,* plaster (1892); *La Danse de l'ours,* plaster; and *Boeuf nivernais,* sandstone of Jeanneney (1914). Also notable is *Fantasia arabe* and a number of other subjects—dogs, chickens, bulls, and deer—some of which may have been exhibited at the Salon before or after World War I.

Prosper Lecourtier also worked in collaboration with Hippolyte Moreau, evidenced by some bronzes that carry the signatures of both artists. The first of these pieces is a group entitled *Piqueur au relais,* on which Lecourtier modeled the dogs.

MUSEUMS
Guéret
Lion rugissant sur un rocher, bronze and marble, 47 cm.
Tarbes, museum Foch
Coq gaulois, gilded bronze, 70 cm (offered to the Foch marshall).

SALES
Arabe sur le sentier de la guerre, 84 cm, Sotheby London, November 8, 1984.
Bouledogue enchaîné, 25 cm, Enghien, March 2, 1980.
Cerf bramant et sa biche, 58 cm (Jollet, founder), Enghien, February 22, 1981.
Chien arrêté devant un lapin, 16.6 cm, Drouot, October 25, 1985, room 4.
Chien basset, 24 cm, Drouot, October 24, 1980.
Chien de meute, 48 cm, Deauville, October 18, 1984.
Deux Chiens de chasse attachés, 65 cm, Rambouillet, November 18, 1984.
Tête de chien, 51 cm, Christie's New York, September 28, 1985.
Chienne et trois chiots, 41 cm, Sotheby New York, April 26, 1986.
Coq français, 38.5 cm (E. Godeau, founder), Enghien, October 19, 1980.
Combat de coqs, 19.5 cm, Enghien, October 19, 1980.
La Fantasia arabe, 80 cm, Drouot, December 14, 1984, room 6; Lokeren, April 20, 1985; Lyon, June 5, 1985; Sotheby London, June 20, 1985.
Ours sur un rocher, 45 cm, Drouot, December 9, 1982, room 8.
Prenez garde au chien!, 45 cm, Drouot, December 3, 1984.

LEDUC, ARTHUR
Torigny-sur-Vire (Manche), March 27, 1848
Antibes, February 29, 1918

This skillful animal sculptor was trained at the école by Lenordez and by Barye. Between 1873 and 1914 he exhibited a rather large number of bronzes at the Salon: *Diane de Poitiers partant pour la chasse* (1877), *Centaure et bacchante* (1879), and *Le Baiser,* an equestrian group, 65 cm; *Harde de cerfs écoutant*

Arthur Leduc,
Trois Enfants montant sur un cheval,
69 cm.

le rapproché, a monumental group placed today in the Luxembourg gardens (1886); *Au bois,* an equestrian study (1887), *Laitière normande* (1888), *Ultimus pro patria spiritus* part of the monument to the dead from Calvados (1889), *Le Baron J. Finot* (1912), and *Un compagnon de Duguesclin,* an equestrian statue (1914). It is also necessary to note some figures and studies in plaster, such as *Porte-Etendard à cheval,* a project for a monument to the armies of Reishoffen (1873), *La Raison du plus fort,* a group of horses (1874), two groups representing hunting scenes (1875), and *Horace Vernet sur la champ de bataille d'Isly,* an equestrian statue (1913).

Leduc also participated, from 1890 to 1907, at the Salon of the Société Nationale des Beaux-Arts with some animals and equestrian portraits, some in plaster, and others, quite numerous, in ceramic sandstone. He also made an equestrian statue of the *Connétable de Richmond* in bronze, destined for the city of Vannes.

The Thiébaut foundry cast the following works in bronze:

Cheval de trait, 41 cm.
Chien poitevin, 33 cm.
Chien vendéen, 27 cm.
Croix de veneur, 42 cm.
Harde de cerfs, 79 and 36 cm.
Plateau orné d'une course de chevaux, 38 x 27 cm.
Saint-Hubert, bas-relief, 139 x 86 and 80 x 50 cm.

Le Porte-Etendard de Reichshoffen was also cast in bronze, 60 cm.

1) Arthur Leduc, Dandy à cheval,
50 cm (1888).

2) Arthur Leduc, Nessus et Déjanire,
gilded bronze, 72 cm.

3) Arthur Leduc, Cheval de labour,
55 cm.

Arthur Leduc,
Sanglier attaqué
par quatre chiens,
65 cm
(1894).

Arthur Leduc,
Jument demi-sang
(1879).

MUSEUMS
Abbeville
Chien en arrêt devant une grenouille, 24 x 46 cm.
Caen
Centaure et bacchante, life size.
Cherbourg
Saint-Hubert.
Sens
Deux Chiens à l'attache, 37 x 43 cm.

SALES
Amazone au lévrier, 70 cm L. (L. Martin, founder),
    Drouot, February 27, 1985.
Cheval de labour au repos, 55 cm, Avignon, April 28,
    1985.
Cheval de trait, L'Isle-Adam, January 27, 1985.
Dandy à cheval, 50 cm (1888), Drouot, September 24,
    1985, room 1.
Nessus et Déjanire, gilded bronze, 72 cm, Saint-Dié,
    December 15, 1985.
Sanglier, 90 x 140 cm (Thiébaut), Senlis, November 11,
    1984 (selling for 300,000 F).
Le Porte-Etendard de Reichshoffen, 60 cm, Belfort, May
    24, 1987 (see reproduction page*). **[LEAVE UNTIL
    LAYOUT HAS DETERMINED PROPER REF. #]***
Sanglier attaqué par quatre chiens, 65 x 46 cm (1894)
    Drouot, September 25, 1984, room 9.
Trois Enfants montant sur un cheval, 69 cm, Castres,
    June 23, 1985; Toulouse, November 17, 1986.

Lefebvre, Hippolyte Jules

Lille, Feburary 4, 1863
Paris, September 22, 1935

A sculptor, an engraver of medals, and a painter,
Lefebvre won the first prize of Rome in sculpture in
1892 with his statue *Adam après la faute*. He studied

at the academic schools of Lille, and then at the Ecole des Beaux-Arts in Paris. Author of a group in stone, *L'Art du XVIIIe siècle* on the facade of the Grand Palais (1900), some equestrian statues in bronze of *Saint Louis,* and of *Jeanne d'Arc* above the portal of the Sacré-Coeur (1924), he produced some very realistic genre scenes and allegories, some busts, and a number of medallions. At the Salon, he debuted in 1886 with a fountain in bronze; notable pieces after that include a statue, *Le Pardon,* representing Christ carrying his cross (1896), a statue entitled *Mignon,* and a group, *Niobé* (1898), all three in marble; a statuette in plaster, *Petit Bouffon* (1902); *Jeunes Aveugles,* marble (1902); *L'Eté,* a statuette in unglazed porcelain from Sèvres (1906); *L'Hiver,* a statue in marble (1907); two statuettes in bronze, *Les Echasses (1908) and Maroussia* (1914); and *Le Printemps,* a group in marble (1909). The Susse editions made in bronze include *Le Porteur d'eau napolitain,* 57 and 33 cm, and the bust of the *Pardon,* 30 cm. A statuette of *Mignon* was cast by Siot-Decauville.

MUSEUMS
Lille
M. Barrois, medallion, 40 x 29 cm.
Croisés dans la tempête implorant la Vierge, medallion, 27 x 22 cm (1901).
Désiré Bloche, plaque, 33 x 24 cm (1901).
Docteur Oui, medallion, 32 x 25 cm (1913).
Eugène Delemer, bâtonnier, medallion, 30 cm diam.
Firmin Rainbeaux, medallion, 32.5 cm diam. (1916).
Itron-Varia Skleirder, medallion, 27 x 23 cm.
Jules Gosselet, géologue, medallion, 33 cm diam. (1910).
Louis Cordonnier, medallion, 35 cm diam.
Lucien Magne, architect, medallion, 34.5 cm diam.
Marie, medallion, 28 cm, diam. (1889).
Sainte Famille, medallion, 29 cm diam.

LEFÈVRE, CAMILLE

Issy-sur-Seine, December 31, 1853
1917

Lefèvre's initiation into sculpture was with wood, which led him first to enter the Ecole des Arts Décoratifs, and finally the Ecole des Beaux-Arts, where he frequented the studio of Cartelier. He made his debut at the Salon in 1879. In 1890, he participated in the foundation of the Société Nationale des Beaux-Arts, where he would henceforth exhibit regularly. He received some commissions for monuments in Paris, particularly the front of the Crédit Lyonnais, some bas-reliefs at the Grand Palais and porte Maillot, and the monument to *Levassor,* which he executed according to a sketch by Dalou.

MUSEUMS
Belfort
Buste de Mme Camille Lefèvre, 35 cm.
Buste de Jules Lermitva, 40 cm.
Buste du docteur Petit, 45 cm.
Buste de Mlle S., 41 cm.
Chambre syndicale de la bijouterie, medallion, 25.5 x 27 cm.
Grand-père Coussery, bas-relief, 28 x 26 cm.
Grand-mère Coussery, bas-relief, 28 x 26 cm.
La Mère de l'artiste, bas-relief, 31.5 x 24.5 cm.
Le Vent, bas-relief, 50 cm diam. (modeled for a medal).
Le Vent, bas-relief, 27.5 cm diam (reverse of the preceding).

LEFÈVRE-DESLONGCHAMPS, LOUIS ALEXANDRE

Cherbourg, November 22, 1849
Paris, February 23, 1893

The first works sent by this artist to the Salon were signed just "Lefèvre;" only in 1882 did he begin to sign his double name. In 1884, he exhibited a monumental group in plaster, *L'Abattoir,* destined to be cast in bronze for the slaughterhouses of La Villette. He also worked for the theatre of Cherbourg and for the city hall of Le Havre. The museum of Cherbourg possesses some of his works in plaster and in marble. Also known by Lefèvre are some bronzes, including *Marguerite à l'église,* 45 cm, modeled after the plaster statue from the 1877 Salon, and *La Science,* 40 cm, cast by Thiébaut.

LEFÈVRE-DEUMIER, MARIE-LOUISE

Argentan, 1820
Paris, April 1877

Wife of the writer Jules Lefèvre-Deumier, Marie-Louise identified herself in different journals under the pseudonym 'Jean de Sologne'. As a sculptor, she was strongly appreciated at the imperial court, and received many commissions from them. However, according to Stanislas Lami, she did not succeed in obtaining the title of "sculptor of the house of the Empress," which she had sought. A number of busts by this artist are known, among which are many of the prince-president *Louis-Napoléon* and of the Empress, as well as some portraits of contemporaries like *Lamartine* and *Mgr Sibour,* archbishop of Paris, some statuettes of the pope *Pie IX,* of the *Reine de Naples,* etc. Two busts in bronze were sent to the Salon, *Matrone romaine* in 1857, and *Alfred Busque* in 1859.

MUSEUMS
Argentan
Buste de Napoléon 1er, 60 cm.
Avignon
Buste de Louis-Napoléon, 81 cm (1851).
Compiègne, château
Buste du prince-président, 59 cm (1851).
Châlons-sur-Marne
Buste de Louis-Napoléon, 81 cm (1851).

LEGENDRE-HERAL, JEAN-FRANÇOIS

Montpellier, January 21, 1796
Marcilly (Seine-et-Marne), September 13, 1851

Very precocious, Legendre-Heral studied from the age of fourteen years at the school of drawing of Lyon, under the direction of Chinard and of Marin. He made his debut at the Salon in 1817 and, beginning the following year, taught at the school of fine arts of Lyon. He worked on different monuments of the city, then left for Rome, finally establishing himself in Paris in 1839. His production would be abundant there. He furnished a number of statues and groups for the churches of Saint-Denis-du-Saint-Sacrement (including a statue of *Saint Pierre*), for Saint-Paul-Saint-Louis, and began one for the front of the Ecole des Mines, which would be completed after his death by his student Chambard. Legendre-Heral's works were conceived with so much precision and attention to detail that he would long be accused of casting directly from natural objects. The museum of Lyon possesses a bronze by this sculptor, *Giotto enfant*.

LEGROS, ALPHONSE

Dijon, May 8, 1837
1911

Beginning in 1851, Legros worked in Paris for a theater decorator. Next he devoted himself especially to engraving and to lithography, though he also practiced painting and sculpture. In 1863, he went to London, where he met Dalou, who had exiled himself at the time of the Commune. Dalou put Legros in contact with some patrons of sculpture, and in 1876, Legros became a professor of drawing at the University College, acquiring a number of students. Four years later, he became a British citizen. His sculpted work, apparently not very abundant, includes some medallions in bronze, and portraits of historical or contemporary people, especially English people.

MUSEUM
Paris, Orsay
Masque de jeune fille, 31 cm.
Torse de jeune femme, 48 cm.
Many small medallions, including those of *Erasme*, 7 cm diam., and of *Titien*, 13.8 cm diam.

SALE
Nue debout, 55 cm, Drouot, November 26, 1984, rooms 5 and 6.

LEHUEDE, MARCEL PIERRE

Le Pouliguen (Loire-Atlantique), January 21, 1886
Cempuis (Oise), April 16, 1918

The museum of Avignon possesses a large medallion in bronze by this sculptor, entitled *Henri Escoffier*, 42 cm diam.

LELIÈVRE, EUGÈNE

Paris, March 13, 1856
January 24, 1945

The Susse foundry cast some clocks and some candy dishes by this little-known sculptor. A pin tray in ornamented, gilded bronze, modeled after a cabbage leaf and a hare, 17 cm L., was sold at the Drouot hotel on December 4, 1981, and a statuette in bronze, *Pékinois faisant le beau*, 15 cm, was also sold there on October 19, 1983, room 9. The same subject exists in patinated metal.

LEMAIRE, GEORGES HENRI

Bailly, January 19, 1853
Paris, 1914

A sculptor and an engraver of fine stones, Georges Henri Lemaire left some subjects made of bronze and of precious materials. Two statuettes, *La Musique* in lapis-lazuli, rock crystal and silvered bronze, 25.5 cm, and *La Poésie* in agate, ivory and silvered bronze, 26 cm, were sold at the Drouot hotel on October 19, 1983.

LEMAIRE, HECTOR

Lille, August 15, 1846
Paris, 1933

A student of the academic schools of Lille, and then of Dumont and of Falguière in Paris, Hector Lemaire stayed in Rome for four years after winning a competition of the Wicar foundation organized by his hometown. Upon returning to France, he made many important works, including the front of the posterior facade of the Petit Palais, symbolizing *Les Heures*. He also made a statue in stone, *Le Soir*, in the gardens of the Tuileries, as well as some works for the Grand Théâtre of Lille and the tomb of Marie d'Orléans in Dreux. From 1869 until his death, he sent to the Salon a number of works, especially in plaster. These included anecdotal or allegorical characters as well as some busts of historical or contemporary people. His principal plasters (some of them later made in marble) shown at the Salon included *Deux Romains jouant à la morra* (1869), *Samson trahi par Dalila* (1878), *La Charité romaine* or *L'Amour filial* (1881), *Le Matin* (1882), *Sauvée!* (1888), *La Roche qui pleure* (1896), *L'Etoile du berger* (1902), *L'Offrande à l'autel de l'Amour* (1904), *Rêve d'amour* (1912), *L'Amour blessé* (1913), etc. He made some rare bronzes, including the bust *Carolus Duran* (1873), the group *Bambini* (1886), a statue of *Duguesclin* (1890), and the group *Le Désir* (1897). Also worthy of note are some marbles, terra cottas, waxes, and, from the Nationale des Beaux-Arts in 1892, a group in bronze, *Rêve d'amour*.

Barbedienne cast the bust of *Hoche* and Susse cast *L'Electricité*, 79 and 37 cm, and *L'Etoile du berger*.

MUSEUMS
Paris, Petit Palais
Enfant au cadran solaire, gilded bronze, 38 cm.
Vannes
La Musique profane, La Musique sacrée, two statuettes, 41 cm.

LEMAIRE, PHILIPPE

Valenciennes, January 9, 1789
Paris, August 2, 1880

Phillipe Lemaire studied first at the Academies of Valenciennes, then at the Academies of Paris, starting in 1816 at the Ecole des Beaux-Arts. He won the grand prize of Rome in 1821, and started his consignments to the Salon ten years later. He was elected member of the Institut in 1845. The classical style of his art and his references to antiquity won him a number of official commissions. His greatest work is the front of the church of the Madeleine, which presents the theme of the *Jugement dernier;* his other works include statues and groups for the church of Notre-Dame-de-Lorette (*L'Espérance*), for the Arc de Triomphe (bas-relief of the *Funérailles du général Marceau*), for the Gare du Nord (allegories of *Calais* and of *Valenciennes*), for the gardens of the Tuileries (*Le Laboureur des géorgiques*) and for the Luxembourg gardens (*Archimadas se préparant à lancer le disque*). Phillipe Lemair is also responsible for diverse works at the courthouse and the stock exchange in Lille, for the city hall of Valenciennes, etc. A number of models by this sculptor belong to the museum of Valenciennes. At the Carnavalet museum in Paris can be found two of his bronzes: *Le Duc de Bordeaux à sept ans*, 115 cm (1827), and *Henri IV*, an equestrian statue (1838) cast by Soyer and Ingé.

Lemaître, Eglantine

Saint-Gervais (Loir-et-Cher), October 6, 1852
December 26, 1920

Under her maiden name, Eglantine Robert-Houdin, this animal artist had nearly solely represented dogs. At the Salon between 1884 and 1907, she exhibited *Coup double, chien de chasse* (1887), *Chien étranglant un renard* (1897), and *Renard défendant sa proie* (1899), among other works. The museum of Blois preserves a small bronze by her, *Chien de chasse couché*, 7 cm. Another bronze, *Deux Chiens de chasse*, 26 cm, was sold by Christie's in New York on September 28, 1985.

Lemire, Charles Gabriel, known as Sauvage

Lunéville, April 24, 1741
Paris, 1827

This sculptor, who directed the modeling studios of the ceramic factory of Niderwiller for twenty years, belongs primarily to the 18th century. However, his participation at the Salon fell between 1809 and 1819, with works including *Le Génie et la Poésie* (1812); *Jeune Berger* and *L'Amour mettant une corde à son arc*, two marbles (1814), the second of which, 125 cm high, belongs to the Louvre museum; *L'Innocence*, marble (1819), etc. Also known are bronze reductions of *L'Amour mettant une corde à son arc* in many dimensions. Some proofs of 52 cm in height were sold by Sotheby in London on November 8, 1984 and in Madrid on October 23, 1985.

Lemot, François Frédéric Baron

Lyon, November 4, 1772
Paris, May 6, 1827

Educated in the classic spirit of the end of the 18th century, Lemot won the grand prize of Rome in 1790. He entered the Institut in 1805, became professor at the Beaux-Arts in 1810, and obtained a number of commissions and distinctions during the course of a career that was nevertheless rather brief. Attributed to him are the equestrian statues of *Louis XIV* for the city of Lyon and that of *Henri IV* for the median of the Pont-Neuf in Paris (1818), as well as the front of the colonnade of the Louvre, face to Saint-Germain-l'Auxerrois (1808). The Carnavalet museum possesses a bronze reduction, 70 cm high, of *Henri IV* on horseback.

Lenoir, Alfred Charles

Paris, May 12, 1850
Paris, July 27, 1920

Some busts, medallions, decorative sculptures, and commemorative monuments comprised the career of this artist, grandson to the famous Alexandre Lenoir, founder of the museum of French monuments (Musée des Monuments Français) during the

Pierre Lenordez, Cheval de course monté, au galop, 32 cm.

Revolution. He worked for the Alexandre III Bridge and made the monument to *Césare Franck* in stone (1891) placed at Samuel-Rousseau Square in Paris. His statue in bronze of *Berlioz*, now at Vintimille Square, was cast during the last war.

MUSEUMS
Paris, Decorative Arts
Monument à la mémoire d'Emile Peyre, 122 cm (1907).
Paris, Orsay
Buste d'Adolphe Moreau, 95 cm (A. Rudier), 1907.
Projet de monument à Prud'hon, 53.5 cm (A. Rudier).

LENOIR, PIERRE CHARLES

Paris, May 22, 1879
Paris, September 9, 1953

A student of his father Alfred Lenoir, then of Falguière and of Peter, this sculptor and medaller executed many commemoratives and monuments to the dead of World War I, as well as some statues,

busts and plaques. He is known for a statuette in bronze, *Fillette assise,* and for a small group, *Les Deux Amies,* which seem to date from the 1920s, as well as for some subjects cast in unglazed porcelain by Sèvres. The museum of Châteauroux possesses two plaques in bronze which had been exhibited at the Salon of 1904: *Bucolique* and *Enfance de Bacchus.* A proof of the *Deux Amies,* 39 cm, was sold at the Drouot hotel, October 19, 1983, and an allegory of *Abondance,* 25 cm (Leblanc-Barbedienne), was sold in New York by Christie's, December 17, 1983.

LENORDEZ, PIERRE

Born in Vaast (near Cherbourg)

Nothing is known of this sculptor but that he exhibited at the Salon from 1855 to 1877, and that to this date he lived in Caen. While he left some

Pierre Lenordez,
L'Etalon "Royal quand même,"
34 x 22 cm.

groups of personages like *Esclave* and *Sultane à cheval fuyant du sérail*, exhibited at the Salon of 1877, most of his work portrayed animals, almost solely horses, in particular of Arabian stallions. A number of waxes and plasters, which may have been presented at the Salon, were made in bronze. Of note is *The Baron, cheval du haras impérial au bois de Boulogne* (wax, Exposition Universelle of 1855), *Etalon et poulinière* (plaster, Salon of 1861), and *Cheval de chasse monté par un piqueur* (plaster, Salon of 1876). In addition to the pieces distributed in public sale, one notable piece is *Trois chevaux de course sur une haie*, 25 cm.

SALES

Chasseur avec son cheval et deux chiens, 48 cm L., Sotheby London, March 26, 1980.
Cheval attaqué par un pithon, 25 x 31 cm, Enghien, March 2, 1980.
Cheval de course, 26 cm, Sotheby London, March 20, 1986.
Cheval de course "Bois Roussel," 31 cm, Sotheby London, March 8, 1984.
Cheval de course normand, 36 cm (Société des Bronzes of Paris), Sotheby London, November 6, 1986.
Cheval de course avec son jockey, au galop, 32 cm, Versailles, June 16, 1984; Enghien, October 6, 1985.
Cheval dessellé, 32 cm, Dijon, February 13, 1983.
Cheval égyptien non sellé monté par Napoléon 1er en 1806, 35.5 cm, Sotheby London, July 5, 1985.
Cheval pur-sang sellé avec levrette, 40 cm, Sotheby London, April 28, 1982.
Cheval "The Ranger", 26 cm, Sotheby London, March 8, 1984.
Etalon et chien, 39.5 cm, Sotheby London, November 6, 1986.

Pierre Lenordez,
Etalon arabe,
46 cm L.

L'Etalon "Gladiateur", 32 cm, Enghien, October 19, 1980.
L'Etalon "Royal quand même", 34 x 22 cm, Bayonne, October 20, 1985.
L'Etalon "Saube box"ST1, 35 cm, Enghien, October 6, 1985.
Le Gagnant du derby, 53 x 52 cm, Versailles, June 16, 1984.
Jument et son poulain, 19.5 x 27.5 cm, Rambouillet, November 7, 1982.

Pierre Lenordez,
Le Gagnant du derby,
53 cm.

LÉONARD, LÉONARD VAN WEYDEVELD, KNOWN AS AGATHON

Lille, August 28, 1841
Paris, January 12, 1923

A.LEONARD

A Belgian artist who became a naturalized French citizen, Léonard entered the Académie des Beaux-Arts of his hometown before exhibiting for the first time in Paris at the Salon of 1868. He was first made part of the Société des Artistes Français, but left it in 1896 for the Société Nationale des Beaux-Arts. He showed his work there until 1914, in the sections for sculpture and for the decorative arts. Starting in 1899, he served as part of the jury which then presided over August Rodin.

Léonard received a small number of commissions from the State, including one for *Hébé* (1899) in marble, but he was notorious during his lifetime as he is today for small subjects representative of the Art Nouveau spirit. Particularly notable are the dances of the *Jeu de l'écharpe*, exhibited in 1897 as a project for a foyer of the dance. They were cast in unglazed porcelain by the Sèvres factory and in bronze by the Susse foundry. These charming young women in long, wide-necked dresses, were proposed to be in patinated or gilded bronze, sometimes with the head, arms and feet in ivory. Each of them was adorned with a different accessory and attitude. Some models were equipped with electricity.

Beyond this well known ensemble, Agathon Léonard produced a number of statuettes, medallions and also small busts of gracious young women, then very much in vogue. At the Salon des artistes français are, among other works, *Amour*, a bust in marble and bronze (1878), *Mignon* and *Marchande de poissons*, two statuettes in bronze (1890), and *Les Rameaux*, a statuette in marble (1894). More prolific was his participation at the Salon de la Nationale des Beaux-Arts. In addition to the models of the *Jeu de l'écharpe* (1897) are a series of busts in bronze: *Le Drame du Vendredi Saint* (1898), *Medjé*, in marble and bronze (1903), *Le Roi des routes* (1904), *Le Vieux Roulier* (1905), *Pilleur d'épaves*, and *Châtelaine du XVe siècle*, this last in marble and bronze (1907). Numerous also are the statuettes in bronze: *Douleur de toujours* (1898), *Les Rameaux*, in ivory and bronze, and *Le Vampire* (1903), *Salomé* and *Danseuse*, in bronze, ivory, enamel and, for the first time, gold and silver (1908), *Danseuse javanaise, Miarka, L'Amour masqué* (1903), etc. A quantity of busts and statuettes in plaster, marble, and ivory are also of note, in which the same type of subjects are featured. Although he cannot be classed among the great masters of his time, Agathon Léonard was, according to Léonce Bénédite, one of "these precious artists who,

Agathon Léonard, Salomé, bronze, ivory, red and turquoise beads, 31.5 cm.

429

Agathon Léonard,
Danseuse nue
à la coupe,
60 cm.

Agathon Léonard,
Danseuse
à l'écharpe,
gilded bronze,
60 cm (Susse).

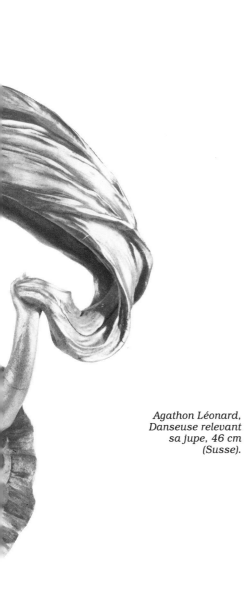

*Agathon Léonard,
Danseuse relevant
sa jupe, 46 cm
(Susse).*

431

in bringing together the sculpture of the goldsmith, of the jewelry, of the curio (trinket), had rejuvenated it, transposed usefully and given it a direct outlet in the contemporary life."

The catalog of Susse editions presents the series of the *Jeu de l'écharpe* as a table centerpiece offered to the Empress of Russia by the president of the Republic.

The following eight pieces were planned in two dimensions, 46 and 23 cm:

Danseuse aux pipeaux.
Danseuse au cothume.
Danseuse à la marguerite.
Danseuse au bracelet.
Danseuse relevant sa jupe.
Danseuse aux cymbales.
Danseuse au tambourin à droite.
Danseuse au tambourin à gauche.

Agathon Léonard,
Danseuse au cothurne,
gilded bronze and ivory,
46 cm (Susse).

Agathon Léonard,
Danseuse au tambourin, 23 cm.

Agathon Léonard,
Danseuse
au cothurne,
46 cm
(Susse).

Agathon Léonard,
Danseuse aux pipeaux,
23 cm.

Alexandre Léonard,
Méhariste,
gilded bronze
and ivory,
24 cm.

The other pieces were cast only in single dimension, with the exception of the last:

Danseuse aux flambeaux à gauche, 61 cm.
Danseuse aux flambeaux à droite, 61 cm.
Danseuse à l'écharpe, pieds invisibles, 60 cm.
Danseuse à l'écharpe, pied gauche levé, 60 cm.
Danseuse à l'écharpe, pied droit levé, 60 cm.
Danseuse à l'écharpe, genou levé, 60, 45 and 31 cm.

A bust of *L'Innocence* was also cast by Susse, 58 and 15 cm, another bust, *Le Lis,* by Siot-Decauville, and a bas-relief, *Sainte Cécile,* by Thiébaut, 100, 47 and 32 cm.

MUSEUMS
Abbeville
Sainte Cécile, bas-relief, 35 x 20.7 cm.
Lille
Le Voeu, 47 cm.
Reims
Danseuse bras droit levé, 26 cm (Susse).

SALES
Angelot au carquiois, bronze and marble, 53 cm, Lille, April 22, 1985.
Danseuse aux pipeaux, 23 cm, Drouot, November 26, 1986, room 9.
Danseuse aux pipeaux, 46 cm, Sotheby Monaco, October 7, 1984.
Danseuse au cothume, 46 cm, Drouot, March 16, 1983, room 9; Sotheby Monaco, October 6, 1985.

Danseuse relevant sa jupe, 23 cm, Drouot, November 26, 1986, room 9.
Danseuse au tambourin, 23 cm, Drouot, May 14, 1986, room 4; Drouot, November 26, 1986, room9.
Danseuse à l'écharpe, 31 cm, Christie's Geneva, November 9, 1986.
Danseuse à l'écharpe, 60 cm, Christie's London, April 17, 1984; Milan, March 13, 1985.
Danseuse nue à la coupe, 60 cm, Toulouse, March 1, 1983.
La Femme chauve-souris, 39 cm, Drouot, December 13, 1982, room 1.

LÉONARD, ALEXANDRE

Paris, March 18, 1821
1877

Perhaps under the influence of Barye, who was one of his masters, Alexandre Léonard specialized in animal art. Between 1852 and 1873, he sent to the Salon some subjects in bronze or in patinaed wax (frequently to be cast in bronze later on). Of particular note among the waxes are *Héron* (1852), *Renard et perdrix* (1853), *Grives combattant* (1859), these last two with a silver patina, *Grives aux aguets* (1861), *Canard sauvage surpris par un renard* (1864), *Arabe surpirs par des lions* (1869), *Combat d'aigles* (1870), and *Poule d'eau* (1873). Among the bronzes, most notable are *Poule picorant* (1864), *Aigle gavant sa proie* and *Le Loup et la cigogne* (both presented at the Exposition Universelle of 1867), *Butor blessé* (Salon of 1867), *Après la chasse* (1869), *Poule d'Amerique du Nord* and *Tétras mâle et femelle* (1870).

Note that the signature of this sculptor, A. Léonard, sometimes led to pieces of his work being attributed to Agathon Léonard. This was the case with his *Méhariste* in gilded bronze and ivory, 24 cm, sold in Enghien on October 24, 1984.

LÉONARD, CHARLES

Born in Lille

Some works in plaster and a bust in pewter entitled *Le Rêve* (1899) were exhibited at the Salon by this sculptor. *Le Rêve* was cast in bronze by Susse in three dimensions, 62, 45 and 29 cm.

LE QUESNE, EUGÈNE

Paris, February 15, 1815
Paris, June, 1887

It was only after obtaining his law degree that Le Quesne entered Pradier's studio in the Ecole des Beaux-Art in 1841. The following year he went to Italy, and from there he sent his first works to the Salon. He won the grand prize for sculpture in 1844, and returned to Rome for five years. It is not surprising that one of Le Quesne's primary inspirations was antiquity. He executed a number of busts, as well as many decorative sculptures for Parisien monuments including the Louvre (the front of the Mollien pavilion), the Opera, the Gare du Nord, and the Palais de

Justice (statues of the *Force, Justice, Innocence,* and *Crime* on the north facade). He also produced statues of famous people for different cities of France, and a work in copper of *Notre-Dame-de-la-Garde* for the Marseille basilica (1870). At the Luxembourg gardens is found his *Faune dansant*, a bronze of 2 meters high cast by Eck and Durand and exhibited at the Salon of 1852. Moreover, he sent a small statue entitled *Baigneuse* to the Salon in 1857, and a statuette entitled *Lesbie* in 1868 (both in bronze). Also among the works Le Quesne sent to the Salon are a plaster entitled *Prêtresse de Bacchus* in 1887, and a bronze casting of the *Faune dansant*.

The following works were made the object of castings by the Susse foundry:

L'Automne, 32 cm.
Didon abandonnée, 35 and 22 cm.
L'Echo, 42 and 28 cm.
Erigone, 42 cm.
Faune dansant, many dimensions not specified.
Femme couchée, 27 cm.
Femme drapée, 27 cm.
Frère et soeur or Enfants à la grenouille, 34 cm.
Jeune Fille à la tortue, 12 cm.
Lesbie, 27 cm.
Nymphe aux deux amours, 100 and 60 cm.
La Peinture and *Le Sculpture*, 44 and 30 cm.

MUSEUMS
Paris, Louvre
Deux Parques, a restoration project of sculptures of the Parthénon, 38 x 22 cm.

SALES
Danseuse, gilded bronze, 75 cm (Susse), Enghien, April 8, 1979.
Faune dansant, 29 cm, Drouot, May 25, 1984, rooms 5 and 6.
Faune dansant, 49.5 cm (Susse), Christie's New York, December 14, 1982.
Pan, 51.5 cm, Sotheby London, June 18, 1982.

LEQUIEN, ALEXANDRE VICTOR

Paris, January 17, 1822
1905

An official portraitist, LeQuien executed a number of busts and statues of historic and contemporary personages, including a bronze bust of *Napoléon III* that was exhibited at the Salon of 1868. Nine replicas were commissioned of it by the administration of the fine arts. At the Salon of 1874 he exhibited a statuette in bronze, *Le Maréchal Ney*. Lequien worked on diverse Parisian edifices, including the city hall of the twelfth district (a statue of *Vigneron*) and the church of the Val-de-Grâce.

MUSEUMS
Ajaccio, Napoléon museum
Buste de Napoléon III, 63 cm.
Compiègne, château
Buste de Napoléon III, 63 cm (1869).

435

Gaston Leroux,
Aïda, 75 cm.

Gaston Leroux,
Guerrier arabe, 95 cm.

Gaston Leroux,
Rébecca, 78 cm.

LEROUX, GASTON

Paris, September 14, 1854
May 25, 1942

The work of Gaston Leroux is dominated by Oriental personages, either contemporary or from antiquity, famous or unknown. One can judge by his consignments to the Salon starting in 1882, starting with the bronzes: *Le Premier Bain* (1887), *Buste d'Othello* (1888), *Jeune Charmeur de serpent* (1889), *Charmeur,* a statuette (1890), *Thaïs,* a statuette in marble and bronze (1903), *Portrait du Dr Moure* and *Après le bain,* two statuettes (1905). It is fitting to mention his works in other materials: *Egyptienne* (1883) and *Marocain* (1884), two statuettes in terra cotta; *La Perle,* a statue in plaster (1891); *Echo,* a statuette in plaster (1906); and *Le Matin,* a statuette in terra cotta (1908). A statue in bronze by Leroux, entitled *Danseuse,* was exhibited at the Nationale des Beaux-Arts in 1892.

SALES

Aïda, bronze polychrome, 57.5 cm, Christie's London, July 18, 1983.
Aïda, 75 cm, Toulouse, May 9, 1985; Avignon, December 6, 1986.

Femme au tambourin assise sur une tête de sphinx, 75 cm, Enghien, March 4, 1984.
Guerrier arabe, 95 cm, Drouot, November 6, 1984, room 1.
Jeune Fille arabe, 45 cm, Drouot, April 27, 1983.
Jeune Orientale, une cruche sur la tête, 74 cm, Christie's New York, September 27, 1986.
La Lecture du Coran, 66 cm, Sotheby London, March 21, 1985.
Rébecca, 75 cm, Fécamp, April 21, 1985; Sotheby London, March 20, 1986.
Romprons-nous ou ne romprons-nous pas?, 72.5 cm, Christie's New York, December 13, 1983.

LETOURNEAU, EDOUARD

Paris, December 23, 1851
June 1907

Student of Frémiet, Letourneau was fond of Oriental subjects and exotic scenes, which he translated principally in wax or in plaster and which he exhibited at the Salon, from 1874 until his death. He is also creast with a number of bronzes, including some groups: *La Part du butin* (Salon of 1881), *La Paix* (1882), and *Au repos* (1885). Among the waxes, made primarily at the beginning of his career, are *Cheval blessé* (1874), *Un moment critique* (1875),

Jeune Fille au rouet, bronze and marble (1903), Fleur de Bretagne and Le Fabliau, two statuettes in gilded bronze and ivory, Contemplation, gilded bronze and marble (1906), Harmonie, a statuette in bronze, marble and onyx (1907), and L'Effort, bronze (1914). The following works in other materials should be noted: Le Nid, a statuette in marble (1889), Après le combat, a group in marble (1890), L'Etoile du berger (1894) and La Vierge au rouet (1895), two statuettes in plaster, La Muse des amours, a statuette in plaster (1899), Pro Patria, a group in marble (1901), Edelweiss (1905), L'Aube (1906), Baigneuse (1908), Caresse (1910), Fleurs de Bretagne (1911), five statuettes inn marble, Phryné (1908), Triomphe d'amazone (1910), two statuettes in ivory, Cyrano de Bergerac, a statuette in wax (1913), etc. A good number of subjects by Henri Levasseur have been cast in bronze, often in many dimensions, in particular by the Société des bronzes of Paris (Gloire au Travail), by Siot-Decauville (Après le combat), and by Thiébaut (a vase, Le Dénicheur, 36 cm, and two statuettes: Retour de l'hirondelle, 84 cm, and Forgeron, 84 cm).

Edouard Letourneau,
Chef indien à cheval, 58 cm.

Combat entre un Mexicain et un Indien (1876), Sentinelle indeinne par un temps de pluie (1878), and Indien donnant le signal (1879). Many plasters are also worthy of note, including Etalon arabe (1883), Mule kabyle (1886), Arabe allant au marché (1901), Judith (1903), La Proie (1905), and Chasseur de sanglier à cheval (1907), etc.

SALES
Cheval arabe sellé, 41 cm, Sotheby London, June 7, 1984.
Chef indien à cheval, 58 cm, Enghien, October 6, 1985; Sotheby London, November 6, 1986.

LEVASSEUR, HENRI
Paris, April 16, 1853
November 3, 1934

Among the numerous consignments by this artist to the Salon, starting in 1881, are a certain number of works in bronze, to which was often added ivory, marble or silver: La Nuit de mai, bronze (1887), Les Rameaux, bronze and gilded silver (1896), La Légende des ruines, bronze and marble (1898), La

Henri Levasseur
Diane chasseresse, 44 cm.

Other statuettes in small groups in bronze have been cast without markings from any founder, including some dancers in bronze and ivory, *Diane*, 71 cm, *L'Etoile du berger*, 90 and 40 cm, *Fleur de Bretagne* (a young woman holding a branch of holly, of which are known some proofs in gilded bronze, 34 cm, in bronze and ivory and also in unglazed porcelain by Sèvres), *Gloire à la Science*, 77 cm, *Hébé sur un aigle*, bronze and marble, 60 cm, *Loïe Fuller*, 38 cm, a bust, *Jeune Femme au lapin*, 57 cm, and finally a *Jeanne d'Arc* in bronze, silver, gold, ivory, fine pearls and rubies, presented to the Exposition Universelle of 1900.

MUSEUM
Strasbourg
Forgeron assis sur son enclume, 112.5 cm (Société des bronzes of Paris).

SALES
L'Amour désarmé, 68 cm, Drouot, June 1, 1983, room 4.
Le Compositeur Boïeldieu, Versailles, September 21, 1986.
Danseuses, four statuettes gilded bronze and ivory, 31 to 36 cm, Drouot, May 14, 1982, room 6.
Diane chasseresse, 44 cm, Drouot, July 7, 1983, room 9.
Diane chasseresse, 72 cm, Versailles, March 6, 1983.
Gloire au Travail, 71 cm, Sotheby London, March 17, 1983.
Le Guerrier blessé, 55 cm (Siot-Decauville), Washington, March 6, 1983.
La Muse et le poète, 61 cm, Drouot, March 23, 1983, room 4.
Napoléon 1er, bust, 62 cm, Christie's New York, February 19, 1985.
Le Songe, 122 cm, Sotheby London, November 10, 1983.

Armand Jules Le Veel,
Grenadier de la Vieille-Garde,
38 cm (Susse).

LEVASSEUR, JULES

Paris, ca. 1831
Paris, April 18, 1888

This sculptor exhibited at the Salon from 1874 to 1887, and is known for some portraits in bust or in medallion, and a certain number in bronze. The Carnavalet museum possesses a medallion in bronze, *Le Général Boulanger*, 38.5 cm diam, dating from 1887.

LE VEEL, ARMAND JULES

Bricquebec, January 26, 1821
Cherbourg, July 26, 1905

The museum of Cherbourg possesses a large number of Le Veel's plasters and bronzes, evidence of the nearly exclusive attraction that the military and heroic subjects held for this artist. Soldiers from centuries past, and famous and glorious personages from the history of France effectively occupied his work. A student of Rude, Le Veel was also an archeologist and collector of faience. He exhibited at the Salon starting in 1850.

The Susse foundry cast the following works:

32e demi-brigade (voltigeur), 82, 37 and 17 cm.
Vieille-Garde (grenadier), 78, 38 and 15 cm.
Huguenot, 60 and 34 cm.
Ligueur, 60 and 34 cm.

MUSEUMS
Bordeaux
32e demi-brigade, 37 cm (Susse).
Cherbourg
Charlemagne à cheval, 100 cm.
Dame du XVIe siècle, 76 cm.
Etude de cheval, 75 cm.
François 1er à cheval, 115, cm.
Frondeur, 53 cm.
Frondeuse, 53 cm.
Hallebardier, 115 cm.
Huguenot, 72.5 cm.
Jeanne d'Arc à cheval, 100 cm.
Jeanne d'Arc à cheval, départ de Vaucouleurs, 93 cm.
Jeanne d'Arc, medallion, 70 x 65 cm.
Lansquenet, 92 cm.
A. Le Veel, autoportrait, medallion, 65 x 61 cm.
Ligueur, 56 cm.
Marceau à cheval, 120 cm.
Porte-Etendard, 115 cm.
Saint Georges à cheval, 107 cm.
Tête de maître d'armes de l'armée d'Afrique, 35 cm.
32e demi-brigade, 82 cm.

Other works by LeVeel include some bronzes found at the museum of Bricquebec.

SALES
Le Tambour, 48 cm, Sotheby London, March 8, 1984.
Vieille-Garde, 38 cm (Susse), Cannes, July 20, 1985.
Vieille-Garde, 78 cm (Susse), Drouot, March 12, 1984, room 14.

Hélène Level,
Enfant jouant
avec un chat,
66 x 105 cm
(Thiébaut frères).

LEVEL, HÉLÈNE

Born in Rio de Janeiro

At the Salon of 1896, this student of Falguière exhibited a group in plaster, *Enfant jouant avec un chat,* and in 1906, a statuette in bronze, *Le Jeu.* A proof in bronze of *Enfant jouant avec un chat,* 66 cm, cast by Thiébaut frères, was sold in Enghien, April 8, 1979.

LÉVÊQUE, EDMOND

Abbeville, July 1, 1814
Paris, January 6, 1875

In Paris from the age of sixteen, Lévêque studied at the Ecole des Beaux-Arts and exhibited at the Salon, from 1833 to 1874, not only sculptures but also some paintings. His work includes mythological subjects, Roman heros, and historical or contemporary people. Of note at the Salon are some statues in marble: *Lesbie* (1852), *Amazone* (1863), *Diane chasseresse* and *Nymphe* (1866, both later placed in the gardens of the Tuileries), and finally a statuette in marble, *L'Enfant au raisin* (1867). There were apparently few bronzes, but a small group is known, *Les Deux Esclaves,* 50 cm, of which a model was sold in Enghien, October 16, 1983.

LÉVY, CHARLES OCTAVE

Paris, ?
Paris, 1899

Lévy exhibited some statuettes at the Salon between 1873 and 1898. These include, in plaster, *Source* (1888) and *La Paix* (1898); in marble, *Naïade* (1889) and *Le Réveil* (1896); in bronze, *Faneur* and

Charles Lévy,
Salomé,
83 cm.

at the Salon starting in 1893. He also exhibited at the Salon d'automne after the war of 1914-1918.

The Barbedienne house cast many subjects by L'Hoëst, including *Porteuse de Rebbia,* 50 cm., *Danseuse orientale,* 43 cm., and *Bédouine au marché,* 50 cm. According to the Barbedienne file in the national archives, the proofs of these three works, still in stock, were given to Mme L'Hoëst when Barbedienne ceased activity in 1954 The bronzes cast of two other subjects are indicated as having been preserved, at the same time, by M. Leblanc-Barbedienne: *Jeune Fellah à la cruche,* 48 cm and *Bédouine en marche,* 20 cm. For its part, the Thiébaut foundry cast *Coquetterie,* 74 cm, from a plaster statue exhibited at the Salon of 1896. Susse cast *La Grande Caravane,* also called *Famille berbère revenant du marché,* 40 x 80 cm.

Eugène L'Hoëst,
La Grande Caravane,
40 x 80 cm (Susse).

Charles Lévy,
Le Faneur,
100 cm.

Captif (1890). A certain number of his works were cast in bronze, sometimes in many dimensions, in particular *Salomé,* 82 cm, *Vénus et Cupidon,* 76 cm, and *Le Faneur,* 100, 75, 50 and 25 cm.

SALES
Le Faneur, 75 cm, Lokeren, October 19, 1985.
Salomé, 82 cm, Enghien, October 16, 1983; Morlaix, August 13, 1984; Sotheby London, November 8, 1984; Lyon-Villeurbanne, March 17, 1986; Clermont-Ferrand, April 24, 1986.

L'HOËST, EUGÈNE

Paris, July 12, 1874
December 24, 1937

A sculptor and medal-engraver, L'Hoëst included in his work a number of busts, allegorical compositions and genre scenes evoking the Orient. Enrolled at the Ecole des Beaux-Arts in 1891, he participated

MUSEUMS
Angers
Three busts: *Le Docteur Montprofit*, 55 cm, *Femme
arabe* and *Joueur de Desbouka.*
Paris, Orsay
Jeune Fellah porteuse d'eau, 48 cm (Cairo, 1910).
Porteur d'eau à Louqsor, 49 cm (Cairo, 1910).

SALES
La Grande Caravane, 40 x 80 cm (Susse), Enghien,
March 4, 1984; Drouot, June 12, 1985, room 7;
L'Isle-Adam, September 29, 1985.
Nubien porteur de couffins, 48 cm (Barbedienne),
Chartres, June 2, 1984; Drouot, October 25, 1985,
room 4.
Trois Musiciens arabes, 39 x 78 cm (Barbedienne 6/
25), Enghien, October 16, 1983.

LIENARD, PAUL

Paris, 1849
Cannes, December 1900

Lienard's bust in marble of *Fragonard*, 70 cm,
was installed in 1877 in a public garden in Grasse;
a statue in marble of *Lord Brougham* was installed in
1879 in Cannes. This student of Duret also exhibited

two plasters at the Salon of 1866, *A la fontaine* and
Baigneuse. He also sculpted some animal subjects.
A small group in bronze, *Epagneul au faisan*, 23 cm,
was sold in Enghien, October 10, 1982.

LOISEAU-BAILLY, GEORGES

Faix-Sauvigny-le-Bois (Yonne), February 16,
1858
Paris, February 6, 1913

Loiseau-Bailly was the author of busts and statues of his contemporaries, allegorical or mythological works, and Oriental figures, which inspired him
to travel to Italy and Tunisia in 1890. He also made
some medallions, plaques, and diverse ornamented
objects in relief: tobacco cans, bouquet carriers,
ashtrays, sugar bowls, etc. At the Salon, where he
exhibited from 1879 to his death, notable works
include: *Pêcheuse d'écrivisses*, a statue in bronze
(1882); *Petite Morvandelle*, a bust in bronze (1886);
Quinze Ans (1887), *Esclave* (1905), *Océanide* (1909),
Après le bain (1910), four statuettes in bronze, the
last gilded; *Fatma*, a bust in bronze; and *Vendangeur*,
a statuette in bronze (1913). He also made many
busts in gilded bronze, including *Nègre, La Source,
Fillette*, etc., and two statuettes in plaster, *Printemps*
and *Flore* (1907). Some works by Loiseau-Bailly
seem to have been cast, among others a statuette of
Graziella, 35 cm high.

LOISEAU-ROUSSEAU, PAUL LOUIS
EMILE

Paris, April 20, 1861
Paris, 1927

A number of trips to Africa inspired Loiseau-
Rousseau to portray typical people from this conti-
nent, big game hunts, and Oriental scenes. He was
also interested in bullfighting and in people from the
Middle Ages and the Renaissance. It seems as if
some of his important works were not executed in
final versions; however, a number of bronzes, often
incorporating all sorts of other materials, appeared
rather frequently among his consignments to the
Salon starting in 1886. These included *Colombine*, a
statuette in bronze (1888); *Les Adieux de Cléopatre*,
a group in bronze, ivory, gold, and precious stones,
and *Harpiste égyptienne*, a statuette in bronze and
silver (1896); *Salem, Nègre du Soudan*, a bust in
marble and bronze (1897); *Le Supplice de la croix* and
Musicien nègre, two statues in marble and bronze
(1898); *Jeune Hollandaise*, a bust in marble and
bronze (1899); *Le Lierre*, bas-relief in bronze (1903);
République de Cuba, a bust in bronze (1904); *Esclave*,
a statuette in bronze (1905); *Béatrice*, a bust in
bronze, marble and onyx, and *Femme du Moyen Age*,
a bust in gilded bronze and onyx (1906); *Pénitente*,
a statuette in gilded bronze and ivory, and *Châtelaine*,
a bust in gilded bronze and unglazed porcelain
(1907); *Nègre*, a bust in bronze, marble and onyx
(1908); *Patricienne*, a bust in bronze and marble

(1909); *Après le bain, La Source,* and *Fillette,* two statuettes and a bust in gilded bronze, and *Nègre,* a bust in bronze, marble and stone (1910); *Ouled-Naïl,* a statuette in gilded bronze (1911); *Taureau,* bas-relief in bronze (1914); as well as diverse small objects, paperweights, and jewelry cases in gilded bronze.

It is also necessary to mention some other works, including *Crispin* (1890), *Etude d'enfant* (1900), *Musique champêtre* (1901), and *Bébé* (1902), all statuettes in plaster; *Yamina, danseuse arabe* (1899), *La Source* (1904), and *Pudeur et Esclave* (1908), all in marble; *Femme au serpent* (1910) in ivory and onyx; *Chasse au taureau* (1886), a group in terra cotta; and finally, some statues and groups in plaster primarily treating African themes.

MUSEUMS
Amiens
Buste de Nègre du Soudan, marble and bronze, 62 cm (1897).
Tourcoing
Musicien nègre, marble and bronze.

The museums of Chambéry, Compiègne (Vivenel museum), Dijon, Nice and Reims each possesses a proof of the haut-relief piece *Picador et taureau,* 44 x 70 cm. The museum of Nice also preserves a group entitled *Cavalier arabe attaqué par un fauve.*

SALES
Arabe, inkwell in bronze and alabaster, Blois, December 16, 1985.
Châtelaine au coffret, onyx pedestal, 18.5 cm, Drouot, December 7, 1983, room 14.
Cheval, 17.5 cm, Sotheby London, November 7, 1985.

LOMBARD, HENRI EDOUARD

Marseille, November 21, 1855
Paris, July 23, 1929

Lombard began exhibiting at the Salon in 1878, and won Rome's grand prize in 1883. He became a professor at the Ecole des Beaux-Arts, and sculpted statues and diverse monuments, particularly works with religious character. Attributed to him is a statue entitled *Vérité* for the Palais de Justice, *l'Eté* at the gardens of the Tuileries, a caryatid on the facade of the Crédit Lyonnais, and the group entitled *Paix* above the porch of the Grand Palais. Also notable is *Léda et le cygne,* a group in bronze.

LONGEPIED, LOUIS EUGÈNE

Paris, August 10, 1849
Paris, October 13, 1888

This sculptor worked on the city hall of Paris, and made the statue of *Philosophie* on the facade of the Sorbonne. He is known for a number of bronzes, including *Flocinière, harponneur napolitain,* 105 cm (Salon of 1884), the bust of *Félix Faure* (1885), and the statue of *Danton,* 307 cm, destined for the city of Arcis-sur-Aube (1888).

The Thiébaut foundry produced a bronze adition of *L'Immortalité,* 45 cm, from the group presented in plaster at the Salon of 1882 and in marble to the Salon of 1886. The museum of Epinal possesses a proof of this work of 74 cm high.

LORIEUX, JULIEN

Paris, December 31, 1876
Toul, April 30, 1915

J. LORIEUX

A student of Falguière and of Mercié at the Beaux-Arts, Lorieux won two grand prizes in Rome (one for medal-engraving and one for sculpture) before his premature death at the time of the First World War. In addition to some busts and medals, in 1913 he exhibited his master work at the Salon, a group in marble entitled *La Sainte-Catherine.* This piece was then bought by the city of Paris and made the object of a reduction cast in bronze. Lorieux is also the creator of a group in marble entitled *La Chute des feuilles* (Salon of 1907), placed in a park of Mont-de-Marsan. The museum of the Petit Palais in Paris possesses a bronze of 49.5 cm high representing a couple embracing, entitled *Printemps* (1909).

LORMIER, EDOUARD

Saint-Omer, January 22, 1847
Paris, June 7, 1919

Lormier went to Paris at the age of fifteen, entering first the Petite Ecole, and then the Beaux-Arts in the studio of Jouffroy. Very highly regarded in the North, he received commissions for many commemorative monuments: *Jacqueline Robin,* the heroine of Saint-Omer, for that city, *La Victoire de 1793* for Dunkerque, and *Aux sauveteurs* for Calais, among others. His work, very eclectic, also included some personages from local history as well as historical, literal or allegorical scenes. In addition to a number of busts (the majority in bronze) Lormier exhibited a number of pieces at the Salon, starting in 1866: *La Charité,* a group in stone for the hospice of Boulogne-sur-Mer (1885), *Fille d'Eve* and *Incroyable,* a statue and a statuette in plaster (1890), *Merveilleuse,* a statuette in plaster (1891), *Rêverie,* a statuette in bronze (1893), *Le Sauveteur,* a statue in bronze for the monument of Calais (1897), *Mort pour la patrie,* haut relief in bronze for a monument of Boulogne (1898), *Le Devoir,* a group in bronze (1909), *A la gloire de Watteau,* a group in bronze (1910), *En détresse* (1911) and *Pensive* (1912), two statuettes in plaster, and others. Many works by Lormier, including *Incroyable,* have been cast in bronze. For its part, the Susse foundry cast *Le Sauveteur* in three dimensions, 70, 50 and 29 cm.

MUSEUMS
Boulogne-sur-Mer
Frédéric Sauvage en prison, bas-relief, 74 x 80 cm (1881).

Julien Lorieux,
La Sainte-Catherine,
according to the marble
from the Salon of 1913.

Périgueux
Buste de Fulbert Dumonteil, écrivain périgourdin, 73 cm
(Montagutelli, founder).
Saint-Omer
Charles Laporterie, medallion, 60 cm diam. (1871).
Jacqueline Robin sur sa barque, bas-relief, 45 x 85 cm.

LOUIS-NOËL, HUBERT, KNOWN AS
NOËL LOUIS

Rumenghem (near Saint-Omer), April 1, 1839
Paris, 1925

Louis-Noël pursued the course of the Academic school of Saint-Omer while he was very young, and then, in 1859, began to study under François Jouffroy at the Ecole des Beaux-Arts of Paris. He debuted at the Salon in 1863, with some works in an academic style. A particularly productive artist, he exhibited there very regularly, contributing a number of busts and statues, portraits of historic people, contemporaries and saints. He worked on many monuments in the north of France, including the courthouse in Saint-Omer, the Hesdin hospital, and the church of Notre-Dame-des-Ardents in Arras. He sculpted many statues or projects of statues for Nancy (*Jacques Callot*), Angers (*David Angers*), Colmar (*Bartholdi*), and finally for Bapaume (a bronze entitled *Général Faidherbe*, considered one of his master works). Among his consignments to the Salon, a number of bronzes are memorable: *Notre-Dame-des-Ardents,* a statuette (1877), *David d'Angers,* a statue (1880), *L'Abbé Halluin,* a statue (1896), *Le Général Dupas,* a statue for Evian (1901), *Monsigny*, a statue (1905), and *Sainte Philomène*, a statuette (1912); some busts and medallions ought also to be taken into consideration. He produced moreover some statuettes in bronze: *Femme drapée tenant un masque*, 29.5 cm, *Femme apppuyée à une amphore*, and the very 'antique-y' *Rébecca*, 70 cm, among others.

MUSEUMS
Boulogne-sur-Mer
L'Abbé Halluin, reduction of a monument of Arras, 71 cm (1896).
Henri Dupuis, medallion, 19.5 cm diam.
Saint-Omer
Auguste Deschamps de Pas, medallion, 15 cm diam.

The museums of Arras, Boulogne-sur-Mer, and Saint-Omer preserve also a number of plaster works by this sculptor.

LOYSEL, JACQUES

Courcelles (Indre-et-Loire), May 29, 1867
Paris, November 1925

Loysel made his debut at the Salon in 1892 with a statue in plaster, *Ariane, ma soeur*. Next came some statuettes: *La Grande Névrose* (1896) and *Baigneuse* (1898), both in marble; *Etudes* (1899), in plaster; *Femme écartant son voile* and *Sur les rochers* (1914), both in alabaster; *La Source* (1906), in stone; and in bronze, *Le Golf* (1909), *Danseuse* (1912), and four figures entitled *Mouvements de danses grecques* (1913). Two other statuettes in bronze, *Un modèle se présente* and *Chien et chat* (Bingen cast), were exhibited at the Salon d'automne in 1904.

MUSEUM
Reims
Femme nue se chachant le visage, 35 cm.
Femme nue avec un chat, 34.2 cm.
Femme nue debout, 35.6 cm.

SALES
Danseuse, Blois, October 15, 1984.
Femme la poitrine découverte, 38.5 cm, Avignon, December 6, 1986.
Le Troubadour, 61 cm (Société des bronzes of Paris), Enghien, April 27, 1980.

Jacques Loysel,
Femme la poitrine découverte,
38.5 cm.

MABILLE JULES LOUIS

Valenciennes, August 14, 1843
Paris, June, 1897

A student of his hometown's academies and of the Beaux-Arts of Paris, Mabille worked on some monuments in Paris and Valenciennes. He produced busts as well as statues and anecdotal groups, a certain number of which were exhibited at the Salon between 1868 to 1896. Of particular note are a statuette in plaster, *Petit Tambour de bataillons scolaires* (1886), and a statue in bronze entitled *L'Amour blessé* (1889) for Monceau Park. The museum of Dunkerque possesses a statuette in bronze, *Vénus et l'amour*, 60 cm, sold at Andelys, October 31, 1982.

MACÉ, ÉMILE LOUIS

Born in Angers

This student of Cavellier worked in Angers and exhibited some busts and some medallions at the Salon between 1883 and 1896. At the museum of his hometown are found the busts in bronze of *J. Daillère*, 75 cm (1888) and *A. Maillé*, the latter cast by Gonon.

MADRASSI, LUCA

Tricessimo (Italy), June 8, 1848
1919

The Italian Madrassi went to Paris to study at the Ecole des Beaux-Arts, and assumed French nationality. Very imaginative, he executed a number of busts, statuettes, statues, and some groups, principally allegorical or genre. Some bronzes number among his consignments at the Salon, including two statues entitled *Puck* (1887) and *Pro Patria* (1912), cast by Goldscheider, and three groups entitled *Madeleine*, 80 cm (1880), *La Paix* (1893), and *Le Baiser* (1901). Also included in his Salon consignments are a number of bronze statuettes, including

Jules Louis Mabille,
Vénus et l'Amour, 60 cm.

445

Luca Madrassi,
L'Etoile du berger,
90 cm.

Luca Madrassi,
Lutin des bois,
104 cm.

Luca Madrassi,
Projet d'avenire,
78 cm.

Luca Madrassi,
Femme sur un nuage,
80 cm.

Lutteur (1898), *Le Lys* (1910), *Mercure* in gilded bronze, *Provocation* (1913), *La Défense, Tireur à l'arc* (1914), and three statuettes in marble and bronze: *Pensée lointaine* and *La Côte d'azur* (1905), and *L'Aurore* (1906). Also of note are some statuettes: *Naissance de Vénus* (1882), *Le Printemps* (1885), *Une leçon* (1888), *Prélude* (1889), and *Terpsichore, muse de la danse* (1899), all in plaster; *Hiver* (1889), *Maternité* (1890), and *La Fatalité* (1891), all in marble. A certain number of works by Madrassi have been cast in bronze.

SALES
Couple d'amoureux, 84 cm, Christie's New York, March 1, 1983.
L'Etoile du berger, 90 cm, Barcelonnette, July 20, 1985.
Femme à la coupe chevauchant un aigle, 78 cm, Drouot, July 3, 1981.
Femme nue, bras levés, 80 cm, Barcelonnette, July 20, 1985; Douai, November 16, 1986.

Jeune Femme debout, 68.5 cm, Sotheby London, March 26, 1980.
Jeune Fille les yeux bandés or the *Colin-Maillard,* 80.5 cm, Sotheby London, November 25, 1982.
Jeune Homme, bust, 34 cm, Drouot, March 28, 1985.
Lutin des bois, 83 cm, Saint-Quentin, December 19, 1982.
Lutin des bois, 104 cm, Sotheby London, November 6, 1986.
Nymphe, 129.5 cm, Christie's New York, May 17, 1983.
Projet d'avenir, 78 cm, La Flèche, November 16, 1986.
Zodiaque, 101 cm, Orléans, May 15, 1982.

MAILLARD, AUGUSTE

Paris, June 15, 1864
August 19, 1944

From this sculptor and engraver of medals, a student of Dalou and of Falguière, best known are some portraits in bust, medallion, statue and statuette form, which he exhibited at the Salon beginning in 1885. He also made many monuments to the dead, including those of Asnières and of Brest. Also of note is a statue in bronze, *Défense du sol* (1896), and the bust in bronze of *Coquelin aîné*. (1904). An equestrian statue, *Le maréchal Joffre*, appeared at the exposition devoted to the famous soldier, at the château of Vincennes in 1984. The museum of Orsay possesses a bronze bust of the artist's father, 45 cm, executed in 1899 and cast by Jaboeuf et Cie (Jaboeuf and Co.).

MAILLARD, CHARLES

Cholet, June 29, 1876
Corné (Maine-et-Loire), August 4, 1973

Maillard's consignments to the Salon, starting in 1904, included some bas-reliefs and figures, for the most part in terra cotta. He produced a number of models of animals, some of which would be reproduced in unglazed porcelain by Sèvres, or in bronze. Maillard's *Lièvre aux écoutes*, in bronze, appeared at

Charles Maillard,
L'Enfant au chat, 62 cm.

the Salon of 1907. A statuette, *Enfant au chat*, also in bronze, was sold at the Drouot hotel, March 30, 1983, and another proof, 62.5 cm high, was sold in New York by Sotheby, April 26, 1986.

MAILLET, JACQUES LÉONARD

Paris, July 12, 1823
Paris, February 14, 1895

This sculptor was awarded the first grand prize of Rome in 1847, after having studied first under the direction of Feuchère, and then of Pradier. He stayed in Rome for five years, and then debuted at the Salon in 1853. He worked on many Parisien churches, the Louvre, the city hall, and the Opera. His work, influenced by scenes from antiquity or the Bible, also includes some small terra cottas and models for goldsmiths. In 1859, he exhibited one of his major works at the Salon, a plaster entitled *Agrippine portant les cendres de Germanicus*, the marble version of which was placed in Paris's Monceau Park in 1893. Also at the Salon appeared some bronzes: *Jeune Syracusaine* in 1857, *Un chasseur* in 1864, *Buste de Charles Christofle*, 65 cm, for the tomb of the famous goldsmith at the Père-Lachaise in 1865, and *Buste d'enfant* in 1874.

MUSEUMS
Calais
Agrippine portant les cendres de Germanicus, reduction, 40 cm.
Périgueux
Le Jeune Chasseur, 217 cm (Salon of 1864)

MAILLOL, ARISTIDE

Banyuls, December 8, 1861
Banyuls, September 24, 1944

Not until he was forty years old was one of the most highly reputed sculptors of the first half of the 20th century able to devote himself fully to his art. According to biographer Waldemar George, Maillol was descended from a family of a rural origin, the son of a cloth merchant and grandson of an old sailor, and spent a sad childhood and boyhood amidst unbelievable poverty. Coming to Paris in 1881 to study painting, he was admitted to the Ecole des Beaux-Arts, though in the end he entered the studio of Cabanel and Gérôme. He lived in misery. In 1889, he made the acquaintance of Bourdelle, poor like himself, and inclined to welcome him. In 1893, he opened a tapestry studio in Banyuls and married one of his workers. Finally, in 1896, he exhibited his first sculptures at the Salon de la Société Nationale des Beaux-Arts: three in wood and one in wax, made under the influence of Gauguin. He installed his first studio in Villeneuve-Saint-Georges, met Picasso, frequented the Nabis, and pursued, always in destitution, his works of tapestry, sculpture, and ceramics. He modeled in particular some terra cottas which appear in certain paintings by his friends Bonnard and Vuillard. The merchant Ambroise Vollard bought some of them and organized an exposition of Maillol's works in 1902. He won a certain success in the artistic community, but remained ignored by the public at large.

In 1903, Maillol established himself in Marly-le-Roi and exhibited a relief in plaster, *La Femme au bain,* at the Nationale des Beaux-Arts. Two years later, a monumental event marked the end of his misery: Rodin introduced him to a German collector, the Count Harry Kessler, who became his patron. That same year, Maillol became friends with Matisse and devoted himself exclusively to sculpture, exhibiting an allegory of the *Méditerranée* at the Salon d'Automne. In 1907, he sculpted in Cagnes a portrait of Auguste Renoir, which in turn incited Renoir to try sculpture himself.

Maillol's notoriety spread henceforth more and more, principally abroad. In France, a certain number of his works were too far ahead of their time, and provoked veritable polemics against their "modernism" and their audacity of conception. This was the case was *L'Action enchaînée*, a monument to *Auguste Blanqui,* inaugurated in Puget-Théniers in 1908. It remained the case with Maillol's monument *Paul Cézanne,* which was refused by the city of Aix-en-Provence, but was placed in the Tuileries in 1929.

After the World War I, Maillol pursued a brilliant career, sculpting monuments to the dead in Banyuls and Port-Vendre as well as a quantity of other works, such as the monuent to *Debussy* (1935), *Les Trois Nymphes* (1936-1938), *L'Air* from the monument *Mermoz* for the city of Toulouse (1940), and *La Rivière* (1943), among others. A number of his great bronzes were placed on the lawns of the Carrousel in 1964, thanks both to a donation by Mme Dina Vierny, the artist's favorite model from 1934 to 1944, and to the decision of André Malraux, then minister of Cultural Affairs.

From the very beginning of his sculpting career, Maillol's work displayed a self-assured maturity; it essentially focused on the female body, presented with an astounding unity. Of a Mediterranean temperment, Maillol was fond of full, robust forms, architectural but still graceful, far removed from any agitations, and posed in tragic attitudes plagiarized from Rodin. "In him," wrote his friend Maurice Denis, "were combined two successive traditions, the fifth century Greek and the 18th century Christian, two arts which portrayed idealized types of humanity though the plenitude and simplicity of forms." In fact, Maillol focused his attention first and foremost on a purely formal heritage. Breaking with 19th century tradition, his works were destitute of all literary, political, mythological or social refer-

*Aristide Maillol,
Eve à la pomme, 1898-1899,
58 cm (Valsuani).*

Aristide Maillol,
Baigneuse debout les bras derrière le dos,
1902, 79 cm.
Dina Vierny Collection, Paris.

ences. Certain themes return incessantly in his production, particularly that of the squatting woman, which he drew, painted, weaved, and sculpted, and which would become *La Vague*, then *La Nymphe*, and finally *La Méditeraranée* (Cf. catalog from the exposition file*Maillol, La Méditerranée*, from the Museum of Orsay, 1986-1987).

Aristide Maillol practiced the direct cut only moderately, and in the 1900s had made a number of terra cottas. But, insisted Mme Dina Vierny, he was especially impassioned by bronzes, "correcting" them himself, always searching for perfection. Each model was executed in the dimension previewed for the casting; none of his monumental works was reproduced by reduction. His bronzes were cast by the lost wax method or in sand, in greatly reduced castings (except for some rare exceptions—six numbered models and some proofs by the artist), by Rudier, C. Valsuani, Godard, Bingen and Cotenoble. Some works were sold to the merchant Ambroise Vollard while Maillol lived in poverty, and these pieces were subjected to unlimited, unnumbered castings.

Mme Dina Vierny, to whom the family of Maillol transferred his rights in 1952, devoted her untiring activity to the defense of the sculptor. In 1977 she created a foundation, of which one of the objectives was to open a Maillol museum in the hotel Bouchardon, rue de Grenelle. The list below notes the bronzes cast from the principal works conceived before 1914:

1895
Femme vêtue accroupie (princess Bibesco), 15 cm.
Jeune Fille accroupie se coiffant, 17 cm.
Nabis nue, 29 cm.
Nabis vêtue, 22 cm.
La Vague, relief, 29 cm.

1896
Les Deux Femmes assises, 13 cm.
Femme nue assise, 27 cm.
L'Homme et la femme, 17 cm.
L'Homme et la femme, 24 cm.
La Lavandière, 12 x 28 cm.
La Parisienne, 24.1 cm.
Petite Vénus sans bras, 36 cm.

1898-1899
Buste de femme, 30.5 cm.
Eve à la pomme, 58 cm.
La Pendule, 51.5 cm.

1900
Baigneuse debout, 63 cm.
Baigneuse debout, 80 cm.
Baigneuse debout les deux mains aux épaules, 120 cm.
Baigneuse debout se coiffant, 28 cm.
Baigneuse se voilant les yeux, 24.5 cm.
Les Deux Lutteuses, 20 cm.
Femme accroupie, 20 cm.
Femme au chignon or *Baigneuse debout*, 66 cm.
Femme au crabe, 16.5 cm.
Jeune Fille accroupie, 17 cm.
Jeune Filel agenouillée, 25.5 cm.

Aristide Maillol,
La Pudique, 1900, 17 x 21 cm.
Dina Vierny Collection, Paris.

Jeune Fille agenouillée, 85 cm.
Jeune Fille assise se tenant la jambe, 21.2 cm.
Jeune Fille au chignon pointu, 16 cm.
Léda, 29 cm.
La Pensive, 15.5 cm.
La Pudique, 17 x 21 cm.
Tête de femme, 30.5 cm.
Torse à la chemise, 21 cm.
Torse d'Eve, 43.2 cm.

1900-1905
La Méditerranée, 1st state, 118 x 142 cm (1900-1902).
La Méditerranée, study, 17.8 cm (1905).
La Méditerranée, study of a torso, 64.2 cm (1905).
La Méditerranée, 104 cm (1902-1905).
La Méditerranée, diverse studies, 15, 17, 18, 20.5 cm
    (1902).

1902
Baigneuse debout les bras derrière le dos, 79 cm.
Femme assuse, 28 cm.
Petite Pensée habillée, 13 cm.
La Nuit, 105 cm.
Etude pour la Nuit, 17.5 cm (1908).

1904-1906
L'Action enchaînée, sans bras, 2nd state, 220 cm
    (1905).
L'Action enchaînée, torso, 130 cm (1905).
L'Action enchaînée (monument to Auguste Blanqui),
    220 cm (1905-1906).
L'Action enchaînée, torso 25.5 cm (1904).
L'Action enchaînée, torso, 14 cm (1905).
L'Action enchaînée, sans bras, 33 cm (1905).
Baigneuse accroupie, 99 x 103 cm (1904).
Le Désir, relief, 119 cm (1906-1908).
La Nymphe, 24.5 cm (1905).
Femme à la colombe, 25.4 cm (1905).

1907
Le Cycliste, 98 cm.
Femme assise (statuette represented by Renoir), 20.6
    cm.
Jeune Fille debout se coiffant, 37.5 cm.
Tête de Renoir, 43 cm.

1910-1911
L'Eté, 162 cm.
Flore, 167 cm.

451

Aristide Maillol,
Jeune Fille assise,
1900, 18 cm.

Flore nue, 170 cm.
Petite Flore nue, 61 cm.
Petite Flore drapée, 60 cm.
L'Ile-de-France, torso, 1st state, 8.5 cm.
L'Ile-de-France, torso, or *Jeune Fille qui marche dans l'eau*, 125 cm.
La Jeunesse, 116 cm.
Pomone, 163 cm.
Le Printemps, torso, 148 cm.
Le Printemps, 171 cm.
Torse, 20 cm.
Torse sur le dauphin, 17.1 cm.

1912-1914
Monument à Paul Cézanne, study, 14 x 23 cm (1912).
Monument à Paul Cézanne, study, 17 x 30 cm (1914).

MUSEUMS
Albi
Vénus au collier, 175 cm.
Bagnols-sur-Cèze
Les Lutteuses, 18 cm (1900; edition Vollard).
Calais
Jeune Fille à la draperie.

Lyon
Femme nue debout, Torse de femme, Vénus.
Montpellier
La Femme qui marche dans l'eau, 125 cm (Valsuani No2).
Orléans
Figure centrale des trois nymphes, 56 cm.
Paris, museum Maillol
This museum possesses the largest group of the sculptor's plasters, marbles, terra cottas, bronzes, drawings, tapestries, and ceramics, with the exception of certain monumental pieces that can be seen most notably on the lawns of the Carrousel.
Paris, Orsay
Baigneuse bras levés, 122 cm (1900; Rudier).
Baigneuse debout, 78 cm (1900; Rudier).
Le Cycliste, 98.5 cm (1907; Godard).
Femme accroupie, 19.5 cm (Rudier).
La Méditerranée, 1st state, 118 x 142 cm.
La Montagne, sketch, 27.5 x 28.8 cm (1935; Rudier 1/6).
Pomone drapée, 176 cm (1921; Godard).
Torse de femme, 66 cm (1900).
Torse du Printemps, 148 cm (Godard).

Aristide Maillol,
L'Action enchaînée,
study without arms
for the monument to
Auguste Blanqui,
second state, 220 cm
(1905). Dina Vierny
Collection, Paris.

Perpignan
Eve à la pomme, 58 cm (Rudier).
Poitiers
Femme nue assise, 22 cm (1900).
La Pudique, 22 cm (1900).
Saint-Denis de la Réunion
Les Deux Soeurs, 51 cm.
Saint-Tropez
Baigneuse or *Jeune Fille à la draperie*, 174 cm (1910; Rudier).
Femme se coiffant, 81 cm (1919; Rudier).
   The museum possesses some other, more recent works, including the *Nymphe* of 1936, 156 cm.
Strasbourg
Baigneuse, 67.
Baigneuse se coiffant, 27 cm.
Femme nue assise sur un rocher, 21.5 cm.
Les Deux Lutteuses, 18 cm (1900).
Troyes, museum of modern Art
Femme nue debout, 66 cm (1900).
Femme nue à la draperie, 68 cm (1900).

   Some bronzes by Maillol appear in a number of other museums, as many in France as abroad.

*Aristide Maillol,
Les Deux Lutteuses, 1900, 19 cm
(Godard 2/6).*

*Aristide Maillol,
La Nymphe,
1905, 24.5 cm.
Dina Vierny Collection, Paris.*

SALES

L'Action enchaînée, study, 31.8 cm (1905; Rudier 1/6), Sotheby London, June 30, 1983.

Auguste Renoir, bust, 40 cm (1907; Rudier), Christie's New York, November 13, 1985.

Baigneuse à l'écharpe, 33 cm (1919; Valsuani 1/6), Christie's New York, May 17, 1984.

Baigneuse aux bras levés, 160 cm (1898; Rudier cast 5/6 around 1930), Christie's New York, November 13, 1985 (sold for 325,000 dollars).

Baigneuse se coiffant, 35 cm (1919-1920; Rudier 6/6), Christie's New York, May 16, 1985.

Baigneuse debout, 66 cm (cast to 12 models), Munich, May 31, 1983.

Baigneuse se coiffant, avec draperie, coude levé, 76.5 cm (Valsuani 5/6), Zurich, May 26, 1984.

Baigneuse debout, 78.5 cm (Rudier 3/6), Sotheby New York, november 15, 1984.

Eve à la pomme, 59 cm (1899; Rudier), Sotheby London, June 25, 1986.

Femme accroupie, 19.5 cm (Rudier), Christie's New York, November 20, 1986.

Femme assise, 26 cm (1902, cast to 4 models), Christie's New York, May 17, 1984.

Femme assise, 22 cm, Drouot, June 18, 1985, rooms 5 and 6.

Femme à la colombe, 24.5 cm (1905; Rudier cast 3/6 of 1927), Sotheby New York, May 16, 1984.

Flore, 160 cm (one of the 8 models by Godard, 1914-1918), Christie's New York, November 13, 1984.

Flore drapée, torso, 63 cm (1910; Valsuani 6/6), Christie's New York, November 14, 1984.

Le Jeune Homme, 31.5 cm (1908; Valusani cast 2/6, 1930), Sotheby New York, May 16, 1984.

Les Deux Lutteuses, 19 cm (1900; Rudier), Sotheby London, June 25, 1986; (Godard 5/6), Sotheby New York, May 16 1984; (Godard 2/6), Sotheby New York, November 15, 1984; (Godard), Sotheby London, December 4, 1985.

Monument à Cézanne, study, 20.3 cm, Christie's New York, November 20, 1986.

La Nuit, 17.5 cm (1902; Rudier 3/6), Sotheby New York, November 17, 1983.

Torse à la chemise, 21.5 cm (1900), Cologne, June 2, 1984.

Torse de Vénus, 114 cm (1920; Rudier 4/6), Christie's New York, November 12, 1985 (270,000 dollars).

MAINDRON, HIPPOLYTE

Champtoceaux (Maine-et-Loire), December 16, 1801
Paris, March 21, 1884

While working on the front of the Panthéon, Maindron collaborated with David d'Angers, whose studio he frequented. For that monument, he also executed two groups in marble, *Clovis baptisé par saint Remi* and *Sainte Geneviève désarmant Attila.* He also worked on the Louvre, the Palais de Justice, the Tribunal de Commerce, the Pont-Neuf, the Palais de Fontainebleau, and the cathedral of Sens, and furnished groups and statues to a number of French cities. In 1834, he debuted at the Salon with a plaster, *Jeune Berger piqué par un serpent,* followed, in 1839, by another plaster entitled *Velleda,* which enjoyed considerable success—the marble would be placed in the Luxembourg gardens. These pieces were followed in the Salon by a statue in bronze of *Aloys Senefelder, inventeur de la lithographie* (1863), and a statuette in bronze of the actor *Bocage* presented at the Exposition Universelle of 1900, etc. With the exception of the statue of *Velleda,* it seems that the works of Maindron have been rarely cast in bronze of small dimensions.

MUSEUMS

Châlons-sur-Marne
Le Duc de La Rochefoucauld-Liancourt.
Paris, Decorative Arts
Jeune Femme debout tenant un châle, 44 cm (Eck and Durand).
Paris, Carnavalet
Jean Georges Eck, fondeur, medallion, 20 cm diam.
Paris, Louvre
Benjamin Fillon, medallion, 20.5 cm diam. (1856).

MAIRE, JEAN-BAPTISTE

Gerné-Fontaine (Doubs), August 15, 1789
Gerné-Fontaine, December 18, 1859

Maire exhibited at the Salon only in 1819, 1822, and 1824. A number of stone or marble busts and some medallions (for the most part portraits of celebrities of Franche-Comté) constitute the bulk of this sculptor's work. The museum of Avignon possesses a small medallion in bronze, 11 cm diam., entitled *Napoléon 1er* and dated 1814.

MALISSARD, GEORGES

Anzin (Nord), October 3, 1877
April 13, 1942

The horse (with or without a rider) and other animals constitute this sculptor's preferred theme. After the war of 1914-1918, Malissard received commissions for many equestrian statues: *Le Roi de Belgique Albert 1er, Le Roi d'Espagne Alphonse XIII,* and the marshals *Pétain, Lyautey, Foch* and *Joffre.* At the Salon, starting in 1908, he sent particularly some bronzes: *Violon II, étalon pur-sang* and *Vieux Cheval de chasse usé* (1908), *La Jument Marinette* and *La Jument Flûte* (1909), *Un étalon* and *La Jument Riveraine* (1910), *La Comtesse R. de B. à cheval* (1912), *Eléphant d'Asie* and *Madame Jean Stern à cheval* (1913), *En vedette, cuirassier sous le vent* (1914), etc. Many works by Malissard were cast by Valsuani.

SALES

Jockey et chevaux à l'entraînement, 38 x 60 cm, Christie's Amsterdam, June 16, 1983.

Homme en chapeau, à cheval, 51 cm (Valsuani), La Flèche, November 24, 1985.

Le Maréchal Foch à cheval, 51 x 54 cm, Drouot, March 17, 1982; Sotheby London, March 8, 1984; Drouot, December 6, 1984, room 5.

Miss Ruth Roach dans Wild West Rodeo (1924), Drouot, January 31, 1983, room 7.

MARCELLIN, JEAN ESPRIT

Gap, May 24, 1821
Paris, June 22, 1884

A student of Rude and then of the Ecole des Beaux-Arts, Marcellin worked on the Louvre, the Tuileries, the churches Saint-Gervais and the Sorbonne, for the prefecture of Marseille (front), and for the city of Gap. He exhibited some remarkable works at the Salon, beginning in 1845: *Le Berger Cyparisse*, marble (1850), *Cypris allaitant l'Amour*, marble (1853), *Bacchante se rendant au sacrifice*, marble (1869 and Exposition of 1878), *La Jeunesse captivant l'Amour* (1885), as well as some statuettes in wood: *Le Petit Maraudeur*, and *Le Premier Bijou* (1865). A bronze, *Jeune Femme et l'Amour*, 53 cm, was sold in London by Sotheby, November 7, 1985.

MARCELLO, ADÈLE D'AFFRY, DUCHESSE, KNOWN AS CASTIGLIONE COLONNA

Fribourg (Switzerland), July 6, 1836
Castellamare (near Naples), July 14, 1879

This painter, designer and sculptor sojourned in Rome from 1853 to 1854, marrying the Duke of Castiglione Colonna; she also lived in Paris and in the suburbs of Fribourg in Switzerland. Later she returned to Rome, where she met Carpeaux in 1861.

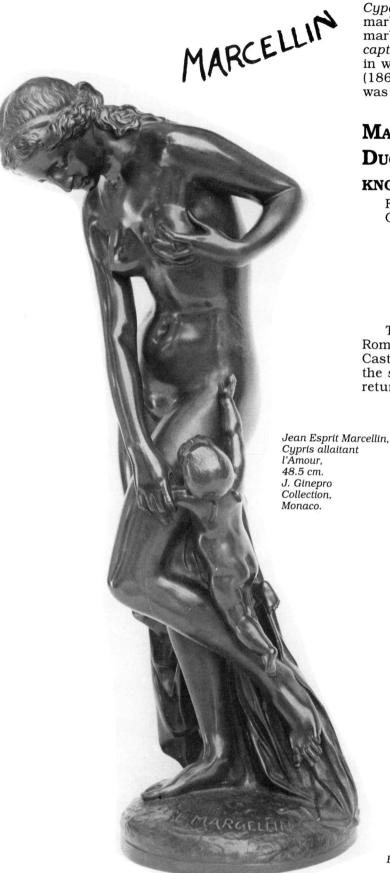

Jean Esprit Marcellin, Cypris allaitant l'Amour, 48.5 cm. J. Ginepro Collection, Monaco.

Marcello, Buste de femme à la tresse, 56 cm.

In Fribourg she established the foundation which carries her name and which possesses a large part of her production. She exhibited at the Salon of Paris starting in 1863, and her works enjoyed an incontestable success. Many of her bronzes were cast by Barbedienne or Thiébaut frères and are preserved today at the foundation Marcello, at the museum of Fribourg, or in a number of other museums and private collections. Notable are the castings by Barbedienne of a bust entitled *Bianca Capello*, 34 cm, and *Gorgone*, 103, 50 and 40 cm, and by Thiébaut of *La Pythie*, 80 and 47 cm (according to the bronze of the Opera of Paris).

MUSEUMS

Among the bronzes preserved by the foundation Marcello of Fribourg are *Bianca Capello*, bust, 85.5 cm (Barbedienne), *Le Chef abyssin*, bust, 105 cm, *Marie-Antoinette au Temple*, bust, 94 cm.

At the museum of Art and of Histoire of Fribourg, of note are *La Belle Hélène*, 42 cm (Barbedienne), *Portrait de Carpeaux*, 66 cm (1875), and *La Pythie*, 122 cm (Thiébaut).

Other bronzes appear at the Bethnal Green museum in London (*La Gorgone*) and at the Philadelphia Museum of Art (*La Pythie*).

SALES

Buste de femme à la tresse, 56 cm, Lille, November 25, 1985.

MARCHEGAY, GUSTAVE

Saint-Germain-de-Prinçay (Vendée), August 25, 1859
1932

This animal sculptor (and watercolorist) specialized exclusively in the representation of fish. The museum of Orsay possesses two statuettes by him in bronze: *Perche*, 14 x 25 cm, and *Truite*, 12 x 13.5 cm.

MARÉCHAL, RENÉ AMBROISE

Paris, February 1, 1818
Rome, October 9, 1847

The winner of the first prize of Rome in 1843, this sculptor died prematurely while still resident student at the villa Médicis. Attributable to him, from the Salon of 1842, are a small model of a statue of *Marie-Amélie, reine des Français* and some mythological or religious works sent from Rome. The museum of decorative arts possesses two bronze statuettes of dancers dating from before his departure for Italy: *Marie Taglioni dans le ballet d'Endymion*, 43 cm (cast by Eck and Durand around 1840) and *Louise Fitzjames* (1842).

MARIE, DÉSIRÉ PIERRE LOUIS

Born in Anisy (Calvados)

This sculptor exhibited at the Salon only in 1861 and 1863, this last year a statue in bronze, *Suzanne au bain*. The château of Compiègne possesses a small bust in bronze, *L'Impératrice Eugénie*, 32 cm (1859).

MARIOTON, CLAUDIUS

Paris, February 2, 1844
Paris, April 26, 1919

Marioton

Part of Marioton's abundant production of busts, medallions, and anecdotal subjects appeared at the Salon. He was a regular exhibitor there from 1873 until his death, showing a wide selection of pieces in bronze, sometimes accompanied by other materials.

Claudius Marioton,
Diogène, 80 cm
(E. Colin, founder).

In particular, there are some statuettes: *Coquette précoce*, 90 cm (1880); *Tyrtée et les cerises* (1887); *Refrain du printemps*, silvered bronze and marble (1888); *Phébé*, silvered bronze (1889); *Clytie* (1890); *Bûcheron* and *David vainqueur*, gilded bronze and marble (1894); *Arbalétrier du XVe siècle*, gilded bronze and marble (1902); *La Canne*, gilded bronze (1909); and *La Gloire*, gilded bronze and marble (1912). Also notable, and all in bronze, are: *Diogène* (1885); *Le Travail guidant la Fortune* (1888); *La Rosée*, water lily lamp in gilded bronze and porphyry (1892); and *Groupe d'enfants*, another lamp in gilded bronze, marble and crystal (1896). Also noteworthy are *Ondine* (1886), and *Byzance* (1891), two statuettes in gold and silver, the second adorned by ivory, enamel, precious stones, and two statues in plaster, *L'Amour faisant tourner le monde* (1879) and *Le Plaisir* (1880).

Diverse works by Claudius Marioton were made the object of editions in bronze, firstly his *Diogène*, which seems to have known a certain success and which was cast in many dimensions by the founder E. Colin. *L'Amour faisant tourner le monde* was cast by Thiébaut in two dimensions, 79 and 40 cm. Also known are an edition of *Plaisir*, 70 cm high.

MUSEUM
Paris, Decorative Arts
Diogène, 54 cm.

SALES
Diogène, 80 cm (E. Colin), Drouot, June 1, 1983, room 4; New York, September 27, 1986.

MARIOTON, EUGÈNE

Paris, April 7, 1857
September 19, 1933

Brother to Claudius Marioton as well as a sculptor and a prolific medal-engraver, Eugène enjoyed a strong reputation for nearly fifty years, producing a number of allegorical subjects, antique and genre scenes, and some portraits, which he exhibited at the Salon starting in 1882. He showed there a number of bronzes, including busts, medallions, statues and groups such as *Gloria Patrix* (1886), *L'Avenir* (1887), *Frères d'armes* (1890), *Zéphire* (1894), *Le Retour* (1903), *Eros enfant* (1904), *Hyménée* (1912). Some statuettes are of especial note: *La Force protégeant le Droit* (1899), *Fleur des champs* (1901), *Méditation* and *Devoir civique* (1902), *La Danse* (1903), *Le Travail* (1905), *Premier frisson* (1906), *Danseuse pompéienne* (1907), and *Muse des eaux* (1908), all in gilded bronze, *Gloire au travail* (1909), *La Victoire* (1910), *L'Abeille* (1911), *La Chanson*, (1912), *Mignon* and *La Vaillance* (1913), *Jockey vainqueur* and *Premier Berceau* (1914), etc.

Rather numerous works by Eugène Marioton have been produced in bronze, such as (cast by Jollet) *La Victoire*; (cast by Colin's) *Fleur des champs*, *Méditation*, *La Danse*, a bust of *Manon*, and *La Musique*; (cast by Siot-Decauville) *Charmeur de serpent*, also called *Fascinator* and *Belluaire*; and (without indication of a founder) *Devoir civique*, *Le Retour du vainqueur*, 91 cm, *Jeanne d'Arc debout en bergère*, and *L'Inspiration*, 92.5 cm.

*Eugène Marioton,
La Danse, 83 cm
(E. Colin, founder).*

SALES
Belluaire, 50 cm (Siot-Decauville), Sotheby London, November 8, 1984.
Belluaire, 84 cm, Valenciennes, December 1, 1986.

Eugène Marioton,
Esméralda.

Eugène Marioton,
Fascinator,
52 cm.

459

Eugène Marioton,
Le Couvre-feu,
78 cm.

Le Couvre-feu, bronze and ivory, 33.5 cm, Drouot, November 28, 1984, room 13.
Le Couvre-feu, 78 cm, Dijon, March 25, 1984.
La Danse, 83 cm, Sotheby London, June 12, 1986.
Esméalda, Evreux, December 14, 1986.
Fascinator, 32.5 cm, Drouot, June 21, 1985.
Femme embrassant un enfant, 50 cm, Sotheby London, April 28, 1982.
Femme à la lyre, 83 cm, Drouot, June 21, 1985.
Femme jouant de la double-flûte, 100 cm, Sotheby London, March 20, 1986.
Femme de la Belle Époque, bust in gilded bronze, 22.5 cm (E. Colin), Sotheby Monaco, October 6, 1985.
Le Gladiateur, 41 cm, Lokeren, June 1, 1985.
Le Guerrier vainqueur, 50 cm, Sotheby London, November 8, 1984; Fontainebleau, June 2, 1985.
Le Moissonneur, 49 cm (Siot-Decauville), Lokeren, April 20, 1985.

MAROCHETTIE, BARON CHARLES

Turin, January 1805
London, 1868

Enrolled in the studio of Bosio in Paris, Marochettie failed to win the prize of Rome but nonetheless went back to study in his native Italy. Upon returning to France, he received some important commissions. In 1834, he sculpted a very large bas-relief in stone, *La Bataille de Jemmapes* (17 m. L.) for the Arc de Triomphe of the Etoile, and *L'Apothéose de sainte Madeleine*, a group in marble for the high altar of the church of the Madeleine. In 1837, he sculpted an equestrian statue in bronze of Emmanuel-Philibert de Savoie for a square in Turin; this piece was to be considered his masterpiece. In 1841—the year in which he acquired French citizenship—he sculpted the *Archange Gabriel* in stone for the gable of Saint-Germain-l'Auxerrois. In 1844, he completed the work *Duc d'Orléans équestre* in bronze, originally destined for the court of the Louvre. Leaving for England at the time of the revolution of 1848, Marochettie executed many monuments and statues there, including *Reine Victoria équestre* for Glasgow and *Richard Coeur de Lion* for Westminster Palace.

The catalog of Susse editions lists a statuette of *Emmanuel-Philibert de Savoie*, 60, 40 and 20 cm, *Saint Louis à genoux*, 40 cm, *Charles 1er équestre*, 100, 50, 35 and 18 cm, *Le Chevalier Bayard*, 100 cm, and a pair entitled *Sodlats porte-torchère*, 100, 70 and 45 cm.

Le Duc de Wellington à cheval, 42.5 cm, was sold in London by Christie's on April 13, 1983.

MARQUE, ALBERT

Nanterre, July 14, 1872

Marque participated in different salons, in particular at the Salon de la Nationale des Beaux-Arts from 1899 to 1904. Notable here are some groups, especially of children. These include, from 1902 *Femme et enfant*, *Les Amants*, and *Femme inquiète*, all in bronze, and *Jeune Penseur*, in bronze and marble. Also of note is a statuette in bronze, *Femme se coiffant*. Two bronzes appear at the museum of Lyon: *Enfant à la grappe* and *Maternité*.

MARQUESTE, LAURENT

Toulouse, June 12, 1848
Paris, April 5, 1920

Marqueste

A court sculptor, winner of the first prize of Rome in 1871, and a member of the Institut in 1900, Marqueste began as a student of Jouffroy and Falguière. His production, very abundant, responded to multiple commissions and won him a number of distinctions. He worked on the city hall (*L'Art*, statue

Laurent Marqueste,
Renommée,
gilded bronze,
49.5 cm.

in bronze on the principal facade), the Galerie d'Anatomie, the Jardin des Plantes (*Le Dressage des chevaux*, haut-relief in bronze on the lateral facade), the Sorbonne, the train station of Orsay, and the Alexandre III Bridge. In the gardens of the Tuileries, he erected the monument *Waldeck-Rousseau*, and also finished the bronze *Etienne Marcel équestre* started by Idrac and placed in front of the lateral facade of the city hall. Starting on 1874, he sent to the Salon some busts of personalities, allegories, people and mythological groups, the majority in plaster or marble. He also sent some busts in bronze (*Falguière, Banjamin Constant*, and *Camille Saint-Saëns*) and a sketch, *L'Enlèvement de Déjanire* (1906). It seems that very few works by Marqueste were made the object of castings in bronze, with the exception of a statuette entitled *Cupidon* by Siot-Decauville and *Renommée*, of which some proofs in bronze and ivory also exist.

MUSEUMS
Montpellier
Buste de M. Ricome, 57 cm.
Rouen
Cupidon, 105 cm.
Toulouse
Buste de Benjamin Constant, 50.5 cm.
Buste de Falguière, 51.7 cm.

MARQUET DE VASSELOT, COMTE, ANATOLE DE

Paris, June 16, 1840
Neuilly-sur-Seine, April 1904

This son of a lawyer was twenty-five years old when he started to study painting with Bonnat and sculpture with Jouffroy. He decided to devote himself to the latter, and exhibited first at the Salon des Artistes français from 1866 to 1894; he switched to

Comte de Marquet
de Vasselot,
Mon Petit Charlot,
48 cm
(Paris 1887).

the Nationale des Beaux-Arts in 1895, but returned to the Artistes français in 1900. His significant works include a quantity of busts and statues of historic or contemporary people. Among the works shown at the Salon were quite a number of bronzes: a portrait in medallion of *Madame Marquet de Vasselot* (1867), a bust entitled *Le Souffle suprême* (1885), a statuette entitled *Jean-Jacques Rousseau* (1886), and some other statues: *Poveretto* or *Petot Joueur de musette*, 112 cm (1880), *Un ymagier du roy* (1883), *Un mineur*, destined for the mines of Bruay (1884), *Un rabbin* (1886), *Lamartine assis* (presented at Lamartine Square in 1886), *Mon Petit Charlot* (1887). At the Salon de la société Nationale des Beaux-Arts, Marquet de Vasslot showed the statues of *Jean-Jacques Rousseau* in 1897 and of the *Marquis de Morès* in 1898.

After a contract was established in 1892, some works by Maruqet de Vasslot were cast by Barbedienne, particularly *Poveretto* and a small bust of *Balzac,* 19 cm. The museum of Valenciennes possesses the *Poveretto* bronze of 112 cm cast by Barbedienne. Another bronze, *Mon Petit Charlot,* 122 cm (by Bingen, founder), was sold by Sotheby in London, November 6, 1986.

MARS-VALLET, MARIUS, KNOWN AS VALLET

Chambéry, November 5, 1896
Chambéry, March 15, 1957

The son of a marbler and a student of Falguière, this sculptor and medaller exhibited at the Salon from 1892 to 1896, and at the Nationale des Beaux-Arts starting in 1896. Of note are some bronzes: *Sur une piste,* bronze and marble, in 1895; *Ondine,* 1897; *Dans l'Eden,* (Eve) in 1902, *Aux lueurs de l'incendie de Rome, Néron,* statuette, in 1913. Mars-Vallet received some official commissions, in particular one for a statue of *Jean-Jacques Rousseau* for Chambéry and a monument to *Garnier* for Hong Kong. In 1904, he was named curator of the museum of fine arts of his hometown. Around the end of his life, in 1948, he gave thirty-one of his statues to this museum. He also became the curator of the Savoisien museum in 1940.

The Siot-Decauville foundry cast, in bronze, a feminine statuette entitled *Wuilfride,* which was a portrait of the famous Sarah Bernhardt. Also noteworthy is a lamp entitled *Loïe Fuller portant deux torche,* 36 cm, a model of which has been noted in an American collection.

Among the works given to the museum of Chambéry are three bronzes: *Eve,* 60 cm, *L'Ingénieur Domergue,* medallion, 40 cm diam, and *Le Peintre Benoît Molin,* bust, 61 cm.

MARZOLFF, ALFRED

Strasbourg, 1867—?

This sculptor and medaller studied in Munich, then exhibited at the Salon of Paris. The museum of Strasbourg preserves his bust of the painter *Hornecker,* 56 cm, dated 1894.

MASSÉ, RENÉ CHARLES

Génelard (Saône-et-Loire), 1856
Troyes

Massé worked first in Paris, but in 1890 moved to Brienne-le-Château, where in 1901 he founded a studio for terra cotta and sandstone work. This studio was shortlived, and Massé established himself next in Troyes, where he would reside until his death. This artist's work focused on some Oriental subjects, some of them cast in regule, particularly *Deux Orientaux porte-torchère,* 130 cm high. Massé sent to the Salon some busts as well as a statue in plaster entitled *Les Saltimbanques* (1893).

MASSON, CLOVIS

Paris, March 7, 1838
September 10, 1913

An animal sculptor and a student of Barye, Masson participated regularly at the Salon from 1867 to 1909, almost exclusively with plasters and waxes representing big game and deer. Among the plasters, one can note: *Chasse au tigre dans l'Inde* (1867), *Kabyle surpris par un lion* (1868), *Sanglier surpris par un lion* (1869), and *Une rencontre au centre de l'Afrique* (1876). A number of waxes can be noted, including *Famille de chevreuils* (1880), *Cheval arabe* (1887), *Gorille terrassant un lion* (1894), *Le roi boit* (1905), etc. Three bronzes are also noteworthy: *Combat de cerfs* (1890), *Jeune Chien de berger* (1891), *Chevreuil au débuché,* (1900). The Thiébaut foundry cast *Eléphant,* 20 cm, *Lion à la source,* 16 cm, *Lion en chasse,* 18 cm, *Tigre à l'affût,* 10 cm, *Tigre grimpant,* 21 cm, *Tigre sur sphinx,* 15 cm. The Susse foundry is responsible for castings of *Chevreuil au débuché,* 34 cm, *Chienne et ses petits,* 30 and 7 cm, *Chatte,* 35 cm, and *Groupe de canards,* 9 cm. At the museum of Nîmes can be found a bronze by Masson entitled *Chevreuil au débuché.*

SALES

Cerf, 30 cm, Sotheby London, June 7, 1984.
Les Cerfs, Fontainebleau, June 3, 1984.
Cerf et biche, 63.5 cm (Société des bronzes de Paris), Sotheby London, June 12, 1986.
Cheval percheron, 67 cm (Susse), Dijon, November 27, 1983.
Chien de chasse à l'arrêt, 27.5 cm, Versailles, October 21, 1984.
Chien tenant un faisan, 42 x 65 cm, Drouot, May 27, 1983, room 10.
Groupe de chiens, Drouot, January 16, 1985.
Combat de cerfs, 44 x 60 cm, Drouot, November 23, 1983, rooms 5 and 6.
Deux Faisans, 58.5 cm, Sotheby London, March 20, 1986.
Lion blessé, 33 cm, Grenoble, April 26, 1982.
Lion couché, Fontainebleau, October 7, 1984.
Lion et lionne, 35 cm, Drouot, June 6, 1984, room 2.
Lionne, 29.5 cm L., Drouot, December 20, 1983, room 10.
Lionne couchée, 13 x 35 cm, Drouot, May 27, 1983, room 4.
Tigre à l'attaque, 30 cm, Drouot, December 9, 1982, room 8.

Clovis Masson,
Lion, 33.5 x 37 cm (1882).

MASSON, JULES EDMOND
Paris, June 3, 1871
December 1932

The son and student of Clovis Masson, this sculptor and engraver in medals practiced animal art like his father, with a preference for Oriental scenes and for equestrian figures of historic people. Starting in 1890, he sent to the Salon a number of waxes, plasters and bronzes, such as: *Taureau espagnol* and *Ane marocain* (1894), *Pro Patria* (1900), *Un accident* and *Après le combat (cerfs)*, the latter in bronze and marble (1906), *La Lutte pour la vie* (1908), *Une belle pièce (braques Saint-Germain)* and *Perdreau* (1909), *Napoléon 1er à cheval* and *En arrêt, groupe de chiens* (1913), etc.

Also noteworthy are *Charles le Téméraire équestre* (1898) and *Chasse au sanglier* (1912) in plaster, as well as some equestrian figures in wax: *Duguesclin* (1899), *Fauconnier arabe* (1901), *Attila* (1903), *Charlemagne* (1904), *Rapt* (1908), and *Jehanne d'Arc* (1910).

Many works exhibited at the Salon were indicated as having been made the object of castings in bronze: *Après le combat* by Frédéric Goldscheider, *Napoléon 1er à cheval* and *En arrêt* by C. Lumineau. From the Susse foundry can be found *Duguesclin équestre*, *Napoléon 1er équestre*, 45 cm, and *Buste de Napoléon 1er,* 16 cm.

Clovis Masson,
Combat de cerfs,
44 x 60 cm.

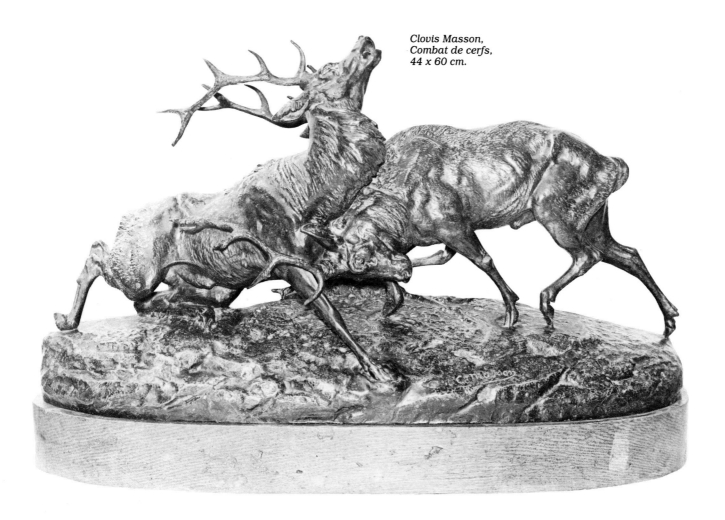

463

MUSEUMS
Dijon
Siège de Paris, maquette of a horse, 26 x 44 cm (1884).
Trompette de cavalerie à cheval, 54 cm.
Troyes
Duguesclin à cheval, 47 cm.

SALES
Cerf et deux biches, 68 cm, Brussels, March 1, 1984.
Deux Canetons se disputant une grenouille (Susse),
     Reims, October 26, 1986.
Deux Chiens de chasse, 39.5 cm, Christie's London,
     July 17, 1984.
Deux Chiens courant, 54 cm, Versailles, November 14,
     1982.

Massoule, André

Epernay, November 5, 1851
Paris, June 19, 1901

The author of busts, medallions and statues of contemporary or historical people, Massoule executed two groups in hammered copper representing some genies with fish in 1900, for the Alexandre-

André Massoule,
Guerrier portant une épée,
57 cm.

André Massoule,
Guerrier forgeant ses armes,
54 cm.

III Bridge. His notable works at the Salon, where he exhibited from 1878 to 1899, include a statue in stone of *Maréchal de Catinat* for the city hall (1881), *Un ancêtre*, a bronze statue of a warrior carrying a sword, destined for the square at the Invalides (1884), *Jeanne d'Arc écoutant ses voix*, a statuette in bronze (1890), *L'Aurore et la Rosée*, a vase in marble (1896), and *Naïade*, a statuette in marble (1899). Thiébaut frères cast two statuettes in bronze: *Distraite*, 40 cm, and *L'Ancêtre*, 75, 57, 40 and 25 cm. Furthermore, Massoule furnished some models of vases for the Sèvres factory.

SALES
Guerrier forgeant ses armes, called also *Vercingétorix*,
     57 cm, Auch, December 21, 1986.
Guerrier portant une épée, 57 cm, Auch, June 29, 1986.
Guerrier romain, 76 cm, Drouot, February 18, 1983,
     room 7; Christie's New York, October 18, 1983.
Pro aris et focis, 69 cm, Christie's New York, June 14,
     1983.

MATISSE, HENRI

Le Cateau-Cambraisis, December 31, 1869
Nice, November 3, 1954

Matisse

In the beginning, Matisse studied law, and worked with a lawyer. In 1890, however, he entered the Académie Julian (then the Ecole des arts décoratifs), finally enrolling in the Beaux-Arts in 1893, to work in the studio of Gustave Moreau. He decided to devote himself to painting. He became adept, the most highly reputed artist of the fauvist movement. Eventually he returned to more structured compostions, but they always remained inundated with color. The chapel of the Dominicans of Vence, opened in 1951, remains one of his most well-known works. This famous painter was also a drawer of prodigious cleverness, an engravor, a lithographer—and a sculptor.

Matisse executed about seventy sculptures "...to rest myself from painting in which I had made all this that I could for the moment...This was in order to organize my sensations, in order to look for a method which absolutely agreed with me. When I had found it in scultpure, this served me for painting." (*Ecrits et propos sur l'art, 1972*).

In 1899, while still enrolled in night courses at Paris's municipal school of sculpture, Matisse executed his first work, *Jaguar dévorant un lièvre,* modeled in Barye's style. In 1900, he frequented the studio of the Grande Chaumière who directed Bourdelle, and started to work on a figure entitled *Le Serf.* He attempted, without success, to enter the studio of Rodin, whose influence was clearly evident in this work. In 1908, Matisse founded his original school where he taught painting and sculpture.

Practicing especially the modeling of clay, Matisse did not strive for precise, realistic models, but rather for an emotional reaction from the spectator. He *suggested*, rather than *described,* the tension or the grace of his personages, the rhythm of the forms and gestures, relying on large, flat areas on which the light and the shadows played. His figures, especially those of the first period from 1900 to 1910 (making up approximately half of his plastic work) are usually of reduced format. "A sculpture," he wrote, "must incite us to handle it as an object...Plus the sculpture is small, and the essence of the form must impose itself." (*Ecrits et propos sur l'art*). Except for the *Jaguar dévorant un lièvre* and a statuette of a horse, his works represent only some isolated human figures. A single exception is the group of the *Deux Négresses.* Some series have been encountered, with variants or successive states, in particular that of *Jeannette,* executed between 1910 and 1913. Many of Matisse's sculptures appear occasionally in his paintings.

The sculpted works by Matisse, for the most part, have been cast in bronze in editions of ten (plus a model for the artist). The majority were produced

Henri Matisse,
Deux Négresses,
47 cm (1908).

by Valsuani, while some of them were made by Costenoble or Georges Rudier. A number of complete ensembles of these bronzes have been exhibited many times, particularly in 1974 at the Matisse museum in Nice, in 1975 at the National Museum of Modern Art, in 1984-1985 at the Hayward Gallery in London and at the City Art Gallery of Leeds. The chronological list which follows refers to the catalogs from the expositions of Nice and Paris (Valsuani castings except where indicated otherwise).

Before 1905

Profil de femme, medallion (1894), 25.4 cm diam. Cast alone to three models.
Jaguar dévorant un lièvre, according to Barye (1899-1901), 23 cm.
Buste ancien (1900), 62 cm.
Le Serf (1900-1903), 92 cm.
Le Cheval (1901), 17 cm.
Madeleine, first state on round terrace (1901), 59.5 cm.
Madeleine, second state on square terrace, (1903), 59.5 cm.
Profil d'enfant, bas-relief (1903), 12.8 x 9.2 cm.
L'Écorché, according to Puget (1903), 23 cm.
Nu assis, bras sur la tête (1904), 35 cm.
Nu cambré (1904), 22.5 cm.

1905

Nu à la chemise relevée, appuyé sur les mains, 13.5 cm.
Tête d'enfant, Pierre Matisse, 16 cm.
Tête d'enfant, Pierre Manguin, 13 cm.
Rosette (la pipe), 10.8 cm.

1906

Nu couché à la chemise, 14 cm.
Nu debout, fillette (Costenoble), 48 cm.
Nu debout, bras sur la tête, 29 cm.
La Vie, torso with head, 23 cm.
Petite Tête au ne camus, 13 cm.
Petite Tête aux cheveux striés, 11.5 cm.
Buste de filette, Marguerite, 16 cm.
Tireur d'épine, 19 cm.

1907

Tête de faune, 14 cm.
Petite Tête au peigne, called *Tête dorée*, 9.5 cm.
Tête au collier 15 cm.
Nu couché avec terrasse, 34 cm.

1908

Petit Nu accroupi, avec deux bras (Costenoble), 15 cm.
Petit Nu accroupi, sans bras droit, 12 cm.
Petit Torse accroupi, 8 cm.
Deux Négresses, 47 cm.
Nu assis, main droite à terre, 18.7 cm.
Nu debout, bas-relief, 23 x 11.5 cm.
Figure décorative, femme assise, 73 cm.

1909

Etude de pied, 27 cm.
Torse debout, 25 cm.
Nu assis, bras derrière le dos, 29.5 cm.
La Serpentine, 56.5 cm.

1910-1930

Nu de dos I, bas-relief (Valsuani, 1909), 189 cm.
Nu de dos II, bas-relief (Georges Rudier, 1913), 188 cm.
Nu de dos III, bas-relief (Georges Rudier, 1916-1917), 189 cm.
Nu de dos IV, bas-relief (Georges Rudier, 1930), 189 cm.

1910-1913

Jeannette, first state, 35 cm.
Jeannette, second state, 26.5 cm.
Jeannette, third state, 60 cm.
Jeannette, fourth state, 61.5 cm.
Jeannette, fifth state, 58 cm.

Henri Matisse,
*Nu assis, main droite à terre,
Olga*, 19 cm (1908).

1910-1918

Grand Nu accroupi, Olga (1910), 43 cm.
La Danse (1911), 41 cm.
Tête de marguerite (1915), 32 cm.
Nu assis, bras autour des genoux or *Vénus assise* (1918), 23 cm.
Vénus accroupie (1918), 26 cm.
Nu couché au plochon (1918), 13.4 cm.

After 1920

Grand Nu assis bras levé (1923-1925), 84 cm.
Petit Nu au canapé (1924), 23.5 cm.
Henriette, grosse tête, first state (1925), 29.5 cm.
Henriette, grosse tête, second state (1927), 32 cm.
Henriette, grosse tête, third state (1929), 40 cm.
Nu couché II (1927), 29 x 51.5 cm.
Nu couché III (1929), 18.5 x 46.5 cm.
Petit Torse (1929), 9 cm.
Petit Torse mince (1929), 8 cm. Cast alone to three models.
Le Tiaré (1920), 20 cm.
Le Tiaré (1933), 20 cm.
Vénus à la coquille I (1930), 31 cm.
Vénus à la coquille II (1932), 34 cm.
Nu assis bras levé (1949), 25.7 cm.
Crucifix de la chapelle de Vence (1949), 46.5 cm.
Nu debout, Katia, called *La Taille cassée* (1950), 45 cm.

MUSEUMS
Le Cateau-Cambraisis, musée Matisse
Jaguar dévorant un lièvre, 23 cm (Valsuani 0/10).
Madeleine II, 59.5 cm (Valsuani 0/10).
Nu de dos I, bas-relief, 189 cm (Valsuani 0/10).
Le Serf, 92 cm (Valsuani).
Nice, musée Matisse
This museum possesses the ensemble of bronzes by the artist thanks to the donation made in 1978 by Mme Jean Matisse, his daughter-in-law.
Paris, musée d'Art moderne de la ville
Henriette II, grosse tête, 32 cm (1927; Valsuani 8/10).
Nu assis, bras derrière le dos, 29.5 cm (1909; Bingen-Costenoble 1/10).
Nu couché, 34 x 50 cm (1907; C. Valsuani 1/10).
Nu de dos I, bas-relief, 189 x 116 cm (1909; C. Valsuani 1/10).
Nu de dos II, bas-relief, 188 x 116 cm (1913; Georges Rudier 3/10), cast after 1948).
Nu de dos III, bas-relief, 189 x 114 cm (1916-1917; Georges Rudier 7/10).
Nu de dos IV, bas-relief, 189 x 114 cm (1930; Georges Rudier 2/10).

Many foreign museums preserve bronzes by Matisse, in particular the Hermitage museum in Leningrad, American museums in Baltimore, Chicago, New York (Museum of Modern Art), and San Francisco, and the Tate Gallery 'in London.

SALES
Cheval, sketch, 16.2 cm (1901; C. Valsuani 9/10), Sotheby New York, November 19, 1986.
Deux Négresses, 47 cm (1908; C. Valsuani 8/10), Sotheby New York, November 13, 1985.
L'Ecorché, 23 cm (around 1902; Valsuani 7/10), Christie's New York, May 17, 1984.
Femme accroupie, 14 cm (C. Valsuani), Zurich, June 2, 1983.
Figure décorative, 71.5 cm (1908; C. Valsuani 2/10); Sotheby New York, November 13, 1985 (price of adjudication: 950,000 dollars).
Henriette III, grosse tête, 40 cm (C. Valsuani 3/6), Christie's New York, May 14, 1986.
Jeannette, first state, 32.5 cm (1910-1913; C. Valsuani 1/10), Sotheby New York, November 13, 1985.
Nu accroupi, 19 cm, (No4), Sotheby New York, May 18, 1983.
Nu debout bras levés, 26 cm (1906; C. Valsuani 6/10), Sotheby New York, May 15, 1985.
Petit Nu accroupi, deux bras, 15.2 cm (1908; C. Valsuani 6/10), Sotheby New York, November 19, 1986.
Petit Nue accroupi sans bras, 12.1 cm (1908; C. Valsuani 1/10), Sotheby New York, November 19, 1986.
Tête d'enfant, Pierre Matisse, relief (No 5), 12.6 x 10 cm, Sotheby New York, November 14, 1985.
Tête de Marguerite, 32 cm (Valsuani No5), Christie's New York, May 16, 1984.
Le Tireur d'épines, 19 cm (around 1906; C. Valsuani 5/10), Sotheby New York, November 19, 1986.
Vénus assise, 23 cm (1918; C. Valsuani 7/10), Sotheby London, May 18, 1983.

MAURETTE, HENRI MARIE
Toulouse, September 21, 1834
Toulouse, June 6, 1898

Maurette spent a numbner of years in Paris, and then returned to Toulouse as a professor at the school of fine arts. He exhibited at the Salon at least from 1861 to 1894, showing busts in bronze and figures in plaster such as *Joueur de lyre* (Salon of 1861) and *Le Chevrier* (Salon of 1873). The museum of Toulouse preserves a bronze by this sculptor entitled *Portrait de l'intendant Viguier,* 76 cm.

MAYER, NICOLAS
Paris, May 31, 1852
After 1939

Like his teacher Cordier, Mayer frequently joined marble with bronze in his works, and, also like Cordier, made busts of Arab or African people. Among his principal works exhibited at the Salon were *Un duel,* a group in plaster (1887), *Mabrouka, souvenir de Gabès,* a statue in plaster (1888), *Buste d'Arabe,* in marble and bronze (1889), *Réveil,* a statue in marble (1891), *Skieur,* a statuette in bronze and marble (1909), and *Buste de Nègre,* in bronze and marble (1910). *Un duel* was cast in bronze, as was a statuette symbolizing *Aurore.*

MEISEL, JOSEPH
Born in Austria—?
Paris, 1914

Meisel exhibited at the Salon de la Société Nationale des Beaux-Arts from 1904 to 1906, primarily showing busts. In the last year, he exhibited two allegories, *Atteinte mortelle* in plaster, and *Seule* in bronze. The museum of Beauvais preserves two of his works in bronze: *Buste de Madame Meisel,* 21 cm, and *Le Centaure,* 31 cm.

MEISSONIER, ERNEST
Lyon, February 21, 1815
Paris, January 31, 1891

Meissonier was a painter, famous during his lifetime particularly for his military scenes, but he also left a certain number of statuettes. They are nearly all equestrians, in which the attitudes and minute techniques of his paintings are also in evidence. Originally, he molded these sculptures as models in wax or plastic paste to serve as studies for his canvases. They could not have been made before 1860, since they primarily portray military subjects, which Meissonier started to paint only after having followed Napoléon III's campaign from Italy in 1859. Two among them are dated 1884 and 1890. Meissonier also produced works portraying animals, focusing particularly on observation of the horse; he made some equestrian portraits greatly admired for their surprising precision. Among his many works, *Le Voyageur* is without doubt the most remarkable and the most widespread; it is also known by three other titles: *Officier de l'Empire dans la tourmente, Napoléon en Russie,* and *Le Maréchal Ney.*

Eight of Meissonier's nineteen sculptures were cast in bronze by Siot-Decauville. They are:

Cheval au repos, 43 x 53 cm.
Cheval blessé (study for the canvas of the siege of Paris), 27 x 44 cm.
Cheval de trompette, 37 x 45 cm.
Cosaque, 20 x 21 cm.
Cuirassier, 52 x 63 cm.
Hussard, 22 x 20 cm.
Napoléon 1er, 1814, 40 x 38 cm.
Le Voyageur, 50 x 55 cm.

Other statuettes cast in bronze (without indication of founder) include *Le Général Duroc à Castiglione, Héraut de Murcie à cheval, Muse dansant,* and *Homme nu.*

MUSEUMS
Bordeaux
Cheval au trot, 40 x 60 cm (Siot-Decauville).
Cuirassier à cheval au galop, 53 x 62 cm (Siot-Decauville).
Napoléon 1er à cheval, 38.5 x 37 cm (Siot-Decauville).
Le Voyageur, 49 x 60 cm (Siot-Decauville).
Châteauroux
Napoléon 1er à cheval, 39 x 37 cm (Siot-Decauville).
Dijon
Cheval blessé, for the canvas of the seige of Paris, 26 cm.
Héraut de Murcie à cheval, 54 cm.
Modèle de cheminée en marble et bronze, 36 x 60 cm.
Grenoble
Cheval blessé, 27 x 44 cm.
Le Général Duroc à cheval à Castiglione, 49 cm.
Gladiateur à l'épée, 29 cm.
Héraut de Murcie à cheval, 54 cm.
Muse dansant, 23 cm.
Lille
Officier de l'Empire dans la tourmente, 49 x 60 cm (Siot-Decauville).

Ernest Meissonier,
Napoléon 1er à cheval, 40 x 38 cm
(Siot-Decauville).

Lyon
Cheval blessé
Homme nu avec glaive et bouchlier
Héraut de Murcie
Paris, Orsay
Muse dansant, 21 cm (Bingen).
Reims
Le Voyageur, 49 cm (Siot-Decauville).
Riom
Le Général Duroc à Castiglione, 54 cm.

SALES
Cheval au galop, 36 x 61 cm (Siot-Decauville No2), Rambouillet, May 17, 1987 (see reproduction on page 651).
Cosaque à cheval, 20 cm (Siot-Decauville), Morlaix, May 2, 1985.
Cuirassier à cheval, 49 cm (Siot-Decauville), Christie's London, July 18, 1983.
Le Général Duroc à Castiglione, 56 cm (note of Mme Meissonier: "last maquette by my husband, 1890"), Enghien, October 6, 1985.
Officier de l'Empire dans la tourmente, Gien, November 22, 1981.

MELINGUE, ÉTIENNE MARIN
Caen, April 16, 1808
Paris, March 27, 1875

A well-regarded dramatic actor, Melingue also worked for some time painting miniature portraits at Guadeloupe. Returning to Paris, he practiced both painting and sculpture while pursuing a theatrical career in Ambigu, at the Gaîté-Lyrique and Odéon theaters, etc. Except for some decorative work for the church of la Madeleine, his sculpted pieces include primarily statuettes and busts of actors, writers, poets, historic people, as in the works *Corneille, Molière, La Fontaine, Racine, Lamartine, Rabelais,* and *Ambroise Paré*. Works portraying actors include *Duprez dans le rôle de Guillaume Tell* and *Bouffé dans le rôle du Gamin de Pairs, Malfilâtre, poète caennais du XVIIIe siècle,* as well as *François 1er, Charles Quint, Le Grand Frédéric* and *Satan.*

A number of these statuettes were cast in bronze. The Susse foundry, for its part, cast the following:

D'Aguesseau assis, 40 cm.
Ambroise Paré, 37, 25 and 19 cm.
Colbert assis, 40 cm.
Corneille debout, 44, 30 and 12 cm.
Dupré dans le rôle de Guillaume Tell, 40 cm.
François 1er, 45 and 12 cm.
La Fontaine debout, 44, 30 and 12 cm.
Le Grand Frédéric à cheval, 45 and 18 cm.
Molière debout, 44, 30 and 12 cm.
Rabelais assis, 40 and 10 cm.
Racine debout, 44, 30 and 12 cm.
Saint-Georges, 48 cm.
Shakespeare assis, 28, 20 and 6 cm.

MUSEUMS
Caen
Corneille, 30 cm
Molière, 30 cm
Hébé, silvered bronze, 40 cm
Histrion, demi-nature.
Paris, Decorative Arts
Bouffé dans le rôle du Gamin de Paris, 25 cm.
Paris, Carnavalet
Bouffé dans le rôle du Gamin de Paris, 25 cm.
Ledru-Rollin, 57 cm.

MÈNE, PIERRE JULES

Paris, March 25, 1810
Paris, May 21, 1879

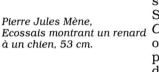

Mène, the most famous animal sculptor after Barye, first started to work at the establishment of his father, who was a metal-turner. Although attracted very early to sculpture and to animals, Mène had to practice small jobs related to his vocation in order to support himself after his marriage in 1832. After spending a long time at the Jardin des Plantes to execute some sketches and also, it is said, some small models of animals, he made his debut at the Salon of 1838 and become popular very quickly. His *Chien étranglant un renard* foreshadows an infinity of statuettes and groups in which the horse was preponderant, though many scenes of hunts, deer, dogs, birds, and barnyard animals also appeared. Practically no big game can be seen in Mène's work.

*Pierre Jules Mène,
Ecossais montrant un renard
à un chien, 53 cm.*

*Pierre Jules Mène,
Chasse en Ecosse,
la prise du renard,
50 cm.*

*Pierre Jules Mène,
Valet de chasse Louis XV
sans chiens, 65 cm.*

*Pierre Jules Mène,
Valet de chasse Louis XV
avec cinq chiens,
67 x 74 cm.*

Pierre Jules Mène,
Valet de chasse Louis XV
avec trois chiens, 67 cm.

Beginning in 1837, Mène worked (as Barye had) at his own foundry, casting first his own works, and later those of his son-in-law, the sculptor Auguste Cain. Mène became absorbed in the meticulous work of casting and chiseling, and some of his bronzes were cast extensively. After his death (and Cain's, in 1894) the Susse foundry acquired the rights to reproduce the models, and produced posthumous proofs marked "Susse foundeur éditeur, Paris."

Among the bronzes by Mène which seem to have been the most in demand and which are most frequently seen today are, first, the *Groupe de chevaux arabes.* Today, the best-known single piece from this group *L'Accolade;* the original model of which was exhibited at the Salon of 1852, and the first casting in bronze at the Salon of 1853 (according to a pattern often resumed by this artist).

Other successful works include *La Prise du renard, Chasse en Ecosse, Le Vainqueur du derby* (of

Collection complète

des

Bronzes d'Art

DE

P.-J. MÈNE

ET DE

AUG. CAIN

Sujets de Chasse — Animaux

⤫

SUSSE FRÈRES, Fabricants-Éditeurs

PARIS

Boulevard de la Madeleine	31, Rue Vivienne, 31
13 & 15	PLACE DE LA BOURSE
—	—
Téléphone : 251-52	Téléphone : 126-10

*Catalog of bronzes
by Pierre Jules Mène,
cast by Susse at the
end of the 19th century.*

P. J. MÈNE

FIGURES & ANIMAUX

Nos		Prix bronze
1	VALET DE CHASSE (Louis XV) ET SA HARDE. .	1500 fr.
	hauteur 67 c., longueur 74 c., profondeur 42 c.	
2	CHASSE EN ÉCOSSE (La Prise du Renard). . . .	1500 »
	h. 50 c., l. 68 c., p. 40 c.	
3	PICADOR A CHEVAL.	1000 »
	h. 72 c., l. 59 c., p. 29 c. Doré. . . .	1650 »
4	FAUCONNIER ARABE A CHEVAL (Chasse au Faucon), (Argenté 1200 fr. — Doré 1650 fr.). .	1000 »
	h. 75 c., l. 39 c., p. 26 c.	
5	VENEUR LOUIS XV A CHEVAL.	800 »
	h. 64 c., l. 54 c., p. 25 c.	
6	GROUPE CHIENS EN DÉFAUT (Valet Louis XV).	500 »
	h. 45 c., l. 47 c., p. 24 c.	
7	VALET DE LIMIER	400 »
	h. 47 c., l. 37 c., p. 22 c.	
8	CHASSEUR AFRICAIN, No 1.	600 »
	h. 64 c., l. 55 c., p. 23 c.	
8bis	CHASSEUR AFRICAIN, No 2.	350 »
	h. 48 c., l. 38 c., p. 19 c.	

9	TORÉADOR-MATADOR		350 »
	h. 52 c., terrasse ronde 22 c.		
10	VALET DE CHIENS TENANT DEUX GRIFFONS ÉCOSSAIS.		450 »
	h. 50 c., terrasse ronde 30 c.		
11	FAUCONNIER ARABE A PIED.		350 »
	h. 65 c., terrasse ronde 22 c.		
12	ÉCOSSAIS MONTRANT UN RENARD A UN CHIEN.		400 »
	h. 53 c., terrasse ronde 31 c.		

— 2 —

Nos		Prix bronze
13	JOCKEY VAINQUEUR DU DERBY	250 fr.
	h. 36 c., l. 43 c., p. 22 c.	
14	AMAZONE, No 1.	225 »
	h. 45 c., l. 41 c.	
15	AMAZONE, No 2.	100 »
	h. 26 c., l. 24 c.	
16	JOCKEY A CHEVAL, No 1.	200 »
	h. 42 c., l. 42 c.	
17	JOCKEY A CHEVAL, No 2	100 »
	h. 25 c., l. 24 c. Argenté.	150 »

CHASSES

Nos		Prix bronze
18	GRANDE CHASSE AU CERF (Cerf attaqué par 4 Chiens), No 1	800 fr.
	h. 39 c., l. 70 c., p. 35 c.	
19	CHASSE AU CERF (Cerf et 3 Chiens), No 2. . . .	300 »
	h. 28 c., l. 40 c., p. 20 c.	
20	CHASSE AU SANGLIER (Sanglier pris par 4 Chiens)	400 »
	h. 28 c., l. 48 c., p. 22 c.	
21	CHASSE AU RENARD (Renard pris par 2 Chiens)	350 »
	h. 27 c., l. 49 c., p. 27 c.	
22	CHASSE AU CANARD (Canard et 2 Chiens épagneuls-griffons)	300 »
	h. 26 c., l. 45 c., p. 24 c.	
23	CHASSE AU LIÈVRE DANS LES VIGNES. . . .	225 »
	h. 21 c., l. 40 c., p. 20 c.	
24	CHASSE AU LAPIN (Groupe Chiens au terrier)	250 »
	h. 20 c., l. 37 c., p. 18 c. Argenté	350 »
25	CHASSE A LA PERDRIX.	225 »
	h. 22 c., l. 42 c., p. 22 c.	

CHEVAUX

Nos		Prix bronze
26	GRANDE JUMENT DE CHASSE AVEC PETIT CHIEN GRIFFON.	800 fr.
	h. 44 c., l. 69 c., p. 32 c.	

— 3 —

Nos		Prix bronze
27	GROUPE CHEVAUX ARABES, No 1	550 fr.
	h. 45 c., l. 68 c., p. 24 c.	
28	GROUPE CHEVAUX ARABES, No 2	350 »
	h. 35 c., l. 54 c., p. 23 c.	
29	GROUPE CHEVAUX ARABES, No 3	150 »
	h. 20 c., l. 34 c., p. 14 c.	
30	GROUPE CHEVAUX ARABES, No 4	30 »
	h. 07 c., l. 13 c.	
31	JUMENT NORMANDE ET SON POULAIN	450 »
	h. 44 c., l. 60 c., p. 24 c.	
32	JUMENT NORMANDE SEULE	250 »
	h. 44 c., l. 49 c., p. 18 c.	
33	JUMENT ARABE ET SON POULAIN, No 1. . . .	300 »
	h. 30 c., l. 50 c., p. 24 c.	
34	JUMENT ARABE ET SON POULAIN, No 2. . . .	100 »
	h. 17 c., l. 27 c.	

Nos		Prix bronze
35	JUMENT ARABE ET SON POULAIN, Nº 3.... h. 08 c., l. 15 c.	50 »
36	JUMENT ARABE (Nedjibé), AVEC HARNACHEMENT... h. 28 c. i. 45 c., p. 20 c.	200 »
37	JUMENT ARABE (Nedjibé), Nº 2. h. 17 c., l. 26 c.	70 »
38	JUMENT A L'ÉCURIE JOUANT AVEC UN CHIEN h. 25 c., l. 47 c., p. 18 c.	250 »
39	CHEVAL DE COURSE........ *180* ~~200~~	»
	h. 30 c., l. 41 c.	
40	CHEVAL ATTAQUÉ PAR UN LOUP, Nº 1.... h. 37 c., l. 31 c., p. 15 c.	200 »
41	CHEVAL ATTAQUÉ PAR UN LOUP, Nº 2.... h. 16 c., l. 14 c.	50 »
42	CHEVAL LIBRE, Nº 1....... h. 30 c., l. 38 c., p. 18 c.	200 »
43	CHEVAL LIBRE, Nº 2....... h. 19 c., l. 21 c.	75 »
44	CHEVAL DE SPAHI AU PIQUET...... h. 27 c., l. 38 c., p. 16 c.	150 »
45	CHEVAL AU PALMIER....... h. 28 c., l. 38 c., p. 14 c.	180 »
46	CHEVAL A LA BARRIERE (Djinn), Nº 1.... h. 29 c., l. 39 c., p. 15 c.	180 »

— 4 —

Nos		Prix bronze
47	CHEVAL A LA BARRIÈRE (Djinn), Nº 2... h. 20 c., l. 25 c.	90 fr.
48	CHEVAL A LA BARRIÈRE, Nº 3........	20 »
49	CHEVAL BRETON...... h. 36 c., l. 36 c., p. 15 c.	200 »
50	JUMENT ANGLAISE (Rédinha)...... h. 30 c., l. 35 c., p. 43 c.	150 »
51	CHEVAL ARABE (Ibrahim), Nº 1....... h. 32 c., l. 37 c., p. 14 c.	150 »
52	CHEVAL ARABE (Ibrahim), Nº 2...... h. 20 c., l. 23 c.	70 »
53	CHEVAL ARABE Ibrahim), Nº 3...... h. 11 c., l. 13 c.	30 »
54	CHEVAL ARABE (Ibrahim), Nº 3, JAMBE LEVÉE h. 11 c., l. 13 c.	30 »
55	CHEVAL PERCHERON........ h. 13 c., l. 16 c.	40 »
56	CHEVAL EFFRAYÉ (MIGNONNETTE).......	20 »

CHIENS

Nos		Prix bronze
57	GROUPE CHIENS AU REPOS (Race Saintongeoise) h. 26 c., l. 44 c., p. 22 c.	250 fr.
58	CHIEN GARDANT DU GIBIER........ h. 31 c., l. 36 c., p. 22 c.	200 »
59	CHIENS BASSETS FOUILLANT UN TAILLIS.. h. 18 c., l. 38 c.	225 »
60	CHIENNE DE MEUTE AVEC SES PETITS... h. 21 c., l. 34 c., p. 18 c. Argenté....	200 » 250 »
61	GROUPE CHIENS AU TAILLIS....... h. 45 c., l. 35 c., p. 15 c.	120 »
62	GROUPE PETITS CHIENS EN DÉFAUT..... b. 14 c., l. 34 c., p. 14 c.	120 »
63	CHIEN ÉPAGNEUL-GRIFFON SAISISSANT UN CANARD.......... h. 15 c., l. 43 c., p. 16 c.	150 »
64	CHIEN BRAQUE SAISISSANT UN LIÈVRE... h. 17 c., l. 35 c., p. 16 c.	125 »

— 5 —

Nos		Prix bronze
65	CHIEN GRIFFON ET DEUX PIGEONS..... h. 18 c., l. 28 c., p. 16 c.	120 fr.
66	CHIEN AU FOUET (Warwick)........ h. 20 c., l. 28 c.	120 »
67	CHIEN LIMIER..... h. 24 c., l. 32 c., p. 14 c.	150 »
68	CHIEN BRAQUE PORTANT UN LIÈVRE. *Nº 1* . h. 21 c., l. 30 c., p. 13 c.	140 »
69	CHIEN ÉPAGNEUL (Sylphe)...... h. 22 c., l. 31 c., p. 15 c.	120 »
70	CHIENNE FRANÇAISE (Bellotte)...... h. 23 c., l. 32 c., p. 12 c. Argenté...	120 » 160 »
71	CHIEN BRAQUE (Trim)...... h. 19 c., l. 28 c.	120 »
72	CHIEN BRAQUE ASSIS GARDANT UN LAPIN.. h. 20 c., l. 25 c.	70 »
73	CHIEN ÉPAGNEUL ANGLAIS (Médor)..... h. 45 c., l. 28 c.	100 »
74	CHIEN ÉTRANGLANT UN RENARD...... h. 43 c., l. 30 c.	90 »
75	CHIEN BASSET A JAMBES TORSES. h. 43 c., l. 32 c.	90 »
76	CHIENNE HALETANTE (Milla)...... h. 45 c., l. 31 c.	80 »
77	CHIEN BRAQUE (Marly)...... h. 20 c., l. 28 c.	100 »
78	CHIEN BRAQUE (Tac)...... h. 12 c., l. 32 c.	90 »
79	CHIEN BRAQUE (Tom)...... h. 45 c., l. 29 c.	60 »
80	CHIEN BRAQUE (Low)...... h. 13 c., l. 23 c.	50 »
81	CHIEN BRAQUE SEUL, Nº 1...... h. 21 c., l. 30 c.	100 »
82	CHIEN BRAQUE SEUL, Nº 2...... h. 45 c., l. 20 c.	50 »
83	CHIEN BRAQUE SEUL, Nº 3...... h. 9 c., l. 14 c.	30 »
84	CHIEN BRAQUE SEUL, Nº 4......	15 »
85	CHIEN BRAQUE, Nº 2, AVEC CANARD.... h. 14 c., l. 20 c.	50 »

— 6 —

Nos		Prix bronze
86	CHIEN BRAQUE, Nº 2, AVEC LIÈVRE.... h. 14 c., l. 20 c.	50 fr.
87	CHIEN ÉPAGNEUL FRANÇAIS (Fabio), Nº 1.. h. 17 c., l. 32 c.	125 »
88	CHIEN ÉPAGNEUL (Fabio), Nº 2........ h. 41 c., l. 20 c.	60 »
89	CHIEN ÉPAGNEUL (Fabio), Nº 3........ h. 7 c., l. 14 c.	30 »
90	CHIEN ÉPAGNEUL (Fabio), Nº 4........	15 »
91	LÉVRIER ESPAGNOL, Nº 1, SEUL...... h. 22 c., l. 29 c.	80 »
92	LÉVRIER ESPAGNOL, Nº 2, SEUL...... h. 43 c., l. 18 c.	40 »
93	LÉVRIER ESPAGNOL, Nº 3, SEUL...... h. 9 c., l. 13 c.	25 »
94	LÉVRIER ESPAGNOL, Nº 4, SEUL......	15 »
95	LÉVRIER ESPAGNOL, Nº 2, AVEC LIÈVRE... h. 13 c., l. 18 c.	50 »
96	GROUPE LÉVRIER ET KING'S CHARLES... h. 16 c., l. 25 c.	75 »
97	GROUPE CHIENS (Mignonnette).....	30 »
98	GROUPE DE DEUX LEVRETTES JOUANT A LA BOULE.......... h. 46 c., l. 22 c.	75 »
99	LEVRETTE JOUANT A LA BOULE (Jiji).... h. 46 c., l. 17 c.	45 »

No		Prix bronze
100	LEVRETTE (Giselle) JOUANT AVEC UNE BOULE . . . . h. 40 c., l. 15 c.	30 »
101	CHIEN GRIFFON ASSIS . . . . h. 17 c., torrasse ronde 14 c. Argenté	70 » 100 »
102	CHIEN GRIFFON-TERRIER COUCHÉ . . . . . h. 40 c., l. 24 c.	50 »
103	CHIEN GRIFFON (Casca).	30 »
104	CHIEN BASSET (Trompette) . . . . h. 41 c., l. 27 c.	80 »
105	CHIEN ÉPAGNEUL (Sultan) . . . . h. 12 c., l. 23 c.	50 »
106	CHIEN COURANT (Wagram). . . . . h. 17 c., l. 24 c.	45 »

— 7 —		
Nos		**Prix bronze**
107	CHIEN COURANT BLESSÉ. . . . . h. 13 c., l. 30 c.	50 fr.
108	CHIEN RATIER (Tom) . . . . h. 14 c., l. 20 c.	50 »
109	CHIEN RATIER LÉCHANT SA PATTE. . . . . h. 12 c., l. 13 c.	30 »
110	LEVRIER A L'ÉVENTAIL (Plock) . . . . h. 17 c., l. 19 c.	45 »
111	CHIENNE (Bachette) . . . . h. 12 c., l. 27 c.	60 »
112	CHIENNE ÉPAGNEUL (Diane)	30 »
113	CHIENNE (Lutine)	30 »
114	CHIENNE (Frisette)	30 »
115	CHIEN KING'S CHARLES	25 »

CERFS, BICHES, DAIMS

Nos		Prix bronze
116	GROUPE CERFS COMBATTANT, No 1 . . . . . . h. 30 c., l. 59 c., p. 27 c.	350 fr.
117	GROUPE CERFS COMBATTANT, No 2 . . . . . . h. 17 c., l. 37 c., p. 15 c.	150 »
118	CERF A LA BRANCHE, No 1 . . . . h. 36 c., l. 38 c., p. 15 c.	150 »
119	CERF A LA BRANCHE, No 2 . . . . h. 22 c., l. 25 c.	80 »
120	CERF A LA BRANCHE, No 3	15 »
121	CERF DAGUET. . . . . h. 35 c., l. 31 c., p. 12 c.	120 »
122	CERF SE FROTTANT A UN ARBRE. . . . . . . h. 19 c., l. 18 c.	90 »
123	CERF COMMUN . . . . h. 17 c., l. 18 c.	50 »
124	CERF MUNTJAC . . . . h. 13 c., l. 19 c.	50 »
125	CERF EFFRAYÉ	30 »
126	CERF DROIT.	15 »
127	CERF TÊTE TOURNÉE.	15 »

— 8 —		
Nos		**Prix bronze**
128	GROUPE DE CERFS . . . . h. 13 c., l. 19 c.	50 fr
129	GROUPE DE DAIMS . . . . h. 9 c., l. 17 c.	50 »
130	DAIM DEBOUT.	30 »
131	DAIM COUCHÉ.	30 »
132	BICHE EFFRAYÉE.	30 »
133	BICHE EFFRAYÉE COUCHÉE	30 »
134	BICHE AXIS COUCHÉE	30 »

PATURAGES

Nos		Prix bronze
135	VACHE ET SON VEAU No 1 . . . . h. 30 c., l. 45 c., p. 23 c.	350 fr.

136	VACHE ET SON VEAU No 2 . . . . h. 23 c., l. 36 c., p. 18 c.	175 »
137	VACHE ET SON VEAU No 3 . . . . h. 14 c., l. 22 c.	100 »
138	TAUREAU NORMAND, No 1 . . . . h. 24 c., l. 36 c., p. 14 c.	170 »
139	TAUREAU NORMAND, No 2 . . . . h. 15 c., l. 24 c.	75 »
140	BÉLIER MÉTIS. . . . . h. 21 c., l. 24 c.	75 »
141	BREBIS ALLAITANT SON AGNEAU . . . . . . h. 15 c., l. 24 c.	75 »
142	MOUTON DES VOSGES, DEBOUT . . . . h. 21 c., l. 23 c.	70 »
143	MOUTON DES VOSGES, COUCHÉ. . . . . . . h. 15 c., l. 24 c.	70 »
144	BOUC, No 1 . . . . h. 20 c., l. 25 c.	70 »
145	BOUC, No 2 (de l'Inde) . . . . h. 13 c., l. 14 c.	50 »
146	BOUC, No 3 . . . . h. 12 c., l. 15 c.	30 »
147	CHÈVRE ET CHEVREAU . . . . h. 24 c., l. 24 c., p. 13 c.	100 »

— 9 —		
Nos		**Prix bronze**
148	FAMILLE DE CHÈVRES . . . . h. 14 c., l. 22 c.	75 fr.
149	CHÈVRE BROUTANT. . . . . h. 16 c., l. 25 c.	60 »
150	CHÈVRE DE L'INDE . . . . h. 11 c., l. 13 c.	50 »
151	CHÈVRE COUCHÉE	30 »
152	CHÈVRE JAMBE LEVÉE.	30 »
153	PETITE CHÈVRE (Mignonnette)	15 »

PLAQUES ET PLANCHETTES
(NATURE MORTE)

Nos		Prix bronze
154	PLAQUE CHEVREUIL ET HÉRON (avec cadre noyer). . . . . h. 44 c., l. 33 c.	100 fr.
155	PLAQUE TÊTE DE CERF (avec cadre). . . . . h. 38 c., l. 29 c.	90 »
156	PLAQUE RENARD (avec cadre) . . . . h. 38 c., l. 29 c.	90 »
157	PLAQUE LIÈVRE ET FAISAN (avec cadre) . . . h. 40 c., l. 26 c.	70 »
158	PLAQUE CHÊNE LIÈVRE ET POISSON. . . . . h. 35 c., l. 25 c.	50 »
159	PLAQUE CHÊNE CANARD ET BÉCASSE. . . . h. 35 c., l. 25 c.	50 »
160	PLANCHETTE FAISAN MORT	30 »
161	— LIÈVRE MORT	30 »
162	— COQ MORT	30 »
163	— LAPIN MORT	30 »

DIVERS

Nos		Prix bronze
164	PAIRE DE VASES, SUJETS DE CHASSE . . . . h. 43 c., l. 16 c.	500 fr.

— 10 —		
Nos		**Prix bronze**
165	JAGUAR ET CAÏMAN. . . . . h. 18 c., l. 41 c., p. 22 c.	250 fr.
166	GROUPE DE CHEVREUILS, No 1 . . . . h. 27 c., l. 35 c., p. 20 c.	200 »
167	GROUPE DE CHEVREUILS, No 2	30 »
168	CHEVREUIL AUX AGUETS. . . . . h. 24 c., l. 27 c., p. 12 c.	90 »

169	CHEVREUIL BUVANT	75 »
	h. 18 c., l. 23 c., p. 12 c.	
170	CHEVREUIL *N°1*	25 »
171	CHEVREUIL *N°2*	15 »
172	JEUNE CHEVREUIL (Carabit)	40 »
173	JEUNE CHEVREUIL	25 »
174	GROUPE RENARDS ET FAISAN	125 »
	h. 19 c., l. 32 c., p. 15 c.	
175	FAMILLE DE RENARDS	125 »
	h. 17 c., l. 33 c., p. 19 c.	
176	GROUPE DE RENARDS	45 »
177	RENARD ET COQ	70 »
	h. 11 c., l. 25 c.	
178	RENARD D'ISLANDE ASSIS	50 »
179	RENARD HALETANT	50 »
180	RENARD DEBOUT	25 »
181	RENARD A LA BARRIÈRE	30 »
182	RENARD COUCHÉ	25 »
183	RENARD	15 »
184	SANGLIER SEUL	120 »
	h. 21 c., l. 37 c., p. 15 c.	
185	CHAMOIS SAUTANT, N° 1	90 »
	h. 22 c., l. 30 c., p. 11 c.	
186	CHAMOIS SAUTANT N° 2	30 »
	h. 11 c., l. 14 c.	
187	CHAMOIS	15 »
188	RATON LAVEUR ÉTRANGLANT UN CANARD . .	80 »
	h. 11 c., l. 25 c.	
189	CHATTE ET SES PETITS	80 »
	h. 12 c., l. 22 c.	
190	CHAT	15 »

— 11 —

Nos		Prix bronze
191	POULE ET SES POUSSINS	50 fr.
192	POULE HUPPÉE	25 »
193	POULE ORDINAIRE	15 »
194	GROUPE DE LAPINS (Porte-Allumettes)	45 »
195	GROUPE DE LAPINS	30 »
196	LAPIN AU REPOS	15 »
197	LAPIN ALLONGÉ	15 »
198	GROUPE DE CANARDS	30 »
199	FAMILLE DE CANARDS	35 »
200	CANARD DROIT	15 »
201	CANARD BUVANT	15 »
202	CANARD MORT	15 »
203	GROUPE DE PIGEONS	35 »
204	PANTHÈRE ET GAZELLE	40 »
205	PANTHÈRE SEULE	30 »
206	JAGUAR DU BRÉSIL	35 »
207	TASSEAU AUX OISEAUX	35 »
208	TASSEAU AUX ÉCUREUILS	35 »
209	GAZELLE DE L'ALGÉRIE	25 »
210	GAZELLE DU DÉSERT BUVANT	25 »
211	FAISAN DROIT	30 »
212	FAISAN TOURNÉ	30 »
213	COQ DEBOUT	25 »
214	LIÈVRE AU REPOS	25 »
215	PERDRIX (Mignonnette)	15 »
216	PERDRIX MORTE	15 »
217	BÉLIER COUCHÉ	30 »

which there exist many versions), *Jument normande et son poulain* (also in many versions), and *Valet de chiens à cheval menant sa harde*, also called *Le Piqueux au tricorne*, etc. Certain models were cast with some variants, while others were separated— for example, one work shows a Scottish hunter approaching a fox with just a single dog, since his horse and the other dogs were removed from the original piece. Other examples of this are a sculpture of a single Norman mare, abandoned by her colt, or an Arab falconer on foot, without his horse. Personages appear frequently in the work of Mène, but almost always in the company of some animals. Solitary human figures, as in the *Toréador*, are exceptional.

Here, in chronological order, are the most typical works exhibited at the Salon by Mène. All, except where indicated otherwise, are in bronze:

Chien et renard (1838)
Cheval attaqué par un loup (1840)
Un renard d'Islande et un coq (1841)
Une panthère de Constantine et une gazelle (1841)
Ibrahim, cheval arabe ramené d'Egypte (1843)
Cerf attaqué par trois chiens (1844)
Taureau normand (1845)
Deux Levrettes jouant avec une boule, plaster (1848)
Dijinn, cheval à la barrière (1849)
Chasse au sanglier (1850)
Chevaux arabes or *L'Accolade* (1853)
Jument jouant avec un chien (1859)
La Prise du renard, chasse en Ecosse, wax (1861; model in silver exhibited in London in 1862, in Paris in 1867)
Jockey à pied or *Vainqueur du derby* (1863)
Mme L. montant Monte-Cristo, cheval anglais pur-sang (1867)
Jument normande et son poulain (1869)
Valet de chiens à cheval menant sa harde (1870)
Veneur Louis XV à cheval (1872)
Chasse au lièvre (1872)
Chasse au faucon (1874)
Picador (1877)
Toréador (1878)
Chasseur africain (1879)
Valet de limiers à pied, wax (1879).

Mène does not seem to have received any but a very few official commissions, nor does he seem to have solicited them. He was first establised at the outskirts of the Temple before installing himself at 9 Rue de l'Entrepôt, in Marais. Here, wrote Stanislas Lami, he associated himself with a number of artists who were drawn to him by his affable character and his open attitude to all manifestations of art.

As we have already noted, the complete collection of works by Mène was cast after his death by Susse. One can see here the reproductions from the catalog published by this foundry.

MUSEUMS
Agen
Cheval arabe.
Béziers
Groupe de chevaux arabes, 33 x 54 cm (Barbedienne).
Compiègne, château
Fauconnier arabe, 63 cm.
Ibrahim, cheval arabe, 20 cm.
Dijon
Djinn, étalon arabe, 30 x 44 cm.
Jument et son poulain, 30 x 49 cm.
Fontainebleau, château
La Chasse en Ecosse, prise du renard, 55 x 73 cm.
Guéret
Deux Chevaux, 33 cm.

1) Pierre Jules Mène, *Valet de limier*, 71 cm.

2) Pierre Jules Mène, *Amazone*, 26 cm (1865).

3) Pierre Jules Mène, *Jockey vainqueur du derby*, 36 cm.

4) Pierre Jules Mène, *Fauconnier arabe à pied*, 65 cm.

5) Pierre Jules Mène, *Chasseur africain à cheval*, 48 cm.

6) Pierre Jules Mène, *Fauconnier arabe à cheval*, 75 cm.

④

⑤

⑥

477

Marseille
Au terrier, group, 20 cm.
Chien courant, 20.5 cm.
Epagneul, 15 cm.
Montpellier
Chèvre et chevreau, 23 cm.
Morlaix
Le Fauconnier arabe, 76.5 cm.
Nantes
Valet de chasse, cinq chiens, 65 cm.
Nîmes
Brebis et agneau, 14.8 cm.
Chatte et ses petits, 10 x 22 cm.
Chien d'arrêt, 11.6 x 23 cm.
Chien tenant un lièvre, 20 x 30.8 cm.
Combat de deux cerfs, 28 x 59.4 cm.
Jument et poulain cabré, 16.9 x 26 cm.
Levrette, 22.2 cm.
Vache et son veau, 14 x 23 cm.
Paris, Decorative Arts
Chèvre broutant, 15 x 25 cm.
Deux Chiens en arrêt (épagneul et braque), 21 x 41.5 cm.
Paris, Carnavalet
Trois Chiens au terrier, 20 x 38 cm.
Paris, Petit Palais
Kemlen-Handani, jument arabe et son poulain.
Reims
Chien, 20 x 30.5 cm.
Rouen
Cerf forcé, 30 x 43.5 cm.
Sanglier attaqué par des chiens, 27 x 47.5 cm.
Toulon
Fauconnier arabe.

SALES
Human figures
L'Amazone, 45 cm, Sotheby London, July 5, 1985.
La Chasse au renard en Ecosse, 50 cm, Drouot, March 14, 1984; Christie's New York, April 16, 1985; Enghien, October 6, 1985; Chrstie's London, May 15, 1986.
Chasseur africain à cheval, 50 cm, Epernay, March 29, 1986.
Fauconnier arabe à cheval, 75 cm, Bourg-en-Bresse, March 2, 1986; Avignon, June 1, 1986; Sotheby London, November 6, 1986.
Fauconnier arabe à cheval, 75 cm (Barbedienne), Tourcoing, July 19, 1986; La Flèche, October 26, 1986; Lyon, December 3, 1986.
Fauconnier arabe à cheval, ivory head, hands and legs, 51 cm, Drouot, November 26, 1984.
Fauconnier arabe à pied, 67 cm, Vierrières-le-Buisson, December 15, 1985; Vitry-le-François, February 23, 1986; Saint-Germain-en-Laye, May 25, 1986; Neuilly, June 15, 1986.
Jockey à cheval, 28 cm, L'Isle-Adam, November 9, 1986.
Jockey à cheval, 43 cm, Drouot, January 10, 9185; Enghien, October 6, 1985; Drouot, November 7, 1985, room 1.
Le Picador à cheval, 70 cm (Barbedienne), Dijon, March 18, 1984; Sotheby London, March 20, 1986.
Le Piqeuex or *Valet de limiers avec deux chiens*, 52 cm, Drouot, June 28, 1985, room 1; Argentan, June 25, 1986.
Le Piqueux, avec un chien, 40 cm, Drouot, June 28, 1985, room 1.
Le Vaingueur du derby, 43 cm, Bourg-en-Bresse, October 19, 1985; Sotheby London, November 6, 1986.
Valet de chasse Louis XV et sa harde, 71 cm, Dijon, November 27, 1983.
Veneur de l'époque Louis XV, 62 x 52 cm, L'Isle-Adam, November 27, 1985; Sotheby London, March 20, 1986.
Horses
L'Accolade, groupe de chevaux arabes, 20 x 33.5 cm, Versailles, April 21, 1985; Angers, June 11, 1985; Christie's London, May 15, 1986; Sotheby London, November 6, 1986.

Pierre Jules Mène,
Le Cheval libre, 31 cm.

Pierre Jules
Mène,
*Jument à l'écurie
Jouant avec un chien*,
25 x 47 cm.

*Pierre Jules Mène,
Grande Jument de chasse,
44 x 69 cm.*

*Pierre Jules Mène,
Ibrahim, cheval arabe,
32 cm.*

*Pierre Jules Mène,
"Djinn," cheval à la barrière,
29 x 40 cm.*

*Pierre Jules
Mène,
Cheval
au palmier,
28 x 38 cm.*

479

Pierre Jules Mène,
L'Accolade,
groupe de chevaux arabes,
45 x 68 cm.

Pierre Jules Mène,
Jument et son poulain
au panier, 8 x 15 cm.

Pierre Jules Mène,
Jeument normande
et son poulain,
44 x 60 cm.

Pierre Jules Mène,
Jument arabe
et son poulain cabré,
17 cm (Susse).

L'Accolade, 33 cm, L'Isle-Adam, April 28, 1985;
    Enghien, October 6, 1985; Washington, December
    8, 1985; Drouot, Janurary 31, 1986, room 1;
    Sotheby London, November 6, 1986.
L'Accolade, 45 cm, Dijon, March 18, 1984; Versailles,
    June 16, 1984; Christie's London, September 25,
    1986.
Cheval arabe sellé, 29 cm, Rambouillet, November 18,
    1984; Sotheby London, July 5, 1985.
Le Cheval libre, 32 x 34 cm, Tours, December 3, 1984;
    Agen, September 23, 1985.
Cheval aux palmes, 72 cm, Sothebvy London, June 15,
    1985.
Cheval percheron, 35 cm, Dijon, March 18, 1984.
Djinn, étalon arabe or Cheval à la barrière, 19 cm,
    Versailles, October 20, 1985; Sotheby London,
    April 20, 1986; Nantes, June 24, 1986.
Djinn, étalon arabe, 30 cm, Lokeren, February 16,
    1985; Epinal, December 8, 1985; Sotheby London,
    March 20, 1986; Drouot, April 7, 1986, room 7.
Etalon barbe, 30 x 26 cm, Agen, March 22, 1986.
Etalon barbe à la barrière, 28 x 42 cm, Agen, March 22,
    1986.
Ibrahim, cheval arabe, 31 cm, Lokeren, February 16,
    1985; L'Isle-Adam, July 7, 1985.
Jument jouant avec un chien, 25 cm, Sotheby London,
    March 21, 1985; Enghien, October 6, 1985.
Jument et son poulain, 45 x 58 cm, Christie's London,
    May 15, 1986.
Jument et son poulain, 29 x 50 cm (Barbedienne),
    Drouot, October 28, 1985, room 15.
Jument et son poulain cabré, 16.5 cm, Dijon, March 18,
    1984.
Jument et son poulain cabré, 30.5 cm, Sotheby London,
    November 8, 1984.
Jument et son poulain cabré, 45 cm, Christie's London,
    April 3, 1985.

481

Jumetn et son poulain devant elle, 45 cm, Sotheby London, November 8, 1984; Drouot, June 20, 1985, room 9; Auxonne, December 14, 1986.

Grande jument de chasse, 44 x 68 cm, Argentan, May 26, 1986.

Dogs

Chien d'arrêt, 22 cm L., Drouot, May 25, 1984, rooms 5 and 6.

Chien attaquant un renard, 21 cm, Brussels, June 17, 1985; Nantes, November 6, 1985.

Chien de chasse levant une perdrix, 22 cm, Drouot, September 25, 1984, room 9.

Chien de chasse tenant un lièvre, 21 cm (Company of bronzes from Brussels), Lokeren, February 25, 1984.

Chien tête tournée, 20 cm, L'Isle-Adam, November 9, 1986.

Deux Chiens de chasse, 25 cm, Troyes, March 10, 1985; Bergerac, December 13, 1986.

Deux Chiens de chasse levant une perdrix, 22 cm, Versailles, December 16, 1984.

Deux Chiens sur un cerf, 33 x 45 cm, Bergerac, December 13, 1986.

Trois Chiens attaquant un cerf, 30 cm, Rambouillet, December 8, 1985.

Trois Chiens auprès d'un terrier, 38 cm L., Brussels, December 12, 1984.

Epagneul, 14 x 28 cm, Drouot, October 25, 1985, room 13; Agen, November 23, 1985.

Levrettes à la boule, 22 cm, Drouot, October 22, 1985, room 13; Pont-Auderner, July 6, 1986.

Levrette et son petit, 15.5 cm, Rambouillet, November 18, 1984.

Lévrier espagnol, 22.5 cm, Sotheby London, November 8, 1984.

Lévrier et King Charle à l'éventail, 16.5 cm, Drouot, December 14, 1984, room 6; Autun, May 18, 1986.

Pointer guettant, 12.5 x 26 cm, Christie's London, May 15, 1986.

Deer, etc.

Deux Antilopes, 27 cm, Christie's London, July 17, 1984.

Cerf, 36 cm, Drouot, November 26, 1985, room 8.

Cerf à la branche, 35 cm, Bordeaux, March 22, 1984; Orléans, December 8, 1984.

Cerf attaqué par des chiens or *Grande Chasse au cerf,* 40 x 63 cm, Dijon, March 18, 1984; Sotheby London, March 20, 1986; Enghien, March 29, 1987.

Pierre Jules Mène,
Deux Levrettes jouant avec une boule,
16 x 22 cm.
J. Ginepro Collection, Monaco.

Pierre Jules Mène,
Lévrier et King's Charles à l'éventail,
16 x 25 cm.

Pierre Jules Mène,
Levrette jouant avec une boule,
10 x 15 cm (Susse).

Cerf et biche, Gien, June 22, 1986.

Combat de cerfs, 29 x 60 cm, Dijon, November 4, 1984; Sotheby London, March 20, 1986.

Chevreuil, gilded bronze, 21 cm, Drouot, December 20, 1983, room 10.

Couple de chevreuils, Auch, December 7, 1986.

Other animals

Agneau tétant sa mère, 13.5 cm, Avignon, March 23, 1986.

Biques et oies, 19 cm, Drouot, March 27, 1984, room 8.

Deux Lièvres, 9 cm, Sotheby London, June 7, 1984.

Lionne et caïman, 18 x 42 cm, Sotheby London, November 8, 1984; Aubagne, April 20, 1986.

Loup attaquant un cheval, 37 cm, Sotheby London, November 7, 1985.

Renard, 11.5 cm, Sotheby London, November 8, 1984.

Sanglier, 21 cm, Rambouillet, November 18, 1984; Epinal, December 14, 1986.

Sanglier au fermé avec quatre chiens, 26 x 45 cm, Drouot, March 20, 1985, room 4.

Taureau debout, 24 cm, Saint-Germain-en-Laye, May 25, 1986.

Pierre Jules Mène,
Chien épagneul anglais,
15 x 28 cm.

Pierre Jules Mène,
Chien limier à l'attache, 24 x 32 cm.

Pierre Jules Mène,
Chien épagneul,
22 x 31 cm.

Pierre Jules Mène,
Chien braque à la feuille, 12 x 23 cm.

Pierre Jules Mène,
Chien braque portant un canard,
14 x 20 cm.

Pierre Jules Mène,
Deux Chiens à l'arrêt devant une perdrix,
21.5 x 40.5 cm.

Pierre Jules Mène,
Renard gueule ouverte, 11 x 22 cm.

Pierre Jules Mène,
Trois Chiens au terrier, chasse au lapin,
20 x 37 cm.

Pierre Jules Mène,
Deux Epagneuls-griffons
saisissant un canard, 26 x 45 cm.

Pierre Jules Mène,
Cerf attaqué
par trois chiens,
28 cm.

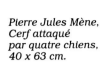

Pierre Jules Mène,
Cerf attaqué
par quatre chiens,
40 x 63 cm.

Pierre Jules Mène,
Cerfs combattant,
17 x 37 cm.

Pierre Jules Mène,
Cerf à la branche,
36 cm.

Pierre Jules Mène,
Brebis allaitant son agneau, 15 cm.

Pierre Jules Mène,
*Chèvre et chevreau,
24 cm.*

Pierre Jules Mène,
Le Bouc, 20 x 25 cm.

Pierre Jules Mène,
Les Deux Canards, 6 x 13 cm.

MENGIN, PAUL EUGÈNE

Paris, July 5, 1853
April 18, 1937

Twin brother of the sculptor and portrait painter Charles Auguste Mengin, Paul Eugène began exhibiting busts, allegorical figures, feminine statuettes, and animals at the Salon starting in 1873. A certain number of bronzes are noteworthy: *Jeunesse*, a bust (1890), *Sirène*, a statuette (1896), *Amour et Jeunesse* (1898), *Maternité* (1900), *Famille de jaguars* and *Etude de bouc* (1901), *Ours blanc* (1902), *Etude de biches* (1903), *Etude de singe* and *Petit Coq* (1905), and *Rêverie au champ*, a statuette (1909). His works in other materials include *Mignon*, a statuette in marble (1894), *Faneuse*, a statuette in marble (1904), *La Nuit*, a statuette in marble (1911), and *Semeuse d'étoiles*, a small group in plaster (1913), etc.

The catalog from the Susse foundry listed castings of the following works:

L'Amour aux aguets, 71, 55, 43 cm.
Innocente, 76 and 50 cm.
Mignon, 93, 78, 66, 57, 26 cm.
Mignon, bust, 45, 35, 28, 21 cm.
Mignon, seal (postmark), 8 cm.
Le Premier Berceau, 63 and 42 cm.
Le Puits qui parle, 150, 112, 95 cm.
Semeuse d'étoiles, 90 cm.

MUSEUMS
Dijon
Une biche, 25 cm.
Narbonne
Maternité, 64 cm.

Pierre Jules Mène,
Lionne
et caïman,
18 x 41 cm.

SALES
Femme à la mandoline, 73 cm, Christie's Oklahoma (United States), September 24, 1981.
Femme à la mandoline, gilded bronze, 54 cm (Susse), Drouot, December 2, 1983, room 5.
Mignon, 81 cm (Susse), Sotheby Chester, July 21, 1983.

MENGUE, JEAN-MARIE

Bagnères-de-Luchon, December 31, 1855
Bagnères-de-Luchon, October 31, 1949

The major works by this sculptor include *Icare*, a statue in marble sent to the Salon of 1887, and *Caïn et Abel*, a group in marble exhibited in 1896. Other significant pieces include *La Source des Pyrénées*, a statue in plaster (1889), *Abandonnées!*, a group in stone, and *Les Foins*, a statuette in marble (1891), *Mandolineta*, a statuette in plaster (1895), *Dans les champs*, (1897), *Océanide, Femme au lys* (1901), two statuettes in marble, and *Rêverie*, a bust in marble and bronze (1904), *Espagnol*, a statuette in bronze (1909), *Suzanne*, a statuette in marble, and *Méditation*, a bust in bronze (1912), etc. At the Susse house are found the bronze castings of a statuette entitled *Repos des champs*, 63 and 32 cm.

MENN, CHARLES LOUIS

Geneva, March 16, 1822
May 10, 1894

A student of Pradier and of Etex, Menn exhibited at the Salon in 1852 and 1859. He is responsible for a number of busts destined for theatres in Geneva. The museum of Avignon possesses a haut-relief in bronze, 24 x 19 cm, representing *Félicien David* (1845).

MENNESSIER, LOUIS CHARLES JUSTIN

Metz, August 8, 1815
Novare (Italy), June 13, 1859

A career soldier and a student of the Ecole de Saint-Cyr, Mennessier also practiced sculpture. From 1840, he executed a group entitled *La Porte Saint-Pancrace*, followed by some statuettes, the majority in plaster: *Tirailleur de Vincennes, Le Zouave* (1842), *L'Assaut, Le Coup de feu, Charles Nodier assis, Le Duc d'Orléans, Le Duc d'Aumale, Le Prince de Joinvile* (1844), *Le Duc de Nemours, Wallace, Ravenwood, Quiberon, Saint Louis, Chevalier banneret* (1847), *Le Vieux Veneur, Mousquetaire de 1720, Revers, Le Grenadier*, and *Le Carabinier*. In a garrison in Africa, he sculpted *La Halte* (1857), then *La Change, Un grenadier* (1859), and *Un cavalier de Marengo*.

A certain number of these statuettes, including *Le Tireailleur de Vincennes*, 30 cm, and *Le Zouave*, 30 cm, were sold to Susse in order to be produced in bronze. Some others, among which are *Le Carabinier*,

Un cavalier de Marengo, Le Grenadier, La Halte, and *Le Mousquetaire,* were cast by the founder Daubrée. After the disappearance of Mennessier, mortally wounded on the battlefield of Magenta, Daubrée sold the models in his possession to Susse.

MUSEUMS
Paris, Decorative Arts
Le Duc d'Aumale, 49 cm (1843; Susse).
Le Duc de Joinville, 48 cm (1844; Susse).
Le Duc de Nemours, 48 cm (1845).

MERCIÉ, ANTONIN

Toulouse, October 30, 1845
Paris, December 14, 1916

A. MERCIÉ

A student of Jouffroy and of Falguière at the Ecole des Beaux-Arts, Mercié won the first grand prize of Rome with his *Thésée vainqueur du Minotaure,* at the age of twenty-three. In 1872, he sent the plaster model of his *David vainqueur* from Rome to the Salon, to win the medal of first class. Simultaneously, he received the cross of the Légion d'honneur, making him unique in the annals of the villa Médicis. Upon his return to Paris in 1874, he began a long and brilliant career, marked by innumerable commissions: funereal monuments, including those for Louis-Philippe and the queen Marie-Amélie for the royal chapel of Dreux (1886), commemorative monuments, statues, and ornamental sculptures.

By the time he was thirty years old, Mercié was already famous. His *Gloria Victis,* exhibited in plaster at the Salon of 1874 and in bronze the following year, experienced an extraordinary success. At 2.20 meters high, this work exalted the heroism and the patriotic sentiments enflamed by the disasters of 1870. The statue would be reduced by the Colas procedure and cast in a number of models, like the *David vainqueur* and a number of other works.

Displaying a predilection for patriotic subjects, Mercié is also the author of the *Quand même!,* the famous group in bronze erected on the Place d'Armes in Belfort in 1884, and of the *Jeanne d'Arc relevant l'épé de la France,* of Domrémy (1902). Also attributed to him is the statuette in bronze of the *Victoire,* placed in 1875 in the hands of Napoléon 1er of the Vendôme Column, to replace the version by Chaudet which was found there before 1871. Other works include *David avant le combat* in marble (Salon of 1876), the *Génie des arts,* a monumental haut-relief in hammered copper substitued above the window of the Carrousel in 1977, a portrait of Napoléon III on horseback cast by Barye, the colossal statue *Renommée* which surmounted the dome of the old Trocadéro (1878), the two large statues in bronze entitled the *Gloire* and the *Douleur,* sculpted for the tomb of the painter Paul Baudry at Père-Lachaise (1889), the monument of *Gounod* at Monceau Park (1897) and that of the poet *Armand Sivestre,* at the

Place du Canada (1905), without counting the front of the Sorbonne symbolising the *Sciences* and the large bas-relief in marble, *L'Histoire,* for the tomb of Jules Michelet, also at the Père-Lachaise (1879).

Antonin Mercié also exhibited at the Salon a bust in bronze of *Dalila* (1872), and some statuettes: *David avant le combat* (1876), *Judith* (1880), *La Peinture* (1890), *La Toilette de Diane* (1891), and *Psyché sur le rocher,* (1898) (all in marble), and *Eveil de l'Afrique* (1897), *Siegfried* (1902), *Waterloo* (1907), and *Michel-Ange* (1912) (all in bronze).

In 1880, Antonin Mercié began to practice painting as well, but it was his work as a sculptor that continued to collect the most distinctions and honors. He joined the Institut in 1891, and was named president of the Société des Artistes Français in 1913, three years before his death. In his works can be discerned a certain sensitivity to lifelike qualities of movement, a veritable exuberance common to the group of artists from the southwest mistakenly called the School of Toulouse (*ecole de Toulouse*).

Antonin Mercié,
Buste de Dalila, 68 cm.
Musée Hébert, Paris.

*Antonin Mercié,
Gloria Victis,
92.5 cm.*

Antonin Mercié,
David vainqueur, 92 cm
(Barbedienne).

Antonin Mercié,
Quand même!, 105 cm
(Barbedienne).

The success obtained by the works of Mercié justified the production of a number of editions in bronze. It is thus that Barbedienne recorded into his catalog the following subjects:

David avant le combat, 80 and 48 cm.
David vainqueur, 110, 92, 73, 46 cm.
Giotto dessinant, 16 cm.
Gloria Victis, 317, 185, 140, 105, 62 cm.
Quand même!, 125, 107, 85, 64 cm.
Buste de Dalila, 67, 42, 29 cm.

Thiébaut cast *La Fortune*, 75 and 57 cm, and *Diane au bain*, 98 and 49 cm, while *Judith* was produced in five dimensions by Goupil.

MUSEUMS
Châlons-sur-Marne
Gloria Victis, 317 cm, 1891 (Thiébaut).
Cherbourg
Gloria Victis, 136 cm.
Dijon
Buste de Dalila, 68 cm (Rome 1871).
Montpellier
David vainqueur, 69 cm (two proofs).
Paris, Decorative Arts
La Fortune, 46.5 cm (Thiébaut).
Paris, musée Hébert
Buste de Dalila, 68 cm.
Paris, Orsay
David vainqueur, 185 cm (Thiébaut).
Gloria Victis, sketch, 80 cm.
Paris, Petit Palais
Gloria Victis, 31.5 cm.
Rouen
Gloria Victis, 136 cm.
Toulouse
Gloria Victis, 185 cm.
Troyes
David vainqueur, 70 cm (Barbedienne).
Valenciennes
Quand même!, 127 cm (Barbedienne).

SALES
Angelot assis, 25.5 cm, Sotheby New York, April 26, 1986.
La Danse de l'almée, according to Gérôme, gilded bronze, 43 cm (Goupil, founder), Drouot, December 2, 1983, room 5.
David vainqueur, 50 cm (Barbedienne), Christie's New York, March 13, 1984.
David vainqueur, 61.5 cm (Barbedienne), Sotheby London, November 6, 1986.
David vainqueur, 73 cm (Barbedienne), Drouot, May 23, 1984, rooms 5 and 6; Nantes, April 23, 1986; Rennes, November 4, 1986.
David vainqueur, 92 cm (Barbedienne), Sotheby London, June 20, 1985; Sotheby London, March 20, 1986; Saint-Etienne, September 21, 1986.
David vainqueur, 110 cm (Barbedienne), Sotheby London, June 12, 1986.
Diane chasseresse, 111 cm (Siot-Decauville, sole proof), Christie's London, September 25, 1986.
Gloria Victis, 90 cm, Lokeren, October 20, 1984; Enghien, December 2, 1984; Sotheby London, March 21, 1985; Sotheby New York, April 26, 1986.
Gloria Victis, 105 cm, Saint-Dié, March 25, 1984; Sotheby London, June 12, 1986.
Gloria Victis, 140 cm, Brussels, October 14, 1985.
Quand même!, 107 cm (Barbedienne), dedicated to Paul Déroulède, Amiens, November 14, 1985.

MERCULIANO, JACQUES

Naples, September 29, 1859
November, 1935

This Italian sculptor, who became a naturalized French citizen, started his career in Naples and pursued it to Paris in 1889. He sculpted a number of busts, but focused primarily on animal subjects. At the Salon, he exhibited in 1899 a study in plaster,

Jacques Merculiano,
Chien d'équipage, 25 x 34 cm (1912).

Jacques Merculiano,
Lionne à sa toilette, 50 cm.

Jacques Merculiano,
Lionne prêtre à bondir, stone pedestal, 38 x 50 cm.

Lion attaqué, after which he showed works done almost exclusively in bronze: *Tigre poursuivi* and *Lion et lionne* (1907), *Rivaux,* a group of lions, and *Lion approchant sa proie* (1908), *Rivalité,* a group of tigers (1909), and *Lévriers russes* (1912 and 1914), etc. The majority of his works were cast by C. Valsuani.

SALES
Chien d'équipage, 25 x 34 cm (1912), Nice, December 15, 1982.
Lionne prête à bondir, 38 x 50 cm, Enghien, February 22, 1981; Morlaix, March 5, 1984.

MÉRITE, ÉDOUARD PAULU

Le Neubourg (Eure), March 7, 1867
1941

Works by this animal artist appear to be veritable scientific documents, due to their realism and minute, almost infinitesimal detail. A student of Frémiet and of Barrias, Mérite became a professor of animal drawing at the Museum of Natural History. He traveled to Africa and the Polar regions with the expeditions of the duke of Orléans. His first works described the domestic animals of our regions, but after his travels he began to sculpt (and paint and draw, as well) the animals he had seen in faraway countries. His studio in Rueil abounded in curious objects and ethnographic documents which he had brought back with him. (Cf. catalog from one of the sales of his collection, 1959).

Some of Mérite's significant works appeared at the Salon, including *Caresse féline* and *Singe* (1898), *Chimpanzé fétiche* (1911) (all bronzes), and *Combats*

de chacals (1901), *Lionceaux et marabout du Soudan* (1902), *Dans la brousse, Vieux Lion et cynocéphale, Jeune Lionne et cynocéphale* (1904), and *Une alerte* (1907) (all plasters), as well as *Chevreuils,* haut-relief (1908).

The studio collection of Edouard Mérite was dispersed during the course of a number of public sales at the Drouot hotel in the 1950s and 1960s.

MUSEUMS
Le Mans
Chimpanzé fétiche, 72 cm.
Paris, Orsay
Sarcelles, galvanoplasty Christofle, 28 cm.

SALES
Bécasse, 20 cm, Enghien, October 10, 1982.
Ours polaire, 9.5 x 18 cm, Enghien, October 19, 1980.

MERLIEUX, LOUIS PARFAIT

Paris, November 27, 1796
Paris, September 8, 1855

Merlieux entered the Ecole des Beaux-Arts in 1812, and in 1820 began work at the Museum of Natural History, where he was assigned to reconstitute some prehistoric animals with the aid of fossils. Next Merlieux worked on fountains for the Place de la Concorde and for that of the Archbishop (Archevêché). He also worked on the altarpiece for Notre-Dame, for which he made the statues of the Virgin with child, the three archangels and the twelve apostles. Merlieux is also the author of a group in bronze, *Hercule étouffant Antée* (1821) and of diverse busts of contemporaries including bronzes of *Cuvier,* exhibited at the Salon of 1827, and of

Charles Michel de l'Epée, for the Institut des sourds-muets (Institute of deaf-mutes) in Paris. The museum of Brives posseses also a bust in bronze, *Pierre André Latreille, entomologiste*, 50 cm, dated from 1833.

Meunier, Constantin

Etterbeck (Belgium), April 12, 1831
Ixelles (Belgium), April 4, 1905

One of the best-known members of the 19th century Belgian school, this sculptor, painter, and engravor has nonetheless been included in this list of French sculptors because of the numerous works he exhibited in Paris, both at the Salon des Artistes Français and at the Société Nationale des Beaux-Arts. His sculptures, like his paintings, are almost entirely devoted to representations of the mining world. At the Artistes Français, he exhibited only three times, *Le Marteleur* in 1886, *Le Puddleur* (two statues in plaster) in 1887, and *Un Supplicié*, a bust in bronze, in 1888.

Among his works at the Nationale des Beaux-Arts between 1890 and 1905 are a number of bronzes: *Buste de pudleur, Marteleur, Pêcheur boulonnais, Débardeur du port d'Anvers, Souffleur de verre* (1890), *Christ Mineur, Le Grisou, Abatteur* (1891), *Ecce homo, Le Faucheur, La Glèbe*, haut-relief, *L'Enfant prodigue* (1892), *Pudleur*, bas-relief, *Mineur à la sorie du puits*, bas-relief, *La Douleur*, a study for *Le Grisou, Vieux Cheval de mine* (1893), *Pudleur* (1894), *Le Père Damien, Juin* (1895), *Laboureur* (1896), *Hercheuse*, a worker pushing a wagon (1898), *Buste d'homme du peuple* (1902), *Buste de Charles Cottet* and *Tête de vieux mineur* (1903), *Mineur* (1904), and *Philosophie*, a bust (1905).

The list of Meunier's bronzes preserved in museums provides a record of their dimensions. The majority of them are found at the Constantin Meunier Museum in Brussels and at the museum of Bochum (Cf. the 1970 catalog of the Constantin Meunier Exposition at the Bergbau Museum in Bochum, Federal Germany).

MUSEUMS
Bochum
La Femme du peuple, 72 cm.
Grand Mineur, 53.5 cm (1900).
Hercheuse, 71 cm (1888).
Mineur à la hache, 54 cm (1900).
Mineur à la hache, 44.5 cm (1901).
Mineur à la veine, 35 cm (1892).
Remonte des mineurs, 55 cm (1892).
Le Retour de la mine, 59 cm.
Vieux Cheval de mine, 38 cm (1890).
Brussels
Autoportrait, 81 cm (1904).
Dans le blés, 58 cm.
Le Débardeur, 120 cm (1893).
Le Désespéré, 30 cm (1904).
Ecco homo, 56 cm (1890).
L'Enfant produgue, 39 cm (1895).
Fille du peuple, 47 cm (1887).
Le Grisou, 27 cm (1893).
Hercheuse à la pelle, 48 cm (1888).
L'Industrie, 135 cm (around 1901).
Le Marteleur, 120 cm (1886).

*Constantin Meunier,
Paysan buvant, 49 cm
(Peterman, founder, Brussels).
Musée d'Orsay.*

493

Constantin Meunier,
Les Puddleurs, bas-relief, 50 x 49 cm
(Van Aerschodt, founder, Louvain).
Musée d'Orsay.

Constantin Meunier,
Débardeur du pon d'Anvers,
bust,
57.5 cm.

Mélancolie, 73 cm (1898).
Mineur à la lanterne, 53 cm (1901).
Le Naufragé, 35 cm (1890).
Ophélie, 36 cm.
Puddleur, 50 cm (1890).
Puddleur au repos, 39 cm (1890).
Le Supplicié, 71.5 cm (1887).
Le Tailleur de pierre, 33 cm (1898).
La Vieille Bûcheronne, 40 cm (1891).

Calais
Le Marteleur, 50 cm.
Paris, Orsay
Buste du peintre Charles Cottet, 50 cm (Verbeyst, Brussels).
Débardeur du port d'Anvers, 50 cm (Petermann, Brussels).
La Glèbe, haut-relief, 45 x 45 cm (Petermann, Brussels).
L'Industrie, haut-relief, 70 x 90 cm (Petermann, Brussels).
Paysan debout buvant, 49 cm (Petermann, Brussels).
Puddleur, bas-relief, 49 x 50 cm (Vam Aerschodt, Louvain).

SALES
L'Enfant prodigue, 44 cm, Cologne, December 1, 1982.
Les Forgerons, haut-relief, 48 x 48 cm, Drouot, June 29, 1984, room 7.
Hercheuse, 48 cm, Cologne, December 8, 1984.
Maternité, 46 cm (Verbeyst, founder), Sotheby London, December 14, 1983.
Le Mineur, 46 cm, Brussels, December 10, 1984.
Le Mineur, 54 cm, Lokeren, April 14, 1984.
La Moisson, bas-relief, 61.5 x 83 cm (Petermann), Drouot, April 25, 1986, room 6.
Ouvrier à la carrière, 59 cm, Anvers, October 23, 1984.
Le Porteur, 47 cm, Lokeren, October 19, 1985.
Le Rameur, 35 cm, Sotheby London, April 28, 1982.

MICHEL, GUSTAVE

Paris, September 29, 1851
Paris, 1924

Virtually forgotten today, this sculptor and medaller was a student of Jouffroy, and was very successful during his lifetime, both in France and abroad. The formal beauty of his works is gratifying; a certain serenity emmanates from within their infusion of vitality. Many of Michel's works are allegories, sculpted with the harmonious traits of feminine figures. In Paris Michel worked on the facade of the Opera-Comique, the Alexandre-III Bridge, the Bridge of Bir-Hakeim (eight groups in casting of the *Forgerons* and of the *Nautes,* 1906), the Palais Galliera, and the church of the Sacré-Coeur (the large *Christ en prière* of the gable). He is the author of the statue *Automne* and the monument of *Jules Ferry* in the gardens of the Tuileries. He sent a number of medals to the Salon (and similarly, to the expositions of 1889 and 1900) as well as some bronzes: *Circé* (1886), *Amour vainqueur* (1887), *David devant Goliath* (1890), *Source limpide* (1902) and *La Musique* (1905), two statuettes in gilded bronze, etc. He also sent some works in plaster, including *Un ruisseau* (1877), *L'Aveugle et le paralytique* (1883), *La Fortune enlevant son bandeau* (1888), *L'Aurore* (1893), *La Pensée* (1894), *La Forme se dégageant de la matière* (1900), and *Extase de l'Infini* (1904). Some statuettes in marble should also be mentioned: *Rêverie d'automne* (1895), *Parmi les fleurs* (1903), *Tritons* (1905), and *L'Aube* (1906).

A number of works by Gustave Michel were cast by the Sèvres factory. Furthermore, the Susse foundry has distributed the following:

La Musique, 88, 73 and 64 cm.
La Pensée, 70 and 35 cm.
Buste de la Pensée, 48, 31 and 24 cm.
Source limpide, 46 cm.

Siot-Decauville cast *Vers la lumière* and a trophy cup of tritons. A contract for castings was also signed by the sculptor with Barbedienne in 1893. A proof in gilded bronze of *La Pensée*, 35 cm, cast by Susse, was sold at the Drouot hotel on December 2, 1983, room 5.

MILLET, AIMÉ

Paris, September 28, 1819
Paris, January 14, 1891

A painter and sculptor, and the son of a miniaturist, Millet received his initial training in his father's studio. He worked for Viollet-le-Duc before entering first the Ecole des Arts Décoratifs and then the Ecole des Beaux-Arts in the studio of David d'Angers. *L'Apollon*, a 7.50 cm high bronze surmounting the gable of the scene of the Opera of Paris, and *Vercingétorix*, embossed copper 6 meters high standing in Alise-Sainte-Reine in the Côte-d'Or, represent only a small part of Millet's official commissions. In addition to the Opera, he participated in the decoration of the Louvre, the city hall (figures of the *Seine* and of the *Marne* flanking the clock), some churches, many buildings ornamented with caryatids, etc. His abundant production includes portraits in bust and in medallion of historic and contemporary people, a numbner of allegorical, mythological or religious groups, and some commemorative or funereal monuments. He exhibited at the Salon starting in 1840. His works do not seem to have been cast in bronze, with the exception of a reduction of *Vercingétorix* nearly fifty centimeters high. The museum of Decorative Arts in Paris possesses a medallion, *Portrait du sculpteur Klagmann*, while the museum of Petit Palais holds a statuette of *Justice*, 99 cm. Another bronze, *François de Châteaubriand*, 50 cm (1875) appears at the museum of Reims.

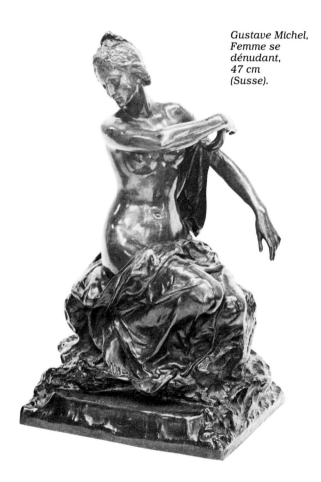

Gustave Michel,
Femme se dénudant,
47 cm
(Susse).

MOIGNIEZ, JULES

Senlis, 1835
Saint-Martin-du-Tertre, May 29, 1894

This sculptor started his career at the Exposition Universelle of 1855, where he presented a plaster entitled *Chien braque arrêtant un faisan*. He seems to have been particularly attracted to fowl, which undoubtably explains his studies with one of his elders, bird specialist Paul Comoléra. Meanwhile, in addition to his herons, pheasants, swallows, egrets, sparrows, and chickens, Moigniez modeled some other animals: dogs, gazelles, mares, and colts. He also made some hunting scenes: *Chasse au tigre*, and *Chasse au sanglier*, and some scenes with mounted race horses. He exhibited regularly at the Salon from 1859 to 1892, and was very successful not only in France, but abroad as well—in Great Britain and the United States principally—where he sold half of his production. His bronzes were cast by his father, a metal-gilder, who opened a foundry with this intention. His castings were of excellent quality, with a variety of patinas. Certain very original patinas were strongly sought after, particularly some of the gilded patinas. However, the plastic qualities of some of Moigniez's work did not rank with the work of the genre's best artists. He can be reproached for a excess of detail, born of overly-finicky, over-worked chiseling. His work is redeemed, however, by a certain elegance of attitudes.

Moigniez sent plasters as well as bronzes to the Salon. The latter appeared especially before 1870, including among others *Chien braque arrêtant un faisan* (1859), a work acquired by the State for the château of Compiègne, *Héron* and *Portrait d'un chien King Charle* (1861), *Tiercelet, oiseau de proie*, silvered bronze (1863), *Faisan et belette* (1864), *Compagnie de perdrix*, silvered bronze (1865), *Aigrette* (1866), *Combat de moineaux* (1867), and *Coq défendant sa famille* (1869).

Jules Moigniez,
Epagneul au faisan,
30 x 40 cm.

Jules Moigniez,
Chien de chasse tenant un lièvre,
32 x 42 cm.

J. Moigniez

Jules Moigniez,
Trois Chiens de chasse
devant un terrier,
33 x 52 cm.

Jules Moigniez,
Basset, 29 cm L.

Jules Moigniez,
Chien de chasse,
32 x 19 cm.

Jules Moigniez,
Epagneul rapportant un faisan,
32 cm.

Jules Moigniez,
Braque de Weimar
arrêtant un faisan,
89 cm
(1855; Susse).

①

②

1) *Jules Moigniez, Sanglier courant, 26 x 40 cm.*

2) *Jules Moigniez, Le Cheval "Chief Baron," 37 cm (Goelzer, founder).*

3) *Jules Moigniez, Cheval de course et son jockey, 34 cm.*

4) *Jules Moigniez, Cerf dix-cors.*

5) *Jules Moigniez, L'Accolade, 36 cm.*

6) *Jules Moigniez, Chevreuils à l'abreuvoir, 25 x 27 cm.*

③

④

⑤

⑥

*Jules Moigniez
Biche
et son petit.*

*Jules Moigniez,
Coq attaquant
une belette,
75 cm.*

After that, he became sick and stopped sculpture, but his bronzes continued to be cast until the beginning of the 20th century by Auguste Gouge, who succeeded Moigniez's father as the head of the foundry. A statuette, *Perdrix blessée,* was cast by Susse in three dimensions, 23, 17 and 13 cm.

MUSEUMS
Compiègne, château
Chien braque arrêtant un faisan, 90 x 117 cm.
Mont-de-Marsan
Chien courant basset tirant au vent, 48.5 cm.

SALES
Une aigrette, 53 cm, Sotheby London, March 21, 1985.
L'Accolade, 36 cm, Bourg-en-Bresse, March 2, 1986.
Basset, 29 cm L., Drouot, July 7, 1983, room9.
Deux Bécasses, 24 cm, Christie's London, September 25, 1986.
La Becquée, silvered bronze, 11 x 18 cm, Drouot, July 7, 1983, room 9.
Biche et son petit, Drouot, May 21, 1984.
Braque de Weimar débusquant un faisan, 89 x 110 cm, Rambouillet, July 27, 1986.
Deux Braques attaquant un sanglier, 30 cm, Enghien, October 10, 1982.
Cheval de course et son jockey, 34 cm, L'Isle-Adam, April 28, 1985; Sotheby London, July 5, 1985.
Deux Chevaux de course, Lyon, March 11, 1985.
Chien à l'arrêt, 28 cm, Grenoble, June 25, 1984.
Chien de chasse, 39 cm L., Lyon, June 18, 1985.
Chien et lapin, 18 cm, L'Isle-Adam, December 9, 1984.
Chien-loup et tortue, 35 cm, Sotheby London, November 7, 1985.
Chien rapportant un lièvre, 32 x 42 cm, Vitry-le-François, July 20, 1986.
Trois Chiens devant un terrier, 16 cm, Sotheby London, March 8, 1984; Lyon, June 18, 1985.
Coq, 75 x 46 cm, Perpignan, March 31, 1984.
Le Coq de bruyère, 53 cm, Lyon, June 5, 1985.
Epagneul au faisan, 30 x 40 cm, Drouot, June 4, 1984.
Faisan, 46 cm, Bourgoin-Jallieu, October 19, 1986.
Faisan sur un rocher, 49.5 cm, Sotheby London, November 8, 1984.

Jules Moigniez,
L'Aiglon,
24.5 x 27.5 cm.

Joueur de polo, L'Isle-Adam, September 14, 1986.
Lion assis, 22 cm, Enghien, October 10, 1982.
Mérinos né à Wideville, 30 cm, Sotheby London, March 20, 1986.
Mon étoile, 32.5 cm, Sotheby London, July 5, 1985.
Deux Oiseaux se bécotant, 20 x 27 cm, Agen, October 19, 1985.
Pointer tenant un lièvre and *Setter tenant un faisan*, two groups, 42 cm, Christie's London, January 22, 1986.
Sanglier, 26 x 40 cm, Dijon, November 4, 1984.
Setter à l'arrêt sur une poule faisane, 90 cm (Susse), Enghien, October 10, 1982.

MOINE, ANTONIN

Saint-Etienne, June 30, 1796
Paris, March 18, 1849

A sculptor, painter, and lithographer, Antoine Moine participated at the Salon from 1831 to 1848, and worked on different edifices including the fountains of the Place de la Concorde, the Chambre des députés, and the church Saint-Gervais. The Susse house cast and exhibited a certain number of his statuettes, which were greatly appreciated by the public:

Don Quichotte, 34 and 12 cm.
Enfant qui pleure, 6 cm.
Enfant qui rit, 6 cm.
Esméralda, 40 cm.

Jules Moigniez,
La Becquée, silvered bronze,
11 x 18 cm.

Jules Moigniez,
Le Grand Héron,
52 cm.

501

Femme au faucon, 42 and 11 cm.
Général Bonaparte, 20 cm.
Kléber, 20 cm.
Napoléon 1er équestre, 45 and 18 cm.
Phébus, 40 cm.
Sancho, 34 and 12 cm.
Sonneur d'olifant, 42 and 11 cm.

The Thiébaut foundry cast a work entitled *Pêcheur endormi* in two dimensions, 24 and 16 cm.

MOLCHNECHT, DOMINIQUE OR MAHLKNECHT

Gröden (Tyrol), November 13, 1793
Paris, May 17, 1876

This student of Canova exhibited some busts, groups and mythological, religious or historical statues at the Salon between 1831 and 1857, and became a naturalized French citizen in 1848. The works he showed had been commissioned for diverse edifices, including the Church des Invalides and the cathedrals of Versailles and Metz. Statues of *Duguay Trouin*, executed for the city of Dinan, and of *Duguesclin*, for Dinan and Nantes, are also credited to this artist. The museum of Toulouse preserves one small statue in bronze, *Le Duc de Bordeaux*, 120 cm high.

MOMBUR, JEAN OSSAYE

Ennezat (Puy-de-Dôme), 1850
1896

This sculptor participated regularly at the Salon from 1878 to 1898, showing diverse busts, some of which were in bronze: *J. Bargoin* (1872), and *Salneuve*, a former jusdtice of the peace (1892), and a statue in bronze entitled *Paysanne d'Auvergne* destined for Montrouge Square in Paris (1883). The museum Bargoin of Clermont-Ferrand possesses no less than four busts in bronze of *Salneuve*, in heights of 74, 75, 82 and 110 cm.

MONARD, LOUIS DE

Autun, January 31, 1873
Paris, July 15, 1939

Born into a family of soldiers, Monard seemed destined for a career in the army. However, his love of nature, animals, horseback riding and hunting, together with an artistic temperment, incited him to devote himself to painting and, more particularly, to sculpture. An uncle in Paris introduced him to some painters and sculptors, namely Rodin and Bartholomé. Monard began to model animals, which at first served as preparatory studies for his canvases (on his property at Bois-le-Roi, near Fontainebleau, Monard raised horses and billy goats). In 1900 his first works appeared, including *Sanglier aux écoutes*. He exhibited at the Artistes français from 1902 to 1904, then at the Société Nationale des Beaux-Arts. Among his bronzes are *Terrier griffon*,

Sanglier (1902), *Taquinerie, Camaraderie, L'Aigle* (1903), *Jument pur-sang* and *Cob, cheval* (1904),*Etalon boulonnais* and *Pur-sang au pas* (1905), *Le Chasse à l'aigle, Groupe de chiens bâtards vendéens, Tête de chien bâtard vendéen, Fox-terrier rapportant un écureuil* (1908), *Chien de meute à l'attache, Chien de meute aboyant* (1909), *Fox-terrier retournant un crabe, Chien de meute hurlant au perdu, Jument de chasse* (1910), *Henri IV à Ivry, Etalon de gros trait breton, Sur la voie froide* (1911), *Jeune bouc luttant* (1912), and *Etalon ardennais de gros trait* (1914), etc.

While enjoying a good reputation among a rich clientele, Louis de Monard was attentive to maintaining the quality of his bronzes, which were executed into just a few castings. He signed many contracts with Eugène Houdebine, Adrien A. Hébrard, Valsuani, and Rudier. Certain works were also cast in unglazed porcelain by the Sèvres factory. Some portraits of contemporary personalities appeared also in this sculptor's work, and some monumental groups such as the bronze monument to dead aviators (1912) for the Church of the Invalides (today at the Ecole de l'Air de Salon-de-Provence). In 1914, Monard enlisted to provide camouflage in the army. He met other artists there, including Forain, Dunoyer de Segonzac, and Georges d'Espagnat. After the war, Monard's style evolved to reflect a greater sobriety and a stronger classical influence. He became more interested in exotic animals, which he studied in different zoological parks. He executed a number of other monumental works, such as the monument to the dead of Bois-le-Roi, the group of *Vautours* for the square of the Batignolles in Paris, and finally, his last sculpture, *La Lionne et ses lionceaux* for the city of Luchon.

M. Jacques Thomas, Monard's biographer, gave a number of the artist's works to the museums of Autun, Vannes and Vernon, and published a catalog of his production (*Bulletin de la Société d'histoire de l'art français*, 1983). Thanks to this work, it is possible to draw up a list of the principal castings made by different foundries with, in some cases, the number of proofs cast.

Bronzes made by Houdebine
Camaraderie, jument et deux chiens (1903), 37 x 50 cm.
La Chasse de l'aigle (1906), 144 x 58 cm.
Cheval en liberté (around 1900), 13 x 24 cm.
Cheval surpris (around 1900), 31 x 25 cm.
Cheval dans la prairie or *Au trot* (1904), 27 x 31 cm.
Craintive mais grincheuse or *Chienne griffon irlandaise* (1901).
L'Etalon, cheval cabré maintenu par un homme (1902), 59 x 52 cm.
Fox-terrier brisant un os (1908), 22 x 32 cm.
Fox-terrier grondant (1908), 25 x 32 cm.
Fox-terrier rapportant un écureuil (1908), 31 x 37 cm.
Jument au caveçon (1904), 41 x 46 cm.
Prise de longe (1902), 30.5 x 46.5 cm.
Sanglier aux écoutes (around 1900), 15 x 25 cm.
Taquinerie, jument et petit chien (1903), 37 x 39 cm.

Bronzes made by Hébrard
Chien de meute aboyant au cerf (1908).
Groupe de chiens bâtards vendéens (1908).
Tête de chien de meute (1908), 31 cm.
Cob irlandais (1904), 25.5 x 30.5 cm, 25 proofs.
Etalon ardennais (1906), one proof around 1932.
Etalon boulonnais (1905), 49 x 60 cm, 15 proofs.
Fox-terrier assis (1905), 15.5 x 10 cm, 20 proofs.
Fox-terrier retournant un crabe (1909), 37 x 75 cm and
24 x 50 cm.
Irish-terrier étranglant un lapin, 4 proofs.
Jument de chasse (1910).
Pur-sang au pas (1904), 40 x 67 cm, 15 proofs.

Bronzes made by Valsuani
Chevaux broutant (1927), 17 x 15.5 cm, 2 proofs.
Chien de meute couché (around 1909), 3 proofs.
Cob irlandais (1904), 25.5 x 30.5 cm, 1 proof in 1953.
Etalon boulonnais, first sketch (1905), 2 proofs.
Jeune Fille au chevreau (1924), 21 x 8.5 cm, 2 proofs.
Jument rentrant au pré (1927), 27 x 28 cm, 2 proofs.
Sanglier aux écoutes (around 1900), 15 x 25 cm, 2
proofs.
Sur la voie froide, chien humant le sol (1910), 37 x 49
cm.
Vautour, 33 x 12 cm.

Bronzes made by Rudier
La Chasse du centaure (1923), 3 proofs.
Chien de meute hurlant au perdu (1910), 26 x 13 cm, 2
proofs.
Etalon ardennais (1906), one proof in 1913.
Fox-terrier retournant un crabe (1914), 9 x 28 cm, 15
proofs.

M. Jacques Thomas notes in addition some recent castings made by Susse in 1983, including *Cob irlandais* and *Chimpanzé*, as well as some castings indicated without the name of the founder:

L'Aigle (1903), 16.5 cm.
Chevreau broutant (1919), 35 x 32.5 cm, 5 proofs.
Chevreau se grattant (1919), 33 x 38 cm, 3 proofs.
Condor, 12 proofs cast in 1929.
Etalon de gros trait breton (1911), 9 proofs.
Vautour penché or *Petit vautour* (around 1912), 20 x 14
cm, 2 proofs.

MUSEUMS
Autun
Diane forçant une biche, 32 cm.
Mouflon à manchettes, 46 cm (Valsuani).
Boulogne-sur-Mer
Cheval boulonnais, 49 cm (Hébrard 2/10).
Dijon
Chevreau couché, 8 x 12 cm.
Sanglier, 15 x 25 cm.
Paris, Orsay
Coupe des grands planeurs (eagle, vulture, condor),
22.5 cm, reduction of the funereal monument of
the sculptor at the cemetery of Bois-le-Roi.
Paris, Petit Palais
Henri IV à Ivry, 114 cm.
Valenciennes
Cheval, prise de longe, statuette.

The museums of Autun, of Dijon, of Vannes and of Vernon also possess a number of plasters.

SALES
Cheval, 41.5 cm, Sotheby London, March 17, 1983.
Chien terrier et crabe, 25.5 cm (Hébrard), Sotheby
London, March 20, 1986.
Coupe des grands planeurs cast of silver, 22.5 cm,
Drouot, May 19, 1982, room 1.

MONCEL, ALPHONSE EMMANUEL, THE COUNT OF PÉRIN

Paris, September 7, 1866
April 7, 1930

A sculptor and medaller, Moncel Alphonse Emmannuel exhibited at the Salon starting in 1886, showing some allegorical works and genre scenes. He also showed portraits of contemporaries, and historical or fictional characters, such as *Pâtre phrygien*, plaster (1887), *Le Poète Alain Chartier*, marble (1892), *Le Lierre*, marble (1895), *Monsieur Gaston Pâris* of the Académie Française, a statuette in bronze (1899), *L'Enigme*, a statuette in oxidized

*Alphonse Emmanuel de Moncel,
La Porteuse d'eau, 46 cm
(Barbedienne).*

bronze (1905), *Monsieur Combes*, a statuette in bronze (1910), *Les Trois Mousquetaires*, a small group in bronze (1914), as well as some busts including *Alexandre Dumas fils*.

Also known are Alphonse Emmanuel Moncel's statuette of *Alain Chartier*, cast in bronze, 70 cm, and *La Porteuse d'eau*, cast in three dimensions by Barbedienne, in patinated bronze as well as in gilded bronze. *La Proteuse d'eau*, 46 cm (Barbedienne), was sold at the Drouot hotel, April 16, 1984, room 1.

MONGINOT, CHARLOTTE

Paris, December 18, 1872—?

This artist started exhibiting at the Salon in 1895 (she resigned from the Société des Artistes Français in 1948), showing notably some statues in plaster such as *Colette et son canard* (1895), *Un faucheur* (1897), *Titan foudroyé* (1901), *Martyre!* (1902), *La Douleur et le Temps* (1904), *Taquinerie* (1905), *Une fille d'Eve* (1908), etc. Some statuettes in bronze include *Le Bruit de la mer* (1899), *Eclosion* (1911), *Retour des vignes* and *Premier Ouvrage* (1912),

Fleurs des champs, passage difficile, La Bande joyeuse, Pêche miraculeuse (1914); and finally, a statuette in plaster, *Victoire* (1899). There are also some marbles: *Pauvre Amour* (1909), *Le Ralliement* and *Vers l'avenir* (1913), and *L'Age heureux* (1914). Some of these works were made the object of editions in bronze, among others *Jeune Femme à la grenouille*, 21 x 12 cm and *Skieuse*, 28 cm. A small group in gilded bronze and ivory, *Quatre Enfants sur une luge*, 24 cm, was sold in London by Sotheby, June 18, 1982.

MONIER, ÉMILE

Paris, July 10, 1883—?

The museum of Troyes preserves three works in bronze by this sculptor and engravor in medals: *Monsieur P. Marquez, conseiller général*, a plaque of 14.5 x 12 cm (1903), *Profil de femme*, a plaque of 15 x 10 cm, and *Sommeil*, a medallion, 7.5 cm diam.

Auguste Moreau, Sélèné or l'Aurore (on a clock), 89 cm.

Auguste Moreau, La Semeuse, 56 cm.

Auguste Moreau, Fillette au parapluie or Il pleut!, 48 cm.

*Auguste Moreau,
Jeune Fille
jouant
avec deux amours,
70 cm.*

*Auguste Moreau,
L'Automne,
45 cm.*

*Auguste Moreau,
Jeune Femme
à l'oiseau,
83 cm.*

MONTEGUT, JEANNE DE CONSTANTIN

Born in Beaumont (Dordogne)

Belonging to an old family from Périgord, this artist made her debut at the Salon in 1880 with a bust in bronze, *Le Docteur Galy, ancien conservateur du musée,* 62 cm (Jaboeuf and Bezout, founders) which belongs specifically to the museum of Périgueux.

MOREAU, AUGUSTE LOUIS MATHURIN

Dijon, 1834
Malesherbes, November 11, 1917

auguste Moreau

The third son of sculptor and painter Jean-Baptiste Moreau, Auguste Louis Mathurin Moreau initiated himself to sculpture along with his older brother Mathurin. In 1861, he made his debut at the Salon, where he would exhibit regularly and abundantly until 1913. His subjects were primarily genre scenes, pastorals, and allegories; his style was realistic and graceful, revealing his relation to the other members of the Moreau dynasty. The similitude of names sometimes provokes confusion in the attribution of certain works signed without first initials.

A number of bronzes (statuettes and small groups, unless noted otherwise) appeared among Auguste Moreau's consignments to the Salon: *Pandore* (1863), *Le Message* (1880), *Les Enfants égarés* (1881), *La Charmeuse,* bust (1882), *Les Adieux, Le Retour des hirondelles* (1883), *Charmeuse, Le Char de l'Amour* (1890), *Le Premier Bijou, Les Grapilleurs* (1892), *Le Lever de l'Aurore* (1893), *Fleur de mer, Victrix enfant,* this latter work in bronze and gold (1897), *Amour triomphant* (1900), *La Source* (1901), *Au clair de lune,* a statue of a woman (1902), *La Fée des mers* (1903), *Ismaël,* a bust, *Les Contes de l'aïeule, Enfant sur la grève* (1905), *Eros enfant* (1907).

Also of note are some small groups and statuettes in marble, such as *L'enfant aux fauvettes* (1878), *Le Baiser* (1880), *Le Printemps* (1881), *La Source* (1885), *La Première Flèche* (1894), *Jeureux Pêcheur* (1895), *Enfant dans les blés* (1901), *La Grande Soeur,* group of children (1907), *Le Baiser d'amour* (1908), *Enfant dans les fleurs* (1912), *Enfant à la chèvre* (1913).

*Auguste Moreau,
Amour à l'arc,
50 cm.*

*Auguste Moreau,
Amour décochant
une flèche,
57 cm.*

It is necessary to note some figures in plaster: *Les Adieux* (1882), *Alerte* (1885), *Pêcheur d'écrevisses* (1902), *Le Baiser de la vague* (1906), some others in terra cotta, and finally two statuettes in pewter: *Eglantine* and *Attraits dangereux* (1896).

A number of Auguste Moreau's subjects, very popular at the time, were cast in bronze. Their titles vary between exposition catalogs and listings from public sales, so connecting individual pieces with works exhibited at the Salon is not easy. Here are bronzes noted at diverse times on the market:

Alerte, 30 cm.
Amour envoyant des baisers, 64 cm.
Amour triomphant or *Amour vainqueur*, 68 cm (cast by Susse).
Apollon, 135 cm.
La Brise (a young girl waving a scarf), 63 and 52 cm.
Cendrillon, 72 cm.
Enfant jouant avec une poule, 77 cm.
Fillette au canard, *Fillette au parapluie*, 48 cm.
Flore, 54 cm.
Heureux Pêcheur, 23 cm.

Ino et Mêlicerte, 130 cm.
Jeune Femme à la vague, 90 cm.
Le Lever de l'Aurore, 80 and 65 cm.
Le Message, 75 cm.
Naïade au trident, 60 cm.
La Pêcheuse de crevettes, 62 cm.
Psyché enfant or *Petite Fille à l'oiseau*, 70 and 55 cm.
Le Retour des hirondelles, 85 cm.
Rose de mai, 83 cm (model in regule, 50 cm).
Vase porté par un amour, 25 cm.
Victrix enfant, cast by Eugène Blot.

Furthermore, Harold Bermann (*Bronzes, Sculptors and Founders, 1974-1981*) made note of a number of original molds originating from a French foundry, acquired after World War II by American founder J.B. Hirsch, and reused thereafter to make new castings. According to Bermann, many works by Auguste Moreau appeared among these American editions, namely *Le Cadeau*, 68 cm, *Cupidon*, 71 cm, *Deux Enfants*, 50 cm, *Fontaine et ruisseau*, 37.5 cm, *Jeune Paysanne*, 58 cm, *Pan*, 75 cm, *Petit Amour*, 33 cm.

Auguste Moreau,
Enfant jouant
avec une poule,
77 cm.

Auguste Moreau,
Les Deux Enfants,
50 cm.

Auguste Moreau,
Trois Enfants
à la pampre.

MUSEUMS
Bordeaux
Enfant moissonneur, 55 cm
Dijon
L'Amour guettant des papillons, bas-relief, 21 x 13 cm.
Cupidon, 31 cm.
Ismaël, bust, 35 cm.
Madame Olivet-Moreau, bas-relief in silver, 30 x 20 cm.
Gray
La Boudeuse, 58 cm (A. Normand, founder).
Reims
Amour à l'oiseau, 28 cm.

SALES
Amour ailé envoyant des baisers, 63 cm, Drouot, April
    17, 1984, room 2.
Amour à l'arc, 50 cm, Drouot, October 10, 1985, room
    7.
Amour décochant des flèches, 57 cm, Lille, November
    25, 1985.
Angelot au tambourin, Epernay, April 6, 1985.
L'Aurore, 67 cm, Sotheby London, March 20, 1986;
    Meaux, May 25, 1986.
L'Automne, 45 cm, Nancy, May 4, 1986.

507

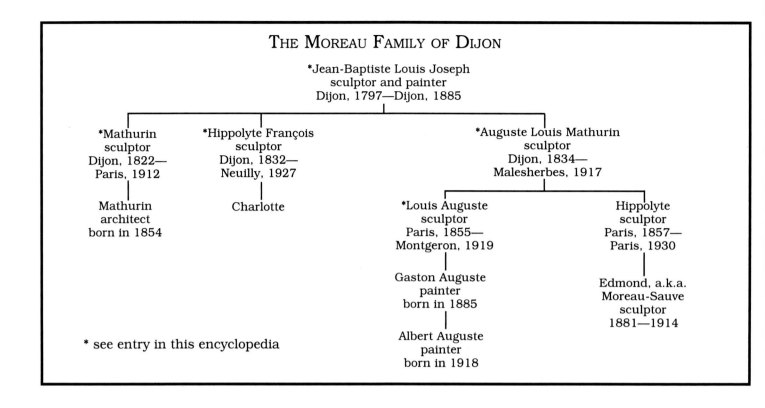

THE MOREAU FAMILY OF DIJON

*Jean-Baptiste Louis Joseph
sculptor and painter
Dijon, 1797—Dijon, 1885

*Mathurin
sculptor
Dijon, 1822—
Paris, 1912

Mathurin
architect
born in 1854

*Hippolyte François
sculptor
Dijon, 1832—
Neuilly, 1927

Charlotte

*Auguste Louis Mathurin
sculptor
Dijon, 1834—
Malesherbes, 1917

*Louis Auguste
sculptor
Paris, 1855—
Montgeron, 1919

Gaston Auguste
painter
born in 1885

Albert Auguste
painter
born in 1918

Hippolyte
sculptor
Paris, 1857—
Paris, 1930

Edmond, a.k.a.
Moreau-Sauve
sculptor
1881—1914

* see entry in this encyclopedia

Baigneuse à la libellule, 26.5 cm, Lokeren, October 20, 1984.
Enfant au canard, 63 cm, Drouot, October 19, 1984, room 1.
Enfant à la poule, 77 cm, Joigny, March 23, 1986.
Les Deux Enfants, Granville, April 3, 1986.
Enfants autour d'un nid, 68 cm, Fontainebleau, June 29, 1985.
Il pleut!, 48 cm, Douamenez, March 28, 1982.
Jeune Femme, Saint-Etienne, November 22, 1986.
Jeune Femme appuyée à un tronc d'arbre, 68.5 cm, Sotheby London, March 8, 1984.
Jeune Femme à la vague, 95 cm, Versailles, December 11, 1983.
Jeune Fille à la mandoline, 56 cm, Cologne, June 29, 1984.
Naissance de Vénus, 92 cm, Sotheby London, November 6, 1986.
Premier Pas, mère et enfant, 46.7 cm, Christie's New York, September 27, 1986.
Rose de mai, 77 cm, Drouot, November 20, 1985.
Sélènê (pedestal clock), 89 cm, Tours, June 17, 1985.
La Semeuse, 56 cm, Villeurbanne, March 10, 1982.
Vici, 44 cm, Drouot, November 9, 1984, room 6.

MOREAU, FRANÇOIS CLÉMENT

Paris, October, 1831
Paris, June 12, 1865

Although apparently not a member of the Dijonaisse Moreau family, this artist nonetheless left some gracious figures and groups of children, often with animals, and some allegorical subjects, which were greatly appreciated during his lifetime. At the Salon, where he exhibited from 1853 until his death, François Moreau exhibited works including *Jeune Fille endormie,* a statue in marble (1857), *Pandore,* a statuette in marble (1859), and two statues in plaster, *La Première Ivresse* (1864) and

Aristophane (1865). An edition in bronze of this last work was made by Thiébaut in two dimensions, 58 and 42 cm.

MOREAU, HIPPOLYTE FRANÇOIS

Dijon, 1832
Neuilly-sur-Seine, 1927

The second son of Jean-Baptiste Moreau, Hippolyte Moreau went to work in Paris under the direction of Jouffroy and exhibited his first work at the Salon in 1859. The best of his work includes charming full figures of children and young women, mostly allegorical, often with the same subjects as used by Hippolyte's brother Auguste.

A few of the bronzes among his consignments at the Salon are *Uno bevitore,* a statue of 199 cm high (1880), *Sortie de l'école,* a group (1886), and *Mireille,* a statuette (1894). There were also a number of marbles, especially some statuettes: *L'Iris* (1886), *Le Rêve* (1887), *Avril* (1888), *Dans les blés, Le Chant de l'alouette* (1889), *Départ des hirondelles* (1891), *Hésitation* (1892), *Chrysanthème* (1893), *Les Cerises* (1894), *Le Ruisseau, Le Crépuscule* (1895), *La Vague* (1896), *Oiseau blessé* (1899), *Dans la vague* (1900), *Fleur de lotus* (1902), *Le Printemps, Le Chant de la mer* (1903), *L'Aurore* (1905), *Faneuse* (1906), and *Le Nid* (1914). Later, notable works include a series of groups in marble: *Première Caresse* (1905), *Traîtrise d'amour* (1907), *Innocence* and *Imprudence* (1908), *Leçon de chant, Tendre Aveu* (1909), *Premier Bijou, Bataille de fleurs* (1910), *Le Secret, Couronnement de l'Amour* (1911), *Age heureux* and *Convoitise* (1912), and *Un maraudeur* (1913).

Among Hippolyte Moreau's works cast in bronze are: *L'Aurore,* 35 cm, *Le Chant de l'alouette,* 45 cm, *Le Chant de la mer,* 45 cm, *Consolation,* 30 cm,

1) Hippolyte Moreau, Ballerine jouant de la mandoline.

2) Hippolyte Moreau and Prosper Lecourtier, Piqueur au relais, 80 cm (Société des bronzes de Paris).

3) Hippolyte Moreau, Jeune Fille à la mandoline or Mignon, 120 cm.

4) Hippolyte Moreau, Couple de jeunes bûcherons, 49 cm.

5) Hippolyte Moreau, Les Deux Soeurs, 75 cm.

L'Echo, 45 cm, *L'Eté et l'Hiver,* 48 cm, *Femme aux sequins,* 80 cm, *Fillette au crabe,* 31 cm, *Passage du gué,* 58 cm, *Le Printemps,* 92 cm, *Le Rêve,* 78 cm, and *Le Secret,* 55 cm. Finally, in a departure from his usual style, Hippolyte Moreau made the bronze *Piqueur au relais,* a figure frequently available in public sale. Cast by the Société des Bronzes de Paris, this group also carries the signature of the animal sculptor Prosper Lecourtier, who probably sculpted the dogs.

MUSEUMS

Chambéry

Le Semeur, 35 cm.

Dijon

This museum possesses a number of plasters and terra cottas as well as some bronzes, including *Un buveur* and *Le Printemps.*

SALES

L'Aurore, nu couché, 47.6 cm (C. Valsuani 10), Christie's New York, November 19, 1986.

Chasseur et son chien, 47.5 cm, Cologne, March 31, 1984.

Couple de jeunes bûcherons, 49 cm, Douai, November 15, 1986.

Le Crépuscule, 72 cm, Sotheby London, June 12, 1986.

Les Deux Soeurs, 75 cm, Troyes, October 21, 1984.

Jeune Fille à la mandoline, 120 cm, Fontainebleau, January 29, 1984.

Jeune Fille à la rose, 65.5 cm, Troyes, November 23, 1986.

Paysanne et ses poules, 42 cm, Drouot, November 28, 1985, rooms 5 and 6.

Piqueur au relais (with P. Lecourtier), 48 cm, Rambouillet, March 9, 1986.

Piqueur au relais, 80 cm, Drouot, May 11, 1983; Drouot, April 3, 1985; Arles, June 16, 1985; Sotheby London, November 7, 1985.

Le Réveil, 82 cm, Washington, June 9, 1985; Madrid, October 23, 1985.

Le Secret, 71 cm, Christie's New York, October 16, 1984.

MOREAU, JEAN-BAPTISTE LOUIS JOSEPH

Dijon, 1797
Dijon, 1855

The father of three highly reputed sculptors, Mathurin, Hippolyte and Auguste Moreau, Jean-Baptiste himself was a painter and sculptor. He is best known for restoring the famous Tombs of the Dukes (*Tombeaux des Ducs*) of Bougogne, damaged during the Revolution and today preserved at the museum of Beaux-Arts of Dijon. This museum collected many works by Jean-Baptiste Moreau, including a group in bronze entitled *Céphale et Procris,* 100 cm, donated by the artist's oldest son, Mathurin.

MOREAU, LOUIS AUGUSTE

Paris, April 23, 1855
Montgeron, October 18, 1919

Taught by his father Auguste Moreau and by his uncle Mathurin Moreau, as well as by Aimé Millet, Dumont and Thomas, Louis Auguste Moreau made decorative sculptures for some monuments of Rochefort, statues, allegorical groups (including a certain number in bronze), and busts of contemporaries. He began exhibiting at the Salon in 1877, and

*Louis Auguste Moreau,
Diane, 54 cm.*

showed some statuettes in bronze, including *Alerta* and *Pêcheuse* (1888), *Surprise* (1890), *David* (1891), *La Jeunesse* (1892), *La Flûte enchantée* (1893), *Futur Musicien* (1895), *Légende de Sémiramis,* ornamented by jewelry (1901), *Vigilantia* (1908), *Le Défi* (1909), *Le Triomphe* (1910), and many figurines of *Algériennes* in 1913. Also in bronze are two busts, *Esclave* (1884) and *Captif* (1905), and some groups, *Pris dans ses filets* (1891), *Nuit d'été* (1894), and *Zéphyr et la vague,* in bronze and marble (1901). Some subjects were presented in plaster, including *Giotto* (1880), *Psyché* (1882), *Sylvain jouant avec un ours* (1886), *Enfant au crabe* (1887), and *La Source tarie* (1889), as well as a statuette entitled *Judith* and a vase in pewter (1896).

An edition of the statuette *Alerta* has been found in proof form, 80 cm high. Some other works by Auguste Moreau were also cast; there exist some castings in composition of *Futur Musicien,* 35 cm.

Finally, according to Harold Bermann (*Bronzes, Sculptors and Founders*), castings of many works by Louis Moreau were executed in America from original molds acquired in France after World War II (see also Auguste Moreau).

MUSEUMS
Périgueux
Gloire à la musique, 78 cm.

SALES
Les Adieux, regule, 83.5 cm, Barcelona, June 20, 1983.
Amour envoyant des baisers, 63.5 cm, Lyon, March 24, 1982.
La Brise, 67 cm, Enghien, March 7, 1982.
Le Char de l'Aurore, 33 cm, Christie's New York, December 13, 1983.
Chérubin au tambourin, 47 cm, Sotheby London, November 25, 1982.
Diane, 54 cm, Sotheby London, June 12, 1986.
Naissance de la perle, 66 cm, Sotheby London, November 10, 1983.
Persée et Andromède, 96 cm (Raingo frères, founders), Sotheby London, November 25, 1982.
SalammbôST1, gilded bronze, 73.5 cm, Christie's London, November 8, 1984.
La Voie lactée, 91 cm, Milan, December 16, 1982.
A pair of vases, decorated in relief by cherubs and aquatic landscape, 24 cm, Reims, October 26, 1986.

MOREAU, MATHURIN
Dijon, November 18, 1822
Paris, February 14, 1912

An expert at portraying feminine grace, Mathurin Moreau sculpted figures, genre scenes, and allegories with an amiable and lighthearted realism. Pieces fitting this description dominated his extensive collection of bronze works, to which should be added a number of official commissions. The son and a student of Jean-Baptiste Moreau, Mathurin entered Paris's Ecole des Beaux-Arts when he was nineteen years old, and studied there under the direction of Ramey and Dumont. He won the second prize of Rome in 1842 with *Diomède enlevant le palladium*, and showed his work for the first time at the Salon in 1848, where he obtained a number of distinctions. Around 1850, he worked for the foundry of Val d'Osne, creating a number of models for statues destined to be cast in iron In later years he became one of that foundry's administrators.

Mathurin Moreau's work includes some commemorative monuments, tombs, a number of statues and busts of personalities, and some ornamental sculptures. He worked for the churches of Saint-Augustin and of the Trinité, for the Opera, the palais de Justice, the city hall, the Tuileries, the pavillion of Marsan at the Louvre, the gare du Nord, one of the fountains of the Théâtre Plaza (the statue of the *Nymphe fluviale*), among others. His work also includes a large quantity of statues, statuettes and groups in pleasant decorative themes, which were quite successful in their time.

Mathurin Moreau sent quite a number of bronzes to the Salon: *La Fée aux fleurs*, a group of 140 cm high (1853), *L'Etude* and *Fileuse* (1859), *La Méditation* (1861), *Le Printemps* (1865), *Primavera* (1872), *Circé*, a statuette (1873), *Ismaël* and *Candeur*, two busts (1875), *Rêverie*, a statuette (1883), *Protection de l'enfance* (1892), *Les Armes d'Achille* (1898), *Le Torrent* (1901), *Marguerite d'Anjou*, a group for the monument of Angers, and *Gramme*, a statue for the

Mathurin Moreau,
Jeune Femme se coiffant,
62 cm.

Mathurin Moreau,
La Source, 70 cm.

Mathurin Moreau,
Baigneuse à la cruche,
74 cm.

Mathurin Moreau,
L'Aurore.

Mathurin Moreau,
Libellule,
85 cm.

513

1) *Mathurin Moreau, Graziella, 73 cm.*

2) *Mathurin Moreau, Grappilleuse, 70 cm.*

3) *Mathurin Moreau, Fillette lisant, 75 cm.*

4) *Mathurin Moreau, L'Immortalité, 83 cm.*

5) *Mathurin Moreau, Deux Jeunes Filles enlacées, 57 cm.*

Mathurin Moreau,
Vénus et l'Amour,
80 cm.

Mathurin Moreau,
Groupe
de trois enfants
or Bacchus jeune,
85 cm
(Susse).

Mathurin Moreau,
Jeune Femme
guettant avec
ses deux enfants,
45 cm.

tomb of the Belgian electrician at Père-Lachaise (1902), *Le Rêve* and *Gloire au travail* (1903), and lastly four statuettes: *La Mutalité* and *Fleuve* (1906), *Première Fleur* (1907), and *La Source de jouvence* (1909). In the category of statuettes and small groups in marble, it is necessary to note also: *Baigneuse* (1876), *Phryné* (1878), *La Vigneronne* (1884), *La Vague* (1887), *Jeanne d'Arc* (1891), *Jeune Fille à la vasque* (1894), *Sorie de bain* (1899), *La Jeunesse* (1905), and *Passage du gué* (1911).

The majority of these works and many others never exhibited at the Salon have been cast in bronze by different founders, as evidenced by pieces appearing on the market and in museums. It is difficult, though, to identify them because the titles vary widely. Of note, however, are some editions made by Susse:

La Charmeuse, 82, 66 and 55 cm.
Jeune Fille à la fontaine, 100, 80 and 65 cm.
Le Réveil du Printemps, 83, 65 and 55 cm.
La Source, plate, 46 cm L.
Triomphe de la jeunesse, 85 cm.

Also known are some bronzes cast by E. Colin, including *Moissonneuse*, 50 cm, and *Jeune Fille assise*, 73 cm. Godeau is known to have produced *Jeune Femme nue assise*, 48 cm, and Berneaux cast editions of *Femme portant une hotte*, 50 cm, among others.

MUSEUMS
Caen
La Fileuse, 130 cm (Victor Paillard, a Parisian founder, 1862).
Dijon
Autoportait, medallion, 26 cm diam.
Les Exilés, 39 cm.
La Fée aux fleurs, 146 cm (Gonon; Salon of 1853).
Femme tenant une branche d'olivier, 33 cm.
Figure funéraire tenant un sablier, 33 cm.
Génie funéraire, 32 cm.
Ismaël, bust, 75 cm

*Mathurin Moreau,
Le Rhône,
58 cm.
J. Ginepro
Collection,
Monaco.*

*Mathurin Moreau,
Le Porcher
or La Toilette
du cochon,
silvered bronze,
21 cm
(Christofle edition).
J. Ginepro
Collection,
Monaco.*

Mathurin Moreau,
L'Echo,
62 cm.

Le Jongleur, 32 cm.
Madame Mathurin Moreau, 38 cm (1896).
La Pudeur, 42 cm.
Thévenot, directeur de l'école normale de Dijon, bust, 82 cm (1869).
La Vendangeuse, 90 cm.
    This museum also possesses a number of small groups and statuettes in terra cotta.

Paris, Decorative Arts
La Toilette du cochon, 23.5 cm.

Reims
La Paix victorieuse de la Tempête, gilded bronze, 98 cm.

SALES

L'Aurore, Drouot, December 20, 1985, room 9.
Bacchus enfant et deux amours, 85 cm (Susse), Drouot, November 28, 1984.
Diane, 54 cm, Anvers, December 4, 1985.
Diane au bain, 68 cm (Société des bronzes de Paris), Sotheby London, June 12, 1986.
L'Echo, 47.5 cm, Christie's New York, March 13, 1984.
L'Echo, 62 cm, Christie's New York, October 16, 1984.
Femme et enfant, Granville, April 30, 1986.
La Fileuse, 73 cm, Drouot, May 3, 1985, room 4.
Femme et deux enfants, 73 cm, Carcassonne, May 9, 1982.
Fillette lisant, 75 cm, Troyes, October 21, 1984.
Le Génie des sciences, 76 cm, Rodez, September 28, 1985.
Immortalité, 88 cm, Epernay, March 19, 1986.
Les Javeleuses, Brussels, November 21, 1984.
Jeune Femme nue assise sur un rocher, 48 cm, Drouot, April 16, 1984, room 2.
Jeune Femme nue assise sur un rocher, 80 cm, Morlaix, August 5, 1985; Sotheby London, June 12, 1986.
Jeune Femme et deux chérubins, 81 cm, Sotheby London, March 20, 1986.
Jeune Fille assise, 73 cm (E. Colin), Drouot, January 23, 1984, room 1.
Deux Jeunes Filles enlacées, 57 cm, Limoges, May 11, 1986.
Jeune Paysanne et dénicheur d'oiseaux, 85 cm, Drouot, November 28, 1986, room 14.
Joueuse de lyre, 58 cm, Nancy, November 18, 1984.
Joueuse de lyre, 85 cm, (Susse), Drouot, November 28, 1984.
Léda et le cygne, Pontoise, May 26, 1984.
La Libellule, 80 cm, Sotheby London, March 20, 1986; Christie's New York, September 27, 1986.
Marie de Médicis, 101.5 cm, Christie's New York, September 24, 1984.
Orphée, 98 cm, Enghien, March 24, 1985.
Psyché, 84 cm, Christie's New York, February 19, 1985.
Le Printemps, 45 cm, Vienna, November 24, 1985.
Le Retour de Diane, 73 cm, Troyes, June 24, 1984.
La Source, 62 cm, Orléans, October 17, 1985; Epernay, December 15, 1985.
Les Trois Amis, 61 cm, Sotheby New York, April 26, 1986.

MOREAU-VAUTHIER, AUGUSTIN JEAN, CALLED MOREAU

Paris, May 8, 1831
Paris, January 17, 1893

    Son of a tabletier, Moreau-Vauthier enjoyed practicing sculpture in ivory, with which he debuted at the Salon in 1857. At the time, his works were signed "Moreau;" it was only in 1865 that he adopted the name "Moreau-Vauthier" to distinguish himself from other sculptors carrying his last name. He was also fond of precious materials—gold, silver, stone, and enamel—which he frequently incorporated in his figures, allegorical and mythological groups, and portraits. He exhibited at the Salon works including *Le Petit Buveur*, bronze (1865), *Baigneuse*, marble

Augustin Moreau-Vauthier, Jeune Homme à la cornemuse.

(1866), *Il Zampognaro*, portraying a young Italian herdsman, bronze (1896), *L'Amour*, bronze (1872), *L'Amour*, a statue in ivory, marble, gold, silver and precious stones (1875), *Bethsabée*, marble (1876), *Néréide*, marble (1877), *La Fortune*, bronze (1879), *L'Amour captif*, a statuette in marble, 85 cm (1880), *La Fortune*, a group in ivory, enamel, onyx and silver (1881), *Jeune Faune*, bronze (1882), *Molière*, bronze, and *Andromède*, ivory, enamel, stones and precious metals (1883), *La Peinture*, a statuette in ivory and gold plate (1885), *Jeune Orientale*, a bust in ivory (1886), *Pascal enfant*, plaster (1888), *Gavroche*, bronze (Exposition Universelle of 1889), *Tête florentine*, a bust in bronze and ivory (1892), *Molière*, a statuette in ivory and gold plate (1893).

    Many works by Moreau-Vauthier have been cast in bronze. Those by Barbedienne are *La Fortune*, 130, 85, 69, 51, 43, and 34 cm, and *Pacal enfant*. Others by Thiébaut are *L'Amour vainqueur*, 76, 36, 22 and 12 cm, *Néréide*, 72 and 29 cm, and *Pifferaro*, 73 and 37 cm. The museum of Reims possesses a statue in bronze entitled *Cupidon*, 141 cm.

SALES

L'Amiral Courbet, bust, 34 cm (Barbedienne), Drouot, October 19, 1983, room 9.
Femme assise sur une coquille, 72 cm (Thiébaut), Sotheby London, June 17, 1986.
La Fortune, 51 cm (Barbedienne), Drouot, December 20, 1983, room 10.
La Fortune, 86 cm (Barbedienne), Christie's New York, October 16, 1983.
Jeune Homme à la cornemuse, Valenciennes, November 26, 1984.
    Also of note is *Cupidon*, a silver subject ornamenting a clock, mounted on a lapis-lazuli pedestal, Belfort, March 10, 1985.

MOREAU-VAUTHIER, PAUL
Paris, November 26, 1871
Poitiers, February 2, 1936

Taught by his father Augustin Moreau-Vauthier and by Thomas, this artist was especially known for an emotional monument entitled *Victimes des révolutions*, erected in 1909 in Gambetta Square, against the wall of the cemetery of the Père-Lachaise. Moreover, an earlier project in plaster, which he exhibited at the Salon in 1902, is entitled *Le Mur* (the wall). Paul Moreau-Vauthier also produced some genre figures, allegories, busts, and statuette portraits. Starting in 1894, he showed works at the Salon, including three small bronze groups from 1910: *Danseuses espagnoles, Toréadors* and *Boxeurs*. He made many monuments to victims of World War I.

MUSEUMS
Dijon
Buste de Morel-Retz, peintre et caricaturiste dijonnais, 55 cm (Salon of 1886).
Nantes
Danseuse de Séville, 17 cm (Séville 1909).
Paris, Orsay
Toréador à Séville, 18 cm (Séville 1909).
Reims
L'Amour, 135 cm.

SALES
L'homme enfourchant sa machine volante échappe à l'attraction de la terre, 23 cm L. (1910; Susse), Paris, Palais des Congrès, June 5, 1983.

MOREL, LOUIS
Essoyes (Aube), November 30, 1887
Troyes, March 29, 1975

A student of Injalbert, Louis Morel made his debut at the Salon in 1906. In 1918, he replaced Richard Guino at the side of Renoir, modeling three bas-reliefs for Renoir: two versions of *Danseuse au tambourin*, and *Le Joueur de flûteau*. Morel's collaboration with the famous artist would not continue, however. Two large figures in bronze carrying Morel's signature, representing *Marie Stuart* and the Queen *Elisabeth*, 105 cm, are noted as being sold in England in 1887. The museum of Troyes preserves many works by this sculptor, including three bronzes: *Masque d'éphèbe*, 43 cm, *Buste de Madame Farjon*, 55 cm, and *Tête de Christ*, 28.5 cm.

MORIA, BLANCHE
Paris, May 7, 1859
November 25, 1926

A sculptor and an engraver of medals, Blanche Moria participated at the Salon from 1883 to 1925, leaving some figures of Breton peasants. A statue in bronze entitled *Quelle Vérité?* was noted at the Exposition Universelle of 1900. A bust in bronze, *Vieille Femme*, 58 cm, is found at the museum of Grenoble.

MORICE, LÉOPALD
Nîmes, 1846
Paris, July 1920

Morice was the author of the monument of the *République*, inaugurated in 1883 on the plaza of the same name in Paris. The Barbedienne house cast his work *Les Joies du foyer*, 90 and 66 cm. One model of this work was exhibited at the Salon of 1895.

MORIS, LOUIS MARIE
Paris, 1818
After 1883

This sculptor, who exhibited at the Salon from 1857 to 1883, produced primarily equestrian figures of historic people, such as *François 1er* in bronze, 100 cm, *Abderame dit le Juste, fondateur du royaume de Cordoue*, a statuette in wax (Salon of 1857), and three statues in plaster: *Napoléon 1er* (1864), *Vercingétorix* (1865), and *Etienne Marcel* (1883). The effigy of the artist, life-size and in bronze, ornaments the tomb of the Moris family at Père-Lachaise (plaster at the Salon of 1882). Many of his works have been cast in bronze, including *Napoléon 1er*, 50 cm, *François 1er*, 85 cm, and *Groupe de chasseurs*, 35 cm.

SALES
Chasseur et ses deux chiens, Sotheby London, March 8, 1984.
Noble Dame espagnole à cheval et son soupirant, 36 cm, Sotheby London, February 9, 1979.

MOUCHON, LOUIS EUGÈNE
Paris, August 30, 1843
Montrouge, March 3, 1914

Mouchon produced mostly medals and medallions, which he sent to the Salon from 1876 to 1912. One of his medallions in bronze, *Portrait de Léon Bourgeois*, 10.2 cm diam. (1897) belongs to the museum of Châlons-sur-Marne.

MOULIN, HIPPOLYTE ALEXANDRE
Paris, June 12, 1832
Charenton, June 1884

Moulin studied at the Ecole des Beaux-Arts starting in 1855, and then improved and worked alone, supporting himself by teaching some courses. He participated at the Salon from 1857 to 1878, contributing a number of busts of contemporaries, including those of *Henri Monnier* (Salon of 1870) and of *Barye*, some scenes with an antique air about them, and some genre scenes. His best-known work, *Une trouvaille à Pompéi*, in bronze, was exhibited in 1864; a group, *Faune et faunesse*, also in bronze, was shown in 1866 (and again at the Exposition Universelle of 1900). Of note also is a statuette in plaster, *Heureux de vivre* (1868), and a group in marble, *Un secret d'en haut*, 170 cm (1875), which is found lately in the Jardins du Carrousel.

Thiébaut cast this artist's works entitled *Une trouvaille à Pompéi*, 82, 73, 40 cm, and *Ganymède*, 80 and 42 cm; Barbedienne cast a statuette of *Michel-Ange*, 72 cm. Also known are the reductions in bronze of *Un secret d'en haut*, 50 cm, *Faune et faunesse*, 12.5 cm, and *Buste d'Henri Monnier*, 21 cm.

The bronze of *Trouvaille à Pompé*, 188 cm, cast by Jacquier (1863), belongs to the museum of Orsay.

MOULY, FRANÇOIS JEAN JOSEPH

Clermont-Ferrand, September 22, 1846
August 25, 1886

Despite achieving success at a very young age, François Jean Joseph Mouly killed himself near Bordeaux at the age of forty. His work includes some busts and medallions, as well as a number of statues which were exhibited at the Salon starting in 1876. In 1883 Mouly sent to the Salon his bronze entitled *Jeune Femme*, and, in 1886, sent the plaster model of *Vercingétorix*, which would be made in bronze and inaugurated in Bordeaux in 1890. This work received only modest recognition—a mere honorable mention—which was the beginning of Mouly's descent towards suicide. A reduction in bronze of 103 cm in height is found at the city hall of Riom.

The museum of Clermont-Ferrand preserves a bronze of 220 cm in heigh cast by Gruet, entitled *Faune dansant* (1879).

MOUTONI, ANTOINE, KNOWN AS MOUTON

Lyon, 1765—?

Only a portion of this artist's works were sculpted during the 19th century, but his years of exhibition at the Salon did span from 1810 to 1817. He is the author of some of the bas-reliefs from the Vendôme Column, and of a statue of the carbineer for the triumphal arch of the Carrousel. At the château of Fontainebleau is found a Moutoni statuette in bronze of 44 cm in height entitled *Napoléon 1er assis consultant une carte*.

MULOT, ALBERT FÉLIX

Le Havre, March 24, 1847
Paris, November 6, 1922

A painter of landscapes and seascapes, Mulot also practiced sculpture, which he learned with Tony Noël. Among his works is a group entitled *Le Renard et les raisins*, exhibited in plaster at the Salon of 1889, and in marble the following year. Other known works include *L'Enfant à la source*, *Armide*, *Le Sommeil de Léda*, etc. The museum of Orsay possesses a small bronze, *Femme arabe au cimietière*, 34 cm, cast by Bingen and Costenoble.

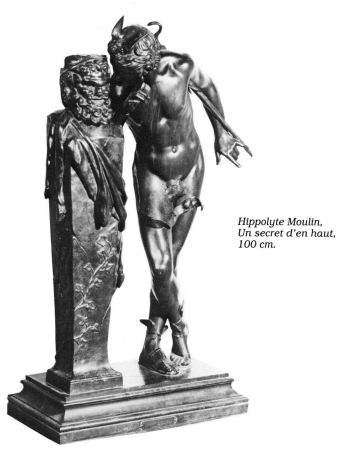

Hippolyte Moulin, Un secret d'en haut, 100 cm.

Hippolyte Moulin, Une trouvaille à Pompéi, 183 cm. Musée d'Orsay.

N

NANNINI, RAPHAËL

Born in Florence

A student of the academy of his hometown, Nannini exhibited at the Salon starting in 1904. Of particular note there are two statuettes in plaster, *La Poésie* in 1907 and *Amateur* in 1909, as well as a bronze, *Tigre et serpent* in 1911.

SALES
Buste de Beethoven, 23 cm, Drouot, October 19, 1983, room 9.
Cavalier de l'Empire, 67 cm, Deauville, May 4, 1986.
Hussard à cheval, 42 cm, Sotheby London, June 12, 1986.
Mimi Pinson, silvered bronze, 18 cm, Drouot, June 23, 1980.
Napoléan équestre, bronze and ivory, 67.5 cm, Christie's New York, May 18, 1982; Deauville, May 4, 1986.

NAVELLIER, ÉDOUARD

Paris, March 26, 1865
Laroche-Migennes (Yonne), March 30, 1944

The son of a printer and grand-nephew of the sculptor Jouffroy, this self-taught artist was first schooled in painting. He turned to animal sculpture after a visit to the Jardin des Plantes, where he was fascinated by the animals. Navellier later studied the large grass-eating animals at the zoo of Anvers. His work appeared at the Salon des Artistes Français starting in 1895, and in 1903 he began to exhibit at the Salon d'Automne, where his work was the object of a retrospective in 1945. He made a number of very precise, realistic bronzes, for the most part of average size. Among his consignments to the Salon are: *Vieux Cerf aux écoutes*, 26 cm, cast by Colin and Co. (1898), *Kangourou géant mâle* (1899), *Eléphant aux prises avec un crocodile*, 22.5 cm (1901), *Boeuf zébu de Madagascar* (1902), *Il passe, éléphant piétinant des pélicans*, 30 cm, chiseled and patinated by the artist (1903), *Chien Colley*, 15 cm, *Brebis du littoral*, 14 cm (1906), *Ane braillant*, 35 cm, cast, chiseled and patinated by the artist (1907), *Buffle de Kerabo*, 14 cm, cast, chiseled and patinated by the artist (1908), *Ben-Mocktar, méhariste en vedette*, 37 cm, chiseled by the artist (1910), *Rhinocéros de l'Inde*, 20.5 cm, chiseled and patinated by the artist (1911), and *Alzonne, pur-sang*, 35 cm (1914).

Raphaël Nannini,
Napoléon 1er équestre,
bronze and ivory,
67.5 cm.

At the Salon d'Automne, the same subjects were presented along with some others, including *Bison d'Amérique* (1904). All were designated as having been chiseled and patinated by the artist. Navellier continued to pursue his activity after the war of 1914-1918.

The works of Navellier seem to have been cast in rather restrained editions. A model of *Bison d'Amérique*, 32 cm, cast by Valsuani and numbered 1/8, was shown at the Paul Ambroise Gallery in

*Edouard Navellier,
Le Pur-sang "Alzonne,"
35 cm.*

*Edouard Navellier,
Bison d'Amérique, 32 cm
(Valsuani 1/8).*

*Edouard Navellier,
Il passe!
or Eléphant
piétinant
des pélicans,
30 cm.*

Comte de Nieuwerkerke, Combat du duc de Clarence et du chevalier de Fontaine, 30 cm (1838).

Paris in 1875. Some other bronzes appeared at the exposition of antiques at the Louvre in 1983. These include: *Eléphant aux prises avec un crocodile*, 26 cm, *Eléphant et pélicans*, 50 cm, *Eléphant et son petit*, 30 cm, *Jeune Lionne à la boule*, 20.5 cm (1919), *Méhariste*, 37 cm, *Rhinocéros courant*, 33.5 cm (1918), *Rhinocéros de l'Inde*, 20.5 cm, and *Zébu de Madagascar*, 30 cm.

MUSEUMS
Paris, Orsay
Chat couché, 9.5 cm.
Chevreuil couché, 12.8 cm.
Il passe, éléphant piétinant des pélicans, 30 cm (1898-1902).
Vieux Cerf aux écoutes, 36.5 cm (1896).
Rouen
Boeuf zébu de Madagascar (before 1902).

SALES
Alzonne pur-sang 35 cm, Orléans, December 8, 1984.
Rhinocéros, 23 cm (Scudéri 3/8), Enghien, October 6, 1986.

NIEUWERKERKE, COUNT OF ALFRED ÉMILIEN O'HARA

Paris, April 16, 1811
Gattajola (Italy), January 16, 1892

It is not surprising that this artist had a double career with the government, both as an administrator and as an official sculptor; he served as the general director of French museums in 1849, the superintendent of the Beaux-Arts and a member of the Institut in 1863, a senator in 1864, and, more-over, was a friend of prince Napoléon, who became the emperor Napoléon III. Nieuwerkerke's work includes a number of busts and equestrian statues of historic or contemporary people, including a bust in marble of the *Comte de Ganay*, which which he debuted at the Salon in 1842, *Guillaume 1er le Taciturne*, an equestrian group inaugurated at La Haye in 1845, *Isabelle la Catholique à cheval* (1847), *René Descartes* in bronze for the city of La Haye-Descartes (1848), *Napoléon 1er équestre*, 4.30 m for La Roche-sur-Yon (1854), a marble statue of the *Maréchal Catinat couché* for the church of Saint-Grantien (1860), busts of *Napoléon III* and of *L'Impératrice Eugénie*, etc. His most famous work remains the group entitled *Combat de deux chevaliers au XVe siècle*, exhibited at the Susse house from 1839, known afterwards under the title *Combat du duc de Clarence et du chevalier de Fontaine*, after an episode from the 100 Years War.

The Count (Comte) of Nieuwerkerke had been the patron of many artists, including Rude, Carpeaux, and Frémiet. After the defeat of 1870 and the fall of the empire, he left France in order to establish himself in Italy at the château of Gattajola, near Lucques.

In the Susse foundry catalog, the following editions appear:

Combat du duc de Clarence et du chevalier de Fontaine, 50 and 25 cm.
Guillaume le Taciturne, 60, 40 and 20 cm.
Homme d'armes, 64 cm.
Napoléon 1er équestre, 26 cm.

523

MUSEUMS

Ajaccio, Napoléon museum
Napoléon 1er à cheval, 26 cm.
Beauvais
Henri IV à cheval, statuette.
Compiègne, château
L'Impératrice Eugène, bust, 14 cm.
Napoléon 1er à cheval, 58.5 cm (Susse).
Napoléon III, bust, 13.5 cm.
Paris, Carnavalet
Le Duc d'Orléans à cheval, 32.5 cm.

SALES

Cavalier, 89 cm (1843; Eck and Durand), Drouot, October 26, 1983, room 7.
Combat du duc de Clarence et du chevalier de Fontaine, silvered bronze, 30 cm, Saint-Germain-en-Laye, October 26, 1986 (sold with two candelabrums).
Guillaume le Taciturne, 80 x 90 cm, Christie's London, May 15, 1986.

NIVET, ÉMILE ERNEST

Levroux (Indre), October 7, 1871
Châteauroux, February 5, 1948

This old practician of Rodin was a discreet and little-known artist, committed to translating the simple, laborious life of the peasantry. He sent primarily plasters to the Salon starting in 1897, including Paysanne tricotant (1897), Fileuse du Berry

Tony Noël,
Les Gladiateurs, 49 cm
(Thiébaut).

(1898), Le Faucheur (1903), Moissonneuse au repos (1908), and Semeur (1913), among others. He contributed just a single bronze, Paysanne cousant (1911). He maintained his activity between the two world wars.

MUSEUM

Châteauroux
Le Bricolin, 50 cm (Barbedienne) modeled from the plaster from the Salon of 1899.
Tricoteuse assise, 30 cm (Barbedienne).

NOCQUET, PAUL ANGE

Brussels, April 2, 1877
Long Island, April 4, 1906

This sculptor and painter undertook some of his studies in Paris, where he made the acquaintance of Rodin, and then established himself in New York in 1903. At the museum of Châteauroux appears a group in bronze cast by Hébrard, Hommes déplaçant un rocher, 33.5 x 67 cm.

NOËL, LOUIS

Born in Saint-Omer

The château of Compiègne possesses a bust by this artist, Le Général Faidherbe, 63 cm high and dated 1891.

NOËL, EDME ANTONY PAUL, KNOWN AS TONY

Paris, January 27, 1845
Palaiseau, October 3, 1909

Though he won the first grand prize of Rome in 1868 with Thésée vainqueur du Minotaure, Noël always refused the opportunities, and remained little-known by the public. He exhibited regularly at the Salon starting in 1872, debuting with a statuette in plaster of Marguerite de Faust. Next, in 1875, he showed Le Rétiaire, a bronze of 110 cm high which would be placed at the square of the Temple. In 1878 he showed La Méditation, a statue in marble for the garden of Ranelagh, and in 1888 showed Les Gladiateurs, a group in marble. At the Société Nationale des Beaux-Arts, where he also exhibited beginning in 1891, Noël showed a statue in bronze, Orphée (1891), and a statuette in marble, Jeune Fille mauresque (1895). Tony Noël is also the author of a group of the Musique on the facade of the Grand Palais, of diverse commemorative monuments, and of terra cottas (a number of which are owned by the museum of the Petit Palais, in Paris).

Thiébaut cast Les Gladiateurs in bronze, 47 cm, and Orphée, 79 cm. At the Siot-Decauville house can be found Baigneuse mauresque, La Comédie, Judith, and La Méditation. An edition of Danseuse pompéienne was made in unglazed porcelain by the Sèvres factory. The bust in bronze of the painter Hébert, 51 cm, appears in Paris at a museum devoted Noël.

A group in bronze, Les Gladiateurs, 47 cm (Thiébaut), was sold in Tarbes on June 7, 1984.

Georges Omerth,
Soldat écossais, Soldat anglais,
21 cm.

OGÉ, PIERRE MARIE FRANÇOIS

Saint-Brieuc, March 24, 1849
Paris, June 5, 1913

The opera *Gaust* by Gounod seems to have fascinated Ogé, for many of his sculptures evoke it and its author. A student of his own father and of Carpeaux, Ogé executed some statues for the city of Saint-Brieuc, in particular for the cathedral, as well as diverse statuettes representing *Marguerite*, a statuette in terra cotta entitled *Virginie* exhibited at the Salon of 1886, a plaster, *Souvenir à Gounod* (1894), and two statuettes also in plaster, *Libellule* (1903) and *Sommeil de la Walkirie* (1907), etc.

Some bronzes have been cast of his works, including *Graziella*, 35 cm, *Le Lierre, Nymphe*, 82 cm, *Souvenir à Gounod*, 100 cm, *Virginie*, 47 cm, etc. The Susse foundry cast *Marguerite* in four dimensions, 120, 80, 60 and 45 cm.

SALES
Marguerite, 60 cm (Susse), Tours, November 24, 1986.
Marguerite, Virginie, two statuettes, 45 cm, Christie's New York, June 19, 1984.

OLIVA, ALEXANDRE JOSEPH

Saillagouse (Pyrénées-Orientales), September 4, 1823
Paris, February 23, 1890

Oliva produced busts of historic or contemporary people almost exclusively, portraying such subjects as *Colbert, Philibert Delorme, Jean Goujon, Nicolas Poussin, Rembrandt, Dumont d'Urville, MacMahon, Napoléon III*, and *L'Impératrice Eugénie*, in different materials and often for public monuments. The bust of *Ferdinand de Lesseps* was cast in bronze by Barbedienne in three dimensions, 78, 44, and 32 cm.

MUSEUMS
Compiègne, château
Buste de l'abbé Deguerry, 35 cm.
Besançon
Buste de Rembrandt, 85 cm (Salon of 1853).

OMERTH, GEORGES

Practically nothing is known of this sculptor, not even his nationality, but his bronzes—often statuettes of children—appeared in rather large numbers on the market. They frequently incorporated ivory, and date visibly from the first years of the 20th century.

MUSEUMS
Reims
Jeune Hollandaise tenant une oie, gilded bronze, 25 cm.

SALES
Danseuse orientale tenant une coupe, bronze and ivory, 40.5 cm, Brussels, March 27, 1985.
Fillette portant un appareil photo, gilded bronze and ivory, 17 cm, Drouot, May 17, 1984, room 7.
Jeune Garçon à la canne, bronze and ivory, marble pedestal, 20 cm, Drouot, February 27, 1985.
La Semeuse, gilded bronze and unglazed porcelain, 29.5 cm, Drouot, November 28, 1984, room 13.

Comte d'Orsay,
Le Duc de Wellington,
41 cm.

ORLÉANS, MARIE CHRISTINE D'
Palerme, April 12, 1813
Pise, January 6, 1839

Marie Christine D'Orléans, the Duchess of Wurtemberg and youngest daughter of Louis-Philippe, studied drawing with Ary Scheffer and sculpture with David d'Angers. The painter Posper Lafaye made a portrait of her in his studio at the Tuileries, which now belongs to the museum of the Versailles. During the course of her very brief life, Orléans sculpted some busts, statuettes and statues; the best-known of these, the *Jeanne d'Arc debout en prière*, was executed in marble in 1837, and is now found at the museum of the Versailles.

This work won considerable success in its day. Some castings in bronze are found in Orléans and at Domrémy. The statue was cast by Susse in seven dimensions, 75, 60, 50, 42, 25, 20 and 15 cm.

ORSAY, ALFRED COMTE D'
Paris, February 4, 1801
Paris, August 4, 1852

Son of a general from the Empire, and an officer himself, Orsay studied sculpture in Florence and would also live in London. He exhibited his works at the Salon of Paris starting in 1845 and at the Royal Academy of London from 1843 to 1848. He was named director of the Beaux-Arts in 1852 by the prince-president Louis-Napoléon. He produced some equestrian figures, including the statue of Napoléon 1er (plaster at the Salon of 1845), and a statuette of *Wellington*. There exist in England some proofs in bronze, gold and silver of this work. At the Salon of 1849, he exhibited a statuette in bronze of *Napoléon 1er*, a model of which he would offer to the city hall of Ajaccio. A proof of *Napoléon équestre*, 75 cm, was sold on two different occassions, both at the end of the 19th century in Florence. Some busts by this artists are known, in particular those of *Prince Napoléon* and *Alphonse de Lamartine*.

MUSEUMS
Ajaccio, museum Napoléonien
Napoléon 1er équestre, 83 cm (1856).
Compiègne, château
Buste du prince Napoléon, 29 cm (1851).
Versailles, château
Buste de Lamartine, 80 cm.

SALES
Le Duc de Wellington équestre, 41 cm, Christie's London, September 25, 1986.

OSBACH, JOSEPH
Lunéville?
1898

Of a number of works in plaster that this sculptor sent to the Salon between 1873 and 1892, notable are the following subjects: *La Toilette* (1875), *L'Amour et la Jeunesse* (1877), *Le Dénicheur d'aiglons* (1881), *Rêverie* (1883), and *L'Aurore* (1891). At the museum of Amiens is a bust in bronze entitled *Gaultier de Rumilly, député de la Somme*, 63 cm.

OTTIN, AUGUSTE LOUIS MARIE
Paris, November 11, 1811
Paris, December 1890

A student of David d'Angers at the Beaux-Arts, Ottin won the first prize of Rome in 1836 with a bas-relief in plaster, *La Mort de Socrate*. He produced a number of portraits in bust and in medallion of famous people, as well as some decorative statues and groups for different monuments. Monuments showing his works include the Louvre, the city hall, the Gare du Nord, the Opera, some churches including the Dôme des Invalides, as well as the Bourse of Marseille (statues in marble of *France* and of the *Ville de Marseille*). He sent to the Salon a bust in bronze of *Ingres* in 1842 and, the same year, *Hercule présentant à Eurysthée les pommes du jardin des Hespérides,* a group in marble which was placed in the Luxembourg gardens. Next came *Chasseur indien surpris par un boa,* a group in bronze (1857), and, at the Exposition Universelle of 1867, *La Lutte moderne, le coup de hanche,* a group in bronze of 145 cm high. This work, presented at the Grand Palais in 1986 at an exposition of 19th century sculpture, was made part of the museum in the Rue de Barentin. Ottin is also the author of the group of *Polyphène surprenant Acis et Galathée;* the first character is portrayed in bronze, the others in marble, and the work ornaments the Médicis Fountain in Paris. Ottin also made two statues, *Le Commerce* and *L'Industrie,* cast in bronze for a fountain in the Square of the Arts-et-Métiers, and finally a colossal statue in bronze of *Henri IV* for Châtillon-sur-Seine. At the château of Fontainbleau is found a bronze of large dimensions cast by Victor Thiébaut and representing an *Indien à cheval surpris par un boa.*

OUDINÉ, EUGÈNE ANDRÉ

Paris, January 3, 1810
Paris, April 12, 1887

The winner of Rome's prize for engraving medals in 1831, Oudiné became attached to the administrations of Timbre and of Monnaie and produced numerous commemorative medals. He also sculpted some busts and statues of contemporary or historical people and worked for the Louvre, the Tuileries and some Parisian churches. At the Salon of 1837, he successfully exhibited the plaster *Gladiateur blessé,* which he had ordered to be sent from Rome. In 1843 a group in marble appeared entitled *La Charité* and, in 1848, a statue in marble, *Psyché.* The works by Oudiné appear in many French musuems. The group of *La Charité* was cast in bronze by Barbedienne in three dimensions, 45, 30, and 22 cm.

OURY, LOUIS

Born in Montauban

Noted at the Salon starting in 1888, Oury exhibited there some busts in plaster and in terra cotta, two busts in bronze, *Mon Père* and *Paysanne bretonne* (1892), and some genre figures in plaster: *Pierrot* (1893), *Feuilles mortes* (1897), *Baiser de la Mort* and *Droit au but* (1898), *Coquetterie* (1899), etc. The museum of Montauban possesses a bust of a man in bronze signed by this artist. Another bronze, *Premier Frisson,* was sold in Nantes on November 24, 1984.

Louis Oury,
Premier Frisson.

Ferdinand Pautrot,
Cavalier arabe
guettant,
50 cm.

PAILLET, CHARLES

Moulin-Engilbert (Nièvre), March 31, 1871
1937

Paillet, an animal sculptor and a student of Gardet, exhibited at the Salon starting in 1897, showing such pieces as *Singe cynocéphale,* a statue in bronze cast by Thiébaut Frères (1898), *Vautour,* a group in plaster (1903), *Chienne au sucre,* in bronze and marble (1908), *Troupe d'artistes,* a group in bronze, *Combat de coqs,* in bronze and marble (1909), *Chat et perroquet,* a small group in bronze (1911), *Jeune Chien jouant,* bronze (1913), etc.

In 1921, Paillet signed with Barbedienne a contract of sale "in all propriety" of a group, *Chien et chat,* entitled also *Les Deux Amis.* A proof of this group, 53 x 58 cm, belongs to the museum of the Petit Palais in Paris.

SALES

Chien et chaton, 62 cm, Christie's New York, March 13, 1984.
Danseuse aux cymbales et ours, 23.5 cm, Enghien, December 2, 1984.
Deux Chevreaux, 49 cm, Rambouillet, November 7, 1982.
Deux Chevreaux jouant, Versailles, June 16, 1984.
Eléphant assis, gilded bronze, 12 cm, Drouot, December 2, 1983, room 5.
Grand Cerf royal, gilded bronze, 58 cm, Drouot, January 22, 1981, rooms 5 and 6; Rambouillet, November 7, 1982.

PARIS, AUGUSTE

Paris, 1850
Colombes, March 25, 1915

Auguste Paris first made statuettes and groups such as the *Danton* in bronze from the Boulevard Saint-Germain in Paris (1891), but when he was stricken with paralysis in his legs he was forced to sculpt in small dimensions. He then began to produce busts, medallions, medals, plaques, statuettes, vases, and objects in diverse materials, including bronze, tin, and silver. Of a number of his consignments to the Salon, notable are *Le Temps et la Chanson,* a group in marble (1885) of which a reduction in bronze would appear the following year, *1789!* or *Liberté de 1789,* a statue in bronze cast by

Thiébaut (1888; also shown at the Exposition Universelle of 1889), *Etienne Marcel,* an equestrian statue in bronze (1889), and finally three statuettes in bronze: *L'Eternael Moqueur* (1899), *L'Echassier* (1901), and *La République* (1905).

The Susse foundry cast *La Chanson,* 77, 57, 45 and 35 cm, *Orphée et Eurydice,* 125, 90 and 72 cm, and *Le Temps et la Chanson,* 80 cm. For its part, Thiébaut issued *La Liberté* in 68 cm of height.

A statuette in bronze, *Soldat colonial,* 47 cm, belongs to the museum of Reims. A proof in bronze of a group *Le Temps et la Chanson,* 80 cm, was sold in Saint-Quentin on December 19, 1982.

PARIS, RENÉ

Paris, November 26, 1881
1970

An animal sculptor, René Paris participated at the Salon while still very young, debuting in 1897 with a group in wax entitled *Tigre et marcassin.* Of further note are some waxes: *Lionne rugissant* (1898), *Lion couché* (1899), *Diane, chienne de la brigade fluviale* (1903), and then some small bronzes: *Le Professeur Desbonnet* (1903), *Le Comte de N. à cheval* (1905), *Vedette cosaque, A two years old's canter, Sous la pluie* (1908) *Finasseur, cheval pur-sang, Clyde, chaval pur-sang, Sur le quai* (1909), *Dans les brisants* (1911), *Vache bretonne, Lion, Lévrier de course* (1912), *Dans la lande, Jument bretonne, Jeune Génisse* (1913), etc. A statuette of *Jockey à cheval,* 32 cm, was cast in bronze by Thiébaut. In addition, some other bronzes (particularly of horses) are noteworthy for having been presented in diverse exhibitions at the beginning of the century: *Chevreuil forcé, Childwick, étalon pur-sang, Au départ, Jeune Basset d'Artois, Le Pansage, La Tentrée du vainqueur, Travail à la longe, Setter,* and *Vache,* as well as many equestrian portraits.

SALES

Le Cosaque, 45 cm, Brussels, November 12, 1984.
Cheval de course avec son jockey, 21 cm, Sotheby London, March 26, 1985.

Auguste Paris,
Le Temps et la Chanson,
80 cm.

Le Cheval "Kargal", 44 cm L, Drouot, June 12, 1981.
Au départ, 20.5 cm, Sotheby London, July 5, 1985.
Galop, 34 cm L., Göteborg, November 9, 1983.
L'Haltérophile, régule, 46 cm, Drouot, February 26, 1982,
room 11.
Veau, 14 cm (Valsuani), Sotheby London, March 8, 1984.

PASSAGE, ARTHUR MARIE GABRIEL, COUNT

Frohen-le-Grand (Somme), June 24, 1838
Frohen-le-Grand, February 1, 1909

Born (and eventually to die) at the château of
Bernaville in Frohen, Passage initially began a career in the military while studying sculpture with
Barye and Mène. He was a second lieutenant in
Maubeuge when he exhibited for the first time at the
Salon of 1865. It was at this time that he decided to
devote himself entirely to his art. He made a relatively small number of statuettes and small groups,
principally of animals and often of horses and riders.
His bronzes, very well-researched, were offered from
time to time in public sale, particularly the *Cheval à
l'entraînemnet, avec son lad courant à ses côtés,*
which was cast in many dimensions. Also notable
among his works from the Salon are *La Mort du
chevreuil,* wax (1865), *Franc-Picard, cheval de steeple-*

Comte Arthur du Passage,
Jument de chasse
sanglée par un lad,
24 x 50 cm.

Comte Arthur
du Passage,
Le Contrebandier
or Cavalier
guettant, 56 cm.

Comte Arthur du Passage,
Cheval à l'entraînement
avec son lad,
45 cm.

Comte Arthur
du Passage,
Cheval marchant
et son lad,
33 cm (1885).

Comte Arthur du Passage,
Deux Chiens de chasse,
26.5 cm.

Comte Arthur du Passage,
Le Piqueux,
100 x 130 cm
(Boudet, fondeur).

chase, wax (1866), *Steeple-chase, le saut de la barrière*, plaster (1867), *Jument de chasse sanglée par un lad*, bronze (1893), *Gaulois rapportant un sanglier*, wax, (1874), according to a bas-relief from the triumphal arch of Orange, *Gaulois revenant de la chasse*, bronze (1875), *Jeanne d'Arc remettant son étendard à Dieu*, silvered bronze (1877), *Le Relais*, bronze (1878), *Cheval de chasse au trottoir*, bronze, 75 x 105 cm (1881), etc. The Count of Passage also furnished journals with some sketches of the sport, such as *La Vie parisienne* and *L'Art et la Mode*. He is not mentioned among Salon exhibitors after 1893, though an important group entitled *Le Veneur* or *Le Piqueux* (sold in Paris in 1983) is dated 1899. Aside from the bronzes recently appearing in those public sales noted below, some significant works include *Le Dressage*, 43 x 62 cm, *A l'entraînement*, 33 x 44 cm, and *Lièvre courant*, 6 x 13 cm.

MUSEUMS
Amiens
Piqueux mettant à la voie, 95 x 135 cm.

SALES
Brocard attaqué par deux chiens, proof from the park life-size, Rambouillet, June 16, 1985 (knocking down 201,000 F).
Cavalier guettant, 61 cm, Valenciennes, November 26, 1984.
Cheval sanglé par son lad, 24 cm, Calais, November 10, 1985; Rambouillet, July 6, 1986.
Cheval à l'entraînement, 33 cm, Drouot, February 19, 1986; Sotheby London, March 20, 1986.
Cheval à l'entraînement, 45 cm, Dijon, November 27, 1983; Sotheby London, July 5, 1985; Rambouillet, July 6, 1986.
Cheval marchant et son lad, 33 cm (1885), Drouot, July 22, 1986.
Chiens de chasse, two statuettes, 26.5 cm, Rambouillet, November 18, 1984.
Le Contrebandier, 56 cm (Colin, founder), Rambouillet, May 27, 1984.
Lièvre courant, 8 cm, Enghien, July 3, 1983.
Le Piqueux, 100 x 130 cm (1899; Boudet, founder), Drouot, December 12, 1983, room 9; Rambouillet, February 15, 1987.

PAULIN, PAUL

Chamalières (Puy-de-Dôme), July 13, 1852
Neuilly-sur-Seine, October 22, 1937

The busts of famous painters and great art aficianados, largely Paulin's friends, constitute the bulk of work by this sculptor, a dentist by profession. He first exhibited at the Salon des Artistes Français from 1882 to 1889, starting in 1901 at that of the Nationale des Beaux-Arts. Noteworthy there a number of busts, often in bronze, including those of *Renoir* (1903), *Claude Monet*, and *Léonce Bénédite* (1911), *Raffaëli* (1912), *Léon Bérard, Ernest Laurent, Armand Guillaumin*, and *Gustave Hoche* (1913), etc. Of note also are some statuettes in bronze: *Baigneuse* (1902), *Le Docteur J.* (1904), *Le Repos*, and *Le Printemps* (1904), both cast by Brame, as well as a bas-relief in gilded bronze representing *Deux Soeurs* (1910) and two statuettes in plaster: *Jeune Fille se coiffant* (1908) and *Etude de nu* (1909).

An exposition of Paul Paulin's sculptures took place in Clermont-Ferrand in 1983. It reunited works borrowed from private collectors with those given to the city's museum by the artist's son, M. Pascal Paulin. A number of bronzes plaques were exhibited, as well as the bronzes *Baigneuse assise*, 29.5 cm, cast by Eugène Blot, and *Baigneuse couchée*, 11.5 x 28 cm. Also shown were a number of busts, including *Guillaumin*, 70 cm, cast by Hébrard, *Le bourg*, 20 cm, also cast by Hébrard, and *Mme Paulin*, 38 cm.

MUSEUMS
Cagnes-sur-Mer, Les Collettes
Buste de Renoir, 46 cm (1904).
Paris, Decorative Arts
Femme nue assise, 26 cm (1901).
Femme nue accroupie, 25.5 cm (1903).
Paris, Carnavalet
Buste de Pierre Beaudin, political man, 62 cm.
Paris, Orsay
Buste de Degas à 50 ans, 48 cm.
Buste de Degas à 72 ans, 49 cm.
Buste de Guillaumin, 64 cm (1902).
Buste de Paul Jamot, 53 cm (1922).
Buste de Claude Monet, 63 cm (1910).
Buste d'Etienne Moreau-Nélaton, 62 cm (1914).
Buste d'Antonin Personnaz, 45.5 cm.

Paris, Petit Palais
Buste d'Armand Guillaumin, 53 cm.
Buste d'Auguste Renoir, 32 cm.
Pau
Buste de Léon Bérard, 56 cm.
Buste d'Edgar Degas, 56 cm.

SALES
Portrait d'Edgar Degas, 46.5 cm (1907; Montagutelli, founder), Sotheby London, December 7, 1983.

PASSAGE, CHARLES MARIE, VISCOUNT

Frohen-le-Grand (Somme), June 28, 1848
Boulogne-sur-Mer, January 26, 1926

Younger brother of the Count Arthur of Passage, Charles Marie of Passage was devoted exclusively to animal sculpture. His work, which he began to exhibit at the Salon in 1874, includes birds, as well as some portrtayals of prey and predators: wild boar, deer, hunting dogs, falcons, etc. Among his bronzes are *Bécasses* (1874), *Faucon terrassant un pigeon voyageur* (1876), *Le Braconnier* (1879), and *Combat de cerfs*, a group in iron and bronze (1894). The works in plaster are the most numerous: *Bull-terrier agaçant une fouine prise au piège* (1875), many hunting groups (1879), *Renard étranglant un coq* (1881), *Combat de sangliers* (1882), *Brocard et chevrette au lancer* (1885), *Gunnor et Flag, chiens du grand prix à l'exposition de Paris* (1887), *La Lutte pour la vie, chien de rue* (1890), *Sanglier et braconnier* (1897), and *Milord et Diane*, bas-relief (1903), etc.

PAUTROT, FERDINAND

Poitiers, 1832
1874

An animal sculptor, Pautrot participated at the Salon from 1861 to 1870. There he showed a number of groups, for the most part in bronze, representing primarily dogs, but also some birds: *Epagneul et sarcelles, Epagneul et lièvre* (1863), *Renard pris au piège* (1864), *Perdreaux et belette, Chien braque et renard* (1866), *Bécassines, Grives* (1867), *Sarcelles* (1869), *Chatte et ses petits, Faisan argenté de Chine* (1870). One can also note, in addition to the pieces recently sold at auction, the following bronzes: *Les Deux Bécasses*, 26 cm, *Coqs de bruyère*, 69 cm, *Coq faisan*, 87 cm, *Coq et deux singes*, 68 cm, *Couple de faisans*, 76 and 46 cm, *Deux Oiseaux de marais*, 54 cm, *Dog assis tenant un lapin*, 30.5 cm, *Epagneul tenant un oiseau*, 31 cm, *Jument et son poulain*, 40 cm, *Poule faisane*, 9.5 cm, and *Setter assis tenant un canard*, 30.5 cm.

SALES
Bécasse, 10 cm, Enghien, February 22, 1981.
Cavalier arabe guettant, 50 cm, Enghien, October 16, 1983; Drouot, December 14, 1984, room 6; Enghien, April 28, 1985; Sotheby London, November 6, 1986 **(see reproduction page* 528).**
Cheval au serpent, 31 cm, Sotheby London, November 6, 1986.

Ferdinand Pautrot,
Epagneul assis tenant un oiseau,
31 cm.

Chien de chasse, silvered bronze, 19 cm, Sotheby London, March 8, 1984.
Chien de chasse tenant un canard sauvage, 45 cm, Sotheby London, July 6, 1984.
Chien debout, 10 cm, Sotheby London, July 6, 1984.
Faisan de l'Himalaya, 86 cm, Christie's Santa Fe, July 2, 1985.
Faisans, two statuettes, 25.5 cm, Christie's London, May 15, 1986.
Deux Faisans et leurs petits, 71 cm, Sotheby New York, April 26, 1981.
La Grouse, 28.5 cm, Drouot, March 20, 1985, room 4.
Jument et poulain, 40.5 cm, Sotheby London, July 5, 1985.
Loup attaquant un coq de bruyère, 20 cm, Lille, April 21, 1986.
Loup dévorant une proie, 7 x 14 cm, Enghien, June 21, 1981.
Oiseau sur une branche, 16.5 cm, Enghien, February 22, 1981.
Oiseau s'envolant, 17 cm, Enghien, Feburary 22, 1981.
Perdreau, 22.5 cm, Enghien, Feburary 22, 1981.
Perdrix, 20 cm, Bergerac, January 15, 1986.
Pointer tenant sa proie, Setter tenant sa proie, two groups, 22 cm, Sotheby London, March 20, 1986.
Renard pris au piège, 64 cm (1860), Rambouillet, July 27, 1986.

PAUTROT, JULES

Born in Vernon

Jules Pautrot studied under Ferdinand Pautrot, but it is not known whether he was the son or the younger brother of his teacher. He exhibited only twice at the Salon, in 1874 with a group in plaster entitled *Lutte de faucons*, and in 1875 with the same work in bronze and a plaster entitled *Héron et couleuvre*. Fowl seem to have been his favorite subject. The museum of Cambrai possess a small group in bronze by this artist entitled *Faisans*, 30.5 cm.

PAVIE, JEAN

1876
Toulouse, July 26, 1928

A certain number of works by this animal sculptor have been cast by the Sèvres factory. Occasional human figures appeared in his works, as in a small group representing *Jeune Fille avec une biche*.

MUSEUMS
Angers
Oie de Toulouse, statuette.
Grenoble
Isard, 18 cm.

SALES
L'Ane, 17 x 25 cm (Valsuani), Enghien, June 21, 1981.

PECH, GABRIEL ÉDOUARD BAPTISTE

Albi, May 21, 1854
Saint-Loup-Cammas (Haute-Garonne), December 2, 1930

A student of Jouffroy, Falguière and Mercié, Gabriel Pech exhibited at the Salon starting in 1883, showing statues of historic or contemporary people as well as some allegories: *Dernière Vision*, plaster (1883), *Guy d'Arezzo*, marble (1887), *Jean-Baptiste Dumas*, bronze for the city of Alès (1888), *Sophocle dansant*, plaster (1890), *La Danse*, bronze (1893), *Un grand secret*, plaster (1896; marble in 1898), *Pierrot*

Ferdinand Pautrot,
Jument et
son poulain,
40.5 cm.

Ferdinand Pautrot,
Chien assis
tenant un lapin,
30 cm.

Ferdinand Pautrot,
Renard pris
au piège,
64 cm
(Paris 1860).

à la lune, plaster (1899), *L'Amiral Jaurès*, bronze for the city of Graulhet (1903), *Désolation*, plaster (1907), and *Charles Perault*, marble for a monument at the Tuileries (1908), etc. Pech also made the monument to *Edith Cavell*, inaugurated in the Tuileries in 1920 and destroyed by the Germans in 1940, as well as the monuments of *Jean Jaurès* in Carmaux and in Castres.

Un grand secret was cast by Susse in two dimensions, 67 and 48 cm. The museum of Albi possesses a bust in bronze of *Jean Jaurès*, 64.5 cm, as well as his mortuary mask, also in bronze.

PECOU, JEAN WILLIAM

Bordeaux 1854-?

A sculptor and medal-engraver, Pecou left in particular some portraits in medallion and in bust. One particular bronze bust represents the *Général Riu*, 85 cm, and belongs to the Montpellier museum.

PEENE, AUGUSTIN

Bergues, May 20, 1853
Meudon, May 1913

This artist obtained the second prize of Rome in 1881. Among his known works are six statues executed for the facade of the city hall of Dunkerque, a statuette in bronze entitled *Diane* exhibited at the Salon in 1890, and a statue in marble entitled *Madeleine au réveil* for the Salon of 1893. The museum of Lille possesses a medallion in bronze, *Portrait de L.J. Blondeau*, 31 x 28 cm.

PEIFFER, AUGUSTE JOSEPH

Paris, December 4, 1832
1886

Mythological and allegorical subjects presented in the guise of graceful feminine figures are typical of the work by Peiffer, a student of Klagmann. His consignments to the Salon from 1865 to 1878 include *Psyché*, a statuette in bronze (1865), *Daphnis*, a group in plaster (1873), and finally his best-known work, *Les Hirondelles*, a statue in marble (1878). The Susse foundry cast a bust of *Hirondelle*, 37 and 25 cm, and a statuette, *Les Hirondelles*, 94, 69, 60, 46 and 25 cm. Also known are a bust of a young girl entitled *Papillon*, 28 cm, and two statuettes, *La Musique* and *Diane chasseresse*. The Carnavalet museum in Paris possesses a statuette by this artist in bronze, *Jean-Jacques Rousseau*, 37 cm high. A small group, *Enfant et chien setter*, 33 cm, was sold in Oklahoma (United States) by Christie's on September 24, 1981.

*Henri Peinte,
Sarpédon,
85 cm.*

PEINTE, HENRI

Cambrai, August 24, 1845
Paris, December 1912

Not a very prolific artist, Peinte exhibited at the Salon between 1877 and 1889, showing some bronzes of mythological inspiration. The best-known, *Sarpédon*, is a statue for a public garden in Cambrai (1878), followed by *Orphée endormant Cerbère* (1888). The reductions of these two works, also in bronze, were presented at the Salon in turn, respectively in 1888 and 1889. They would be cast by Siot-Decauville, the *Sarpédon* in 85, 62, 42 and 30 cm high. Some proofs of *Orphée endormant Cerbère* have been sold in dimensions of 88, 70, and 29 cm.

MUSEUMS
Cambrai
Orphée endormant Cerbère, 247 cm (Siot and Perzinka, founders).
Sarpédon, 207 cm (Hohwiller, founder).
Maubeuge
Sarpédon, 14 x 16.5 cm.

SALES
Sarpédon, 85 cm, Vendôme, February 23, 1985.

contribution to the Salon was *Une pousse de champignon* (1905). Also of note is a group in plaster, *La Grande Soeur*, exhibited in 1903. This work has been cast by Thiébaut in two dimensions, 54 and 44 cm; Thiébaut also cast a bust, 48, 39 and 17 cm. Susse cast a bas-relief entitled *Repos en Egypte*, 53 x 35 cm, 41 x 27 cm and 24 x 16 cm, a little table bell ornamented with a young boy, 18.5 cm, and a vase entitled *Enfant effrayé*, 23 cm. Pernot also furnished some models to the Sèvres factory.

PERRAUD, JEAN

Monay (Jura), April 26, 1819
Paris, November 2, 1876

Perraud won the first prize of Rome in 1847. He sent his works to the Exposition Universelle of 1855, and then, until his death, to the Salon. A sculptor or works on a very large scale, he obtained a number of

Edouard Pépin,
Jeune Cireur
de chaussures
arabe,
65 cm.

PÉPIN, ÉDOUARD

Paris, 1853—?

This student of Cavelier exhibited at the Salon starting in 1878. He left a statue of *Madame Vigée-Lebrun* at the city hall of Paris, and a caryatid on the facade of the Crédit Lyonnais.

SALES
La Gloire au travail, 75 cm, L'Agle, May 31, 1986.
Jeune Cireur de chaussures arabe, 65 cm, Drouot, November 28, 1986, room 14.

PERNOT, HENRI

Gand, March 10, 1859
1937

Though of French nationality, Pernot studied at the school of fine arts of Brussels. He exhibited at the Salon des Artistes Français starting in 1895, showing in particular some statuettes. Those in marble include *Piège à loup* (1898), *Le Crabe* (1901), and *Rêve fleuri* (1914); the plasters include *Coquetterie du dimanche* and *Porteuse de pain* (1908); his bronze

Edouard Pépin,
La Gloire au travail, 75 cm.

official commissions for the Louvre, the Palais de Justice, the Gare du Nord, the Opera (the group *Drame lyrique*, located on the facade), etc. He was also the creator of many statues and groups erected in the gardens, including *Adam après sa chute* (Exposition of 1855) for Fontainebleau, *L'Enfance de Bacchus*, in bronze, for the garden of the Galliera Palace, and *Le Jour*, a group in marble for the Avenue de l'Observatoire (Salon of 1875). A bust in bronze of *Berlioz* appeared at the Salon of 1868. *L'Enfance de Bacchus*, or *Eduction de Bacchus*, was cast by Thiébaut in three dimensions, 113, 78 and 57 cm. A proof belongs to the museum of Valence.

PERRAULT-HARRY, ÉMILE

Paris, August 9, 1878
October 1938

An animal sculptor, Perrault-Harry started exhibiting dogs (and sometimes other animals and allegorical scenes) at the Salon in 1901. He also furnished some models to the Sèvres factory. Among his consignments are a notable group in wax entitled *Chien et rat* (1901), some plasters entitled *Etude de chien bulldog* (1902), *Chiens courants* (1905), and *Passage de bédouins* (haut-relief), and a pair of statuettes entitled *Tunisiennes* (1907). Perrault-Harry is also responsible for *La Mort du cerf* (1912), *Le Chien de garde, Le Chevreau qui danse* (1913), *Ours blanc en marche* and *Ours blanc et pingouins* (1914); a statue in stone entitled *Danois au soleil* (1903); a group in marble entitled *Renard du Sahara;* and finally a marble and bronze piece entitled *Chien danois* (1909). After the First World War, Perrault-Harry pursued a career in preserving the very classical style handed down from the 19th century. A statuette in bronze, *Eléphant*, 18 cm, cast by Hébrard, belongs to the museum of Orsay. *Cigogne*, 13.3 cm (Siot-Decauville) was sold in New York by Christie's on March 26, 1983.

PERREY, LÉON AUGUSTE

Paris, August 24, 1841
Paris, March 19, 1900

Son and student of the sculptor Aimé Perrey, Léon Auguste Perrey produced busts in different materials, medallions in bronze, and some genre scenes. He worked on some Paris landmarks (the Louvre, the city hall, the Trocadéro, and the Saint-Eustache church), for the Château de Pierrefonds, and for the cathedral of Vannes. His best-known work, *Un joueur de toupie* (as a statue in marble at the Salon of 1865, and as a statuette in bronze at that of 1868), became the object of an edition in bronze by Thiébaut (39 cm). Also noteworthy are the following: *Jeune Pêcheur*, marble (Salon of 1869); *Tondeur de moutons*, a group in bronze sent to Tunis (1882); an allegory in bronze entitled *Le Génie de la charité*; the work *L'Histoire et la Reconnaissance* for the tomb of M. Boucicaut at the Montparnasse cemetery (1887); and *Jeune Moulière* (Exposition Universelle of 1900) of which would be cast a statuette in bronze, etc.

PERRON, CHARLES THÉODORE

Paris, October 16, 1862
December 2, 1934

Perron's best-known work, *L'Epave*, a statue in marble inspired by a François Coppée poem, was exhibited at the Salon of 1897. Also attributed to him are *Espièglerie*, a statue in marble, and *Surprise*, a group in bronze, both sent to the Salon of 1899. He is lastly known for a number of decorative groups inspired by the Art Nouveau style.

MUSEUMS
Dunkerque
Doux Rêve, 85 x 48 cm (Salon of 1900).
Poitiers
Buste de Béhanzin, 85 cm (1899).

SALES
Défense du drapeau, 72 cm, Barcelona, Novmeber 14, 1979.
Diane, statuette in régule, 39 cm, Doruot, Feburary 27, 1981.
Faneuse and *Forgeron*, two statuettes, 48 cm, Sotheby London, April 28, 1982.

PETER, VICTOR

Paris, December 20, 1840
March 29, 1918

Victor Peter, an animal sculptor, painter and medal-engraver, studied with Falguière. He produced mostly statuettes and small groups, as well as many plaques, medallions and medals. In a larger format, he worked for the city hall and the Grand Palais. For the latter monument, he made one of the two equestrian groups in bronze which flank the entrance on the Avenue Franklin-Roosevelt, entitled *La Science en marche en dépit de l'Ignorance*. Also in Paris, in the Square of Saint-Lambert, two others of his works can be found: *Chien*, in stone, and a bronze group portraying the *Oursons*.

Peter, who worked as a craftsman with Dubois, Falguière, Mercié, and Rodin, participated at the Salon des Artistes Français from 1873 to 1914, with an interruption between 1891 and 1898, during which he exhibited at the Salon de la Société Nationale des Beaux-Arts. Among his consignments (the majority of which were in bronze) are the follwing: *Chien et chienne*, bas-relief (1873); *Lion de Zanzibar* (1875); and a series of nine bas-reliefs, including *Chèvre, Lion, Taureau, Chienne, percheron*, etc. (1881). Further consignments include *Fauvette, chienne d'arrêt*, a plaque (1883); *La Poésie provençale*, bas-relief (1889); *Maternité, lionne et ses petits* and *Gazelle*, plaque (1892); and *Les Deux Amis, Arabe et son cheval* (Exposition of 1900). Before 1914, Peter made a large number of plaques in bronze or in plaster, some of them in metal, representing all sorts of animals. Of further note is a small group in marble, *Jeune Ours jouant*, exhibited at the Salon of 1901.

The following works have been cast by Thiébaut: *Lièvre*, 15 cm, *Lionne et lionceaux*, 35 and 17 cm, *Ours*, 11 cm, and *Rat à l'oeuf*, 9 cm.

The Susse foundry distributed editions of these works by Peter: *Chat et tortue*, 9 cm., *Deux Amis*, 59, 40, 26 and 16 cm, *Lion et rat*, 37, 24, and 12 cm, *Lionceau de l'Atlas*, 19 cm, and *Ourson jouant*, 55, 34 and 21 cm.

Some bronzes by Peter were also put out by Hébrard, in particular the following medallions and plaques: *Cheval, la tête baissée*, 7.5 x 10.5 cm, and *Coq*, 14 x 10 cm, etc.

MUSEUMS
Angers
Chien épagneul, bas-relief, 8 cm (according to the marble from the Salon of 1886).
Chienne d'arrêt, bas-relief, 8 cm (according to the marble from the Salon of 1886).
Avignon
Maternité, lionne et ses lionceaux, 31 x 74 cm (Thiébaut).
Cahors
Maternité, lionne et ses lionceaux, 17 x 36 cm.
Château-Thierry
Le Lion et le rat, 12 x 20 cm (Susse).
Clermont-Ferrand
Antilope, bas-relief, 20 x 30 cm.
Lille
Deux Amis, 40 cm.
Paris, Orsay
Chien d'arrêt, 32 cm.
Epagneul gordon, 35 cm.
Many plaques and medals representing some animals
Rennes
Maternité, lionne et ses lionceaux.
Toulon
Deux Amis, Arabe et son cheval, 58 x 62 cm.
Troyes

This museum possesses some medals as well as the following plaques:
Antilope, 9.5 x 9.5 cm.
Canard, 5 x 7 cm.
Canard et escargot, 5.5 x 9.5 cm.
Cane et canetons, 8 x 9.5 cm.
Chèvre et arbuste, 10.5 x 9.5 cm.
Chèvre avec longe, 7 x 9.5 cm.
Chevreau, 5.5 x 8.5 cm.
Epagneul gordon, 7 x 12.5 cm.
Lion, 9.5 x 15.5 cm.

The museums of Agen, Bayonne, Dijon, Narbonne, and Rennes, as well as the national Library, possess a certain number of medallions and plaques representing animals and portraits.

PETIT, JEAN

Besançon, February 9, 1819
Paris, March 6, 1903

Jean Petit studied successively in his hometown's school of drawing, the Ecole des Arts Décoratifs of Paris, and the Beaux-Arts, where he frequented the studio of David d'Angers. He obtained the second prize of Rome in 1839 and exhibited at the Salon from 1844 to 1885. A good portraitist, he executed some statues, busts, medallions of historic and contemporary people, and allegorical or mythological compositions. These works were executed for such locations as the château of Fontainebleu, the Granvelle Palace in Besançon, and (in Paris) the Tuileries, the Opera, the Louvre, and the city hall.

The museum of Gray possesses a medallion in bronze, *Le Baron Martin de Gray*, 25 cm diam. (1851).

PETITOT, LOUIS MESSIDOR LEBON

Paris, June 23, 1794
Paris, June 1, 1882

Louis Petitot was first taught by his father, Pierre Petitot, and then by Cartellier, whose daughter he would marry. He won the first prize of Rome in 1814 with a work on the subject of *Achille blessé à mort retirant la flèche de sa blessure*. His best-known work, *Louis XIV à cheval*, a bronze of 5.60 m high, stands at the center of the Cour d'Honneur at the château of Versailles (but please note that the horse in that work was sculpted by Cartellier). Petito received a number of official commissions for the Louvre, the triumphal arch of the Carrousel, the Chambre des Députés, the Concorde Plaza (allegories of *Marseille* and of *Lyon*), the Carrousel Bridge (*L'Abondance, L'Industrie, La Ville de Paris*, and *La Seine*, sculpted for the old bridge in 1846 and replaced on the new one), the Bourse, the Saint-Sulpice church, etc. Petitot began exhibiting at the Salon in 1819, and presented a marble, *Jeune Chasseur blessé par un serpent*, in 1828.

At the château of Versailles is found a reduction in bronze, 134 cm high, of the *Louis XIV équestre* from the Cour d'Honneur.

PÊTRE, CHARLES

Metz, March 27, 1828
Bourges, October 1907

Born to a family of modest means, Pêtre went to Paris in 1847 thanks to a scholarship from his hometown. He entered the Beaux-Arts in the studio of the sculptor Toussaint, and then returned to Metz to teach at the municipal school of drawing. In 1854 he made a statue in bronze of the *Maréchal Ney*, to be accompanied on the esplanade in 1872 by a new bronze, entitled *La Source*. In 1873, Pêtre began to teach at the College of Nancy and, in 1881, became director of the school of fine arts of Bourges. He also worked for different cities, in particular Neufchâteau in the Vosges, to which he furnished a statue in bronze of *Jeanne d'Arc* in 1857.

MUSEUMS
Metz
Buste de A. Rolland (Barbedienne), 1849.
Nancy
Jeune Femme riant, bust, 50 cm (1864).
Le Maréchal Ney, reduction of the statue from the esplanade of Metz, 59 cm.

PEYNOT, ÉMILE EDMOND

Villaneuve-sur-Yonne, November 22, 1850
Paris, December 13, 1932

Peynot studied sculpture with Jouffrey and debuted at the Salon in 1876. He exhibited there regularly, and over the course of a long career he obtained a number of distinctions in France as well as in different foreign countries. In 1880, he won the grand prize of Rome. He collaborated in the decoration of monuments and public squares. In Paris he is credited with a number of decorative works for the Petit Palais, the Opera-Comique, and the Lyon train station. His consignments to the Salon include a number of busts and some widely varied subjects. Among the bronzes are *Une fileuse* (1882), *Marchand tunisien, Pro Patria* (1887), *Buste de sénateur romain* (1894), *Eternelle Lutte* (1898), and *Le Travail* (1901). Peynot also worked for the park of the château of Vaux-Le-Vicomte, at which he exhibited two projects in plaster in 1888 and 1889, *Triton et enfants* and *Naïade,* and a marble in 1892, *Les Quatre Parties du monde.*

Some of Peynot's works were cast in bronze by Susse, including *Christophe Colomb debout,* 93 and 62 cm, and *Buste de Christophe Colomb,* 22 cm. Another statuette, *Marchand tunisien* or *Marchand d'armes arabe,* 60 cm, carries the mark of the founder Tassel. The museum of Sens possesses some works by this artist.

SALES

Jeune Arabe vérifiant son arme, 67.5 cm, Christie's London, January 22, 1986.
Le Ramoneur, 70 cm, Sotheby London, November 6, 1986.

①

②

③

1) Emile Edmond Peynot, Jeune Arabe vérifiant son arme, 67.5 cm.

2) Emile Edmond Peynot, Le Ramoneur, 70 cm.

3) Emile Edmond Peynot, Le Moteur et la Renommée.

PEYRE, CHARLES RAPHAËL

Paris, June 1, 1872
January 3, 1949

This sculptor, a student of Falguière and of
Mercié, preferred symbolic or allegorical subjects,
and exhibited at the Salon beginning in 1893. Of
note are some statuettes in gilded bronze such as
Lys (1901) and *Douleur* (1905), and some plasters:
Salammbô (1893), *Saint Jean-Baptiste enfant* (1894),
Extase enfantine (1896), *Après la bacchanale* (1899),
Offrande à Vénus (1906), *La Nymphe à la vague*
(1907), *Bataille de fleurs* (1909), *Vendangeur* (1913),
etc. Thiébaut also cast an inkwell decorated with
figures of children, 20 x 30 cm.

MUSEUM
Compiègne, château
Napoléon III, medallion, 19.5 cm diam.

SALES
Deux bouffons dansant, gilded bronze and ivory, 47 cm,
    Christie's New York, December 31, 1984.
Le Couronnement de l'Amour, 76.5 cm, Christie's Okla-
    homa (United States), September 24, 1981.
L'Enfant et la brebis, 20 x 44 cm (Susse), Drouot, March
    1, 1982, room 10.
Fillette et agneau, 44 cm, Drouot, March 4, 1983, room 1.
Trois Enfants dansant, 62 cm, Sotheby London, March
    20, 1986.

Charles Raphaël Peyre,
Trois Enfants dansant, 62 cm.

PEYROL, FRANÇOIS AUGUSTE HIPPOLYTE

Paris, June 10, 1856
Neuilly-sur-Seine, December 24, 1929

Some genre scenes, animals (big game, dogs,
and horses), and portraits of his close relatives made
up the production of this artist. Son of the sculptor
and founder Hippolyte Peyrol and of Juliette Bonheur,
the youngest sister of Rosa and Isidore Bonheur,
François Peyrol studied with these family members
before debuting at the Salon of 1881 and exhibiting
there regularly. He sent some bronzes to the Salon,
including *Vercingétorix devant César* (1889, reduction of a plaster exhibited in 1883), *Protection* (1890),
Tigre à l'affût and *Tigre et crabe* (1891), *Chienne
setter* (1895), *Vénus marine* (1897), *Cheval* (1905),
Renard (1906), *Tigre dévorant un faon de cerf* (1912),
and *Lion marchant* (1913). His consignments to the
Salon included many other works in plaster and in
marble, on similar themes. Also known by him are
some portraits of Isidore and Rosa Bonheur, including a medallion in bronze for the monument raised
in Rosa's memory at Fontainebleau.

A bronze, *Lionne à l'affût,* 20 cm, is found at the
Arts Africains et Océaniens Museum in Paris.

PEZIEUX, JEAN ALEXANDRE

Lyon, June 17, 1850
Epinay-sur-Seine, September 1898

Jean Alexandre Pezieux studied under Jouffroy
and Tony Noël at the Ecole des Beaux-Arts. The Siot-
Decauville foundry cast his statuette entitled *Jeune*
Berger, a reduction of the marble exhibited at the
Salon of 1894 (entitled at the time *Oh! Jeunesse*);
today this piece is shown at the Galliera Palace. A
group in bronze, *Non omnes morimur,* has recently
been located in Parmentier Square in Paris.

PICASSO, PABLO, ALSO CALLED RUIZ

Malaga (Spain), October 25, 1881
Mougins, April 8, 1973

Though most of this artist's work must be categorized as 20th century, it was not untouched by
the 19th. For a long time, his works of sculpture were
obscure; indeed, he kept most of them in his studio.
Many are cubist constructions, assemblages of iron
or ceramics, and collages of diverse materials. A
catalog of plastic works drafted in 1971 by Werner
Spiess noted at least 664 titles, even when omitting
the ceramics. Among these works are some bronzes;
executed in the first years of the 20th century, they
remained close to the realistic tradition of the preceding century.

Picasso was attracted even in his his early boyhood to the modeling of clay, and frequently visited
his sculptor friends in Barcelona around 1896, as

541

Pablo Picasso,
Le Fou, 40 cm
(earlier casting in 1939).

well as in Paris, where he installed himself definitively in 1904. It was at this time that he made his first forays into sculpture, influenced, perhaps, by the art of Rodin. These first pieces were cast in a small number of bronze models, generally by the founder Valusani. Picasso's early works in bronze, in the chronological order indicated by Werner Spiess, include:

Femme assise, 14 x 8 cm (Barcelona 1902).
Tête de chanteur aveugle, 13 cm (Barcelona 1902).
Tête de picador au nez cassé, 18.5 cm (Barcelona 1903).
Le Fou, bust according to the wax, 40 cm (Paris 1905).
Tête de femme, Alice Derain, 27 cm (Paris 1905).
Tête de femme, Fernande, 34 cm (Paris 1906).
Femme se coiffant, according to a ceramic, 42 cm (Paris 1906).
Tête de femme, bas-relief according to a copper, 12.5 x 6 cm (Paris 1906).
Buste d'homme, according to a ceramic, 16.5 x 22 cm (Paris 1906).

In 1907, Picasso's sculptures began to show evidence of his research into cubism and other movements. These pieces must be incontestably categorized as 20th century art.

MUSEUMS
Paris, city museum of modern art
Le Fou, bust, 40 cm.
Tête de femme, 34 cm.

Troyes, museum of modern art
Le Fou, bust, 40 cm.
Paris, Picasso museum
Tête de femme, Fernande, 34 cm.
Femme se coiffant, 42 cm.
Le Fou, bust, 40 cm.

SALES
Le Fou, bust, 40 cm (cast around 1958; numbered on 12), Christie's New York, November 19, 1986.
Tête de femme, Alice Derain, 27 cm (Valsuani 00), Sotheby New York, May 12, 1982.

PICAULT, ÉMILE LOUIS
Paris, August 24, 1833
1915

The abundant work of this sculptor appeared regularly at the Salon starting in 1863, and included allegories, warriors, figures exalting patriotic virtue (often accompanied by Latin or French mottoes), heroes, and some historic or mythological personages. He sent to the Salon some bronzes, including *Le Supplice de Tantale* (1867), *Persée délivrant Andromède*, 90 cm (1880), *Le Génie du progrès* and *Nicolas Flamel* (1885), *Le Cid* (1886), *La Naissance de Pégase*, and two medallions, *Joseph expliquant les songes du pharaon* and *L'Agriculture* (1888). Picault also sent to the Salon the bronzes *Le Bourgeois gentilhomme* (1890), *Le Génie des sciences* (1894), *Le Génie des arts* (1895), *Le Livre* (1896), *Le Drapeau "ad unum"* (1898), *Vox progressi* (1903),

Emile Louis Picault,
Le Porteur d'eau,
66 cm
(made in Tunis).

and *Bellérophon* (1906). Also of note are some statuettes in plaster: *Jason* (1879), *Andromède* (1892), *Prométhée dérobant le feu du ciel* (1894), *La Vaillance* (1896), *Vertus civiques* (1897), *Le MInerai* (1902), *La Forge* (1905), *Science et Industire* (1909), and *Propter gloriam* (1914).

In his work *Bronzes, Sculptors and Founders*, Harold Bermann notes a large number of works cast, sometimes in many dimensions, by different foundries including Colin and Houdebine. Susse cast *Le Génie du travail* (inscription: "On the field of the labor, the victory is fecund") in three dimensions: 125, 80 and 53 cm.

Among recent pieces dispersed at auction are some bronzes by Picault, listed below, which appeared on the market at different times:

Le Devoir, 56 cm.
Dom César de Basan, 59 cm.
Le Drapeau "ad unum," 82 cm.
Eugénie, 69 cm,
Excelsior (Houdebine) 90 cm.
Ganymède, 87 cm.
Galilée, 63 cm.
Le Génie de l'étude, 86 cm.
Le Génie de la lumière, 93 cm.
L'Inspiration, 128 cm.
Janissaire, 26.5 cm.
Musicien du XV siècle, 26.5 cm.
Pax et Labor, 80 and 56.5 cm.
La Pensée, 93 and 68 cm.
Le Penseur, 45 cm.
Post Pugnam, 32 cm (in metal) and 80 cm (in bronze).
Prêtre égyptien.
Prêtresse égyptienne, 72 cm.
Le Progrès, 78 cm.
Pro jure, 34 cm.

E. PICAULT

Emile Louis Picault,
Le Penseur.

Emile Louis Picault,
Don César de Basan,
84.5 cm.
J. Ginepro Collection,
Monaco.

Emile Louis Picault,
Pro Jure,
34 cm.

543

Le Provocateur, 85, 65 and 45 cm.
Retour de pêche, 76 cm.
Le Semeur d'idées, 92 and 45 cm.
La Sérénade or the *Ménestrel*, 60 and 47 cm,
Soldat au mousquet, 47 cm.
La Source du Pactole, 75 cm.
Virtutes civicae, 70 cm.

MUSEUMS
Chambéry
Le Semeur d'idées, 45 cm.
Clermont-Ferrand
Hébé, 93 cm.
Maubeuge
Le Devoir (inscription: "Honor Patria"), 45 cm.

SALES
Ad Unum, 85 cm, Lokeren, October 19, 1985.
Ad Unum, 123 cm, Christie's New York, June 19, 1984.
La Cigale, 53 cm, Drouot, May 19, 1982.
Le Déclin du jour, 87 cm, Lokeren, February 16, 1985.
Dénicheur d'aigles, 97 cm, Christie's New York, March 13, 1984.
Escholier du XIVe siècle, 64 cm, Lokeren, April 20, 1985.
Excelsior, group of two personages, 91 cm, Christie's New York, September 27, 1986.
Le Fauconnier et son chien, 77.5 cm, Sotheby London, March 21, 1985.
Femme de pêcheur, 76 cm, Tarbes, November 3, 1985.
Le Génie du travail, 90 cm (Susse), Lokeren, October 19, 1985.
Le Génie du travail, 115 cm (Susse), Christie's New York, June 19, 1984.
Le Grand Pharaon, 72 cm, Enghien, October 16, 1983.
Le Guerrier, 42 cm, Douai, May 13, 1984.
Homme avec rameau d'olivier, 90 cm, Vienne, April 19, 1986.
Jeune Femme à l'épée, 77.5 cm, Sotheby London, March 21, 1985.
Mémoria, 62 cm, Charleville, March 3, 1985.
Ménestrel, 78 cm, Sotheby London, March 20, 1986.
Des mystérieuses profondeurs elle apporte à l'homme l'étincelle divine, 94 cm (Colin), Drouot, July 1, 1986, room 15.
Orientale à l'épée, 97 cm, Sotheby New York, September 1986.
Pax et Labor, 73 cm, Brussels, December 10, 1984.
Le Penseur, 46 cm, Lokeren, April 30, 1985.
Le Penseur, 74 cm, Lokeren, June 1, 1985.
Persée et Pégase, 95 cm, Sotheby London, November 6, 1986.
Le Porteur d'eau, 66 cm, Saint-Etienne, November 18, 1985.
La Science éclairant le monde, 99 cm, Drouot, October 19, 1983, room 9.
Le Semeur d'idées, 80 cm, Chartres, December 11, 1983.
La Source du Pactole, 80 cm, Lokeren, June 1, 1985.
Le Souvenir, 63 (Colin), Drouot, June 14, 1985.
Valentinien 1er empereur et les exécuteurs de ses hautes oeuvres, 71 cm, Christie's London, July 17, 1984.
La Victoire, 112 cm, Sotheby Chester, March 29, 1984.

PIGALLE, JEAN-MARIE

Paris, May 19, 1792
Paris, 1857

Entering the Ecole des Beaux-Arts in 1810, Jean-Marie Pigalle exhibited at the Salon from 1814 to 1850. He left some busts, medallions and statuettes of famous people. The busts in bronze of the *Empereur Alexandre de Russie* and of the *Roi de Prusse* were sent to the Salon of 1815. He also produced a series of statuettes, also in bronze, of great writers, including Molière, Racine, Corneille, Pascal, and La Fontaine. It is not believed that this artist has any family ties to the famous sculptor Jean-Baptiste Pigalle.

The museum of Dijon possesses a bronze statuette by this artist entitled *Bossuet*, 37 cm, dated 1828; the museum of Carnavalet in Paris has a proof of *Mirabeau à la tribune*, 60 cm high.

PILET, LÉON

Paris, 1836
Paris, 1916

Many statuettes portraying musicians, dancers, Oriental people, and children were made by this sculptor and medal-engraver, who exhibited his elaborately realistic works at the Salon from 1861 to 1914. Among his statuettes are *L'Amour discret*, in marble (1894), *Baigneuse*, in marble and bronze (1913), and some plasters, *Une vision* (1901), *Après le partage* and *Guerrier de Mérovée* (1902), *La Musique* and *Prêtresse de l'île de Sein* (1904), *La Paix armée* (1908), *Maraudeur* (1911), *Danseuse hindoue* (1913), and *Marée montante* (1914). Also of note are two statues in bronze, *Joueur de flûte* (1877) and *Jeune Gaulois en vedette* (1894), and two statues in marble, *Bethsabée* (1883) and *Coup de vent* (1888).

*Léon Pilet,
Jeune Esclave assise,
67 cm.*

Alfredo Pina,
L'Effort suprême,
28.5 x 96 cm
(Valsuani).

A number of editions in bronze, rather limited it seems, were cast of certain works by Pilet. These include some proofs of *La Musique*, 39 cm, *Cléopâtre*, 59 cm, *Baigneuse, Bellone, L'Enfant à la tortue,* and *Japonaise.*

SALES
Le Fauconnier, 40 cm, Enghien, March 4, 1984.
Jeune Esclave assise, 67 cm, Roanne, June 16, 1984.

PINA, ALFREDO
Milan, December 13, 1887
Mesves (Nièvre), December 22, 1966

A student of the Brera Academy in Milan, Alfredo Pina obtained the grand prize for sculpture, and worked and exhibited at first in Italy. He next went to France and set himself up in a studio in Sceaux. Very strongly influenced by Rodin, Pina made his debut at the Salon of 1912 with a bust in bronze entitled *Vieux Romain*. In 1914, he exhibited two bronzes, a statuette entitled *La Douleur* and a group entitled *Victor Hugo*, both cast by Montagutelli. During the First World War, he sojourned in Montpellier, where he sculpted a bust of *Beethoven*. Upon returning to Paris, he lived in Montparnasse. Starting in 1920, he frequently went to Nièvre. Two years later, while pursuing his work, he established residence permanently in Mesves and became a naturalized French citizen. Many of his sculptures were cast in bronze. In addition to the proofs dispersed at auctions during the course of recent years,

Alfredo Pina,
Tête de Gorgone, 47 cm.

545

Alfredo Pina,
Homme à genoux
sur un rocher,
43 cm.

Alfredo Pina,
La Source,
73 cm
(Panini, founder).

the following are of note: *Le Baiser*, 37 cm, *Beethoven*, bust, 56 cm, *Femme assise*, 23.5 cm, *Homme nu assis*, 30 cm, *Homme s'étirant* or *Homme enchaîné*, 43 cm, and *Léda*, *Négresse portant un couffin*.

MUSEUMS
La Charité-sur-Loire
Buste d'homme âgé, 59 cm.
Montpellier
Beethoven, head, 45 cm.

SALES
Adolescent, bust, 49 cm, Rambouillet, March 15, 1984.
L'Amour assouvi, 94 cm (Valsuani), Versailles, May 25, 1984.
L'Archer, bronze and stone, 54 cm, Drouot, September 26, 1986, room 8.
Bacchus, bust, 41 cm, Drouot, February 6, 1984.
Jeune Bacchus, bust, 29 cm (Valsuani), Drouot, February 6, 1984.
Le Baiser, 46 cm (Valsuani), Versailles, June 12, 1985.
Beethoven, head, 17.5 cm, Christie's London, May 15, 1986.
Beethoven, head, 69 cm, Drouot, March 7, 1986, room 10.
Buste d'homme, 28 cm (Marcel Guillemard, founder), Drouot, November 9, 1984, room 6.
Couple à genoux enlacé, Saint-Maur, December 12, 1985.
L'Effort suprême, 28.5 x 96 cm (Valsuani), Drouot, January 23, 1984, room 4, Versailles, May 27, 1984.
Gorgone, head, 47 cm, Drouot, January 23, 1985.
Homme et femme, 96 cm L. (Valsuani), Drouot, May 25, 1984, room 5 and 6.
Homme à genoux sur un rocher, 43 cm, Drouot, December 9, 1983.
Jeune Fille, bust, 40 cm (Valsuani), Drouot, December 13, 1985, room 16.
Le Printemps, bust of a young girl, 24 cm, Troyes, September 22, 1985.
La Source, 73 x 24 cm (Pannini, founder), Drouot, May 20, 1983, room 7.
Tireur à l'arc, Dijon, April 27, 1986.

PINEDO, ÉMILE
Paris, January 4, 1840
May, 1916

Pinedo

A sculptor and medal-engraver, Pinedo also practiced casting, a domain in which he succeeded his father in 1865. As a sculptor, he made his debut at the Salon of 1870. He seemed to prefer sculpting feminine figures and Oriental people. His bronzes are highly reputed and of a very good quality.

SALES
Arabe en marche, 34 cm, Sotheby London, March 8, 1984; Christie's London, June 7, 1984.
Départ pour la Mecque, 48 cm, Sotheby London, November 8, 1984.
L'Esclave, 60 cm, Drouot, October 19, 1983, room 9.
Femme nue sur un coussin devant une psyché, gilded bronze, 34 cm, Sotheby Monaco, December 7, 1981; Drouot, April 16, 1984, room 2.
Guerrier arabe sur un dromadaire, 33 cm, Sotheby London, March 21, 1985.
Guerrier arabe sur un dromadaire, 76 cm, Sotheby London, June 20, 1985.

Emile Pinedo,
L'Esclave, 60 cm.

PIRON, EUGÈNE DÉSIRÉ

Dijon, April 30, 1875
Aix-en-Provence, November 16, 1928

This artist was especially fascinated by nymphs and female fauns, portraying them often before putting an end to his days. At the Salon, where he started to exhibit in 1899, works of note include *Jeune Faunesse*, a statue in marble (1907), two statuettes in bronze, portraits of the painter *Carolus Durand* and of the ambassador *C. Barrère* (1908), a group entitled *Les Druides*, in travertin (1909), *Faunesse*, a statue in bronze. Other contributions include *Faune et nymphe*, a group in plaster (1910), *Jeune Faunesse*, this time in bronze (1911), and *Diane*, a statue in plaster (1912). Piron won the prize of Rome in 1903.

MUSEUMS
Dijon
La Faunesse aux pipeaux (Rome 1906), 135 cm (placed in the garden of Arquebuse).
Masque tenu par la main d'un faune, 47 cm.
Tête de nymphe, 30 cm (these two last works come from the monument of Alexis Piron in Dijon, destroyed in 1942).

SALES
Faunesses dansant, five statuettes, from 27 to 32 cm, Drouot, December 19, 1986, room 7.
Narcisse, 54 cm, Sotheby Johannesbourg, July 3, 1984.

MUSEUMS
Lille
Le Premier Pas, 137 cm (F. Tassel, founder).

SALES
Charmeuse de serpents, 90 cm, Enghien, March 4, 1984; Enghien, April 28, 1985.
Chasseur du XVIe siècle et ses deux dogues, 65 cm, Sotheby London, June 12, 1986.
Couple dansant, 66 cm, Sotheby New York, April 26, 1986.
Femme aux fleurs et aux oiseaux, Etampes, September 23, 1984.
Guerrier oriental à l'étendard, 141 cm, Enghien, June 26, 1983 (sold for 400,000 F).
La Pensée, 143 cm, Drouot, March 23, room 3.

POITEVIN, PHILIPPE

Saint-Maximin, January 21, 1831
Marseille, September 15, 1907

After his studies at the Ecole des Beaux-Arts and a sojourn of nearly a dozen years in Paris, Poitevin returned to Marseille and worked for the Longchamp Palace. He exhibited at the Salon at least as early as 1855, showing busts and medallions as well as

PLÉ, HENRI HONORÉ

Paris, March 2, 1853
Paris, January 31, 1922

Proud and powerful masculine figures, often heroes from history or from mythology, occupy an important part of this sculptor's eclectic production. Endowed with genuine talent, he exhibited his works at the Salon starting in 1877, sending a number of bronzes: *Cicéron*, a statuette (1877), *Cyparisse* (1881), *Femme de Mequinez*, a bust (1884), *Le Premier Pas* (1885), *Patriam familiae proetulit* (1886), *L'Inspiration* (1887), some statuettes, *Triomphator* (1888), *Un joli rêve* (1892), *Méditation* (1893), *Le Dolmen, Sortie d'église, Le Voeu, Le Pardon* (1902), and finally a group, *Le Chemin de l'école* (1914). Some noteworthy works in plaster or in marble are: *Colombella* (1881), *Vainqueur! Mexicain du XVIe siècle* (1885), *Le Prix du tournoi* (1887), *Cigale* (1894), *Echo des bois* (1896), *Ronde des blés* and *Frisson* (1899), *Notre Maître à tous* (1900), *Fleur d'eau* (1901), *Shakespeare* (1904), *Les Hirondelles, Rêverie, Diane, La bise est venue, Combat de coqs*, five statuettes (1905), *Pureté*, (1908), and *Baiser d'Avril* (1914).

Many works by Plé were cast in bronze. Thiébaut cast *Cyparisse*, 78 and 40 cm, and Barbedienne cast two vases: *Le Dénicheur* or *Grimpeur*, 41 cm, and *La Voie lactée*, 34 and 22.5 cm, and two statuettes, *Le Futur Avocat*, 58, 41, 28 and 15 cm, and *Premier Pas*, 85, 68, 53 and 39 cm, as well as a floor lamp with six lights, *Femme à la vasque*, 110 cm. Of further note is *David vainqueur*, 63 cm, *Femmes aux oiseaux* (Colin, founder), 84 cm, *Le Grand Veneur*, 59 cm, and *Le Triomphateur*, 55 and 98 cm, etc.

Henri Honoré Plé,
a Charmeuse de serpents,
90 cm.

Henri Honoré Plé,
La Pensée,
143 cm.

Henri Honoré Plé,
Guerrier oriental à l'étendard,
135 cm.

Eugène Désiré Piron,
Cinq Faunesses dansant,
27 to 32 cm.

Joseph Pollet,
Une heure de la nuit,
46 cm.
Fabius frères Collection,
Paris.

personages and genre scenes: *Jeune Chasseur excitant un chien et un faucon,* a statue in plaster (1863), *L'Enfant au nid* and *Jeune Fille à l'aiguille,* 110 cm, two marbles (1867), and *Daphnis et Chloé,* a group in marble, 88 cm, (1875).

MUSEUMS
Marseille
Le Joueur de billes, 76 cm (Salon of 1859).
Le Joueur de toupie, 91 cm (Salon of 1861).

POLLET, JOSEPH
Palerme, 1814
Paris, December 31, 1870

Pollet

Born in Sicily to French parents, Pollet traveled widely and worked in different countries. He started to sculpt in Italy, and then went successively to Paris, Brussels, and again to Italy before establishing himself permanently in Paris. He focused on executing busts in plaster and in marble, including many of *Napoléon III* and of the *Impératrice Eugénie,* as well as some statues, including that of the *Duc de Brabant,* for Brussels. Provided with a number of official commissions, he also worked for the palace of Saint-Cloud, for diverse minsters, for the Opera, the Louvre, the Sainte-Clotilde basilica, the churches of Saint-Eustache and Sainte-Elisabeth (a bas-relief pietà for the facade). In addition to some busts, between 1846 and 1869 the Salon showed his works entitled *Une heure de la nuit,* a statue in marble (1850, bronze at the Exposition Universelle of 1855), and *Eloa, la soeur des anges,* a group in bronze inspired by a work of Alfred de Vigny (1863). *Une heure de la nuit* was cast in many dimensions by the founder Colin and by Labroue.

MUSEUMS
Grenoble
Une heure de la nuit, 34 cm (E. de Labroue, founder).
Reims
Une heure de la nuit, 53 cm.
Rouen
Eloa, la soeur des anges, 152 cm (Salon of 1863).

POMPON, FRANÇOIS
Saulieu, May 9, 1855
Paris, May 6, 1933

It was only at the Salon d'Autumn of 1922, with his work entitled *Ours blanc,* that this famous, sixty-seven year old animal sculptor was truly discovered by the public at large, despite a career that was already quite full. The son of a cabinetmaker, Pompon had started at a very young age to work with a marbler in his hometown. From the age of fifteen, he studied at the school of fine arts in Dijon. At twenty, he entered the Ecole des Arts Décoratifs in Paris. Soon faced with the challenge of supporting himself, he began to sculpt funerary monuments and building facades. He engaged himself as craftsman with different sculptors, including Antonin Mercié, Saint-Marceaux, Falguière, and, in 1889, Rodin. Though he would eventually undergo a radical departure from Rodin's style, the great sculptor nevertheless once said to Pompon, "You will be a great artist," upon seeing one of his first works. Pompon also made the acquaintance of Sarah Bernhardt, whom he aided in her own works of sculpture.

In 1879, Pompon started to exhibit a certain number of busts at the Salon, but it was, he said, the zoomorphic capital of a column from the Roman church in Saulieu which determined his calling as an animal sculptor. Like many other artists, he frequented the Jardin des Plantes; around 1900, animals (rare in his earlier work) increasingly replaced the human figure. His consignments to the Salon included some plasters and only a few bronzes: one statue entitled *Cosette,* in 1890, a bust in 1898, *Poule cayenne* and *En prière* in 1906, and *Coq* in

Pompon

François Pompon,
Poule,
une patte levée,
27 cm
(1908; Hébrard).

1907. During the course of these same years, Pompon's artistic personality asserted itself. The forms freed themselves of all details, becoming smooth, polished, and pared down, sometimes evoking the sculptures of ancient Egypt. Pompon's sculptures reflect no anatomical research, with positions frozen as if in a snapshot, presented in a spare, calm, and simple style reflecting the artist's own temperment, and completely opposite to Rodin's style.

By 1922 the acclaim that Pompon received, as noted above, permitted him to work entirely for himself. It was at this stage that he made some of his most important works. One of them, *Le Cerf,* a large bronze of 2.59 m in height, was erected on the plaza of Arnheim in Holland. Another bronze, *Le Taureau* (1933), was erected in Saulieu.

Numerous are the works by Pompon which were cast in bronze by the lost wax technique, mainly by Valsuani and Hébrard. Some proofs by Valsuani were numbered up to twelve. The growing success of this artist, however, also prompted other founders to cast proofs of bad quality, really bad copies and fakes.

Thanks to a gift from the sculptor, the museum of Dijon possesses about three hundred of his works in plaster, terra cotta and bronze. Noted below are the bronzes for which models were executed before 1920. Some models of these bronzes belong to the museum of Dijon (*), while others figured in an exposition at the Laurenceau Gallery in 1962.

Before 1900
*Homme assis, père de l'artiste, 21 cm.
*Maman en prière, 30 cm.
*Berthe Pompon, femme de l'artiste, head unfinished, 22 cm.
1900
*Monsieur de Saint-Marceaux, 21 cm.
1904
*Kaddour, petit chien assis, sketch, 8 cm.
*Maternité, 25 cm.
Around 1905
*Femme pensive, 17 cm.
1906
*Dromadaire, sketch, 15 cm.
*Girafe, sketch, 20 cm.
1907
*Bison, 20 x 25 cm.
*Coq, 29 cm.
1908
*Coq, weather vane, 47 cm.
*Jeune Oie marchant, 26 cm.
*Truie, sketch, 7 x 12 cm.
1909
Coq endormi, 23 cm.
1910
Jeune coq déplumé courant.
Pintade.
1911
*Canard debout, 19 cm.
*Canard sortant de l'eau, 16 cm.
*Cochon du Yorkshire, 12 x 16 cm.
*Dindon, 25 cm.
*Poule d'eau, 27 cm.

François Pompon,
Coq endormi,
23 x 30 cm
(Valsuani).

François Pompon,
Jeune Oie
marchant,
25 cm
(1908).

552

François Pompon,
Pintade marchant, 20 cm
(1910).

Paris, Orsay
Bison, 16.5 x 23 cm (1907).
Canard debout, 19 cm (1911).
Cigogne (or *Grive*), 17.3 cm (1921).
Femme pensive, 17 cm.
Hippopotame, 14 x 22.5 cm (1918).
Jeune Chouette, 19 cm (1918).
Marabout, 15.3 cm (1925).
Panthère, 14 x 22.5 cm (1925).
Perdreau, 25 cm (1923).
Poule d'eau, 27 cm (1911).
The museum possesses an important ensemble of plasters.

Paris, Petit Palais
Dindon, 24 cm.
Taureau, 137 x 220 cm.

Vernon
Caille, 22.5 cm. (Valsuani).
Cane, 15 cm (Valsuani).
Marabout.

Vire
Poule, 24.5 cm (1911).
Foulque, 28 cm (1913).

Some works are noted in different museums, particularly in Sauleu, in Rouen, in Algiers (*L'Ours,* bronze, 21 cm).

SALES
Bouledogue, 30 cm, 1931 (Valsuani), Drouot, November 29, 1985, room 9.
Canard sur l'eau, 14.5 cm, 1911 (Hébrard), Drouot, May 31, 1985, rooms 5 and 6.
Cerf, 58 cm (Valsuani), Bourg-en-Bresse, March 2, 1986; Rambouillet, July 27, 1986.
Chat assis jouant avec sa queue, 17.5 cm (Valsuani), Brussels, December 8, 1986.
Chouette, 27 cm (Valsuani), Rambouillet, June 8, 1986.
Le Cochon, 12 cm (C. Valsuani), Drouot, June 27, 1983.
Coq dormant, 23 cm, 1909 (Hébrard No3), Drouot, May 31, 1985, rooms 5 and 6.

1913
*Foulque, 28 cm.
*Jeune Coq, 26 cm.
Pélican.
1918
*Chouette, 18 cm.
Hippopotame, 14 cm.
1919
Coq sur drapeau, for a monument to the dead, 16 cm.

Also known are some castings in silver: *Génisse,* 12 cm, and *Veau,* 11 cm (1909), and *Dinde,* 9 cm (1911).

The museum of Dijon also preserves some proofs in bronze of more recent works. Here are listed a selection of bronzes belonging to other museums, and some bronzes dispersed in public sale (without specification of dates).

MUSEUMS
Boulogne-sur-Mer
Coq, 29 cm (1907).
Calais
Pintade (1910).
Chalon-sur-Saône
Bison, 20 cm.
Dijon
(see above)
Lyon
Poule d'eau.
Sanglier.

François Pompon,
Canard, 18 cm
(1911; Valsuani 11/12).

François Pompon,
La Truie, 10.5 x 21 cm
(1908; Hébrard No5).

Le Corbeau, 38.5 cm (Valsuani), Drouot, June 15, 1984.
Grand-Duc (Valsuani), Versailles, June 18, 1986.
Grue couronnée, 27 cm, 1926 (Valsuani), Drouot, May 31, 1985, rooms 5 and 6; Bourg-en-Bresse, March 2, 1986; Rambouillet, March 9, 1986.
Lionne marchant, 15 cm, Brest, May 20, 1984; Rambouillet, March 9, 1986.
L'Oie, 18 cm, Rambouillet, December 8, 1985.
L'Oie, 25.5 cm, (Hébrard), Bourg-en-Bresse, March 2, 1986; Drouot, November 27, 1986, rooms 1 and 7.
Jeune Oie marchant, 25 cm, 1908 (Valsuani), Drouot, March 4, 1984; Zurich, November 9, 1985; (Valsuani 4/12), Drouot, December 13, 1985, room 15; Drouot, April 18, 1986, room 5.
Ours, 24 x 45 cm (Valsuani), Bourg-en-Bresse, March 2, 1986; Lyon, March 10, 1986 (taking 112,000 F).
Ours blanc, 12.5 cm (Valsuani), Drouot, June 27, 1983.
Ours blanc or Ours polaire, 24 x 44 cm, 1922 (Valsuani), Orléans, May 11, 1985; Drouot, May 31, 1985, rooms 5 and 6 (138,000 F); Rambouillet, June 8, 1986; Enghien, November 23, 1986.
Panthère, 61 cm L. (Valsuani); Rouen, December 16, 1984.
Panthère marchant, 13 x 35 (Valsuani), Drouot, March 4, 1984; Zurich, June 8, 1985; Christie's Geneva, November 10, 1985.
Grande Panthère, 24 x 84 cm (Valsuani), Drouot, May 31, 1985, rooms 5 and 6 (166,000 F).
Pintade marchant, 20 cm (Hébrard), Versailles, March 17, 1985; Drouot, November 28, 1985, rooms 5 and 6.
Poule (Valsuani 7/12), Enghien, November 24, 1985.
Poule d'eau, 27 cm, 1925 (Valsuani 1/12), Enghien, November 23, 1986.
Le Rhinocéros, 15.5 x 18 cm (Valsuani), Drouot, November 27, 1986, rooms 1 and 7.
Sanglier, 24 cm (Valsuani), Drouot, May 31, 1985, rooms 5 and 6 (110,000 F).
Tourterelle, 23.5 cm, 1908 (Valsuani), Drouot, May 31, 1985, rooms 5 and 6.
La Truie, 11 cm (Hébrard), Rambouillet, July 27, 1986.

PONSCARME, FRANÇOIS JOSEPH HUBERT
Belmont-les-Monthureux (Vosges), May 20, 1827
Malakoff, February 27, 1903

A sculptor and medal-engraver, Ponscarme went to Paris at the age of eighteen and worked at various jobs before being able to devote himself entirely to his art. He obtained the second prize of Rome for engraving in medals in 1855. At the Salon, where he debuted two years later, he primarily exhibited medals. Drawing inspiration from the masters of the Renaissance, he was considered one of the renovators of this discipline. Above all a portraitist, Ponscarme also made some busts and medallions. The museum of Epinal possesses nearly a dozen medallions in bronze, portraying the artist's contemporaries. One medallion, *Portrait de Charles Ernest Beulé,* 18 cm diam, belongs to the museum of Angers.

POTET, LOYS
Nantes 1866—?

This artist exhibited some plasters at the Salon, in particular pieces representing people from the Bible, including *Abel* in 1892, and *Tobie rendant la vue à son père* in 1895. Some bronzes appeared on the market, including an inkwell in gilded bronzed ornamented by a *Naïade sur un rocher,* 36 x 15 cm, and a small group, *La Chasse au tigre* (or *au léopard*), 45 cm.

PRADIER, JEAN-JACQUES, KNOWN AS JAME
Geneva, May 23, 1790
Bougival, June 4, 1852

Pradier

Working in the realm between academicism and romanticism, Jean-Jacques Pradier situated himself closer to the first, though he did not accept rules that were too sterile. If he often found inspiration from antiquity, he readily interpreted it in the amiable and sensual manner of neo-classical sculptors from the end of the Old Regime. The 1986 Paris exhibition *Stautes de chair,* which was devoted to him, permitted a rediscovery of an artist in full possession of his art, with an extraordinary sureness of hand and a rare skill. Meticulous and spiritual, he was particularly appreciated during his lifetime for his countless, elegant feminine statuettes, among which are the twelve *Victoires* from the tomb of Napoléon I at the Invalides.

Born to a Protestant family from Toulouse, Pradier followed the courses of the Geneva school of drawing, going to Paris in 1807 and entering the Ecole des Beaux-Arts the following year. He obtained the first prize of Rome in 1813, and stayed for four years at the Villa Médicis. Upon returning to Paris, he made his debut at the Salon of 1819 and acquired a reputation very quickly. He returned to Rome for a year in 1823, and went there again in 1841. In the meantime, after a liaison with Juliette Drouet, he was married in 1833 to Louis d'Arcot, from whom he would separate in 1845. In his studio, he reunited himself with a number of artists, sculptors, painters, musicians, and writers. A member of the Institut

James Pradier,
Femme à l'urne, 40 cm (Susse).
Susse Founder Collection, Arceuil.

James Pradier,
La Négresse aux calebasses,
45.5 cm.
Fabius frères Collection,
Paris.

555

and a professor at the Ecole des Beaux-Arts, Pradier became the most renowned sculptor during the reign of Louis-Philippe. He was nicknamed "the last of the Greeks," perhaps explaining why certain critics, particularly Baudelaire, who judged his works at the Salon of 1846, considered his "a cold and academic talent."

During the course of his career, Pradier received a number of official commissions. In Paris, he made two stone statues for the Fountain of Molière (*La Comédie légère* and *La Comédie sérieuse*), a statue of the *Industrie* for the Bourse, works for the Luxembourg and the Palais Bourbon, four renowned pieces in bas relief for the Arc de Triomphe de l'Etoile, statues of *Lille* and of *Strasbourg* for Concorde Plaza, and the cast iron piece *Amazone* for the Cirque d'Hiver. He is also the author of two works in stone placed in the gardens of the Tuileries, *Prométhée enchaîné* and *Phidias*, and of a bronze entitled *Saint Louis*, 3 meters high, for the city of Aigues-Mortes. In the last years of his life, Pradier took many trips to Nîmes so thast he could construct the remarkable Fontaine de l'Esplanade, installed in 1851.

Of a number of consignments to the Salon, some marbles of note are *Psyché* (1824), the *Prométhée* from the Tuileries (1827), *Les Trois Grâces* (1831), *Phryné* (1845), *Nyssia* (1848), *La Toilette d'Atalante* (1850), and *Sapho assise* (1852). Some noteworthy bronzes include the bust of *Louis-Philippe* (1834), a statue of *Sapho debout* (1848), and *Médée et Pandore* (1850).

Very prolific, Pradier practiced commercialized and edition sculpture during his lifetime, using different materials and a quantity of fashionable subjects. For the bronzes, he entered into some contracts with different founders, who continued to distribute his works after his death. Moreover, during the liqudation sale of his studio after his death, held on July 26-28, 1852, and then in 1881, in a legal sale between his heirs, some models were sold with the rights of reproduction in all materials. It is impossible to index all of these editions because of their abundance. Furthermore, the catalog from the exhibition *Statues de chair* guards against the studio copies, castings from other molds, and counterfeits which were brought to light even during the lifetime of the artist.

James Pradier,
La Toilette d'Atalante,
32 cm (Susse).

Bronzes cast by Susse
Cornélie, 35 and 28 cm.
Danseuses aux fleurs, 44 cm (two versions, nude and dressed).
Danseuses aux fleurs (figures separated from the preceding group).
Diane accroupie, 20 cm.
Diane endormie (assise), 25 cm.
Enfant aucygne, 100, 55 and 40 cm.
L'Esclave, 32 cm.
Femme couchée rêvant (paperweight).
Femme nue endormie (paperweight).
Femme ôtant sa chemise, 32 cm (cast during the lifetime of the artist).
Femme au panier, 32 cm.
Femme au perroquet, 39 cm (cast during the lifetime of the artist).
Femme à l'urne, 32 cm.

Hébé, 50 and 35 cm.
Lesbie tenant un perroquet, 35 cm.
La Mère de famille, 35 cm.
Napoléon 1er, 30 cm.
Nyssia, 32 cm (reduction slightly different from the marble of 1848).
Phyrné, 60, 40 and 12 cm (cast during the lifetime of the artist; the same subject was mounted in clock).
Pradier en buste, 28 cm.
Le Premier Pas de Bacchus, 45 and 38 cm (the same subject mounted on a clock, 45 cm).
Sapho assise, 75, 35, 28 and 22 cm (cast during the lifetime of the artist).
Sapho, bust, cast in many dimensions (for inkwell and for a clock).
La Toilette d'Atalante, 78, 25 and 22 cm.

Bronzes cast by Thiébaut
Femme ôtant sa chemise (without the column).
La Prière, episode from cholera in Palerme, 37 cm.
Vénus à la coquille, naissance de l'Amour, 17 and 9 cm.

Bronzes cast by Thiébaut, Fumière and Gavignot successors (in 1898), in addition to the preceding subjects
Danseuse africaine au tambourin, 31 cm.
La Prière, arrangement with Gothic pre-dieu, 38 cm.

Bronzes cast by Barbedienne
Flore au serpent, 29 cm.
La Toilette d'Atalante, three dimensions.

Bronzes cast by E. de Labroue
L'Etoile du soir.
Pandore.
Phryné.
Vénus et l'Amour.

Many other editions of Pradier's works were made, but it is not always possible to be certain of the founder's name or the importance of the castings. Again, the catalog of the Statues de Chair Exhibition, already cited, indexes and comments on the following subjects:

Anacréon et l'Amour, sketch sold with rights of reproduction after the decease of the sculptor.
Bayadère assoupie sur des coussins; a proof in bronze, 16 cm, is known.
Bacchante et l'Amour, edition in bronze made around 1850 by Duplan and Salles, founders.
Chloris, a reduction in bronze, 29 cm, in a private collection.
Danaïde, some proofs in bronze noted.
Le Gardon, one of the figures sitting from the Fontaine de l'Esplanade in Nîmes; reduction cast around 1875 by Boyer and Rolland, founders.
Homère et son guide, some recutions in bronze, 41.5 cm.
John Pradier, fils du sculpteur or *Enfant au chien,* 24 cm, model sold in 1852 with rights of reproduction in bronze.
Léda et le cygne, some proofs in bronze known at the end of the 19th century (one model in silver, gold, ivory and turquoise belongs to a German collector).

James Pradier, Sapho, 45.5 cm (1848). J. Ginepro Collection, Monaco.

James Pradier, Le Duc d'Orléans, 34 cm. Musée du Louvre.

Médée, some proofs in bronze in two dimensions, 92 and 45 cm.

Le Moineau de lesbie, cast by Boyer and Rolland around 1875.

Nymphe des eaux, one of the figures sitting by the Fontaine de l'Esplanade in Nîmes; reduction around 1875 by Boyer and Rolland.

Odalisque assise, some proofs known in 51 cm height (the Brooklyn Museum possesses a model of 29 cm height.

Pandore, model and molds sold with rights with rights of reproduction.

La Poésie légère, a number of reductions, with some variantes, certain castings by Boyer and Rolland, 50 and 35 cm.

Rêverie, one of the figures stting by the Fontaine de l'Esplanade in Nîmes; reduction around 1875 by Boyer and Rolland.

La Sagesse repoussant les traits de l'Amour, sketch sold with rights of reporduction after the death of the sculptor.

Sapho debout, an edition in bronze, 45 cm (a proof in silver, 86 cm, belongs to the Bowes museum.)

Vénus à la coquille, bronzes by Duplan and Salles.

Some other bronzes are known only by a single model, and do not seem to have been made the object of entire editions. There is one bust of note entitled *Le Duc d'Orléans*, 34 cm, of which many proofs have been found.

MUSEUMS

Aix-en-Provence
Buste du peintre Victor Chavet, 34 cm.
Angers
Sapho, statuette, 71 cm.
Chartres
La Naissance de l'Amour or *Vénus à la coquille*, 13 cm.
Nîmes
Jules Canonge, bust, 54 cm.
Jean Reboul, bust, 47 cm (Simonet, founder), 1849.
Lyon
Odalisque.
Paris, Decorative Arts
Femme au bas, 22.5 cm.
La Négresse aux callebasses, 32 cm.
Petit Garçon à la pèlerine, John Pradier, 25 cm.
Phryné remettant ses voiles, 67 cm.
Vénus et l'Amour, 25 cm (E. de Labroue, founder).
Paris, Carnavalet
Le Duc d'Orléans, medallion, 25 cm diam. (Simonet, founder).
Isaac Strauss, directeur des bals de l'Opera, medallion, 24 cm diam.
Paris, Louvre
Le Duc d'Orléans, bust, 34 cm.
Maxime du Camp, bust, 53 cm (1850).
Phryné nue dansant, 31 cm.

The museum of Art and of History of Geneva possesses an important collection of works by Pradier, particularly plasters. Among the bronzes held there are:

Anacréon et l'Amour, 75 cm (Gonon, founder).
Augustin-Pyramus de Candolle, bust, 82 cm (Gonon).
Danseuse africaine au tambourin, 51 cm.
Danseuse avec fleurs, 46 cm.
Le Duc d'Orléans, medallion, 25 cm diam (Simonet, founder).
Homère et son guide, 41.5 cm.
Marie-Amélie reine de France, 45 cm. (1846).
Pandore, gilded bronze, 40.5 cm.
La Pêche, 52 cm.

La Prière, 38 cm (Fumière, founder).
Phryné mettant ses voiles, 40 cm.
La Sagesse repoussant les traits de l'Amour, 87 cm (Gonon).

SALES
Enfant et cygne, 109 x 72 cm (Susse), Christie's London, September 29, 1986.
La Luxure, Drouot, February 22, 1986, room 8.
La Toilette d'Atalante, 32.5 cm (Sussez), Christie's London, May 15, 1986.
Vénus et l'Amour, 96.5 cm, Sotheby London, June 17, 1986.

PRÉAULT, AUGUSTE

Paris, October 6, 1810
Paris, January 11, 1879

AUG PREAULT

Resisting the commercial career for which he was intended, Préault initially entered the studio of an ornamental sculptor, and then the studio of David d'Angers. D'Angers, wrote Stanislas Lami, soon released Préault because of his lack of attention, his exuberance and his grandiose theories. Préault had a very restless, romantic temperament, wrote Lami, and sought to attract attention through witticisms. He apprenticed himself to another sculptor, Antonin Moine, and debuted at the Salon in 1833. The following year, the jury accepted only one large bas-relief, *La Tuerie*, from among his consignments; its exacerbated style revealed his avant-garde nature to the public, a reputation which henceforth sustained him. The Salon rejected all of his other works in 1833, as they would continue to do until 1849.

Thanks to David d'Angers, who maintained their friendship, Préault obtained some government and private commissions. Of particular note is the very moving *Christ en croix* in wood from the church Saint-Gervais, a number of statues for the facade of this same church, as well as for the church of Saint-Paul-Saint-Louis; also significant are the *Cavalier gaulois* in stone for the Pont d'Iéna (1849), and many funeral monuments: *Le Silence*, a mask in demironde bosse, in marble for the tomb of Jacob Roblès at the Père-Lachaise (1848), the medallion in bronze of *Mme Paul Meurice*, 50 cm diam., also at the Père-Lachaise (1856), some reliefs in bronze for the tomb of the actor Rouvière at the Montmartre cemetery (1866), the medallion in bronze of *Adam Mickiewicz* at the Montmorency cemetery (1868), another of *Paul Huet*, 42 cm diam, a statue in marble of *Clémence Isaure* at the Luxembourg gardens, and a statue in bronze of the *Général Marceau*, 3 meters high, destined for the city of Chartres (1851). Also attributable to him are some groups of a social character—*Les Mendiants, La Famine, La Misère*—the realism of which was not lucky enough to please the Salon jury. Préault also made busts and a number of medallions, for the most part in bronze, representing some of his contemporaries. Among his notable bronzes are *Douleur*, a statuette exhibited at the Salon begin-

Auguste Préault,
La Tuerie,
bas-relief,
109 x 140 cm.
Musée de Chartres.

ning in 1849, *Ophélie*, a large bas-relief, 75 x 200 cm (Salon of 1876), two haut-reliefs entitled *Buste d'Arabe* and *Buste de Peau-rouge*, (40 x 50 cm and 44 x 40 cm, respectivley), and finally *La Honte* (exhibited in 1900).

MUSEUMS
Auxerre
Le Silence, medallion in haut relief, 38 cm diam.
Blois
Alfred Julien, medallion, 40 cm diam. (1874).
Lélia, medallion, 54 cm diam.
Soldat gaulois, medallion, 60 cm diam.
Tête d'enfant, medallion 50 cm (1896).
Caen
L'Acteur Etienne Mélingue, medallion.
Chartres
La Tuerie, large bas-relief.
Lille
This museum possesses nearly forty medallions in bronze.
Paris, Carnavalet
Two medallions: *Léopald Leclanché*, 17.5 cm diam. and *Tullie Blum*, 41.5 cm diam.
Paris, Louvre
Two medallions: *Alphonse David*, 19 cm diam. and *Delacroix*, 35 cm diam.
Paris, Orsay
Dante, medallion, 95 x 86 cm (Eck and Durand).
Ophélie, bas-relief, 75 x 200 cm (1876; Thiébaut).
Virgile, medallion, 95 x 85.5 cm (1855; Eck and Durand).
Rouen
Théodore Géricault, medallion, 35 cm diam.
Toulouse
Aulus Vitellius, medallion in haut-relief.

PRESIER, ÉDOUARD

Strasbourg, October 1, 1877- ?

Presier studied in Paris and in Munich, and after the First World War sculpted a number of monuments to the dead in Alsace. He is the author of a statuette entitled *Homme au baluchon*, 30 cm, which the museum of Strasbourg possesses.

PREVOT, EDMOND

Bordeaux, 1848
Bordeaux, 1892

Working in Bordeaux, Prevot produced medals, busts, and a number of genre scenes, which he exhibited at the Salon from 1876 to 1892. At the museum of Bordeaux, a bronze entitled *Homme nu foulant au pied un serpent*, 100 cm, is exhibited.

PRINTEMPS, JULES LOUIS

Lille?
March, 1899

A student of Jouffroy, Printemps produced a number of busts and debuted at the Salon of 1878. One of them—*Portrait de J.-B. Trystram*—was cast as a 72 cm bronze by Barbedienne, and belongs to the museum of Dunkerque.

PROUVÉ, VICTOR

Nancy, August 15, 1858
Sétif, 1943

Prouvé was one of the masters of Art Nouveau. Working simultaneously as a historical painter, sculptor, medal-engraverer, decorator, and lithographer, he would become the director of the school of fine arts of Nancy. His bronzes are few in number. One among them, a large cup symbolizing *La Nuit*, 45.5 x 79 cm, was exhibited at the Grand Palais in 1986; it belongs to the museum of the school in Nancy, which possesses a number of other works by the Prouvé. Another cup, entitled *Offrande*, portrays a nude woman, 27.5 cm, and was sold in Enghien on October 28, 1979.

PUECH, DENYS

Gavernac (Aveyron), December 3, 1854
Rodez, December 9, 1942

An official artist, Puech held a number of distinguished titles, was made a member of the Institut in 1905, and served as the director of the Villa Médicis in Rome from 1921 to 1933. A sculptor and medal-engraver, he studied with Jouffroy, Chapu and Falguière before debuting at the Salon in 1875. He received a certain number of commissions, including the statue *Musique* for the facade of the Opera-Comique, the monument to the explorer *Francis Garnier* at the square of the Observatoire, and that of *Gavarni* at the plaza of Saint-Georges. He exhibited a number of busts at the Salon, as well as some groups and statues. Among these are *Jeune Homme au poisson*, marble (1884), *Jeune Marin*, a statue in bronze designed for a monument for the Chilean Navy (1885), *La Seine*, haut-relief in plaster (1887), *La Muse d'André Chénier*, marble (1890), *Etoile du soir*, plaster (1891), *L'Enfant au poisson*, marble (1899), *L'Aurore*, marble (1901), *L'Enfant au dauphin*, marble (1913), and *La Princesse Gagarine Stourdza peignant*, a statuette in gilded bronze (1914), etc.

A haut-relief of the *Seine* was cast in bronze, 25 x 62 cm, by Thiébaut; *La Sirène*, 80 cm, was cast by Barbedienne; and another statuette, *Le Livre d'or*, 90, 65 and 52 cm, was cast by Susse.

MUSEUMS
Bayonne
Léon Bonnat, 51 cm.
Nice
Jeune Fille nue assise à sa toilette.
Paris, Orsay
Amour et dauphin.
Rodez
Baigneuse, 57 cm (Rome 1929).
Madame Denys Puech (princesse Gagarine Stourdza), 105 cm (1913; C. Valsuani).
Madame Denys Puech, bust, 67 cm (1908; C. Valsuani).
Désespérée, long woman, 40 cm (Rome 1922).
La Femme au lys, 95 cm (Rome 1930).
Héro pleurant Léandre, 75 cm (1929).
Peintre tenant sa palette, 2nd proof, 1915 (C. Valsuani).
Projet de groupe funéraire, 30 cm (Carvilla, founder).
Sommeil de l'étoile, 112 cm (Colin, founder).
Tobie retirant les poissons de l'eau, 112 cm (1922).

SALES
La Seine, 23.5 x 72 cm (Fumière, founder), Drouot, December 13, 1985, room 15.

QUENARD, ARMAND PIERRE LOUIS

Allonnes (Maine-et-Loire), January 25, 1865
November 26, 1925

A sculptor, medal-engraver, and chiseler, Quenard sent some busts, medallions, and a certain number of statuettes in bronze to the Salon, from 1897 until his death. These works include *Abel* and *Bacchante* (1899), *Plume de paon* (1900), *Singe sajou mort* (1903), *Emilie Guyon de la Comédie française* (1905), *Chez le bijoutier* (1908), *Football* (1909), *Espiègle* (1910), *Charmeuse de lézard* (1911) (these last four in gilded bronze), and *Une trouvaille* (1913), etc. The *Singe sajou mort*, 46 cm L., was cast by the foundry of Vincennes.

MUSEUM
Paris, Carnavalet
Emilie Guyon, de la Comédie française, 36.5 cm.

SALES
La Dame de qualité, bronze and ivory, 34 cm, Brussels, December 12, 1984.
Jeune Femme au miroir, 60 cm, Enghien, March 4, 1984.

QUILLIVIC, RENÉ

Plouhinec (Finistère), May 13, 1879
Paris, April 8, 1969

Subjects inspired by Brittany dominate the work of this sculptor, who made many monuments to the dead for his home province after the First World War. A student of Mercié, Quillivic participated in different salons from the beginning of the twentieth century. At the Artistes Français, he is noted for two busts in plaster entitled *Ma mère* and *Veuve d'Audierne* in 1905, a statue in bronze called *Brodeuse de Pont-l'Abbé* in 1908, *Petite Mignonne* and *Les Binious de Pont-l'Abbé*, a statue and a group in bronze, in 1909, and a bronze statuette entitled *Mère kabyle* in 1913. Quillivic also sculpted some statues in granite.

RAFFAËLLI, JEAN-FRANÇOIS

Paris, April 20, 1850
Paris, February 29, 1924

Though he began as a theater actor, Raffaëlli became a painter and engraver after studying in the studio of Gérôme. The best-known and best-appreciated phase of his painted work portrays Parisian scenes and countrysides. He also produced some sculptures. In a sale of his works, which he organized at the Drouot Hotel on June 21, 1894, two bronzes made as unique pieces appeared, entitled *M. et Mme Denis* and *Profil de cantonnier*. In 1891 he exhibited two bronzes at the Salon de la Nationale des Beaux-Arts: a bas-relief, *Le Rémouleur*, cast by Gruet, and a bust entitled *Vieux*, cast by Gonon. Lastly, in 1912, he presented another bronze, *Tête de petit bourgeois*, a unique proof by Gruet.

SALES
Le Cheminot, bust, 18 cm, Saint-Maur, December 7, 1986.
La Discussion politique, (bust similar to the preceding, with arms), 25 cm, Drouot, October 12, 1984, room 1.

Jean-François Raffaëlli,
La Discussion politique,
25 cm.

RAMBAUD, JOSEPH PIERRE

Allevard (Isère), 1852
October, 1893

A student of Jouffrey and of Chapu, Rambaud sent statues of historic personages, genre scenes, and allegories.to the Salon from 1878 until his death. His bronze work *Agrippa d'Aubigné*, 147 cm, exhibited in 1892, was cast by Siot-Decauville. This bronze is found at the museum of Angers.

RAMEY, ÉTIENNE JULES

Paris, May 23, 1796
Paris, October 29, 1852

Étienne Jules Ramey started to sculpt under the direction of his father, Claude Ramey, and then entered the Ecole des Beaux-Arts at a very young age. In 1815 he obtained the first prize of Rome with his work *Ulysse reconnu par son chien*, and stayed at the Villa Médicis for five years. He later succeeded Cartellier as a professor at the Beaux-Arts, and took Houdon's place in the Institut in 1828. His sculpture includes works of an allegorical, mythological, or religious nature, some of which were destined to be monuments at the Sorbonne, the Louvre, the churches of Madelaine, Saint-Vincent-de-Paul, and Saint-Germain-en-Laye, and the arc de triomphe for the entrance to Aix in Marseille. At the Salon of 1822 Ramey exhibited a statue in marble entitled *L'Innocence pleurant un serpent mort* and a group in

*Ernest Rancoulet,
Deux Femmes
et l'Amour,
79 cm.*

*Ernest Rancoulet,
Jeune Berger dansant,
22 cm.
J. Ginepro Collection,
Monaco.*

plaster entitled *Thésée combattant le Minotaure*. This work, presented in marble in 1827, is found in the Tuileries. A small bronze of the same subject, 30 cm, belongs to the Bonnat museum of Bayonne.

RANCOULET, ERNEST

Born in Bordeaux

This artist participated at the Salon for a number of years, starting in 1870. He is known for works cast in bronze, most likely in rather limited castings: *Elégantes*, two statuettes of 41 cm height, *Joueur de violoncelle*, *Jeune Danseur*, *Jeune Danseuse*, and *Jeune Vendangeuse* (79 and 50 cm), etc.

MUSEUM
Reims
Vendangeuse or *Jeune Femme à la hotte*, 106 cm.

SALES
Alceste et Cerbère, 87 cm, Christie's New York, September 27, 1986.
Femme jouant des cymbales and *Homme jouant des cymbales*, 21 cm, Drouot, January 17, 1985, room 7.
Deux Femmes drapées à la lyre, avec l'Amour, 79 cm, Sotheby London, October 12, 1986.
Hercule, Athéna et Cerbère, 86.5 cm, Sotheby London, March 21, 1985.
La Poésie, 67 cm, Stockholm, April 20, 1983.
Retour du printemps, and *La Nuit, tout repose*, two statuettes, 56 cm, Sotheby London, November 10, 1983.

RAPHAËL, FRANCE EMMA

Amsterdam, July 13, 1877
1962

France Emma Raphaël prefered to practice the art of the direct cut on stone and on wood. Starting in 1900, she exhibited her works in different Salons, signed with her single name. She is known for such bronzes as *Femme assise lisant*, 29 cm, and a group entitled *Toboggan* portraying four people on a bobsled, in gilded bronze and marble, 42 cm.

RÉCIPON, GEORGES

Paris, January 17, 1860
1920

Two colossal quadriges in hammered copper, audaciously projecting at wide angles from the facade of the Grand Palais, bear witness to the talent of this under-appreciated artist, whose work is representative of Art Nouveau sculpture. He is also the author of the nymphs of the *Seine* and of the *Néva*, likewise in hammered copper, which ornament the Alexandre-III Bridge. He began exhibiting works at the Salon in 1879, including two groups in plaster entitled *Tyrtée* (1879) and *Le Convalescent* (1882), and the following bronzes: *La Harpe et l'épée* (1892), *Cheval emballé* (1894), busts entitled *Notre Amie* (1896) and *Jean-Léon Gérôme* (1903), a haut-relief called *Chevalier normand combattant une chimère* (1909), the statuette *Leçon de choses*, (1910), and *Psyché ayant dérobé les armes de l'Amour* (1914). A small subject in iron in the shape of a horse, *Porte-bonheur*, was cast by Susse and passed rather frequently in public sale. The museum of Beauvais possesses a medallion in bronze entitled *Yvonne Récipon enfant*, 19.7 cm (1894).

RENARD DE BUZELET, ADRIENNE

Metz, 1797
1881

The museum of Lille possesses a bas-relief in bronze entitled *Cerf et quatre biches dans un paysage*, 28 x 33 cm, by Renard de Buzelet. This piece was featured at the Exposition Universelle of 1867.

Georges Récipon,
Porte-bonheur or La Chance,
gilded and silvered bronze,
15 x 11 cm (Susse).
J. Ginepro Collection, Monaco.

RENOIR, AUGUSTE

Limoges, February 25, 1841
Cagnes, December 3, 1919

Towards the end of his life, from 1913 to 1918, Renoir made nearly twenty sculptures, despite the fact that he could scarcely use his paralysed hands. In actuality, Renoir made these works through the hands of another—the young sculptor Richard Guino (1890-1973), one of Maillol's students. A judgement dating November 13, 1973 (the year of Guino's death) conceded to Guino the title of co-author for these works, but this does not diminish the fact that the whole world recognizes the manner, style, and spirit of Renoir in these works.

The sculptures by this famous painter were often modeled after his canvases or drawings, at the request of the merchant Ambroise Vollard, and with the assistance of Guino. A kind of intimate communion was established between the artist and his practitioner—Renoir, a stick in his hand, gave brief indications with his gestures, while Guino followed the instructions to craft small models before undertaking works in their final dimensions.

After Guino's departure in 1918, Renoir attempted to execute some works with sculptor Louis Morel, before abandoning sculpture permanently.

Renoir's father, a tailor, went to Paris to establish himself in 1844, and Auguste Renoir began working at the age of thirteen in a ceramic studio, where he painted flowers on plates. Soon he began to participate in the decoration of Parisian cafes. He entered the Ecole des Beaux-Arts in 1862, but remained there for only two years. He made the acquaintance of Monet, Sisley, Bazille, and then Cézanne, Degas, and the painters of the Barbizon. After the work of 1870, although Charles Durand-Ruel had become his marketer, Renoir pursued the career for which he is now known: as one of the most famous masters of impressionism. Renoir worked in Paris, in Essoyes, near Troyes on a property owned by his wife, and finally in Cagnes, where he retired in 1898, already suffering from rheumatism of the joints.

In 1908, after meeting Maillol in Essoyes, Renoir executed his two first sculpted works. These pieces—a bust and a medallion portraying his youngest son Claude (known as Coco)—were destined to be the only sculptures ever modeled by Renoir's own hands. Renoir was constantly preoccupied with trying to resolve the problems of volume and monumentality in his canvases, but it was five years before he again approached three-dimensional work. This engendered the sculptures made under his direction by the hand of Richard Guino, starting in 1913. Many of them would be cast in bronze by Rudier before being cast by other founders.

Auguste Renoir,
Coco, medallion, 26 cm diam.
(C. Valsuani).

Auguste Renoir and Richard Guino,
Petite Vénus debout sur socle
au Jugement de Pâris,
84 cm.

During his lifetime, Renoir entered into a contract with C. Valsuani for a limited and numbered edition of some of his works. Some new editions—numerous, it is said—were made after his death, and even today. Some very recent castings exist, moreover dated regularly. It is necessary to note that all bronze proofs carrying the double signature of both Renoir and Guino are necessarily dated after the judgement of 1973. Connoisseurs of Renoir's bronzes and other works must be on guard against fradulent castings.

Below is a chronological list of Renoir sculptures that were cast in bronze:

Works made by Renoir alone
Coco, medallion (1908), 26 cm diam., cast by Valsuani to 10 models; another edition Valsuani numbered to 30.
Coco, bust (1908), 28 cm, cast by Valsuani (some proofs numbered to 6).

Works made by Renoir and Richard Guino
Petite Vénus debout (1913), 60 cm, cast by Valsuani; another edition by Susse (some proofs dated 1983 numbered to 8).
Tête de Vénus, 15.5 cm; a proof marked C. Valsuani noted in public sale in the United States; recent edition by Susse (some proofs dated 1983 numbered to 8).
Grande Vénus debout or *Vénus victrix* (1915), 180 cm; edition by Susse (a proof dated 1984 numbered to 8).

Auguste Renoir,
Coco, bust, 28 cm
(C. Valsuani HC 2).

Auguste Renoir
and Richard Guino,
Mère et enfant
or Maternité,
55 cm
(1916; A. Rudier).

Auguste Renoir and Richard Guino,
Etude pour la Maternité, 30 cm
(A. Rudier).

Grand Jugement de Pâris (1916), 73 x 91 cm, cast by Vollard; a proof numbered to 3 in a Swiss collection.

Buste de Pâris, 63 cm; some proofs signed A. Rudier, numbered to 6.

Mère et enfant or *Maternité*, Mme Renoir and her son Pierre (1916), 54 cm, cast by Rudier and by Valsuani; another edition by Susse (proofs dated 1983, numbered to 8).

Mère et enfant or *Maternité*, study, 32 cm; casting by Valsuani and Rudier.

Le Feu or *Petit Forgeron* or *Jeune Berger* (1916), 33 cm, cast by Valsuani (some proofs numbered to 10); posthumous edition of 10 models cast by Renou and Poyet; another edition by Susse (some proofs of 60 cm high, dated 1983 and numbered to 8).

Buste de Madame Renoir (1916), 60 cm, cast by Valsuani in 20 models; other castings by Renou and Poyet; other castings by Susse in 1983.

L'Eau or *Petite Laveuse accroupie* or *Jeune Baigneuse* (1916), 32 cm, cast by Vollard; another edition by Susse in 1983 (some proofs in 34 and 27 cm numbered to 8).

L'Eau or *Grande Laveuse accroupie* or *Grande Baigneuse* (1917), 123 cm, cast by Vollard in 6 models; other editions by Susse in 1983.

Danseuse aux voiles, 64 cm, cast by Valsuani in 20 models.

Pendule hymne à la vie, 71 cm, cast by the merchant Alfred Daber in 8 models, cast by Bisceglia.

Works made in 1918 by Renoir and Louis Morel:

Danseuse au tambourin I, bas-relief, 58 cm, cast by Valsuani.

Danseuse au tambourin II, bas-relief, 57 cm, cast by Valsuani in 20 models.

Joueur de flûteau, bas-relief, 58 cm, cast by Valsuani in 20 models.

MUSEUMS

Cagnes-sur-Mer
The villa of the Collettes, where Renoir lived, owns many sculpted works including some bronzes:
Buste de Coco, 22 cm.
Le Petit Forgeron, 33 cm (Valsuani).
La Petite Laveuse, 32 cm (Valsuani).
Maternité, 54 cm (Valsuani).
Madame Renoir, bust, 60 cm.
Venus victrix, 180 cm.

Grenoble
Le Berger Pâris, bust, 78 cm.

Lyon
Madame Renoir, bust, 60 cm.

Paris, Orsay
L'Eau or *Petite Laveuse*, 33 cm.
Le Feu or *Petit Forgeron*, 32 cm (Valsuani 4/10).
La Grande Laveuse accroupie, 123 cm.
Hymne à la vie, clock, 71 cm (Bisceglia).
Tête de Coco, medallion, 21.5 cm diam. (Valsuani 5/30).

Paris, Petit Palais
Grande Vénus debout, 180 cm.

Saint-Denis de la Réunion
La Petite Laveuse, 26 cm.

Auguste Renoir and Richard Guino,
Le Feu or Petit Forgeron, 28 cm
(Valsuani).

L'Eau or Petite Laveuse accroupie,
27 cm.

Auguste Renoir and Richard Guino,
L'Eau or Grande Laveuse accroupie, 123 cm
(1917; Susse EA 4/4, 1983 casting).

SALES

(These works appear in chronological order).

Coco, head in medallion, 26 cm diam (Valsuani), Drouot, June 18, 1985, rooms 5 and 6; Rambouillet, October 20, 1985; Drouot, November 25, 1985, rooms 5 and 6; L'Isle-Adam, December 1, 1985; Rambouillet, October 12, 1986.

Coco, bust, 28 cm (Valsuani), Saint-Dié, May 13, 1984; Drouot, July 11, 1985, rooms 5 and 6; Sotheby London, December 4, 1985; Saint-Maur, March 2, 1986; Lyon, December 14, 1986.

Coco, bust with piédouche, 41.5 cm, Saint-Maur, May 11, 1986 (for 115,000 F).

Petite Vénus debout, 60 cm (Valsuani), Sotheby New York, November 15, 1984; Versailles, March 2, 1986; Drouot, June 26, 1986 (310,000 F).

Tête de Vénus, 15.5 cm (C. Valsuani), Washington, June 10, 1984.

Tête de Vénus, 39.5 cm (A. Rudier), Christie's New York, May 15, 1986.

Grande Vénus debout or *Vénus victrix,* 180 cm (Susse EA 4/4, 1984), Enghien, June 17, 1984; (Susse), Christie's New York, November 13, 1985 (fetching 220,000 dollars).

Buste de Pâris (A. Rudier 3/6), Drouot, March 18, 1986, rooms 1 and 7.

Maternité, 54 cm (Valsuani), Drouot, February 3, 1986, room 2; Saint-Maur, October 26, 1986.

Maternité, 54 cm (Susse EA 4/4, 1983), Enghien, June 17, 1984.

Maternité, study, 32 cm (Valsuani), Drouot, June 12, 1985, rooms 5 and 6; Rouen, December 15, 1985.

*Auguste Renoir
and Richard Guino,
Buste de Pâris, 63 cm
(1915; A. Rudier 3/6).*

*Auguste Renoir
and Richard Guino,
Buste de Mme Renoir,
60 cm
(1916;
Susse EA 4/4
1983 casting).*

*Auguste Renoir,
Joueur de flûteau,
bas-relief,
58 x 41 cm
(executed by
Louis Morel in 1918;
Valsuani casting).*

*Auguste Renoir,
Danseuse
au tambourin I,
bas-relief,
58 x 40 cm
(executed by
Louis Morel
in 1918;
Valsuani casting).*

*Auguste Renoir
and Richard Guino,
L'Eau or
Petite Laveuse accroupie,
34 cm.*

Maternié, study, 32 cm (A. Rudier), Rambouillet, December 15, 1985.

Le Feu or the *Petit Forgeron,* 33 cm (Valsuani), Saint-Maur, December 7, 1986.

Buste de Madame Renoir, 60 cm (C. Valsuani 15/20), Sotheby London, November 6, 1986.

Buste de Madame Renoir, 60 cm (Susse, 1983), Enghien, June 17, 1984.

L'Eau or *Petite Laveuse,* 27 cm (Valsuani), Saint-Maur, December 7, 1986.

L'Eau or *Petite Laveuse,* 34 cm (Susse 5/8), Enghien, November 25, 1984.

L'Eau or *Grande Laveuse,* 123 cm (Susse EA 4/4, 1983), Enghien, June 17, 1984 (545,000 F).

Danseuse aux voiles, 64 cm (C. Valsuani HC III, 1964), Sotheby London, March 26, 1986; (Valsuani 6/20, 1964), Christie's New York, May 15, 1986.

RICHARD, ALFRED PIERRE

Paris, ?
Paris, April 1884

This artist is known for a number of fantasy portraits, genre scenes, and busts. At the Salon, where he exhibited from 1867 until the time of his death, his notable exhibitions include the plasters *Prèmiere Coquetterie* (1867), *Jeune Pêcheur* (1869), *Idécise* (1870), Le Retour du bois (1881), and *Chien français* (1883), as well as a group in bronze entitled *La Halte, chameaux et chameliers* (1882). Two other works are noted as having been cast in bronze, *Arlequin* and *Colombine,* 60 cm.

RICHÉ, LOUIS

Paris, May 29, 1877
May 12, 1949

Louis Riché,
Couple de lions,
52 cm.

Cats were this artist's favorite theme, though he did sculpt some human figures as well. Of note at the Salon, where he began to participate when he was nineteen, are a good number of bronzes: *Jeune Chat jouant* (1899), *Etude de chats,* bronze and lithographic stone (1903 and 1904), *Algériennes* (1904), *Petit Grouope de chats* (1906), *Etude de chats,* marble and bronze (1910), *Bacchante au bouc,* a statuette cast by Fumière and Co. (1911), *Chat s'étirant,* a statuette cast by Goldschider (1912), *Prélude, lion et lionne* (1913), and *Chiens policiers,* a group cast by Jollet, (1914). Some works in wax, plaster, or marble complete the list of his consignments, particularly many groups of lions and lionesses, as well as five groups of cats in silver, cast by Risler and Carré and exhibited at the Salon of 1909. Riché continued to exhibit animal subjects between the two world wars. The catalogs of the Thiébaut foundry note the following editions:

Chat allongé, 4.5 x 17 cm.
Chat assis, 15 cm.
Chat endormi, 8.5 x 17 cm.
Bacchante au bouc, 39 cm.

One can also note some other subjects in bronze, including *Bouc,* 27 cm, *Ours assis,* 15.5 cm, *Ours polaire,* 28 cm, *Deux Panthères,* 69 and 34 cm, and *Deux Renards alsaciens* (Colin, founder), 52 cm, etc.

MUSEUMS
Bordeaux
Chat endormi, 14 x 27 cm (before 1905).
Lion au repos, 15 x 30 cm (before 1905).
Nîmes
Bacchante, statuette.
VALENCE
Chat guettant un papillon.

SALES
Chat assis, 24 cm (Susse), Drouot, December 2, 1983. room 5.
Chat debout, 23 cm (Valsuani), Enghien, October 10, 1982.
Lévrier, 19 x 22 cm, Rambouillet, March 25, 1984.
Couple de lions, 52 cm, Enghien, October 6, 1985.
Deux Panthères, 34 cm, Sotheby London, November 8, 1984.

RICHEFEU, CHARLES ÉDOUARD

Paris, January 7, 1868
January, 1945

This sculptor's work consists of portraits—especially figures of soldiers—and military scenes from the first Empire. Starting in 1902, he sent to the Salon some statuettes in bronze representing contemporaries, and a work entitled *1804* (1910). He also sent some groups, likewise in bronze: *La Charge, dragons du premier Empire* (1909), *Le Père François, grenadier de la garde* (1910), an important group including many people entitled *Charge du 1er régiment des grenadiers de la garde impériale* (1913), today in possession of the museum of the Armée in Paris. Richefeu continued to exhibit, always in the same spirit, until the Second World War.

One subject in gilded and patinaed bronze, *Vive l'empereur!*, 35.5 cm (Thiébaut-Fumière, founder), was sold at the Drouot Hotel, December 14, 1984, room 6.

RICHER, DOCTEUR PAUL

Chartres, January 17, 1849
December 1933

Richer's reputation was greatly enhanced by his activities as a scholar and doctor, and by the publications illustrated with his original drawings. Endowed with a real talent for sculpture, he made some full-length statues, including *Le Premier Artiste* in bronze (1890), today in the Jardin des Plantes, and the statue in stone of the doctor *Alfred Vulpian* (1928), located on the Rue Antoine-Dubois in Paris, in the sixth district. Richer's work also includes some masculine figures of athletes, sportsman, and workers, often treated in an impressionistic spirit, as well as some plaques, medals and diverse decorative objects. Starting in 1878, he showed works at the Salon including a certain number of bronzes: *Premier Artiste* (1891), *Bûcheron* (1894), *Le Semeur* (1896), *Forgeron* (1898), *Faucheur* (1903), *Décrépitude* (1913), and a statuette in silvered bronze entitled *Jean-Paul Laurens* (1914). The sculptor also presented some works in plaster: *Un gymnaste* (1887), *Le Moissonneur* (1888), a bas-relief entitled *Départ pour les champs* and *Cancalaise* (1897), *Football* (1899), and *Lancement du poids* (1901).

The Susse foundry cast the following works:

Aux champs, 42 and 21 cm.
Bûcheron, 61 and 29 cm.
Forgeron, 76 and 37 cm.
Le Semeur, 61 and 29 cm.
Jardinière La Moisson, 60 cm.
Jardinière Les Pommes, 17 cm.
Jardinière Les Raisins, 17 cm.
Plat Faucheur, 33 cm.
Plat Moisson, 39 cm.
Plat Rentrée des gerbes, 39 cm.
Plat Semeur, 39 cm.
Vase Buveur, 35 cm.
Vase Le Cidre, 35 cm.
Vase Le Vin, 32 cm.

A statuette of *Faucheur* may have been cast by Goldscheider in two dimensions.

SALES
Le Mineur, 40 cm (Susse), Drouot, December 6, 1982, room 1.
Le Semeur, 29 cm (Susse), Drouot, June 13, 1983, room 10.

RINGEL D'ILLZACH, JEAN DÉSIRÉ

Illzach (Bas-Rhin), September 29, 1847
Strasbourg, July 28, 1916.

Especially well-known by this artist are a large number of medallions, the majority in bronze, preserved in different museums. They are portraits of well-known contemporaries—writers, musicians, actors, sculptors, scholars, and political men. However, Ringel d'Illzach also made statues and groups portraying a variety of people, genre scenes, and allegories, which he exhibited at the Salon des Artistes Français from 1873 to 1889, and at the Nationale des Beaux-Arts from 1890 to 1913. Among the bronzes (disregarding the medallions) are three statues, *Flûtiste* (1878), *Liberté* (1881), and Perversité (1890), and two busts entitled *La Victoire* and *La Défaite,* made of bronze, wax, iron, brass, and crystal (1902). Another statue in bronze, *La Saga,* was cast during the last war, and was placed in the Luxembourg gardens. Ringel d'Illzach's principal bronze medallions have an average diameter of 17 to 18 cm. They are listed below, along with some of the museums in which they apppear:

Arago—Sète.
Emile Augier—Avignon, Bordeaux, Lille.
Savorgnan de Brazza—Sète.
Eugène Chevreul—Avignon, Bordeaux, Lille.
Engelbert Dolfuss, homme politique autrichien—Bordeaux.
Jean Dolfuss de Mulhouse—Lille, Toulon.
Alexandre Dumas fils—Avignon, Bordeaux, Lill, Sète.
Alexandre Falguière—Avignon.
Léon Gambetta—Avignon, Bordeaux, Lille, Paris/ Carnavalet, Sète.
François Jules Edmond Got—Avignon, Bordeaux.
Edmond de Goncourt—Bordeaux, Sète.
Charles Gounod—Avignon, Bordeaux, Sète.
Jules Grévy—Bordeaux, Lille, Sète, Toulon.
Eugène Guillaume—Bordeaux, Lille.
Ludovic Halévy—Avignon, Bordeaux, Toulon.
Victor Hugo—Avignon, Lille, Sète.
Eugène Labiche—Bordeaux.
Ferdinand de Lesseps—Bordeaux.
Ferdinande de Lesseps—Bordeaux, Lille, Toiulon.
Léon Lhermitte—Bordeaux, Lille, Toulon.
Louis Pasteur—Avignon, Bordeaux, Lille, Toulon.
Général Francis Pittie—Bordeaux.
Ernest Renan—Avignon, Lille, Toulon.
Rodin—Bordeaux, Lille, Nîmes.
Francisque Sarcey—Avignon.
Auguste Vacquerie—Sète, Toulon.

Other medallions in bronze include *Sarah Bernhardt, Coquelin, Général Galifet, Massent, Maurice Rollinet, Victorien Sardou, Emile Zola,* etc.

RISPAL, JULES LOUIS

Bordeaux, 1872
Piquey, 1910

Rispal exhibited the majority of his busts and medallions in different materials at the Salon from 1893 to 1910. Two statuettes are also of note, the first a plaster entitled *L'Architecture* exhibited at the Salon of 1902, and the second a marble entitled *Fleurs des ruines* shown at the Salon of 1910. A large medallion in bronze, *Paul Bert*, 30.8 x 27.9 cm, belongs to the museum of Bordeaux.

RIU, EUGÈNE

Montpellier, July 15, 1832
Paris, January 24, 1895

An officer in the military destined to finish his career as a general, Riu was also attracted to sculpture. Passing through Rome with his regiment in 1859, he received lessons from Flaguière, who was staying at the Villa Médicis. Riu also worked with Ponscarme and Hiolle, participating at the Salon for the first time in 1869. After a ten-year interruption, he again began to send pieces to the Salon, until 1894. In 1893, after retiring, he was elected to the Parliament from Blois. His sculpted work consists primarily of medallions. One in bronze, *Portrait de Gambetta*, cast by Barbedienne with a diameter of 16 cm, is found at the museum Gambetta in Sèvres. Another, *Le Président Chapu*, 15 cm diam., belongs to the museum of Blois.

RIVIÈRE, JEAN

Toulouse, December, 1853
1924

This sculptor was trained at the school of fine arts in Toulouse. His bronze statuette *Nu allongé*, 27 x 44 cm, numbered I/IV, was sold at the Drouot Hotel on March 22, 1985 (fetching a price of 36,000 F).

RIVIÈRE, THÉODORE

Toulouse, September 1857
Paris, November 9, 1912

RIVIERE

Allegory, mythology, and history (especially the character of Salammbô) dominated this artist's work. An architect as well as a sculptor, Rivière studied under Jouffroy, Falguière and, for five years, Mercié. His irresistible attraction to eastern subjects manifested itself when he visited Tunisia in 1890, and he taught drawing there for some time. It was upon returning to France, in 1894, that one of his statues of *Salammbô* was noticed both by the critics and by the public. Later, he made some symbolic works and portraits of celebrities, before sculpting statues and monuments destined for Indochina. He also investigated the use of materials, gladly mixing marble, ivory, onyx, bronze, silver, and gold (cf. catalog of sale *L'Art en marge des grands mouvements*, Drouot Hotel, March 28, 1979). Among his consignments to the Salon, where eastern subjects dominated, are *Nubien*, a statuette in plaster (1880), two statuettes in plaster entitled *Orientale après la danse du sabre* (1882) and *Baigneuse* (1886), two bronzes entitled *Djinn* (1889) and *L'Eléphant d'Amilcar* (1893), a small group in marble and bronze entitled *Ultimum feriens, épisode du Salammbô de Gustave Flaubert* (1894), a small group in bronze and ivory entitled *Salammbô chez Matho* (1895), two small groups in bronze, marble, and ivory entitled *Le Voeu* (1896) and *Charles VI et Odette* (1897), and a piece made with marble, ivory, silver, gold, and precious stones entitled *Fra Angelico* (1898).

The following editions were made by Susse:

Eve, 20 cm, *Loïe Fuller*, 27 cm, *Pasteur*, 33 cm, *Salammbô chez Matho*, 41 cm, and *La Vigne*, 54 cm. Some works by Théodore Rivière were also cast by P. Bingen, E. Colin, and A. Rudier.

MUSEUMS
Bayonne
Bonaparte premier consul, en pied, 37 cm.
Nancy
La Funèbre Trouvaille, 42 cm.

Théodore Rivière,
Salammbô chez Mathô,
bronze and ivory, 41 cm.

Paris, Decorative Arts
Charles VI et Odette de Champdivers, bronze and ivory, 41.5 cm (1897).
Madame Alice Théodore Rivière, 39 cm (1903).
Paris, Orsay
Brodeuse tunisienne, bronze and ivory, 37 cm (Salon of 1901).
Entrée de Roghi prisonnier à Fès, 63 x 268 cm (A. Rudier).
Gypaète, bird, bronze and granite, 19.5 cm.
Salammbô chez Matho, bronze and ivory, 40 cm (Bingen).
Ultimum feriens (épisode du *Salammbô* by Flaubert), bronze and marble, 77 cm.
Reims
Deux Danseuses, 21 cm.
Nymphe et satyre, 30 cm.

SALES
L'Eléphant fureur de Baal, 24.5 cm (Siot-Decauville), Enghien, December 11, 1983.
Marian, silvered bronze, 15.5 cm, Enghien, December 11, 1983.
Le Médecin, 30 cm, Drouot, May 16, 1984, room 9.
Paon branché, 34 cm, Enghien, March 21, 1982.
Salammbô chez Matho or *Carthage*, gilded bronze, 41 cm (Susse), Christie's New York, March 26, 1983.
Salammbô chez Matho, silvered bronze, 55.5 cm, Munich, November 16, 1984.
Salammbô chez Matho, bronze and ivory, 41 cm, Sotheby Monaco, October 6, 1985.

ROBERT, ÉLIAS

Etampes, June 6, 1821
Paris, April 29, 1874

A student of David d'Angers and of Pradier, Robert produced statues and monumental groups such as *La Justice*, a bronze of 2.2 meters in height for the Saint-Michel fountain, *Le Drame*, a 2.5 meter statue in stone for the theater of Châtelet, and *Geoffroy Saint-Hilaire*, a statue for the city of Etampes. He made sculptures for the Louvre, the Opera and other Parisian monuments, as well as a number of caryatids for the Philadelphia Academy of Music. His most colossal monument (27 m) is a statue of the emperor *Pedro IV* in Lisbon, with the sovereign in gilded bronze., and some figures in marble representing *Prudence, Force, Justice* and *Tempérance*. Elias Robert also made a number of busts and figures such as *L'Enfant-dieu*, a statue in marble (Salon of 1847), the medallion in bronze of *Madame Delafontaine*, 45 cm diameter, for her tomb at the Montparnasse cemetery, *La Fortune*, a 2 meter statue in bronze (Salon of 1857), a bust in bronze of the *Docteur Vigla*, 60 cm, at the Montparnasse cemetery, etc. *L'Enfant-dieu* or *Enfant assis* was cast in bronze by A. D. Delafontaine, 24 cm. A number of plasters by this artist were noted at the museum of Etampes.

SALES
Buste de femme, 23 cm, Drouot, October 28, 1985, room 15.
L'Innocence, 57 cm, Drouot, January 14, 1987, room 1.
Mercure assis, 41 cm (Susse), Christie's New York, May 17, 1983.

ROBERT, MARC

March 26, 1875—?

A student of Falguière and of Mercié, Marc Robert stopped appearing at the Société des Artistes Français in 1935. The Thiébaut house cast his work

Les Vendanges, a bronze of 68 cm in height. Another bronze, *Gladiateur et lion*, 51 cm, ws sold by Christie's in Oklahoma on September 24, 1981.

ROBINET, PIERRE ALFRED

Paris, 1814
Paris, April 8, 1878

A student of Pradier, Ramey, and David d'Angers, Robinet exhibited at the Salon from 1835 to 1877, showing primarily busts of contemporaries and statues. He also worked for the Louvre, the churches of Saint-Roch and Saint-Jacques-du-Haut-Pas, and for the cathedral of Senlis. He sojourned in Jersey from 1873 to 1876, and received a commission for a monument to be raised on the island. He sent a statue entitled *Le Génie du commerce*, designed for this monument, to the Salon of 1877.

MUSEUMS
Amiens
Le Docteur Dubois d'Amiens, bust modeled after a plaster from the Salon of 1853, 87 cm.
Paris, Carnavalet
Delphine Gay, dame de Girardin, statuette, 42 cm (1856).
Reims
Marigny de Pigny, medallion, 10.8 cm diam.

ROCHE, FERNAND MASSIGNON, ALSO CALLED PIERRE

Paris, 1855
Paris, January 18, 1922

This artist, a sculptor, medal-engraver, and ceramicist, was a student of Dalou and of Rodin. Known for portraying the strength and power of vigorous athletes, he also addressed the turn-of-the-century charm of Loïe Fuller. His best-known accomplishments are *L'Effort*, a group in lead and sandstone, 170 cm, from the Luxembourg gardens, the *Avril* in bronze from the Galliera gardens, and three terra cotta figures ornamenting the porch of the church Saint-Jean-de-Montmartre. At the Salon de la Société Nationale des Beaux-Arts, he showed many projects of fountains, *La Loïe Fuller* in marble, a lead relief entitled *La Femme de Loth* (1899), a statue in bronze entitled *Victorieuse* (1910), and two sketches in plaster, *L'Envolée* and *Sirène* (1912).

MUSEUMS
Paris, Decorative Arts
La Loïe Fuller dansant, 54.5 cm (1897).
Paris, Orsay
La Fée Morgane, bronze and lead, 83 cm (1904).

ROCHET, LOUIS

Paris, August 24, 1813
Paris, January 21, 1878

Louis Rochet, a student of David d'Angers, earned recognition from a bronze group he made in collaboration with his brother Charles, *Charlemagne et ses preux* from the square of Notre-Dame in Paris. He is also the author of many public statues and mouments, such as the bronze *Bonaparte à l'école de Brienne*, inaugurated in 1855 in Paris, the statues of *Notre-Dame de Savoie* near Chabéry, and *Guillaume-le-Conquérant* for Falaise. Rochet went to Rio de Janeiro in 1856, and made for that city a bronze equestrian statue of *Don Pedro 1er*, the founder of independent Brazil.

Louis Rochet's work *Bonaparte à Brienne* was exhibited in plaster at the Salon of 1853, and in marble at the Exposition Universelle of 1855. In addition to the bronze of Brienne, a replica in silvered bronze was presented to the Salon in 1859 and to the Exposition in 1900, and a casting of it was made in galvanoplasty. A copy in marble was made of it by Charles Rochet in 1880, and some reductions in bronze would be cast by Susse in three dimensions, 78, 43 and 27 cm.

In 1870, Louis Rochet sent to the Salon a group in gilded and silvered bronze entitled *Cassandre poursuivi par Ajax;* in 1874 he sent the 75 cm plaster model of *François 1er équestre;* and finally, in 1876, he sent another group in bronze, entitled *Mercure et Bacchus.* Besides his activity as a sculptor, Rochet was also interested in the languages of the Far East, so much so that he published the *Manuel de la langue chinoise* in 1846, and *Sentences, maximes et proverbes mandchous et mongols* in 1875.

RODIN, AUGUSTE

Paris, November 12, 1840
Meudon, November 17, 1917

A. Rodin

One would like to avoid comparisons between the most highly regarded artists whose genius would inevitably render them far superior to the rest. Thus it is with Rodin. Few today could dispute that he is the best of all late nineteenth century sculptors, or even one of the best of all time. His works have vigor, dynamism, and sensuality; their characteristically impressionistic rendering of nuances and strength today receives unanimous approval .

However, there are few artists who have faced such fierce adversaries, inspired such polemics, or incurred so much slander and injury during their lifetimes as Rodin; likewise, few artists have known such glory. Rodin's talent was so powerful and his art so original that he was not understood by the

Auguste Rodin,
Le Lion qui pleure,
28 x 33 cm.

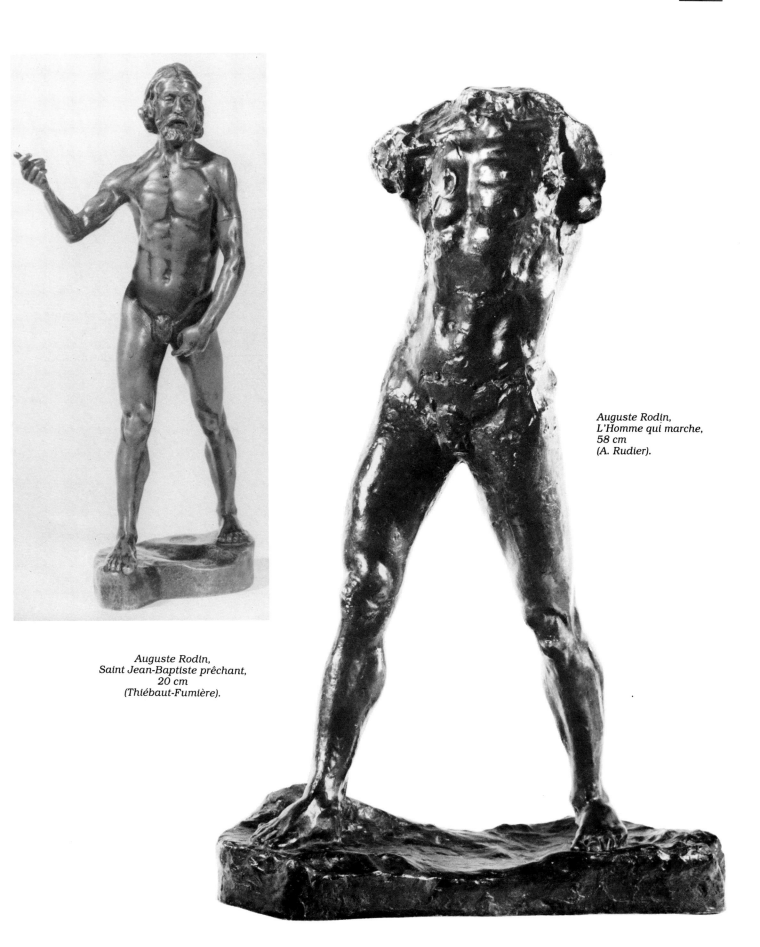

*Auguste Rodin,
Saint Jean-Baptiste prêchant,
20 cm
(Thiébaut-Fumière).*

*Auguste Rodin,
L'Homme qui marche,
58 cm
(A. Rudier).*

Auguste Rodin,
L'Eternel Printemps,
64 cm
(A. Rudier).

"mandarins" of the art world—the representatives of official doctrine, the members of the Institut who were steeped in the sacrosanct rules of Academicism. They refused him admittance to the Ecole des Beaux-Arts three times and waged many press campaigns against him, but nonetheless failed to deprive France of the admirable museum which now carries his name. His talent was so powerful, and his art so original, that after a certain time he overturned all of the obstacles, bursting forth onto the international scene and attracting collectors from all over the world to his studio.

The son of a minor civil servant who worked at police headquarters, Auguste Rodin was born on the Rue de l'Arbalète in Paris. From his earliest youth, he displayed a strong attraction for drawing—but none for his studies, which began at his neighborhood elementary school and continued at a boarding school directed by his uncle in Beauvais. At seventeen, Rodin's parents decided to enroll him into the Petite Ecole, where he received some lessons from Carpeaux. Rodin drew, painted, and modeled clay with passion, frequenting the Louvre and the Muséum (where he met the son of Barye and, on another occassion, the famous animal sculptor himself). Rodin also worked in the open air, in the market, and in the street.

After his triple failure to gain admittance to the Ecole des Beaux-Arts, according to Bernard Champigneulle, the eighteen-year-old Rodin had to

Auguste Rodin,
Jean d'Aire nu,
103 cm
(A. Rudier).

*Auguste Rodin,
Torse de femme,
9.5 cm.*

*Auguste Rodin,
Jean d'Aire,
46 cm
(L. Persinka).*

*Auguste Rodin,
La Métamorphose
d'Ovide,
33 cm.*

look for employment; he would remain in these straits for nearly twenty years. He executed some obscure works with a number of ornamentalists, jewelry makers, and sculptors. In 1862, the death of his adored sister Maria provoked a spiritual crisis, and Rodin entered the Fathers of the Saint-Sacrement as a novice. At this time, he sculpted the bust of father Pierre-Julien Eynard, his spiritual director. It was his second work, the first being the bust of his father, Jean-Baptiste Rodin, executed two years earlier. Then, realizing that he lacked a religious vocation, Rodin resumed his tasks as a craftsman.

THE FIRST WORKS

A freezing cold studio, remodeled in an old stable in the Gobelins quarter, saw the birth of the plaster mask of *L'Homme au nez cassé;* Rodin sent it to the Salon in 1864, only to be refused by the jury. The piece was finally admitted to the Salon in 1875, this time as a marble, under the title *Portrait de M.B.* It was really just a portrait of Bibi, an old man of the quarter who served as a model for artists. That same year, still in the Gobelins quarter, Rodin prepared himself to to enter the studio of the sculptor Carrier-Belleuse, for whom he would work anonymously for six years. During this time in the quarter, the artist fell in love with a small dressmaker, Rose Beuret, who became his lifetime companion. Two years later, she gave him a son whom he did not acknowledge, and who carried only his first name. It was only eighteen days before her death, in 1917, that Rose Beuret would become Mme Rodin.

During the war of 1870-1871, Rodin, who had been invalided out of military service, was called to Brussels by Carrier-Belleuse. He stayed there until he made a trip to Florence and Rome in 1875, during which he was profoundly impressed by Michelangelo, whose influence can be seen on a large number of Rodin's works.

In the capital of the youthful country of Belgium, as well as in Anvers, Rodin worked with a sculptor friend, Joseph Van Rasbourg, and executed portraits, furnished models for the Societé des Bronzes, and finally finished a statue in plaster, after eighteen years of labor. This was the first of a long series of works which established Rodin's renown, at the price of some hard battles. The statue was originally called *Le Vaincu,* and then *L'Homme qui s'éveille à la nature;* it would eventually go by the title *L'Age d'airain.*

L'Age d'airain was Rodin's first important work, and also inspired the first campaign of disparagment. First exhibited in 1877 to the Brussels artistic community, cites Ionel Jianou, its extraordinary realism was so surprising that the newspaper *L'Etoile belge* asked if it had been molded directly from a living model. Accused of such gimmickry, Rodin became embittered, all the more so because the same insinuations were taken up when *L'Age d'airain* was exhibited at the Salon of Paris that same year. Paul Dubois took up Rodin's defense with a letter also signed by Chapu, Falguière, Carrier-Belleuse, and some other well-known and respected artists, assuring that *L'Age d'airain* was certainly an original work, "created by a young sculptor with a great future." Cast in bronze, *L'Age d'airain* would finally be purchased by the State in 1880.

Auguste Rodin,
Andrieu d'Andrès, 46 cm
(A. Rudier).

A.Rodin

Auguste Rodin,
Jean de Fienne,
46 cm
(A. Rudier).

Auguste Rodin,
Pierre de Wissant,
46 cm
(A. Rudier).

Auguste Rodin,
Torse d'homme,
25 cm.

Auguste Rodin,
Eustache de Saint-Pierre,
46 cm
(A. Rudier).

It was also in 1877 that Rodin undertook a tour of France which would leave him with unforgettable memories. He returned dazzled by the vision of cathedrals, which he later visited frequently. He devoted a book to them, published in 1914.

THE GATES OF HELL

It is impossible to enumerate all the works which followed in succession during Rodin's forty years of truly intensive production. The best that can be done is to mention the most important works, or those numerous ones which inspired some incident or polemics.

In 1878, Rodin participated in the competition for a monument to the Republic for the traffic circle of the Défense in Courbevoie; Barrias won the competition, but Rodin's project, entitled *L'Appel aux armes*, was not even kept by the jury. The following year, Rodin was again forced to take a job, this time with the Sèvres factory, to which he furnished some figurine models. Nontheless, he exhibited a bust of his *Saint Jean-Baptiste* at the Salon; this, notes Georges Grappe in his 1944 catalog from the Rodin Museum, permitted him to obtain his first award in France, a third-place medal awarded, apparently, only at arm's length.

The era of great commissions and glory finally started in 1880, though neither the difficulties nor the hostility of Rodin's unshakable opponents ceased. First, at the command of the Under-Secretary of State at the Beaux-Arts, Rodin started a gigantic work inspired by Dante, entitled *La Porte de l'Enfer*, or "The Gates of Hell." It was intended for a museum of decorative arts to be constructed on the bank of the Seine, at the site of the Cour des Comptes, which was burned down at the time of the Commune. A studio was allotted to Rodin in a marble warehouse on the Rue de l'Université. However, it was soon decided that the museum of decorative arts would be installed in the pavillion of the Marsan at the Louvre instead, rendering Rodin's commission futile. The sculptor nevertheless continued to work on it until his death. The inital plans were profoundly modified. The work ceased to be limited to the specifications of the gate. It was, wrote Ionel Jianou, "a world in itself" which linked no fewer than 186 figures, some of which were extracted from their context to become some of Rodin's most famous sculptures: *Le Baiser, Le Penseur, Fugit Amor, Le Fils prodigue, La Vieille Heaulmière, L'Eternelle Idole, Adam, Eve, La Danaïde, Les Trois Ombres*, etc. They were presented to the public, sometimes in different dimensions, at the occasion of several salons and exhibitions. The central figure of the tympanum from the *Porte de l'Enfer, Le Penseur*, in bronze of small format, was exhibited in 1888 in Copenhagen, where it received almost no notice. Re-cast in bronze, but this time in the large size of 2 meters, the piece was placed in 1906 in front of the Panthéon before being relocated to the garden of the Rodin Museum in 1922. As for *Baiser*, presented at the Universal Exposition of Chicago in 1893, it had to be enclosed in a special room in order not to shock the Puritans.

THE BOURGEOIS OF CALAIS

The notoriety of Rodin spread at the same time as his worldly connections did. He made the acquaintance of politicians, writers, and artists. When Rodin

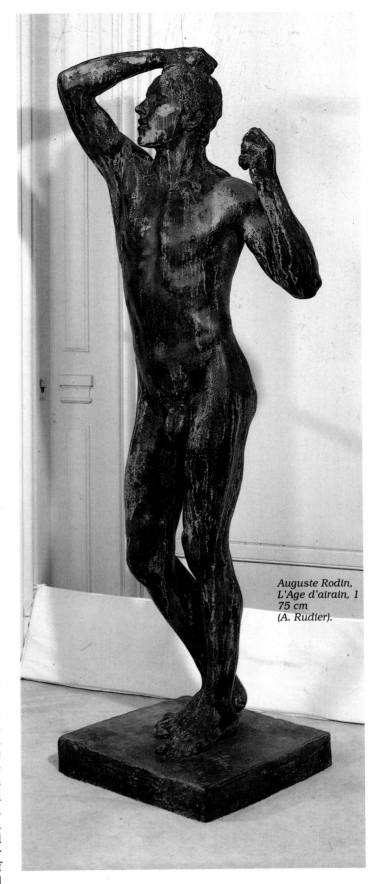

Auguste Rodin, L'Age d'airain, 1 75 cm (A. Rudier).

travelled to England in 1881, his friend Alphonse Legros, the painter, introduced him to London society, just as he had introduced Dalou ten years earlier. Rodin's activity became such that he rented a new studio at 117 Rue de Vaugirard, though he continued to work in the studio on the Rue de l'Université as well. It was there that the talented Camille Claudel came as a practitioner in 1885; she would become his model and, for a time, his companion.

Auguste Rodin's second great undertaking, the group *Bourgeois de Calais* on the reverse of the *Porte de l'Enfer,* was finished and put in place. The city council had originally envisioned commemorating the heroic act of its citizens with a statue of a single one of them, Eustache de Sinat-Pierre. Rodin proposed in 1884 to make a group of six for the same price. He obtained the commission (though not easily) and multiplied the studies of heads, torsos, hands, and feet of each of the people, first nude and then dressed. Finished in plaster in 1886, the group was exhibited three years later at the Georges Petit Gallery, where it received very mixed reviews. In 1895 the work in bronze was inaugurated in Calais, in a presentation conforming little with the wishes of the sculptor (his wishes have been respected in the present-day presentation; the piece is without a pedestal).

Like many of the master's works, *Monument à Victor Hugo*, commissioned in 1889 for the interior of the Panthéon, suffered through a number of shifts of fortune. It too required multiple studies and projects, concluding with a group in which the famous poet is seated, surrounded by muses, though the commission had specified that he be standing. Its nudity, moreover, was severely criticized. In 1890 the director of the Beaux-Arts commissioned a second *Victor Hugo,* again for the Panthéon, and this time standing, but this work was never completed. The original sculpture was modified by Rodin, who made it in marble, without the muses. It was accepted despite all its difficulties, but for the Luxembourg gardens rather than the Panthéon. Because the Luxembourg was already crowded with statues, however, in 1909 it was placed in the Jardin du Palais Royal, before being transfered to the Rodin Museum in 1935. In a final twist, Georges Rudier cast a bronze in 1964, modeled from the original plaster (with the muses), in order to be erected at the intersection of the Avenue Victor-Hugo and the Avenue Henri-Martin in Paris.

THE BALZAC AFFAIR

In 1891, a year after founding the Société Nationale des Beaux-Arts with Dalou and the painter Meissonier, Rodin received a commission from the Société des Gens de Lettres ("Society of Men of Letters") for a statue of Balzac. This commission was destined to raise a hurricane with which the preceding tempests could not even compare. It is true that Rodin, already immersed in the troubles of his *Porte de l'Enfer* and *Victor Hugo*, hardly facilitated matters, completely unconcerned that the society had to give him an extension of eighteen months to present his project. As always, out of careful perfectionism and honesty, he broadened his studies; he made sketches and models, one after the other. Time passed, and the intrigue grew. The Société des Gens de Lettres was divided into two groups—the sculptor's

Auguste Rodin,
Le Penseur,
7.5 cm
(A. Rudier).

Auguste Rodin,
L'Athlète américain,
43 cm
(A. Rudier).

Auguste Rodin,
Buste de Balzac,
30 cm
(Georges Rudier).

Auguste Rodin,
Balzac nu,
study,
legs spread by
a support,
75 cm.

Auguste Rodin,
Tête de Balzac,
18 cm.

Auguste Rodin,
Le Baiser,
61 cm
(Barbedienne).

advocates and the sculptor's adversaries. The melee went public in 1898, when the project in plaster was finally presented at the Salon de la Société Nationale des Beaux-Arts.

"As there was a Dreyfus affair," wrote Bernard Chamigneulle, "...there was a Rodin affair." Rodin's massive silhouette of Balzac, clothed in his legendary chamber robe, astonished some and outraged others. Campaigns of hate and injury broke out: "An impudent act by some master of monkey business...The Michael-Angelo of the goiter...A scandulous lump for the one who signed it and shameful for French art...A mistake by a man of genius.." "One has the right to be surprised," wrote *Illustration* for its part, "that the artist took close to three years to look for the address of Balzac's tailor. The author of the *Comédie humaine* then lived in a sack?" This aspect of the work provoked great agita-tion, which Ionel Jianou summed up perfectly in his work on Rodin: "Those who searched in the statue of Balzac for the faithful description of anatomy or face according to the classical rules had reason to be disappointed. Their mistake was in not seeing that this form, which was sufficient in and of itself, embodied the genius of Balzac in a different, more expressive way."

With all that happened, the worn-out sculptor withdrew his work from the Salon and decided to keep it himself, despite the offers to buy it from many of his admirers. During this time, the Société des Gens de Lettres commissioned Falguière to execute another statue of Balzac. This new, very discreet and academic statue was unveiled on the Avenue Friedland in 1902, after the death of its author. Eventually Rodin too died, but more than twenty

Auguste Rodin,
Je suis belle
or L'Enlèvement,
75 cm.

Auguste Rodin,
Baigneuse assise,
also called Zoubaloff,
36 cm.

Auguste Rodin,
La Danaïde,
22 x 41 cm.

years passed before *his* version of Balzac was unveiled, at the intersection of the Boulevard Raspail and the Boulevard Montparnasse in 1939. At long last, Rodin's *Balzac* was cast in bronze, and today it is Rodin who is acclaimed.

GLORY

At the end of the 19th century, Rodin exhibited his works in different cities throughout Europe and the United States. At the time of the Exposition Universelle of Paris in 1900, he obtained the authorization to raise his own pavilion at the Alma plaza, where he exhibited a hundred and seventy sculptures and a large number of drawings and watercolors. His success was indescribable. The scandal of *Balzac* had made Rodin notorious; museums and collectors worldwide sought out his works, bringing him fortune. Today, a Rodin Museum has been established in Philadelphia, and some particularly important pieces of his work are on display at the museum of the Légion of Honnor of San Francisco and at the Museum of Occidental Art in Tokyo.

After renting a house in Bellevue in 1894, Rodin acquired the Villa des Brillant in Meudon two years later, a place eagerly visited by the greats of this world. Rodin undertook diverse works there, and in the garden he remounted a part of the facade of the Château d'Issy, recovered from its demolition. Inside the house, Rodin accumulated all sorts of antique objects, sculpture from different eras, and canvases by contemporaries including Renoir, Van Gogh, Monet, and Carrière.

During the last years of his life, Rodin applied himself increasingly to the study of the human body in all its positions, making countless drawings and sketches in clay. In 1908, he rented a studio on the Rue de Varenne, on the first floor of a magnificent 18th century Biron hotel, which he just barely saved from demolition. Not long after Rodin moved in, the occupants of the hotel (a number of artists) were evicted so that the site could be cleared. It was then that the idea of a Rodin Museum was born, energetically defended by Rodin's friend and admirer Judith Cladel. Rodin supported this idea, and proposed to bequeath his works and his collections to the State—if they would permit him to live out the rest of his life in the hotel on the Rue de Varenne. With this, a number of new press campaigns were released by his adversaries, primarily members of the Intstitut. At the Chambre, a deputy attacked him as "the artist who has dedicated himself to trying to scandalize all the world;" another called him "demented, hallucinated, possessed, convulsive and a mystificator." Reason reasserted itself, and in 1916, even in the midst of a full-blown war, the Chambre des Députés and then the Sénat voted by a large majority to establish the museum. One year later, on November 17, 1917, Rodin died at the Villa des Brillants. He

Some of the great masterpieces which highlighted Rodin's career, as well as a number of his reductions, sketches, fragmentary studies, and projects, were cast in bronze during his lifetime and after his death. Some monumnetal sculptures were the objects not of 'editions' proper but of repeated castings in bronze. The catalog of Rodin's work drawn up by Ionel Jianou in 1967 notes at least eighty-eight known versions of *L'Age d'airain*, 1.75 m, nine proofs of *L'Homme qui marche*, 2.25 m, and a study and ten 2-meter proofs of the *Saint Jean-Baptiste*. The *Porte de l'Enfer*, which measures at least 6.35 m, has been made in four models, the group of the *Bourgeois de Calais*, originally 2.10 m, in nine models, and the statue of *Balzac*, 3 m, in eight.

While it is easy to appreciate the quality of Rodin's bronzes, differences can be noted even among those produced during the artist's lifetime, depending upon the casts and the founders who executed them. Much less is known about the number of proofs made for each subject cast. Again, the notion of limited castings had not yet become the custom. Rodin cast some bronzes in great number, responding to constant demand from a widespread clientele. He did not hesitate to mechanically enlarge or reduce the most sought-after subjects, to isolate and extract characters from certain groups (the *Porte de l'Enfer* and the *Bourgeois de Calais* in particular), or to regroup figures from older works to create new ones with a method called 'marcottage'. He entrusted the completion of the models to his studio specialists and to a number of founders he employed. Moreover, he signed contracts for the edition of several hundred models for some of his works. There is also a tenacious legend with variations according to which he exercised minute control over every detail of the execution of all his bronzes. It can be stated with certainty that it would not have been physically possible to supervise the casting of most of them in person.

This was the case even with the patina. Mme Monique Laurent, curator of the Rodin museum, described the long collaboration—between 1900 and 1915—between Rodin and Jean-François Limet, the artist's favorite patinator. Limet, established in the north in Cayeux, received bronzes sent directly to him from the foundries. In his correspondence, Limet informed Rodin of the quality of the proofs that the sculptor had clearly never seen. Limet himself, shipped the finished pieces to the clientele.

Auguste Rodin,
La Petite Faunesse, 23.5 cm
(Georges Rudier No8, of 12).

was buried in the garden beside his wife, who had preceded him by some months. Close to the tomb was raised the statue of the *Penseur* ("The Thinker").

RODIN AND BRONZE

Rodin practiced cutting stone or marble directly very little. He most often entrusted this work to craftsmen, contenting himself to guide and supervise them. The names of some of these artisans became famous: Jules Desbois, the Schnegg brothers, Fagel, Baffier, Escoula, Haou, Peter and especially Camille Claudel, Antoine Bourdelle, Charles Despiau, and François Pompon. Instead of working in stone or marble, Rodin had a notable preference for bronze, or more precisely, for the clay which was made into casting models, as well as for the plaster which Rodin used as an intermediary stage.

Sometimes, however, Rodin attentively followed the execution and finish of bronzes commissioned by important buyers. Sometimes these buyers even demanded the exclusitivity of the model, in other words a unique casting, or, at least, personalized with several special details.

The archives preserved by the Rodin Museum enumerate, among the suppliers of the sculptor, twenty-eight different founders. Of particular note is the Compagnie des Bronzes from Brussels, with

Auguste Rodin,
Faunesse à genoux,
53 cm
(A. Rudier).

Auguste Rodin,
Polyphème,
25 cm
(Thiébaut frères).

which Rodin contracted for the edition of the busts *Dosia* and *Suzon* while travelling in Belgium in 1875 (these works have been sold in five different dimensions just in the last thirty years). Also noteworthy are Gruet Jr., who worked for Rodin from 1880 to 1883; his eldest son, Adolphe Gruet, who worked from 1891 to 1895; Pierre Bingen, from 1884 to 1889; Griffoul and Lorge, from 1887 to 1894; J.-B. Griffoul, from 1895 to 1898; Léon Persinka, from 1896 to 1901; Furnière and Gavignot, Thiébaut's successors, who cast the *Saint Jean-Baptiste prêchant* and the *Jeunesse triomphante* in four dimensions, in virtue of the contracts established in 1898; Leblanc-Barbedienne, who obtained, also in 1898, a twenty-year contract for the edition in four sizes, by Collas reduction, of the *Baiser* and the *Eternel Printemps*.

Finally, Eugène Rudier started working for Rodin in 1902, continuing to use the seal of his father, Alexis Rudier, who had died in 1897. Thus was born another legend claiming that Alexis Rudier was the principal founder for Rodin. In reality, in the documents preserved by the museum, there is no proof of collaboration between the two men.

All this already represents a respectable number of models on which the founders did not always affixed their seal. It is necessary to also consider some clandestine proofs. It has been said that, at certain times, Rodin payed the foundersbadly. They then compensated for their losses by casting some supplementary proofs—of excellent quality, so it seems—and selling them directly. Moreover, In 1919, one of them, Montagutelli, was implicated in a

1) Auguste Rodin, L'Eternelle Idole, study, 17.5 cm (Rudier No3, casting 1959).

2) Auguste Rodin, Le Succube, 13.5 cm.

3) Auguste Rodin, Petite Vénus, jambes écartées, 21 cm.

4) Auguste Rodin, La Jeunesse triomphante, 48 cm (Thiébaut-Fumière).

process, at the same time for some bronzes cast without authorization and—even more serious—for counterfeiting certain works.

THE RODIN MUSEUM AND THE BRONZES

After Rodin's death, the museum which had served as trustee of the his donation to the state became his heir. Possessing almost all of the 'good hollow' molds and some original plasters, it continued the castings that Rodin himself had initiated. These castings were executed by Eugène Rudier until his death in 1952. Because Eugène Rudier had preserved the seal of his father Alexis, it is impossible to know if any bronze carrying that seal were made before or after Rodin's death. It is also known that Rudier's studio made some castings during World War II for the German forces of the occupation. It is thus that the fourth proof of the *Porte de l'Enfer,* today at the Kunsthaus of Zurich, was commissioned by the sculptor Arno Brecker for the Count of the German government. In short, the nature and the number of Rodin bronzes cast by the museum from its beginnings in 1919 until 1945 remain very unclear, because of the museum's lack of archives .

In 1946, a decision was made to systematically limit the number of castings to twelve proofs. Since the bronzes made during Rodin's lifetime and after his death had not been numbered, however, it is scarcely possible to determine how many proofs of each subject have been cast. It seems that the twelve-cast maximum has not always been respected, during this period, especially as the date of the cast was not set in the bronze but only mentioned on the certificate. Fortunately, starting in 1968, the date and the number of the proof have been engraved in the bronze next to the mark of the founder and the copyright of the museum.

Investigations into some public and private collections have revealed that the best-known works were all produced in these series of twelve, and in even greater numbers. They can no longer be cast into new proofs. On the other hand, the museum still exploits the original unedited plasters—studies, variants, unknown works, and abandoned projects—that had been preserved in the studio of Meudon (where Rodin died in 1917) and which had never been cast in bronze. This time, the number of proofs is rigorously controlled, and each of them, following the decree of March 3, 1981, is numbered from 1/8 to 8/8; four others marks, the Roman numerals I/IV to IV/IV, were reserved for cultural organizations, including the museum itself.

"The Board of Directors of the museum," wrote Mme Monique Laurent, "asked themselves if they had the right to exploit the works which Rodin himself had never distributed. There is, in fact, a letter from the sculptor which directed the decision. In 1916, he had written to Léonce Bénédite, the first curator of the museum: "I would like, as much as is permitted the resources of my right as the artist, for my works which exist only in plaster in Meudon to be made into bronze, in order to give a definitive aspect to the ensemble of my work."

*Auguste Rodin,
Enfants au lézard,
39 cm.*

Many founders work today for the Rodin museum. Among them are Georges Rudier, nephew and successor of Eugène, who replaced the Alexis Rudier seal in 1953 with his own. Another, the foundation Coubertin, has made large pieces including the *Porte de l'Enfer,* cast in 1977 for an American collector. Also employed by the Rodin Museum today is the foundry of Susse and Godard.

Lastly, though the work of Auguste Rodin fell into the public domain in 1982, the unedited plasters from Meudon are protected for nearly fifty years after the year of their discovery; thus, the Rodin Museum still owns the exclusive rights to them.

CASTINGS AND EDITIONS

The catalog of Rodin's works contained in Ionel Jianou and Cécile Goldscheider's 1967 published work have allowed the compilation of an alphabetical list of those Rodin works that were cast in many bronze models. As proved by the frequent appearance at sales and auctions of subjects missing from the aforementioned book, this list is neither exhaustive nor definitive. A number of bronzes were cast during the course of these latter years by the Rodin museum, particularly for American clients. For the works mentioned below, the number orf proofs cast varies widely, and for new castings can still vary widely up to the number of 12, as prescribed by the 1981 law. For this reason, it is sufficient to note the original date of each item, as well as the dimensions of the most current proofs cast; the works marked (*) were made part from the sketches, studies or fragments of the *Porte de l'Enfer*.

Adam (1880), 192 cm.
Adèle, torso (1882), 15 cm.
Alphonse Legros, bust (1881), 29 cm.
L'Age d'airain (1876-1880), 66, 110, 175 cm.
L'Appel aux armes or La Défense (1878), 116 and 235 cm.
L'Athlète américain (1903), 43.5 cm.
Madame Auguste Rodin (1891), 27 cm.

Baigneuse aux sandales (around 1899), 42 cm.
Grande Baigneuse accroupie (around 1886), 19 cm.
Petite Baigneuse accroupie or *Femme au crabe* (around 1886), 20 cm.
Le Baiser (1886), 71 and 86 cm. Between 1898 and 1918, a Barbedienne edition was produced in four dimensions: 49 proofs of 73 cm, 65 proofs of 61 cm, 108 proofs of 38 cm, 93 proofs of 24 cm.
Balzac (1892-1897), 300 cm.
    Diverse studies for the *Balzac* include:
—*Tête*, 17 cm.
—*Tête*, last state, 19 cm.
—*Nu, jambes écartées, bras droit tendu en avant*, 27 and 41 cm.
—*Nu, jambes écartées, support entre les jambes, bras croisés*, 75.
—*Habillé, robe de chambre avec col*, 106 cm.
Baudelaire, head (1898), 20 cm.
Bellone (1878), 80 cm.
Les Bénédictions (1894), 90 cm.
Benoit XV, head (1915), 26 cm.
Les Bourgeois de Calais (1884-1895), 210 cm.

Auguste Rodin,
Frère et soeur, 38.5 cm
(A. Rudier).

    Some fragmentary studies of different personages of this group were cast, in particular:
—*Andrieu d'Andrès*, 46 cm.
—*Eustache de Saint-Pierre*, 46 cm.
—*Eustache de Saint-Pierre*, study of nude, 98 cm.
—*Eustache de Saint-Pierre*, head, 7 cm.
—*Jean d'Aire*, 46 cm.
—*Jean d'Aire vêtu*, 190 cm.
—*Jean d'Aire*, head, 6.5, 14.5 and 26 cm.
—*Jean de Fiennes*, 46 cm.
—*Jean de Fiennes*, head, 8 cm.
—*Pierre de Wissant*, 46 cm.
—*Pierre de Wissant*, nude, without head, 190 cm.
—*Pierre de Wissant*, head, 8, 11 and 33 cm.
—*Pierre de Wiassant*, monumental head, 86.5 cm.

* *Le Désespoir*, figure sitting, left leg raised (1889), 17 cm.
Dosia, bust (1875), cast in five dimensions by the Compagnie des bronzes of Brussels.
* *La Douleur* (1882), 22 and 37 cm.
* *La Douleur* (1887), 19 cm.

Camille Claudel (1884), 27 cm.
* *Cariatide à la pierre* (1881), 44 and 130 cm.
* *Cariatide à l'urne* (1883), 50 and 125 cm.
* *Celle qui fut la belle Heaulmière* (1885), 51 cm.
Cérès, according to Mrs Russel (1896), 22.5 cm.
Couronnement de la maquette de la tour du Travail (1894), 28 and 53 cm.
Le Cri (1898), 26 cm.

L'Enfant au lézard (1881), 39 cm.
* *L'Enfant prodigue* (before 1889), 55 and 140 cm.
L'Esclave aveugle (around 1885), 13 cm.
L'Eternelle Idole (1890), 17.5 and 30 cm.
L'Eternel Printemps (1884), 24, 52 and 65 cm. Between 1898 and 1918, Barbedienne produced an edition in four dimensions: 58 proofs of 64 cm, 33 proofs of 52.5 cm, 83 proofs of 40 cm, 63 proofs of 23 cm.
Eugène Guillaume (1903), 34 cm.
* *Eve* (1881), 70 and 170 cm.

* *Danaïde* (1885), 23 and 35 cm.
Danseur, small head, Nijinsky (1912), 6 cm.
* *Le Désespoir* (1889), 34 cm.

Auguste Rodin,
Le Peintre,
project for the monument
in Bastien-Lepage,
36.5 cm.

Exhortation (1903), 40 cm.
Falguière, bust (1897), 43 cm.
* *Faunesse debout* (1884), 62 cm.
* *Faunesse à genoux* (1884), 55 cm.
* *Petite Faunesse* or *Petite Bretonne* (1882), 16 cm.
* *Femme accroupie* (1882), 32 and 84 cm.
Femme assise, torso (1890), 13 and 51 cm.
Figure volante (1890), 21.5 cm.
La France, after Camille Claudel (1884), 48 cm.
Frère et soeur (1891), 39 cm.
* *Fugit Amor* (before 1887), 45 cm.

Le Génie funéraire, head, for the monument of Puvis of
    Chavannes (1891), 14 cm.
George Wyndman (1903), 50 cm.
George Clemenceau (1911), 48 cm.
Gustave Geffroy, bust (1905), 34 cm.

Gustave Mahler (1909), 34 cm.
Hanako, mask (1908), 16 cm.
Hanako, head, 17 cm.
Hanako, head with chignon, 31 cm.
Henri Rochefort, bust (1884), 57 cm.
Henri Rochefort, large bust (1884), 75 cm.
L'Homme qui marche, study for *Saint Jean-Baptiste* (1877),
    84 and 225 cm.
L'Homme qui marche, torso, 53 cm.
L'Homme au nez cassé, mask (1864), 24 cm.
L'Homme au nez cassé, head, 8.8, 14.5, 19.5, 27 cm.
L'Homme à une oreille (around 1885), 14 cm.
* *L'Homme qui tombe* (1882), 69 cm.
Les Illusions reçues par la terre (1895), 55 cm.
Iris éveillant une nymphe (around 1885), 36 cm.
Iris messagère des dieux, study of female nude without
    head, one leg raised (1890), 20, 46 and 95 cm.
Iris, head (1891), 10 and 60 cm.
Jean-Paul Laurens (1881), 56 cm.

593

* *Je suis belle* or *L'Enlèvement* (1882), 75 cm.
Jeune Fille aux écoutes (1878), 65 cm.
Jeune Fille aux fleurs dans les cheveux (around 1868), 52 cm.
La Jeune Mère (around 1885), 39 cm.
La Jeunesse triomphante (1894), 53 cm; 19 proofs made by Furnière, successor of Thiébaut (contract of 1894).
Jules Dalou, bust (1883), 52 cm.
Le Lion qui pleure (1881), 28 cm.
Main crispée droite (around 1890), 46 cm.
La Main de Dieu (1898), 15, 32, 68 cm.
La Main de Rodin tenant un petit buste, 25 cm.
Marcelin Berthelot, head (1906), 30 cm.

* *La Martyre* (1885), 13, 19, 40 cm.
* *La Méditation* (1885), 78 and 158 cm.
* *La Métamorphose d'Ovide* or *Volupté* or the *Jeune Fille et la mort* (before 1886), 33 cm.
Mignon (1869), 40 cm.
Minerve au casque, after Mrs. Russel (1896), 50 cm.
La Mort d'Adonis, sketch (1889), 28 cm.
Mouvement de danse, different steps (1910-1913), sketches in different dimensions, from 25 to 71 cm.

Océanides (1910), 53 cm.
* *L'Ombre* (1880), 98 and 192 cm.
Orphée (1892), 150 cm.

Auguste Rodin,
La Main de Rodin tenant un torse de femme, 25 cm.

Pallas au casque, after Mrs. Russel (1896), 60 cm.
* *Le Penseur* (1880), 37.5, 69 and 200 cm.
Pierre Julien Eymard, bust (1863), 59 cm.
Pierre Julien Eymard, head, 15 cm.
* *La Pleureuse*, mask for the lintel of the Gates of Hell *(La Porte de l'Enfer)* (1889), 30 cm.
* *Polyphème* (1888), 25 cm.
La Porte de l'Enfer (1880-1917), 635 cm.
Les Premières Funérailles or the *Purgatoire*, sketch (1900), 61 cm.
Puvis de Chavannes, bust (1891), 50 cm.
Pygmalion et Galatée, nude woman standing (1889), 36.5 cm.

Le Rieur, head (1889), 13 cm.
J.-B. Rodin père, bust (1860), 41 cm.
Mrs. Russel, bust (1888), 43 cm.

Saint Jean-Baptiste prêchant (1878), 200 cm.
Saint Jean-Baptiste prêchant, bust, 20 cm; four proofs by Fumière.
Saint Jean-Baptiste prêchant, bust, 50 cm; twelve proofs by Fumière, five proofs by Rudier.
Saint Jean-Baptiste prêchant, bust, 79 cm; five proofs by Fumière.
Saint Jean-Baptiste, head cut off (1887), 3.5, 11 and 20 cm.
Le Sculpteur et sa muse (1895), 67 cm.
Séverine or the *Mulâtresse*, head (1893), 16 cm.
* *Les Sirènes* (before 1888), 26 cm.
Le Succube (1890), 13.5 cm.
Suzon, bust (1875), cast in five dimensions by the Compagnie des bronzes of Brussels.

La Terre (1884), 20 and 46 cm.
* *Torse d'homme* (1882), 28 and 35 cm.
* *Petit Torse debout* (1882), 23 cm.
* *Les Trois Faunesses* (1882), 16 cm.
* *Les Trois Ombres* (1880), 98 and 192 cm.

Victor Hugo, bust (1883), 48 and 56 cm.
Victor Hugo, small bust on a piédouche with fallen branches (around 1885), 38 cm.
Victor Hugo, head (around 1886), 18 cm.
Victor Hugo, large bust (1897), 70 cm.

MUSEUMS
Aix-les-Bains
Baigneuse aux sandales, 42 cm.
Roméo et Juliette (1902), 70 cm.

Auguste Rodin,
Main gauche d'Eustache de Saint-Pierre,
27 cm.

Albi
Balzac, mask, 32 cm.
Angers
Mignon, bust, 53 cm (Rudier).
Belfort
Polyphème, 25 cm (cast by Camille Lefèvre after the plaster given to him by Rodin).
Besançon
L'Eternel Printemps, 64 cm (Griffoul et Lorge, founders).
Victor Hugo, bust, 38.5 cm.
Boulogne-sur-Mer
L'Enfant prodigue, 59 cm.
Pierre de Wissant, 45 cm.
Bourges
Eve, Fugit Amor, Le Minotaure, and *Buste de Georges Hecq.*
Calais
Andrieu d'Andrès, 61 cm (Susse, copyright Rodin Museum 1973).
Eustache de Saint-Pierre nu, 97 cm (G. Rudier, copyright Rodin Museum 1965).
Eustache de Saint-Pierre, second maquette, 68.5 cm (Susse, copyright Rodin Museum 1973).

Eustache de Saint-Pierre, definitive state, 42 cm (Godard, copyright Rodin Museum 1981).
Jacqes de Wissant, second maquette, 68.3 cm, (Susse, copyright Rodin Museum 1973).
Pierre de Wissant, second maquette, 68.7 cm (Susse, copyright Rodin Museum 1973).
Pierre de Wissant nu avec tête et bras, 196 cm (G. Rudier).
Jean d'Aire, second maquette, 68.5 cm (Susse, copyright Rodin Museum 1973).
Jean de Flennes, second maquette, 71.2 cm (Susse, copyright Rodin Museum 1973).
Camille Claudel, head, 24.5 cm (Rudier).
Omer Dewavrin, bust, 25 cm (G. Rudier).
Châlons-sur-Marne
La Beauté, 69 cm.
L'Eveil de l'humanité, 63 cm.
Colmar
Georges Clemenceau, 48 cm.

Dijon
L'Age d'airain, 180 cm (Rudier).
Alphonse Legros, 32 cm (Rudier).
Eugène Guillaume, sculptor, 35 cm.
Tête de femme pleurant, 21 cm.
La Toilette de Vénus.
Douai
L'Enfant prodique, 138 cm.

Guéret
Le Baiser, 61 cm (Barbedienne).
Eve, 74 cm (Rudier).

Lille
Andrieu d'Andrès, 43 cm.
Eustache de Saint-Pierre, 46 cm.
Jean d'Aire, 47 cm.
Jean de Fiennes, 46 cm.
Pierre de Wissant, 45 cm.
Lyon
L'Age d'airain, 175 cm.
Cariatide à l'urne, 170 cm.
Eve, 170 cm.
L'Homme qui marche, 225 cm.
Masque de Madame Rodin.
L'Ombre, 192 cm.
La Petite Ombre.
Victor Hugo, 48 cm.

Montauban
Le Penseur, 69 cm.
Morlaix
Gustave Geffroy, 41 cm (Rudier cast 1927).

Nantes
Dalou, bust, 53 cm.
Jean-Paul Laurens, 58 cm.
Victor Hugo écoutant les sirènes, 69 cm.
Nice
L'Age d'airain.
Victor Hugo, head, 17 cm.

Orléans
L'Ombre, 98 cm.

Paris, Decorative Arts
Femme accroupie soulevée par une vague, plaque, 30 x 26.5 cm (modeled after the bas-relief from the Hotel Fenaille in Neuilly).
Jeune Fille, bust.
Satyre et nymphe, 33 cm.
Paris, Carnavalet
Masque mortuaire de Blanqui, silvered bronze, 26 cm.
Paris, Orsay
L'Age d'airain, 178 cm (Thiébaut).
Alphonse Legros, bust, 41 cm.
Bellone, bust, 77.5 cm (A. Rudier).

Auguste Rodin,
Tête de Rose Beuret, 37 cm
(1880-1882; A. Rudier).

Auguste Rodin,
Tête de femme pleurant, 20.5 cm.

Dalou, bust, 54.5 cm (A. Rudier).
Eugène Guillaume, bust, 49 cm.
Faune et nymphe, 32.6 cm (A. Rudier).
Fugit Amor, 39 cm.
Gustave Geffroy, bust, 43 cm.
Homme couché, study, 8 x 25.5 cm.
L'Homme qui marche, 213 cm (A. Rudier).
Homme au nez cassé, 39 cm.
Jean-Paul Laurens, bust, 58 cm (F. Rudier, Griffoul et Cie
    (and Co.), founders).
Puvis de Chavannes, bust, 51 cm (A. Rudier).
Rochefort, bust, 75 cm (A. Rudier).
Saint Jean-Baptiste, 204 cm (Gruet).
Victor Hugo, bust, 39 cm.
Victor Hugo, heroic bust, 70.6 cm.
Paris, Petit Palais
Alexandre Falguière, bust, 44 cm.
Alphonse Legros, head, 30 cm.
L'Homme qui marche, torso, 53 cm.
Le Succube, 13.5 cm.
Paris, Rodin Museum
        This museum possesses almost all of the sculptor's
works, as much in marble and plaster (in Meudon) as
in bronze. The majority of bronzes were part of the
donation of 1916. Some of them have been cast since.
Paris, Victor Hugo Museum
Victor Hugo, large bust, 70 cm.
Pau
Madame Rodin, head, 26 cm.
Poitiers
L'Homme au nez cassé, 11.7 cm (Rudier).
Narcisse or *Adolescent désespéré*, 30.4 cm.
Riom
La Jeune Mère, 39 cm.
Saint-Etienne
Danaïde, 35 cm.
Strasbourg
Gustave Mahler, head, 32.2 cm.

Auguste Rodin,
La Luxure, 35 cm
(A. Rudier 3/6).

Toulouse
Jean-Paul Laurens, bust, 58 cm.
Tours
Balzac, bust, 32 cm (Rudier).
L'Homme au nez cassé, 12.5 cm.

Some bronzes and other works by Rodin are shown also in a number of museums, in particular in the United States: New York's Metropolitan Museum of Modern Art, Philadelphia's Rodin Museum, and San Francisco's California Palace of the Legion of Honour, as well as in the museums of Baltimore, Boston, Cleveland, Detroit, Washington, etc. The city of Dallas has seven open-air Rodin monuments. Other notable museums showing Rodin's work include those of Algiers, London (the Victoria and Albert Museum and the National Gallery), Manchester, Anvers, Copenhagen (Ny Carlsberg Glyptothèque), Stockholm, Zurich, Prague, Moscow (Pouchkine Museum), Budapest, Montréal, Tokyo (Museum of Occidental Art), etc.

SALES
Adam, 19.2 cm (Susse), Sotheby New York, May 15, 1984.
Adèle, torso, 42.5 cm (G. Rudier), Christie's New York, May 17, 1984.
L'Age d'airain, 66 cm (A. Rudier), Christie's, May 16, 1984; Sotheby, November 13, 1985.
L'Age d'airain, 110 cm (A. Rudier), Chartres, November 24, 1985; Enghien, April 13, 1986 (sold for a million francs).
L'Age d'airain, 175 cm (A. Rudier), Sotheby New York, May 15, 1984 (240,000 dollars).
L'Amour qui passe, 38 cm, Sotheby London, December 4, 1985.
Baigneuse Zoubaloff, 36.5 cm (A. Rudier), Sotheby New York, November 14, 1985.

Auguste Rodin,
Tête de l'homme au nez cassé, 30 cm.

597

Baigneuse Zoubaloff, head, 9.3 cm (A. Rudier), Christie's New York, November 20, 1986.

Le Baiser, 24 cm (Barbedienne), Rambouillet, March 9, 1986; Drouot, March 26, 1986, room 9; Christie's New York, May 15, 1986; Sotheby London, June 25, 1986.

Le Baiser, 38 cm (Barbedienne), Drouot, September 27, 1986; Versailles, June 11, 1986; Rambouillet, November 30, 1986 (sold for 301,000 F); Sotheby London, December 3, 1986.

Le Baiser, 61 cm (Barbedienne), Dijon, April 27, 1986; Sotheby London, May 25, 1986; Enghien, November 23, 1986.

Le Baiser, 24 cm (Rudier), Drouot, March 7, 1985, room 1; Drouot, April 14, 1986, rooms 5 and 6.

Le Baiser, 72 cm (inscribed "First proof"), Sotheby London, December 3, 1986.

Le Baiser, 85 cm (G. Rudier, Rodin Museum 1970), Sotheby New York, May 15, 1984.

Balzac, study, 106 cm (G. Rudier No 10/Rodin Museum 1981), Christie's New York, May 15, 1985.

Balzac, study, 106 cm (G. Rudier No 6/Rodin Museum 1974), Sotheby New York, May 14, 1986.

Balzac, bust, 30 cm (G. Rudier/Rodin Museum 1960), Versailles, December 8, 1985.

Balzac, head, 18 cm (A. Rudier), Drouot, November 19, 1986, room 12; Saint-Maur, December 7, 1986.

Les Bénédictions, 90 cm (G. Rudier/Rodin Museum 1955), Sotheby New York, May 15, 1985.

Benoît XV, head, 26 cm, Sotheby London, June 25, 1985.

Bibi-la-purée, head, Lyon, December 1, 1985.

Les Bourgeois de Calais, maquette, 33 cm (Godard No 1/Rodin Museum), Sotheby New York, May 14, 1986.

Andrieu d'Andrès, 46 cm (A. Rudier), Drouot, December 8, 1983, rooms 5 and 6; Sotheby London, June 26, 1984.

Eustache de Saint-Pierre, 46 cm (A. Rudier), Saint-Dié, March 23, 1986; Le Touquet, May 18, 1986.

Eustache de Saint-Pierre, head, 33 cm, Drouot, June 18, 1985, rooms 5 and 6.

Eustache de Saint-Pierre, hand, 27 cm, Calais, June 23, 1985.

Jean d'Aire nu, 103 cm (A. Rudier), Enghien, June 14, 1981.

Jean d'Aire, 46 cm (A. Rudier/Rodin Museum around 1930), Drouot, May 21, 1984, rooms 5 and 6.

Jean d'Aire, 46 cm (L. Persinka), Montpellier, May 25, 1985; Enghien, April 13, 1986.

Jean d'Aire, colossal head, 60 cm (G. Rudier No 7/Rodin Museum 1981), Sotheby New York, November 19, 1986.

Jean de Fiennes, 46 cm (A. Rudier), Saint-Brieuc, December 9, 1984; Limoges, October 19, 1986.

Pierre de Wissant, 46 cm (A. Rudier), Drouot, June 10, 1985, room 10; Le Touquet, May 18, 1986; Limoges, October 19, 1986.

Pierre de Wissant, head, 33 cm, Christie's London, December 2, 1985.

Cariatide à la pierre, 44 cm (A. Rudier), Sotheby New York, May 15, 1985.

La Cathédrale, 25 cm (G. Rudier, 5/12), Sotheby London, December 3, 1985.

La Chutte d'Icare, 32 cm (A. Rudier), Christie's New York, November 14, 1984.

Le Cri, 26 cm (G. Rudier/Rodin Museum), Drouot, April 16, 1986.

Danaïde, 22 cm (A. Rudier 3/8), Clermont-Ferrand, April 24, 1986.

Danaïde, 33 cm, San Francisco, February 28, 1985; Rambouillet, November 30, 1986.

Le Désespoir, 28 cm (A. Rudier), Drouot, March 25, 1984, rooms 5 and 6.

Dosia, bust, 38 cm (Company of bronzes of Brussels (Compagnie des bronzes)), Sotheby New York, May 14, 1986.

La Douleur, head, 24 cm (G. Rudier/Rodin museum 1956), Sotheby New York, November 19, 1986.

L'Eternelle Idole, 17.5 cm (Rudier No 3, 1959), Drouot, February 9, 1987, room 1.

L'Eternel Printemps, 23 cm (Barbedienne), Drouot, April 29, 1985; Sotheby London, May 15, 1985; Sotheby New York, May 14, 1986; Christie's New York, November 20, 1986.

L'Eternel Printemps, 40 cm (Barbedienne), Drouot, March 25, 1984, rooms 5 and 6; Lyon, November 19, 1985; Christie's New York, October 9, 1986.

L'Eternel Printemps, 52.5 cm (Barbedienne), Christie's New York, May 16, 1985.

L'Eternel Printemps, 64 cm (Barbedienne), Christie's London, December 2, 1985; Sotheby London, December 4, 1985; Enghien, November 23, 1986 (sold for 500,000 F).

L'Eternel Printemps, 65 cm (A. Rudier), Drouot, , June 26, 1986, rooms 5 and 6 (sold for 825,000 F).

L'Eternel Printemps, 67.5 cm (carries the seal of the founders Méroniez-Radice), Drouot, June 11, 1986, room 9.

L'Eternel Printemps, 74.5 cm, Dijon, April 27, 1986.

Eugène Guillaume, bust, 34 cm (A. Rudier), Sotheby New York, October 18, 1984.

Faunesse à genoux, 53 cm (A. Rudier), Sotheby London, June 26, 1985; Drouot, April 9, 1987, rooms 5 and 6.

Femme accroupie, 32 cm (A. Rudier), Sotheby London, December 4, 1984.

Femme nue assise, 50 cm (G. Rudier No 12/Rodin museum 1959), Christie's New York, November 13, 1985.

Femme pleurant, head, 20.5 cm, Rambouillet, November 30, 1986.

Femme penchée en avant, 21 cm, Drouot, June 17, 1985, rooms 5 and 6.

Fugit Amor, 48 cm (G. Rudier/Rodin Museum), Christie's New York, November 13, 1985.

Frère et soeur, 38.5 cm (A. Rudier), Drouot, May 21, 1984; Sotheby London, June 25, 1986.

La Fuite, 33.5 cm (E. Godard No 11/Rodin Museum 1972), Sotheby London, October 22, 1986.

Galatée, study, 28 cm (E. Godard 8/12/Rodin Museum 1981), Sotheby New York, October 18, 1985.

Le Génie funéraire, head, 14 cm (Rodin Museum 1960), Sotheby New York, October 18, 1985.

Hanako, head, 31 cm (G. Rudier/Rodin Museum 1962), Sotehby New York, November 19, 1986.

L'Homme qui marche, 84 cm (A. Rudier/Rodin museum), Drouot, June 23, 1986, rooms 5 and 6.

L'Homme qui marche, torso (Coubertin No 11/Rodin Museum 1980), Sotheby New York, May 15, 1986.

L'Homme au nez cassé, head, 8.5 cm, Berne, June 20, 1985; Christie's New York, May 15, 1986.

L'Homme au nez cassé, head, 25 cm (Rudier), Sotheby London, June 25, 1986; Saint-Dié, December 14, 1986.

Iris, study without head, 19.5 cm (A. Rudier), Drouot, March 13, 1985, room 9.

Iris messagère des dieux, small study, 15 cm (E. Godard No 9/Rodin Museum 1971), Sotheby New York, November 19, 1986.

Jeanne d'Arc nue, 205 cm (Coubertin 6/8/Rodin Museum 1982), Sotheby New York, May 14, 1985 (220,000 dollars).

Jeune Fille confiant son secret à Isis or *Le Bon Génie,* 23 cm, Drouot, June 12, 1985, room 9.

Jeune Fille confiant son secret à Isis, study, 12 cm (A. Rudier), Sotheby New York, June 7, 1984.

Jeune Fille aux fleurs dans les cheveux, 49 cm (Coubertin/Rodin Museum 1980), Sotheby New York, May 15, 1985.

La Jeune Mère, 37 cm, Sotheby New York, November 15, 1984.

La Jeunesse triomphante, 48 cm (Thiébaut-Furnière), Fécamp, November 30, 1986 (sold for 200,000 F).

Le Lion qui pleure, 28 cm, Drouot, September 27, 1984, room 11.

Main, 13.5 cm (E. Godard No 12/Rodin Museum 1977), Sotheby London, Ocotber 22, 1986.

Main gauche, deux doigts repliés, 18 cm (A. Rudier), Drouot, March 15, 1985, rooms 5 and 6.

Main gauche, 31 cm, Versailles, June 11, 1986.

Main gauche sur phalanges, 28 cm, Brussels, September 15, 1986.

Main gauche ouverte, 34.5 cm, Brussels, September 15, 1986.

Grande Main gauche, 33.5 cm (A. Rudier), Christie's New York, November 20, 1986.

Grande Main gauche, 38 cm (Barbedienne), Sotheby London, December 3, 1986.

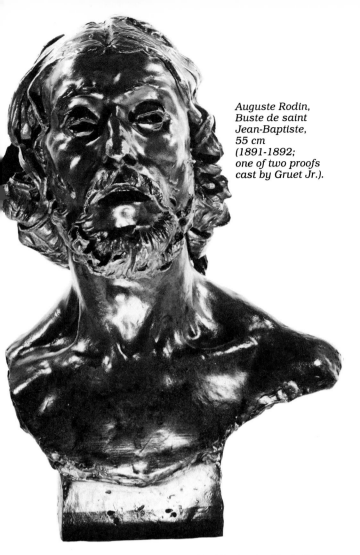

*Auguste Rodin,
Buste de saint
Jean-Baptiste,
55 cm
(1891-1892;
one of two proofs
cast by Gruet Jr.).*

Grande Main droite, 32 cm (A. Rudier), Christie's New York, November 20, 1986.
La Main de Dieu, 16.5 cm, L'Isle-Adam, April 28, 1985.
La Méditation, sans bras, 146 cm (Coubertin 4/8), Sotheby New York, May 15, 1984.
Les Métamorphoses d'Ovide, 33 cm, Christie's New York, November 20, 1986.
Mouvement de danse, 33 cm (A. Rudier), Drouot, June 18, 1985, rooms 5 and 6.
L'Ombre No 1, 31.5 cm (A. Rudier), Sotheby London, June 27, 1984.
Le Penseur, 37.5 cm (A. Rudier), Paris Crédit Municipal, June 12, 1986; Enghien, June 19, 1986; Brussels, September 15, 1986; Limoges, October 19, 1986; Sotheby London, December 2, 1986.
Le Penseur, 69 cm (A. Rudier), Sotheby London, March 25, 1986; Sotheby New York, November 18, 1986.
Le Penseur, 74 cm (G. Rudier, Rodin Museum 1955, Sotheby New York, May 14, 1985.
Roméo et Juliette, 69.2 cm (A. Rudier), Sotheby New York, November 19, 1986.
Rose Beuret, mask, 26 cm, Drouot, March 19, 1984.
Saint Jean-Baptiste, 50 cm (Thiébaut-Fumière), Christie's New York, February 16, 1984.
Saint Jean-Baptiste, bust, 55 cm (Gruet the younger), Enghien, March 24, 1984.
Les Sirènes, 43.8 cm (L. Persinka), Christie's New York, November 20, 1986.
Suzon, 26 cm (Compagnie des Bronzes of Brussels), Lokeren, April 20, 1985.
Suzon, 33 cm (Compagnie des Bronzes of Brussels), Christie's London, March 26, 1985.
Suzon, 40 cm (Compagnie des Bronzes of Brussels), Lokeren, February 16, 1985.
Tête de femme pleurant, 20.5 cm, Rambouillet, November 30, 1986.
Torse d'homme, 14 cm (A. Rudier), Drouot, December 5, 1985, room 1.
Torse d'homme, 25.5 cm, Sotheby London, June 25, 1986.
Torse de jeune femme, 89 cm (A. Rudier), Christie's New York, May 14, 1986.

Triton et Néréide sur un dauphin (G. Rudier No2/Rodin Museum 1963), Sotehby London, June 25, 1986.
Les Trois Faunesses, 23.5 cm (G. Rudier), Sotheby London, October 1985.
Vénus bras levés, 49.5 cm (G. Rudier 12/12, Rodin Museum 1962), Drouot, March 18, 1986, rooms 1 and 7.
Petite Vénus jambes écartées, 21 cm, Calais, November 10, 1985.
Victor Hugo et les muses, 36.9 cm (L. Persinka), Christie's New York, May 16, 1985.

ROGER, FRANÇOIS
Rambervillers (Vosges), February 14, 1843
August 19, 1898

Roger's consignments to the Salon, which fell between 1873 and 1889, include some busts and statues. One of these, *Le Bilboquet*, was exhibited in plaster in 1880, and again, in bronze, in 1886. Bronze reductions of this work were cast in many dimensions.

ROGER-BLOCHE, PAUL
Paris, March 31, 1865
1943

This artist, who studied under the direction of Cavelier and of Barrias, consigned a rather large number of bronzes to the Salon. These include *L'Enfant* and *Jeune Fille d'Assise*, a group and a statuette (1899), *Léon Lhermitte*, a statuette (1900), *Le Froid*, a group of 185 cm height for the city of Manosque, *La Faim* and *Apprenti* (1905), *Le Départ* (1906), *Souvenir, La Camomille, Boîte au lait, L'Anniversaire* (1907), *Flirt*, and *Bouquet de roses* (1908). Also of note is a statuette in marble, *Rêve de gloire* (1894) and some plasters: *Dans les nuages* (1896), *L'Accident* (1909), and *Le Sommeil* (1914).

Works cast by Susse include *L'Enfant*, 39 and 29 cm, *Le Froid*, 34 and 16 cm, and *Dans les nuages*, 79 cm. Also notable, by an unspecified founder, is *Bouquet d'anniversaire*, 36 cm.

MUSEUMS
Calais
La Faim, 150 cm (F. Gruet Jr., founder, 1904).
Paris, Orsay
Jeune Fille d'Assise, 56 cm (Salon of 1899).
Léon Lermitte, 39 cm (Salon of 1900).
Paris, Petit Palais
La Faim, 105 x 125 cm (1904).
Reims
Jeune Fille d'Assise, 56 cm.
Saint-Etienne, Amis du Vieux Saint-Etienne
L'Apprenti, homme tenant une masse, 165 cm (1903).

ROINÉ, JULES ÉDOUARD
Nantes, October 24, 1857
April 11, 1916

Roiné

Roiné worked in New York from 1886 to 1894, and then in Paris. The museum of Mâcon owns a figure in bronze entitled *Persée*.

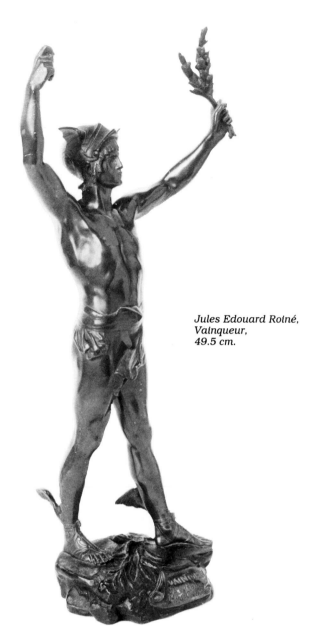

Jules Edouard Roiné,
Vainqueur,
49.5 cm.

François Laurent Rolard,
Monnaie de singe,
87.5 cm
(Société des bronzes
de Paris).

ROLARD, FRANÇOIS LAURENT

Paris, January 26, 1842
Paris, October 1, 1912

After studying at the Ecole des Beaux-Arts, Rolard produced a large number of busts and medallions as well as some figures. Some of these works were made for the open air, like *Monnaie de singe* (Salon of 1884), a bronze for Montholon Square in Paris, or *Le Sauvetage* (Salon of 1886), a bronze for the park of the Buttes-Chaumont. Also found at the Salon of 1875 is a statuette of *Aristide Boucicaut, Fendeur d'échalas* (1890), a statuette of *Diane* (1892), *L'Archer Aster* (1893), *Laitière normande* (1910), *Le Conventionnel René Levasseur*, a statue destined to the city of Mans (1911), all in bronze. It was Rolard's group entitled *Monnaie de singe*, representing a monkey on the back of a man holding a hoop, which seems to have become most successful. Also known

are other reductions of different dimesions, carrying the seal of the Société des Bronzes of Paris. One proof of 87.5 cm in height was sold in Biarritz on October 20, 1985.

ROMAGNESI, ANTOINE JOSEPH MICHEL

Paris, around 1782
Paris, April 9, 1852

A sculptor and lithographer from a family of artists, Romagnesi was also the modeler for a famous goldsmith of the Empire, Auguste. His date of birth is not known exactly, and he is sometimes confused with a certain Louis Alexandre Romagnesi, born in Orléans in 1776. Antoine Romagnesi exhibited at the Salon from 1808 to 1831, and received a number of official commissions, as many under the Empire as under the Restoration. Attributed to him is a work entitled *Minerve protégeant l'enfance du roi de Rome*, as well as some busts of *Louis XVIII, Comte d'Artois* (Salon of 1814), *Duchesse d'Angoulême*, and *Wellington*. The museum of Blois preserves a bust in bronze of *Louis XVIII*, 70 cm.

ROSSOLIN, AGNÈS L.

Born in Denmark, April 20, 1872

A naturalized French citizen, Agnès Rossolin was a student of Rodin and of the painter Fernand Sabatté. At the Salon, she exhibited some bronzes cast by Montagutelli, including a bust of the painter *Fernand Sabatté* in 1911 and a bust of *Orphée* in 1913. She pursued her activity between the two world wars, and is listed among the members of the Société des Artistes Français until 1939. The museum of the Petit Palais owns a 38 cm bust in bronze by Rossolin, portraying the painter *Fernand Sabatté*.

ROTY, LOUIS OSCAR

Paris, June 11, 1846
Paris, March 23, 1911

Roty's most famous work is none other than the *Semeuse*, pictured on some pieces of silver used from 1897 to 1914, recaptured on the postage stamps and, again today, on certain pieces of money. Considered one of the master medal-craftsmen of the 19th century, Roty obtained the prize of Rome in this discipline in 1875, became a member of the Institut, and obtained a number of other awards. He is also the author of plaques. An exhibition of his works took place in 1985 at the museum of Courbevoie.

MUSEUMS
Lille
Pictura, plaque, 19 x 13 cm.
Versailles, château
Léon Gambetta, medallion, 16 cm diam.

The museum of Bayonne preserves a series of medals by this sculptor.

ROUBAUD, LOUIS

Cerdon (Ain), February 29, 1828
Paris, April 11, 1906

Roubaud entered the Beaux-Arts in 1855 and debuted at the Salon in 1861. He worked for different monuments of Paris (the city hall, church of Notre Dame of Bercy) and of Grenoble (facade of the museum), and made the colossal statue of Pope Urbain II for the city of Châtillon-sur-Seine. Two statues in bronze of note at the Salon are *L'Hiver* (1873) and *La Vocation* (1888 and Exposition Universelle of 1889). His last work, *La Douleur*, a funereal statue in marble, was exhibited at the Salon of 1905. The museum of Mâcon owns the bronze of *La Vocation*.

ROUILLARD, PIERRE LOUIS

Paris, January 16, 1820
Paris, June 2, 1881

An animal sculptor and a student of Cortot, Rouillard generally treated his subjects in a more academic style than a number of his colleagues. Entering the Ecole des Beaux-Arts at the age of seventeen in 1837, he debuted at the Salon that same year. While he mainly exhibited plasters there, he also sent some bronzes and works in different materials, including zinc, silver, and cast iron (these made by the foundry of Val-d'Osne). He was granted some commissions for the Louvre, the Opera, and the Tribunal of Commerce, and made the *Cheval* in cast iron, 3.55 m., which used to appeared in front of the old Trocadéro, and which stands henceforth on the square of the Musée d'Orsay. Also among Rouillard's works is an equestrian statue of *François de la Rochefoucault*, the marshall of France under François I, sculpted for the Château d'Esclimont. Among his most typical works exhibited at the Salon are *Dromadaire*, plaster (1838), *Chien roquet culbutant un chat*, bronze (1842), *Chasse au sanglier*, terra cotta (1842), *Lion algérien* and *Tête de lion marocain*, plasters (1848), *Renard et lapins*, bronzed plaster (1852), *Vache*, bronze (1869), *Tigre*, bas-relief in bronze, 45 x 55 cm, for the Galerie d'Anatomie of the Jardin des Plantes (1872), *Combat de taureaux*, oxydized silver (1874), and *Porcs et porcher*, a group in silver executed in collaboration with Mathurin Moreau (1881). A group in bronze entitled *Chien et chat se battant* belongs to the museum of decorative arts of Paris. A proof of the same subject, 20 x 33 cm, was sold in Vichy on November 26, 1983.

ROULLEAU, JULES PIERRE

Libourne, October 16, 1855
Paris, March 30, 1895

Roulleau worked first as a stone cutter before entering the the studios of Cavelier and of Barrias at the Beaux-Arts. In 1878, Roulleau sent his first works to the Salon, and in 1882 sent a statue in bronze of *Lazare Carnot*, 3 m, made for the city of Nolay in Côte-d'Or. Then he consigned two statuettes to the Salon, bronzes entitled *Hébé* in 1882 and *Léon Gambetta* in 1888, and finally, in 1890, a statue in marble entitled *Léda*, 2.1 m. Also significant is the monument to *Théodore de Banville* from the Luxembourg gardens (1892) and the *Jeanne d'Arc équestre* cast in 1893 for the city of Chinon.

Three works by Roulleau were cast by the Thiébaut house: *Hébé*, 66 and 54 cm, *Moissonneuse*, haut-relief, 109 cm, and *La Victoire*, 97 and 49 cm.

ROUSAUD, ARISTIDE CHARLES LOUIS

Rivesaltes (Eastern Pyrenees), February 7, 1868
Paris, February 12, 1946

A student of Falguière and of Rodin, Rousaud exhibited at the Salon between the two world wars. The museum of Narbonne possesses a statuette in bronze by Rousaud, entitled *Saint Jean-Baptiste*, 27 cm, dated from 1904. A small bronze, *Taureau et enfant*, 24 cm, was sold in Enghien on October 19, 1980.

ROUSSEL, PAUL

Paris, October 23, 1867
Paris, January 1, 1928

Winning the first prize of Rome in 1895, Roussel served his apprenticeship with Cavelier, Barrias and Coutan. A number of his most remarkable works were sent to the Salon, including *La Mer*, a bas-relief in plaster (1896), *Farfalla*, bronze (1897), *L'Etoile du berger*, marble (1901), *Nonia, danseuse de Pompéi*, a statue in plaster (1906; a reduction in bronze exhibited in 1908), *La Tentation*, a statuette in marble and bronze (1906), *La Pomme*, a statue in ivory, marble and bronze (1908), *Coupe Michelin pour l'aviation*, bronze (1909), *Apollon*, a statue in plaster (1910), *Le Petit Poucet*. Roussel also sent the Salon three busts, *Sablaise*, *Les Cerises*, and *La Jeune Mère*, all bronzes (1911), and *Les Tout Petits*, a group in marble (1914), among others. Roussel also sculpted an official bust of the *République* as well as some monuments to the dead.

The Susse foundry cast some of Roussel's works in bronze, including *Le Papillon*, 61 cm, and a vase entitled *Fée aux roseaux*, 31 cm.

A statuette, *Eve*, 44.5 cm (Hohwiller, founder) appeared at the Musée d'Orsay in Paris. Another, in gilded bronze, *Diane*, 38 cm, was sold at the Drouot Hotel on April 10, 1981.

ROZE, ALBERT

Amiens, August 4, 1861
Amiens, Ocotber 17, 1952

Albert Roze was only twelve years old when he entered the school of drawing in Amiens, and at eighteen, a scholarship allowed him to go to Paris. He stayed there for twelve years, but was unable to win the grand prize of sculpture. He went to Rome nevertheless in 1891, and stayed there for two years. Upon returning to France, he was named director of the Ecole des Beaux-Arts of Amiens, a post he occupied for thirty years. Similarly, he held the position of director at the museum of Picardie for twenty-six years, devoting himself to safeguarding its riches during the course of the second world war. He scultped a number of works for Amiens and the Picardie, particularly the famous virgin of the Basilica of Albert which, in 1914, after a bombardment, would remain suspended in the emptiness. The museum of Amiens possesses three bronzes by this sculptor: *Buste de son père*, 59 cm, dating from 1927, *Tête d'homme*, 66 cm, and *Tête de vieille Picarde*, 38 cm (A. Rudier).

ROZET, RENÉ

Paris, May 14, 1858
1939

Statuettes and groups of children were apparently the favorite subject of this sculptor, who exhibited at the Salon from 1876 to 1935. Around 1900, the Thiébaut house cast his works entitled *Enfant assis sur un coussin*, 14 cm, and *Girandole Louis XV avec enfant*, 75 cm. Also known are a group of three children in bronze intended for a candelabrum or floor lamp.

Paul Roussel,
Eve or La Pomme, 44.5 cm (Hohwiller).
Musée d'Orsay.

RUBIN, AUGUSTE

Grenoble, March 6, 1841
1909

With the exception of some (mainly female) figures, Rubin primarily made objects of decoration, plates, cups, lamps, etc., all diversely ornamented. A small lamp in bronze, sylphide form, 25 cm, was sold by Sotheby in Monte-Carlo in 1978.

RUDE, FRANÇOIS

Dijon, January 4, 1784
Paris, November 3, 1855

F. RUDE

Though he was born in a quiet environment like his contemporary David d'Angers, Rude had a more spirited, romantic temperament, which closed the doors of the Académie to him. In this "vigorous tailor of images...[this] unfortunate candidate at the Institut," said M. Pierre Pradel, waged "the eternal debate between realism and academicism."

All the authors note the independence of Rude, his revolt against official teachings, his power of expression, his realism, and his research into elaborate movement which bordered on expressionism. These qualities literally burst through his most famous group, a work so universally known that it obscures the rest of Rude's work: Le Départ des volontaires de 1792, also called La Marseillaise from the Arc de Triomphe de l'Etoile.

A child of the people, Rude worked in the paternal ironworks in Dijon while he was very young. He entered Dijon's school of fine arts when he was sixteen, and there his teacher, François Devosge, exercised considerable influence on the young artist. On Devosge's recommendation, Rude went to Paris in 1807. He travelled with another native Bourguignon, Vivant-Denon, then the director of the Beaux-Arts, who prompted the young man to first enter the studio of Gaulle and then the studio of Cartellier. He was still working under the ideals of classicism when he won the first grand prize of Rome in 1812 with his Aristée pleurant ses abeilles. In 1815, he went to Belgium in the company of a Dijonnais, M. Frémiet, who was exiled because of his Bonapartist opinions. In Brussels, where he stayed for twelve years, Rude married Sophie Frémiet, his friend's daughter. He became the official court sculptor for the new king of the Netherlands, Guillaume I.

Upon returning to Paris in 1827, Rude established himself on the Rue Denfer and, at the Salon, exhibited his Mercure rattachant sa talonnière, a plaster which caused him to be compared to the greatest classicists; the bronze would later be exhibited at the Salon of 1834 and at the Exposition Universelle of 1855. Nevertheless, the movement and suppleness of forms began to appear in this piece, and in 1833, Rude's 77 cm marble entitled Petit Pêcheur napolitain, full of life and emotion, upset the supporters of academicism. A modern subject and not mythological: it was, according to the description of one of his biographers, Henri Drouot, "a new step forward". Throughout the monarchy of July, from 1830 to 1848, Rude created a number of statues of historic and contemporary people, which served as pretexts for his research into movement, life, and truth. Among his most remarkable pieces in Paris, it is necessary to mention the extraordinary effigy in bronze of Godefroy Cavaignac at the Montmartre cemetery (1847) and Maréchal Ney, also in bronze, at the Observatory Plaza (1853), as well as a group in bronze entitled Le Christ, la Vierge et saint Jean (2 m, Eck and Durand casting) for the high altar of the church of Saint-Vincent-de-Paul. In the provinces, works of note include a portrayal of Louis XIII à l'âge de seize ans, cast in silver by Eck, Richard and Durand in 1842 for the château de Dampierre, and Le Réveil de Napoléon, a large 2.5 m bronze made for the park of Fixin in the Côte-d'Or (1847).

The main work of Rude is still the great masterpiece of Romantic sculpture, Le Départ des volontaires, which he made in 1835-1836 and which did not fail to confuse and shock some of the public with its spirit, enthusiasm, power, and audacity of conception. One can only regret today that Rude did not make the ensemble of four groups for which it was to have been the precursor.

The museum of fine arts and the Rude museum of Dijon gather an important collection of original works and castings from this brilliant sculptor. Several of his many sketches in plaster and a number of replicas and reductions had been cast in bronze, apparently in small numbers. Notable among these bronzes are the following: Thésée, 29 cm, cast from the statuette Rude had presented to Vivant-Deneon while arriving in Paris in 1807; Eurydice mordu par le serpent, cast in 1830 by Delafontaine after an older model; Le Petit Pêcheur napolitain, cast in bronze by Eck and Durand after the plaster of 1831; a reduction of the Mercure rattachant sa talonnière, executed after the original for the cabinet of M. Thiers; Hébé et l'aigle de Jupiter, a reduction of a marble started in 1852 and finished after his death by his nephew Paul Cabet. Finally, the head of the Marseillaise, for which Mme Rude had posed, was executed in plaster to one-third of the size. It was also cast in bronze, and more than any other work it characterized the style of François Rude. It justified the comments made by M. Pierre Pradel in the catalog written for the exposition at the centenial of Rude's death, held in Dijon in 1955: "Rude captured the passing reactions of man, eternalized forever an amazement, a contortion, a moment of confusion."

Some works by Rude were also made the object of more important editions by the following founders:

Barbedienne executed Le Petit Pêcheur napolitain in three dimensions, 32, 24 and 16 cm. A contract was drawn up with Rude on May 23, 1843 anticipating the drafting of a reduction of the effigy of Godefroy Cavaignac, using the Collas procedure. Susse also cast Le Petit Pêcheur napolitain in three dimensions, 35, 28 and 20 cm.

Thiébaut cast the bust of the Christ, 76, 55, 38 and 22 cm, and Hébé, 68 cm.

François Rude,
Hébé et l'aigle,
76.5 cm
(Thiébaut).
J. Ginepro Collection,
Monaco.

François Rude,
Tête de la Marseillaise,
46 cm.

MUSEUMS
Dijon
Aristée déplorant la perte de ses abeilles, 90 cm
 (Delafontaine).
Eurydice mordu par le serpent, 87 cm (Delafontaine).
Lutteur au repos déposant son ceste, 40 x 46 cm.
Mercure rattachant sa talonnière, 117 cm (Eck and Durand).
Napoléon mort veillé par l'aigle, first maquette for the
 monument of Fixin, 29 x 54 cm.
Petit Pêcheur napolitain, 77 cm (Eck and Durand).
Vieux Guerrier, head, 64 cm (cast from *Départ des*
 volontaires of the Arc de triomphe).
Nice
Tête de la Marseillaise.
Paris, Louvre
Hébé et l'aigle de Jupiter, 78 cm (reduction of the group
 made by Cabet).
Mercure rattachant sa talonnière.
Thésée, 29 x 42 cm (dated 1802).
Toulouse
Le Connétable de Luynes, 102 cm.
Valence
Petit Pêcheur napolitain, statuette.

SALES
Léda et le cygne, 75 cm, Nantes, December 17, 1986.
Tête de la Marseillaise, 46 cm, Enghien, October 24, 1982.

François Rude,
Pêcheur napolitain,
31.5 x 34 cm
(Barbedienne).
J. Ginepro Collection,
Monaco.

RUILLÉ, COUNT HENRI GEOFFROY DE LA PLANCHE

Angers, January 17, 1842
1922

Nothing is known of this sculptor—not even his given name—with the exception of some rare, very good quality bronzes on the subject of horses, more precisely the art of horseback riding. Research has turned up a few references to this sculptor.

The Count of Ruillé exhibited some works at the Salon, principally in plaster, from 1884 to 1921. The pieces were almost entirely oriented to horses, races, and equestrian portraits. Ruillé's participation in the Salon can be judged by the following pieces, which were among his consignments there: *Le Dernier Effort, steeple chase* (1887), *La Rentrée du vainqueur* (1888), *Cheval d'attelage* (1889), *Emballée* and *Portraait d'un général à cheval* (1890), *Le Pas espagnol* (1893), *Une arrivée* (1894), *Une intrépide* (1898), *Chevaux de poste* (1901), *Amazone* (1904), *Après la charge* (1905), *Chasseur du 1er Empire* (1906), *Murat à Eylau* (1907), *Au manège* (1909), *Amazone* (1912), and *Hussard du 1er Empire, Chevaux en liberté* (1914).

It is unlikely that all of this artist's works were cast in bronze, because they appear only very rarely in public sale—and then, almost exclusively, the piece is either one representing two race horses in full action (perhaps *Une arrivée* from the Salon of 1894), or a particularly original work entitled *La Courbette et la croupade.*

SALES

L'Amazone, 51 cm, Sotheby London, June 7, 1984; Christie's London, May 15, 1986.
Cavalier sur un cheval cabré, 57 cm, Belfort, May 24, 1987 **(see reproduction page* 652).**

Comte de Ruillé,
La Courbette et la croupade,
59 x 38 cm.

Deux Chevaux au galop, 9 cm (Valsuani), Sotheby London, July 5, 1985.
Deux Chevaux de course et leurs jockeys, 41 cm, Enghien, March 29, 1987.
Deux Chevaux de course sautant un obstacle, 51 cm, Sotheby London, November 8, 1984.
La Courbette et la croupade, 59 cm, Enghien, October 10, 1982.

Comte de Rullé
*L'Entraînement
des jockeys,
41 x 72 cm.*

SABOURAUD, DOCTEUR RAYMOND

A doctor, a great art lover, and a collector all in one, Sabouraud started to sculpt around 1880 and exhibited at the Salon d'Automne. His works—studies of nude dancers in different positions, clothed women, and figures of slaves—have a great liberty of expression reminiscent of the impressionist manner. Sabouraud also produced a certain number of busts, in particular portraits of doctors. His activity continued into the 1930s. The Orsay museum owns a bronze by this artist dating from 1889, cast by Valsuani, entitled *Manfred, homme nu debout*, 29 cm, as well as some other bronzes made between the two world wars: *Jeune Fille assise sur le sol* (1931), *Le Rut*, 31.5 cm (1929), and *Titan foudroyé*, 15.5 cm (Siot-Decauville).

SACHOT, OCTAVE

Born in Montigny-Lencoup (Seine-et-Marne)

A sculptor and an engraver of medals, Sachot contributed to the Salon between 1861 and 1878. The museum of Mans preserves a medallion in bronze by Sachot, entitled *Profil d'homme*, 25 cm diam., dated 1870.

SAINT-ANGEL, PIERRE CHARLES GABRIEL DE

Born in Montbreton (Gironde)

An animal sculptor, Saint-Angel began participating at the Salon in 1868. The Thiébaut house cast a number of works by this artist, including *Vache broutant*, 32 cm L, *Vache se léchant le dos*, 26 cm L, *Vache se léchant le pied*, 26 cm L, and *Vache et son veau*, 32 cm L.

SAINT-MARCEAUX, RENÉ DE

Reims, September 23, 1845
Paris, April 23, 1915

The son of a wholesaler in Champagne, Saint-Marceaux was attracted to sculpture from the age of eighteen, and went to the Beaux-Arts in Paris in

René de Saint-Marceaux,
Arlequin, silvered bronze, 100 cm
(Barbedienne).
J. Ginepro Collection, Monaco.

especially *Arlequin* in 1883. One meter in height, amusing and witty, *Arlequin* became extraordinarily popular among the majority of art lovers, though a few found it too realistic. A bronze would be cast of it and presented at the Exposition of 1889, with equal success. Furthermore, it was made the object of multiple editions. Saint-Marceau exhibited another piece at the Salon, in 1890: a statuette in painted stone entitled *La Dame de pique,* modeled after a game ticket.

In 1892, Saint-Moreaux abandoned the Artistes Français for the Société Nationale des Beaux-Arts, where he was a prolific exhibitor. Of note there was a statue in marble in 1893, entitled *Première Communion.*

Barbedienne, after arranging contracts in 1880 and in 1893, cast the *Arlequin* in six dimensions, 103, 85, 69, 51, 43 and 34 cm, as well as *Première Communion.*

St MARCEAVX

René de
Saint-Marceaux,
L'Arlequin,
69 cm.

René de
Saint-Marceaux,
La Danseuse,
47.5 cm
(C. Valsuani).
J. Ginepro Collection,
Monaco.

order to study in Jouffroy's studio. He made his debut at the Salon in 1868, beginning a career highlighted by a number of successes. In 1869, and again in 1872, Saint-Marceaux went to Italy, specifically to Florence, where he immersed himself in the works and styles of the great Renaissance masters. Later, between 1874 and 1879, he traveled to Spain and Morocco. In 1905, he was elected to be a member of the Institut, replacing the sculptor Paul Dubois. Very talented, Saint-Marceaux produced masks, busts and statues of famous personages, genre scenes, allegories, and commemorative monuments. In the gardens of the Champs-Elysées is found his statue in marble of *Alphonse Daudet,* and in Malesherbes Square, a very "belle époque" statue in stone portraying *Alexandre Dumas fils* (1906).

But it was at the Salon that Saint-Marceaux earned his renown, with three successive marble works: *La Jeunesse de Dante* in 1869, *Le Génie gardant le secret de la tombe* in 1879, and finally and

Thiébaut cast *La Dame de pique*, 76 and 43 cm, and Susse cast the *Génie gardant le secret de la tombe*, 90, 69, 52 and 33 cm. There also exist some castings by Valsuani, as well as many bronzes which do not carry the seal of the founder.

MUSEUMS

Lyon
Le Rhône et la Saône, sketch.
Nancy
La Dame de pique, statuette.
Paris, Decorative Arts
Femme drapée devant un temple grec, monument à Jules Maciet, bas-relief, 128 x 81 cm (1912).
Paris, Carnavalet
Buste de Clairin, 39 cm (1897).
Paris, Orsay
Buste de Dagnan-Bouveret, 36 cm (1892).
Buste de J.-L. Forain, 57.6 cm (1913).
The museum of Orsay possesses some busts and some masks in terra cotta. The museum of the Petit Palais preserves a number of terra cottas.
Paris, Musée postal
Maquette du monument de l'Union postale Universelle de Berne.
Reims
Arlequin, reduction, 34 cm (1879).
Le Baiser, sketch, 35.5 cm.
Bénitier, 20 cm (C. Valsuani).
Jean Boldini, head, 40 cm (1903).
Eternelle Renaissance d'Amour, rough draft, 36.5 cm (Valsuani).
Eternelle Renaissance d'Amour, 29.5 cm (Valsuani).
Fille de ferme, 73 cm (1885).
Génie gardant le secret de la tombe, 17 x 19.5 cm.
Homme d'Etat au chapeau, sketch, 10.6 cm (C. Valsuani).
Homme d'Etat au chapeau, 28 cm (C. Valsuani).
Léda, sketch, 20.5 cm (C. Valsuani).
Maternité, sketch, 17 cm (C. Valsuani).
Mousse de champagne, jeune fille nue tenant un cep (Barbedienne, according to the plaster of 1888).
La Musique, dans une niche, gilded bronze and marble, 15 x 4 cm.
Paysanne, 16.8 cm (C. Valsuani).
Le Premier Baiser, sketch, 18 cm (C. Valsuani).
Vichy
Arlequin.

SALES

Arlequin, 51 cm, Sotheby New York, January 9, 1985.
Arlequin, 69 cm, Dijon, October 23, 1983; Drouot, May 24, 1984, room 9.
Arlequin, 85 cm, Limoges, November 23, 1985.
(The original plaster of *Arlequin*, 170 cm (1879) was sold for 250,000 F on December 3, 1985 at the Drouot Hotel).
Jeune Femme à l'éventail, 61 cm, Sotheby London, November 8, 1984.

SALMON, ÉMILE FRÉDÉRIC

Paris, June 15, 1840
Forges-les-Eaux, June 12, 1913

An animal sculptor primarily influenced by Barye more than by any of his other masters, Salmon also produced allegories and some watercolors. The son of a medal-engraver, Salmon debuted at the Salon in 1859 with a memorable plaster called *Vache couchée*; in later Salon exhibitions he showed two bronzes, *Levrette* in 1864 and *Chien terrier en arrêt* in 1865, and a group in wax entitled *Après la bataille* in 1867.

SALMSON, JEAN JULES

Paris, July 18, 1823
Coupvray (Seine-et-Marne), May 7, 1902

Son of a medallion engraver, Salmson made his debut at the Salon in 1859 then worked on various Parisian monuments: the Opera, the Tuileries, and the Tribunal de Commerce, as well as for the city hall of la Rochelle. He also made the monument to *Saussure et Balmat*, in bronze, inaugurated in Chamonix in 1887. After the war of 1870 Salmon went to London, and then to Geneva, where he directed the Ecole d'Art Industriel beginning in 1876. He produced a number of statuettes of famous

Jean Jules Salmson,
Femme arabe portant un vase,
58 cm.

Salmson

people, including *Shakespeare, Hamlet, Byron, Van Dyck, Walter Scott, Rubens, Washington, Charle 1er, Marie Stuart,* and *Jean-Jacques Rousseau,* among others. At the Salon, he exhibited bronzes including the following: *La Dévideuse,* a work greatly inspired by antiquity (1863), groups entitled *Phryné devant l'aréopage* and *Laïs et Démosthène* (1870), *Chute des Titans,* a shield, 60 cm diam (1891); at the Exposition Universelle of 1900 he showed a statuette in bronze entitled *Femme à la marguerite.* Also noteworthy in this sculptor's production are some portraits in medallion form and some Oriental sbujects. Among his works cast in bronze are *La Dévideuse, Chef arabe à pied,* 55 and 30 cm, *Femme arabe porteuse d'eau,* 55 and 30 cm, *Femme à la marguerite, Fillette à l'oiseau, Italien* and *Italienne, La Musique,* 63 cm, *Pandore, Phryné devant l'aréopage, Retour des champs, Laïs et Démosthène,* as well as the busts of *Charlotte Corday* and the *Princesse de Lamballe.*

MUSEUMS
Angers
Les Titans, shield, 60 cm diam.
Paris, Orsay
La Dévideuse, 121 cm (Salon of 1863)

SALES
Arabe debout, 56 cm, *Femme arabe,* 63 cm, Sotheby London, March 21, 1985.
Femme arabe revenant de la fontaine, 58 cm, Enghien, June 20, 1983.
Guerrier arabe, 59 cm, Enghien, June 20, 1983.
Jeune Fille et génie ailé, 81 cm, Sotheby London, March 20, 1986.
Milton, Shakespeare, two statuettes, 58 cm, Christie's New York, March 13, 1984.

SANCHEZ, ALBERT ERNEST

Paris, April 24, 1878—?

This student of Falguière, Mercié and Gardet participated at the Salon from 1904 to 1923. His work seems essentially devoted to the portrayal of animals, and includes some appropriately small-sized bronzes representing small animals. Pieces of Sanchez's work were cast by Valsuani, Hébrard (*L'Escargot,* 6 cm), and Thiébaut (*Souris,* 9 x 13 cm). Though the founder is unknown, Sanchez's works *Coquelet à l'escargot, Coquelet au serpent,* and *Poussin à l'escargot* are also noteworthy.

SALES
Lévrier couché, 21.5 x 43 cm (1913; Valsuani), Drouot, June 14, 1985.
Oisillon mordu par un serpent, 12 x 16 cm, Enghien, March 7, 1992.

Jean Jules Salmson, Guerrier arabe, 59 cm.

SANSON, JUSTIN CHRYSOSTOME

Nemours, August 8, 1833
Paris, November 2, 1910

Le Danseur de Saltarelle, reproduced often under many diverse names, is the highlight of the work of Justin Sanson, who obtained the first grand prize of Rome in 1861. Cast in bronze by Thiébaut, 168 cm high, *Le Danseur* was exhibited at the Salon of 1866 and placed in the Jardin de Diane in Fontainebleu, reappearing in 1869 as a bronze reduction under the name of *Danseur romain.* Also notable is another bronze, *Chanteur napolitain* from the Salon of 1882, and some plasters: *Suzanne au bain* in 1868, *Souvenir d'Ischia* in 1895, *Diane* in 1896, and *Coquetterie* in 1910. Sanson also executed some statues for the decoration of the Louvre, the Tuileries, the Opera, the city hall, the church of Saint-François-Xavier, and the courthouse of Amiens, as well as a *Piéta* in bronze for the church of Nemours.

MUSEUMS
Amiens
L'Architecte amiènois J.B. Herbault, medallion, 42 cm diam.
Le Géologue autrichien Edouard Suess, bust, 59 cm.
Chambéry
Danseur romain, reduction of the *Danseur de Saltarelle,* 55 cm.
Nemours
Danseur de Salterelle (1865).
Suzanne (1866).
The museum also preserves some plasters and some marbles by this artist.

SALES
Danseur romain, 72 cm, Sotheby London, November 8, 1984.

SANTA COLOMA, EMMANUEL
Bordeaux, 1826
1886

An animal sculptor, Santa Coloma exhibited at the Salon between 1863 and 1870, principally showing horses and equestrian figures. Notable among others are *Cheval d'attelage* (1863) and *Cavalier espagnol* (1864), both in bronze, *Cavalier, Lion* (1866), *Cheval irlandais* (1867), and *Napoléon III à Solférino* (1868), etc.

The museum of Bordeaux preserves one statuette, entitled *Cavalier espagnol,* 52 cm in height. A small group, *Chevaux emballés,* 58 cm (1865) was sold in Enghien on October 6, 1985.

SAPPEY, PIERRE VICTOR
Grenoble, February 11, 1801
Grenoble, 1856

A sculptor and an architect, Sappey entered the Beaux-Arts in 1825. He exhibited only once at the Salon, in 1831, and then returned to Grenoble to be named professor at the municipal school of fine arts. He worked primarily for his hometown (a fountain at Grenette Plaza) and for different cities of the region, including Valence (a statue in bronze of *Championnet,* 4 m.), Chambéry, and Uriage. The museum of Grenoble possesses many of his works, including a medallion portrait in bronze presumed to be *Benjamin Rolland,* 18 cm diam.

SAUVAGE, PIERRE
Abbeville, April 11, 1821
Vichy, June 20, 1883

A bronze by this sculptor entitled *La Nymphe Amanthéa avec une chèvre,* 64 cm, was sold in London at Sotheby's on March 17, 1983.

SAUVAGEAU, LOUIS
Paris, July 22, 1822—?

Sauvageau's participation at the Salon began in 1848 and ended in 1874. He worked in almost every genre—mythological, allegorical, religious, and animal—and produced statues as well as bas-reliefs, busts, and medallions, often in terra cotta. Some bronzes which appeared on the market occassionally were *Cavalier chassant le tigre,* 63 cm, *Enfant,* after Pigalle, *Femme et Amour* symbolizing *L'eau,* 82 and 41 cm, *Femme et Amour* symbolizing *Le feu,* 82 and 41 cm, *La Femme au perroquet,* 59 cm, *Marchande d'amour,* etc. Two bronzes, *L'Eau* and *Le Feu* (also called *L'Automne* and *L'Hiver*) were sold in London at Sotheby's on April 28, 1982.

SAVINE, LÉOPALD
Paris, March 6, 1861
October 7, 1934

Numerous feminine figures in genre and allegorical scenes are typical of Savine's production. He exhibited at the Salon starting in 1888, sending

Louis Sauvageau, Cavalier chassant le tigre, 63 cm.

mainly plasters such as *Tête de vieillard* and *Tête d'enfant* in 1894. He also sent *Fileuse* in 1886, *Après la danse* in 1889, *La Moisson* in 1890, *Tireuse d'arc* in 1891, *Fleur de blé* in 1895, *Désolation* in 1906, *Au Maroc, La Prière* and *Yassmina* in 1913, etc. In bronze, the only works noted are some busts, including *Lygie* (1902), and one statue, *Découragement* (1905).

A certain number of works by Savine have been cast in bronze, among them the busts of *Lygie* and of *Jeune Fille aux cheveux ornés de fleurs*, 51 cm.

SALES

Femme étendue dans les bagues, 22 cm L., Drouot, December 2, 1983, room 5.
Femme au paon, gilded bronze, 39 cm, Drouot, March 4, 1983, room 1.
Petit Buste de femme, 16 cm, Drouot, June 12, 1981.
La Nymphe du lac, bust in gilded bronze, 50 cm (Louchet, founder), Drouot, December 3, 1984, rooms 5 and 6.
Porte-bouquet au paon, 39 cm, Enghien, March 29, 1981.

SCHIFF, MATHIAS

Rettel-lès-Sierck (Moselle), 1862
Nancy, November 1886

A painter and sculptor, Schiff is particularly known for producing busts, a certain number of them in bronze, including *Victor Poirel*, 78 cm, exhibited at the Salon in 1884, and a portrait of the Baron *Guerrier de Dumast* from 1885. The museum of Nancy possesses the bust of *Victor Poirel*, as well as a small (50 cm) group in bronze, the first project for an equestrian statue entitled *Duc René II de Lorraine*, erected on the plaza of Saint-Epvre in 1883.

SCHNEGG, GASTON

Bordeaux, August 4, 1866
Paris, November 25, 1953

The son of an antique cabinetmaker, Schnegg went to Paris in 1884, entered the Beaux-Arts, and worked for Rodin along with his older brother, Lucien. Gaston Schnegg began exhibiting works at the Salon des artistes Français in 1887, and in 1894 started to participate in the Salon de la Nationale des Beaux-Arts. In addition to some busts of relatives, he was fond of portraying children. There is record of some consignments of bronzes: *Maternité* (1904), *La Dîme* (1905), *La Leçon de couture* and *Groupe d'enfants* (1909). Editions of certain works have been made in ceramic, plaster, and bronze. Among the bronzes are *Bourgeois et savant* (after a group sculpted in wood), *Le Chant*, a group of three people, *La Dîme*, 31 cm, *La Leçon de couture*, 34 cm, *Maternité*, 39.5 cm, and *Sainte-Famille*, 12.5 x 16 cm (after the bas-relief in stone exhibited in 1898).

MUSEUMS
Bordeaux
Les Jumeaux, group of children, 35.5 cm (1908).
Sainte-Famille, bas-relief, 34.5 x 43.5 cm (1894).
La Tempête, 28.5 cm (1898).
A number of works by Gaston Shnegg were given to the museum by the sculptor's daughter in 1984.
Cherbourg
Maternité, 39 cm.

SCHNEGG, LUCIEN

Bordeaux, April 19, 1864
Paris, December 22, 1909

Lucien Schnegg's work is composed essentially of busts of his family and friends, medallions, and statuettes of young children and young women in innocent forms. This sculptor was first trained as a

Lucien Schnegg,
La Grande Soeur
or *Les Deux Soeurs*,
24 cm.
J. Ginepro Collection,
Monaco.

*Lucien Schnegg,
Femme agenouillée,
les coudes au sol,
16 x 27 cm
(Lamy casting).
J. Ginepro Collection,
Monaco.*

decorator in Bordeaux before leaving for Paris to work in Falguière's studio. With his brother Gaston, he worked as an assistant to Rodin. Soon, he gathered the master's other practicians around him to form what would be called "the band of Schnegg." Lucien exhibited first at the Artistes Français from 1887 to 1890, principally showing busts and medallions in plaster and terra cotta. In 1892, he began to show at the Société Nationale des Beaux-Arts, to which he sent some bronzes, busts, and diverse subjects such as *Torse de jeune femme* (1904), *La Jeune Heaulmière* (1905), *Adolescent* (1907), *Enlèvement* (1909) and, posthumously titled, a head and a statuette of *Aphrodite, Le Baiser, L'Arrestation, Adolescent, Grande Soeur, La Vigne, Torse de Vénus,* and *Vénus* (1910). He also showed some statuettes in marble, including *Jeune Bacchante* (1894), and plasters including *La Terre promise* (1908) and *Junon* (1909). Some works by Schnegg were made in faience by Théodore Deck.

In an exposition entitled *La Bande à Schnegg* organized at the Bourdelle museum in 1974, some of Schnegg's bronze proofs appeared. Among the pieces preserved today at the Musée d'Orsay (see below), of especial note are *Le Baiser,* 38 cm, *Enlèvement,* 33.5 cm, *Femme nue,* 43 cm, *Femme nue debout tenant son genoux,* 49.5 cm, *Le Grand-Père,* 46 cm, *La Grande soeur,* 24 cm, *Louise Schnegg, fille de l'artiste, enfant,* 26 cm, *Petit Nu féminin,* 30 cm, and *La République,* 102 cm.

MUSEUMS
Bordeaux
Buste de Jane Poupelet, 26 cm (around 1890).
Paris, Orsay
Aphrodite penchée. 42 cm.

Aphrodite, petite tête, 15.2 cm.
Aphrodite, torso, 31 cm.
Autoportrait, 42 cm.
Les Deux Soeurs, 33.5 cm.
Femme agenouillée, les coudes au sol, 16 cm.
La Jeune Heaumière, 43 cm.
Paris, Petit Palais
Adolescent, 46.5 cm.
Aphrodite, 41 cm (dated 1905).

SCHOENEWERK, ALEXANDRE PIERRE
Paris, February 16, 1820
Paris, July 22, 1885

Schœnewerk

A protégé encouraged by the princess Mathilde, Schoenewerk was very successful under the Second Empire, but eventually went mad and took his own life. A student of David d'Angers, he remained very influenced by Italy and by classical antiquity. He produced a number of busts and statues for the decoration of the Louvre, the Tuileries, the city hall, the Opera, some gardens of the old Trocadéro (allegories of *Europe* in bronze, today located on the square of the Musée d'Orsay), and the church of the Sorbonne. He debuted at the Salon in 1841 with *Agar,* a statue in plaster, and then exhibited, in succession, the bronze statuettes *Madame Rouart* (1849) and *Rêverie* (1853), the bronze groups *Bacchante faisant danser un enfant* (1852), *L'Amour vaincu* (Exposition of 1855), and *L'Enlèvement de Déjanire*, a colossal group cast by Thiébaut for the city of Rouen (1870), *Cet âge est sans pitié*, formerly in the Square of the Temple in Paris (1880). He also showed some works in marble: *Au bord d'un ruisseau Jeune Pêcheur* (1861), *Jupiter et Léda* (1863), *Enfant au cytgne* (1870), *La Jeune Tarentine* (1872), *Jeune Fille à la fontaine* (1873), *Hésitation* (1876), and *Au matin* (1879). Some works in bronze have been noted on the market: *Andromède sur le rocher*, 55 cm, *Bacchante assise*, 40.5 cm, *Femme allongé vêtue à l'antique*, 15 x 30 cm, and *Femme assise vêtue à l'antique*, 30 cm.

SALES
Femme cueillant des fleurs, 41 cm (L. Marchant, editor), Christie's London, June 15, 1986.
Jeune Femme assise à la lyre, 33 cm, Sotheby London, November 7, 1985.
Jeunes Femme drapées à l'antique, two statuettes, 52 cm, Sotheby London, April 28, 1982.

SCHROEDER, JEAN-LOUIS DÉSIRÉ
Paris, December 24, 1828
Paris, 1898

A student of Rude and of Dantan Sr., Schroeder produced a number of busts, statues, and allegorical groups such as *L'Amour attristé*, in marble (Salon of 1852), and *La Chute des feuilles*, in marble, 32 cm (1859, with a reduction in bronze at the Salon of 1866), *Le Baume maternel*, a group in bronze (1863), *Le Prince impérial*, a statuette in terra cotta (1870), *Tête de vieillard*, in bronze (1884), *Bouquetière pompéienne* (1892) and *La Prière* ('897), two statuettes in plaster. Schroeder worked on the Louvre, the Trocadéro, the city hall, the churches of Saint-Augustin, Saint-Etienne-du-Mont, Saint-Eustache, and other monuments. The museum of Dijon preserves Schroeder's *Tête de vieillard* in bronze, 40 cm (1884), as well as a number of his statuettes and groups in terra cotta.

Alexandre Pierre Schoenewerk,
Femme cueillant des fleurs, 41 cm
(L. Marchand, editor).

SCHULTZ, ALBERT
Strasbourg, April 15, 1871
1953

Schultz executed some statues for buildings in his hometown as well as many effigies in Alsace. The museum of Strasbourg possesses the following works by this artist:

Les Ailes du moulin, 24 cm.
Alsacienne allant à l'eglise, 42.5 cm.
Alsacienne à la grenoiuille, 19.5 cm.
Alsacienne au lapin, 22 cm.
Alsacienne aux poussins, 27.5 cm.
L'Automne or the *Vendangeurs*, 25.5 x 35 cm (Susse).
Bergère, 24 cm.
Coq du pont du Rhin, 35 cm.

L'Eté or the *Moissonneurs*, 25 x 35.5 cm (Susse).
La Faneuse, 43.5 cm.
Gänseliesel, gilded bronze, 40.5 cm.
La Géante de Nideck, 27 cm.
L'Hiver or the *Bûcherons*, 25.5 x 35.5 cm (Susse).
Jeanne d'Arc brisant son épée, 41 cm.
Léda, 40 cm.
Mercure, 81 cm (Susse).
Phryné, 40 cm (Montagutelli).
Portrait d'Albert Schultz, relief, 18 x 11.6 cm (1894).
Le Printemps or the *Taille des arbres*, 25 x 35 cm (Susse).
Sainte Cécile, 43 x 45 cm.
La Vanneuse, 49 cm.
Le Voleur de poules, 41 x 58 cm (Valsuani).

SEGOFFIN, VICTOR JOSEPH
Toulouse, March 5, 1867
Paris, October 17, 1925

Specializing in busts of painters, this student of Cavalier and Barrias also produced some allegorical and mythological works, as well as some small subjects in bronze which were well-appreciated in their day. Strongly influenced by Barrias, and to a lesser degree, by Rodin and Falguière, Segoffin won the grand prize of Rome in 1897, after seven fruitless attempts. At the Salon, where he debuted in 1890, his works of particular note included *Mauvais Génie*, plaster (1892), *Semeur de mondes*, plaster (1896), *Judith et Holopheme*, pewter (1898), *Le Temps et le Génie*, a group in bronze (1908), *Vercingétorix*, a statue in bronze for the Panthéon (1912), etc. A statuette entitled *Danseuse aux tambourins* or *aux cymbales* was cast by Susse in many dimensions. The group *Judith et Holopherne* was also cast in bronze, 108 cm (Cf. sale catalog *En marge des grands courants*, Drouot Hotel, March 28, 1974). Also noteworthy are *Tête de femme criant*, 45 cm, cast by Andro (Drouot Hotel, 1976) and a statue entitled *L'Extase*, 180 cm, cast by Rudier (Enghien, 1980).

MUSEUMS
Beaune
Félix Ziem, head, 36 cm (1907).
Bordeaux
Homme criant, mask, 90 cm.
Dijon
Félix Ziem, head, 36 cm.
Mont-de-Marsan
Buste de Monsieur D. (Hohwiller, founder; 1899).
Homme criant, 16 cm (1891).
Paris, Carnavalet
Femme nue called *Sorcière*, 48 cm.
Paris, Orsay
Félix Ziem, bust, 36 cm (1905; Hohwiller).
Harpignies, bust, 71.5 cm.
Homme criant, mask, 46 cm (1905).
Léon Bonnat assis, 38 cm (1921).
Léon Bonnat, bust, 62.5 cm (1909).
Paris, Petit Palais
Félix Ziem, bust, 37 cm (1906).
Félix Ziem, medallion, 36 cm diam. (1912).
Harpignies, bust, 69 cm (1909).
Léon Bonnat, bust, 28 cm (1909).
Toulouse
La Danse sacrée, torso, 63.8 cm.
La Danse sacrée, head, 16 cm.
Le Génie vainqueur du Temps, 51 cm.
Judith et la tête d'Holopherne, 107 cm.
La Suppliante, 58.6 cm.
Vercingétorix, 77.5 cm.
La Victoire, from the monument to the dead of the Ecole polytechnique, 48 x 80.7 cm.
Valenciennes
Harpignies, 51 cm (1906).

SALES
Danseuses aux cymbales or *Fureur*, 61 cm (Susse No. 26), Rouen, November 28, 1982.
Danseuses aux cymbales, 117 cm (Susse), Enghien, December 11, 1983; Semur-en-Auxois, February 17, 1985.

SERRES, PROVIN

Gaillac (Tam), March 8, 1840—?

Serres exhibited at the Salon from 1879 to 1902, sending *Un sauveteur*, a statue in plaster (1879), *Les Deux Joueurs*, a group in bronze (1889), *Léda*, a group in plaster (1894), among others. A statuette in bronze entitled *Pan et une jeune femme*, 48 cm, was cast by the Société des Bronzes of Paris, and appeared in a sale at Sotheby's in London on March 20, 1986

SEYSSES, AUGUSTE

Toulouse, August 22, 1862
July, 1946

A sculptor and engraver in medals who studied under Falguière, Seysses exhibited at the Salon starting in 1884. He showed some busts and medallions representing contemporaries, as well as allegories, mythological subjects, and a number of animals. Notable among his plasters are *Naïade* (1888), *Mierille* (1889), *Jeune Femme jouant sur une tortue* (1891), *La Mort de Sapho* (1895), *L'Eternelle Idole* (1899), *Une confidence* (1903), *Le Soir de la vie* (1907), and *La Proie, lion et bélier* (1914); his marbles include *Pro Libertate* (1894), *La Curée* (1895), *La Pudeur* (1900), *Le Lys* (1903), *Circé* (1904), and *L'Enchanteresse*, a bust (1909); finally, his bronzes include *Triomphe de Diane*, a group (1896), *Phryné*, a statuette (1899), *Eléphant Egypte*, a statuette (1905), *Portrait d'Achille Anglade*, a statuette in gilded bronze (1907), *Pierre Debauge*, a statuette in bronze and silver (1908), etc. Also credited to Seysses are the stone statues of the *Théâtre* and of the *Dessin* placed above the porch of the Grand Palais, and a group in marble, *Le Retour* (Salon of 1898), destined for the botanical gardens of Toulon. The Susse foundry cast *Eléphant d'Afrique*, 24 and 15 cm, *Triomphe de Diane*, 98, 74 and 49 cm, and *La Vérité*, 110 cm.

Also known from this artist's work are diverse proofs in bronze, some of which he exhibited at the Société des Artistes Animaliers: *La Chasse à l'ours*, 80 cm, *Combat de lions*, *La Femme aux lys*, 79 cm, *Groupe d'éléphants*, *Jeune Captif*, *Jeune Ourson*, *Lionne traînant un cygne*, 24 x 49 cm (cast by Valsuani), *Phryné*, 45 cm.

The museum of the Petit Palais in Paris owns a bronze by this sculptor entitled *La Proie, lion et bélier*, 37 cm in height.

SALES
Diane chasseresse, 74 cm, La Flèche, November 16, 1986.
Eléphant d'Afrique trompe levée, 19 cm (Susse, founder), Sotheby London, April 28, 1982.

SICARD, FRANÇOIS

Tours, April 21, 1862
Paris, 1934

Before obtaining the prize of Rome in 1891, Sicard had worked as a craftsman with his master, Barrias, executing sculptures in marble for him. A talented portraitist whose figures were highly regarded for their realism, his works remaining in Paris include *Le Bon Samaritain* in the Tuileries, *George Sand* at the jardin du Luxembourg, *Sarah*

Bernhardt en Phèdre at the Malesherbes plaza, and a group in stone entitled*La Nuit* on the lateral facade of the Grand Palais. He also sculpted the caryatids at the city hall of Tours, a large fountain in Sydney, and diverse commemorative monuments. Among his consignments to the Salon, starting in 1887, are a bronze entitled *La Touraine courannant ses enfants* (1887), then *Agar,* haut relief in marble (1897), *Le Bon Samaritain,* marble (1898), *Pour la patrie,* plaster (1901), *OEdipe vainqueur du sphinx,* a group in bronze (1903), *George Sand,* marble (1905), *Eve,* plaster (1907), and, both in marble, *La Nuit* (1908) and*Danse de l'écharpe* (1914).

Many works by Sicard were cast in bronze, primarily at the Thiébaut house, which executed *L'Honneur,* 80, 53 and 34 cm, *Buste de l'Honneur,* 39 and 26 cm, and *Saint-Michel,* 118 and 88 cm. Siot-Decauville produced editions of *Agar.*

MUSEUMS
Paris, Orsay
Oedipe et le sphinx, 80.5 cm (1903).
Victor Laloux, architecte, plaque, 22 x 17 cm (1910).
Tours
Paysan allumant sa pipe.
Victor Laloux, architecte, plaque, 22 x 17 cm.
Tours, Museum of Compagnonnage
Le Charpentier.

SALES
La Charmeuse de serpent, 53 cm (Barbedienne), Enghien, April 28, 1985.
Oedipe et le sphinx, gilded and patinated bronze, 65 cm, Drouot, March 23, 1984, room 1.
La Victoire, 90 cm (Fumière), on the pedestal column, Drouot, December 3, 1984, rooms 5 and 6.

SIGNORET-LEDIEU, LUCIE
Nevers, 1858
1904

A statue in bronze of *Jeanne d'Arc* by this artist was installed in 1902 in Saint-Pierre-le-Moutier in the Nièvre. Signoret-Ledieu also exhibited a number of plasters at the Salon starting in 1878, including the following busts: *L'Innocence,* (1878), *Mignon enfant* (1879), *Le Soir* and *Jeune Esclave* (1881). She also made some statues and statuettes: *Aux champs* (1883), *Ruth* (1887), *Myphe* (1889), *L eTravail et l'étude* (1892), and *Salomé* (1897). Three busts in bronze are also notable: *Femme* (1887), *Coquetterie* (1894), and *Sans-gêne* (1897), as well as a statuette entitled *La Fileuse* (1886), which would be cast by Thiébaut. Also known are some proofs in bronze of the *Nymphe,* 65 cm, and of the *Source,* 69 and 88 cm. The museums of Chambéry and of Dijon each possesses a proof of the *Fileuse,* 77 cm high.

SALES
Diane chasseresse, 48 cm, Barcelona, March 15, 1983.
Nymphe de Diane, 86 cm, Sotheby London, November 10, 1983.
La Source, 88 cm, Sotheby London, March 20, 1986.

SIMART, PIERRE CHARLES
Troyes, June 27, 1806
Paris, May 27, 1857

Though he seemed to be destined to follow his father's path into carpentry, Pierre Simart prefered sculpture, and entered the Beaux-Arts in 1824. Winning the first prize of sculpture in 1833, he went to Rome, where Ingres (then director of the Académie de France) lavished advice on him, making him study and revere the sculpture of antiquity. Simart started to exhibit at the Salon in 1831, but experienced difficult beginnings. His first important commission did not come until 1840, and he did not gain a strong reputation until several years after that. He was elected to the Institut in 1852 to replace Pradier.

Simart's production includes scenes of allegory, mythology, and history, sculpted in a very classical style. His major work is the tomb of Napoléon I in the crypt of the Invalides—a statue of the emperor in imperial costume, and ten bas-reliefs in marble (three of which were finished by his colleagues). Simart also worked on the Louvre (a pediment of the Sully pavilion), the old city hall, the columns of the Trône (winged figures in haut-relief symbolising *La Justice* and *L'Abondance*), the château of Dampierre, the cathedral of Troyes, and, also in Troyes, the Saint-Pantaléon church (four bas-reliefs in bronze for the pulpit: *La Foi, L'Espérance, La Charité,* and *La Libéralité*). Seventy-one works by the sculptor were given by his widow to the museum of Troyes. The Carnavalet Museum in Paris preserves a medallion in bronze entitled *Portrait de l'architecte Visconti,* 24 cm diam., cast by Eck and Durand.

SOLDI-COLBERT, ÉMILE ARTHUR, KNOWN AS SOLDI
Paris, May 27, 1846
Rome, March 14, 1906

The son of a German professor of Danish origins, Soldi-Colbert became a sculptor, an engraver of medals and cameos, and an art writer, and would also handle some archeological excavations in Italy. In 1869 he won the first prize of Rome in medal-engraving, and in 1872 began exhibiting at the Salon. He contributed a number of busts in marble, some statues, and finally, in 1873, a relief in bronze entitled *Gallia,* 77 x 67 cm, today owned by the Musée d'Orsay. One bronze representing a dancer and entitled *Pas de danse,* 83 cm, was sold in Enghien on December 2, 1984.

SOLIVA, LOUIS
Born in Paris

Practically nothing is known about this animal artist, who is noted in the Salon's catalogs in the latter years of the 19th century. He exhibited a study in bronze entitled *Singe assis se tenant la tête* in 1893, later to be cast by Siot-Decauville. In 1895, there was a group in pewter, *Singe saoul,* and finally two studies in plaster, *Lionne* in 1897 and *Ours* in 1900. A statuette of Soliva's *Eléphant chargeant* also carries the seal of Siot-Decauville.

SOMME, THÉOPHILE FRANÇOIS

Nancy, September 7, 1871
August 4, 1952

Some busts, genre scenes, and allegories, most often executed in plaster, were exhibited by this sculptor at the Salon starting in 1893: *Orphée mourant* (1898), *Dénicheur d'aigles* (1899), *Le Celte* (1900), *L'Eveil* (1901), *La Fin d'un rêve* (1902), *Contemplation* (1904), *Le Livre* (1906), *Vers la terre* (1908), *Résignée* (1913), *Vers le progrès* (1914). Somme's works in bronze sometimes incorporated other materials, like his bust *Rêverie*, in bronze, marble, gold and precious stones, presented to the Salon in 1905. Many works by this artist have been cast in bronze, including *Dénicheur d'aigles*, 94 cm. The museum of Toulon preserves a bust entitled *Portrait de Madame B.*, 60 cm in height.

Soldi-Colbert,
Pas de danse,
83 cm.

E. Soldi Colbert

François Sicard,
La Charmeuse de serpent,
53 cm
(Barbedienne).

617

SALES

Dénicheur d'aigle, 94 cm, Lokeren, April 20, 1985.

Egyptienne, bronze and ivory, 18 cm, Drouot, March 8, 1981.

Femme au manchon, bronze and ivory, 25 cm, Drouot, April 10, 1981.

Guerrier soulevant une pierre, 30 cm, Sotheby London, June 12, 1986.

Héroïne, bronze and ivory, 30 cm, Drouot, May 18, 1981.

Inspiration, gilded bronze and ivory, 42 cm, Drouot, December 7, 1983.

Jeune Bretonne en prière, bronze and ivory, 25 cm, Brest, May 15, 1983.

Jeune Femme debout, gilded bronze and ivory, 32 cm, Sotheby London, March 21, 1985.

SOULES, FÉLIX

Eauzé (Gers), October 12, 1857
Eauzé, March 1904

L'Aurore, a group in stone surmounting the lateral facade of the Grand Palais, on the Champs-Elysée side, carries the signature of this artist. After some studies at the school of fine arts in Toulouse, Soules went to work in Paris under the direction of Jouffroy and Falguière. He debuted at the Salon in 1881 and obtained the second prize of Rome in 1887. His work is composed of antique subjects, some genre scenes, and allegories: *Vainqueur,* a statuette in plaster (Salon of 1885), *Enlèvement d'Iphigénie par Diane,* a group in bronze (1890; marble in 1892), *Joueuse de boules,* a statuette in marble (1894), *Bacchante à la chevre,* a group in marble (1896), and *La Ville de Mont-de-Marsan,* a group in bronze (1903), etc. *L'Enlèvement d'Iphigénie* was cast by Siot-Decauville.

A bust entitled *Le Président Fallières,* 5.3 cm, cast by Montagutelli, belongs to the museum of Périgueux.

STEINER, LEOPALD

Paris, March 7, 1853
December, 1899

The son of a sculptor and a student of Jouffroy at the Beaux-Arts, Léopald Steiner left some allegorical groups, genre scenes, and busts and statues of great men, including *Ledru-Rollin, Berryer, Rouget-de-l'Isle,* etc. He is also the author of the gilded bronze work *Renommée de l'Industrie,* which surmounts one of the pillars of the Left Bank's Alexandre-III Bridge; he also made the sculpted decorations for diverse châteaux and certain hotels, and a 2 meter high bronze group entitled *Berger et Sylvain* in Briançon, etc. Of note at the Salon is *La Cigale,* a statuette in marble (1887), *Jeune Homme au chat,* a statuette in bronze (1891), and a number of statuettes in plaster or in terra cotta representing contemporaries. Some works by Steiner have been cast in bronze by different founders, such as Eugène Blot, Susse, and Thiébaut. Thiébaut also cast *Berger et Sylvain,* 91 and 63 cm, *Candélabre Louis XIV,* 95 cm, *Cupidon ravisseur,* 68 cm, and *Petite Blanchisseuse,* 22 cm. There are some proofs of *Jeune Homme au chat,* 63 and 46 cm, *Paysanne et enfant,* 85 cm (cast by Eugène Blot), a portrayal of a clock entitled *La Rosée,* 104 cm, and *La Tentation,* etc.

*Léopold Steiner,
Berger et Sylvain, 91 cm
(Thiébaut frères).*

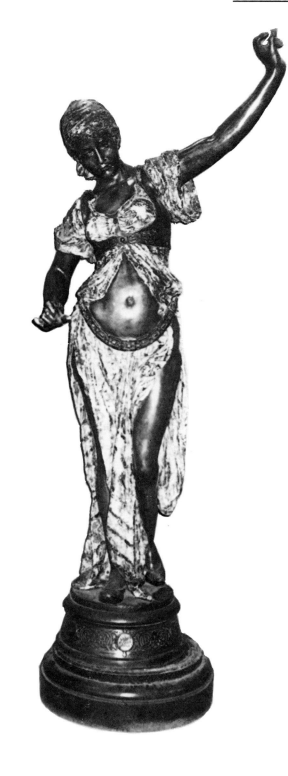

Léopold Steiner,
Femme orientale,
painted regule, 210 cm.

Léopold Steiner,
Escrimeur, 65 cm.

SALES

Berger et Sylvain (Thiébaut), 91 cm, Sotheby London, November 6, 1986.

Escrimeur, 65 cm, Sotheby London, June 12, 1986.

Hébé, 94 cm (Colin, founder), Christie's London, September 25, 1986.

Jeune Homme marchant, dressed in the style of antiquity, Brest, March 20, 1986.

Femme orientale, painted regule, 210 cm, Bordeaux, October 23, 1986 (sold at 62,000 F).

STEINLEN, THÉOPHILE ALEXANDRE

Lausanne, November 10, 1859
Paris, December 14, 1923

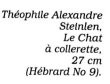

Of Swiss origin, Steinlen came to Paris at the age of nineteen and was naturalized to French citizenship in 1901. A painter, watercolorist, and an illustrator in different journals (such as *Le Gil Blas illustré* and *Le Chat noir*), he was a sculptor as well,

though this part of his work is much less well-known. However, his subjects are the same—particularly his favorite, cats. He sculpted just as he drew or painted, portraying cats of every breed, in all positions. Most were cast in bronze, often by Hébrard, as is evidenced by the numerous pieces passed in public sale and possessed by museums.

MUSEUMS
Gray
Chat accroupi, 20.5 cm.
Paris, Decorative Arts
Chat faisant le gros dos, 12 cm (Hébrard, founder).
Paris, Orsay
Chat abyssin assis, 14 cm.

Théophile Alexandre Steinlen, Chat angora assis, 12 cm (Hébrard).

Théophile Alexandre Steinlen, Le Chat à collerette, 27 cm (Hébrard No 9).

Alexandre Stella,
Petit Mendiant,
26.5 cm.

Alexandre Stella,
Le Marchand
d'esclaves,
83 cm.

Alexandre Stella,
Allégorie du vin,
92 cm.

Chat angora assis, 7 cm.
Chat angora couché sur un canapé, 16 cm.
Chat couché sur le sol, 9 cm (Hébrard).
Chat regardant l'extrémité de ses pattes, 10 cm.
Tête couchée aux longs cheveux, 4 x 6.7 cm.
Tête de femme, bouche ouverte, 8.8 cm.
Tête d'homme, 8 cm.
Saint-Etienne
Maternité, 43 cm.

SALES
Chat, 12.5 cm (Hébrard), Drouot, November 28, 1985, rooms 1 and 7.
Chat angora assis, 12.5 cm (Hébrard No4), Sotheby London, March 29, 1984; Drouot, April 18, 1986, room 5.
Chat assis, 27.5 cm (Hébrard No6), Drouot, April 18, 1986, room 6 (price at auction: 100,000 F).
Chat couché, 8.5 x 24 cm, Drouot, February 6, 1984, room 7; Drouot, March 10, 1984, room 8.
Tête de chat, 6.5 cm, Valenciennes, April 9, 1984.

STELLA, ALEXANDRE

Born in Paris

STELLA

Alexandre Stella exhibited at the Salon between 1878 and 1885, contributing portraits of historical personages and genre scenes, mostly in plaster. These include *Louis XIV* and *Molière,* two bas-reliefs (1878), a statue of *Rabelais* (1880), and the following additional bas-reliefs: *Tentation* (1881), *Le Droit du seigneur* and *La Dîme du seigneur* (1885). Stella is known to have produced a single statue in bronze, *Le Printemps,* in 1881. A statuette in bronze, *Le Marchand d'esclaves,* 83 cm, was sold in Etampes on September 23, 1984.

STRAETEN, GEORGES VAN DER

Gand, December 21, 1856—?

Though of Belgian nationality, this artist lived in Paris for a long time, and began exhibiting at the Salon in 1885. He produced a number of portraits, some fanciful busts of young women, and gracious feminine figures which often evoke the amiable style of 18th century sculptors, particularly Watteau. His plaster consignments to the Salon include a bust exhibited in 1886 entitled *Le Drame*, some statuettes entitled *Fantaisie* (1887), *Une merveilleuse* (1888), and *Fantaisie Watteau* (1911), a number of statues and groups including *Embrasse!* (1889), *Le Printemps* (1890), *Sous l'Empire* (1893), *Amour maternel* (1896), *Mondaine* (1899), and *Liseuse Empire* (1910), and finally some statuettes in bronze and ivory cast by F. Goldscheider: *Mimi* and *Rêverie* (1909), and *Innocence* and *Menuet* (1910).

Many founders, including the Société des Bronzes of Paris, Pinédo, and Goldscheider, have cast the works of Van der Straeten in rather large numbers, with different dimensions and under very varied titles. Of note, among others, are a number of feminine busts, including *Jeune Femme à la coiffe*, 70 cm, *Elégante assise* (E. Blot), 24.5 cm, *Colombine* and *Le Croissant de lune*, cast in bronze and in composition, 76 cm.

The museum of Maubeuge preserves a bust by Van der Staeten in bronze, *La Source*, 40.5 cm, cast by the Société des Bronzes of Paris.

SALES

Gentleman rider, 39 cm (Société des Bronzes of Paris), Sotheby London, March 20, 1986.
Jeune Femme, 25 cm (Blot, founder), Lokeren, April 20, 1985.
Jeune Femme assise sur une corne d'abondance, 68.5 cm, Sotheby London, November 7, 1985.
Jeune Femme en robe du soir, 33 cm, Poitiers, Ocotber 22, 1983.
Buste de jeune femme, bronze, ivory and marble, 22 cm, Barcelona, March 26, 1985.
Buste de jeune femme, 59 cm (Société des Bronzes of Paris), Sotheby London, November 8, 1984.

SYAMOUR, MARGUERITE

Bréry (Jura), August 10, 1857
1945

Marguerite Syamour lived and worked in Bréry for most of her life, until the beginning of the 1930s. Her production includes some busts and statues of historical personages or of contemporaries (including a statue of *Voltaire* for the city of Saint-Claude, and of *Gagneur* for Poligny), as well as mythological and allegorical groups. A plaque in bronze entitled *Pour Auguste Brézeux*, 21.8 x 14.2 cm., is preserved at the museum of Avignon.

Georges van der Straeten,
Trois bustes de jeunes femmes,
17 to 19 cm.

T

TARRIT, JEAN

Châtillon-sur-Chalaronne (Ain), December 31, 1865

Tanger, May 2, 1950

Though he first portrayed subjects drawn from domestic French fauna, starting in 1910 this sculptor switched to personages and scenes from Morocco, where he had settled. He produced a certain number of plasters, which he exhibited at the Salon: *Enfant à la bulle de savon* (1896), *Chant du matin* (1898), *Chatte et ses petits* (1902), *L'Effort*, haut-relief (1907), and *Laitière normande* (1909). Additionally, there are some statuettes in wood entitled *Chiffonnière* (1901), *Enfant aux chats* (1905), and *Jeunes Chats* (1910); a group in stone entitled *Aveugles marocains à Tanger* (1913); two bronzes entitled *Route de Fez, Marocain revenant du marché* and *Porteur d'eau marocain* (1914), and other works. The small group representing a *Chatte et ses petits* was exhibited in sandstone at the Société Nationale des Beaux-Arts in 1903.

A bronze by Tarrit, *Dromadaire allaitant son petit*, 38 cm (Motte Frères No. 6), was sold in Enghien on June 26, 1983. A statuette in regule, *Porteur d'eau marocain*, 27.5 cm, passed in sale at the Drouot Hotel on June 27, 1983 in room 6.

TASSEL, EDMOND LOUIS CHARLES

Born in Evreux

This sculptor exhibited a statuette in plaster entitled *Le Passage du ruisseau* at the Salon of 1890. Some castings of this piece are known, in bronze of 55 cm high.

TATTEGRAIN, GEORGES GABRIEL

Péronne (Somme), November 5, 1845
Amiens, December 16, 1916

A poet and sculptor with a profound attachment to the Picard region, Tattegrain worked in Amiens and began exhibiting his works at the Salon in 1877. He produced numerous busts, portraits of contemporaries, imaginary personages, and regional types, such as *Moissonneur de Picardie, Travailleur,* and *Vieille Femme picarde* (a bust in terra cotta at the Salon of 1878), *Jeune Escholier du XV siècle,* etc. The museum of Amiens possesses a bust in bronze entitled *Hector Crinon, poète picard,* 53 cm, modeled after a plaster presented to the Salon of 1892.

TEGNER RUDOLF

Copenhagen, July 12, 1873
1950

This Danish artist exhibited his works at the Salon de Paris in the first years of the 20th century and after the First World War. He had them cast in Paris as well, most frequently by Colin. The Salon catalog of 1921 notes that Tegner presented a bronze entitled *Hercule tuant l'hydre de Lerne,* 90 x 86 cm in that year. Tegner lived with the Danish silversmith Georg Jensen on the Rue Saint-Honoré. A bronze entitled *Le gladiateur vaincu,* 86 cm (Colin, founder), was sold at the Drouot Hotel on May 13, 1985, room 4. Another bronze, *Hercule tuant l'hydre de Lerne,* 90 cm, was sold at the Drouot Hotel on December 7, 1983, room 14.

TERROIR, ALPHONSE CAMILLE

Marly (Nord), November 12, 1875
October 15, 1955

A painter and sculptor, Terroir studied first at the academies of Valenciennes, and then in Paris under Barrias and Coutan. Winning the prize of Rome in 1902, he produced some religious works and funerary figures, often for monuments to the dead and showing Italian influence. In 1908 he sent a group to the Salon entitled *Adam et Eve,* and a bas-relief entitled *Seul dans la vie,* both in marble. Then, in 1909, he sent *L'Orphelin,* a group in stone made for a Valenciennes garden in 1911, a bronze head of *Adam* in 1912, a group in stone called *Vision antique* in 1913, *L'homme devant la mort se recueille,* also in

Rudolf Tegner,
Le Gladiateur vaincu, 86 cm (Colin).

stone, etc. He continued consigning at the Salon after World War I, with, for example, a statue in bronze entitled *Recueillement* (1924), modeled after his *L'Homme devant la mort* (1913). The museum of Carnavalet in Paris possesses a bust of a woman in bronze, 66 cm high.

A bronze by Terroir entitled *Homo Faber,* 40 cm, was cast by Susse, and was sold at the Drouot Hotel on March 7, 1984 in room 7.

THABARD, ADOLPHE MARTIAL

Limoge, November 13, 1831
Clamart, December 2, 1905

Thabard, a student of Duret, had been trained especially for ornamental sculpture, both exterior and interior. He participated in the restoration of a number of monuments, including the Palais Royal, the Louvre, the city hall, the Saint-Eustache church, and the church of the Sorbonne. He is also the author of a monumental group, *Le Génie de la force,* for a bridge in Budapest. He participated at the Salon starting in 1863 with the following notable pieces: *Le Charmeur,* a statue in marble of 140 cm in height (1875), *L'Amour au cygne,* marble (1884 and Exposition Universelle of 1889), *Narcisse et Léda,* a sketch in bronze (1888), and *La Poésie,* a statue in marble (1891).

A bronze of 68 cm in height, *Pan assis,* was sold in London at Sotheby's on November 6, 1986.

THAREL, LÉON

Tôtes (Seine-Maritime), circa 1858
1902

Tharel's consignments to the Salon were essentially genre scenes, including the plaster *A la pêche aux crevettes,* the bronze *Pifferaro* (1885), *Cosette* in plaster and *Sans soucis* in marble (1886), *Le Dénicheur de nids* (1888) and *Premier Sourire* (1890), both in plaster, *Souvenir* in stone and *Turenne enfant* in plaster (1893), and another plaster entitled *La Dernière Rose* (1897).

Sans soucis (a young seated violinist) was cast in bronze by Susse in three dimensions, 35, 26 and 18 cm.

SALES

Jeune Violoniste assis, 30.5 cm, Christie's Oklahoma, September 24, 1981.
Jeune Violoniste assis, 27.5 cm, Cologne, October 26, 1984.

THEUNISSEN, CORNEILLE HENRI

Anzin (Nord), November 6, 1863
Paris, December, 1918

On the northern lateral facade of the Grand Palais, Theunissen sculpted a vast bas-relief representing *Les Arts et les Sciences rendant hommage au nouveau siècle.* Studying first of the academies of Valenciennes and then under Cavelier at the Ecole des Beaux-Arts of Paris, this artist is also the author of busts and medallions, often in bronze, some genre scenes, and commemorative monuments in the north

of France (including *Défense de Saint-Quentin contre les Espagnols en 1557*, inaugurated in 1897). Memorable among his consignments to the Salon between 1883 and 1914 are some statuettes in bronze, including *Joueuse de violon* (1886), *L'Architecte Prosper Bobin* (1903), and *Le Violoncelliste Raymond Marthe* (1907), as well as two statuettes in sandstone of Muller entitled *Première Communiante* and *En avant* (1896) and a bust in oak of the painter *Harpignies* (1901). A statuette in bronze entitled *Rêverie aux champs* is held in a private collection.

MUSEUMS
Roubaix
Buste de Victor Champier (1908).
Tourcoing
Buste d'Edouard Sasselange, 50 cm (1896).

THIÉBAUT, HENRI LÉON

Paris, 1855
January 12, 1899

Working simultaneously as a founder, an editor for very highly reputed art bronzes, and a sculptor, Thiébaut exhibited some portraits in bust or in medallion at the Salon between 1878 and 1898. A

Adolphe Martial Thabard,
Pan assis, 68 cm.

Corneille Henri Theunissen,
Rêverie au champ
or Moissonneuse au repos,
52 cm (Susse).
J. Ginepro Collection, Monaco.

certain number of them were in bronze, as were a number of other forms: a vase entitled *La Mer* in 1894, a sketch entitled *Coquillage* in 1895, and *Onze Clochettes et grelots pour bicyclettes et voitures à pneumatiques* in 1898. At the beginning of the century, the Thiébaut house (where Henri Léon would later be succeeded by Fumière and Gavignot) cast the vase *La Mer* in 68 cm of height.

THOMAS, ÉMILE

Paris, February 6, 1817
Neuilly-sur-Seine, January 2, 1882

A student of Pradier at the Beaux-Arts, Émile Thomas exhibited at the Salon from 1843 to 1874, sojourning in Rome around 1846. He received numerous commissions, for statues of saints and historic people, and for busts of contemporaries including *Champollion, Alexandre Dumas fils, Théophile Gautier,* and *James Pradier.* Thomas worked for the cathedral of Arras and for many churches in Paris: *Sainte-Elisabeth, Saint-Louis-d'Antin, Saint-Séverin, Saint-Sulpice,* and *La Trinité.* The château of Compiègne possesses a small bust by this artist entitled *Napoléon III,* 27.5 cm.

THOMAS, GABRIEL JULES

Paris, September 10, 1824
Paris, March 8, 1905

Gabriel Thomas's teachers (Ramey and Dumont at the Ecole des Beaux-Arts) instilled their student with a regard for antiquity, to which he would remain faithful all his life. The son of sculptor Alexis Thomas, Gabriel won the first prize of Rome in 1848 with *Philoctète partant pour le siège de Troie.* After his stay at the Villa Médicis, he exhibited at the Salon for the first time in 1857. Very prolific, he participated in the decoration of numerous buildings, including the Louvre, the Tuileries, the Opera, the Galliéra Palace, the Gare du Nord, the city hall, the Grand Palais (executing the group of the *Arts Graphiques*), the churches of Saint-Etienne-du-Mont (the *Martyre de saint Etienne* in the tympanum) and Saint-François-Xavier (the tympanum), as well as the cathedral of Marseille and the casino of Monte-Carlo. A 165 cm high statue representing *L'Adolescence* was cast in bronze for the city of Guillestre. At the foot of the stairwell of the Jardin des Plantes' zoology gallery stands one of his groups in bronze, cast by Thiébaut, entitled *L'Homme au serpent.* In 1875, Thomas was elected to the Institut to replace Barye. He became a teacher at the Beaux-Arts in 1884.

Thomas executed a number of busts, medallions, and mythological and allegorical scenes. Of note among his works are some bronzes, including *Virgile,* after the plaster from the Salon of 1861, *Lucien Bonaparte,* a statue destined for the monument of the Bonaparte family in Ajaccio, the bust of the architect *Paul Abadie,* exhibited at the Salon of 1880, and another bust portraying a member of the Institut, *L. Ginain* (1885), etc.

MUSEUMS
Bayonne
Buste d'homme chauve aux favoris, 27 cm (Eck and Durand, founders 1857).
Grenoble
Portrait d'Irvoy, medallion, 45 cm diam.
Morlaix
Virgile, 70 cm (Thiébaut).

THOMAS-SOYER, MATHILDE

Troyes, August 19, 1858
Brinon-sur-Sauldre (Indre), July 20, 1940

The daughter of a magistrate, Mathilde Thomas-Soyer studied sculpture with Chapu and Cain, essentially devoting herself to animal art, with a very marked predilection for portraying dogs. Starting in 1879, she participated very regularly at the Salon. She exhibited some subjects in plaster, including *Vache terrassant un loup whi vient d'égorger son veau* (1879), *Cheval russe attaqué par des loups,* 135 cm (1880), *Chiens perdus, étude de lévriers russes,* 110 cm (1881), *Chasseur et braconnier, Chien d'arrêt et chien de berger,* 110 cm (1882), *En vedette* (1883), *Au chenil* (1886), *A bout de force, étude d'âne* (1888), *Bataille de chiens* (1892), *Hérault d'armes du XVe siècle* (1894), *Chien et vipère* (1896), *Au bord du terrier* (1897), *Alerte, laie et marcassins* (1898), *Etude de chiots* (1900), *Double arrêt, setter et loverock* (1902), *Préméditation, Chat* (1904), *Le Repos, attelage de chiens* (1906), *Chevaux* (1909), *Deux Gendarmes* (1912), *Etude d'ours* (1913), etc. Some works, a certain number of them first exhibited in plaster, were also presented in bronze: *La Chèvre Amalthée* (1886), *Le Guet, étude de chat* (1891), *Retour des champs* (1894), and *Down, chien* (1914).

Many subjects by Mathilde Thomas-Soyer were cast in bronze. Some carry the seal of Thiébaut, including *En vedette, sentinelle à cheval,* 59 cm, *Lévrier barzoi,* 26 cm, and *Deux chiens attachés ensemble,* 14 cm. Marked by Siot-Decauville is the bronze *Chat à l'arrêt,* 6 cm.

SALES
Deux chiens attachés ensemble, 14 cm (Thiébaut), Sotheby London, April 28, 1982.
Le Cuirassier à cheval, 58 cm, Madrid, October 23, 1985.
En vedette, 58 cm (Thiébaut), Sotheby London, July 7, 1984.

THOMIRE, PIERRE PHILIPPE

Paris, December 5, 1751
Paris, June 9, 1843

A chiseler who had followed in his father's footsteps, Thomire is considered the greatest specialist in bronze of furnishings of the first Empire. In 1776, after studying with the equally famous Gouthière, Thomire founded a universally reputed studio which collaborated with the greatest cabinetmakers and the Sèvres factory to work for Louis XVI and Napoléon I, and then again for the Bourbons after 1815. At

Pierre Nicolas Tourgueneff, Grenadier et Hussard du premier Empire, 61 cm.

certain times, the studio employed many hundreds of workers. In 1823, Thomire retired from the business, leaving his enterprise to his sons-in-law, whom he had taken as partners.

This unrivaled artist also practiced sculpture, an art he had been initiated into by Houdon and Pajou at the Académie of Saint-Luc. In particular, he made some bronzes based on sculptures from the 18th century, particularly those by Pigalle, as well as some allegorical figures intended for centerpieces, clocks, and candelabras. In 1811, he completed the coronation bower for the king of Rome. Finally he left some busts of contemporaries, principally in bronze, including diverse members of his family. A certain number of these busts were exhibited at the Salon between 1810 and 1834, as was Thomire's self-portrait in profile (a medallion). Also shown at the Salon was his bronze self-portrait bust (1813), cast by Eck and Durand in 58 cm, and placed on his tomb at the Montmartre cemetery.

MUSEUMS
Paris, Decorative Arts
Bacchante drapée dans une peau de lion, 48 cm.
André Anatole Allar enfant, bust, 23 cm (1832).
Hippolyte Beauvisage-Thomire, the artist's grandson, bust, 37 cm (1832).

TOURGUENEFF, PIERRE NICOLAS
Paris, April 2, 1853
Paris, March 21, 1912

Born into a family originally from Russia, Tourgueneff was a student of Frémiet. Like his master, he could be categorized among the animal sculptors because of his portraits of horses and dogs. Also attributed to him, however, are some equestrian figures of horses and riders, mostly portraying the military of Tourgueneff's own time or of the First Empire. His works have been cast in bronze, exclusively by the Susse foundry. A number of these works, particularly some statuettes, were exhibited in bronze at the Salon, where he started participating regularly in 1880. This is the case with *Loys, comte de Nassau*, an equestrian statue (1884), *Veneur à cheval du XIVe siècle* (1885), *Le Patron* (1886), *Francarcher du XVe siècle* (1887), *Etalon percheron* (1890), *Gardeuse d'oies* (1891), *Madame X. à cheval* (1893), *Red Lancer* (1895), *Cavalier de 1806* (1899), *Le Vieux*, equestrian group and *Téméraire III, pur-sang* (1903), *Pierre-le-Grand à cheval* (1906), *Jument poulinière pur-sang* (1907), *Mademoiselle V. Nimidoff, de l'Opera* (1908), and *Alexandre III de Russie*, an equestrian statue for the museum of

Saint-Petersburg (1910). Of further note among many other similar subjects are plasters including *Visapour, étalon russe*, 20 x 90 cm (1880), *Yermak, conquâte de la Sibérie en 1583*, an equestrian statue (1884), *Pasteur dans la steppe*, an equestrian statue (1886), *Halage* (1887), *Fille d'Eve* (1888), *En grand' garde* (1890), *La Charge* (1892), *Chevaux de labour* (1896), *Jument et son poulain* (1898), *Grenadier de la garde consulaire* and *Chasseur d'Afrique*, two equestrian statuettes (1901), *Dans la prairie, jument pur-sang* (1905), and *Diane chasseresee à cheval* (1910).

The catalog published by Susse at the beginning of the 20th century listed the twenty-four following works, cast in patinated bronze, some also in gilded bronze:

Archer, 73 and 37 cm.
Chasseur en vedette, 38 cm.
Cheval anglais, 47 cm.
Cheval Cob, 23 cm.
Cheval demi-sang, 48 cm.
Cheval au dressage, 31 cm.
Cheval Norfolk, 32 cm.
Cheval de selle, 31 cm.
Chien barbet assis (scotch terrier), 16 cm.
Chiens bassets, group, 12 cm.
Chien à l'escargot, 6 cm.
Chien griffon basset (à la piste), 11 cm.
Chien de police, 19 and 10 cm.
Tête de chien, 23 and 6 cm.
Tête de chien, seal, 7 cm.
Cuirassier à la charge, 46 cm.
Dogue, 19 and 12 cm.
Dragon en vedette, 40 cm.
Grenadier de la garde, 62 cm.
Hussard 1806, 61 cm.
Jument Thérésa, 17 cm.
Groupe de deux juments, 41 cm.
Poulinière, 28 cm.
Retour du labour, 50 cm.

MUSEUMS
Paris, Orsay
Chevaux de halage, 48 x 69.5 cm (1903).

SALES
L'Anon, 24 x 21 cm (Susse), Enghien, Feburary 22, 1981.
Cheval, Drouot, October 15, 1986, room 16.
Chien Couché, 19 x 39 cm (Susse), Enghien, February 22, 1981.
Grenadier et Hussard du premier Empire, two statuettes, 61 cm, Orléans, March 28, 1987.

TOURNOIS, JOSEPH

Chazeuil (Côte-d'Or), May 18, 1830
Paris, 1891

Tournois studied first in Dijon, and then at the Ecole des Beaux-Arts of Paris in the studio of Jouffroy. He went to Rome after winning the grand prize of sculpture with *Ulysse blessé à la chasse par un sanglier*. At the Salon, where he exhibited starting in 1868, some bronzes are noteworthy: *Bacchus*

inventant la Comédie, a statue of 170 cm cast by Victor Thiébaut (1869), *Joueur de palet,* 138 cm (1870), *Persée,* a replica of the marble exhibited in in 1875, and *Buste de Henner* (1892). A statue of *François Rude,* also in bronze, was presented to the Exposition Universelle of 1889. The museum of Dijon possesses a larger than life bronze representing *Persée.*

TOUSSAINT, ARMAND

Paris, April 7, 1806
Paris, May 24, 1862

Toussaint, both a sculptor and a medaller, won the second prize of Rome in 1832 and debuted at the Salon in 1836. His work consists of diverse ornamental sculptures for the Louvre, the churches of Notre-Dame and Saint-Sulpice, the basilica of Sainte-Clotilde, and the Marseille stock exchange; he is also known for a colossal bust in marble of *David d'Angers*—his master at the Beaux-Arts—for the museum of Angers, as well as for some groups and historical people. In addition, he made figures in stone polychrome, which replaced the 16th century originals on Paris's Palais de Justice clock in 1851. Barbedienne cast some works by this artist, including *Deux Esclaves prote-lumières,* 112 and 70 cm, and a medallion, *Laissez venir à moi les petits enfants,* 39, 31, 19 and 13 cm diam.

Two candelabras ornamented with statuettes of eastern people, 120 cm, was sold in Enghien on October 16, 1983.

TRODOUX, HENRI

Born in Saint Petersburg

Born to French parents, Trodoux served his apprenticeship at the school of fine arts in his hometown. He lived and worked there approximately from 1835 to 1855, participating most notably in the decoration of the Palais d'Hiver. For several years he exhibited at the Salon of Paris, primarily with animal or exotic subjects, in particular, a work in silvered bronze entitled *Bécasse* (1874), and two plaster statue-candelabras, entitled *Bison de l'Ouest* and *Femme orientale* (both 1876), as well as some busts and some medallions.

SALES
Dog jouant avec une souris, 10.5 x 17 cm, Enghien, June 21, 1981.
Oiseau d'eau, 24 cm, Enghien, February 22, 1981.

TROUBETZKOY, PRINCE PAUL

Intra, Italy, February 16, 1866
Suna, near Intra, February 12, 1938

Rare are the artists with such international lives and notoriety. Born in Italy to an American mother and a Russian father descended from a large aristocratic family, Troubetzkoy first married a Swede, and after her decease, married an Englishwoman; his only son was born in Finland. Troubetzkoy also

Armand Toussaint, Personnages orientaux, pair of candelabrum, 120 cm, (F. Barbedienne). See reproduction in color from a similar proof page 15.

Paul Troubetzkoy

Prince Paul Troubetzkoy,
Jeune Femme assise,
38 cm.

Prince Paul Troubetzkoy,
Danseuse jambe droite levée,
35 cm (Valsuani).

Prince Paul Troubetzkoy,
Jeune Femme assise,
sketch.

Prince Paul Troubetzkoy,
Mère et enfant,
sketch, 37.5 cm.

631

lived and worked, (according to his biographer M. John S. Grioni, in *Gazette des Beaux-Arts*, May 1985), in Italy, Paris, London, Russia, Egypt, the United States (where he spent the years of World War I), and Sweden—thus explaining both the success he had all over Europe and beyond the Atlantic, as well as the widespread dispersal of his works in a number of museums and private collections. In Paris he won the grand prize of sculpture at the Exposition Universelle in 1900. He located his studio in Neuilly—for though he traveled widely, he lived primarily in France—and it was frequented by the most conspicuous artists and personalities. He visited the shores of Lake Majeur frequently, and established residence there permanently in 1932.

A sculptor and an engraver, Troubetzkoy represented animals, horsemen, dancers, intimate scenes, and a number of portraits of contemporaries, including the members of the Russian aristocracy. His sculptures frequently evoke feminine fashions from the beginning of the century. Influenced by Rodin, he devoted himself to seizing the movement, the positions, the fleeting effects and emotions, using a style that can only be categorized as impressionistic. Very popular, he entrusted the production of his works in bronze to nearly fifteen founders, principally in France by Valsuani and others including Hébrard. He earned a great deal of money, but, a tireless gambler, he lost just as much. He had the most popular models cast frequently, in great number and according to his needs, each proof carrying the date of the casting rather than the date of the original model.

After Troubetzkoy's death, the plasters and bronzes from his studio were given to the small Italian community where he was born.

The bronzes of Paul Troubetzkoy appear in rather large numbers on the market. Among the proofs dispersed to auctions in recent years (see below), of particular note are *Amazone*, an equestrian group, 47 cm (1896), *Bédouin au dromadaire* 27 cm (1896), *Le Docteur Bruyère*, Hébrard casting, 47 cm (1907), *Carlo Bugatti debout*, 45.5 cm (1889), *Cheval au galop*, 52 cm L., *Chien assis*, 25 cm, *Le Cow-boy galopant*, Valsuani casting, 30 x 41 cm, *La Danse, danseuse jambe droite levée*, Valsuani casting, 35 cm, *Danseuse dans le rôle de Cléopatre*, 58 cm (1909), *Danseuse espagnole*, Valsuani casting, 51 cm, *La Danseuse Pavlova dans Bacchanale*, Valsuani casting, 52 cm (1910), *Jeune Femme assise*, 38 cm (many versions), *Jeune Fille allongée sur un lit*, Valsuani casting, 22 cm, *Le Gaucho à cheval* (1911), *Guerrier Peau-Rouge à cheval*, 40.5 cm, *Lancier italien à cheval*, 60 cm, *Lapon, son renne et ses chiens* (Moscow 1899), 36 x 82 cm, *Lévrier couché* 12 x 39 cm (1909), *Mère et enfant*, sketch, 82 cm, *Paul Heller debout*, 58 cm, *La Baronne Robert de Rothschild assise*, 46 cm (1911), *Rodin debout*, 52 cm, *La Troika épuisée*, 27 x 59 cm (1900), and *Vache se léchant* (1887), 21.5 cm.

MUSEUMS
Paris, Orsay
Jeune Femme assise, Mme Anernheimer après le bal, 53 cm (1898).
Monument d'Alexandre III, sketch, 55 cm (1905; Hébrard).
Le Comte Robert de Montesquiou assis au lévrier, 56 cm (Valsuani; 1907).
Tolstoï à cheval, 50 cm (1899).

Some bronzes by Troubetzkoy are displayed in many foreign museums, in particular at the Russian museum of Leningrad and at the Tretiakov Gallery of Moscow.

*Prince Paul Troubetzk[oy]
Tolstoï à cheval,
50.5 cm.*

*Prince Paul Troubetzkoy,
Jeune Fille debout
tenant sa natte,
44 cm.*

*Prince Paul Troubetzkoy,
Cavalier arabe au galop,
25 x 39 cm (Valsuani).*

*Prince Paul Troubetzkoy,
Jeune Fille à demi nue
se coiffant,
49 cm.*

*Prince Paul Troubetzkoy,
Lapon, son renne
et ses chiens,
36 x 82 cm.*

SALES

Ballerine, 35 cm, Milan, October 30, 1984.
Carlo Bugatti, 44 cm (Milan 1899), Drouot, July 2, 1984, room 10.
Cavalier arabe au galop, 25 x 39 cm (posthumous font, A. Valsuani), Saint-Maur, March 2, 1986.
Danseuse jambe droite levée, 35 cm (Valsuani), Compiègne, June 2, 1985; Granville, November 3, 1985; Versailles, February 16, 1986.
Elégante assise, 44.5 cm (1897), Christie's New York, April 29, 1984.
Femme assise, 38 cm, Lille, October 22, 1984.
Fillette au chien, Rambouillet, October 12, 1986.
Indien debout, 53 cm (1916), Christie's New York, March 27, 1985.
Une Japonaise, 57 cm (Hébrard), Sotheby London, June 13, 1984.
Jeune Femme mains aux hanches (1930), Nice, June 28, 1986.
Jeune Fille debout tenant sa natte, 44 cm, Saint-Maur, March 8, 1987.
Jeune Fille à demi-nue se coiffant, 49 cm, Drouot, November 14, 1986.
Loup, 31 x 17.7 cm, Milan, March 27, 1984.
Marie Clark de Brabant, 37.5 cm, Christie's New York, May 24, 1984.
Mère et enfant, 37.5 cm, Drouot, April 21, 1985 (sold for 90,000 F).
Rodin en pied, 50 cm (A. Valsuani), Saint-Maur, May 11, 1986; Granville, June 13, 1986.
Tolstoi à cheval, 50.5 cm (Robecchi, founder; 1901); Saint-Maur, October 26, 1986.
Le Traîneau, 26 cm, Drouot, April 4, 1984, room 1.

TRUFFOT, ÉMILE LOUIS

Valenciennes, July 26, 1843
Paris, December 26, 1896

Enrolled in the Ecole des Beaux-Arts at the age of nineteen, Truffot made his debut at the Salon one year later. His work is almost entirely devoted to eastern and Far Eastern people and scenes, evident themes in his consignments to the Salon. In addition to a number of busts displayed there, his most notable Salon bronzes (often exhibited first in plaster) include *L'Amour et la Folie* (1876), two busts entitled *Lotha la Nubienne* and *Yoki la Japonaise* (1880), *Amazone libyenne* (1883), *Esméralda* (1886), and *Le Berger Jupile luttant avec un loup enragé*, a group destined to for the Institut Pasteur (1889). Some animal subjects appeared at the end of his career, including a group in bronze entitled *Chaude Ouverture, chien de chasse et lièvre* (Salon de 1892), as well as the plasters *Caresse de fauve* (1892), *Un braconnier, renard tenant un faisan* (1893), and *Flagrant Délit* (1894).

The Siot-Decauville foundry cast Truffot's *Chaude Ouverture* and *Un braconnier*. There are some proofs of this latter work known in many dimensions, including 56 x 90 and 40 x 60.

The museum of Puy owns Truffot's group in bronze entitled *Berger Jupille*, 73 cm, dated 1877.

TRUPHÈME, ANDRÉ FRANÇOIS JOSEPH

Aix-en-Provence, March 23, 1820
Paris, January 22, 1888

Mythological and allegorical subjects, genre scenes, and numerous statues and busts of historic people came from the studio of this sculptor, who worked for different cities, particularly Aix-en-Provence (sculpting the statue of *Mirabeau* for the courtyard of its city hall) and Marseille. In Paris, Truphème participated in the decoration of many buildings, including the Louvre, the city hall, the Opera, the church of the Trinité, and the Sainte-Clotilde basilica. He came to the capitl at the age of twenty, and entered the Beaux-Arts in 1846. He sent a statuette in bronze of *André Chénier* to the Exposition Universelle of 1855, and a marble statue entitled *Jeune Fille à la source* to the Exposition of 1855. At the Salon, where he debuted in 1850, his notable works include *Ils n'ont plus de mère*, a statuette in marble (1859), and *La Rêverie*, a statuette in terra cotta (1872).

The Thiébaut foundry cast *Jeune Fille aux poussins*, 37 cm (probably the statuette entitled *Ils n'ont plus de mère* at the Salon of 1859). A reduction of the statue of *Mirabeau* was also cast in bronze. A model of this work, 46 cm, was sold in London by Sotheby on March 8, 1984.

Emile Louis Truffot,
Un braconnier, 56 x 90 cm
(Siot-Decauville).

TURCAN, JEAN

Arles, September 13, 1846
Paris, January 3, 1895

Turcan's best-known work, *L'Aveugle et le paralytique*, won the gold medal at the Salon of 1888. A replica in bronze was inaugurated in 1901 in front of the school of fine arts in Marseille. A student of Cavelier and winner of the second grand prize of Rome in 1876, this sculptor, who died in poverty, exhibited at the Salon from 1878 to 1893. As late as 1883, he contributed a work entitled *Porteuse d'eau* in bronze. One of his works, *Le Chasseur et la fourmi*, was cast by Thiébaut, 52 cm. Of further note is a small group in bronze, *Les Lutteurs*, 28 cm.

MUSEUMS
Semur-en-Auxois
Le Chasseur et la fourmi, 90 cm.
Tête de jeune fille, study, 27 cm.
Vannes
Les Lutteurs, 27 cm.

V

VACOSSIN, GEORGES LUCIEN
Granvilliers (Oise), March 1, 1870
August 31, 1942

The dog is the favorite subject of Vacossin, an animal sculptor who exhibited at the Salon from 1902 to 1937. After 1900, the Thiébaut house produced editions in bronze of *Chien assis*, 20 cm, *Chien couché*, 14 x 24 cm, *Deux Chiens*, 20 cm, and *Chiot et escargot*, 20 and 12 cm. Certain sculptures were also cast by the Sèvres factory.

SALES
Chien d'arrêt, 23 cm L., Drouot, May 3, 1985, room 4.
Le Chien et le crapaud, 32 cm, Sotheby London, March 17, 1983.
Loup à l'affût sur un rocher, 42 cm, Christie's Oklahoma, September 24, 1981.
La Victoire, 75 cm, Drouot, March 14, 1985, room 1.

VALETTE, HENRI
Bâle, September 16, 1877
1962

Valetter spent his childhood in Montpellier, where he started to model small animals and birds. He remained faithful to the animal genre, sculpting a few of subjects in small format, as well as some busts and feminine figures with the grace of 18th century styles. The Drouot Hotel sale of his studio on December 16, 1981 included some plasters and terra cottas. Valette, a friend of fellow animal sculptor Henri de Monard, also sculpted a number of monuments to those killed in the First World War. Bronzes were cast (particularly by the Susse house) from a certain number of his works: *Biche couchée*, 19 x 28 cm, *Chevreaux affrontés*, book ends, *Chien briard*, 25 cm, *Chouette*, a door knocker (Susse), 23 cm, *Goret* (Susse), 6.5 cm, *Moineau* (Susse), 12.5 cm, *Taureau poitevin*, 25 cm, *Tête d'enfant*, 30 cm, etc.

The museum of Vernon possesses two small bronzes by this artist, *Pékinois*, 9 cm, and *Poussin*, 6.5 cm.

SALES
Three bronzes were sold at the Drouot Hotel on June 16, 1982, room 8: *Goret*, 6.5 cm (Susse), *Le Lévrier*, 24 cm (Montagutelli; 1908), and *Taureau romain*, 7 cm

VALTON, CHARLES
Paris, January 26, 1851
Chinon, May 21, 1918

Valton's *La Lionne blessée*, pierced with arrows, was reproduced in many models, and is undoubtedly much more famous than the artist himself. Valton, an animal sculptor and a student of Barye and Frémiet, became well-acquainted with the Jardin des Plantes at the age of fifteen. He exhibited regularly at the Salon from 1868 to 1914, first showing some plasters and waxes, but after 1880 almost exclusively showing small groups in bronze, often incorporating other materials. THe majority of his works portrayed big game, especially lions and lionesses. Among his plasters are *Lionne du Sénégal* (1868), *Renard étranglant un lapin* (1869), *Jaguar* (1870), *Lion du Sénégal* (1874), *Tigre jouant* (1878), and *Lion et lionne dormant* (1882).

The following works were exhibited in bronze: *Deux cailles se disputant une guêpe* (1879), *Lion rugissant* and *Lionne bâillant* (1880), *Chienne danoise et ses petits* (1883), *Un taureau échappé* (1884), *Tigre et tigresse* (1886), *Attelage de boeufs nivernais* (1887), *Au champ, fermière et vache* (1888), *La Lionne blessée*, inspired by an Assyrien bas-relief and *Cheval de halage et marinier* (1889), *Etude de lion*, a reduction of a plaster exhibited in 1883, and *Vache à l'étable* (1890), *La Belle Petite Lydie, chienne, et Jeune Chèvre dans des racines* (1892), *Tigre* (1893), *Jaguar* (1894), *Un loup sur une piste dans la neige* (1895); four works in bronze and marble entitled *Un dromadaire méhari* (1896), *Un Indien sur son éléphant* (1897), *Chien Saint-Bernard* (1898), and *Grue cendrée* (1901); a subject in bronze, onyx and ivory entitled *L'Hippopotame* (1903); some more patinated bronzes, including *Un cerf de France* (1897), *Une lutte au Colisée, tigre et bestiaire* (1902), *Lion, Panthère, Ours, Daim, Lionne* (1905), *Panthère aux aguets, Panthère en colère, Sanglier couché* (1906), *Lionne et ses petits* (1909), *Lionne assise, Panthère dormant,*

*Charles Valton,
Lionne et ses lionceaux,
21 cm.*

Lynx d'Abyssinie, Vautour (1911), *Lionne et lionceaux en présence d'un danger, Lionne mangeant, Girafe mangeant* (1912), and *Cerf et biche* (1913).

Despite the great number of works Valton exhibited at the Salon, it does not seem that any extensive editions were produced, and only a few bronzes by Valton appear in public sale or with antique dealers. The Siot-Decauville foundry cast, in addition to *Lionne blessée*, the works *Vache au champ* and *Lion après le repas. Tigre au repos*, 11 cm, appears in the catalog of Barbedienne.

Other bronzes of note, without unspecified founders, are among the pieces recently sold at auction: *Grand Cerf bramant*, 46 cm, *Cheval, antérieur droit levé*, 9.5 cm; numerous types of dogs including *Deux Chiens de chasse*, 36 cm, *Deux Chiens attaquant un oiseau*, 49.5 cm, *Passez au large! bouledogue*, 11.5 and 46.5 cm, *Saint-Bernard*, 9.5 cm, *Eléphant*

*Charles Valton,
Les Deux Lionnes,
20 x 34 cm.*

*Charles Valton,
Lionne blessée,
55 x 88 cm
(Siot-Decauville).*

Charles Valton,
Cheval arabe, antérieur gauche levé,
40 cm.

indien, 18 cm, *Lion léchant sa patte, Lion et homme,*
Lionne couchée, Loup, 58 cm, *Pur-sang arabe,* 9.5
cm, etc., and *Cheval arabe, postérieur gauche levé,*
cast in bronze or in patinated metal, 47 cm. Some
editions were produced in ceramic by the Sèvres
factory.

The museum of Mont-de-Marsan possesses a
small group in bronze, *Lionne et lionceaux,* 21 x 39
cm.

SALES
Le Chamelier, 38 cm, Enghien, March 4, 1984.
Cheval arabe, 40 cm, Douai, November 16, 1986.
Deux Chevaux, 49 cm, Sotheby London, November 7,
  1985.
Les Deux Lionnes, 20 x 34 cm, La Roche-sur-Yon, Febru-
  ary 14, 1987.
Eléphant marchant, 18 cm, Sotheby London, June 7,
  1984.
Lionne allongée, 12.5 x 22 cm, Nogent-le-Rotrou, July 22,
  1984.
Lionne blessée, 55 x 85 cm (Siot-Decauville), Le Raincy,
  June 15, 1985; Dijon, April 27, 1986.
Méhariste et son dromadaire, 32 cm, Enghien, June 26,
  1983.
Méhariste et son dromadaire, another version, 38 cm,
  Enghien, March 4, 1984.
Deux Panthères combattant, 22 cm (Colin), Sotheby Lon-
  don, March 20, 1986.
Passez au large! chien, 29.2 cm, Christie's New York,
  September 27, 1986.

VARENNE, HENRI FRÉDÉRIC
Chantilly, January 24, 1860
Tours, March 1933

Busts, medallions, numerous figurines of women
and children, portraits, religious subjects and genre
scenes make up the very varied work of this sculptor
who, after having worked in wood, perfected his
skills in the studio of Cain. He also executed some
statues for different monuments in Tours, including
the cathedral. His first consignments to the Salon in
1886 included the plaster *Tête de saint Jean-Baptiste,*
followed, in 1888, by the plaster *Buste de*
Méphistophélès; in 1892, he sent two statues in
plaster entitled *Il m'aime!* and *Charmeuse de ser-*
pents, and in 1893, another statue in plaster entitled
Fin d'un rêve. In 1895, Varenne contributed the
marble *Christ au tombeau du XV siècle* and a *Portrait*
de bébé in gilded bronze; in 1903, a statuette of
Quasimodo in lithographic stone, etc. In addition to
a number of editions by Sèvres, some of Varenne's
works were cast in bronze, particularly the two
statuettes entitled *Joueuses de tennis,* 17 cm, by the
Thiébaut house, and two other statuettes in gilded
bronze entitled *La Parisienne de 1810* and *La*
Parisienne de 1830, 15 cm, by Susse.

MUSEUMS
Blois
Andromède, 60 x 28 cm.
Cavalier arabe, 17 x 16 c.
La Douleur, femme assise, 26 x 18 cm.
Femme en toilette du XVIII siècle, 19 cm.
Femme en toilette d'époque Marie-Antoinette, 18 cm.
Femme en toilette 1830, 16 cm (A. Rudier).
Femme en toilette 1854, 17 cm.
Flamant, 30 x 35 cm.
Ganymède, project for a fountain in Buenos Aires, 22 cm.
Jeune Femme en toilette 1911 (A. Rudier), 17 cm.
Marabout, 32 x 10 cm.
Madame Nobel, bust, 8.5 cm.
Nymphe dansant, 94 x 40 cm.
Trompette à cheval, 17 x 16 cm.
Vautour, 25 x 15 cm.
Cariatide, femme, 37 cm.
Cariatide, femme, 43 cm.
Vase, décor en relief, 35 cm.
Vase, décor de deux personnages thibétains, 20 cm.
Paris, Petit Palais
Tête de Christ, gilded bronze, 25 cm.
Tours
Tendresse maternelle, gilded bronze (1895).

SALES
La Lorette, gilded bronze, 17 cm (Susse), Drouot, March 4,
  1983, room 1.

VARNIER, PIERRE HENRI LÉON
Bourg-lès-Valence (Drôme), 1826
Fin, 1890

This artist sculpted funereal figures as well as
diverse groups and decorative statues for the Louvre, the Tuileries, and the Opera. In addition to some
busts, he sent a statue in plaster of *Ambroise Paré*
and a statuette in bronze entitled *Courtisane* to the
Salon in 1857, the year of his debut. Later he sent a
statue in marble, *Chloris* (1865), a reduction in
bronze of the *Ambroise Paré* (1867), a statuette in
plaster, *La Marquise de Sévigné* (1874), and another
statue in plaster, *Nycea* (1877). The statuette of
Ambroise Paré was cast by Barbedienne, 20 cm.

VATINELLE, URSIN JULES

Paris, August 23, 1798
Paris, September 16, 1881

The winner of the grand prize of Rome in medal-engraving in 1819, Vatinelle also engraved cameos and sculpted. The museum of Aix-en-Provence possesses three of his works in bronze: a small group, *Ma Pecorella, chienne allaitant ses petits*, 25 x 37 cm, and two busts, *P.F. Giraud, statuaire*, 34 cm, and *J.-B. Grittot de Fontenis, amateur d'art*, 33 cm.

VAUDREY, PIERRE

Lyon, February 15, 1873—?

This artist specialized in funeral sculpture, and has many works in the Père-Lachaise cemetery, but appears more frequently in the registers of the Société des Artistes Français, starting in 1947. A statue in bronze entitled *Jeune Homme et son chien* (1905), 160 cm, carrying Vaudrey's signature and cast by A. Butteau, was sold at the Drouot Hotel on June 17, 1984, room 9 (fetching a price of 68,000 F).

VELAY, AMÉDÉE JOSEPH

Born in Laval

This artist, painter and sculptor was still living in 1912. The museum of Caen possesses a medallion in bronze representing a life-size portrait of *Emile Augier*.

VERAY, JEAN-LOUIS

Barbentane (Bouches-du-Rhône), June 11, 1820
Barbentane, November 9, 1881

Admitted to the Ecole des Beaux-Arts in 1842, Veray exhibited at the Salon from 1853 to 1861, and then, again, between 1880 and 1884, as well as at the Exposition Universelle of 1855. Of note are *La Poésie*, a statuette in terra cotta (1853), *La Moissonneuse endormie*, a statue in plaster, and *L'Arlésienne*, a bust in plaster (1855, and in bronze at the Salon of 1856), *Louis de Balbes, seigneur de Crillon*, a statue in bronze of 3.3 m high made for the city of Avignon (1857), and finally two statuettes in plaster entitled *Fauconnier* and *La Reine de Naples* (1861). A bust in bronze, *Le Comte de Chambord*, 38 cm (1872), was sold at the Drouot Hotel on May 7, 1980.

MUSEUMS
Avignon
Arlésienne en costume du pays, 63.5 cm (Thiébaut; 1854).
Louis de Balbes dit le brave Crillon, reduction of the bronze of 1857, 81 cm (Thiébaut).

VERLET, RAOUL

Angoulême, September 7, 1857
Paris, December, 1923

Very visible during his lifetime, Raoul Verlet was made a member of the Institut in 1910. In Paris remains his monument *Guy de Maupassant* at Monceau Park (1897), a statue entitled *L'Eloquence* at the Palais de Justice, and a group entitled *Les Arts* above the portal of the Grand Palais. He exhibited at the Salon from 1880 to 1914, showing a number of busts and statues of personalities, along with some figures—including one of the most well known, *La Douleur d'Orphée*, in plaster (1887; the bronze, erected at Malesherbes Plaza in Paris, was destroyed in 1942) and a statuette in marble entitled *Danseuse* (1891). He also made a statue in bronze of *Adrien*

Pierre Vaudrey,
Jeune Homme et son chien, 160 cm
(1905; A. Butteau founder).

Dubouché for the museum which carries his name in Limoges (1899), some groups in marble including *La Terre* (1909), *La Fille prodigue* (1910), and *La Fleur et le ruisseau* (1911), a group in bronze entitled *La Jeunesse et l'Amour* (1913), and a statuette in bronze entitled *La Rose* (1914).

Many works by Raoul Verlet have been cast in bronze, particularly one of the figures from the monument of Guy de Maupassant, entitled *La Rêverie*, 40 cm, which was produced by Thiébaut. At the Barbedienne house were produced editions of *La Danseur*, 62 cm, and *La Douleur d'Orphée*, also called *Orphée et Cerbère*, 125, 100, 82 and 63 cm. Also of note, from an unspecified founder, is *La Jeunesse et l'Amour*, 34 cm.

MUSEUMS
Angoulême
Buste de M. de Nerville, 68 cm (1886).
Dijon
Buste de Guillebot de Nerville, inspecteur général des mines de la Côte-d'Or, 64 cm (1886).
Louviers
La Douleur d'Orphée, 125 cm.

SALES
La Douleur d'Orphée, 82 cm (Barbedienne), Madrid, October 23, 1985; Fontainebleau, November 10, 1985; Sotheby London, November 6, 1986.
La Douleur d'Orphée, 100 cm (Barbedienne), Sotheby London, March 20, 1986.
La Douleur d'Orphée, 125 cm (Barbedienne), Lokeren, June 1, 1985.
Hercule combattant le monstre Géryon, 82 cm, Fontainebleau, November 10, 1985.

Raoul Verlet,
Orphée et Cerbère,
82 cm
(Barbedienne).

VERMARE, ANDRÉ CÉSAR

Lyon, November 27, 1869
Ile-de-Bréhat (Côtes-du-Nord), August 7, 1949

This artist, son of the sculptor André Vermare, was a great admirer of the Renaissance. He studied first at the school of fine arts in Lyon, and then in the studio of Falguière in Paris. He won the first prize of Rome in 1898 with *Adam et Eve retrouvant le corps d'Abel*, and then stayed for three years at the Villa Médicis. He executed some allegorical and mythological groups and statues, participated in the decoration of diverse monuments in Lyon, Saint-Etienne, and even Québec after World War I. His religious works ornament many churches in Lyon, Paray-le-Monial, and other cities of France. His *Jeanne d'Arc debout portant son étendard* gave rise to many replicas. He began exhibiting at the Salon in 1892, and in 1902 one of his most typical works appeared there, the bas-relief in plaster entitled *Le Rhône et la Saône*, the marble of which ornaments the Palais du Commerce in Lyon. He also sent to the Salon the bust in bronze of Lyon architect *Tony Garnier*, in 1904; in 1906 he sent to Paris's Trousseau Square a bronze group entitled *Vendanges*, which was destroyed during the Occupation. In 1908 he sent four bronzes—a bust, *Printemps*, and three figures, *Berger romain*, *Terraccinella*, and *Saint Jean*; in 1910 he sent a statuette in bronze entitled *Bacchante et bouc* and in 1911 a statue in marble, *Pierrot*, etc.

In addition to the editions of certain works by Vermare in unglazed porcelain by Sèvres, there exist some castings in gilded bronze of the *Pierrot*, 41 cm, in patinated bronze of the *Jeanne d'Arc*, 40 cm, and, editions in composition, also of *Jeanne d'Arc*.

VERNIER, ÉMILE

Paris, October 16, 1852
Paris, September 9, 1927

This sculptor and medal-engraver exhibited at the Salon starting in 1876, and served as president of the Société des Artistes Français from 1905 to 1910. His plaque in gilded bronze entitled *Femme couchée dans les joncs*, 30 cm L., was sold at the Drouot Hotel on December 2, 1983.

The museum of Bordeaux possess a bronze by Vernier, *Fernand Mazerolle, directeur de la Gazette numismatique*, 14 x 10.5 cm.

VERNON, FRÉDÉRIC CHARLES VICTOR DE

Paris, November 17, 1858
Paris, October 28, 1912

Frédéric Vernon was both a sculptor and a medal-engraver. Aside from some noteworthy medals, most significant among his works are a number of commemorative plaques and medallions, with exceedingly few works in ronde bosse. The museum of Lille possesses a medallion, *Gallia*, 15 cm diam, and three plaques, portraits of *Boutry*, 17.5 x 12 cm (1891), *G. Charpentier*, 17.5 x 12 cm (1890), and *Rosa*, 24.5 x 15.5 cm (1888).

VERSCHNEIDER, JEAN

Lyon, August 29, 1872
December 20, 1943

Verschneider started to exhibit at the Salon in 1905, showing subjects obviously inspired by Roman antiquity, and others with symbolism that sometimes became very elaborate. Primarily, these pieces are in plaster: *Annibal enfant* (1905), *Vainqueur, gladiateur romain* (1906), *Fils d'amilcar* (1908), *Méfiance* (1910), *La Nuit consolatrice* (1911), *Les Pommes d'or* (1912), *Sous le soleil*, and *L'Orage* (1914). Of further note are two statuettes in bronze, entitled *L'Entrée dans l'arène* (1910) and *L'Effort* (1913). Among the proofs in bronze cast from Verschneider's works are *Femme casquée debout sur un rocher* (entitled *France*), 68 cm, *Petite Femme courbée*, 35.5 cm, *Buste d'homme*, 32.5 cm, etc. A group in bronze, *Lion et son dompteur*, 42 cm, was sold in Nantes on November 24, 1984.

VIDAL, HENRI

Charenton (Val-de-Marne), May 4, 1864
Paris, 1918

This student of Mathurin Moreau left some busts, medallions, and statues in plaster. Also known are a few bronzes: *La Fortune et le jeune enfant*, exhibited at the Salon of 1899, and *Cain*, a statuette, sent to the Exposition Universelle of 1900. He also produced some animal bronzes. A statuette in gilded bronze, *Lion rugissant*, 18 cm, was sold at the Drouot Hotel on December 2, 1983, room 5.

VIDAL, LOUIS, ALSO CALLED NATAVEL

Nîmes, December 6, 1831
Paris, May 7, 1892

Jean Verschneider,
Lion et son dompteur, 42 cm.

Despite encroaching blindness (as a result of a serious eye disease contracted in his youth), Henri Vidal continued to model clay and exhibit his animal sculptures at the Salon. According to Stanislas Lami, Vidal's former teacher Barye would retouch all his works, which were often signed "Vidal aveugle," that is, "Vidal the Blind." A number of them were bought by the princess Mathilde, the Rothschilds, and other patrons of the arts. In 1888, Vidal became a professor of modeling at the Ecole Braille. In 1892 he died at the Hôpital des Quinze-Vingt (Cf. *L'Estampille*, November 1971).

In 1855, Vidal begtan sending some plasters and some bronzes to the Salon. Among the bronzes are *Panthère couchée* (1855), *Biche couchée* and *Lionne* (1859), *Taureau* and *Cerf mourant* (1863), *Cheval arabe* (1869), *Daim* (1870), *Grand Lion du Sénégal* (1875), *Cerf* (1877), *Gazelle algériene* (1880), *Traveller, cheval de course anglais* (1881), and *Kob, cheval anglais* (1882). Certain subjects by Louis Vidal were

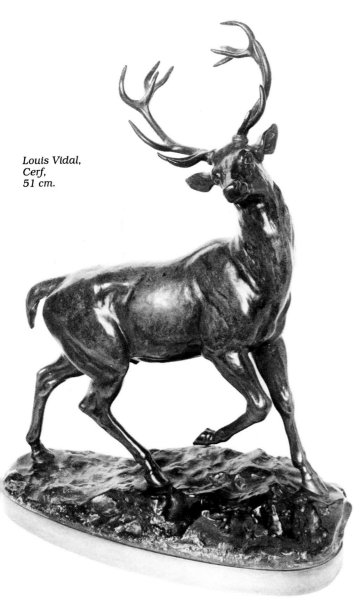

Louis Vidal,
Cerf,
51 cm.

VIGNON, NOÉMIE CONSTANT, ALSO KNOWN AS CLAUDE

Paris, 1828
Nice, April 10, 1888

An author of books and of Salon reviews, and a student of sculpture under Pradier, Noémie Vignon exhibited from 1852 to 1864 under the name 'Noémie Constant'. In 1864 she decided to go by the name 'Claude Vignon' instead, and worked under this name for the rest of her life . She worked on the decoration of the Louvre, the Tuileries, and the fountain of Saint-Michel (the central bas-relief), and on the church of Saint-Denis-du-Saint Sacrement (the four haut-relief figures from the porch: *La Force, La Justice, La Prudence* and *La Tempérance*). At the Salon, she exhibited most notably a statue in marble entitled *L'Enfance de Bacchus* (1853) and some bronzes including *Bacchus enfant* in 1869, and *Le Pêcheur à l'épervier* in 1882. Another marble of note presented at the Exposition Universelle of 1867 is *Daphné changée en laurier*, 210 cm, and a bust in bronze, *Autoportait*, dated from 1880. This piece was eventually placed on the artist's tomb at Père-Lachaise.

VIGOUREUX, PIERRE

Avallon, April 4, 1884
Nogent-sur-Marne, October 24, 1965

This student of Lemaire debuted at the Salon in 1906, and worked primarily between the two world wars. It is thus that his *Vendangeuse* in stone was erected in 1937 on the terrace of the Museum of Modern Art in Paris. Before 1914, he exhibited some allegorical figures in plaster at the Salon, entitled *Refuge, Résignation, Sur les grèves, La Poésie du passé,* and *L'Aube,* among others.

SALES
Léda et le cygne, Auxerre, April 8, 1984.
Léda et le cygne, 43.5 cm (Pannini, founder), Drouot, December 4, 1985, room 15.

VILLANIS, EMMANUEL

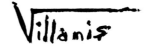

Born in Lille, France to Italian parents (though other sources say he was born in Italy), Villanis worked in France and began exhibiting at the Salon in 1886. Strongly influenced by Art Nouveau, he produced innumerable works, mostly representing feminine figures. The majority were cast in bronze and in various tinted metals, often in many dimesions, and indeed in many versions. Nonetheless, before 1914 he exhibited at the Salon only a single bust in bronze, entitled *Judith* (1898), and some plasters such as the statue *L'Esclave* (1890), the busts *Saint-Saë* and *Galatée* (1894), and the statues *L'Adultère* and *La Guerre* (1897 and 1900, respectively).

made into rather important castings, including some proofs of *L'Antilope*, 25 cm, *Cerf*, 60.5 cm, *Chamois*, 25 cm, *Enfant tenant un chien*, 43 cm, *Lion rugissant*, 36 and 17.5 cm, and *Le Pur-sang*, 29 cm, etc.

MUSEUMS
Angoulême
Cerf blessé, 38 cm (1880).
Bordeaux
Cerf mourant, 25 cm.
Nantes
Lionne d'Améique, 20 cm.
Nîmes
Cerf mourant, 25 cm.
Taureau.

SALES
Cerf dix-cors, 50 cm, Versailles, June 16, 1984.
Lièvre effrayé, 8.5 cm, Rambouillet, November 18, 1984.
Lion marchant, 35 cm, Drouot, July 7, 1983, room 9; Christie's London, May 15, 1986.

*Emmanuel Villanis,
L'Otage à la colonne,
painted metal.*

*Emmanuel Villanis,
Le Talisman, 60 cm.*

*Emmanuel Villanis,
Sapho, 93 cm.*

A number of proofs in bronze signed by Villanis can be noted: *Ballerine sur les pointes*, 32.5 cm, *La Captive*, 55 cm, (portraying an eastern woman, chained; another version of the same subject exists, bearing the seal of the Société des Bronzes of Paris, 73 cm), *Enfant pêcheur*, 64 cm, *Femme arabe esclave assise*, 42 cm, *Femme au faisan*, 50 cm L, *Femme nue en marble sur un coquillage en bronze*, 39 x 42 cm, *Gaulois vaincu* (Barbedienne casting), 83 cm L, *Gitane à la mandoline*, 60 cm, *L'Histoire, femme assise*, 48 cm, *Judith*, 70 cm, *Lygie*, 52 cm, *Mademoiselle Lange*, 29 cm, *L'Otage, femme attachée à une colonne*, 100 and 55 cm, *La Peinture*, 70 cm, *Prise du Corsaire, femme orientale, les poignets enchaînés*, 86 cm, *Sapho, femme jouant de la lyre*, 85, 72 and 60 cm, *La Sculpture*, 52 cm, *Soleil*, 98 cm, and *Talisman*, 34 cm.

To this list must be added a quanity of busts of young women and girls of different dimensions, most notably those pieces entitled *Capture*, 62 cm, *Diane*, 41 cm, *Esméralda* (bronze polychrome), 57 cm, *Faralla*, 37.5 and 12.5 cm, *Galatée*, 77 cm, *Lalla*

*Emmanuel Villanis,
Esclave à vendre,
30 cm*

*Emmanuel Villanis,
Jeune Femme
sur un coquillage,
39 cm.*

643

Roukh, 21 cm, *Lola,* 50 cm, *Lucrèce,* 37 cm, *Mauresque,* 56 cm, *Mignon,* 56.5 and 35 cm, *Saïda,* 48 and 22 cm, *Sapho,* 40 and 30 cm, *La Sibylle* (gilded bronze), 52 cm, *Tanagra,* 42 and 32 cm, *Walkyrie,* 80, 65, 45 and 25 cm, etc. Also of note are some castings made in composition, including *La Fourmi* (in green paint) 54 cm, and *Joueur de boules* (polychrome), 18 cm.

MUSEUMS
Troyes
La Sibylle, bust, 35.5 cm.

SALES
Esméralda, gilded bronze, 38 cm, Sotheby London, March 8, 1984.
Femme à la lyre, Parthenay, may 25, 1985.
Jeune Danseuse au tambourin, 73 cm, Sotheby London, June 12, 1986.
Jeune Femme sur un coquillage, 39 cm, Rouen, February 3, 1985.

Emmanuel Villanis,
Buste de Javotte,
60 cm.

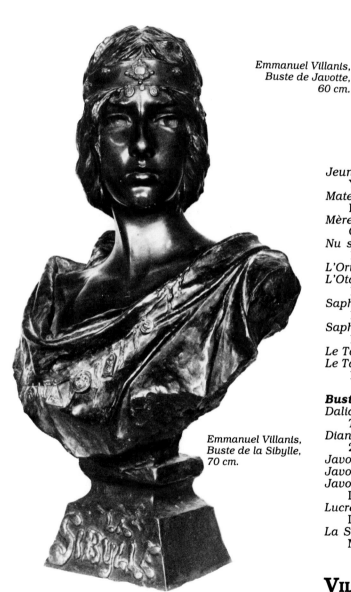

Emmanuel Villanis,
Buste de la Sibylle,
70 cm.

Jeune Fille dansant, 31 cm (Roman Bronze Works, New York), New York, June 12, 1985.
Maternité, 38 cm (Roman bronze works, New York), Sotheby London, December 18, 1985.
Mère et enfant, 26 cm (Roman bronze works, New York), Christie's New York, December 6, 1985.
Nu symbolisant le soleil, 106 cm, Drouot, October 26, 1983.
L'Orient, 50 cm, Christie's London, March 20, 1984.
L'Otage à la colonne, metal paint, Arles, December 1, 1985.
Sapho, 72 cm, Saint-Brice-sous-Forêt, September 30, 1984.
Sapho, 93 cm, Chartres, April 28, 1985; Agen, June 29, 1985.
Le Talisman, 60 cm, Lorient, November 8, 1986.
Le Tambourin, 36 cm, Drouot, November 28, 1984, room 13.

Busts:
Dalida, 42.5 cm, *Fille de Bohême,* 46 cm, *Mignon,* 57 cm, *Thaïs,* 19.5 cm, Sotheby London, November 6, 1986.
Diane, 36.5, *Mignon,* 36.5 cm, Christie's London, January 22, 1986.
Javotte, 60 cm, Saint-Etienne, March 24, 1986.
Javotte, 27 cm, Drouot, March 28, 1984, room 1.
Javotte, 61 cm, *Lydia,* 60 cm, *Lucrèce,* 54 cm, Sotheby London, June 12, 1986.
Lucrèce, 37 cm (Société des Bronzes of Paris), Sotheby London, March 20, 1986.
La Sibylle, 70 cm, Bordeaux, March 25, 1984; Meaux, March 16, 1986.

VILLENEUVE, JACQUES

Bassan (Hérault), January 1, 1865
Paris, February 1933

This sculptor is known for an allegorical statue entitled *L'Art industriel,* which ornaments the corner facade of the Grand Palais, next to the Cours la

Reine. He made his debut at the Salon in 1895, and exhibited a number of bronzes there, including statuettes entitled *Patrie* (1907) and *Eveil* (1914), and statues and groups entitled *Prométhée* (1908), *A la gloire de la République* (1909), *La Rose passe* and *Bataille de fleurs* (1913). Previously, Villeneuve had exhibited plasters in which animals figured prominently: *Poule et couleuvre* (1895), *Bouc et enfants* (1902), etc. Finally, in 1909, he presented a centerpiece entitled *Vendanges fleuries*, cast in silver by Valsuani. A group in bronze, *Prométhée enchaîné*, 110.5 cm, was sold by Christie's on September 24, 1981 in Oklahoma (United States).

MUSEUMS
Dax
Les Trois Grâces, 87 cm.
Montpellier
Caïn, 45 cm (Exposition of 1900).

VINCENT, CHARLES

Rouen, April 1, 1861
July, 1918

A student of Falguière and Mercié, Charles Vincent began sending his work to the Salon in 1901, showing allegories including *La Rosée* (1903) and figures including *Le Berger* (1905 in plaster, 1906 in bronze). Editions of this last work were also produced in ceramic, by the Sèvres factory. A proof in bronze, 61 cm, cast by Hohwiller, belongs to the museum of Guéret. Another, 44 cm high, cast by Jaboeuf and Rouard, was sold by Christie's on September 24, 1981 in Oklahoma (United States).

Charles Vital Cornu,
Fracasse, 38 cm.

VITAL, CORNU CHARLES

Paris, 1851
June 29, 1927

Allegorical figures, genre scenes, and portraits (as many in ronde bosse as in decorative relief appliqued on vases) are the essence of this artist's work. He exhibited at the Salon starting in 1876. His bronzes include *Le Ricochet*, 125 cm (1881), *Toréador* (1888), *Muscadin* (1889), *Consolation humaine* (1904), *Tendresse humaine* (1905), *Dans la vie* and *Buste de Quentin Bauchard* (1906), etc. His plasters include *Abandonnée* (1883), *Fierté guerrière* (1885), *Belles Vendanges* (1886), *Pro scienta, pro patria* (1890), *Douleurs humaines* (1902), *Douceurs nocturnes* (1903), *Trésor maternel* (1907). Among the marbles are *Archimède* and *Crépescule* (1893), *Le Spleen* (1897), *Douce Langueur* (1898), *La nature s'éveille* (1901), etc.

It is important to note that Vital Cornu signed his works without leaving a space between the two parts of his name. Early readings of this signature led certain sale catalogs to call him by the name "Vitallony."

The Susse foundry cast the following works in bronze:

Crépuscule, 69 and 33 cm.
Jardinière Sommeil, 28 cm.
Vase Anémone, 40 and 30 cm.
Vase Digitale, 29 cm.
Vase Lassitude, 24 cm.
Vase Paradis perdu, 41 cm.
Vase Soleil, 31 cm.
Vase Sommeil, 39 and 28 cm.
Broc Le Vin (Salon of 1896).

Works by Vital Cornu were distributed by some other founders, including Thiébaut (*Souvenir de Venise*, 82 cm), the Société des Bronzes of Paris

Charles Vital Cornu,
Victoire triomphante, 120 cm
(Société des bronzes de Paris).

(*Victoire triomphante*), and Siot-Decauville (*Le Spleen*).

Victoire triomphante has been sold on many occasions, including sales by Christie's in Oklahoma on September 24, 1981, 119.5 cm; by Drouot on February 25, 1983, room 9; and by Romans on May 12, 1985.

VITALLONY

see Vital Cornu

VOULOT, FÉLIX

Altkirch (Haut-Rhin), May 7, 1865
1926

Voulot was fond of allegorical subjects, which he treated in a graceful, lifelike manner. He began exhibiting them at the Artistes Français in 1886 and at the Nationale des Beaux-Arts in 1895. At the latter, he showed bronzes entitled *Jeunesse* (1897), *Vers le bonheur, Coquetterie,* and *Danseuse* (1902), and *Le Printemps* (1907). Other typical bronzes by Vaulot are *Triade antique* and *Coup de vent.* Many of his works were cast in bronze, apparently in limited editions; these works include *Caresse maternelle,* 18 cm, *Danseuse* and *Deux Soeurs* (Hébrard, founder), and *Le Printemps,* 42 cm.

MUSEUMS
Altkirch
Jeunesse and *Vers le bonheur,* two statuettes, 25 cm.
Bordeaux
Jeunesse, 57 cm (E. Gruet Jr., founder).
Strasbourg
Caresse maternelle, 20 cm.

VOYEZ, ÉMILE

Paris—?
Paris, 1895

Voyez exhibited at the Salon from 1873 to 1892. The works he showed there primarily include busts in different materials. A figure in bronze entitled *Avant l'assaut,* 65 cm high, was sold in Detroit on September 18, 1983.

WAAGEN, ARTHUR

Born in Mernel (Eastern Prussia)

Waagen Saul

This sculptor is known to have specialized in eastern people and animals, but few of his works are known besides those which appear sporadically on the market and those that were exhibited at the Salon. Two Waagen plasters entitled *Faisans* and *Un vandale* were shown at the Salon in 1869 and 1887 respectively, and two bronze statuettes entitled *L'Oracle des fleurs* and *Le Retour des champs* were shown there in 1870. Some of his works were cast in bronze, in particular *Kabyle au retour de la chasse*, a group known in proofs of diverse dimensions. It carries the seal of the editor L. Martin, and is sometimes designated under other titles, including *Chasseur arabe* and *Cavalier aux chiens*.

SALES

Kabyle au retour de la chasse, 41 cm (Martin), Christie's New York, October 18, 1983.
Kabyle au retour de la chasse, 69 cm (Martin), Drouot, January 31, 1984; Drouot, Feburary 3, 1984, room 7; Sotheby London, March 21, 1985.
Kabyle au retour de la chasse, 90 cm (Martin), Sotheby London, November 7, 1985; Lyon, October 20, 1986.
Kabyle au retour de la chasse, 118 cm (Martin), Rouen, December 15, 1985 (knocking down 165,000 F).
Groupe de chasseurs arabes et trois chiens, 110 cm (Martin), Brusells, March 1, 1983.

Arthur Waagen,
Kabyle au retour de la chasse, 110 cm
(Martin, founder).

WADERE, HENRI

Colmar, July 2, 1865
Munich, February 27, 1950

Wadere worked in Paris and Colmar and exhibited at the Salon, producing an abundant number of sculptural works. At the museum of Strasbourg is found a bust of a woman in bronze entitled *Guilia*, 50 cm, dated 1902.

WARD, HERBERT

London, 1863
Paris, August 7, 1919

While still very young, Herbert Ward traveled to Australia, New Zealand, and, with the explorer Stanley, to Africa. When he became a sculptor, writer, and painter, Ward was inspired by these travels to portray various people of the black races. He exhibited at the Royal Academy of London and at the Salon of Paris. His works are shown in many museums of the world—including some in Great Britain, South Africa, the United States, and France. Among his bronzes which apparently were not cast into major series are *Le Tailleur d'idoles* (1906), *Chef de tribu* (1908), *Sauvage allumant du feu*, *Sorcier dansant*, *Guerrier congolais*, *Femme et deux enfants congolais*, and *Masque de jeune fille congolaise*.

MUSEUMS
Paris, Orsay
Homme de l'Ariwiai, head, 54.5 cm.
Jeune Fille Bâ-Kongo, head, 57.2 cm.

SALES
Jeune Africaine, 43.5 cm, Drouot, November 6, 1984, room 1.

WATRINELLE, ANTOINE GUSTAVE
Verdun, October 24, 1828
Ouistreham, June 1913

After winning the second prize of Rome in 1858 with a work entitled *Achille saisissant ses armes*, Watrinelle worked for different Parisian buildings, including the Opera, Notre-Dame, and the church Saint-Merri, as well as for the cathedral of Valence. His bronze statue of *David*, 157 cm, from the Salon of 1869, belongs to the museum of Epinal.

WEIGELE, HENRI
Schierbach (Haut-Rhin), September 20, 1858
Neuilly, 1927

The Orsay museum possesses one statuette by this artist, a work in gilded bronze entitled *Hippolyte Alfred Chauchard assis*, 49 cm, executed before 1910.

WEITMEN, CLAUDE JEAN-BAPTISTE
Albertville, February 28, 1867
Albertville, November 3, 1918

Weitman was educated first in Lyon, and then in Paris at the Ecole des Beaux-Arts. Between 1891 and 1912 he sent a number of busts to the Salon, as well as some figures in plaster: *Caïn* (1894), *Eve* (1898), *Le Paradis perdu* (1901), and *La Cigale* (1906). He also sent a terra cotta entitled *Bacchus enfant* to the Salon in 1907. The museum of Chambéry possesses some works by this artist, including a bust in bronze of the deputy *Pierre Blanc*, 75 cm, exhibited at the Salon of 1894.

WILLEME, AUGUSTE FRANÇOIS
Givonne (Ardennes)—?
Roubaix, February, 1905

This artist is known for his invention of photosculpture, very successful shortly after its completion in 1860. The procedure permits artists

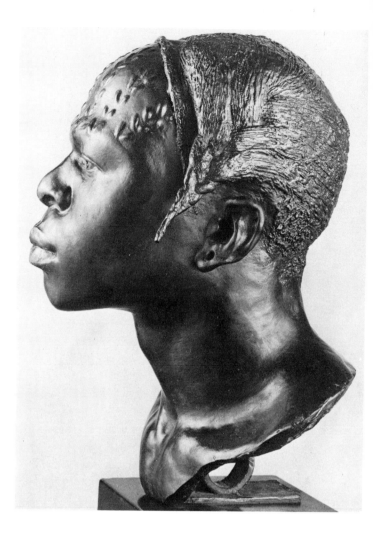

Herbert Ward,
Tête d'homme de l'Ariwiai, 54.5 cm.
Musée d'Orsay.

like Willeme to sculpt with the aid of a pantograph, using the negatives of photographs of an object taken from all angles. The Carnavalet museum possesses many of Willeme's statuettes portraying actors, including *J.B. Bressant*, 46 cm, *Louis Delaunay, du Français*, 44 cm, *Leroux, du Français*, 44 cm, and *Provost*, 45 cm.

WITTMANN, ERNEST
Sarre-Union (Bas-Rhin), September 24, 1846

Very early on, Wittmann was attracted by the common people of Lorraine, and modeled some small subjects in clay portraying them. He frequented the school of fine arts in Nancy and devoted himself to painting before returning to sculpture around 1888. He exhibited in Lorraine and in Paris,

(1)

(4)

(2)

(3)

(5)

1) Ernest Wittmann, Le Chiffonnier, 40.5 cm.

2) Ernest Wittmann, Le Faucheur aiguisant sa faux, 37 cm.

3) Ernest Wittmann, Le Bûcheron, 37 cm.

4) Ernest Wittmann, Paysan au fagot, 31 cm.

5) Ernest Wittmann, Deux Paysans marchant, 32 cm.

but did not participate at the Salon. His figurines, very realistic and close to Art Nouveau, reflected the social tendencies of the era and frequently represented peasants at work. In 1907, he established himself in Rupt-sur-Moselle, where he pursued his career as sculptor. A number of his works were cast in bronze and in sandstone (gritstone) by the Mougin brothers, ceramists in Nancy.

On December 7, 1977, a sale of works by Wittmann took place at the Drouot Hotel rive gauche. The following bronzes appeared in the catalog: *Le Bûcheron*, 47 cm, *Bûcheron*, 37 cm, *Le Lieur de fagots*, 28 cm, *Le Clochard*, 29.5 cm, *Le Chemineau* (Andro, founder in Paris), 36 cm, *Le Chiffonier*, 40.5 cm, *Le Terrassier*, 44 cm, *Le Porte-faux* (Andro, founder), 34.5 cm, *Le Faucheur aiguisant sa faux*, 37 cm, *Le Porteur de petit bois*, 26 cm, *Les Vieux* (1903), 40 cm L, *En revenant du marché*, 32 cm, *Homme en pied* (1912), 30 cm, *L'Homme des champs*, and *L'Eplucheur de pommes de terre*.

Some of Wittmann's statuettes were cast in sandstone by the Mougins, and were put up for public sale at the Drouot Hotel on March 27, 1985 (*L'Homme à la hotte*, *Le Bûcheron*, *Couple marchant*, *Le Terrassier*, *Le Paysan à la pipe*, and *L'Homme au baluchon*).

MUSEUMS
Nancy
Couple de vieillards, *Homme les mains derrière le dos*, *Homme portant une hotte*, and *Homme un sac sur l'épaule*.
Nancy, museum of the art school
Faucheur s'essuyant le front.

SALES
Couple de vieillards sur un banc, 30 cm (Bisceglia, founder), Epinal, March 24, 1985; Drouot, February 3, 1986, room 2.
Paysan au fagot, 31 cm, Epinal, March 24, 1985.
Deux paysans marchant, Epinal, March 24, 1985.
Terrassier à la pelle, Drouot, February 3, 1986, room 2.

WLÉRICK, ROBERT
Mont-de-Marsan, 1882
Paris, 1944

Wlérick's forms are characteristically well-balanced, full, and calm like those of his compatriot Despiau. Wlérick was among Rodin's practicians and was a member of the "band of Schnegg." A son and grandson of cabinetmakers, he studied sculpture at the school of fine arts in Bordeaux from 1899 to 1904 before establishing himself in Paris in 1906. His work was produced, for the most part, between the two world wars. However, three plasters made before 1914 (and which were translated into bronze) merit attention, especially since he destroyed many of the works from his youth. The first of these was one of his best-known works, the bust of the *Petite Landaise*, 40 cm, which he exhibited at the Nationale des Beaux-Arts in 1912 and which Rodin would compare to a Donatello. A number of different founders, including Montagutelli, Thinot, and Valsuani, cast this work in bronze, using the lost wax method. Executed in 1913, the 32 cm bust of *Madame Wlérick* was cast in bronze in many models; proofs numbered up to eight are known. Finally, there are records indicating that a small 11 cm head entitled *Jeunesse* was cast in ten models by Valsuani. Wlérick also sculpted the equestrian statue of the marshall Foch located in the Trocadéro Plaza, a statue which would be finished after his death by his student Raymond Martin.

MUSEUMS
Proofs in bronze of the *Petite Landaise* are shown at the museums in Bordeaux (cast by Montagutelli), Mont-de-Marsan, and Poitiers as well as in the museums of Algiers and Stockholm. The Poitiers museum's model was cast by Valsuani in gilded bronze (using the lost wax method) in 1966, with the agreement of the sculptor's family. Valsuani also made a casting for Poitiers of a gilded bronze bust of *Madame Wlérick*.

*Ernest Wittmann,
Le Lieur de fagots,
28 cm.*

YON, CHARLES
Dijon, 1803
Paris, 1851

The museum of Dijon possesses Charles Yon's bronze bust of *Lazare Carnot*, 80 cm, which was exhibited at the Salon of 1847.

1) Ernest Wittmann, L'Homme des champs.

2) Ernest Wittmann, Le Chemineau, 36 cm (Andro, founder).

3) Ernest Meissonier, Cheval au galop, 36 x 61 cm (Siot-Decauville, No 2).

①

③

②

1) Arthur Leduc, *Le Porte-étendard de Reichshoffen*, 60 cm, according to a project for a monument to cavalry soldiers.

2) Comte de Ruillé, *Cavalier sur un cheval cabré*, 57 cm.

3) Raoul Larche, "In nomine patris et filii et spiritus sancti," 95 cm.

══FOUNDERS DICTIONARY══

Information concerning 19th century founders is incomplete and quite fragmented; almost all of them disappeared, and their archives are either lost or inaccessible. The activities of a good number of them are known only by the existence of bronzes carrying their mark. Because of this, the archives of the Rodin Museum, with commentary and explanations from its curator Mme Monique Laurent, are very precious. There is some additional information furnished by M.C.B. Metman in his thesis for the Ecole du Louvre, entitled *La Petite Sculpture d'édition au XIXe siècle* (1944).

BARBEDIENNE

Born in 1810 in Saint-Martin-de-Fresnay in Calvados, Ferdinand Barbedienne went to Paris at the age of thirteen. He was placed as an apprentice with a saddler, and then worked in different wall-paper shops before establishing himself independently on the Rue Notre-Dame-de-Lorette in 1833. He made the acquaintance of Achille Collas, who had invented a cylinder for the impression of painted canvases and then completed an apparatus intended to mechanically reduce statues. In 1838, the two men entered into a partnership and started to manufacture bronzes. At first they produced reductions of antiques, including the *Vénus de Milo,* and then sought out models made by living artists. Their first casting contract was signed with Rude on March 22, 1843.

After enduring grave difficulties during the revolution of 1848, the firm began to increasingly expand its activities. They worked for a number of renowned sculptors, producing works of note including Rude's standing pose of Godefroy Cavaignac, the works of Clésinger (for whom they served as the exclusive founders), works by David d'Angers and many other artists, as well as some personal objects, chandeliers, and fireplace accessories. Barbedienne's head office was henceforth established at 30 Boulevard Poissonnière, and his studios at 63 Rue de Lancry. By the time that Achille Collas died in 1859, Barbedienne employed some three hundred workers and possessed a specialized studio for casting bronze monuments.

The absence of Collas left Ferdinand Barbedienne the sole master of the business. An excerpt from an 1866 Barbedienne catalog explained that "the licenses, machines, and models that had belonged to the Société A. Collas and Barbedienne became the exclusive propriety of the Barbediene house. The mathematical reductions...continued under the sole direction of M.F. Barbedienne."

The success of Barbedienne's editions was considerable, as was his production. Though interrupted by the war of 1870 (when he had to furnish seventy canons for the Défense Nationale), he resumed with even greater strength when peace returned. Ferdinand Barbedienne assumed the presidency of the Réunion of bronze-makers from 1865 to 1885. After the death of Barye in 1876, Barbedienne bought one hundred and twenty-five models by Barye at a sale, and cast them in a number of models marked with his initials. He exported a significant portion of his manufacturings, though rumor says all of them. When Barbedienne died on March 21, 1892, the number of his workers exceeded six hundred. He was buried at Père-Lachaise, and on his tomb was placed a sculpted bust of him made by Alfred Boucher.

Gustave Leblanc, the nephew Ferdinand Barbedienne had taken as a partner, succeeded him under the name of Leblanc-Barbedienne. Leblanc signed a contract with Rodin to ensure the company's exclusive right to cast *Eternel Printemps* and *Baiser* for twenty years. Furthermore, in 1895 he executed the casting of the first proofs of the *Bourgeois de Calais.* Whether busy with small editions or with monumental castings, the company was always very successful. Leblanc made use of agencies in the United States and Great Britain, and opened a branch in Berlin in 1913. After World War I, he worked notably on some commemorative monuments, and made innumerable editions of works by Emmanuel Frémiet, and (from 1929 to 1952) busts by Daumier. Leblanc's activity finally ended on December 31, 1954.

Cmte. des Fondeurs Barbedienne Père-Lachaise
Mm CHATS, buste auteur com... figure...
De ... aux Ateliers

1880

DÉPARTEMENT DES SCULPTURES
DU MUSÉE DU LOUVRE

~~GRAPHIQUES~~

Autorisation du Département

Paris. — 30, boulevard Poissonnière.

BRONZES D'ART

F. BARBEDIENNE

RÉCOMPENSES OBTENUES DANS LES EXPOSITIONS UNIVERSELLES
DE LONDRES, DE PARIS ET DE VIENNE

A PARIS 1878
GRAND PRIX
GRANDE MÉDAILLE D'OR
DIPLOME D'HONNEUR
VINGT-HUIT MÉDAILLES DE COOPÉRATEURS

A VIENNE 1873
DEUX DIPLOMES D'HONNEUR
UNE MÉDAILLE DE PROGRÈS
VINGT-CINQ MÉDAILLES DE COOPÉRATEURS

A PARIS 1867
JURÉ RAPPORTEUR (HORS CONCOURS)

A LONDRES 1862
TROIS MÉDAILLES POUR EXCELLENCE

A PARIS 1855
GRANDE MÉDAILLE D'HONNEUR

A LONDRES 1851
DEUX GRANDES MÉDAILLES (COUNCIL MEDALS)

REDUCTION MATHÉMATIQUE
ACHILLE COLLAS
(Inventeur)
GRANDE MÉDAILLE D'HONNEUR

A PARIS 1855

COOPÉRATEURS
Trois Médailles de 1re classe
DÉCERNÉES A
MM. MANGUIN, architecte; CH. GILBERT, directeur du travail; E. PHŒNIX, sculpteur.

Quatre Médailles de 2e classe	Quatre Mentions honorables
DÉCERNÉES A MM.	DÉCERNÉES A MM.
LECOMPTE, contre-maître ciseleur.	LEROUVILLOIS, ciseleur.
LEBLANC, » monteur.	MAXIME BETTE, monteur.
GUYON, » menuisier-ébéniste.	BICHON, menuisier-ébéniste.
BLUGEOT, » de la réduction.	BESSON, menuisier-ébéniste.

Une Médaille pour excellence
A M. CONSTANT-SEVIN, sculpteur-ornemaniste de la Maison. (LONDRES 1862.)

LES ATELIERS DE LA MAISON
Fonderie, Fabrication des bronzes, Dorure, Émaillerie, Marbrerie et Réduction
Sont situés RUE DE LANCRY, 63.

SEULS AGENTS EN ANGLETERRE
MM. JACKSON ET GRAHAM
30 to 38, Oxford street
LONDRES, W

— 8 —

GÉNIE DU REPOS ÉTERNEL
Le marbre antique est au musée du Louvre, à Paris.

	fr.
La réduction aux 2 cinquièmes . . .	350 P. 20f
Hauteur, 0.75 c.; largeur, 0.22 c.	
La réduction aux 3 dixièmes . . .	195
h. 0.55 c., l. 0.16 c.	
La réduction aux 2 dixièmes . . .	125
h. 0.36 c.; l. 0.11 c.	

CUPIDON EN HERCULE
Le marbre antique est au musée du Louvre, à Paris.

La grandeur originale	1,100
h. 0.94 c.	

GÉNIE ADORANT
Le marbre antique est au musée royal de Berlin.

La réduction aux 2 cinquièmes . . .	225 P. 15f
h. 0.54 c.; l. 0.13 c.	
La réduction aux 2 dixièmes . . .	80
h. 0.27 c.; l. 0.07 c.	

TIREUR D'ÉPINE
Le bronze antique est au musée du Vatican, à Rome.

La réduction aux 2 cinquièmes . . .	225 P. 15f
h. 0.32 c.; l. 0.24 c.	
La réduction aux 3 dixièmes . . .	130
h. 0.24 c.; l. 0.18 c.	
La réduction aux 2 dixièmes . . .	80
h. 0.16 c.; l. 0.12 c.	

— 9 —

CUPIDON (ESSAYANT SON ARC)
Le marbre antique est au musée du Louvre, à Paris.

	fr.
La réduction aux 2 cinquièmes . .	250
Hauteur, 0.55 c.; largeur, 0.20 c.	
La réduction aux 2 dixièmes . . .	95
h. 0.26 c.; l. 0.11 c.	

L'AMOUR ET PSYCHÉ (GROUPE)
Le marbre antique est au musée Capitolin, à Rome.

La réduction à la moitié	500
h. 0.61 c.; l. 0.34 c.	
La réduction aux 2 cinquièmes . .	350
h. 0.50 c.; l. 0.19 c.	
La réduction aux 3 dixièmes . . .	230
h. 0.39 c.; l. 0.14 c.	
La réduction au huitième	80
h. 0.17 c.; l. 0.06 c.	

ENFANT A L'OIE
Le marbre antique est au musée du Louvre, à Paris.

La réduction aux 2 cinquièmes . .	250 P. 15f
h. 0.37 c.; l. 0.36 c.	
La réduction aux 3 dixièmes . . .	140
h. 0.26 c.; l. 0.20 c.	
La réduction aux 2 dixièmes . . .	75
h. 0.18 c.; l. 0.13 c.	
La réduction plus petite	45
h. 0.09 c.; l. 0.08 c.	

JOUEUSE D'OSSELETS
Le marbre antique est au musée royal de Berlin.

La réduction aux 2 cinquièmes . .	190 P. 15f
h. 0.17 c.; l. 0.28 c.	
La réduction au tiers	160
h. 0.26 c.; l. 0.24 c.; p. 0.18 c.	
La réduction aux 3 dixièmes . . .	125
h. 0.20 c.; l. 0.19 c.	
La réduction aux 2 dixièmes . .	65
h. 0.14 c.; l. 0.13 c.	

Pages from a Ferdinand Barbedienne catalog
around 1880.

— 20 —

	fr.
VASE CLODION. — N° 1, l'un	300
Hauteur, 0.48 c.; largeur, 0.27 c.	
— — N° 2, l'un	200
h. 0.35 c.; l. 0.19 c.	
— — N° 3, l'un	150
h. 0.28 c.; l. 0.16 c.	
COLLECTION DE COUPES, VASES, etc.	»
VASE AGRICULTURE	300
h. 0.27 c.; l. 0.24 c.	

LES PARQUES
(Groupe tiré du fronton du Parthénon)

Dont les marbres originaux sont au musée Britannique, à Londres.

RESTAURATION DUDIT GROUPE
Par M. Clésinger.

La réduction n° 1 . . .	1,600
h. 0.58 c.; l. 0.92 c.	
La réduc. aux 2 cinq .	1,250
h. 0.51 c.; l. 0.76 c.	
La réd. aux trois dix.	650
h. 0.36 c.; l. 0.56 c.	
La réd. aux deux dix .	425
h. 0.30 c.; l. 0.45 c.	

CÉRÈS ET PROSERPINE
(Groupe tiré du fronton du Parthénon)

Dont les marbres originaux sont au musée Britannique, à Londres.

RESTAURATION DUDIT GROUPE
Par M. Clésinger.

Réduction aux 3 cinquièmes	2,200
h. 0.90 c.; l. 0.65 c.	
Réduction aux 2 cinquièmes.	»
h. 0.60 c.; l. 0.45 c.	
Réduction aux 3 dixièmes. .	550
h. 0.40 c.; l. 0.36 c.	
Réduction aux 2 dixièmes. .	350
h. 0.30 c.; l. 0.22 c.	

— 21 —

ŒUVRES MODERNES

MOISE, PAR MICHEL-ANGE

Le marbre original est dans l'église de San-Pietro in Vincole, à Rome.

	fr.
La réduction aux 9 vingtièmes . .	2,200
Hauteur, 1.12 c.; largeur, 0.41 c.; profondeur, 0.49 c.	
La réduction aux 9 vingt-cinquièmes	»
h. 0.91 c.; l. 0.82 c.; p. 0.37 c.	
La réduction aux 2 cinquièmes. . .	1,250
h. 0.82 c.; l. 0.34 c.; p. 0.35 c.	
La réduction aux 3 dixièmes. . . .	700
h. 0.61 c.; l. 0.25 c.; p. 0.26 c.	
La réduction au quart	500
h. 0.49 c.; l. 0.20 c.; p. 0.21 c.	
La réduction aux 2 dixièmes. . . .	350
h. 0.41 c.; l. 0.16 c.; p. 0.18 c.	
La réduction aux 3 vingtièmes. . .	250
h. 0.37 c.; l. 0.15 c.; p. 0.16 c.	
La réduction plus petite.	140
h. 0.24 c.; l. 0.10 c.; p. 0.11 c.	

SIX STATUES DES TOMBEAUX DES MÉDICIS
Les marbres sont à Florence.

LAURENT DE MÉDICIS (PENSEROSO)

La réduction n° 1	1,200
h. 0.92 c.; l. 0.35 c.; p. 0.37 c.	
La réduction n° 2	800
h. 0.74 c.; l. 0.26 c.; p. 0.30 c.	
La réduction n° 3	650
h. 0.61 c.; l. 0.23 c.; p. 0.24 c.	
La réduction n° 4	500
h. 0.54 c.; l. 0.20 c.; p. 0.22 c.	
La réduction n° 5	350
h. 0.46 c.; l. 0.17 c.; p. 0.19 c.	
La réduction n° 6	250
h. 0.37 c.; l. 0.13 c.; p. 0.14 c.	
La réduction n° 7	130
h. 0.25 c.; l. 0.09 c.; p. 0.10 c.	
La réduction n° 8	120
h. 0.23 c.; l. 0.08 c.; p. 0.09 c.	

— 34 —

MADELEINE, PAR CANOVA
Le marbre est à Gênes.

	fr.
La réduction aux 2 cinquièmes. . .	300
Hauteur, 0.36 c.; largeur, 0.28 c.	
La réduction aux 3 dixièmes. . . .	180
h. 0.26 c.; l. 0.20 c.	
La réduction aux 2 dixièmes. . . .	120
h. 0.18 c.; l. 0.14 c.	

SALMACIS (NYMPHE), PAR LE BARON BOSIO
Le marbre est au musée du Louvre, à Paris.

La réduction aux 2 cinquièmes. . .	250
h. 0.33 c.; l. 0.30 c.	
La réduction aux 3 dixièmes. . . .	175
h. 0.24 c.; l. 0.23 c.	
La réduction aux 2 dixièmes. . . .	70
h. 0.19 c.; l. 0.16 c.	

JEUNE INDIENNE, PAR LE BARON BOSIO
Le marbre est au ministère de l'intérieur.

La réduction aux 2 cinquièmes. . .	250
h. 0.25 c.; l. 0.40 c.	
La réduction aux 3 dixièmes. . . .	175
h. 0.20 c.; l. 0.29 c.	
La réduction aux 2 dixièmes. . . .	75
h. 0.15 c.; l. 0.20 c.	

HENRI IV (ENFANT), PAR LE BARON BOSIO
Une fonte en argent est au musée du Louvre, à Paris.

Grandeur originale	»
La réduction aux 2 cinquièmes. . .	225
h. 0.50 c.; l. 0.15 c.; p. 0.16 c.	
La réduction aux 3 dixièmes. . . .	140
h. 0.36 c.; l. 0.14 c.; p. 0.12 c.	
La réduction aux 2 dixièmes. . . .	80
h. 0.24 c.; l. 0.09 c.; p. 0.08 c.	

VÉNUS (ENDORMIE), PAR LE BARON BOSIO
Inédit.

La réduction aux 2 cinquièmes. . .	300
h. 0.21 c.; l. 0.70 c.	
La réduction aux 3 dixièmes. . . .	175
h. 0.15 c.; l. 0.50 c.	
La réduction aux 2 dixièmes. . . .	90
h. 0.11 c.; l. 0.33 c.	

— 35 —

CLÉOPATRE (COUCHÉE)
PAR M. DANIEL

	fr.
La réduction aux 2 cinquièmes. . .	500
Hauteur, 0.25 c.; largeur, 0.61 c.	
La réduction aux 2 dixièmes. . . .	225
h. 0.17 c.; l. 0.31 c.	

PETIT PÊCHEUR A LA TORTUE
PAR M. RUDE

Le marbre est au musée du Louvre, à Paris.

La réduction aux 2 cinquièmes. . .	250
h. 0.33 c.; l. 0.35 c.	
La réduction aux 3 dixièmes. . . .	175
h. 0.24 c.; l. 0.26 c.	
La réduction aux 2 dixièmes. . . .	90
h. 0.16 c.; l. 0.17 c.	

LA PRIÈRE, PAR M. JALEY
Le marbre est au musée du Louvre.

La réduction aux 2 cinquièmes. . .	200
h. 0.27 c.; l. 0.21 c.	
La réduction aux 3 dixièmes. . . .	140
h. 0.27 c.; l. 0.16 c.	
La réduction aux 2 dixièmes. . . .	65
h. 0.18 c.; l. 0.11 c.	

GIOTTO (DESSINANT)
PAR M. MERCIER

La réduction aux 2 dixièmes. . . .	55
h. 0.16 c.; l. 0.15 c.	

FÉNELON, PAR DAVID D'ANGERS
(DE L'INSTITUT)

Le marbre est à Cambrai.

La réduction aux 2 cinquièmes. . .	800
h. 0.54 c.; l. 0.86 c.	
La réduction aux 2 dixièmes. . . .	250
h. 0.27 c.; l. 0.42 c.	
La réduction au septième.	160
h. 0.20 c.; l. 0.33 c.	

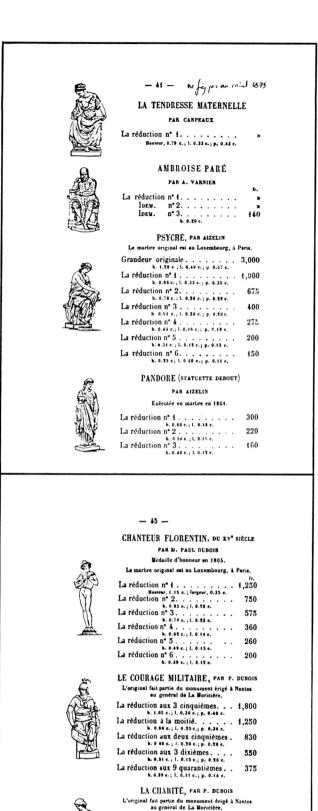

— 40 —

VOLTAIRE (STATUE ASSISE), PAR HOUDON

Le marbre original est dans le foyer de la
Comédie française, à Paris.

	fr.
La réduction n° 1	2,000
Hauteur, 0.80 c.; l. 0.35 c.; p. 0.59 c.	
La réduction n° 2	1,250
h. 0.65 c.; l. 0.31 c.; p. 0.47 c.	
La réduction n° 3	850
h. 0.53 c.; l. 0.25 c.; p. 0.37 c.	
La réduction n° 4	550
h. 0.45 c.; l. 0.21 c.; p. 0.32 c.	
La réduction n° 5	325
h. 0.32 c.; l. 0.15 c.; p. 0.23 c.	
La réduction n° 6	210
h. 0.22 c.; l. 0.11 c.; p. 0.16 c.	

AMBROISE PARÉ

PAR DAVID D'ANGERS

Grandeur d'exécution	250
h. 0.49 c.; l. 0.16 c.	
La réduction n° 1	140
h. 0.29 c.; l. 0.11 c.	
La réduction n° 2	90
h. 0.23 c.; l. 0.09 c.	
La réduction n° 3	65
h. 0.16 c.; l. 0.06 c.	

PÉNÉLOPE, PAR M. CAVELIER

Le marbre, qui a remporté le prix d'honneur,
appartient à M. le duc de Luynes.

Grandeur de la composition originale.	2,500
h. 0.95 c.; l. 0.55 c.; p. 0.75 c.	
La réduction n° 1	950
h. 0.62 c.; l. 0.35 c.; p. 0.54 c.	
La réduction n° 2	360
h. 0.36 c.; l. 0.22 c.; p. 0.28 c.	
La réduction n° 3	270
h. 0.31 c.; l. 0.17 c.; p. 0.26 c.	
La réduction n° 4	200
h. 0.25 c.; l. 0.14 c.; p. 0.20 c.	
La réduction n° 5	125
h. 0.16 c.; l. 0.09 c.; p. 0.14 c.	

— 41 — ne figure pas au raint 1875

LA TENDRESSE MATERNELLE

PAR CARPEAUX

La réduction n° 1	»
Hauteur, 0.79 c.; l. 0.33 c.; p. 0.43 c.	

AMBROISE PARÉ

PAR A. VARNIER

	fr.
La réduction n° 1	»
IDEM. n° 2	»
IDEM. n° 3	140
h. 0.20 c.	

PSYCHÉ, PAR AIZELIN

Le marbre original est au Luxembourg, à Paris.

Grandeur originale	3,000
h. 1.29 c.; l. 0.49 c.; p. 0.57 c.	
La réduction n° 1	1,000
h. 0.86 c.; l. 0.33 c.; p. 0.35 c.	
La réduction n° 2	675
h. 0.76 c.; l. 0.26 c.; p. 0.29 c.	
La réduction n° 3	400
h. 0.51 c.; l. 0.20 c.; p. 0.20 c.	
La réduction n° 4	275
h. 0.43 c.; l. 0.16 c.; p. 0.18 c.	
La réduction n° 5	200
h. 0.31 c.; l. 0.12 c.; p. 0.13 c.	
La réduction n° 6	150
h. 0.25 c.; l. 0.10 c.; p. 0.11 c.	

PANDORE (STATUETTE DEBOUT)

PAR AIZELIN

Exécutée en marbre en 1864.

La réduction n° 1	300
h. 0.60 c.; l. 0.18 c.	
La réduction n° 2	220
h. 0.50 c.; l. 0.15 c.	
La réduction n° 3	160
h. 0.40 c.; l. 0.12 c.	

— 44 —

ORPHÉE, PAR AIZELIN

L'original en marbre appartient à l'État.

La réduction	»
La réduction aux 2 cinquièmes . .	»
Hauteur, 0.35 c.	
La réduction	»
La réduction au quart.	»
h. 0.53 c.	

DERNIERS JOURS DE NAPOLÉON Iᵉʳ

PAR V. VÉLA

Exécuté en marbre en 1867.

Grandeur originale	1,700
h. 0.56 c.; l. 0.30 c.; p. 0.52 c.	
La réduction n° 1	650
h. 0.43 c.; l. 0.23 c.; p. 0.39 c.	
La réduction n° 2	280
h. 0.27 c.; l. 0.16 c.; p. 0.26 c.	
La réduction n° 3	200
h. 0.19 c.; l. 0.10 c.; p. 0.17 c.	

ŒUVRES DE M. PAUL DUBOIS

SAINT JEAN, PAR M. PAUL DUBOIS

La réduction n° 1	1,000
h. 1.20 c.; l. 0.34 c.	
La réduction n° 2	550
h. 0.95 c.; l. 0.26 c.	
La réduction n° 3	400
h. 0.80 c.; l. 0.22 c.	
La réduction n° 4	300
h. 0.64 c.; l. 0.18 c.	
La réduction n° 5	180
h. 0.36 c.; l. 0.12 c.	

— 45 —

CHANTEUR FLORENTIN, DU XVᵉ SIÈCLE

PAR M. PAUL DUBOIS

Médaille d'honneur en 1865.

Le marbre original est au Luxembourg, à Paris.

	fr.
La réduction n° 1	1,250
Hauteur, 1.15 c.; largeur, 0.35 c.	
La réduction n° 2	750
h. 0.93 c.; l. 0.28 c.	
La réduction n° 3	575
h. 0.76 c.; l. 0.23 c.	
La réduction n° 4	360
h. 0.62 c.; l. 0.18 c.	
La réduction n° 5	260
h. 0.49 c.; l. 0.15 c.	
La réduction n° 6	200
h. 0.39 c.; l. 0.12 c.	

LE COURAGE MILITAIRE, PAR P. DUBOIS

L'original fait partie du monument érigé à Nantes
au général de La Moricière.

La réduction aux 3 cinquièmes. . .	1,800
h. 1.03 c.; l. 0.30 c.; p. 0.40 c.	
La réduction à la moitié.	1,250
h. 0.86 c.; l. 0.25 c.; p. 0.34 c.	
La réduction aux deux cinquièmes.	830
h. 0.68 c.; l. 0.20 c.; p. 0.26 c.	
La réduction aux 3 dixièmes. . . .	550
h. 0.51 c.; l. 0.15 c.; p. 0.20 c.	
La réduction aux 9 quarantièmes. .	375
h. 0.39 c.; l. 0.11 c.; p. 0.14 c.	

LA CHARITÉ, PAR P. DUBOIS

L'original fait partie du monument érigé à Nantes
au général de La Moricière.

La réduction aux 3 cinquièmes. . .	1,800
h. 0.96 c.; l. 0.31 c.; p. 0.35 c.	
La réduction à la moitié.	1,250
h. 0.80 c.; l. 0.27 c.; p. 0.29 c.	
La réduction aux 2 cinquièmes. . .	900
h. 0.64 c.; l. 0.21 c.; p. 0.23 c.	
La réduction aux 3 dixièmes. . . .	590
h. 0.46 c.; l. 0.16 c.; p. 0.18 c.	
La réduction aux 9 quarantièmes. .	410
h. 0.36 c.; l. 0.12 c.; p. 0.13 c.	

— 46 —

ÉTUDE ET MÉDITATION

PAR PAUL DUBOIS

L'original fait partie du monument érigé à Nantes
au général de La Moricière.

La réduction aux 3 cinquièmes. . .	1800
Hauteur, 0.95 c.; l. 0.38 c.; p. 0.44 c.	
La réduction à la moitié.	1250
h. 0.80 c.; l. 0.30 c.; p. 0.36 c.	
La réduction aux 2 cinquièmes. . .	900
h. 0.64 c.; l. 0.24 c.; p. 0.29 c.	
La réduction aux 3 dixièmes. . . .	590
h. 0.48 c.; l. 0.18 c.; p. 0.22 c.	
La réduction aux 9 quarantièmes. .	410
h. 0.36 c.; l. 0.14 c.; p. 0.17 c.	

LA PRIÈRE

PAR PAUL DUBOIS

L'original fait partie du monument érigé à Nantes
au général de La Moricière.

La réduction aux 3 cinquièmes . . :	1550
h. 0.97 c.; l. 0.35 c.; p. 0.25 c.	
La réduction à la moitié.	1050
h. 0.82 c.; l. 0.30 c.; p. 0.30 c.	
La réduction aux 2 cinquièmes. . .	640
h. 0.65 c.; l. 0.23 c.; p. 0.13 c.	
La réduction aux 3 dixièmes	430
h. 0.49 c.; l. 0.18 c.; p. 0.15 c.	
La réduction aux 9 quarantièmes. .	325
h. 0.37 c.; l. 0.13 c.; p. 0.13 c.	

JEANNE D'ARC, PAR CHAPU

Le marbre original est au Luxembourg, à Paris.

Grandeur originale	4,500
h. 1.17 c.; l. 0.83 c.	
La réduction n° 1	1,000
h. 0.72 c.; l. 0.53 c.	
La réduction n° 2	750
h. 0.60 c.; l. 0.45 c.	
La réduction n° 3	540
h. 0.47 c.; l. 0.29 c.	
La réduction n° 4	340
h. 0.36 c.; l. 0.25 c.	
La réduction n° 5	250
h. 0.30 c.; l. 0.21 c.	
La réduction n° 6	180
h. 0.23 c.; l. 0.17 c.	

— 47 —

LA JEUNESSE, PAR CHAPU.

Le marbre original est au monument d'Henri Regnault,
aux Beaux-Arts, à Paris.

La réduction n° 1	1,500
Hauteur, 1.18 c.	
La réduction n° 2	1,100
h. 0.93 c.	
La réduction n° 3	575
h. 0.60 c.	

DAVID, AVANT LE COMBAT

PAR MERCIÉ

Grandeur de l'original	500
h. 0.80 c.; l. 0.27 c.; p. 0.29 c.	
La réduction n° 1	250
h. 0.45 c.; l. 0.14 c.; p. 0.15 c.	

DAVID, VAINQUEUR DE GOLIATH

PAR MERCIÉ

La réduction n° 1	1,250
h. 1.10 c.; l. 0.27 c.	
La réduction n° 2	800
h. 0.92 c.; l. 0.23 c.	
La réduction n° 3	550
h. 0.73 c.; l. 0.18 c.	

GLORIA VICTIS, PAR MERCIÉ

L'original appartient à la Préfecture de la Seine.

Grandeur de l'original.	»
h. 3.17 c.	
La réduction aux 3 cinquièmes. . .	6000
h. 1.90 c.	
La réduction aux 9 vingtièmes. . .	3200
h. 1.40 c.	
La réduction aux 3 dixièmes. . . .	2100
h. 0.95 c.	

— 60 —

DEUX FEMMES, STYLE RENAISSANCE

(FIGURES DEBOUT, PORTE-LUMIÈRES)

PAR E. GUILLEMIN

	fr.
Grandeur n° 1	3700
Hauteur, 1.50 c.; largeur, 0.38 c.	
Grandeur n° 2	2200
h. 1.20 c.; l. 0.30 c.	

DEUX FEMMES JAPONAISES

(FIGURES DEBOUT, PORTE-LUMIÈRES)

PAR E. GUILLEMIN

Grandeur n° 1 . . . . . la paire.	2,000
h. 1.20 c.; l. 0.30 c.	
Grandeur n° 2 . . . . . IDEM.	

FEMMES ALGÉRIENNES

(FIGURES DEBOUT, PORTE-LUMIÈRES)

PAR FULCONIS

Grandeur originale, la paire.	6200
h. 2.00 c.; l. 0.57 c.	
La réduction aux 3 cinquièmes.	3000
h. 1.20 c.; l. 0.34 c.	
La réduction à la moitié. . . .	»
h. 1.00 c.; l. 0.26 c.	

N. B. Les prix ci-dessus avec un brandon au gaz; lesdites torchères peuvent s'exécuter avec
un bouquet de plusieurs feux, dont le prix varie suivant le nombre de lumières et la richesse
de l'ornementation.

ENFANTS GRIMPEURS

(TORCHÈRES, 4 FEUX AU GAZ)

PAR GUILLEMIN

Grandeur originale, la paire	1,800
h. 1.35 c.; l. 0.18 c.	

— 61 —

LA VICTOIRE, PAR CARRIER-BELLEUSE

Figure debout, porte-lumières sur colonne marbre.

	fr.
Grandeur originale	3,250
Hauteur, 2.25 c.	

ANIMAUX

GROUPE DE LEVRETTES

Le marbre antique est au musée du Vatican, à Rome.

La réduction aux 2 cinquièmes. . .	120
h. 0.20 c.; l. 0.22 c.	
La réduction aux 3 dixièmes. . . .	90
h. 0.15 c.; l. 0.16 c.	
La réduction aux 2 dixièmes. . . .	65
h. 0.10 c.; l. 0.11 c.	

LEVRETTE (SEULE)

Le marbre original est au musée du Louvre, à Paris.

La réduction aux 2 cinquièmes. . .	90
h. 0.22 c.; l. 0.28 c.	
La réduction aux 3 dixièmes. . . .	60
h. 0.17 c.; l. 0.21 c.	
La réduction aux 2 dixièmes. . . .	40
h. 0.11 c.; l. 0.14 c.	

AIGLE

Le marbre antique est au musée du Vatican, à Rome.

La réduction aux 7 neuvièmes. . . .	325
h. 0.50 c.	
La réduction aux 3 cinquièmes. . .	180
h. 0.36 c.; l. 0.28 c.	
La réduction au tiers	75
h. 0.22 c.; l. 0.17 c.	
La réduction au quart.	35
h. 0.16 c.; l. 0.11 c.	

The Barbedienne company published a certain number of commercial catalogs in which were listed bronze castings of antique or contemporary works in many dimensions. The selection was considerable, from sculptures of the Parthenon to Michaelangelo's *Moïse,* from full- and half-size versions and details of the baptismal doors in Florence to Bosio's *Henri IV,* from the *Chanteur Florentin* by Paul Dubois to *Mozart enfant* by Barrias, and from busts by David d'Angers to works by Aizelin, Carrier-Belleuse, Clésinger, and Gardet, not to mention the clocks, lights, decorative furnishings, and 'mantelpiece artworks' decorated with enamel and other precious materials. In the catalogs published before 1875 appeared the heading "Dépot de la collection Barye" (deposit of the Barye collection). After this date and the purchase of the sculptor's models, Barbedienne devoted an entire catalog to him.

Here, as an example, is an excerpt from one of the innumerable contracts Ferdinand Barbedienne arranged with sculptors. This one was concluded on January 1, 1879, with Ernest Louis Barrias.

"Monsieur Barrias yields, before those present, to M. Barbedienne who accepts, the exclusive right to reduce a statue of Bernard Palissy by means of the Achille Collas procedure [...] and to reproduce as he would understand it the reductions of the above-mentioned statue; M. Barrias created moreover a series of small models entitled *Enfant sur torue, Enfant à l'escargot, Enfant au panier, Enfant à l'amphore, Enfant au coquillage et crabe, Amphore femme ailée, Vase aux lianes,* and *les Deux Soeurs,* of which he also yields the exclusive right of reproduction to M. Barbedienne who accepts [...] The present right is granted for a period of twenty-five years to start on this day."

The passage continues,

"M. Barbedienne commits himself to owe to M. Barrias twenty percent of the net proceeds and effects of the sale of each of the reductions and reproductions..."

In his report on the art bronzes and bronze furnishings presented at the Chicago Exposition in 1893, Albert Susse, mourning the disappearance of Ferdinand Barbedienne, asessed well the notoriety of the famous founder, not hesitating to consider Barbedienne "... the pride of the nation [...] who had carried the splendor of our industry so loftily to all international competitions."

BARYE, ANTOINE LOUIS

This famous sculptor opened his original foundry in 1838 to cast his own works. Despite serious setbacks between 1845 and 1857, the foundry remained active until Barye's death in 1875. (See the heading devoted to this artist in the dictionary of sculptors.)

BINGEN, PIERRE

Born in 1842, Pierre Bingen worked first in residence for some silversmiths before giving himself up to casting bronzes. He was particularly interested in the lost wax procedure. In the 1880s, he established himself at 74 Rue des Plantes and furnished Rodin with nearly a dozen pieces in small dimensions. Carrier-Belleuse, Falguière, Cordier, Barrias, and Dalou were among his clients. For Dalou, Bingen started casting the *Triomphe de la République,* but had to abandon it because the cost was too high. This work was finally made by Victor Thiébaut. Bingen lived at 8 Villa Ciollet in 1900, during which period can be found mention of his successors, Bingen Jr and Costenoble.

BISCEGLIA, MARIO

Coming from Italy at the beginning of the 20th century, this founder established himself in Malakoff, near Paris, and worked regularly for Henri Bouchard and a number of other artists. His activity continued until 1962, after which he sold his studios to Emile Godard. A certain number of seals carry the phrase "Bisceglia frères."

BLOT, EUGÈNE

A manufacturer of "art zinc" was documented in 1874 under the trade name Blot and Drouard. In 1878 they exhibited many of his imitation bronzes, a certain number of them reproductions of works by Guillemin and Dumaige. At the end of the 19th century, Eugène Blot (undoubtedly the son of the original founder) worked as an editor of bronzes and owned an exhibition gallery at 5 Boulevard de la Madeleine. There could be found some canvases of the great impressionist painters, lamps, curios, and some bronzes by Constantin, Meunier, Hoetger, Jouant, Van der Staeten, Roger-Bloch, and Camille Claudel; all of the bronzes had been cast by Eugène Blot. He particularly admired Camille Claudel, for whom he cast works in limited and numbered castings. Adapting a phrase from Mirbeau, Blot wrote later the Claudel "is to Rodin as Berth Morizot is to Manet." In 1937 and 1938, after retiring from the business, Eugène Blot yielded "the rights of manufacturing and casting many models of the statues" mentioned above to Leblanc-Barbedienne. He indicated at this time that he was formerly the editor of art at 11 Rue Richepanse and that his factory was found at 84 Rue des Archives.

COLIN, EMILE

Emile Colin worked in the second half of the 19th century for a number of renowned artists, including Carrier-Belleuse, Feuchère, Fratin, Pradier, Théodore Rivière, Mathurin Moreau, Mindron, and Charpentier. He sent a bronze clock and some marble vases decorated with bronze to the 1893 Chicago Exposition, in addition to some sculptures. The Colin foundry was located at 29 Rue de Sévingé in 1843, and then at 17 Rue des Tournelles starting in 1914. Around 1930, the foundry operated a shop at 12 Avenue Victor-Emmanuel-III.

COLLAS, ACHILLE

Paris, 1795
Paris, 1859

The inventor of diverse machines to variegate colors for the imprinting of calico, Collas completed a procedure of reduction of the statues based on the pantograph and, in 1838, went into business with the famous founder Ferdinand Barbedienne. His first reduction, a statuette in bronze of the *Vénus de Milo*, 90 cm high, drew the attention of founders and sculptors when it was first exhibited in 1839. His invention (and other similar creations made simultaneously by different inventors, including Sauvage) was originally used for producing immense numbers of bronze reproductions in the second half of the 19th century. In 1867, the international jury of the Exposition Universelle posthumously eulogized Achille Collas, unhesitatingly comparing him to Gutenberg.

DAUBRÉE, ALFRED

Daubrée owned a goldsmith's shop in Nancy before establishing himself as merchant of art bronzes and jewelry at the Paris address of 85 Rue Montmartre in the 1850s. He cast a certain number of works by Fratin, Cumberworth, Menessier, Michel Pascal, and Kampf. He used a number of intermediaries to sell his bronzes, which only rarely carried his mark. Starting in 1860, he lived at 48 Boulevard de Strasbourg, and by 1881 had moved to 12 Boulevard de Strasbourg. At the time of the Exposition Universelle of 1867, Daubrée was noted among the reputed founders of the time. His son succeeded him after his death in 1885.

DEBRAUX

Sometimes called "Debraux d'Englures," this founder began participating in expositions of industrial products in 1834. He was the first manufacturer to be titled as an "editor of art," in 1839. He was then established on the Rue de Castiglione, and owned a store at 17 Rue d'Astorg. In 1837 he made the cast for the statue by Emmanuel-Philibert of Savoie, of Marochettie, for a square in Turin. His studio also cast other works for this sculptor as well as a number of other artists, including Gechter, Fauginet, and Barye. In 1852, the commercial directories mention this foundry for the last time under the trade name "Veuve Debreaux." However, its name appeared again in 1858, in the *Magasin pittoresque* for some castings in bronze by contemporary sculptors.

DELAFONTAINE

As early as the 18th century, there was a bronze factory managed by a master founder by the name of Jean-Baptiste Maximilien Delafontaine, born in 1750.

His son, Pierre Maximilien (1774-1860), succeeded him. Their factory was first located at 13 Rue d'Orléans, and, beginning in 1824, at 10 Rue Neuve-de-l'Abbaye. The succession apparently continued from father to son; Auguste Maximilien Delafontaine operated the business at 46 Rue Bonaparte in the 1840s, until the company moved to 10 Rue de l'Université in 1870. This period, while the firm was under Auguste Maximilien's direction, was its most fecund. Simply an editor, he entrusted the execution of bronzes to the Molz foundry on the Rue de Rennes. Resuming the contracts arranged by Duret with the founder Quesnel, he cast *Le Danseur napolitain, Le Vendangeur improvisant, Jeune Pêcheur dansant la tarentelle, La Tragédie, La Comédie* and some other subjects by the great sculptor around 1855. His catalog of "bronzes of art and of furnishings" offered some works by other artists (including Pradier), reproductions of antique statues, and diverse objects d'art and furniture. At the posthumous sale of Barye's works in 1876, Auguste Maximilien Delafontaine bought a certain number of models, particularly of dogs, of which he made some editions. Pursuing his activities, his son Henri Maximilien succeeded him in 1884 and in turn published his own catalog, noting the company's possession "of the greatest part of the work by Duret" and the edition of works by numerous other sculptors such as Cavelier, Pradier, Elias Robert, Guillaume, Mathurin Moreau, some collections of animals by Barye and Jacqumart, some reductions of sculptures from antiquity, the Renaissance, and the 17th and 18th centuries, and finally some objects of furniture and decoration. Henri Maximilien Delafontaine sold his business and retired in 1905.

DENIÈRE

The Denière factory of art bronzes began at 15 Rue Vivienne during the 1820s, primarily producing furnishings, chandeliers, candelabras, etc. The manufacturing studios were situated at the Rue d'Orléans (later renamed the Rue Charlot). Denière, Sr. had belonged to the Union des Fondeurs of Paris in 1818. He participated in exhibitions of industrial products, particularly in 1839, with some objects made in collaboration with his son (who joined the Union des Fondeurs in 1847). He furnished the duke of Orléans with an ornamented centerpiece, consisting of figures by Cavelier, Klagmann and some other sculptors; this centerpiece was sold at the same time as the collection of the prince in 1852. The Denière house acquired a tremendous notoriety, and his stand at the Exposition Universelle of 1855 attracted many customers. Beginning around 1855, the company operated under the direction of Denière's son Guillaume. Similarly, he presented numerous works at the Exposition de l'Union Centrale des Beaux-Arts Appliqués à l'Industrie in 1874, including candelabras made up of Clodion figures, vases ornamented with cloisonné enamel, busts in marble by Carrier-Belleuse, etc. The house also cast some statuettes by the Carrier-Belleuse, and executed the gilded bronze casting of the group *Apollon* by Aimé Millet, which surmounts the great gable of the stage from the Opera. Princes and kings figured among Denière's wealthy clientele, and he remained active until the end of the century, always at the same addresses.

ECK AND DURAND

After separating from Quesnel, the founder Louis Richard (see the entry for Richard and Quesnel) established himself at 15 Rue des Trois-Bornes. In 1838 he entered into partnership with a chisel-worker named Jean Georges Eck and a molder named Durand. Their business then took flight, thanks to the reputation for quality their castings earned. Shortly after 1840, fifty-three year old Richard retired, leaving Eck and Durand alone. The Richard, Eck and Durand foundry became the Eck and Durand foundry, and produced a large number of works. Some of these were very well-known, including bronzes by David d'Angers, the doors from the church of the Madeleine de Triqueti, a silver version of Rude's *Louis XIII à l'age de size ans* for the château of Dampierre, and (again from Rude) the *Réveil de Napoléon* for the parc de Fixin in the Côte-d'Or. They also produced some well-known statuettes of actresses and famous people sculpted by Barre, the *Molière* by Bernard Seurre for the Molière fountain in Paris, and the dragons of the fountain Saint-Michel that had been sculpted by Jacquemart.

In 1863, at the death of Jean Georges Eck, Durand retired. The studios were sold, and a number of models were redeemed by Victor Thiébaut.

FEUCHÈRE

In 1784, the chiseler Jean-François Feuchère reactivated his father's foundry at 57 Rue Saint-Martin, and began executing works for diverse royal residences. In 1800, he transported his studios to 25 Rue Notre-Dame-de-Nazareth, where he produced mainly chandeliers, fireplace garnitures, and other furnishings. Before 1820, they were noted as chiseler/gilders, suppliers to His Majesty. They produced some statuettes, for the most part copies of sculptures from antiquity or from the 17th and 18th centuries. From 1841 to 1860, there are records of one Armand Feuchère (perhaps the son of Jean-François Feuchère) whose store was located at 7 bis Rue du Grand-Prieuré, and whose factory at 20 Rue Crussol.

FUMIÈRE AND GAVIGNOT

(See Thiébaut)

GODARD

The origin of this foundry, though it is still in business in Malakoff near Paris, remains obscure. The foundry was opened at the end of the 19th or the beginning of the 20th century by Désiré Godard. In 1928, it's location was noted at 18 and 20 Rue Charles-Friedel in the twentieth district. Emile Godard succeeded his father and, in 1962, acquired the old Bisceglia foundry in Malakoff. He established his studios there, although the quarters on the Rue Charles-Friedel were still used for about fifteen years more. The Godard foundry executed some bronzes by Carpeaux, Bourdelle, Maillol, and Picasso, among others. It also worked for the Rodin museum, practicing the art of casting by the lost wax technique as well as by sand casting.

GOLDSCHEIDER

At the end of the 19th century and until the First World War, the Parisian and Viennese art editor Frédéric Goldscheider distributed bronzes, as well as some terra cottas and marbles. He worked for a number of sculptors, including Alloiuard, Carlier, Carrier-Belleuse, Félix Charpentier, Injalbert, Loiseau-Rousseau, Moreau-Vauthier, Marqueste, and Tony Noël. He lived at 45 Rue de Paradis and owned a retail store at 28 Avenue de l'Opera. After the war, an Arthur Goldscheider appeared on the Rue de Paradis, an art editor noted as running a "House franco-teque." Van der Straeten was one of the sculptors whose work was cast by the Goldscheider house at this time.

GONON

Honoré Gonon (1780-1850), who established his foundry in 1810 in the Saint-Martin suburbs, excuted many official commissions under the Empire, including some of the bas-reliefs of the Vendôme column. The equestrian statue of *Henri IV* on the Pont-Neuf, sculpted by François Lemot in 1818, was produced by Gonon's studios as well. He soon became impassioned over the lost wax procedure, very seldom used at that time, and in 1829 began to manage a foundry "of art objects difficult to make" with his two sons in Buttes-Chaumont. The castings in lost wax made by Gonon and his sons were particularly well-reputed. Among the most famous are those made for Barye (*Tigre dévorant un gavial, Lion au serpent,* and the centerpiece for the duke of Orléans) and some works by other great sculptors like Pradier, David d'Angers, and Duret (the *Pêcheur napolitain*). Honoré Gonon, who did not practice casting himself, retired in 1840. He was succeeded by one of his sons, Eugène Gonon (1814-1892), who was also a sculptor (see entry devoted to him). Located first at 80 Rue de Sèvres, and then at 18 Rue Pérignon, Eugène Gonon continued to cast by the lost wax method, working in particular for Pradier, Barye, Frémiet, Gérôme, Dalou, and Ernest Christophe. In addition, he worked for Rodin, who passed some commissions to him between 1882 and 1885.

GOUGE, AUGUSTE

Resuming work at the sculptor Jules Moigniez's old foundry at 124 Rue Vieille-du-Temple in the 1880s, Auguste Gouge continued to cast works there through the beginning of the 20th century. The foundry seems to have become inactive a short time after 1920.

GRAUX-MARLY

This firm was active during the second half of the 19th century, first on the Boulevard du Temple, and then at 8 Rue du Parc-Royal beginning in 1860. In

1880, the sons of M. Graux-Marly were noted as successors to their father. They produced some bronze furnishings, clocks, and ornamented candelabras in the Clodion style, as well as in Russian, Byzantine, and Persian styles, decorated with enamel. They also cast reproductions of sculptures from antiquity and the Renaissance as well as some models by Barye, Carpeaux, Frémier, Carrier-Belleuse and other contemporary artists.

GRIFFOUL

This founder worked first in partnership with François Rudier, as evidenced by some invoices dated 1881 preserved by the Rodin Museum. Next he formed the firm Griffoul and Lorge, located at 6 Passage Dombasle, which furnished Rodin with one hundred and five bronzes including *Le Baiser, Le Printemps, Ugolin, Faunesse à genoux, Eve, Cariatide à la pierre,* and *Le Génie de la guerre,* between 1887 and 1894. In addition to some works for other artists, the castings for Rodin continued to be executed by Jean-Baptiste Griffoul—eighteen pieces between 1895 and 1898—and then with Auguste Griffoul, who made twenty-one bronzes between June, 1898 and March, 1899. At the end of 1899, Auguste Griffoul went to the United States, opening a prosperous foundry named of A. Griffoul and Bros Co. in Newark.

GRUET

This foundry executed works for different sculptors, but especially for Rodin; a brief history of their work with the famous sculptor can be compiled from museum archives. Gruet, Jr., who was established at 195 Rue du Maine around 1880, furnished thirteen castings to Rodin, including the first version of *Saint Jean-Baptiste.* Three other bronzes were delivered to him between 1889 and 1890, but this time under the sole name of Gruet; later, between 1891 and 1895, twenty-four bronzes, including *Le Baiser,* were delivered to his oldest son, Adolphe Gruet, at the same address. Adolphe Gruet soon abandoned casting for the art of rendering patinas, but by the turn of the century E. Gruet, Jr. (from his establishment at 44 Bis Avenue de Châtillon) was also working for Rodin.

HÉBRARD, ADRIEN A.

Born in 1865, this extremely well-reputed founder doubled as a very shrewd businessman, an expert in evaluating the talent of young artists. He possessed a gallery at 8 de la Rue Royale, where he organized exhibitions and presented the works of his protégés. He had studios at 73 Avenue de Versailles, where he frequently practiced casting not only by the lost wax technique but also by sand. He cast works by Carpeaux, Dalou (including numerous bronzes from the terra cottas and plasters at the Petit Palais, mostly in numbered castings of ten, though some were special unique editions), Falguière, Jules Desbois, Bourdelle, Bugatti (with whom he signed a contract of exclusivity in 1904, when the sculptor was still a minor), Degas (casting twenty-two editions of each of the bronzes between 1919 and 1920, after the artist's death), Pompon, Joseph Bernard, and a quantity of other artists. He does not seem to have worked for Rodin, though he did desire to. The Hébrard house disappeared in 1937, with the death of its founder.

HOHWILLER

The Hohwiller foundry was opened in 1906 by an Alsacian. His son and widow maintained the firm until 1965. This house worked for many famous sculptors, including Henri Bouchard.

HOUDEBINE

This small business was founded in 1845 by a workman, and can be traced until about 1910 through the following trade names and addresses: Henri Houdebine et Cie., at 3 Rue de la Perle in the 1850s; Henri Houdebine and V.F. Blumberg, at 44 Rue Saint-Louis-au-Marais (later renamed Rue de Turenne) around 1860; Henri Houdebine, at 64 Rue de Turenne, 1865-1880; Houbedine & Son at the same address, around 1890; and finally E. Houdebine, at the end of the 19th and in the first years of the 20th century.

The Houdebine house participated in many universal expositions—in 1878 and 1889 in Paris, and in 1893 in Chicago, sending candelabras and fireplace accessories in an Italian Renaissance style as well as some sculptures. Around 1900, the Houbedine house cast a number of works by Dalou and other artists, including Bofill, Mars-Vallet, Picault, and Monard.

LABROUE, E. DE

This founder, whose activity seems to have been of a short duration, was established at 10 Rue des Filles-du-Calvaire. His name appears just once, at the time of the Expositions Universelle of 1855, at which he presented some chandeliers, candelabras, statuettes, and groups in bronze. He cast a number of works by Pradier (*Vénus et l'Amour, Phryné, L'Etoile du soir, Pandore,* etc.), Carrier-Belleuse (*Albert Dürer, Rembrandt, Dante, L'Arioste, Le Highlander,* and *Le Zouave*), Feuchère, Polet, Michel-Pascal, Lequesne, and many others.

LEROLLE FRÈRES

These brothers succeeded their father in 1836, and one year later cast a work by Dantan Jr. entitled *Madame Alexis Dupont dans le pas styrien.* After 1850, they also began practicing the techniques of galvanoplastic gilding and silvering, and produced some subjects in imitation bronze. In 1863, they were still cited as makers of art bronzes, and participated with a very significant showing at the Exposition des Beaux-Arts appliqués à l'industrie, exhibiting a quantity of furnishings and some individual statuettes.

MARCHAND, LÉON

Founded in 1822, this factory of art bronzes was located at 57 Rue de Richelieu around 1850. It was accompanied by an important exhibition gallery which, according to the numbers from L'Illustration of 1860, was well-stocked in bronze furnishings, candelabras, vases, fireplace accessories, statuettes, and groups. Among other works cast by Marchand is the group entitled Cléopâtre et Lesbie by Cumberworth.

MATIFAT, C.

Noted as early as 1840, C. Matifat seems to have produced some small bronzes and furnishings. In 1873, he made two important castings—L'Enfant des Abruzzes, a bronze of 130 cm high modeled after the plaster sent to Rome by Allar, and the fountain from the Paris Observatoire with Carpeaux's group Quatre Parties du monde and Frémier's horses, dolphins, and tortoises. For his work, Matifat earned 60,000 F, much more than the two sculptors combined.

MÈNE, PIERRE JULES

The famous animal sculptor (see the entry devoted to him) opened his original foundry in 1837 in order to edit his own works. It was first located at 129 Rue du Temple, but moved in 1842 to 7 Faubourg du Temple, and finally, around 1857, to 21 Rue de l'Entrepôt-du-Marais. He also cast the bronzes of his son-in-law, Auguste Cain, another animal sculptor, who worked with him at the foundry. The work of their studio was reputed to be of excellent quality, and customers were well- assured that the two artists chiseled their bronzes themselves. After the death of Mène in 1879, Cain continued casting until his own death in 1894. The two sculptors' models were then acquired by the Susse foundry, which in turn cast the pieces themseslves. Some were also sold to Barbedienne.

MOIGNIEZ

This foundry on the Rue Charlot was opened around 1850 by a metal gilder who sought to cast the works of his son, the animal sculptor Jules Moigniez. The bronzes he produced had a reputation for the finesse of their casting and the quality of their patinas. The trade name "Moigniez fils," adopted in 1860, indicates that the sculptor himself had undertaken its direction. In 1870, however, the foundry was moved to 124 Rue Vieille-du-Temple under the direction of F. Dietsh, Jules Moigniez's successor.

Auguste Gouge became the final proprietor of the endeavor around 1890, casting bronzes by Moigniez until the beginning of the 20th century.

PAILLARD, VICTOR

While still a child, Victor Paillard learned chiseling with Denière, and opened his own business of "art and furniture bronzes" in the 1830s, at 105 Boulevard Beaumarchais and at 6 Rue Saint-Claud. He first made small objects, then some candelabras, clocks, groups, and statuettes. He appeared for the first time at the Exposition des Produits de l'Industrie in 1839. He worked for a number of sculptors, including Feuchère, Pradier, Barye, Carrier-Belleuse, Préault, and Kalgman. According to his biographer Mme Christiane Frain de la Gaulayrie, in 1855 he employed nearly one hundred workers and offered to his clientele more than four hundred models, as many in bronze as in imitation zinc. He himself created some statuettes of young children and of lovers, with which he ornamented diverse objects, including inkwells, flat candlesticks, and andirons. His castings were usually marked by the initials "VP" surmounted by a closed crown. He died in 1886 at the age of eighty-one. Most of his models were sold in 1890.

PERSINKA, LÉON

A founder and chiseler established at first at 29 Rue de Montreuil in Versailles, and then at 11 and 13 of the same street, Léon Persinka executed a number of castings for Rodin between 1896 and 1902, including Iris messagère des dieux, L'Appel aux armes, two proofs from L'Age d'airain, and some reductions of people from the Bourgeois de Calais. He was unable, however, the secure a position as Rodin's exclusive founder. Some bronzes by other artists carry the mark of this founder.

PEYROL, HIPPOLYTE

An old student of Barye, this founder (1830-1891) set up his workshop at 14 Rue de Crussol. He cast the works of Isidore and Rosa Bonheur, whose sister, Juliette Bonheur, he had married in 1852. Until the 1920s, Peyrol's foundry pursued its activity under the same name. It is also noted as specialist in animal bronzes by Isidore and Rosa Bonheur.

PINEDO

Before 1850, the Pinedo house was located at 25 Rue de Bretagne, though it would pursue its activity at different addresses until the 1930s. In 1855, L. Pinedo operated at 110 Rue Saint-Louis-au-Marais. His son, who was also sculptor (see the entry devoted to him), succeeded him in 1865 under the trade name "Emile Pinedo fils," producing art bronzes and furnishings from his studios at 18 Boulevard du

*Some examples of founders'
seals and signatures.*

663

Prince-Eugène and 49 Rue de Bondy. Starting in 1880, the Pinedo house (with no indication of a first name) was located at 40 Boulevard du Temple. It produced some groups, statuettes, busts, candelabras, and all sorts of furnishings. At the exposition in Chicago in 1893, Pinedo's bronzes were particularly appreciated by the public for their polychrome patinas. Among the sculptors cast by Pineda were Hiolin (*Au loup !*), Leroux (*Aïda*), Debut, (*Le Porteur d'eau*), Meissonier (numerous busts of *Napoléon 1er*), Van der Straeten, Pépin, etc.

QUESNEL

A short time after separating from the founder Richard (see entry under this name), E. Quesnel installed himself at 22 Rue des Amandiers-Popincourt and pursued the casting of Duret's works, among which was *L'Improvisateur*, exhibited at the Salon of 1839. He appeared in 1844 under the trade name Quesnel et Cie., situated at 112 Rue de Richelieu, with a store full of vases, statuettes and art bronzes located at 15 Rue de la Paix. Most notably, he offered works by Pradier and by Duret there. It seems that after being ruined by the revolution of 1848, Quesnel yielded his business to his son. Thus there is record of a company called L. Quesnel et Cie, located at 22 Rue des Amandiers-Popincourt, until it moved to 25 Rue des Trois-Bornes in 1852. His activity ended around 1855, at which time he transferred his contracts with Duret to the founder Delafontaine.

RAINGO FRÈRES

The Raingo business was founded in 1813, and around 1830 it appeared at 8 Rue de Touraine. The four Raingo brothers were first recognized as clockmakers, but in 1841, at 11 Rue de Saintonge, they added art bronzes and furnishings to their repertoire. As of 1860, the Raingo house furnished bronzes to the emperor and empress, and owned an important store of exhibition pieces at 102 Rue Vieille-du-Temple. They stayed at this address until the 1930s. At first they made reproductions of antiques, and then proceeded to works by contemporary artists, cast in a small number of models (not really editions). Among the artists whose work was cast by Raingo Frères are Pradier, Carrier-Belleuse, and Auguste Moreau.

RICHARD AND QUESNEL

After having worked separately, the founder Louis Richard and the chiseler E. Quesnel went into partnership in 1826. Their studio, located at 11 Rue Aux-Fèves and 2 Rue de la Folie-Méricourt, produced subjects in bronze, some clocks, medals, and optical instruments. They worked on commission for different sculptors. In 1834, at the Exposition des Produits de l'Industrie, they presented a casting in bronze of the *Pêcheur dansant la tarentelle*, by Duret, for whom the first work was cast the following year by Gonon. In 1835, they were indicated as founders at 13 Rue des Enfants-Rouges, but separated around 1836. E. Quesnel (see the entry under this name)

continued to live for some time at 13 Rue des Enfants-Rouges. Louis Richard established himself at 15 Rue des Trois-Bornes, and went into partnership three years later with Eck and Durand (see entries under these names). Bronzes signed with the name Richard alone are rare. He is, however, cited as David D'Angers' favorite founder for casting medallions.

ROLLAND, A.

The successor of Boyer, Sr. and Rolland, this founder was established at 10 and 12 Rue de l'Asile-Popincourt and used the Sauvage procedure to produce some reductions of antique statues. In 1884, he proceeded to cast a large group by the sculptor Auguste Cain entitled *Rhinocéros attaqué par des tigres*, which was placed in the gardens of the Tuileries.

RUDIER

There were plans for a foundry to be opened in the second half of the 19th century by three brothers: Victor, François and Alexis Rudier. Apparently, however, their association did not last; in 1881 some invoices listed François Rudier as the head of Griffoule et Cie. at 41 Rue Vavin, and then in 1883, of François Ruder et Cie. In particular, this foundry worked for Rodin, to whom it furnished one hundred and fifteen bronzes between 1881 and 1904. For the most part, these pieces seem to carry neither the seal nor the signature of the founder.

Alexis, on the other hand, opened his own foundry in 1874. His production became very important, but he probably did not work for Rodin, although a large quantity of Rodin bronzes do carry the mark of Alexis Rudier. After Alexis's death in 1897, first his widow and then his son Eugène Rudier preserved the signature (see the entry devoted to Rodin) for the still very active foundry, which worked for a number of sculptors. At the beginning of the century, the company was established at 45 Rue de Saintonge, and starting in 1902, Rodin entrusted to Eugène the casting of some of the sculptor's works. Soon, Eugène Rudier became Rodin's principal founder, indeed the exclusive founder as of 1913. He would later remain the founder for the Rodin museum.

Eugène Rudier stayed at 45 Rue de Saintonge, maintaining his studios at 37 Rue Olivier-de-Serres. Among the innumerable editions that he made in addition to Rodin's pieces are nearly twenty proofs of Daumier's *Ratapoil* from 1925, and, around 1935, ten proofs of the second version of Daumier's *Emigrants*. Eugène Rudier also worked for Renoir, Bourdelle and Maillol. He continued to use the mark of his father Alexis until his own death in 1952, at which time the personnel and material of his foundry were dispersed among many firms. For his part, Eugène's nephew Georges Rudier opened his own foundry at Châtillon-sous-Bagneux. In 1955, he cast ten proofs of the first version of the *Emigrants* by Daumier.

SAUVAGE, PIERRE LOUIS FRÉDÉRIC

Boulogne-sur-Mer, 1786
Paris, 1857

Pierre Sauvage's reducer of statues, for which he obtained a patent in 1832, was used extensively by the Susse foundry. The iron and bronze instrument that he invented is preserved at the Industrial Museum of Boulogne-sur-Mer.

SIOT-DECAUVILLE

Founded by M. and Mme Siot-Decauville, this firm was directed around 1860 by Edmond Siot-Decauville (1841-1908). His exhibition salon and shop was located at 24 Boulevard des Italiens, and his foundry at 8 and 10 Rue Villehardoin. The company kept the same addresses until 1920. Indicated as a founder of bronze and pewter, their catalogs advertised bronze editions of artwork by a number of reputed artists, including Gérôme (a large portion of his work), Gardet (a number of animals), Meissonier, A. Mercié, Bartholomé, Marqueste, Marioton, Récipon, Fix-Masseau, Injalbert, Vital-Cornu, Agathon Léonard, Valton, and Larche, as well as a number of furnishings, lighting elements, and office accessories. In 1890, the foundry cast twenty numbered models of the *Ratapoil* by Daumier, and in 1893, of five proofs of the second version of *Emigrants* by the same artists. For a number of years after 1920, the Siot-Decauville foundry was housed at 63 Avenue Victor-Emmanuel-III, where they sold statuettes and objects d'art cast in bronze through the lost wax method.

SOCIÉTÉ DES BRONZES DE PARIS

From the last quarter of the 19th century until the 1930s, this foundry was located at 41 Boulevard du Temple and at 14 Rue Béranger. Their manufacturing studios were found at 117 Boulevard Voltaire. They made some castings for sculptors including Van der Straeten.

SOYER AND INGÉ

Established at 28 Rue des Trois-Bornes, this foundry practiced casting bronzes in large dimensions, like Dumont's *Génie de la liberté* for the column of July in 1835 and his half-size reduction for the Salon the following year, Phillipe Lemaire's *Henri IV équestre*, and the reduction of Suerre's *Napoléon 1er*. The partnership Soyer and Ingé seemed to stop its activity in 1843. Soyer, who had already been recognized for chiseling Bosio's silver *Henri IV* in 1824, then cast by Odiot, exhibited some "galvanic bronzes" under his own name in 1844.

SUSSE

Susse is the only great foundry from the first half of the 19th century which even now remains in business. Originally from Lorraine, in 1758 Jean Susse went to Paris, where he practiced a number of different professions, including being the supplier of Menus-Plaisirs for the king. In 1806, Nicolas and Michel Victor Susse, undoubtedly Jean Susse's sons, established a stationery store at the Panoramas. They also sold some statuettes in plaster and in bronze, though it is possible that in this domain they were merely agents of the manufacturers. Susse started, however, to cast some bronzes, publishing a six-page catalog of leslie in 1839. This same year, the name of Susse was mentioned for the first time at the Exposition des Produits de l'Industrie. It seems that, beginning in 1830, the firm was directed by the sons of Michel Victor Susse, Victor (1806-1860) and Amédée (1808-1880). They opened a second store at the Plaza of the Bourse, where in 1841 they showed "Artistic bronzes for clocks, candelabras, statuetes, etc." Some years later, the commercial catalogs note a manufacturing workshop located at 12 Rue de Ménilmontant. The trade name of the firm was accompanied by a description of its products: "Statuettes, historical groups, a gallery of saints...A founder for Pradier, Marochetti, Nieuwerkerque, Mélingue, etc. A founder of reductions of antiques by the mechanical procedure of Sauvage." On June 14, 1841, Victor and Amédée Susse signed a contract with Pradier, now the oldest known contract of edition. In 1847, they obtained the authorization to use the Sauvage procedure of reduction, similar in principle to that of Achille Collas.

Many artists, in addition to those who were just noted, appeared in the Susse catalogs published under the Second Empire. Found there, among others, are the names of Cumberworth, Coinchon, Duret, Jacqumart, Antonin Moine, Moigniez, etc. Moreover, on the second floor on the premises of the Plaza of the Bourse were exhibited some modern canvases and drawings, works of cabinetry, objects in gilded bronze, mounted porcelains, and diverse curios, and on the mezzanine were some children's toys. Still, the original enterprise was not abandoned: the first floor hosted the stationary store and departments for leather goods and colorful boxes.

After Victor died in 1860, Amédée Susse remained alone for the rest of his life. Albert Susse suceeded him in the direction of the firm, serving between 1880 and 1922. He gave a new impetus to the firm, developed the foundry so extensively that it took precedence over all other activities, and at the beginning of the 20th century opened a luxurious store at 13 Boulevard de la Madeleine, while continually manintaining the shops at the Plaza of the Bourse (31 Rue Vivienne). The catalogs from this era most notably list the complete and exclusive editions of the works of Mène, Cain, Tourgueneff, and Lanceray, as well as editions of works by countless other artists: Barrias (including the famous *Nature se dévoilant dvant la Science)*, Dalou, Agathon Léonard and his series of dancers from the *Jeu de l'écharpe*, Mongin, Théordore Rivière, Hector Lemoire, Falguière, Mathruin Moreau, and Paul Richer, etc. The catalogs also list clocks, candelabras, cups, inkwells, and flat candlesticks. The continuity of the company was maintained Albert Susse's son, Jacques Susse, and then by his grandson, André, who died in 1961, and finally by André's widow, who kept it up until the 1970s. In our day, the foundry has preserved its reputation for high quality, pursuing its activity in Arcueil, practicing both sand-casting and casting from the lost wax technique.

CATALOGUE

DES·

MODÈLES EN BRONZE ET PLASTIQUES

ANCIENS ET MODERNES

ÉDITÉS PAR LA MAISON SUSSE FRÈRES

PRIZE MEDAILLE
EXPOSITION UNIVERSELLE

MÉDAILLE ANGLAISE.
LONDRES.

PREMIÈRE MÉDAILLE
EXPOSITION UNIVERSELLE

MÉDAILLE FRANÇAISE
PARIS.

FABRIQUE DE BRONZES D'ART POUR PENDULES ET AMEUBLEMENT

OEUVRES DE PRADIER, CUMBERVORTH, MÉLINGUE, ANTONIN MOINE, DURET, COMTE DE NIEUVERKERKE,
MAROCHETTI, LEQUESNE, COINCHON, MOIGNEZ, ETC.

EXPOSITION PUBLIQUE AU 1ᵉʳ ÉTAGE.

Maison Susse Frères

Brevetée de LL. MM. l'Empereur et l'Impératrice et du Roi des Pays-Bas,

PLACE DE LA BOURSE

PARIS.

du 12 5ᵧ
D. 2608

3 2608

*Pages from a Susse frères (Susse brothers) catalog,
at the time of the Second Empire.*

CHEFS-D'ŒUVRE

PROVENANT

FRANÇAIS

ANCIENS

DES MUSÉES

ET ÉTRANGERS

Réduits

PAR LE PROCÉDÉ MÉCANIQUE ET MATHÉMATIQUE

DE SAUVAGE

Numéros d'ordre.	No de grandeur.	Hauteur.		ARTISTE ou Provenance.	Sujet.	Prix EN Bronze.	Prix EN Plâtre. Stérlué.	
		m.	c.			Francs.	Fr.	C.
1	1re Grandeur.	1	»	VATICAN (ROME).	APOLLON DU BELVÉDÈRE.	800		
2	2e —	»	60	Do	Do	250		
3	3e —	»	40	Do	Do	120		
4	4e —	»	12	Do	Do	25		
5	1re Grandeur.	1	»	MUSÉE DU LOUVRE.	DIANE A LA BICHE.	800		
6	2e —	»	60	Do	Do	250		
7	3e —	»	40	Do	Do	120		
8	4e —	»	12	Do	Do	25		
9	1re Grandeur.	1	»	MUSÉE DU LOUVRE.	VÉNUS DE MILO.	550	20	»
10	2e —	»	60	Do	Do	190		
11	3e —	»	40	Do	Do	70	10	»
12	4e —	»	12	Do	Do	25		
13	1re Grandeur.	1	»	GALERIE DE FLORENCE.	VÉNUS DE MÉDICIS.	800	25	»
14	2e —	»	60	Do	Do	250		
15	3e —	»	40	Do	Do	125	12	50
16	4e —	»	12	Do	Do	25		
17	1re Grandeur.	1	»	MUSÉE DU LOUVRE.	POLYMNIE.	800	25	»
18	2e —	»	60	Do	Do	250		

1

#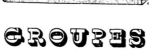

STATUETTES ET FIGURES ÉQUESTRES

POUR PENDULES ET AMEUBLEMENT

PAR LES ARTISTES MODERNES

Numéros d'ordre.	N° de grandeur	Hauteur.	ARTISTE.	Sujet.	Prix EN Bronze.	Prix EN Plâtre. Stériné.	
		m. c.			Francs.	Fr.	[C.
83	1re Grandeur.	» 58	AUG. BARRE.	MARIE DE BOURGOGNE (Figure équestre).	375	50	»
84	2e —	» 35	D°	D°	200		
85	3e —	» 48	D°	D°	70		
86		» 60	DE BEAUMONT.	NÉGRESSE PORTANT UNE TORCHÈRE.	250		
87		» 25	ÉTIENNE BENJAMIN.	PÊCHEURS DE CREVETTES PORTANT UN PANIER.	75		
88		» 25	D°	D°	75		
89	1re Grandeur.	» 31	BOITEL.	NAPOLÉON EN PIED.	75	10	»
90	2e —	» 23	D°	D°	40		
91	3e —	» 12	D°	D°	25		
92		» 16	FLATERS.	VÉNUS DANS UNE COQUILLE.	200	12	50
93		» 16	D°	VÉNUS AVEC TUNIQUE DANS LA COQUILLE.	200	12	50
94	1re Grandeur.	» 25	CUMBERVORTH.	ODALISQUE COUCHÉE (D'après INGRES).	225	12	50
95	2e —	» 10	D°	D°	55	5	»
96		» 25	D°	ODALISQUE COUCHÉE HABILLÉE.	250		
97		» 30	D°	JEUNE FILLE A L'OISEAU.	75		
98		» 25	D°	LE COMTE DE PARIS ET L'ANGE GARDIEN.	250	25	»
99	1re Grandeur.	» 25	D°	JEUNE FILLE ENDORMIE ET L'ANGE GARDIEN.	250	25	»

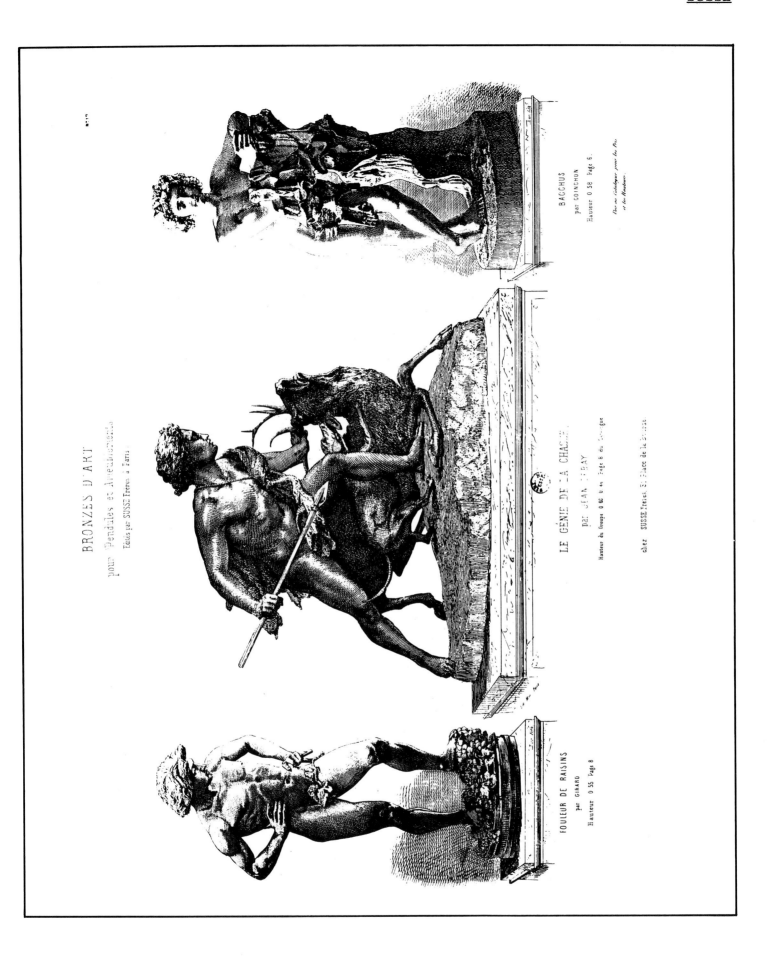

BRONZES D'ART

pour Pendules et Ameublements

Édités par SUSSE Frères à Paris

BACCHUS
par COINCHON
Hauteur 0 58 Page 6

Voir au Catalogue pour les Prix
et les Hauteurs

LE GÉNIE DE LA CHASSE
par JEAN FRAY

Hauteur du Groupe 0 60 0 41 Page 8 du Catalogue

chez SUSSE Frères, 3, Place de la Bourse

FOULEUR DE RAISINS
par GIRARD
Hauteur 0 55 Page 8

PRIX-COURANT

BRONZES D'ART

SUSSE FRÈRES

FABRICANTS ÉDITEURS

31, RUE VIVIENNE — PLACE DE LA BOURSE

13-15, BOULEVARD DE LA MADELEINE

PARIS

Exposition au 1er

Ascenseur

TÉLÉPHONES
Bourse 126-10
Madeleine 251-52

Catalogue des bronzes édités par Susse frères,
début du XXᵉ siècle.

NOMS DES ARTISTES	NUMÉROS D'ORDRE	DÉSIGNATION DES ŒUVRES	Nᵒˢ DES MODÈLES	PRIX BRONZE OU ÉTAIN	PRIX BRONZE DORÉ	DIMENSIONS Hauteur	DIMENSIONS Longueur	DIMENSIONS Profondeur	PAGE DE L'ALBUM
		A							
L. BOTTÉE.	1	Amour à l'affût 51	1	1.500	2.500	·83·	·50·	·28·	4
	2	— 40	2	850	1.200	·67·	·34·	·22·	
	3	— 21	3	450	750	·42·	·31·	·17·	
P. MENGIN.	4	Amour aux aguets	1	900	»	·71·	·47·	·27·	6
	5	—	2	600	»	·55·	·43·	·23·	
	6	—	3	450	»	·43·	·40·	·21·	
A. BOUCHER.	7	Amour boudeur 50	1	850	1.200	·47·	·42·	·27·	19
	8	— 4	2	450	800	·32·	·30·	·19·	
	9	—	3	150	250	·16·	·15·	·10·	

NOMS DES ARTISTES	NUMÉROS D'ORDRE	DÉSIGNATION DES ŒUVRES	Nᵒˢ DES MODÈLES	PRIX BRONZE OU ÉTAIN	PRIX BRONZE DORÉ	DIMENSIONS Hauteur	DIMENSIONS Longueur	DIMENSIONS Profondeur	PAGE DE L'ALBUM
L. GRÉGOIRE.	10	Amour charmeur.	1	650	»	·67·	·22·	·22·	
	11	—	2	350	»	·48·	·17·	·17·	
	12	—	3	180	»	·31·	·12·	·12·	
Aᵗᵉ MOREAU.	13	Amour vainqueur	»	650	»	·68·	·40·	·18·	19
RUFFIER.	14	Amour sur livre.	»	150	200	·12·	·15·	·10·	
	15	— sur fer à cheval . .	»	125	150	·10·	·18·	·15·	
MÉLINGUE.	16	Ambroise Paré.	1	275	»	·37·	·28·	·21·	24
	17	—	2	150	»	·25·	·19·	·14·	
	18	—	3	90 70	»	·19·	·14·	·10·	
DEGEORGE.	19	Aristote (Jeunesse d'). . .	1	2.000	»	·80·	·52·	·53·	8
	20	—	2	900	»	·60·	·32·	·38·	
	21	—	3	500	»	·40·	·21·	·25·	
	22	—	4	300	»	·30·	·16·	·19·	
P. RICHER.	23	Aux Champs. 16	1	500	»	·52·	·29·	·20·	11
	24	—	2	200	»	·21·	·18·	·10·	
DURET	25	Ange Gabriel	1	150	»	·38·	·12·	·09·	
	26	—	2	80	»	·25·	·08·	·06·	
	27	— Saint-Michel	»	150	»	·38·	·12·	·09·	
LEDRU.	28	Appliques Libellule 2 lum . . .	»	350	600	»	·35·	·20·	16
A. ROSE.	29	Accordée de Village (Plaquette).	»	sᵗ velours	50	»	·23·	·16·	
V. PETER.	838	Assiette Âge heureux	1	100	»	»	·30·	·30·	14
	839	—	2	70	»	»	·24·	·24·	
	840	— d'or.	1	100	»	»	·30·	·30·	14
	841	—	2	70	»	»	·24·	·24·	
LEDRU.	842	— Aurore.	»	60	»	»	·23·	·23·	
		B							
P. RICHER.	30	Bûcheron 15	1	450	»	·61·	·22·	·22·	11
	31	—	2	200	250	·29·	·11·	·11·	
ROCHET Fᵉˢ.	32	Bonaparte (à l'École de Brienne).	1	650	»	·78·	·25·	·24·	4
	33	—	2	250	»	·43·	·14·	·14·	
	34	—	3	125	»	·27·	·09·	·09·	
GAUDEZ.	35	Benvenuto-Cellini	1	1.200	»	·80·	·32·	·32·	19
	36	—	2	800	»	·64·	·28·	·28·	
	37	—	3	500	»	·52·	·21·	·21·	
BARRE.	38	Berryer (à la tribune)	1	300	»	·44·	·16·	·16·	
	39	—	2	150	»	·30·	·10·	·10·	
DALOU.	40	Botteleur	»	125	»	·11·	·08·	·08·	
	41	Botteleuse.	»	125	»	·11·	·08·	·08·	3
	42	Bineur debout	»	90	»	·14·	·08·	·06·	
	43	Balayeuse (bas-relief). . .	»	»	»	»	»	»	
	44	Bardeur	»	»	»	»	»	»	
	45	Bûcheron —	»	»	»	»	»	»	
	46	Baguier crabe	»	120	150	·06·	·11·	·09·	
	47	Bas-relief Les Châtiments (av. cad.)	»	300	»	·33·	·23·	»	3
	48	— Mirabeau —	»	450	»	·26·	·60·	»	3
	49	— Fraternité !	»	600	»	·44·	·28·	»	3
BARRIAS.	50	Bas-relief L'Étude . Pendule	+	1.800		15	16		
	51	— Nuitsatum							
	52	— La Jeunesse	+	900	»	15	50	»	
	53	— 1		500		58	36		
LELIÈVRE.	54	Bonbonnière pivoine	»	100	150	·09·	·11·	·11·	
	55	— chardons . . .	»	100	»	·07·	·15·	·15·	
LEDRU.	56	Bougeoir pavot	»	150	225	·15·	·20·	»10	16
	57	— Réveil	»	120 175	175	·09·	·20·	·13·	
	58	— Sommeil	»	120	175	·06·	·21·	·13·	
	59	— Poisson	»	»	»	·12·	·23·	·07·	
ROBERT Fᵉˢ.	60	Bouts-de-table Coquetterie . . .	»	simples. 450 riches.	600	·35·	·15·	»	13
P. MENGIN.	61	Buste Mignon	1	400 420	»	·45·	·28·	·17·	
	62	—	2	225	350	·35·	·22·	·12·	
	63	—	3	150	250	·28·	·18·	·10·	
	64	—	4	80	150	·21·	·12·	·07·	
BARRIAS.	65	Buste Jeunesse	»	100	175	·22·	·12·	·07·	1
	67	— Jeune fille de Bou-Saada .	1	450	550	·37·	·27·	·16·	1
	68	—	2	250	350	·28·	·19·	·11·	
	69	—	3	150	200	·19·	·13·	·08·	
G. MICHEL.	70	Buste Pensée 16	1	450	600	·48·	·35·	·20·	20
	71	—	2	250	350	·31·	·23·	·13·	
	72	—	3	150	250	·24·	·18·	·10·	
PEIFFER.	73	Buste Hirondelle	1	225	350	·37·	·21·	·10·	22
	74	—	2	100	200	·25·	·14·	·06·	
PEYNOT.	75	Buste Christophe Colomb	1	250	»	»	»	»	
	76	—	2	180	»	·22·	·24·	·13·	
A. LÉONARD.	77	Buste Innocence	1	800	1.500	·58·	·33·	·24·	5
A. LÉONARD.	78	Buste Innocence	2	»	»	»	»	»	
	78 bis	—	3	175	260	25	·10·	·08·	
HOUDON.	79	Buste Diane	1	750	»	·70·	·39·	·21·	13
	80	—	2	400	1.000	·60·	·35·	·18·	

NOMS DES ARTISTES	N° D'ORDRE	DÉSIGNATION DES ŒUVRES	N° DES MODÈLES	PRIX BRONZE OU ÉTAIN	PRIX BRONZE DORÉ	Hauteur	Longueur	Profondeur	PAGE DE L'ALBUM
	81	—	3	225	700	48	28	13	
	82	—	4	100		28	17	09	
	83	—	5	75		18	11	06	
L. DESCHAMPS.	84	Buste Moissonneuse	1	1.500		73	62	45	5
	85	—	2						
	86	—	3						
	87	—	4						
BEYLARD.	88	Buste Jeanne d'Arc	1	200		31	16	08	
MASSON.	89	Buste Napoléon Ier	1	75	100	16	09	06	
Ch. LÉONARD.	90	Buste Le Rêve	1	600	1.000	62	34	20	22
	91	—	2	300	500	45	24	15	
	92	—	3	200	300	29	15	09	
BEER.	93	Buste Luther enfant	1	150		30	15	12	
GRÉGOIRE.	94	Buste Alsace	1	400		48			18
	95	—	2	300		44			
	96	—	3	200		34			
	97	—	4	100		28			
	98	—	5	75		20			
	99	— Lorraine	1	400		48			18
DE St-MARCEAUX.	100	Buste Génie gardien du Secret	1	250		33	23	23	22
	101	—	2						
CARLÈS.	102	Buste Junon	1	450	600	60	37	18	9
	103	—	2	300	400	48	31	15	12
FONTAINE.	104	Buste Liseron	1	150		27	15	11	
	105	—	2						
Hte LEFEBVRE.	106	Buste Le Pardon	1	400		30	20	22	20
HOUDON.	107	Buste Saint Bruno	1						
	108	—	2	150		24	10	10	
DANTAN.	109	— Beethoven	1	300		45	24	13	
	110	—	2	40		17	10	16	
	111	— Gluck	2	40		17	10	16	
	112	— Mozart	2	40		17	10	16	
	113	— Haydn	2	40		17	10	16	

C

NOMS DES ARTISTES	N° D'ORDRE	DÉSIGNATION DES ŒUVRES	N° DES MODÈLES	PRIX BRONZE OU ÉTAIN	PRIX BRONZE DORÉ	Hauteur	Longueur	Profondeur	PAGE DE L'ALBUM
CROISY.	114	Chasseur à pied	1	800		65	40	27	18
	115	—	2	400		50	30	20	
	116	—	3	200		33	19	12	
CROISY.	117	Chanzy (Général)	1	1.200		1	28	28	
	118	—	2	650		69	20	20	
	119	—	3	300		40	12	12	
JACQUEMART.	120	Christ debout	1	200		46	16	10	
	121	—	2	100		30	10	10	
	122	—	3	50		13	06	04	
Mathurin MOREAU.	123	Charmeuse	1	1.200		82	30	30	7
	124	—	2	650		66	24	24	
	125	—	3	425		55	20	20	
Aug PARIS.	126	La Chanson	1	600		77	23	23	10
	127	—	2	300		57	17	17	
	128	—	3	200		45	13	13	
	129	—	4	160	250	35	09	09	
	843	Le Chant du Départ (bas-relief d'après Rude)	1	18.000		2 25	1 40	40	
			2	4.000		1 30	90	24	
Vital CORNU.	130	Crépuscule	1	600	1.200	69	23	23	15
	131	—	2	200	350	33	10	10	
PEYNOT.	132	Christophe Colomb	1	2.000		93	55	36	6
	133	—	2	850		62	37	24	
MÉLINGUE.	134	Cornélie	1	200		40	14	14	
	135	—	2	100		30	10	10	
L. GRÉGOIRE.	136	Clairon! La Charge!	1	300		51	16	16	18
DE NIEUWERKERKE.	137	Combat (Duc de Clarence)	1	1.200		50	60	15	21
	138	—	2	500 300		25	30	10	
	138bis	Homme d'armes	1	500	700	64	16	16	21
LANCERAY.	139	Chasse à courre (Huntsman)		650		60	72	17	
	140	—		500		43	40	17	
	141	Cheval Orloff		150		27	32	10	
BARYE.	142	Cerf debout	0	1.200		77	97	41	23
	143	—	1	250		42	50	22	
	144	—	2	120		25	28	13	
	145	—	3	60		18	18	08	
	146	— au Jaguar	1	300		33	48	25	23
	147	—	2	150		19	27	15	
	148	—	3	75		12	17	09	
	149	— couché	1	250		45	44	28	23
	150	—	2	120		17	23	17	
	151	—	3			11	16	11	
MASSON.	152	Chevreuils au débuché	4	400		34	43	25	16

NOMS DES ARTISTES	N° D'ORDRE	DÉSIGNATION DES ŒUVRES	N° DES MODÈLES	PRIX BRONZE OU ÉTAIN	PRIX BRONZE DORÉ	Hauteur	Longueur	Profondeur	PAGE DE L'ALBUM
	153	Chienne et petits	1	200		30	43	25	
	154	—	2	35		07	12	06	
	155	Chatte —	2	35		06	11	06	
MASSON.	156	Groupe de canards		60		09	14	08	
Vve PÉTER.	157	Chat et Tortue		60	75	09	15	07	
H. LEMAIRE.	158	Chat porte-bouquet		120		20	13	10	
DALOU.	159	Charretier (bas-relief)							
	160	Casseur de pierres		80		10	08	07	3
ALHAMBRA.	161	Coffret à bijoux			350	16	24	17	
BECKER.	162	Coffret à bijoux « Fraisia »				09	20	11	17
GATTI.	163	Chien de meute		120		17	32	15	
CARVIN.	164	Caresse matinale		50	75	11	07	07	
ARNOUX.	164bis	Couteau à papier Violettes		25	40		25		
SABATIER.	165	Couteau à papier Cigale		40	60		25		21
GRANJO.	166	Coupe Retour de chasse		160		13	42	32	
FRÉMIET.	167	— Jeanne d'Arc	1	125		10	42	32	
	168	—	2	100		10	37	27	
	169	— Vestale antique	1	140		10	42	32	
	170	—	2	100		10	37	27	
LEVILLAIN.	171	Coupe Idylle	1	125	175	11	33	33	14
	172	—	2	50	80	09	24	24	
	173	—	3	30	45	07	19	19	
	174	— Diogène		30	45	08	15	15	14
	175	— cinq masques	1	300		14	40	40	14
	176	—	2	200	300	10	34	34	
	177	— Cérès		150		12	42	32	
	178	— Lutteurs	1	125	140	11	30	30	
	179	—	2	55	80	10	24	22	
	180	— Canards		100		10	28	28	
A. ROSE.	181	— L'Accordée de Village		100		10	28	28	17
	182	Cendrier —		25		02	09	09	
LEDRU.	183	Cendrier Étoile du matin		25		01	13	10	
LEVILLAIN.	184	Cendrier Éléments		30	40	02	15	15	
	185	— Idylle		30	40	02	15	15	
	186	— Diogène rond		30	40	03	15	15	
	187	— long		30	60	01	15	07	
	188	— Latone long		30	60	01	14	07	
	189	— Médée long		35	70	01	15	08	
	190	— Amphitrite long		35	70	01	15	08	
Mathurin MOREAU.	190bis	Cendrier La Source —		30	60	01	15	11	
LANSON.	191	Cendrier Jason		40	75	03	16	11	
ARNOUX.	192	Cendrier Violettes		40	80	02	15	15	
BOUCHER.	193	Cendrier Hirondelle blessée		35	70	01	15	11	
LEDRU.	194	Coquille Le Repos		1.500		33	84	39	
	195	— Galliéra	1	800		31	47	26	
	195bis	—	2	350		30	30	17	
	196	— Indiscrète	1	600	900	39	34	24	16
	196bis	—	2	225	300	18	17	10	
	197	— La Perle	1	400	500	14	41	27	
	198	— La Vague	1	400	500	16	45	22	
	198bis	—	2	160	225	08	22	11	
	199	— Lutinerie		65	120	04	21	18	
	200	— Curieuse		60	100	03	20	20	
	201	— Charmeuse		55	100	03	19	16	16
HOUDON.	202	Cachet Voltaire (avec écrin) (1)		60		09	05		22
	203	— Diane	1	70	85	10	05		21
	204	—	2	40	60	07	04		
	205	— Saint Bruno		55	75	10	04		
Jean GOUJON.	206	Cachet Diane de Poitiers (en écr.) (1)		40	60	07	04		
FONTAINE.	207	Cachet Liseron —		100 110		08	04		22
BARRIAS.	208	Cachet Jeune fille de Bou-Saada —			120	08	05		
	209	— Jeunesse			110	09	04		
G. MICHEL.	210	Cachet La Pensée			130	10	07		7
	211	— La Musique							
CARLÈS.	212	Cachet Junon			130	09	06		
	213	—	2		90	07	04		
P. MENGIN.	214	Cachet Mignon			110	08	06		6
DE St-MARCEAUX.	215	Cachet Génie gard. du Secret	1		140	10	06		22
	216	—			110	10	06		
PEIFFER.	217	Cachet Les Hirondelles	1		110	10	06		22
	218	—	2		90	07	04		
LAFRANCE.	219	Cachet Saint Jean enfant —		55	75	09	04		20
Ch. LÉONARD.	220	Cachet Le Rêve —	1		130	11	06		22
	221	—	2		90	08	05		

NOMS DES ARTISTES	NUMÉROS D'ORDRE	DÉSIGNATION DES ŒUVRES	Nᵒˢ DES MODÈLES	PRIX		DIMENSIONS			PAGE DE L'ALBUM
				BRONZE OU ÉTAIN	BRONZE DORÉ	Hauteur	Longueur	Profondeur	
Cathédrale de Nuremberg	222	Cachet La Prière	»		100	» 08	» 04	»	
RUDE.	223	Cachet Pêcheur napolitain	1	55	»	» 10	» 06	»	21
	224	—	2	45	»	» 07	» 04	»	
LANSON.	225	Cachet Jason	»	55	»	» 09	» 03	»	
ROCHET Frᵉˢ	226	Cachet Bonaparte	»	55	»	» 09	» 05	»	
LE VEEL.	227	Cachet Jeanne d'Arc	»	55	»	» 09	» 05	»	20
Princesse Marie d'Orléans.	228	Cachet Jeanne d'Arc buste	»	60	»	» 10	» 06	»	
	229	— statuette	»	60	»	» 10	» 04	»	
BARRIAS.	230	Cachet Jeanne d'Arc prisonn.	»	110	»	» 08	» 04	»	
				argenté					
MELINGUE.	231	Cachet Rabelais (en cr.) (1)	»	70	»	» 10	» 06	»	
	232	— d'Aguesseau	»	70	»	» 10	» 06	»	22
	233	— Ambroise Paré	»	55	»	» 10	» 06	»	22
ANTIQUE.	234	Cachet Cicéron	»	35	»	» 07	» 03	»	
	234	— Démosthènes	»	35	»	» 07	» 03	»	
	236	— Ajax	»	50	»	» 09	» 04	»	22
	237	— Lucius Verus	»	50	»	» 09	» 04	»	
	238	— Henri IV	»	50	»	» 07	» 03	»	
	139	— Ariane	»	45	»	» 08	» 04	»	
	240	— Antinoüs	»	45	»	» 08	» 04	»	
L. GRÉGOIRE.	241	Cachet Alsace	»	50	»	» 07	» 04	»	18
	242	— Lorraine	»	50	»	» 07	» 04	»	18
JACQUEMART.	243	Cachet buste Christ	»	60	»	» 11	» 06	»	
	244	— Vierge	»	60	»	» 11	» 06	»	
L. GRÉGOIRE.	245	Cachet Amour charm. (stat.)	»	90	»	» 10	» 03	»	
MELINGUE.	246	Cachet François Iᵉʳ	»	50	»	» 07	» 03	»	
	247	— Charles-Quint	»	50	»	» 07	» 03	»	
				bronze la paire	la paire				
PRÉVOST.	248	Candélabres Louis XVI, 6 lumières	»	250	450	» 52	» 22	» 22	12
		Pieds marbre nᵒ 114	»	200	»	» 10	» 13	» 13	12
	249	Candélabres Renaissance, 4 lum.	»	250	450	» 52	» 20	» 20	
		Pieds marbre nᵒ 104	»	100	»	» 07	» 11	» 11	
ROBERT Frᵉˢ	250	Candélabres L. XV, vases marbre nᵒ 1, 4 enfants, riches	1	»	5.000	1 »	» 24	»	12
	251	Les mêmes, sans enfants, simples	1	»	3.000	1 »	» 24	»	13
		— 4 enfants, riches	2	»	2.400	» 75	» 27	»	
		— sans enfants —	2	»	1.400	» 75	» 27	»	
CLODION.	252	Candélabres Vases nᵒ 2, 6 lum.	»	»	900	» 66	» 26	»	
		Pieds marbre nᵒ 112	»	»	250	» 12	» 15	»	
	153	Candélabres Vases nᵒ 3, 4 lum.	»	»	600	» 46	» 16	»	
		Pieds marbre nᵒ 104	»	»	100	» 07	» 11	»	
ROBERT Frᵉˢ	263	Candélabres L. XVI, vases m. 1, riches	»	»	5.000	» 98	» 44	»	12
		— — 1, simp.	»	»	3.000	» 98	» 44	»	
	258	— — 2, —	»	»	1.600	» 73	» 32	»	
		— — 2, riches	»	»	2.400	» 73	» 32	»	
LELIÈVRE.	254	Candélabres L. XIV, br. doré —	»	»	1.400	» 70	» 26	»	
ROBERT Frᵉˢ	255	Candélabres L. XVI, vases m côtes dr.	»	»	2.000	» 85	» 38	»	
	256	Candélabres L. XV tout cuivre	1	»	1.800	» 80	» 40	»	24
	261	— —	2	»	950	» 61	» 31	»	
	262	— —	3	»	»	»	»	»	
	257	— Coquetterie, 3 lum. simp.	»	»	450	» 35	» 15	»	13
		— — riches	»	»	600	» 35	» 15	»	
CLODION.	259	Candélabres Bacchantes, 5 lumières	»	»	1.500	» 97	» 42	»	
ROMAIN.	265	— Enfants, 6 —	1	»	1.200	» 78	» 33	»	
		Pieds marbre nᵒ 115	»	»	250	» 12	» 15	»	
	260	Candélabres Enfants, 4 lumières	2	»	600	» 55	» 20	»	
ROBERT Frᵉˢ	264	Candélabres Vases marbre torses	»	»	1.400	» 70	» 30	»	12
		— à bougies, 6 lum.	»	»	1.400	» 70	» 30	»	
		— électriques	»	»	1.600	» 70	» 30	»	
		Les mêmes, Vases marbre unis	»						
		— à bougies	»	»	1.200	» 70	» 30	»	
		— électriques	»	»	1.400	» 70	» 30	»	
LELIÈVRE.	266	Candélabres L. XV, 4 lumières	1	»	950	» 58	» 35	»	13
		— électriques	1	»	1.200	» 58	» 35	»	
	267	— 4 lumières	2	»	650	» 45	» 27	»	
		— électriques	2	»	800	» 45	» 27	»	
		— 4 lumières	3	»	»	»	»	»	
		— électriques	3	»	»	»	»	»	
ROBERT Frᵉˢ	268	Candélabres L. XVI Fleurs des champs	1	»	1.600	» 85	» 44	»	12
		— électr.	1	»	2.000	» 85	» 44	»	
	269	— bougies	2	»	1.000	» 64	» 35	»	
		— électr.	2	»	1.200	» 64	» 35	»	
	270	— bougies	3	»	»	»	»	»	
OUDRY.	271	Candélabres Enfants, 4 lumières	»	»	600	» 58	» 20	»	13
	276	— Cornes d'abondance, 2 lum.	»	»	500	» 35	» 15	»	
		— électr.	»	»	600	» 35	» 15	»	

NOMS DES ARTISTES	NUMÉROS D'ORDRE	DÉSIGNATION DES ŒUVRES	Nᵒˢ DES MODÈLES	PRIX		DIMENSIONS			PAGE DE L'ALBUM
				BRONZE OU ÉTAIN	BRONZE DORÉ	Hauteur	Longueur	Profondeur	
	272	Les mêmes, 3 lumières	»	»	700	» 35	» 20	»	13
		— électriques	»	»	800	» 35	» 20	»	
	275	Candélabres Enfants, cor de chasse, 3 bougies	»	»	600	» 40	» 20	»	13
ROBERT Frᵉˢ	277	Les mêmes, à l'électricité	»	»	800	» 40	» 20	»	
	279	Candélabres L. XVI, bouidoire, 6 lum.	1	»	1.800	» 87	» 40	»	13
		— à l'électricité	1	»	2.200	» 87	» 40	»	
	280	Les mêmes	2	»	1.000	» 67	» 31	»	
		— à l'électricité	2	»	1.250	» 67	» 31	»	
RAMBAUD.	280bis	Candélabres L. XV, 3 bougies	»	»	500	» 33	» 27	»	24
		— à l'électricité	»	»	600	» 33	» 27	»	
		Les mêmes, 4 bougies	»	»	600	» 43	» 30	»	24
		— à l'électricité	»	»	700	» 43	» 30	»	
		D							
Victor PÉTER.	281	Deux Amis	1	1.200	»	» 50	» 61	» 28	14
	282	—	2	600	»	» 40	» 41	» 18	
	283	—	3	300	»	» 26	» 28	» 12	
	283bis	—	4	160	»	» 16	» 17	» 08	
ROGER BLOCHE.	284	Dans les Nuages	1	1.600	»	» 79	» 50	» 40	
CROISY.	285	La Défense du Drapeau	1	3.500	»	1 » 20	1 »	» 45	18
	286	— —	2	2.000	»	» 80	» 75	» 35	
	287	— —	3	1.000	»	» 58	» 55	» 25	
	288	— avec 1 marin	3	1.200	»	» 58	» 65	» 30	
HOUDON.	289	Diane statuette	»	350	»	» 60	» 12	» 12	
A. LÉONARD.	290	Danseuse aux pipeaux	1	450	600	» 46	» 19	» 19	5
	291	—	2	»	»	»	»	»	
	292	—	3	200	250	» 23	» 08	» 08	
	293	— au cothurne	1	450	600	» 46	» 19	» 19	
	294	—	2	300	400	37	»	»	
	295	—	3	200	250	» 23	» 08	» 08	
	296	— chantant	1	450	600	» 46	» 19	» 19	
	297	—	2	»	»	»	»	»	
	298	—	3	200	250	» 23	» 08	» 08	
	299	— à la marguerite	1	450	600	» 46	» 19	» 19	5
	300	—	2	»	»	»	»	»	
	301	—	3	200	250	» 23	» 08	» 08	
	302	— au bracelet	1	450	600	» 46	» 19	» 19	
	303	—	2	»	»	»	»	»	
	304	—	3	200	250	» 23	» 08	» 08	
	305	— relevant sa jupe	1	450	600	» 46	» 19	» 19	5
	306	—	2	»	»	»	»	»	
	307	—	3	200	250	» 23	» 08	» 08	
	308	— aux cymbales	1	450	600	» 46	» 19	» 19	5
	309	—	2	»	»	»	»	»	
	310	—	3	200	250	» 23	» 08	» 08	
	311	— tambourin à droite	1	450	600	» 46	» 19	» 19	
	312	—	2	»	»	»	»	»	
	313	—	3	200	250	» 23	» 08	» 08	
	314	— à gauche	1	450	600	» 46	» 19	» 09	
	315	—	2	»	»	»	»	»	
	316	—	3	200	250	» 23	» 08	» 08	
	317	— aux flambeaux à gauche	1	500	700	» 61	» 25	» 18	5
	318	—	2	»	»	»	»	»	
	319	—	3	»	»	»	»	»	
		— à l'électricité	1	575	750	» 61	» 25	» 18	
	320	— aux flambeaux à droite	1	500	700	» 61	» 25	» 18	5
		— à l'électricité	1	575	750	» 61	» 25	» 18	
	321	—	2	»	»	»	»	»	
	322	—	3	»	»	»	»	»	
	323	— écharpe pieds invisibles	1	500	700	» 60	» 45	» 18	5
		— à l'électr.	1	575	775	» 60	» 45	» 18	
	324	—	2	»	»	»	»	»	
	325	—	3	»	»	»	»	»	
A. LÉONARD.	326	Danseuse écharpe pied gauche levé	1	500	700	» 60	» 45	» 18	
	327	— à l'électr.	1	575	775	» 60	» 45	» 18	
	328	— levé	2	»	»	»	»	»	
	329	— pied droit levé	1	500	700	» 60	» 45	» 18	
	»	— à l'électr.	1	575	775	» 60	» 45	» 18	
	330	—	2	»	»	»	»	»	
	331	—	3	»	»	»	»	»	
	332	— genou levé	1	500	700	» 60	» 45	» 18	
	333	—	2	300	400	» 35	» 32	» 13	
	334	—	3	200	250	» 31	» 20	» 08	
	»	— la même à l'électricité	1	575	775	» 60	» 45	» 18	
	»	— —	2	350	450	» 35	» 32	» 13	
	»	— —	3	250	300	» 31	» 20	» 08	

Left table

NOMS DES ARTISTES	N°s D'ORDRE	DÉSIGNATION DES ŒUVRES	N°s DES MODÈLES	PRIX BRONZE OU ÉTAIN	BRONZE DORÉ	Hauteur	Longueur	Profondeur	PAGE DE L'ALBUM
MASSON.	334bis	Duguesclin équestre		400 300	600.	» 45	» 34	» 12	
LE VEEL.	769	32e Demi-Brigade (Voltigeur)	1	400		» 82	» 22	» 22	10
	770	— —	2	150		» 37	» 12	» 12	
	771	— —	3	50		» 17	» 04	» 04	
		E							
BEER.	338	Escholier XVe siècle	1	550	700	» 71	» 29	» 24	8
	339	—	2	260	375	» 49	» 17	» 14	
Roger BLOCHE.	340	L'enfant!	17 1	600		» 39	» 25	» 32	8
	341		2	350		» 29	» 18	» 24	
Th. RIVIERE.	342	Ève			150	» 20	» 05	» 05	9
Hr LEMAIRE.	343	Électricité	16 1	800	1 400	» 79	» 17	» 17	11
	344		2						
	345		3	225	400	» 37	» 10	» 10	
MAROCHETTI.	346	Emmanuel-Philibert	1	500		» 60	» 55	» 20	
	347		2	250		» 40	» 35	» 15	
	348		3	150		» 20	» 15	» 07	
~~BARYE~~ Barbé	349	L'Empereur		100 150		» 2	» 08	» 08	
Hr LEMAIRE.	350	L'étoile du Berger	1	800 700	75				11
	351		2						
	352		3						
SEYSSES.	355	Éléphant d'Afrique	1	275	350	» 24	» 26	» 13	9
	356		2	150	200	» 15	» 16	» 08	
LEDRU.	357	Encrier la Vague		300	450	» 20	» 28	» 28	
	358	— Curieuse		300	450	» 15	» 43	» 30	
	359	— le Flot		200	300	» 14	» 18	» 27	16
	360	— Nénuphars		300	450	» 15	» 36	» 27	
	361	— Sommeil		300	450	» 16	» 30	» 23	
LEVILLAIN.	362	Encrier Douze Apôtres		50		» 05	» 19	» 19	
	363	— Colombe		100	150	» 05	» 22	» 18	21
	363b	— Penseur de Michel Ange	5	130	150	» 38	» 21		21
	365b		4	250	275	» 32	» 17	» 21	21
	364	— Vase Cratère		100	120	» 15	» 38	» 21	21
V. CORNU.	364	Encrier Anémones		300	450	» 17	» 33	» 25	15
GARDE-MEUBLES.	365	— Louis XV 2 godets		125	150	» 12	» 19	» 12	
DALOU.	366	Encrier Lavoisier sur marbre		700		» 25	» 57	» 28	
GAUDEZ.	367	Encrier Molière sur marbre		600		» 50	» 54	» 30	21
DEGEORGE.	368	Encrier Aristote sur marbre		500		» 35	» 58	» 31	
THAREL.	369	Encrier Sans-Souci, 1 godet		225	250	» 25	» 38	» 33	
	370	— 2 godets		250	275	» 25	» 38	» 26	
DAVID D'ANGERS.	371	Encrier Gutenberg		200	225	» 23	» 35	» 16	
ARNOUX.	372	Encrier Cyclamens		100	225	» 07	» 23	» 19	21
	373	— Violettes		50	100	» 07	» 15	» 15	
DALOU.	374	Encrier Crabe		125	150	» 07	» 15	» 11	
TROUDLE.	375	Encrier Chrysanthèmes		80	150	» 07	» 25	» 12	17
	376	— Chardons		80	150	» 05	» 27	» 12	
MELINGUE.	377	Encrier Ambroise Paré sur marbre		160		» 25	» 38	» 21	
MICHEL.	385	Encrier buste Pensée		350	450	» 32	» 18	» 23	20
BARRIAS.	388	Encrier buste Jeunesse		250	300	» 27	» 40	» 23	20
		F							
P. RICHER.	398	Forgeron	14 1	700		» 76	» 27	» 32	11
	399		2	250		» 37	» 16	» 13	
	400		3						
Roger BLOCHE.	401	Froid (Le)	1	600		» 53	» 25	» 19	8
	402		2	250		» 35	» 16	» 13	
RAMBAUD.	410b	Flambeaux Louis XV, électriques		300		» 28	» 13	» 13	24
	404b	— Louis XVI		200		» 28	» 13	» 13	24
OUDRY.	406	Flambeaux enfant au masque électr.		350		» 30	» 11	» 11	
	407	— au panier		350		» 30	» 11	» 11	
GARDE-MEUBLES.	405	— Louis XV, bas		100		» 11	» 10	» 10	
		G							
DAVID D'ANGERS.	411	Gutenberg	1	300		» 50	» 15	» 15	
	412		2	75		» 16	» 05	» 05	
ASCOLI.	413	Gringoire	1	800		» 50	» 29	» 20	
DE St-MARCEAUX.	414	Génie gardien du secret	1	3.500		» 90	» 50	» 55	4
	415		2	1.600		» 62	» 35	» 45	
	416		3	1.000		» 52	» 26	» 35	
PICAULT.	417	Génie du travail	1	2 000		» 25	» 65	» 45	19
	418	— —	2	800		» 80	» 24	» 22	
	419	— —	3						

Right table

NOMS DES ARTISTES	N°s D'ORDRE	DÉSIGNATION DES ŒUVRES	N°s DES MODÈLES	PRIX BRONZE OU ÉTAIN	BRONZE DORÉ	Hauteur	Longueur	Profondeur	PAGE DE L'ALBUM
DALOU.	420	Glaneuse		60		» 08	» 07	» 05	3
DE NIEUWERKERQUE.	421	Guillaume le Taciturne	1	500		» 60	» 55	» 20	
	422	—	2	250		» 40	» 35	» 15	
	423	—	3	150		» 20	» 15	» 07	
LE VEEL	424	Grenadier (Vieille garde)	1	400		» 78	» 22	» 22	10
	425	— —	2	150		» 41	» 12	» 12	
	426	— —	3	50		» 15	» 04	» 04	
VITAL CORNU.	427	Gourde		80	150	» 15	» 10	» 10	15
	428	Gobelet la Vigne		80	150	» 11	» 06	» 06	15
NON SIGNE.	429	Garniture fumeur azalées		175		» 12	» 30	» 24	
	430	Glace Louis XV	1		300	» 50	» 30	»	
	431	—	2		150	» 25	» 15	»	
		H							
A. BOUCHER.	432	Hirondelle blessée	1	2 000 2 500		» 93	» 41	» 28	2
	433	—	2	1.200		» 80	» 33	» 21	
	434	—	3	800	1.200	» 08	» 30	» 19	
	435	—	15 4	400	7 800	» 46	» 20	» 13	
COMOLERA.	436	Hirondelle volant		50	75	» 18	» 12	» 10	4
PEIFFER.	437	Hirondelles (Les) retour		2.000		» 91	» 38	» 38	4
	438	—	2	1.200		» 69	» 27	» 27	
	439	—	24 3	750	1.200	» 60	» 22	» 22	
	440	—	4	450	600	» 46	» 16	» 16	
	440b	—	5	200	275	» 25	» 09	» 09	
LE VEEL	441	Huguenot	1	400		» 60	» 16	» 16	16
	442	—	2	150		» 34	» 10	» 10	
BOSIO	443	Henri IV enfant	1	150		» 42	» 14	» 14	
	444	—	2	125		» 35	» 10	» 10	
	445	—	3	80		» 25	» 08	» 08	
		I							
GAUTHERIN.	446	Instruction (L') éclairant le monde		600		» 45	» 33	» 25	19
MENGIN.	447	Innocence	44 1	1.200		»	»	»	
	447b	—	2	900		» 76	» 26	» 30	
	447b	—	3	600		» 50	» 20	» 17	
FONTAINE.	448	Inspiration	19 1	650		» 70	» 33	» 22	6
		J							
ARNOUX	449	Jardinière Iris	1	400	600	» 16	» 48	» 26	17
	450	—	2	250	400	» 12	» 35	» 20	
DEBON.	451	Jardinière Tulipes	4	200	350	» 15	» 30	» 25	17
	452	— Muguet, ronde		175	300	» 13	» 25	» 22	
	453	— ovale		200	350	» 13	» 31	» 22	17
	454	— Glycines		350	600	» 13	» 40	» 31	
P. RICHER.	455	Jardinière la Moisson	24	1.200		» 60	» 28	» 32	
	456	— les Pommes	1	400		» 17	» 30	» 25	
	457	— les Raisins	9	400		» 17	» 30	» 25	
ROBERT Fr.	458	Jardinière les Saisons	1	1 500 2 800		» 20	» 71	» 30	
	459	—	2	400	600	» 12	» 44	» 22	
V. CORNU.	460	Jardinière Sommeil	1	1000 900	1 300	» 28	» 72	» 45	15
Princesse Marie d'Orléans	461	Jeanne d'Arc	25'5 1	500		» 75	» 25	» 25	20
	462	—	10'2 2	250		» 50	» 17	» 17	
	463	—	3	160		» 42	» 15	» 15	
0.60 – 350	464	—		125		» 13	» 13		
0.28 – 115	465	—		100		» 11	» 11		
0.20 – 85	466	—		80		» 10	» 10		
0.15 – 65	467	—		65		» 07	» 07		
0.10 – 50	468	—				» 05	» 05		
CHAMPIGNEULLE.	470	Jeanne d'Arc à l'Étendard	12 1	350		» 83	» 17	» 17	
	471	—	2	180		» 52	» 10	» 10	1
BARRIAS.	472	Jeanne d'Arc prisonnière	1	1.600	2 000	»	» 30	» 30	
	473	—	15? 2	600		» 71	» 19	» 19	
	474	—	6'5 3	300		» 33	» 08	» 08	
	475	—	4	200		» 21	» 06	» 06	
	476	—	5	100		»	»	»	
A. LANSON.	477	Jason rapportant la toison d'or (complet)	1	1.600		» 1	» 23	» 23	4
	478	—	2	850	1500	» 75	» 23	» 23	
	479	—	3	500	900	» 50	» 15	» 15	
	480	— 5 (simple)	4		1000	» 31	» 30		
	481	—	1	1.200		» 31	» 30		
	482	— 50	2	650	1 200	» 75	» 23	» 23	
	483	— 13	3		550	350	» 37	» 12	» 12
	484	—	4	250	350	» 37	» 12	» 12	
MATHURIN MOREAU.	335	Jeune fille à la fontaine	1	1.800		» 1	» 45	» 41	7
	336	—	2	1.200		» 80	» 28	» 26	
	337	—	3	700		» 65	» 26	» 21	
BARRIAS.	485	Jeune fille de Bou-Saada	1	3.200		» 70	» 55	» 51	1
	486	—	34 2	1.200	1.600	» 52	» 40	» 36	
	487	—	15 3	600	900	» 31	» 24	» 23	

Left Table

NOMS DES ARTISTES	NUMÉROS D'ORDRE	DÉSIGNATION DES ŒUVRES	N°s DES MODÈLES	PRIX BRONZE OU ÉTAIN	PRIX BRONZE DORÉ	Hauteur	Longueur	Profondeur	PAGE DE L'ALBUM
		L							
LELIÈVRE.	488	Lampe Iris (statuette)	»	250	400	» 30	» 13	» 13	22
	489	— Lever du jour (vase). .	»	150	225	» 22	» 10	» 10	
LELIÈVRE.	490	Lampe Pavot (vase)	»	175	250	» 31	» 12	» 00	
	492	— le Blé — . . .	»	225	300	» 31	» 12	» 00	
	493	— Maïs — . . .	»	200	275	» 31	» 14	» 10	
CLODION.	494	Lampe Bacchante	»	450	»	» 75	» 21	» 21	
COUPRI.	498	Lampe Berce de Chine . . 8	»	450	600	» 60	» 21	» 21	17
ROBERT Fᵒⁿ.	499	Lampe Louis XV rocaille . .	1	650	»	» 65	» 18	» 18	17
	500		2	450		» 60	» 23	» 23	
	501	— Louis XVI fleurs des champs.	1 Pétrole	250 600		» 68	» 21	» 21	5
	502	— —	2 Électrique	350		» 80	» 17	» 17	
	502ᵇⁱˢ	— —	3 Électrique	250		» 50	» 17	» 17	
RAMBAUD.	503	Lampe Louis XVI électrique, riche	»	450		» 70	» 33	» 17	5
	503ᵇⁱˢ	— la même, simple	»	300		» 70	» 33	» 17	
		— Louis XV, électrique .	»	350		» 60	» 30	» 13	
LE VEEL.	504	Liqueur	1	400	»	» 60	» 16	» 16	16
	505		»	150	»	» 35	» 10	» 10	
GAYRARD.	506	Lévrier couché	1	125	»	» 13	» 32	» 15	
	507		2	35	»	» 06	» 15	» 07	
V. PETER.	509	Lionceau de l'Atlas . . .	»	180	250	» 19	» 29	» 12	14
	510	Lion et Rat . . . 29	1	700	»	» 37	» 61	» 27	14
	511	— 10	2	300	»	» 24	» 50	» 18	
	512		3	80	150	» 12	» 20	» 09	
DALOU.	513	Lavoisier 183	1	6.000	»	1 03	» 70	» 65	3
	514	35	2	1.250	1.500	» 51	» 34	» 27	
	515	10	3	500	»	» 29	» 19	» 15	
	516	Liseuse	1	1.200	»	» 57	» 33	» 38	3
	517		2	»	»	»	»	»	
	518		3	»	»	»	»	»	
	519	Lafayette	»	300	»	» 37	» 11	» 11	3
Tᴴ. RIVIÈRE.	520	Loïe Fuller	»	450	»	» 27	» 09	» 12	
DENYS PUECH.	521	Livre d'Or de l'École centrale 61	1	2.000	2.600	» 90	» 43	» 43	2
	522	34	2	1.400	1.700	» 65	» 25	» 25	
	523	19	3	700	900	» 52	» 22	» 22	
		M							
PIERRE OGÉ.	524	Marguerite (jeune fille). . . .	0	2.000	»	1 20	»	»	19
	525		1	650	»	» 80	»	»	
	526		2	400	»	» 60	»	»	
	527		3	250	»	» 45	»	»	
P. MENGIN.	528	Mignon 51	1	1.600	2.200	» 93	» 43	» 42	6
	529		2	1.000	1.500	» 78	» 29	» 29	
	530		3	700	1.200	» 05	» 25	» 25	
	531		4	500	800	» 57	» 21	» 21	
	532		5	200	250	» 26	» 09	» 09	
DALOU.	533	Médaillon le Bineur	»	50	»	» 03	» 15	» 10	
	534	— Retour des champs .	»	35	»	» 03	» 12	» 08	
FONTAINE.	535	Matin (Le)	1	1.200	»	» 60	» 25	» 25	11
DESCHAMPS.	536	Moisson (En)	1	1500		81	46	38	4
	537	—	2	850		»	»	»	
	538	—	3	250		54	17	16	
	539	—	4						
CROISY.	540	Marin	1	700	»	» 68	» 39	» 26	18
	541	—	2	350	»	» 49	» 30	» 17	
	542	—	3	200	»	» 33	» 20	» 12	
	543	Mobile	1	700	»	» 68	» 39	» 26	18
	544	—	2	350	»	» 49	» 30	» 17	
	545	—	3	200	»	» 33	» 20	» 12	
JEANNE ITASSE.	546	Mater Dei (bas-relief). . . .	1	300	400	» 53	» 23	» 09	20
	547	—	2	200	300	» 40	» 20	» 07	
	548	—	3	100	150	» 24	» 16	» 04	
	549	—	4	50	80	» 15	» 10	» 03	
G. MICHEL.	550	Musique (La) 65	1	1800	»	» 88	» 39	» 31	7
	551	—	2	1200	»	» 73	» 29	» 26	
	552	—	3	900	»	» 64	» 24	» 22	
GAUDEZ.	553	Molière enfant . . . Original	10.000		1 30	» 95	» 92	8	
	554	—	2.000		» 78	» 46	» 46		
	555	—	800		» 60	» 35	» 35		
	556	—	400		» 50	» 22	» 22		
CORDONNIER.	557	Marchand de dieux à Pompéi .	»	900	»	» 66	» 35	» 30	4
		N							
BARRIAS.	558	Nature (La) se dévoilant devant la science	1	2.000	3.000	» 97	» 35	» 23	1
	559	— 30	2	1.200	1.800	» 73	» 27	» 18	

Right Table

NOMS DES ARTISTES	NUMÉROS D'ORDRE	DÉSIGNATION DES ŒUVRES	N°s DES MODÈLES	PRIX BRONZE OU ÉTAIN	PRIX BRONZE DORÉ	Hauteur	Longueur	Profondeur	PAGE DE L'ALBUM
	560	— 18	3	800	1.200	» 58	» 20	» 15	
	561	— 10	4	600	900	» 43	» 15	» 10	
	562	— 25	5	250	450	» 24	» 08	» 06	
MASSON.	563	Napoléon Iᵉʳ, équestre . . .	1	500	750	» 55	» 34	» 13	10
BARRE.	564	Napoléon Iᵉʳ, debout. . . .	1	160	400	» 17	» 19	» 7	
	565		2	75		» 15	»	»	
DE MEULWERKERQUE.	566	Napoléon Iᵉʳ, équestre . . .		150		» 26	» 25	» 9	
		O							
Aᵗˢ PARIS.	567	Orphée et Eurydice	1	3.200	»	1 25	» 65	» 41	10
	568	—	2	1.600	»	» 90	» 47	» 31	
	569	—	3	1.000	»	» 72	» 36	» 24	
V. PÉTER.	570	Oursons jouant	1	1.200	»	» 35	» 50	» 33	14
	571	—	2	450	»	» 34	» 31	» 21	
	572	—	3	200	»	» 21	» 19	» 12	
FRÉMIET.	573	Ourse et Finlandais	»	150	250	» 30	» 18	» 15	23
		P							
D'ASTANIÈRES.	574	Pêcheur à la ligne	1	600	»	» 72	» 22	» 22	19
	575	—	2	400	»	» 62	» 20	» 20	
	576	—	3	300	»	» 52	» 17	» 17	
L. GRÉGOIRE.	577	Pêcheuse de crevettes . . .	1	600	»	» 72	» 22	» 22	
	578	— . . .	2	400	»	» 62	» 20	» 20	
	579	— . . .	3	300	»	» 52	» 17	» 17	
CROISY.	580	Patrie!	1	1.200	»	1 11	» 32	» 32	18
	581	—	2	650	»	» 85	» 23	» 23	
	582	—	3	300	»	» 55	» 14	» 14	
	583	—	4	200	»	» 42	» 11	» 11	
PAUL ROUSSEL.	584	Papillon (Le)	»	900	»	» 61	» 15	» 19	
G. MICHEL.	585	Pensée (La) 58	1	2.000	»	» 70	» 40	» 30	7
	586	—	2	600	»	» 35	» 20	» 15	
	587	—	3	»	»	»	»	»	
LAOUST.	588	Pavane (La) 25	1	1.000	»	» 67	» 45	» 31	
	589	—	2	650	»	» 50	» 30	» 23	
MASSON.	590	Petits Poussins	»	60	»	» 09	» 13	» 08	
Cathédrale de Nuremberg.	591	Prière (La)	1	450	700	» 62	» 16	» 16	20
	592	—	2	225	450	» 43	» 10	» 10	
	593	—	3	150	225	» 28	» 07	» 07	
LEFEBVRE.	594	Porteur d'eau Napolitain . . .	1	400	»	» 57	» 17	» 22	
	595	— . . .	2	250	»	» 33	» 07	» 13	
P. MENGIN.	596	Puits qui parle. . . . 76	1	3.500	4500	1 50	» 83	» 47	6
	597	— . . .	2	1.800	2500	1 12	» 65	» 40	
	598	— . . . 31	3	1.200	1800	» 95	» 46	» 31	
RUDE.	599	Pêcheur Napolitain	1	400	»	» 35	» 20	» 38	
	600	—	2	225	»	» 28	» 17	» 30	
	601	—	3	130	»	» 20	» 12	» 21	
Tᴴ. RIVIÈRE.	602	Pasteur	»	300	»	» 33	» 11	» 11	9
Léo LAPORTE.	603	Prix du tournoi, électrique. . .	»	175	300	» 30	» 15	» 13	15
DROPSY.	604	Plaquette Saintes Femmes . . .	»	60 80	85 120	» 12	» 21	» 20	
	605	— tête bretonne .	»	50 70	75 110	» 11	» 15	»	
DALOU.	606	Pudleur bas-relief	»	»	»	»	»	»	
	607	Paveur	»	»	»	»	»	»	
	608	Porteuse de pain bas-relief . .	»	»	»	»	»	»	
	609	— de lait	»	60	»	» 12	» 06	» 06	
P. MENGIN.	610	Premier berceau 36	1	1.000	1.400	» 63	» 44	» 32	6
	611	—	2	600	600	» 42	» 31	» 21	
ARNOUX.	612	Plumier Cyclamens	»	60	»	» 03	» 33	» 12	
MOIGNIEZ.	613	Perdrix blessée	1	150	»	» 28	» 25	» 22	
	614	—	2	100	»	» 17	» 18	» 14	
	615	—	3	50	»	» 13	» 13	» 10	
HANNAUX.	616	Poète et la Sirène (Le) . . .	1	3000	3500	100	88	45	2
	617	— . . .	2	1800	2200	78	73	35	
	618	— . . .	3	1100	1300	56	50	25	
	619	— . . .	4	»	»	»	»	»	
ARTS DÉCORATIFS.	620	Pendule Louis XV rocaille . .	3	»	300	» 35	» 25	» 15	
	621	Pendule enfant flambeau . . .	4	1.000	»	» 65	» 32	» 17	24
	622	— . . . 5	»	600	» 48	» 23	» 13		
	623	— . . . 4	»	250	» 30	» 10	» 07		
OUDRY.	624	Pendule Louis XVI, enfant Colombe	»	700	» 55	» 23	» 16	13	
LELIÈVRE.	625	Pendule Louis XV . . . l	»	850	» 53	» 31	» 22	13	
	626	— . . .	»	450	» 40	» 22	» 13		
	627ᵇⁱˢ	— Watteau . .	»	700	» 50	» 30	» 21	24	
Musée de l'Ermitage.	627	Pendule coquetterie . . .	»	650	900	» 43	» 30	» 20	13
RÉCIPON.	628	Porte-bonheur fer à cheval. . .	1	125	150	» 13	» 21	» 16	21
	628ᵇⁱˢ	— — . . .	2	100	125	» 10	» 15	» 11	

Left table

NOMS DES ARTISTES	N° D'ORDRE	DÉSIGNATION DES ŒUVRES	N° DES MODÈLES	PRIX BRONZE OU ÉTAIN	PRIX BRONZE DORÉ	Hauteur	Longueur	Profondeur	PAGE DE L'ALBUM
LEDRU.	629	Plat la Mer	»	500		» 12	» 85	» 60	
	630	— le Rêve	»	150	300	» 03	» 51	» 37	16
	631	— Étoile du matin	1	150	300	» 03	» 51	» 37	16
	632	—	2	90	150	» 02	» 34	» 24	
	633	— Badinage	»	90		» 03	» 31	» 24	
	634	— la Pêche	»	80	»	» 03	» 31	» 24	16
	635	— jeune mère	»	65	»	» 03	» 28	» 18	
	636	— Libellule	1	150	300	» 04	» 50	» 30	
	637	—	2	80	100	» 03	» 25	» 16	
	638	— l'Onde	1	400		» 04	» 81	» 52	
	639	—	2	175		» 03	» 52	» 37	
	640	—	3	120		» 02	» 35	» 25	
	641	— la Vague	1	400		» 04	» 81	» 16	
	642	—	2	175		» 03	» 52	» 37	
	643	—	3	120		» 02	» 35	» 25	
	644	— Surprise	1	400		» 04	» 81	» 16	
	645	—	2	175		» 03	» 52	» 37	
	646	—	3	120		» 02	» 35	» 25	
LANSON.	647	— Jason	1	150		» 03	» 46	» 33	
	648	—	2			»	»	»	
DESVIGNES.	649	Plat Poésie	1	150		» 05	» 50	» 31	
DESVIGNES.	650	Plat Poésie	2	»		»	»	»	
A. BOUCHER	651	Plat Hirondelle blessée	»	160		» 04	» 46	» 34	
MATHURIN MOREAU	652	Plat la Source	»	140		» 04	» 46	» 34	
P. RICHER.	653	Plat Semeur	»	120		» 04	» 39	» 28	11
	654	— Moisson	»	120		» 04	» 39	» 28	11
	655	— Rentrée des gerbes	»	120		» 04	» 39	» 28	
	656	— Faucheur	»	100		» 03	» 33	» 21	
LEVILLAIN.	658	Plat le Songe	»	150 125		» 02	» 35	» 35	14
	659	— Idylle	1	100		» 02	» 30	» 30	
	660	—	2	70		» 02	» 25	» 25	
	661	Présentoir Latone	»	80		» 03	» 34	» 17	
	662	— Diogène	1	120		» 04	» 39	» 28	14
	663	—	2	60		» 03	» 28	» 12	
	664	— Médée	1	160		» 03	» 41	» 21	14
	665	—	2	70		» 02	» 27	» 14	
	666	— Amphitrite	»	140		» 03	» 39	» 20	
PAUL ROUSSEL.	667	Plat Tarentola	»	300		» 15	» 42	» 25	22

R

NOMS DES ARTISTES	N° D'ORDRE	DÉSIGNATION DES ŒUVRES	N° DES MODÈLES	PRIX BRONZE OU ÉTAIN	PRIX BRONZE DORÉ	Hauteur	Longueur	Profondeur	PAGE DE L'ALBUM
BARRIAS.	668	Renommée	1	1800	2400	167	»	»	
	669	—	2	800	1.500	» 85	» 40	» 52	1
	670	—	3	350	600 700	» 43	» 19	» 26	
	671	—	4	»	»				
	672	Reconnaissance (La)	64 1	2.500		1 03	» 40	» 31	1
	673	—	37 2	1.200	1 800	» 78	» 37	» 23	
	674	—	15 3	600	900	» 52	» 24	» 17	
		Rêverie	10	450	600	» 47	» 20	» 20	
MATHURIN MOREAU	676	Réveil du printemps	1	1.600		» 83	» 32	» 32	7
	677	—	2	1.000		» 65	» 25	» 25	
	678	—	3	600		» 55	» 21	» 21	
FALGUIÈRE.	679	Renommée	47 1	3.000		1 24	» 70	1 30	2
	680	—	14 2	1 200		» 95	» 50	» 95	
	681	—	16 3	650	1.200	» 72	» 35	» 70	
	682	—	6 4	350	600	» 48	» 24	» 48	
MÈNE.	683	Rémouleur porte allumettes	»	75		» 19	» 10	» 15	
PERNOT.	684	Repos en Égypte (bas-relief)	1	300	400	» 53	» 35	» 07	20
	685	— —	2	200	300	» 41	» 27	» 05	
	686	—	3	100	200	» 24	» 16	» 04	
	687	—	4	»	»				
DALOU.	688	Retour des champs	»	90		» 13	» 09	» 06	3
	689	— du bois	»	80		» 13	» 08	» 06	
	690	— de l'herbe	»	60		» 11	» 04	» 06	3
DALOU.	691	Rabatteur de faulx	»	160		» 12	» 10	» 16	3
MENGUE.	692	Repos aux champs	1	500		» 65	» 24	» 24	6
	693	—	2	200		» 32	» 11	» 11	

S

NOMS DES ARTISTES	N° D'ORDRE	DÉSIGNATION DES ŒUVRES	N° DES MODÈLES	PRIX BRONZE OU ÉTAIN	PRIX BRONZE DORÉ	Hauteur	Longueur	Profondeur	PAGE DE L'ALBUM
LAFRANCE.	694	Saint Jean enfant	Original	4.000		» 48	» 52	» 58	20
	695	—	1	550		» 95	» 33	» 30	
	696	—	2	350		» 70	» 30	» 30	
	697	—	3	27 200		» 59	» 26	» 23	
	698	—	4	1/2 140		» 42	» 17	» 16	
	699	—	5	100		» 26	» 10	» 09	
THAREL.	700	Sans-Souci	1	450		» 35	» 28	» 30	19
	701	—	2	250		» 26	» 21	» 27	
	702	—	3	130		» 18	» 15	» 20	

Right table

NOMS DES ARTISTES	N° D'ORDRE	DÉSIGNATION DES ŒUVRES	N° DES MODÈLES	PRIX BRONZE OU ÉTAIN	PRIX BRONZE DORÉ	Hauteur	Longueur	Profondeur	PAGE DE L'ALBUM
LORMIER.	703	Sauveteur	42? 1	1.500		» 70	» 33	» 40	2
	704	—	17? 2	550	900	» 50	» 20	» 28	
	705	—	3	300		» 29	» 12	» 31	
P. RICHER.	707	Semeur (Le)	15 1	500		» 61	» 22	» 31	11
	708	—	2	200	250	» 29	» 10	» 15	
ALLOUARD.	709	Source (La)	15 »	900	1.200	» 49	» 30	» 25	
G. MICHEL.	710	Source limpide	16	750	1.000	» 46	» 28	» 22	7
Th. RIVIÈRE.	711	Salammbô chez Matho	1	600	800	» 41	» 18	» 18	9
	712	—	2	»	»				
Léo LAPORTE.	713	Servante moyen âge	»	250	300	» 34	» 11	» 11	15
LEVASSEUR.	714	Sonnette Surprise	»						
CONVERS.	715	Sonnette Servante	»	60	100	» 12	» 06	» 06	9
LEDRU.	716	Sonnette Naïades	»	60	100	» 13	» 10	» 10	16
PERNOT.	717	Son de la Cloche	7 1	225	350	» 38	» 13	» 19	20
	718	—	2	100	135	» 19	» 06	» 06	
MAROCHETTI.	719	Saint Louis à genoux	»	300		» 50	» 18	» 28	
NON SIGNÉ.	720	Socle marbre et bronze doré	103		600	» 13	» 30	» 30	
	721	— bronze à draperies	104		600	» 13	» 30	» 30	
	722	— marbre Louis XVI	112		450	» 20	» 38	» 30	
	723	Pieds marbre Louis XVI	112		250	» 13	» 18	» 16	
	724	Socle marbre Renaissance	113		450	» 20	» 38	» 30	
	725	Pieds Renaissance	113		250	» 13	» 18	» 16	
	726	Socle marbre Louis XVI dessus rond	114		300	» 15	» 28	» 28	13
	727	Pieds —	114		200	» 10	» 13	» 13	
	728	Socle marbre Louis XVI dessus rond	115		450	» 16	» 34	» 34	
	729	Pieds —	115		250	» 12	» 15	» 15	
	730	Socle marbre Louis XVI carré	116		300	» 15	» 32	» 32	12
	731	Pieds —	116		200	» 12	» 15	» 15	
NON SIGNÉ.	732	Socle marbre Louis XVI carré	116?		250	» 15	» 23	» 23	
	733	— Renaissance	117		300	» 20	» 32	» 32	
	734	Pieds —	117		200	» 12	» 10	» 10	
	735	Socle marbre Louis XV n° 1	118		750	» 24	» 49	» 35	
	736	— n° 2	119		500	» 18	» 35	» 28	
	737	—	120			»	»	»	
	738	—	121			»	»	»	
	739	—	122			»	»	»	
	740	—	123			»	»	»	
	741	Pieds marbre Louis XVI	124		100	» 07	» 12	» 12	

T

NOMS DES ARTISTES	N° D'ORDRE	DÉSIGNATION DES ŒUVRES	N° DES MODÈLES	PRIX BRONZE OU ÉTAIN	PRIX BRONZE DORÉ	Hauteur	Longueur	Profondeur	PAGE DE L'ALBUM
Ate PARIS.	742	Temps et Chanson	1	2.500		» 80	» 48	» 40	10
	743	—	2	1.000		» 60	» 35	» 27	
	744	—	3	700		» 48	» 30	» 26	
BELLOC.	745	Temps futurs	50 1	1.500		» 88	» 35	» 34	2
	746	—	30 2	850		» 65	» 27	» 27	
	747	—	11 3	450		» 44	» 18	» 18	
	748	—	4	250	350	» 29	» 12	» 12	
SEYSSES.	749	Triomphe de Diane	1	1.200		» 98	» 33	» 35	9
	750	—	2	650		» 74	» 25	» 25	
	751	—	3	350		» 49	» 15	» 15	
L. GRÉGOIRE.	752	Tambour! en Avant!	»	300		» 51	» 16	» 16	18
CROISY.	753	Tirailleur	1	600		» 60	» 25	» 25	
	754	—	2	300		» 40	» 18	» 18	
	755	—	3	200		» 30	» 14	» 14	
MATHURIN MOREAU.	756	Triomphe de la Jeunesse	»	1.600		» 85	» 35	» 30	7
DALOU.	757	Travail	1	500		» 61	» 20	» 20	3
	758	—	2	200		» 29	» 10	» 10	
	759	Torse femme nue	»	300		» 49	» 18	» 18	
	760	Terrassier	»	125		» 20	» 07	» 06	
	761	Tonnelier	»	100		» 15	» 06	» 06	
	762	Tueur (bas-relief)	»			»	»	»	
BARRIAS.	353	Tablettes de l'Histoire	1			»	»	»	
	354	—	2	600		» 46	» 29	» 29	1
LELIÈVRE.	763	Tasse et Soucoupe	»	75		» 10	» 15	» 15	

U

NOMS DES ARTISTES	N° D'ORDRE	DÉSIGNATION DES ŒUVRES	N° DES MODÈLES	PRIX BRONZE OU ÉTAIN	PRIX BRONZE DORÉ	Hauteur	Longueur	Profondeur	PAGE DE L'ALBUM
PECH.	764	Un grand secret	1	»	»	» 67	» 31	» 40	
	765	—	41 2	1.200		» 48	» 22	» 28	
	766	—	11 3	900		» 48	» 22	» 28	

V

NOMS DES ARTISTES	N° D'ORDRE	DÉSIGNATION DES ŒUVRES	N° DES MODÈLES	PRIX BRONZE OU ÉTAIN	PRIX BRONZE DORÉ	Hauteur	Longueur	Profondeur	PAGE DE L'ALBUM
BARRAU.	767	Vanneuse	1	400		» 47	» 16	» 16	8
	768	—	2	225		» 31	» 10	» 10	
LE VEEL.	769	Voltigeur (32e demi-brigade)	1	400		» 82	» 22	» 22	10
	770	— —	2	150		» 37	» 12	» 12	
	771	— —	3	50		» 17	» 05	» 05	

NOMS DES ARTISTES	NUMÉROS D'ORDRE	DÉSIGNATION DES ŒUVRES	Nº DES MODÈLES	PRIX		DIMENSIONS			PAGE DE L'ALBUM
				BRONZE OU ÉTAIN	BRONZE DORÉ	Hauteur	Largeur	Profondeur	
DALOU.	772	Vérité méconnue	1	600	..	35	27	30	3
	773	— —	2	250	..	22	12	19	
CUMBERWORTH.	774	Vierge Immaculée	1	200	..	40	15	15	
	775	— —	2	100	..	25	10	10	
BEAUMONT.	776	— et Enfant Jésus	1	200	..	40	15	15	
	777	—	2	100	..	25	10	10	
	778	— de Louis XIII		150	95		10	10	
Léo LAPORTE.	779	Voie lactée	1	"	"	"	"	"	
	780	—	2	450	"	43	"	"	15
	781	—	3	"	"	"	"	"	
Th. RIVIÈRE.	782	Vigne (La)		600	750	54	15	15	9
CONVERS.	783	Victoire (La)		400	500	62	35	32	9
SEYSSES.	784	Vérité (La)	11	1.200	..	1 10	28	31	
DEBON.	785	Vide-poches Anémones		75	125	05	16	15	
LEDRU.	786	Vase Espiègle	36	1.200	..	64	41	39	16
	787	—	2	450	..	40	27	27	
	788	— la Proie	10 1	600	..	45	35	35	16
	789	—	2	450	..	35	27	27	
	790	—	3	250	..	25	18	18	
	791	— Ondine	16	500	..	45	35	35	
	792	— Houblon		450	..	35	27	25	
	793	— Confidence		400	..	35	23	23	
	794	— Écho		350	..	35	28	23	
	795	— Naïades		300	400	35	28	23	16
	796	— Algue		200	300	22	15	15	
	797	— Rêverie		150	250	19	15	12	
Vital CORNU.	787b	Vase Paradis perdu	31	1.000	..	41	59	42	15
	798	— Sommeil	14 1	800	1.200	39	42	33	15
	799	—	10 2	450	600	28	28	23	
	800	— Anémones	1	450	600	40	25	25	
	801	—	2	250	400	30	16	16	
	802	— Pot à eau	10	300	..	32	26	22	
	803	— Digitale		250	350	29	16	16	
	804	— Lassitude		175	250	24	12	12	
	805	— Soleils		150	"	31	13	10	
P. RICHER.	806	Vase le Cidre		300	"	35	21	21	23
	807	— Buveur	10	300	"	35	20	25	
	808	— le Vin		300	400	32	20	18	15
DEBON.	809	Vase Iris	9 1	300	400	44	30	20	23
	810	—	2	160	250	30	20	13	
RÉCIPON.	811	Vase Cache-cache		250	"	35	26	15	23
LEVILLAIN.	812	Vase Diogène		300	500	41	17	17	14
	813	— Cérès		150	"	23	17	15	14
SIMON.	814	Vase Iris petit		60	120	15	07	07	22
LELIÈVRE.	815	Vase Angélique		250	350	27	15	15	22
	816	— le Blé		160	"	22	11	09	
	817	— Chardons		160	"	22	11	09	
808bis	— Maïs		125	175	22	12	12	22	
	818	— Pavot		100	150	21	12	08	22
	819	— Lever du jour		80	125	20	10	10	
	820	— Léda		80	150	21	12	08	
	821	— Violettes		60	100	11	06	06	
	822	— Chèvrefeuille		60	100	11	06	06	
	823	— Colchique	1	50	90	10	09	07	22
	824	—	2	30	50	07	07	05	
	827	— Chrysanthèmes		250	350	26	16	16	
GAUTRUCHE.	824b	Vase Oignon d'Espagne		80	125	24	10	10	22
Paul ROUSSEL.	825	Vase Fée aux Roseaux		250	350	31	11	11	22
BUREAU.	826	Vase Glycines	45	200	300	33	17	15	10
ROSE.	828	Vase Myosotis		1/o 105	1/o 175	21	09	09	17
PERNOT.	829	Vase Enfant effrayé		250	300	23	17	15	24
RAMBAUD.	825b	Vase Marronniers		70	125	18	08	08	22
BECKER.	830	Vase Quatre saisons		150	250	22	11	11	10
	830b	— Crevettes		75	125	11	10	10	
DALOU.	831	Vase Travaux des champs		200	"	18	14	14	3
CROISY.	832	Zouave pontifical	1	"	"	"	"	"	
	833	—	2	650	"	66	22	22	
	834	—	3	300	"	48	20	20	
	835	Groupe zouave et chasseur	1	1.500	"	66	•	•	
	836	— —	2	750	"	53	•	•	
	837	— —	3	400	"	35	•	•	
LANCERAY.	•	Adieux du Cosaque (Les)	1	375	475	41	36		23
	•	—	2	225	300	26	21		
MÊNE.	•	Fauconnier arabe à cheval	•	1.000	1.650	75	59	26	23

THIÉBAUT

This firm started with Charles Cyprien Thiébaut (1769-1830). The son of a tanner, he worked in a small firm, for which he became director in 1787. He later went into partnership with his son Charles Antoine Floréal, born in 1794, who in 1827 would act as the sole director the firm, under the name of Thiébaut Sr. He established himself on the Rue du Faubourg-Saint-Denis and manufactured copper cylinders for the impression of canvases as well as some 'objets d'art'.

In turn, Charles Antoine worked with his own son Victor (b. 1828) under the trade name Thiébaut et fils. They produced some industrial castings and art bronzes. Victor Thiébaut, who was soon left alone with the business, brought the firm to great property. In 1851, he created a foundry for art pieces, from which he initially issued some unrefined castings, which he sent to some other manufacturers (including Barbedienne) for finishing. He started next to produce editions for different sculptors such as David d'Angers (*La Liberté* and the 548 medallions, these latter offered to customers at prices between 7.50 and 30 F), Carpeaux (*Le Pêcheur à la coquille*), Diéboit (*La France rémunératrice*), Falguière (*Le Vainqueur au combat de coqs*), Carrier-Belleuse (*Le Baiser d'une mère*), Paul Dubois, Moulin, Ottin, Cumberworth, and Pradier. He also made some vases, cups, and fireplace fittings. In 1864, he bought back a number of models from the Eck and Durand foundry, which had just stopped all activity. Victor Thiébaut also made some monumental castings, like the *Saint Michel terrassant le dragon* by Duret for the fountain of Saint-Michel, and the *Napoléon 1er* by Dumont for the Vendôme column.

Increasingly afflicted by blindness, in 1870 Victor Thiébaut left his enterprise to his three sons, Victor (1849-1908), Jules (1854-1898), and Henri—who was also a sculptor (1855-1899). After having manufactured arms during the hostilities, in 1877 Thiébaut Frères moved their studios from the Rue du Faubourg-Saint-Denis to 32 Rue de Villiers (the future Rue Guersant), and in 1880 opened a store on 32 Avenue de l'Opera. Among the countless bronzes issued by the foundry during this period, some monumental works are of note: the *Gloria Victis* by Mercié, the monument to the *Défense de Paris* by Barrias, the *Alexandre Dumas père* by Gustave Doré, and from the same artist, the colossal vase of the *Vigne* (today at the museum of San Francisco), *Etienne Marcel* by Idrac finished by Marqueste for the city hall, the *République* by Morice, *Charlemagne* from the Marquet brothers, and the reduction of *Liberté* by Bartholdi for the Grenelle bridge. Thiébaut Frères participated in a number of exhibitions and acquired an international reputation.

Shortly before the death of his two brothers, Victor Thiébaut found himself alone at the head of the firm. He executed the casting of the *Triomphe de la République,* the large group by Dalou erected at the center of the Plaza de la Nation. It was then that he yielded a part of his firm to Fumière and Gavignot. This house, which marked its bronzes "Thiébaut Frères, Fumière and Gavignot successors," continued to produce numerous editions. In 1898, Rodin signed ten-year contracts with the firm for editions of *Saint Jean-Baptiste* and *Jeunesse triomphante* in

THIEBAUT FRÈRES

FUMIÈRE et Cⁱᵉ, Successeurs

Maison fondée en 1789

PARIS

ÉDITIONS D'ŒUVRES

DES PRINCIPAUX ARTISTES FRANÇAIS

ONZE D'AMEUBLEMENT & D'ECLAIRAGE

ND PRIX, Expositions de Paris de 1878 et 1889

HORS CONCOURS, Président du Jury en 1900

Magasins : 32, Avenue de l'Opéra.

Tél. Central 34-74.

APPAREILS D'ÉCLAIRAGE DE TOUT STYLE

INSTALLATION COMPLÈTE D'ÉLECTRICITÉ

LUMIÈRE, SONNERIE, TÉLÉPHONE

SIGNAUX LUMINEUX - FORCE

ENVOI DE DEVIS SUR DEMANDE

Service électrique : 32, Rue Guersant.

Tél. Wagram 11-01.

4

Orphée

par TONY-NOEL ✻. *Grand Prix de Rome.*

Hauteur 0ᵐ74, bronze . . . .   750 fr

bronze doré 1.300

Poëte sur Pégase

par FALGUIÈRE ✻. Membre de l'Institut.

Hauteur 0ᵐ71, bronze . . . .   1.100 fr.

bronze doré 1.800

Original : *Square de l'Opéra*, Paris.

Femme à la Harpe

par DING.

Nº 1. Hauteur 0ᵐ83/0ᵐ92, bronze . . . .   1.650 fr.

Nº 2.   0ᵐ50, avec base marbre .   750

Original : *Musée de Grenoble.*

L'Amour domptant la Force
par INJALBERT ✳, Membre de l'Institut.
Hauteur 0ᵐ45, bronze . . . . 750 fr.
Original : Jardins du Peyroux, Montpellier.

La Victoire
par ROULLEAU ✳, Hors Concours.
Nᵒ 1. Hauteur 0ᵐ97 1ᵐ45, bronze. 2.750 fr.
Nᵒ 2. 0ᵐ49 0ᵐ71 850
Original au Monument Carnot, à Nolay.

La Force domptée par l'Amour
par INJALBERT ✳, Membre de l'Institut.
Hauteur 0ᵐ45, bronze . . . . 750 fr.
Original : Jardins du Peyroux, Montpellier.

many sizes. As for Victor Thiébaut, he sold his foundry in 1901 to Gasne, who was followed first by Malesset, and then by Fulda. In 1919, Fumière (alone this time) bought from Fulda the right to cast using the name of Thiébaut Frères. The firm stopped its activity in 1926 and all the models were sold.

VALSUANI

Originally from Italy, Claude Valsuani began as a workman, and then as a technical director at the Hébard house. In 1899, he started a foundry in Châtillon, and around 1905 established himself at 74 Rue des Plantes in Paris. After his death in Malgrate, Italy in 1923, his son Marcel succeeded him. The Valsuani foundry acquired a great reputation very quickly, particularly for its castings made by the lost wax method. The firm worked for a number of famous artists, including Renoir, Bourdelle, Picasso, Pompon, Despiau, Troubetzkoy, and especially Matisse. In addition, they cast some works by Dalou, Carpeaux, Gauguin, and Daumier. In fact, they began to cast twenty-three figurines for Daumier in 1930, and cast his *Autoportrait* in 1954-1955, *Ratapoil* and *Homme à la perruque* in 1960, and thirty-six busts in 1970. From 1959 to 1968, they also translated many woods by Gauguin into bronze.

Claude Valsuani's brother Attilio Valsuani opened his own foundry in Bagneux in the 1920s.

Vase " Les Hirondelles "
par HINGRE, Médaillé.
Nᵒ 1. Hauteur 0ᵐ62, bronze . . . . . . 1.100 fr.
Nᵒ 2. — 0ᵐ41 — 550

Comba
par GARDET
Nᵒ 1. Hauteur 0ᵐ73
En marbre mo
Nᵒ 2. Hauteur 0ᵐ48
—
En marbre mo
Nᵒ 3. Hauteur 0ᵐ39
—
Original : M

19

Chien Vendéen

Hauteur 0m27, bronze. **225** fr.

Chiens Poitevins

Hauteur 0m33 ; largeur 0m43, bronze. **450** fr.

Croix du Veneur

Hauteur 0m42, bronze. **380** fr.

Harde de Cerfs

Nº **1**. Hauteur 0m79, bronze. **1.100** fr.
Nº **2**. — 0m36 — 380

Original : *Jardins du Luxembourg.*

Œuvres de LEDUC ✱

Médaille de 1re Classe

Cheval de Trait

Hauteur 0m41 ; largeur 0m44, bronze. **380** fr.

Vase " La Mer "

par Henri THIÉBAUT ✱, *Médaillé.*

Hauteur 0m68 ; largeur 0m28, bronze. **1.500** fr.

Original : *Musée du Luxembourg.*

750 fr.
000
850
350
500
450
775

Le Chant

par BARRIAS ✱, de l'Institut.

Nº **1**. Haut. 1m », bronze. **1.750** fr.
Nº **2**. — 0m75 — 800
Nº **3**. — 0m33 — 280
— — doré . 450
Nº **4**. — 0m15, bronze. 200

Original : *Hôtel de Ville de Paris.*

Les Premières Funérailles

par BARRIAS ✱, de l'Institut.

Nº **1**. Haut 0m85, bronze. **3.200** fr
Nº **2**. — 0m71 — 2.350
— — doré . 4.400
Nº **3**. — 0m51, bronze. **1.300**

Original : *Musée du Petit Palais.*

Borne Frontière

par BARTHOLDI ✿, *Médaille d'Honneur.*

Hauteur 0m44/0m48, bronze. **650** fr.

En Vedette

par Mad. THOMAS-SOYER, *Médaillé.*

Hauteur 0m59, bronze . . . . **750** fr.

— — bronze doré **1.100**

Appartient au *Musée des Beaux-Arts.*

La Liberté

par PARIS, *Médaillé.*

Hauteur 0m68/0m80, bronze. **750** fr.

Le Vainqueur

par GREBER ✩ *1re Médaille.*

Nº **1**.	Hauteur 0m84, bronze	**900** fr.
Nº **2**.	— 0m70	. . . . **525**
Nº **3**.	— 0m52	. . . . **380**
Nº **4**.	— 0m38	. . . . **260**

Vers la Gloire

par PETER ✿. *Médaillé.*

Hauteur 0m90, bronze . . . . . **2.000** fr.

Original au Grand-Palais, Paris.

Trouvaille à Pompéi

par MOULIN, *Hors Concours.*

Nº **1**.	Hauteur 0m82/0m98, bronze
Nº **2**.	— 0m73/0m85
Nº **3**.	— 0m40/0m47

Original : Musée du Luxembourg.

══BIBLIOGRAPHY══

General Works
About Edmond, *Voyage à traverse l'exposition des Beaux arts*, Paris, 1855.
Bénézit Emmanuel, *Dictionnaire des peintres, sculpteurs et graveurs*, Paris, 1976.
Benoît Luc, *La Sculpture romantique*, Paris 1928.
Benoît Luc, *La Sculpture française*, Paris, 1945.
Bermann Harold, *Bronzes, Sculptors and Founders*, Chicago, 1974-1980.
Cooper Jeremy, *Nineteenth Century Romantic Bronzes*, London, 1975.
Devaux Yves, *L'Universe des bronzes et des fontes monumentales*, Paris, 1978.
Gonse Louis, *La Sculpture française*, Paris, 1895.
Horswell Jane, *Bronze Sculpture of "les animaliers,"* Woodbridge, 1971.
Kjellberg Pierre, *Le Guide des statues de Paris*, Paris, 1973.
Lami Stanslas, *Dictionnaire des sculpteurs de l'école française du XIXe siècle*, Paris, 1914-1921.
Mackay James, *The Animaliers*, New York, 1977.
Mackay James, *The Dictionnary of western sculptors in bronze*, Woodbridge, 1977.
Metman C.B., *La Petite Sculpture d'édition au XIXe siècle*, thesis from the Ecole du Louvre (School of the Louvre), 1944.
Musée d'Orsay, *Catalogue des nouvelles acquisitions*, Paris, 1983.
Musée d'Orsay, *Catalogue des sculptures*, Paris, 1986.
Payne Christopher, *Animals in Bronze*, Woodbridge, 1986.
Pradel Pierre, *La Sculpture du XIXe siècle au musée du Louvre*, Paris, 1957.
Radcliffe Anthony, *European Bronze Statuettes*, 1966.
Rheims Maurice, *La Sculpture au XIXe siècle*, Paris, 1972.
Savage George, *A Concise History of Bronzes*, London, 1968.
Drouot, L'Art et les enchères (annual).
Le Prix de l'art (annual).
Mayer, *Annuaire international des ventes*.

Catalogs from collective expositions
Salon de la Société des Artistes Français.
Salon de la Société Nationale des Beaux-Arts.
Salon d'Automne.
Expositions Universelles (1855, 1867, 1878, 1889, 1900).
Metamorphose in Nineteenth Century Sculpture, Cambridge/Fogg Art Museum, 1975.
Un siècle d'art animalier, Paris/galerie Paul Ambroise, 1975.
L'Art en France sous le second Empire, Paris/ Grand Palais, 1979.
The Romantics to Rodin; French Nineteenth Century Sculpture from North-American Collections, Los Angeles County Museum, 1980-1981.
De Carpeaux à Matisse; la sculpture française de 1850 à 1914 dans les musées du nord de la France, Calais, Lille, Arras, Boulogne-sur-Mer, Paris/Musée Rodin, 1982-1983.
Sculptures des XIXe et XXe siècles dans les musées de Poitiers, 1983.

La Sculpture française au XIXe siècle, Paris/Grand Palais, 1986.
Nineteenth century French and West European sculpture, New York/Shepherd Gallery, 1985.

Biographical works and catalogs from personal expositions
Saunier Charles, *Barye*, Paris, 1925.
Pivar Stuart, *The Barye bronze*, New York, 1974.
Glenn F. Benge, *A. L. Barye, sculptor of romantic realism*, Philadelphia, 1984.
Exposition *Barye, sculptures, peintures et aquarelles de collections publiques*, Paris/Louvre, 1956-1957.
Exposition *Marguerite de Bayser-Gratry, soixante ans de sculpture*, Paris/galerie Bernheim, 1962.
Retrospective *Joseph Bernard*, Paris/Orangerie, 1932.
Exposition *Joseph Bernard*, Paris/Musée Rodin, 1973.
Exposition *Le Sculpteur Max Blondat*, Beauvais/Musée Départemental de l'Oise, 1979.
Anna Klumpke, *Rosa Bonheur*, Paris, 1908.
Vallier Thérèse, *Henri Bouchard*, Paris, 1943.
Retrospective *Henri Bouchard*, Paris/Ecole des Beaux-Arts, 1963.
Exposition *Donation Henri Bouchard*, Dijon/Musée des Beaux-Arts, 1968.
Exposition *Henri Bouchard, centenaire de sa naissance*, Dijon/Musée des Beaux-Arts, 1975.
Gauthier Maximilien, *Bourdelle*, Paris, 1951.
Descargues Pierre, *Bourdelle*, Paris, 1954.
Jianou Ionel, Dufet Michel, *Bourdelle*, 1975.
Lavrillier Carol-Marc, Dufet Michel, *Bourdelle et la critique de son temps*, Paris, 1979.
Harvey Mary, *The bronzes of Roland Bugatti*, London 1979.
Dejean Philippe, *Bugatti*, Paris, 1981.
Chalom des Cordes Jacques and Fromanger des Cordes Véronique, *Rembrandt Bugatti sculpteur*, Paris, 1987.
Exposition *Rupert Carabin*, Paris/musée Galliéra, 1934-35.
Exposition *L'Œuvre de Rupert Carabin*, Paris/Gallery du Luxembourg, 1974.
Clément-Carpeaux Louise, *La Vérité sur l'œuvre et la vie de Jean-Baptiste Carpeaux*, Paris, 1934-1935.
Exposition *Jean-Baptiste Carpeaux*, Paris/Petit Palais, 1955-1956.
Radcliffe Anthony, *Jean-Baptiste Carpeaux*, Paris, 1969.
Exposition *Sur les traces de Jean-Baptiste Carpeaux*, Paris/ Grand Palais, 1975.
Exposition *Jean-Baptiste Carpeaux, sa famille et ses amis*, Courbevoie/Musée Roybet-Fould, 1975-1976.
Hardy André, Braunwald Anny, *Catalogue des peintures et sculptures de Jean-Baptiste Carpeaux à Valenciennes*, 1978.
Hargrove June Ellen, Life and work of Albert Carrier-Belleuse, New York, 1975.
Pagot-Villerelle Germaine, marchand J.-J., *Pierre Jules Cavelier*, Paris, 1979.
Paris Reine-Marie, *Camille Claudel*, Paris, 1984.
Exposition *Camille Claudel*, Paris/Museé Rodin, Poitiers/Musée Saint-Croix, 1984.

Caillaux Henriette, *Dalou, l'homme et l'oeuvre*, Paris, 1935.

Gobin Maurice, *Caumier sculpteur*, Geneva, 1952.

Exposition *Daumier sculpture*, Cambridge/Fogg Art Museum, 1969.

Passeron R., *Daumier témoin de son temps*, Paris, 1971.

Cherpin Jean, *Daumier et la sculpture*, Paris, 1979.

Exposition *Daumier sculpteur*, Paris/galerie Sagot-Legarrec, 1979.

Cabanne Pierre, Grégoire Michel, Leduc Michel, *Daumier, les bustes de parlementaires*, Paris, 1980.

Join Henri, *David d'Angers, sa vie, son oeuvre, ses écrits et ses contemporains*, Paris, 1878.

Metzger Charles, Chesneau Georges, *Les OEuvres de David d'Angers*, Angers, 1934.

Exposition *David d'Angers et son temps*, Angers/Musée des Beaux-Arts, 1958.

Exposition *David d'Angers*, Paris/Hôtel de la Monnaie, 1966.

Bazin Germain, *Degas sculpteur*, Paris, 1931.

Matt Léonard von, Rewald John *L'OEuvre sculpté de Degas*, Zurich, 1957.

Exposition *The Complete Sculpture of Degas*, London/The Lefevre Gallery, 1976.

Exposition *Degas*, Paris/Centre Culturel du Marais, 1983.

Deshairs Léon, *Charles Despiau*, Paris, 1930.

Exposition *Charles Despiau*, Paris/Musée Rodin, 1974.

Damase K/. *Gustave Doré, peintre et sculpteur, 1979*.

Exposition Gustave Doré, Strasbourg/Musée d'Art Moderne, Paris/Pavillon des Arts, 1983.

Bénédite Léonce, *Alexandre Falguière*, Paris, 1902.

Bougon Jacqueline J. A., *Le Sculpteur animalier Fratin*, 1983.

Fauré-Frémiet Philippe, *Emannuel Frémiet*, Paris, 1934.

Gray Christopher, *Sculptures and ceramics of Paul Gauguin*, Baltimore, 1963.

Clément Charles, *Géricault*, Paris, 1868.

Ackerman Gérald M., *Jean-Léon Gérôme*, Paris, 1986.

Paillard Etienne, *Le Statuaire Guéniot*, Review from the Bas-Poitou, 1966.

Dornand Guy, *Georges Guyot*, 1963.

Exposition *Georges Lacombe, le nabis sculpteur*, Paris/Galerie Pacitti, 1969.

Exposition *Hoetger, oeuvres plastiques des années parisiennes*, Bremen/Wolgangerner, 1977.

Isay Raymond, *Paul Landowski*, Paris, 1931.

Cladel Judith, *Aristide Maillol, sa vie, son oeuvre, ses idées*, Paris, 1937.

Exposition *Hommage à Aristide Maillol*, Paris/Musée National d'Art Moderne, 1961.

George Waldemar, *Aristide Maillol et l'âme de la sculpture*, Paris, 1964.

Chevalier Denys, *Maillol*, Paris, 1970.

Exposition *Maillol*, New York/Solomon-Guggenheim Museum, 1975.

Bessis Henriette, *Marcello sculpteur*, Fribourg, 1980.

Exposition *Marcello*, Paris/Musée Rodin, 1980-1981.

Matisse Henri, *Ecrits et propos sur l'art*, Paris, 1972.

Exposition *Tout l'oeuvre sculpté de Matisse*, Nice/Musée Matisse, 1974.

Exposition *Henri Matisse, dessins et sculptures*, Paris/Musée National d'Art Moderne, 1975.

Exposition *Matisse*, London/Hayward gallery, 1984, Leeds/City Art Gallery, 1985.

Poinso, M.C., *Constantin Meunier*, Paris, 1910.

Exposition *Constantin Meunier*, Bochum (RFA)/Bergbau Museum, 1970.

Exposition *Louis de Monard*, Autun/Musée Rolin, 1973.

Thomas Jacques, *Louis de Monard*, bulletin from the Société d'Histoire de l'Art Français, 1983.

Exposition *Paul Paulin, sculpteur impressionniste*, Clemont-Ferrand/Musée Bargoin, 1983.

Exposition *Hommage à Pablo Picasso, dessins, sculptures, céramiques*, Paris/Petit Palais, 1966.

Penrose Roland, *The Sculptures of Picasso*, New York, 1967.

Spiess Werner, *Les Sculptures de Picasso*, Lausanne, 1971.

Exposition *Sculptures de Pablo Picasso*, New York/Pace Gallery, 1982.

Pavlowski G. de, *Alfredo Pina*, 1929.

Guineau Bernard, *Alfredo Pina*, 1978.

Exposition *François Pompon*, Paris/Galerie Laurenceau, 1962.

Exposition *François Pompon, sculpteur animalier bourguignon*, Dijon/Musée des Beaux-Arts, 1964.

Exposition *Statues de chair, sculptures de James Pradier*, Geneva/Musée d'Art and d'Histoire, 1985, Paris/Musée du Luxembourg, 1986.

Haesaerts Pau, *Renoir sculpteur*, 1947.

Rochet André, *Louis Rochet sculpteur*, Paris, 1978.

Cladel Judith, *Auguste Rodin, sa vie glorieuse, sa vie inconnue*, Paris, 1944.

Grappes Georges, *Catalogue du musée Rodin*, Paris, 1938.

Charbonneaux Jean, *Les Sculptures de Rodin*, Paris, 1949.

Exposition *Rodin inconnu*, Paris/Louvre, 1962-1963.

Jianou Ionel, Goldscheider Cécile, *Rodin*, Paris, 1967.

Champigneulle Bernard, *Rodin*, Paris, 1967.

Tancock John L., *The Sculpture of Auguste Rodin: The collection of the Rodin museum*, Philadelphia, 1976.

Exposition *Rodin, le monument des Bourgeois de Calais dans les collections du musée Rodin et du musée de Calais*, Calais, Paris, 1978.

Exposition *Rodin*, New York/Metropolitan Museum, 1986.

Exposition *Louis Oscar Roty*, Courbevoie/Musée Roybet Fould, 1985.

Exposition *Rude, centenaire de sa mort*, Dijon/Musée des Beaux-Arts, 1955.

Drouot Henri, *Une carrière: Rude*, Paris, 1958.

Faure Elie, *Raymond Sabouraud sculpteur*, Paris, 1929.

Beaunier André, *René de Saint-Marceaux*, Reims, 1922.

Exposition *Gaston Schnegg*, Bordeaux/Galerie des Beaux-Arts, 1986.

Exposition retrospective *Robert Wlérick*, Paris/Petit Palais, 1962.

Exposition *Robert Wlérick*, Bruton Gallery and Museum of Birmingham, 1976.

Reviews and journals

Connaissance des Arts (monthly). Articles of note include "Dalou tiré de l'oubli," by Claude Freignac, May 1964; "Rodin, l'affaire Balzac," by Evelyne Schlumberger, April 1967; "Duo avec Carpeaux," By Henriette Bessis, March 1975; "Rodin, les avatars des Bourgeois de Calais," by François Le Targat, June 1978; "Voir naître un bronze," by Pierre Kjellberg, November 1982, etc.

The Connoiseur (monthly).

L'Estampille (monthly). Numerous articles on sculpture, bronzes and sculptors, the majority signed Jacques Ginépro, in particular in the years 1980 to 1983.

Gazette des Beaux-Arts (monthly).

Gazette de l'hôtel Drouot (weekly).

L' Œil (monthly).

Revue du Louvre (bi-monthly).

PHOTOGRAPH CREDITS

Michel Kempf, Paris : 10, 25 à 41, 47, 55, 60, 61, 63, 66, 67, 73, 80, 87, 99, 109, 136, 173, 174, 178, 179, 183, 221, 252, 280, 291, 297, 301, 302, 313, 328, 345, 347, 354, 361, 365, 366, 385, 390, 391, 392, 395, 416, 417, 437, 439, 459, 462, 503, 515, 517, 525, 543, 550, 555, 600, 621, 622, 640, 663.

Michel de Lorenzo, Monaco : 9, 163, 177, 187, 201, 211, 217, 234, 240, 246, 247, 249, 255, 265, 283, 284, 310, 318, 319, 336, 377, 398, 456, 482, 516, 543, 557, 562, 563, 603, 604, 607, 608, 612, 613, 625.

Réunion des musées nationaux : 93, 96, 212, 251, 264, 268, 273, 296, 315, 368, 379, 382, 488, 493, 494, 520, 557, 559, 605, 648, 678.

Mᵐᵉ Dina Vierny : 450, 451, 452, 453, 454.

Fondation de Coubertin : 89, 92.

Musée Bouchard : 110 à 118, 663.

Ventes publiques : Agen, Armengau : 483, 642. Amiens, Leruste : 367, 490. Angers, Martin, Branger : 276, 305, 415, 515. Argentan, Audhoui : 237, 363. Arles, Holz : 642. Aubagne, Gamet : 411, 486. Auch, Briscadieu : 316, 464. Avignon, Germain, Desamais : 36, 323, 363, 444, 486. Avranches, Poulain : 191, 292. Bayeux, Havard, Bailleul : 84, 85, 191, 531. Beaune, Herry : 36. Belfort, Gauthier : 652. Bergerac, Feydy, Biraben : 505. Biarritz, Carayol : 279, 427, 600. Bordeaux, Vergne Jean dit Cazaux, Dubern : 202, 619, 644. Bourg-en-Bresse, Kohn : 78, 499. Brest, Thierry, Martin, Lesieur : 99, 312, 352, 397, 418, 504. Brive, Kaczorowski : 399. Calais, Pillon : 71, 195, 248, 371, 530, 590, 595. Cannes, Appay, Gairoard, Manon-Gairoard : 295, 358, 438. Carcassonne, Deleau : 515. Castres, Joanny : 421. Charleville-Mézières, Bauer : 543. Chartres, Lelièvre : 105. Clermont-Ferrand, Aguttes : 36. Corbeil-Essonnes, Bonduelle : 13. Deauville, Le Houeller : 370, 521. Dijon, Pichenot, De Vrégille : 75, 459, 476, 598. Dijon, Sadde : 91, 222, 356, 565, 575, 608, 636. Douai, Declerck : 374, 447, 509, 637. Dunkerque, Girard : 138. Enghien, Champin, Lombrail, Gautier : 15, 18, 19, 22, 23, 49, 51, 62, 67, 71, 95, 108, 132, 137, 145, 147, 150, 151, 152, 155, 156, 157, 159, 176, 177, 208, 215, 218, 222, 223, 242, 243, 248, 266, 273, 276, 288, 300, 301, 334, 336, 341, 353, 364, 372, 373, 388, 394, 401, 411, 426, 477, 479, 484, 498, 512, 522, 528, 549, 554, 567 à 570, 576, 577, 581, 582, 583, 585, 588, 597, 599, 604, 606, 609, 617, 628, 629. Epernay, Petit : 512, 514. Epinal, Jivoult : 105, 162, 317, 649. Etampes, Colobert : 621. Evreux, Thion : 459. Fécamp, Wemaere : 590. Fontainebleau, Osenat : 53, 101, 509, 639. Gien, Renard : 168. Granville, Robin : 198, 507. Joigny, Sausverd : 507. La Flèche, Manson : 140, 216, 447. L'Aigle, Blanchetière : 191, 335, 537. La Roche-sur-Yon, Raynaud : 636. Le Havre, Mabille-Vankemmel, Revol : 103. Les Andelys, Cousin : 369, 445. Lille, Singer, Desbuisson : 39, 203, 225, 265, 278, 293, 316, 318, 364, 456, 506, 603. Limoges, Galateau : 514. L'Isle-Adam, Elkaim : 87, 104, 292, 330, 403, 499. Lorient, Guignard : 642. Louviers, Thion : 300. Lyon, Anaf : 158. Lyon, Conan, Auclair-Conan : 36, 470. Lyon, Génin, Leseuil, Rambert : 11. Lyon, Milliarède : 504. Manosque, De Dianous : 446. Meaux, De Corneillan : 220, 252, 278, 293. Melun, Péron : 367, 417. Morlaix, Boscher, Oriot : 335, 491. Nancy, Bailly, Loevenbrück : 338. Nancy, Gautier, Hertz : 194. Nancy, Teitgen, Leroy : 505. Nanterre, Gillet : 225. Nantes, Antonietti : 296. Nantes, Blanche-Trégouet, Boré : 106, 261, 319, 527, 640. Neuilly, Ionesco : 121, 123, 126, 194, 245, 247, 248, 360, 408. Nice, Courchet, Palloc, Jaffet : 347, 483, 492. Nogent-le-Rotrou, Ecklé : 407. Orléans, Maison, Binoche : 41, 168. Orléans, Savot : 60, 79, 470, 485, 522, 627. Palaiseau, Martin du Nord : 205, 477. Paris, Ader, Picard, Tajan : 40, 122, 141, 157, 186, 272, 303, 354, 513, 537, 564, 576, 589, 633. Artus, Gridel, Boscher : 106, 196. Audap, Godeau, Solanet : 193, 194, 201, 253, 578, 580. Binoche, Godeau : 92, 147. Boisgirard : 65, 144, 237, 239, 620. Bondu : 153, 160, 239, 241. Boscher, Gossart : 236, 249, 500, 596. Briest : 65, 146, 210, 454, 568, 580. De Cagny : 246, 274, 479. Cardinet : 506. Chambelland, Giafferi : 70, 192, 293, 301, 342, 343, 410, 496, 531, 575, 579. Charbonneaux : 175, 207, 574. Chayette, Calmels : 56, 98, 217, 218, 219, 317, 339, 403, 494, 499, 501. Cheval : 74, 221, 631. Cornette de Saint-Cyr : 8, 157, 166, 167, 190, 197, 214, 230, 250, 259, 276, 277, 282, 311, 320, 322, 323, 327, 332, 334, 343, 381, 400, 405, 422, 423, 497, 501, 532, 547, 549, 597. Couturier, De Nicolay : 147, 361. Delaporte, Rieunier : 434. Delavenne, Lafarge : 228, 341. Delorme : 171, 509, 546. Dumousset : 374. Gros, Delettrez : 148, 548. Hoebanx, Couturier : 210, 590. Labat : 182, 183, 189, 258, 259, 348, 448, 592, 652. Laurin, Guilloux, Buffetaud, Tailleur : 129, 204, 208, 396, 638. Le Blanc : 408, 412. Libert, Castor : 47, 54, 552. Loudmer : 161, 432, 434, 482, 483, 484, 486, 568, page 4 de couverture. Mathias : 158, 624. Mercier : 545. Millon, Jutheau : 43, 61, 122, 167, 171, 179, 216, 224, 227, 240, 254, 283, 289, 298, 329, 353, 356, 360, 414, 420, 432, 457. Morelle : 649, 650, 651. Néret-Minet, Coutau-Bégarie : 256, 646. Offret : 375. Oger, Dumont : 440. Péchon : 238, 328. Pescheteau-Badin, Ferrien : 311. Poulain : 154, 551. Renaud : 20, 91, 170, 371, 546. Reiunier, Bailly-Pommery : 151, 409, 582. Rogeon : 323, 483, 515. Tilorier : 561. Wapler : 470. Parthenay, Vergnault : 86. Perpignan, Pujol, Jurain : 500. Poitiers, Verhaeghe, Hervoin : 349. Rambouillet, Faure, Rey : 54, 59, 99, 104, 136, 145, 149, 153, 160, 188, 207, 306, 420, 476, 496, 532, 535, 553, 566, 596, 651. Rennes, Gallais, Livinec, Pincemin : 202. Roanne, Engles-Lanfrey : 544. Rouen, Bisman : 643. Rouen, Fournier : 577. Saint-Brieuc, Guichard : 579. Saint-Dié, Guérin : 399, 412, 422, 565. Saint-Etienne, Ballot : 100, 333, 520, 542, 644. Saint-Germain-en-Laye, Loiseau, Schmitz : 40. Saint-Maur, La Varenne-Saint-Hilaire, Lombrail, Teucquam : 63, 275, 290, 567, 620, 632, 633. Saint-Quentin, Debra, Mune : 530. Saumur, Ségeron : 154, 373, 419, 477. Semur-en-Auxois, Machoïr : 326. Tarbes, Adam : 524. Toulouse, Chassaing, Rivet, Fournie : 430. Tours, Odent, Beaumont : 46, 216, 297, 383, 504. Troyes, Pomez, Boisseau : 120, 509, 514. Valenciennes, Ernault, Macaigne : 179, 180, 184, 518. Vannes, Mandart : 344. Vendôme, Rouillac : 536. Versailles, Blache : 483. Versailles, Martin, Desbenoit : 63, 344, 425. Versailles, Perrin, Royère, Lajeunesse : 159.
Christie's Londres : 12, 48, 169, 254, 281, 355, 389, 489, 511, 526, 540, 556, 614.
Sotheby Londres : 119, 125, 127, 139, 200, 209, 223, 226, 231, 232, 270, 302, 362, 367, 413, 416, 433, 434, 437, 446, 462, 510, 540, 541, 542, 562, 618, 625.
Palais des beaux-arts, Bruxelles : 239, 507, 647. De Vuyst, Lokeren : 65.

© SPADEM 1987 : Joseph Bernard : 89, 91, 92 ; Pierre Bonnard : 12, 107, 108 ; Henri Bouchard : 110, 111, 112, 113, 114, 115, 116, 117, 118 ; José Clara : 207, 208 ; Juan Clara : 209 ; Camille Claudel : 210, 211, 212, 213 ; Fix-Masseau : 318, 319 ; Paul Jouve : 394 ; Aristide Maillol : 449, 450, 451, 452, 453, 454 ; Henri Matisse : 465, 466 ; Edouard Navellier : 522 ; Pablo Picasso : 542 ; Jean-François Raffaëlli : 561 ; Théophile-Alexandre Steinlen : 620.

© ADAGP 1987 : Pierre Bonnard : 12, 107, 108 ; Antoine Bourdelle : 121, 122, 123, 124, 125, 126, 127, 128, 129, 130, 132, 133, 134, 135, 136 ; Georges Guyot : 374 ; Paul Jouve : 394 ; François Pompon : 551, 552, 553, 554.

Jean-Baptiste Carpeaux, Le Pêcheur napolitain (detail).